Charlie Calvert's Borland C++Builder™

Charles Calvert

SAMS
PUBLISHING

201 West 103rd Street
Indianapolis, IN 46290

UNLEASHED

This book is dedicated to David Intersimone, in respect for his tireless and enthusiastic advocacy of good technology. His example demonstrates how managers and programmers can survive in an overly commercialized industry without compromising their integrity or their love of what's best in computer science.

Copyright © 1997 by Sams Publishing

FIRST EDITION

International Standard Book Number: 0-672-31022-8

Library of Congress Catalog Card Number: 96-71201

2000   99   98   97   4   3   2   1

Interpretation of the printing code: the rightmost double-digit number is the year of the book's printing; the rightmost single-digit, the number of the book's printing. For example, a printing code of 97-1 shows that the first printing of the book occurred in 1997.

Composed in AGaramond and MCPdigital by Macmillan Computer Publishing

Printed in the United States of America

Trademarks

Publisher and President	*Richard K. Swadley*
Publishing Manager	*Greg Wiegand*
Director of Editorial Services	*Cindy Morrow*
Managing Editor	*Mary Inderstrodt*
Director of Marketing	*Kelli S. Spencer*
Assistant Marketing Managers	*Kristina Perry, Rachel Wolfe*

Acquisitions Editor
Christopher Denny

Development Editor
Richard W. Alvey, Jr.

Software Development Specialist
Brad Myers

Production Editor
Mary Inderstrodt

Copy Editors
Keith Davenport
Chuck Hutchinson
Anne Owen
Kris Simmons

Indexer
Christine Nelsen

Technical Reviewers
Sergio Cardaso
Charles Gallant
Matt Lawrence
John R. Thomas

Editorial Coordinator
Katie Wise

Technical Edit Coordinator
Lynette Quinn

Resource Coordinator
Deborah Frisby

Editorial Assistants
Carol Ackerman
Andi Richter
Rhonda Tinch-Mize

Cover Designer
Tim Amrhein

Book Designer
Gary Adair

Copy Writer
David Reichwein

Production Team Supervisors
Brad Chinn
Charlotte Clapp

Production
Jennifer Dierdorff
Paula Lowell
Tim Osborn
Ian A. Smith

Contents

Acknowledgments

As always, I want to extend my deepest and most heartfelt thanks to my wife Margie. Without her, I doubt if I ever would have gotten interested in computers, nor would I have found the patience and strength to write books about them.

I am the one who writes the text and works out nearly all the sample programs, but there are many other people who helped bring this book to print. My debt is portioned evenly between the technical people at Borland who found time to answer my questions, and the editors at Sams and Borland who helped format the text and search for errors.

A particular debt of gratitude is owed to the expert Borland programmers who took the time to talk theory with me. Getting a good technical answer to a specific question is one thing, but getting the benefit of someone's understanding of the significance and structure of a subject is even more important.

On the BCB side, I want to thank Bruneau Babet, Ellie and Jeff Peters, Roland Fernandez, Lar Mader, John Wiegley, Evan Scott, Matt Lawrence, Peter Sollich, Eli Boling, Dave Wilhelm, Conrad Herman, Taylor Hutt, Sergie Cardosa, John Thomas, and Pete Williams for their help. I want to extend a special thanks to Maurice Barnum for his tireless patience in answering some of the most difficult of my many technical questions.

On the VCL side, I would like to thank Danny Thorpe, Steve Trefethen, Steve Teixeira, Alain Tadros, Allen Bauer, Gary Whizin, Bill Weber, Mark Sikes, Lance Devin, David Intersimone, and Zack Urlocker for all their patience in answering my many questions and for their good work in support of the VCL.

I would like to extend a special thanks to Chuck Jazdzewski for finding time to answer questions and for the tremendous work he has done in making the VCL such a success. The VCL is the result of the output from many talented programmers, but if I were forced to single out the one person who made the biggest contribution, that would have to be Chuck.

Thanks to Kari Marcussen for her talent and help with the art in the DirectX examples. Thanks to John Thomas, Jeff Cottingham, and Stuart Fullmer for their help porting the DirectX components from Object Pascal to C++.

I would like to thank Tamara Meyer, Kurt Hecht, Yolanda Davis, CJ Martin, Ellen Lawson, and Nancy Collins for making my day-to-day life manageable. A special thanks goes to Karen Giles for her good heart and hard work.

As always, I want to thank the people at Sams who work so hard to make these books readable. Chris Denny is the sole of patience and even temper when he deals with me regularly on the phone. Thanks also to Mary Inderstrodt, Rich Alvey, and all the other Sams employees who worked so hard on this book. None of my books would be even half as readable were it not for the efforts of the editors and technicians at Sams who work on layout, structure, and grammar.

Thanks to readers from all around the world whose feedback inspires me to keep writing. Thanks also to everyone in the computer industry who stays in the game because of their love of the technology. In the short term, it appears that money, flash, and marketing are the forces that drive the industry. In the long run, however, the people who really shape the future of computers are the technicians and scientists who write code and dream dreams. I am in the debt of everyone who sits down to write code or who takes the time to discuss programming seriously in books, articles, and newsgroups. There is definitely a worldwide community of programmers who exist outside the boundaries of individual nations. This book is merely a small part of that community's continuous, ongoing dialog.

Charlie Calvert
`users.aol.com/charliecal`
Santa Cruz, CA
March, 1997

About the Author

Charlie Calvert

Charlie Calvert is the author of *Teach Yourself Windows 95 Programming in 21 Days, Delphi 2 Unleashed,* and *Turbo Pascal Programming 101.* His day job is at Borland International, where he works as a manager in Developer Relations. In the past, he has also worked as a journalist and English teacher. He lives with his wife Margie in Santa Cruz, CA.

Tell Us What You Think!

As a reader, you are the most important critic and commentator of our books. We value your opinion and want to know what we're doing right, what we could do better, what areas you'd like to see us publish in, and any other words of wisdom you're willing to pass our way. You can help us make strong books that meet your needs and give you the computer guidance you require.

Do you have access to CompuServe or the World Wide Web? Then check out our CompuServe forum by typing GO SAMS at any prompt. If you prefer the World Wide Web, check out our site at http://www.mcp.com.

> **NOTE**
>
> If you have a technical question about this book, call the technical support line at 317-581-3833.

As the publishing manager of the group that created this book, I welcome your comments. You can fax, e-mail, or write me directly to let me know what you did or didn't like about this book—as well as what we can do to make our books stronger. Here's the information:

Fax: 317-581-4669

E-mail: programming_mgr@sams.samspublishing.com

Mail: Greg Wiegand
Sams Publishing
201 W. 103rd Street
Indianapolis, IN 46290

IN THIS PART

Getting Started

PART

I

Introduction to C++Builder

IN THIS CHAPTER

CHAPTER

1

Overview

In this chapter I introduce Borland C++Builder (BCB) and explain what it is about. I also devote considerable time to explaining the purpose of this book and the philosophy behind my approach to technical writing.

Technical subjects covered in this chapter include

- Creating a simple Multimedia RAD program that plays movies, WAV files, and MIDI files.
- Shutting down the BCB RAD programming tools and writing raw Windows API code instead.
- Creating components dynamically on the heap at runtime.
- Setting up event handlers (closures) dynamically at runtime.
- A brief introduction to using exceptions. This topic is covered in more depth in Chapter 5, "Exceptions."
- A brief introduction to ANSI strings. This subject is covered in more depth in Chapter 3, "C++Builder and the VCL."
- Using the online help.
- Greping through the include and source files that come with the product and with this book.

This chapter includes sample programs or code snippets illustrating all of these concepts. The sample programs for this chapter are found on the CD that accompanies this book in the directory called Chap01. The same pattern is followed for all other chapters. For instance, the code for Chapter 2, "Basic Facts About C++Builder," is in a subdirectory on the CD called Chap02.

Getting in the Mood

Programming is part of an esoteric world where logic is sacred. Even if you understand exactly why a program works, there is still a magical element involved. Things appear and disappear. Objects materialize, and then dematerialize. They do so according to strictly defined logical rules; but still, there is the fact that things appear and disappear right before our eyes.

To be a good programmer, you have to be a wizard. You have to study arcane material, sit up over it until your eyes are bleary, and ponder its meaning, seeking to understand its mysteries. Many people never understand the subtleties of programming. They don't ever penetrate to the inner mysteries of this challenging field.

But think of the joy you feel when you finally figure it out! The profound satisfaction of actually cracking the code, mastering the spells, and seeing through to the inner mystery! The arcane minutiae of programming is part of a subtle, intricate world that can be mastered only by a few dedicated souls who are willing to work hard to get at the inner truth of an algorithm, of an object hierarchy, of a coding technique.

Some products seem to be effective at capturing the essence of the beautiful, mysterious logic that underlies the world of programming. C++ has always had free entry into this realm. C++Builder, however, raises the ante in the C++ world by allowing you to create programs with a powerful set of tools that gracefully augment your programming skills.

BCB is one of the first serious compilers that allows you to pick up objects called components with the mouse and move them around so that you can change the logic of your program visually, rather than solely with code. The core of this technology is component programming—not large, bloated, difficult to create components but small, sleek, easy-to-build components that run at lightning speed, components that appear and disappear before your eyes at the click of a mouse.

Programming is intellectually exciting. At times, it's even—dreaded word—fun! C++Builder puts the excitement back in C++ programming. If you like to write fast programs that are easy and fun to use, this is the right tool for you. Best of all, C++Builder gives you full access to all the advanced features of C++, including templates, name spaces, operator overloading, and the entire Windows API, including cutting-edge APIs such as DirectX, OLE Automation, and ActiveX.

Most of the time, BCB programming is surprisingly easy. On occasion, it's very challenging. It is, however, always interesting and exciting. Let other programmers plod along with boring compilers made by some huge soulless conglomerate full of middle managers who middle-manage their products into one giant, boring access violation. There is something different about BCB. Like its cousin Delphi, it has something of the true spark of the real programmer's art in its sleek lines, in its fast compilation, and in its subtle and artful use of the C++ language.

The Audience for This Book

Throughout this book, I walk a subtle line between extremes. Sometimes the text has pulled me in the direction of system programming, and at other times I have relied on the RAD tools that make BCB so easy to use. At times, I have wanted to find the fastest way to perform a particular task and at others I have wanted to find the clearest, simplest way to perform a task. Almost a third of the book concentrates on database tasks, but I also dig deeply into OOP, component creation, and esoteric Windows APIs such as DirectX.

C++ is the language of choice for programmers obsessed with speed, who long to optimize their programs down to the last clock cycle, and who love to plumb the most intricate depths of the computer. Some C++ programmers feel physical pain when they have to give up clock cycles that could be optimized out given sufficient time. In short, C++ is a language designed for creating operating systems and compilers.

RAD tools, on the other hand, are designed for programmers who have a job to do and want to get it done quickly. These people want a safety net so they don't crash and burn! They are willing to give up clock cycles in return for usable code.

In short, RAD programmers are intent on getting a job done quickly and safely, whereas C++ programmers are traditionally intent on creating the smallest, fastest programs possible.

This book, and BCB as a whole, is about the meeting of these two diverse camps. I am very much aware that many C++ programmers won't like the "smell" of RAD, and that many RAD programmers will be appalled by the ornate subtleties of C++. However, I believe that there is a place where these two groups can meet, and furthermore, I think C++ can provide the high productivity tools that RAD programmers expect, along with the high performance, system-loving, optimized intricacies that true aficionados of C++ demand.

In short, this book is for contemporary programmers who practice their art on the cutting edge of modern programming techniques. That does not mean that this book is about the most technical aspects of C++ and Windows, nor does it mean that this book is about a dangerous, new form of programming that wastes clock cycles indiscriminately. Instead, this book is about techniques that allow systems programmers to get their work done quickly, while allowing RAD programmers to speed up and enhance their programs.

I should perhaps add that a large portion of this book is dedicated to client/server database programmers. Nearly 80 percent of the applications made today involve databases, and this tool will undoubtedly be used very heavily by client/server developers. I go into considerable lengths to talk about the advanced database features found in BCB; I cover SQL, stored procedures, triggers, filters, lookups, and numerous other database techniques.

BCB Versus VB

There is one thing that ought to be made clear right at the start. The programs you write with BCB are comparable in terms of size and performance with the programs you create with OWL or MFC. It would be a mistake to assume that BCB has any of the limitations you find in VB or PowerBuilder, or even in Optima. Anything you can do in MSVC or in BC5 you can also do in BCB, and you can do it with the same, or an increased, degree of subtlety and artfulness.

Both BCB and VB are RAD tools. But that is where the comparison between the two products must end. VB is a nice product, but it is not a serious programming tool. BCB is a very serious programming tool. It is a real C++ compiler that comes with all the bells and whistles.

The presence of RAD tools can lead you to believe that BCB is somehow crippled in terms of performance or capability. However, that is an erroneous conclusion. If you take the time to explore the product in depth, you will find that it lacks nothing in terms of power or capability.

The RAD tools in this package add no real overhead to your programs that you would not find in either OWL or MFC. The VCL is comparable to OWL and MFC in every way, except for the fact that it is much easier to use and much more elegantly designed.

The word *component* can also conjure up images of slow, buggy, hard-to-understand ActiveX controls. BCB components are much faster, much smaller, and much easier to make than ActiveX controls. OLE is a powerful technology—and one that I use quite frequently—but it lacks the subtlety, speed, and elegance of the VCL code that underlies BCB.

A Cautious Approach to Programming

Having gone to some lengths to emphasize the technical depth of BCB, I want to turn around and discuss the relatively conservative approach I take to the art of writing programs.

I have been writing code long enough to have grown suspicious of techniques that are too fancy, too subtle, and too hard to parse, execute, and maintain. As a result, I have adopted the style of programming championed by people who want to write safe, easy-to-maintain programs.

I tend to promote a conservative programming style—and indeed, almost all the good programmers I know use these same techniques, even when writing code that is designed for high performance applications.

A certain degree of caution is necessary if you want to write robust code. When in doubt, I always err on the side of caution.

Does this mean I want you to write slow, bloated code? No, of course not! My goal is to walk that fine line between writing code that is such a high wire act that it can't be maintained, and writing code that is so high-level, so abstracted, that its performance becomes an abomination.

BCB is about the place you can get the maximum in terms of safety, without giving up significant power in terms of speed and flexibility. It's about walking the line between two extremes.

On Using C++

When creating the sample applications for this book, I tried to choose code that walks the middle line between being too cautious and too daring. I tried to take the best ideas from the C++ language and combine them with the benefits of RAD.

I want to get far enough into C++ to leverage its power, without going so far that I spend whole chapters parsing the subtleties of some obscure syntactical corner of the language. I also want to use many high-level, RAD-based tools, but I don't want to rely on them so completely that they overshadow the power of the C++ language.

The goal is to find the middle ground, the artful line that yields the best programs. If I am in doubt, I will err on the side of the RAD programmers who have a job to do. The primary reason for this decision is simply that there are already many great books out there on the intricacies of C++ and on the subtleties of the Windows API. There is no need for another book on those subjects. Instead, I want to show what C++Builder brings to the table.

When exploring BCB, however, I will always keep at least one eye on the system programmer. I know what you want, I believe in your cause, and I want to show you how BCB can help you complete even the subtlest jobs more quickly than traditional environments such as BC5 or MSVC. My promise is that the executables you produce with BCB will be at least as small, and at least as fast as the executables you produce with MFC or OWL. And, if you want, you can cut out BCB's object-oriented tools and produce tiny executables that match anything that you can do with BC5 or MSVC.

I am not trying to create a companion volume to a classic hard-core tome such as the *Zen of Assembly Language, More Effective C++, Undocumented Windows*, the *ARM*, or *Inside Windows*. Books like that have their place, of course, but that is not the kind of programming I want to write about.

Clearly, I am trying to set practical, reasonable goals for this book. However, I don't mean to imply that this is a plodding, methodical book that will never take flight into any interesting subjects. On the contrary, I want to show how you can do fancy, flashy, exciting things with a computer, without having to parse the lowest-level bits in the operating system. If you want to plumb to the lowest depths of the operating system, I will take you right up to the edge, show you how to get started, and then wish you Godspeed. You can use BCB to do some great system programming, but I will leave the specifics of how to proceed to other authors, or to a second book of my own on the subject.

This book contains lots of exciting code on subjects such as multimedia, games, and Internet programming. I concentrate on very high-performance tools such as DirectX and on cutting-edge technologies such as OLE. Unlike other books on these subjects, however, my goal is to show how you can integrate these things into your projects even if you are on a tight schedule and even if you would not normally be inclined to do the kind of spelunking that those names imply.

In my opinion, the kind of programming described in this book is the essence of cutting-edge computer technology (at the time of this writing). The best programmers today use whatever tools they can find to allow them to quickly produce high-performance programs. Plumbing the depths is fun, but it loses some of its appeal when the Internet calls, or when you need to produce an inventory program quickly, or when you want to spice up an application so that your users actually enjoy sitting down to work with one of your creations.

My point is quite simply that today many of the best programmers are specializing, not in plumbing the depths of the operating system, but in producing real-world applications quickly. This is an advanced programming book that assumes a good deal of experience on the part of the reader. However, I want your experience to be not deep and narrow, but broad and expansive.

Humility, Crooked Timber, and the Practical Programmer

In the book *Code Complete* (published by Microsoft Press), Steve McConnell quotes an award-winning paper by Edsger Dijkstra called the "The Humble Programmer." I regard this work as one of the guiding lights of this book.

I would much rather write a humble program that works well than be involved in a flashy, ego-ridden project that is never finished, or that ships two years late. The key to getting things done is to show a little humility.

In particular, if you work under the assumption that any one programmer is perfect, you are doomed to failure. Computers are reliable; programmers make mistakes.

Computers, on the other hand, look remarkably dense when compared to the creativity a good programmer can wield. Machines get a zero on the creativity scale, whereas programmers can be very creative. The key is not to try to make people like computers, but to find the best way to leverage the virtues of both programmers and computers.

If you write code that assumes the programmer is perfect, sooner or later that code will fail. Don't mix up the programmer and the computer. The computer is the one that doesn't make mistakes; the programmer is the one that comes up with ideas.

I write code that assumes I not only can make mistakes, but that I will make mistakes. I write code that shies away from the extremely low-level code that crimps my creative side, and which invites bugs.

The code I like to write assumes that I tend to make errors, and that I should be free to exercise a degree of creativity. Code that is too technical, too cutting-edge, or too clever is code that is prone to bugs and late, sleepless nights.

The right kind of code gets the job done quickly enough to leave programmers still fresh and alert, so that they can exercise creativity in coming up with the best solutions.

Quite often in this book, I will recommend techniques that fly in the face of the advice you undoubtedly get from that hotshot programmer who works down the hall. My problem is not that I fail to appreciate the importance of performance or producing small, fast programs. Rather, I worship at a different shrine, the one that finds the middle ground between code that is too subtle and code that is too abstract, too high-level.

This book is dressed in jeans or cords, good practical shoes, and a tough, but attractive, plaid work shirt. Programmers who like to dress in patent leather shoes and $2,000 suits might make fun of some of my techniques. What I like about the clothes that this book wears is that they are tough, well-suited to a wide variety of conditions, and they look great on a wide range of people.

I don't write for someone who wants to be the best programmer in a group. Instead, I am interested in people who want to make things. I want to get from conception to a finished product, and I don't care if all of the techniques I use aren't the fanciest available. I don't, quite frankly, care all that much about the schedule my manager wants to live by; rather, my goal is to get the job done before I become utterly sick of it. I like to make things. I want to finish the project.

Immanuel Kant is one writer who aptly captured the spirit by which most programmers should live: "Out of timber so crooked as that from which man is made nothing entirely straight can be carved." In other words, don't expect your programs to be perfect, and don't waste time trying to achieve perfection. Aim a little lower, instead. Rather than perfect, shoot for: "It works." Or, at best: "This program is remarkably bug-free!"

Even better, aim for programs that are creative, fun to use, and useful. The strongest suit a programmer can take to a task is creativity. Even the best programmers look like bunglers when compared to the reliability of a computer.

The best programmers also make mistakes with a frightening regularity. I try to accept that fact, accept my limitations, and then find ways to program that are safe! If I have the humility to admit I am not perfect, I can start making programs that work and that get turned in on time!

Once again, I don't really care about my manager's schedule; I care about my schedule. I want to start a project, bring it to fruition, and then move on to the next thing that interests me! I don't want to be stuck working on the same task for years on end!

API Code Versus RAD Code

At this stage, it might be helpful to give a few specific examples of the difference between RAD programming with BCB and traditional Windows programming. My primary point here is to show that BCB can do it all. If you want to write API code, BCB will let you write it. If you want to write OWL code, BCB will let you do that, too. If—heaven forbid—you should even be foolish enough to want to write MFC code (perish the thought!), you can also do that with BCB.

In this section, you will see two sample programs. The first is a traditional RAD application written in BCB, and the second is a standard Windows API program. I will spend a few moments talking about each program and then will use these examples to illustrate just what it is about RAD that I find appealing, as well as explain something about the parts of RAD development that I will focus on in this book.

A Very Short Introduction to the VCL

Reading this text over, I find that I am throwing a number of acronyms around. One that really begs for a short explanation is VCL.

The VCL is the Visual Component Library. It is to BCB what OWL is to BC5, and what MFC is to MSVC. (This is called acronym immersion therapy.) In other words, it is the object-oriented library, or framework, that underlies BCB. The difference between VCL and OWL is that the VCL is based on components, properties, and events, while OWL and MFC have none of these features. In particular, events support something called the delegation model, which is an alternative to simple inheritance.

The VCL fully supports all standard OOP concepts such as inheritance, polymorphism, and encapsulation. What it brings to the party are components, properties, and events. (Events are also known as closures.) One of the goals of this book is to explain components, properties, and events in the clearest possible terms, and to state why I feel this is the proper programming model for this stage of computer programming development.

Perhaps most importantly, the VCL is written in Object Pascal. In fact, it is literally the same code base used by Delphi. Later in this chapter, I will explain a bit more about BCB's relationship to Delphi, and I will explore the subject in detail in the next chapter. For now, you need to know only that the VCL would not be any faster or smaller were it written in C++. Object Pascal has some stark differences from C++, but speed and size are not among them. As explained previously, Object Pascal is a real, compiled, object-oriented language that fully supports true inheritance, polymorphism, and encapsulation. All Object Pascal code that works in Delphi works automatically in C++Builder.

That's all I will say on this subject at this point, though I will spend considerable time defining the VCL and its related programming models more carefully in later chapters. In particular, Chapter 2 and Chapter 3 go into considerable depth on the subject of VCL, how it works, and why it exists.

On Using the Visual Tools

Before I get started with a specific programming example, I want to take a moment to discuss the technique I use when writing about BCB programs. Except for a few places in the first chapters, I will generally skip over detailed descriptions of the visual programming tools.

In this text, I will usually not explain the process of setting up a standard component at all. For instance, if text on a TButton component says OK, Exit, or Close, I will not say Set the `Caption` field of the TButton component to Exit, or Close. Instead, I will assume that you can figure that much out just by looking at the figure that accompanies my description of the program.

As you gain more experience with C++Builder, you will quickly learn how to work with most of the properties associated with components. As a result, I usually do not bother to write detailed explanations about setting up a component, such as that you need to set its `Align` property to `alClient`, or its `Stretch` property to `True`. I assume that you can see that much just from glancing at the figure. Of course, I assume there will be times when you will want to run the programs on disk to see exactly how I have achieved a particular affect.

My point here is that you should be able to glean information of this kind from the manuals that ship with the product or from the online help. You could also turn to a beginning level C++Builder book, such as *Teach Yourself C++Builder in 21 Days* (published by Sams). In the current text, however, I will try to skip over that kind of beginning material, in order to best give you what you expected when you bought an intermediate- to advanced-level book.

I am aware, however, that BCB is a new product and that some introductory material is needed. I will try to keep it to a minimum. In particular, almost all the introductory material occurs in this chapter and the next. After that, I'll assume you know how to use the environment.

A Simple RAD Multimedia Program

 The code for the Multimedia RAD program is shown in Listing 1.1. The entire program is found on the CD that accompanies this book. An explanation of the program follows these listings.

Listing 1.1. The header file for the Multimedia RAD program.

```
//----------------------------------------------------------------
#ifndef MainH
#define MainH
//----------------------------------------------------------------
#include <vcl\Classes.hpp>
#include <vcl\Controls.hpp>
#include <vcl\StdCtrls.hpp>
#include <vcl\Forms.hpp>
#include <vcl\ExtCtrls.hpp>
#include <vcl\MPlayer.hpp>
#include <vcl\Menus.hpp>
#include <vcl\Dialogs.hpp>
//----------------------------------------------------------------
class TForm1 : public TForm
{
__published:  // IDE-managed Components
  TPanel *Panel1;
  TImage *Image1;
  TMediaPlayer *MediaPlayer1;
  TMainMenu *MainMenu1;
  TMenuItem *File1;
  TMenuItem *Load1;
  TMenuItem *Play1;
  TMenuItem *N1;
  TMenuItem *Exit1;
  TOpenDialog *OpenDialog1;
  TMenuItem *Options1;
  TMenuItem *ChangeBackground1;
  void __fastcall Load1Click(TObject *Sender);
  void __fastcall Play1Click(TObject *Sender);
  void __fastcall Exit1Click(TObject *Sender);
  void __fastcall ChangeBackground1Click(TObject *Sender);
private: // User declarations
public:  // User declarations
  virtual __fastcall TForm1(TComponent* Owner);
};
//----------------------------------------------------------------
extern TForm1 *Form1;
//----------------------------------------------------------------
#endif
```

Listing 1.2. The main module for the Multimedia RAD program.

```cpp
/////////////////////////////////////
// File: Main.cpp
// Project: Muli-media RAD
// Copyright (c) 1997 by Charlie Calvert
#include <vcl\vcl.h>
#pragma hdrstop
#include "Main.h"
#pragma resource "*.dfm"
TForm1 *Form1;
__fastcall TForm1::TForm1(TComponent* Owner)
  : TForm(Owner)
{
}
void __fastcall TForm1::Load1Click(TObject *Sender)
{
  if (OpenDialog1->Execute())
  {
    MediaPlayer1->FileName = OpenDialog1->FileName;
    MediaPlayer1->Open();
  }
}
void __fastcall TForm1::Play1Click(TObject *Sender)
{
  try
  {
    MediaPlayer1->Play();
  }
  catch(EMCIDeviceError &E)
  {
    AnsiString S("\rUse the File | Open menu item to select an AVI file.");
    ShowMessage("Bummer: " + E.Message + ". " + S);
  }
}
void __fastcall TForm1::Exit1Click(TObject *Sender)
{
  Close();
}
void __fastcall TForm1::ChangeBackground1Click(TObject *Sender)
{
  AnsiString RootDir(ParamStr(0));
  AnsiString SaveDir = OpenDialog1->InitialDir;
  AnsiString SaveFilter = OpenDialog1->Filter;
  OpenDialog1->InitialDir = ExtractFilePath(RootDir);
  OpenDialog1->Filter = "Picture | *.bmp";
  if (OpenDialog1->Execute())
  {
    Image1->Picture->LoadFromFile(OpenDialog1->FileName);
    Image1->Stretch = True;
  }
  OpenDialog1->InitialDir = SaveDir;
  OpenDialog1->Filter = SaveFilter;
}
```

This program pops up in a window that has a picture of a Mayan temple as a background, as shown in Figure 1.1. From the menu, you can pop up an open file common dialog that will let you select and play either a movie file, WAV file, or MIDI file. You can also browse to select new backgrounds for the main form.

FIGURE 1.1.

The main screen for the Multimedia Adventure program.

The RAD Tasks for Creating the Multimedia Program

To create the program, bring up BCB and select New Application from the File menu. Drop down the following components on the main form:

```
TPanel *Panel1;
TImage *Image1;
TMediaPlayer *MediaPlayer1;
TOpenDialog *OpenDialog1;
```

> **NOTE**
>
> In some RAD programming books, code is presented that shows the exact location of the objects placed on a form. For instance, here are some selections from the text representation of the form for the Multimedia program:
>
> ```
> object Form1: TForm1
>   Left = 244
>   Top = 147
>   Width = 493
>   Height = 388
>   Caption = 'Form1'
>   Menu = MainMenu1
>   object Image1: TImage
>     Left = 0
>     Top = 41
>     Width = 485
> ```

```
      Height = 301
      Align = alClient
      Picture.Data = { Lots of numbers omitted here }
    end
    object Panel1: TPanel
      Left = 0
      Top = 0
      Width = 485
      Height = 41
      Align = alTop
      TabOrder = 0
      object MediaPlayer1: TMediaPlayer
        Left = 192
        Top = 5
        Width = 253
        Height = 30
        TabOrder = 0
      end
    end
    // Menu would appear here
    object OpenDialog1: TOpenDialog
      FileEditStyle = fsEdit
      Filter = 'Movies, Sound, Midi¦*.avi;*.wav;*.mid'
      InitialDir = 'c:\'
      Left = 48
      Top = 48
    end
end
```

You can convert your forms into this kind of text by right-clicking them and selecting View as Text from a popup menu. Conversely, you can translate text into visual forms by right-clicking them and selecting View as Form from a popup menu. You can also convert programs back and forth from text to binary files by running a command-line utility called `Convert.exe`. Finally, you can type the preceding code into a text editor, copy it to the Clipboard, and then paste it onto a BCB form or panel. After the paste operation, you will not see text, but live visual components.

At any rate, I have opted not to use the kind of textual description of a form shown above, primarily because the form itself is available on disk, and secondarily, because a picture of a form, like that shown in Figure 1.2, provides more information than a textual description. I do, however, provide both binary and textual copies of the forms on the CD that accompanies this book.

A Brief Note on Creating Menus

You can add a menu to this program by dropping down a TMenu component, double-clicking it, and filing it out as follows:

```
TMenuItem *File1;  // Popup menu
TMenuItem *Load1;  // menu item
TMenuItem *Play1;  // menu item
```

```
TMenuItem *N1;       // (separator made by entering a dash in the Caption field)
TMenuItem *Exit1;  // menu item
TMenuItem *Options1;              // Popup menu
TMenuItem *ChangeBackground1;  // menu item
```

The text for each of these menu items is the same as the name of the menu item itself, except that the 1 is removed from the end of the name.

FIGURE 1.2.

The Menu Designer as it looks during the construction of the menu for the Multimedia RAD program.

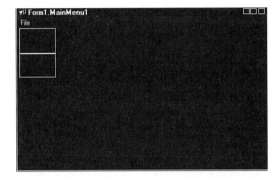

NOTE

I would not normally cover this kind of material in this book, but it might be helpful to hear one description of how to use the C++Builder visual tools in hyper-mode. If you grasp the subtleties of this technique, you will find that you do not need to manually switch back and forth between a form and the Object Inspector. Instead, the environment will move you back and forth automatically between the two tools.

To get started working in hyper-mode, make sure the Menu Designer is closed, because this process works best if you start from scratch. Now bring up the Menu Designer by double-clicking the TMenu object you dropped on the form.

Immediately after double-clicking the item, start typing into the Menu Designer dialog. Don't bring up the Object Inspector. Instead, type directly on the Menu Designer, and watch as the Object Inspector comes up of its own accord. When you want to switch back to the Menu Designer, just press Enter.

For instance, focus the Menu Designer on the first blank menu item and type the word File. Press Enter. Type Open. Press Enter. Type Close. Press Enter. To move over to the next column, press the right arrow key. Type Edit, press Enter, and so on.

You can also select items on the Menu Designer and edit them inside the Object Inspector. However, it is easier to use the hyper-mode method. For more details, see the online help or an introductory book on BCB programming.

You should also go to the Object Inspector for the TImage component and set its Picture property to the bitmap you want to have as the background for the main form. The TImage component should have its Align property set to alClient, and its Stretch property set to True.

You should set the `Filter` property for the `TOpenDialog` component so it looks like the screen shot shown in Figure 1.3. In particular, the text for the property would look like this, if you were filling it out in code rather than via the Object Inspector:

```
OpenDialog1->Filter = "Movies, Sound, Midi | *.avi;*.wav;*.mid";
```

FIGURE 1.3.

The Property editor for the Filter *property of the* TOpenDialog *component.*

Loading a Multimedia File

The following function is called when the user selects the Load menu item from the File menu:

```
void __fastcall TForm1::Load1Click(TObject *Sender)
{
  if (OpenDialog1->Execute())
  {
    MediaPlayer1->FileName = OpenDialog1->FileName;
    MediaPlayer1->Open();
  }
}
```

This code first opens a common dialog to allow the user to select a filename. If the user clicks the OK button in this dialog, the selected filename is assigned to the multimedia component and the component is opened. The act of opening the component "turns on the lights" on the multimedia control itself. In other words, after you open the component, it moves from a grayed-out, inactive state to a colorful, active state.

The VCL and Memory Allocation

Notice that the objects you are working with here are all created on the heap. There is no such thing as a static instance of a VCL component, or indeed, of a VCL object. All VCL objects are created on the heap—that is, you always create a pointer to a VCL object and you don't ever create a static instance of a VCL component. In fact, you can't create a static instance of a VCL object. The compiler won't let you. VCL objects exist on the heap by definition, as will be explained further in the next chapter.

> **NOTE**
>
> My mixing of the words component and object in the previous paragraph is intentional. All VCL components are nothing more than VCL objects with a small amount of overhead added to them so they can appear on the Component Palette. All VCL components are also VCL objects, but not all VCL objects are components. This subject will be explained in depth in the chapters on creating your own components.
>
> You will also find that I use the words class and object interchangeably. Contrary to popular belief, this is not an error. Needless to say, I understand that quite often people use the word *class* to refer to a declaration, and they use the word *object* to refer to an instance of a class. However, this rather fine distinction becomes a bit precious in real life, so I tend to use the words interchangeably unless I have a specific need to make a distinction between the two concepts. When that is the case, I will make it abundantly clear that you need to make a distinction between a class declaration and an object instance.

Notice also that you are not actually responsible for allocating or deallocating memory for VCL components. If you want to, you can explicitly create a component in code. For instance, here is how to dynamically create a TButton control:

```
MyButton = new TButton(this);
MyButton->Parent = this;
MyButton->Caption = "Dynamic Button";
MyButton->Width = 250;
MyButton->Show();
```

This type of code is explored in depth later in this chapter, but if you want to see it in action right away, you can run the DynamicButton program found on the CD-ROM that accompanies this book, in the Chap01 directory. A screen shot of that program appears in Figure 1.4.

FIGURE 1.4.

The DynamicButton program dynamically allocates a button at runtime.

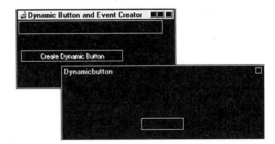

It is also not usually your concern to deallocate the memory associated with a component. BCB has no garbage collection facility. The constructor for TButton shown above assigns this as the owner of the control. That means that the main form for the program is responsible for disposing MyButton, because it has been designated as the owner of the button. (The this pointer is a bit of syntactical hand-waving that allows an object to refer to itself. In this case, Form1 owns TButton, and the identifier this is a way of referring to Form1.) The code in TForm that deallocates MyButton is built into the VCL. You never have to think about it. I will, however, discuss how it works in several parts of this book.

The scheme described here sounds a lot like garbage collection. In fact, if you drop a component on a form from the Component Palette and then run the program and terminate it normally, you will never have to worry about either allocating or deallocating memory for components. This is not a true garbage-collection scheme because you have the option of not passing in a parent to an object when you create it and you can decide to deallocate an object at any time if you want. In other words, many of the memory management chores are taken care of for you, but they do not have to be handled by the system if you would rather do them yourself. This freedom is what I love about BCB, but it also brings responsibility with it.

A true garbage collection scheme would never allow you to make mistakes allocating or deallocating memory. The VCL does not go that far. You can definitely make mistakes with memory management if you are not careful. On the other hand, it should be clear to you that BCB programmers are relieved of many onerous memory management chores. In fact, if you do things right, you rarely have to think about memory management. Part of the job of this book will be to explain how to ensure that you never have to worry about memory management. I will, however, also show you how to take matters into your own hands, if you wish.

A First Glance at Exception Handling

The simple act of opening the TMediaPlay component is not the same as causing the component to play a movie or song. If the users want to play a file that has been loaded into the component, they can push the green button on the TMediaPlayer control. Alternatively, they can select the Play menu item from the File menu:

```
void __fastcall TForm1::Play1Click(TObject *Sender)
{
  try
  {
    MediaPlayer1->Play();
  }
  catch(EMCIDeviceError &E)
  {
    AnsiString S("\rUse the File | Open menu item to select an AVI file.");
    ShowMessage("Bummer: " + E.Message + ". " + S);
  }
}
```

As you can see, this code includes a try..catch block that shoulders some exception-handling chores. If you wanted, you could safely leave the explicit try..catch block out of this code and the VCL would still automatically raise an exception if the user has picked the Play option before loading a file. In that case, the VCL will automatically create an exception that tells the user No MCI Device Open.

For an error built into a programmer's library, the simple strings popped up by the VCL are usually very complete and comprehensible error messages. However, you will probably want to improve on it before showing it to the users of one of your own programs. The code above accomplishes this task by catching the exception, modifying its output string, and then using custom code to display it for the user.

Exceptions in BCB are exactly like exceptions in normal C++ programs, only now your entire program is automatically wrapped in a `try..catch` block and you also have a very rich set of exception classes at your disposal courtesy of the VCL. In particular, you can see that the `Play1Click` method catches an exception class called `EMCIDeviceError`. All VCL exception classes begin with the letter E, so this class might be more readily comprehended as the `MCIDeviceError` exception class, used to raise exceptions that occur when using the `TMediaPlayer` control.

> **NOTE**
>
> The `TMediaPlayer` control is a wrapper around the now somewhat old-fashioned Windows Media Control Interface, or MCI—hence the name `MCIDeviceError`. As you will see, BCB can also use DirectX, DirectMovie, and other advanced multimedia APIs made by companies such as Apple or Intel. In fact, BCB can use any API that works in Windows, but this particular example happens to use the MCI, which is more than adequate for the task at hand.

As will be explained in depth in Chapter 4, "Events," the following code gives you access to a variable named E, of type `EMCIDeviceError`:

```
catch(EMCIDeviceError &E)
```

As you will see in Chapter 3, you can use E to call a number of methods of the `EMCIDeviceError` class. One of these methods is called `Message`, and it returns a human-readable string that can be displayed to the user. I include this string in the text I show to the user, but I add other information including a potential response to the error.

A Brief Introduction to `AnsiStrings`

One pair of lines that have surely caught your eye by this time are the ones that use a new, BCB-specific class called `AnsiString`:

```
AnsiString S("\rUse the File ¦ Open menu item to select an AVI file.");
ShowMessage("Bummer: " + E.Message + ". " + S);
```

The `AnsiString` class is explained in depth in Chapter 3. For now, all I will say is that it provides a type of string that is fully compatible with the Object Pascal strings used by the VCL. In particular, the `AnsiString` class overrides the + operator to support concatenating strings.

Underneath it is a simple string class that most likely calls `strcat` in one of its methods. The use of operator overloading and several other techniques makes it look and act like a Pascal string.

Though it is tempting to use either plain `NULL`-terminated strings, one of the string classes from the `STL`, or one from some other library, you will find that I use `AnsiStrings` almost exclusively in the code that accompanies this book. The primary reason for this is their compatibility with the VCL. However, I am also drawn to their safety and ease of use.

Two-Way Tools: Changing Properties at Runtime

The code in the `ChangeBackgroundClick` method shows how you can manipulate properties either in code, or via the Object Inspector:

```
void __fastcall TForm1::ChangeBackground1Click(TObject *Sender)
{
  AnsiString RootDir(ParamStr(0));
  AnsiString SaveDir = OpenDialog1->InitialDir;
  AsiString SaveFilter = OpenDialog1->Filter;
  OpenDialog1->InitialDir = ExtractFilePath(RootDir);
  OpenDialog1->Filter = "Picture ¦ *.bmp";
  if (OpenDialog1->Execute())
  {
    Image1->Picture->LoadFromFile(OpenDialog1->FileName);
    Image1->Stretch = True;
  }
  OpenDialog1->InitialDir = SaveDir;
  OpenDialog1->Filter = SaveFilter;
}
```

This code changes the `InitialDir` and `Filter` properties of the `TOpenDialog` object at runtime. At first, you might suspect that the only way to manipulate a BCB component is through the Object Inspector. However, everything that you can do visually with BCB also can be done in code.

Of course, I could have saved time writing some code here by placing two `TOpenDialog` controls on the form. However, I do things this way so that

- You can see how BCB's two-way tools work. You can do things two ways: You can write code, or you can do things visually.

- It is also a potentially more efficient use of memory not to have two copies of the object on the form. I would, of course, have to run more tests to be sure that this technique is really saving memory, but the point is that BCB gives you the flexibility to do things as you think best.

The `ChangeBackground1Click` method first saves the current state of the `Filter` and `InitialDir` properties. Then it changes them to values that support the loading of a new bitmap for the background of the form. In particular, the VCL functions called `ParamStr` and `ExtractFilePath` are used to get the initial name of the program as it was passed to the executable by Windows. (There is no need to parse argv; that task is already done for you by `ParamStr`.) The `ExtractFilePath` function strips off the executable name, leaving only the path to the directory where your program was launched. The code then assumes that some bitmaps suitable for a background are available in that directory, which is the case with the code that ships with this book.

The VCL and the Windows API

Notice the `LoadFromFile` method used to initialize the `Picture` property of the `TImage` component:

```
if (OpenDialog1->Execute())
{
  Image1->Picture->LoadFromFile(OpenDialog1->FileName);
  Image1->Stretch = True;
}
```

`LoadFromFile` entirely hides the act of loading a bitmap into memory, getting a handle to it, and passing it to the `TImage` component that can display it to the user.

This capability of components to hide the intricacies of the Windows API from the user is one of the VCL's key strengths. It would be a mistake, however, to view components as black boxes. They are no more black boxes than in any other object you would find in OWL, MFC, or any other OOP library. The whole source to the VCL ships with most versions of BCB and is always available from Borland.

> **NOTE**
>
> The fact that the VCL is in Pascal should not be a great hindrance to most BCB programmers. If you examine the actual source files, you will find that they consist primarily of calls to the Windows API and of calls to other portions of the VCL. Because BCB programmers work with the VCL all day, they should have little trouble reading calls to the VCL that happen to be wrapped in begin..end blocks rather than curly braces. Furthermore, a Windows API call in Object Pascal looks almost exactly like a Windows API call in C++. There is no significant difference in their appearance or performance, as long as you are not confused by minor differences such as the appearance of a := operator where you expect to see a simple = operator. In Chapter 2, "Basic Facts About C++Builder," I will show how you can step into the Pascal code of the VCL with the debugger.

Even more important than the presence of the source to the VCL is the fact that you can use BCB to create your own components. If you see yourself as primarily as a system hacker who wants to be close to the Windows API, you can get as close as you want while creating your own components. In fact, BCB allows you to use the Windows API at any time, and in any way you want.

Needless to say, good VCL programmers use components whenever possible, because they are so robust. If you need to drop to the Windows API, it is often a good idea to wrap up the resulting code in a component and then share it with or other programmers—or, if you prefer, sell it to other programmers.

Tools like Visual Basic or PowerBuilder gave people the mistaken impression that RAD was innately slow and perhaps designed for programmers who didn't really know how to write "real" code. Delphi put the lie to that misconception, but it had to struggle uphill against ignorant prejudices concerning Object Pascal. BCB is not as fully encumbered by that weight as Delphi, and it will show everyone who cares to listen that the fastest way to build small, tight, robust OOP-based programs is through RAD.

Writing RAW Windows API Code with BCB

Having ended the last section on a rather provocative note, it's perhaps time to show the more technical side of BCB programming. The WinAPICode program shown below is written entirely using raw Windows API calls. There are no objects in this program; instead, everything is done in a manner similar to the one Petzold used back when Windows programming was just getting started.

The code shown here does not follow Petzold exactly, in that I use Windowsx and STRICT to help make the code more readable, more maintainable, and more portable. The basic approach, however, is tied very closely to the Windows API. For instance, I have a real WndProc and message loop, and I make calls to old standbys such as CreateWindow, ShowWindow, UpdateWindow, and RegisterClass. The code itself is shown in Listing 1.3.

Listing 1.3. Standard Windows API program that compiles unchanged in BCB.

```
/////////////////////////////////////////
// File: WinAPICode.cpp
// Project: WinAPICode.cpp
// Copyright (c) 1997 by Charlie Calvert
#define STRICT
#define WIN32_LEAN_AND_MEAN
#include <windows.h>
#include <windowsx.h>
#pragma warning (disable: 4068)
#pragma warning (disable: 4100)
static char szAppName[] = "Window1";
static HWND MainWindow;
LRESULT CALLBACK WndProc(HWND hWindow, UINT Message,
                         WPARAM wParam, LPARAM lParam);
BOOL Register(HINSTANCE hInst);
HWND Create(HINSTANCE hInst, int nCmdShow);
// ===================================
// INITIALIZATION
// ===================================
/////////////////////////////////////////
```

continues

Listing 1.3. continued

```c
// The WinMain function is the program entry point.
// Register the Window, Create it, enter the Message Loop.
// If either step fails, exit without creating the window
///////////////////////////////////////
#pragma argsused
int WINAPI WinMain(HINSTANCE hInst, HINSTANCE hPrevInstance,
                   LPSTR lpszCmdParam, int nCmdShow)
{
  MSG  Msg;
  if (!hPrevInstance)
    if (!Register(hInst))
      return FALSE;
  MainWindow = Create(hInst, nCmdShow);
  if (!MainWindow)
    return FALSE;
  while (GetMessage(&Msg, NULL, 0, 0))
  {
     TranslateMessage(&Msg);
     DispatchMessage(&Msg);
  }
  return Msg.wParam;
}
///////////////////////////////////////
// Register the window
///////////////////////////////////////
BOOL Register(HINSTANCE hInst)
{
  /* You can use WNDCLASSEX and RegisterClassEx with WIN32 */
  WNDCLASS WndClass;
  WndClass.style         = CS_HREDRAW | CS_VREDRAW;
  WndClass.lpfnWndProc   = WndProc;
  WndClass.cbClsExtra    = 0;
  WndClass.cbWndExtra    = 0;
  WndClass.hInstance     = hInst;
  WndClass.hIcon         = LoadIcon(NULL, IDI_APPLICATION);
  WndClass.hCursor       = LoadCursor(NULL, IDC_ARROW);
  WndClass.hbrBackground = (HBRUSH)(COLOR_WINDOW+1);
  WndClass.lpszMenuName  = NULL;
  WndClass.lpszClassName = szAppName;
  return (RegisterClass(&WndClass) != 0);
}
///////////////////////////////////////
// Create the window
///////////////////////////////////////
#include <wtypes.h>
__RPC_FAR Sam()
{
  return 0;
}
HWND Create(HINSTANCE hInstance, int nCmdShow)
{
  HWND hWindow = CreateWindowEx(0, szAppName, szAppName,
                     WS_OVERLAPPEDWINDOW,
                     CW_USEDEFAULT, CW_USEDEFAULT,
                     CW_USEDEFAULT, CW_USEDEFAULT,
                     NULL, NULL, hInstance, NULL);
```

```
  if (hWindow == NULL)
    return hWindow;
  ShowWindow(hWindow, nCmdShow);
  UpdateWindow(hWindow);
  return hWindow;
}
// ======================================
// IMPLEMENTATION
// ======================================
#define Window1_DefProc    DefWindowProc
void Window1_OnDestroy(HWND hwnd);
/////////////////////////////////////////
// The window proc is where messages get processed
/////////////////////////////////////////
LRESULT CALLBACK WndProc(HWND hWindow, UINT Message,
                                WPARAM wParam, LPARAM lParam)
{
  switch(Message)
  {
    HANDLE_MSG(hWindow, WM_DESTROY, Window1_OnDestroy);
    default:
      return Window1_DefProc(hWindow, Message, wParam, lParam);
  }
}
/////////////////////////////////////////
// Handle WM_DESTROY message
/////////////////////////////////////////
#pragma argsused
void Window1_OnDestroy(HWND hwnd)
{
  PostQuitMessage(0);
}
```

This program looks like, and indeed is, an old-fashioned Windows program from back before the days of the object frameworks such as OWL or the VCL. It will, however, compile unchanged in BCB. In fact, I did not have to change any of the code or any of BCB's compiler settings in order to create this program.

To get started producing this code from scratch, open up BCB and start a new project. Go to View | Project Manager and remove Unit1 from the project. Now save the file to a directory created specifically for this program.

TIP

I believe you should always create unique directories for each program you create. If you do not take this step, you will never be able to keep the files from this program sorted from files used by other programs you create. To not put a BCB project in its own directory is to go face to face with the forces of chaos.

Go to the View menu again and choose the Project Source menu item. Strip out all the code created for you by BCB and replace it with the code shown above. You are taking control of this project and don't need any help from the BCB or its rudimentary code generation processes.

In the next chapter I will explain in some depth why BCB should not be considered a code generator, a CASE tool, or anything of the kind. I do, however, feel that BCB is primarily an IDE-oriented tool. In this one case, it would not matter much whether you wrote the code inside the IDE or from the command line. However, BCB code is meant to be written, and your programs are meant to be designed, inside the IDE.

This is not the place to get into a lengthy explanation of how the WinAPICode program works. If you are truly curious, it is taken nearly verbatim from one of the early chapters of my book called *Teach Yourself Windows 95 Programming,* published by Sams Publishing. That book covers raw Windows API programming, which is an invaluable skill, even for BCB RAD programmers. However, unraveling the secrets of the Windows API is not the goal of this current book, so I will merely point out a few key passages from the program.

The following code shows the message loop for the WinAPICode program:

```
while (GetMessage(&Msg, NULL, 0, 0))
{
    TranslateMessage(&Msg);
    DispatchMessage(&Msg);
}
```

This is the engine that drives the program, but it is unlike any of the code you see in a standard BCB program. It is not, however, any different from the message loop that appears inside the VCL. I will show you how to step into the code that contains that loop in Chapter 2.

At first, the following code also looks completely foreign to the BCB paradigm:

```
LRESULT CALLBACK WndProc(HWND hWindow, UINT Message,
                                WPARAM wParam, LPARAM lParam)
{
  switch(Message)
  {
    HANDLE_MSG(hWindow, WM_DESTROY, Window1_OnDestroy);
    default:
      return Window1_DefProc(hWindow, Message, wParam, lParam);
  }
}
```

It would, however, be a mistake to assume the VCL knows nothing about Windows procedures. In fact, you can add code to your BCB programs that gets called every time the WndProc for your program or any of its forms gets called. Once again, I am in danger of wandering too far afield, but if you open up Forms.hpp from the include/VCL directory, you will find the following declaration:

```
virtual void __fastcall WndProc(Messages::TMessage &Message);
```

This call is one of the methods of TForm. As you can see, it is declared virtual, so you can override it in any of your own programs if you want. By doing so, you place yourself directly inside the window procedure for your form. This is an extremely powerful technique, but is one that most programmers will never need to utilize. However, it is good to know that it is available if you need it. I give an example of how to override this method in Chapter 4.

NOTE

The TMessage structure that is passed to the WndProc method of TForm contains all the fields that are passed to a standard Windows procedure:

```
struct TMessage
{
  unsigned int Msg;
  union
  {
    struct
    {
      unsigned short WParamLo;
      unsigned short WParamHi;
      unsigned short LParamLo;
      unsigned short LParamHi;
      unsigned short ResultLo;
      unsigned short ResultHi;
    };
    struct
    {
      long WParam;
      long LParam;
      long Result;
    };
  };
};
```

All the information is there, if you need it. However, my point is that there are few cases in BCB programming in which it is necessary to get down to this level. Once again, this subject will be taken up later in greater depth. In particular, I discuss TMessage and related structures in Chapter 4.

In this section of the chapter, I have shown that BCB allows you to get down to the raw Windows API level if you want. There is, of course, nothing involving the Windows API you cannot do in BCB, just as there was nothing involving the Windows API that you could not do in either BC5 or Delphi. It would be silly and fruitless to try to hunt for exceptions. Callbacks, pointers to pointers, COM, whatever it is you want to do; BCB is up to the challenge. My point in this section is simply to show the great technical depth of this product.

The DynamicButton Program

The DynamicButton program, shown in Listing 1.4, demonstrates how to use code to do all the same tasks you would normally do with the visual tools. Needless to say, I am not showing you this program as an example of how to program VCL projects. Instead, I want to broaden the common base of understanding regarding the way the VCL works. The goal is to demystify the visual tools so that you can see that they do nothing magical or special but only execute code in the background automatically, so that you are spared the laborious task of writing the same lines of code over and over again.

Listing 1.4. The header for the DynamicButton program.

```
/////////////////////////////////////
// File: Main.cpp
// Project: DynamicButton
// Copyright 1997 by Charlie Calvert
#ifndef MainH
#define MainH
#include <vcl\Classes.hpp>
#include <vcl\Controls.hpp>
#include <vcl\StdCtrls.hpp>
#include <vcl\Forms.hpp>
class TForm1 : public TForm
{
__published: // IDE-managed Components
  TButton *CreateDynamicButtonBtn;
  void __fastcall CreateDynamicButtonBtnClick(TObject *Sender);
  void __fastcall DynamicClick(TObject *Sender);
private: // User declarations
  TButton *MyButton;
public: // User declarations
  virtual __fastcall TForm1(TComponent* Owner);
};
//-------------------------------------------------------------------
extern TForm1 *Form1;
//-------------------------------------------------------------------
#endif
```

Listing 1.5. The Main source file for the DynamicButton program.

```
/////////////////////////////////////
// File: Main.cpp
// Project: DynamicButton
// Copyright 1997 by Charlie Calvert
#include <vcl\vcl.h>
#pragma hdrstop
#include "Main.h"
#pragma resource "*.dfm"
TForm1 *Form1;
```

```
__fastcall TForm1::TForm1(TComponent* Owner)
  : TForm(Owner)
{
}
void __fastcall TForm1::DynamicClick(TObject *Sender)
{
  AnsiString S("As you can see, I have an event associated with me. "
               "Also, you can see the other button on the form has been "
               "grayed out. Charlie explains all this in Chapter 1 of "
               "the book. ");
  ShowMessage(S);
}
void __fastcall TForm1::CreateDynamicButtonBtnClick(TObject *Sender)
{
  MyButton = new TButton(this);
  MyButton->Parent = this;
  MyButton->Caption = "Push me: I'm a Dynamic Button";
  MyButton->Width = 250;
  MyButton->Show();
  MyButton->OnClick = DynamicClick;
  CreateDynamicButtonBtn->Enabled = False;
}
```

Here is code that creates a button dynamically:

```
MyButton = new TButton(this);
MyButton->Parent = this;
MyButton->Caption = "Push me: I'm a Dynamic Button";
MyButton->Width = 250;
MyButton->Show();
MyButton->OnClick = DynamicClick;
CreateDynamicButtonBtn->Enabled = False;
```

The first two lines of code duplicate what happens when you drop a component on a form. First, the button is assigned an owner that will take care of memory allocations. Next, the button is assigned a parent, so that Windows will know what surface to draw the button on.

The last sentence contains a very important point. The VCL never does anything more than call standard Windows API functions. It's not as if these objects completely take over Windows and do things mysteriously in some dense black box that cannot be understood. Instead, they wrap simple Windows API calls or wrap entire Windows API classes, such as the button class. Underneath, you just have the same old button that you see in any standard Windows program. The job of the VCL is simply to make it easy for you to use these standard buttons.

The code then sets the Caption and Width for the component. If you wanted, you could also have set the Left, Top, and Height properties of the component.

To make the component visible, simply call its Show method. This will ensure that the object is made visible to the user.

The next-to-last line of code in the method sets up an event handler:

```
MyButton->OnClick = DynamicClick;
```

This line of code is comparable to double-clicking a button at design time to set up an `OnClick` event handler. As you will see in Chapter 4 the whole delegation model is based on the simple task of assigning a method pointer to a method.

Right now it is not terribly important that you understand how events work. Instead, I just want to show you that you do the same things in code that you do with visual tools. In particular, you can create components dynamically, assign values to their properties, and set up events. This is what RAD is all about; the VCL environment makes it easy for you to do these things with visual tools, and the code shown here demonstrates how to do the same task in code.

The only key piece of the RAD puzzle not demonstrated by this program is the art of making components. But that truly is a more complicated subject, and one that I will broach only at the appropriate time.

In the last few sections of this chapter, you have seen a number of programs that demonstrate key features of BCB. I have shown you these programs not so that you can understand them in their entirety but as an introduction to the VCL and to the material covered in this book.

During the course of Chapter 2, the core technical content of this book will be introduced bit by bit. By the time you reach Chapter 3, the story will be in full swing, and it will not let up until the last page. The remainder of this chapter, however, provides overviews of important matters of general interest.

On the Structure and Contents of This Book

I will now go on to give an overview of the contents of this book, as well as highlight certain ideas and programming techniques that permeate most of the rest of the text. Few of the ideas presented in the rest of this chapter are of earth-shattering importance, and you are free to skip them if you are in a hurry. I include them here only to help clarify my purposes in this book and to create a common foundation for the ideas on which the rest of this text will build.

Program Builders Versus Component Builders

An important distinction can be made between people who do low-level work and people who build entire programs. For the moment, let me call the people who do low-level work component builders or tool vendors, and those who do high-level work program builders or program designers.

Suppose you are a program builder and you develop a need to convert files of type PCX to type GIF. There are two things you can do:

1. You could find a book on file formats and start writing the code for converting PCX files to GIF files.

2. You could search the Net, bookstores, and vendors, such as Programmer's Paradise (www.pparadise.com), for components, objects, or libraries that will do this for you.

Here is the moment of truth. What do you want to be: a component builder or a program builder? Most programmers do a little of both, but there comes a time when you have to decide which camp you will call home. You might think that you live in both worlds, but the odds are against it!

Stop and think for a moment about the PCX-to-GIF creation tool. Here are some of the factors you need to take into account:

1. You can't just assume there is only one version of the PCX and GIF file format. Both standards have been around for a long time, and there are undoubtedly several versions of each format.

2. You can't just work with 16-bit color files; you need to be prepared for 8-bit, 16-bit, and 24-bit color—at a minimum! And don't forget that new formats might come out, so you might have to update your code!

3. You have to create code that is reusable and maintainable. You can't just throw this code together. What happens if you need to add a new format to your program? What happens if you need to move from 32-bit Windows to 16-bit Windows? What if you wanted to start supporting OLE automation? You have to structure your code so it can be maintained.

4. Think long and hard about bugs. How clean is your code going to be? What about corrupt PCX files? How about testing on a wide range of systems? What about all the different size bitmaps people might want to make. What if you find that your code works fine under most circumstances, but all of a sudden a user from Germany complains that he wants 1152×864 size bitmaps and that your code is messing up the last 20 rows of pixels. You tested 1024×768, 800×600, and 640×480 bitmaps, but you never thought about 1152×864 bitmaps. In fact, you didn't even know that this was a standard screen size supported by Windows 95 and used by lots of people all over the world! Where are you going to find a computer that can even show screens at that resolution?

Take all the points listed above into consideration. How long is it going to take you to create code that is at least reasonably bug-free and safe? One week? Well, that's probably optimistic. Maybe two weeks? Well, possibly, if you are very good, and if you add in maybe one week more for bug fixes. But let's be realistic. For many programmers, a job of that size might take a month, or even two. That's just to release the beta. Then you enter into another month or two of testing, bug fixing, and updating.

Now, how long is it going to take you to find a component that does the same thing? Maybe you could get one in an hour on the Internet. It might even be free, and it might even come with source. Maybe you will have bad luck—and it might take five hours to find the code, you have to pay some shareware low-level stud $50 for it, and all you get are the binaries. (Bad sign. You *want* that source code!) Or maybe, worst-case scenario, you can't find the code out there anywhere on the Net, and you have to go to Programmer's Paradise (1-800-445-7899, www.pparadise.com) and actually buy the code for some big-time $150 to $200 expenditure!

Think: $150 now, plus three hours to learn the product, means I could have this portion of the code written by tomorrow at noon. Or, maybe I should do it myself and spend four weeks on the project. Four weeks of work is 4×40 hours a week; that's 160 hours. Now suppose the following:

1. I'm a hotshot consultant being paid $100 an hour for my work. 160 hours times $100 is $16,000.

2. I'm a struggling corporate type being paid $25 an hour. 160 hours times $25 is $4,000.

3. I'm a hotshot housewife hacker who has three shareware products on the market. My husband is complaining about being a computer widower, but he kind of likes the extra $15,000 I brought in last year with my products. A month or two of weekends and weeknights hacking the PCX format might finally force a real domestic crisis! After all, there would be no time for dinners out and no time for movies or concerts. Just that darn GIF format! Or, maybe I should just bite the bullet, buy the software tools for $150, and maybe skip having dinner and a movie out this one week. Which is worse, another shoot-out at the domestic corral or maybe that one painful $150 expenditure?

My point here is that being a low-level programmer is not necessarily the intelligent thing to do any longer. It used to be that all the smart people learned to hack the low-level code, and their effort made them very successful. Now, however, the smart people find ways to avoid writing the low-level code!

Of course, if you work day in and day out with components, you need to know how to build them as well as use them. This book will teach you enough about components to show how to create them when you need them. I will cover all the key areas, including the major sticky points that trip up beginners. However, I will not focus on the subject to the exclusion of other, perhaps more important, themes.

The Case for the Low-Level Programmer

The majority of readers of this book will fit into the program builder, component user category. Of course, there are others who will want to take the opposite tack. These are the programmers who want to make programming tools for a living. In particular, if you think about the facts I've outlined above, it must be obvious that there is a market for people who build programming tools.

It happens that I spend a good deal of my professional life talking to programmers who build tools for a living. I've been working at Developer Relations at Borland for several years now. The primary job of Developer Relations is to work with independent software vendors (ISVs) who build tools that can be used with Borland's programming tools.

During my years at Developer Relations, I have met many people who build programming tools for a living. Some of them work alone, some of them work for small companies, and some of them work at large companies and build tools on the side as a moonlighter. Many of them work part-time as writers, part-time as consultants, and part-time as tool vendors.

I understand that there is a thriving market for tool vendors. In fact, I want to say as loudly as possible that if you want to build tools for a living, that is certainly a reasonable goal. It is not necessarily an easy way to make a living and not necessarily a very romantic way to make a living, but it can be done.

The trick, however, is not to get caught in some never-never land between being a program developer and a component or tool developer. Don't start to build a program and then end up spending months building the tools you want to work with! In that way lies madness!

This book shows quite a bit about how to build components, and how to add component editors and property editors to your tools. However, if you want to work full time on components, you should use this book as a starting point and then go on to read *Delphi Component Design,* (Addison Wesley, by Danny Thorpe) and *Delphi Components,* (Coriolis Group, by Ray Kanopka). These guys work in Object Pascal, but they take the VCL down to the bare metal. Of course, I've read those books, so many of the hot techniques these authors cover will be included here. But as a rule, this book is about program building, not about tool building!

Though I cover components in considerable depth, this book is aimed primarily at program builders. Whether you create shareware, work for a corporation, or work as a consultant, the goal of this book is to show you how to use components to create programs.

I will definitely take time to talk about the Web, about what's on the Web, and about how to find things on the Web. I will talk about companies like Programmer's Paradise. I will show you what is available, and I will supply many tools on the CD that comes with this book.

Types of Technical Books

There are three types of technical writing commonly used today:

Reference: These texts contain lists of information. For instance, a common reference book might contain a list of functions in one or more APIs. The reference would state the name of the function, where it can be found, its purpose, and its parameters.

Tutorial: These texts step you through a process. For instance, a tutorial might explain how to create a form by walking you through the process one step at a time. Here is some sample text from an imaginary tutorial: "First create a new form. Now drop a button on the form and use the align dialog to center it at the bottom of the window."

Discursive (explanatory): A discursive, or explanatory, text attempts to explain a concept in plain English. These texts work with concepts and theories and frequently attempt to take complex subjects and explain them in clear, easy-to-understand language.

This book uses all three of the techniques described above, but my primary emphasis is on the third. The decision to focus on this third technique is in part a natural consequence of my own talents and inclinations. However, I have also spent considerable time thinking about how to write technical books, and I have concluded that the discursive technique is the best one to use when explaining complex material such as a compiler.

The problems I have with reference books include the following:

- They are intensely, even painfully, boring to read.

- They present material on paper, even though reference materials are perhaps best kept in online help files. In other words, I think reference texts are slowly being moved from paper to binary format, because binary formats allow the users to search quickly for the specific information they need.

- There is no question that some reference books are invaluable; but as a rule, this technique is not useful when trying to teach someone a new language or product. Reference books don't teach people anything; they are simply a useful tool that can aid a programmer.

For some reason, tutorials are a favorite technique among managers. They appear to be a shortcut to a particular end, and like downsizing, they seem to promise easy profits with little work. Indeed, like layoffs, one can gain a lot from a tutorial in a short period of time. However, tutorials are plagued by the following problem:

- They are brutally boring, though not quite as mind deadening as a reference. You usually know where a tutorial is headed, so there is little sense of surprise or anticipation.

Tutorials force you to constantly move back and forth between a text and your computer. This is a very uncomfortable thing to do. You read a sentence, try something on your computer, and then try to find your place in the text again, only to be immediately torn away and forced to find your train of thought onscreen. I find this an extremely unpleasant and distracting process that I have never managed to pursue for more than an hour at a time. Usually, I find some excuse to escape from a tutorial after about 10 or 15 minutes.

Discursive, or explanatory text, has the following advantages:

- It teaches you the theory behind an idea. After you understand the theory or the concepts behind an idea, you can perform the entire action on your own, unaided. A tutorial might step you through 30 moves to show how a single concept works. Conversely, if you grasp a single concept correctly, you can usually intuit the entire 30-step process needed to bring it to fruition.

- You can read a discursive text straight through without interruption. You need not read a few sentences, go to your computer, and then come back to your text. You can concentrate first on the text and then on the computer, which is more pleasant and palatable.

- Discursive text has some intellectual tension inherent in it, which can, at least on occasion, make it enjoyable to read. For instance, a discursive text can pose a problem and then take you on a small, intellectual excursion while you learn the solution to it. When a matter is posed in this way, the reader has his curiosity peaked and then gets a chance to, as it were, solve the problem with the writer of the book. This creates intellectual tension, excites curiosity, and gets the reader's mind working. In other words, a discursive text can be useful because it is interesting to read, whereas references and tutorials tend to gather dust simply because they are so dreadfully boring.

Once again, I want to emphasize that I use all three techniques in this book. There are many miniature tutorials in this text, and on occasion I will allow my prose to degenerate into a reference if I feel it is helpful. As a rule, however, I try to make this text as interesting as possible and provide you with a book that is at least somewhat compelling to read.

In particular, I am much taken by the power of computer languages and by the intellectual excitement inherent in the act of programming. It's fun to program, and writing code is one of the most intellectually engaging tasks I know. If a subject is this interesting, the text written about it should also capture some of that excitement. The Internet, GDI, DirectX, OLE, and other topics are innately interesting, and I write about them with as much energy and enthusiasm as they engender in the best programmers.

Programming Theory

In keeping with the discursive theory of writing, this book tries to encourage the development of general solutions to technical problems. In short, when solving problems, I often find solutions that work in one instance, but that aren't applicable to general instances. My goal in this book is to look beyond single instances to find the common threads that run through a particular type of programming problem.

To grossly oversimplify the matter, consider the following function:

```
int AddTen(int Value)
{
    return Value + 10;
}
```

This function adds 10 to whatever number you pass into it.

Now consider the following function:

```
int Add(int Value1, int Value2)
{
    Result = Value1 + Value2;
}
```

This function adds two numbers together.

The first function presented above solves one specific problem. The second function solves a general class of problem.

When reduced to an example as simple as the one shown above, it would seem like programmers would always opt for general solutions rather than specific ones. The second function requires two parameters rather than one, but it obviously has considerably more power. As a result, most programmers would choose it over a function like AddTen, which has less flexibility and less power.

Of course, in the real world, there is a much greater temptation to select specific, rather than general, solutions. Some problems are hard to find general solutions for, and as a result, programmers tend to find simple solutions that solve the immediate problem, rather than looking for a more general solution. However, the key point here is that general solutions can be reused, whereas specific solutions are generally good for only one try. It is therefore usually worthwhile spending extra time trying to find general solutions whenever possible. It is also often worth using up one or two clock cycles on a general solution rather than constantly writing custom solutions tailored to speed up individual tasks. In other words, I often prefer a general solution that takes up 50 clock cycles to a hand-crafted solution that takes up 40 clock cycles.

Throughout this book, I often take the time to find general solutions to problems. Sometimes this will make it appear that I am going the long way around when doing something. For instance, the first example above is briefer, more concise. It takes only one parameter rather than two. Isn't it therefore better, more highly optimized, than the second example? Well, in a word, no. Sometimes it's better to write a little more code in order to save room in the long run. One method with two parameters is better than 50 methods with one parameter, even if at first it appears to be the long way around.

About Comments

I tend to avoid using comments in my programs. However, I will occasionally jot notes at the top of a module or right before a potentially complicated or confusing procedure.

I am adamant about not including comments inside a block of code or inside a class declaration, except under the most extreme and unusual circumstances. Code is hard enough to read as it is, but adding comments to the middle of a block of code leads to the worst kind of cognitive dissonance.

As a rule, I limit comments to single block before the implementation of each method, or a longer section at the top of a module. This way, you can view the code without having to simultaneously wrestle with reading comments. When you need the comments, you can scroll up to find them.

RAD Versus the Command Line

Some long-term C programmers find themselves shying away from BCB's components, experts, and other visual programming tools. Indeed, there was a time when it made sense for some programmers to eschew fancy environments and to stick to a "command-line ethic" that involved working mostly with simple text editors and the Make utility. After all, there was a time when the IDE merely helped to simplify the effort involved in learning certain tasks. During that phase, the IDE did not necessarily speed up or improve development; it just made things easier. BCB, however, actually brings tools to the table that outperform anything you can do from the command line.

If you have decided to work in BCB, you have, in a sense, crossed the Rubicon. There is no point in going back to the old command-line way of thinking. BCB is a rapid application development tool, and the correct attitude is to find ways to increase your ability to utilize the IDE, and even to come up with suggestions for how the Borland team can improve the IDE. In fact, you can even create your own experts that will improve the IDE itself.

One of the burdens of this book is to convince even the most recalcitrant command-line programmer that RAD programming, when done right, is every bit as technical and every bit as macho as the old "all I need is Brief and a makefile" way of viewing programming.

> **NOTE**
>
> Brief is an old text-based editor that has always been very popular in the C programming world. Makefiles, of course, are still used in Builder. However, there is rarely a reason why BCB programmers should ever need to write or edit a makefile themselves. BCB uses the make syntax primarily because it is a convenient, text-based way to manage projects. Some members of the BCB team prefer text-based project management to the kind of binary file currently used by Microsoft, and previously used by the Borland C++ products.

The point I'm making in this section is not that programmers should give up the old, hard-core systems view of programming. All of that is very much a part of good RAD environments such as BCB. Everything that you know about the Windows API, assembly language, and the art of memory management applies just as much to BCB as it did to BC5 or MSVC. Good systems programmers are as badly needed in BCB as they were in BC5.

What, then, is the difference between programming BCB and programming BC5 or VC++? One thing that has changed is the number of people who can play the game. In BC5, only a relatively small set of programmers could make the grade. With BCB, more people can manage to acquire true competency in the product.

BCB programmers are divided into two groups. There are the expert system programmers who spend most of their time designing objects and creating components. The second group of programmers are the consumers of these components. It often takes a great deal of skill to create the components, and considerably less skill to use them.

Of course, in many cases, the same programmer will be both a creator and a consumer of components. This means some of the time you will have your systems programmer hat on, and some of the time you will just be a RAD programmer who produces programs in an incredibly short period of time.

The beauty of BCB is that it allows you to wear both hats. When you need to be productive, you can use BCB to put programs together faster and with more ease than any Visual Basic programmer. At other times, you can get back into that command-line ethic and dig into the Windows API, into the system's code.

My personal belief, however, is that 95 percent of the time, the command-line ethic should just be a metaphorical view of the world. You shouldn't literally program at the command line with Brief and a series of makefiles. BCB is bringing that world to a close. But you want to hang onto that tough "I'm a real programmer" attitude. That's something that's very much a part of the BCB programming world.

One final word, just to avoid any misunderstandings: You will find that at times I do program from the command line, and I will discuss techniques for doing so with BCB. In other words, I am an advocate of hard-core Windows API system programming. I have spent much of my C/C++ programming career working from the command line with Brief and a series of makefiles. I believe in that heritage, but I think it is important to recognize the sea of change that BCB is introducing into the programming world. BCB is a RAD tool based inside an IDE, not at the command line.

Of course, part of the fun of the programming world is that it allows people to maintain a sense of identity. I'm sure there will be some successful programmers who never come over to the RAD way of thinking. I'm not saying "Beware, your career is toast unless you get this new visual programming paradigm!" That's not my point at all. However, there is something pretty important going on here, and like Dylan's Mr. Jones, you'll probably be better off if you figure out what it is.

On Builder's Object Pascal Origins

BCB is an unusual product in that it is a C++ tool built on top of an Object Pascal object framework called the Visual Component Library, or VCL. In fact, all of the VCL, and almost all of the IDE, is written not in C++, but in Object Pascal.

The reason for this unusual structure is simply that BCB is built on top of the architecture for the successful Object Pascal–based Delphi product. Delphi solved many of the difficult architectural problems inherent in creating a high-performance, compiled, object-oriented language that could be elegantly hosted in a RAD development environment. It was natural to build BCB on top of this framework, even though it is C++-based and Delphi is Object Pascal–based.

I am well aware of the fact that, for many people, BCB's Object Pascal heritage will be considered a rather serious drawback. For many programmers, a reliance on Object Pascal immediately implies that the product must be both slow and somehow crippled. This is a natural position for a C++ programmer to take, and for those who have never been exposed to Object Pascal, it is perhaps the only possible conclusion to reach.

It happens, however, that I have two great loves in the programming world: C++ and Object Pascal. This puts me in a somewhat unusual position, which is often rather awkward. However, it does give me good credentials for writing this book, and hopefully it qualifies me to at least attempt an explanation of the true nature of the relationship between BCB and Delphi, and between C++ and Object Pascal.

As a big fan of both Object Pascal and C++, I want to take a few moments to clear up some commonly held opinions that I regard as erroneous. Some of the most important of these misconceptions I can simply list in a few short sentences:

- There are many people who think that C++ is better than Object Pascal because it is faster. This is simply untrue. There is no significant difference in speed between the two languages. For instance, the 32-bit version of Delphi uses the same compiler as Borland C++ 5.0 and as BCB itself. Both languages produce the same code; they just express the ideas behind the code somewhat differently. The equality of speed between the two products was equally true in Borland's Windows and DOS implementations of C++ and Object Pascal. This does not mean that you won't find particular cases in which one product is faster than another, but the overall trend is toward two products that have the same performance level.

- It is also untrue that C++ produces smaller, tighter code than Object Pascal. In fact, the advantage in this particular issue probably resides with Object Pascal.

- There are many people who think there are limitations inherent in Object Pascal that make it incapable of performing certain functions. This is also completely untrue. For instance, many people simply assume that you can't express the idea of a pointer to a pointer in Object Pascal. To those who know Object Pascal, the very idea of this objection is ridiculous. Of course, you can express that concept or any other fundamental programming concept in Object Pascal. It's a general purpose programming language just like C++. It's not an innately limited language like Visual Basic.

- Some people think that the Pascal language stopped growing in 1970. Object Pascal is not your father's Pascal any more than C++ is the same language that Kernighan and Ritchie invented those many long years ago, back when the earth's crust was still cooling. In fact, Object Pascal is a much more dynamic language than C++, and it has changed to adopt to the latest programming developments in a way that C++ cannot hope to change, due to the nature of its committee.

Okay, so some of the objections to BCB's reliance on Object Pascal can be eliminated. It does not have an effect on the speed or size of the executables you produce. In fact, if the whole product were written in C++, the code produced by BCB would not be any smaller or faster. Nor does the reliance on Object Pascal mean that BCB is innately incapable of performing certain functions. You can do anything in Object Pascal that you can do in C++, so the VCL is every bit as flexible and powerful as a C++ framework.

Does this then mean that there are no drawbacks to BCB's Object Pascal heritage? Well, I would have to stop short of making quite so bold a claim. There are some problems, some of which are more than minor annoyances, that result from BCB's heritage.

The first and most significant problem is that the VCL is indeed written in Object Pascal, so you have no C++ source that you can peruse to find out how your object framework is put together. This does not mean, however, that there is no source for you to look at. The Object Pascal source ships with the product, and if you have any understanding of Object Pascal, you should be able to read it to see what BCB is doing in the particular cases when you really need to know. You can also link this code into your project and step through it if you desire, as shown in Chapter 2.

You will also find that that VCL sometimes expresses concepts in a manner somewhat foreign to C++ programmers. This can be a bit like listening to a very intelligent foreigner speak English. What they are saying makes sense and might even be rather eloquent; but at times their choice of words, or their word order, or just something about their accent, betrays the fact that they are not native-born English speakers. Ninety percent of the time, this fact might not even be noticeable, but occasionally it will surface.

Xenophobes always tend to assume that the awkwardness they perceive in a foreigner's speech is due to some inherent limitation in that person's culture. From my experience, as someone who knows both C++ and Object Pascal, I find that this type of analysis of the two languages is flawed. For instance, there are some things Object Pascal does better than C++, just as there are some things C++ does better than Object Pascal. And it is only natural that some people will prefer one language to the other, just as someone might prefer French to Spanish, or vice versa. But the truth is that there might be some things that sound wonderful in French that sound rather prosaic in Spanish, but that doesn't mean French is better than Spanish. The issue, of course, is that you can almost always reverse the tables by finding something that sounds wonderful in Spanish, but doesn't sound so good in French.

In short, it's best not to judge these matters too quickly. C++ and Object Pascal are both extremely sophisticated languages, and the marriage between them found in BCB may prove to be a much better match than some suppose. In fact, the ability to pull the best from both languages may prove to be an advantage for the product, rather than a drawback!

To close this section, I should perhaps add that I am not an advocate of either language over the other language. I like both languages equally. C++ has a richness and syntactical fluidity that can make Object Pascal appear quite naked, and, conversely, Object Pascal has a simplicity and elegance that can make C++ appear rather florid and overdone.

Ultimately, I believe the only crime is to be a language bigot who assumes his language is better than the other guy's language due to a classic case of contempt prior to investigation. Almost all the programmers I know who are truly fluent in the latest incarnations of both languages tend to agree with the conclusions I am reaching here. The hardcore Object Pascal and C++ bigots that I have met are usually only truly conversant in one language or the other. And strangely enough, it's always the language that these people know well that they consider best!

Creating Programs Quickly

In the last days of DOS, back in the early '90s, I remember a stage where many of the people I knew were creating great utilities that we could all use. In fact, many of the programs that I ran day to day were utilities that I or my friends had created in C or in Object Pascal.

The introduction of Windows soon put an end to that outpouring of great utilities. Windows was more fun that DOS, and more interesting, but it usually took a good deal of work to create a program that was the least bit useful.

Now, after five or six years of work, Windows is finally at the stage where programmers can again feel as though they are productive when using common programming tools. Using C++Builder, you can put together all kinds of useful applications in a short period of time.

Part of the fun of programming is the ability to create your own programs for your own needs. It's much more fun to use one of your own programs than it is to use a program written by someone else.

C++Builder is one of the set of exciting new tools that puts the fun back in programming. Using this tool, you can create your own applications in days or hours, rather than in months or years. This makes our managers in our assorted corporations happy, but more importantly, it helps us put the fun back in our own jobs.

Most programmers are in the business because they got bitten by the excitement of this profession at some point in their careers. Most of us have been able to stay with the fun for a long time. Some programming experiences, however, can be too much like drudgery and too little like a good time. C++Builder helps make our careers enjoyable. That's a very strong statement, when you come to think about it, but I believe it to be true. The great thing about RAD is not what it does for corporations, but what it does for you, the programmer!

Use the Source, Luke!

Some versions of BCB ship with not only the invaluable header files found in the `include` directory, but also the original Pascal source to the VCL. You should become familiar with both "sources" of information.

The key include files for BCB are in the `../BCB/include/VCL` directory, where the first part of the path references the place where you installed BCB. You should become familiar with all of these files, but as you will see in the next two chapters, two of the most important are the ones called `sysdefs.h` and `dstrings.h`.

My Favorite Program: Grep

BCB ships with a command-line utility program called `Grep.exe`. This humble 73,000-byte program is one of the most useful tools in my programming arsenal. I use it to scan over tens of thousands of lines of source code for examples that I can use.

For instance, suppose I have just finished reading an article on exceptions and I want to add them to my program. Perhaps one of the first lines of code I write looks like this:

```
catch(runtime_error)
```

Unfortunately, when the compiler reaches this line of code, it pops up a message about `runtime_error` being an unknown identifier. Having been down this road a number of times before, I know immediately what is wrong: I need to include a header file in my project that declares `runtime_error`. The question, of course, is which file is it that I need to include?

If I'm lucky, I can put my cursor over the word, press F1, and be taken to an online example that will show me how to use the code and which files to include with my project. However, it's quite possible that

- The online help is broken.
- The online help is incomplete.
- The online help is working and complete in this instance, but this particular reference was apparently written in under 30 seconds by a harried individual who at least shows signs of being under the influence of drugs that might increase a person's production, but at the expense of his or her fundamental reasoning powers.

- The code I'm looking for is from a proprietary library that has no help file.
- I wrote the function or identifier I'm searching on myself, and therefore there is no online help on it.
- This is a beta version of a product, and as a result the documentation is not yet complete.

Of course, the first three options are out of the question for a Borland product—say what?—but the last three occur from time to time. When you are stuck in this kind of situation, Grep is one of the best ways out.

What I normally do is go down to the root include directory for BCB, and type

```
grep -id "runtime_error" *.h*
```

This command causes Grep to search over the include directory, and all subdirectories beneath it, for the string "runtime_error", without regard to case, as it appears in files that have an extension that begins with an H. In particular, the -I switch says search without concern for case, and the -d switch says search in subdirectories. I sometimes add the -1 switch, which tells Grep to just return the names of files that include the string and not to quote any occurrences of the string:

```
grep -lid "runtime_error" *.h*
```

Here is the result of running the first command:

```
File STDEXCEP.H:
class RWSTDExport runtime_error : public exception
    runtime_error (const string& what_arg): exception(what_arg) {;}
class RWSTDExport range_error : public runtime_error
    range_error (const string& what_arg): runtime_error(what_arg) {;}
class RWSTDExport overflow_error : public runtime_error
    overflow_error (const string& what_arg): runtime_error(what_arg) {;}
File STDMUTEX.H:
                runtime_error,
                runtime_error,
                runtime_error,
                runtime_error,
```

Here is the result from running the second command:

```
File STDEXCEP.H:
File STDMUTEX.H:
```

Needless to say, there are many times when I find it useful to Grep across the directories for the sample programs that ship with a product, across the directories for the Microsoft SDK, or across the sample directories in the CD for a book. For instance, if I wanted to see not the declaration for runtime_error but the way it is used in a program, I would Grep across sample directories, looking for *.c* rather than *.h*.

When I am writing a book like this or when I am programming a new API with which I am not familiar, I might use Grep as often as 10 times a day. There are, of course, many Windows–based versions of Grep, and I'm sure there are even some available that will integrate directly into the BCB IDE. However, I rarely use any of these tools for long. For one reason or another, I find it simplest just to use the plain old, humble, command-line version of grep.

If you grep across directories and get many lines in return, use the more command to browse through one page of information at a time:

```
grep -id "WinINet" *.cpp ¦ more
```

If you want, you can also send the output to a text file:

```
grep -id "Windows" *.htm > WebResults.txt
```

Hardware Requirements for Using BCB

BCB needs at least 20MB of memory, and really comes into its own if you have 32MB or more. Trying to use it on Windows NT with less that 32MB of memory is probably too frustrating.

You should have a Pentium 120MHz or higher computer, with at least 100MB of disk space free on the drives where you store BCB and your projects. That is 100MB free after the installation, not before!

If at all possible, you should run at a screen resolution of 1024×768 pixels. 800×600 is probably acceptable in most circumstances, though it is far from ideal. You can also run at 640×480, but you will spend a lot of time shuffling Windows around. (I should know, because I use this resolution a lot when I am on the road. Its appeal wears thin over time.)

In this day and age, you really should try to get not just a good machine, but an ideal machine. At the time of this writing, the ideal machine is a 200MHz Pentium Pro with 64MB of memory and a 4GB SCSI drive. The machines I wrote this book on were 120 and 133MHz Pentiums with 32MB of memory. One was a laptop with 1.2GB of hard drive space, and my home machine has about 3GB of hard drive space. Throughout the whole process, I was shameless enough to long for yet more power, more memory, and more hard drive space. If Ecclesiastes were writing today, I'm sure he would have added: "Of the longing for more MIPS, there is no end. This also is vanity and a striving after wind."

Getting Updates for *C++Builder Unleashed*

If you want to find updates for the code, you can visit my Web site at users.aol.com/charliecal. If AOL stays afloat, and if its rates remain reasonable, it will remain my online headquarters indefinitely. A backup site is www.supersonic.com/calvert.

I am afraid that I reserve the right not to answer questions sent directly to my e-mail address. However, if you cannot find my Web site or if you have a bug to report that is not addressed on my Web site, you can send me e-mail and I will attempt to get some form of answer back to you. If you just want to say hello, to pass the time of day, or to rag on me regarding some portion of this book, of course you should feel free to write, and I will try to respond if at all possible.

Every effort is made to assure that the code in this book works correctly. However, if you see something in the book that does not look exactly right, check the CD to see if it is corrected in the electronic version. If that still doesn't look right, check my Web site. If all else fails, send me mail.

Be sure to find the readme file on the CD and to examine it carefully. You should find both a text-based and an HTML-based version of the readme file.

You can write me at ccalvert@wpo.borland.com, 76711.533@compuserve.com, charliecal@aol.com, or 71601.1224@compuserve.com. If you want to send a binary file to me via the Internet, write to ccalvert@corp.borland.com. I tend not to answer technical questions sent to me by mail, but I can give you updates on the location of my Web site and about where to search on the site for answers to your question.

My Web site contains links to places of interest on the Web, including other major BCB or Delphi Web sites and to vendors of BCB components. If you have never visited a really hot, privately maintained, product-specific Web site, you are missing out on one of the more valuable and interesting aspects of contemporary programming. Programmers who can somehow carve some free time out of their schedules often create fantastic Web sites with lots of free components, tech tips, and news of general interest. I personally don't have time for that kind of endeavor, but I try to list links to the most important of these sites on my Web pages.

Adapting to the Tides of Change

To sum up this introductory chapter, it might be helpful to simply focus on the subject of change. Clearly this book is very different from most C++ programming books. Instead of concentrating on the C++ language or on the Windows API, I am focusing on components, databases, games, and on the Web. Furthermore, I am saying that I am doing this because I believe this is the best, even the mainstream, way to build programs in these waning years of the twentieth century. If I am right about all this, that means that the programming industry is changing.

There will probably be a time when the waves of rapid change that have been washing over the computer industry will at last subside. But for now, and for the foreseeable future, we can look forward to change and then even more change.

C++Builder is part of one of the big waves of change that have come washing up on our shores of late. This is a RAD-based tool with powerful component and database capabilities. This is a more powerful tool than what we had before, but it is also a new tool for most users, and that means we have lots to learn.

During these times of change, the only way to survive is simply to adapt to the idea of living in a constantly shifting landscape. In fact, it's not a landscape at all, but a shifting sea of technology that looks different depending on the flow of the tide, the force of the wind, and the hour of the day.

Those who don't take the risk inherent in changing tools will find that others get the jump on them. With C++Builder, most developers can turn out programs at least twice as fast, and often three or four times as fast, as they could with Borland C++ or Microsoft C++. Furthermore, there will be no price to pay in terms of the size or performance of your final program. This product represents a huge change in the way we think about programming.

The fundamental idea we need to grasp is that components are now the core around which our programs are built. At one point it was procedures and functions; then it was objects, and now it is components. Undoubtedly, the future will bring yet more changes, but this is what we need to learn now.

If there is any doubt, I should perhaps add that I believe C++Builder, and its sister tool, Delphi, are the best programming tools on the market today. They aren't just better than Borland C++, Microsoft Visual C++, or Visual Basic, they are three or four times better. Four or five years from now, I expect that tools like Borland C++ and Visual C++ will play the same role in the market that Assembler plays today. Visual Basic will probably still be widely used, but it is unlikely that it will ever catch up with the flexibility and performance of C++Builder or Delphi.

In short, I am an extremely dedicated adherent of C++Builder. I am completely serious in saying that I think this is the best way to program C++ in today's world. Furthermore, I have made every effort to ensure that this book captures what is best in this product and shows you how it can be used to create the best, cutting-edge development tools that simultaneously impress users and solve a wide range of problems.

Summary

In this chapter you learned a few facts about BCB, and quite a bit about my approach to writing this book. There will be a few more general-interest comments in the next chapter, but most of the material in the remaining portions of this book focuses on hardcore programming issues. This chapter is the place where I set the mood and the tone for the book. The rest of the material focuses in on the core task of writing code!

Before closing, I should perhaps point out that over the last few years, I have spent many long hours using C++Builder's sister product, Delphi. My long experience with Delphi means that I have, literally, more than three and one half years of experience using a product that is very similar to C++Builder. Just how similar the two products really are will become clear over the course of the next three chapters.

I believe that my Delphi-based experience helps me focus on what is best in C++Builder. The opinions I have about this remarkable product have not been reached hastily. They have been forged through years of experience.

I have now spent about six months with BCB, and I can say that it is a product that lives up to the Delphi name, and that surpasses that product in many ways. This is a great tool, which has really changed the way I think about writing code.

There is a lot of material to study in this book and lots of hard work ahead. But don't be so rushed that you never take the time to see what's exciting and artful about this product. Programming is a lot of work, but it is also a lot of fun. Right now C++Builder exists on the cusp of what's best and most exciting in the programming world. Learn how to use the product, but also take a little time to admire the sheer elegance of its execution. I have found that it always pays off to take the time to see beneath the surface of a product, to see not only how it works, but why it works!

Basic Facts About
C++Builder

IN THIS CHAPTER

CHAPTER 2

This chapter and the next five cover the basic facts that everyone needs to know about BCB. Important subjects included in this chapter are as follows:

- The IDE
- Projects
- The VCL
- Core VCL Technologies: Components, Properties, and Events
- Stepping into the Pascal source for the VCL
- The syntax of the VCL
- An overview of the component architecture
- A brief look at Run Time Type Information (RTTI)

This introduction to BCB continues in the next chapter, where I cover the new Borland additions to the C++ language and introduce several key BCB classes such as AnsiStrings and Sets. These special classes emulate features of Object Pascal. Then, in Chapter 4 you will have a look at events. Chapter 5 focuses on exceptions, Chapter 6 on using Delphi code in BCB, and Chapter 7 on graphics programming with the VCL. The latter chapter will complete my introduction to the VCL and to the syntax that is common to almost all BCB programs.

When reading this chapter, you need to remember the basic philosophy of this book. My goal here is not to plumb the depths of C++, the VCL, the Windows API, or any other hardcore technical syntax. Instead, I want to show you how to quickly build real-world applications without losing touch with the underlying Windows architecture. In these chapters there are many times when I make a pass over very complicated subjects such as C++ constructors, templates, rules of precedence, the GDI, and so on. I am, of course, aware that these are sticky subjects that take many pages to cover appropriately. However, you will not find in-depth discussions of these subjects in this book, for there are many other volumes dedicated to those topics. Furthermore, the goal of this book is to show how to use RAD tools and high-level objects to perform complicated tasks quickly, easily, and safely.

C++ is already at least 10 times faster than interpreted languages such as Visual Basic, Java, or PowerBuilder. If slowing down performance by five percent yields a 10- or 20-fold increase in reliability or ease of use, I think it is worth it to play a somewhat more cautious game. In my opinion, it is better to be nine times faster and nearly as safe as an interpreted tool than it is to be 10 times faster and 10 times more dangerous than an interpreted tool. That last 5 or 10 percent that you can eke out of the language by using every imaginable trick just isn't worth it, except in a few unusual circumstances such as compilers, operating systems, and game engines. Even in those cases, it is still probably best to use the relatively small and fast OOP-based techniques outlined in this book.

This particular chapter is unique in that it covers a number of technical subjects that are not very complex. Everything in this chapter is here because I either

■ Think that you have to know it in order to complete BCB programs.

■ Think that you have to know it in order to feel at all comfortable inside the BCB programming environment.

Don't worry if you find most of the material in this chapter a bit too simplistic. There is some basic material that almost has to be covered in a book of this type, and once I get it out of the way, I will move on to more interesting subject matter in the next chapters.

It's time now to get started with an overview of the BCB environment, project management, the VCL, and the basic syntax used by BCB programmers. When you have completed this and the next five chapters, you should have all the knowledge you need to begin a robust, broad exploration of the all the exciting features found in BCB.

Creating C++Builder Projects

C++Builder has a project manager that you can access from the View menu. You can use this tool to add files to a project or to remove files from a project.

You can add files with the following extensions to your project, and C++Builder will compile and/or link them automatically, as shown in Table 2.1:

Table 2.1. Files you can add to a BCB project.

Type of File	Description
CPP	C++ Source module. OWL and MFC are treated in the appendices.
C	C Source module.
PAS	Any Pascal module that will compile in Delphi 2.01.
RC	Resource script.
RES	Resource file.
OBJ	Compiled C++, C, or PAS file.
LIB	C or C++ Library file.
DEF	Module Definition file.

You can use the IDE to produce Windows executables, DLLs, or console applications:

■ To create a 32-bit Windows executable, you need do nothing. The default behavior of the IDE is to generate this type of executable.

- To create a DLL, go to File | New and select DLL from the Object Repository. Click OK. Everything else is automatic. I discuss exporting functions from a DLL in several later chapters of the book, including Chapter 26, "Extending an Internet Server with ISAPI." In a word, the key to exporting a method from a DLL is to use `__declspec(dllexport)`, as described in Chapter 26 and in the comments at the top of the file `ISAPI1.CPP` from Chapter 26.

- To create a console application, go to the Options | Project | Linker option from the menu and select Console Application. If you want to create a console application as a quick way to produce text output, you should consider using the BCB `TMemo`, `TListBox`, and `TEdit` controls instead. I can output text to these controls at least as quickly as I can use `printf` or `cout`. I find these components are more useful than outputting text to the command line, because they support concepts like scrolling and saving their contents to a file or the clipboard.

> **NOTE**
>
> Delphi programmers need to remember that it is not enough merely to #include a C, CPP, or PAS file in a module of an existing project. You also have to add the file itself to the project using the Project Manager or the Add to Project menu choices or speed buttons. Delphi's linker assumed that you would not reference a file from your uses clause unless you wanted it to be part of your project. C++Builder, for better or worse, makes no such assumption. You must incorporate the new file into your makefile listing, or it will not be linked into your project.

BCB projects are managed in a standard C++ makefile. The easiest way to get something into your makefile is through the project manager. Editing the makefile itself is not recommended, but C++ experts will find there are some changes to your project that can only be made by editing the makefile.

Most of the important changes which can be made to a makefile are configurable through the Options | Project or Options | Environment menu choices. The developers of BCB do not expect you to find many occasions when you will need to edit the makefile. I believe the primary reason the makefile exists is that the team grew tired of trying to manage a binary project file.

The Microsoft C++ team, on the other hand, recently grew tired of trying to manage a text-based project file! This is probably one of those cases where developers have a choice between two evils.

If you are trying to manage projects that consist of multiple executables and DLLs, you will almost certainly find the current BCB project manager inadequate. Borland C++ 5.02 will support compiling C++Builder projects. You will therefore want to consider using the advanced tools in BC 5.02 for managing huge projects.

BC5 also supports a powerful scripting language not available in BCB. As a result, I think some programmers will find a combination of BC5 and BCB to produce the ultimate C++ programming environment.

Having made my pitch to that special group of programmers who are managing massive projects, I want to end this section by stating that I find BCB includes everything I need and considerably more. The goal of this book is to talk about completing high quality projects as quickly and efficiently as possible. If that is your goal, stick with BCB and with third-party tools tailored for this environment. BCB is the ideal tool for creating C++ applications. It is state of the art and leagues ahead of any other C++ environment that is planned or available at the time of this writing.

BCB File Extensions

In the last section, in Table 2.1, I list the types of files you can include in C++Builder. Most of these files will be generated automatically for you by the compiler, and I list them here just so you will know why they exist and what they do. In this section, I will talk about all the important files that become part of your project.

Table 2.2 lists the key extensions in BCB projects.

Table 2.2. File types used in a BCB project.

File extension	Description	File type
RC	Source for resource file.	Text
RES	Resource file. There will usually be one RES file with the same name as your project that contains only an icon. It's best to leave this file alone.	Binary
CPP, C	C++ source file.	Text
PAS	Delphi 2.01 source file.	Text
H or HPP	C++ header file.	Text
DSK	The location of files on the desktop.	Text
DFM	Binary file containing form definition. Use CONVERT.EXE to translate into text.	Binary

continues

Table 2.2. continued

File extension	Description	File type
MAK	The project makefile in text format.	Text
TDS	Turbo debugger symbols.	Binary
ILX	Incremental linker symbols.	Binary

When browsing this table, take special notice of the incremental linker files. These four files, all of which begin with ILX, are huge. They are the key files needed to produce BCB's incredibly fast link times. If you turn incremental linking off, as explained later in this chapter, these files will disappear. Turning incremental linking off means that your compilation and link times will be from 5 to 10 times slower than they are with incremental linking turned on.

The `include` and `lib` Directory Paths Issue

There are, confusingly enough, two places where you can designate the paths to your `include` and `lib` files. One is located in the Options | Project | Directories/Conditionals menu choice, and the second is located in the Options | Environment | Library section. These pages are shown below in Figures 2.1, 2.2, and 2.3. There is also a Path for Source option in the Options | Environment | Preferences page.

FIGURE 2.1.

The Options menu leads to the Project dialog where you can set paths for your project.

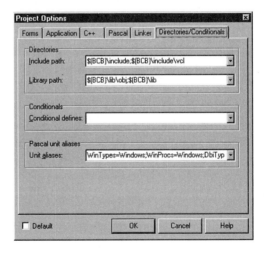

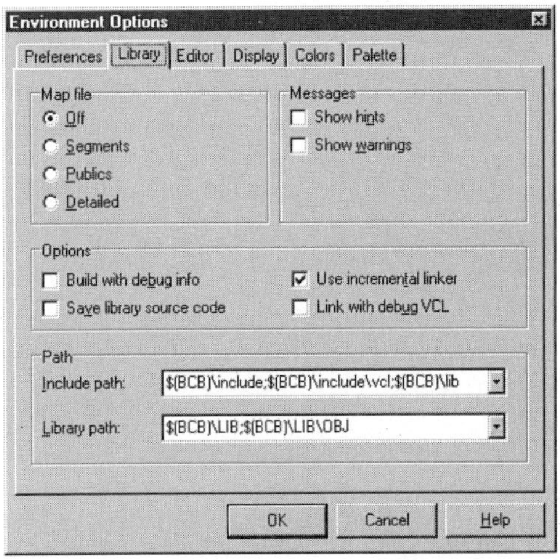

FIGURE 2.2.

The Options menu is also the gateway to the Environment dialog where you can find the Library page.

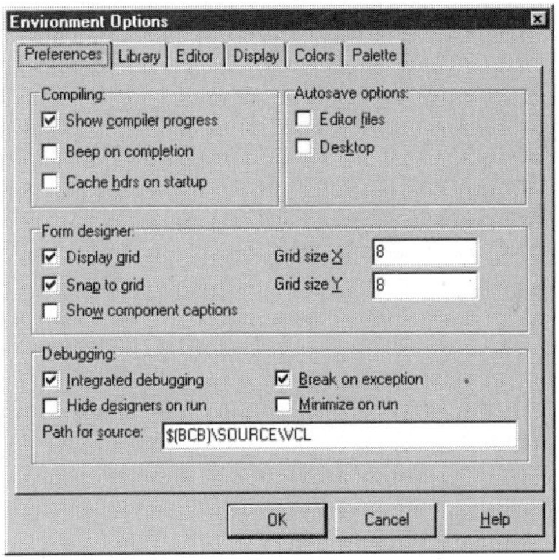

FIGURE 2.3.

The Options | Environment | Preferences page gives you a place to add the path to modules you include in your projects.

The BCB macro shown in the Path statements from Figures 2.1 through 2.3 resolves into the path that points to your current installation of BCB. This kind of information is stored in the Registry under `HKEY_CURRENT_USER/Software` and `HKEY_LOCAL_MACHINE/Software`. For instance, see the `RootDir` entry in `HKEY_LOCAL_MACHINE/Software/C++Builder/1.0`. To view the Registry, select Run from the Windows Start menu, type in the word `RegEdit`, and press the Enter key.

As a rule, you make changes specific to one project in the Options | Project dialog, and make global changes that you want reflected in all programs in the Options | Environment dialog. Use the Path for Source to include any directories that contain utility code that you use frequently.

As a rule, additions to these various path statements are made automatically when you add modules to your project through the Project Manager. However, there are times when I need to go in and explicitly edit one of these options.

Remember that if you are adding a component to the Component Palette, you have to add the path to that component in the Options Environment dialog or the Component Palette will not load. This addition to the Path statement will be made automatically if you add a component from inside the IDE. If you add the component from the command line by recompiling CMPLIB32.CCL, you need to update the Library path statement yourself. If you are using DLLs from inside a component, make sure the DLL is in a directory that is on your global DOS/Windows path. For instance, you might consider putting it in the Windows or Windows/System directory.

> **NOTE**
>
> The question of whether to call a C module used in a BCB program a unit or a module is something of an open matter in BCB. My inclination is to call it a module, because that is traditional C usage, but BCB seems to refer to them as units. To be utterly frank, this is the kind of issue that doesn't really grip me all that deeply. In particular, I'm sure you will have no trouble understanding me regardless of which term I use. As a result, you will hear me referring to C modules as either modules or units, depending more on whim than on any clearly defined practice.

Working in the IDE

Here are some tips for working inside the IDE. I'll make this section brief, because I don't want to waste time on issues like this in a book that is clearly aimed at experienced programmers. However, this is a new environment, so it might help to share a few tips.

Whatever you do, be sure that you understand that this tool is meant to be used from inside its IDE. This is not a command-line environment!

> **NOTE**
>
> I'm sure that most programmers who investigate the matter will see that the command-line approach makes no sense with BCB. If that sentence strikes a sour note with you, all I ask is that you don't develop contempt prior to investigation. In my opinion, this IDE has something so powerful to offer that it finally makes command-line programming obsolete. With

BC5, and even with MSVC, I usually worked from the command line. I was one of the last of the hardcore C++ command-line junkies. With BCB, however, I have changed my ways. I'm totally sold on this environment, and would never consider going back to the command line except for a few rare situations.

Tips on Manipulating Controls

Here are a few tips for using the visual tools. If you are new to the environment, you should boot up BCB and follow along when reading these time-saving tips.

When dropping controls on a form, do the following:

■ Use the Control key plus the arrow keys to move the location of a component one pixel at a time. In particular, drop a component such as a button on a form. Select it with the mouse. Hold down the Control key and press the left arrow key.

■ Repeat the previous steps, only this time use Shift plus the arrow keys to resize a component one pixel at a time.

■ Hold down the Shift key when selecting a component from the Component Palette if you want to drop multiple copies of it on a form without having to go back to the palette. Click the "arrow" icon at the far left of the Component Palette to break out of this process.

■ Become familiar with the Align and Size options from the Edit menu. Quickly drop down five buttons on a form, each one below the last, without taking the time to carefully align their right and left sides. Hold down the Shift key, then select the five buttons with the mouse by clicking on each one. Now use the Align dialog from the Edit menu to align the tops or sides of all the selected controls.

■ A second technique for selecting a large group of components is to click on the main form and hold down the left mouse button while dragging over several components. When you let up the mouse, you will find the components are selected. If the components you want to select are resting on top of another control such as a panel, then you will need to hold the control button down before and during the process of dragging the mouse.

■ When designing a form, make it as large as you want. Then, when you have everything in place, use the Scale option from the Edit menu to make your form as small as you want, while still keeping each item on the form in proportion.

■ Right-click a component, as shown in Figure 2.4, to bring up a menu that lets you change the size, alignment, tab order, scaling, or creation order.

FIGURE 2.4.

Right-clicking a TTable
*object to bring up a list
of custom options.*

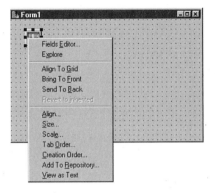

Making the Most of the IDE

Here are some tips on using the IDE:

- Right-click almost anything in the IDE to bring up a menu to configure the component or tool you are currently using. For instance, right-click the colorful toolbar at the top left of the environment. Select Properties from the popup menu to bring up the Toolbar editor. Now drag a colorful button from the toolbar onto the Toolbar editor and grab another button from the ToolBar editor and drag it back onto the toolbar. I sometimes delete the Trace, Trace Into, and Pause buttons from the extreme right of the toolbar and replace them with Copy, Cut, and Paste buttons or with compiler buttons such as Make, Build All, and Compile Unit.

- Notice that you can view the Project Source and Project Makefile from the View menu. The project source contains the WinMain() or main() block for your code. You rarely will need to edit this code. Its contents are usually configurable from the Options | Project menu. For instance, you can change the code in the Project Source from Forms page of the Options | Project menu.

- Check out the Project Manager, which is also available from the View menu.

- You can lock the controls on a form by selecting the Lock Controls option from the Edit menu. If you have spent some time working on a form and want to be sure that it does not accidentally get changed, select Lock Controls, and it will not be possible to move the controls on that form, or any other, until you deselect this option.

- If you want to set the text on the editor page to read only, right-click the editor page and select Read Only.

- Watch out for the AutoScroll property of a form. This is set to true by default, but it can bite back if you leave it set to true and then move your form to a different resolution. For instance, if you move from 640×480 to 800×600, you generally should not have AutoScroll set to true, especially if your form is populated with a large number of controls.

- Use the `Position` property of a form to decide whether the form should first appear in the screen center, at the place where you positioned it at design time, or at a default location defined by Windows.

- Use the `WindowState` property of a form to decide if the form should first be shown minimized, maximized, or at normal size.

- Before releasing a project to the public, check out its appearance in at least three different resolutions and make sure at least one of them toggles the font from Small Fonts to Big Fonts, or vice versa. (You can change Windows' resolution by right-clicking the desktop, selecting Properties, and going to the settings page. Make sure you change between Big Fonts and Small Fonts during your testing!)

Project Options

Other than the path-related issues covered in the last section, there are only a few options that you need to know about when programming BCB. The rest of the setup-related issues are handled for you automatically by the environment.

All the options you choose in the Project and Environment dialogs are written to the Registry. If you want to write custom programs that change these settings, you can learn how to proceed by reading the sections on the Registry in Chapter 13, "Flat-File, Real-World Databases."

The Options | Project menu has six pages in it:

Forms: This page is discussed in depth later in the chapter when I discuss the Project Source file for the ShapeDem program in the section called "Creating Forms." The core functionality on this page addresses the question of which unit will be the main module for your application—that is, which will come up first when you start the program. A secondary issue addressed in this page is whether a form will have memory allocated for it automatically at startup, or whether you want to create it explicitly at some point during your application's runtime. Forms listed in the left-hand list box shown on this form are created automatically; those on the right-hand list box must be created explicitly by the developer. The following code will create a form, show it to the user, and delete it:

```
Form2 = new TForm2(this);
Form2->ShowModal();
delete Form2;
```

This code would not work unless the header for Form2 was included in the module that wanted to call the code quoted here:

```
#include "unit2.h"
```

Application: This is where you can set up the icon or help file for your project. This is an intuitive process; click Help in the dialog if you have questions.

C++: This is where you can set the Debug and Release compiler options. You can also do a small amount of fine-tuning here, but this book hardly ever steps beyond recommending that you use the Debug option in development and the Release version when you ship. I almost never have occasion to do more than choose the simple binary Debug or Release option, except for occasionally toggling the precompiled headers option.

Pascal: Here is where Pascal aficionados can fine-tune their code. I would recommend leaving all these options untouched unless you have a specific reason to change them. If you want to get involved in this page, the first level of advice is to turn Range and Stack checking on only during debug cycles, and to turn Optimizations on only when you ship.

Linker: This is where you can decide to produce a Windows or console application, an EXE, or a DLL. This is also the place where you can toggle the incremental linker on and off. In development, you probably want the incremental linker on to speed compilation; when you ship, you should test the size of your executables when it is off and when it is on, and ship the smallest version.

Directories / Conditionals: The key features of this page were covered earlier in this chapter. Note that this is also where you can define conditionals. The whole subject of unit aliases is an Object Pascal–specific issue that enables you to create an alias for the name of a unit. For instance, the 16-bit version of Delphi kept all the Windows API calls in a unit called `WinProcs.pas`, and all the Windows types in a unit called `WinTypes.pas`. When the big segment sizes of 32-bit Windows became available, the two units were consolidated into one called `Windows.pas`. To remove the burden of having to change the uses (`#include`) statements in a Pascal file, the developers enabled you to create aliases. The most common alias told the compiler to use `Windows.pas` whenever it saw a request to include the `WinTypes` or `WinProcs` units.

As you can see, I don't put a lot of weight on fine-tuning the settings for your project. If you flip through these pages and see the small number of options available, you can see that the developers were not very concerned about this issue either. One of the major goals of BCB is to make C++ once again a mainstream language. The programming world used to be much simpler than it is today. Now we are all expected to know about OLE, MAPI, the Internet, multimedia, or other cutting-edge technologies. I invest my time in learning these valuable new technologies, and ask little more of my compiler than that it link quickly and easily and automatically produce small, tight code.

Environment Options

There are six pages in the Options | Environment menu choice. I play with many of these options all the time because they do nothing more than tweak the appearance or feel of the IDE. You aren't going to accidentally mess up the link process in your program or add 500KB to the size of an executable by tweaking one of these options. Feel free to set them as you please. Following is a list of the options I often play with during development.

There are some choices that are listed in both the Environment Options pages and the Project Options pages. If you make a change in the Project pages, you are changing an option for just that one project, while if you make the change in the Environment page, you are changing things globally for the entire environment. Local options always override global options.

Preferences: In the preferences page I always set Show Compiler Progress to true so that I can tell how far along I am in the compile cycle. I set AutoSave to true for Desktop files so that the environment will remember which project I was working on and which files I had open in the IDE. I also frequently tweak Break On Exception, depending on whether or not I want to catch problems in my code (turn it on) or just test to see if exceptions are popping up as expected at runtime (turn it off). This is also where you can turn integrated debugging on and off and change the path, as described above in the section on setting the project path.

Library: This is where you can set the path for `include` and `lib` files, as described previously. You can also globally decide for all projects whether or not to use the incremental linker. If you are adding components to the Component Palette, you should set Save Library source code to true so that you can build the Component Palette from the command line to save time or to repair a damaged Component library.

Editor: I discuss this page in a later section called "Feeling at Home in the IDE." It is here you can customize the behavior of the editor. All the major third-party editors (CodeWright, SlickEdit, MultiEdit) have some customizations for BCB, but none of them can get into the environment to the degree to which you, I, and they would like. Hopefully, improvements will come in this area in later releases.

Display: I discuss this page in a later section called "Feeling at Home in the IDE." It is here you can choose the keystroke emulation and font for the editor.

Colors: I discuss this page in a later section called "Feeling at Home in the IDE." It is here you can customize the colors of the editor. It particular, it enables you to switch between different color schemes or customize the colors for each element in the language, such as string, identifiers, integers, and so on. Like all the settings mentioned in these pages, the results of your decisions are written to the Registry. The Address2 program from Chapter 13 shows how you could write custom programs that tweak the Registry. For instance, you could write a program that automatically switched between four or five additional color schemes.

Palette: If you want to change the order in which components appear in the Component Palette, this is the place to make your changes. You can also reach this page by right-clicking the Component Palette and choosing Properties. It is pretty hard to do any serious damage to the environment using this page, but if you feel you need help, just press the Help button on the dialog itself.

2

BASIC FACTS ABOUT C++BUILDER

As you can see, most of the options on these pages address only aesthetic or habit-based preferences regarding how the IDE works. From a development point of view, the key issues involve incremental linking, paths, and saving the source for the Component Palette. Make sure you understand those important issues before moving on to the next topic of discussion.

Feeling at Home in the IDE

To help make the IDE comfortable, you might go to the Options | Environment | Editor page, shown in Figure 2.5.

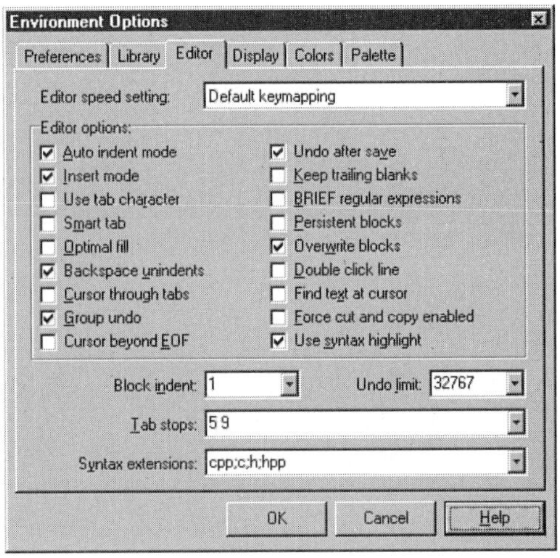

FIGURE 2.5.

The Options menu gives you access to the Environments dialog where you find the Editor page.

From the Editor page you can make the following changes:

- Turn the Use tab character option on or off, depending on your liking. (I prefer to turn it off, so I always know exactly what my code will look like regardless of the editor or tab settings I happen to use.)

- Decide what tab stops you want to use. I set mine to 3 and 5.

- Choose the Editor speed setting you want. You can choose between the Default keymapping, IDE Classic, Brief, or Epsilon emulations.

- Go to the Colors page and set the colors you want to use in the editor.

- Consider setting Undo after save to true so that you can keep a buffer of changes you make, even after you save.

- There are third-party tools such as SlickEdit, MultiEdit, and CodeWright that have some degree of integration with C++Builder. However, none of these products is able to work as closely with the IDE as one would like, due to limitations in the current Tools API for BCB.

Converting Forms to Text and Back

Everything you can do in BCB through the visual tools you can also do in code. The visual tools are just a means of expediting the programming process. They do not supplant code, they complement it. This is what the Borland marketing department means when they talk about "two way tools." The are two different ways to approach some parts of a BCB project: in code or by using the RAD tools.

If you right-click a form, you can select the View as Text menu item to convert a form to text. To convert back, just right-click the text version of the form.

BCB also ships with a command-line utility called Convert that will convert DFM files to text, or text to DFM files. At the command line type either

```
convert MyForm.dfm
```

or

```
convert MyForm.txt
```

The first example converts a binary form to a text form with the extension TXT, and the second example reverses the process.

If you have 4DOS on your system, you can use the following command to convert all the DFM files in a branch of subdirectories from DFM to text files:

```
global /I convert *.dfm
```

This command will iterate through all the subdirectories below your current position and convert all the files in those directories to text. If you are concerned about archiving files, this is a good way to proceed. In particular, a text file is a much more robust storage medium than a binary file. If you lose one byte of a binary file, it may become worthless. Losing one byte from a text file rarely causes any serious mischief.

If you have one form and want to paste all or part of it into a second form, you can select multiple objects from the first form, choose Edit | Copy, focus the second form, and then paste the selections from the first form into it. If you want, you can have an intermediate step where you paste the items from the first form into a text editor such as Notepad, edit them, and then paste them onto a form.

NOTE

If you are a Delphi programmer and want to port a form from Delphi to BCB, you might consider using the technique outlined in the last paragraph as a way to proceed. Of course, you can compile your Delphi forms directly in BCB, but if you want to port them, just cutting and pasting to the clipboard is a good way to proceed.

Here is a what a BCB button looks like in text form:

```
object Button1: TButton
  Left = 96
  Top = 16
  Width = 75
  Height = 25
  Caption = 'Button1'
  TabOrder = 0
end
```

To get this code, I Alt+Tabbed out of my word processor over to BCB, selected a button on a form, and chose Edit | Copy from the menu. I then Alt+Tabbed back to my word processor, and chose Edit | Paste. During the process the Windows button was automatically converted to text.

Here is a second version of the button code that has been slightly modified:

```
object MyButton: TButton
  Left = 1
  Top = 16
  Width = 75
  Height = 25
  Caption = 'My Button'
  TabOrder = 0
end
```

As you can see, I have changed the name of the button from `Button1` to `MyButton`, and I have changed the `Caption` and `Left` properties. Now I can select this text in my word processor, Alt+Tab over to BCB, select and form, and choose Edit | Paste to paste it back into the form. However, this time it has a new name, a new location, and new caption.

This is what is meant by a two-way tool. I can edit the form using the visual tools, or I can edit it in a word processor. It works in two different ways, depending on my current needs.

> **NOTE**
>
> When working with forms, remember that the currently selected component will be the target for a Paste operation. For instance, if I have selected a TButton object, and I chose Paste, BCB will attempt to make the control currently in the clipboard into a child of the button. In most cases, this is not what I want. Instead, I should first select a form or a panel, and then paste the controls onto that object. You also want to make sure the object you are pasting into is big enough to receive the control or controls you are about to dump from the Clipboard.

You have now made it through the first section of this chapter. In the next section I am going to switch my approach from a "hot tips" format to a more discursive style. If you want more information of the type you have seen so far in this chapter, you should look in the online help or pick up a book aimed at introductory BCB programming issues. Everyone has to know the kind of information I have been ladling out in the last few pages, and indeed it is vital information, but it is not the subject matter of this book. I have included this much only because I feel many of the issues addressed here are not immediately obvious when you first open BCB, and yet you absolutely have to know these facts in order to get any serious work done in the environment.

Core Technology: Components, Properties, Delegation

Many people are confused about Borland C++Builder. They are not used to the idea of having a RAD tool that works with C++, and they don't know quite what to make of it when they see it.

Some people think they are seeing a code generator; others think this is a visual tool meant for programmers who don't want to write code. Some people think they have found a great tool for building databases, and others a tool for prototyping applications.

There is some truth to all of these ideas, yet they all miss the mark if your aim is to find the essence of Borland C++. The core pieces of the technology are threefold:

- Right up front you have components and properties.
- Buried a little deeper you have the delegation model, which involves events and method pointers.
- Tying the whole picture together are exceptions and a very sophisticated RTTI system located in a file called `TYPINFO.HPP`. Most programmers rarely have to deal with this side of the product, but it is part and parcel of what makes the tool possible in its current form.

These are things that lie at the core of C++Builder. Don't let anyone else lead you astray with tales about prototyping or about BCB being a replacement for PowerBuilder. This tool may in fact perform those roles at times, but that's not what it is all about.

> **NOTE**
>
> It may be that from a commercial perspective the majority of programmers will find the database support to be the most valuable aspect of this tool. Indeed, I spend a large portion of this book covering that subject. However, the emphasis on databases is market-driven, while the technological core of the product lies elsewhere.

To get at the heart of BCB, you have to understand components, you have to understand the delegation model, and you have to understand RTTI. In particular, the first two points are essential to an understanding of how this product works, while the third helps you understand why it works.

You have, no doubt, either already noticed or have heard talk about the fact that BCB has some proprietary extensions to C++. These extensions are there to support the creation and use of components as well as the associated concepts of properties and events that make components so powerful.

There was no way to create a product like BCB without extending C++ to support components, properties, and the delegation model. This is a better way to program, and there is no force in the world that can suppress it. I have no problem at all asserting that in five years time, all compilers will support these features and most programmers will use them by two years from now (1999).

Let me say it one more time, because this is so crucially important: What's key is the component model, and its reliance on properties and events. *Components, properties, the delegation model.* Those are the things that stand at the heart of this technology. The three tools make it easy to build databases or multimedia applications. To say that the tool is primarily about building games or databases or Web sites is putting the cart before the horse. The tool is primarily about components, properties, and the delegation model. The other strengths of the tool fall out more or less automatically once the ground work has been laid.

Why the VCL?

Now that you know something about the environment in which BCB exists, it's time to dig a little deeper and start examining the VCL object model used by BCB. The VCL (Visual Component Library) is an object-oriented library designed to ease the process of creating visual components.

> **NOTE**
>
> When I say that BCB uses the VCL, I mean for the phrase to be taken in at least two distinct ways. BCB uses the VCL in the sense that the physical IDE is literally built into VCL, and also in the sense that we, as BCB programmers, use the VCL as the object model of choice when creating applications. Borland is not asking you to do anything they wouldn't do. Delphi is built into the VCL. BCB is built into the VCL, and much of Latte, the new Java product, is built into the VCL. The VCL is the tool of choice for people who have a choice.

Many C++ programmers who come to C++Builder find themselves wondering why the VCL exists in the first place. What was wrong with OWL or with MFC? Why should there be yet another object framework?

The simple answer is that visual programming, RAD, needed a whole new framework with new features. RAD relied on new concepts such as event handlers, properties, property editors, components, component editors, experts, forms, and a slew of other features. The language that implemented these new syntactical elements also desperately needed improvements in the areas of streaming, string handling, object initialization, and referencing.

These features simply were not available in either the C++ or Object Pascal versions of OWL. As a result, a new framework was created that supported these features; it is called the VCL, or Visual Component Library. The name goes a long way toward explaining why OWL could never do this job correctly. This is an object-oriented library built around visual components, and visual components do not have even the most oblique reference anywhere in OWL or MFC. They are a completely new entity and required their own object-oriented framework.

Having said that, I should add that VCL is closely related to OWL, just as the current version of OWL is closely related to the 16-bit version of OWL from which it grew. If you know OWL, you will find much in VCL that is familiar. Indeed, even MFC is a good background for understanding VCL. However, this is a fundamentally different kind of beast, one that is built around a new concept called a visual component.

NOTE

I am aware, of course, that ActiveX is another specification for building visual components. The difference between ActiveX and the VCL is that the VCL is specifically designed to be used with advanced programming languages such as C++ or Object Pascal. ActiveX was designed to be used in a broader context featuring a wide variety of languages and operating systems. ActiveX is more powerful than VCL, but it is also much bigger, much more complex, and slower.

Come on Charlie, Tell Us What You Really Think!

To conclude this brief introduction to the long discussion of the VCL found in this chapter, I feel it is important to explicitly state that I am aware that many hardcore C++ programmers will not automatically greet the VCL and its occasional bits of nonstandard C++ syntax with open arms. When writing this chapter, I am conscious of the need both to explain the VCL and also explain exactly why the VCL exists.

I want to make it absolutely clear that I am one hundred and ten percent committed to the VCL, and have absolutely no doubt that it represents the correct model for programming at this point in the ongoing development of programming tools and languages. I will occasionally make statements that explicitly justify some part of the VCL in the face of possible criticisms. These statements do not in any sense represent doubts in my own mind about the VCL. I prefer the VCL to OWL or MFC, and I am absolutely certain that all of the extensions to the C++ language that it introduces are necessary and represent significant advances for the language.

I am aware that some readers have large quantities of legacy OWL and MFC code that they want to preserve. I do not take those needs lightly and feel it is my obligation to state explicitly why changes have been made to the C++ object model.

BCB enables you to use MFC and OWL code, but the only reason this feature exists is to support legacy code. I personally do not think either MFC or OWL is the best choice any longer for large programming projects. The introduction of the component, property, delegation model offers such vast improvements in our ability to write code, that I don't think it's advisable to use OWL or MFC simply because of the poignant weight of all that legacy code. This is not a criticism of these two excellent object frameworks. The point is simply that they do not support components, properties, or events, and without that support they don't meet my current needs. I simply cannot imagine that anyone else who works with BCB for any significant length of time could possibly come to any other conclusion.

I am aware, however, that this is a controversial subject. Over the last four years I have been using the VCL almost every day. Most of that experience is on the Delphi side, but I have also been using BCB every day for about five months at the time of this writing. During the last four years, I have had many occasions to also use MFC and OWL. After my first six months with the VCL, there was never one single time that I went back to MFC or OWL without the feeling that I was using a much loved but outdated system that lacked fundamental features that have become a necessary part of what I believe to be the best contemporary programming model. This doesn't mean that I won't use OWL or MFC if it has an existing object in it that I find appealing, but only that I prefer to use the VCL if that is an option. Indeed, in most cases, the VCL provides for all my needs.

If a language or programming model does not support properties, components, and delegation, I personally find it lacking, no matter how many other fine features it may present to the user. VCL is the right way to go, and it would be absurd to read my occasional arguments on its behalf as representative of doubts in my own mind about this programming model.

In a sense, my job would be easier if the VCL were harder to use. It was very frustrating for me to realize that I had to start leaving behind all that detailed knowledge about OWL in order to use a system that was so much simpler to use. Wasn't there something that the VCL was missing? Didn't there have to be a catch? How could the solution to so many long-term problems turn out to be so simple?

Well, I believe that there isn't a catch, and that the VCL does everything that OWL or MFC did, but does it better. Of course, OWL and VCL have tremendous depth in terms of the number of objects in the existing hierarchy, which is one reason why BCB supports them. You will find, however, the VCL has great depth itself, and that it supports all the features, if not all the objects, found in MFC and OWL. In other words, if you find that a particular object you used in OWL is not part of VCL, you could either use the existing object or create a new one that does the same thing in the VCL. The VCL supports all the features of OWL, but may not at this time have duplicates of all its objects. Furthermore, there is tremendous existing third-party support for the VCL that helps fill in some of the gaps.

For good measure, the VCL adds some new tricks regarding components, properties, and events that can't be found in either OWL or MFC. The kicker, of course, is that the VCL produces code that is at least as fast and small as OWL or MFC, but it is literally about ten times easier to use.

Let me give it to you straight. Back in the old days I loved OWL and thought it was the greatest thing I had ever seen. I used it all the time and was a fanatical adherent of that programming model. I now use VCL for everything, and go back to OWL or MFC only when I absolutely must. To my eyes, the support for components, properties, and events makes VCL clearly better than OWL or MFC in the same sense that OWL was clearly better than structured programming. If you love OWL, it is sad to hear this kind of thing, but components, properties, and events simply bring something new to the table that OWL and MFC simply can't emulate.

It is hard to accept the rate at which programming languages are evolving at this time. The burden this places on programmers is immense. The size of this burden is one of the key reasons I advocate, again and again, doing things the simplest, easiest, safest way. You have enough to worry about without trying to figure out the last picayune details of constantly changing standards!

The learning curve associated with the onrush of progress, our attachment to legacy code, a sentimental attachment to the ANSI committee (of all things!)—none of these represent a reason to stick with an outdated technology when a clear advancement in programming tools appears. I obviously have a involvement with Object Pascal. But I am also a long-term (10 years) C++ programmer, and I know about the deep attachment we all feel to the rules of this language, and I know what a huge improvement OWL and MFC represent over structured programming. However, things have changed again, and personally, I love it! VCL is wonderful. I never waste two seconds thinking about going back to the old way of doing things.

NOTE

One final note on this subject ought to go out to readers of my *Teach Yourself Windows* and *Teach Yourself Windows 95 Programming* books. Those books talk about straight C Windows API programming (*a la* Petzold) without the aid of any object framework. I do not believe there is anything in this book that makes the material in those books obsolete.

To be a good Windows programmer you still have to know the Windows API, and you still have to know about message loops and window procedures. Indeed, in *Delphi 2 Unleashed,* I went on for several hundred pages about material of that sort. I do not include any of that kind of material in this book because there are many C++ programming books that cover that material. (There were not any, as far as I knew, Pascal books that covered that material, which is why I included it in *Delphi 2 Unleashed.*)

Needless to say, I think you ought to use the VCL to write contemporary Windows programs. However, if you also know the Windows API, you can become a great VCL programmer. If you don't know the Windows API, you will always be at a loss when using some features of the VCL, at least until such time as Windows becomes a true object-oriented operating system.

Do you have to know OWL or MFC to become a great VCL programmer? No. Do you have to know the Windows API in order become a great VCL programmer? Absolutely! The Windows API material found in my *Teach Yourself...* books has a very long life from a technical, if not a commercial, point of view. Assuming that Java does not take over the world, a knowledge of the Windows API is always invaluable to a contemporary programmer.

Remember, however, that even the glorious VCL has a shadow over it, in the form of Java. I never get too bogged down in the details of the VCL or any other framework, because I never know when this rapidly changing programming world is going to enter another period of mind-numbing change in which the slow ones get left behind!

The Windows API is the only really complex programming paradigm that is worth learning in depth, because all the others are likely to change over time. The fact that the VCL is easy to use is not just a nice feature, it's a necessity in this contemporary programming world where the only constant is change. I should perhaps add that the reason you use the VCL instead of the raw Windows API is because you get your work done in about one-tenth the time. If you use OWL or MFC, your code will be much bigger than if you use raw Windows API code, but you will also have a better chance of getting your work done on time. If you want another four- or five-fold increase in productivity, use the VCL.

Using the VCL

Now that you have heard an advertisement for the VCL, it might help to provide a few more basic examples illustrating some of the virtues of this programming system. These are very simple examples that are a bit atypical of the type of code you will see in this book, or even in the latter portions of this chapter. I feel, however, that these basic examples are useful when illustrating some of the key features of RAD programming with the VCL. Their presence ensures that everyone understands the benefits of visual programming with the VCL.

I will, however, use these basic examples to explore some fairly complex aspects of the VCL, and especially of the code that executes just before and after the main form of your application is made visible. In particular, I will look at the code in the project source file for a typical BCB application that uses the VCL.

The first program I want to discuss uses a standard Delphi component called TShape. If you open up BCB and drop the TShape component on a form, you will see that it draws a simple white rectangle on the screen.

Of course, the TShape object can perform more than this one simple trick. For instance, if you pull down the list associated with the Shape property in the Object Inspector, you see that you can easily work with ellipses, circles, squares, and other assorted shapes. Furthermore, if you expand the Brush property, you can change the shape's color. The Pen property enables you to change the width and color of the outline of a TShape object.

NOTE

Don't forget that you can expand properties that have a plus sign (+) next to them by double-clicking the property's name. A Color property always has a dialog associated with it. To bring up the dialog, double-click the area to the right of the Color property. This area is called the property editor. (Later in the book I will show how to create your own property editors and how to use existing property editors.) Select a color from the dialog, click the OK button, and the color you chose automatically takes effect.

As just described, it's trivial to change the major characteristics of a TShape object at design time. However, I spoke earlier about BCB supporting two-way tools. Anything that you do with the visual tools you can also do in code. It is, of course, a little more work to make the same changes at runtime that you made at design time, but the basic principles are still simple. The SHAPEDEM and SHAPEDEM2 programs on the CD that accompanies this book show you how to proceed.

NOTE

I try to avoid it, but you might find a few places in the sample programs where I hard-code in the path to a file. You will probably have to edit these paths to get the program to run on your system.

I go to a great deal of effort to ensure that the code that accompanies this book works correctly. If you are having trouble running any particular program, check the readme files found on the CD that accompanies this book. If you still can't get the program running, go to my Web site and see if there is an update, hint, or bug report available. My Web site is `users.aol.com/charliecal`.

At its core, the SHAPEDEM program consists of nothing more than a TShape object placed on a form, along with two scroll bars and a menu. What's interesting about the program is the ease with which you can change the size, color, and shape of the TShape object at runtime.

You can find the code for the program in Listings 2.1 through 2.3. Remember that if you want to view the source for the project file in your application, you can select the View | Project Source menu item.

Listing 2.1. The code for SHAPEDEM.CPP.

```
#include <vcl.h>
#pragma hdrstop

USEFORM("Main.cpp", Form1);
USERES("ShapeDem.res");

WINAPI WinMain(HINSTANCE, HINSTANCE, LPSTR, int)
{
  Application->Initialize();
  Application->CreateForm(__classid(TForm1), &Form1);
  Application->Run();

  return 0;
}
```

Listing 2.2. The header for the main unit in SHAPEDEM.

```
#ifndef MainH
#define MainH
#include <Classes.hpp>
#include <Controls.hpp>
#include <StdCtrls.hpp>
#include <Forms.hpp>
#include <ExtCtrls.hpp>
```

```cpp
#include <Dialogs.hpp>
#include <Menus.hpp>

class TForm1 : public TForm
{
__published:
  TShape *Shape1;
  TScrollBar *ScrollBar1;
  TScrollBar *ScrollBar2;
  TColorDialog *ColorDialog1;
  TMainMenu *MainMenu1;
  TMenuItem *Shapes1;
  TMenuItem *ShapeColor1;
  TMenuItem *FormColor1;
  TMenuItem *Shapes2;
  TMenuItem *Rectangle1;
  TMenuItem *Square1;
  TMenuItem *RoundRect1;
  TMenuItem *RoundSquare1;
  TMenuItem *Ellipes1;
  TMenuItem *Circle1;
  void __fastcall ShapeColor1Click(TObject *Sender);
  void __fastcall FormColor1Click(TObject *Sender);
  void __fastcall Rectangle1Click(TObject *Sender);
  void __fastcall ScrollBar1Change(TObject *Sender);
  void __fastcall ScrollBar2Change(TObject *Sender);
  void __fastcall FormResize(TObject *Sender);
private:
public:
  virtual __fastcall TForm1(TComponent* Owner);
};

extern TForm1 *Form1;

#endif
```

Listing 2.3. The code for the main unit in SHAPEDEM.

```cpp
#include <vcl.h>
#pragma hdrstop
#include "Main.h"

#pragma resource "*.dfm"
TForm1 *Form1;

__fastcall TForm1::TForm1(TComponent* Owner)
  : TForm(Owner)
{
  Shape1->Left = 0;
  Shape1->Top = 0;
}

void __fastcall TForm1::ShapeColor1Click(TObject *Sender)
{
```

continues

Listing 2.3. continued

```cpp
  if (ColorDialog1->Execute())
    Shape1->Brush->Color = ColorDialog1->Color;
}

void __fastcall TForm1::FormColor1Click(TObject *Sender)
{
  if (ColorDialog1->Execute())
    Form1->Color = ColorDialog1->Color;
}

void __fastcall TForm1::Rectangle1Click(TObject *Sender)
{
  Shape1->Shape = TShapeType(dynamic_cast<TMenuItem*>(Sender)->Tag);
}

void __fastcall TForm1::ScrollBar1Change(TObject *Sender)
{
  Shape1->Width = ScrollBar1->Position;
}

void __fastcall TForm1::ScrollBar2Change(TObject *Sender)
{
  Shape1->Height = ScrollBar2->Position;
}

void __fastcall TForm1::FormResize(TObject *Sender)
{

  ScrollBar1->Max = ClientWidth - (ScrollBar2->Width + 1);
  ScrollBar2->Max = ClientHeight - (ScrollBar1->Height + 1);
  ScrollBar1->Left = 0;
  ScrollBar2->Top = 0;
  ScrollBar2->Left = ClientWidth - ScrollBar2->Width;
  ScrollBar2->Height = ClientHeight;
  ScrollBar1->Top = ClientHeight - ScrollBar1->Height;
  ScrollBar1->Width = ClientWidth - ScrollBar2->Width;
}
```

In the next few paragraphs, you'll hear a discussion of how to change the color of the form, the shape shown on the form, and the size and shape of the object itself.

When you run the SHAPEDEM program, it looks like the screen shot shown in Figure 2.6. Use the program's scrollbars to change the size of the figure in the middle of the screen. Use the menu to select a new shape for the object and to bring up a dialog that enables you to change the color of either the form or the shape.

FIGURE 2.6.

You can use the scrollbars and buttons to change the appearance of the SHAPEDEM program's form.

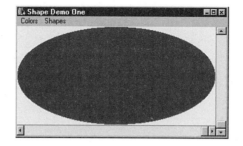

The Project Source: Where Pascal Meets the C

Before getting into any details about how the ShapeDem program works, it might be helpful to take one moment to look at the project source. You can access the project source from the View menu.

This is the place in the book I have chosen to give you a close look at how Borland blended its Pascal and C++ technology into one product. I will not show much Object Pascal code in this book, but you will see quite a bit in the next few pages.

At the top of the project source you see code that brings in the VCL:

```
#include <vcl/vcl.h>
#pragma hdrstop
```

In many programs, you will not have to add any other include statements to your program other than this one, except when you want to include other units from your current project, and even that can be automated through the File Include Unit Hdr menu option. That's not a hard and fast statement; I only mean to imply that you don't tend to spend a lot of time adding include statements unless you want to access obscure features of the Windows API. Many other include statements will be added to your header files, however, when you drop components down on a form.

The pragma statement shown here tells the compiler that you only want to have the VCL in your precompiled headers. Any additional files should be recompiled each time you do a build or a make. This is done for the sake of efficiency, because your own header files are likely to change on a regular basis.

The next few lines tell the project manager to bring in forms or resources:

```
USEFORM("Main.cpp", Form1);
USERES("ShapeDem.res");
```

You would not normally add this kind of code yourself, but would ask the visual tools to insert it for you. In this case, the tool you would use is the Project Manager from the View menu. However, you don't have to use the Project Manager; you can make this changes manually if you wish, and the Project Manager will pick up on your work.

Here is the `WinMain` block for your program:

```
WINAPI WinMain(HINSTANCE, HINSTANCE, LPSTR, int)
{
  Application->Initialize();
  Application->CreateForm(__classid(TForm1), &Form1);
  Application->Run();

  return 0;
}
```

As you can see, BCB assumes you won't be using any of the parameters passed to it. In particular, the VCL provides a global variable called `HInstance`, which provides the `HInstance` for your application. The `HPrevInstance` variable is never used in Win32 programming. Parameters passed to your program are available in the form of a VCL function called `ParamStr`, and a variable called `ParamCount`. To get at the name and path of your executable, access `ParamStr(0)`, to get at the first parameter passed to it, access `ParamStr(1)`, and so on. `ParamCount` contains the number of parameters passed to your executable. For instance, the following code pops up a message box showing the name and path of your executable:

```
void __fastcall TForm1::Open1Click(TObject *Sender)
{
  ShowMessage(ParamStr(0));
}
```

NOTE

Wary C++ programmers may be concerned about the fact that the VCL has gotten at the `HInstance` and program parameters before they reached `WinMain`. Don't worry, there is no huge subsystem underlying your entire program! However, a few things do happen before `WinMain` is called, just as a few things happen in all C++ compilers before `WinMain` is called.

This is a case where it might help to talk about how Object Pascal handles program startup. Object Pascal simply did not support `WinMain` on the grounds that it was faster and more convenient to perform processing of `HInstance` and the program parameters without setting up a stack frame for a function call. The Object Pascal system is faster and more efficient because you don't have to push things on the stack before calling a function named `WinMain`. On the other hand, the overhead of calling `WinMain` with four parameters is hardly significant in the face of the time it takes to load a contemporary Windows program into memory. Of course, BCB provides a `WinMain` for you so you will be able to compile standard C++ programs without modification.

The key point to notice here is that the VCL provides extra support for you without affecting the performance of your program and without changing the way that C++, or standard Windows programs, operate. This is the right way to handle the interface between C++ and Object Pascal. No changes to C++, no impact on performance, no changes to the standard Windows programming model, and yet additional features are provided for the programmer in terms of `ParamStr` and the global `HInstance`.

After getting to `WinMain`, the program uses the pre-initialized `Application` object to get your program up and running:

```
Application->Initialize();
Application->CreateForm(__classid(TForm1), &Form1);
Application->Run();
```

I will discuss each of these calls in their own sections of this chapter. Brace yourself, because I am going to step you through the Object Pascal code that underlies each of these calls.

Initializing the Application

The first call in `WinMain` performs some initialization:

```
Application->Initialize();
```

The two most important tasks performed by this code involve OLE and database code. If there is database programming in your application, the database code starts an object called `TSession`. If there is OLE code in your program, the program may call a method that updates the Registry automatically so that your program is a properly registered automation server. If the code uses neither technology, nothing happens in the call to initialize.

Here is the code for the `Initialize` method of `TApplication` as it appears in `Forms.pas`:

```
procedure TApplication.Initialize;
begin
  if InitProc <> nil then
    TProcedure(InitProc);
end;
```

If you want to step through this code, simply copy `Forms.pas`, `Controls.pas`, `Classes.pas`, and `VCL.INC` from the `BCB\SOURCE\VCL` subdirectory into your project directory and add `Forms.pas`, `Controls.pas`, and `Classes.pas` to your C++ project. To add the files, bring up the Project Manager from the View menu, click the plus button, and use the drop-down list from the Files of Type section to browse for files with a `.pas` extension. Next, select `Forms.pas`, `Classes.pas`, and `Controls.pas`, and close the Project Manager. This technique is probably preferable to bringing in the source to the whole VCL by adding the `CBuilder\SOURCE\VCL` to the include or library path for your project.

When you step through this Object Pascal code in the BCB integrated debugger, you will find that `InitProc` is never called, because it is set to `NULL` unless you bring in database code or OLE automation code. Needless, to say, it takes one line of assembly code to test for `NULL`, so there is no significant overhead involved here other than the call to the `Initialize` method itself.

Here is the code at the bottom of the `OLEAuto` unit that would initialize `InitProc` if you used `OLEAutomation` in your program:

```
initialization
begin
  OleInitialize(nil);
  VarDispProc := @VarDispInvoke;
```

```
  Automation := TAutomation.Create;
  SaveInitProc := InitProc;
  InitProc := @InitAutomation;
end;

finalization
begin
  Automation.Free;
  OleUninitialize;
end;

end.
```

This call starts by initializing OLE and then setting up a dispatch point for use when making calls into IDispatch. Next, it allocates memory for the Automation object, calls its constructor, and finally points InitProc at the proper method after saving the previous value of the function pointer. Of course, none of this code will be called unless you are using OLE Automation in your program through the routines found in the OleAuto unit.

Creating Forms

The second call in WinMain creates the MainForm for your application:

```
Application->CreateForm(__classid(TForm1), &Form1);
```

You already have the Forms unit linked into the project, so you can step into this code without any further work. However, if you want to get into more detail here, you can also add Classes.pas and Controls.pas to your project. However, there are very few users of the VCL who really need to know what happens in either controls or classes.

Here is the call to CreateForm:

```
procedure TApplication.CreateForm(InstanceClass: TComponentClass; var Reference);
var
  Instance: TComponent;
begin
  Instance := TComponent(InstanceClass.NewInstance);
  TComponent(Reference) := Instance;
  try
    Instance.Create(Self);
  except
    TComponent(Reference) := nil;
    raise;
  end;
  if (FMainForm = nil) and (Instance is TForm) then
  begin
    TForm(Instance).HandleNeeded;
    FMainForm := TForm(Instance);
  end;
end;
```

The vast majority of this code does nothing but initialize variables or check for errors.

The base VCL object is called `TObject`. All VCL objects descend from `TObject` by definition. It is impossible to create a VCL object that does not descend from `TObject`, because any object that does not descend from `TObject` is not part of the VCL. The call to `TObject.NewInstance` does nothing more than allocate memory for an object and return a pointer to it, as you can see from viewing this call in `System.pas`:

```
class function TObject.NewInstance:TObject;
asm
        PUSH    EDI
        PUSH    EAX
        MOV     EAX,[EAX].vtInstanceSize
        CALL    _GetMem
        MOV     EDI,EAX
        MOV     EDX,EAX
        POP     EAX
        STOSD                                   { Set VMT pointer }
        MOV     ECX,[EAX].vtInstanceSize        { Clear object }
        XOR     EAX,EAX
        PUSH    ECX
        SHR     ECX,2
        DEC     ECX
        REP     STOSD
        POP     ECX
        AND     ECX,3
        REP     STOSB
        MOV     EAX,EDX
        POP     EDI
end;
```

Needless to say, this is probably the only place you will ever see anyone allocate memory for an object by calling `NewInstance`. As a rule, the constructor for an object will call `NewInstance` automatically. Here is the standard code for creating an object:

```
TMyObject *MyObject = new TMyObject();
```

This will call `NewInstance` for you automatically, and it would be madness to proceed in any other fashion.

NOTE

`TObject.NewInstance` is what is called in Object Pascal a class method and what C++ implements as a static method. Class methods and static methods can be called without an object instance; that is, they can be called before you allocate memory for an object or call its constructor. Class methods could have been implemented as functions that are associated with a class, and indeed, there is no significant difference between a function associated with a class and a class method. However, it is syntactically useful from the user's point of view to include them in a class declaration, because it makes the association between the class and the method obvious. In other words, class methods are aesthetically

continues

continued

pleasing, and they help you create logical, easy-to-read code. Besides `NewInstance`, the following methods of `TObject` are all class methods: `ClassName`, `ClassNameIs`, `ClassParent`, `ClassInfo`, `InstanceSize`, `InheritsFrom`, `MethodAddress`, and `MethodName`.

These methods are segregated out of the BCB declaration for `TObject` and declared as a class with the somewhat intriguing name `TMetaClass`. This metaclass is a trick that allows C++ to get along with the VCL and its associated RTTI. `TMetaClass` plays no significant role in standard BCB programming and is designed primarily for the use of the compiler team itself. You may have occasion to use this metaclass when working with RTTI, but as a rule, it lies outside the realm of standard BCB programming. If you have the time and inclination to pursue this matter, the whole class is declared and implemented in `SYSDEFS.H`.

For instance, the `ClassType` method of `TObject` returns a variable of type `TClass`, and `TClass` is defined as a pointer to `TMetaClass`. You can use variables of this type to perform the same kinds of comparisons you would perform on standard C++ classes with `typeid`.

The most important call in `TApplication CreateForm` is to `Instance.Create(Self)`. It is the call that ends up calling the constructor for the main form, as well as calling the Windows API `CreateWindowEx` function. If you step into this code with the debugger, you will find that it ends up stepping right into the constructor for your main form:

```
__fastcall TForm1::TForm1(TComponent* Owner)
  : TForm(Owner)
{
}
```

The last few lines of code in the `CreateForm` method set the variable `FMainForm` to the current form if it has not already been assigned.

The main form for your application will be the one that appears first when someone launches your executable. As you can see from examining the code in `CreateForm`, the first object passed to `CreateForm` will be the main form for that application:

```
if (FMainForm = nil) and (Instance is TForm) then
begin
  TForm(Instance).HandleNeeded;
  FMainForm := TForm(Instance);
end;
```

Each project that you create can have zero, one, or more forms. You can add forms to a project from the File menu or from the File | New menu choice. If you add three forms to a project, this is what the project source looks like:

```
Application->Initialize();
Application->CreateForm(__classid(TForm1), &Form1);
Application->CreateForm(__classid(TForm2), &Form2);
Application->CreateForm(__classid(TForm3), &Form3);
Application->Run();
```

In this case, Form1 will be the main form for the application. If you change the order of these statements, another form could become the main form:

```
Application->Initialize();
Application->CreateForm(__classid(TForm3), &Form3);
Application->CreateForm(__classid(TForm1), &Form1);
Application->CreateForm(__classid(TForm2), &Form2);
Application->Run();
```

In the preceding code, Form3 is now the main form for the application.

Normally, I do not edit the project source for my application directly. Instead, I go to the Options | Project menu item and use the Forms page from the Project Options dialog to make these kinds of changes. Once again, this is a two-way tool, and you can do things visually via the Project Options dialog or you can do things manually in code. It's up to you to make the decision.

Calling Run: Finding the Message Loop

The last call in WinMain is to the Run method:

```
Application->Run();
```

TApplication.Run does a few initialization chores, and then calls a method called HandleMessage that in turn calls ProcessMessage:

```
function TApplication.ProcessMessage: Boolean;
var
  Handled: Boolean;
  Msg: TMsg;
begin
  Result := False;
  if PeekMessage(Msg, 0, 0, 0, PM_REMOVE) then
  begin
    Result := True;
    if Msg.Message <> WM_QUIT then
    begin
      Handled := False;
      if Assigned(FOnMessage) then FOnMessage(Msg, Handled);
      if not IsHintMsg(Msg) and not Handled and not IsMDIMsg(Msg) and
        not IsKeyMsg(Msg) and not IsDlgMsg(Msg) then
      begin
        TranslateMessage(Msg);
        DispatchMessage(Msg);
      end;
    end
    else
      FTerminate := True;
  end;
end;
```

This is the standard message loop that lies at the bottom of all Windows applications. As you can see, it calls TranslateMessage and DispatchMessage just like every other message loop in every other Windows application.

The HandleMessage routine that calls ProcessMessage also ends up calling a method named Idle. If you hook the OnIdle handler to TApplication, you can get a chance to perform background tasks while your application is running. It is generally not a good idea to respond to OnIdle events unless you are absolutely positive you know what you are doing. On the other hand, I would not suggest starting up a second PeekMessage loop in your application, so if you have to do background processing, I would indeed do it in response to OnIdle.

You now know what happens when a VCL application is first launched. I've shown it to you in such depth for two reasons:

- You need to know this information if you are going to use BCB for serious work. You have to understand how your application is launched, where the message loop is, and how forms are allocated.

- There has to be some time when you actually see the place where C++ and Object Pascal meet. So now you've seen it. The point I hope you take home from this is that there just plain isn't any real difference between C++ and Object Pascal. There may be a difference between ANSI C and ANSI Pascal, but C++ and Object Pascal are the same. Certainly there is no significant difference in the way the two languages perform or in the capabilities of the two languages. It should also now be obvious that the compiler just doesn't care which language you use. I mix and match C++ and Object Pascal all the time. I know both languages well enough so half the time I am not even conscious of which language I'm using. You can find a language bigot on every street corner. What's rare is to find someone who can look beneath the surface and see that at bottom the two languages are virtually identical. The differences are almost all superficial, and they tend to cancel each other out. C++ does some things better than Object Pascal, and Object Pascal does some things better than C++. Who cares? The point is they are both great languages. Now you can use them both together without penalty, so you can take the best from both worlds.

Creating the ShapeDem Program

It's time now to come back to the original purpose of this section of the chapter, which is to examine the ShapeDem program. To create the program yourself, start by dropping down a TMainMenu and a TColorDialog. The TColorDialog is found on the Dialogs page of the Component Palette, while the TMenu is on the Standards page. Now create a menu heading called Options and beneath it two menu items with captions that read Shape Color and Form Color.

> **NOTE**
>
> I briefly introduced using the Menu Designer in Chapter 1. Remember that you can get help on most (in a perfect world it would be all) BCB components, code elements, or tools by selecting the item in question and pressing F1.

After closing the menu designer, double-click the menu item you made called `Form Color` to create a method in the editor that looks like this:

```
void __fastcall TForm1::FormColor1Click(TObject *Sender)
{
  if (ColorDialog1->Execute())
    Form1->Color = ColorDialog1->Color;
}
```

When you run the program, the code shown here pops up the `ColorDialog`, as shown in Figure 2.7.

FIGURE 2.7.

The Color Dialog gives the user an easy way to select a valid color at runtime.

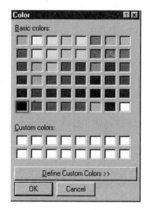

If the user clicks the OK button in the form, the following line of code is executed:

```
Form1->Color = ColorDialog1->Color;
```

This line of code sets the `Color` property for `Form1` to the color that was selected by the user inside of `ColorDialog1`.

The technique just shown can be used to change the color of the `TShape` object. All you need to do is drop down a `TShape` object from the additional page, and then associate some code with the Shape Color menu item:

```
void __fastcall TForm1::ShapeColor1Click(TObject *Sender)
{
  if (ColorDialog1->Execute())
    Shape1->Brush->Color = ColorDialog1->Color;
}
```

What could be simpler?

You should now run the SHAPEDEM program so that you can see how easy it is to change the color of the elements on the form. Of course, you don't have to give the user the exclusive right to control all the elements of your program. Sometimes you can take the initiative. For instance, you could change the color of your form or of an element on your form in order to focus the user's attention on a particular part of the screen.

Notice that the code written here is all but self-documenting. Anyone with even the slightest acquaintance with programming can just glance at this procedure and determine what it does. Assuming you have more than a passing acquaintance with programming, here is how to translate the code into English: "If the user clicks on a visual element on Form1 that is called ShapeColor1, that visual element will delegate an activity to Form1. That activity consists of popping up a color dialog and asking the user to make a selection. If the user chooses the OK button, the color of Shape1 is set to the color selected in the TColorDialog object."

What do I mean when I say that the ShapeColor menu item "delegates" an activity to Form1? Well, this means that the ShapeColor TMenuItem object does not itself handle being clicked, but instead allows the form to decide what happens when someone clicks it. It delegates the job to the main form.

The delegation model works through events, which are listed in the Object Inspector on the page sitting next to the properties for an object. Some people call events closures, though I regard that as a very technical term with certain platform-specific ramifications that I have never fully explored. As a result, I will usually play it safe and call events nothing more than events and leave it at that. The delegation model is implemented through events, and events are explored in depth in Chapter 3, "Events," and Chapter 4, "Exceptions."

In the beginning, it is probably simplest to think of events as being similar to standard Windows messages, such as WM_CREATE, WM_COMMAND, or WM_VSCROLL. Indeed, handling standard Windows messages is one of the functions of events. However, you will see that events can also delegate to another control tasks that you usually could not handle unless you subclassed a component such as an edit control, or else descended from an object that wrapped a control, as you would in OWL or MFC.

Perhaps an acceptable first crack at defining events would be to say that: "Events allow you to delegate tasks from one component to another component so that you do not have to subclass the first component, nor respond inside a window procedure to messages that the first control generates. In particular, events are usually delegated by the controls on a form to the form itself."

The advantages of the delegation model are threefold:

- They do not force you to subclass a control, nor inherit from a class in order to override one of its properties. For instance, you can change an edit control's behavior without subclassing the control or descending from an OWL or MFC type object that wraps the control.

- They enable you to forgo the ugly, lengthy, and confusing switch statement found in standard window procedures.

- It provides for contract-free programming. You can do whatever you want in an event handler. There are no rules binding what you can and cannot do inside an event handler. Any code you can write legally elsewhere in a program you can also write in an event handler.

It makes sense that it should not be very difficult to change the color of an object found on one of the forms you create. But using scrollbars to change its shape at least appears to be a more difficult task. In fact, experienced Windows programmers know that using scrollbars in a Windows program can be a fairly difficult task, one that requires you to trap and parse a number of messages in a complex switch statement. BCB, however, reduces the entire task of responding to a scrollbar to a single line of code.

To get started, first drop two scrollbars on the screen and set the Kind property of one of them to sbHorizontal, and the Kind property of the other to sbVertical. Now, turn to the events page of the Object Inspector and create a method for the OnChange event of each scrollbar. Fill in the methods with two lines of code so that they look like this:

```
void __fastcall TForm1::ScrollBar1Change(TObject *Sender)
{
  Shape1->Width = ScrollBar1->Position;
}

void __fastcall TForm1::ScrollBar2Change(TObject *Sender)
{
  Shape1->Height = ScrollBar2->Position;
}
```

The code shown here sets the Width and Height of the TShape object to the current position of the thumb on the scrollbar. Clearly it is extremely easy to write BCB code that performs a task, which would be relatively complex to execute if you had to work directly with the Windows API. The VCL always makes you feel as though you are working directly with an object, and tries to hide the complexities that are introduced by the Windows API or by standard object frameworks.

> **NOTE**
>
> Note in particular that you don't have to first set a property of a control and then ask it to redraw itself! This magic is the result of the set method associated with the Height property of Shape1. I will explore the Set and Get methods of properties later in this chapter.

You use the program's menu to change the shape of the TShape component. In particular, a portion of the main menu for the program should have the following items on it:

```
Rectangle1: TMenuItem
Tag = 0
Caption = 'Rectangle'
Square1: TMenuItem
Tag = 1
Caption = 'Square'
RoundRect1: TMenuItem
Tag = 2
Caption = 'RoundRect'
RoundSquare1: TMenuItem
Tag = 3
Caption = 'RoundSquare'
```

```
Ellipes1: TMenuItem
Tag = 4
Caption = 'Ellipse'
Circle1: TMenuItem
Tag = 5
Caption = 'Circle'
```

The Tag field is a special field associated with all components that can be set to an integer value. The VCL has no use for this field; it is designed explicitly for you to use as you wish, for whatever purpose you want.

All six menu items should be associated with the same event handler through their OnClick method. You can create the original handler by open up the Menu Designer, turning to the Events page in the Object Inspector, and double-clicking the OnChange event. If you then select the OnChange event for the other menu items, you will see that it opens up into a combo box from which you can select all the compatible events. For each of the other five menu items, select the event you created for the first menu item. The event itself should look like this:

```
void __fastcall TForm1::Rectangle1Click(TObject *Sender)
{
  Shape1->Shape = TShapeType(dynamic_cast<TMenuItem*>(Sender)->Tag);
}
```

I will explain what this code means over the course of the next few paragraphs.

> **NOTE**
>
> Just now I said that the events that appear in the drop-down combo for the Events page of the Object Inspector must be compatible with a particular event. This means that they must have the same signature, which is yet another term that needs explanation! The signature of an event is found in the header for the method handler associated with a particular event, and in particular it is represented by the parameters passed to the handler. For instance, the signature for the Rectangle1Click method is represented by the fact that it is a method that returns nothing and which accepts a single parameter of type TObject *. Methods that look like this are of type TNotifyEvent. Here is the declaration for TNotifyEvent as it appears in CLASSES.HPP:
>
> ```
> typedef void __fastcall (__closure *TNotifyEvent)(System::TObject* Sender);
> ```
>
> When you see this signature for an event, you can assume that Sender contains an instance of the object that sent the event. For instance, in the case currently under consideration, it is a TMenuItem that sent the event, and the specific TMenuItem that sent the message is passed in the Sender parameter.

The items in the menu designate each of the possible shapes the `TShape` component can assume. You can find these words listed in the online help under the listing for `TShapeType`. Or, if you want to go back to the original source code, you find the following enumerated type:

```
enum TShapeType { stRectangle, stSquare, stRoundRect,
                  stRoundSquare, stEllipse, stCircle }
```

> **NOTE**
>
> You can also access the names of the members of enumerated type by using the `GetEnumName` and `GetEnumValue` functions from the `TypInfo` unit, which is pronounced "tip-info."

In this particular case, you need to write only one line of code in response to the event that occurs when a user clicks a `TMenuItem`:

```
Shape1->Shape = TShapeType(dynamic_cast<TMenuItem*>(Sender)->Tag);
```

This line of code sets the `Shape1->Shape` property to the shape that the user has selected in the combo box. The code works because of the correspondence between the ordinal members of an enumerated type and the numerical value you assigned to the `tag` property of a menu. In other words, the first element in an enumerated type has the value zero, as does the first `tag` property.

You know, and I know, that the `Sender` variable contains an instance of the `TMenuItem` item class. However, the wonders of polymorphism allow BCB to declare this variable to be of type `TObject`. That way, a `TNotifyEvent` can accept objects of any type. (Polymorphism will be addressed later in the book in Chapter 21, "Polymorphism.")

The programmer's knowledge of the `Sender` parameter needs to be shared with the compiler. In other words, you and I need to have some way of telling the compiler that the object is not really of type `TObject`, but that it is a just a polymorphic disguise for a `TMenuItem`. This is an important step because the `TObject` class does not have a `Tag` field, and the `TMenuItem` class does have a `Tag` field. In this case, it is absolutely necessary to get at the `Tag` field because it contains the code information about the shape the user wants to select.

To cast a `TObject` as a `TMenuItem` you can use the `dynamic_cast` syntax. This syntax can be used as part of RTTI to test whether a component is of a particular type, or it can be used to actually make the cast. In this case I am daring and make the cast without bother to test it first. This is safe in this case because I know the only object that can be passed here is a `TMenuItem`. However, if I wanted to be extra careful, I could write the following:

```
if (dynamic_cast<TMenuItem*>(Sender))
  Shape1->Shape = TShapeType(dynamic_cast<TMenuItem*>(Sender)->Tag);
```

This would ensure that no exceptions were raised if the cast should happen to fail, which it won't in this particular case.

The final part of the ShapeDem program that is worthy of discussion involves making sure that the scrollbars cling to the bottom and right edges of the control. To do this, you need to respond to WM_SIZE messages, which come to BCB programmers under the friendly guise of an OnResize event:

```
void __fastcall TForm1::FormResize(TObject *Sender)
{
  ScrollBar1->Max = ClientWidth - (ScrollBar2->Width + 1);
  ScrollBar2->Max = ClientHeight - (ScrollBar1->Height + 1);
  ScrollBar1->Left = 0;
  ScrollBar2->Top = 0;
  ScrollBar2->Left = ClientWidth - ScrollBar2->Width;
  ScrollBar2->Height = ClientHeight;
  ScrollBar1->Top = ClientHeight - ScrollBar1->Height;
  ScrollBar1->Width = ClientWidth - ScrollBar2->Width;
}
```

This code uses third grade math (the only kind I ever understood!) to ensure that the scrollbars are allowed as tall or as wide as the form, no matter how it is stretched or pulled by the user. Furthermore, it ensures that the Min and Max property for the control ranges from zero to the exact size of the current client window. This ensures that you can use the OnChange event for the scrollbar to make the TShape object as large as the client window, but no larger.

Notice also that the TForm object has properties called ClientWidth and ClientHeight. These properties calculated the client size of the current window; that is, the size of the window minus the menu, caption, and frame. If this was done for you, you would have to write code that looked something like this:

```
int Menu, Caption, Frame;
Caption = GetSystemMetrics(SM_CYCAPTION);
Frame = GetSystemMetrics(SM_CXFRAME) * 2;
Menu = GetSystemMetrics(SM_CYMENU);
ScrollBar1->Left = 0;
ScrollBar2->Top = 0;
ScrollBar1->Max = Width;
ScrollBar2->Max = Height;
ScrollBar2->Left = Width - Frame - ScrollBar2->Width;
ScrollBar2->Height = Height - Frame - Caption- Menu;
ScrollBar1->Top = Height - ScrollBar2->Width - Frame - Caption - Menu;
ScrollBar1->Width = Width - ScrollBar2->Width - Frame;
```

The point here is that without having to know about GetSystemMetrics and all its associated constants, you can still write code that calculates the size of the TShape object down to the last pixel.

A First Look at RTTI and TypInfo

If you look on the disk, you will find a second copy of the ShapeDem program, called ShapeDem2, that uses a combo box as well as a menu to let the user select the current shape of the object. For instance, you can drop down the combo box and pick a shape such as stCircle or stSquare. These shapes have funny-looking Hungarian squiggles prefixed to them because they are taken directly from the source code of the program at runtime rather than typed in by the programmer at design time. In the next few paragraphs I explain how to use that control, primarily because it also contains an interesting description of how to use Run Time Type Information.

You would think that you need to explicitly type in the names of the shapes that appear in the combo box. For instance, you might assume you need to manually type in the words stCircle and stSquare, and so on. These are the same names you see listed in the Object Inspector for the Shape1 object under the property called Shape, and they are the same words that appear in the combo box at runtime. In other words, if you highlight Shape1 on the form and look at the Shape property in the Object Inspector, you find a list of the possible shapes that can be associated with this object. These are the same shapes you should list in the combo box.

As I said earlier, it's not possible to get access to the Object Inspector at runtime. As a result, if you wanted to explicitly type in the names, you would need to first pop open the Property editor for the Items property, and then manually type these names. To get started, first highlight the combo box on the form by clicking it. Then, double-click the right side of the Items property in the Object Inspector, or you can click the [...] button on the Strings property once. This pops up a String list editor, as shown in Figure 2.8.

FIGURE 2.8.

The String list editor enables you to type in a set of default names that appear in a combo box.

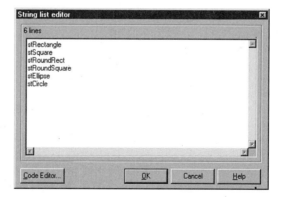

> **NOTE**
>
> In the bottom-left corner of the String list editor is a button that says "Code Editor." If you press this button you can edit your list inside the regular editor for the IDE. This can be especially useful with SQL query statements, which actually provide syntax highlighting. You access the SQL list editor from inside a TQuery component as explained in Chapter 10, "SQL and the TQuery Object."

The actual items that you would type into the String list editor are shown next. Be sure to type them in exactly as shown, and in the identical order.

```
stRectangle
stSquare
stRoundRect
stRoundSquare
stEllipse
stCircle
```

Now when you run the program, the user can drop down this list and select a shape. Here is the code associated with the OnClick event for the combo box:

```
void __fastcall TForm1::ComboBox1Change(TObject *Sender)
{
  Shape1->Shape = TShapeType(ComboBox1->ItemIndex);
}
```

As you can see, there is no significant difference between this code and the code written in response to a click on the shapes listed in the menu. Of course, in this case you don't have to perform a dynamic cast, but that is a mere bagatelle.

The interesting thing about this second version of the ShapeDem program is the code that appears in the constructor for the form:

```
__fastcall TForm1::TForm1(TComponent* Owner)
  : TForm(Owner)
{
  int i;

  PPropInfo PropInfo = GetPropInfo(PTypeInfo(ClassInfo(__classid(TShape))),
  "Shape");

  for (i = 0; i < 6; i++)
    ComboBox1->Items->Add(GetEnumName(PropInfo->PropType, i));

  ... // Code irrelevant to this example omitted here.
}
```

This code uses RTTI to retrieve the names of the enumerated type that underlies the Shape property for the TShape object.

All VCL classes are illuminated with type information. You can find out virtually anything you want about these published properties of a class at runtime merely by asking through one or more of the functions in the TypInfo unit.

RTTI is an essential part of RAD programming because there must be a way for the Object Inspector to query an object about its published properties. For instance, the Object Inspector has to list the names of the TShapeType so that you can select them from the Property editor for the Shape property. The code shown in the constructor for the main form of this application uses the same technique to retrieve this information that the Object Inspector uses. It would not do to have BCB developers type in this information manually before releasing the project because the Object Inspector must be able to retrieve this information for any component, including the ones that you create or find after purchasing the product.

Are classes illuminated with RTTI larger than non-illuminated classes? You bet! RTTI is bought at a price. However, it is a price that I am willing to pay for two reasons:

- It makes RAD possible, as described previously in the text that explains how the property types are listed in the Property editor.

- It enables me to query objects at runtime. Querying objects at runtime gives me the ability to create generic code that will work automatically, regardless of the type of object I pass to it. For instance, the RTTI example using `dynamic_cast` shown previously explains how you can safely test the type of an object before performing an action on it. You will see many examples of that type of code in this book, including cases where you can pass an entire form to a routine, and ask that routine to perform some function on all the controls of a certain type on that form. Generic code of that type can be tested once and then used over and over again with multiple objects. The ability to talk to an object and ask it its type gives us the ability to manage objects automatically. This can be especially useful in Ole Automation, and particularly in DCOM. For instance, you can start wandering about on a network, looking for objects. If you find one, you can use RTTI to ask it questions about itself, and to query its capabilities!

Using the RGB Function

In this section I take a very quick look at a second program that uses many of the same controls from the first program. This is just an example, but it is interesting in that it involves using at least one simple Windows API function, or rather, macro. It's important to understand that you can, of course, call the Windows API whenever you want.

Whenever a TShape component is painted, its interior and border are drawn in particular, pre-defined colors. By default, these colors are white and black, respectively. More specifically, the interior of the ellipse is filled with the color of the currently selected brush. You can change this color by making an assignment of the following type:

```
Shape1->Brush->Color = MyNewColor;
```

The RGBSHAPE program on your disk shows how you can get very specific control over the colors of an object that you paint to the screen. The letters RGB stand for red, green, and blue; each of the these colors makes up one of the colors passed to the Windows API RGB macro itself:

```
COLORREF RGB(
   BYTE   bRed,    // red component of color
   BYTE   bGreen,  // green component of color
   BYTE   bBlue    // blue component of color
   );
```

The parameters passed to this function describe an intensity to be assigned to one of these three colors. These numbers always exist within a range between 0 and 255.

If you pass the RGB function the following parameters, it will return a long integer representing the color red:

```
void __fastcall TForm1::Button1Click(TObject *Sender)
{
  int Red;

  Red = RGB(255, 0, 0);
  Shape1->Brush->Color = TColor(Red);
}
```

The `Color` property of a `TBrush` object is of type `TColor`, but `TColor` is nothing but an enumerated type ranging over all the possible values that can be returned by the RGB macro.

> **NOTE**
>
> You can call the entire Windows API from inside BCB. However, most of the time your calls to the Windows API will be mapped through `WINDOWS.HPP`, which is a wrapper around the Pascal version of these calls.
>
> The Object Pascal team did not translate all the headers for the Windows API. As a result, when you call some of the more obscure or some of the most recent Windows API functions, you may have to explicitly include the header files for these calls. For instance, there is no Pascal translation of the headers for DirectX. As a result, you must include `DDRAW.H`, and so on in your project if you want to make calls to `DirectDraw` or other DirectX functions. The vast majority of Windows API calls are in `WINDOWS.HPP`, however, and that unit is included in all your projects automatically, so you don't have to `#include` anything in your projects.
>
> Needless to say, all Windows API calls are just mappings into a DLL, and it doesn't matter one wit whether you are mapped into the call through Pascal or C++. The compiler does the exact same thing in both cases, and there is no difference in performance, size, and so on.

Here's how you get the colors green and blue:

```
Green = RGB(0, 255, 0);
Blue = RGB(0, 0, 255);
```

If you combine these three colors in various ways, you can produce particular shades. For instance, if you drop a button into a form and respond to a click on the button with the following code, you draw a bright yellow ellipse on the screen:

```
Shape1->Brush->Color = RGB(255, 255, 0);
Shape1->Shape = stEllipse;
```

To achieve the color gray, pass in the following parameters:

```
Gray = RGB(127, 127, 127);
```

To get a fleshlike color, enter

```
Skin = RGB(255, 127, 127);
```

You see how it works. Remember that the first parameter controls the amount of red in the final color, the second the amount of green, and the third the amount of blue. RGB: red, green, blue!

The RGBSHAPE program has a TShape component, three labels, three scrollbars, and three edit controls.

The RGBSHAPE program has only one method:

```
void __fastcall TForm1::ScrollBar1Change(TObject *Sender)
{
  Shape1->Brush->Color = RGB(ScrollBar1->Position,
                             ScrollBar2->Position,
                             ScrollBar3->Position);

  Edit1->Text = IntToStr(ScrollBar1->Position);
  Edit2->Text = IntToStr(ScrollBar2->Position);
  Edit3->Text = IntToStr(ScrollBar3->Position);
}
```

This method first uses the current positions of the scrollbars to assign a color the TShape objects brush. To make this work correctly, I set the Max property for each scrollbar to 255. When the color has been drawn on the screen, I show the actual numbers passed to the scrollbar in the edit components.

The point of the RGB program is to give you a graphical representation of the way the RGB function works. You might also find that this program helps you choose colors that you want to use in your own programs.

NOTE

When working with the RGBSHAPE program, some users may find that Windows cannot create pure tones for some colors, but instead creates a kind of patchwork that approximates the shade described by the parameters passed to the RGB function. However, you can generally get pure tones if you set each of the parameters to 0, 128, or 255. Numbers halfway between 0 and 128 also usually produce pure tones. Of course, the actual results you see depend on whether you are using a 16-color card, 256-color card, or some video card that offers many thousands of colors.

You also need to have the correct video drivers in place. For instance, you don't want to be using a powerful video card and get only 16 colors from it simply for want of the right driver! If you suspect your card is not performing correctly, get on the Web, visit the home page of the company that makes your video card or computer, and download the latest drivers. In Windows 95, you can usually simply unzip the drivers into a temporary directory, right click the desktop, and select Properties | Settings | Change Display Type. When Windows asks for your new drivers, simply point it at the directory where you unzipped the files and it will add them to the system automatically. Be sure to test your work before you restart Windows!

Listing 2.4. The code for the main unit in the RGBSHAPE program.

```
#include <vcl.h>
#pragma hdrstop

#include "Main.h"
#pragma resource "*.dfm"
TForm1 *Form1;
__fastcall TForm1::TForm1(TComponent* Owner)
  : TForm(Owner)
{
}

void __fastcall TForm1::ScrollBar1Change(TObject *Sender)
{
  Shape1->Brush->Color = RGB(ScrollBar1->Position,
                             ScrollBar2->Position,
                             ScrollBar3->Position);

  Edit1->Text = IntToStr(ScrollBar1->Position);
  Edit2->Text = IntToStr(ScrollBar2->Position);
  Edit3->Text = IntToStr(ScrollBar3->Position);
}
```

Summary

In this chapter you have been introduced to the basic facts about Borland C++Builder. In particular, you learned about the environment, manipulating components, and some of the basic tricks of RAD programming. You also had a brief introduction to some advanced topics such as RTTI.

By now the boards are clear to head into some more technical subject matter, such as the examination of extensions to the language featured in the next chapter. After that you will look at events, exceptions, graphics, and sharing code with Delphi. By the time you have finished all these sections, you will have a solid base from which you can launch an exploration of how to use BCB to create cutting-edge Windows applications.

There is so much information to give out in a book like this that I sometimes forget to mention how much I love this programming environment. All the information I am presenting here adds up to a tool that is more powerful, more flexible, and easier to use than any other C++ compiler on the market. Furthermore, this is just the 1.0 version of a product that should become the environment of choice for serious programmers during the next few years.

C++Builder and the VCL

CHAPTER 3

IN THIS CHAPTER

In this chapter you will get a look at the interface between BCB and the Object Pascal code found in the VCL. This is a subject you need to understand if you want to take full advantage of the power of Borland C++Builder.

There are very few occasions when BCB programmers have to think explicitly about the fact that the VCL is written in Object Pascal. Most of the time you can forget its Delphi-based heritage without fear of missing out on anything important. There are, however, a few times when Object Pascal affects your programming. Almost all my descriptions of those occasions are concentrated in this chapter. Throughout most of the rest of this book the subject will never even arise.

The material in this chapter is divided into three main sections:

1. Understanding the VCL
2. Changes to the C++ Language
3. Classes created to imitate Object Pascal simple types that do not exist in C++

Understanding the VCL

All VCL objects are referenced as pointers. There is no such thing as a static or local instance of a VCL object. You are always working with a pointer to a VCL object. This is the result of the VCL's origin in the world of Object Pascal.

Delphi sought to simplify its syntax to the greatest degree possible. However, there were several hurdles that had to be crossed before the language could be made accessible to a wide variety of programmers. In particular, something had to be done about the complexity of dealing with pointers.

For various reasons related to performance and wise use of memory, it is usually best to declare an object on the heap, rather than on the stack, particularly if you are still inhabiting the segmented world of 16-bit programming. As a result, the designers of Object Pascal wanted to make it as simple as possible for their users to work with objects that live on the heap.

Rather than inflict pointer syntax on unwary Object Pascal programmers, the creators of the VCL decided that all objects would necessarily be created on the heap, but would support the syntax associated with local objects. In short, they created a world that eliminated pointer syntax for objects altogether. They could afford to do this because they made it impossible to create an object that was not a pointer. All other language types, such as strings, integers, arrays, structures, and floating-point numbers, could be treated either as pointers or as static objects. This rule applied only to objects.

It might help to illustrate this point with examples. Here is hypothetical code for how an Object Pascal programmer might have treated objects according to the standard rules of Pascal:

```
var
  S: ^TObject;
begin
  S := New(Tobject, Create);
  S^.DoSomething;
  S^.Free;
end;
```

The preceding code will not compile in Delphi, but it is an example of how Delphi code might have looked had the developers not done something to simplify matters. In particular, Delphi eliminated some syntactical clutter by enabling you to write the following:

```
var
  S: TObject;
begin
  S := TObject.Create;
  S.DoSomething;
  S.Free;
end;
```

Clearly this is an improvement over the first example. However, both samples produce essentially the same underlying machine code. In other words, both examples allocate memory for the object, call a constructor called `Create`, implicitly call a method called `DoSomething`, call a destructor called `Destroy`, and then `Free` the memory associated with the object. In the second example, all of this can be done without any need to dereference a pointer with the "^" symbol or without making explicit reference to the act of allocating memory. The point being that the compiler knows that the variable `S` has to be a pointer to an object, because Object Pascal forbids the creation of objects that are not pointers.

Clearly, in the Object Pascal world, it made sense to decide that all objects had to be pointers. There is no significant overhead involved with using pointers, and indeed they are often the fastest way to manipulate memory. So why not make this one hard and fast rule in order to make everyone's life simpler?

Translate this same concept into C++, and suddenly the rule doesn't make quite as much sense. In particular, you can only dare go so far when changing the C++ language to accommodate a new paradigm, and you therefore can't reap any of the benefits that adhered to the Object Pascal code shown in the second of the two most recently listed code samples. In other words, C++ reaps no benefits from this rule, while it does tend to limit your choices. In other words, you are no longer free to create VCL objects locally, but must perforce create them on the heap, whether you want to or not.

I will therefore take it as a given that the need to create VCL objects on the heap is not particularly beneficial to C++ programmers. On the other hand, there is no particular hardship inherent in doing so, nor does it force you to endure any hit on the performance of your application. It is therefore merely a fact of life, neither inherently good nor inherently bad. If you find this unduly irksome, you might consider the many other benefits that BCB brings you, and consider this one limitation as a small price to pay for getting the benefit of this product's strengths.

3

C++BUILDER AND
THE VCL

One final, and not at all unimportant, point: Only VCL objects have to be created on the heap. All standard C++ objects can be handled as you see fit. In other words, you can have both static or dynamic instances of all standard C++ objects. It's only VCL objects that must be addressed with pointers and must be allocated on the heap!

Changes to the C++ Language

It's now time to wrap up the introductory portion of this chapter, which provided an overview of the VCL and BCB programming. The next subject on the agenda involves how the VCL has impacted the C++ language and how the C++ language has affected the VCL. It's perhaps simplest to start with a run down of the new features in the C++ language.

I am, of course, aware of how controversial it is to add extensions to C++. However, I personally am only interested in good technology and the quality of the products I use. BCB is a good product, and part of what makes it good is the power of the VCL and the power of the component, property, event model of programming. The new extensions have been added to the language to make this kind of programming possible, and so I am in favor of these changes. The C++ committee has done excellent work over the years, but no committee can keep up with the furious pace of change in this industry.

The following extensions have been added to the language in order to support the VCL and the component, property, and delegation model of programming:

```
_ _declspec(delphiclass | delphireturn)
_ _automated
_ _published
_ _closure
_ _property
_ _classid(class)
_ _fastcall
```

As you can see, all of these keywords have two underscores prefixed to them. In this instance, I have separated the underscores with a single space to emphasize the fact that not one, but two underscores are needed. In your programs, the underscores should be contiguous, with no space between them.

I am going to go through all these new keywords and make sure that you understand what each means. The purpose of each of these sections is not to explain the how, when, where, and why of a particular keyword, but only to give you a sense of what you can and can't do with them. I will also say something about the relative importance of each new piece of syntax. My goal is to create a handy reference for the new keywords, but I will wait until later to explain most of them in real depth. For instance, a lengthy discussion of the __automated keyword appears in Chapter 27, "Distributed COM," which covers DCOM and Automation, and I discuss properties at length in Chapters 19 through 24, which cover creating components.

Automated

The automated keyword is for use in OLE automation classes. Only classes that descend from `TAutoObject` or a descendant of `TAutoObject` would have a use for this keyword.

Here is an example of a class that sports an automated section:

```
class TMyAutoObject : public TAutoObject
{
private:
public:
  virtual __fastcall TMyAutoObject();
__automated:
  AnsiString __fastcall GetName(void) { return "MyAutoObject"; }
};
```

If this class were compiled into a working program, the `GetName` function would be available to other programs through OLE automation. They can call the function and it will return the word `"MyAutoObject"`.

The reason the `GetName` function can be accessed through OLE automation is because it appears in the automated section of an object. Notice that it is also declared `__fastcall`. This is necessary with automated functions. It means the compiler will attempt to pass the parameters in registers rather than on the stack.

The `__automated` directive makes OLE automation programming much easier, but it's effect is limited to this one area. It has no far reaching effect on the whole of the C++ language.

The Published Keyword

In addition to public, protected, and private, C++ now supports two new keywords used to delineate a section in a class declaration where properties that are to appear in the Object Inspector can be declared. If you are creating a component with new properties that you want to appear in the Object Inspector, you should place those properties in the published section. Properties that appear in the published section have very complete RTTI generated for them by the compiler.

It is only legal to use the `__published` keyword in VCL classes. Furthermore, though the compiler may or may not enforce the rule, it is generally not sensible to use the `__published` keyword in objects that do not descend from `TComponent` or from a descendant of `TComponent`. The reasoning here is simply that `TComponent` is a necessary ancestor of all components, and the `__published` keyword exists because it helps to enhance components. The RTTI associated with the `__published` section will have some effect on program performance, so you don't want to use it unless it will be helpful. Therefore, use `__published` only in classes that you want to make into components.

Here is an example of an object that features a published section:

```
class TMyObject : public TComponent
```

```
{
private:
  int FSomeInteger;
protected:
  int AnotherInteger;
public:
  int PublicInteger;
__published:
  __property int SomeInteger={read=FSomeInteger, write=FSomeInteger};
};
```

In this declaration, the property called SomeInteger is published, will be illuminated with RTTI, and will appear in the Object Inspector if you install TMyObject as a component.

The __published directive changes the way I think about classes, and it changes the way I write code. It currently has significance only for VCL classes and for your components. At this time it has no far-reaching implications in regard to the structure of the C++ language. It is just something that aids in the construction of VCL components.

Properties

Properties represent one of the most important, and most beneficial additions to C++ that you will find in BCB. There will be several places in this book where I discuss properties in depth. In this section I simply give you a general outline of the key points regarding this subject.

Properties have four primary purposes:

1. They support a technology that allows you to expose part of an object to visual programmers via the Object Inspector.

2. They provide an excellent means of creating a rigidly defined, and thoroughly correct, interface for an object.

3. They make it easy for you to protect the private data of an object, and the private portions of your implementation.

4. They support a very sophisticated form of RTTI which allows them to be both seen in the object inspector, and to be automatically streamed out to and read from disk without intervention from the programmer. The automatic streaming of objects is one of the great features of the VCL.

Properties can be added to either the public or published section of a class declaration. It makes no sense to put them in either the protected or private sections, because their primary purpose is to provide a public interface to your object.

Here is a declaration for a property:

```
class TMyObject : public TComponent
{
private:
  int FSomeInteger;
__published:
```

```
    __property int SomeInteger={read=FSomeInteger, write=FSomeInteger};
};
```

In this class, `SomeInteger` is a property of type `int`. It serves as the public interface for the private `FSomeInteger` variable.

To declare a property:

- Use the __property keyword.
- Declare the type of the property.
- Add the name of the property.
- Add an equal sign and an open and close curly brace followed by a semicolon.
- Between the curly braces, properties can have read and write sections. These sections are used to designate how to set or get the value of a property. To declare the read section, write the word read followed by an equal sign, and do the same thing with the write section.

It is very common in VCL classes to declare `private` data with the letter `F` prefixed to it. The letter `F` stands for field. It serves as a reminder that this is a `private` variable and should not be accessed from another class.

You can declare a property to be read only or write only:

```
__property int SomeInteger={read=FSomeInteger};
__property int SomeInteger={write=FSomeInteger};
```

The first of these declarations is read only, the second is write only.

Because `FSomeInteger` is private, you might need to provide some means of accessing it from another object. You can and should sometimes use the `friend` notation, but that really violates the whole concept of the `private` directive. If you want to give someone access to your data, but continue to hide the specific implementation of that data, use properties. The preceding code provides one means of giving someone access to your data while still protecting it. It goes without saying that if your property does nothing else but call directly to a variable of the same type in the `private` section, the compiler generates code that gives you direct access to the type. In other words, it doesn't take any longer to directly use a property like `SomeInteger` than it would to use `FSomeInteger` directly. The compiler takes care of the details for you, and uses less code than it would with an inline access function.

> **NOTE**
>
> C++ programmers have long used get and set methods to provide access to `private` data. There is a certain amount of controversy as to whether or not properties add something to the object model outside of their capability to be seen in the Object Inspector.

continues

continued

Here is a second way to state the matter. Given the presence of the Object Inspector, properties clearly play an important role in BCB programming. A second debate, however, would involve the question of whether or not—absent the issue of the Object Inspector—properties add something new to the mix that would not be there if we had only access functions and get and set methods.

One thing I like a great deal about properties is the clarity of the syntax they present to the user. They make it easier to write clear, maintainable code. They also do a very good job of helping you protect the low-level implementation of your object. I recognize, however, that it could be argued that access functions provided sufficient power to accomplish these goals without the aid of properties.

I could safely hide behind the fact that the BCB programming model demands the presence of properties. However, I will stick my neck out on this one and say that I feel properties are an important contribution to C++, and should become part of the language. I recognize, however, that this is the kind of subject that fosters intense controversy, and concede that the debate is not entirely one-sided.

Here is another use of properties that differs from the one just shown:

```cpp
class MyObject : public TObject
{
private:
  int FSomeInteger;
  int __fastcall GetSomeInteger() { return FSomeInteger; }
  void __fastcall SetSomeInteger(int i) { FSomeInteger = i; }
__published:
  __property int SomeInteger={read=GetSomeInteger, write=SetSomeInteger};
};
```

In this class, `SomeInteger` has get and set methods. These get and set methods are associated with a property and should always be declared with the `__fastcall` calling convention.

Get and set methods provide a means of performing calculations or other actions when getting and setting the value of a property. For instance, when you change the `Width` property in a `TShape` object, not only does some internal variable get set, but the whole object redraws itself. This is possible because there is a set method for this property that both sets the internal `FWidth` property to a new value and redraws the object to reflect these changes.

You could perform calculations from inside a get method. For instance, you could calculate the current time in a property designed to return the current time.

The existence of get and set methods represents another important reason for keeping the data of your object `private`, and for not giving anyone else access to it except through properties. In particular, you may change a value in a set or get method or have side effects that you want to be sure are executed. If someone accesses the data directly, the side effects or other changes will not occur. Therefore, you should keep the data `private` and let them access it through a function, and let the function itself be accessed through a property.

Properties can be of a wide variety of types. For instance, they can be declared as AnsiStrings, arrays, sets, objects, or enumerated types. Events, which are a kind of method pointer, are really a type of property, but they behave according to their own peculiar rules and are usually treated as a separate subject from properties.

Properties can be declared to have a default value:

```
__property int SomeInteger={read=GetSomeInteger, write=SetSomeInteger, default=1};
```

This syntax is related only tangentially to the concept of setting a property automatically to a particular value. If you want to give a property a predefined value, you should do so in the object's constructor.

Default is used to tell the VCL whether or not a value should be written out to a stream. The issue here is that streaming can result in producing large files, because so many objects have such large numbers of properties. To cut down on the size of your form files, and on the time spent writing the files to disk, the VCL enables you to declare a default value for a property. When it comes time to stream properties to disk, they will not be streamed if they are currently set to the default value. The assumption is that you will initialize them to that value in the object's constructor, so there is no need to save the value to disk. Many properties are declared to be nodefault, which means they should be streamed to disk.

A property can also have the stored directive. Confusingly enough, this is another means of deciding whether or not a property should be streamed. In this case, it gives you the option of changing whether or not a property can be streamed. For instance:

```
property TColor Color={read Fcolor, write SetColor,
    stored=IsColorStored, default=clWindow};
```

This property calls a method named IsColorStored to determine whether the color should be stored at this time. For instance, if the property is set to have the same value as its parent, there is no need to store it, and IsColorStored returns False. This property will therefore only be stored if IsColorStored returns True and the color is not set to clWindow.

Say what?

Don't worry, most of the time you don't have to get involved with these tricky storage specifiers and their disarming schemes to save disk space. However, there are times when the matter comes to the front, and now you have a place to look to remember what they mean.

Properties play a big role in VCL programming, and furthermore, they can be used in objects that have nothing to do with the VCL. This subject has tremendous potential scope and will affect the way the C++ language as a whole is handled by BCB programmers.

That is all I'm going to say about properties for now. There is an example of creating and using an array property later in this chapter in the section called "Arrays of AnsiStrings."

Events: Understanding Delegation

Most of the time I will refer to closures as events. Technically, a closure is the type of method pointer used in event properties, but I will generally refer to the whole syntactical structure as an event that supports the delegation model.

As you learned in the last section, an event is really a kind of property. The primary difference between a standard property and an event is that the type of an event is a method pointer.

NOTE

Some people refer to events as closures, but it could be argued that the word has a rather stuffy, academic overtone to it. Certainly it is used in some circles in a very strict manner that does not necessarily conform in all its particulars to the way BCB handles events.

Consider the `OnMouseUp` event that is supported by many components and declared in `CONTROLS.HPP`:

```
__property TMouseEvent OnMouseUp = {read=FOnMouseUp, write=FOnMouseUp};
```

Like the `OnMouseUp` property, `FOnMouseUp` is, naturally, also declared to be of type `TMouseEvent`:

```
TMouseEvent FOnMouseUp.
```

So far the syntax used for events seems pretty much identical to that used for all properties. The new code that is specific to the delegation model is the actual declaration for the method pointer used by an event:

```
typedef void __fastcall (__closure *TMouseEvent)(System::TObject* Sender,
  TMouseButton Button, Classes::TShiftState Shift, int X, int Y);
```

All `OnMouseUp` events are of this type. In other words, if an `OnMouseUp` event is not set to `null`, it is set to a method pointer of this type. You can then call the event by writing code of this type:

```
if (FOnMouseUp)
  FOnMouseUp(this, Button, Shift, X, Y);
```

If the event is not set to `null`, call the method associated with the event and pass parameters of a type that conform with the signature of the relevant method pointer. This is called delegating the event.

NOTE

It is generally considered very bad form to return a value from an event. Trying to do so could cause a compiler error, and you should avoid including code of this type in your own programs. The VCL has gone through several iterations now, and returning values from events has worked in some versions and not in others. The team that wrote the VCL, however, asked the DOC team to state explicitly that events should not return values. It usually turns out badly when you get stuck with legacy code that worked in one version, but directly contradicts the desires of the folks who keep the reins in their own hands.

The method associated with the `OnMouseUp` event will look something like this:

```
void __fastcall TForm1::Button1MouseUp(
  TObject *Sender,
  TMouseButton Button,
  TShiftState Shift,
  int X,
  int Y)
{

}
```

I generally call a method of this type an event handler. It handles an event when it is delegated by a component or object.

Most of the time an event is assigned to a method automatically by the compiler. However, you can do so explicitly if you desire, and in fact I do this in several places in my own code. If you want an example, see the Music program from Chapter 16, "Advanced InterBase Concepts." Here is how the assignment would be made from inside the Controls unit:

```
FOnMouseEvent = Button1MouseUp;
```

Code of this type appears everywhere in the VCL, and indeed it is one of the central constructs that drives BCB. This is the heart of delegation programming model. As I have said several times, BCB is primarily about components, properties, and the delegation model. Take events away, and you have some other product altogether. Events radically change the way C++ programs are written. The key effect of events on C++ seems to me to be the following: "In addition to using inheritance and virtual methods to change the behavior of an object, BCB allows you to customize object by delegating events. In particular, VCL objects often delegate events to the form on which they reside."

Like all properties, events work with both standard C++ classes and with VCL classes.

3

C++BUILDER AND
THE VCL

declspec(delphiclass | delphireturn | pascalimplementation)

All the additions to C++ discussed so far are primarily about finding ways to support the VCL. In particular, the new VCL object model has certain benefits associated with it, and so Borland has extended C++ in order to accommodate this new model. The property and event syntax, however, appears to have at least some other implications beyond its simple utilitarian capability to support the VCL. I think you will find the next three changes are very small potatoes compared to properties and events. All they really do is make it possible for BCB to use the VCL, and they don't really have much effect at all on the way we write code.

As you have no doubt gleaned by this time, VCL classes behave in specific ways. For instance, a VCL class can only by instantiated on the heap, and you can only use the __published or __automated keywords with VCL classes.

The majority of the time your own classes can inherit this behavior directly, simply by descending from a VCL class. For instance, here is part of the declaration for TControl

```
class __declspec(pascalimplementation) TControl : public Classes::TComponent
{
  typedef Classes::TComponent inherited;
private:
  TWinControl* FParent;
  … // etc
}
```

As you can see, these classes are declared with the delphiclass or pascalimplementation attribute. This means they are implemented in Pascal, and the headers are the only part that appear in C++ code. If you have an Object Pascal unit that you want to use in a BCB application, the other declarations in the unit will automatically be translated and placed in a C++ header file. The class declarations in that header file will be similar to the one shown here.

However, if you create a descendant of TControl, you don't have to bother with any of this, because the attributes will be inherited:

```
class MyControl : public TControl
{
  // My stuff here
}
```

Class MyControl is automatically a VCL class that can support __published properties and must be created on the heap. It inherits this capability from TControl. As a result, it is implicitly declared pascalimpementation, even though you don't explicitly use the syntax. I don't like to clutter up class declarations with __declspec(pascalimplementation), but it may appeal to some programmers because it makes it clear that the class is a VCL class and has to be treated in a particular manner.

If you want to create a forward declaration for a class with the pascalimplementation attribute, it must have the delphiclass attribute:

```
class __declspec(delphiclass) TControl;
```

This is a forward declaration for the `TControl` class found in `CONTROLS.HPP`. You do not inherit `delphiclass` in the same sense that you do `pascalimplementation`, and so you must use it explicitly in forward declarations!

`delphireturn` is used to tell the compiler to generate a particular kind of code compatible with the VCL when it returns objects or structures from a function. The only place in BCB where this is done is in `SYSDEFS.H` and `DSTRINGS.H`, which is where classes like `Currency`, `AnsiString`, and `Variant` are declared. If you need to return objects or structures to the VCL, you may need to declare your class with this directive. However, there are very few occasions when this is necessary, and most programmers can forget about `delphireturn` altogether.

> **NOTE**
>
> As shown later in this chapter, the `TDateTime` object is declared `delphireturn`. This is necessary because instances of the object can be passed to VCL functions such as `DateTimeToString`.

All of this business about `dephireturn` and `pascalimplementation` has little or no effect on the code written by most BCB programmers. `delphiclass` is slightly more important, because you will likely have occasion to declare a forward declaration for one of your own descendants of a VCL class. This is clearly a case where you can indeed afford to "pay no attention to the man behind the curtain." Most of this stuff is just hand signals passed back and forth between the compiler and VCL, and you can afford to ignore it. Its impact on the C++ programming as a whole is essentially nil.

classid(class)

Use `classid` if you need to pass the specific type of a class to a function or method used by the VCL RTTI routines. For instance, if you want to call the `ClassInfo` method of `TObject`, you need to pass in the type of the class you want to learn about. In Object Pascal you write

```
ClassInfo(TForm);
```

which means: Tell me about the `TForm` class. Unfortunately, the compiler won't accept this syntax. The correct way to pose the question in BCB is

```
ClassInfo(__classid(TForm));
```

Again, this is just the compiler and the VCL having a quiet little chat. Pay no attention to the man behind the curtain. RTTI looks one way in the VCL, another in standard C++. This syntax is used to bridge the gap between the two, and it has no far reaching implications for C++, the VCL, or anyone else. The excitement is all centered around the property and event syntax; this is a mere trifle.

__fastcall

The default calling convention in Object Pascal is called fastcall, and it is duplicated in C++Builder with the __fastcall keyword. __fastcall methods or functions usually have their parameters passed in registers, rather than on the stack. For instance, the value of one parameter might be inserted in a register such as EAX and then snagged from that register on the other side.

The __fastcall calling conventions pass the first three parameters in eax, edx, and ecx registers, respectively. Additional parameters and parameter data larger than 32 bits (such as doubles passed by value) are pushed on the stack.

Delphi-Specific Classes

Not all the features of C++ are available in Object Pascal, and not all the features of Object Pascal are available in BCB. As a result, the following classes are created to represent features of the Object Pascal language that are not present in C++:

```
AnsiString
Variant
ShortString
Currency
TDateTime
Set
```

Most of these classes are implemented or declared in SYSDEFS.H, though the crucial AnsiString class is declared in its own file called DSTRINGS.H.

> **NOTE**
>
> Neither the real nor comp types used in Object Pascal are supported adequately in BCB. Because Pascal programmers often used the comp type to handle currency, they should pay special attention to the section in this chapter on the BCB currency type. The real type is an artifact of the old segmented architecture days when anything and everything was being done to save space and clock cycles. It no longer plays a role in contemporary Object Pascal programming.

I will dedicate at least one section of this chapter to each of the types listed previously. Some important types, such as Sets and AnsiStrings, will receive rather lengthy treatment stretching over several sections.

Many C++ programmers will have questions about the presence of some of these classes. For instance, C++ comes equipped with a great set template and an excellent string class. Why does BCB introduce replacements for these classes? The answer to the question is simply that BCB needed a class that mimicked the specific behavior of Object Pascal sets and Object Pascal strings.

Here are some macros you can use with these classes:

```
OPENARRAY
ARRAYOFCONST
EXISTINGARRAY
SLICE
```

These macros are also discussed in the upcoming sections.

Introducing the AnsiString Class

The C language is famous for its null-terminated strings. These strings can be declared in many ways, but they usually look like one of these three examples:

```
char MyString[100]; // declare a string with 100 characters in it.
char *MyString;     // A pointer to a string with no memory allocated for it.
LPSTR MyString;     // A "portable" Windows declaration for a pointer to a string
```

Declarations like these are such a deep-rooted and long standing part of the C language that it is somewhat shocking to note that they are not as common as they once were. There is, of course, nothing wrong with these strings, but C++ has come up with a new, and perhaps better, way to deal with strings. (I speak of these strings as being exclusive to C, though of course these same type of strings are also used in Object Pascal, where they are called PChars.)

The "old-fashioned" types of strings shown previously cause people problems because it is easy to make memory allocation errors with them or to accidentally omit the crucial terminating zero ('/0') that marks the end of these strings.

These same strings are also famous for their accompanying string library, which includes a series of cryptic looking functions with names like strcpy, strlen, strcmp, strpbrk, strrchr, and so on. These functions, most of which occur in both C++ and Object Pascal, can be awkward to use at times, and can frequently lead to errors if a programmer gets careless.

In this book, I will try to avoid using any of the "old fashioned" C style strings whenever possible. Instead, I will do things the C++ way and use string classes. Most C++ programmers prefer string classes on the grounds that they are easier to use, easier to read, and much less likely to lead to an error involving memory allocation.

In this book there is a fourth reason for using string classes. In particular, a string class called AnsiString provides compatibility with the underlying strings found in the VCL. C++ programmers will find that AnsiStrings are similar to the standard ANSI C++ String class.

AnsiStrings are very easy to use. In fact, many programmers will find that they have an intuitive logic to them that almost eliminates the need for any kind of in-depth explanation. However, AnsiStrings happen to form one of the key building blocks on which a great deal of C++Builder code is based. It is therefore of paramount importance that users of BCB understand AnsiStrings.

3

C++BUILDER AND
THE VCL

The next few sections of the book take on the task of explaining AnsiStrings. To help illustrate this explanation with ready-made examples, you can turn to the UsingAnsiString program found on the book's CD-ROM. This program provides examples of essential AnsiString syntax and shows several tricks you can use when you add strings to your programs.

Working with the AnsiString Class

The AnsiString class is declared in the DSTRING.H unit from the ..\INCLUDE\VCL directory. This is a key piece of code, and one which all BCB programmers should take at least a few minutes to study.

The declaration for the class in the DSTRING.H unit is broken up into several discreet sections. This technique makes the code easy to read. For instance, one of the sections shows the operators used for assignments:

```
// Assignments
    AnsiString& __fastcall operator =(const AnsiString& rhs);
    AnsiString& __fastcall operator +=(const AnsiString& rhs);
```

Another section shows some comparison operators:

```
//Comparisons
    bool __fastcall operator ==(const AnsiString& rhs) const;
    bool __fastcall operator !=(const AnsiString& rhs) const;
    bool __fastcall operator <(const AnsiString& rhs) const;
    bool __fastcall operator >(const AnsiString& rhs) const;
    bool __fastcall operator <=(const AnsiString& rhs) const;
    bool __fastcall operator >=(const AnsiString& rhs) const;
```

Another handles the Unicode-related chores:

```
//Convert to Unicode
    int __fastcall WideCharBufSize() const;
    wchar_t* __fastcall WideChar(wchar_t* dest, int destSize) const;
```

There is, of course, much more to the declaration than what I show here. However, these code fragments should give you some sense of what you will find in DSTRING.H, and of how to start browsing through the code to find AnsiString methods or operators that you want to use.

The rest of the text in this section of the chapter examines most of the key parts of the AnsiString class and shows how to use them. However, you should definitely find time, either now or later, to open up DSTRING.H and to browse through its contents.

AnsiString Class Constructors

AnsiStrings are a class; they are not a simple type like the string type in Object Pascal, which they mimic. Object Pascal or BASIC programmers might find that the next line of code looks a little like a simple type declaration. It is not. Instead, this code calls the constructor for an object:

```
AnsiString S;
```

Here are the available constructors for the AnsiString class:

```
__fastcall AnsiString(): Data(0) {}
__fastcall AnsiString(const char* src);
__fastcall AnsiString(const AnsiString& src);
__fastcall AnsiString(const char* src, unsigned char len);
__fastcall AnsiString(const wchar_t* src);
__fastcall AnsiString(char src);
__fastcall AnsiString(int src);
__fastcall AnsiString(double src);
```

The simple AnsiString declaration shown at the beginning of this section would call the first constructor shown previously, which initializes to zero a private variable of the AnsiString class. This private variable, named Data, is of type char *. Data is the core C string around which the AnsiString class is built. In other words, the AnsiString class is a wrapper around a simple C string, and the class exists to make it easy to manipulate this string and to make the string compatible with the needs of the VCL.

The following simple declaration would call the second constructor shown in the previous list:

```
AnsiString S("Sam");
```

This is the typical method you would use when initializing a variable of type AnsiString.

NOTE

I have included a second example program called UsingAnsiString2, which features a small class that overrides all the constructors for the AnsiString class:

```
class MyAnsiString : public AnsiString
{
public:
__fastcall MyAnsiString(void): AnsiString() {}
__fastcall MyAnsiString(const char* src): AnsiString(src) {}
__fastcall MyAnsiString(const AnsiString& src): AnsiString(src) {}
__fastcall MyAnsiString(const char* src, unsigned char len): AnsiString
    (src, len) {}
__fastcall MyAnsiString(const wchar_t* src): AnsiString(src) {}
__fastcall MyAnsiString(char src): AnsiString(src) {}
__fastcall MyAnsiString(int src): AnsiString(src) {}
__fastcall MyAnsiString(double src): AnsiString(src) {}
};
```

This class is provided so you can step through the constructors to see which ones are being called. For instance, the three constructors shown immediately after this note have been rewritten in the UsingAnsiStrings2 program to use MyAnsiStrings rather than AnsiStrings. This gives you an easy-to-use system for explicitly testing which constructors are being called in which circumstance.

When I come up with a unit like this that may be of some general utility in multiple programs, I usually put it in the utils subdirectory located on the same level as the chapter subdirectories. In other words, I move or copy it out of the directory where the files for the

continues

continued

current program are stored and place it in a subdirectory called `utils` that is on the same level as the directories called `Chap01`, `Chap02`, and so on.

You might need to add this directory to the include search path for your project, or the program might not be able to find the `MyAnsiString.h` unit. To set up the compiler for your system, go to Options | Project | Directories/Conditionals and change the Include Path to point to the directory where `MyAnsiString.h` is stored.

Sometimes I will leave one frozen copy of a unit in the directory where it was first introduced and continue development of the copy of the unit that I place in the `utils` subdirectory. That way, you can find one copy of the file that looks the way you expect it to look in the same directory as the program in which I introduce it, while continuing to develop the code in a separate unit of the same name found in the `utils` directory. Check the `Readme.txt` file on the CD that accompanies this book for further information.

The following are a few simple examples from the UsingAnsiStrings program that show examples of creating and using `AnsiStrings`:

```
void __fastcall TForm1::PassinCString1Click(TObject *Sender)
{
  AnsiString S("Sam");
  Memo1->Text = S;
}

void __fastcall TForm1::PassInInteger1Click(TObject *Sender)
{
  AnsiString MyNum(5);
  Memo1->Text = MyNum;
}

void __fastcall TForm1::PassInaDouble1Click(TObject *Sender)
{
  AnsiString MyDouble(6.6);
  Memo1->Text = MyDouble;
}
```

This code demonstrates several things. The first, and most important point, is that it shows how you can create an `AnsiString` object by initializing it with a string, an integer, or a double. In short, these constructors can automatically perform conversions for you. This means you can usually write code like this:

```
AnsiString S;
int I = 4;
S = I;
ShowMessage(S);
```

When working with C strings, you always have to be careful that the variable you have been working with has been properly initialized. This is not nearly as big a concern when you are working with `AnsiStrings`. Consider the following code:

```
void __fastcall TForm1::InitializetoZero1Click(TObject *Sender)
{
  AnsiString S;
  Memo1->Text = S.Length();
}
```

The first line creates an `AnsiString` class that has a zero length string. The second line performs a completely safe and legal call to one of the methods of this `AnsiString`. This is the type of situation that can be very dangerous in C. Here, for instance, is some code that is likely to blow up on you:

```
char *S;
int i = strlen(S);
```

This code appears to do more or less the same thing as the code in the `InitializetoZero1Click` method. In practice, however, this latter example actually raises an access violation, while the `AnsiString` code example succeeds. The explanation is simply that the declaration of the `AnsiString` class created a real instance of an object called `S`. You can safely call the methods of that object, even if the underlying string has no memory allocated for it! The second example, however, leaves the `char *` declared in the first line completely impotent, with no memory allocated for it. If you want to avoid trouble, you should not do anything with that variable until you allocate some memory for it.

In the last few paragraphs I have outlined an example illustrating what it is I like about the `AnsiString` class. In short, this class makes strings safe and easy to use.

NOTE

It goes without saying that C strings are generally faster than `AnsiStrings`, and that they take up less memory. Clearly, these are important features, and obviously I am not stating that C strings are now obsolete.

The reasoning on this issue is a bit like that we undertake when deciding whether to buy a car or a motorcycle. Cars are more expensive than motorcycles, and they don't let you weave back and forth between lanes when there is congested traffic. On the other hand, drivers of cars are much less likely to end up in the hospital, and cars are much more pleasant to be in during inclement weather. In the same way, `AnsiStrings` aren't as small and flexible as C strings, but they are less likely to crash the system, and they stand up better when you are in a rush or when handled by inexperienced programmers.

This book focuses on ways to quickly write safe, high-performance programs. If that is your goal, use `AnsiStrings`. If you are trying to write an operating system, a compiler, or the core module for a 3D game engine, you should probably concentrate more on speed than I do in this book and should use `AnsiStrings` only sparingly.

Please note that my point here is not that you can't use C++Builder to write highly optimized code, but only that this book usually does not focus on that kind of project.

Sticky Constructor Issues

The `AnsiString` constructors are easy to use, but things can be a bit confusing if you try to think about what is going on behind the scenes. For instance, consider what happens when you pass an `AnsiString` to a function:

```
AnsiString S;
MyFunc(S);
```

If the call to `MyFunc` is by value, not by reference, the constructor for `S` is going to be called each time you pass the string. This is not a tremendous burden on your program, but it is probably a bit more significant weight than you had in mind to impose on your code. As a result, you should pass in the address of the variable in most circumstances:

```
AnsiString S;
MyFunc(&S);
```

Even better, you should construct methods that declare all their string variables as being passed by reference:

```
int MyFunc(AnsiString &S)
{
  S = "The best minds of my generation...";
  return S.Length();
}
```

This is like a var parameter in Object Pascal in that it lets you pass the string by reference without worrying about pointers:

```
void __fastcall TForm1::Button1Click(TObject *Sender)
{
  AnsiString S;
  int i = MyFunc(S);
  ShowMessage(S + " Length: " + i);
}
```

Even when `MyFunc` changes the string, the result of the changes is reflected in the calling module. This syntax passes a pointer to the function, but makes it seem as though you are working with a local stack-based variable on both the caller and calling sides.

Consider the following code samples:

```
MyAnsiString S = "The road to the contagious hospital";
MyAnsiString S1 = AnsiString("If I had a green automobile...");
MyAnsiString S2("All that came out of them came quiet, like the four seasons");
ShowMessage(S + '\r' + S1 + '\r' + S2);
```

It should be clear from looking at this code that the second example will take longer to execute than the third, because it calls two constructors rather than just one. You might also think that the first takes longer than the third. A logical course of reasoning would be to suppose that, at minimum, it would have to call both a constructor and the equals operator. In fact, when I stepped through the code, it became clear that the compiler simply called the constructor immediately in the first example, and that the machine code executed for the first and third examples was identical.

What is the lesson to be learned here? Unless you are writing a compiler, an operating system, or a 3D game engine, just don't worry about this stuff. Of course, if you love worrying about these issues, then worry away. I suppose someone has to. Otherwise, relax. There is almost no way to tell from looking at the code what the compiler is going to do, and 90 percent of the time the compiler is smart enough to generate optimal code unless you explicitly tell it to go out of its way, as I do in the second example.

If you are a beginning- or intermediate-level programmer, someone is going to tell you that you should pull your hair out worrying about optimization issues like this. Personally, I think there are more important subjects to which you can dedicate your time. Eliminating one constructor call might save a few nanoseconds in execution time, but nobody is going to notice it. Learn to separate the petty issues from the serious issues.

Most importantly of all, wait until you have a program up and running before you decide whether or not you have a performance bottleneck. If the program is too slow, use a profiler to find out where the bottlenecks are. Ninety-eight percent of the time the bottlenecks are in a few isolated places in the code, and fixing those spots clears up the problem. Don't spend two weeks looking for every place there is an extra constructor call only to find it improves your performance by less than one percent. Wait till you have a problem, find the problem, and then fix it. If it turns out that you are in a loop, and are making extra constructor calls in the loop, and that by doing some hand waving to get rid of the calls you improve program performance by 10 percent, then great. But don't spend days working on "optimizations" that end up improving performance by only one or two percent.

AnsiString Comparison Operators

Comparison operators are useful if you want to alphabetize strings. For instance, asking if StringOne is smaller than StringTwo is a means of finding out whether StringOne comes before StringTwo in the alphabet. For instance, if StringOne equals "Dole" and StringTwo equals "Clinton", StringOne is larger than StringTwo because it comes later in the alphabet. (At last, a politically controversial string comparison analysis!)

Here are the AnsiString class comparison operators and methods:

```
bool __fastcall operator ==(const AnsiString& rhs) const;
bool __fastcall operator !=(const AnsiString& rhs) const;
bool __fastcall operator <(const AnsiString& rhs) const;
bool __fastcall operator >(const AnsiString& rhs) const;
bool __fastcall operator <=(const AnsiString& rhs) const;
bool __fastcall operator >=(const AnsiString& rhs) const;
int __fastcall AnsiCompare(const AnsiString& rhs) const;
int __fastcall AnsiCompareIC(const AnsiString& rhs) const; //ignorecase
```

The UsingAnsiString program on this book's CD-ROM shows how to use these operators. For instance, the following method from that program shows how to use the equals operator:

```
void __fastcall TForm1::Equals1Click(TObject *Sender)
{
  AnsiString StringOne, StringTwo;
```

```
  InputDialog->GetStringsFromUser(&StringOne, &StringTwo);
  if (StringOne == StringTwo)
    Memo1->Text = "\"" + StringOne + "\" is equal to \"" + StringTwo + "\"";
  else
    Memo1->Text = "\"" + StringOne + "\" is not equal to \"" + StringTwo + "\"";
}
```

Here is an example of using the "smaller than" operator:

```
void __fastcall TForm1::SmallerThan1Click(TObject *Sender)
{
  AnsiString String1, String2;

  InputDialog->GetStringsFromUser(&String1, &String2);
  if (String1 < String2)
    Memo1->Text = "\"" + String1 + "\" is smaller than \"" + String2 + "\"";
  else
    Memo1->Text = "\"" + String1 + "\" is not smaller than \"" + String2 + "\"";
}
```

The `AnsiCompareIC` function is useful if you want to ignore the case of words when comparing them. This method returns zero if the strings are equal, a positive number if the string calling the function is larger than the string to which it is being compared, and negative number if it is not larger than the string to which it is being compared:

```
void __fastcall TForm1::IgnoreCaseCompare1Click(TObject *Sender)
{
  AnsiString String1, String2;

  InputDialog->GetStringsFromUser(&String1, &String2);
  if (String1.AnsiCompareIC(String2) == 0)
    Memo1->Text = "\"" + String1 + "\" equals \"" + String2 + "\"";
  else if (String1.AnsiCompareIC(String2) > 0)
    Memo1->Text = "\"" + String1 + "\" is larger than \"" + String2 + "\"";
  else if (String1.AnsiCompareIC(String2) < 0)
    Memo1->Text = "\"" + String1 + "\" is smaller than \"" + String2 + "\"";
}
```

Consider the following chart:

StringOne	StringTwo	*Result*
England	England	Returns zero
England	France	Return a negative number
France	England	Returns a positive number

Using the Pos Method

The `Pos` method is used to find the offset of a substring within a larger string. Here is a simple example from the UsingAnsiString program of how to use the `Pos` function:

```
void __fastcall TForm1::SimpleString1Click(TObject *Sender)
{
  AnsiString S = "Sammy";
```

```
  Memo1->Text = S;
  int i = S.Pos("mm");
  S.Delete(i + 1, 2);
  Memo1->Lines->Add(S);
}
```

This code creates an `AnsiString` initialized to the name `"Sammy"`. It then searches through the string for the place where the substring `"mm"` occurs, and returns that index so that it can be stored in the variable i. I then use the index as a guide when deleting the last two characters from the string, thereby transforming the word `"Sammy"` to the string `"Sam"`.

Here is a similar case, except that this time code searches for a tab rather than an ordinary substring:

```
void __fastcall TForm1::Pos1Click(TObject *Sender)
{
  AnsiString S("Sammy \t Mike");
  Memo1->Text = S;
  AnsiString Temp = Format("The tab is in the %dth position",
    OPENARRAY(TVarRec, (S.Pos('\t'))));
  Memo1->Lines->Add(Temp);
}
```

The code in this example first initializes the `AnsiString` S to a string that contains a tab, and then searches through the string and reports the offset of the tab: "The tab is in the 7th position." The `Format` function shown here works in the same fashion as `sprintf`. In fact, the following code would have the same result as the `Pos1Click` method shown previously:

```
AnsiString S("Sammy \x009 Mike");
Memo1->Text = S;

char Temp[75];
sprintf(Temp, "The tab is in the %dth position", S.Pos('\t'));
Memo1->Lines->Add(Temp);
```

Escape Sequences in C++

C++ uses a series of escape sequences to represent special characters such as tabs, backspaces, and so on. If you are not familiar with C++, you might find the following table of escape sequences useful:

Human readable name	Escape sequence	Hex representation
Bell	\a	\x007
Backspace	\b	\x008
Tab	\t	\x009
Newline	\n	\x00A
Form Feed	\f	\x00C
Carriage return	\r	\x00D

continues

3

C++BUILDER AND THE VCL

Human readable name	Escape sequence	Hex representation
Double quote	\"	\x022
Single quote	\'	\x027
Backslash	\\	\x05C

Escape sequences are usually placed in single quotes, though in the previous case it would not matter whether I used single or double quotes in the `Pos` statement.

Using hex values has the exact same effect as using escape sequences. For instance, the following code creates identical output to the `Pos1Click` method shown previously:

```
AnsiString S("Sammy \x009 Mike");
Memo1->Text = S;
AnsiString Temp = Format("The tab is in the %dth position",
OPENARRAY(TVarRec, (S.Pos('\x009'))));
Memo1->Lines->Add(Temp);
```

Though some programmers may find it simpler and more intuitive to use the Hex values shown in the last column of the table, the arcane-looking escape sequences cling on in C++ code because they are portable to platforms other than Windows and DOS.

Arrays of `AnsiStrings`

In this section you will see how to declare an array of `AnsiStrings`. The text includes examples of how to access them as standard null-terminated strings, and how to use them in moderately complex circumstances.

The following ChuangTzu program uses some Chinese quotes with a millennium or two of QA under their belt to illustrate the favorite theme of this book:

```
Easy is right. Begin right
And you are easy.
Continue easy and you are right.
The right way to go easy
Is to forget the right way
And forget that the going is easy.
```

This program declares this string as an `AnsiString`, and then passes it to a procedure that can break it down into a series of words. These words are passed back one at a time and added into an array. The array is then displayed in a series of one word lines in a memo control. The program appears in Listings 3.1 and 3.2.

Listing 3.1. The header for the ChuangTzu program.

```
//-------------------------------------------------------------
#ifndef MainH
#define MainH
//-------------------------------------------------------------
#include <Classes.hpp>
```

```cpp
#include <Controls.hpp>
#include <StdCtrls.hpp>
#include <Forms.hpp>
//-------------------------------------------------------------------

class TChuangTzu
{
private:
  int FCount;
  AnsiString FWords[40];
  AnsiString GetWords(int Index);
  void SetWords(int Index, AnsiString S);
public:
  TChuangTzu(){ FCount = 0; }
  __property AnsiString Words[int Index] = {read=GetWords, write=SetWords};
  __property int Count={read=FCount, write=FCount};
};

class TForm1 : public TForm
{
published:
  TButton *Button1;
  TMemo *Memo1;
  void __fastcall Button1Click(
  TObject *Sender);
private:
public:
  virtual __fastcall TForm1(TComponent* Owner);
};
//-------------------------------------------------------------------
extern TForm1 *Form1;
//-------------------------------------------------------------------
#endif
```

3

C++BUILDER AND
THE VCL

Listing 3.2. The main module of the ChuangTzu program.

```cpp
#include <vcl.h>
#pragma hdrstop
#include "Main.h"
#include "codebox.h"
#pragma resource "*.dfm"
TForm1 *Form1;

////////////////////////////////////////
// ChuangTzu /////////////////////////////
////////////////////////////////////////
AnsiString TChuangTzu::GetWords(int i)
{
  return FWords[i];
}

void TChuangTzu::SetWords(int i,const AnsiString s)

{
  FCount++;
  FWords[i]=s;
```

continues

Listing 3.2. continued

```
}

AnsiString StripWords(AnsiString &S, char Token)
{
  AnsiString TokenStr(Token);
  AnsiString Temp1;
  AnsiString Temp2 = S + ' ';

  Temp1 = strtok(S.c_str(), TokenStr.c_str());
  Temp2 = strrev(Temp2.c_str());
  Temp2.SetLength(Temp2.Length() - (Temp1.Length() + 1));
  S = strrev(Temp2.c_str());
  return Temp1;
}

/////////////////////////////////////
// Form1 /////////////////////////////
/////////////////////////////////////

__fastcall TForm1::TForm1(TComponent* Owner)
  : TForm(Owner)
{
}

void __fastcall TForm1::Button1Click(
  TObject *Sender)
{
  TChuangTzu C;
  AnsiString S1;
  int i = 0;
  AnsiString S =
    "Easy is right. Begin right ";
    "And you are easy. "
    "Continue easy and you are right. "
    "The right way to go easy "
    "Is to forget the right way "
    "And forget that the going is easy.";

  do
  {
    S1 = StripWords(S, ' ');
    C.Words[i] = S1;
    i++;
  } while (S1 != "");

  for (i = 0; i < C.Count; i++)
  {
    Memo1->Lines->Add(C.Words[i]);
  }
}
```

The core of this program is the ChuangTzu class definition:

```
class TChuangTzu
{
```

```
private:
  int FCount;
  AnsiString FWords[40];
  AnsiString GetWords(int Index);
  void SetWords(int Index, AnsiString S);
public:
  TChuangTzu(){ FCount = 0; }
  __property AnsiString Words[int Index] = {read=GetWords, write=SetWords};
  __property int Count={read=FCount, write=FCount};
};
```

At the heart of the object is the declaration for an array of 40 AnsiStrings:

```
AnsiString FWords[40];
```

You can access the second member of this array with code that looks like this:

```
FWords[1] = "Let some sad trumpeter stand on the empty streets at dawn."
AnsiString S = FWords[1];
```

The ChuangTzu object provides an array property that gives you access to this private data. There is, of course, no reason why you can't declare an array of AnsiStrings on their own without a supporting object. However, I thought it might be helpful to see how you can use an array in your program without breaking the rule about keeping the raw data of your objects private.

Here is the declaration for the array property:

```
__property AnsiString Words[int Index] = {read=GetWords, write=SetWords};
```

As you can see, it returns an AnsiString and can be indexed with an integer value. (There is nothing to keep you from declaring array properties that are indexed with AnsiStrings!)

Here is the get method for the array:

```
AnsiString TChuangTzu::GetWords(int i)
{
  return FWords[i];
}
```

Notice that it takes a single integer as a parameter and returns an AnsiString.

Here is the set method for the array:

```
void TChuangTzu::SetWords(int i,const AnsiString s)
{
  FCount++;
  FWords[i]=s;
}
```

This function takes both an integer and a string as parameters. In order to call this method, you write

```
ChuangTzu.Words[i] = "peace proclaims olives of endless age."
```

3

C++BUILDER AND THE VCL

Here you can see the integer that is passed to SetWords, as well as a quote from Shakespeare's 107 sonnet that is passed in the second parameter. The FCount variable is used to track the number of entries in the array. Note that properties provide an improvement over get and set methods by letting you use simple array syntax.

Here is an example of how to declare a large AnsiString that extends over several lines:

```
AnsiString S =
    "Easy is right. Begin right ";
    "And you are easy. "
    "Continue easy and you are right. "
    "The right way to go easy "
    "Is to forget the right way "
    "And forget that the going is easy.";
```

The StripWords function is used to peel off words from this quote one at a time, starting at the front:

```
AnsiString StripWords(AnsiString &S, char Token)
{
  AnsiString TokenStr(Token);
  AnsiString Temp1;
  AnsiString Temp2 = S + ' ';

  Temp1 = strtok(S.c_str(), TokenStr.c_str());
  Temp2 = strrev(Temp2.c_str());
  Temp2.SetLength(Temp2.Length() - (Temp1.Length() + 1));
  S = strrev(Temp2.c_str());
  return Temp1;
}
```

There are two interesting things about this function. The first shows how to concatenate strings with the plus operator, and the second shows how to use standard C string functions on an AnsiString.

Notice the bit of syntax that adds a space onto the end of the string passed to the function:

```
AnsiString Temp2 = S + ' ';
```

You can always use the plus operator to append or prefix information to an AnsiString. This eliminates any need for you to use the strcat function, though strcat is a likely candidate for the routine inside the AnsiString implementation that actually performs the concatenation.

NOTE

The reason I append a space onto the end of this string is to ensure that the AnsiString object that underlies this C string makes a unique copy of it. If I simply assign the two strings without changing them, the call to strrev or strtok will affect both strings!

Note also that AnsiStrings support the += operator. Therefore you don't have to write S = S + "Sam", but can write S += "Sam".

I do, however, use standard C functions to tokenize and reverse the strings:

```
Temp1 = strtok(S.c_str(), TokenStr.c_str());
Temp2 = strrev(Temp2.c_str());
Temp2.SetLength(Temp2.Length() - (Temp1.Length() + 1));
```

What the function does here is not important. Just notice that I can get at the underlying null-terminated string with the c_str() method of the AnsiString class. Once I have access to the underlying string, I can pass it to any of the standard C functions such as strrev, strcat, strtok, and so on.

To get the length of a string, call the Length method of the AnsiString class:

```
int I = MyString.Length();
```

I have gone on at some length about the AnsiString class because it is used extensively throughout this book and throughout most BCB programs. The key fact to remember is that AnsiStrings are compatible with the VCL. For instance, you can assign an AnsiString directly to a VCL control:

```
AnsiString S("Doubting the filching age will steal his treasure");
Edit1->Text = S;
```

You can also assign a regular C string to a VCL control, but that is because the VCL string is represented on the C++ side as an AnsiString, which can have its constructor called by a null-terminated string:

```
char S[] = {"Till either gorge be stuffed or prey be gone"};
Memo1->Text = S;
```

NOTE

This time the quote is from Shakespeare's Venus and Adonis, with this seemingly gruesome line appearing in the following context:

```
Till either gorge be stuffed or prey be gone
Even so she kiss'd his brow, his cheek, his chin,
And where she ends she doth anew begin.
```

The bard's point being, I suppose, that her appetites were large.

In fact, you can take advantage of these constructors and assign an integer directly to a VCL control:

```
Memo1->Text = 2;
```

This is considerably more freedom than the strongly typed Object Pascal language would ever give you liberty to pursue.

Exploring SYSDEFS.H

This chapter is largely about the places where C++ and the VCL are woven together. Most of the code that is used to accomplish this end is found in SYSDEFS.H. SYSDEFS.H is the place where the developers put most of the core system code needed to allow BCB to use the VCL native types. In particular, if there was some element of Object Pascal not supported by C++ that played a role in the VCL, solutions to that problem were mapped out in this file. The only major exception to this rule is DSTRINGS.H, where the AnsiString class is declared.

> **NOTE**
>
> SYSDEFS.H is to some degree a testament to the power of the C++ language. It features classes and templates that emulate features of Object Pascal that Delphi relies on the compiler to implement. The advantage of having the compiler implement these features is that it is possible to pick and choose exactly what kind of syntax you want to use. Thus the elegance and simplicity of the Object Pascal language. On the other hand, the extraordinary richness and flexibility of the C++ object model is highlighted beautifully by the work done in SYSDEFS.H.

The following classes appear in SYSDEFS.H:

```
class __declspec(delphireturn) Currency : public CurrencyBase
class __declspec(delphireturn) TDateTime : public TDateTimeBase
class __declspec(delphiclass) TObject
class TMetaClass
class __declspec(delphireturn) Set
class TVarArray
class TVarData
class TVarRec
template<class T> class OpenArray
class __declspec(delphireturn) Variant: public TVarData
class AutoCmd
class NamedParm
class Procedure: public AutoCmd
class Function: public AutoCmd
class PropertySet: public AutoCmd
class PropertyGet: public AutoCmd
typedef class TMemoryManager *PMemoryManager;
class THeapStatus;
```

Some of these classes, such as TObject and TMetaClass, have already been discussed at length. Other classes such as Procedure, Function, PropertyGet, and PropertySet are part of the guts of the BCB-VCL interface, and are not worth discussing in this context. But a few of these classes, notably Set, Currency, TDataTime, Variant, and TMemoryManager play an important role in standard BCB programming, and will therefore be covered in the next few pages. I will also take a look at TVarRec and OpenArray, because they play an important supporting role in the object model.

Formatting Text

In the next three sections, called TDateTime, TCurrency, and OpenArrays, I explore some of the ways you can format text before presenting it to the user. You should read through all three sections to get a feeling for some of the options supplied by BCB.

Many tools for formatting text have been contributed by third-party VCL vendors. There are many sites on the Web that provide links to third-party toolmakers. To get started, visit the Link section of my Web site: users.aol.com/charliecal, or go to www.borland.com.

TDateTime

The VCL comes equipped with a number of functions for working with the current date or time, as shown by this excerpt from the online help:

Date	Returns the current date
DateTimeToStr	Converts a value from time format to a string
DateTimeToString	Converts a value from time format to a string
DateToStr	Converts a value from date format to a string
DayOfWeek	Returns the current day of the week
DecodeDate	Decodes the specified date
DecodeTime	Decodes the specifies time
EncodeDate	Returns values specified in date format
EncodeTime	Returns values specified in time format
FormatDateTime	Formats a date and time using the specified format
Now	Returns the current date and time
StrToDate	Coverts a string to a date format
StrToDateTime	Converts a string to a date/time format
StrToTime	Converts a string to a time format
Time	Returns the current time
TimeToStr	Converts a time format to a string

There is also a TDateTimeField that is used in database programming.

Many of these functions work with an object type called TDateTime that is found in the SYSDEFS.H unit. Most of the rest of this section is dedicated to exploring the uses of the TDateTime type. This type exists in order to provide compatibility with the VCL routines listed at the beginning of this section.

The following method shows two different ways of outputting the current date:

```
void __fastcall TForm1::CurrentDate1Click(TObject *Sender)
{
  TDateTime Date1, Date2 = Now();
  AnsiString S;

  DateTimeToString(S, "dddd, mmmm dd, yyyy", Date1.CurrentDate());
  S += "\r" + Date2.FormatString("dddd, mmmm dd, yyyy");

  ShowMessage(S);
}
```

The code shown in the CurrentDate1Click method outputs the following text inside a RichEdit control:

```
Tuesday, January 07, 1997
Tuesday, January 07, 1997
```

> **NOTE**
>
> The TRichEdit control from the Win95 page of the Component Palette provides supports for the RTF format. There is no set limit on the amount of text you can display in a TRichEdit control, and it supports the use of multiple fonts and colors inside a single control. There are also routines for saving the loading and saving the contents of the control, and for printing.

I initialize the first of the two TDateTime objects with the default constructor, which automatically sets the date to Saturday, December 30, 1899. Then set asks this object to retrieve the current date (not the default date), which it passes to me in the form of a TDateTime object:

```
static TDateTime __fastcall CurrentDate();
```

A raw TDateTime object is obviously not something I can show to the user, so I use the VCL DateTimeToString routine to convert it into a string:

```
DateTimeToString(S, "dddd, mmmm dd, yyyy", Date1.CurrentDate());
```

This routine takes a string in the first parameter, a format string in the second parameter, and a TDateTime record in the third parameter.

> **NOTE**
>
> If you look in SYSDEFS.H, you will see that TDateTime is declared delphireturn. That is because this object needs to conform to the expectations of VCL routines such as DateTimeToString. In other words, this is a classic example of what use the BCB team made of delphireturn.

The second TDateTime object shown in this example is set equal to the current date during its construction:

```
TDateTime Date2(Now());
```

Notice that I pass the VCL routine called Now to the TDateTime constructor. Now returns a variable of type TDateTime that is initialized to the current date and time. You can then use the FormatString method of the TDateTime object to retrieve the current string:

```
S += "\n" + Date2.FormatString("dddd, mmmm dd, yyyy");
```

The FormatString method takes the same type of format string passed to DateTimeToString.

Format strings are documented in the online help, but the basic idea behind them is that if you pass in two letters, you get a number back; pass in three letters, and you get an abbreviation back; and pass in four letters, and you get a whole word back:

```
dd => 01
ddd => Sun
dddd => Sunday
```

The following method displays the current time in a specified format:

```
void __fastcall TForm1::CurrentTime1Click(TObject *Sender)
{
  TDateTime Date(Now());
  RichEdit1->Text = Date.FormatString("h:nn:ss am/PM");
}
```

The result will look something like this:

```
12:27:56 PM
```

In this case, the PM is in large letters because I wrote it that way in the format specifier. Had I written am/pm, the resulting string would have looked like this: 12:27:56 pm. The rest of the format specifiers works like this:

```
h => No leading zero
hh => Prefix a leading zero
```

In short, if you pass in one letter, you get back a string with no leading zero; if you pass in two, a leading zero will be added automatically. Notice that you pass in an n to specify the format for minutes. This is because m has already been used for months.

Here is a table listing the various specifiers you can use:

Format specifier	Item
s	Seconds
m	Minutes
h	Hour

continues

Format specifier	Item
d	Day
m	Month
y	Year
am/pm	Format for time
c	Uses ShortDateFormat and LongTimeFormat
t	Uses ShortTimeFormat
tt	Uses LongTimeFormat
ddddd	Display date using ShortDateFormat
dddddd	Display date using LongDateFormat

The various date and time formats shown in the last items will be explained in just one moment.

The DateTimeString., DateString, and TimeString methods of the TDateTime object do not require that you provide format specifiers. Here, for instance, is an example of how to use the DateTimeString method:

```
void __fastcall TForm1::DateandTime1Click(TObject *Sender)
{
  TDateTime Date(Now());
  RichEdit1->Lines->Add(Date.DateTimeString());
}
```

On my system, the code shown here produces the following result:

```
1/7/97 12:31:24 PM
```

The format used in this case is global to the system. You can change these settings by working with a series of global variables found in SYSUTILS.HPP:

```
extern System::AnsiString CurrencyString;
extern unsigned char CurrencyFormat;
extern unsigned char NegCurrFormat;
extern char ThousandSeparator;
extern char DecimalSeparator;
extern unsigned char CurrencyDecimals;
extern char DateSeparator;
extern System::AnsiString ShortDateFormat;
extern System::AnsiString LongDateFormat;
extern char TimeSeparator;
extern System::AnsiString TimeAMString;
extern System::AnsiString TimePMString;
extern System::AnsiString ShortTimeFormat;
extern System::AnsiString LongTimeFormat;
extern System::AnsiString ShortMonthNames[12];
extern System::AnsiString LongMonthNames[12];
extern System::AnsiString ShortDayNames[7];
extern System::AnsiString LongDayNames[7];
```

On my system, these values are preset as follows:

```
CurrencyString: $
CurrencyFormat: 0
NegCurrFormat: 0
ThousandSeparator: ,
DecimalSeparator: .
CurrencyDecimals: 2
DateSeparator: /
ShortDateFormat: M/d/yy
LongDateFormat: dddd, MMMM dd, yyyy
TimeSeparator: :
TimeAMString: AM
TimePMString: PM
ShortTimeFormat: h:mm AMPM
LongTimeFormat: h:mm:ss AMPM
ShortMonthNames: Jan
ShortMonthNames: Feb
ShortMonthNames: Mar
ShortMonthNames: Apr
ShortMonthNames: May
ShortMonthNames: Jun
ShortMonthNames: Jul
ShortMonthNames: Aug
ShortMonthNames: Sep
ShortMonthNames: Oct
ShortMonthNames: Nov
ShortMonthNames: Dec
LongMonthNames: January
LongMonthNames: February
LongMonthNames: March
LongMonthNames: April
LongMonthNames: May
LongMonthNames: June
LongMonthNames: July
LongMonthNames: August
LongMonthNames: September
LongMonthNames: October
LongMonthNames: November
LongMonthNames: December
ShortDayNames: Sun
ShortDayNames: Mon
ShortDayNames: Tue
ShortDayNames: Wed
ShortDayNames: Thu
ShortDayNames: Fri
ShortDayNames: Sat
LongDayNames: Sunday
LongDayNames: Monday
LongDayNames: Tuesday
LongDayNames: Wednesday
LongDayNames: Thursday
LongDayNames: Friday
LongDayNames: Saturday
```

For instance, the following code changes the nature of the current `ShortDateFormatString`:

```
void __fastcall TForm1::SetShortDateFormattoMMMMDDDDYYYY1Click(TObject *Sender)
{
  RichEdit1->Text = Now();
  ShortDateFormat = "MMMM/DDDD/YYYY";
  RichEdit1->Lines->Add(Now());
}
```

The text displayed by calling this function is as follows:

```
1/7/97 1:30:21 PM
January/Tuesday/1997 1:30:21 PM
```

The first block of text shows the default behavior, and the second block shows what happened after I made a few subtle changes to the system.

The system initializes the date and time strings to the choices you make in Windows. You can see the current Windows settings by calling `GetLocaleInfo`. Changes you make are written to the system registry if you send a `WM_INICHANGE` message to your own nonconsole mode application.

The following lines of code show how you can compare two times using the greater than operator:

```
void __fastcall TForm1::SetTimeOne1Click(TObject *Sender)
{
  FTimeOne = Now();
  RichEdit1->Text = FTimeOne.TimeString();
}

void __fastcall TForm1::SetTimeTwo1Click(TObject *Sender)
{
  FTimeTwo = Now();
  RichEdit1->Lines->Add(FTimeTwo.TimeString());
}

void __fastcall TForm1::CompareOnetoTwo1Click(TObject *Sender)
{
  AnsiString S;

  if (FTimeOne > FTimeTwo)
    S = FTimeOne.TimeString() + " > " + FTimeTwo.TimeString();
  else
    S = FTimeTwo.TimeString() + " > " + FTimeOne.TimeString();
  RichEdit1->Lines->Add(S);
}
```

The first method shown here sets a global object called `TimeOne` to the current time. The second method sets a second global object to the current time. After calling the two functions at a two-second interval, you can end up with the objects initialized to two different times:

```
2:10:29 PM
2:10:31 PM
```

You can then use the third function to compare them using the > operator:

```
2:10:31 PM > 2:10:29 PM
```

You can also use the ++ operator on the current time to increment the day by one:

```
void __fastcall TForm1::CompareTwotoOne1Click(TObject *Sender)
{
  int i;

  RichEdit1->Lines->Add(FTimeOne.DateTimeString());
  FTimeOne++;
  RichEdit1->Lines->Add(FTimeOne.DateTimeString());
}
```

Here is the output in the RichEdit control after a run off all four functions:

```
2:13:03 PM
2:13:05 PM
2:13:05 PM > 2:13:03 PM      // First call to compare
1/7/97 2:13:03 PM
1/8/97 2:13:03 PM
2:13:03 PM > 2:13:05 PM      // Second call to compare
```

As you can see, calling the ++ operator incremented the day by one. After incrementing the values, a second call to the compare function showed that FTimeOne is now larger than FTimeTwo. Even though it is still two seconds smaller than date two, it is now a day later, and hence larger.

This should give you some sense of what you can do with the TDateTime type. This has not been an exhaustive investigation of what can be done, but if you now open up SysDefs.h, you should have no trouble following the drift of the declaration for the other methods in the TDateTime object. The code samples shown in this section are from a program found on disk called, in a flight of poetic fancy, DateTime1.

TCurrency

I will now spend a few minutes looking at TCurrency. After the rather lengthy investigation of TDateTime that you just saw, there should not be much need to examine this object in-depth, because it follows the same general patterns of logic you saw in the previous section.

When following this discussion, remember that the primary reason the type exists is for compatibility with the VCL. In particular, the TCurrency type, like the TDateTime type, is used in database programming. For instance, there is a TCurrencyField and a TDateTimeField available for database programmers. The principles behind the field types are examined in detail throughout the lengthy database section of this book, Chapters 8 through 18, and particularly in Chapter 11, "Working with Field Objects."

The Currency type is a wrapper around the built in __int64 type. The compiler probably will not support assigning large numbers directly to a variable of type Currency:

```
Currency C = 5000000000000; // This probably won't work
```

3

You can, however, pass in a string that holds a large number. Consider the following method:

```
Currency C = void __fastcall TForm1::Button1Click(TObject *Sender)
{
  Currency C("500000000000000");

  AnsiString S = C;
  Edit1->Text = S;
  Edit2->Text = Format("%m", OPENARRAY(TVarRec, (C)));
}
```

This method initializes a variable of type currency to a large number with a string. Most of the time large numbers will be entered by the user in an edit control, so this is a reasonable way to proceed.

Once you have an instance of a Currency type, you can display it directly to the user or assign it to a TCurrencyField from a database table. Notice that you can assign a string directly to a Currency field, and vice versa. When translating a currency type to a string, the result does not produce a formatted result string. Instead, you see a plain number:

500000000000000

If you want to display the string with proper formatting, use the Format function, as shown in the Button1Click method:

$500,000,000,000,000.00

I will describe the Format function, and OpenArrays, in the next section of this chapter, called "Working with OpenArrays." Note that some of the database controls will automatically display a currency type with formatting, depending in part on their attributes and the contents of the Data Dictionary.

The currency type will handle numbers in the following range:

-922337203685477.5808..922337203685477.5807

That is, it can handle between 19 and 20 digits.

There are many operators in the Currency class for performing mathematical operations. For instance, the following syntax is valid:

```
Currency C1 = 25000, C2 = 5000, C3;
C1 += C2;
C1 = C2 / 9;
C3 = (C1 % C2);
C3 = (C1 + C2) / C1 + (C1 % C2);
```

It's interesting to note that these operations are performed on objects, and not on simple types. This is an excellent example of the power of C++ and the amazing things you can do with operator overloading. If you are not used to C++, you should spend a few moments contemplating the fact that C1, C2, and C3 are objects, with methods and functions, and not just simple built-in types like integers or floats. You should open up SysDefs.h to see a list of all the supported syntax used by the Currency object.

MaskEdits and Other Issues

The native VCL `TMaskEdit` control deserves at least a few sentences of comment during this discussion of formatting strings. This component is a descendant of `TEdit` that enables you to control the kinds of characters that are entered into the control.

The key to the `TMaskEdit` component is the `EditMask` property, which enables you to enter a string that uses several special characters to define what the user can legally enter into the edit area.

There is a property editor associated with the `EditMask` property. In this editor, you can find a number of default masks, as shown in Figure 3.1. However, on many occasions, none of these masks will suit your purpose.

FIGURE 3.1.

The property editor for the `EditMask` *property.*

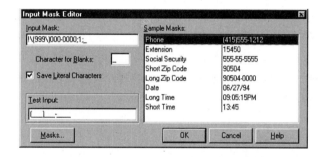

I could, for instance, enter the following string as an `EditMask`:

```
######;0;_
```

The purpose of this string is to ensure that the user can enter only numeric values. In particular, these numeric values represent the number of widgets that the user wants to sell.

To understand the `EditMask` property, you need to study the entry associated with it in the online help. Here, you see all the characters that can be used to define a mask, along with a description of the effects associated with each character. I quote most of this list later in this section.

In the online help for the `EditMask` property, you will find that a pound sign (#) enables you to enter only numbers, spaces, and plus and minus characters. Notice, however, that there is also a `0` character, which requires that you enter a number in each location marked with that character. The question, then, is which special character should you use: # or `0`?

In some cases, the `0` character is *not* what you want, because it forces the user to enter values. For instance, the following code forces the user to enter a six-digit number, one for each of the zeroes you place in the mask:

```
000000;0;_
```

The preceding mask would enable you to enter the number 123456, but it would reject 123. If you want to give the user the freedom to enter a number of any size up to 999,999, you should use the # character rather than the 0 character. One way to sum this matter up is as follows: The 0 character means that the user has to fill in that place with a number, while the # character enables the user to fill in that space with either a number or a blank space.

The zero that appears after the semicolon in the previous string specifies that the mask entered is not saved as part of the data. If I had placed a 1 here, the mask would have been saved. In this particular case, there are no mask characters to either save or discard, so it doesn't matter what I placed in this location. The phone mask, shown previously in Figure 3.1, contains two parentheses that would be affected by this value.

Finally, the very end of the previous mask includes an underscore. This value is used to specify what will be used to designate the space character.

Notice that each field of the mask is separated from the last by a semicolon. Each mask consists of three fields, which were described earlier.

The MaskEdit component is available from the Additional page of the Component palette. Notice that you can click a button in the EditMask dialog found in the EditMask property editor in order to load country-specific strings.

NOTE

The following lists format specifiers you can use in the TMaskEdit control:

!   If an ! character appears in the mask, leading blanks don't appear in the data. If an ! character is not present, trailing blanks don't appear in the data.

>   If a > character appears in the mask, all characters that follow are in uppercase until the end of the mask or until a < character is encountered.

<   If a < character appears in the mask, all characters that follow are in lowercase until the end of the mask or until a > character is encountered.

<>   If these two characters appear together in a mask, no case checking is done and the data is formatted with the case the user uses to enter the data.

\   The character that follows a \ character is a literal character. Use this character when you want to allow any of the mask special characters as a literal in the data.

L   The L character requires only an alphabetic character only in this position. For the US, this is A-Z, a-z.

l   The l character permits only an alphabetic character in this position, but doesn't require it.

A   The A character requires an alphanumeric character only in this position. For the US, this is A-Z, a-z, and 0-9.

a   The a character permits an alphanumeric character in this position, but doesn't require it.

c The c character requires a character in this position.

c The c character permits a character in this position, but doesn't require it.

0 The 0 character requires a numeric character only in this position.

9 The 9 character permits a numeric character in this position, but doesn't require it.

The # character permits a numeric character or a plus or minus sign in this position, but doesn't require it.

: The : character is used to separate hours, minutes, and seconds in times. If the character that separates hours, minutes, and seconds is different in the International settings of the Control Panel utility on your computer system, that character is used instead of :.

/ The / character is used to separate months, days, and years in dates. If the character that separates months, days, and years is different in the International settings of the Control Panel utility on your computer system, that character is used instead of /.

; The ; character is used to separate masks.

_ The _ character automatically inserts a blank the edit box. When the user enters characters in the field, the cursor skips the blank character. When using the EditMask property editor, you can change the character used to represent blanks. You can also change this value programmatically. See the following table.

Remember that many of the database objects such as the TDateTime field provide automatic formatting for you.

This is also an area where you might consider turning to third-party products. For instance, Turbo Power Software has an excellent library called Orpheus that provides many fine controls and routines for automatically formatting strings. You should, however, explore the market thoroughly, because there are many fine products out there for handling this type of problem. In particular, many controls are found on the Web. You can visit my Web site to find links to sites that specialize in components. (users.aol.com/charliecal).

Working with OpenArrays

The VCL supports a concept called an array of const. This type will enable you to pass in a variable number of parameters. Think for a moment of the sprintf function:

```
int sprintf(char *buffer, const char *format[, argument, ...]);
```

The last argument of this function can contain multiple parameters. OpenArrays provide the same functionality in Object Pascal. In short, they enable you to pass a variable number of parameters to a function.

3

Here is an Object Pascal code segment declared to accept an array of `const`:

```
function Format(const Format: string; const Args: array of const): string;
```

The `Format` function acts almost exactly like `sprintf`. Its first parameter contains a string with various format specifiers in it, and its second parameter consists of an array containing multiple values to be formatted. The format specifiers used by `Format` are essentially the same as those you would use in `sprintf`. After all, the whole point of adding the function to the Object Pascal language was simply to duplicate the functionality of `sprintf` inside Object Pascal. Here is the way a call to `Format` looks in Object Pascal:

```
var
  S, Name: string;
  Age: Integer;
begin
  Name = GetName;
  Age = GetAge;
  S := Format("My name is %s and I am %d years old", [Name, Age]);
end;
```

All this is good and well, but you might object that C++ already has support for this kind of syntax through `sprintf`. That is correct, but you will find many VCL database routines that use arrays of `const` for various purposes. There are no standard C++ equivalents of these routines, as they exist only in the VCL. In other words, the C++ and Object Pascal implementations of this functionality differ in their details, even though the interface to the user is similar. As a result, special C++ classes need to be created to duplicate this built-in Object Pascal type.

While you may or may not find the `Format` routine itself useful, you will definitely need to know about arrays of `const` if you want to work with the VCL, and particularly if you want to do any database programming. For instance, the following database routines all use arrays of `const`: `FinkKey`, `FindNearest`, `SetRange`, `AddRecord`, `SetKeyFields`, `AppendRecord`, `InsertRecord`, `SetFields`, `AssignValue`, and `DBErrorFmt`. Clearly, this is a subject that you need to understand.

Here is the declaration for the `Format` function as it appears in `SYSUTILS.HPP`:

```
extern System::AnsiString __fastcall Format(const System::AnsiString Format,
  const System::TVarRec *Args, const int Args_Size);
```

As you can see, this function takes not two, but three parameters. You will not, however, pass all three parameters into this function, nor will you pass them into any of the database routines shown previously. Instead, you use a macro called `OPENARRAY`, which enables you to call VCL functions that use arrays of `const` with a reasonable degree of ease.

NOTE

As I am sure you have noticed already, this particular subject is not exactly the garden spot of C++Builder. We are definitely in the low-rent district right now, and so perhaps a few more words of explanation are necessary.

Object Pascal originally had no support for functions that took a variable array of parameters. As the spec for Delphi developed, it became clear that there had to be a solution to this problem. The language needed to support functions that took a varying array of parameters because various database calls demanded this functionality. In particular, routines that dealt with keyed fields needed varying numbers of parameters depending on the number of fields present in a composite key.

An array of const was the solution the Object Pascal team came up with for this problem. On the Delphi side, this is a elegant solution that enables you to write simple, easy-to-read code. However, this is not the same solution that the C and C++ languages used when resolving a similar problem. As a result, arrays of const are implemented in an entirely different manner than either the variadic arguments such as you find in sprintf, or the standard C++ practice of function overloading. There was, in short, no common ground between the two languages when it came to this subject.

Hence you find your self wandering down this dark alley, where OpenArrays meet the array of const. I won't make myself look foolish by trying to claim that the solution found here is elegant, but it is usable. Given the nature of the problem the BCB team had thrust upon them, the solution seems reasonable to me.

I also do not feel that this particular low-rent district is typical of BCB neighborhoods. I love BCB components, properties, and events. These are areas where the tool really shines. Open arrays, on the other hand, are at best nothing more than a satisfactory solution to a difficult problem.

One important point to note about the BCB environment, however, is that you can use function overloading in some cases, OPENARRAYS in other cases, or switch to Object Pascal code and use elegant and concise solution provided by an array of const. This environment provides a rich set of tools from which you can pick and choose. Because you have access to the tools available in two different languages, there is no other programming environment on the market that even comes close to the richness of features found in BCB.

Here is a routine that uses both open arrays and sprintf to solve the same problem:

```
void __fastcall TForm1::Button1Click(TObject *Sender)
{
  char S[150];

  if (MoreInput->ShowModal() == mrOk)
  {
    sprintf(S, "Hello, my name is %s, and I'm %d years old.",
      MoreInput->Name, MoreInput->Age);
    Edit1->Text = S;

    Edit2->Text = Format("Hello, my name is %s, and I'm %d years old.",
      OPENARRAY(TVarRec, (MoreInput->Name, MoreInput->Age)));
  }
}
```

In showing your comparative examples of `sprintf` and `Format`, this function makes use of a second form called `TMoreInput`. I will discuss this form in the next section of the chapter. For now, however, I will forgo discussing multiform projects, and will concentrate instead on using `OpenArrays`.

As you can see, it doesn't really take any more code to use `Format` and `OPENARRAY` than it does to use `sprintf`. In fact, both techniques have their disadvantages. The `sprintf` method requires you to declare a temporary variable, the `Format` method gives you a good dose of the wordy `OPENARRAY` macro. However, neither technique is particularly difficult to implement.

When using `OPENARRAY`, you usually pass `TVarRec` as the first argument of the macro, and then pass a comma-delimited set of variables in the second argument. The entire second argument should be set off by parentheses. Here are a few rather artificial examples of how to use the macro:

```
OPENARRAY(TVarRec, (1))
OPENARRAY(TVarRec, (1, 2))
OPENARRAY(TVarRec, (1, 2, 3))
```

And so on, up to, but not beyond, 18. The point is that you pass the variables you want to have processed in the second argument to the macro. You can pass any type in this section, because the macro itself doesn't care. The method that is using the macro may not be so forgiving, however, so you need to put some thought into the code you write. For instance, `Format` takes only certain types of parameters, and there would be no point in passing something to `OPENARRAY` that the `Format` function could not process. The same holds true of `sprintf`. There would be no point in passing the wrong type of parameter to it, because the format specifiers handle only certain types.

The `OPENARRAY` macro itself is very simple:

```
#define OPENARRAY(type, values) \
    OpenArray<type>values, OpenArrayCount<type>values.GetHigh()
```

As you can see, it takes two separate object templates to make the array work. (In fact, `TVarRec` is a third object, so it takes three objects in all to bring this business home for dinner.) If you are interested, you can open up `SysDefs.h` and see how this technology is implemented. For the purposes of this book, however, I will simply say that this is one of those cases where you should "pay no attention to the man behind the curtain." I just let the macro do its work and concentrate instead on the parts of the program that are under my jurisdiction.

That is all I'm going to say about `OpenArrays`. As I conceded earlier, this is not really the garden spot of BCB programming. However, the code I've shown you does get the job done. In particular, the point of this `OpenArray` business is that it enables you to pass a variant number of parameters to a function. This is a pretty slick trick in itself, and some programmers will probably be able to find occasions when they can use this technology for their own purposes. Its main value, however, is simply that it enables you to use the parts of the VCL that are expecting an `array of const`.

Using Two Forms in One Program

The sample function shown above called `Button1Click` has a line in it where a second form is launched:

```
if (MoreInput->ShowModal() == mrOk)
```

The program uses this second form to retrieve the name and age input from the user.

Popping up a form to get information from a user is a common task in BCB, so I should perhaps take a moment to explain how it works.

To get started, you should use the File menu, or some other tool, to create a second form for your project. Save it into the same directory where your current project is located. Add two edit controls labeled `Name` and `Age` to the second form, and place two `TBitBtns` on the form, as shown in Figure 3.2. Use the `Kind` property of the `BitBtns` to make one an OK button and the second a Cancel button. Notice that the `ModalResult` property of the OK `TBitBtn` is automatically set to `mrOk`, and the `ModalResult` property of the Cancel `TBitBtn` is automatically set to `mrCancel`.

FIGURE 3.2.

The form for the `TMoreInput` *dialog has two labels, two edit controls, and two* `TBitBtns`.

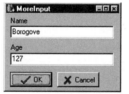

Now create two properties that users of the form can use when they need to access the input from the user:

```
class TMoreInput : public TForm
{
  // Code omitted here
private:
  AnsiString FName;
  int FAge;
public:
  virtual __fastcall TMoreInput(TComponent* Owner);
  __property int Age={read=FAge, write=FAge};
  __property AnsiString Name={read=FName, write=FName};
};
```

As you can see, the `Age` and `Name` properties front for two `private` variables of the object. These variable are assigned to the user's input if the user presses the OK button:

```
void __fastcall TMoreInput::OkBtnClick(TObject *Sender)
{
  Name = Edit1->Text;
  Age = Edit2->Text.ToInt();
}
```

It is now time to go full circle and look back at the stripped-down version of the function that makes use of this dialog:

```
void __fastcall TForm1::Button1Click(TObject *Sender)
{
  if (MoreInput->ShowModal() == mrOk)
  {
    Edit2->Text = Format("Hello, my name is %s, and I'm %d years old.",
      OPENARRAY(TVarRec, (MoreInput->Name, MoreInput->Age)));
  }
}
```

The `Button1Click` method calls the `TForm` `ShowModal` method to launch the dialog. If the user presses the OK button, the input is retrieved from the `TMoreInput` dialog through the officially designated properties. This enables you to use the private data of `TMoreInput` without forcing `TMoreInput` to refrain from ever changing its implementation. For instance, `TMoreInput` could someday use a `struct` that contains both the `Name` and `Age` fields, but could continue to give users of the form access to data through the `Name` and `Age` variables.

If you are interested in this program, you can find it on disk in the `Chap02` directory as a file called `OpenArrays1`. The program itself is simple, but it gives a good illustration of how to use a second dialog to retrieve information from the user. This is a common task that will see many variations run on it in different parts of this book.

Working with the Set Object

Sets are used widely in BCB. Here for instance, is the `MsgDialog` routine, which is called frequently but requires some knowledge of sets before you can use it correctly:

```
AnsiString S("While Lust is in his pride, no exclamation \n"
             "Can curb his heat or rein his rash desire.");

MessageDlg(S, mtInformation, TMsgDlgButtons() << mbOK, 0);
```

The VCL makes heavy use of sets, so there are a number of places in standard BCB database or interface code where you will need to take advantage of the syntax you see here. The goal of the next few pages of this chapter is to explore the BCB Set class and reveal its inner workings.

Sets are easy to understand if you just take a few minutes to absorb their syntax. This is, however, one of those subjects that you have to master if you want to use BCB. In fact, you will find many parts of BCB cumbersome if you don't understand this template class.

Here is a "pseudo template" for the header of the set class designed to help you see how these sets are structured:

```
Set<Type, MinimumValue, MaximumValue>
```

More precisely, here is the more formal header declaration from `SysDefs.h`:

```
template<class T, unsigned char minEl, unsigned char maxEl>
```

To declare a set, you write the word Set followed by an open bracket, the type of your set, and its minimum and maximum values. For instance, if you want to create a set of all small letters, you would write

```
Set<char, 'a', 'z'> SmallLetters;
```

To create the set of all numbers between 0 and 9, you might write

```
Set<int, 0, 9> SmallNumbers;
```

In the first case, MySet does not consist of the letters a and z, but of a, z, *and* all the letters between them. In other words, the letter a is the smallest value in the set and the letter z is the maximum value in the set, as shown previously in the formal declaration for the template class.

Both SmallLetters and SmallNumbers are declarations of objects. Often, you don't want to create a new object, but create a new object type with the typedef keyword:

```
typedef Set<int, 0, 9> TSmallNumbers;
```

Now you have a type you can work with, and can therefore declare separate instances of this type:

```
TSmallNumbers SmallNumbers1;
TSmallNumbers SmallNumbers2;
```

The point here is that the first numeric set declared previously, the one called SmallNumbers, is an instance of an object, while TSmallNumbers is the declaration for a type.

3

C++BUILDER AND THE VCL

NOTE

I'm going to break a rule of this book and spend a few moments on standard C syntax. In particular, I'm going to look at typedefs, because this is an important and easily misunderstood part of the language. The typedef keyword enables you to declare a type within a particular scope. Unfortunately, the #define directive performs a function similar to the typedef keyword, even though the two pieces of syntax have different ways of implementing the result.

For instance, the following two lines have the same effect on your code:

```
typedef float REAL;
#define float REAL
```

One asks the compiler to do its work for it, while the second asks the preprocessor to do the work. The result, however, is similar. That is, they give you a new "type" to work with called REAL.

I try to keep some order in my code by always using typedef to declare types, while I generally use #define only to declare constants. No one is perfect, and I probably break that rule from time to time, but I try to follow it with some regularity.

continues

continued

A typedef has effect only within a particular scope. I generally declare types in the header for a unit, unless I want to limit the scope of the type to a particular method or function, in which case I declare the type inside that method or function.

I will not go into this subject any further in this book, nor is the discussion included here meant to be exhaustive. If you want additional information on the typedef keyword, you should turn to a primer on C++. For this book all you need to know is that typedefs provide a way of declaring your own types within a particular scope. I never use it for any other purpose, and I try never to use any other technique for declaring types.

Now that you know the basic facts about sets, it's time to look at some programs that give them a workout. These are important examples, so I will feature them in their own section of the chapter.

Two Sample Programs for Working with Sets

The sample program shown in Listings 3.3 and 3.4, called NumberSets, gives you a look at the basic syntax for creating sets. It is followed by a second sample program, called SetBasics, that shows how to create the union, intersection, and difference of two sets.

NOTE

The Set sample programs used in this book originally included some sample components that are found in the Examples directory that ships with BCB. These components were found in Delphi on a page called Samples, but are not installed by default in BCB. If you go into the Examples\Controls directory, you will find an explanation of how to install these components.

In particular, the spin edit control can be a useful tool to use in this kind of program. Check the CD that accompanies this book for an update on this issue and how it affects these programs.

Listing 3.3. The header for the NumberSets program.

```
//------------------------------------------------------------
#ifndef MainH
#define MainH
//------------------------------------------------------------
#include <vcl\Classes.hpp>
#include <vcl\Controls.hpp>
#include <vcl\StdCtrls.hpp>
#include <vcl\Forms.hpp>
```

```
#include <vcl\Spin.hpp>
//-------------------------------------------------------------------------
typedef  Set<int, 0, 9> TSmallNum;

class TForm1 : public TForm
{
__published:
  TButton *AddToSetABtn;
  TListBox *ListBox1;
  TSpinEdit *SpinEdit1;
  TButton *RemoveFromSetBtn;
  void __fastcall AddToSetABtnClick(TObject *Sender);

  void __fastcall RemoveFromSetBtnClick(TObject *Sender);
private:
  TSmallNum NumSet;
  void __fastcall ShowSet(TSmallNum ANumSet, int ListBoxNum);
public:
  virtual __fastcall TForm1(TComponent* Owner);
};
//-------------------------------------------------------------------------
extern TForm1 *Form1;
//-------------------------------------------------------------------------
#endif
```

3

C++BUILDER AND
THE VCL

Listing 3.4. The main form for the NumberSets program.

```
#include <vcl\vcl.h>
#pragma hdrstop
#include "Main.h"
#pragma resource "*.dfm"
TForm1 *Form1;

__fastcall TForm1::TForm1(TComponent* Owner)
  : TForm(Owner)
{
}

void __fastcall TForm1::ShowSet(TSmallNum ASmallNum, int ListBoxNum)
{
  AnsiString S("Set <");

  for (int i = 0; i < 275; i++)
  {
    if (ASmallNum.Contains(i))
      S += "'" + AnsiString(i) + "',";
  }
  S.SetLength(S.Length() - 1);
  S += ">";
  if (S.Length() == 5)
    S = "NULL Set";

  switch (ListBoxNum)
  {
    case 1:
```

continues

Listing 3.4. continued

```
        ListBox1->Items->Add(S);
        break;

    default:
        ShowMessage("Error specifying listbox");
    }
}

void __fastcall TForm1::AddToSetABtnClick(TObject *Sender)
{
    int i = SpinEdit1->Text.ToInt();

    NumSet << i;

    ShowSet(NumSet, 1);
}

void __fastcall TForm1::RemoveFromSetBtnClick(TObject *Sender)
{
    int i = SpinEdit1->Text.ToInt();
    NumSet >> i;

    ShowSet(NumSet, 1);
}
```

NumberSet works with a simple set containing the numbers between 0 and 9:

```
typedef  Set<int, 0, 9> TSmallNum;
TSmallNum NumSet;
```

The main function of the program is to show how to move items in and out of a set. The AddToSetABtnClick method retrieves the number the user places in a TSpinEdit control:

```
int i = SpinEdit1->Text.ToInt();
```

It then uses the << operator to insert the new number into the set:

```
NumSet << i;
```

A similar method shows how to move information out of the set:

```
int i = SpinEdit1->Text.ToInt();
NumSet >> i;
```

The most complicated code in the program involves a method called ShowSet that creates a picture of the set and shows it to the user. The heart of the ShowSet method uses the Contains method of BCB's Set class to see if a particular element is contained in the set:

```
if (ASmallNum.Contains(i))
```

Contains returns True if the element is part of the set, and it returns False if the element is not in the set. The results of this effort are shown to the user in a TListBox, as illustrated in Figure 3.3.

FIGURE 3.3.

The NumberSet program creates a visual image of a set so you can get an accurate feeling for how sets work.

The SetBasics program takes the principles used in the NumberSet example and pushes them a little further so you can get a clear sense of what it means to create the intersection, union, or difference of two sets. (See Figure 3.4.) The code for the program is shown in Listing 3.5 and 3.6.

FIGURE 3.4.

The SetBasics program shows how to find the union, difference, or intersection of two sets.

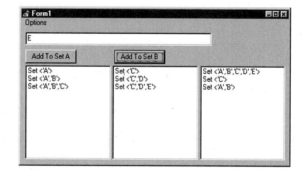

Listing 3.5. The header for the SetBasics program.

```
//--------------------------------------------------------------
#ifndef MainH
#define MainH
//--------------------------------------------------------------
#include <vcl\Classes.hpp>
#include <vcl\Controls.hpp>
#include <vcl\StdCtrls.hpp>
#include <vcl\Forms.hpp>
#include <vcl\Menus.hpp>
//--------------------------------------------------------------

typedef Set <char, 'A', 'z'> TLetterSet;

class TForm1 : public TForm
{
__published:
  TEdit *Edit1;
  TButton *AddToSetABtn;
  TListBox *ListBox1;
  TButton *AddToSetBBtn;
```

continues

Listing 3.5. continued

```
  TListBox *ListBox2;
  TListBox *ListBox3;
  TMainMenu *MainMenu1;
  TMenuItem *Options1;
  TMenuItem *Union1;
  TMenuItem *Intersection1;
  TMenuItem *Difference1;
  void __fastcall AddToSetABtnClick(TObject *Sender);
  void __fastcall AddToSetBBtnClick(TObject *Sender);
  void __fastcall Union1Click(TObject *Sender);
  void __fastcall Intersection1Click(TObject *Sender);
  void __fastcall Difference1Click(TObject *Sender);
private:
  TLetterSet LetterSetA;
  TLetterSet LetterSetB;
  void __fastcall ShowSet(TLetterSet ALetterSet, int ListBoxNum);
public:
  virtual __fastcall TForm1(TComponent* Owner);
};
//--------------------------------------------------------------
extern TForm1 *Form1;
//--------------------------------------------------------------
#endif
```

Listing 3.6. The main form for the SetBasics program.

```
#include <vcl\vcl.h>
#pragma hdrstop

#include "Main.h"

#pragma resource "*.dfm"
TForm1 *Form1;


__fastcall TForm1::TForm1(TComponent* Owner)
    : TForm(Owner)
{
}

void __fastcall TForm1::ShowSet(TLetterSet ALetterSet, int ListBoxNum)
{
  AnsiString S("Set <");

  for (int i = 0; i < 275; i++)
  {
    if (ALetterSet.Contains(char(i)))
      S += "'" + AnsiString(char(i)) + "',";
  }
  S.SetLength(S.Length() - 1);
  S += ">";

  if (S.Length() == 5)
    S = "NULL Set";
```

```
  switch (ListBoxNum)
  {
    case 1: ListBox1->Items->Add(S); break;
    case 2: ListBox2->Items->Add(S); break;
    case 3: ListBox3->Items->Add(S); break;
  default:
    ShowMessage("Error specifying listbox");
  }
}

void __fastcall TForm1::AddToSetABtnClick(TObject *Sender)
{
  AnsiString S(Edit1->Text);
  char ch = S[1];

  LetterSetA << ch;

  ShowSet(LetterSetA, 1);
}

void __fastcall TForm1::AddToSetBBtnClick(TObject *Sender)
{
  AnsiString S(Edit1->Text);
  char ch = S[1];

  LetterSetB << ch;

  ShowSet(LetterSetB, 2);
}

void __fastcall TForm1::Union1Click(TObject *Sender)
{
  TLetterSet Union;

  Union = LetterSetA + LetterSetB;

  ShowSet(Union, 3);
}

void __fastcall TForm1::Intersection1Click(TObject *Sender)
{
  TLetterSet Intersection;

  Intersection = LetterSetA * LetterSetB;

  ShowSet(Intersection, 3);
}

void __fastcall TForm1::Difference1Click(TObject *Sender)
{
  TLetterSet Difference;

  Difference = LetterSetA - LetterSetB;

  ShowSet(Difference, 3);
}
//------------------------------------------------------------------
```

The SetBasics program uses a set of char instead of a set of integers:

```
typedef Set <char, 'A', 'z'> TLetterSet;
```

The code for moving elements in a set has not changed significantly from the NumberSet example:

```
void __fastcall TForm1::AddToSetABtnClick(TObject *Sender)
{
  AnsiString S(Edit1->Text);
  char ch = S[1];

  LetterSetA << ch;

  ShowSet(LetterSetA, 1);
}

void __fastcall TForm1::AddToSetBBtnClick(TObject *Sender)
{
  AnsiString S(Edit1->Text);
  char ch = S[1];

  LetterSetB << ch;

  ShowSet(LetterSetB, 2);
}
```

The difference here, of course, is that two sets are being used, and that you can only add elements to each set.

NOTE

Just before the release of C++Builder, the team changed the way the first character of an AnsiString is accessed. It is now indexed at the first position in the array, rather than at position zero:

```
char ch = S[1];  // First character of string
char ch = S[0];  // References nothing, incorrect reference!
```

This change came so late in the product cycle that I may not reference it correctly in all cases where the subject is brought up in this text. However, I should have caught all references in the code that appears on the CD-ROM that accompanies this book.

Once you have created two sets that interest you, you can press a button on the applications form to see the union, difference, or intersection of the sets. Here, for instance, is how to create the intersection of two sets:

```
void __fastcall TForm1::Intersection1Click(TObject *Sender)
{
  TLetterSet Intersection;

  Intersection = LetterSetA * LetterSetB;
```

```
    ShowSet(Intersection, 3);
}
```

The * operator of the Set template is used to perform the operation. You use the + operator to find the union of two sets and the - operator to show the difference between two sets:

```
Union = LetterSetA + LetterSetB;
Difference = LetterSetA - LetterSetB;
```

The main form for the program is shown in Listing 3.6.

Suppose you have two sets that look like this:

```
<'A', 'B', 'E'>     <'B', 'G'>
```

The union of the sets would look like this: `<'A', 'B', 'E', 'G'>`.

The intersection would look like this: `<'B'>`.

The difference, if you subtracted the second from the first, would look like this: `<'A', 'E'>`.

You can experiment with the program further if you want to see more about creating the intersection, union, or difference of two sets. If you look in SysDefs.h or in the online help, you will see that there are also operators that enable you to test for equality or to see if one set is larger than another.

A Few Additional Points about Sets

You can add multiple items to a set with the following syntax:

```
NumSet << 2 << 3 << 5;
```

Here, for instance, is a real-world case of adding or removing items from a TNavigator control:

```
FMyNavigator->VisibleButtons =
    TButtonSet() << nbFirst << nbLast << nbNext << nbPrior;
```

In general, sets are very easy to use, though their syntax is not particularly inviting at first glance. Once again, it is important to remember that this Set class is meant for use with the VCL. The Set class in SysDefs.h is not a general purpose set class, and it is not meant as a substitute for the code you find in the Standard Template Library.

As with much of the code shown in this chapter, the key point that justifies the existence of the Set class is its compatibility with certain features of the VCL. Two such features have been illustrated in the last few pages. The first illustrative example is the preceding FMyNavigator code, and the MsgDialog code shown back at the beginning of this discussion of sets:

```
MessageDlg(S, mtInformation, TMsgDlgButtons() << mbOK, 0);
```

`TMsgDlgButtons` is a set class. It has the following declaration:

```
enum TMsgDlgBtn { mbYes, mbNo, mbOK, mbCancel, mbAbort,
                  mbRetry, mbIgnore, mbAll, mbHelp };

typedef Set<TMsgDlgBtn, mbYes, mbHelp>  TMsgDlgButtons;
```

It should now be obvious how to use this set. The elements of the set consist of all the items in the `TMsgDlgBtn` enumerated type. The set itself ranges from a low value of `mbYes` to a high value of `mbHelp`. If you wanted All and Ignore buttons on a `MessageBox`, you could write the following code to display it to the user:

```
MessageDlg(S, mtInformation, TMsgDlgButtons() << mbAll << mbIgnore, 0);
```

The second parameter to `MessageDlg` contains a value from the following enumerated type:

```
enum TMsgDlgType { mtWarning, mtError, mtInformation, mtConfirmation, mtCustom };
```

Use the Source, Luke!

You might notice that I frequently refer directly to the various header files that ship with BCB. Getting to know as much as possible about the source for the VCL and for BCB is a worthwhile endeavor. There are times when I use the Tool menu to make it even easier to get at source files that I use a lot.

You can configure the Tools menu in BCB to run any program you like. As a result, I sometimes ask it to start Notepad (also known as Visual Notepad) or some other editor with the source from a key header file in it. To do this

1. Open the Tools menu and select Configure.
2. In the Title field, give your new menu item a name, such as `SysDefs`.
3. In the Program field, enter the name of the executable you want to run, such as Notepad, Visual SlickEdit, CodeWright, or MultiEdit.
4. Set up a working directory, which is usually the place where the include files are located: `g:\bcb\include\vcl`.
5. Pass in the name of the file you want to launch in the Parameters field.
6. Click the Close button.

The way this process looks in action is shown in Figure 3.5.

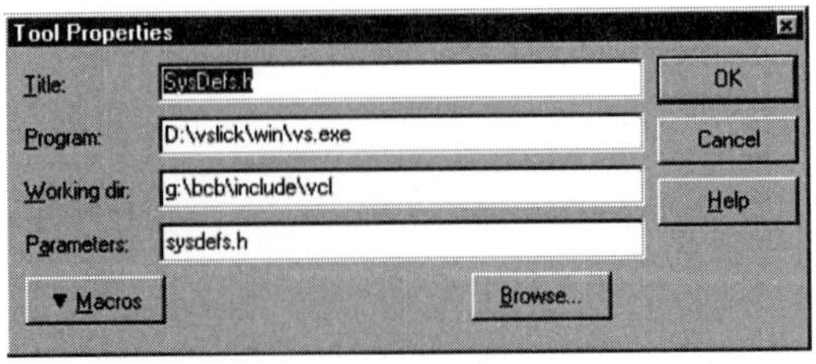

FIGURE 3.5.

Using the Tools menu to create a means for automatically opening a header file whenever you need it.

If possible, and especially if you are using Windows 95, you should find a real editor to use with large header files. Good ones include Visual SlickEdit from MicroEdge, MultiEdit from American Cybernetics, and CodeWright from Premia.

Getting the Heap Status

To understand what is happening in your program, you should become familiar with the `THeapStatus` class from `SYSDEFS.HPP`:

```
class THeapStatus {
  public:
    Cardinal TotalAddrSpace;
    Cardinal TotalUncommitted;
    Cardinal TotalCommitted;
    Cardinal TotalAllocated;
    Cardinal TotalFree;
    Cardinal FreeSmall;
    Cardinal FreeBig;
    Cardinal Unused;
    Cardinal Overhead;
    Cardinal HeapErrorCode;
} ;
```

To retrieve an instance of this type, you can call `GetHeapStatus`:

```
THeapStatus HeapStatus = GetHeapStatus();
```

The values retrieved by a call to `GetHeapStatus` tell you about the condition of the heap for your program. They do not refer to global memory for the machine on which your program is running. This call will probably fail if made from inside a DLL.

Variants

Variants are an OLE-based type in the VCL that can be assigned to a wide range of variable types. Some people jokingly refer to variants as a typeless type, because it can be used to represent a string, an integer, an object, or several other types.

The following is a simple procedure that illustrates the flexible nature of variants:

```
void __fastcall TForm1::BitBtn1Click(TObject *Sender)
{
  Variant V;
  V = 1;
  V = "Sam";
}
```

This procedure compiles fine under BCB. As you can see, you are allowed to assign both a string and an integer to the same variant variable.

The following procedure is also legal:

```
void __fastcall TForm1::BitBtn1Click(TObject *Sender)
{
  Variant V;
  V = 1;
  Caption = "Sam" + V;
}
```

The attempt to assign Edit1.Text to a variant concatenated with a string would have been flagged as a type mismatch by Delphi because a variant in Object Pascal takes on some of the attributes of an integer after being assigned to that type. The Variant class implemented in SYSDEFS.H, however, allows this kind of behavior and handles it properly.

Underneath the surface, variant types are represented by a 16-byte structure found in SYSDEFS.H. At the time of this writing, that structure looks like this:

```
class TVarData {
  public:
    Word VType;
    Word Reserved1;
    Word Reserved2;
    Word Reserved3;
    union {
      Smallint VSmallint;
      Integer VInteger;
      Single VSingle;
      Double VDouble;
      CurrencyBase VCurrency;
      TDateTimeBase VDate;
      PWideChar VOleStr;
      Ole2::IDispatch* VDispatch;
      Integer VError;
      WordBool VBoolean;
      Ole2::IUnknown* VUnknown;
      Byte VByte;
      Pointer VString;
      PVarArray VArray;
      Pointer VPointer;
    };
};
```

Notice that this is a union; that is, the various types represented in the switch statement are overlaid in memory. The structure ends up being 16 bytes in size because the VType field is 2 bytes; the three reserved fields total 6 bytes; and the largest of the types in the variant section is the double, which is 8 bytes in size. (2 + 6 + 8 = 16.) Once again, the switch statement in the declaration is not a list of separate fields, but a list of different ways to interpret the 8 bytes of data contained in the second half of the space allocated for the record.

The following are the declarations for the values used with variants:

```
#define varEmpty (unsigned char)(0)
#define varNull (unsigned char)(1)
#define varSmallint (unsigned char)(2)
#define varInteger (unsigned char)(3)
```

```
#define varSingle (unsigned char)(4)
#define varDouble (unsigned char)(5)
#define varCurrency (unsigned char)(6)
#define varDate (unsigned char)(7)
#define varOleStr (unsigned char)(8)
#define varDispatch (unsigned char)(9)
#define varError (unsigned char)(10)
#define varBoolean (unsigned char)(11)
#define varVariant (unsigned char)(12)
#define varUnknown (unsigned char)(13)
#define varByte (unsigned char)(17)
#define varString (unsigned short)(256)
#define varTypeMask (unsigned short)(4095)
#define varArray (unsigned short)(8192)
#define varByRef (unsigned short)(16384)
```

> **NOTE**
>
> When you study these declarations, it's important to understand that the VCL defines a certain set of behavior to be associated with variants, but might not guarantee that the implementation will remain the same from version to version. In other words, you can almost surely count on the fact that assigning both a string and an integer to the same variant will always be safe. However, you might not necessarily be sure that variants will always be represented by the same constants and record shown previously. To check whether these implementations have been blessed as being permanent, refer to your VCL documentation.
>
> If I were writing the documentation for the VCL, I might decide not to show you the specific record shown previously because these kinds of details might change in later versions of the product, just as the internal representation for long strings might change. However, in this book I do not claim to be defining the language in a set of official documents. Instead, I am explaining the product to you, using the techniques that seem most useful. In this particular case, I think it helps to see behind the scenes and into the particulars of this implementation of the Variant type. Whether or not this will become a documented fact or an undocumented trick is not clear at the time of this writing.

It should be clear from the preceding code examples that knowing what type is represented by a variant at a particular moment can be important. To check the variant's type, you can use the VarType function, as shown here:

```
void __fastcall TForm1::BitBtn1Click(TObject *Sender)
{
  int AType;
  Variant V;

  AType = VarType(V);
  // Additional code
}
```

In this example, the `Integer` variable `AType` will be set to one of the constants shown previously. In particular, it will probably be assigned to `varEmpty`, because in the preceding example this variable has not yet been assigned to another type.

If you want to get a closer look at a variant, you can typecast it to learn more about it, as shown in the following example:

```
void __fastcall TForm1::BitBtn1Click(TObject *Sender)
{
  Variant V;
  TVarData VarData;
  int AType;

  V = 1;
  VarData = TVarData(V);
  AType = VarData.VType;
}
```

In this particular case, `AType` will be set to the same value that would be returned from a call to `VarType`.

To understand more about how all this works, see Listing 3.7 and 3.8, in which you can find the code for the VarDatas program. This code sets a single variant to a series of different values and then examines the variant to discover the current value of its `VType` field.

Listing 3.7. The VarDatas program lets you examine variant types. Here is the header file for the main form of the program.

```
/////////////////////////////////////////
// Copyright (c) 1997 by Charlie Calvert
//
#ifndef MainH
#define MainH
#include <vcl\Classes.hpp>
#include <vcl\Controls.hpp>
#include <vcl\StdCtrls.hpp>
#include <vcl\Forms.hpp>

class TForm1 : public TForm
{
__published:
  TButton *bVariantPlay;
  TListBox *ListBox1;
  void __fastcall bVariantPlayClick(TObject *Sender);
private:
  void ShowVariant(Variant &V);
public:
  virtual __fastcall TForm1(TComponent* Owner);
};
extern TForm1 *Form1;
#endif
```

Listing 3.8. The main source file for the VarDatas program includes a routine that returns a string stating the type of a variant.

```cpp
///////////////////////////////////////
// Copyright (c) 1997 by Charlie Calvert
//
#include <vcl\vcl.h>
#pragma hdrstop
#include "Main.h"
#pragma resource "*.dfm"
TForm1 *Form1;

__fastcall TForm1::TForm1(TComponent* Owner)
  : TForm(Owner)
{
}

AnsiString GetVariantType(Variant &V)
{
  TVarData VarData;
  AnsiString S;

  VarData = TVarData(V);
  switch (VarData.VType)
  {
    case varEmpty: S = "varEmpty"; break;
    case varNull:  S = "varNull";  break;
    case varSmallint: S = "varSmallInt";  break;
    case varInteger: S = "varInteger";  break;
    case varSingle: S = "varSingle"; break;
    case varDouble: S= "varDouble"; break;
    case varCurrency: S = "varCurrency"; break;
    case varDate: S = "varDate"; break;
    case varOleStr: S = "varOleStr"; break;
    case varDispatch: S = "varDispatch"; break;
    case varError: S = "varError"; break;
    case varBoolean: S = "varBoolean"; break;
    case varVariant: S = "varVariant"; break;
    case varUnknown: S = "varUnknown"; break;
    case varString: S = "varString"; break;
    case varTypeMask: S = "varTypeMask"; break;
    case varByRef: S = "varByRef"; break;
    case varByte: S = "varByte"; break;
    case varArray: S = "varArray"; break;
    default:
      S = "Error";
  }
  return S;
}

void TForm1::ShowVariant(Variant &V)
{
  AnsiString S, Temp;

  if ((VarIsEmpty(V) == True) || (VarIsNull(V) == True))
  {
    Temp = "Null";
    S = Format("Value: %-15s  Type: %s",
```

continues

Listing 3.8. continued

```
      OPENARRAY(TVarRec, (Temp, GetVariantType(V))));
  }
  else
  {
    Temp = V;
    S = Format("Value: %-15s   Type: %s",
      OPENARRAY(TVarRec , (Temp, GetVariantType(V))));
  }
  ListBox1->Items->Add(S);
}

void __fastcall TForm1::bVariantPlayClick(TObject *Sender)
{
  Variant V;

  ShowVariant(V);
  V = Null;
  ShowVariant(V);
  V = 1;
  ShowVariant(V);
  V = "Sam";
  ShowVariant(V);
  V = 1.25;
  ShowVariant(V);
}
```

A typical run of this program is shown in Figure 3.6.

FIGURE 3.6.

The VarDatas program uses the TVarData *structure to examine how variants are put together.*

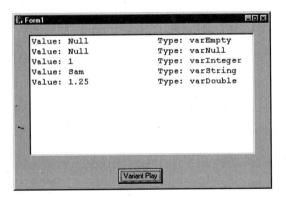

The data shown in the list box in Figure 3.6 represents the value and internal representation of a single variant that is assigned a series of different types. It's important to understand that Variant can't simultaneously represent all types, and can instead at any one moment take on the characteristics of only one particular type.

The code that assigns different types to a variant is easy to understand, as is shown here:

```
void __fastcall TForm1::bVariantPlayClick(TObject *Sender)
```

```
{
  Variant V;

  ShowVariant(V);
  V = Null;
  ShowVariant(V);
  V = 1;
  ShowVariant(V);
  V = "Sam";
  ShowVariant(V);
  V = 1.25;
  ShowVariant(V);
}
```

The code that reports on the current type of a variant is somewhat more complex, but still relatively straightforward, as shown next:

```
AnsiString GetVariantType(Variant &V)
{
  TVarData VarData;
  AnsiString S;

  VarData = TVarData(V);
  switch (VarData.VType)
  {
    case varEmpty: S = "varEmpty"; break;
    case varNull:  S = "varNull";  break;
    case varSmallint: S = "varSmallInt";  break;
    case varInteger: S = "varInteger";  break;
    case varSingle: S = "varSingle"; break;
    case varDouble: S= "varDouble"; break;
    case varCurrency: S = "varCurrency"; break;
    case varDate: S = "varDate"; break;
    case varOleStr: S = "varOleStr"; break;
    case varDispatch: S = "varDispatch"; break;
    case varError: S = "varError"; break;
    case varBoolean: S = "varBoolean"; break;
    case varVariant: S = "varVariant"; break;
    case varUnknown: S = "varUnknown"; break;
    case varString: S = "varString"; break;
    case varTypeMask: S = "varTypeMask"; break;
    case varByRef: S = "varByRef"; break;
    case varByte: S = "varByte"; break;
    case varArray: S = "varArray"; break;
    default:
      S = "Error";
  }
  return S;
}
```

This code first converts a variant into a variable of type TVarData. In doing so, it is merely surfacing the true underlying type of the variant. However, a variable of type TVarData will not act the same as a variable of type Variant. This is because the compiler provides special services for variants that it would not provide for a simple record type such as TVarData.

It's important to note that there are at least two ways to write the first lines of code in this function. For instance, I could have written

```
AnsiString GetVariantType(Variant &V)
{
  AnsiString S;

  switch (VarType(V))
  {
    case varEmpty: S = "varEmpty"; break;
    case varNull:  S = "varNull";  break;
    // Code omitted
  }
}
```

This code works the same as the code shown in the actual program found on the CD-ROM.

However you decide to implement the function, the key point is that variants can take on the appearance of being of a certain type. The chameleon-like behavior of `Variant` is sparked by the type of variable to which it is assigned. If you want, you can think of a variant as a chameleon that hides itself from view by assuming the coloration of the variable to which it is assigned. A variant is never of type `Variant`; it's always either empty, `NULL`, or the type of the variable to which it is assigned. In the same way, a chameleon has no color of its own but is always changing to adapt its color to the environment around it. Either that, or it is unborn, dead, nonexistent, or has no color at all!

The following routines can all be used with variants. To learn more about these routines, look in the online help.

```
extern void __fastcall VarClear(Variant &V);
extern void __fastcall VarCopy(Variant &Dest, const Variant &Source);
extern void __fastcall VarCopyNoInd(Variant &Dest, const Variant &Source);
extern void __fastcall VarCast(Variant &Dest, const Variant &Source, int VarType);
extern int __fastcall VarType(const Variant &V);
extern Variant __fastcall VarAsType(const Variant &V, int VarType);
extern bool __fastcall VarIsEmpty(const Variant &V);
extern bool __fastcall VarIsNull(const Variant &V);
extern AnsiString __fastcall VarToStr(const Variant &V);
extern Variant __fastcall VarFromDateTime(TDateTime DateTime);
extern TDateTime __fastcall VarToDateTime(const Variant &V);
```

Here are some routines to use with Variant arrays.

```
extern Variant __fastcall VarArrayCreate(const int *Bounds, const int Bounds_Size,
                                         int VarType);
extern Variant __fastcall VarArrayOf(const Variant *Values, const int Values_Size);
extern void __fastcall VarArrayRedim(Variant &A, int HighBound);
extern int __fastcall VarArrayDimCount(const Variant &A);
extern int __fastcall VarArrayLowBound(const Variant &A, int Dim);
extern int __fastcall VarArrayHighBound(const Variant &A, int Dim);
extern void * __fastcall VarArrayLock(const Variant &A);
extern void __fastcall VarArrayUnlock(const Variant &A);
extern Variant __fastcall VarArrayRef(const Variant &A);
extern bool __fastcall VarIsArray(const Variant &A);
```

Before closing this section, I want to make it clear that variants are not meant to be used broadly in your program whenever you need to work with a variable. I have no doubt that some people will in fact program that way, but I want to emphasize that the developers didn't really want variants to be used that way. This is mainly because they have some overhead associated with them that can slow down the compiler. Some tricks performed by variants, such as string manipulation, happen to be highly optimized. However, you should never consider a variant to be as fast or efficient as a standard C type.

Variants are almost certainly best used in OLE and database applications. In particular, variants were brought into the language because they play a role in OLE automation. Furthermore, much of the structure and behavior of variants is defined by the rules of OLE. These unusual types also prove to be useful in database applications. As a rule, there is so much overhead involved in referencing any value from a database that a little additional variant manipulation code is not going to make a significant difference.

Working with Text Files

Some of the best features of C++Builder are not immediately obvious to you when you first start working with the tool, or even after you have been working with the tool for awhile. For instance, C++Builder has a built in type called a `TStringList` that all but makes obsolete the concept of a text file. This class is so easy to use, and so powerful, that there are few occasions when you would want to open a text file using `fopen`. It's important to note that manipulating text files is not really the central purpose of the `TStringList` class; however, it performs this task so well that there is little need to ever resort to using `fopen`, `fclose`, and other similar commands.

Before looking at how you would use to `TStringList` to open a text file, it might be helpful to point out the places in BCB where this class is most often used, as well as a few other features of the class.

The `TStringList` class is a descendant of the abstract class `TStrings`. There are no instances of the `TString` class in BCB, because this is an abstract type. However, the `TStringList`, `TListBox->Items`, `TComboBox->Items`, `TMemo->Lines`, `TRichEdit->Lines` and `TQuery->VCL` classes all descend directly from `TStrings`. This means you can assign instances of these classes to one another.

You can, for instance, create an instance of the `TStringList` class and assign it to a `TListBox->Items` object:

```
TStringList *MyStringList = new TStringList;
MyStringList->Add("Some text");
MyStringList->Add("More text");
ListBox1->Items = MyStringList;
```

If you write code like this, `ListBox1` will end up showing two items in it, with the first being `"Some text"`, and the second being `"More text"`.

You can write the contents of any string list to file by using the `SaveToFile` method, and you can read the list back using `LoadFromFile`. There are also `SaveToStream` and `LoadFromStream` methods:

```
MyStringList->SaveToFile("C:\\Sam.txt");
MyStringList->LoadFromFile("C:\\Sam.txt");
```

TStringLists have a sort property that can enable you to sort them instantly. You can also associate an object with each string in the TStringList using the InsertObject method.

Given the presence of all this flexibility in one simple-to-use object, it does not really make sense to use any other tool for handling lists of strings. It is definitely worth taking time to explore this object and to see what it can do for you.

New Compiler Switches

I will spend little time in this book talking about how to pass switches to the compiler. That subject simply is of no interest to programmers whose primary goal is rapid application development. However, even under ideal conditions, there may be times when a programmer may have to take off their RAD hat and put on their Systems programming hat. So, if you absolutely need to start tweaking the compiler, here are some new BCC32.EXE switches culled from the online help:

New BCC32.EXE switches:

- -Vx switch for truly empty (0 length) structs
- -He switch (extern types in .OBJs)
- -Hs switch (smart-cached headers)

New BCC32.EXE pragmas:

- #pragma link "obj" (object file dependencies)
- #pragma resource "res" (resource file dependencies)
- #pragma anon_struct on (for support of VCL variant records)

New switches for the Pascal DCC32.EXE compiler:

- -jp switch: creates Borland C++ compatible .OBJ files
- -jph switch: creates C++Builder compatible header (.HPP) files from Object Pascal unit files (.DCL)
- -jphn switch: uses the Object Pascal unit name as the enclosing C++ namespace for both .OBJs and .HPPs that are generated
- -n switch: specify .DCU output directory
- -nh switch: specify .HPP output directory
- -no switch: specify .OBJ output directory

Tips On Using the Visual Tools

One of the biggest problems with BCB forms is getting them to look correct in all the possible resolutions. There is probably no surefire method for achieving these ends. However, there are some tips that I have found that help.

When I build forms I almost always set the AutoScroll property to False. If you do not do this, your form will always stay the same size, which means that the edges of your form will be obscured in some resolutions. To avoid this, you would have to resize the form to fit around the edges of your controls when you changed resolutions.

Whatever approach you take, you simply have to view your form in at least three or four different modes before releasing it to the public. In particular, be sure to switch back and forth between Large Fonts and Small Fonts when you change resolutions. If you are a complete perfectionist, you may decide that the only solution is to have two sets of forms, one for use with Small Fonts, and the other for use with Large Fonts.

Some people have a definite knack for designing good-looking forms. If you find someone who can do this, ask them to critique your forms or even to help you design them. If you find forms that you like, study them. Use whatever tricks you can find to help you create decent-looking forms. Try to leave some whitespace on your forms if you can, and make sure controls line up vertically and horizontally whenever possible.

Summary

In this chapter you saw an overview of all the key areas in which BCB and the VCL meet. This is a complicated, yet extremely important aspect of the product.

I'm sure it tried your patience at times to have to go through so much dry material. However, if you have this subject firmly under your belt, you are ready to begin a serious study of BCB. You now know a good deal about how this product is put together, and why it was constructed in this particular fashion. This is the kind of knowledge for which there is no substitute. You simply have to know these kinds of things about a product before you can take advantage of its best features.

BCB is a tool for using components and objects to make applications. Any type of application you can conceive of creating can be made better in Borland C++Builder than it can with any other C/C++ compiler. What do I mean by better? I mean that it can be put together faster, with a better chance of having the right design, and with fewer bugs. In order to get that power, BCB had to tap into the VCL. In this chapter you saw how it was done.

One of the most important themes of this chapter was the central role played by components, properties, and events in the BCB programming model. This product does a lot of great things, but the key features that make it all possible are the support for components, properties, and events. Much of the groundwork for that support was laid out in this chapter.

Events

IN THIS CHAPTER

CHAPTER 4

In this chapter you take a look at the basic facts about the BCB delegation model. Events are fundamental to the use of this programming environment, and you will never be able to do serious work in BCB without understanding them.

Subjects covered in this chapter include

- Using the mouse and the keyboard
- Responding directly to Windows messages such as WM_KEYDOWN or WM_MOUSEMOVE
- Custom event structures such as TWMMouse or TMessage
- Menus and menu IDs
- Setting up a WndProc in a VCL application
- Responding to WM_COMMAND messages

This chapter is not designed to be difficult, but rather to hit the highlights of each of these subjects so you can understand how to use events in your own programs. By the time you are through with this chapter, you should have a thorough understanding of the BCB delegation model and will know how to use events in your own program. Additional material on events is included in the chapters that cover creating components.

Events: The BCB Delegation Model

The two central ideas behind the type of RAD programming of which BCB partakes are components and delegation. Components are treated at length in Part IV of this book, called "Creating Components." This is where I will talk about delegation.

Delegation is an alternative to inheritance. It's a trick to allow you to receive the same benefits as inheritance but with less work.

Delegation is not entirely original with RAD programming; however, it is taken much further in this paradigm than elsewhere. A part of classic windows programming that supports delegation is the way you handle standard WM_COMMAND messages.

Think for a moment about standard Windows programming as it appeared before RAD rewrote the book on Windows programming. I'm talking the Windows programming of Petzold, or of my *Teach Yourself Windows 95 Programming in 21 Days* (Sams Publishing) book. Suppose that in a standard Windows program you have a button that responds to a particular event, say a message click. You usually handled that click inside the WM_COMMAND section of the window procedure (WndProc). Windows was delegating the event from the button to your WM_COMMAND handler. In other words, Windows did not force you to subclass the button class in order to respond to clicks on a button.

This is the central idea behind the delegation model in BCB. In C++Builder, if you drop a button on a form, you can set up an OnClick event handler to handle clicks on the button. The great advantage this system has over the standard Windows model is ease of use. BCB will create the message handler for you, asking that you write only the code that responds to the event.

Specifically, it fills in the class definition with a declaration for your event in the header:

```
class TForm1 : public TForm
{
__published:
  TButton *Button1;
  void __fastcall Button1Click(TObject *Sender); // DECLARATION HERE!
private:
public:
  virtual __fastcall TForm1(TComponent* Owner);
};
```

And it creates the even handler itself in your CPP file:

```
void __fastcall TForm1::Button1Click(TObject *Sender)
{
}
```

This is what is meant by the delegation model in BCB. What is radical about the VCL's use of the delegation model is that it appears everywhere. All sorts of components support the model and enable you to use it to do all sorts of things that required subclassing in standard Windows programming and in OWL or MFC.

One of the primary goals of the delegation model is to allow the main form in your application to handle code that you would have had to use inheritance to handle in OWL or MFC. In the inheritance model you had to override a constructor to change the way an object was initialized. In BCB, you just respond to an OnCreate event. If you want to modify the things a user can type into an edit control, you don't have to subclass the control; instead, you just respond to OnKeyDown events.

Delegation is easier than inheritance. It enables neophytes who don't understand inheritance a way to get up to speed quickly. More importantly, it enables programmers to get their work done quickly without a lot of repetitive typing.

Of course, if you want to use inheritance, it is available. In fact, inheritance is used all the time in BCB. The point is not to eliminate a powerful technique like inheritance, but to give you an alternative to use in the vast majority of cases where inheritance is overkill.

The Delegation Model and Contract-Free Programming

The delegation model supports something called contract-free programming. In some semiliterate circles this has also been known as "contractless" programming.

The idea behind contract-free programming is that there is no contract between the developer of a component and the user of a component as to what can and can't be done inside an event handler.

A classic example of a contract-bound program is found in Windows when you handle WM_KILLFOCUS message. There are some things you can and cannot do in response to this message. For example, if you change the focus during your response to this message, you can crash

Windows. There is a contract between you and Windows not to change the focus while responding to this message. Learning all the things you can and cannot do in response to a message is a long, error-prone, and frustrating process.

BCB supports contract-free programming, which means you can do whatever you want while responding to an event. BCB is religious in pursuit of this goal. In my code, I strive to achieve this same goal, though I admit that I have been known to cheat. When I do so, however, I severely limit the usability of my components.

The Basics of the Delegation Model

Event-oriented code is one of the central tenets of Windows programming. Some rapid-application development environments attempt to hide users from this feature altogether, as if it were something so complicated that most programmers couldn't understand it. The truth is that event-oriented programming is not, in itself, particularly complex. However, some features of the way it is implemented in Windows can be confusing under certain circumstances.

BCB gives you full access to the event-oriented substructure that provides Windows with a high degree of power and flexibility. At the same time, it simplifies and clarifies the way a programmer handles those events. The end result is a system that gives you complete access to the power of Windows while simultaneously protecting you from unnecessary complexity.

These next few sections cover the following topics:

- Event-oriented programming basics
- Responding to mouse events or key events
- Accessing the information passed in events
- The basics of sets, which are used frequently in BCB event handlers
- Circumventing BCB message handling tools and directly capturing messages
- Creating WM_COMMAND handlers and finding the IDs of the components used in a program

To be really good at programming Windows, you need to be able to look at these subjects from both the perspective of a RAD programmer and of a Windows API programmer. That is, you need to know the VCL inside out, and you need to know the Windows API inside out. This chapter concentrates on the VCL side of that equation, whereas the other side is featured in books such as *Teach Yourself Windows 95 Programming in 21 Days* (Sams Publishing) and *Programming Windows* (Microsoft Press). Put both perspectives together and you can go on to create your own VCL components or you can design elegant, well-structured Windows programs.

Before starting, let me reiterate that BCB hides much of the complexity of Windows programming. However, the developers did not want to prevent programmers from accessing any portion of the Windows API. By the time you finish reading this section of the chapter, you should be able to see that BCB gives you access to the full range of power provided by an event-oriented system.

BCB Events

BCB makes it easy to handle keyboard and mouse events. Suppose, for instance, you wanted to capture left mouse clicks in the main form of your program. Here's how to get started. Create a new project and name it EVENTS1.MAK.

In the Object Inspector for the main form, choose the Events Page and double-click the area to the right of the OnClick property. Create the following function:

```
void __fastcall TForm1::FormClick(TObject *Sender)
{
  MessageDlg("The delegation model says hello.", mtInformation,
            TMsgDlgButtons() << mbOK, 0);
}
```

This code tells Windows that a dialog box should appear every time the user clicks the left mouse button in the form. The dialog box is shown in Figure 4.1.

FIGURE 4.1.

The dialog box displayed by the EVENTS1 program when you click the left mouse button inside the main form.

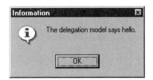

The previous code presents one of the simplest possible cases of responding to an event in a BCB program. It is so simple, in fact, that many programmers write this kind of code without ever understanding that they are writing event-oriented code. In this case, BCB programmers get the event secondhand, because VCL massages the event before passing it on to the main form. Nonetheless, this is real event-oriented programming, albeit in a very simplified manifestation.

As you saw back in the section on the Windows API, the operating environment notifies you not only of the event, but of several related bits of information. For instance, when a mouse-down event is generated, a program is informed about where the event occurred and which button generated the event. If you want to get access to this kind of relatively detailed information, you should turn to the Events Page for the form and create an OnMouseDown handler:

```
void __fastcall TForm1::FormMouseDown(TObject *Sender, TMouseButton Button,
  TShiftState Shift, int X, int Y)
{
  if (Shift.Contains(ssRight))
  {
    Canvas->Brush->Style = bsClear;
```

4

EVENTS

```
    Canvas->TextOut(X, Y, "* Button");
  }
}
```

This method writes text to the form every time the user clicks the right mouse button. It sets the brush to bsClear style to make the background of text transparent.

To test this method, run the program and click the right mouse button in several different locations in the form. You'll see that each spot you click is marked, as shown in Figure 4.2.

FIGURE 4.2.

When you click the right mouse button in the form of the EVENTS1 program, the location of the event is recorded.

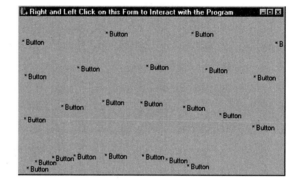

The Canvas->TextOut function prints text to the screen at the location specified by the variables X and Y. Both of these variables are supplied to you by BCB, which received them in turn from the operating system. The X variable tells you the column in which the mouse was clicked, and the Y variable tells you the row.

As you can see, BCB makes it simple for you to respond to events. Furthermore, not only mouse events are easy to handle. You can respond to keypresses in a similar manner. For instance, if you create a method for the OnKeyDown property on the Events Page for the form, you can show the user which key was pressed on the keyboard whenever the EVENTS1 program has the focus:

```
void __fastcall TForm1::FormKeyDown(TObject *Sender, WORD &Key,
  TShiftState Shift)
{
  MessageDlg(Key, mtInformation, TMsgDlgButtons() << mbOK, 0);
}
```

In the preceding code, the MessageDlg function will pop up the ASCII value associated with a keystroke. In other words, BCB and the operating system both pass you not an actual letter like A, B, or C, but the number associated with the key you pressed. On PCs, the letter A is associated with the number 65. It wouldn't be appropriate for BCB to perform this translation for you automatically, because some keys, such as the F1 or Enter key, have no letter associated with them. Later in this chapter you learn how to use OnKeyDown events to respond sensibly to keypresses on special keys such as F1, Shift, or Caps Lock.

Besides OnKeyDown events, BCB also lets you respond to keyboard activity through the OnKeyPress event:

```
void __fastcall TForm1::FormKeyPress(TObject *Sender, char &Key)
{
  AnsiString S("OnKeyPress: " + AnsiString(Key));
  MessageDlg(S, mtInformation, TMsgDlgButtons() << mbOK, 0);
}
```

You can see that this event is similar to an OnKeyDown event. The difference is that the Key variable passed to OnKeyPress events is already translated into a char. However, OnKeyPress events work only for the alphanumeric keys and are not called when special keys are pressed. In short, the OnKeyPress event is the same as a WM_CHAR event.

The code for the EVENTS1 program is shown in Listing 4.1. Get the program up and running and take whatever time is necessary to be sure it all makes sense to you. There is no point in trying to be a Windows programmer if you don't understand events.

Listing 4.1. The main form for the EVENTS1 program.

```
//////////////////////////////////////
// Copyright (c) 1997 by Charlie Calvert
//
#include <vcl.h>
#pragma hdrstop
#include "Main.h"
#pragma resource "*.dfm"
TForm1 *Form1;
__fastcall TForm1::TForm1(TComponent* Owner)
  : TForm(Owner)
{
}
void __fastcall TForm1::FormMouseDown(TObject *Sender, TMouseButton Button,
  TShiftState Shift, int X, int Y)
{
  if (Shift.Contains(ssRight))
  {
    Canvas->Brush->Style = bsClear;
    Canvas->TextOut(X, Y, "* Button");
  }
}
void __fastcall TForm1::DelegateMe(TObject *Sender)
{
  MessageDlg("The menu says hello.", mtInformation,
            TMsgDlgButtons() << mbOK, 0);
}
void __fastcall TForm1::FormClick(TObject *Sender)
{
  MessageDlg("The delegation model says hello.", mtInformation,
            TMsgDlgButtons() << mbOK, 0);
}
void __fastcall TForm1::FormKeyPress(TObject *Sender, char &Key)
{
```

4

EVENTS

continues

Listing 4.1. continued

```
  AnsiString S("OnKeyPress: " + AnsiString(Key));
  MessageDlg(S, mtInformation, TMsgDlgButtons() << mbOK, 0);
}
void __fastcall TForm1::FormKeyDown(TObject *Sender, WORD &Key,
  TShiftState Shift)
{
  MessageDlg(Key, mtInformation, TMsgDlgButtons() << mbOK, 0);
}
```

After this introduction to event-oriented programming, it's time to step back and see some of the theory behind the code. After explaining something of how the system works, this chapter goes on to give examples of how to take full advantage of Windows event-oriented code base.

Understanding Events

Event-oriented programming isn't unique to Windows, nor is it a chore that can be handled only by an operating system. For instance, any DOS program could be based around a simple loop that keeps running the entire time the program is in memory. Here is a hypothetical example of how such code might look:

```
do
{
  CheckForMouseEvent(Events);
  CheckForKeyPress(Events)
  HandleEvents(Events);
} while (!Events.Done);
```

This code represents a typical event-oriented loop. A simple do..while statement checks for keyboard and mouse events and then calls HandleEvents to give the program a chance to respond to the events that are generated by the user or the operating system.

The variable called Events might be a record with a fairly simple structure:

```
struct TEvent {
  int X, Y;
  TButton MouseButton;
  int Key;
  bool Done;
};
```

X and Y give the current location of the cursor, and Key contains the value of the top event in the key buffer. The TButton type might have a declaration that looks like this:

```
enum TButton {ButtonLeft, ButtonRight};
```

These structures permit you to track where the mouse is, what state its buttons are in, and what keys the user has pressed. Admittedly, this is a simple type of event structure, but the principles involved mirror what is going on inside Windows or inside other event-oriented systems such as Turbo Vision. If the program being written was an editor, pseudo-code for the HandleEvent for the program might look like this:

```
void HandleEvent(TEvent: Events)
{
  switch(Events.Key)
  {
    case "A..z":
      WriteXY(Events.X, Events.Y, Events.Key);
      break;
    case EnterKey:
      Write(CarriageReturn);
      break;

    case EscapeKey:
      Events.Done = TRUE;
      break;
  }
}
```

Given the preceding code, the program would go to location X,Y and write the letter most recently pressed by the user. If the Enter key was pressed, a carriage return would be written to the screen. A press on the Esc key would cause the program to terminate. All other keypresses would be ignored.

Code like this can be very powerful, particularly if you're writing a program that requires animation. For instance, if you need to move a series of bitmaps across the screen, you want to move the bitmap a few pixels and then check to see whether the user has pressed a button or hit a keystroke. If an event has occurred, you want to handle it. If nothing occurred, you want to continue moving the bitmap.

I hope the short code samples shown here give you some feeling for the way event-oriented systems work. The only piece that's missing is an understanding of why Windows is event-oriented.

Microsoft made Windows event-oriented in part because multiple programs run under the environment at the same time. In multitasking systems, the operating system needs to know whether the user has clicked in a program or whether the click was in the desktop window. If the mouse click occurred in a window that was partially hidden behind another window, it is up to the operating system to recognize the event and bring that window to the foreground. Clearly, it wouldn't be appropriate for the window itself to have to be in charge of that task. To ask that much would place an impossible burden on the programmer who created the window. As a result, it's best for the operating system to handle all the keystrokes and mouse clicks, and to then pass them on to the various programs in the form of events. Any other system would force every programmer to handle all the events that occurred when his or her program had the focus, and to manipulate the entire operating system in response to certain mouse events or keystrokes, such as Alt+Tab.

In short, Windows programmers almost never directly monitor the hardware or hardware interrupts. Instead, the operating system handles that task. It passes all external events on to individual programs in the form of messages. In a typical event-oriented system, the operating system continually polls the hardware in a loop and then sends each event off to its programs in the form of some kind of event structure or event variables. This is the same kind of activity you saw in the brief code snippets shown earlier.

You have seen that Windows handles mouse and keyboard events, and passes them on to the appropriate window. The message that is generated in these cases gets sent to the default window function, which, as you know, is called `DefWindowProc`. `DefWindowProc` is analogous to the `HandleEvent` function shown earlier.

The important point to understand is that Windows messages contain the information that drives the entire operating environment. Almost everything that happens inside Windows is a message; if you really want to tap into the power of BCB, you need to understand how these messages work.

One of the tricky parts of Windows event-oriented programming is extracting information from the `WPARAM` and `LPARAM` variables passed to the window function. In most cases, BCB frees you from the necessity of performing this task. For instance, if you create an event for the `OnMouseDown` property, BCB directly tells you the `X` value and `Y` value where the event occurred. As a programmer, you don't have to struggle to get the event and its associated values. As you will see in the next section, everything about the event is shown to you in a simple and straightforward manner.

> **NOTE**
>
> `WPARAM` and `LPARAM` are the types of the parameters passed to a standard `WndProc` as is declared in `WinUser.h`:
>
> `typedef LRESULT (CALLBACK* WNDPROC)(HWND, UINT, WPARAM, LPARAM);`
>
> These variables are usually given names such as `wParam` and `lParam` or `WParam` and `LParam`:
>
> `WndProc(HWND hWnd, UINT Message, WPARAM wParam, LPARAM lParam);`
>
> You will find that I sometimes refer to these parameters by type in all caps, and sometimes as variable identifiers with mixed caps and small letters. In all cases, I am referring to the same variables passed to the user from the system. Even in the discussion of the `TMessage` type, which occurs later in the chapter, I am still referring to these same parameters, only in a slightly different context. Specifically, `TMessage` is a VCL type that contains exact copies of these parameters. The `X` and `Y` parameters passed to an `OnMouseDown` event are not exact copies of `WPARAM` and `LPARAM`, but variables designed to display information originally contained in `WPARAM` or `LPARAM` after they have been parsed by the VCL.

Using Sets to Track Messages

Rather than ask you to parse the LPARAM and WPARAM parameters, BCB performs this chore for you and then passes the information on in the form of parameters:

```
void __fastcall TForm1::FormMouseDown(
  TObject *Sender,
  TMouseButton Button,
  TShiftState Shift,
  int X,
  int Y)
```

This is by far the most convenient way for you to handle events. BCB can also give direct access to the values sent to you by the operating system. That is, you can handle WPARAM and LPARAM directly if you want. After you have studied the EVENTS2 program and learned more about sets, I'll show you exactly how to get at that raw data.

Take a moment to consider the Shift parameter shown in the FormMouseDown header. Shift is declared to be of type TShiftState:

```
enum Classes_1 { ssShift, ssAlt, ssCtrl, ssLeft, ssRight, ssMiddle, ssDouble };
typedef Set<Classes_1, ssShift, ssDouble>  TShiftState;
```

TShiftState is a set, that is, it's an instance of the Set template class from SYSDEFS.H. To find out whether a particular element is a member of the set passed to you by BCB, you can perform simple tests using the Contains method:

```
ShiftKey->Checked = Shift.Contains(ssShift);
ControlKey->Checked = Shift.Contains(ssCtrl);
LeftButton->Checked = Shift.Contains(ssLeft);
RightButton->Checked = Shift.Contains(ssRight);
```

This code asks whether the element ssRight is in the set passed to you via the Shift variable. If it is, the code sets the state of a TCheckBox component.

Here is how you can declare a set at runtime:

```
TShiftState LeftShift;
LeftShift << ssLeft << ssShift;
```

Given this set, the Contains operator returns True if you ask about ssLeft or ssShift.

Besides the important Contains method, there are three key operators you can use with the Set class:

```
+    Union
-    Difference
*    Intersection
```

All three of these operators return a set, whereas Contains returns a Boolean value. The SETSEXP program, shown in Listing 4.2, shows how to work with these key elements of the Set template class.

4

EVENTS

Listing 4.2. The SETEXP program shows how to use operators to track the members of sets such as TShiftState.

```cpp
////////////////////////////////////
// Copyright (c) 1997 by Charlie Calvert
//
#include <vcl.h>
#pragma hdrstop
#include "Main.h"
#pragma resource "*.dfm"
TForm1 *Form1;
__fastcall TForm1::TForm1(TComponent* Owner)
  : TForm(Owner)
{
}
void TForm1::CheckState(TShiftState Shift)
{
  ShiftKey->Checked = Shift.Contains(ssShift);
  ControlKey->Checked = Shift.Contains(ssCtrl);
  LeftButton->Checked = Shift.Contains(ssLeft);
  RightButton->Checked = Shift.Contains(ssRight);
}
void __fastcall TForm1::UnionClick(TObject *Sender)
{
  AnsiString Operators[3] = {"+", "*", "-"};
  TShiftState FinalSet;
  TShiftState LeftShift;
  TShiftState LeftCtrl;
  LeftShift << ssLeft << ssShift;
  LeftCtrl << ssLeft << ssCtrl;

  switch (TOptType(dynamic_cast <TBitBtn*>(Sender)->Tag))
  {
    case otUnion:
      FinalSet = LeftShift + LeftCtrl;
      break;
    case otIntersection:
      FinalSet = LeftShift * LeftCtrl;
      break;
    case otDifference:
      FinalSet = LeftShift - LeftCtrl;
      break;
  }
  CheckState(FinalSet);
  Label2->Caption = Operators[dynamic_cast<TBitBtn *>(Sender)->Tag];
}
void __fastcall TForm1::Label4MouseDown(TObject *Sender, TMouseButton Button,
  TShiftState Shift, int X, int Y)
{
  CheckState(Shift);
}
```

The SETEXP program shows how you can read and manipulate sets. In particular, you work with sets of type TShiftState. When you are finished studying the program, you will have all the knowledge you need to work with BCB sets.

The main form for the SETEXP program consists of four checkboxes, two panels, four labels, and three bitbtns, as shown in Figure 4.3. The four checkboxes are placed on top of the first panel, and the fourth label is placed on the top of the second panel.

FIGURE 4.3.

The SETEXP program's main form enables you to manipulate variables of type TShiftState.

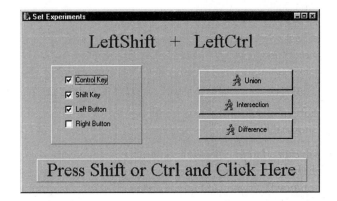

SETEXP tells you whether the Shift or Ctrl keys are pressed when the mouse is clicked, and it tells you whether the user pressed the right or left mouse button. The code also shows how to use the Intersection, Union, and Difference operators.

The key method in the SETEXP program looks at a variable of type TShiftState and displays its contents to the user through the program's radio buttons:

```
void TForm1::CheckState(TShiftState Shift)
{
  ShiftKey->Checked = Shift.Contains(ssShift);
  ControlKey->Checked = Shift.Contains(ssCtrl);
  LeftButton->Checked = Shift.Contains(ssLeft);
  RightButton->Checked = Shift.Contains(ssRight);
}
```

This code takes advantage of the fact that Contains returns a Boolean variable, and the Checked property of a radio button is also declared to be of type Boolean. As a result, you can test to see whether a particular element is part of the Shift set. If it is, you can easily set the Checked state of a radio button to record the result. For example, in the preceding code, if ssShift is part of the current set, the Shift Key radio button is checked.

Two different routines pass variables of type TShiftState to the CheckState method. The first routine is called whenever the user clicks in the panel at the bottom of the program or the label that rests on the panel:

```
void __fastcall TForm1::Label4MouseDown(TObject *Sender, TMouseButton Button,
  TShiftState Shift, int X, int Y)
{
  CheckState(Shift);
}
```

This code passes the Shift variable on to CheckState, which displays the contents of the variable to the user. For instance, if the Shift key is being held down and the right mouse button is pressed, Label4MouseDown is called. Label4MouseDown then passes the Shift variable to CheckState, and CheckState causes the ShiftKey and RightButton controls to be checked. The other two radio buttons are left unchecked.

There are three bitbtns on the right side of the main form. They are labeled Union, Intersection, and Difference. Clicking any of these buttons demonstrates one of the non-Boolean set operators. All three buttons have their OnClick event set to the following function:

```
void __fastcall TForm1::UnionClick(TObject *Sender)
{
  AnsiString Operators[3] = {"+", "*", "-"};
  TShiftState FinalSet;
  TShiftState LeftShift;
  TShiftState LeftCtrl;
  LeftShift << ssLeft << ssShift;
  LeftCtrl << ssLeft << ssCtrl;

  switch (TOptType(dynamic_cast <TBitBtn*>(Sender)->Tag))
  {
    case otUnion:
      FinalSet = LeftShift + LeftCtrl;
      break;
    case otIntersection:
      FinalSet = LeftShift * LeftCtrl;
      break;
    case otDifference:
      FinalSet = LeftShift - LeftCtrl;
      break;
  }
  CheckState(FinalSet);
  Label2->Caption = Operators[dynamic_cast<TBitBtn *>(Sender)->Tag];
}
```

The UnionClick method declares three variables of type TShiftState. Two of these variables are used to create sets that are used by the rest of the SetBtnClick method:

```
LeftShift << ssLeft << ssShift;
LeftCtrl << ssLeft << ssCtrl;
```

The first line assigns the LeftShift variable to a set that contains the values ssLeft and ssShift. The next line assigns the LeftCtrl variable to a set that contains ssLeft and ssCtrl. The rest of this method enables the user to see the union, intersection, and difference of these two sets.

The switch statement in the middle of the SetBtnClick method detects which of the three bitbtns the user clicked. This is the old, time-honored technique featuring the use of an enumerated type and the assignment of zero-based ordinal values to the Tag field of each button.

If the user clicks the Union button, the FinalSet variable is set to the union of the LeftShift and LeftCtrl variables:

```
FinalSet = LeftShift + LeftCtrl;
```

A click on the Intersection button executes the following code:

```
FinalSet = LeftShift * LeftCtrl;
```

The difference of the sets is calculated if the user clicks the Difference button:

```
FinalSet = LeftShift - LeftCtrl;
```

After the `switch` statement ensures the selection of the proper operator, the `FinalSet` value is passed to `CheckState` and its contents are displayed to the user. For instance, if the user clicks the Union button, the LeftButton, ShiftKey, and ControlKey radio buttons are all checked. The Intersection button causes the LeftKey to be checked, and the Difference button causes the ShiftKey to be checked. Here is another way of looking at the work accomplished by these operators:

```
[ssLeft, ssShift] + [ssLeft, ssCtrl] = [ssLeft, ssShift, ssCtrl];
[ssLeft, ssShift] * [ssLeft, ssCtrl] = [ssLeft]
[ssLeft, ssShift] - [ssLeft, ssCtrl] = [ssShift]
```

To help the user understand exactly what is happening, the current set operation is displayed at the top of the form. For instance, if the user clicks the Union button, the following expression is shown to the user:

```
LeftShift + LeftCtrl
```

Throughout a run of the program, the words `LeftShift` and `LeftCtrl` are displayed to the user in a pair of `TLabels`. A third label displays +, -, or *, depending on the current state of the program:

```
Label2->Caption = Operators[dynamic_cast<TBitBtn *>(Sender)->Tag];
```

In this code, `Operators` is an array of three strings that contains the operators that return a set:

```
AnsiString Operators[3] = {"+", "*", "-"};
```

The SETEXP program gives you enough information that you should be able to work with the sets that are passed to BCB event handlers. The code shown here defines the way sets are usually handled in all BCB programs. However, you can actually directly manipulate the raw data that represents a BCB set. Techniques for performing these manipulations are shown in the `GetShift` method, which is part of the program examined in the next section of this chapter. You can also review the information on sets in Chapter 3.

Tracking the Mouse and Keyboard

You now know enough to begin an in-depth study of the main event handlers used by BCB forms and controls. The EVENTS2 program, shown in Listings 4.3 through 4.5, enables you to trace the occurrence of all the keyboard or mouse interrupts generated during the run of a program.

Listing 4.3. The EVENTS2 header and main form provide a detailed look at how to track events.

```cpp
//---------------------------------------------------------------------------
#ifndef MainH
#define MainH
//---------------------------------------------------------------------------
#include <Classes.hpp>
#include <Controls.hpp>
#include <StdCtrls.hpp>
#include <Forms.hpp>
#include <ExtCtrls.hpp>
//---------------------------------------------------------------------------
class TForm1 : public TForm
{
__published:
  TPanel *Panel1;
  TLabel *Label1;
  TLabel *LMouseMove;
  TLabel *Label3;
  TLabel *LMouseDown;
  TLabel *Label5;
  TLabel *LKeyDown;
  TLabel *Label7;
  TLabel *LKeyUp;
  TLabel *Label9;
  TLabel *LMouseUp;
  TLabel *Label11;
  TLabel *LWidth;
  TLabel *Label13;
  TLabel *LHeight;
  TLabel *LSpecialMouse;
  TLabel *Label16;
  void __fastcall FormResize(TObject *Sender);
  void __fastcall FormPaint(TObject *Sender);
  void __fastcall FormMouseUp(TObject *Sender, TMouseButton Button,
                              TShiftState Shift, int X, int Y);
  void __fastcall FormKeyUp(TObject *Sender, WORD &Key, TShiftState Shift);
  void __fastcall FormKeyDown(TObject *Sender, WORD &Key, TShiftState Shift);
  void __fastcall FormMouseMove(TObject *Sender, TShiftState Shift, int X,
  int Y);
  void __fastcall FormMouseDown(TObject *Sender, TMouseButton Button,
                                TShiftState Shift, int X, int Y);

private:
MESSAGE void MyMouseMove(TWMMouse &Message);
public:
  virtual __fastcall TForm1(TComponent* Owner);
BEGIN_MESSAGE_MAP
  MESSAGE_HANDLER(WM_MOUSEMOVE, TWMMouse, MyMouseMove);
END_MESSAGE_MAP(TForm);
};
//---------------------------------------------------------------------------
extern TForm1 *Form1;
//---------------------------------------------------------------------------
#endif
```

Listing 4.4. The EVENTS2 main form provides a detailed look at how to track events.

```cpp
/////////////////////////////////////
// Copyright (c) 1997 by Charlie Calvert
//
#include <vcl.h>
#pragma hdrstop
#include "Main.h"
#include "VKeys1.h"
#include "Binary.h"
#pragma resource "*.dfm"
TForm1 *Form1;
__fastcall TForm1::TForm1(TComponent* Owner)
  : TForm(Owner)
{
}
void TForm1::MyMouseMove(TWMMouse &Message)
{
  TForm::Dispatch(&Message);
  LSpecialMouse->Caption = "X " + IntToStr(Message.XPos) +
                           " Y " + IntToStr(Message.YPos);
}
void __fastcall TForm1::FormResize(TObject *Sender)
{
  LHeight->Caption = IntToStr(Width);
  LWidth->Caption = IntToStr(Height);
}
void __fastcall TForm1::FormPaint(TObject *Sender)
{
  Canvas->Font->Name = "New Times Roman";
  Canvas->Font->Size = 48;
  Canvas->TextOut(1, Panel1->Height, "Mouse Zone");
}
void __fastcall TForm1::FormMouseUp(TObject *Sender, TMouseButton Button,
                                    TShiftState Shift, int X, int Y)
{
  LMouseUp->Caption = "X " + IntToStr(X) + " Y " +
                      IntToStr(Y) + " " + GetShift(Shift);
}
void __fastcall TForm1::FormKeyUp(TObject *Sender, WORD &Key, TShiftState Shift)
{
  LKeyUp->Caption = GetKey(Key) + " " + GetShift(Shift);
}
void __fastcall TForm1::FormKeyDown(TObject *Sender, WORD &Key,
  TShiftState Shift)
{
  LKeyDown->Caption = GetKey(Key) + " " + GetShift(Shift);
}
void __fastcall TForm1::FormMouseMove(TObject *Sender, TShiftState Shift, int X,
                                      int Y)
{
  LMouseMove->Caption = "X " + IntToStr(X) + " Y " +
                        IntToStr(Y) + " " + GetShift(Shift);
}
void __fastcall TForm1::FormMouseDown(TObject *Sender, TMouseButton Button,
                                      TShiftState Shift, int X, int Y)
{
  LMouseDown->Caption = GetShift(Shift);
}
```

Listing 4.5. The VKeys unit is used by the EVENTS2 program.

```cpp
//////////////////////////////////////
// Vkeys.cpp
// Project Name: Events2
// Copyright (c) 1997 by Charles Calvert
//
#include <vcl.h>
#pragma hdrstop
#include "VKeys1.h"
AnsiString MessageArray[5] =
  {"WM_CHAR", "WM_KEY", "WM_MOUSEMOVE", "WM_MOUSEDOWN", "WM_MOUSEUP"};
AnsiString ButtonArray[3] =
  {"mbLeft", "mbRight", "mbCenter"};
AnsiString ShiftArray[8] = {"ssShift", "ssAlt", "ssCtrl", "ssLeft",
                            "ssRight", "ssMiddle", "ssDouble", "ssUnknown"};
AnsiString GetShift(TShiftState State)
{
  int B = 0, i;
  AnsiString S;
  for (i = 0; i <= 7; i++)
  {
    if (State.Contains(i))
      S = S + " " + ShiftArray[i];
  }
  return S;
}
AnsiString GetKey(WORD K)
{
  AnsiString S;
  switch (K)
  {
    case VK_LBUTTON: S = "VK_LButton"; break;
    case VK_RBUTTON  : S = "VK_RBUTTON"; break;
    case VK_CANCEL   : S = "VK_CANCEL"; break;
    case VK_MBUTTON  : S = "VK_MBUTTON"; break;
    case VK_BACK     : S = "VK_BACK"; break;
    case VK_TAB      : S = "VK_TAB"; break;
    case VK_CLEAR    : S = "VK_CLEAR"; break;
    case VK_RETURN   : S = "VK_RETURN"; break;
    case VK_SHIFT    : S = "VK_SHIFT"; break;
    case VK_CONTROL  : S = "VK_CONTROL"; break;
    case VK_MENU     : S = "VK_MENU"; break;
    case VK_PAUSE    : S = "VK_PAUSE"; break;
    case VK_CAPITAL  : S = "VK_CAPITAL"; break;
    case VK_ESCAPE   : S = "VK_ESCAPE"; break;
    case VK_SPACE    : S = "VK_SPACE"; break;
    case VK_PRIOR    : S = "VK_PRIOR"; break;
    case VK_NEXT     : S = "VK_NEXT"; break;
    case VK_END      : S = "VK_END"; break;
    case VK_HOME     : S = "VK_HOME"; break;
    case VK_LEFT     : S = "VK_LEFT"; break;
    case VK_UP       : S = "VK_UP"; break;
    case VK_RIGHT    : S = "VK_RIGHT"; break;
    case VK_DOWN     : S = "VK_DOWN"; break;
    case VK_SELECT   : S = "VK_SELECT"; break;
    case VK_PRINT    : S = "VK_PRINT"; break;
    case VK_EXECUTE  : S = "VK_EXECUTE"; break;
```

```
      case VK_SNAPSHOT   : S = "VK_SNAPSHOT"; break;
      case VK_INSERT     : S = "VK_INSERT"; break;
      case VK_DELETE     : S = "VK_DELETE"; break;
      case VK_HELP       : S = "VK_HELP"; break;
      case VK_NUMPAD0    : S = "VK_NUMPAD0"; break;
      case VK_NUMPAD1    : S = "VK_NUMPAD1"; break;
      case VK_NUMPAD2    : S = "VK_NUMPAD2"; break;
      case VK_NUMPAD3    : S = "VK_NUMPAD3"; break;
      case VK_NUMPAD4    : S = "VK_NUMPAD4"; break;
      case VK_NUMPAD5    : S = "VK_NUMPAD5"; break;
      case VK_NUMPAD6    : S = "VK_NUMPAD6"; break;
      case VK_NUMPAD7    : S = "VK_NUMPAD7"; break;
      case VK_NUMPAD8    : S = "VK_NUMPAD8"; break;
      case VK_NUMPAD9    : S = "VK_NUMPAD9"; break;
      case VK_MULTIPLY   : S = "VK_MULTIPLY"; break;
      case VK_ADD        : S = "VK_ADD"; break;
      case VK_SEPARATOR  : S = "VK_SEPARATOR"; break;
      case VK_SUBTRACT   : S = "VK_SUBTRACT"; break;
      case VK_DECIMAL    : S = "VK_DECIMAL"; break;
      case VK_DIVIDE     : S = "VK_DIVIDE"; break;
      case VK_F1         : S = "VK_F1"; break;
      case VK_F2         : S = "VK_F2"; break;
      case VK_F3         : S = "VK_F3"; break;
      case VK_F4         : S = "VK_F4"; break;
      case VK_F5         : S = "VK_F5"; break;
      case VK_F6         : S = "VK_F6"; break;
      case VK_F7         : S = "VK_F7"; break;
      case VK_F8         : S = "VK_F8"; break;
      case VK_F9         : S = "VK_F9"; break;
      case VK_F10        : S = "VK_F10"; break;
      case VK_F11        : S = "VK_F11"; break;
      case VK_F12        : S = "VK_F12"; break;
      case VK_F13        : S = "VK_F13"; break;
      case VK_F14        : S = "VK_F14"; break;
      case VK_F15        : S = "VK_F15"; break;
      case VK_F16        : S = "VK_F16"; break;
      case VK_F17        : S = "VK_F17"; break;
      case VK_F18        : S = "VK_F18"; break;
      case VK_F19        : S = "VK_F19"; break;
      case VK_F20        : S = "VK_F20"; break;
      case VK_F21        : S = "VK_F21"; break;
      case VK_F22        : S = "VK_F22"; break;
      case VK_F23        : S = "VK_F23"; break;
      case VK_F24        : S = "VK_F24"; break;
      case VK_NUMLOCK    : S = "VK_NUMLOCK"; break;
      case VK_SCROLL     : S = "VK_SCROLL"; break;
    default:
      S = K;
    }
    return S;
}
```

4

EVENTS

EVENTS2 shows how to extract the full content of a message sent to you by BCB. The main form for the program (shown in Figure 4.4) provides information on a wide range of mouse and keyboard-generated events.

FIGURE 4.4.

The EVENTS2 program tracks key Windows events as they occur.

To use the program, simply compile and run it. Click the mouse in random locations and strike any of the keys on the keyboard. Just rattle away; you won't do any harm unless you press Ctrl+Alt+Del. Every time you move the mouse, click the mouse or strike a key; the exact nature of the event that occurred is shown in the main form of the program. For instance, if you move the mouse, its current location is shown on the form. If you press the F1 key while the Ctrl key is pressed, those keys' values are displayed on the form.

If you don't have the `MyMouseMove` function defined, the `FormMouseMove` event handler in the `EVENTS2` window tracks the current location of the mouse and the state of its buttons. It does this by responding to `OnMouseMove` events:

```
void __fastcall TForm1::FormMouseMove(TObject *Sender, TShiftState Shift, int X,
  int Y)
{
  LMouseMove->Caption = "X " + IntToStr(X) + " Y " +
                        IntToStr(Y) + " " + GetShift(Shift);
}
```

The method for tracking the X and Y values is fairly intuitive. X stands for the current column, and Y stands for the current row, with columns and rows measured in pixels. Before these values can be shown to the user, they need to be translated into strings by the `IntToStr` function. Nothing could be simpler than the techniques used to record the current location of the mouse.

The technique for recording the current shift state, however, is a bit more complex. As you saw earlier, the elements of this set track all the possible states of the Shift, Alt, and Ctrl keys, as well as the mouse buttons.

The `Set` class makes it a simple matter to create a function that will find all the currently selected elements of a variable of type `TShiftState`:

```
AnsiString GetShift(TShiftState State)
{
  int B = 0, i;
  AnsiString S;
```

```
for (i = 0; i <= 7; i++)
{
  if (State.Contains(i))
    S = S + " " +  ShiftArray[i];
}
return S;
}
```

The preceding code takes advantage of the following constant array:

```
AnsiString ShiftArray[8] = {"ssShift", "ssAlt", "ssCtrl", "ssLeft",
                            "ssRight", "ssMiddle", "ssDouble", "ssUnknown"};
```

More specifically, the code checks to see whether the first possible element of the set is active, and if it is, `"ssShift"` is added to the string returned by the function. If the next element in the enumerated type underlying the set is present, the string `"ssAlt"` is added to the string returned by the function, and so on. As you move through the elements in the underlying enumerated type, you get a picture of the current state of the mouse and keyboard. For instance, if the Shift and Ctrl keys are pressed, as well as the right mouse button, the string returned by the function looks like this:

```
ssShift ssCtrl ssRight
```

Trapping Virtual Keys

When keys are pressed in a Windows program, two different messages can be sent to your program. One message is called WM_KEYDOWN, and it is sent whenever any key on the keyboard is pressed. The second message is called WM_CHAR, and it is sent when one of the alphanumeric keys is pressed. In other words, if you press the A key, you get both a WM_KEYDOW and a WM_CHAR message. If you press the F1 key, only the WM_KEYDOWN message is sent.

OnKeyPress event handlers correspond to WM_CHAR messages, and OnKeyDown events correspond to WM_KEYDOWN events. That's why OnKeyPress handlers are passed a Key variable that is of type char, and OnKeyDown handlers are passed a Key variable that is of type WORD.

When you get a WM_KEYDOWN message, you need to have some way of translating that message into a meaningful value. To help with this chore, Windows declares a set of virtual key constants that all start with vk. For example, if you press the F1 key, the Key variable passed to an OnKeyDown event is set to VK_F1, in which the letters vk stand for virtual key. The virtual key codes are found in the WINDOWS unit and also in the online help under Virtual Key Codes.

You can test to see which virtual key has been pressed by writing code that looks like this:

```
if (Key == VK_CANCEL)
  DoSomething();
```

This code simply tests to see whether a particular key has been pressed. If it has, the code calls the DoSomething function.

To help you understand virtual keys, the GetKey method from the VKEYS unit returns a string stating exactly what key has been pressed:

```
AnsiString GetKey(WORD K)
{
  AnsiString S;
  switch (K)
  {
    case VK_LBUTTON: S = "VK_LButton"; break;
    case VK_RBUTTON   : S = "VK_RBUTTON"; break;
    case VK_CANCEL    : S = "VK_CANCEL"; break;
    case VK_MBUTTON   : S = "VK_MBUTTON"; break;
    case VK_BACK      : S = "VK_BACK"; break;
    case VK_TAB       : S = "VK_TAB"; break;
    case VK_CLEAR     : S = "VK_CLEAR"; break;
    case VK_RETURN    : S = "VK_RETURN"; break;
    case VK_SHIFT     : S = "VK_SHIFT"; break;
    case VK_CONTROL   : S = "VK_CONTROL"; break;
    case VK_MENU      : S = "VK_MENU"; break;
    case VK_PAUSE     : S = "VK_PAUSE"; break;
    case VK_CAPITAL   : S = "VK_CAPITAL"; break;
    case VK_ESCAPE    : S = "VK_ESCAPE"; break;
    case VK_SPACE     : S = "VK_SPACE"; break;
    case VK_PRIOR     : S = "VK_PRIOR"; break;
    case VK_NEXT      : S = "VK_NEXT"; break;
    case VK_END       : S = "VK_END"; break;
    case VK_HOME      : S = "VK_HOME"; break;
    case VK_LEFT      : S = "VK_LEFT"; break;
    case VK_UP        : S = "VK_UP"; break;
    case VK_RIGHT     : S = "VK_RIGHT"; break;
    case VK_DOWN      : S = "VK_DOWN"; break;
    case VK_SELECT    : S = "VK_SELECT"; break;
    case VK_PRINT     : S = "VK_PRINT"; break;
    case VK_EXECUTE   : S = "VK_EXECUTE"; break;
    case VK_SNAPSHOT  : S = "VK_SNAPSHOT"; break;
    case VK_INSERT    : S = "VK_INSERT"; break;
    case VK_DELETE    : S = "VK_DELETE"; break;
    case VK_HELP      : S = "VK_HELP"; break;
    case VK_NUMPAD0   : S = "VK_NUMPAD0"; break;
    case VK_NUMPAD1   : S = "VK_NUMPAD1"; break;
    case VK_NUMPAD2   : S = "VK_NUMPAD2"; break;
    case VK_NUMPAD3   : S = "VK_NUMPAD3"; break;
    case VK_NUMPAD4   : S = "VK_NUMPAD4"; break;
    case VK_NUMPAD5   : S = "VK_NUMPAD5"; break;
    case VK_NUMPAD6   : S = "VK_NUMPAD6"; break;
    case VK_NUMPAD7   : S = "VK_NUMPAD7"; break;
    case VK_NUMPAD8   : S = "VK_NUMPAD8"; break;
    case VK_NUMPAD9   : S = "VK_NUMPAD9"; break;
    case VK_MULTIPLY  : S = "VK_MULTIPLY"; break;
    case VK_ADD       : S = "VK_vkADD"; break;
    case VK_SEPARATOR : S = "VK_SEPARATOR"; break;
    case VK_SUBTRACT  : S = "VK_SUBTRACT"; break;
    case VK_DECIMAL   : S = "VK_DECIMAL"; break;
    case VK_DIVIDE    : S = "VK_DIVIDE"; break;
    case VK_F1        : S = "VK_F1"; break;
    case VK_F2        : S = "VK_F2"; break;
    case VK_F3        : S = "VK_F3"; break;
    case VK_F4        : S = "VK_F4"; break;
```

```
      case VK_F5        : S = "VK_F5"; break;
      case VK_F6        : S = "VK_F6"; break;
      case VK_F7        : S = "VK_F7"; break;
      case VK_F8        : S = "VK_F8"; break;
      case VK_F9        : S = "VK_F9"; break;
      case VK_F10       : S = "VK_F10"; break;
      case VK_F11       : S = "VK_F11"; break;
      case VK_F12       : S = "VK_F12"; break;
      case VK_F13       : S = "VK_F13"; break;
      case VK_F14       : S = "VK_F14"; break;
      case VK_F15       : S = "VK_F15"; break;
      case VK_F16       : S = "VK_F16"; break;
      case VK_F17       : S = "VK_F17"; break;
      case VK_F18       : S = "VK_F18"; break;
      case VK_F19       : S = "VK_F19"; break;
      case VK_F20       : S = "VK_F20"; break;
      case VK_F21       : S = "VK_F21"; break;
      case VK_F22       : S = "VK_F22"; break;
      case VK_F23       : S = "VK_F23"; break;
      case VK_F24       : S = "VK_F24"; break;
      case VK_NUMLOCK   : S = "VK_NUMLOCK"; break;
      case VK_SCROLL    : S = "VK_SCROLL"; break;
    default:
      S = char(K);
    }
    return S;
}
```

This function is really just a giant case statement that checks to see whether the Key variable is equal to any of the virtual keys. If it is not, the code assumes that it must be one of the standard keys between A and Z. (See the else clause in the code to see how these standard keys are handled.)

As explained in the last paragraph, the virtual key codes do not cover normal letters such as A, B, and C. In other words, there is no value VK_A or VK_B. To test for these letters, just use the standard ASCII values. In other words, test whether Key is equal to 65, or whether char(key) = 'A'. The point here is that these letters already have key codes. That is, the key codes for these letters are the literal values A, B, C, and so on. Because these are perfectly serviceable values, there is no need to create virtual key codes for the standard letters of the alphabet, or for numbers.

To see the value as a number, make the default section of the code look like this:

```
S = K;
```

Then if you press the A key, you get back 65. If you want to see the letter 'A' instead, write the following:

```
S = char(K);
```

You probably won't have much use for the GetKey routine in a standard BCB program. However, it is useful when you are trying to understand virtual keys and the OnKeyDown event. As a result, I have included it in this program.

4

EVENTS

Handling Events Directly

If you look at the bottom of the EVENTS2 form, you see that there is a special event that tracks the position of the mouse. The EVENTS2 program tracks the mouse movements in two different ways because I wanted to show you that you can get information about the mouse either by responding to OnMouseMove events or by directly tracking WM_MOUSEMOVE messages.

Here is how you declare a function that is going to directly capture a message:

```
class TForm1 : public TForm
{
__published:
    ... // Declarations omitted
private:
MESSAGE void MyMouseMove(TWMMouse &Message);
public:
    virtual __fastcall TForm1(TComponent* Owner);
BEGIN_MESSAGE_MAP
    MESSAGE_HANDLER(WM_MOUSEMOVE, TWMMouse, MyMouseMove);
END_MESSAGE_MAP(TForm);
};
```

The declaration shown here tells BCB that you want to respond directly when the operating system informs your program that the mouse has moved. In other words, you don't want the BCB VCL to trap the message first and then pass it on to you in an OnMouseMove event. Instead, you just want the message sent straight to you by the operating system, as if you were working with one of the Windows API programs shown earlier in the book. In short, you're telling the VCL: "Yes, I know you can make this task very simple and can automate nearly the entire process by using visual tools. That's nice of you, but right now I want to get the real event itself. I have some reason of my own for wanting to get very close to the metal. As a result, I'm going to grab the message before you ever get a chance to look at it!"

Here's the code for the MyMouseMove function:

```
void TForm1::MyMouseMove(TWMMouse &Message)
{
  TForm::Dispatch(&Message);
  LSpecialMouse->Caption = "X " + IntToStr(Message.XPos) +
                           " Y " + IntToStr(Message.YPos);
}
```

You can see that the code begins by calling the Dispatch method inherited from TObject. If you didn't make this call, the program would still run, but the OnMouseMove event would never be sent to the FormMouseMove function. It isn't an error if you don't pass the message back to BCB. You can either keep the message for yourself or pass it on, as you prefer.

If you omit the call to Dispatch from the MySpecialMouse function, the FormMouseMove method in the EVENTS2 program is no longer called. In other words, you are directly trapping WM_MOUSEMOVE messages and not passing them on to the VCL. As a result, the VCL does not know that the event occurred, and FormMouseMove is not called.

The explanation in the last paragraph might not be easy to grasp unless you actually experiment with the EVENTS2 program. You should run the program once with the default version of the MyMouseMove method, and once with the call to Inherited commented out:

```
void TForm1::MyMouseMove(TWMMouse &Message)
{
  // TForm::Dispatch(&Message);
  LSpecialMouse->Caption = "X " + IntToStr(Message.XPos) +
                           " Y " + IntToStr(Message.YPos);
}
```

Notice that when you run the program this way, the OnMouseMove message at the top of the form is left blank.

If you look at the header for the MyMouseMove function, you can see that it is passed a parameter of type TWMMouse. As you recall, the TWMMouse record, found in MESSAGES.PAS, looks like this:

```
struct TWMMouse
{
  unsigned int Msg;
  long Keys;
  union
  {
    struct
    {
      Windows::TSmallPoint Pos;
      long Result;
    };
    struct
    {
      short XPos;
      short YPos;
    };
  };
};
```

If you break out both of the options shown in this variant record, you can further simplify this record by writing

```
struct TWMMouse
{
  unsigned int Msg;
  long Keys;
  Windows::TSmallPoint Pos;
  long Result;
};
```

or

```
struct TWMMouse
{
  unsigned int Msg;
  long Keys;
  short XPos;
  short YPos;
};
```

For most users, one of these two views will be the most useful way to picture the record.

4

EVENTS

The same information is present in a TWMMouse record that you would find if you responded to an OnMouseMove or OnMouseDown event. If appropriate, you can find out the row and column where the mouse is located, what key is pressed, and what state the Shift, Alt, and Ctrl keys are in. To pursue this matter further, you should look up WM_MOUSEMOVE and WM_MOUSEDOWN messages in the online help.

TWMMouse plays the same role in a BCB program that message crackers from WINDOWSX.H play in a C++ program. In other words, they automatically break out the values passed in lParam or wParam parameters of the WndProc. However, if you want, you can pass a variable of type TMessage as the parameter sent to the WM_MOUSEMOVE message handler.

Because TMessage and TWMMouse are both the same size, BCB doesn't care which one you use when trapping WM_MOUSEMOVE events. It's up to you to decide how you want to crack the wParam and lParam parameters passed to the WndProc.

In this section, you have learned something about directly handling Windows messages. When you write code that captures messages directly, you are in a sense reverting back to the more complicated model of programming found in Borland C++ 5.x. However, there are times when it is helpful to get close to the machine; BCB lets you get there if that is what you need to do.

Menu IDs, Handling WM_COMMAND, Finding TForm's WndProc

In standard Windows programming, as it was conducted before the appearance of visual tools, one of the most important messages was WM_COMMAND. This message was sent to a program every time the user selected a menu item or a button, or clicked almost any other control that is part of the current program. Furthermore, each of the buttons, menu items, and other controls in a program had a special ID, which was assigned by the programmer. This ID was passed to WM_COMMAND handlers in the wParam variable.

BCB handles WM_COMMAND messages in such a way that you almost never have to think about them. For instance, you can get clicks on a button or menu by using the delegation model. Standard BCB controls still have IDs, but BCB assigns these numbers automatically, and there is no obvious way for you to learn the value of these IDs.

Despite BCB's capability to simplify this aspect of Windows programming, there are still times when you want to get down to the bare bones and start handling WM_COMMAND messages yourself. In particular, you will want to find a way to discover the ID associated with a particular command, and you will want to trap that ID inside a WM_COMMAND handler.

The MENUDEF program gives a general overview of how to handle WM_COMMAND messages. The program enables you to discover the ID used by a series of menu items and then enables you to trap these IDs when they are sent to a WM_COMMAND handler in the form of a TMessage.wParam variable.

As a bonus, the program also shows how to use the TForm WndProc method, which lets you set up your own window function that receives all the messages sent to your form. It is extremely rare that you would ever need to override this virtual method in your own programs, but I show you how to do it just so you will understand a little more about how the VCL operates. You should be warned that this is a dangerous method to override, because it might come into existence before your controls are initialized and ready for use and might disappear after the controls have been disposed. For instance, I check for WM_CLOSE messages, and once I get one, I don't try to show you any more messages coming into the WndProc. Needless to say, you would crash your program immediately if you overrode this method and did not call its ancestor.

Figure 4.5 shows the form for the MENUDEF program. Here are the menu items that you can't see in Figure 4.5:

```
Caption = 'File'
   Caption = 'Open'
   Caption = 'Close'
   Caption = 'Exit'
Caption = 'Edit'
   Caption = 'Cut'
   Caption = 'Copy'
   Caption = 'Paste'
```

FIGURE 4.5.

The MENUDEF program uses a TMemo, *a* TButton, *and a* TMainMenu *control.*

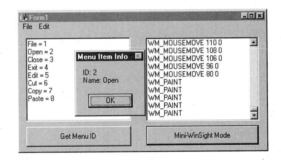

The code for the MENUDEF program is in Listings 4.6 and 4.7. You can see that it features two standard BCB event handlers, as well as a WM_COMMAND handler and the overridden WndProc virtual method.

Listing 4.6. The MENUDEF program shows how to retrieve the ID of a BCB menu item.

```
#ifndef MainH
#define MainH
#include <Classes.hpp>
#include <Controls.hpp>
#include <StdCtrls.hpp>
#include <Forms.hpp>
#include <Menus.hpp>
class TForm1 : public TForm
{
__published:
  TMemo *Memo1;
  TButton *MenuID;
  TMainMenu *MainMenu1;
  TMenuItem *File1;
  TMenuItem *Open1;
  TMenuItem *CLose1;
  TMenuItem *Exit1;
  TMenuItem *Exit2;
  TMenuItem *Cut1;
```

```
    TMenuItem *Copy1;
    TMenuItem *Paste1;
    TListBox *ListBox1;
    TButton *MiniWinSight;
    void __fastcall MenuIDClick(
    TObject *Sender);
    void __fastcall MiniWinSightClick(
    TObject *Sender);
private:
 MESSAGE void WMCommand(TMessage &Message);
 int TotalMenuItems;
 int MenuItemArray[100];
protected:
   virtual void __fastcall WndProc(Messages::TMessage &Message);
public:
   virtual __fastcall TForm1(TComponent* Owner);
BEGIN_MESSAGE_MAP
   MESSAGE_HANDLER(WM_COMMAND, TMessage, WMCommand);
END_MESSAGE_MAP(TForm);
};
extern TForm1 *Form1;
#endif
```

Listing 4.7. The MENUDEF program uses a TMemo, a TButton, and a TMainMenu control.

```
///////////////////////////////////////
// Copyright (c) 1997 by Charlie Calvert
//
#include <vcl.h>
#pragma hdrstop
#include "Main.h"
#pragma resource "*.dfm"
TForm1 *Form1;
static bool ShowMessages = FALSE;
__fastcall TForm1::TForm1(TComponent* Owner)
  : TForm(Owner)
{
  int i;
  TotalMenuItems = 0;
  for (i = 0; i < ComponentCount; i++)
    if (dynamic_cast<TMenuItem *>(Components[i]))
    {
      MenuItemArray[TotalMenuItems] =
        dynamic_cast<TMenuItem*>(Components[i])->Command;
      TotalMenuItems++;
    }
}
void TForm1::WMCommand(TMessage &Message)
{
  int i,j;
  AnsiString S1(IntToStr(Message.WParam)), S3;
  for (i = 0; i < TotalMenuItems; i++)
    if (Message.WParam == MenuItemArray[i])
    {
```

continues

Listing 4.7. continued

```cpp
      for (j = 0; j < ComponentCount; j++)
      {
        if (dynamic_cast<TMenuItem*>(Components[j]))
          if (dynamic_cast<TMenuItem*>(Components[j])->Command ==
              MenuItemArray[i])
            S3 = dynamic_cast<TMenuItem*>(Components[j])->Caption;
      }
      S1 = "ID: " + S1 + "\rName: " +  S3;
      MessageBox(Handle, S1.c_str(), "Menu Item Info", MB_OK);
    }
  TForm::Dispatch(&Message);
}
void __fastcall TForm1::MenuIDClick(TObject *Sender)
{
  int Command, i;
  AnsiString Name;
  Memo1->Lines->Clear();
  for (i = 0; i < ComponentCount; i++)
  {
    if (dynamic_cast<TMenuItem*>(Components[i]))
    {
      Command = dynamic_cast<TMenuItem*>(Components[i])->Command;
      Name = dynamic_cast<TMenuItem*>(Components[i])->Caption;
      Memo1->Lines->Add(Name + " = " + IntToStr(Command));
    }
  }
}
void __fastcall TForm1::MiniWinSightClick(
  TObject *Sender)
{
  ShowMessages = True;
}
void ShowMsg(AnsiString &S)
{
  if (Form1->ListBox1)
    Form1->ListBox1->Items->Add(S);
  if (Form1->ListBox1->Items->Count > 6)
    Form1->ListBox1->TopIndex = Form1->ListBox1->Items->Count - 5;
}
void HandleMessages(TMessage &Msg)
{
  AnsiString S;
  switch(Msg.Msg)
  {
    case WM_PAINT:
      S = "wm_Paint";
      ShowMsg(S);
      break;
    case WM_MOUSEMOVE:
      S = IntToStr(Msg.LParamLo) + " " + IntToStr(Msg.LParamHi);
      S = "WM_MOUSEMOVE " + S;
      ShowMsg(S);
      break;
    case WM_LBUTTONDOWN:
      S = IntToStr(Msg.LParamLo) + " " + IntToStr(Msg.LParamHi);
      S = "WM_LBUTTONDOWN" + S;
```

```
      ShowMsg(S);
      break;
    case WM_RBUTTONDOWN:
      S = IntToStr(Msg.LParamLo) + " " + IntToStr(Msg.LParamHi);
      S = "WM_RBUTTONDOWN" + S;
      ShowMsg(S);
      break;
/*    case WM_NCHITTEST: // Uncomment WM_NCHITTEST to see a flurry of messages.
      S = "WM_NCHITTEST";
      ShowMsg(S);
      break; */
    }
}
void __fastcall TForm1::WndProc(Messages::TMessage &Message)
{
  if (Message.Msg == WM_CLOSE)
    ShowMessages = FALSE;
  if (ShowMessages)
    HandleMessages(Message);

  TForm::WndProc(Message);
}
```

The MENUDEF program has two features:

- If you click the button at the bottom of the main form, the program's memo control displays a list of all the items in the menu, along with their IDs.

- If you click any of the menu items, a message box appears stating the name of the menu item and its ID.

Here is the code that grabs the ID of all the menu items and displays the ID along with the menu item's caption in a TMemo:

```
void __fastcall TForm1::MenuIDClick(TObject *Sender)
{
  int Command, i;
  AnsiString Name;
  Memo1->Lines->Clear();
  for (i = 0; i < ComponentCount; i++)
  {
    if (dynamic_cast<TMenuItem*>(Components[i]))
    {
      Command = dynamic_cast<TMenuItem*>(Components[i])->Command;
      Name = dynamic_cast<TMenuItem*>(Components[i])->Caption;
      Memo1->Lines->Add(Name + " = " + IntToStr(Command));
    }
  }
}
```

The code begins by clearing the current contents of the memo control. It then iterates through all the components on the form and finds any of them that are of type TMenuItem. The next step is to get the ID and the caption of the menu items. To get the ID, you need only reference the Command property of the TMenuItem component. The caption can be retrieved the same way, and then you can add this information to the list box.

The use of a `dynamic_cast` in the previous code demonstrates BCB's capability to work with Run Time Type Information (RTTI). RTTI enables you to test the type of a particular variable and respond accordingly. For instance, in this case the program simply asks whether a particular component is of type `TMenuItem`; if this Boolean question returns `True`, the program examines the component in more depth.

The remaining code in the program captures the IDs of the menu items in an array and then responds to `WM_COMMAND` messages generated by clicks in one of the program's menu items. As explained earlier, the code displays a message box stating that the menus are not yet functional. In the caption of the menu box, you can read the ID of the control that was clicked.

The code that captures the menu items in an array occurs in a `Forms` constructor:

```
__fastcall TForm1::TForm1(TComponent* Owner)
  : TForm(Owner)
{
  int i;
  TotalMenuItems = 0;
  for (i = 0; i < ComponentCount; i++)
    if (dynamic_cast<TMenuItem *>(Components[i]))
    {
      MenuItemArray[TotalMenuItems] =
        dynamic_cast<TMenuItem*>(Components[i])->Command;
      TotalMenuItems++;
    }
}
```

This code is almost identical to the `MenuIDClick` method, except that the IDs of the `TMenuItems` are stored in an array rather than being shown in a `TMemo`. The declaration for the array looks like this:

```
int MenuItemArray[100];
```

The declaration for the `WM_COMMAND` handler should be familiar to you by this time:

```
MESSAGE void WMCommand(TMessage &Message);
BEGIN_MESSAGE_MAP
  MESSAGE_HANDLER(WM_COMMAND, TMessage, WMCommand);
END_MESSAGE_MAP(TForm);
```

Here, the message directive tells the compiler that this is a dynamic method and the offset in the dynamic method table is established by the `WM_COMMAND` constant.

The `WMCommand` method compares the values sent in `Message.wParam` to the values in the `MenuItemArray`. If it finds a match, it displays the message box previously described.

```
void TForm1::WMCommand(TMessage &Message)
{
  int i,j;
  AnsiString S1(IntToStr(Message.WParam)), S3;
  for (i = 0; i < TotalMenuItems; i++)
    if (Message.WParam == MenuItemArray[i])
    {
```

```
      for (j = 0; j < ComponentCount; j++)
      {
        if (dynamic_cast<TMenuItem*>(Components[j]))
          if (dynamic_cast<TMenuItem*>(Components[j])->Command ==
            MenuItemArray[i])
            S3 = dynamic_cast<TMenuItem*>(Components[j])->Caption;
      }
      S1 = "ID: " + S1 + "\rName: " + S3;
      MessageBox(Handle, S1.c_str(), "Menu Item Info", MB_OK);
    }
  TForm::Dispatch(&Message);
}
```

This code calls the Windows API `MessageBox` function rather than `MessageDlg`.

Here is the code that overrides the window function:

```
void __fastcall TForm1::WndProc(Messages::TMessage &Message)
{
  if (Message.Msg == WM_CLOSE)
    ShowMessages = FALSE;
  if (ShowMessages)
    HandleMessages(Message);

  TForm::WndProc(Message);
}
```

The `TMessage` struct looks like this:

```
struct TMessage
{
  unsigned int Msg;
  union
  {
    struct
    {
      unsigned short WParamLo;
      unsigned short WParamHi;
      unsigned short LParamLo;
      unsigned short LParamHi;
      unsigned short ResultLo;
      unsigned short ResultHi;
    };
    struct
    {
      long WParam;
      long LParam;
      long Result;
    };
  };
};
```

This structure has all the information in it that you would get if you were inside a standard windows function. For all intents and purposes, you are inside a standard window function. (See `TApplication.Create` in the Pascal source, as well as the `TForm` object, for more information.)

At this stage I could begin a 400- or 500-page analysis of window functions, messages, and the structure of the Windows operating system. (That was pretty much what I did in *Teach Yourself Windows 95 Programming in 21 Days* (Sams Publishing), so there is a source for this kind of information if you want it.) However, this book is not about that kind of material, so I will leave this method hanging and let you explore it to the degree to which the subject matter calls you. Remember, however, that this method can be dangerous to handle, as it is active even when the controls on your form have not been created, and it is still active after they have been destroyed.

One final point about working with the IDs of a control: If you build the interface of your program and then don't change its menus or any other aspect of its interface, the IDs that BCB associates with each control will (at least theoretically) remain the same throughout the development of your application. This might give some people the idea of using the `MenuIDClick` method, shown earlier, as a temporary response to a click on one of your controls and the storing of the output to a file. Thereafter, you would hope to know the ID associated with each of your controls and could handle them in a `WM_COMMAND` routine. This technique is theoretically possible, but I wouldn't recommend it as part of the framework for any serious application. In short, if you have to know the ID of a particular control, I would determine it in the `FormCreate` method, thereby ensuring that the ID is correct for that build of your program.

Summary

In this chapter you learned how to handle events using the standard BCB delegation model. You saw that when the need arises, you can circumvent this system and handle events directly by employing message maps. You can also pass messages back to the system by calling the inherited `Dispatch` method. Events represent one of the most important subjects in BCB programming, and you probably shouldn't move on until you have a good idea of what's going on in the EVENTS2 program.

This chapter also explained that you can handle `wParam` and `lParam` variables directly. Furthermore, BCB gives you a way to parse the information passed with events, so that you can place a custom record as the parameter to a message handler. For instance, if Windows conceals a set of X and Y coordinates inside the high or low words of `wParam`, BCB enables you to define a custom record that automatically breaks up `wParam` into two separate variables called X and Y. This is the same functionality that is found in the message crackers provided in `WINDOWSX.H`. The `TWMMouse` record discussed earlier is one of these records; `TMessage` is another. If you want, you can create your own records that parse the information associated with standard BCB events or with events that you create yourself. You are not limited to custom BCB handlers such as `TMessage` or `TWMMouse`.

Exceptions

IN THIS CHAPTER

CHAPTER 5

In this chapter you learn how to add error handling to your programs. This is done almost entirely through a mechanism called *exceptions.*

In particular, the following subjects are covered:

- Exception-handling theory
- Basic exception classes
- `try..catch` blocks
- Raising and reraising exceptions
- Creating your own exception classes
- Saving error strings in resources and retrieving them with `LoadString`
- Internationalizing your program with string tables
- Using the destructor of an object to ensure that code is executed even after an exception occurs. (Delphi and Java programmers should note that this is how C++ gets the functionality found in `try..finally` blocks.)
- Overriding the default exception handler

To a large degree, BCB and the VCL make it possible for you to write programs that almost entirely ignore the subject of error checking. This is possible because exceptions are built into most classes and stand-alone routines and will be thrown automatically whenever something goes wrong. Furthermore, your entire program is automatically wrapped inside a `try..catch` block. Professional programmers, however, will want to go beyond even this level of safety and add additional error checking to their code, or else change the default error handling performed by BCB. Also, your programs might need to throw their own errors, so you will need to add and throw new exception classes.

This explanation of exceptions is not meant to replace chapters on that subject in standard books on C++ programming. Instead, I will concentrate on handling exceptions in VCL-based programs.

BCB does a great job of seamlessly surfacing Pascal-based VCL exceptions in your C++ code. As far as BCB programmers are concerned, there is no difference between an exception that occurs in a block of Pascal code and an exception that occurs in C++ code.

I believe exceptions are the correct model for reporting errors in any application. Because exceptions play such a big role in all VCL programs, this is a topic of which you should have at least a minimal understanding.

The Theory Behind Exceptions

Exceptions enable you to designate specific areas of your code designed to handle errors. In particular, you can "guard" whole sections of code in such a way that if errors occur inside them, the problem will be handled in a different area by a set of routines designed explicitly for that purpose. This technique covers nested functions, too, so you can begin a guarded block, step in through six or seven levels of function calls, and then, if something goes wrong, bounce directly back out to a single area in your code designed to handle error conditions. The goal is to do as much as possible to relieve the burden of writing error-handling routines so that you can concentrate on other, more important, goals.

> **NOTE**
>
> Right at the start, it's important to recognize the difference between BCB exceptions, which cover language issues, and hardware exceptions, which involve hardware and hardware interrupts. You can (and BCB often does) wrap a hardware exception inside a BCB exception and handle the event that way, but hardware exceptions are different than BCB exceptions.
>
> For instance, running out of paper in a printer causes a hardware exception. Your code doesn't get an exception in this case, but a component might throw an exception if the situation is detected. Raising the exception does not cause the hardware error; it already exists outside the program.

Traditionally, error handling has been a matter of one area of code setting flags and then a second area of code responding appropriately. For instance, if you tried to open a file that does not exist, a flag would be set and other portions of your code could detect the condition by checking the flag. Under the new system, instead of a flag being set, an exception is thrown.

The easiest way to start appreciating the advantages that exceptions bring to your code is to imagine a situation in which three different levels of code are called. Suppose, for instance, that you wanted to display data in a grid, where the data in question is stored in a text file. You might have the following set of calls, all nested inside each other:

```
int DisplayDataInGrid();
  int RetrieveData();
    int OpenFile();
    int ReadFile();
    int CloseFile();
```

In this scenario, `DisplayDataInGrid` calls `RetrieveData` and `RetrieveData` calls `OpenFile`, `ReadFile`, and `CloseFile`. After `CloseFile` was called, control would return to `DisplayDataInGrid`, and the actual data would be shown to the user.

If something went wrong during the time the file was being opened, `OpenFile` would have to pass that information back to `RetrieveData`. `RetrieveData` would have to include code ensuring that `ReadFile` and `CloseFile` didn't get called; then it would have to pass the error condition back to `DisplayDataInGrid`. In turn, `DisplayDataInGrid` would have to ensure that it did not try to display data that was never retrieved correctly. This whole process of passing information in a daisy chain forces you to write complicated, confusing, and error-prone code.

As a child, you might have played a game called "telephone." In particular, you might have had a teacher, camp counselor, or friend who arranged a large group of people in a circle and then whispered something to the person on his or her left. That person in turn whispered the message to someone on his left, and so on, until the message went all the way around the circle. When the message had made the whole trip, its meaning almost always ended up changing radically from its initial conception. The same thing can happen in a program if you use the daisy chain method of conveying error conditions. The worst case, of course, is when one link in the chain is broken altogether and the rest of the code continues merrily on its way, oblivious of the fact that something serious has gone wrong.

Exceptions don't use the daisy chain theory of error processing. Instead, if an exception is thrown in the function OpenFile, the code automatically unwinds back to DisplayDataInGrid, where you can write code that handles the error. Exceptions automatically pop functions and data off the stack, and they automatically ensure that no other routines behind or in front of it are called until the code is found that is intended to handle the exception.

> **NOTE**
>
> In Java and Object Pascal, when code is being popped off the stack during an exception, the compiler checks for one particular block of code that needs to be executed, even if an exception has occurred. This special code is enclosed in try..finally blocks. C++ has no support for try..finally blocks. Instead, you can put your cleanup code in the destructor of your local objects. The destructor will be called even if an exception has occurred.

In BCB, if an exception occurs and you do not handle it explicitly, a default exception handler will process the exception. Most exceptions are not handled explicitly.

When the VCL default exception handler is invoked, it displays a message dialog describing the exception to the user, and then your program resumes its normal processing of Windows messages. Your program does not return to the code that threw the exception. When an exception is thrown, special compiler-generated code checks the most recently entered try block on the call stack for a suitable exception handler. If that try block has no exception handlers suitable for the current exception, the next outward try block is checked, and so on, until an exception handler is found or it reaches the default exception handler. Normal program execution resumes at the next statement following the code that handles the exception.

If you have a strong background in C++, it might take a while to get used to the idea that your VCL programs are automatically encased in exception-handling code. The standard C++ code you write will not partake of this benefit, but you can easily add exception handling to that code if you want it.

I believe that if you combine the increased robustness given to you by exceptions with the benefit of having to write fewer lines of code, you come up with a clear winner. In fact, I would say that the VCL's built-in, exception-handling capabilities are one of the great benefits of the system.

As stated earlier, the VCL, and any related Object Pascal functions supported by BCB, are all guaranteed to be wrapped in exception handlers. This is not true of the standard C++ routines and objects that you might call. In my mind, this is a reason to turn to the VCL whenever possible, and to use other routines only when necessary. Exception handling is part of good contemporary programming practice, and I believe that it will remain part of it into the foreseeable future.

If the basic idea behind exceptions does not yet quite make sense to you, just forge ahead anyway, and I think it will become clear in time. The previous few paragraphs lay out the theory behind a fairly simple set of syntactical routines. Play with the syntax for a while, using the following descriptions as a guide, and then if you want, come back and read the theory a second time.

Exception Classes

BCB comes with a rich set of built-in exception classes meant for handling a wide range of exceptions. You can easily create your own exception classes for handling the key events in your program that might be susceptible to error. Here is the base class for BCB exception handling, as it is declared in SYSUTILS.HPP:

```
class __declspec(delphiclass) Exception;
class __declspec(pascalimplementation) Exception : public System::TObject
{
  typedef System::TObject inherited;
private:
```

```
  System::AnsiString FMessage;
  int FHelpContext;
public:
  __fastcall Exception(const System::AnsiString Msg);
  __fastcall Exception(const System::AnsiString Msg,
    const System::TVarRec *Args, const int Args_Size);
  __fastcall Exception(int Ident);
  __fastcall Exception(int Ident, const System::TVarRec *Args,
    const int Args_Size);
  __fastcall Exception(const System::AnsiString Msg, int AHelpContext);
  __fastcall Exception(const System::AnsiString Msg,
    const System::TVarRec *Args,
    const int Args_Size, int AHelpContext);
  __fastcall Exception(int Ident, int AHelpContext);
  __fastcall Exception(int Ident, const System::TVarRec *Args,
    const int Args_Size, int AHelpContext);
  __property int HelpContext = {read=FHelpContext, write=FHelpContext, nodefault};
  __property System::AnsiString Message =
    {read=FMessage, write=FMessage, nodefault};
public:
  /* TObject.Destroy */ __fastcall virtual ~Exception(void) { }
};
```

A quick perusal of this declaration reveals that all exceptions have a message that can be displayed to the user. You can pass in this message through a number of different constructors, and you can retrieve it through the Message property.

> **NOTE**
>
> On the off-chance that you are new to C++, I might add here that C++ classes sometimes have multiple constructors because you may have more than one way in which you want to create a class. Sometimes you might want to initialize a class by passing in one type of string, and another time you might want to pass in a second type of string or perhaps an integer. To give you the flexibility you need, C++ enables you to declare multiple constructors. Needless to say, you still call only one constructor when creating a class; it's just that you have a choice of which constructor you want to choose. Unlike Object Pascal, all these constructors have the same name, which is identical to the class name.

Here are some additional built-in exceptions, all quoted directly from SYSUTILS.PAS:

```
class __declspec(delphiclass) EIntError;
class __declspec(delphiclass) EInOutError;
class __declspec(delphiclass) EOutOfMemory;
class __declspec(delphiclass) EDivByZero;
class __declspec(delphiclass) ERangeError;
class __declspec(delphiclass) EIntOverflow;
class __declspec(delphiclass) EMathError;
class __declspec(delphiclass) EInvalidOp;
class __declspec(delphiclass) EZeroDivide;
class __declspec(delphiclass) EOverflow;
class __declspec(delphiclass) EUnderflow;
class __declspec(delphiclass) EInvalidPointer;
```

```
class __declspec(delphiclass) EInvalidCast;
class __declspec(delphiclass) EConvertError;
class __declspec(delphiclass) EAccessViolation;
class __declspec(delphiclass) EPrivilege;
class __declspec(delphiclass) EStackOverflow;
class __declspec(delphiclass) EControlC;
class __declspec(delphiclass) EVariantError;
class __declspec(delphiclass) EPropReadOnly;
class __declspec(delphiclass) EPropWriteOnly;
class __declspec(delphiclass) EExternalException;
```

You can see that there are exception classes for divide-by-zero errors, file I/O errors, invalid type casts, and various other conditions both common and obscure.

The preceding list, however, is far from complete. Many other exceptions classes are declared in other modules of the VCL. To get a feeling for their complete scope, you should use the online help or browse the source files in the Include/VCL directory.

Basic Exception Syntax

When working with the code presented in this chapter, you will be raising a lot of exceptions. If you set Options | Environment | Preferences | Break on Exception to True, exceptions thrown by your program will cause the debugger to take you as near as possible to the place in your code where the exception occurred. Only after you start running again will you see the error message as it will be reported to the user. As a result, you should probably keep Break on Exception set to False except when you explicitly want to step through your code during an exception.

The SIMPEXP program, referenced in Listing 5.1, gives four examples of how to throw and handle exceptions in BCB. The first two examples shown are of the simplest possible kind, and are meant to get you started with the concepts involved in this process. The latter two examples in this program are a bit more complex, but are still relatively straightforward. The main form for the program is shown in Figure 5.1.

FIGURE 5.1.

The main form for the SIMPEXP program.

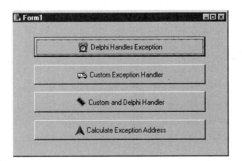

Remember to turn Optimizations off when running this program. You can find the Optimizations settings in the Project | Options | Compiler menu option.

Listing 5.1. The SIMPEXP program demonstrates basic techniques for handling exceptions.

```
/////////////////////////////////////////
// Copyright (c) 1997 by Charlie Calvert
//
#include <vcl.h>
#pragma hdrstop
#include "Main.h"
#include "codebox.h"
#pragma resource "*.dfm"
TForm1 *Form1;
__fastcall TForm1::TForm1(TComponent* Owner)
  : TForm(Owner)
{
}
void __fastcall TForm1::DelExceptClick(
  TObject *Sender)
{
  int i = 4, j = 0, k;
  k = i / j;

  ShowMessage(k);
}
void __fastcall TForm1::UserExceptClick(TObject *Sender)
{
  int i = 4, j = 0, k;
  try
  {
    k = i / j;
    ShowMessage(k);
  }
  catch(EDivByZero &E)
  {
    MessageDlg("Awe Shucks! Another division by zero error!",
              mtError, TMsgDlgButtons() << mbOK, 0);
  }
}
void __fastcall TForm1::DeclareClick(TObject *Sender)
{
  int i;
  AnsiString S;
  try
  {
    i = StrToInt("Sam");
    ShowMessage(i);
  }
  catch(EConvertError &E)
  {
    AnsiString S("Class where error occurred: " + this->ClassName());
    AnsiString S1("Type of error: " + E.ClassName());
    MessageDlg(S + '\r' + S1 + '\r' + E.Message, mtError,
      TMsgDlgButtons() << mbOK, 0);
  }
}
```

```
// Address2 String is in the CodeBox unit that ships w/ the book's CD
// in the UTILS subdirectory
void __fastcall TForm1::CalcAddClick(
  TObject *Sender)
{
  float k;
  try
  {
    k = StrToFloat("Sammy");
    ShowMessage(k);
  }
  catch(EConvertError &E)
  {
    MessageDlg(E.Message + '\r' +
      " Error Address: " + Address2Str(ExceptAddr),
      mtError, TMsgDlgButtons() << mbOK, 0);
  }
}
```

This program contains four TBitBtns that, when pressed, throw exceptions. In the first case, the code lets BCB's built-in routines handle the exception; in the rest of the examples, a custom error handler is invoked.

Here is the simplest way to throw and handle an exception:

```
void __fastcall TForm1::DelExceptClick(
  TObject *Sender)
{
  int i = 4, j = 0, k;
  k = i / j;

  ShowMessage(k);
}
```

The code shown here causes a divide-by-zero error, and it will automatically pop up the dialog shown in Figure 5.2. Notice that the ShowMessage code never gets executed, because the exception occurs before you reach that part of your code. In this case, it would not cause a serious problem if ShowMessage were executed, but you don't want it to execute because it would report nonsense to the user. The benefit this code provides for you is therefore twofold:

- ■ It automatically reports a reasonable error.
- ■ It saves you the trouble of writing error-handling code that would ensure that ShowMessage was not executed in case of an error.

FIGURE 5.2.

The default mechanism for handling a divide-by-zero error.

The error message shown in Figure 5.2 is useful to programmers because it provides an address you can use in the Search | Find Error menu choice. However, it is not a particularly friendly message to send to a user of your program.

The following code demonstrates how to set up a try..catch block that gives you a place to handle an error:

```
void __fastcall TForm1::UserExceptClick(TObject *Sender)
{
  int i = 4, j = 0, k;
  try
  {
    k = i / j;
    ShowMessage(k);
  }
  catch(EDivByZero &E)
  {
    MessageDlg("Awe Shucks! Another division by zero error!",
               mtError, TMsgDlgButtons() << mbOK, 0);
  }
}
```

The code that you want to test appears right after the reserved word try. In this case, all that goes on in this section is that you force a divide-by-zero error. When the error occurs, the code after the word catch is executed. In this section, you designate that you want to handle EDivByZero messages explicitly, and you do so by popping up an error message.

Once again, you will notice that the ShowMessage code is never executed, which is what you want, because it would only report nonsense to the user. Needless to say, the size of the block of code that needs to be skipped does not matter. Nor does it matter how deep into a series of function calls your code might go. For instance, instead of simply raising a divide-by-zero error on the top level, your code might call a second function. That function could in turn call another function, and so on, for six, ten, or however many levels of nested calls. If any of the routines in that block throw an EDivByZero error, the code would automatically jump to the MessageDlg shown in the preceding code.

Or, to state the same fact somewhat differently, if the code looked like this:

```
j = 0;
try
{
k = i / j;
DoSomething;
DoSomethingElse;
DoThis;
DoThat;
ShowMessage(k);
}
catch(EDivByZero &E)
{
MessageDlg("Awe Shucks! Another division by zero error!",
           mtError, TMsgDlgButtons() << mbOK, 0);
}
```

then `DoSomething`, `DoSomethingElse`, `DoThis`, and `DoThat` would never be executed. Instead, the code would jump immediately from the division statement to the `catch` section.

You can combine the convenience of having BCB report an error with the luxury of being able to define your own error strings:

```
void __fastcall TForm1::DeclareClick(TObject *Sender)
{
  int i;
  AnsiString S;
  try
  {
    i = StrToInt("Sam");
    ShowMessage(i);
  }
  catch(EConvertError &E)
  {
    AnsiString S("Class where error occurred: " + this->ClassName());
    AnsiString S1("Type of error: " + E.ClassName());
    MessageDlg(S + '\r' + S1 + '\r' + E.Message, mtError,
      TMsgDlgButtons() << mbOK, 0);
  }
}
```

The `StrToInt` function shown here will throw an `EConvertError` because it cannot convert the string `"Sam"` into an integer.

In this code, BCB is in effect enabling you to map an identifier onto the already existing exception object instance that was thrown. This is not a variable declaration, because no new storage is being allocated. It's simply giving you a convenient way to access the exception object instance so that you can extract additional information carried by the object instance, such as the error message string `E.Message`.

In this case, `Message` returns the string that BCB would associate with this error. To understand where `Message` comes from, refer to the declaration of `TException` shown previously. Note also that you need to work with the address of the `EConvertError`, because this is a VCL class and must be passed by reference:

```
catch(EConvertError &E)
```

This is what you want, anyway, because it is cheaper to pass around pointers than to pass around an actual copy of the object. You should not, however, allocate memory for an exception class before passing it, because that is a dangerous thing to do during an error condition.

After you have access to the `message` associated with an exception, you can add your own information to it. For instance, in this case I snag the name of the object whose method is raising the exception, as well as the name of the `Exception` class itself, thereby helping me know right away where the problem has occurred and why:

```
AnsiString S("Class where error occurred: " + this->ClassName());
AnsiString S1("Type of error: " + E.ClassName());
MessageDlg(S + '\r' + S1 + '\r' + E.Message, mtError,
TMsgDlgButtons() << mbOK, 0);
```

The string created in these lines of code is shown in Figure 5.3.

FIGURE 5.3.

*An exception that shows
a string created in part
by BCB and in part by
the programmer.*

You also might want to display the actual address at which an exception is thrown. The VCL `ExceptAddr` function returns this address:

```
void __fastcall TForm1::CalcAddClick(
  TObject *Sender)
{
  float k;
  try
  {
    k = StrToFloat("Sammy");
    ShowMessage(k);
  }
  catch(EConvertError &E)
  {
    MessageDlg(E.Message + '\r' +
               " Error Address: " + Address2Str(ExceptAddr),
               mtError, TMsgDlgButtons() << mbOK, 0);
  }
}
```

This code displays the regular error message associated with an `EConvertError` exception, and then immediately converts the result of the `ExceptAddr` function into a string so that you can see that it returns the same address displayed by a BCB exception. You can use this address in the Search | Find Error menu option, which will take you to the place in your code where the error occurred.

To convert a pointer into a string, you can use the following function from the `CodeBox` unit:

```
AnsiString Address2Str(void *Addr)
{
  return Format('%p', OPENARRAY(TVarRec, (Addr)));
}
```

This function uses the `Format` routine to perform a routine string operation that returns a string version of an address.

In this section, you learned how to handle simple exceptions. The actual logistics of handling these situations can be quite complex at times, but you are now armed with the basics needed to go into battle and wage war with the compiler. Note that I arranged the examples in this section in order of increasing complexity, where the first two are more typical of the code you will use in most programs, and the latter two are useful when you want to use advanced techniques.

Why Exceptions Are So Great

For some reason, when I first saw exceptions, I was confused by them. The syntax was simple enough, but I couldn't figure out exactly how I was supposed to use the darn things. My only consolation was that I saw so many others flounder in the same sea.

If you are feeling a little confused by what you have just seen of exceptions, try to cut through the fog created by their newness and remember that exceptions are really simple. They do two wonderful things:

1. Pop up error messages automatically.
2. Help you avoid accidentally executing any sensitive code after an error occurs.

If you are confused by an exception, try asking these two questions:

1. What error is being reported for me automatically?
2. What sensitive code is or can be protected by this exception?

In the preceding examples, the answer to the first question is this: either an `EDivByZero` or `EConvertError` message is being reported automatically, without my necessarily having to do any work. The answer to the second question is that a call to `ShowMessage` is being protected. Therefore, `ShowMessage` will only be called when it has valid data to show the user.

That's it! If you can grasp those two simple concepts, you know the most important facts about exceptions. At their core, exceptions are very simple and very useful.

Given the extreme simplicity and extraordinary benefits associated with this subject, there is only one big question left: Why doesn't everyone use exceptions all the time? Why do so many people regard this simple and helpful tool as something rather advanced and murky?

The biggest impediment to the acceptance of exceptions is simply that people haven't yet gotten in the habit of wrapping their entire program inside a `try..catch` block. If you don't take that one step, exceptions can be a minefield that might cause your program to shut down unexpectedly. However, if you do wrap your whole program in a well-constructed `try..catch` block, this tool will do an incredible amount of good work for you with little effort on your part.

One of the great benefits of BCB is that all standard BCB programs automatically exist inside a well-constructed `try..catch` block. (Console applications don't necessarily have this same benefit.) Furthermore, the entire VCL, and most of the routines that support it, also make good use of exceptions. For instance, the `StrToInt` function you saw earlier throws its own exceptions. But I am getting ahead of myself, because there is more territory to cover before talking about raising your own exceptions.

> **NOTE**
>
> It's important to understand that you should not use exceptions indiscriminately. There is a difference between wrapping a program in a `try..catch` block and filling it up with thousands of `try..catch` blocks. There is some overhead involved in this process, so you should use it with a degree of discretion.

The main point is to understand that exceptions are at heart very simple. Furthermore, they exist primarily to make your life as a programmer considerably simpler.

Throwing Exceptions

I want this part of the book to focus primarily on what BCB and the VCL bring to standard exception-handling practice. However, it might be helpful to show a few bits of syntax that highlight some of the particular features of C++ exception handling.

Consider the SimpleExcept program (distinct from the SIMPEXP program shown previously) found in Listing 5.2. This program highlights some of the basic facts about exceptions in C++. For an in-depth discussion of this subject, you should turn to a book on the C++ language. The main form for the SimpleExcept program is shown in Figure 5.4.

FIGURE 5.4.

The SimpleExcept program raises many different kinds of exceptions.

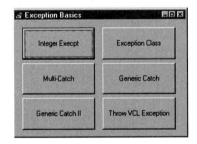

Listing 5.2. The SimpleExcept program shows a few basic features of C++ exception-handling syntax.

```
///////////////////////////////////////
// File: Main.cpp
// Project: SimpleExcept
// Copyright (c) 1997 by Charlie Calvert
/*
  This code provides a few very simple examples of basic
  exception syntax.
*/
#include <vcl\vcl.h>
#pragma hdrstop
#include "Main.h"
#pragma resource "*.dfm"
TForm1 *Form1;
```

```
__fastcall TForm1::TForm1(TComponent* Owner)
  : TForm(Owner)
{
}
void __fastcall TForm1::IntegerExecptBtnClick(TObject *Sender)
{
  try
  {
    throw 23;
  }
  catch(int ErrorCode)
  {
    ShowMessage(ErrorCode);
  }
}
void __fastcall TForm1::ExceptionClassBtnClick(TObject *Sender)
{
  try
  {
    int i = StrToInt("Sam");
  }
  catch(Exception &A)
  {
    ShowMessage("Info: " + A.Message);
  }
}
void __fastcall TForm1::MultiCatchBtnClick(TObject *Sender)
{
  try
  {
    int i = StrToInt("Sam");
  }
  catch(int ErrorCode)
  {
    ShowMessage("int: " + ErrorCode);
  }
  catch (WORD Sam)
  {
    ShowMessage("WORD: " + AnsiString(Sam));
  }
  catch(Exception &A)
  {
    ShowMessage("Exception: " + A.Message);
  }
  catch(EConvertError &B)
  {
    ShowMessage("EConvertError: " + B.Message);
  }
  catch(EDatabaseError &C)
  {
    ShowMessage(C.Message);
  }
}
void __fastcall TForm1::GenericCatchBtnClick(TObject *Sender)
{
  try
  {
    StrToInt("Sam");
```

continues

Listing 5.2. continued

```
  }
  catch (...)
  {
    ShowMessage("Something went wrong");
  }
}
void __fastcall TForm1::GenericCatchIIBtnClick(TObject *Sender)
{
  try
  {
    throw 12;
  }
  catch(EExternalException &E)
  {
    ShowMessage(E.Message);
  }
}
```

This very simple-minded program shows some of the things you can do with exceptions in C++.

Here is a very simple-minded way to throw an exception:

```
void __fastcall TForm1::IntegerExecptBtnClick(TObject *Sender)
{
  try
  {
    throw 23;
  }
  catch(int ErrorCode)
  {
    ShowMessage(ErrorCode);
  }
}
```

The throw statement shown here causes an exception to be thrown. The catch statement catches the error. Needless to say, the variable ErrorCode will be set to the integer value thrown during the exception, which is 23.

The problem with this example is that it is so stripped-down as to appear a bit mysterious. The first point to grasp when looking at this code is that exceptions are not caused by errors—they are caused by using the throw keyword. When you use exceptions, the errors that occur are still the same old boring errors that C++ programmers have been looking at for years. The only difference here is that after the exception occurs, you can notify the user of your routine or object that something has gone wrong by using the keyword throw.

The simplest type of object you can throw is of type int, as shown here. Of course, as you have already seen, it is usually more helpful to throw an object rather than a simple integer. The advantage, of course, is that objects can speak to you and can be queried, while integers are a bit mute and faceless.

Compare the previous `IntegerExceptionButtonClick` with this method:

```
void __fastcall TForm1::ExceptionClassBtnClick(TObject *Sender)
{
  try
  {
    int i = StrToInt("Sam");
  }
  catch(Exception &A)
  {
    ShowMessage("Info: " + A.Message);
  }
}
```

Code inside of `StrToInt` throws an exception if an error occurs. If it did not explicitly use the `throw` keyword (or at least its Pascal equivalent), the exception would not occur. There is nothing mysterious about exceptions; they occur because someone used a `throw` expression in their code.

You have seen that you can pass different types of variables to a catch statement:

```
void __fastcall TForm1::MultiCatchBtnClick(TObject *Sender)
{
  try
  {
    int i = StrToInt("Sam");
  }
  catch(int ErrorCode)
  {
    ShowMessage("int: " + ErrorCode);
  }
  catch (WORD Sam)
  {
    ShowMessage("WORD: " + AnsiString("Sam"));
  }
  catch(Exception &A)
  {
    ShowMessage("Exception: " + A.Message);
  }
  catch(EConvertError &B)
  {
    ShowMessage("EConvertError: " + B.Message);
  }
  catch(EDatabaseError &C)
  {
    ShowMessage(C.Message);
  }
}
```

This code is loaded down with a series of catch statements:

```
catch(int ErrorCode)
catch (WORD Sam)
catch(Exception &A)
catch(EConvertError &B)
catch(EDatabaseError &C)
```

The question is which statement, or statements, will be called?

The first part of the answer is that only one catch statement will be called unless you rethrow the error. I will talk about reraising errors later in the chapter. The second half of the question, however, still remains. Which statement will execute?

As you know, the error which occurs in this program is of type EConvertError:

```
int i = StrToInt("Sam");
```

Given the nature of the error, it should be obvious that neither of the first two options will be executed. The object thrown is not of type int, and it is not of type WORD. It therefore will bypass these two catch statements with nary a nod.

You might think, however, that the code would also skip the Exception catch block and go directly to the EConvertError exception. This is not what happens. Instead, the Exception catch block is executed because the rules of polymorphism dictate that an EConvertError can be assigned to one of its parent objects. As you saw earlier, EConvertError is a child of Exception.

Given this information, the logical way to arrange the code in this method is as follows:

```
catch(int ErrorCode)
catch (WORD Sam)
catch(EConvertError &B)
catch(EDatabaseError &C)
catch(Exception &A)
```

This code will first try to find a match in the first four catch statements, and if that fails, it will come to rest in the Exception catch statement, because that is a generic resting place for VCL exceptions.

Of course, not all exceptions are VCL exceptions. For instance, exceptions of type WORD or int are not VCL exceptions.

There are some things you can do to spread a really wide net for catching exceptions. The following examples show how to use the ellipses syntax in a catch expression to trap generic exceptions of any type:

```
void __fastcall TForm1::GenericCatchBtnClick(TObject *Sender)
{
  try
  {
    StrToInt("Sam");
  }
  catch (...)
  {
    ShowMessage("Something went wrong");
  }
}
```

This catch block will trap whatever exception comes its way. It is the broadest and safest possible net, but it is also not very helpful when it comes to telling you exactly what went wrong.

To flag down at least some additional information, you can include `except.h` in your program and use the following syntax:

```
void __fastcall TForm1::GenericCatchBtnClick(TObject *Sender)
{
  try
  {
    throw 12;
  }
  catch (...)
  {
    ShowMessage("Something went wrong");
    ShowMessage(__throwExceptionName);
  }
}
```

This code uses `throwExceptionName` to find the name of the type of exception that was thrown. In this case, it will report that you have an exception of type `int`. Not a great or wondrous fact, but at least it is a start if you are trying to figure out what went wrong. `__throwExceptionName` might not work with VCL exceptions, but it will work with standard C++ exceptions.

Here is a VCL exception class that might be of some use when you are trying to track down exceptions:

```
void __fastcall TForm1::GenericCatchIIBtnClick(TObject *Sender)
{
  try
  {
throw 12;
  }
  catch(EExternalException &E)
  {
    ShowMessage(E.Message);
  }
}
```

This VCL exception class will handle the error that has occurred, even though it is not a standard VCL error.

I've walked right up to the edge of the point beyond which I do not want to go in this book. From here, keen-sighted readers can no doubt catch sight of some generic C++ vistas that contain innumerable questions concerning subtle matters of correct syntactical usage. For more information, you should turn to a book on the C++ language. My goal in this book is to stick to simple syntax that is easy to use, and to avoid digging into potential minefields, no matter how interesting the terrain may appear.

My suggestion is to not yield to the temptation to do anything fancy with exceptions. Just use them to report errors, and do so by throwing standard VCL exception classes or descendants of standard VCL exception classes. If you follow these rules, you will reap benefits and avoid trouble.

Throwing VCL Exception Classes

Here is an example from the SimpleException program of how to throw a VCL exception:

```
void __fastcall TForm1::ThrowVCLExceptionClick(TObject *Sender)
{
  try
  {
    throw Exception("VCL class");
  }
  catch(Exception &E)
  {
    ShowMessage(AnsiString(E.ClassName()) + " " + E.Message);
  }
}
```

The throw statement in this method automatically creates an instance of the Exception class and calls its constructor with a simple string. You can, depending on your needs, place anything in this string.

Notice that there are other constructors for automatically formatting strings and for retrieving strings that are stored in the program's executable. For instance, if you have a string table, you can automatically retrieve an item from that table by number using the following constructor of the Exception class:

```
__fastcall Exception(int Ident);
```

In this code, Ident is the ID of a string in a resource linked into your application.

Here is a constructor designed to enable you to format input with a string stored in a resource:

```
__fastcall Exception(int Ident, const System::TVarRec * Args, const int Args_Size);
```

For instance, here is an example of using a string from a string table in conjunction with a format statement:

```
throw Exception(12, OPENARRAY(TVarRec, (12, "Value out of range!")));
```

If the string stored in the resource table looked like this

```
Custom Error %d: %s
```

then the string shown to the user would be

```
Custom Error 12: Value out of range!
```

An example of raising this kind of error is found in the ResError program, discussed later in this chapter. The source for the program is found in the ResError directory of the CD-ROM that accompanies this book.

Understanding the VCL Exception Classes

In the section of this chapter called "Exception Classes," I showed you a long, but not exhaustive, list featuring the names of a number of VCL exception classes. Here, to refresh your memory, are some of the declarations from that list:

```
class __declspec(delphiclass) EIntError;
class __declspec(delphiclass) EInOutError;
class __declspec(delphiclass) EOutOfMemory;
class __declspec(delphiclass) EDivByZero;
```

The interesting thing about all these classes is that they descend from a single root class called Exception. The declaration for class Exception was quoted in full in the section of this chapter called "Exception Classes."

I've already said that one of the great things BCB does for you is wrap your whole program in a try..catch block. A second great BCB benefit, of almost equal importance, is this class hierarchy. Of course, none of this would matter if C++ was not such a strong language with the capability to support a wide range of powerful features.

As you have seen, it's possible to create exceptions that pass nothing but an integer to a catch block:

```
catch (int)
{
}
```

This syntax can be useful under certain circumstances, but you are much better off if you receive an entire exception class inside a catch block. That way you can call the methods of that class in order to find out exactly what is wrong, or to perform other tasks that might be helpful to you.

For instance, if you are not sure of the exact name of the error class which is being thrown, you can always throw the error intentionally and check its ClassName inside a catch block that catches all VCL exceptions:

```
catch(Exception &E)
{
AnsiString S(this->ClassName());
AnsiString S1(E.ClassName());
MessageDlg(S + '\r' + S1, mtError, TMsgDlgButtons() << mbOK, 0);
}
```

This code reports the class in which the exception occurred, and then on the next line, the class that threw the exception. For instance, it might post the following lines inside the MessageDlg:

```
TForm1
EConvertError
```

The key point here is that polymorphism is being put to work to the programmer's great benefit. All VCL exception classes descend from class Exception, so the rules of polymorphism dictate that you can pass them to a catch block that takes a parameter of type Exception. Furthermore, when you call the methods of the class passed to you, polymorphism will ensure that the method called is not necessarily of type Exception, but of the type passed to you.

The previous code correctly reports that the class name of the exception is EConvertError, even though the type of the class is declared to be of type Exception. In other words, due to the wondrous rules of polymorphism, an exception of type EConvertError could be passed to you through a variable of type Exception.

Creating and Raising Your Own Exceptions

In this section, I show how you can create your own exceptions and how to throw exceptions when errors occur. The code explored in this section is from the MyExcept program shown in Listing 5.3. The form for the program has three buttons and an edit control. The main form for the MyExcept program is shown in Figure 5.5.

FIGURE 5.5.

The main form for the MyExcept program.

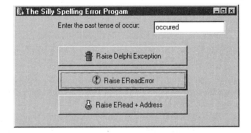

Listing 5.3. The header for the MyExcept program shows how to create a custom exception.

```
///////////////////////////////////////
// Main.h
// Project: MyExcept
// Copyright (c) 1997 by Charlie Calvert
//
#ifndef MainH
#define MainH
#include <Classes.hpp>
#include <Controls.hpp>
#include <StdCtrls.hpp>
#include <Forms.hpp>
#include <Buttons.hpp>

class ESillySpellingError: public Exception
{
  public:
  __fastcall ESillySpellingError(const AnsiString Msg)
    :Exception(Msg) {}
};
```

```
class TForm1 : public TForm
{
__published:
  TLabel *Label1;
  TBitBtn *ERead;
  TBitBtn *EReadAddr;
  TBitBtn *RaiseException;
  TEdit *Edit1;
  void __fastcall RaiseExceptionClick(
  TObject *Sender);
  void __fastcall EReadClick(
  TObject *Sender);
  void __fastcall EReadAddrClick(
  TObject *Sender);
private:
public:
  virtual __fastcall TForm1(TComponent* Owner);
};

extern TForm1 *Form1;

#endif
```

Listing 5.4. The MyExcept program shows how to throw standard and custom exceptions.

```
//////////////////////////////////////
// Main.cpp
// Project: MyExcept
// Copyright (c) 1997 by Charlie Calvert
//
#include <vcl.h>
#pragma hdrstop
#include "Main.h"
#include "codebox.h"
#pragma resource "*.dfm"

TForm1 *Form1;

__fastcall TForm1::TForm1(TComponent* Owner)
  : TForm(Owner)
{
}

void __fastcall TForm1::RaiseExceptionClick(
  TObject *Sender)
{
  StrToInt("23a");
}

void __fastcall TForm1::EReadClick(
  TObject *Sender)
{
  throw EReadError("EReadError has occurred");
}
```

continues

5

EXCEPTIONS

Listing 5.4. continued

```
AnsiString GetAddr()
{
  void *P;
  P = Form1->MethodAddress("EReadAddrClick");
  return Address2Str(P);
}

void __fastcall TForm1::EReadAddrClick(TObject *Sender)
{
  AnsiString S = Edit1->Text;
  if (UpperCase(S) == "OCCURED")
  {
    S = "A Silly Spelling error has occured! "
        "The correct spelling is occuRRed, not occuRed! ";
    throw ESillySpellingError(S + "\rAddress: " +GetAddr());
  }
}
```

To use this program, just press any of the three buttons on the form. The third button won't throw an exception unless the edit control is set to the misspelled string occured.

Exceptions occur because they are explicitly thrown. For instance, here is another version of the StrToInt routine:

```
int Str2Int(AnsiString S)
{
  int i = atoi(S.c_str());
  if (i == 0)
    throw EConvertError("Cannot convert " + S + " to an int");
  return i;
}
```

This function uses the atoi function to convert a string into an integer. If all is successful, the function result is set equal to the transmuted string. If there is a problem, the value returned from atoi is zero. When an error condition exists, the Str2Int routine throws an EConvertError and passes in a string that explains what has gone wrong.

> **TIP**
>
> Obviously, the previous function would not work correctly if you passed in "0" or "00", and so on, as a string. If you need a secure function, use StrToInt.

EConvertError is a built-in BCB type meant to be used in situations where an error occurs in a conversion routine. If you look in SYSUTILS.HPP, you will find that BCB uses this exception quite a bit, but tends to throw it through the good graces of the ConvertError routine.

There is nothing in BCB that forces you to use a particular class of exceptions in a particular situation. For instance, in the following method I throw an EReadError, even though nothing has gone wrong in the program:

```
void __fastcall TForm1::EReadClick(TObject *Sender)
{
  throw EReadError("EReadError has occurred");
}
```

As you saw earlier, exceptions are triggered when you use the reserved word throw and then construct an instance of a particular type of exception. In and of themselves, exceptions have nothing to do with errors, and indeed you could use them for some entirely different purpose. In other words, exceptions are a good means of reporting errors, but they do not occur because an error occurs; they occur because you use the reserved word throw!

Many of the exception classes that are built into BCB may be useful to you at times. For instance, you might need to convert some variable from one type to another; or there may be an occasion when you need to read some value. If errors occur during such tasks, it would make sense to throw an EConvertError or an EReadError. That way, the code that depends upon your conversion routines doesn't have to worry about what to do when the conversion routines fail. On failure, they will throw an exception and will never return bad data or error codes to the caller. That can go a long way toward simplifying your code.

Despite the usefulness of many of BCB's built-in exception classes, there are many occasions when you are going to need to create exception classes of your own. To do so, you should first declare a new class:

```
class ESillySpellingError: public Exception
{
  public:
    __fastcall ESillySpellingError(const AnsiString Msg)
      :Exception(Msg) {}
};
```

This code states that class ESillySpellingError is a descendant of type Exception. You can create as many constructors for your class as you think you need, or you can simply copy the constructors from one of the classes in the SYSUTILS.HPP file and do a search and replace on the class name.

I created ESillySpellingError for the quixotic reason of desiring to finally squelch permanently a spelling error that I have made many times in my life. In particular, I tend to misspell the past tense of the word *occur*:

```
void __fastcall TForm1::EReadAddrClick(TObject *Sender)
{
  AnsiString S = Edit1->Text;
  if (UpperCase(S) == "OCCURED")
  {
    S = "A Silly Spelling error has occured! "
        "The correct spelling is occuRRed, not occuRed! ";
    throw ESillySpellingError(S + "\rAddress: " +GetAddr());
  }
}
```

Hopefully, writing about the error in this book will help me remember that there are two Rs in the word—not just one! (My plan seems to have worked, but alas, there are so many other words that I misspell!)

At any rate, you can see that it is easy to create your own exceptions and to throw them. Whenever you feel that you need to describe a new type of error, you can do so by just creating the simple type shown in the preceding code. If you want, you can create more complex exception types. For instance, the BCB `EInOutError` adds an `ErrorCode` to its object declaration. You can then reference this error code in a `catch` block:

```
try
  ..
catch(EInOutError &E)
{
  Code = E.ErrorCode;
}
```

Remember that the need for different types of errors becomes evident not when you are raising them, but in the `catch` portion of `try..catch` blocks. You might want to handle a particular type of error explicitly and let other errors be handled by the default handler. To do this, you must have a variety of different exception classes to throw so that your exception handlers can be set up to distinguish between the different error situations.

The lazy man's way to raise an exception is simply to write

```
throw Exception("Another lazy man error has occured!");
```

This technique works fine in many cases. However, it is best to create your own exception classes so that you can create `try..catch` blocks that work only with a specific type of error.

For more on creating your own exception classes, see the ResError program shown later in this chapter. ResError has an example in it of using a constructor for a custom `Exception` class that grabs a string from a string table and uses the `format` function to customize the string when displaying it to the user.

Rethrowing an Exception

The `AutoThrowClick` method from the ThrowAgain program shows how to rethrow an exception:

```
void __fastcall TForm1::ThrowItAgainSamClick(TObject *Sender)
{
  int k;
  try
  {
    k = StrToInt("Sam");
    ShowMessage(k);
  }
  catch(...)
  {
```

```
        ShowMessage("Something went wrong");
        throw;
    }
}
```

Rethrowing an exception involves nothing more than using the `throw` keyword. The preceding example intentionally creates an `EConvertError error`, shows a message to the user, and rethrows the exception. If you run the program, you will first see the custom error message I have devised and then the standard `EConvert` error message. Most of the time you would not want to show two error messages, and I have written this kind of code only so you can see exactly what is happening when you run the program.

Rethrowing an exception enables you to get the best of both worlds. You get to perform some custom handling and allow BCB to automatically inform the user exactly what has gone wrong.

In many cases, it is a good idea to rethrow an exception, because you cannot be sure that all the handling necessary for dealing with the error is complete. In fact, it is often a good idea to let the system handle exceptions automatically without interfering in any way. If you do need to step into the process by writing a `try..catch` block, you should give serious thought to rethrowing the exception in case some other routine needs to know about it. The great beauty of exceptions is that things often work best if you just forget about handling errors altogether!

Exceptions and Destructors

Despite the note on which I ended the last section, there are certain types of situations in which you need to ensure that a particular block of code is executed even if something goes wrong in the code that precedes it. For instance, you may allocate memory, perform several actions, and finally intend to deallocate the memory. However, if an exception is thrown between the time you allocate memory and the time you want to deallocate the memory, the code that deallocates the memory might never get executed. In Java and Object Pascal, this situation is handled with `try..finally` blocks. C++ does not support that syntax, but it has another technique you can use instead.

Here is a second way to think about this whole situation. As you know, a `try..catch` block can cause the execution pointer for your program to jump from the place that an error occurs directly to the place where you handle that error. That is all well and good under most circumstances, and indeed, as I said at the end of the last section, it is usually best to let this process occur unattended. However, there are times when you want to make sure that some code between the error and the exception handler is executed regardless of circumstances. The code shown in Listings 5.5 through 5.7 shows how to proceed. The program is run in a simple form that contains a button and an edit control.

Listing 5.5. The AllObjects program shows how to handle memory allocations.

```
/////////////////////////////////////
// Copyright (c) 1997 by Charlie Calvert
//
#ifndef MainH
#define MainH
#include <Classes.hpp>
#include <Controls.hpp>
#include <StdCtrls.hpp>
#include <Forms.hpp>
class TMyObject
{
public:
  TMyObject(void);
  ~TMyObject(void);
  void SayHello(void);
  void BlowUp(void);
};
class TForm1 : public TForm
{
__published:
  TButton *NoCareTaker;
  TButton *CareTaker;
  TButton *CareTakeWithTryExcept;
  void __fastcall NoCareTakerClick(
  TObject *Sender);
  void __fastcall CareTakerClick(
  TObject *Sender);
  void __fastcall CareTakeWithTryExceptClick(
  TObject *Sender);
private:
public:
  virtual __fastcall TForm1(TComponent* Owner);
};
extern TForm1 *Form1;
#endif
```

Listing 5.6. The AllObjects program shows how to handle memory allocations (continued).

```
/////////////////////////////////////
// Copyright (c) 1997 by Charlie Calvert
//
#include <vcl.h>
#pragma hdrstop
#include "Main.h"
#include "CareTaker1.h"
#pragma resource "*.dfm"
TForm1 *Form1;
TMyObject::TMyObject(void)
{
  ShowMessage("TMyObject constructor called");
}
TMyObject::~TMyObject(void)
{
  ShowMessage("TMyobject destructor called!");
```

```
}
void TMyObject::BlowUp(void)
{
  throw(42);
}
void TMyObject::SayHello(void)
{
  ShowMessage("MyObject says hello");
}
__fastcall TForm1::TForm1(TComponent* Owner)
  : TForm(Owner)
{
}
// In this method the destructor for TMyObject is NOT called
void __fastcall TForm1::NoCareTakerClick(TObject *Sender)
{
  TMyObject *MyObject = new TMyObject;
  MyObject->SayHello();
  MyObject->BlowUp();
  delete MyObject;
}
// In this method the destructor for TMyObject is called
void __fastcall TForm1::CareTakerClick(
  TObject *Sender)
{
  TCareTaker<TMyObject> MyCareTaker;
  TMyObject *MyObject = MyCareTaker.GetObject();
  MyObject->SayHello();
  MyObject->BlowUp();
}
void __fastcall TForm1::CareTakeWithTryExceptClick(
  TObject *Sender)
{
  TCareTaker<TMyObject> MyCareTaker;
  TMyObject *MyObject = MyCareTaker.GetObject();
  try
  {
    MyObject->SayHello();
    MyObject->BlowUp();
  }
  catch(int i)
  {
    ShowMessage("The secret of the universe revealed: " + AnsiString(i));
  }
}
```

Listing 5.7. The caretaker module contains a useful template class that ensures the memory allocated for an object will be destroyed.

```
/////////////////////////////////////
// Copyright (c) 1997 by Charlie Calvert
//
#ifndef CareTaker1H
#define CareTaker1H
template<class T> class TCareTaker
```

continues

Listing 5.7. continued

```
{
  T* Pointer;
public:
  TCareTaker()
  {
    ShowMessage("CareTaker constructor called.");
    Pointer = new T;
  }
  ~TCareTaker(void)
  {
    ShowMessage("CareTaker destructor called.");
    delete Pointer;
  }
  T *GetObject(void)
  {
    return Pointer;
  }
};
#endif
```

The key point to grasp about the AllObjects program is that it consists entirely of objects. This is important because of a simple rule of C++ exception handling: Local objects whose constructors are called successfully before an exception occurs will have their destructor called.

> **NOTE**
>
> The word "successfully" in the last sentence of the previous paragraph is very important! This system won't work if an exception occurs midway through the call to a constructor.
>
> Again, I am on the edge of entering a dark and murky C++ underworld. Rather than burden myself with pages of exegesis on the correct way to cross the river Styx, I will step away from this subject by simply advising you not to allow exceptions to occur inside a constructor.
>
> If you have something delicate to do, don't do it in a constructor! It's not that C++ has no means of dealing with that type of situation; I just think it's wiser to play it safe. The goal is to get programs written, not to find the Shadow Land and spend time poking around therein!

The thing I like about this rule regarding exceptions and destructors is that it encourages programmers to make everything an object. I've been using objects pretty much every day for the last eight or nine years, and the more I see of them, the more I like them. Objects are the right paradigm, and coding practices that encourage their use are probably worth cultivating.

The AllObjects program contains a simple object called TMyObject:

```
class TMyObject
{
```

```
public:
  TMyObject(void);
  ~TMyObject(void);
  void SayHello(void);
  void BlowUp(void);
};
```

The implementation for this object is very straightforward:

```
TMyObject::TMyObject(void)
{
  ShowMessage("TMyObject constructor called");
}
TMyObject::~TMyObject(void)
{
  ShowMessage("TMyobject destructor called!");
}
void TMyObject::BlowUp(void)
{
  throw(42);
}
void TMyObject::SayHello(void)
{
  ShowMessage("MyObject says hello");
}
```

The constructor and destructor simply report on whether or not they have been called. The SayHello method just pops up a simple message. The BlowUp method raises an exception.

I use the TMyObject class three times in the program. The first time, I call it in order to show the problem that needs to be fixed:

```
void __fastcall TForm1::NoCareTakerClick(TObject *Sender)
{
  TMyObject *MyObject = new TMyObject;
  MyObject->SayHello();
  MyObject->BlowUp();
  delete MyObject;
}
```

This method allocates an instance of TMyObject on the heap, calls SayHello, and finally steps into the whirlwind by calling BlowUp. BlowUp will raise an exception, which means that the code executing after the call to BlowUp will never be called. In particular, the memory allocated for MyObject will never be freed.

The solution to this problem is simply to put the sensitive code you want to have executed inside the destructor for a local object whose constructor was called before the exception occurs.

One generic way to solve this type of problem is to create a bare-bones template class that handles memory allocation:

```
template<class T> class TCareTaker
{
  T* Pointer;
public:
  TCareTaker()
  {
```

```
    ShowMessage("CareTaker constructor called.");
    Pointer = new T;
  }
  ~TCareTaker(void)
  {
    ShowMessage("CareTaker destructor called.");
    delete Pointer;
  }
  T *GetObject(void)
  {
    return Pointer;
  }
};
#endif
```

I called this class TCareTaker because it takes care of memory allocations and deallocations for you. Calling the class is extremely simple:

```
void __fastcall TForm1::CareTakerClick(TObject *Sender)
{
  TCareTaker<TMyObject> MyCareTaker;
  TMyObject *MyObject = MyCareTaker.GetObject();
  MyObject->SayHello();
  MyObject->BlowUp();
}
```

The first line of code allocates memory for an instance of TMyObject. The second line retrieves the instance, and the rest of the code calls the methods of the object. There is no need to explicitly deallocate the memory used by TMyObject, because it will be deleted for you automatically by TMyCareTaker the moment before TMyCareTaker goes out of scope:

```
~TCareTaker(void)
{
ShowMessage("CareTaker destructor called.");
delete Pointer;
}
```

Notice also that it does not take any more lines of code for you to use this technique than it does to allocate the memory for TMyObject the normal way. Of course, there is overhead associated with this process, but it does not take up any more of your time to use it.

The important part of this code hangs on the fact that TCareTaker is a template with a destructor. The fact that TMyObject is also a class is largely irrelevant to the main argument of this example. I made TMyObject a class simply so you can visibly see its destructor being called when you step through the code or run the program. The important object in this example, however, is the minimal implementation of TCareTaker.

Streams, Exceptions, and Freeing Memory

In the last section you learned the basics about how to use the destructor of an object to ensure that certain code will be executed even after an exception has been thrown. The CareTaker example used to illustrate the point is valuable in that it shows how to handle memory allocations. However, there are other situations besides memory allocations where you need to ensure that code will be executed.

The example presented in this section still involves memory allocation, but it also focuses on the issue of ensuring that files are properly opened and closed even if an exception occurs. The source for the program is shown in Listings 5.8 and 5.9.

The main reason I am providing this second example of how to use destructors to your advantage in exception handling is simply that it is a relatively "classic" example of how to wrap up a process inside an object. Here, the delicate act of opening and closing a file could become troublesome, so the program wraps the process up inside an object.

Listing 5.8. The StreamException program shows how to guard code involving streams.

```
/////////////////////////////////////
// Main.h
// Copyright (c) 1997 by Charlie Calvert
//
#ifndef MainH
#define MainH
#include <Classes.hpp>
#include <Controls.hpp>
#include <StdCtrls.hpp>
#include <Forms.hpp>
class TFileObject
{
  AnsiString FFileName;
  TFileStream *FMyFile;
public:
  TFileObject(AnsiString S);
  ~TFileObject();
  void OpenFile();
  AnsiString GetData(AnsiString &S);
  void BlowUp();
};
class TForm1 : public TForm
{
__published:
  TButton *Button1;
  TMemo *Memo1;
  void __fastcall Button1Click(
  TObject *Sender);
private:
public:
  virtual __fastcall TForm1(TComponent* Owner);
};
//-----------------------------------------------------------
extern TForm1 *Form1;
//-----------------------------------------------------------
#endif
```

Listing 5.9. The StreamException program shows how to guard code that performs file IO.

```
//////////////////////////////////////
// Main.cpp
// Copyright (c) 1997 by Charlie Calvert
//
#include <vcl.h>
#pragma hdrstop
#include "Main.h"
#pragma resource "*.dfm"
TForm1 *Form1;
//////////////////////////////////////
// TFileObject ////////////////////////
//////////////////////////////////////
TFileObject::TFileObject(AnsiString S)
{
  FFileName = S;
  FMyFile = NULL;
}
TFileObject::~TFileObject()
{
  ShowMessage("Freeing memory associated with stream!");
  FMyFile->Free();
}
void TFileObject::OpenFile()
{
  FMyFile = new TFileStream(FFileName, fmOpenRead);
}
AnsiString TFileObject::GetData(AnsiString &S)
{
  S.SetLength(FMyFile->Size + 1);
  FMyFile->Read(S.c_str(), FMyFile->Size);
  S[FMyFile->Size] = '\0';
  return S;
}
void TFileObject::BlowUp()
{
  throw EInOutError("Exception raised in method BlowUp!");
}
//////////////////////////////////////
// TForm1 /////////////////////////////
//////////////////////////////////////
__fastcall TForm1::TForm1(TComponent* Owner)
  : TForm(Owner)
{
}
void __fastcall TForm1::OpenFileBtnClick(TObject *Sender)
{
  AnsiString S;
  TFileObject FileObject("c:\\autoexec.bat");
  FileObject.OpenFile();
  Memo1->Lines->Add(FileObject.GetData(S));
  FileObject.BlowUp();
}
```

The reason for concern in the process of opening and closing a stream does not really have much to do with the act of allocating memory for the stream. Nor, in fact, is there much reason to be concerned that something might go wrong when you open the stream:

```
FMyFile = new TFileStream(FFileName, fmOpenRead);
```

BCB has all the bases covered in this case, and if you pass in a bogus filename while opening a stream, it will clean things up for you.

The issue in this example, then, is not really memory allocation per se, but only that you want to be sure that the stream is closed up once the process is finished. In other words, something might go wrong while you are reading the stream, or during some other related part of the process. For instance, in a real-world programming example, you might process the data in the stream, with a good chance that an exception will be raised during the processing of the data.

The purpose of the example shown here is to show how to use a destructor to ensure that the memory for the TFileStream object will be deallocated even if something goes wrong while reading from the file. In particular, if something goes wrong during the execution of this block of code:

```
S.SetLength(FMyFile->Size + 1);
FMyFile->Read(S.c_str(), FMyFile->Size);
S[FMyFile->Size] = '\0';
return S;
```

you can still be sure that the stream will be deallocated:

```
FMyFile->Free;
```

The mechanism that ensures that the Free method gets called is nothing more than a simple destructor. This is a common use of the power of destructors in exception handling, and it is one you should be sure you understand.

The preceding code also demonstrates how to open up a simple TFileStream object and read in some data. The newly collected data is then displayed to the user through the auspices of the TMemo object. Once the stream is no longer needed, it is destroyed by a call to Free.

The Create method for a stream takes two parameters. The first is a string specifying the name of the file you want to read. The second is a constant that informs the system what kind of operation you want to perform. The following are the constants associated with BCB streams, as found in the online help:

fmOpenRead	Open the file for reading only
fmOpenWrite	Open the file for writing only
fmOpenReadWrite	Open the file for reading or writing
fmShareExclusive	Open the file, disallowing other applications to open it for reading or writing
fmShareDenyWrite	Open the file, disallowing other applications to open it for writing

5

EXCEPTIONS

fmShareDenyRead	Open the file, disallowing other applications to open it for reading
fmShareDenyNone	Open the file, disallowing other applications to open it for exclusive use
fmCreate	Create a new file, replacing any existing file with the same name

Streams have several methods associated with them, including generic Read and Write methods, and custom methods that enable you to easily read or write a component to a stream. These latter routines are called ReadComponent and WriteComponent; they will be discussed in some depth in Chapters 19 through 24, which cover objects and components. Streams also have a Size property that reports on the size of the file being read, and a Position property, which identifies your current position in the stream. For further information, see the online help entries for both TFileStream and TStream.

Replacing the Default Exception Handler

You might want to override the default exception handler for a BCB program either because you want to customize your program or because you want to be sure some things happen, regardless of how your program ends. BCB provides an event called OnException in the Application class that can be used for this purpose. A sample program, called OnExcept, demonstrates how to use this event. The code for the program is in Listing 5.10. The form for this program consists of two buttons, one called DivByZero and the other called ReadError.

Listing 5.10. The OnExcept program creates a generic error handler for all exceptions in your program.

```
#include <vcl.h>
#pragma hdrstop
#include "Main.h"
#pragma resource "*.dfm"
TForm1 *Form1;
__fastcall TForm1::TForm1(TComponent* Owner)
  : TForm(Owner)
{
  Application->OnException = HandleExcepts;
}
void __fastcall TForm1::ReadErrorClick(
  TObject *Sender)
{
  throw EReadError("Read Error");
}
void __fastcall TForm1::DivByZeroClick(
  TObject *Sender)
{
  throw EDivByZero("Exception of type EDivByZero");
}
void __fastcall TForm1::HandleExcepts(TObject *Sender, Exception *E)
{
```

```
//  if (typeid(E) = typeid(EDivByZero) then
     MessageDlg("Custom OnException: " + E->Message, mtError,
       TMsgDlgButtons() << mbOK, 0);
}
```

The OnExcept program will handle all exceptions in a single routine defined by the programmer. It is not meant as an example of how to write exceptions or how to construct a program. However, it does provide advanced programmers with an illustration of how to use the OnException event.

The OnException property for TApplication is declared like this:

```
__property TExceptionEvent OnException =
  {read=FOnException, write=FOnException};
```

Here is the declaration for TExceptionEvent:

```
typedef void __fastcall (__closure *TExceptionEvent)
  (System::TObject* Sender, Sysutils::Exception* E);
```

Normally, the code for an OnXXX handler is created for you automatically when you click the Events page of the Object Inspector. In this case, however, TApplication never appears in the Object Inspector, so you must manually create the call as a method of TForm1:

```
class TForm1 : public TForm
{
__published:
  TButton *DivByZero;
  TButton *ReadError;
  void __fastcall ReadErrorClick(
  TObject *Sender);
  void __fastcall DivByZeroClick(
  TObject *Sender);
private:
  void __fastcall HandleExcepts(TObject *Sender, Exception *E);
public:
  virtual __fastcall TForm1(TComponent* Owner);
};
```

After declaring the function, you can assign it to the TApplication OnException property in the TForm1 constructor:

```
__fastcall TForm1::TForm1(TComponent* Owner)
  : TForm(Owner)
{
  Application->OnException = HandleExcepts;
}
```

The HandleExcepts method will now be called when an exception occurs, as long as you don't declare any intervening try..catch blocks. In the example shown here, the HandleExcepts function explicitly handles EDivByZero errors but responds to all other errors through a generic handler:

```
void __fastcall TForm1::HandleExcepts(TObject *Sender, Exception *E)
{
```

5

EXCEPTIONS

```
//  if (typeid(E) = typeid(EDivByZero) then
    MessageDlg("Custom OnException: " + E->Message,
      mtError, TMsgDlgButtons() << mbOK, 0);
}
```

Needless to say, it is usually not a good idea to create OnException handlers. You should use them only if you are absolutely sure you know what you are doing and why you want to do it. Otherwise, you can end up destroying the carefully created try..catch block that wraps your programs. The built-in exception-handling capabilities in BCB programs are invaluable aids, and you should be careful not to undermine them.

Using Resources to Track Error Strings

Internationalization issues are discussed briefly in this section, as well as the mechanics of using string tables.

If you look carefully at the Pascal version of the SysUtils unit, you will see that the developers of the VCL rarely hard coded a string into the code that throws exceptions. Instead, the VCL constantly calls functions with names such as LoadStr or FmtLoadStr. These functions call the Windows API routine LoadString, which retrieves a string from a resource:

```
int LoadString(
    HINSTANCE  hInstance,   // handle of module containing string resource
    UINT   uID,             // resource identifier
    LPTSTR  lpBuffer,       // address of buffer for resource
    int  nBufferMax         // size of buffer
   );
```

The LoadString function is akin to the LoadResource function:

> Instance: HInstance variable of the current module. This variable is declared and assigned automatically by the system. You don't have to do anything but use the variable, which is passed on to you *gratis* by both Windows and BCB. (You can load strings from a resource DLL simply by using the DLL's module handle for the Instance parameter to LoadString.)

> ID: A number referencing a particular string in a string resource.

> Buffer: A buffer to hold the string.

> BufferMax: The maximum size of the string to be placed in the buffer.

Listings 5.11 through 5.14 show how to put this function to work. In a well-designed program, this code will save room in your executables and help when it comes time to internationalize an application. You can see the main form for this program in Figure 5.6.

FIGURE 5.6.

The simple main form for the ResError program has four bitmap buttons on it.

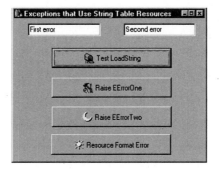

Listing 5.11. The ResError program shows how to read error strings from a resource file.

```
/////////////////////////////////////
// Main.h
// Project: ResError
// Copyright (c) 1997 by Charlie Calvert
//
#ifndef MainH
#define MainH
#include <Classes.hpp>
#include <Controls.hpp>
#include <StdCtrls.hpp>
#include <Forms.hpp>
#include <Buttons.hpp>
class ErrorOne;
class ErrorOne: public Exception
{
  typedef Sysutils::Exception inherited;
public:
    __fastcall ErrorOne(const System::AnsiString Msg): Exception(Msg) {}
};
class ErrorTwo;
class ErrorTwo: public Exception
{
  typedef Sysutils::Exception inherited;
public:
    __fastcall ErrorTwo(const System::AnsiString Msg): Exception(Msg) {}
    __fastcall ErrorTwo(int Ident, const System::TVarRec * Args,
    const int Args_Size): Exception(Ident, Args, Args_Size) {}
};
class TForm1 : public TForm
{
__published:
  TBitBtn *TestLoadStr;
  TBitBtn *RaiseErrorOne;
  TEdit *Edit1;
  TEdit *Edit2;
  TBitBtn *RaiseErrorTwo;
  TBitBtn *ResourceFormatBtn;
  void __fastcall TestLoadStrClick(
  TObject *Sender);
  void __fastcall RaiseErrorOneClick(
  TObject *Sender);
```

continues

Listing 5.11. continued

```
  void __fastcall RaiseErrorTwoClick(
  TObject *Sender);
  void __fastcall ResourceFormatBtnClick(TObject *Sender);
private:
public:
  virtual __fastcall TForm1(TComponent* Owner);
};
extern TForm1 *Form1;
#endif
```

Listing 5.12. The main module for the ResError program.

```
/////////////////////////////////////
// Main.cpp
// Project: ResError
// Copyright (c) 1997 by Charlie Calvert
//
#include <vcl.h>
#pragma hdrstop
#include "Main.h"
#pragma resource "*.dfm"
#include "resmain.inc"
TForm1 *Form1;
__fastcall TForm1::TForm1(TComponent* Owner)
  : TForm(Owner)
{
}
#define Max 150
AnsiString GetError(int ID)
{
  AnsiString S;
  S.SetLength(Max);
  LoadString((HINSTANCE)HInstance, ID, S.c_str(), Max);
  return S;
}
void __fastcall TForm1::TestLoadStrClick(TObject *Sender)
{
  Edit1->Text = GetError(ErrorOneStrID);
  Edit2->Text = GetError(ErrorTwoStrID);
}
void __fastcall TForm1::RaiseErrorOneClick(TObject *Sender)
{
  throw ErrorOne(GetError(ErrorOneStrID));
}
void __fastcall TForm1::RaiseErrorTwoClick(TObject *Sender)
{
  throw ErrorTwo(GetError(ErrorTwoStrID));
}
void __fastcall TForm1::ResourceFormatBtnClick(TObject *Sender)
{
  throw ErrorTwo(ResFormatStrID,
    OPENARRAY(TVarRec, (3, "Number too large!")));
}
```

Listing 5.13. The RESMAIN.INC file lists the errors used by the ResError program.

```
#define ErrorOneStrID 1
#define ErrorTwoStrID 2
#define ResFormatStrID 3
```

Listing 5.14. The RESMAIN.RC file can be converted in a RES file by typing BRCC32 -r RESMAIN.RC at the DOS prompt.

```
#include "resmain.inc";
STRINGTABLE
{
  ErrorOneStrID, "First error"
  ErrorTwoStrID, "Second error"
  ResFormatStrID, "Custom Error %d: %s \rRaised by ResError Program!"
}
```

The ResError program loads error strings from a resource and displays them to the user when an exception is thrown. One button on the main form of the program is used to test whether the strings found in the resource can be retrieved, and the other two buttons actually throw exceptions.

> **NOTE**
>
> String tables can help you during development and during maintenance by enabling you to change strings in one place and see the changes reflected throughout your program. Needless to say, this technique can be very useful when you are trying to create multiple versions of a program for internationalization purposes.
>
> When foreign languages are involved, you might store your string resources in a DLL so that you can change the strings without having to recompile your main program. In short, you can create DLLs that contain nothing but string resources. Each DLL will contain strings from a different language so that you have a version that is French, another that is German, and so on. You can then ship a different DLL with the products that you ship to different countries. When using these DLLs, call LoadString, but pass in the HInstance of the DLL where the string is stored. One way to get this HInstance is by calling LoadLibrary explicitly, rather than letting the system call it for you. The value returned by the call to LoadLibrary can be passed to LoadString:
>
> ```
> HINSTANCE LoadLibrary(
>   LPCTSTR  lpLibFileName // address of filename of executable module
>   );
> ```
>
> Note also that the string resources in your EXE can be removed and replaced without recompiling the EXE. All you have to do is use BRCC32.EXE to tack the new resources onto the precompiled EXE.

To create a string resource, you could use the following syntax in an RC file:

```
STRINGTABLE
{
  1, "First error"
  2, "Second error"
  3, "Custom Error %d: %s \rRaised by ResError Program!"
}
```

1, 2, and 3 are the IDs of the strings, and the strings themselves are shown in double quotes.

Notice, however, that ResError does not hard-code numbers into its string table:

```
#include "resmain.inc";
STRINGTABLE
{
  ErrorOne, "First error"
  ErrorTwo, "Second error"
  ResFormatStrID, "Custom Error %d: %s \rRaised by ResError Program!"
}
```

Instead, it uses constants that are declared in RESMAIN.INC:

```
#define ErrorOneStrID 1
#define ErrorTwoStrID 2
#define ResFormatStrID 3
```

You can, of course, simply add an RC file to a project in order to have it compile automatically. Alternatively, you can compile an RC file into a RES file by typing this line at the DOS prompt:

```
brcc32 -r resmain.rc
```

BRCC32.EXE expects your RC script to use #include to reference the include file. Of course, you reference the same include file in a BCB program by writing the following:

```
#include "resmain.inc"
```

NOTE

Windows 95 can make life miserable for denizens of the command line. In particular, programs are sometimes installed in deeply nested paths that contain long filenames. For instance, the default location of BCB is installed in the C:\PROGRAM FILES\BORLAND\BCB32 subdirectory. Given this rather bleak scenario, the correct command line for compiling the RES file would be as follows:

```
c:\progra~1\borland\BCB32\bin\brcc32.exe -r resmain.rc
```

The issue here, of course, is that the directory PROGRAM FILES is referenced as shown under DOS 7.0, though it may be referenced differently on your system. Note that 4DOS for Windows 95 supports long filenames. Without command-line support for long filenames, the best approach may be for you to create a batch file with the preceding line in it. (See GO.BAT on the CD that ships with this book.)

Or, alternatively, you can install BCB into a different directory. For instance, on my home machine, BCB is in G:\BCB. Besides help with command-line activities, a second great advantage of this system is that it helps you load the include files quickly into the editor without typing a long path each time you need to peruse a few lines of syntax.

I should perhaps add that I do not mean to encourage you to work from the command line. If you have a resource file you want to add to a project, use the IDE to help you manage your resource. It's good to know how to use the command line when necessary, but it's almost always simplest and safest to do things from inside the IDE. The goal of this product is to make C++ a standard again, and the best way to do that is to keep things as simple as possible.

Once you have created a RES file and an include file, you can load the strings into your program with a relatively simple routine:

```
AnsiString GetError(int ID)
{
  AnsiString S;
  S.SetLength(Max);
  LoadString((HINSTANCE)HInstance, ID, S.c_str(), Max);
  return S;
}
```

`LoadString` is part of the Windows API, so it works with NULL-terminated strings. Notice that once again, I avoid hard-coding numbers into the program, and instead declare a constant called `Max`. Even if you reference a number only once, it's still a good habit to declare it as a constant. The reasoning, of course, is that you can change the number in one place and be sure that all references to that number will change.

The following excerpt from `SYSUTILS.RC` shows a portion of a string table used by BCB to aid in reporting errors:

```
#include "sysutils.inc"
STRINGTABLE
{
  SInvalidInteger, "'%s' is not a valid integer value"
  SInvalidFloat, "'%s' is not a valid floating point value"
  SInvalidDate, "'%s' is not a valid date"
  SInvalidTime, "'%s' is not a valid time"
  SInvalidDateTime, "'%s' is not a valid date and time"
  STimeEncodeError, "Invalid argument to time encode"
  SDateEncodeError, "Invalid argument to date encode"
  SOutOfMemory, "Out of memory"
  ...
}
```

Notice that this table obviously relies on `Format` and related functions to enable the program to insert data into a string before showing it to the user.

The following constants are excerpted from a BCB source file called SYSUTILS.INC and are used as IDs that reference the errors in the string table shown previously:

```
const
  SInvalidInteger = 65408;
  SInvalidFloat = 65409;
  SInvalidDate = 65410;
  SInvalidTime = 65411;
  SInvalidDateTime = 65412;
  STimeEncodeError = 65413;
  SDateEncodeError = 65414;
  SOutOfMemory = 65415;
  ...
```

These string constants end up being linked into most of your programs, so you might want to open up SYSUTIL.RC and see if you can use any of them in your own code. The const syntax shown here is the Pascal equivalent of #include.

The ResError program shows an example of using the Format function in an exception:

```
void __fastcall TForm1::ResourceFormatBtnClick(TObject *Sender)
{
  throw ErrorTwo(ResFormatStrID,
    OPENARRAY(TVarRec, (3, "Number too large!")));
}
```

The parameters passed into this function are formatted with the following string from the program's resource:

```
"Custom Error %d: %s \rRaised by ResError Program!"
```

As a result, the user ends up seeing a string that looks like this:

```
Custom Error 3: Number too large!
Raised by ResError Program
```

The constructor called here internally uses the Format function from the VCL, as shown by the following pseudocode:

```
AnsiString S = Format("Custom Error %d: %s \rRaised by ResError Program!",
  OPENARRAY(TVarRec, (3, "Number too large!")));
```

Summary

In this chapter you learned about exceptions. Exceptions are a vital part of all well-written programs. However, you should remember that BCB declares a large number of exceptions for handling the errors that occur in your program. As a result, many errors will be handled gracefully without your intervention. For instance, the error popped up in the first EDivByZero example shown in this chapter is perfectly suitable for many programs. That exception was thrown without you having to write special error-handling syntax. Often the best advice when using exceptions is just to step out of the way and let the process work automatically without your intervention.

Exceptions are one of the most important parts of BCB's syntax, and you should dedicate considerable time to learning how they work. Overall, the mechanics of exceptions are fairly simple. However, there is an art to learning exactly when and how to use exceptions. Gaining a skill in this art takes time, and will in most cases evolve over a period of months or years rather than hours or days. However, the basic idea behind exceptions is extremely simple, and given the structure of the VCL it is unlikely they will cause serious problems in your programs. As a result, there is no reason why you can't plunge right in and start using them in your programs immediately. If you find later that you have used them more than necessary, it is a simple matter to remove them.

In this chapter I have concentrated on how exceptions work in BCB. If you want additional information on this interesting topic, you should get a good book on the C++ language. The redoubtable Scott Meyers, in his excellent book *More Effective C++*, takes a long hard look at the dark side of exceptions. I don't agree with all his conclusions, but if you want a balanced view of the subject, you might use his cautious approach as a counterbalance to my enthusiasm for this subject.

Sharing Code Between Delphi and C++Builder

CHAPTER 6

C++Builder and Delphi have a unique relationship that enables programmers to easily share code between the two environments. Almost anything you write in Delphi can easily be used in C++Builder, and some of the code you write in C++Builder can be used in Delphi. As a result, programmers can work in either C++ or Delphi, depending on their skill level or inclination.

Despite their similarity, each has capabilities:

- Delphi's ease of use enables a wide range of programmers to quickly produce high performance, robust components, objects, and applications.
- C++Builder, on the other hand, allows the best programmers to write code in a language known for its flexibility, subtlety, and wide acceptance.

Because you can share code between the two environments, programmers can use the tools that best suit their current needs. Then later on they can swap the code back and forth between the two environments.

This chapter has somewhat unusual origins, in that I created it originally as a white paper for use on Borland's Web sites. I have decided to include it in this book without extensive revisions because it covers an important topic in a fairly short space. Readers with good ears will hear a rather different tone in this chapter than you find in the other sections of this book.

Because of its origins, this chapter does not contain as many sample programs as most of the chapters in this book. However, if you look in the Chap06 directory on the *C++Builder Unleashed* CD-ROM, you will find a few programs illustrating the main points of this chapter.

This chapter is divided into two main sections. The first part contains a summary of the techniques for sharing code between the two environments. The second, and longer, section of the chapter contains a more technical analysis of the methods for sharing code between C++Builder and Delphi.

Benefits of Sharing Code Between C++Builder and Delphi

This section lists some of the key benefits gained when you share code between Delphi and C++Builder. These items are listed in no particular order:

- Programmers can work in either C++ or Delphi. You don't have to worry that code written with one tool will not be accessible from inside the other tool. Instead, you can concentrate on finding the fastest way to create usable modules, and then link them in to either C++Builder or Delphi, depending on the needs of your engineers. Of course, the route from Delphi to C++Builder is much more open than the route from C++Builder to Delphi, but it is possible to move in either direction.

■ Sharing code between Delphi and C++Builder also promotes code reuse. You can write an object once for a Delphi project, and then reuse it, unchanged, in a C++ project. There is no performance or size penalty associated with writing code in Delphi rather than C++. Anything you might have heard about C++ being significantly faster than Object Pascal is simply untrue.

■ Delphi is extremely easy to use. It offers programmers a simple, easy-to-understand syntax. Companies can allow inexperienced programmers to work in Delphi without fear that their code cannot also be used in C++ projects. You can therefore have some of your team working full-time in C++, and the rest of the team working full-time with the much easier to use Delphi language. The efforts of both programmers can then be combined into a single, high-performance executable.

■ Because Delphi is so easy to use, it is often the language of choice during projects that have tight deadlines. Even your best programmers might prefer to use Delphi when they are rushed, or when they want to create high-performance programs as easily as possible. Any modules or objects created on these types of projects can then later be linked in to C++ projects. This means that there is no penalty associated with using Delphi, even if you are primarily a C++ shop.

Technical Highlights

This section of the chapter contains an overview of the key points you need to know about sharing code between C++Builder and Delphi. It consists of two subsections called

Overview: Using Delphi Code in C++Builder

Overview: Using C++ Code in Delphi

When you are through reading these sections, you will have a general feeling for how, and to what degree, you can share code between Delphi and C++Builder. In subsequent sections, I will review most of these points in more detail.

Before beginning, you should note that Delphi uses Object Pascal, which is widely taught in many schools. C++Builder uses C++, which is probably the most widely used language in corporate America. Most programmers will know one, if not both, of these languages.

Overview: Using Delphi Code in C++Builder

C++Builder does not care whether the units you add to your project are written in C++ or in Delphi. It will compile either type of unit as if it were native to C++Builder.

As a general rule, any Delphi 2.01 unit you create that compiles in Delphi should compile unchanged in C++Builder. There are a few Delphi syntactical elements that will not be accepted by C++Builder. However, these are minor exceptions, and you will generally find that all your Delphi 2.01 or Delphi 2.0 code will compile unchanged in C++Builder. After all, the entire VCL is written in Object Pascal, and it compiles fine under BCB. The VCL consists of many thousands of lines of code, and contains almost any imaginable Object Pascal construct.

In particular, the following types of code will compile in C++Builder:

1. Delphi forms
2. Delphi units containing objects
3. Delphi units containing procedures, functions, constants, structures, arrays, and so on
4. Delphi components

You usually do not have to change your Delphi units at all to link them in to C++Builder. There is no need to change the code, to create header files, or to massage your code in any way. You can mix the types of code listed previously in any way you like. For instance, you can link in to C++Builder one Delphi unit that contains the following:

- A form
- An object
- Some functions
- A component

The unit can contain any combination of the preceding types, or of any other valid Object Pascal types. These types can appear in any combination. For instance, a Pascal unit can contain only an object, or it can contain both an object and a form. You can link in as many Pascal units as you like, with each containing any combination of the above objects. There is no limit on the number of Delphi units you can add to a C++Builder project.

To link Delphi code into C++Builder you simply choose Add to Project from the menus and then browse for files that end in PAS. Once you have added one or more Delphi units to your project, they will compile and link seamlessly with the rest of your C++ code. You may edit only the source code of the units while they are open inside of C++Builder. You cannot edit the forms. You can, however, create a descendant of a Pascal form and then edit that descendant.

Besides the simple techniques outlined previously, advanced programmers can also link Delphi code into C++ by using one of the following techniques:

1. Delphi dynamic link libraries (DLLs) can be easily added to your C++ projects.
2. You can use COM and OLE to add Delphi 2.0 or Delphi 3.0 objects to C++Builder. In particular, you can add Delphi objects to C++Builder through

    OLE Automation.

    The basic rules of COM, including dual interfaces.

    Creating Delphi ActiveX controls that you use in C++Builder.

Sharing Code Between Delphi and C++Builder

CHAPTER 6

247

6

SHARING CODE
BETWEEN DELPHI
AND C++BUILDER

3. Delphi and C++Builder share the same Virtual Method Tables (VMTs). This means you can create an object in Delphi and use it in C++Builder through the technique outlined in the section called "Mapping Virtual Method Tables." This technique is very similar to what happens when you create a dual interface in OLE Automation.

Overview: Using C++ Code in Delphi

C++ supports some syntactical elements such as multiple inheritance and function overloading that make it difficult to directly link all C++Builder code into Delphi. However, you can still use C++ code in Delphi projects through the following techniques:

1. COM and OLE. Delphi fully supports both OLE Automation and dual interfaces.

2. DLLs.

3. Direct linking of C++Builder units containing functions. (Note that Delphi supports OBJ files.)

The most convenient of the preceding techniques is the first, especially if your C++ COM objects support type libraries. Delphi 97 has full support for type libraries, and you will be able to generate Delphi units directly from a type library. This means that you can link C++ COM objects that support type libraries directly into Delphi without having to write any extra code. All the necessary files for linking in C++ COM objects that support type libraries will be generated automatically by Delphi.

DLLs are a powerful means of sharing code between Delphi and C++Builder. Virtually any C++Builder function that you create can be placed in a DLL and called directly from Delphi. Delphi supports all the common calling conventions such as CDECL, PASCAL, and STDCALL. You can access an object written in C++ from inside Delphi simply by reversing the technique described in the section titled "Mapping Virtual Method Tables."

It is possible, under certain circumstances, to link C++ OBJ files directly into Delphi. This is a powerful technique that can be very useful in certain circumstances. However, there are limitations on what you can do with this technology, and it should not be viewed as a primary means of porting code between the two environments.

Summary of Techniques for Sharing Code

Before closing this section of the chapter, it might be helpful to review some of the key points mentioned so far.

C++Builder has virtually no limitations on its capability to use Delphi 2.01 code. You can simply link your Pascal units directly into C++Builder without modifying them in any way. They will then compile into the same small, tight, high-performance machine code you would expect if you wrote them in C++.

If you use both C++Builder and Delphi in a single project, you can promote code reuse while simultaneously leveraging the skills of all your programmers. Your best engineers can work in C++, where they can take advantage of that language's flexibility. Inexperienced programmers, those who prefer Object Pascal, and programmers who are rushed, can work in Delphi. With this division of labor, all the programmers on your team will be productive immediately.

The key point is that the technology outlined in this chapter enables your programmers to work in either C++ or Delphi without fear that the code will not be available for use in all your C++ projects.

A More Technical Analysis

You have now completed the overview of the techniques for sharing code between C++Builder and Delphi. For most programmers, this is where the chapter starts to get interesting. The subject matter in the following sections starts out with the simplest techniques, and becomes increasingly complex as the chapter nears its conclusion.

Ground Rules for Linking Delphi Code into C++Builder

You have already learned that you can link Delphi code directly in to C++Builder projects. In this section, I explain how this is possible, and put to rest any fears you might have about this kind of project.

First, I will lay down three key ground rules:

1. You cannot mix C++ and Delphi code in the same unit. You have to create separate units (modules) for each type of code.

2. It's best if you have the Pascal source to the unit you want to use. You cannot link a Pascal binary file (DCU) in to a C++Builder project. You can, however, link in BCB OBJ files made from Pascal source. In other words, you must have either the Pascal source for the unit or an OBJ made in BCB. You can't use a DCU file. Third parties that don't want to distribute source to their tools can simply recompile once in BCB and then distribute the resultant binary OBJ files.

3. You cannot edit the visual part of a Pascal form while it is open in C++Builder. You can, however, edit the source. If you create a descendant of the Pascal form, you can edit the descendant object with the visual tools.

Furthermore, you should note that a Pascal unit cannot usually be the project file for a C++Builder application. However, if one small module is written in C++, and everything else in the project is written in Object Pascal, the project is still, by definition, a C++Builder project, even though the code is 98 percent written in Object Pascal. The Entities program from Chapter 28, "Game Programming," is an example of this kind of project.

Sharing Code Between Delphi and C++Builder

CHAPTER 6

249

6

SHARING CODE
BETWEEN DELPHI
AND C++BUILDER

Here is a detailed description of the simple steps needed to link a Delphi unit in to a C++Builder project:

1. First, choose the Project | Add to Project menu option.
2. When the Add to project dialog appears, pull down the Files of type combo box at the bottom of the dialog. You will then be able to select files of type CPP, PAS, C, RES, OBJ, or LIB, as shown in Figure 6.1. You should select PAS.
3. Browse for the Pascal source file you want and add it to your project. After you have selected the file you want to use, you can click OK to add it to your project and proceed exactly as you would if this were a C++ file.

FIGURE 6.1.

Selecting a Pascal file to add to your C++ project.

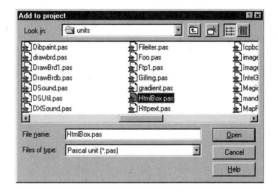

The header file for your unit will be generated automatically. You don't have to do anything to the unit to use it in a C++Builder project. An example of this type of project is found on the CD that accompanies this book, in the Chap06 directory, in a project called Test1.

Linking a Delphi Component in to a C++Builder Project

If you want to use a Delphi component in a C++ project, you would normally want to first add it to the Component Palette. You do this through the same basic technique you would use to add a C++Builder component written in C++. In particular

1. Choose Component | Install from the menu.
2. Select the Add button from the Install Components dialog, as shown in Figure 6.2.
3. Use the Add Module dialog to enter or browse for the name of the PAS file you want to use—that is, for the PAS file that contains the registration procedure for your Delphi component.
4. After selecting the module, click the OK button in the Install Components dialog. C++Builder will then recompile CMPLIB32.DLL, thereby adding your component to the Component Palette.

FIGURE 6.2.

*Adding a Pascal
component to a
C++Builder project.*

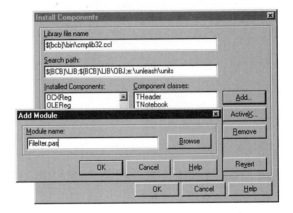

Adding a Pascal Component to a C++Builder Project

After you have integrated a Delphi component into C++Builder, you can then treat it exactly
as if it were a native C++Builder component. That is, you can drop it onto a form and manipulate its methods with the object inspector. If you need to reference any of the components
methods, properties, or events in your C++ code, you should use C++ syntax. The details of
this syntax can be surmised by viewing the header file created when you added the component
to the Component Palette.

A sample Delphi component called TSmiley is available in the Utils subdirectory. This component was written by the great Nick Hodges. It is not only one of the first components ever
written in Delphi, but it is also the world's most famous and most highly acclaimed Truly Useless
Component. TSmiley is a mission-critical component designed for use in distributed n-tier
applications created by Fortune 500 companies. All its functionality can be accessed through
the Mood property, which can be set to various values such as smHappy, smSad, smIndifferent,
smShades, and smTongue.

Some Theory on Linking Object Pascal and C++Builder Code

Delphi is an Object Pascal–based language, while C++Builder is obviously a C++-based language. How is it possible to link Pascal directly into a C++ project?

A good way to begin your exploration of this issue is to understand that Delphi 2.0, Delphi
3.0, BCB, and Borland C++ 5.X use the same compiler. The difference is simply in how the
language is parsed. Delphi parses Object Pascal, tokenizes it, and then passes it on to the compiler. Borland C++ 5.X and BCB parse C++, tokenize it, and then pass it on to the compiler.
Underneath the hood, Delphi 2.0, C++Builder, and Borland C++ are very similar tools. The
difference is in how the syntax of the language looks before it is parsed and tokenized.

Delphi sometimes finishes its compile and link cycles faster than Borland C++ simply because
Pascal is easier to parse, and because Delphi supports a simpler and more flexible type of binary

Sharing Code Between Delphi and C++Builder

Chapter 6

251

6

SHARING CODE
BETWEEN DELPHI
AND C++BUILDER

file (DCUs are easier to make than OBJs). Of course, the incremental linker found in C++Builder does much to eliminate this difference in performance.

Because C++Builder uses the same compiler as Delphi, the road is obviously at least halfway open to finding compatibility between Delphi and C++. The next stone on the path is laid by C++Builder's advantageous use of the Delphi VCL.

C++Builder uses the Delphi VCL in all of its standard projects. It therefore needs to understand Delphi's types, objects, and syntax. This was made possible in part by the fact that Object Pascal is similar in structure to C++, but supports a subset of the features available in C++. (There are some features of Object Pascal, such as sets, not supported by C++, but these are relatively minor roadblocks that can be overcome through a judicious use of templates and classes.)

The converse of the logic in the last paragraph is not true. There is no need for Delphi to parse C++. Furthermore, Object Pascal is, in a sense, a subset of C++. It is therefore easier for C++Builder to adapt to the features of Delphi than it is for Delphi to support certain esoteric features of C++ such as multiple inheritance or function and operator overloading.

Object Pascal is not radically different from C++ in the sense that BASIC is radically different from C++. Serious languages like Object Pascal and C++ are part of the same family of tools, whereas cute and cuddly Visual Basic is from an altogether different planet.

C++Builder and Delphi share a common heritage in the way they construct objects, handle variable types, and define methods. In particular, a Delphi object's VMT is identical in structure to a C++ object that uses single inheritance. Furthermore, Delphi supports all the calling conventions, such as CDECL, PASCAL, and STDCALL, that are used with C++ functions and methods. Therefore, there is no difference in the structure of a Delphi function or method and a C++ function or method. They look the same on the assembler level, as long as C++ is not using any "advanced features," such as function overloading. (Remember that by default, 32-bit Object Pascal uses the fastcall calling convention, which means that it passes some parameters to functions in registers. This same convention is supported by C++Builder, or you can explicitly use a different convention if you like.)

Finally, there is a direct parallel between most C++ types and the standard Delphi types. For instance, a C++ `int` is identical to a Delphi `Integer`. Other types, such as strings, are either identical, or very similar. For instance, a C++ `char *` (`LPSTR`) is identical to a Delphi `PChar`. Furthermore, a Delphi string is fully compatible with a `char *`, and the C++Builder `AnsiString` type is designed to be compatible with, and to mimic, a Delphi `string`. This parallel structure continues throughout the two languages, and includes complex types such as structures (records) and arrays. (What C++ calls a union, Delphi calls a variable record, and so on.)

There are, however, some differences between the languages. For instance, Delphi does not support templates, C++Builder does not support `try..finally` blocks or `with` statements, and each language implements exception handling and RTTI slightly differently. These differences are significant, but they do not represent an impenetrable barrier erected between Delphi and C++Builder.

In this section you have seen that Delphi and C++Builder both use the same compiler and support a similar syntax and style of programming. These are the key elements that make it possible to share code between C++Builder and Delphi.

Using COM to Link Delphi Code in to C++Builder

The last few sections have shown that it is trivial to link Delphi units and components directly in to C++Builder. Another great way to share code between the two tools is through COM and OLE. You might want to use COM and OLE if you want to share your code not only between Delphi and C++Builder, but also between Delphi and Visual Basic, or other OLE aware tools such as Word, Excel, Visual C++, and so forth.

There are three key ways to link Delphi COM objects into C++Builder:

1. Use OLE Automation or dual interfaces.
2. Use Delphi 3.0 to create ActiveX controls, and then load the ActiveX controls on the C++Builder Component Palette.
3. Write raw COM or OLE code to link in Delphi objects.

The first two methods are supported automatically by C++Builder. The third method requires you to dig into the details of OLE.

One simple way to link in Delphi objects through COM is to use OLE Automation. C++Builder fully supports OLE Automation, and it provides a simple technique for accessing the methods of an automation object.

Automation objects can be accessed in one of two fashions: You can access them through a COM `IDispatch` interface or through dual interfaces. C++Builder has built-in support for `IDispatch` through the `CreateOleObject` VCL function and the `Variant` template class. This is the simplest method for accessing automation objects, and it is the one you should use unless speed is an extremely important issue for you.

For instance, suppose you have a Delphi 3.0 `IDispatch` interface that exports the following methods:

```
ITest = interface(IDispatch)
  ['{1746E520-E2D4-11CF-BD2F-0020AF0E5B81}']
  function Get_Value: Integer; safecall;
  procedure Set_Value(Value: Integer); safecall;
  function Get_Name: WideString; safecall;
  procedure Set_Name(const Value: WideString); safecall;
  procedure Prompt(const text: WideString); safecall;
  procedure VarTest(var v1, v2, v3: Variant); safecall;
  property Value: Integer read Get_Value write Set_Value;
  property Name: WideString read Get_Name write Set_Name;
end;
```

Assume further that the DLL that contains this interface is referenced in the Registry in association with a `CLSID` that has a `ProgID` called `"TestLib.Test"`.

Sharing Code Between Delphi and C++Builder

CHAPTER 6

253

6

SHARING CODE
BETWEEN DELPHI
AND C++BUILDER

Here is how you can retrieve the interface and call the `Prompt` method from inside C++Builder:

```
void __fastcall TForm1::Button1Click(TObject *Sender)
{
  Variant V = CreateOleObject("TestLib.Test");
  V.OleProcedure("Prompt", "Beware the Jabberwock, my son!");
}
```

This code first retrieves an instance of `IDispatch` inside a variant. It then uses a method of the `Variant` class to call the `Prompt` method from the Delphi interface.

Here is how you would call the `VarTest` method:

```
void __fastcall TForm1::Button1Click(TObject *Sender)
{
  Variant V1, V2, V3;
  Variant V = CreateOleObject("TestLib.Test");
  V1 = 5;
  V2 = "Beware the Jubjub bird, and shun the frumious Bandersnatch!";
  V3 = V;
  V.OleProcedure("VarTest", V1, V2, V3);
}
```

Delphi users looking at this code should note that a `Variant` is a C++ class declared in `Sysdefs.h`. It is not a simple type as it is when used inside Delphi. This subject is covered in depth in Chapter 3, "C++Builder and the VCL."

If you want to use dual interfaces in C++Builder, you can get fast access to automation objects that reside in a DLL. You can also access local servers, that is automation objects in an executable, more quickly via dual interfaces, but the built-in overhead with local servers is so great that the improvement in speed given by dual interfaces is less noticeable.

There are no built-in tools for accessing dual interfaces in C++Builder. Obviously, it will be possible to use them (after all, you can do anything in C++), but you will have to lay the groundwork yourself. (The basic technique is similar to the one outlined shortly in the section titled "Mapping Virtual Method Tables.")

> **NOTE**
>
> I cannot ship an example of this kind of code with this book because Delphi 3.0 had not shipped when we went to press.

Using Delphi ActiveX Controls in C++Builder

C++Builder has built-in support for ActiveX controls. You can load them into the environment and use them just as if they were native components. To get started, do the following:

1. Choose Component | Install from the menu.
2. In the Install Components dialog, select the OCX button to bring up the Import OLE Control dialog.

3. All the registered components on your system will appear in the Import OLE Control dialog, as shown in Figure 6.3. If you want to register a new component, select the Register button in the Import OLE Control dialog.

4. After selecting the control you want to import, press the OK button.

5. Your new control will now be listed at the bottom of the Installed Components dialog, and an interface source file will be placed in the LIB directory.

6. Press OK to recompile CMPLIB32 and add your control to the Component Palette. By default, the new ActiveX control will appear in the OCX page of the Component Palette.

FIGURE 6.3.

The registered components as seen when adding an ActiveX control to BCB.

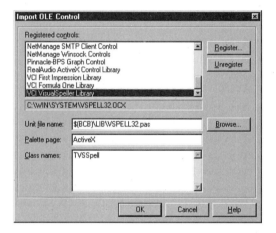

If you don't want to use the previously shown automated method, you can also use the C++ language to build your own OLE containers. This is, of course, a difficult process, and the technique outlined earlier is usually infinitely preferable. Don't forget that you can use the tools in Borland C++ to create OLE containers, and then link that code in to your C++Builder project either directly or through libraries or DLLs.

Using the Windows API to Link in Delphi COM and OLE Objects

Delphi 3.0 is an extremely powerful tool for creating COM and OLE objects. You can use it to build automation objects, dual interfaces, ActiveX controls, and all manner of simple (or complex) COM objects.

C++Builder does not have the built-in support for COM that you find in Delphi 3.0. However, it does have access to all the OLE code you find in Borland C++ 5.x, the Windows SDK, the MSDN, or in commercially available books and libraries. It will access most of the key OLE code found in MFC or the new ActiveX Template Library.

The following is a definition for a simple Delphi COM object that will compile in either Delphi 2.0 or Delphi 3.0. For that matter, it will also compile fine under BCB.

```
const
  CLSID_ITable: TGUID = (D1:$58BDE140;D2:$88B9;D3:$11CF;D4:($BA,$F3,$00,$80,$C7,
                                                           $51,$52,$8B));
type
  ITable = class(IUnknown)
  private
    FRefCount: LongInt;
    FObjectDestroyed: TObjectDestroyed;
    Table: TTable;
  public
    constructor Create(ObjectDestroyed: TObjectDestroyed);
    destructor Destroy; override;
    function QueryInterface(const iid: TIID; var obj):
      HResult; override; stdcall;
    function AddRef: Longint; override; stdcall;
    function Release: Longint; override; stdcall;
  { interface }
    procedure Open; virtual; stdcall;
    procedure Close; virtual; stdcall;
    procedure SetDatabaseName(const Name: PChar); virtual; stdcall;
    procedure SetTableName(const Name: PChar); virtual; stdcall;
    procedure GetStrField(FieldName: PChar; Value: PChar);
      virtual; stdcall;
    procedure GetIntField(FieldName: PChar; var Value: Integer);
      virtual; stdcall;
    procedure GetClassName(Value: PChar); virtual; stdcall;
    procedure Next; virtual; stdcall;
    procedure Prior; virtual; stdcall;
    procedure First; virtual; stdcall;
    procedure Last; virtual; stdcall;
    function EOF: Bool; virtual; stdcall;
  end;
```
Here is the same interface as it would be declared inside a C++ project:
```
class IDBClass : public IUnknown
{
public:
    STDMETHOD(QueryInterface) (THIS_ REFIID, LPVOID*) PURE;
    STDMETHOD_(ULONG,AddRef)  (THIS) PURE;
    STDMETHOD_(ULONG,Release) (THIS) PURE;
    // Interface
    STDMETHOD_(VOID, Open) (THIS) PURE;
    STDMETHOD_(VOID, Close) (THIS) PURE;
    STDMETHOD_(VOID, SetDatabaseName) (THIS_ LPSTR Name) PURE;
    STDMETHOD_(VOID, SetTableName) (THIS_ LPSTR Name) PURE;
    STDMETHOD_(VOID, GetStrField) (THIS_ LPSTR FieldName, LPSTR Value)
      PURE;
    STDMETHOD_(VOID, GetIntField) (THIS_ LPSTR FieldName, int * Value)
      PURE;
    STDMETHOD_(VOID, GetClassName) (THIS_ LPSTR Name) PURE;
    STDMETHOD_(VOID,  Next) (THIS) PURE;
    STDMETHOD_(VOID,  Prior) (THIS) PURE;
    STDMETHOD_(VOID,  First) (THIS) PURE;
    STDMETHOD_(VOID,  Last) (THIS) PURE;
    STDMETHOD_(BOOL,  EOF) (THIS) PURE;
};
```

This code is shown on the CD that accompanies this book in the program called ComTable. Given the preceding definition, you could write the following C++ code to use the Delphi object in C++:

```cpp
#pragma argsused
void Window1_OnLButtonDown(HWND hwnd, BOOL fDoubleClick, int x, int y, UINT
keyFlags)
{
  char CR[2] ="\r";
  HRESULT hr;
  PIDBClass P;
  LPSTR S, Temp;
  CoInitialize(NULL);
  hr = CoCreateInstance(CLSID_IDBClass, NULL, CLSCTX_INPROC_SERVER,
                        IID_IUnknown, (VOID**) &P);
  if (SUCCEEDED(hr))
  {
    S = (char *)malloc(1000);
    Temp = (LPSTR)malloc(100);
    P->SetDatabaseName("DBDEMOS");
    P->SetTableName("COUNTRY");
    P->Open();
    strcpy(S, "Countries and their capitals: ");
    strcat(S, CR);
    strcat(S, CR);
    while (!P->EOF())
    {
      P->GetStrField("NAME", Temp);
      strcat(S, Temp);
      strcat(S, ": ");
      P->GetStrField("CAPITAL", Temp);
      strcat(S, Temp);
      strcat(S, CR);
      P->Next();
    }
    MessageBox(hwnd, S, "COUNTRY TABLE", MB_OK);
    P->Release();
    free(S);
    free(Temp);
  }
}
```

This code is found on disk in the program called CRunTable. Clearly this technique takes a bit of work, but it is not overly difficult. If you understand something about COM objects, it provides a viable method for sharing code between Delphi and C++.

In the ComTable directory on the CD that accompanies this book, you will find two sample programs: one called ComTable and the other called CRunTable. ComTable is a Delphi DLL that contains the COM object shown earlier in this section of the chapter. You can compile this program with Delphi 2.0 or with the command-line version of the Delphi compiler called DCC32.EXE that ships with C++Builder.

In the same directory as the source for ComTable, you will find a file called Win32.reg, which can be used to register ComTable with the system. In this file you will find an entry called

Sharing Code Between Delphi and C++Builder

CHAPTER 6

257

6

SHARING CODE
BETWEEN DELPHI
AND C++BUILDER

InProcServer that will have a path to ComTable.dll hardcoded into it. You will have to edit this path to point to the place on your system where ComTable.dll resides. You can load the Win32.reg program into the Windows utility called RegEdit.exe or go to a DOS window, change to the ComTable directory, and type START WIN32.REG.

After compiling and registering ComTable, you can use BCB to compile and run CRunTable. Click once with the left mouse button on the surface of this application to load the Delphi COM object. CRunTable happens to be a Windows API program rather than a standard BCB RAD program, but the core code that launches the COM object also works in a standard BCB program. An sample BCB program of this type called BCBRunTable can be found on the CD that accompanies this book.

The code found in ComTable provides a good example of how to construct a simple COM object. Unfortunately, there isn't enough room in this book to discuss this topic in any depth. If you want to learn more about this subject, read my book *Delphi 2 Unleashed* (published by Sams), or go to www.microsoft.com and download the COM specification, which turns out to be a surprisingly readable document.

Using DLLs to Link Delphi Code in to C++Builder

C ++Builder can easily access a Delphi DLL containing functions and procedures. If you want to access a Delphi object implemented inside a DLL from C++Builder, you should read the following section called "Mapping Virtual Method Tables."

If you have a Delphi DLL that you can call from inside a Delphi 2.01 project, you do not need to change it at all to call it from inside C++Builder. To get started, take the Delphi unit that lists the methods in your DLL and add it to your C++ project. C++Builder will automatically compile the unit and generate a C++ header file. In particular, you should link the unit using the techniques described previously in the section called "Ground Rules for Linking Delphi Code in to C++Builder."

You will not be able to access data declared in your DLL without first calling a function or procedure. This same limitation applies to all DLLs, regardless of the language used to implement them.

DLLs are useful when you have a large project that you want to divide into several modules. By placing code in DLLs, you can divide your projects into several binary files that can be loaded in and out of memory at will.

Mapping Virtual Method Tables

Delphi objects stored in a DLL are normally out of reach of Ebony projects. However, there is a way to get at them by matching the VMT of the Delphi object to the VMT of a virtual abstract, or "PURE," C++ object.

An example of this type of program is found on the CD that accompanies this book in the directory called ObjectsInDLL. The code for this project is described in the remainder of this section of the chapter. To run the program, use Delphi or the copy of DCC32.exe that ships with BCB to compile ObjectLib.dpr:

```
dcc32 -b ObjectLib.dpr
```

Then load the GetObject project into BCB and compile and run the program. After the program is launched, you can press the button in the BCB program in order to call one of the methods in the Object Pascal DLL.

Consider the following Delphi declaration:

```
TMyObject = class
  function AddOne(i: Integer): Integer; virtual; stdcall;
  function AddTwo(i: Integer): Integer; virtual; stdcall;
end;
```

A virtual abstract version of the same object could be declared in C++ like this:

```
class __declspec(pascalimplementation) TMyObject: public TObject
{
public:
  virtual _stdcall int AddOne(int i) = 0;
  virtual _stdcall int AddTwo(int i) = 0;
};
```

To match up the VMT of the C++ object to the VMT of the Pascal object, all you need to do is retrieve a pointer to the object from the DLL. One way to do this is to export a function from the DLL that is designed for this explicit purpose:

```
function CreateObject(ID: Integer; var Obj): Boolean;
var
  M: TMyObject;
begin
  if ID = ID_MyObject then begin
    M := TMyObject.Create;
    Result := True
  end else begin
    M := nil;
    Result := False
  end;
  Pointer(Obj) := M;
end;
exports
  CreateObject name 'CreateObject';
```

You can call this method from the Ebony project with the following code:

```
typedef Boolean (_stdcall *LPCreateObject)(int ID, void *obj);
void __fastcall TForm1::Button1Click(TObject *Sender)
{
  TMyObject *MyObject;
  LPCreateObject CreateObject;
  HANDLE hlib = LoadLibrary("OBJECTLIB.DLL");
  CreateObject = (LPCreateObject)GetProcAddress(hlib, "CreateObject");
```

```
    if (CreateObject(1, &MyObject))
    {
      int i = MyObject->AddOne(1);
      ShowMessage((AnsiString)i);
    }
    FreeLibrary(hlib);
}
```

The code shown here first declares a pointer to a function with the same signature as the CreateObject routine in the DLL. It then calls the standard Windows API functions LoadLibrary and GetProcAddress in order to retrieve a pointer to CreateObject. If the call succeeds, you can call CreateObject, return the address of the object you want to call, and then call one of its methods.

Notice that all the methods in the Pascal object are declared virtual. This is necessary because you want to match up the VMTs, or Virtual Method Tables, of the two declarations. If the methods weren't declared virtual, there would be no Virtual Method Table and the ploy would not work. You can declare nonvirtual methods in your object if you want, but you will not be able to call these methods from C++.

Note also that the order of the methods you declare is very important. The names of the methods you want to call are not important to the C++ implementation; all that matters is the order in which the methods are declared.

You can use this same technique, or one like it, to export any object from a Delphi DLL into a C++Builder or Borland C++ project. You do not have to use GetProcAddress and LoadLibrary, but could instead import a Delphi unit that exports CreateObject directly into your C++Builder project. However, I use GetProcAddress in this example because it forces you to imagine the exact steps necessary to make this process work. In other words, it forces you to think about the addresses that are being shared between the DLL and the BCB project.

Summary

In this chapter you have learned that C++Builder has an unprecedented capability to access the code from its sister product, Delphi. As a rule, you can simply link Delphi code directly into your C++Builder projects without any additional work on your part. It is no harder to link Object Pascal code into C++Builder than it would be to link Object Pascal code into a Delphi project!

The types of code that can be shared between Delphi and C++Builder include forms, components, ActiveX controls, and simple methods and functions. You can simply link this code directly into your projects without any extra work.

This chapter also examined using OLE or DLLs to share code between C++Builder and Delphi. OLE can be useful if you want to share code with not only C++Builder, but also with other, non-Borland environments such as Word, Visual Basic, or Excel. DLLs are a great way to share code if memory management issues are significant. In particular, you can load and unload DLLs from memory during the life of your project.

Graphics

IN THIS CHAPTER

CHAPTER 7

This chapter covers the basics of graphics programming in the VCL. The VCL encapsulates the Windows Graphics Device Interface, or GDI. GDI programming can be a subtle and dangerous process. The VCL tames this technology and makes it extremely easy to use.

In the following pages you will learn about:

- The TCanvas object
- Painting shapes on the screen
- Working with colors
- Working with bitmaps
- Working with metafiles
- Drawing fractals
- Working with fonts

It's important to understand that the basic graphics functionality presented here is a far cry from the sophisticated tools you find in the DirectX programs seen in Chapter 28, "Game Programming." This is just the basic functionality needed to present standard Windows programs. However, the material presented in this chapter is useful in most standard Windows programs, and it is part of the core knowledge that all VCL programmers should possess. In particular, it shows how the VCL encapsulates and simplifies Windows GDI programming.

Graphics.Hpp

The core of the VCL graphics support is found in Graphics.Hpp. The following objects can be found in this file:

Object	Description
TCanvas	This is the basic graphics object used to paint shapes on a form or other surface. It is the primary wrapper around the GDI.
TBrush	This is the object used to designate the color or pattern that fills in the center of shapes such as rectangles or ellipses.
TPen	This is the object used for drawing lines, and as the outline for rectangles or ellipses.
TPicture	This is the generalized, high-level VCL wrapper around "pictures" such as bitmaps, metafiles, or icons.
TMetaFileCanvas	This is the drawing surface for a metafile.
TMetaFile	This is the VCL wrapper around a windows metafile.
TBitmap	This is the VCL wrapper around bitmaps.
TIcon	This is the VCL wrapper around icons.
TGraphicsObject	This is the base class for TBrush, TFont, and TPen.
TGraphic	This is the base class for TMetaFile, TBitmap, and TIcon.

Many of these objects are explored in the next few pages. In particular, I demonstrate how to use bitmaps and pens and show how to draw basic geometric shapes to the screen. You also see how to work with bitmaps and metafiles.

After the TFont object, the next most important graphics object in the VCL is TCanvas. This is a wrapper around the Windows GDI, or Graphics Device Interface. The GDI is the subsystem Windows programmers use to paint pictures and other graphics objects. Most of the content of Graphics.Hpp is aimed at finding ways to simplify the GDI so that it is relatively easy to use.

Two other important graphics-based objects not found in Graphics.Hpp are TImage and TPaintBox. Both of these components are covered in this chapter.

The TColor Type

Almost all the graphics objects use the simple TColor type. This is one of the building blocks on which the whole graphics system is laid.

For most practical purposes, a variable of type TColor is synonymous with the built in Windows type COLORREF. However, the actual declaration for TColor looks like this:

```
enum TColor {clMin=-0x7fffffff-1, clMax=0x7fffffff};
```

If you know the COLORREF type, you can see that it is similar to the TColor type. In a sense, the TColor type is nothing but a set of predefined COLORREFs.

The Windows palette system enables you to define three different colors, Red, Green, and Blue, where each color has 255 different shades. These colors are specified in the last three bytes of the 4-byte long value used to represent a variable of type TColor.

Here is what the three primary colors look like:

```
Canvas->Brush->Color = 0x000000FF;  // Red
Canvas->Brush->Color = 0x0000FF00;  // Green
Canvas->Brush->Color = 0x00FF0000;  // Blue
```

You worked with these colors, and combinations of these colors, in the RGBShape program from Chapter 2, "Basic Facts about C++Builder."

Of course, it's not convenient to have to write out these numbers directly in hex. Instead, you can use the RGB macro:

```
Canvas->Brush->Color = RGB(255, 0, 0);  // Red
Canvas->Brush->Color = RGB(0, 255, 0);  // Green
Canvas->Brush->Color = RGB(0, 0, 255);  // Blue
```

You can, of course, combine red, green, and blue to produce various shades:

```
RGB(255, 0, 255); // Purple
RGB(255, 255, 0); // Yellow
RGB(127, 127, 127);  // Gray
```

The VCL also provides a series of constants you can use to specify common colors. clBlack, for instance, has the same internal number you would obtain from the following code:

```
COLORREF clBlack = RGB(0, 0, 0);
```

Here are some declarations from GRAPHICS.HPP:

```
#define clBlack  TColor(0)
#define clMaroon TColor(128)
#define clGreen  TColor(32768)
#define clOlive  TColor(32896)
```

If you want to experiment with this system, you can create a new project in BCB, drop a button on the main form and run some changes on a method that looks like this:

```
void __fastcall TForm1::Button1Click(TObject *Sender)
{
  Canvas->Brush->Color = 0x0000FFFF;
  Canvas->Rectangle(0, 0, 200, 200);
}
```

This code will draw a bright yellow rectangle in the upper right corner of the main form. Try changing the values of the Brush color to 0x00FF0000, to RGB(255, 0, 255), to clBlue, and so on. If you get tired of drawing rectangles, you can switch to ellipses instead:

```
Canvas->Ellipse(0, 0, 200, 200);
```

I talk more about drawing shapes with a canvas later in the chapter.

Most of the time you will pick colors from the Color property editor provided by most components. For instance, you can double click the Color property for a TForm object to bring up a TColorDialog. However, there are times when you need to work with the TColor type directly, which is why I have explained the topic in some detail.

The Canvas Object

All forms, and many components, have a canvas. You can think of a canvas as being the surface on which graphics objects can paint. In short, the metaphor used by the developers here is of a painter's canvas.

This TCanvas object is brought into the core component hierarchy through aggregation, which means in many cases that you access its features via a field of an object such as a TForm or TImage object. For instance, you can write the following:

```
Form1->Canvas->TextOut(1, 1, "Hello from the canvas");
```

This statement writes the words "Hello from the canvas" in the upper-left corner of a form. Notice that you do not have to access or reference a device context directly in order to use this method.

Of course, most of the time you are accessing Form1 from inside of Form1, so you can write

```
Canvas->TextOut(1, 1, "Hello from the canvas");
```

However, you cannot write

```
Form1->TextOut(1, 1, "Hello from the canvas");
```

This is because the Canvas object is aggregated into Form1. TCanvas is not brought in through multiple inheritance. Furthermore, the aggregation does not attempt to wrap each of the methods of TCanvas inside methods of TForm. Aggregation is discussed in more detail in Chapters 19, "Inheritance," and 20, "Encapsulation."

The Canvas object has several key methods that all VCL programmers should know:

Arc	Draw an arc
Chord	A closed figure showing the intersection of a line and an ellipse
CopyRect	Copy an area of one canvas to another
Draw	Draw a bitmap or other graphic on a canvas
Ellipse	Draw an ellipse
FillRect	Fill a rectangle
FloodFill	Fill an enclosed area
FrameRect	Draw a border around a rectangle
LineTo	Draw a line
MoveTo	Draw a line
Pie	Draw a pie-shaped object
Polygon	Draw a multisided object
PolyLine	Connect a set of points on the canvas
Rectangle	Draw a rectangle
RoundRect	Draw a rectangle with rounded corners
StretchDraw	Same as Draw, but stretches the object to fill an area
TextHeight	The height of a string in the current font
TextOut	Output text
TextRect	Output text in a defined area
TextWidth	The width of a string in the current font

The following properties of the Canvas object are important:

```
Font
Brush
Pen
Pixels
```

The following events can be important to some very technical programmers:

```
OnChange
OnChanging
```

If you know the Windows API, many of these methods will be familiar to you. The big gain from using the Canvas object rather than the raw Windows GDI calls is that the resources you use will be managed for you automatically. In particular, you never need to obtain a device context, nor do you have to select an object into a device context.

In some cases, you will get better performance if you write directly to the Windows GDI. However, it's a mistake to assume that you will always get better by doing so. For instance, the VCL graphics subsystem will cache and share resources in a sophisticated manner that would be very difficult to duplicate in your own code. My personal opinion is that you should use the VCL graphics routines whenever possible, and only turn to the raw Windows API when you run up against an area of graphics not covered by the VCL.

The DrawShapes program demonstrates how easy it is to use the TCanvas object in a program. This application delineates the outlines of a simple paint program that has the capability to draw lines, rectangles, and ellipses. A screen shot of the program is shown in Figure 7.1, and the source for the program appears in Listings 7.1 and 7.2.

FIGURE 7.1.

The DrawShapes program shows how to create the lineaments of a simple paint program.

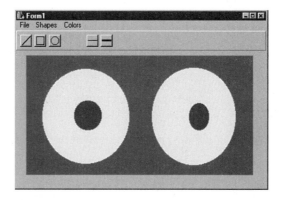

Listing 7.1. The header file for the DrawShapes program declares an enumerated type and several simple fields.

```
//////////////////////////////////////
// Main.cpp
// DrawShapes Example
// Copyright (c) 1997 by Charlie Calvert
//
#ifndef MainH
#define MainH
#include <vcl\Classes.hpp>
#include <vcl\Controls.hpp>
#include <vcl\StdCtrls.hpp>
```

```cpp
#include <vcl\Forms.hpp>
#include <vcl\Menus.hpp>
#include <vcl\ExtCtrls.hpp>
#include <vcl\Buttons.hpp>
#include <vcl\Dialogs.hpp>
enum TCurrentShape {csLine, csRectangle, csEllipse};
class TForm1 : public TForm
{
__published:
  TMainMenu *MainMenu1;
  TMenuItem *File1;
  TMenuItem *Open1;
  TMenuItem *Save1;
  TMenuItem *N1;
  TMenuItem *Rectangle1;
  TMenuItem *Shapes1;
  TMenuItem *Rectangle2;
  TMenuItem *Ellipse1;
  TMenuItem *Colors1;
  TMenuItem *Brush1;
  TMenuItem *Pen1;
  TPanel *Panel1;
  TSpeedButton *SpeedButton1;
  TSpeedButton *SpeedButton2;
  TSpeedButton *SpeedButton3;
  TSpeedButton *SpeedButton4;
  TMenuItem *Lines1;
  TColorDialog *ColorDialog1;
  TSpeedButton *SpeedButton5;
  void __fastcall FormMouseDown(TObject *Sender, TMouseButton Button,
                        TShiftState Shift, int X, int Y);
  void __fastcall FormMouseUp(TObject *Sender, TMouseButton Button,
                        TShiftState Shift, int X, int Y);
  void __fastcall FormMouseMove(TObject *Sender, TShiftState Shift, int X,
                        int Y);
  void __fastcall SpeedButton1Click(TObject *Sender);
  void __fastcall Brush1Click(TObject *Sender);
  void __fastcall Pen1Click(TObject *Sender);
  void __fastcall SpeedButton5Click(TObject *Sender);
private:
  TRect FShapeRect;
  TColor FPenColor;
  TColor FBrushColor;
  bool FDrawing;
  TCurrentShape FCurrentShape;
  int FPenThickness;
  void __fastcall DrawShape();
public:
  virtual __fastcall TForm1(TComponent* Owner);
};
extern TForm1 *Form1;
#endif
```

Listing 7.2. The main form for the DrawShapes program shows how to draw shapes on a canvas.

```cpp
////////////////////////////////////////
// Main.cpp
// DrawShapes Example
// Copyright (c) 1997 by Charlie Calvert
//
#include <vcl\vcl.h>
#pragma hdrstop
#include "Main.h"
#pragma resource "*.dfm"
TForm1 *Form1;
__fastcall TForm1::TForm1(TComponent* Owner)
: TForm(Owner)
{
  FDrawing= False;
  FCurrentShape = csRectangle;
  FBrushColor = clBlue;
  FPenColor = clYellow;
  FPenThickness = 1;
}
void __fastcall TForm1::FormMouseDown(TObject *Sender, TMouseButton Button,
                                      TShiftState Shift, int X, int Y)

{
  FShapeRect.Left = X;
  FShapeRect.Top = Y;
  FShapeRect.Right = - 32000;
  FDrawing = True;
}
void __fastcall TForm1::FormMouseUp(TObject *Sender, TMouseButton Button,
                                    TShiftState Shift, int X, int Y)

{
  FDrawing = False;
  FShapeRect.Right = X;
  FShapeRect.Bottom = Y;
  Canvas->Pen->Mode = pmCopy;
  DrawShape();
}
void __fastcall TForm1::DrawShape()
{
  Canvas->Brush->Color = FBrushColor;
  Canvas->Pen->Color = FPenColor;
  Canvas->Pen->Width = FPenThickness;
  switch (FCurrentShape)
  {
    case csLine:
      Canvas->MoveTo(FShapeRect.Left, FShapeRect.Top);
      Canvas->LineTo(FShapeRect.Right, FShapeRect.Bottom);
      break;
    case csRectangle:
      Canvas->Rectangle(FShapeRect.Left, FShapeRect.Top,
                        FShapeRect.Right, FShapeRect.Bottom);
      break;
    case csEllipse:
      Canvas->Ellipse(FShapeRect.Left, FShapeRect.Top,
                      FShapeRect.Right, FShapeRect.Bottom);
      break;
    default:
```

```
      ;
  }
}
void __fastcall TForm1::FormMouseMove(TObject *Sender,
                                  TShiftState Shift, int X, int Y)
{
  if (FDrawing)
  {
    Canvas->Pen->Mode = pmNotXor;
    if (FShapeRect.Right != -32000)
      DrawShape();
    FShapeRect.Right = X;
    FShapeRect.Bottom = Y;
    DrawShape();
  }
}
void __fastcall TForm1::SpeedButton1Click(TObject *Sender)
{
  FCurrentShape = TCurrentShape(dynamic_cast<TSpeedButton *>(Sender)->Tag);
}
void __fastcall TForm1::Brush1Click(TObject *Sender)
{
  ColorDialog1->Color = FBrushColor;
  if (ColorDialog1->Execute())
    FBrushColor = ColorDialog1->Color;
}
void __fastcall TForm1::Pen1Click(TObject *Sender)
{
  ColorDialog1->Color = FPenColor;
  if (ColorDialog1->Execute())
    FPenColor = ColorDialog1->Color;
}
void __fastcall TForm1::SpeedButton5Click(TObject *Sender)
{
  FPenThickness = dynamic_cast<TSpeedButton *>(Sender)->Tag;
}
```

This program enables you to draw lines, rectangles, and ellipses on the main form of the application. You can select the type of shape you want to work with through the menus or by clicking on speed buttons. The program also lets you set the color of the shapes you want to draw and specify the width and color of the border around the shape.

Pens and Brushes

When setting the color of a shape, you need to know that the filled area inside a shape gets set to the color of the current Brush for the canvas. The line that forms the border for the shape is controlled by the current Pen.

Here is how to set the current color and width of the Pen:

```
Canvas->Pen->Color = clBlue;
Canvas->Pen->Width = 5;
```

If you want to change the color of the Brush, you can write the following code:

```
Canvas->Brush->Color = clYellow;
```

I don't work with it in this program, but you can assign various styles to a Brush, as defined by the following enumerated type:

```
TBrushStyle { bsSolid, bsClear, bsHorizontal, bsVertical,
    bsFDiagonal, bsBDiagonal, bsCross, bsDiagCross };
```

By default, a Brush has the bsSolid type.

To set the style of a Brush, you would write code that looks like this:

```
Canvas->Brush->Style = bsSolid;
```

Brushes also have Color and Bitmap properties. The Bitmap property can be set to a small external bitmap image that defines the pattern for Brush.

There is only one method of the TBrush object that you would be likely to use. This method is called Assign, and it is used when you want to copy the characteristics of one brush to another brush.

Pens have all the same properties as Brushes, but they add a Width and Mode property. The Width property defines the width of the Pen in pixels, and the Mode property defines the type of operation to use when painting the Pen to the screen. These logical operations will be discussed further in just a few moments.

Rubber Banding

Before reading this section, fire up the DrawShapes program and practice drawing ellipses and rectangles onscreen so you can see how the rubber-band technique works. If for some reason you can't run the DrawShapes program, open up Windows Paint and draw some squares or circles by first clicking the appropriate icon from the Tools menu. Watch the way these programs create an elastic square or circle that you can drag around the desktop. Play with these shapes as you decide what dimensions and locations you want for your geometric figures.

These tools appear to be difficult for a programmer to create, but thanks to the Windows API, the code is relatively trivial. Following are the main steps involved, each of which is explained in-depth later in this section:

1. When the user clicks the left mouse button, DrawShapes "memorizes" the x and y coordinates of the WM_LBUTTONDOWN event.

2. As the user drags the mouse across the screen with the left button still down, DrawShapes draws a square or circle each time it gets a WM_MOUSEMOVE message. Just before painting each new shape, the program blanks out the previous square or circle. The dimensions of the new shape are calculated by combining the coordinates of the original WM_LBUTTONDOWN message with the current coordinates passed in the WM_MOUSEMOVE message.

3. When the user generates a `WM_LBUTTONUP` message, DrawShapes paints the final shape in the colors and pen size specified by the user.

Although this description obviously omits some important details, the outlines of the algorithm should take shape in your mind in the form of only a few relatively simple, logical strokes. Things get a bit more complicated when the details are mulled over one by one, but the fundamental steps should be relatively clear.

> **NOTE**
>
> In the previous numbered list, I give the names of the messages that generate VCL events. For instance, a `WM_LBUTTONDOWN` message generates an `OnMouseDown` event, the `WM_MOUSEMOVE` message generates an `OnMouseMove` event, and so on. I'm referring to the underlying messages because it is a good idea to remember the connection between VCL events and their associated Windows messages.

Zooming in on the details, here's a look at the response to a `WM_LBUTTONDOWN` message:

```
void __fastcall TForm1::FormMouseDown(TObject *Sender, TMouseButton Button,
  TShiftState Shift, int X, int Y)
{
  FShapeRect.Left = X;
  FShapeRect.Top = Y;
  FShapeRect.Right = - 32000;
  FDrawing = True;
}
```

FormMouseDown saves the location on which the mouse was clicked in the first two fields of a TRect structure called FShapeRect. FShapeRect is declared as a field of TForm1. I set the Right field of the TRect structure to a large negative number so I know that this is the first time that I need to start tracking the user's mouse movements. This is necessary because the very first shape I draw needs to be treated as a special case.

The last thing done in the FormMouseDown method is to set a private variable of TForm1 called FDrawing to True. This lets the program know that the user has started a drawing operation.

After the left mouse button is pressed, the program picks up all `WM_MOUSEMOVE` messages that come flying into DrawShape's ken:

```
void __fastcall TForm1::FormMouseMove(TObject *Sender,
                                      TShiftState Shift, int X, int Y)
{
  if (FDrawing)
  {
    Canvas->Pen->Mode = pmNotXor;
    if (FShapeRect.Right != -32000)
      DrawShape();
    FShapeRect.Right = X;
    FShapeRect.Bottom = Y;
    DrawShape();
  }
}
```

The first line of the function uses one of several possible techniques for checking to see if the left mouse button is down. If the button isn't down, the function ignores the message. If it is down, the function gets the device context, sets the Pen's drawing mode to pmNotXor, memorizes the current dimensions of the figure, draws it, and releases the device context.

The Mode property of a TPen object sets the current drawing mode in a manner similar to the way the last parameter in BitBlt sets the current painting mode. You can achieve the same effect by directly calling the Windows API function called SetROP2. In this case, DrawShape uses the logical XOR and NOT operations to blit the elastic image to the screen. This logical operation is chosen because it paints the old shape directly on top of the original image, thereby effectively erasing each shape:

- If you XOR a square to the screen, the square will show up clearly.
- If you XOR that same image again in the same location, the image will disappear.

Such are the virtues of simple logical operations in graphics mode.

NOTE

Aficionados of graphics logic will note that the logical operation employed by DrawShapes is a variation on the exclusive OR (XOR) operation. This variation ensures that the fill in the center of the shape to be drawn won't blot out what's beneath it. The Microsoft documentation explains the difference like this:

```
R2_XOR:         final pixel = pen ^ screen pixel
R2_NOTXORPEN : final pixel = ~(pen ^ screen pixel)
```

This code tests to see whether the pixels to be XORed belong to a pen.

Don't waste too much time worrying about logical operations and how they work. If they interest you, fine; if they don't, that's okay. The subject matter of this book is programming, not logic.

If you were working directly in the Windows API, you would work with a constant called RT_NOTXORPEN rather than pmNotXor. I have to confess that the VCL's tendency to rename constants used by the Windows API is not a very winning trait. Granted, the people in Redmond who came up with many of those identifiers deserve some terrible, nameless, fate, but once the damage had been done it might have been simpler to stick with the original constants. That way people would not have to memorize two sets of identifiers, one for use with the VCL, and the other for use with the Windows API. You cannot use the Windows constants in place of the VCL constants, as the various identifiers do not map down to the same value.

Despite these objections, I still think it is wise to use the VCL rather than writing directly to the Windows API. The VCL is much safer and much easier to use. The performance from most VCL objects is great, and in many cases it will be better than what most programmers could achieve writing directly to the Windows API.

Notice that `FormMouseMove` calls `DrawShape` twice. The first time, it passes in the dimensions of the old figure that needs to be erased. That means it XORs the same image directly on top of the original image, thereby erasing it. Then `FormMouseMove` records the location of the latest WM_MOUSEMOVE message and passes this new information to `DrawShape`, which paints the new image to the screen. This whole process is repeated over and over again (at incredible speeds) until the user lifts the left mouse button.

In the `DrawImage` function, `Metaphor` first checks to see which shape the user has selected and then proceeds to draw that shape to the screen using the current pen and fill color:

```
void __fastcall TForm1::DrawShape()
{
  Canvas->Brush->Color = FBrushColor;
  Canvas->Brush->Style = bsSolid;
  Canvas->Pen->Color = FPenColor;
  Canvas->Pen->Width = FPenThickness;
  switch (FCurrentShape)
  {
    case csLine:
      Canvas->MoveTo(FShapeRect.Left, FShapeRect.Top);
      Canvas->LineTo(FShapeRect.Right, FShapeRect.Bottom);
      break;
    case csRectangle:
      Canvas->Rectangle(FShapeRect.Left, FShapeRect.Top,
                        FShapeRect.Right, FShapeRect.Bottom);
      break;
    case csEllipse:
      Canvas->Ellipse(FShapeRect.Left, FShapeRect.Top,
                      FShapeRect.Right, FShapeRect.Bottom);
      break;
    default:
      ;
  }
}
```

This code sets the current `Pen` and `Brush` to the values chosen by the user. It then uses a `switch` statement to select the proper type of shape to draw to the screen. Most of these private variables such as `FPenColor` are set by allowing the user to make selections from the menu. To see exactly how this works, you can study the code of the application.

Notice that when drawing these shapes, there is no need to track the HDC of the current `Canvas`. One of the primary goals of the `TCanvas` object is to completely hide the HDC from the user. I discuss this matter in more depth in the next section of the chapter, "To GDI or not to GDI."

The final step in the whole operation occurs when the user lifts his finger off the mouse:

```
void __fastcall TForm1::FormMouseUp(TObject *Sender, TMouseButton Button,
                                    TShiftState Shift, int X, int Y)
{
  FDrawing = False;
  FShapeRect.Right = X;
  FShapeRect.Bottom = Y;
```

```
Canvas->Pen->Mode = pmCopy;
DrawShape();
}
```

This code performs the following actions:

- A flag is set stating that the user has decided to stop drawing.
- The final dimensions of the shape are recorded.
- The mode for the Pen is switched from pmNotXor to the default value, which is pmCopy.
- The final image is painted to the screen.

The code that paints the final shape takes into account the colors and the pen thickness that the user selected with the menus.

Well, there you have it. That's how you draw shapes to the screen using the rubber-band technique. Overall, if you take one thing at a time, the process isn't too complicated. Just so you can keep those steps clear in your mind, here they are again:

- Remember where the WM_LBUTTONDOWN message took place.
- Draw the shape each time you get a WM_MOUSEMOVE message.
- Draw the final shape when you get a WM_LBUTTONUP message.

That's all there is to it.

To GDI or not to GDI

The VCL will never cut you off completely from the underlying Windows API code. If you want to work at the Windows API level, you can do so. In fact, you can often write code that mixes VCL and raw Windows API code.

If you want to access the HDC for a window, you can get at it through the Handle property of the canvas:

```
MyOldPenHandle = SelectObject(Canvas->Handle, MyPen->Handle);
```

In this case you are copying the Handle of a Pen object into the HDC of the TCanvas object.

Having free access to the Handle of the TCanvas object can be useful at times, but the longer I use the VCL, the less inclined I am to use it. The simple truth of the matter is that I now believe that it is best to let an object of some sort handle all chores that require serious housekeeping. This course of action allows me to rely on the object's internal logic to correctly track the resources involved.

If you are not using the VCL, whenever you select something into an HDC, you need to keep track of the resources pumped out of the HDC by the selection. When you are done, you should then copy the old Handle back into the HDC. If you accidentally lose track of a resource, you can upset the balance of the entire operating system. Clearly, this type of process is error-prone and best managed by an object that can be debugged once and reused many times. My options, therefore, are to either write the object myself or use the existing code found in the VCL. In most cases, I simply take the simplest course and use the excellent TCanvas object provided by the VCL.

When I do decide to manage an interaction with the GDI myself, I often prefer to get hold of my own HDC and ignore the TCanvas object altogether. The reason I take this course is simply that the TCanvas object will sometimes maintain the Canvas's HDC on its own, and I therefore can't have complete control over what is happening to it.

Here is a simple example of how to use the GDI directly inside a VCL program:

```
HDC DC = GetDC(Form1->Handle);
HFONT OldFont = SelectObject(DC, Canvas->Font->Handle);
TextOut(DC, 1, 100, "Text", 4);
SelectObject(DC, OldFont);
ReleaseDC(Form1->Handle, DC);
```

If you look at the code shown here, you will see that I get my own DC by calling the Windows API function GetDC. I then select a new font into the DC. Notice that I use the VCL TFont object. I usually find it easier to manage Fonts, Pens, and Brushes with VCL objects than with raw Windows API code. However, if you want to create your own fonts with raw Windows API code, you are free to do so.

Here is an example of creating a VCL Font object from scratch:

```
TFont *Font = new TFont();
Font->Name = "Time New Roman";
Font->Size = 25;
Font->Style = TFontStyles() << fsItalic << fsBold;
HDC DC = GetDC(Form1->Handle);
HFONT OldFont = SelectObject(DC, Font->Handle);
TextOut(DC, 1, 100, "Text", 4);
SelectObject(DC, OldFont);
ReleaseDC(Form1->Handle, DC);
delete Font;
```

This code allocates memory for a Font object, assigns some values to its key properties, and then copies the Handle of the Font object into the current DC. Notice that I still have to save the old Font handle and copy it back into the DC when I am done with it. This is the type of operation that I prefer to have handled by an object. When I am done with the example code shown here, I delete the Font object I created.

Examples such as the ones you have just seen show that you can use the Windows API by itself inside a VCL graphics operation, or you can combine VCL code with raw GDI code. The course you choose will be dictated by your particular needs. My suggestion, however, is to use the VCL whenever possible, and to fall back on the Windows API only when strictly necessary. The primary reason for this preference is that it is safer to use the VCL than to write directly to the Windows API. It is also easier to use the VCL than the raw Windows API, but that argument has a secondary importance in my mind.

Using TImage, Saving and Loading Bitmaps

If you work with the DrawShapes program for awhile, you will find that it has several weaknesses that cry out for correction. In particular, the program cannot save an image to disk, and it cannot repaint the current image if you temporarily cover it up with another program.

Fixing these problems turns out to be remarkably simple. The key functionality to add to the program is all bound up in a single component called TImage. This control provides you with a Canvas on which you can draw, and gives you the ability to convert this Canvas into a bitmap.

The BitmapShapes program, shown in Listing 7.3, shows how to proceed in the creation of an updated DrawShapes program that can save files to disk, and can automatically redraw an image if you switch back to the main form from another program.

Listing 7.3. The main module for the BitmapShapes program.

```
/////////////////////////////////////////
// Main.cpp
// DrawShapes Example
// Copyright (c) 1997 by Charlie Calvert
//
#include <vcl\vcl.h>
#pragma hdrstop
#include "Main.h"
#pragma resource "*.dfm"
TForm1 *Form1;
__fastcall TForm1::TForm1(TComponent* Owner)
: TForm(Owner)
{
  FDrawing= False;
  FCurrentShape = csRectangle;
  FBrushColor = clBlue;
  FPenColor = clYellow;
  FPenThickness = 1;
}
void __fastcall TForm1::FormMouseDown(TObject *Sender, TMouseButton Button,
                                 TShiftState Shift, int X, int Y)

{
  FShapeRect.Left = X;
  FShapeRect.Top = Y;
  FShapeRect.Right = - 32000;
  FDrawing = True;
}
void __fastcall TForm1::FormMouseUp(TObject *Sender, TMouseButton Button,
                                TShiftState Shift, int X, int Y)

{
  FDrawing = False;
  FShapeRect.Right = X;
  FShapeRect.Bottom = Y;
  Image1->Canvas->Pen->Mode = pmCopy;
  DrawShape();
}
void __fastcall TForm1::DrawShape()
```

```
{
  Image1->Canvas->Brush->Color = FBrushColor;
  Image1->Canvas->Brush->Style = bsSolid;
  Image1->Canvas->Pen->Color = FPenColor;
  Image1->Canvas->Pen->Width = FPenThickness;
  switch (FCurrentShape)
  {
    case csLine:
      Image1->Canvas->MoveTo(FShapeRect.Left, FShapeRect.Top);
      Image1->Canvas->LineTo(FShapeRect.Right, FShapeRect.Bottom);
      break;
    case csRectangle:
      Image1->Canvas->Rectangle(FShapeRect.Left, FShapeRect.Top,
        FShapeRect.Right, FShapeRect.Bottom);
      break;
    case csEllipse:
        Image1->Canvas->Ellipse(FShapeRect.Left, FShapeRect.Top,
        FShapeRect.Right, FShapeRect.Bottom);
      break;
    default:
      ;
  }
}
void __fastcall TForm1::FormMouseMove(TObject *Sender,
                                      TShiftState Shift, int X, int Y)
{
  if (FDrawing)
  {
    Image1->Canvas->Pen->Mode = pmNotXor;
    if (FShapeRect.Right != -32000)
      DrawShape();
    FShapeRect.Right = X;
    FShapeRect.Bottom = Y;
    DrawShape();
  }
}
void __fastcall TForm1::SpeedButton1Click(TObject *Sender)
{
  FCurrentShape = TCurrentShape(dynamic_cast<TSpeedButton *>(Sender)->Tag);
}
void __fastcall TForm1::Brush1Click(TObject *Sender)
{
  ColorDialog1->Color = FBrushColor;
  if (ColorDialog1->Execute())
    FBrushColor = ColorDialog1->Color;
}
void __fastcall TForm1::Pen1Click(TObject *Sender)
{
  ColorDialog1->Color = FPenColor;
  if (ColorDialog1->Execute())
    FPenColor = ColorDialog1->Color;
}
void __fastcall TForm1::SpeedButton5Click(TObject *Sender)
{
  FPenThickness = dynamic_cast<TSpeedButton *>(Sender)->Tag;
}
void __fastcall TForm1::Save1Click(TObject *Sender)
{
```

continues

Listing 7.3. continued

```cpp
    if (SaveDialog1->Execute())
    {
      Image1->Picture->SaveToFile(SaveDialog1->FileName);
    }
  }
void __fastcall TForm1::Open1Click(TObject *Sender)
{
  if (OpenDialog1->Execute())
  {
    Image1->Picture->LoadFromFile(OpenDialog1->FileName);
  }
}
void __fastcall TForm1::Exit1Click(TObject *Sender)
{
  Close();
}
```

The key change from the DrawShapes program is that all of the Canvas operations are performed on the Canvas of a TImage control rather than directly on the Canvas of a form:

```cpp
Image1->Canvas->MoveTo(FShapeRect.Left, FShapeRect.Top);
Image1->Canvas->LineTo(FShapeRect.Right, FShapeRect.Bottom);
```

A TImage control is designed explicitly for the type of operations undertaken by this program. In particular, it maintains an internal bitmap into which images are automatically drawn.

When it comes time to save the picture you have created, you can do so with one line of code:

```cpp
void __fastcall TForm1::Save1Click(TObject *Sender)
{
  if (SaveDialog1->Execute())
  {
    Image1->Picture->SaveToFile(SaveDialog1->FileName);
  }
}
```

Loading a file into memory from disk is also a simple one-line operation:

```cpp
void __fastcall TForm1::Open1Click(TObject *Sender)
{
  if (OpenDialog1->Execute())
  {
    Image1->Picture->LoadFromFile(OpenDialog1->FileName);
  }
}
```

Both of the preceding calls assume that you have dropped a TOpenDialog onto the main form of your application. The TOpenDialog object is extremely easy to use, so you should have no trouble learning how to use it from the online help.

> **NOTE**
>
> When I opt not to explain an object such as `TOpenDialog`, my intention is not to ignore the needs of this book's readers, but rather to avoid inserting boring, repetitive information into the book. If you really crave a reference other than the online help for this kind of information, you should check the bookstore for introductory texts that cover this kind of material.

If you want a bit more flexibility, and desire to have a separate `TBitmap` object which you can use for your own purposes, it is easy to create one from the image you created with this program. To proceed, just create a `TBitmap` object, and then use the `Assign` method to copy the picture from the `TImage` control to your bitmap:

```
Graphics::TBitmap *Bitmap = new Graphics::TBitmap();
Bitmap->Assign(Image1->Picture->Graphic);
Bitmap->SaveToFile(SaveDialog1->FileName);
delete Bitmap;
```

In this example I save the bitmap to file and then delete the object when I am through with it. In the context of the current program, this doesn't make a great deal of sense. However, code like this demonstrates some of the functionality of the `TBitmap` object. I qualify the reference to `TBitmap` with `Graphics.Hpp`, because there are two `TBitmap` declarations in the header files included in most BCB programs.

Working with Metafiles

Bitmaps are very convenient and are often the best way to work with graphic images. However, BCB also lets you work with enhanced metafiles.

Metafiles are collections of shapes drawn into a device context. Internally, they are little more than a list of GDI calls that can be played back on demand to create a picture. Metafiles have two big advantages over bitmaps:

- They are very small. The same image that might take hundreds of KB to save in bitmaps can often be saved in a metafile of just 10 or 20 thousand bytes.
- Because metafiles consist of a series of shapes, you can, at least potentially, iterate through the list of shapes in a picture and edit them one at a time. This can give you a very powerful ability to precisely edit the contents of a picture.

The disadvantage of metafiles is that they must consist only of a series of GDI calls. As a result, you can't easily transform a photograph or a scanned image into a metafile. Metafiles are best defined as a simple way of preserving text, or as a simple means of storing a series of fairly simple shapes such as a line drawing. In the hands of a good artist, however, you can get metafiles to show some fairly powerful images. (See Figure 7.2.)

FIGURE 7.2.

A grayscale version of a colorful metafile that ships with Microsoft Office shows some of the power of this technology.

There are two types of metafiles available to Windows users. One has the extension .WMF, and is primarily designed for use in the 16-bit world. The second type of file has the extension .EMF, for Enhanced Metafile. These latter types of files are designed for use in the 32-bit world. I find them much more powerful than their 16-bit cousins.

The code shown in the forthcoming MetaShapes program is designed to work only with enhanced metafiles. BCB will save a file as a regular metafile if you give it an extension of .WMF, and it will save it as an enhanced metafile if you give it an extension of .EMF. When using BCB, it is best to stick with enhanced metafiles. If you have some .WMF files you want to use with BCB, you might want to find a third-party tool that will convert your .WMF into an .EMF.

The MetaShapes program is very similar to the DrawShapes and BitmapShapes programs. It has the same capabilities as the BitmapShapes program in terms of its capability to save and preserve images, only it works with metafiles rather than bitmaps. Metafiles are many times smaller than standard .BMP files.

There is no TImage control for metafiles, so you have to do a little more work to make this system function properly. In particular, you have to explicitly open a metafile and then draw directly into it, as shown in Listing 7.4 and 7.5.

Listing 7.4. The header for the MetaShapes program.

```
/////////////////////////////////////
// Main.h
// MetaShapes Example
// Copyright (c) 1997 by Charlie Calvert
//
#ifndef MainH
#define MainH
#include <vcl\Classes.hpp>
#include <vcl\Controls.hpp>
#include <vcl\StdCtrls.hpp>
#include <vcl\Forms.hpp>
#include <vcl\Menus.hpp>
#include <vcl\ExtCtrls.hpp>
#include <vcl\Buttons.hpp>
```

```cpp
#include <vcl\Dialogs.hpp>

enum TCurrentShape {csLine, csRectangle, csEllipse};

class TForm1 : public TForm
{
__published:
  TMainMenu *MainMenu1;
  TMenuItem *File1;
  TMenuItem *Open1;
  TMenuItem *Save1;
  TMenuItem *N1;
  TMenuItem *Exit1;
  TMenuItem *Shapes1;
  TMenuItem *Rectangle2;
  TMenuItem *Ellipse1;
  TMenuItem *Colors1;
  TMenuItem *Brush1;
  TMenuItem *Pen1;
  TPanel *Panel1;
  TSpeedButton *SpeedButton1;
  TSpeedButton *SpeedButton2;
  TSpeedButton *SpeedButton3;
  TSpeedButton *SpeedButton4;
  TMenuItem *Lines1;
  TColorDialog *ColorDialog1;
  TSpeedButton *SpeedButton5;
  TMenuItem *New1;
  TPaintBox *PaintBox1;
  TSaveDialog *SaveDialog1;
  TOpenDialog *OpenDialog1;
  void __fastcall FormMouseDown(TObject *Sender, TMouseButton Button,
                                TShiftState Shift, int X, int Y);
  void __fastcall FormMouseUp(TObject *Sender, TMouseButton Button,
                              TShiftState Shift, int X, int Y);
  void __fastcall FormMouseMove(TObject *Sender, TShiftState Shift, int X,
                                int Y);
  void __fastcall SpeedButton1Click(TObject *Sender);
  void __fastcall Brush1Click(TObject *Sender);
  void __fastcall Pen1Click(TObject *Sender);
  void __fastcall SpeedButton5Click(TObject *Sender);
  void __fastcall New1Click(TObject *Sender);
  void __fastcall Exit1Click(TObject *Sender);
  void __fastcall PaintBox1Paint(TObject *Sender);
  void __fastcall FormDestroy(TObject *Sender);
  void __fastcall Save1Click(TObject *Sender);
  void __fastcall Open1Click(TObject *Sender);
private:
  TRect FShapeRect;
  TColor FPenColor;
  TColor FBrushColor;
  bool FDrawing;
  TCurrentShape FCurrentShape;
  int FPenThickness;
  TMetafile* MyMetafile;
  TMetafileCanvas* MyCanvas;
  void __fastcall DrawShape();
public:
```

continues

Listing 7.4. continued

```
  virtual __fastcall TForm1(TComponent* Owner);
};

extern TForm1 *Form1;

#endif
```

Listing 7.5. The MetaShapes program shows how to draw into a metafile and save it to disk.

```
//////////////////////////////////////
// Main.cpp
// MetaShapes Example
// Copyright (c) 1997 by Charlie Calvert
//
#include <vcl\vcl.h>
#pragma hdrstop
#include "Main.h"
#pragma resource "*.dfm"

TForm1 *Form1;

__fastcall TForm1::TForm1(TComponent* Owner)
: TForm(Owner)
{
  FDrawing= False;
  FCurrentShape = csRectangle;
  FBrushColor = clBlue;
  FPenColor = clYellow;
  FPenThickness = 1;
  MyMetafile = new TMetafile;
  MyCanvas = new TMetafileCanvas(MyMetafile, PaintBox1->Canvas->Handle);
}

void __fastcall TForm1::FormMouseDown(TObject *Sender, TMouseButton Button,
                                      TShiftState Shift, int X, int Y)

{
  FShapeRect.Left = X;
  FShapeRect.Top = Y;
  FShapeRect.Right = - 32000;
  FDrawing = True;
}

void __fastcall TForm1::FormMouseUp(TObject *Sender, TMouseButton Button,
                                    TShiftState Shift, int X, int Y)

{
  if (FDrawing)
  {
    FDrawing = False;
    FShapeRect.Right = X;
    FShapeRect.Bottom = Y;
    PaintBox1->Canvas->Pen->Mode = pmCopy;
    MyCanvas->Pen->Mode = pmCopy;
    DrawShape();
  }
```

```
}

void __fastcall TForm1::DrawShape()
{
  PaintBox1->Canvas->Brush->Color = FBrushColor;
  PaintBox1->Canvas->Brush->Style = bsSolid;
  PaintBox1->Canvas->Pen->Color = FPenColor;
  PaintBox1->Canvas->Pen->Width = FPenThickness;

  MyCanvas->Brush->Color = FBrushColor;
  MyCanvas->Brush->Style = bsSolid;
  MyCanvas->Pen->Color = FPenColor;
  MyCanvas->Pen->Width = FPenThickness;

  switch (FCurrentShape)
  {
    case csLine:
      MyCanvas->MoveTo(FShapeRect.Left, FShapeRect.Top);
      MyCanvas->LineTo(FShapeRect.Right, FShapeRect.Bottom);
      PaintBox1->Canvas->MoveTo(FShapeRect.Left, FShapeRect.Top);
      PaintBox1->Canvas->LineTo(FShapeRect.Right, FShapeRect.Bottom);
      break;

    case csRectangle:
      PaintBox1->Canvas->Rectangle(FShapeRect.Left, FShapeRect.Top,
                                   FShapeRect.Right, FShapeRect.Bottom);
      MyCanvas->Rectangle(FShapeRect.Left, FShapeRect.Top,
                          FShapeRect.Right, FShapeRect.Bottom);
      break;

    case csEllipse:
      PaintBox1->Canvas->Ellipse(FShapeRect.Left, FShapeRect.Top,
                                 FShapeRect.Right, FShapeRect.Bottom);
      MyCanvas->Ellipse(FShapeRect.Left, FShapeRect.Top,
                        FShapeRect.Right, FShapeRect.Bottom);
      break;

    default:
      ;

  }
}

void __fastcall TForm1::FormMouseMove(TObject *Sender,
                                      TShiftState Shift, int X, int Y)
{
  if (FDrawing)
  {
    PaintBox1->Canvas->Pen->Mode = pmNotXor;
    MyCanvas->Pen->Mode = pmNotXor;
    if (FShapeRect.Right != -32000)
      DrawShape();
    FShapeRect.Right = X;
    FShapeRect.Bottom = Y;
    DrawShape();
  }
}
```

continues

Listing 7.5. continued

```cpp
void __fastcall TForm1::SpeedButton1Click(TObject *Sender)
{
  FCurrentShape = TCurrentShape(dynamic_cast<TSpeedButton *>(Sender)->Tag);
}

void __fastcall TForm1::Brush1Click(TObject *Sender)
{
  ColorDialog1->Color = FBrushColor;
  if (ColorDialog1->Execute())
    FBrushColor = ColorDialog1->Color;
}

void __fastcall TForm1::Pen1Click(TObject *Sender)
{
  ColorDialog1->Color = FPenColor;
  if (ColorDialog1->Execute())
    FPenColor = ColorDialog1->Color;
}

void __fastcall TForm1::SpeedButton5Click(TObject *Sender)
{
  FPenThickness = dynamic_cast<TSpeedButton *>(Sender)->Tag;
}

void __fastcall TForm1::New1Click(TObject *Sender)
{
  delete MyCanvas;
  delete MyMetafile;

  MyMetafile = new TMetafile;
  MyCanvas = new TMetafileCanvas(MyMetafile, 0);
  InvalidateRect(Handle, NULL, True);
}

void __fastcall TForm1::PaintBox1Paint(TObject *Sender)
{
  delete MyCanvas;
  if (MyMetafile)
    PaintBox1->Canvas->Draw(0,0,MyMetafile);
  MyCanvas = new TMetafileCanvas(MyMetafile, PaintBox1->Canvas->Handle);
  MyCanvas->Draw(0, 0, MyMetafile);
}

void __fastcall TForm1::FormDestroy(TObject *Sender)
{
  delete MyCanvas;
}

void __fastcall TForm1::Exit1Click(TObject *Sender)
{
  Close();
}

void __fastcall TForm1::Save1Click(TObject *Sender)
{
  if (SaveDialog1->Execute())
```

```
  {
    delete MyCanvas;
    MyMetafile->SaveToFile(SaveDialog1->FileName);
    MyCanvas = new TMetafileCanvas(MyMetafile, 0);
    MyCanvas->Draw(0, 0, MyMetafile);
  }
}

void __fastcall TForm1::Open1Click(TObject *Sender)
{
  if (OpenDialog1->Execute())
  {
    FShapeRect = Rect(0, 0, 0, 0);
    delete MyCanvas;
    TFileStream *Stream = new TFileStream(OpenDialog1->FileName, fmOpenRead);
    MyMetafile->LoadFromStream(Stream);
    MyCanvas = new TMetafileCanvas(MyMetafile, PaintBox1->Canvas->Handle);
    MyCanvas->Draw(0, 0, MyMetafile);
    PaintBox1->Canvas->Draw(0, 0, MyMetafile);
    Stream->Free();
  }
}
```

This program works just like the BitmapShapes program shown previously, in that it lets you draw colored shapes to the screen and then save them to file. A screenshot of the program is shown in Figure 7.3.

FIGURE 7.3.

The MetaShapes program in action.

When working with metafiles, you need to create both a TMetafile object and a TMetafileCanvas object.

```
MyMetafile = new TMetafile;
MyCanvas = new TMetafileCanvas(MyMetafile, PaintBox1->Canvas->Handle);
```

Notice that the TMetafileCanvas is explicitly associated with a particular TMetafile object. Specifically, the TMetaFile object is passed in as the first parameter of the TMetaFileCanvas object's constructor. These two classes are designed to work in tandem, and both pieces must be present if you want to create a metafile.

Here is a simple example of how to draw into a `TMetafile` canvas:

```
MyCanvas->Ellipse(FShapeRect.Left, FShapeRect.Top,
                  FShapeRect.Right, FShapeRect.Bottom);
```

This code looks exactly like any other call to the `TCanvas::Ellipse`, only this time I am writing into a `TMetafileCanvas` rather than a form's `Canvas`.

NOTE

The VCL preserves the `Canvas` metaphor in a wide variety of contexts, such as when you are working with metafiles or bitmaps. This enables you to learn one set of commands, and to then apply them to a wide variety of objects. As you will see later in the book, this type of functionality derives in part from a judicious and intelligent use of polymorphism.

Basing a suite of objects on one model enables users to quickly get up to speed on new technologies. The underlying code for creating bitmaps is very different from the code for creating metafiles. But the `TCanvas` object enables you to treat each operation as if it were nearly identical. People who are interested in object design should contemplate the elegance of this implementation.

If you only want to display a metafile, you can work solely with the `TMetafile` object. However, if you want to create metafiles, to draw images into a metafile, you need a `TMetafileCanvas` object. You can draw directly into a `TMetafileCanvas`, but when you want to display the image to the user, you need to delete the object so that its contents will be transferred into a metafile that can be displayed for the user:

```
delete MyCanvas;
PaintBox1->Canvas->Draw(0,0,MyMetafile);
```

In this code I am using a `PaintBox` as the surface on which to display the metafile. The code first deletes the `TMetafileCanvas`, thereby transferring the painting from the `TMetafileCanvas` to the `TMetafile`. This implementation is, I suppose, a bit awkward, but once you understand the principle involved, it should not cause you any serious difficulty.

There is no particular connection between metafiles and the `TPaintBox` object. In fact, I could just as easily have painted directly into a `TForm`. The reason I chose `TPaintBox` is that it enables me to easily define a subsection of a form that can be used as a surface on which to paint. In particular, part of the form in the `MetaShapes` program is covered by a `TPanel` object. To make sure that the user can see the entire canvas on which he will be painting, I used a `TPaintBox`.

If you are interested in these matters, you might want to open up `EXTCTRLS.HPP` and compare the declarations for `TPaintBox` and `TImage`. Both of these controls are descendants of `TGraphicControl`, and both offer similar functionality. The big difference between them is that `TImage` has an underlying bitmap, while `TPaintBox` has a simpler, sparer architecture.

By now it has probably occurred to you that there is no simple means for displaying a metafile to the user at the time it is being created. In particular, you can't show it to the user without first deleting the TMetafileCanvas. To avoid performing this action too often, I simply record the user's motions into both the TMetafileCanvas and the Canvas for the main form:

```
PaintBox1->Canvas->Brush->Color = FBrushColor;
 ... // Code ommitted
MyCanvas->Brush->Color = FBrushColor;
 ...// Code ommitted
switch (FCurrentShape)
{
  case csLine:
    MyCanvas->MoveTo(FShapeRect.Left, FShapeRect.Top);
    MyCanvas->LineTo(FShapeRect.Right, FShapeRect.Bottom);
    PaintBox1->Canvas->MoveTo(FShapeRect.Left, FShapeRect.Top);
    PaintBox1->Canvas->LineTo(FShapeRect.Right, FShapeRect.Bottom);
    break;
    ... // etc
```

This duplication of code, while bothersome, is not really terribly costly in terms of what it is adding to the size of my executable. Needless to say, I use this technique so that the user can see what he or she is painting.

If the user flips away from the program and covers it with another application, I need to re-paint the image when the user flips back to MetaShapes:

```
void __fastcall TForm1::PaintBox1Paint(TObject *Sender)
{
  delete MyCanvas;
  PaintBox1->Canvas->Draw(0,0,MyMetafile);
  MyCanvas = new TMetafileCanvas(MyMetafile, PaintBox1->Canvas->Handle);
  MyCanvas->Draw(0, 0, MyMetafile);
}
```

As you can see, this code deletes the TMetafileCanvas and then paints the current image to the screen. I then create a new TMetafileCanvas and paint the contents of the current metafile into it:

```
MyCanvas->Draw(0, 0, MyMetafile);
```

This same process occurs when I load a metafile from disk:

```
void __fastcall TForm1::Open1Click(TObject *Sender)
{
  if (OpenDialog1->Execute())
  {
    delete MyCanvas;
    TFileStream *Stream = new TFileStream(OpenDialog1->FileName, fmOpenRead);
    MyMetafile->LoadFromStream(Stream);
    MyCanvas = new TMetafileCanvas(MyMetafile, PaintBox1->Canvas->Handle);
    MyCanvas->Draw(0, 0, MyMetafile);
    PaintBox1->Canvas->Draw(0, 0, MyMetafile);
  }
}
```

In this code, I delete the contents of any current TMetafileCanvas, not because I want to draw it, but because I want to create a new, blank surface on which to paint. I then load a metafile from disk and create a new TMetafileCanvas into which I can paint the contents of the freshly loaded metafile:

```
MyCanvas->Draw(0, 0, MyMetafile);
```

Finally, the program plays the contents of the metafile back to the user:

```
PaintBox1->Canvas->Draw(0, 0, MyMetafile);
```

When you are playing back fairly large metafiles, you can sometimes see the shapes being painted to the screen one at a time. This helps to illustrate the fact that metafiles are literally just lists of GDI calls with their related parameters and device contexts carefully preserved. There are calls available that enable you to walk through these lists and delete or modify individual items. However, I do not take the code in this program quite that far. If you master this process, however, you have the rudiments of a CAD or sophisticated drawing program on your hands.

The only thing left to discuss is saving metafiles to disk, which turns out to be a simple process:

```
void __fastcall TForm1::Save1Click(TObject *Sender)
{
  if (SaveDialog1->Execute())
  {
    delete MyCanvas;
    MyMetafile->SaveToFile(SaveDialog1->FileName);
    MyCanvas = new TMetafileCanvas(MyMetafile, 0);
    MyCanvas->Draw(0, 0, MyMetafile);
  }
}
```

This code deletes the current TMetafileCanvas, thereby assuring that the TMetafile object is up-to-date. It then makes a call to the TMetafile::SaveToFile method. Finally, it creates a new TMetafileCanvas and draws the contents of the current metafile into it, which enables the user to continue editing the picture after the save.

That is all I'm going to say about metafiles. Admittedly, this is a somewhat esoteric subject from the point of view of many programmers. However, metafiles are a useful tool that can be a great help if you want to save text, or a series of images, in a small, compact file.

When I talk about saving text to a metafile, remember that all calls to draw text on the screen are simply calls into the Windows GDI. You can therefore save these calls in a metafile. Many fancy programs that enable you to quickly scroll through large volumes of text are using metafiles as part of their underlying technology.

Working with Fonts

The raw Windows API code for working with fonts is quite complex. The VCL, however, makes fonts easy to use.

You have already seen an example of using the TFont object. The basic idea is simply that a TFont object has eight key properties called Color, Handle, Height, Name, Pitch, PixelsPerInch, Size, and Style. It is a simple matter to create a TFont object and change its properties:

```
TFont *MyFont = new TFont();
MyFont->Name = "BookwomanSH";
MyFont->Size = 24;
MyFont->Style = TFontStyles() << fsBold;
Form1->Font = MyFont;
```

In this case, the programmer has no obligation to delete the TFont object, because its ownership is assumed by the form in the last line. If you did not pass the ownership of the object over to the Form, you would need to explicitly delete the Font when you were through with it:

```
delete MyFont;
```

Most of the time, if you want to give the user the capability to select a font at runtime, you should use the TFontDialog from the dialogs page of the Component Palette. However, you can iterate through all the fonts on your system by using the Fonts field of the TScreen object.

The TScreen object is used primarily for keeping track of the active forms in your application and the current cursor. However, you can also use it for iterating through all the available fonts on the system. These fonts are kept in a TStringList object that is accessible through a property called Fonts:

```
ListBox1->Items = Screen->Fonts;
```

The screen object is created automatically by the VCL, and is available to all applications as a global object.

Besides the screen fonts, some programmers might also be interested in accessing the available printer fonts. These can be accessed through an object called TPrinter, which is kept in a module called PRINTERS.HPP:

```
TPrinter *Printer = new TPrinter();
ListBox2->Items = Printer->Fonts;
delete Printer;
```

The BCBFonts program from this book's CD-ROM gives a simple example of how to iterate through all the fonts on the system so the user can pick and choose from them. The source code for the program is shown in Listing 7.6.

Listing 7.6. The main module for the BCBFonts program shows how to view a list of the currently available fonts.

```
/////////////////////////////////////
// Main.cpp
// Project: BCBFonts
// Copyright (c) 1997 by Charlie Calvert
//
```

continues

Listing 7.6. continued

```cpp
#include <vcl\vcl.h>
#include <vcl\printers.hpp>
#pragma hdrstop
#include "Main.h"
#pragma resource "*.dfm"
TForm1 *Form1;
__fastcall TForm1::TForm1(TComponent* Owner)
: TForm(Owner)
{
  ListBox1->Items = Screen->Fonts;
  TPrinter *Printer = new TPrinter();
  ListBox2->Items = Printer->Fonts;
  delete Printer;
  Panel4->Font->Size = TrackBar1->Position;
  ListBox1->ItemIndex = 0;
  Panel4->Caption = ListBox1->Items->Strings[0];
}
void __fastcall TForm1::ListBox1Click(TObject *Sender)
{
  if (ListBox1->ItemIndex != -1)
  {
    Panel4->Font->Name = ListBox1->Items->Strings[ListBox1->ItemIndex];
    Panel4->Caption = Panel4->Font->Name;
  }
}
void __fastcall TForm1::TrackBar1Change(TObject *Sender)
{
  Panel4->Font->Size = TrackBar1->Position;
}
```

This program has two list boxes. At program startup, the first list box is initialized to display all the fonts currently available on the system. The right-hand list box shows all the fonts currently available on the printer. As a rule, you don't need to worry about coordinating the two sets of fonts, because Windows will handle that problem for you automatically. However, if you are having trouble getting the right fonts on your printer when working with a particular document, you might want to compare these two lists and see if any obvious problems meet the eye.

If you select a font from the first list box in the BCBFonts program, its name will appear in the caption of a TPanel object shown at the bottom of the program. The Caption for the panel will use the font whose name is currently being displayed, as shown in Figure 7.4. At the bottom of the BCBFonts program is the TTrackBar object, which enables you to change the size of the current font.

FIGURE 7.4.

The BCBFonts program gives samples of all the fonts on the system.

Working with Fractals

The graphics code shown so far in this section has been fairly trivial. The last program I show in this chapter ups the ante a bit by showing how you can create fractals, using the VCL graphics objects. This code should make it clear that the VCL tools are quite powerful, and can be put to good use even in fairly graphics-intensive programs.

 The sample program on the CD, Fractals, is where you can find all of the code discussed in this section of the chapter. The source for the program is shown in Listings 7.7 through 7.13.

Listing 7.7. This program shows how to use fractals to draw various shapes.

```
////////////////////////////////////////
// Main.cpp
// Project: Fractals
// Copyright (c) 1997 by Charlie Calvert
//
#include <vcl\vcl.h>
#pragma hdrstop
#include "Main.h"
#include "Ferns.h"
#include "Squares1.h"
#include "Mandy.h"
#pragma resource "*.dfm"
TForm1 *Form1;
__fastcall TForm1::TForm1(TComponent* Owner)
  : TForm(Owner)
{
}
```

continues

Listing 7.7. continued

```
//-------------------------------------------------------------------
void __fastcall TForm1::Ferns1Click(TObject *Sender)
{
  FernForm->ShowModal();
}
void __fastcall TForm1::Squares1Click(TObject *Sender)
{
  SquaresForm = new TSquaresForm(this);
  SquaresForm->ShowModal();
  SquaresForm->Free();
}
void __fastcall TForm1::Mandelbrot1Click(TObject *Sender)
{
  MandelForm = new TMandelForm(this);
  MandelForm->ShowModal();
  delete MandelForm;
}
//-------------------------------------------------------------------
```

Listing 7.8. This header is for a form that draws a fractal fern.

```
///////////////////////////////////////
// Ferns.h
// Project: Fractals
// Copyright (c) 1997 by Charlie Calvert
//
#ifndef FernsH
#define FernsH
#include <vcl\Classes.hpp>
#include <vcl\Controls.hpp>
#include <vcl\StdCtrls.hpp>
#include <vcl\Forms.hpp>
#include <vcl\ExtCtrls.hpp>
class TFernForm : public TForm
{
__published:
  TTimer *Timer1;
  void __fastcall Timer1Timer(TObject *Sender);
  void __fastcall FormResize(TObject *Sender);
private:
  void DoPaint();
  float  x, y;
  int MaxIterations;
  int Count;
  int MaxX;
  int MaxY;
public:
  virtual __fastcall TFernForm(TComponent* Owner);
};
extern TFernForm *FernForm;
#endif
```

Listing 7.9. This form draws a fractal that looks like a fern.

```cpp
//////////////////////////////////
// Ferns.cpp
// Project: Fractals
// Copyright (c) 1997 by Charlie Calvert
//
#include <vcl\vcl.h>
#pragma hdrstop
#include "Ferns.h"
#pragma resource "*.dfm"
TFernForm *FernForm;
typedef float TDAry[4];
TDAry a = {0, 0.85, 0.2, -0.15};
TDAry b = {0, 0.04, -0.26, 0.28};
TDAry c = {0, -0.04, 0.23, 0.26};
TDAry d = {0.16, 0.85, 0.22, 0.24};
TDAry e = {0, 0, 0, 0};
TDAry f = {0, 1.6, 1.6, 0.44};
__fastcall TFernForm::TFernForm(TComponent* Owner)
  : TForm(Owner)
{
  Count = 0;
  x = 0;
  y = 0;
}
void TFernForm::DoPaint()
{
  int k;
  float TempX, TempY;
  k = random(100);
  if ((k > 0) && (k <= 85))
    k = 1;
  if ((k > 85) && (k <= 92))
    k = 2;
  if (k > 92)
    k = 3;
  TempX = a[k] * x + b[k] * y + e[k];
  TempY = c[k] * x + d[k] * y + f[k];
  x = TempX;
  y = TempY;
  if ((Count >= MaxIterations) || (Count != 0))
   Canvas->Pixels[(x * MaxY / 11 + MaxX / 2)]
                [(y * - MaxY / 11 + MaxY)] =  clGreen;
  Count = Count + 1;
}
void __fastcall TFernForm::Timer1Timer(TObject *Sender)
{
  int i;

  if (Count > MaxIterations)
  {
    Invalidate();
    Count = 0;
  }
  for (i = 0; i <= 200; i++)
    DoPaint();
}
```

continues

Listing 7.9. continued

```
void __fastcall TFernForm::FormResize(TObject *Sender)
{
  MaxX = Width;
  MaxY = Height;
  MaxIterations = MaxY * 50;
```

Listing 7.10. The header for the Squares form.

```
///////////////////////////////////////
// Squares.h
// Project: Fractals
// Copyright (c) 1997 by Charlie Calvert
//
#ifndef Squares1H
#define Squares1H
#include <vcl\Classes.hpp>
#include <vcl\Controls.hpp>
#include <vcl\StdCtrls.hpp>
#include <vcl\Forms.hpp>
#include <vcl\ExtCtrls.hpp>
#define BoxCount 25
class TSquaresForm : public TForm
{
__published:
  TTimer *Timer1;
  void __fastcall Timer1Timer(TObject *Sender);
  void __fastcall FormShow(TObject *Sender);
  void __fastcall FormHide(TObject *Sender);
private:
  void DrawSquare(float Scale, int Theta);
public:
  virtual __fastcall TSquaresForm(TComponent* Owner);
};
extern TSquaresForm *SquaresForm;
#endif
```

Listing 7.11. A form that draws a hypnotic series of squares.

```
///////////////////////////////////////
// Squares.cpp
// Project: Fractals
// Copyright (c) 1997 by Charlie Calvert
//
#include <vcl\vcl.h>
#include <math.h>
#pragma hdrstop
#include "Squares1.h"
#pragma resource "*.dfm"
TColor Colors[BoxCount];
```

```cpp
typedef TPoint TSquarePoints[5];
TSquarePoints Square =
    {{-100, -100},{100, -100},{100, 100},
     {-100, 100},{-100, -100}};
TSquaresForm *SquaresForm;
__fastcall TSquaresForm::TSquaresForm(TComponent* Owner)
  : TForm(Owner)
{
  int X;
  Randomize;
  Colors[1] = TColor(RGB(random(255), random(255), random(255)));
  for (X = 2; X <= BoxCount; X++)
    Colors[X] = TColor(Colors[X-1] + RGB(random(64), random(64), random(64)));
}
void TSquaresForm::DrawSquare(float Scale, int Theta)
{
  int i;
  float CosTheta, SinTheta;
  TSquarePoints Path;
  CosTheta = Scale * cos(Theta * M_PI / 180);   // precalculate rotation & scaling
  SinTheta = Scale * sin(Theta * M_PI / 180);
  for (i = 0; i <= 4; i++)
  {
    Path[i].x = (Square[i].x * CosTheta +  Square[i].y * SinTheta);
    Path[i].y = (Square[i].y * CosTheta -  Square[i].x * SinTheta);
  }
  Canvas->Polyline(Path, 4);
}
void __fastcall TSquaresForm::Timer1Timer(TObject *Sender)
{
  int i;
  float Scale = 1.0;
  int Theta = 0;
  SetViewportOrgEx(Canvas->Handle, ClientWidth / 2, ClientHeight / 2, NULL);
  Canvas->Pen->Color = clWhite;
  for (i = 1; i <= BoxCount; i++)
  {
    DrawSquare(Scale, Theta);
    Theta = Theta + 10;
    Scale = Scale * 0.85;
    Canvas->Pen->Color = Colors[i];
  }
  for (i = BoxCount - 1; i >= 1; i—)
    Colors[i] = Colors[i - 1];
  Colors[0] = TColor(RGB(Colors[0] + random(64),
                Colors[0] + random(64),
                Colors[0] + random(64)));
}
void __fastcall TSquaresForm::FormShow(TObject *Sender)
{
  Timer1->Enabled = True;
}
void __fastcall TSquaresForm::FormHide(TObject *Sender)
{
  Timer1->Enabled = False;
}
```

Listing 7.12. The header for the form that draws the Mandelbrot set.

```cpp
///////////////////////////////////////
// Mandy.h
// Project: Fractals
// Copyright (c) 1997 by Charlie Calvert
//
#ifndef MandyH
#define MandyH
#include <vcl\Classes.hpp>
#include <vcl\Controls.hpp>
#include <vcl\StdCtrls.hpp>
#include <vcl\Forms.hpp>
#include <vcl\ExtCtrls.hpp>
class TMandelForm : public TForm
{
__published:
  TTimer *Timer1;
  void __fastcall FormMouseDown(TObject *Sender, TMouseButton Button,
  TShiftState Shift, int X, int Y);
  void __fastcall FormMouseUp(TObject *Sender, TMouseButton Button,
  TShiftState Shift, int X, int Y);
  void __fastcall FormResize(TObject *Sender);
  void __fastcall Timer1Timer(TObject *Sender);
  void __fastcall FormDblClick(TObject *Sender);
  void __fastcall FormMouseMove(TObject *Sender, TShiftState Shift, int X, int Y);
private:
  int FDepth;
  float FXRange;     // The width and height of the
  float FYRange;     // mandlebrot plane. Starts at 3.
  int FScrOrgX;
  int FScrOrgY;
  int FScrMaxX;
  int FScrMaxY;
  float FBaseOrgX;
  float FBaseOrgY;
  bool FQuitDrawing;
  void GetOriginsAndWidths(float &XOrg, float &YOrg, float &XMax, float &YMax);
  float Distance(float X, float Y);
  void Calculate(float X, float Y, float &XIter, float &YIter);
  int GetColor(int Steps);
  TRect FShapeRect;
  bool FDrawing;
  void SetBoundary(int ScrX, int ScrY, int ScrX1, int ScrY1);
  void SetMouseDownPos(int ScrX, int ScrY);
  void SetMouseUpPos(int ScrX1, int ScrY1);
  bool Run();
public:          // User declarations
  virtual __fastcall TMandelForm(TComponent* Owner);
  void __fastcall DrawShape();
};
extern TMandelForm *MandelForm;
#endif
```

Listing 7.13. A simple form for drawing the Mandelbrot set.

```cpp
//////////////////////////////////////
// Mandy.cpp
// Project: Fractals
// Copyright (c) 1997 by Charlie Calvert
//
#include <vcl\vcl.h>
#include <math.h>
#pragma hdrstop
#include "Mandy.h"
#pragma resource "*.dfm"
TMandelForm *MandelForm;
__fastcall TMandelForm::TMandelForm(TComponent* Owner)
  : TForm(Owner)
{
  FXRange = 3;
  FYRange = 3;
  FBaseOrgX = -2.25;
  FBaseOrgY = -1.5;
  Width = 550;
  Height = 400;
  FDrawing = False;
}
void TMandelForm::GetOriginsAndWidths(float &XOrg, float &YOrg, float &XMax, float
                                      &YMax)
{
  float VOrgX, VOrgY, VMaxX, VMaxY;
  float XPercent, YPercent;
  float MaxXPercent, MaxYPercent;
  VOrgX = FScrOrgX;
  VOrgY = FScrOrgY;
  VMaxX = FScrMaxX;
  VMaxY = FScrMaxY;
  XPercent = VOrgX / Width;
  YPercent = VOrgY / Height;
  MaxXPercent = VMaxX / Width;
  MaxYPercent = VMaxY / Height;
  XOrg = (XPercent * FXRange) + FBaseOrgX;
  YOrg = (YPercent * FYRange) + FBaseOrgY;
  XMax = (MaxXPercent * FXRange) + FBaseOrgX;
  YMax = (MaxYPercent * FYRange) + FBaseOrgY;
  FBaseOrgX = XOrg;
  FBaseOrgY = YOrg;
  FXRange = XMax - XOrg;
  FYRange = YMax - YOrg;
}
float TMandelForm::Distance(float X, float Y)
{
  if ((X != 0.0) && (Y != 0.0))
    return sqrt(pow(X, 2) + pow(Y, 2));
  else
    if (X == 0.0)
      return abs(Y);
    else
      return abs(X);
};
```

continues

Listing 7.13. continued

```
void TMandelForm::Calculate(float X, float Y,
                            float &XIter, float &YIter)
{
  float XTemp, YTemp;
  XTemp = pow(XIter, 2) - pow(YIter, 2) + X;
  YTemp = 2 * (XIter * YIter) + Y;
  XIter = XTemp;
  YIter = YTemp;
}
// Steps won't be larger than FDepth.
int TMandelForm::GetColor(int Steps)
{
  int TopVal= 16777215; // RGB(255,255,255)
  float Variation;
  int Val;
  Variation = TopVal / FDepth;
  Val = Variation * Steps;
  return Val;
}
void TMandelForm::SetBoundary(int ScrX, int ScrY, int ScrX1, int ScrY1)
{
  FScrOrgX = ScrX;
  FScrOrgY = ScrY;
  FScrMaxX = ScrX1;
  FScrMaxY = ScrY1;
};
void TMandelForm::SetMouseDownPos(int ScrX, int ScrY)
{
  FScrOrgX = ScrX;
  FScrOrgY = ScrY;
}
void TMandelForm::SetMouseUpPos(int ScrX1, int ScrY1)
{
  FScrMaxX = ScrX1;
  FScrMaxY = ScrY1;
  if ((FScrMaxX - FScrOrgX) > 10)
    Run();
}
void __fastcall TMandelForm::DrawShape()
{
  Canvas->Rectangle(FShapeRect.Left, FShapeRect.Top,
    FShapeRect.Right, FShapeRect.Bottom);
}
void __fastcall TMandelForm::FormMouseDown(TObject *Sender, TMouseButton Button,
                                           TShiftState Shift, int X, int Y)
{
  if (Shift.Contains(ssRight))
    FQuitDrawing = True;
  else
    SetMouseDownPos(X, Y);
  FShapeRect.Left = X;
  FShapeRect.Top = Y;
  FShapeRect.Right = - 32000;
  FDrawing = True;
}
```

```cpp
void __fastcall TMandelForm::FormMouseUp(TObject *Sender, TMouseButton Button,
                                         TShiftState Shift, int X, int Y)
{
  FDrawing = False;
  FShapeRect.Right = X;
  FShapeRect.Bottom = Y;
  Canvas->Pen->Mode = pmCopy;
  DrawShape();
  SetMouseUpPos(X, Y);
}
bool TMandelForm::Run()
{
  int i, j, Steps;
  float XStep, YStep, XPos, YPos, XOrg, YOrg;
  float XMax, YMax, XIter, YIter;
  bool Done;
  if (FDepth < 1)
    FDepth = 50;
  InvalidateRect(Handle, NULL, True);
  GetOriginsAndWidths(XOrg, YOrg, XMax, YMax);
  XStep = (XMax - XOrg) / Width;
  YStep = (YMax - YOrg) / Height;
  for (i = 0; i <= Width; i++)
    for (j = 0; j <= Height; j++)
    {
      XPos = XOrg + i * XStep;
      YPos = YOrg + j * YStep;
      XIter = 0.0;
      YIter = 0.0;
      Steps =0;
      Done = False;
      do {
        Calculate(XPos, YPos, XIter, YIter);
        Steps++;
        if (Distance(XIter, YIter) >= 2.0)
          Done = True;
        if (Steps == FDepth)
          Done = True;
      } while (!Done);
      if (Steps < FDepth)
        SetPixel(Canvas->Handle, i, j, GetColor(Steps));
      Application->ProcessMessages();
      if (FQuitDrawing)
        break;
    }
  return True;
}
void __fastcall TMandelForm::FormResize(TObject *Sender)
{
  SetBoundary(0, 0, ClientWidth, ClientHeight);
}
void __fastcall TMandelForm::Timer1Timer(TObject *Sender)
{
  Timer1->Enabled = False;
  Run();
}
void __fastcall TMandelForm::FormDblClick(TObject *Sender)
{
```

continues

Listing 7.13. continued

```
  FQuitDrawing = True;
}
void __fastcall TMandelForm::FormMouseMove(TObject *Sender, TShiftState Shift,
                                           int X, int Y)
{
  if (FDrawing)
  {
    Canvas->Pen->Mode = pmNotXor;
    if (FShapeRect.Right != -32000)
      DrawShape();
    FShapeRect.Right = X;
    FShapeRect.Bottom = Y;
    DrawShape();
  }
}
//------------------------------------------------------------------------
```

When this program is launched, you see the opening form shown in Figure 7.5. The menu for this form will let you select secondary forms that draw fractal ferns (Figure 7.6), squares (Figure 7.7), and a rather hastily thrown together version of the Mandelbrot set (Figure 7.8).

FIGURE 7.5.

The main form for the Fractals program features a bitmap made in Caligari's TrueSpace program.

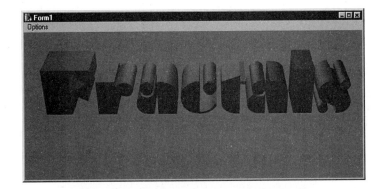

FIGURE 7.6.

A fractal fern drawn with VCL code.

Figure 7.7.

These squares are animated and appear to be swirling away from the user.

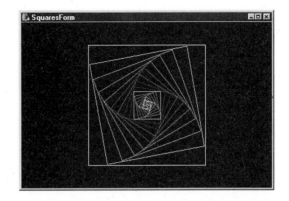

Figure 7.8.

You can draw a square on the form with the mouse to zoom in on any part of the Mandelbrot set.

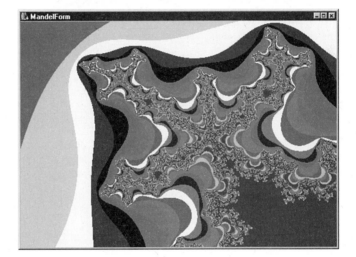

This book is not about mathematics, so I will not give an in-depth explanation of any of these forms. Instead, I will simply give a quick overview of each of the major forms from the program. The key point to grasp is simply that you can use the VCL to create programs that create rather elaborate graphics.

The Fern form uses a global variable called Count to check the depth of detail to which the fern is drawn. When the detail reaches a certain point, the image is erased, and the drawing is begun anew.

The output for the Fern program is handled by a single routine found in the DoPaint method that draws a point to the screen:

```
Canvas->Pixels[(x * MaxY / 11 + MaxX / 2)]
  [(y * - MaxY / 11 + MaxY)] =  clGreen;
```

A `Timer` component dropped on the form calls the `DoPaint` method at periodic intervals. By laboriously drawing pixels to the screen, one at a time, the `DoPaint` method slowly builds up a fractal image of a fern. Needless to say, it is the array-based math in the program that calculates where to draw the pixels so that the fern takes on a "life of its own." The `Squares` form creates the illusion that it is animating a set of squares by rotating them one inside the next, so that they appear to be receding into the distance as they spin away from the user. In fact, the code only calculates how to draw the squares once, and then animates the palette with which the squares are colored:

```
for (i = 1; i <= BoxCount; i++)
{
  DrawSquare(Scale, Theta);
  Theta = Theta + 10;
  Scale = Scale * 0.85;
  Canvas->Pen->Color = Colors[i];
}
for (i = BoxCount - 1; i >= 1; i—)
  Colors[i] = Colors[i - 1];
Colors[0] = TColor(RGB(Colors[0] + random(64),
              Colors[0] + random(64),
              Colors[0] + random(64)));
```

The first loop shown here draws each square in a different color from an array of 25 different colors:

```
#define BoxCount 25
TColor Colors[BoxCount];
```

The second loop shown above shifts each color up the array by one notch. The final statement sets the first element in the array to a new color.

When you watch the program in action, each color appears to be racing away from the user down through the swirling maze of squares. Of course, the squares themselves aren't really moving; it's just that the colors assigned to them change with each iteration of the main loop in the program.

The `Mandy` form uses standard code to draw the Mandelbrot set. The user can then left-click at one point and drag a square across a portion of the set that he or she would look to see in more detail. When the user lets go of the left mouse button, the highlighted part of the image will be redrawn at a high magnification.

The whole point of the Mandelbrot set, of course, is that there is no end to the degree of detail with which you can view it. Of course, in this version, if you zoom in close enough, some of the detail gets lost. You could add code to the program that would fix this problem, but the current implementation should provide enough fun for most users.

I provide only minimal code that checks all the possible errors the user could make, such as clicking once on the form in the same spot:

```
void TMandelForm::SetMouseUpPos(int ScrX1, int ScrY1)
{
  FScrMaxX = ScrX1;
  FScrMaxY = ScrY1;
  if ((FScrMaxX - FScrOrgX) > 10)
    Run();
}
```

Here you can see that I check to make sure there is at least 10 pixels of difference between the location where the user clicked the mouse and the location where he let go of the mouse. This helps to protect the user from feeding invalid data to the routines that calculate the area to draw. However, this code is not foolproof, and you might find yourself in a situation where the code is taking a ridiculously long time to finish its calculations. In that case, you can just double-click the form to stop the drawing.

You have already seen the rubber band technology used to draw a square on the form that delineates the next frame to be viewed. The code that performs that function for the MandyForm is taken verbatim from the DrawShapes program shown earlier in this chapter.

Summary

In this chapter you have had an overview of graphics programming with the VCL. I have made no attempt to cover all facets of this subject, but hopefully you now have enough information to meet most of your needs.

Key subjects covered in this chapter include the TCanvas object, used for drawing shapes or words on a form or component surface. You also saw the TFont, Tbrush, and TPen objects, which define the characteristics of the shapes or letters drawn on a component. The TMetaFile and TBitmap objects were also introduced, though I never did do anything with the simple and easy-to-use TIcon object. The last section of the chapter had a bit of fun drawing flashy images to the screen.

One related subject that was not covered in this chapter is the TImageList object. If you are interested in this subject, you might want to look at the KdAddExplore program found on the CD-ROM that accompanies this book. The program should be in the Chap14 directory. The TImageList component provides a means of storing a list of images in memory while taking up the minimum possible amount of system resources. It is much less expensive to store five images in an image list than it would be to use five separate bitmaps in your program.

IN THIS PART

Relational Databases

II

PART

Database Basics and Database Tools

CHAPTER

8

This chapter provides an introduction to BCB database programming. I start by showing how to create aliases and simple database applications, and then move on to a discussion of various conventions that I use when programming databases. Next, I discuss key database tools that ship with BCB, and close with a discussion of getting ODBC and TCP/IP set up on your system.

In subsequent chapters I move on to a discussion of advanced client/server issues. I am covering such basic material as you find in this chapter in a book on intermediate-to-advanced programming because there are so many C++ programmers who are new to the database world. If you have much experience in C++ desktop and systems programming, but little database experience, you should take the time to work through this chapter. BCB makes this subject easy to master, and once you have database tools at your fingertips, you will be surprised how many uses you can find for them. This is especially true in the data-centric, Internet-based world most programmers live in these days.

More advanced database programmers should also read this chapter, because I include an overview of the BCB database architecture. All serious developers need to be concerned with matters covered in this chapter such as Object Repositories, business rules, the proper use of TDataModule, and so on.

More specifically, the subjects covered in this chapter include introductions to the following:

- The TTable, TQuery, and TDataSource objects. The discussion of these subjects will show you how to connect to tables with and without SQL.
- The tools available for creating aliases.
- The Object Repository, Database Explorer, and SQL Monitor.
- The TDataModule keeps your form clear of database objects, and it consolidates your database code and rules in a single object that can be shared in multiple applications. In particular, it enables you to place nonvisual components, and particularly nonvisual database components, on a special window that remains hidden at runtime. This window can be stored in the Object Repository and can be used to specify business rules that can be reused by a wide range of projects and programmers.
- The last part of this chapter covers the different means for accessing data from inside BCB. For instance, you can use the BDE, ODBC, and SQL Links. In this section you learn about the difference between Paradox, dBASE, InterBase, Oracle, and Sybase, as well as other related matters.
- The chapter ends with a discussion of using ODBC, and of setting up TCP/IP on your system.

After you have covered the basics in this chapter, the next step is to move onto the in-depth discussions of these topics found in the next few chapters. In particular, the next chapter covers the TTable object in depth, and the following chapter covers the SQL-based TQuery object.

Here is an overview of what lies ahead:

- Chapter 8: This chapter, which covers database basics, including introductions to `TTable` and `TQuery`
- Chapter 9: An in-depth look at `TTable` and `TDataSet`
- Chapter 10: An in-depth look at `TQuery` and an introduction to SQL programming

Subsequent chapters in this section of the book cover intermediate and advanced database topics. For instance, you will find more material on the database tools in general and on CASE tools in particular, in Chapters 17 and 18.

The logic behind arranging things this way is to enable you to first get an introduction to BCB and databases, and to then dig into the subject once you understand the issues involved. This way I can keep the simplest subject matter out of the latter chapters so they can focus on relatively serious programming issues.

If you are interested primarily in design issues, you can safely skim through this chapter, looking only for the parts that interest you. If you have not built a BCB database program before, you should read this entire chapter through from beginning to end.

On Setting Up the Database Tools

BCB comes ready to run Paradox, dBASE, and local InterBase tables. If you have the client/ server version of the product, it comes with the full InterBase server. The client/server product also lets you access any DB2, Informix, MS SQL Server, Sybase, and Oracle you have available. The very first version of BCB does not ship with built-in support for Access or FoxPro, but if you have Delphi 3.0 installed on your system, you can get access to these features automatically.

> **NOTE**
>
> The issue here is that BCB 1.0 ships with an older version of the BDE than Delphi 3.0, because the new version of the BDE was not available at BCB ship time. If you can get the most recent version of the BDE, BCB will work with it automatically, which means you can get at Access tables. You can sometimes download the BDE directly from the Borland Web site at www.borland.com. If you can't get the most recent version of the BDE, you can use ODBC to, as they say, access "Access."
>
> It does not matter that BCB shipped with an earlier version of the BDE than the one you may be running on your system. The BDE was designed to handle this type of situation, and it is entirely regular. I use the most recent version of the BDE with my copy of BCB, and I never have any hint of trouble.

8

DATABASE BASICS
AND DATABASE
TOOLS

The primary way to access data from BCB involves the BDE, or Borland Database Engine. This engine, which is explained in more depth near the end of this chapter, is the backbone of the BCB database tools.

Paradox, dBASE, and Access tables can be reached directly from the BDE. To access the other databases, you also need SQL Links, which is a product that ships with the client/server version of Delphi.

One simple way to find out what database access you have from your system involves dropping down a TDatabase object on a form and examining its DriverName property in the Object Inspector. This property contains a list of the installed drivers on your system. For instance, all the databases listed earlier in this section appear in this Property Editor on my system. (Paradox and dBASE tables are accessed through the driver labeled "Standard.")

If you are having trouble accessing some or all databases from your system, the best remedy is usually to do a complete uninstall and a complete reinstall. The local database systems ought to work automatically out of the box without any effort on your part. For instance, I have probably installed BCB 50 times on a variety of systems, and I have always been able to reach Paradox or dBASE tables immediately after installation.

Users of the BDE should be aware that BCB ships with a tool called the BDE Configuration utility. This application can be accessed from the Start menu. You can use this tool to make sure the BDE itself is running correctly. As a rule, if the BDE is not running, you will not be able to access databases from inside of BCB.

Database Basics

To create a simple database application, start by placing a TTable, a TDataSource, and a TDBGrid component on a form, as shown in Figure 8.1.

FIGURE 8.1.

TTable, TDataSource, *and* TDBGrid *arranged on a form.*

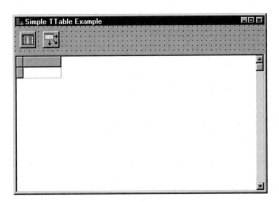

Wire these three controls together by completing the following simple steps:

1. Connect the `DataSource` property of the `TDBGrid` to `DataSource1`.
2. Connect the `DataSet` property of the `TDataSource` control to `Table1`.

After completion of these steps, the three components are hooked together and can communicate with one another.

Connecting the `TTable` object to a table that resides on disk is a three-step process:

1. Set the `DatabaseName` property either to a valid alias or, in the case of Paradox or dBASE, to the subdirectory where your data resides. For the example currently under discussion, you can set the `DatabaseName` property to the `BCDEMOS` alias, which is created by default during BCB's installation. Alternatively, you could type `c:\CBuilder\demos\data` into the DatabaseName Property Editor, where you might need to change some aspects of this path depending on where you choose to install BCB.
2. Set the `TableName` property to the name of the table you want to view; for instance, you might choose the `CUSTOMER.DB` table. The Property Editor drops down a list of available tables, so there is no need for you to type anything; the whole job can be done with the mouse.
3. Set the `Active` property, found at the very top of the Object Inspector, to `true`.

When you are done, the Object Inspector should look as it does in Figure 8.2.

FIGURE 8.2.

The Object Inspector after connecting to a table called Customer, *using an alias called* BCDEMOS.

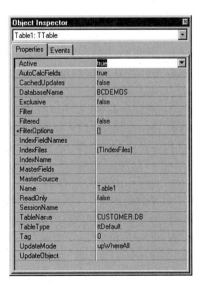

8

DATABASE BASICS AND DATABASE TOOLS

If you have completed all these steps properly, you should now be looking at the data from the table you chose, as shown in Figure 8.3. To take this process one step further, you can compile and run the program and then begin browsing and editing your data.

FIGURE 8.3.

Simple form displaying the contents of CUSTOMER.DB.

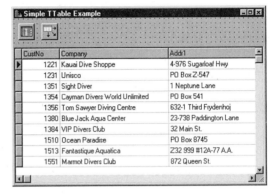

If you want to simplify the task of browsing through the data in your application, you can go back into design mode and add the TDBNavigator control to the program. To hook this control into the loop, all you need to do is set its DataSource property to DataSource1. Now you can run the program and begin iterating through the records with the navigator, as shown in Figure 8.4. In Figure 8.4, most of the functionality of the TDBNavigator has been turned off by manipulating its VisibleButtons property. For instance, a navigator can automatically enable you to edit, insert, delete, post, cancel, and refresh. All those capabilities have been disabled and hidden in the form shown here by manipulating the VisibleButtons property of TDBNavigator.

FIGURE 8.4.

A simple database program with a TDBNavigator *control.*

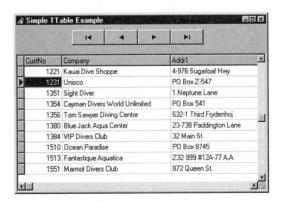

A program like the one described here is found on the CD-ROM that accompanies this book as `Simple.cpp`. Programs like this are the bread and butter of the database world. You might even find it useful to create several programs of this type, just be to be sure you can do it quickly and easily with little thought. BCB database programmers work with the `TTable`, `TDataSource`, and `TDBGrid` objects on a regular basis, and the basics of their operation should be as easy as tying your shoe.

Naming and Architectural Conventions

In this section I lay out a number of conventions that I generally abide by in programming projects. Before beginning, I should emphasize that these are merely conventions. There are no hard and fast rules in this area, and you should feel free to follow my suggestions only to the degree that they suit your taste. In fact, you will find that I myself do not follow these conventions one hundred percent of the time, though I generally conform to them when I am not feeling too rushed. I also have included legacy code in this book in which I did not adopt the techniques that I currently believe are best. In some cases, I have updated the legacy code, but some sample programs still use old conventions.

When arranging tables on a data module, I usually follow some simple naming conventions. If I attach a `TTable` object to a table called `Customer`, I will call the `TTable` object `CustomerTable`. The data source attached to that table will generally be called `CustomerSource`.

8

DATABASE BASICS
AND DATABASE
TOOLS

> **NOTE**
>
> An alternative technique, called Hungarian notation, would name all `TTable` objects `tblXXX`, where the *XXX* is the name of the table you want to use: `tblCustomer`, `tblBioLife`, and so on. You could then prefix `ds` before the table name to designate the name of the data source: `dsCustomer`, `dsBioLife`, and so on. This was the technique I used in the past, but which I no longer believe to be best.
>
> The Hungarian system enables you to automatically group all the objects shown in the Object Inspector according to type. If all the tables begin with `tbl`, they will appear together in the Object Inspector.
>
> Despite this advantage, I have decided against Hungarian notation on the grounds that it tends to make even simple code appear a bit abstruse. Recondite code has a certain emotional appeal, but it is not the effect I want to strive for in a book that champions the virtues of clear, easy-to-read logic.
>
> In general, I try to avoid systems that force me to use hard to read abbreviations, or that clutter up the beginnings of words. In particular, I find an identifier like `dsCustomer` unpleasant because it makes the type of the variable appear more important than the name of the variable. This system also makes it hard to read the identifier, because you have to mentally
>
> *continues*

continued

skip over the first syllable before getting to the key piece of information contained in the name.

Of course, my least favorite naming convention abbreviates both the type and the variable name:

```
DDSURFACEDESC       ddsd;
HBITMAP             hbm;
RGBQUAD *           prgb;
```

Incredibly, these samples are taken from source code distributed by a major software company in order to promote a new API. I am at least tempted to believe that the people who came up with these variable names were trying to be funny, or perhaps just to pull someone's leg. At any rate, these are classic examples of naming conventions that I try to avoid.

So, in this book, it will generally be `CustomerTable`, and not `tblCustomer`. If you prefer some other system, you should feel free to pursue your tastes. After all, many of the best programmers use Hungarian notation on a regular basis. In fact, in the world of C++, my tastes probably represent a minority opinion.

In simple projects that have only one data module, I will usually call the files associated with the data module `DMod1.cpp` and `DMod1.h`. The `TDataModule` object itself I usually rename to `TDMod`. In more complex projects that have multiple data modules I might rename the data module to something more meaningful such as `TDModAddress`, and I might then save the file under the name `DModAddress1.cpp`.

Please note that my convention is to name the file in which a data module or form is stored as the same name as the data module or form, except that I append a `1` to it. Thus the file in which a data module called `TDMod` is stored will be called `DMod1`. This prevents name conflicts between the object name and the filename. If I have a form called `TAddress`, I will save it in a file called `Address1.cpp`. The one exception to the previous rule is that I tend to name the main module of a project `Main.cpp`, and I then usually keep the main form default name of `Form1`.

Please understand that I have included this section more as a courtesy than out of a desire to attempt to force my tastes on someone else. I want you to know and understand the conventions I use, but you should feel free to use the techniques that you feel work best.

Enough on naming conventions. It's time now to move on to a related, but slightly different matter regarding the proper use of data modules.

Using the TQuery Object

You can create a BCB SQL statement by using a TQuery component in the following manner:

1. Drop down TQuery, TDataSource, and TDBGrid objects on a form and wire them together.

2. Assign an alias to the DatabaseName property of the TQuery object. For instance, use the BCDEMOS or DBDEMOS alias. These aliases are created automatically by BCB and Delphi, respectively, during installation.

3. Use the SQL property to enter a SQL statement such as Select * from Country.

4. Set the Active property to True. If you completed each step correctly, and if the BDE is set up correctly, the grid should now contain the records from the Country table.

If you're working with local data, you can substitute a fully qualified subdirectory path for an alias. When using the latter method, it's best if you don't include the actual name of a table, but only the subdirectory in which one or more tables exist. In my opinion, however, it is almost always better to work with an alias rather than specify the path directly in the DatabaseName property.

That's all I'm going to say about TQuery for now. Later in this chapter I discuss the SQL monitor tool that comes with BCB. In subsequent chapters I begin using SQL statements more heavily. I find it easier to use TTable than TQuery for many basic database operations. However, as I discuss matters of increasing complexity throughout the database section of this book, I will rely more and more on SQL.

The Data Module

Earlier in this chapter, you placed a TTable and TDataSource component on the same form with your visual components. When you ran the program, the icons representing these components disappeared. However, they are visible at design time and have a tendency to clutter up the form. Partially out of a desire to eliminate this clutter, BCB features a component called a TDataModule, which can be used to store nonvisual controls such as TTable and TDataSource. A program on disk called SimpleTable shows how to use the TDataModule component.

To get started working with TDataModules, first begin a new application. Next, choose File | New and select the Data Module component from the New page of the New Items dialog, as shown in Figure 8.5. You can also choose to create a data module directly from the New Data Module option on the File menu. You should, however, get used to using the Object Repository as it plays a big role in BCB programming.

FIGURE **8.5.**

Selecting the
TDataModule
component from the
New Items dialog.

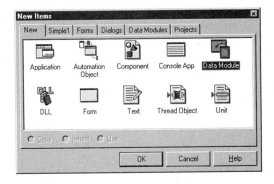

> **NOTE**
>
> A TDataModule is not the same thing as a form. For instance, if you look in its ancestry you will see that it is a direct descendant of TComponent.
>
> When you first see a TDataModule object, there is a tendency to view it as merely a special kind of form, which is, to some degree, true, at least in a very nontechnical sense. However, the hierarchy for a TForm component looks like this:
>
> ```
> -TComponent
>   -TControl
>     -TWinControl
>       -TScrollingWinControl
>         -TForm
> ```
>
> The hierarchy for a TDataModule, on the other hand, looks like this:
>
> ```
> -TComponent
>   -TDataModule
> ```
>
> Clearly, TForms and TDataModules are two very different beasts, despite some apparent similarities between them.
>
> The header file that contains the declaration for the TDataModule class is FORMS.HPP. If you have the Pascal source to the VCL, the TDataModule object is found in FORMS.PAS.

After adding a TDataModule object to your application, take a moment to save your code. You might save Unit1 as MAIN.CPP and Unit2 as DMOD1.CPP. Click Form1, open the File menu, and choose the Include Unit Header expert from the menu. In the Include Unit dialog, select DMod1 and press OK. This is a simple way of automatically inserting an #include directive at the top of Unit1. In particular, the following changes are made to your code:

```
#include <vcl\vcl.h>
#pragma hdrstop
#include "Main.h"
#include "DMod1.h" // This directive references the data module
#pragma resource "*.dfm"
```

You can, of course, type in the #include directive without using the small expert found on the File menu. There is no particular advantage in using the expert other than its ease of use.

Remember, however, that if you want to include a unit in your project, it is generally not enough to simply add a header file to a unit. You must also be sure the unit has been explicitly added to your project. In the case discussed here, there is no need to explicitly add Unit2 (a.k.a. DMod1) to the project, because it was done automatically when you first created the unit.

> **NOTE**
>
> This is a time when some programmers may need to force themselves to abandon the old "command-line" attitude, and to instead embrace a visual tool that can help make you more productive. As always, the choice is yours, but if the visual tools are easier to use, and if they make you more productive, you should consider using them. Command-line programming has an honorable place in this world, but it is generally not part of the attitude that makes for good RAD programmers.
>
> Let me tack on one additional piece of information to this note. If you want to add a module to a project without using the project manager, and without editing a makefile, you can use the following syntax:
>
> ```
> #pragma link "dmod1.obj"
> ```
>
> This syntax can be very useful when adding components to the component palette. See the FTP2.cpp module in the Utils directory from the CD-ROM that ships with this book for an example of using this approach.

Arrange Form1 and DataModule2 on the screen so you can view them both at the same time. Drop a TTable and TDataSource component on the data module, as shown in Figure 8.6.

FIGURE 8.6.

Form1 and DataModule2 arranged on the screen so that you can easily view them both at the same time.

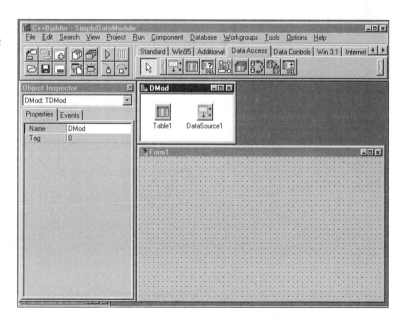

> **NOTE**
>
> For various reasons I snapped my screen shots for this book at 640×480 resolution. Needless to say, I don't usually run BCB at that resolution. 1024×768 is probably a more reasonable size when working with an environment like this, though even higher resolutions would be better. 800×600 is tolerable, but I still feel the pinch when working at that low a resolution.

Wire the TDataSource to the TTable object, and set the DatabaseName of the TTable object to BCDEMOS and the TableName to BioLife. Set the Active property of the TTable object to True.

Right-click the TTable object and bring up the Fields Editor. Right-click the Fields Editor, and bring up the AddFields dialog. Make sure all the fields in the dialog are selected, which is the default behavior for the tool. Click the OK button.

The Fields Editor now contains a list of all the fields in the BioLife table. To add these fields to your form, simply click one or more fields, hold the left mouse button down, and drag the fields onto the form. For instance, select the Graphics field, making sure that it is the only one highlighted. Now drag it onto the form. When you let go of the left mouse button, the Graphics field will automatically display itself in a TDBImage component. Drag over several other fields, and create a form that looks something like the image in Figure 8.7.

FIGURE 8.7.

Some of the fields of the
BioLife table arranged
in visual controls on a
TForm object.

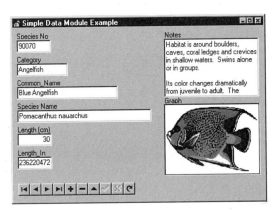

If you want to drag multiple fields over at the same time, perform a multiselect operation in the Fields Editor, just as you would in a list box. Now drag all the fields over to the main form at once. Most likely they will scroll on past the bottom of your form when you insert them, but you can fix this easily enough by aligning them as you like with the mouse.

The TDBImage component, where the picture of the fish is displayed, may be in some disarray when you first insert the components on the form. To straighten things out, select the TDBImage component, go to the Object Inspector, and set the Stretch property to True.

A sample program illustrating these principles ships on the CD-ROM that accompanies this book. It is called SimpleDataModule.

The Purpose of `TDataModule`

Now that you know how to use the `TDataModule`, let me add a few words on its significance. This component's primary purpose is to provide a place where you can define the means for accessing a set of tables. However, it is also a place to put business rules, and a place to create reusable means of accessing data.

Client/server database programmers often want to put all the rules for accessing data on the server side. Indeed, BCB supports this paradigm, and you can use stored procedures, views, and other advanced database technologies to whatever degree you want when accessing SQL databases. However, you also have the ability to define a set of rules that live on the client side, inside a `TDataModule`. You can then use the Object Repository from the File | New menu choice to store this form in a place where it can be reused by multiple programmers. To put a form in the Object Repository, right-click it and chose Add to Repository from the menu. I discuss the Object Repository in more depth later in this chapter.

There is no simple way to decide when it is best to put rules on the server side or when it is best to put them inside a `TDataModule`. Often the best solution is to use a combination of the two techniques. Put things on the server side when that is simplest, and store things on the client side when you think the power of C++ and its strong debuggers will be useful to you.

There is considerable complexity in the whole set of related subjects that involve designing databases, creating business rules, and creating metadata such as stored procedures on a server. Many of these topics will be explored in considerable depth in the next few chapters. However, a thorough examination of these topics requires considerably more scope than I have in this book.

Conventions Regarding the Use of `TDataModules`

When working with database code, I often prefer to put my `TTable`, `TQuery`, and `TDatasource` objects in a `TDataModule`, rather than placing them on a form. In other words, I think there are architectual reasons for using `TDataModules` rather than placing tables directly on a form.

There are several interrelated advantages to this scheme, most of which have to do with proper design issues. In particular, the scheme outlined previously enables me to do the following:

- Separate my database code and my GUI code. In an ideal situation, all the front-end code is in my form, and all the database code is in the `TDataModule`.

■ Protect the data in database code. It can sometimes be bad practice to directly access any of the methods or fields of an object from inside another object. Instead, you can present a series of public properties and methods as the interface for an object. There is, however, nothing wrong with accessing the properties of a `TTable` and `TQuery` object through pointer notation. In other words, the rules of aggregation state that it is acceptable and safe to write `DMod->Table1`, rather than trying to hide `Table1` behind methods of `TDMod` that wrap the object and hide it from sight.

■ Promote reuse. By isolating the database code in the `TDataModule`, and by protecting the data associated with my database code, I am creating a robust object that can be reused in multiple programs. In particular, several programs may want to access data in the same manner. By using a `TDataModule` correctly, you can encapsulate your data, and its associated rules, inside a single related object that can be reused in multiple programs. This is one way to create a set of reusable business rules that can be shared by multiple members of your team, or by multiple programmers.

I will often use the constructor of a `TDataModule` or its `OnCreate` event to open up the tables or data modules used in a project:

```
void __fastcall TDModBioLife::DModBioLifeCreate(TObject *Sender)
{
  BioLifeTable->Open();
}
```

This is the proper and ideal way to do things. I want to stress, however, that it is also correct from an OOP standpoint to access the same table from inside your main form through the `scoping` operator:

```
void __fastcall TForm1::Button1OnClick(Tobject *Sender)
{
  DMod->BioLifeTable->Open();
}
```

You can use either technique, depending on your needs. Most of the time, you will use the second technique shown here, the one that uses `scoping` operators. There are, however, some good arguments in favor of using the first method. In particular, the first technique is pure from an OOP point of view in that it completely hides the details of what goes on in the `TDMod` object.

One problem with the rigorous technique illustrated by the first example is that it can add complexity to simple programs. If you only need to access one table, and only need one `TDataSource` object, even the simple act of creating a data module can seem like overkill. Going even further and insisting that the code for manipulating the table also reside in the `TDataModule` can then seem almost absurdly roundabout and abstruse.

In the type of simple database projects that you will see in this chapter, it is possible to forgo the use of data modules altogether and to instead place the `TTable` and `TDataSource` objects directly on your main form. However, I will generally use a `TDataModule` even in such simple cases simply because it is the best way to architect an application. The point is to get in the habit of doing things the right way, because ultimately, in large scale projects, decisions such as this do matter.

> **NOTE**
>
> Data modules can be used not only for data controls, but for all nonvisual controls. You can, for instance, place a TMenu object on a data module, and then add the data module's header file to your main form, thereby accessing the TMenu object through the Object Inspector. The problem with this technique, of course, is that the methods you want to access from the menu are not always going to be located in the data module. Another issue is that your form and the data module will then be bound together, at least to some degree.

Remember that one of the key features of data modules is that they provide a place to store a set of business rules. You can create tables and queries, link them together, and use code to define rules regarding the way they work. To replicate these rules in multiple projects, simply reuse the data module that contains them.

The Object Repository

In the last section, I said that data modules can help promote reuse of code. BCB has a specific mechanism called an Object Repository that can help with this process. In particular, Object Repositories are a place where you can store data modules and forms so that they can be reused in multiple applications. If you define a set of business rules in a data module, you can save it to the Object Repository and reuse it in multiple projects. This helps you propagate the rules and promote conformity to them across a wide range of projects.

The simplest way to introduce you to the Object Repository is to just lead you step-by-step through the process of using it. After you have seen how it works, I will take a moment to explain its significance.

Save the program you created in the last section as follows:

1. Save Unit1 as `Main.cpp`.
2. Save Unit2 as `DModBiolife.cpp`.
3. Save the project file as `Biolifeapp`.
4. Rename the table and data source to `BioLifeTable` and `BioLifeSource`.
5. Select the data module and use the Object Inspector to rename it from `DataModule2` to `DModBioLife`.

Right-click the data module and select Add To Repository. Fill in the Add To Repository dialog by setting the Title, Description, and Author fields as you see fit. In the Page drop-down combo, select Data modules. Use the Browse button to select an icon from the `..BCB\images\icon` subdirectory, or from any place else where you might have some icons stored.

Start a new project. Choose File | New. This time, instead of choosing the Data module component from the New page, select the Data modules page and choose the `DModBioLife` component that you just finished creating. When it appears on the screen, you will see that it contains a `TTable` and `TDataSource` component. The components are wired together, and the `TTable` object is set to the `BioLife` table with its `Active` property set to `True`.

To access this table from `Form1`, you must first employ the Include Unit Header menu option from the File menu to add `Unit2` to the uses clause in `Unit1`. Go to the DataControls page of the Component Palette, and drop down a `TDBGrid` object on `Form1`. In the Object Inspector, drop down the `DataSource` property of the `TDBGrid` object, and you will see the `TDataSource` object from the `DModBioLife` module listed. Select this item, and the grid will automatically fill up with data.

If you drop down a `TDBEdit` control instead of a `TDBGrid` control, you proceed the same way, except that you will need to fill in not only the `DataSource` property in the Object Inspector, but also the `DataField` property. There is no need to type information into the `DataField` property, because it will automatically contain a list of the available fields in the `BioLife` table.

The true significance of the Object Repository is only hinted at by this example. The importance of this tool is made more obvious if you have six or seven tables dropped onto a data module. You might then define several relationships between the tables and add other related code. For instance, you might have some one-to-many relationships established, possibly a many-to-many relationship established, and you might have several filters, lookups, and several calculated fields defined.

Altogether, a data module of this type might encapsulate several sets of business rules defining exactly how tables should be accessed and how they relate to each other. The ability to save all this work in the repository, and to then automatically reuse it in multiple projects, is extremely valuable. I am, however, getting ahead of myself. Discussions of filters, lookups, calculated fields, and other database issues occur in various places over the next few chapters.

The Database Explorer

In addition to the data module, another key tool to use when working with databases is the Database Explorer. You can access the Database Explorer by choosing the Database | Explore menu item. The Explorer is a stand-alone executable, so you can also access it from the Windows Start button on the taskbar. You can use the Explorer even if BCB is not running, but BCB and the Explorer work best in conjunction with one another.

Once you have loaded the Explorer, make sure you have selected the Databases page and not the Dictionary page. Click the `BCDEMOS` node to expose the `Tables` node. Now click the little plus sign before the Tables node. A list of all the tables in the database will appear. Select the BioLife table and choose the Data page to view the contents of the table, as shown in Figure 8.8.

FIGURE 8.8.

Exploring the BioLife *table in the Database Explorer.*

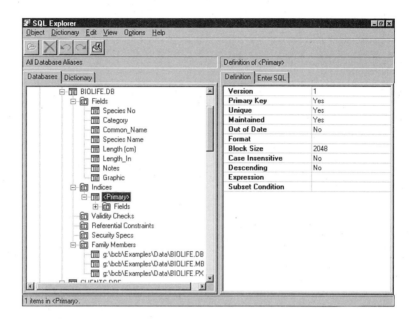

Click the little plus symbol in front of the BioLife.db node, and you will see a list of properties for the BioLife table. The properties listed are Fields, Indices, Validity Checks, Referential Constraints, Security Specs, and Family Members. You can expand each of these nodes to view their properties. For instance, if you select the Fields node, you will see a list of all the fields in the table. As you select each individual field, you will see a description of its primary characteristics.

NOTE

The Database Explorer provides a means for viewing the text of stored procedures and triggers. You cannot edit these values, but you can view their code.

The Database Explorer is a fairly complex tool with a number of powerful traits, many of which will undoubtedly be expanded in future versions of the product. In particular, you should note that it contains a DataDictionary that enables you to define a new alias or modify existing aliases.

At this stage, I want to show you only one key trait of the Database Explorer. Arrange your screen so you can view both the Explorer and Form1 at the same time. Select the BioLife table

8

DATABASE BASICS
AND DATABASE
TOOLS

in the Explorer with the mouse, and then drag and drop it onto Form1. If you want, you can experiment further by expanding the BioLife node in the Explorer and dragging and dropping individual fields of the table onto Form1, just as you did when using the Fields Editor.

If you start a new application, and then drag and drop the BioLife table onto Form1 from the Explorer, you will find that the TTable and TDataSource objects are placed on Form1. If you want to move them off the form, you can add a TDataModule object to the project, and then select both the TTable and TDataSource objects and choose Edit | Cut from the menu. Now select the TDataModule object and choose Edit | Paste. Make sure Form1 contains a reference (#include) to the unit that contains the TDataModule, and then hook up the grid to the TDataSource object in the TDataModule. This sounds like a fairly complicated process when written out, but you can perform this task in just a few seconds using BCB's visual tools.

Once again, the last few paragraphs have done nothing more than introduce you to the Database Explorer. This is a complex tool that will prove useful to you in many different ways, some of which might not even have been apparent to its creator. For now, the key point to grasp is that it gives you an overview of all the data in a database and enables you to drag and drop fields and tables onto your forms.

Working with the SQL Monitor

The SQL Monitor is an advanced tool that enables you to see exactly what SQL statements are being generated by your application when you are running queries against SQL databases such as InterBase. The SQL Monitor only works when you are using an ODBC connection or SQL links to access real databases such as InterBase, Oracle, Sybase, or Informix. In other words, it is not useful when you are using the TTable object, or when you are accessing Paradox or dBASE tables.

There is no trick to using the SQL Monitor. If it ships with your version of BCB, you can simply select the SQL monitor from the Database menu, run your program, and then browse through the SQL Monitor to see the specific statements generated by your program.

Here is code produced from a simple SQL request for all the rows from the Customer table from the IBLOCAL alias. Note that in this case I am using an InterBase table. InterBase is an ANSI 92 SQL-compatible database server:

```
1     18:49:40  SQL Prepare: INTRBASE - select * from Customer
2     18:49:40  SQL Vendor: INTRBASE - isc_dsql_allocate_statement
3     18:49:40  SQL Vendor: INTRBASE - isc_start_transaction
4     18:49:40  SQL Vendor: INTRBASE - isc_dsql_prepare
5     18:49:40  SQL Vendor: INTRBASE - isc_dsql_sql_info
6     18:49:40  SQL Vendor: INTRBASE - isc_vax_integer
7     18:49:40  SQL Transact: INTRBASE - XACT (UNKNOWN)
8     18:49:40  SQL Vendor: INTRBASE - isc_commit_retaining
9     18:49:40  SQL Execute: INTRBASE - select * from Customer
10    18:49:40  SQL Vendor: INTRBASE - isc_dsql_execute
11    18:49:40  SQL Stmt: INTRBASE - Fetch
12    18:49:40  SQL Vendor: INTRBASE - isc_dsql_fetch
```

```
13      18:49:40  SQL Stmt: INTRBASE - Fetch
14      18:49:40  SQL Vendor: INTRBASE - isc_dsql_fetch
15      18:49:40  SQL Stmt: INTRBASE - Fetch
16      18:49:40  SQL Vendor: INTRBASE - isc_dsql_fetch
17      18:49:40  SQL Stmt: INTRBASE - Fetch
18      18:49:40  SQL Vendor: INTRBASE - isc_dsql_fetch
19      18:49:40  SQL Stmt: INTRBASE - Fetch
20      18:49:40  SQL Vendor: INTRBASE - isc_dsql_fetch
21      18:49:40  SQL Stmt: INTRBASE - Fetch
22      18:49:40  SQL Vendor: INTRBASE - isc_dsql_fetch
23      18:49:40  SQL Stmt: INTRBASE - Fetch
24      18:49:40  SQL Vendor: INTRBASE - isc_dsql_fetch
25      18:49:40  SQL Stmt: INTRBASE - Fetch
26      18:49:40  SQL Vendor: INTRBASE - isc_dsql_fetch
27      18:49:40  SQL Stmt: INTRBASE - Fetch
28      18:49:40  SQL Vendor: INTRBASE - isc_dsql_fetch
29      18:49:40  SQL Stmt: INTRBASE - Fetch
30      18:49:40  SQL Vendor: INTRBASE - isc_dsql_fetch
31      18:49:40  SQL Stmt: INTRBASE - Fetch
32      18:49:40  SQL Vendor: INTRBASE - isc_dsql_fetch
```

All this information can be a bit overwhelming at times. To simplify the output from the SQL Monitor, select Options | Trace Options from the SQL Monitor menu. The dialog shown in Figure 8.9 is launched. You can then select just the first two, or perhaps only the second option. The output from the same test run previously then looks like this:

```
2       04:54:44  Log started for: Project1
3       04:55:02  SQL Prepare: INTRBASE - select * from customer
4       04:55:03  SQL Execute: INTRBASE - select * from customer
```

Now you see only the prepare and execute statements, which is probably all the information you needed. A screen shot of the SQL Monitor with this simple information in it is shown in Figure 8.10.

Once again, the SQL Monitor is only for use with powerful databases such as InterBase or Oracle. I will present in-depth discussions of InterBase later in this section of the book.

FIGURE 8.9.

The SQL Monitor Trace Options dialog is accessible from one of the program's speed buttons.

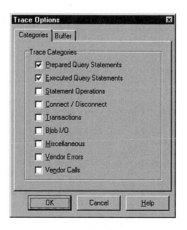

FIGURE 8.10.

The SQL Monitor showing prepared and executed SQL statements.

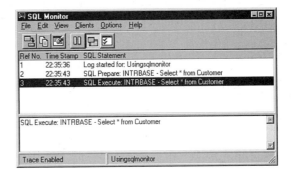

Understanding the BDE and Aliases

The BDE is the Borland Database Engine, which used to be called IDAPI. This engine is the gateway to all the databases accessed from BCB, except under certain unusual circumstances.

The BDE gives you direct access to Paradox and dBASE tables. If you own a copy of Paradox or dBASE, you already have the BDE installed on your system. The brains behind these two products is the BDE. Paradox and dBASE are merely wrappers around the BDE, in much the same way that the BCB IDE is a wrapper around a C++ compiler.

Besides giving you access to Paradox and dBASE, the BDE also uses Borland's SQL Links technology to give you fast access to client/server databases. In particular, BCB ships with SQL Links drivers for InterBase, Oracle, Sybase, MS SQL Server, DB2, and Informix.

The list of available client/server databases changes depending on the version of the BDE you are using. To check the current list, open up the BDE Configuration application that ships with BCB and look at the available list of drivers. (See Figure 8.11.)

FIGURE 8.11.

The Borland Database Configuration utility (BDECFG32.exe) provides a list of available SQL Links drivers.

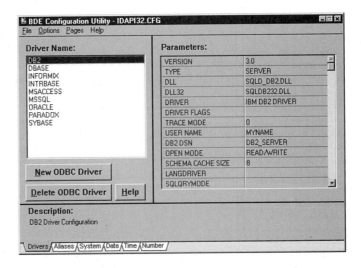

The BDE Configuration utility lists the actual files that contain the SQL Links drivers. For instance, the SQL Links driver for Oracle is called SQLORA32.dll. The driver for InterBase is called SQLINT32.dll, and so on, as shown in Table 8.1.

Table 8.1. DLLs associated with various SQL drivers.

Database	SQL Links driver names
DB2	SQLDB232.dll
Informix	SQLINF32.dll
InterBase	SQLINT32.dll
MS SQL	SQLMSS32.dll
Oracle	SQLORA32.dll
Sybase	SQLSSC32.dll

The mere presence of the preceding DLLs is not enough, however, to connect you to a client/ server database. You will also need to be running a network protocol such as TCP/IP, and you will need local drivers and tools for the database supplied by the database vendor. The next section of this chapter discusses setting up TCP/IP on your computer.

Each vendor will have a different set of local drivers and tools for you to use. For instance, if you want to connect to Oracle, you need to install the Oracle SQL Net tools.

Your copy of BCB comes with a local version of InterBase. If you look at the right-hand portion of the taskbar at the bottom of your copy of Windows 95 or Windows NT, you should see the green and gray icon for the InterBase Server Properties applet. Other InterBase applets include the InterBase Server Manager (IBMGR32.exe) and InterBase Windows SQL (WISQL32.exe). (When reading these cryptic and inadvertently humorous 8/3 executable names, you should break the abbreviations up like this: IB-MGR-32.exe, not like this: IBM-GR-32.exe.)

If you are running BCB, your connection to InterBase will be set up automatically during program install. However, if you want to connect to Oracle, Sybase, or some other SQL server, you can be in for a rather complicated ordeal. The difficult part of these installs is almost always setting up the third-party tools. Borland's half of the equation is usually automatic, and occurs without effort on your part during BCB's install.

To get connected to Oracle or Sybase, the first thing to do is close BCB and all the Borland tools, and consult the manuals for your server. They will show you how to get the server set up, how to test the connection, and how to run some tools for managing your database. Once this part of the procedure is over, you can launch BCB, and you should be able to connect right away after establishing an alias. Aliases are described in the next section of this chapter, and in-depth in several of the upcoming chapters, including Chapter 15, "Working with the Local InterBase Server." They are also discussed in the readme file from the CD that accompanies this book. Of course, you have to have the client/server version of Delphi to connect to these databases.

There is a Sams Publishing book called the *Database Developer's Guide with Delphi 2* (Ken Henderson, ISBN 0-672-30862-2), which goes into considerable depth on connecting to most of the major servers. The portion of the book you want to see is Chapter 24, "Delphi's Database Drivers Demystified." Almost anything this book says about Delphi databases will apply equally to BCB's databases. Delphi and BCB are sister and brother tools, and their approach to databases is almost identical.

I will, however, go to some lengths to ensure you are properly connected to InterBase, when I introduce that topic in Chapter 15. Until that time, there is no need for you to be connected to InterBase while reading this book. I should add, however, that connecting to InterBase is a simple task that should have been done for you automatically during the install of BCB. To check whether you are properly connected, try using the IBLOCAL alias set up by the install program for connecting to an InterBase table called Employee.gdb.

Aliases

You can create aliases inside any one of three tools:

- The SQL Explorer accessed through the Database | Explore menu option. From inside this tool, choose Object | New to create an alias.

- The Database Desktop. This is a stand-alone program installed by default in the Program Files\Borland\Database Desktop directory. Choose Tools | Alias Manager from the DBD menu to create an alias.

- The BDECFG32.exe program found in the directory where the BDE is installed. Turn to the Alias page in this program to create an alias.

Both Paradox and InterBase aliases are created automatically when you install BCB. You can study these aliases as guides when creating your own aliases. Also see the readme files on the CD that accompanies this book, and the section on creating ODBC aliases near the end of this chapter.

Various installation programs, such as Wise from Great Lakes Business Software (www.glbs.com, Tel (313) 981-4970, Fax (313) 981-9746) and InstallShield, can create aliases for you automatically. If you need to add aliases to a client machine during installation, you should let one of these programs handle it for you. They will also automate the installation of the BDE. InstallShield Express ships in the ISX directory found on some versions of the BCB CD.

Some Notes on Installing TCP/IP

In this section I briefly discuss the process of setting up TCP/IP on a Windows 95 machine. The process should be nearly identical on a Windows NT 4.0 machine, though the dialogs might have a slightly different name or appearance.

TCP/IP is the protocol of choice when connecting to client/server databases. It ships automatically with the 32-bit Windows products. To see if it is installed on your system, open the Control Panel and launch the Network applet. If you have TCP/IP installed, it will show up on the Configuration page of this applet, as shown in Figure 8.12.

FIGURE 8.12.

The TCP/IP information from the Control Panel.

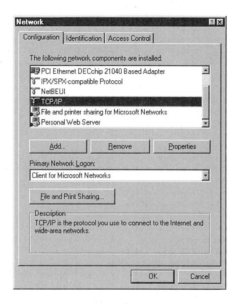

If TCP is not installed, you should push the Add button on the Configuration page and bring up the Select Network Component Type dialog. Select Protocol from the list of drivers, and again choose the Add button. In the Select Network Protocol dialog, choose Microsoft in the left-hand list box, and TCP/IP in the right-hand list box. Windows will then install the necessary software, which may require the use of your Windows Install CD-ROM.

You will probably also have to specify an IP address, subnet mask, gateway, and DNS server. This information can be garnered from your network administrator. If you are working on a small local network with Windows machines that you have set up in your office or home, you can ignore the DNS server, and can make up your own IP address, subnet mask, and gateway. For instance, the following numbers would do, as long as you are not connected to the real Internet, and are only talking to the machines in your home or office:

```
IP Address: 143.186.186.2
Subnet mask: 255.255.255.0
Gateway: 143.186.186.1
```

The other machines on your network should have the same subnet and gateway, but the IP address should be unique. For instance, the next machine should have an IP address of 143.186.186.3, and then 143.186.186.4, and so on. Remember, don't make up your own numbers if you are connected to the real Internet! If you have an Internet connection, contact your network administrator or Internet service provider (ISP).

NOTE

If you are appalled by my suggestion that people make up their own IP addresses, you should remember that many people connect their machines without being on the Internet. I do this all the time with two laptops when I am on the road showing BCB and Delphi. I also have a network at home with machines on it that are never connected directly to the Net.

I want to stress, however, that if you are connected to the Internet, it is very simple to ask your IS department for an IP address for your computer. There are plenty of IP addresses in this world, and everyone can afford to have several for their own use.

To check whether you are connected properly, open up a DOS window and try to ping one of the machines in your network. Ping is a built-in application that ships with Windows 95 and Windows NT. If you installed TCP/IP as explained previously, ping will be set up on your machine.

To get started, you can try to ping yourself:

```
Ping 143.186.186.2
```

Here is a built-in address for referencing your own machine:

```
Ping 127.0.0.1
```

Or you can try to ping one of the other machines in your network:

```
Ping 143.186.186.3
```

Here is the result of successful session:

```
c:\4dos>ping 143.186.186.2
Pinging 143.186.186.2 with 32 bytes of data:
Reply from 143.186.186.2: bytes=32 time=55ms TTL=32
Reply from 143.186.186.2: bytes=32 time=1ms TTL=32
Reply from 143.186.186.2: bytes=32 time=1ms TTL=32
Reply from 143.186.186.2: bytes=32 time=1ms TTL=32
c:\4dos>
```

Here is the result of a failed session:

```
c:\4dos>ping 143.186.186.3
Pinging 143.186.186.3 with 32 bytes of data:
Request timed out.
Request timed out.
Request timed out.
Request timed out.
c:\4dos>
```

Failed sessions usually occur because your machine is not configured properly or else the wires connecting you to the network are not set up correctly. (For instance, you might have forgotten to plug into the network!)

If you are attached to the Internet and have a DNS server, you can try to ping one of the big servers on the Net:

```
Ping compuserve.com
```

Here is successful session:

```
c:\>ping compuserve.com
Pinging compuserve.com [149.174.207.12] with 32 bytes of data:
Reply from 149.174.207.12: bytes=32 time=298ms TTL=239
Reply from 149.174.207.12: bytes=32 time=280ms TTL=239
Reply from 149.174.207.12: bytes=32 time=333ms TTL=239
Reply from 149.174.207.12: bytes=32 time=332ms TTL=239
c:\>
```

Pinging compuserve.com is the same thing as pinging 149.174.207.12. In fact, it's the job of the DNS server (the Domain Name Server) to resolve a human-readable name such as compuserve.com into an IP address.

If you want to create a human-readable IP address on a local office or home network, you can edit the HOSTS files that ship with Windows 95 or Windows NT. Under Windows 95, you will find a sample HOSTS file called Hosts.sam in your Windows directory. Here is what this file looks like:

```
# Copyright (c) 1994 Microsoft Corp.
#
# This is a sample HOSTS file used by Microsoft TCP/IP for Chicago
#
# This file contains the mappings of IP addresses to host names. Each
# entry should be kept on an individual line. The IP address should
# be placed in the first column followed by the corresponding host name.
# The IP address and the host name should be separated by at least one
# space.
#
# Additionally, comments (such as these) may be inserted on individual
# lines or following the machine name denoted by a '#' symbol.
#
# For example:
#
#      102.54.94.97     rhino.acme.com          # source server
#       38.25.63.10     x.acme.com              # x client host
127.0.0.1 localhost
```

You can rename this file to HOSTS. with no extension, and then add your own list of IP address to it:

```
143.186.186.3 MarysPC
143.186.186.4 MikesPC
```

After doing this, you can ping the other machines with a human-readable name:

```
ping maryspc
```

Connecting to ODBC

ODBC is a popular means of connecting to databases. For many developers, ODBC plays the same role in their development that the BDE plays in the life of Borland developers. ODBC is so popular that Borland has added a high-performance ODBC socket to the BDE that enables you to access data through ODBC.

> **NOTE**
>
> It's important to understand that ODBC is not a database, but only a means of accessing a database. ODBC is a standard for creating drivers; it is a not a type of data. For instance, Borland developers commonly use SQL Links to connect to Oracle or Sybase. If you wanted, you could also use ODBC drivers in lieu of SQL Links, though this is usually not a wise thing to do because ODBC is often slow, while SQL Links are usually fast.

The main appeal of ODBC is its popularity. There are ODBC drivers for connecting to nearly every database imaginable. If Borland does not ship with drivers for the data you want to access, the logical thing to do would be to search for ODBC drivers and then use them from BCB through the ODBC socket layer currently under discussion in this section of the chapter.

Some copies of BCB ship with an ODBC driver for InterBase. Because this driver is readily available, I will use it as the model for this discussion.

To get started using ODBC, you should close down your Borland tools, open up the Windows Control Panel, and start one of its applets called, quite poetically, "32 Bit ODBC." This applet can be used to manage the ODBC connections on your machine.

As shown in Figure 8.13, on the bottom-right corner of the applet is a button with the word Driver on it, and another one right above it with the word Add on it. If you click either button you can see a list of the drivers available on your system.

FIGURE 8.13.

The 32-Bit ODBC application.

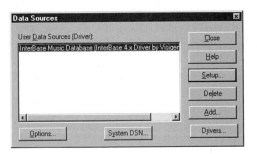

On my system one of the available drivers is called InterBase 4.X driver by Visigenic (*.gdb). If I selected this button in the Add dialog, the dialog shown in Figure 8.14 would appear.

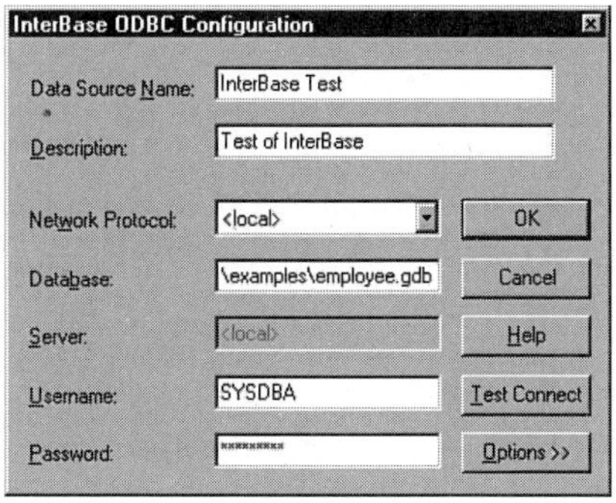

FIGURE 8.14.

*The dialog used for
configuring an ODBC
connection.*

To set up a connection to the Employee.gdb table through the local InterBase server, I fill out
the fields of the dialog, as shown in Figure 8.14. The database field of the dialog might have a
path in it that looks like this:

```
c:\program files\borland\intrbase\examples\employee.gdb
```

The rest of the fields should look like this:

```
Data Source Name: InterBase Test
Description: Test of InterBase
Driver: Local
DataBase: c:\program files\borland\intrbase\examples\employee.gdb
User Name: SYSDBA
Password: masterkey
```

You should enter SYSDBA as the user name, and enter masterkey as the password. After entering
all this information, you should be able to connect to the table by pressing the Test Connect
button. However, you may not be able to run this test until you first press OK in the dialog,
and then bring the dialog back up by pressing the Settings button from the main screen of the
32-Bit ODBC applet.

If all is working correctly, you can now bring up the BDE Configuration utility that ships with
Borland C++Builder. On the drivers page pick New ODBC Connection to bring up the dialog for creating a new BDE connection, as shown in Figure 8.15. Fill in the fields as follows:

```
SQL_Link_Driver:  ODBC_Test2
Default ODBC Drive: InterBase 4.x Driver by Visigenic
Default Data Source Name: InterBase Test.
```

After creating the driver for the ODBC test, switch to the Alias page of the BDE Configuration Utility. Select New Alias and type in ODBCTest1. Set the Alias type to ODBC_Test2. Click
OK, save your work from the File menu, and exit BDECFG.exe.

If BCB is already running, close it down. Now start up BCB and drop a TTable object on the
main form. Select ODBCTest1 from the list of available aliases in the DatabaseName property. Now
proceed as you normally would, selecting a TableName and attaching a TDataSource and TDBGrid
object to the table. When prompted for a password, enter SYSDBA as the Username and masterkey

as the password. If you want, you can relaunch the BDE configuration program and set the user name for this alias permanently to SYSDBA.

In the summary presented here, I have hardcoded in the names of the various drivers and aliases you create. You can, of course, name the alias anything you want, just as you can enter whatever names you want in the Data Source Name and Description fields of the ODBC Configuration dialog in the 32-Bit ODBC applet from the Control Panel.

FIGURE 8.15.

The dialog for creating a new ODBC.

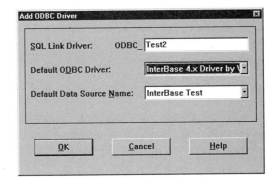

Summary

In this chapter you have learned some of the fundamental facts you need to know to start accessing databases from BCB. In particular, you have learned about the following:

- The basics of using TTable and TQuery
- The TDataModule object
- The SQL Monitor and Database Explorer
- TCP/IP and ODBC connectivity

Now that the groundwork has been laid, the next few chapters start digging into the objects that BCB uses to access databases. As a rule, this is not a particularly difficult subject, but there is a good deal of information that needs to be covered.

Once you have the facts that you need at your fingertips, you can start building real databases with BCB. C++Builder is one of the premier tools in the industry for accessing data, so you should be prepared to find yourself quickly writing powerful database applications that can be used by hundreds of people at one time.

Using TTable and TDataSet

CHAPTER 9

In this chapter, you learn some of the basics about accessing database tables using the `TTable` object. In particular, the chapter covers the fundamental information you need to access tables without using SQL. An examination of using SQL to access tables begins in the next chapter.

In the examples given here, you will be explicitly working with local Paradox tables, but nearly everything explained in this chapter applies equally to dBASE files or to files located on a SQL server such as InterBase or Oracle. I decided to run these examples against Paradox tables because I wanted to keep this chapter as simple as possible. Large portions of this book work exclusively with SQL databases, but this chapter sticks to the world of local tables.

Looking a little more deeply at the content of this chapter, you can expect to find information on the following:

- The `TTable` object, which provides the fastest and simplest access to tables.
- The `TQuery` object, which is the gateway to the flexible and powerful world of SQL.
- The `TDataSet` object, an ancestor of `TTable` and `TQuery`, which provides the core functionality for accessing tables and the records that lie within them.
- The `TField` object, which gives you access to the fields in a table or dataset. This object has powerful descendants such as `TStringField` and `TIntegerField`, all of which can be created automatically by a visual tool called the Fields Editor.
- The `TDataSource` object, which serves as an intermediary between data-aware controls and the `TTable` and `TQuery` objects.
- The `TDBGrid` object, which provides a simple and easy way to display the contents of tables to the user. The `TDBGrid` object supports editing, deletion, and insertion. It also has support for drop-down lists in lookup fields, and the capability to assign colors to a column, row, or individual field. I visit this control more in Chapter 11, "Working with Field Objects."
- The `TDBEdit` component, which enables you to display a single field from a single record and to edit or insert the data for that field.
- Filtering on nonkeyed fields.
- The `TDatabase` component, which can be handy when you need to optimize the way you connect to a server.
- Connecting to a database without using any visual tools. BCB supports something called two-way tools, which enable you to do things either visually or in code. Most of this chapter takes the visual route, but you can work entirely in code if you want or if you have some special need that requires that approach. This chapter ends with a lengthy explanation of how to take this rather unusual approach to BCB database programming.
- The order in which database events occur. This is an important subject, which has to be mastered by serious database programmers.

Here is a second way to categorize some of the objects discussed in this chapter:

- Nonvisual: TTable, TQuery, TDataSet, TField, and TDatabase
- Visual: TDBGrid and TDBEdit
- Link (also nonvisual): TDataSource

This latter view of the major database components breaks them down into two major categories. The nonvisual components enable you to open, close, edit, and otherwise manipulate tables, records, and fields. The visual components display the tables to the user so he or she can view or edit them. The powerful TDataSource object forms a link between the visual and nonvisual database controls. You might want to think of the nonvisual controls as being the intelligent heart of the BCB database tools, while the visual controls are the less intelligent outward show. The nonvisual controls manipulate the data; the visual controls display it.

The overriding purpose of this chapter is to give you a good overview of the basic facts about using a BCB database class called TDataSet. TDataSet is the driving force behind both the TTable and TQuery objects. It is the root class from which they are both descended. A third component, called TStoredProc, is also descended from TDataSet. It will be discussed in more depth in Chapters 15, "Working with the Local InterBase Server," and 16, "Advanced InterBase Concepts," both of which deal with InterBase.

Specific information about other database issues will be presented in subsequent chapters. For instance, the TQuery object will be treated in depth in the next chapter, and more detailed explanations of TDBGrid, TField, TStringField, and TIntegerField are found in Chapter 11.

Understanding the TDataSet Class

In the last chapter you were introduced to the Database Explorer, the SQL Monitor, and TDataModule. It is now time to start digging into some of the technical details of the TTable object. Learning something about these details will go a long way toward helping you understand the structure of the database tools supplied by BCB.

TTable and TQuery inherit most of their functionality from TDataSet. As a result, the TDataSet class is one of the most important database objects. To get started working with it, you need to concentrate on the hierarchy shown in Figure 9.1.

TDataSet contains the abstractions needed to directly manipulate a table. TDBDataSet knows how to handle passwords and other tasks directly associated with linking to a specific table. TTable knows how to handle indices and the specific chores associated with linking two tables in a one-to-many relationship.

As you will see in the next chapter, TQuery has a deeply rooted and complete knowledge of how to process SQL statements. The TStoredProc object is on the same level of the hierarchy as TTable and TQuery. It is used to process the stored procedures in a SQL database.

Figure 9.1.

The core hierarchy for TTable *and* TQuery.

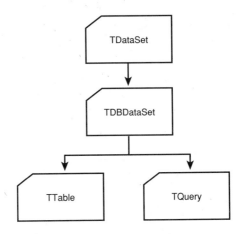

The methods of the TDataSet object enable you to open and navigate a table. Of course, you will never directly instantiate an object of type TDataSet. Instead, you will usually be working with TTable, TQuery, or some other descendant of TDataSet. The exact way this system works, and the precise significance of TDataSet, will become clear as you read through this chapter.

On the most fundamental level, a dataset is nothing more than a set of records, each containing x number of fields and a pointer to the current record.

On many occasions, a dataset has a direct, one-to-one correspondence with a physical table that exists on disk. However, at other times, you may perform a query or other action that returns a dataset that contains either a subset of one table or a join between multiple tables. The text that follows, however, sometimes uses the terms dataset and table interchangeably if it helps to simplify the explanation of a particular concept.

You will normally instantiate an object of type TTable or TQuery in order to access the functionality of TDataSet. Because of this relationship, the code in the next few sections will always assume the existence of an instance of class TTable. Remember, however, that the functions under discussion are part of TDataSet, unless the text specifically states otherwise. In other words, much of what I say here applies to both TQuery and TTable, since both of these objects descend from TDataSet.

It's now time for you to begin a direct exploration of TDataSet. As you become familiar with its capabilities, you will begin to understand exactly how BCB accesses the raw data saved to disk as a database. The key point to remember is that nearly every time a BCB programmer opens a table, he or she will be using a class such as TTable or TQuery, both of which are merely thin wrappers around TDataSet.

Opening and Closing Datasets

The simplest thing you can do with a TDataSet is open or close it. This is therefore an appropriate starting point for an exploration of datasets. In the sections that follow, you will drill down deeper and learn more about the thorough access to databases provided by BCB.

If you are writing code rather than working through the Object Inspector, there are two different ways to open or close a dataset. You can write the following line of code:

```
Table1->Open();
```

Or, if you prefer, you can set the Active property equal to True:

```
Table1->Active = True;
```

There is no difference between the effect produced by these two statements. The RTL call to Open, however, ends up setting Active to True, so it may be ever so slightly more efficient to use the Active property directly.

Just as there are two ways to open a table, there are also two ways to close a table. The simplest way is to call Close:

```
Table1->Close();
```

Or, if you want, you can write the following:

```
Table1->Active = False;
```

Once again, there is no substantial difference between these two calls. You should note, however, that Close and Open are functions, while Active is a property.

In this section, you have learned about two methods:

```
void __fastcall Open(void);
void __fastcall Close(void);
```

You also learned about one property:

```
__property System::Boolean Active;
```

It is definitely worthwhile opening up DB.HPP, finding the class declaration for TDataSet, and examining the methods shown here as well as some of the other ones included in this large object. Remember, most of the rest of this chapter is dedicated to an examination of TDataSet.

Navigational Routines

After opening a dataset, the next step is to learn how to move about inside it. The following rich set of methods and properties from TDataSet provides all the tools you need to access any particular record inside a dataset:

```
void __fastcall First(void);
void __fastcall Last(void);
void __fastcall Next(void);
void __fastcall Prior(void);
property System::Boolean Bof;
property System::Boolean Eof;
System::Integer_fastcall MoveBy(System::Integer Distance);
```

Experienced programmers will find these functions very easy to use. Here is a quick overview of their functionality:

■ Calling Table1->First() moves you to the first record in a table.

■ Table1->Last() moves you to the last record.

■ Table1->Next() moves you one record forward, unless you are at the end of a table.

■ Table1->Prior() moves you one record back, unless you are at the beginning of the table.

■ You can check the Bof or Eof properties in order to see if you are at the beginning or the end of a table.

■ The MoveBy() function moves you *x* number of records forward or backward in a table. There is no functional difference between calling Table->Next and calling Table->MoveBy(1). Furthermore, calling Table->Prior has the same effect as calling Table->MoveBy(-1). In fact, Next and Prior are one-line functions that call MoveBy, exactly as shown here.

Most of these properties and methods are demonstrated in the sample program found on the CD-ROM accompanying this book as Navy.dpr. You can open this example directly, or construct it piece by piece by following the description that follows.

To get started using these navigational routines, you should perform the following steps:

1. Place a TTable, TDataSource, and TDBGrid on a form.

2. Hook the grid to the data source and the data source to the table.

3. Set the DatabaseName property of the table to the DBDEMOS alias, or type in the path to the demos subdirectory (..\BCB 2.0\demos\data).

4. Set the TableName property to the CUSTOMER table.

If you are having trouble completing these steps, refer to Navy.dpr.

If you run a program that contains a `TDBGrid` control, you will find that you can iterate through the records in a dataset by manipulating the scrollbars on the edges of the grid. You can gain the same functionality by using the `TDBNavigator` component. However, there are times when you want to move through a table programmatically, without the use of the built-in visual tools. The next few paragraphs explain how this process works.

Place two buttons on a form and label them Next and Prior, as shown in Figure 9.2.

FIGURE 9.2.

The Prior and Next buttons in `Navy.dpr` *enable you to maneuver through a database.*

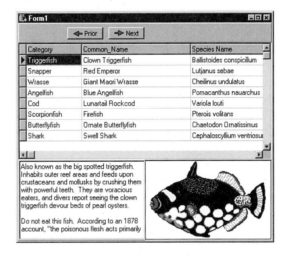

Double-click once on the Next button to create an `OnClick` method, and fill it in like this:

```
void __fastcall TForm1::bbNextClick(TObject *Sender)
{
  BioLife->Next();
}
```

Perform the same action with the Prior button, so that the function associated with it looks like this:

```
void __fastcall TForm1::bbPriorClick(TObject *Sender)
{
  BioLife->Prior();
}
```

Now run the program and click the two buttons. You will find that they easily let you iterate through the records in a dataset.

Now drop down two more buttons and label them First and Last, as shown in Figure 9.3.

Do the same thing for the calls to `Table->First` and `Table->Last` as you did with `Next` and `Prior`:

```
void __fastcall TForm1::bbFirstClick(TObject *Sender)
{
  BioLife->First();
}
void __fastcall TForm1::bbLastClick(TObject *Sender)
{
  BioLife->Last();
}
```

Nothing could be more straightforward than these navigational functions. `First` takes you to the beginning of a dataset, `Last` takes you to the end, and the `Next` and `Prior` functions move you one record forward or backward.

Checking for the End or Beginning of a Dataset

`TDataSet`'s `Bof` is a read-only Boolean property used to check whether or not you are at the beginning of a dataset. The `Bof` property returns `True` on three occasions:

■ After you first open a file

■ After you call `TDataSet->First()`

■ After a call to `Prior` fails

The first two items listed should be obvious. Specifically, when you open a dataset, BCB places you on the first record, and when you call `First`, BCB again moves you to the beginning of the dataset. The third item, however, requires a little more explanation: After you have called `Prior` enough times to get to the beginning of a file, and have then tried one more time and found that the call failed, `Bof` will return `True`.

The following code shows a common method for using Prior to get to the beginning of a file:

```
void __fastcall TForm1::bLastToFirstClick(TObject *Sender)
{
  ListBox1->Items->Clear();
  tblAnimals->Last();
  while (!tblAnimals->Bof)
  {
    ListBox1->Items->Add(tblAnimals->Fields[0]->AsString);
    tblAnimals->Prior();
  }
}
```

The code shown here is from the BofAndEof program found on the CD-ROM that comes with this book. In this case the ListBox Add method is called on the current record and then on every other record between the end and beginning rows of the dataset. The loop continues until a call to Table->Prior fails to move you back any further in the table. At that point Bof returns True and the program breaks out of the loop.

If your dataset is connected to a data source, you can optimize a loop like the one shown previously by setting DataSource1.Enabled to False before beginning the loop, and then resetting it to True after the loop is finished. These two lines of code enable you to iterate through the table without having to update the visual tools at the same time.

Everything said previously about Bof also applies to Eof. In other words, the code that follows provides a simple means of iterating over all the records in a dataset:

```
void __fastcall TForm1::bFirstToLastClick(TObject *Sender)
{
  ListBox1->Clear();
  tblAnimals->First();
  while (!tblAnimals->Eof)
  {
    ListBox1->Items->Add(tblAnimals->Fields[0]->AsString);
    tblAnimals->Next();
  }
}
```

The classic error in cases like this is to enter into a while or repeat loop but to forget to call Table->Next:

```
do
{
  ListBox1->Items->Add(tblAnimals->Fields[0]->AsString);
} while (!tblAnimals->Eof);
```

If you accidentally wrote code like this, your machine would appear to lock up. You could break out of the loop only by pressing Ctrl+Alt+Del and asking Windows to kill the current process. Also, this code could cause problems if you opened an empty table. Because the code uses a do loop, the ListBox Add method would still be called once, even though there was nothing to process. As a result, it's better to use while loops rather than do loops in situations like this.

9

**USING TTABLE
AND TDATASET**

Eof returns True in the following three cases:

- If you open an empty dataset
- If you call `Table->Last`
- If a call to `Table->Next` fails

> **NOTE**
>
> Iterating through tables as described in the last few paragraphs is a common process on local databases, but it is not as popular a technique to use with SQL servers. In particular, most client/server databases expect you to process individual records, or sets of records, but not to treat a table as a series of contiguous rows. This is rather a fine point to put on the discussion at this stage of the game, but it is something to keep in mind if you intend to move directly into processing large amounts of data on a server. If you must perform this kind of operation on a real server, it is probably best to do so from inside a stored procedure.

The last navigational routine that I want to cover is called `MoveBy`. `MoveBy` enables you to move *x* number of records forward or backward in a dataset. If you want to move two records forward, you would write the following:

```
tblAnimals->MoveBy(2);
```

And if you wanted to move two records backward, you would write this:

```
tblAnimals->MoveBy(-2);
```

When using this function, you should always remember that when you are working on a network, datasets are fluid entities, and the record that was five records back a moment ago may now be back four records, or six records, or who knows how many records. In other words, when you are on a network, someone on another machine may delete or add records to your database at any time. If that happens, `MoveBy` might not work exactly as you expect. One solution to this "fluidity" problem is to use the Bookmark functions mentioned later in this chapter.

> **NOTE**
>
> `Prior` and `Next` are simple one-line functions that call `MoveBy`. If you have the source, look up `TDataSet.Next` in `DB.PAS`. The `TDataSet` object is a beautifully written wrapper around the core functionality in the BDE.

After reading the last two sections, you should have a good feeling for how to move around in a dataset. The navigational commands you have been learning about are very easy to use. Take the few moments necessary to be sure you understand them, because they are likely to be part of your day-to-day BCB programming experience.

Fields

On most occasions when you want to programmatically access the individual fields of a record, you can use one of the following properties or methods, all of which belong to TDataSet:

```
__property TField *Fields[System::Integer Index];
__property System::Integer FieldCount;
__property System::Variant Value;
TField *__fastcall FieldByName(const System::AnsiString FieldName);
```

The Fields property is one of the most important single syntactical elements of the VCL. It consists of an array of TField objects, each of which is automatically assigned to a separate field in a table. For instance, if a table called Address had five fields called Name, Address, City, State and Zip, BCB would automatically create five field objects when you accessed the Address table. You don't have to do anything to create these field objects; they are given to you automatically.

The Fields array for the hypothetical Address table mentioned in the last paragraph would have five members. Fields[0] would access the Name field, Fields[1] would access the Address field, and so on.

The TField object is declared in DB.HPP. This is an extremely powerful, and fairly complex object, which is worth your while to study in depth. For instance, here are some of the methods of the TField object:

Assign	Assigns one field to another.
Clear	Sets the field to NULL.
FocusControl	Sets the focus of the form to the first control that hosts the field.
GetData	Gets raw data from a field in a buffer. Contrast with AString, AsInteger.
SetData	Sets the field to raw data held in a pointer. Contrast with AsString or AsInteger.
IsValidChar	Tests to see if a character is within the range of valid values for a particular field.

Here are some of the properties associated with a TField object:

AsBoolean	Conversion property, can be used to read or set the value of a field as a Boolean value.
AsDateTime	Conversion property, can be used to read or set the value of a field as a date.
AsFloat	Conversion property, can be used to read or set the value of a field as Float.

9

USING TTABLE AND TDATASET

AsString	Conversion property, can be used to read or set the value of a field as a string.
AsInteger	Conversion property, can be used to read or set the value of a field as an Integer.
Calculated	Read only Boolean property, tells whether a field is calculated.
DataSet	Assign a dataset to a field, or read what dataset is associated with a field.
EditMask	Define a mask limiting the valid characters used by a field.
Value	The standard means for accessing the value of a field.
FieldName	The name of the underlying field in the database.
Visible	Boolean property toggles whether or not a field is visible.

Most of the properties and methods listed previously are discussed in the next few pages of this book. For now you can just review the functionality previously outlined in a general way, so that you can get some sense of what the TField class is about. Remember, the previous list is far from exhaustive. It is meant merely to introduce some of the key features of the object.

The TField object also has a number of useful descendant classes with names such as TStringField and TIntegerField. These child objects are discussed in Chapter 17, "Printing: QuickReport and Related Technologies."

The FieldCount property returns an integer that specifies the number of fields in the current record structure. If you wanted a programmatic way to read the names of these fields, you could use the Fields property:

```
{
  AnsiString S(Table->Fields[0]->FieldName);
}
```

If a record had a first field called CustNo, the preceding code would put the string "CustNo" in the variable S. If you wanted to access the name of the second field in the example, you could write this:

```
S = Table->Fields[1]->FieldName;
```

In short, the index passed to Fields is zero-based, and it specifies the number of the field you want to access, where the first field is number zero, the second is referenced by the number one, and so on.

If you want to find out the current contents of a particular field from a particular record, you can use the Fields or FieldByName property, or you could access the entire table as an array of fields. To find the value of the first field of a record, index into the first element of the Fields array:

```
S = Table->Fields[0]->AsString;
```

Assuming that the first field in a record contains a customer number, the code shown would return a string such as '1021', '1031', or '2058'. If you wanted to access this variable as an integer value, you could use AsInteger in place of AsString. Similar properties of Fields include AsBoolean, AsFloat, and AsDate.

If you want, you can use the FieldByName function instead of the Fields property:

```
S = Table->FieldByName("CustNo")->AsString;
```

As used in the examples shown here, both FieldByName and Fields return the same data. The two different syntaxes are used solely to provide programmers with a flexible and convenient set of tools for programmatically accessing the contents of a dataset. When in doubt, use FieldByName because it won't be affected if you change the order of the fields in your table.

NOTE

I'll add a note here for Delphi programmers who may be a bit confused by the tack I am taking on this subject. In Delphi, you can also treat TTable as a variant array, which will let you access the fields of a table with the following syntax:

```
S := Table1['CustNo'];
```

This is obviously a considerable improvement over the FieldByName method. However, this syntax is not supported in BCB.

It might be helpful to take a few moments to discuss a set of routines from the FieldObject program found on the disk that accompanies this book. These routines illustrate the most common ways to access the value of a field.

The vValueClick routine shows the default means for setting or getting the value of a field:

```
void __fastcall TForm1::bValueClick(TObject *Sender)
{
  ShowMessage(tblOrders->FieldByName("TaxRate")->Value);
}
```

This is the standard way to get at a field. You use the AsString or AsInteger properties for conversion, but when you just want to get at the type of a field, you can use the Value property. However, the issue of conversion can sometimes raise its head at strange moments, so it is helpful to note that properties such as AsInteger and AsString exist.

In the `TField` object, the `Value` property is declared as being of type `Variant`, which means it will handle most type conversions for you automatically. This is illustrated in the previous example, where the `TaxRate` field, which is of type `Float`, is converted for you automatically to a string. Note, however, that descendants of `TField`, such as `TStringField`, may explicitly declare the `Value` field as an `AnsiString`:

```
__property System::AnsiString Value;
```

> **NOTE**
>
> Remember that Object Pascal treats properties and methods with the same name differently than C++. In particular, there is no function or method overloading in Object Pascal.

Here are some other illustrations of how to use the `TField` object:

```
void __fastcall TForm1::bAsStringClick(TObject *Sender)
{
  ShowMessage(tblOrders->FieldByName("TaxRate")->AsString);
}
void __fastcall TForm1::bAsIntegerClick(TObject *Sender)
{
  int i = tblOrders->FieldByName("TaxRate")->AsInteger;
  ShowMessage(static_cast<AnsiString>(i));
}
void __fastcall TForm1::bAsFloatClick(TObject *Sender)
{
  float f = tblOrders->FieldByName("TaxRate")->AsFloat;
  ShowMessage(static_cast<AnsiString>(f));
}
```

Three of the four routines shown here from the FieldObject program produce the same output. The odd man out in this group is the `bAsIntegerClick` method, which displays the value as an `Integer`, rather than as a floating-point number. For instance, if the value of the `TaxRate` field in the current record was 4.5, three of the methods shown here would display the string `"4.5"`. The `bAsIntegerClick` method, however, would display the string as simply `"4"`. The difference here is simply due to the fact that the `AsInteger` property automatically converts a floating point number to an int.

More Information on the `Fields` Property

The Fielder program that ships on this book's CD-ROM demonstrates some simple ways to use the `Fields` property of `TDataSet`. If you want to construct the program dynamically, place a `TTable`, two buttons, and two list boxes on a form, as shown in Figure 9.4. Hook up the `TTable` object to the CUSTOMER table that ships with BCB.

FIGURE 9.4.

The Fielder program shows how to use the Fields *property.*

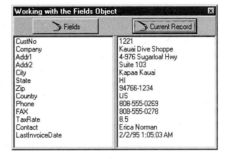

Double-click the Fields button and create a method that looks like this:

```
void __fastcall TForm1::bbFieldsClick(TObject *Sender)
{
  int i;
  ListBox1->Clear();
  for (i = 0; i < tblCustomer->FieldCount; i++)
    ListBox1->Items->Add(tblCustomer->Fields[i]->FieldName);
}
```

This method starts by clearing the current contents of the first list box, and then it iterates through each of the fields, adding their names one by one to the list box. Notice that the for loop shown here counts from 0 to one less than FieldCount. If you don't remember to stop one short of the value in FieldCount, you will get a "List Index Out of Bounds" error, because you will be attempting to read the name of a field that does not exist.

If you enter the code correctly, you will fill the list box with the names of all the fields in the current record structure. BCB provides other means to get at the same information, but this is a simple, programmatic way for you to access these names at runtime.

In the Fielder example, you can associate the following code with the second button you placed on the program's form:

```
void __fastcall TForm1::bbCurRecordClick(TObject *Sender)
{
  int i;
  ListBox2->Clear();
  for (i = 0; i < tblCustomer->FieldCount; i++)
    ListBox2->Items->Add(tblCustomer->Fields[i]->AsString);
}
```

This code adds the contents of each of the fields to the second list box. Notice that once again, it is necessary to iterate from zero to one less than FieldCount. The key point here is that the indices to Fields is zero-based.

9

USING TTABLE
AND TDATASET

> **NOTE**
>
> Much of the functionality of TField can be achieved with visual tools. In particular, you can manipulate fields with the Fields Editor, which you can access by clicking once with the right mouse button on the top of a TTable or TQuery object. This subject is explored in more depth in Chapter 9. However, good programmers know how to use both the methods of TDataSet and the Fields Editor. Furthermore, the Fields Editor can be used to best advantage if you understand how to enhance its functionality with some of the code you are learning about in this chapter.

In this section and the one previous to it you learned how to access the fields of a record. In the next section you will see how to use this knowledge when you want to append, insert, or edit records in a dataset.

Changing Data

The following methods enable you to change the data associated with a table:

```
void __fastcall Post(void);
void __fastcall Insert(void);
void __fastcall Edit(void);
void __fastcall Append(void);
void __fastcall Delete(void);
void __fastcall Cancel(void);
```

All these routines are part of TDataSet, and they are inherited and used frequently by TTable and TQuery.

The preceding list is hardly exhaustive. For instance, here are a few more related methods of TDataSet:

```
    void __fastcall AppendRecord(const TVarRec *Values, const System::Integer
                           Values_Size);
void __fastcall ClearFields(void);
    void __fastcall InsertRecord(const TVarRec *Values, const System::Integer
                           Values_Size);
void __fastcall FetchAll(void);
void __fastcall UpdateRecord(void);
void __fastcall ApplyUpdates(void);
void __fastcall CommitUpdates(void);
void __fastcall CancelUpdates(void);
```

The point here is not that you need to learn all these methods right away. Rather, I would concentrate on the first list, the one that include Post, Insert, and so on. This first list is meant to be a fairly careful selection of the most commonly used methods. Many programmers will never need to use any other methods than those in the first list. But it is helpful to know that the TDataSet object has considerable depth, and if you need customized functionality, you can generally find it in the TDataSet object itself.

NOTE

There are, of course, times when some programmers might need to do something to a database that is not covered in the VCL. In those cases, your next resort after TDataSet might well be the BDE itself. In particular, you should use the Borland Database Engine, found in BDE.HPP, or in a separate package available from Borland.

Whenever you want to change the data associated with a record, you must first put the dataset you are using into edit mode. As you will see, most of the visual controls do this automatically. However, if you want to change a table programmatically, you need to use the functions listed previously.

Here is a typical sequence you might use to change a field of a given record:

```
Table1->Edit();
Table1->FieldByName("ShipToContact")->Value = "Lyle Mayes";
Table1->Post();
```

 The first line shown places the database in edit mode. The next line assigns the string "Lyle Mayes" to the field labeled "ShipToContact". Finally, the data is written to disk when you call Post. See the SimpleEdit program on the CD-ROM accompanying this book for an example of this code in action. When looking at that programming, you might note that I have double-clicked the grid control in order to edit its properties. Working with the grid control will be explained in more depth later in this chapter.

The very act of moving on to the next record automatically posts your data to disk. For instance, the following code has the same effect as the code shown previously, plus it moves you on to the next record:

```
Table1->Edit();
Table1->FieldByName("ShipToContact")->Value = "Lyle Mayes";
Table->Next();
```

Calls to First, Next, Prior, and Last all perform Posts, as long as you are in edit mode. If you are working with server data and transactions, the rules explained here do not apply. However, transactions are a separate matter with their own special rules, as explained in Chapter 15, "Working with the Local InterBase Server." (Both local tables and SQL servers support transactions, but I cover this subject in the chapter on the InterBase server because it is usually considered an intermediate or advanced database topic.)

Even if you are not working with transactions, you can still undo your work at any time, as long as you have not yet either directly or indirectly called Post. For instance, if you have put a table into edit mode, and have changed the data in one or more fields, you can always change the record back to its original state by calling Cancel. For instance, you can edit every field of a record, and then call the following line to return to the state you were in before you began editing:

```
Table->Cancel();
```

Here is an excerpt from the SimpleEdit program that shows three button response methods that enable you to enter data and then cancel or post your changes. This code is still not robust enough for a shipping programming, but it gives you a good idea of how to proceed if you don't want to include much error checking.

```
void __fastcall TForm1::bEditClick(TObject *Sender)
{
  AnsiString S;

  if (InputQuery("Enter Contact Dialog", "Enter Name", S))
  {
    DMod->tblOrders->Edit();
    DMod->tblOrders->FieldByName("ShipToContact")->Value = S;
  }
}
void __fastcall TForm1::bCancelClick(TObject *Sender)
{
  DMod->tblOrders->Cancel();
}
void __fastcall TForm1::bPostClick(TObject *Sender)
{
  DMod->tblOrders->Post();
}
```

I say this code is not really robust. For instance, I do not check to see if the dataset is in edit or insert mode before calling Post. This kind of error checking is covered later in this chapter, and several times in the next few chapters. Despite its lack of error checking, the simple methods shown here should give you a good idea of how to proceed in your own programs.

> **NOTE**
>
> The InputQuery method shown in the bEditClick method is used to retrieve a string from the user. The first parameter is the title of the dialog used to retrieve the string, the second the prompt asking for a string, and the third the string to be retrieved. InputQuery is a Boolean VCL function. It is usually best to zero out the string passed in the third parameter before showing it to the user.

There are also cancel, edit, and insert buttons on the TDBNavigator control. You can use this control to work with a dataset without having to write any code.

There are two methods, called Append and Insert, which you can use whenever you want to add another record to a dataset. It obviously makes more sense to use Append on datasets that are not indexed, but BCB won't throw an exception if you use it on an indexed dataset. In fact, it is always safe to use either Append or Insert whenever you are working with a valid dataset.

On your disk you will find a simple program called Inserts, which shows how to use the Insert and Delete commands. To create the program by hand, first use a TTable, TDataSource, and TDBGrid to open up the COUNTRY table from the demos subdirectory. Then place two buttons on the program's form and call them Insert and Delete. When you are done, you should have a program like the one shown in Figure 9.5.

FIGURE 9.5.

The Inserts program knows how to insert and delete a record from the COUNTRY *table.*

> **NOTE**
>
> To spice up the Inserts program, you can drop a panel on the top of the form and then add the buttons to the panel. Set the panel's Align property to alTop, and set the TDBGrid's Align property to alClient. If you run the program, you can then maximize and resize the form without damaging the relationship between the various visual components.

The next step is to associate code with the Insert button:

```cpp
void __fastcall TForm1::FInsertClick(TObject *Sender)
{
  FCountry->Insert();
  FCountry->FieldByName("Name")->Value = "Erehwon";
  FCountry->FieldByName("Capital")->Value = "Nowhere";
  FCountry->FieldByName("Continent")->Value = "Imagination";
  FCountry->FieldByName("Area")->Value = 0;
  FCountry->FieldByName("Population")->Value = 0;
  FCountry->Post();
}
```

The function shown here first puts the table into insert mode, which means that a new record filled with blank fields is automatically inserted into the current position of the dataset.

9

USING TTABLE
AND TDATASET

After inserting the record, the next job is to assign strings to one or more of its fields. There are, of course, several different ways to enter this data. Using the current program, you could simply type the information into the current record in the grid. Or, if you wanted, you could place standard edit controls on the form and then set each field equal to the value the user has typed into the edit control:

```
Table1->FieldByName('Name')->Value = Edit1.Text;
```

If you place a table in edit mode, or if its TDataSource object has AutoEdit set to True, you can use data-aware controls to insert information directly into a record.

The intent of this chapter, however, is to show you how to enter data programmatically. Therefore you are presented with an example in which information is hardwired into the code segment of the program:

```
FCountry->FieldByName("Name")->Value = "Erehwon";
```

> **NOTE**
>
> One of the interesting (or perhaps "frustrating" would be a more appropriate word) byproducts of this technique is that pressing the Insert button twice in a row automatically triggers a "Key Violation" exception. To remedy this situation, you must either delete the current record or manually change the Name and Capital fields of the newly created record.
>
> You should recall that you can pass either a string or a number into a field when using the Value property. The Value property is of type Variant, and so you can, to a considerable degree, ignore type issues in this situation. For instance, there is no need to write code that looks like this:
>
> ```
> void __fastcall TForm1::FInsertClick(TObject *Sender)
> {
>   FCountry->Insert();
>   FCountry->FieldByName("Name")->AsString = "Erehwon";
>   FCountry->FieldByName("Capital")->AsString = "Nowhere";
>   FCountry->FieldByName("Continent")->AsString = "Imagination";
>   FCountry->FieldByName("Area")->AsInteger = 0;
>   FCountry->FieldByName("Population")->AsInteger = 0;
>   FCountry->Post();
> }
> ```
>
> Instead of calls to AsString and AsInteger, you can just use Value.

Looking at the code shown previously, you will see that the mere act of inserting a record and of filling out its fields is not enough to change the physical data that resides on disk. If you want the information to be written to disk, you must call Post.

After calling Insert, if you change your mind and decide to abandon the current record, you should call Cancel. As long as you do this before you call Post, everything you have entered is discarded, and the dataset is restored to the condition it was in before you called Insert.

One last related property that you should keep in mind is called CanModify. A table might be set to ReadOnly, in which case CanModify would return False. Otherwise CanModify returns True and you can enter edit or insert mode at will. CanModify is itself a read-only property. If you want to set a dataset to read-only, you should use the ReadOnly property, not CanModify.

In this section, you have learned how to use the Insert, Delete, Edit, Post, Cancel, and Append commands. Most of the actions associated with these commands are fairly intuitive, though it can take a little thought to see how they interact with the Fields property.

Using SetKey or FindKey to Search through a File

If you want to search for a value in a dataset, you can call on five TDataSet methods, called FindKey, FindNearest, SetKey, GotoNearest, and GotoKey. These routines assume that the field you are searching on is indexed. You should note that the BCB includes two methods for searching for values in a table. The SetKey, GotoNearest, and GotoKey methods comprise one technique, and FindKey and FindNearest comprise a second technique. I discuss both techniques in the next few paragraphs.

 This book's CD-ROM contains a demonstration program called Search that shows how to use these calls. You should open up this program and run it once to see how it works, or else follow the steps shown here to create the program yourself.

> **NOTE**
>
> There is actually a third method for searching for values in a table. I demonstrate that technique in the upcoming section from this chapter called "Filtering with the OnFilterRecord Event." The technique in question uses a series of routines called FindFirst, FindLast, FindNext and FindPrior. Unlike the routines used in this section, FindFirst and the like are not tied to the index fields of your table.

To create the Search program, place TTable and TDataSource objects on a data module, and TDBGrid, TButton, TLabel, and TEdit controls on a form. Arrange the visual controls so the result looks like the image shown in Figure 9.6. Be sure to set the caption of the button to Search, and then to wire the database controls so you can view the Customer table in the grid control.

FIGURE 9.6.

The Search program enables you to enter a customer number and then search for it by pressing a button.

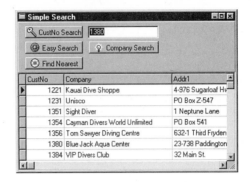

One set of functionality for the Search program is encapsulated in a single method that is attached to the Search button. This function retrieves the string entered in the edit control, searches the CustNo column until it finds the value, and finally switches the focus to the record it found.

In this program, I observe more carefully the rules of object-oriented programming. In particular, I create a data module, store the non-visual database tools on it, and then create methods for manipulating the data within the data module itself, rather than inside the object for the main form. This has only theoretical benefits in a simple program like Search. However, in a more complex program, this shows the way to create a single data module—with some built in rules and functionality—that can be reused in multiple programs. It also shows how to create programs that are easy to maintain, and easy to understand.

In particular, the main form contains a method response routine for the Search button that looks like this:

```
void __fastcall TForm1::bSearchClick(TObject *Sender)
{
    DMod->Search(Edit1->Text);
}
```

In its turn, the data module has a search method that looks like this:

```
void TDMod::Search(AnsiString S)
{
  tblCustomer->SetKey();
  tblCustomer->Fields[0]->AsString = S;
  tblCustomer->GotoKey();
}
```

As you can see, the TDMod object protects its data and exposes its functionality to the outside world through a single easy-to-call method. This way, TDMod could totally change the internal technique it has for searching through a table without forcing you to modify the TForm1 object in any way.

The first call in this function sets Table1 into search mode. BCB needs to be told to switch into search mode simply because you use the Fields property in a special way when BCB is in search mode. Specifically, you can index into the Fields property and assign it to the value you want to find.

In the example shown here, the CustNo field is the first column in the database, so you set the Fields index to zero. To actually carry out the search, simply call Table->GotoKey(). GotoKey is a Boolean function, so you could write code that looks like this:

```
if (!Table->GotoKey)
  DatabaseError("Error searching for data!");
```

The DatabaseError routine might raise a database exception of some kind.

If you are not sure of the value you are looking for, call Table->GotoNearest. GotoNearest will take you to the numerical or string value closest to the one you specify.

The FindKey and FindNearest routines perform the same function GotoKey or GotoNearest, but they are much easier to use. Here, for instance, is the technique for using FindKey:

```
tblCustomer->FindKey(OPENARRAY(TVarRec, (S)));
```

In this case, S is assumed to be a valid AnsiString containing a CustNo for which you want to search.

Here's how FindNearest looks:

```
tblCustomer->FindNearest(OPENARRAY(TVarRec, (S)));
```

When using FindKey or FindNearest there is no need to first call SetKey or to use the FieldByName property. (Needless to say, internally FindKey and FindNearest end up calling SetKey and FieldByName, before making calls to either GotoKey or GotoNearest.)

FindKey and FindNearest take an array of values in their sole parameter. You would pass multiple parameters to FindKey or FindNearest if you have a table that was indexed on multiple fields. In this case, the Customer table has a primary index on one field, called CustNo. But if it had multiple fields in the primary index, you could specify one or more of the values for these fields in this parameter:

```
tblCustomer->FindNearest(OPENARRAY(TVarRec, (S1, S2, S3)));
```

This is one of those cases where Object Pascal provides a built in, easy-to-use method for working with a dynamically created array of values, while there is no such native type in C++. C++, of course, is nothing if not flexible, and it is rare that you cannot find a way to make the language conform to your desires. For instance, in this case, one simple way for C++ to accommodate the VCL's request for a dynamically constructed array of values is by using the OPENARRAY macro and its associated template class from Sysdefs.h.

If you are not searching on the primary index of a file, you must use a secondary index and specify the name of the index you are using in the IndexName property for the current table. For instance, the `Customer` table has a secondary index called `ByCompany` on the field labeled `Company`. You would have to set the `IndexName` property to the name of that index if you wanted to search on that field. You could then use the following code when you searched on the `Company` field:

```
void TDMod::CompanySearch(AnsiString S)
{
  tblCustomer->IndexName = "ByCompany";
  tblCustomer->FindNearest(OPENARRAY(TVarRec, (S)));
}
```

Remember: This search will fail unless you first assign the correct value to the `IndexName` property. Furthermore, you should note that `IndexName` is a property of `TTable` and would therefore not automatically be included in any direct descendant of `TDataSet` or `TDBDataSet` that you might create yourself. In particular, it's not part of `TQuery`. Indeed, none of the functions discussed in this section are part of `TQuery`.

The previous code is flawed, or at least could be flawed in some cases, in that any attempt to search on the `CustNo` field after a call to `CompanySearch` would fail, because the table would no longer be indexed on the `CustNo` field. As a result, you might want to save the old index in a temporary variable so it can be restored at the end of the function:

```
void TDMod::CompanySearch(AnsiString S)
{
  AnsiString Temp(tblCustomer->IndexName);
  tblCustomer->IndexName = "ByCompany";
  tblCustomer->FindNearest(OPENARRAY(TVarRec, (S)));
  tblCustomer->IndexName = Temp;
}
```

A neat trick you can use with the `FindNearest` method involves performing an incremental search across a table. Start a new project and get things rolling quickly by simply dragging the `Country` table off the Database Explorer and onto `Form1`. You will end up with a `TTable`, `TDataSource`, and `TDBGrid` on the form, with the `TTable` hooked up to the `Country` table. Put a panel on the top of the form and set its `Align` property to `alTop`. Set the `Align` property of the `TDBGrid` for the `Country` table to `alClient`.

Place a `TEdit` component on the panel and create an `OnChange` event with the following code attached to it:

```
void __fastcall TForm1::Edit1Change(TObject *Sender)
{
  tblCountry->FindNearest(OPENARRAY(TVarRec, (Edit1->Text)));
}
```

Run the program. When you type into the edit control, you will automatically begin incrementally searching through the table. For instance, if you type `C`, you will go to the record for Canada, if you type `Cu`, you will go to the record for Cuba.

The incremental search example is available on disk as the IncrementalSearch program. It's perhaps worth pointing out that this program is interesting in part because it shows how you can use the built-in features of BCB to easily implement additional features that were never planned by the developers. For instance, there is no Incremental Search component in BCB. However, if you need to build one, the tools come readily to hand.

Filtering the Records in a Dataset with ApplyRange

The next two sections cover two different ways to filter data. Of these two techniques, the second is preferable on several counts; so if you are in a hurry, you can skip this section. The key difference between the two methods is that the one explained in this section uses keyed fields, while the next technique will work on any type of field. The technique used in the next section is very highly optimized, but the conservatives in the crowd might find the technique outlined in this section appealing because it relies on indexes, which are a tried and true database technology, guaranteed to execute in a highly optimized manner.

The ApplyRange function lets you set a filter that limits the range of the records you view. For instance, in the Customers database, the CustNo field ranges from just over 1,000 to a little under 10,000. If you wanted to see only those records that had a customer number between 2000 and 3000, you would use the ApplyRange method from TTable and two related routines. When using this method, you must work with a field that is indexed. (As explained in the next chapter, you can perform this same type of operation on a nonindexed field by using a TQuery object rather than TTable object. You can also use the technique explained in the next section of this chapter for searching on non-keyed fields.)

Here are the four methods of TTable that make up the suite of routines you will use when setting up filters:

```
void __fastcall ApplyRange(void);
void __fastcall SetRangeEnd(void);
void __fastcall SetRangeStart(void);
void __fastcall CancelRange(void);
```

To use these functions, perform the following steps:

1. Call SetRangeStart and then use the Fields property to designate the start of the range.

2. Call SetRangeEnd and use the Fields property a second time to designate the end of the range you are specifying.

3. The first two actions prepare the filter; now all you need to do is call ApplyRange, and the new filter you have specified will take effect.

4. If you want to undo the effects of a call to ApplyRange or SetRange, you can call the CancelRange function.

The Ranger program, which is located on the CD-ROM that comes with this book, shows you explicitly how to use these functions. To create the program, drop a TTable, TDataSource, and TDBGrid onto a form. Wire them up so that you can view the CUSTOMERS table from the demos subdirectory. You need to set Table->Active to True. Next, drop two labels on the form and set their captions to Start Range and End Range. Place two edit controls next to the labels. Finally, add a single button with the caption ApplyRange. When you are done, you should have a form like the one shown in Figure 9.7.

FIGURE 9.7.

The Ranger program shows how to limit the number of records from a table that are visible at any one time.

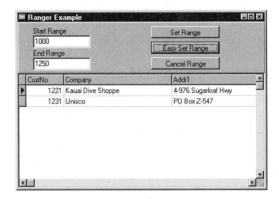

The SetRangeStart and SetRangeEnd functions enable you to declare the first and last members in the range of records you want to see. To get started using the functions, first double-click the button labeled SetRange, and then create a function that looks like this:

```
void __fastcall TForm1::bbSetRangeClick(TObject *Sender)
{
  DMod->SetRange(StrToInt(eStart->Text), eEnd->Text.ToInt());
}
```

This code shows two different ways to translate a string value into an integer value. The first technique calls a stand-alone VCL method named StrToInt, the second technique uses a method of the AnsiString class.

Once again, the TForm1::bbSetRangeClick function merely calls a method of TDMod that does all the real work:

```
void TDMod::SetRange(int AStart, int AnEnd)
{
  tblCustomer->SetRangeStart();
  tblCustomer->Fields[0]->AsInteger = AStart;
  tblCustomer->SetRangeEnd();
  tblCustomer->Fields[0]->AsInteger = AnEnd;
  tblCustomer->ApplyRange();
}
```

The TDMod::SetRange function first calls SetRangeStart, which puts the table into range mode and blanks out the records seen in the TDBGrid control. Once in range mode, the program next expects you to specify the beginning range, which in this case you grabbed from the first edit control. Setting the end range for the program involves following a similar pattern. First you call SetRangeEnd, and then you pass it an appropriate value culled from the second Edit control back on the main form.

Note that you can use the Fields property to specify the actual range you want to use:

```
Table->Fields[0]->AsInteger = AStart;
```

This use of the Fields property is obviously a special case, since the syntax shown here is usually used to set the value of a field, not to define a range. This special case comes into effect only after you have put Table1 into range mode by calling SetRangeStart.

The final step in the function just shown is the call to ApplyRange. This is the routine that actually puts your request into effect. When the call to ApplyRange ends, the table is no longer in range mode, and the Fields property returns to its normal functionality.

If you want to undo the results of a call to ApplyRange, you can call the CancelRange function:

```
Table->CancelRange();
```

A typical run of the program might involve the user typing in the number 4000 in the first edit control and the number 5000 in the next edit control. After entering the data, clicking the ApplyRange button would put the request into effect.

So far, you have learned how to filter the data from a table so that you view only a particular range of records. The steps involved are threefold:

1. Call SetRangeStart and specify the beginning value in the range of records you want to see.
2. Call SetRangeEnd and specify the ending value in the range of records you want to see.
3. Call ApplyRange in order to view the results of your request.

BCB also provides a shorthand method calling the SetRangeStart, SetRangeEnd, and ApplyRange methods. This technique is featured in both the Ranger and Ranger2 programs. The conceit behind the Ranger2 program is to place a Windows 95 track bar control at the top of the form, and to enable the user to move the thumb on the track bar in order to select a range of values to view:

```
void __fastcall TForm1::TBarChange(TObject *Sender)
{
  int i = TBar->Position * 1000;
  int j = i + 1000;
  DMod->SetRange(i, j);
}
```

TBarChange is called whenever the thumb on the track bar moves. The valid range of values on the track bar are 1 to 10. The code multiplies current position on the track bar times 1,000 to get the start of the range, and adds 1,000 to this value to get the end range. The theory here is that the track bar measures the range in increments of 1,000.

The TBarChange method calls the SetRange method of TDMod:

```
void TDMod::SetRange(int AStart, int AFinish)
{
  tblCustomer->SetRange(OPENARRAY(TVarRec, (AStart)), OPENARRAY(TVarRec,
(AFinish)));
}
```

This TTable SetRange method takes two OpenArray templates, the first to cover the starting range, the second to cover the ending range. The idea here is that the table might be indexed on multiple fields, and you can use an OpenArray to specify the values associated with more than one field, if needed.

Filtering with the OnFilterRecord Event

The OnFilterRecord event enables you to set up filters on fields even if they are not keyed. You can use this event in two different ways.

The first technique involves setting the TTable Filtered property to True. When you do this, you will see only the records that are designated by the formula defined in the OnFilterRecord event. For instance, if you had a State field in your dataset and the OnFilterRecord event said to accept only records from New Hampshire, you would see only the records from New Hampshire when Filtered was set to True.

The second technique enables you to search for records even when Filtered is set to False. For instance, if you set up an OnFilterRecord event that accepted only records from New Hampshire, you could call Table->FindFirst to find the first of these records, and Table->FindNext to find the next one, and so on. There are also FindPrior and FindLast properties that you can use with the OnFilterRecord event. The key point to remember is that as long as the OnFilterRecord event is implemented correctly, you can use FindFirst, and so on, even when Filtered is not set to True.

 An example of the OnFilterRecord event is shown in the Filter program found on this book's CD-ROM. The rest of this section describes how to create that program from scratch.

To see the OnFilterRecord event in a live program, start by dragging the Country table off the Database Explorer onto a blank form or data module from a new project. (It sometimes helps to close the Database Explorer after the drop operation, rather than trying to switch between the two tools by changing their focus.) Drop down a panel and set up the Align property for the panel and for the TDBGrid as explained in the previous examples from this chapter.

Place a TCheckBox object on the panel and set its caption to Filtered. Associate the following method with the OnClick event for the checkbox:

```
void __fastcall TForm1::FFilterClick(TObject *Sender)
{
  FCountry->Filtered = FFilter->Checked;
}
```

This code ensures that the table will be filtered whenever the checkbox is checked.

Use the Fields Editor for the Table1 object to create field objects for all the fields in the database. Drag the Continent field off the Fields Editor onto the form, as shown in Figure 9.8.

FIGURE 9.8.

The main form for the Filter program includes a grid, a panel, a checkbox, a TDBEdit *control, and a button.*

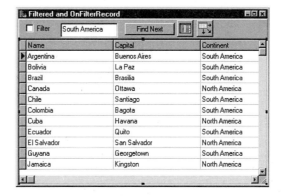

Turn to the Events page for the TTable object, and associate the following code with the OnFilterRecord event:

```
void __fastcall TForm1::FCountryFilterRecord(TDataSet *DataSet, Boolean &Accept)
{
  Accept = tblCountry->FieldByName("Continent")->AsString == "South America";
}
```

This code states that the OnFilterRecord event will accept all records where the Continent field of the Country table contains the word "South America". The Continent field will have either the value North America or South America in it. If you click the checkbox to turn the filter on, you will see only the records from South America. In short, the filter will automatically accept only those records whose Continent field matches the value "South America".

If you wanted, you could change the code so that it always filtered on the value currently in the Continent field:

```
void __fastcall TForm1::FCountryFilterRecord(TDataSet *DataSet, Boolean &Accept)
{
  Accept = tblCountry->FieldByName("Continent")->AsString == DBEdit1->Text;
}
```

For this code to work, you must drop down a DBEdit control, and hook it up to the Continent field of the Country table.

It's important to note that the Accept field of the OnFilterRecord event is a Boolean value. This means that you can set up any kind of a Boolean statement in order to set the value of this field. For instance, in addition to the = operator, you could also use the following operators: <>, >, or <'.

The FindNext, FindFirst, and FindPrior functions are extremely easy to use. For instance, if you wanted to find the next record in the database that satisfied the requirements specified in the OnFilterRecord event, you could write the following code to be fired in response to clicking a button:

```
void __fastcall TForm1::FFindNextClick(TObject *Sender)
{
    tblCountry->FindNext();
}
```

The other functions work exactly the same way. This is a Boolean function that will return False if the search fails. Remember that these methods work even if the Filtered property of the TTable object is set to False.

Using the Refresh Function

As you already know, any table that you open is always subject to change. In short, you should regard a table as a fluid, rather than as a static, entity. Even if you are the only person using a particular table and even if you are not working in a networked environment, there is always the possibility that the program you are running may have two different ways of changing a piece of data. As a result, you should always be aware of the need to update, or refresh, your current view of a table. Furthermore, BCB will not always update data after you perform an action in the background. As a result, you may need to update data by performing a refresh, particularly after certain kinds of delete operations.

The Refresh function is related to the Open function because it retrieves the data, or some portion of the data, associated with a given table. For instance, when you open a table, BCB retrieves data directly from a database file. Similarly, when you refresh a table, BCB goes out and retrieves data directly from a table. You can therefore use this function to update a table if you think it might have changed. It is faster, and much more efficient, to call Refresh than to call Close and then Open.

> **NOTE**
>
> In a networked environment, refreshing a table can sometimes lead to unexpected results. For instance, if a user is viewing a record that has been deleted, it will seem to disappear out from under the user the moment the program calls Refresh. Similarly, if another user has edited data, a call to Refresh can result in data dynamically changing while a user is viewing it. Of course, it is unlikely that one user will change or delete a record while another is viewing it, but it is possible. As a result, you should use calls to Refresh with caution.

Bookmarks

It is often useful to mark a particular location in a table so that you can quickly return to it when desired. BCB provides this functionality through three methods of TDataSet that use the metaphor of a bookmark. When you use these functions, it is as if you have left a bookmark in the dataset, and you can therefore turn back to it quickly whenever you want:

```
void __fastcall FreeBookmark(System::Pointer Bookmark);
System::Pointer __fastcall GetBookmark(void);
void __fastcall GotoBookmark(System::Pointer Bookmark);
```

As you can see, the GetBookmark call returns a variable of type pointer, which is in fact just a pointer to a Bookmark. A Bookmark pointer contains enough information to enable BCB to find the location to which it refers. Therefore, you can simply pass this bookmark to the GotoBookmark function, and you will immediately be returned to the location with which the bookmark is associated.

It's important to note that a call to GetBookmark allocates memory for the bookmark, and so you must remember to call FreeBookmark before you exit your program and before every attempt to reuse a bookmark. For instance, here is a typical set of calls for freeing a bookmark, setting a bookmark, and moving to a bookmark:

```
void __fastcall TForm1::bMarkClick(TObject *Sender)
{
  if (Bookmark == NULL)
    Bookmark = DataMod->tblCountry->GetBookmark();
}

void __fastcall TForm1::bReturnClick(TObject *Sender)
{
  if (Bookmark != NULL)
  {
    DataMod->tblCountry->GotoBookmark(Bookmark);
    DataMod->tblCountry->FreeBookmark(Bookmark);
    Bookmark = NULL;
  }
}

void __fastcall TForm1::FormDestroy(TObject *Sender)
{
  DataMod->tblCountry->FreeBookmark(Bookmark);
}
```

The code shown here is excerpted from a program called Bookmark, which comes with the CD-ROM that accompanies this book. In the declaration for TForm1, a variable called Bookmark is declared in the private section. Every time the MarkClick function is called, the first step is to be sure the Bookmark is freed. It is never a mistake to call FreeBookmark, because the function checks to make sure Bookmark is not set to NULL. After de-allocating any existing copies of the Bookmark, a new one is allocated. You can then call GotoBookmark and repeat the cycle.

Bookmarks are powerful features that can be of great benefit under certain circumstances. The developers of BCB, for instance, used bookmarks frequently in order to develop the database components. They often have several different bookmarks open at the same time.

> **NOTE**
>
> Most of the features surfaced in `TDataSet` are built into the BDE. For instance, filters, searching for keys, and bookmarks are available to anyone who uses the BDE. What the developers of BCB have done is surface these features so that they can be easily accessed using object-oriented programming techniques. The calls from the BDE are available to people who purchase the Borland Database Engine from Borland or to patient BCB spelunkers who spend some time with `BDE.hpp`.

More on TDataSet and TTable

`TTable` adds several frequently used properties to `TDataSet`:

```
__property System::Boolean ReadOnly;
// From TTable
__property System::Boolean Exclusive;
__property System::AnsiString MasterFields;
__property DB::TDataSource *MasterSource;
__property System::AnsiString TableName;
```

Of the properties shown here, the most common ones are probably `TableName` and `ReadOnly`. You can use the `TableName` property to specify the table you want to open, and you can set the `ReadOnly` property to `True` or `False` depending on whether you want to allow the user to change the data in a dataset. Neither of these properties can be used when a table is active.

The `Exclusive` property lets you open up a table in a mode that guarantees that no other user will be able to access it at the same time. You will not be able to set `Exclusive` to `True` if another user is currently accessing the table.

The `MasterSource` property is used to specify a `TDataSource` from which the current table needs to obtain information. For instance, if you linked two tables in a master/detail relationship, the detail table can track the events occurring in the first table by specifying the first table's data source in this property. This technique is demonstrated in the following section on linked cursors.

Creating Linked Cursors

Linked cursors enable programmers to easily define a one-to-many relationship. For instance, it is sometimes useful to link the CUSTOMER and ORDERS tables so that each time the user views a particular customer's name, he or she can also see a list of the orders related to that customer. In short, the user can view one customer's record, and then see only the orders related to that customer.

To understand linked cursors, you first need to see that the CUSTOMER table and the ORDERS table are related to one another through the CustNo field. This relationship exists specifically because there needs to be a way to find out which orders are associated with which customer.

 The Links program on the book's CD-ROM demonstrates how to create a program that uses linked cursors. To create the program on your own, place two tables, two data sources, and two grids on a form. Wire the first set of controls to the CUSTOMER table and the second set to the ORDERS table. If you run the program at this stage, you should be able to scroll through all the records in either table, as shown in Figure 9.9.

FIGURE 9.9.

The Links program shows how to define a relationship between two tables.

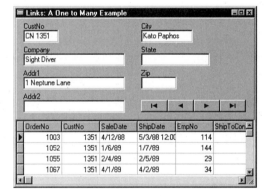

The next step is to link the ORDERS table to the CUSTOMER table so that you view only those orders associated with the current customer record. To do this, you must take three steps, each of which requires some explanation:

1. Set the MasterSource property of Table2 to DataSource1.
2. Set the MasterField property in Table2 to CustNo.
3. Set the IndexName property of Table2 to ByCustNo.

If you now run the program, you will see that both tables are linked together, and that every time you move to a new record in the CUSTOMER table, you can see only those records in the ORDERS table that belong to that particular customer.

The MasterSource property in Table2 specifies the DataSource from which Table2 can draw information. Specifically, it allows the ORDERS table to know which record currently has the focus in the CUSTOMER table.

The question then becomes this: what other information does `Table2` need in order to properly filter the contents of the `ORDERS` table? The answer to this question is twofold:

1. It needs the name of the field that links the two tables.
2. It needs the index of the field in the `ORDERS` table that is going to be linked to the `CUSTOMER` table.

In order to correctly supply the information described here, you must first ensure that both the `CUSTOMER` table and the `ORDERS` table have the correct indexes. Specifically, you must ensure that there are indexes on both the `CustNo` field and the `CustNo` field in the `ORDERS` table. If the index in question is a primary index, there is no need to specifically name that index, and therefore you can leave the `IndexName` field blank in both tables. However, if either of the tables is linked to the other through a secondary index, you must explicitly designate that index in the `IndexName` field of the table that has a secondary index.

In the example shown here, the `CUSTOMER` table has a primary index on the `CustNo` field, so there is no need to specify the index name. However, the `ORDERS` table does not have a primary index on the `CustNo` field, and so you must explicitly declare it in the `IndexName` property by typing in or selecting the word `CustNo`.

NOTE

To simplify the process described previously, the developers put in a dialog that appears when you click the `MasterFields` property. This dialog simplifies the process and helps to automate the task of setting up a link between two tables.

In particular, to use the MasterFields dialog, start a new project and drag the `Customer` and `Orders` tables off the Explorer onto the main form. Arrange the grids with the `Customer` grid on top and the `Orders` grid beneath it. Set the `DataSource` property of the `Orders` TTable object to the `TDataSource` object associated with the `Customer` table.

Pop up the MasterFields dialog and make sure the Available Indexes is set to Primary Index. Click the `CustNo` field in both Detail Fields and MasterFields list boxes. Click Add. The two fields will appear in the Joined Fields list box. At this stage, you are all done, so you can click the OK button.

Some indexes can contain multiple fields, so you must explicitly state the name of the field you want to use to link the two tables. In this case, you should enter the name `CustNo` in the `MasterFields` property of `Table2`. If you wanted to link two tables on more than one field, you should list all the fields, placing a pipe symbol between each one:

```
Table->MasterFields := "CustNo ¦ SaleData ¦ ShipDate";
```

In this particular case, however, I'm guilty of a rather shady bit of expediency. In particular, the statement shown here makes no sense, because the `SaleData` and `ShipDate` fields are neither indexed nor duplicated in the CUSTOMER table. Therefore, you should only enter the field called CustNo in the MasterFields property. You can specify this syntax directly in a property editor, or else write code that performs the same chore.

It's important to note that this section covered only one of several ways you can create linked cursors using BCB. Chapter 10, "SQL and the TQuery Object," describes a second method that will appeal to people who are familiar with SQL. The Database Expert provides a third means of achieving this end. As you have seen, the Database Expert is an easy-to-use visual tool. The Query Builder is yet a fourth way of creating a one-to-many relationship between two tables. Like the Database Expert, the Query Builder is a visual tool that can save you much time. However, it's best not to rely entirely on visual tools, because there are times when you might feel limited by their functionality. In such cases, you will be glad if you understand the underlying technology. That way you can get the job done yourself without being forced to wrestle with the limitations of a particular tool.

TDataSource Basics

Class TDataSource is used as a conduit between TTable or TQuery and the data-aware controls such as TDBGrid, TDBEdit, and TDBComboBox. Under most circumstances, the only thing you will do with a TDataSource object is to set its DataSet property to an appropriate TTable or TQuery object. Then, on the other end, you will also want to set a data-aware control's DataSource property to the TDataSource object you are currently using.

> **NOTE**
>
> Visual tools such as TDBEdit or TDBGrid all have a DataSource property that connects to a TDataSource object. When reading this chapter, you need to distinguish between a visual control's DataSource property and the TDataSource object to which it is attached. In other words, the word DataSource can be a bit confusing. I try to refer to a TDataSource object as a data source, and to refer to the DataSource property as a DataSource. You should, however watch the context in which these words are used, and be aware of the rather subtle distinctions in meaning surrounding this issue.

A TDataSource also has an Enabled property, and this can be useful whenever you want to temporarily disconnect a table or query from its visual controls. This functionality might be desirable if you need to programmatically iterate through all the records in a table. For instance, if a TTable is connected to a data-aware control, each time you call TTable.Next, the visual control needs to be updated. If you are quickly going through two or three thousand records, it can take considerable time to perform the updates to the visual controls. In cases like this, the best thing to do is set the TDataSource object's Enabled field to False, which will enable you to iterate through the records without having to worry about screen updates. This single change can improve the speed of some routines by several thousand percent.

The AutoEdit property of TDataSource enables you to decide whether or not the data-aware controls attached to it will automatically enter edit mode when you start typing inside them. Many users prefer to keep AutoEdit set to True, but if you want to give a user more precise control over when the database can be edited, this is the property you need. In short, if you set AutoEdit to False, you have essentially made the table read-only.

Using TDataSource to Check the State of a Database

The events belonging to TDataSource can be extremely useful. To help illustrate them, you will find a program on the CD-ROM that comes with this book called Dsevents that responds to all three TDataSource events. This program shows an easy way to set up a "poor man's" data-aware edit control that automatically shows and posts data to and from a database at the appropriate time.

This example works with the COUNTRY database and it has a TTable, TDataSource, five edits, six labels, eight buttons, and a panel on it. The actual layout for the program is shown in Figure 9.10. Note that the sixth label appears on the panel located at the bottom of the main form.

FIGURE 9.10.

The Dsevents program shows how to track the current state of a table.

TDataSource has three key events associated with it:

```
OnDataChange
OnStateChange
OnUpdateData
```

A TDataSource OnStateChange event occurs whenever the current state of the dataset changes. A dataset always knows what state it's in. If you call Edit, Append, or Insert, the table knows that it is now in edit mode, and that fact is reflected in the value held in the TDataSource State property. Similarly, after you Post a record, the database knows that it is no longer editing data, and it switches back into browse mode. If you want more control, the next section in this chapter explains that a dataset also sends out messages just before and just after you change states.

The dataset has nine possible states, each of which are captured in the following enumerated type:

```
enum TDataSetState { dsInactive, dsBrowse, dsEdit, dsInsert,
                     dsSetKey, dsCalcFields, dsUpdateNew,
                     dsUpdateOld, dsFilter };
```

During the course of a normal session, the database will frequently move back and forth between browse, edit, insert, or the other modes. If you want to track these changes, you can respond to them by writing code that looks like this:

```
void __fastcall TForm1::dsCountryStateChange(TObject *Sender)
{
  AnsiString S;

  switch (tblCountry->State)
  {
    case dsInactive:
      S = "Inactive";
      break;
    case dsBrowse:
      S = "Browse";
      break;
    case dsEdit:
      S = "Edit";
      break;
    case dsInsert:
      S = "Insert";
      break;
    case dsSetKey:
      S = "SetKey";
      break;
  }
  StatusBar1->Panels->Items[0]->Text = S;
}
```

In this code, I am using a TStatusBar object to report the state of the dataset to the user. To use a TStatusBar object, first drop one on a form and then double-click on the editor for the TStatusBar Panels property to bring up the Status Bar Panel Editor. Create a new panel in the Status Bar Panel Editor and set its text to Browse, or to some other string. You now have one panel the text of which you can change with the following line of code:

```
StatusBar1->Panels->Items[0]->Text = S;
```

It's time now to stop talking about the OnStateChange event and to move on to the OnDataChange event. OnDataChange occurs whenever you move on to a new record. In other words, if you call Next, Previous, Insert, or any other call that is likely to lead to a change in the data associated with the current record, an OnDataChange event will get fired. If someone begins editing the data in a data-aware control, an OnResync event occurs.

Dsevents has one small conceit that you need to understand if you want to learn how the program works. Because there are five separate edit controls on the main form, you need to have some way to refer to them quickly and easily. One simple method is to declare an array of edit controls:

```
TEdit *Edits[5];
```

9

USING TTABLE AND TDATASET

To fill out the array, you can respond to the forms `OnCreate` event:

```
void __fastcall TForm1::FormCreate(TObject *Sender)
{
  int i;
  for (i = 0; i <= 4; i++)
    Edits[i] = (TEdit*)FindComponent("Edit" + IntToStr(i + 1));
  tblCountry->First();
}
```

The code shown here assumes that the first edit control you want to use is called `Edit1`, the second is called `Edit2`, and so on.

Given the existence of this array of controls, it is very simple to use the `OnDataChange` event to keep them in sync with the contents of the current record in a dataset:

```
void __fastcall TForm1::dsCountryDataChange(TObject *Sender, TField *Field)
{
  int i;

  if (FUpdating)
    return;
  for (i = 0; i <= 4; i++)
    Edits[i]->Text = tblCountry->Fields[i]->AsString;
}
```

This code iterates through each of the fields of the current record and puts its contents in the appropriate edit control. Whenever `Table->Next` is called, or whenever any of the other navigational methods are called, the function shown previously gets a chance to strut onto the stage. Its primary *raison d'etre* is to ensure that the edit controls always contain the data from the current record.

Whenever `Post` gets called, you will want to perform the opposite action. That is, you will want to snag the information from the edit controls and tuck them away inside the current record. To execute this chore, simply respond to `TDataSource.OnUpdateData` events, which are generated automatically whenever `Post` is called:

```
void __fastcall TForm1::dsCountryUpdateData(TObject *Sender)
{
  int i;
  for (i = 0; i <= 4; i++)
    tblCountry->Fields[i]->Value = Edits[i]->Text;
}
```

The Dsevents program switches into edit mode whenever you type anything in one of the edit controls. It manages this sleight of hand by responding to `OnKeyDown` events:

```
void __fastcall TForm1::Edit1KeyDown(TObject *Sender, Word &Key,
      TShiftState Shift)
{
  if (dsCountry->State != dsEdit)
    tblCountry->Edit();
}
```

This code demonstrates how to use the `State` variable of a `TDataSource` object to find out the current mode of the dataset.

Tracking the State of a Dataset

In the last section, you learned how to use TDataSource to keep tabs on the current state of a TDataSet and to respond just before certain events are about to take place.

Using a TDataSource object is the simplest way to perform all these functions. However, if you would like to track these events without using TDataSource, you can respond to the following rather intimidating list of events from TDataSet, all of which are naturally inherited by TTable or TQuery:

```
__property TDataSetNotifyEvent BeforeOpen;
__property TDataSetNotifyEvent AfterOpen;
__property TDataSetNotifyEvent BeforeClose;
__property TDataSetNotifyEvent AfterClose;
__property TDataSetNotifyEvent BeforeInsert;
__property TDataSetNotifyEvent AfterInsert;
__property TDataSetNotifyEvent BeforeEdit;
__property TDataSetNotifyEvent AfterEdit;
__property TDataSetNotifyEvent BeforePost;
__property TDataSetNotifyEvent AfterPost;
__property TDataSetNotifyEvent BeforeCancel;
__property TDataSetNotifyEvent AfterCancel;
__property TDataSetNotifyEvent BeforeDelete;
__property TDataSetNotifyEvent AfterDelete;
__property TDataSetNotifyEvent OnNewRecord;
__property TDataSetNotifyEvent OnCalcFields;
__property TFilterRecordEvent OnFilterRecord;
__property TOnServerYieldEvent OnServerYield;
__property TUpdateErrorEvent OnUpdateError;
__property TUpdateRecordEvent OnUpdateRecord;
__property TDataSetErrorEvent OnEditError;
__property TDataSetErrorEvent OnPostError;
__property TDataSetErrorEvent OnDeleteError;
```

Most of these properties are self-explanatory. The BeforePost event, for instance, is functionally similar to the TDataSource->OnUpdateData event that is explained and demonstrated previously. In other words, the Dsevents program would work the same if you responded to DataSource1->OnUpdateData or to Table->BeforePost. Of course, in one case you would not need to have a TDataSource on the form, while the other requires it.

All of these events are associated with methods that have a particular signature. For instance, most of them are of type TDataSetNotifyEvent. A TDataSetNotifyEvent is declared like this:

```
typedef void _C!astcall (__closure *TDataSetNotifyEvent)(TDataSet *DataSet);
```

Or, to make the matter more comprehensible, here is the code BCB generates for an AfterClose event:

```
void __fastcall TForm1::tblCountryAfterClose(TDataSet *DataSet)
{
}
```

9

**USING TTABLE
AND TDATASET**

To work with these properties, you should see the EventOrd program found on the CD-ROM that accompanies this book, and shown below in Figure 9.11. This program is better experienced in action, rather than explained in words here on the page. The main point of the program is to notify you when any major event associated with a table occurs. If you play with the program for some time, you will begin to get a good feeling for the events associated with a table, and for the order in which they occur.

> **NOTE**
>
> When I first wrote this program, I learned a number of things about VCL databases that had not been clear to me from prior experience. There is nothing like seeing the events being fired to start to get a sense of how the VCL really works! So I would strongly recommend spending some time with this program.

FIGURE 9.11.

The EventOrd program tracks the events that occur in a TTable-*based database application.*

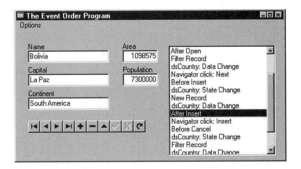

The EventOrd program responds to all the published events that can occur on a TTable object. Each method response event does nothing more than report the event by posting a string to list box. Here, for instance, is the response to the NewRecord event:

```
void __fastcall TDataMod::tblCountryNewRecord(TDataSet *DataSet)
{
  HandleDataEvent("New Record");
}
```

The HandleDataEvent pops the string into the list box and makes sure that the most recently added items in the list box are always visible:

```
void __fastcall TDataMod::HandleDataEvent(char * S)
{
  Form1->ListBox1->Items->Add(S);
  Form1->ListBox1->ItemIndex = Form1->ListBox1->Items->Count - 1;
}
```

The main form for the application has a simple method that will write the contents of the list box to disk:

```
void __fastcall TForm1::WriteListBoxDataToDisk1Click(TObject *Sender)
{
  if (OpenDialog1->Execute())
    ListBox1->Items->SaveToFile(OpenDialog1->FileName);
}
```

Here, for instance, is a short run from the program:

```
Before Open
Filter Record
dsCountry: State Change
dsCountry: Data Change
After Open
Filter Record
dsCountry: Data Change
Navigator click: Next
Filter Record
dsCountry: Data Change
Navigator click: Next
Before Insert
dsCountry: State Change
New Record
dsCountry: Data Change
After Insert
Navigator click: Insert
Before Cancel
dsCountry: State Change
Filter Record
dsCountry: Data Change
After Cancel
Navigator click: Cancel
```

The preceding list records what happens when

■ A table is opened

■ The TDBNavigator Next button is pressed twice

■ The TDBNavigator Insert button is pressed

■ The TDBNavigator Cancel button is pressed

Unfortunately, the TDBNavigator OnClick method occurs after the changes are recorded in the dataset. For instance, the last six events in the record look like this:

```
Before Cancel
dsCountry: State Change
Filter Record
dsCountry: Data Change
After Cancel
Navigator click: Cancel
```

They actually occurred in the following order:

```
Navigator click: Cancel
Before Cancel
dsCountry: State Change
Filter Record
dsCountry: Data Change
After Cancel
```

The point is that I clicked the navigator Cancel button, and then the other events occurred, in the order shown. However, BCB gives priority to the database events, and then reports the OnClick event.

If you do a lot of database programming, you really need to know the order in which certain events occur. Outlining all that information in these pages is not likely to be particularly helpful to most readers. To learn about this information, it's best just to watch the events occur and to trace their history. So fire up the OrdEvents program and see what you can learn from it.

Working with TDatabase

While you are learning the basics of connecting to a table, you should also look at the TDatabase object, which exists primarily to give you a means of staying connected to a database even if you are continually opening and closing a series of tables. If you use TDatabase, you can be connected to Oracle, InterBase, or other servers without ever opening any tables. You can then begin opening and closing tables over and over without having to incur the overhead of connecting to the database each time you call Open.

The TDatabase object also enables you to start server-based applications without specifying a password, and it gives you access to transactions. Besides the information in this chapter, more information on TDataBase appears in the discussion of the Transacts program, which is covered at the end of Chapter 15, "Working with the Local InterBase Server."

To use the TDatabase object, first drop it on to a form or data module. Set the AliasName property to DBDEMOS. Create your own DatabaseName, such as MyDBDemos. Set Connected to True. Drop down a TTable object and set its DatabaseName property to MyDBDemos. The issue here is that you created a "new database" when you dropped the TDatabase object on the form and filled in its fields as shown previously. Therefore you can select the name of this database from the drop-down list for the TTable DatabaseName property.

After connecting the table to the TDatabase object, you can work with the TTable object exactly as you would under normal circumstances. For instance, you could connect it to the BioLife table, as shown in the DatabaseObject program found on the CD-ROM that accompanies this book.

If you double-click a TDatabase object, you bring up the component editor for this object, shown in Figure 9.12. Inside the component editor you can discover the default values for many of the database parameters passed in the BDE alias for this database.

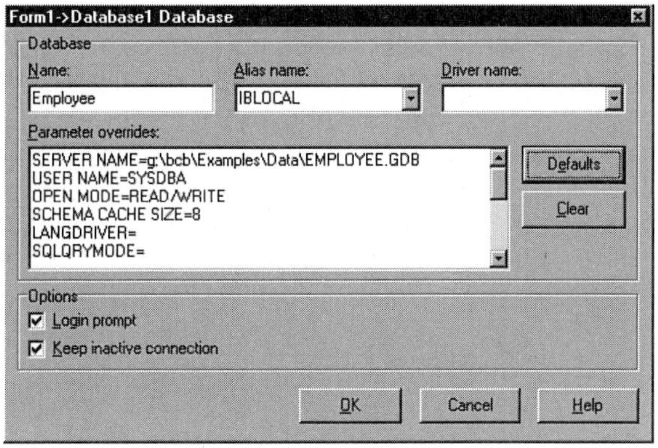

FIGURE 9.12.

The component editor for the TDataBase *object displaying information about a connection to an InterBase table.*

In this section your learned about the TDatabase object, which can be used to optimize code that is continually connecting and disconnecting from tables that belong to one database. Throughout the rest of this chapter and the next, the TDatabase object will play only a minor role. However, these components come into their own when you are connecting to SQL data as described in Chapter 15.

Connecting to a Database without Visual Tools

Everything that you do in BCB with the visual tools can also be done in code. The visual tools are just an easy way to write code; they do not do anything special that you can't also do in code. In fact, the code came first, and then the visual tools were added to make it easier for you to create programs. The key to BCB is the way its language conforms to the metaphors of visual programming without causing you any undo overhead.

> **NOTE**
>
> It would not be true, of course, to say that BCB has no overhead as a result of its concessions to the world of visual programming. For instance, all objects that reside on the Component Palette inherit at least some code that makes them able to be manipulated visually. In other words, they descend not directly from TObject, but from TComponent.
>
> The amount of this code is small compared to what you see in a product like PowerBuilder. In particular, it is nearly identical in size and kind to the code associated with an OWL or MFC object. In short, BCB components are really just normal objects with a few extra methods. As a result, they are much smaller than most ActiveX controls or than controls you see in other products. Furthermore, the principles of inheritance allow most of the code to be reused over and over by multiple objects. In other words, you get the hit the first time you bring up a form, but other forms, or subsequent objects dropped on a form, just reuse the same objects used by the TForm object.
>
> *continues*

continued

To help drive this point home, I should perhaps point out that a typical small BCB application with five or six components on it is about 200KB in size. Many of the ActiveX controls that I have used are at least that large. In other words, it would not be unusual to find that five ActiveX controls added over a megabyte to the size of your application's install image. BCB controls, on the other hand, frequently added no more than five or ten KB to the size of your executable.

An exception is the presence of the first database control you drop on a form, which usually adds about 200KB to your executable. You should note, however, that because of inheritance, subsequent database objects do not increase the size of your application by nearly so large a percentage. Big database applications with four or five forms and thirty or forty database controls are frequently some 500–700KB in size. That's big by the old standards of DOS, but not large by today's standards.

If you want to write code that is completely independent of the visual tools, you have to add some include directives to the header file for your form. For instance, to use a TTable object, you should add the following code to your header file:

```
#include <vcl\DBTables.hpp>
#include <vcl\DB.hpp>
```

Here is an example of how to connect to a TTable object without using any visual tools:

```
void __fastcall TForm1::Button1Click(TObject *Sender)
{
  TTable *MyTable = new TTable(this);
  MyTable->DatabaseName = "DBDEMOS";
  MyTable->TableName = "COUNTRY";
  MyTable->Open();
  ShowMessage(MyTable->Fields[0]->AsString);
  MyTable->Free();
}
```

Of course, this code would not work if I did not first drop down a TButton object and create an OnClick event for it with the visual tools. But I am not using any visual tools when working with the database.

In this example, the first line of code creates an instance of a TTable object. This is the equivalent in code of dropping a TTable object onto a form from the Component Palette. Notice that you pass in this to the object's constructor in order to give the object an owner. In particular, Form1 is being assigned as the owner of the object, and is therefore responsible for freeing the object at shutdown time. If you passed in NULL in this parameter, you would have to call Free or Delete in the last line of code. I chose to do this anyway, in large part because I am declaring TTable as a local variable that lives on the stack created for this one function. It therefore makes sense to destroy the object at the end of the function, though the VCL would in fact still clean up the memory for me when the form is destroyed. However, if I declared MyTable as a field of

Form1, it would make sense just to let Form1 call Free on the object at program shutdown, which is what I do in the other examples included in this section.

The next three lines of code do what you would normally do with the Object Inspector. That is, you first fill in the DatabaseName and TableName properties, and then you call Open, which is the equivalent of setting Active to True.

After opening the table, you are free to access its code in any way you want. You could, for instance, iterate through the records in a table, as explained later in this chapter, or you could even connect the table to a data source, and the data source to a TDBGrid or TDBEdit control.

An example of this type of program is available on disk as a program called TABLESWITHOUTVISUALTOOLS.MAK, found in the NOVISUALTOOLS directory. The code for the program is shown in Listings 9.1 and 9.2.

Listing 9.1. The main source file for the TablesWithoutVisualTools program.

```
//---------------------------------------------------------------
#include <vcl\vcl.h>
#pragma hdrstop
#include "Main.h"
//---------------------------------------------------------------
#pragma resource "*.dfm"
TForm1 *Form1;
//---------------------------------------------------------------
__fastcall TForm1::TForm1(TComponent* Owner)
  : TForm(Owner)
{
}
//---------------------------------------------------------------
void __fastcall TForm1::Button1Click(TObject *Sender)
{
  TTable *MyTable = new TTable(this);
  MyTable->DatabaseName = "DBDEMOS";
  MyTable->TableName = "COUNTRY";
  MyTable->Open();
  ShowMessage(MyTable->Fields[0]->AsString);
  MyTable->Free();
}
```

Listing 9.2. The header file for the TablesWithoutVisualTools program.

```
//---------------------------------------------------------------
#ifndef MainH
#define MainH
//---------------------------------------------------------------
#include <vcl\Classes.hpp>
#include <vcl\Controls.hpp>
#include <vcl\StdCtrls.hpp>
#include <vcl\Forms.hpp>
#include <vcl\DBTables.hpp>
```

continues

Listing 9.2. continued

```
#include <vcl\DB.hpp>
//-----------------------------------------------------------------
class TForm1 : public TForm
{
__published:    // IDE-managed Components
  TButton *Button1;
  void __fastcall Button1Click(TObject *Sender);
private:        // User declarations
public:         // User declarations
  virtual __fastcall TForm1(TComponent* Owner);
};
//-----------------------------------------------------------------
extern TForm1 *Form1;
//-----------------------------------------------------------------
#endif
```

If you also wanted to connect to TDatabase object without using any visual tools, you can do so as follows:

```
void __fastcall TForm1::bOpenTableClick(TObject *Sender)
{
  FMyDatabase = new TDatabase(this);
  FMyDatabase->AliasName = "DBDEMOS";
  FMyDatabase->DatabaseName = "MyDBDemos";
  FMyDatabase->Connected = True;
  FMyTable = new TTable(this);
  FMyTable->DatabaseName = FMyDatabase->DatabaseName;
  FMyTable->TableName = "COUNTRY";
  FMyTable->Open();
  DataSource1->DataSet = FMyTable;
}
```

For this code to work, you need to do several things. In particular, you would need to add DB.HPP and DBTABLES.HPP to your header file for your main form, and you would need to edit the declaration for your TForm1 class so that it looked like this:

```
class TForm1 : public TForm
{
__published:
  TButton *bOpenTable;
  TDBGrid *DBGrid1;
  TDataSource *DataSource1;
  void __fastcall bOpenTableClick(TObject *Sender);
private:                            // User declarations
  TDatabase *FMyDatabase;           // Add field for database
  TTable *FMyTable;                 // Add field for table
public:                             // User declarations
    virtual __fastcall TForm1(TComponent* Owner);
};
```

Notice the addition of the TDatabase and TTable data items. These are added so that the objects are available for use in the bOpenTableClick function.

I have also added `TDBGrid` and `TDataSource` to the project and hooked up my database to them. I do this in order to show that there is absolutely no difference between creating a `TTable` and `TDatabase` object in code and doing it with the visual tools. As you can see, you can hook up the visual tools to the code based objects with just a single line of code:

```
DataSource1->DataSet = FMyTable;
```

In particular, this line of code defines exactly what happens logically when you connect a data source to a table using the visual tools.

In this next example, absolutely everything is done from scratch. No visual database objects are used, and even the `Alias` is created on the fly. All the visual database controls are created on the fly, assigned locations on the form, attached to the database, and made visible:

```cpp
void __fastcall TForm1::bCreateClick(TObject *Sender)
{
  FMyDatabase = new TDatabase(this);
  FMyDatabase->DatabaseName = "AnyName";
  FMyDatabase->DriverName = "STANDARD";
  FMyDatabase->Params->Add("path=g:\\cs\\examples\\data");
  FMyDatabase->Connected = True;
  FMyTable = new TTable(this);
  FMyTable->DatabaseName = FMyDatabase->DatabaseName;
  FMyTable->TableName = "BioLife";
  FMyTable->Open();
  FMyDataSource = new TDataSource(this);
  FMyDataSource->DataSet = FMyTable;
  FMyEdit = new TDBEdit(this);
  FMyEdit->DataSource = FMyDataSource;
  FMyEdit->Parent = this;
  FMyEdit->Visible = True;
  FMyEdit->DataField = "Common_Name";
  FMyImage = new TDBImage(this);
  FMyImage->Parent = this;
  FMyImage->BoundsRect = Bounds(0, 100, 300, 150);
  FMyImage->DataSource = FMyDataSource;
  FMyImage->DataField = "Graphic";
  FMyImage->Stretch = True;
  FMyImage->Visible = True;
  FMyNavigator = new TDBNavigator(this);
  FMyNavigator->Parent = this;
  FMyNavigator->BoundsRect = Bounds(0, 50, 100, 25);
  FMyNavigator->VisibleButtons =
    TButtonSet() << nbFirst << nbLast << nbNext << nbPrior;
  FMyNavigator->DataSource = FMyDataSource;
  FMyNavigator->Visible = True;
}
```

Needless to say, this code would not work unless the database objects were declared in the class declaration for `TForm` or in some other legal location:

```cpp
class TForm1 : public TForm
{
__published:    // IDE-managed Components
    TButton *bCreate;
    void __fastcall bCreateClick(TObject *Sender);
```

```
private:          // User declarations
  TDatabase *FMyDatabase;
  TTable *FMyTable;
  TDataSource *FMyDataSource;
  TDBEdit *FMyEdit;
  TDBImage *FMyImage;
  TDBNavigator *FMyNavigator;
public:           // User declarations
    virtual __fastcall TForm1(TComponent* Owner);
};
```

In this case all variables declared in the private section are database objects used in the
bCreateClick method shown previously.

The key lines to focus on are the ones that define the Alias for the TDatabase object:

```
FMyDatabase->DatabaseName = "AnyName";
FMyDatabase->DriverName = "STANDARD";
FMyDatabase->Params->Add("path=g:\\bcb\\examples\\data");
```

The first thing to notice about this code is that it hard-codes the path to my version of BCB
into the application. You will, of course, probably have to edit this path before running the
application.

You can see that the database object is given a DatabaseName, but no AliasName is declared. Instead,
a DriverName is specified. This is an either/or proposition. You declare the AliasName, in which
case the driver is specified inside the Alias, or else you explicitly declare the DriverName, which
means that no externally defined Alias will be used.

Selecting the STANDARD driver is another way of saying you want to use a Paradox table. If you
resort to the visual tools, you can see that this is a drop-down list of items, so you can see what
other drivers are available on your system. As a rule, you will have available STANDARD drivers,
dBASE drivers, and a list of SQL Links drivers such as Oracle, Sybase, and so on.

If no externally defined Alias will be used, how does the TDatabase object perform its function? How does it know which database you want to reference? How does it know the details
about the database such as server name, user name, and database name? The solution to this
quandary is supplied by the Params property, which can be used to define all the data that
normally appears in an Alias. (This is the same property you explored earlier in this chapter
when you double-clicked a TDataBase object to bring up the TDatabase component editor.)

In the case of Paradox tables, the only information that you need to fill concerns the path to
the database. However, there are additional fields that will need to be covered if you want to
connect to a client/server database. The Params property is of type TStrings, which means you
can treat it more or less as you would any TStringList object, or as you would the Items property for a TListBox.

Notice that when you create visual database controls, you need to specify both the owner and
the parent of the control:

```
FMyEdit = new TDBEdit(this);
FMyEdit->Parent = this;
```

In this case, both the owner and the parent are the main form. The Owner is responsible for deallocating the memory associated with the object, and the Parent is a field used by Windows so it will know where to draw the control.

If you are working in code rather than using the visual tools, you still have complete control over the object. For instance, I can define how many buttons will be visible on a TDBNavigator control:

```
FMyNavigator->VisibleButtons =
    TButtonSet() << nbFirst << nbLast << nbNext << nbPrior;
```

In this case, the VisibleButtons property is of type TButtonSet. In C++, sets are emulated through objects. If you want to add a member to the set, you use the overloaded << operator. In this case I am turning on the First, Last, Next, and Prior buttons, and leaving the other buttons uninitialized.

Before closing this section, I should make one final point. In all these examples, I am assuming that a TSession object has been created. This will indeed happen automatically, so long as you have a TApplication object initialized in your application. The DatabaseAlias application and all standard BCB applications initialize the TApplication object in WinMain:

```
WINAPI WinMain(HINSTANCE, HINSTANCE, LPSTR, int)
{
    Application->Initialize();
    Application->CreateForm(__classid(TForm1), &Form1);
    Application->Run();
    return 0;
}
```

If you don't have this kind of code in your application (for instance, if you have created a console application), you will have to explicitly create the TSession object yourself. Code for doing this is shown later in the book in the chapter on ISAPI programming, "Extending an Internet Server with ISAPI."

In this section you have learned something about creating database objects in code rather than with the visual tools. One drawback to this section is that it makes BCB database programming appear fairly difficult. The other side of the coin, of course, is that you don't have to manipulate the database tools this way. In fact, you will usually use the speedy visual tools to do in a few seconds what is done previously in code. It is, however, important to know that you can do all forms of database programming in code if you so desire.

Summary

In this chapter, you have learned how to use the TDataSet, TField, TDBDataSet, TTable, TDatabase, and TDataSource classes. This material is very much at the heart of the BCB database machinery, so you should be sure you understand how it works.

9

USING T**ABLE**
AND T**DATA**S**ET**

The key points to remember are as follows:

- TDataSet encapsulates the basic actions you will perform on a table.
- TField is a property of TDataSet that enables you to access the contents or name of each field in a record.
- TDBDataSet gives you the capability to associate a dataset with a given table.
- TTable encapsulates all the functionality of a dataset, but it also gives you access to table-specific chores such as setting indexes or creating linked cursors.
- TDataSource forms a link between TTable or TQuery and any of the data-aware components such as TDBEdit or TDBGrid. TDataSource also contains three useful events that keep you informed about the current state of the database.

In the next chapter, you will learn about the TQuery object and SQL. SQL is especially useful when you want to access the advanced capabilities associated with servers and server data.

SQL and the TQuery Object

CHAPTER 10

This chapter is about queries. It's a subject that lies at the heart of client/server programming, so this is one of the more important chapters in the book.

The material will be broken down into the following main sections:

- Using the TQuery object
- Using SQL with local and remote servers to select, update, delete, and insert records
- Using SQL statements to create joins, linked cursors, and programs that search for individual records

The acronym SQL stands for Structured Query Language, and is usually pronounced *sequel* or by saying each letter (*Ess Que El*). Whichever way you choose to pronounce it, SQL is a powerful database language that is easily accessible from within BCB but is distinct from BCB's native language. BCB can use SQL statements to retrieve tables from a database, to perform joins between tables, to create one-to-many relationships, or to request almost any feature that your server can provide.

BCB ships with two SQL engines, one built into the BDE for use with Paradox and dBASE, and the other built into InterBase. In addition, you can also gain access to other SQL databases such as MS SQL Server, Sybase, Oracle, DB2, and Informix. As a rule, the InterBase SQL engine is more powerful than the one built into Paradox or dBASE tables, but they both provide a wide range of services. The key point, however, is that you can perform SQL queries even if you're working on a stand-alone machine and don't have access to a server.

BCB provides support for pass-through SQL, which means that you can compose SQL statements and then have them sent directly (with one or two exceptions) to an Oracle, Sybase, InterBase, or other server. Pass-through SQL is a powerful feature for two reasons:

1. Most servers can process SQL statements very quickly, which means that you can use SQL on remote data to get an extremely fast response to your requests.
2. You can compose SQL statements that ask a server to perform specialized tasks unavailable through BCB's native language.

In the last chapter, you learned a lot about how BCB works internally and how to utilize its native capabilities. Now it's time to see how BCB interacts with the database tools that exist either on your current machine or on a network.

If you have never used the TQuery object before, you should review the section on that control found in Chapter 8, "Database Basics and Database Tools," which gives an overview of all the fundamental database tools found in BCB. This chapter focuses on one of those tools—TQuery— and explains it in some depth.

This chapter isn't intended to be a SQL primer, but rather a description of the TQuery object and the basic tasks you can perform with it. Even if you don't know anything about SQL, this chapter will still be helpful to you, and you'll end up learning a number of basic facts about how to compose a SQL statement. However, for a detailed analysis of the language, you should turn to one of the many books and public documents available on this subject. For instance, I am partial to *The Practical SQL Handbook,* Bowman et al, Addison Wesley. You also can refer to the handy reference in the online help for the WISQL utility. Additional information is available in the form of a LOCALSQL.HLP file that ships with BCB. (Open help, press Alt+F+O, and then choose LOCALSQL.HLP. You need to be in a help file for this to work, not in the Index or Content section. Alternatively, you may have to browse to the ..\BCB\help subdirectory to find this file.)

The SQL Property

The SQL property is probably the single most important part of TQuery. You can access this property from the Object Inspector during design time or programmatically at runtime. In Chapter 6 you saw how to access the SQL property at design time, so the next few sections concentrate on ways to manipulate it programmatically.

Most people want to access the SQL property at runtime in order to dynamically change the statement associated with a query. For instance, if you want to issue three SQL statements while your program is running, there's no need for you to place three TQuery components on your form. Instead, you can just place one on the form and simply change its SQL property three times. The most efficient, most powerful, and simplest means of doing this is through parameterized queries, which are explained in the next section. However, this chapter first examines the basic features of the SQL property and then covers more advanced topics, such as parameterized queries.

The SQL property is of type TStrings, which means that it is a series of strings kept in a list. The list acts very much as if it were an array, but it's actually a special class with its own unique capabilities. If you want to find out everything you can about the SQL property, you should study the class TStrings or TStringList. (Don't try to implement a standalone version of the abstract TString class, but instead work with TStringList.) A brief description of TStringList appeared in Chapter 3, "C++Builder and the VCL," near the end of the chapter in the section called "Working with Text Files."

When using TQuery programmatically, you should first close the current query and clear out any strings that might already be residing in the SQL property:

```
Query1->Close();
Query1->SQL->Clear();
```

It's always safe to call Close. If the query is already closed, the call will not cause an error.

The next step is to add the new strings that you want to execute:

```
Query1->SQL->Add("Select * from Country");
Query1->SQL->Add("where Name = 'Argentina'");
```

You can use the Add property to append from one to *X* number of strings to a SQL query, where *X* is limited only by the amount of memory on your machine. Clearly I could have used one statement to add the short SQL command shown in the last two lines of code; however, I wanted to give you an example of how to add multiple, or very long, strings to the SQL property.

To ask BCB to process the statement and return a cursor containing the results of your query, you can issue the following statement:

```
Query1->Open();
```

Note that Open is the command you should give when you want to return rows from a table. If you don't want to get any data back—for instance, if you are deleting or inserting data—you should call ExecSQL rather than Open. The ExecSQL command will be considered in more depth later in this chapter.

Whenever you want to change a SQL statement, you can simply go through the process outlined previously a second time. In particular, you can close the current Query, then Clear it, and pass a new string to the Add property:

```
CountryQuery->Close();
CountryQuery->SQL->Clear();
CountryQuery->SQL->Add("Select * from Country");
CountryQuery->Open();
```

In this case, CountryQuery is a variable of type TQuery. I tend to append the word Query to my TQuery objects, just as a I append table after a TTable object.

The sample program called EASYSQL demonstrates this process. EASYSQL is shown in Figure 10.1.

FIGURE 10.1.

The EASYSQL program shows how to issue multiple queries from a single TQuery object.

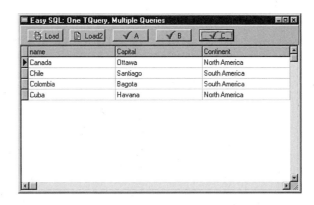

The EASYSQL program uses a feature of local SQL that lets you use case-insensitive wild cards. For instance, the following SQL statement returns a dataset containing all the records in which the Name field begins with the letter C:

```
Select * from Country where Name like 'C%'
```

The following syntax enables you to see all the countries that have the letter C embedded somewhere in their name:

```
Select * from Country where Name like '%C%';
```

Here's a statement that finds all the countries whose name ends in the letters ia:

```
Select * from Country where Name like '%ia';
```

If you want to compose a series of statements like the preceding one, you can expedite matters by using either parameterized queries, sprintf, or the VCL Format function. These techniques will all be explained in this chapter.

One of the most powerful features of the SQL property is its ability to read text files containing SQL statements directly from disk. This feature is also demonstrated in the EASYSQL program.

Here's how it works. There are several files with the extension SQL in the EASYSQL subdirectory. These files contain SQL statements such as the ones shown previously. The EASYSQL program has a Load button that enables you to select one of these text files and then run the SQL statement stored in that file. Be sure that the DatabaseName property for your TQuery object is assigned an alias before you try this code. In particular, I work with the DBDEMOS alias in all these examples.

The Load button has the following response method for its OnClick event:

```
void __fastcall TForm1::bbLoadClick(TObject *Sender)
{
  if (OpenDialog1->Execute())
  {
    TStringList *StringList = new TStringList();
    StringList->LoadFromFile(OpenDialog1->FileName);
    DMod->RunQuery(StringList);
    StringList->Free();
  }
}
```

The DMod RunQuery method looks like this:

```
void TDMod::RunQuery(TStringList *StringList)
{
  CountryQuery->Close();
  CountryQuery->SQL = StringList;
  CountryQuery->Open();
}
```

The LoadClick method first loads the OpenDialog component and enables the user to select a file with a SQL extension. The code checks to see whether the user has selected a file. If a file has been selected, the current query is closed, and the selected file is loaded from disk and displayed to the user.

OpenDialog1 has its Filter property set to the following value:

```
OpenDialog1->Filter = "SQL(*.SQL)¦*.SQL"
```

As a result, it lists only files that have an SQL extension, as shown in Figure 10.2.

FIGURE 10.2.

The Open dialog from the EASYSQL program enables you to select a prepared SQL statement from an ASCII file stored on disk.

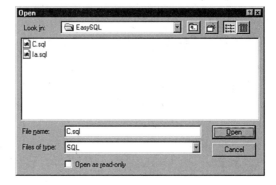

The `LoadFromFile` function enables you to load an entire text file at runtime by issuing a single command. The trick, then, is to store SQL statements in text files and load them at runtime. Because the `SQL` property can contain an essentially unlimited number of strings, there is no practical limit to the size of the SQL statement that you could load in this fashion. You can use this technique to quickly execute a series of very complex SQL statements.

> **NOTE**
>
> In this example, I happen to create a `StringList` and then pass it into the `RunQuery` function. Alternatively, you could simply pass a filename to the `RunQuery` function and let it use the `LoadFromFile` method of the `TQuery` SQL object:
>
> ```
> void __fastcall TForm1::bbLoad2Click(TObject *Sender)
> {
>   if (OpenDialog1->Execute())
>     DMod->RunQuery2(OpenDialog1->FileName);
> }
> void TDMod::RunQuery2(AnsiString S)
> {
>   CountryQuery->Close();
>   CountryQuery->SQL->Clear();
>   CountryQuery->SQL->LoadFromFile(S);
>   CountryQuery->Open();
> }
> ```
>
> This latter technique is probably the better of the two for this particular case, but it is important for you to understand that the `SQL` property consists of a string list, so I include both techniques in this chapter.

In this section, you have seen two methods of changing the `SQL` property at runtime. The first technique enables you to add strings to the `SQL` property, run a query, change the strings, and run the query again. The second technique enables you to load one or more statements from a file. The `LoadFromFile` technique is obviously quite elegant. The first technique can be very powerful at times, but it can be a bit awkward if all you want to do is change one word in a

SQL statement. In the next section, you'll learn about how you can eliminate this awkwardness by using parameterized queries.

TQuery and Parameters

BCB enables you to compose a flexible form of query statement called a *parameterized query*. A parameterized query enables you to substitute variables for single words in the where or insert clause of a SQL statement. These variables can then be changed at any time throughout the life of the query. (If you're using local SQL, you'll be able to make substitutions on almost any word in a SQL statement, but this same capability is not included on most servers.)

To get started using parameterized queries, consider again one of the simple SQL statements listed earlier:

```
Select * from Country where Name like 'C%'
```

To turn this statement into a parameterized query, just replace the right side of the like clause with a variable called NameStr:

```
select * from County where Name like :NameStr
```

In this SQL statement, NameStr is no longer a predefined constant, but instead can change at either design time or runtime. The SQL parser knows that it is dealing with a parameter instead of a constant because a colon is prepended to the word NameStr. That colon tells BCB that it should substitute the NameStr variable with a value that will be supplied at some future point.

It's important to note that the word NameStr was chosen entirely at random. You can use any valid variable name in this case, just as you can choose a wide range of identifiers when you declare a string variable in one of your programs.

There are two ways to supply variables to a parameterized SQL statement. One method is to use the Params property of TQuery to supply the value at runtime. The second is to use the DataSource property to supply information from another dataset at either runtime or design time. Here are the key properties used to accomplish these goals:

```
__property TParams *Params;
TParam *__fastcall ParamByName(const System::AnsiString Value);
void __fastcall Prepare(void);
```

Both TParam and TParams are objects found in DBTABLES.HPP. It is not particularly important for you to understand how those objects work.

When you substitute bind variables in a parameterized query by using the Params property, you usually take four steps:

1. Make sure the table is closed.
2. Ready the Query object by issuing the Prepare command (optional, but highly recommended).

3. Assign the correct values to the `Params` property.

4. Open the query.

Here's a sample code fragment showing how this might be done in practice:

```
void TDMod::NewParameterizedQuery(AnsiString S)
{
  CountryQuery->Close();
  CountryQuery->Prepare();
  CountryQuery->ParamByName("NameStr")->AsString = S;
  CountryQuery->Open();
}
```

If you're not familiar with parameterized queries, the preceding code might appear a bit mysterious. To understand it thoroughly, you'll need to do a careful line-by-line analysis. The simplest way to begin is with the third line, because it is the `Params` property that lies at the heart of this process.

`Params` is an indexed property that uses a syntax similar to the `Fields` property from `TDataSet`. For instance, you can access the first bind variable in a SQL statement by referring to element `0` in the `Params` array:

```
CountryQuery->Params->Items[0]->AsString := S;
```

Or, if you prefer, you can use `ParamByName` instead:

```
CountryQuery->ParamByName("NameStr")->AsString = S;
```

There is a classic trade-off here, in that `Params->Items` usually executes somewhat faster than `ParamByName`, because there is no string handling involved in tracking down the referenced parameter. However, `ParamByName` is safer, because your code would not break simply because the order of the fields was changed.

If you combine a simple parameterized SQL statement such as this

```
select * from Country where Name like :NameStr
```

with the `Params` statements shown previously, the result is the following SQL statement:

```
select * from Country where Name like 'Argentina'
```

What's happened here is that the variable `:NameStr` has been assigned the value `Argentina` by the `Params` property, thereby enabling you to complete a simple SQL statement.

If you have more than one parameter in a statement, you can access them by changing the index of the `Params` property:

```
Params->Items[1]->AsString = "SomeValue";
```

So far, you've seen that a parameterized query uses bind variables, which always begin with a colon, to designate the places where parameters will be passed. With this concept in mind, you can move on to the other lines in the previous code fragment.

Before you use the Params variable, you should first call Prepare. A call to Prepare causes BCB to parse your SQL statement and ready the Params property so that it's prepared to accept the appropriate number of variables. This is particularly important if you are about to enter a loop where the same Query will be executed over and over. If you try to assign a value to the Params variable without first calling Prepare, your code will still work, but the routine may not be as highly optimized. The issue here is that in a loop, BCB will have to call internally at each iteration, rather than having it called once by the programmer before the loop begins. There is also an UnPrepare statement that you should use if you are very concerned about taking up database resources.

After you've called Prepare and assigned the correct values to the Params variable, you should call Open to complete the binding of the variables and produce the dataset that you hope to find. In this particular case, given the input shown previously, the dataset includes the contents of the record where the name field is set to Argentina.

In the Examples subdirectory, you'll find a program called EASYSQL2 that demonstrates how to use parameterized queries. The EASYSQL2 program performs a function very similar to the one shown earlier in the first EASYSQL program. However, this new version shows how parameterized queries can be used to increase the flexibility of a SQL statement.

To create the program, place TQuery, TDataSource, TDBGrid, and TTabSet components on a form, or in a program that uses both a form and data module. Hook up the data controls and set the query's DatabaseName property to the DBDEMOS alias. Fill in the tabset so that it lists the alphabet from *A* to *Z*, as shown in Figure 10.3.

FIGURE 10.3.

The EASYSQL2 program shows how to use parameterized queries.

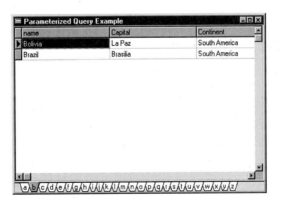

Enter the following string in the SQL property for the query component:

```
select * from Country where Name like :NameStr
```

Now all that's left to create is a response method for the OnChange property of the tabset:

```
void __fastcall TForm1::TabSet1Change(TObject *Sender, Integer NewTab,
                            Boolean &AllowChange)
{
```

```
AnsiString S(UpperCase(TabSet1->Tabs->Strings[NewTab]) + "%");
DMod->NewParameterizedQuery(S);
}
```

The `NewParameterizedQuery` method is shown and explained a few paragraphs back in this same section of the chapter.

The code shown here follows the four simple steps outlined previously. This is what the code does:

1. Closes the query
2. Prepares the `Params` property
3. Assigns a string to the `Params` property
4. Executes the resultant SQL statement by calling `Query1.Open`

The actual string assigned to the `Params` property consists of one of the letters of the alphabet plus the `%` symbol. A typical query produced by this method might look like this:

```
Select * from Country where Name like 'C%'
```

The end result, then, is that the EASYSQL2 program lets you view the contents of the table in alphabetical sequence. Press the tab labeled A, and you see only those records in the database for which the first letter of the `Name` field begins with an A. Press the B tab, and you see only those items with a first letter of B.

The important point, of course, is that you were able to produce the previous program by writing only six lines of C++ code, plus one line of SQL:

```
Select * from Country where Name like :NameStr
```

This combination of SQL and BCB's native language provides maximum power and flexibility when you want to produce your own applications.

> **NOTE**
>
> In the last chapter, I showed you how to write this same type of program using the `TTable` object rather than the `TQuery` object. The question then becomes, which one is better?
>
> Well, there is no definitive answer to this question. If you come from the client/server world and have been writing SQL statements for years, you will almost certainly prefer the `TQuery` object. If you come from the C++ world, you will probably prefer the `TTable` component because you are likely to find SQL awkward to write, at least at first.
>
> In general, `TTable` is easier to use, and less prone to error, so it is a good choice in many cases. I certainly use it a great deal in my own programs.
>
> If you are running against large SQL databases, you can use `TQuery` to optimize your code for maximum performance. There is at least some merit to the idea that you can use `TTable` when working with local data, but consider using `TQuery` if you are running against SQL

server data, and particularly if you are working with a large SQL database. Most SQL servers were designed around the idea that users will access records one at a time, or in small groups. The concept of treating an entire table as a series of rows—which is the fundamental theory behind the TTable object—can run against the grain of some servers, particularly when they are carrying a large load.

Finally, I should add that no one can hope to do any serious contemporary database development without understanding something about SQL. SQL is a vital part of the client/ server world, and if you don't understand how to use the TQuery object, your viability as a professional client/server programmer would be seriously, perhaps hopelessly, impaired. In general, a good database programmer has to be an expert in SQL, just as a good systems programmer should be an expert in C++ or Object Pascal.

Further examples of parameterized queries are found on the CD-ROM that accompanies this book as PARAMS2 and PARAMS3. The PARAMS2 program is particularly interesting because it shows how to work with two parameterized variables at once. In particular, it makes the following request: "Show me all the records where the Size field is above X, and the Weight field is above Y", where Size and Weight are fields defining the size and weight of the animals listed in the table. In other words, it lets you list animals by their size and weight.

To create the PARAMS2 program, drop a query, data source, and DBgrid on a form, and place two list boxes and TDBImage above the grid, as shown in Figure 10.4. Use TLabel objects to put the word Size above the first list box, and the word Weight above the second list box. Set the DataSource property of the TDBImage control to DataSource1, and type the word BMP in the editor for its DataField property.

FIGURE 10.4.

The form for the PARAMS2 program, as it appears at runtime.

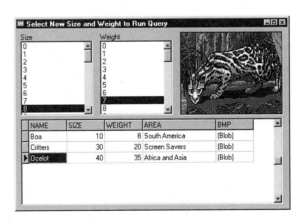

The SQL statement used in the PARAMS2 program looks like this:

```
select * from Animals
  where
    Animals."Size" > :Size and
    Animals."Weight" > :Weight
```

To satisfy the two parameters specified in this SQL statement, you should create the following method:

```
void TDMod::RunQuery(int Box1, int Box2)
{
  sqlAnimals->Close();
  sqlAnimals->Prepare();
  sqlAnimals->Params->Items[0]->AsInteger = Box1;
  sqlAnimals->Params->Items[1]->AsInteger = Box2;
  sqlAnimals->Open();
}
```

The OnClick events for both list boxes should be set to this simple routine, which calls TDMod::RunQuery:

```
void __fastcall TForm1::ListBox1Click(TObject *Sender)
{
  DMod->RunQuery(ListBox1->Items->Strings[ListBox1->ItemIndex].ToInt(),
                 ListBox1->Items->Strings[ListBox2->ItemIndex].ToInt());
}
```

When you run the PARAMS2 program, both list boxes are automatically filled with numbers that range from 0 to 42. By selecting a value from the first list box, you specify the size of the animal you want to find. By selecting one from the second list box, you select its weight. Using both values together, you are able to resolve both parameterized variables, thereby effectively selecting a range of animals to view. For instance, select 4 in the Size list box, and then iterate through the choices 2, 4, 6, 8, and 10 in the Weight list box.

As a final touch, the PARAMS2 program displays a picture of the animals in question in the TDBImage control. The blob field of the table that contains the picture is called BMP. The TDBImage control asks only that you set its DataSource property to a valid TDataSource object and its DataField property to the name of the blob field you want to display. In this case, the DataSource is DataSource1, and the blob field is called BMP. (See Listings 10.1 and 10.2.)

Listing 10.1. The PARAMS2 program shows how to work with a parameterized query that has two fields.

```
//--------------------------------------------------------------------------
#include <vcl\vcl.h>
#pragma hdrstop
#include "Main.h"
#include "DMod1.h"
//--------------------------------------------------------------------------
#pragma resource "*.dfm"
TForm1 *Form1;
//--------------------------------------------------------------------------
__fastcall TForm1::TForm1(TComponent* Owner)
  : TForm(Owner)
{
}
//--------------------------------------------------------------------------
void __fastcall TForm1::FormCreate(TObject *Sender)
{
```

```
  int i;
  AnsiString S;
  for (i = 0; i < 40; i++)
  {
    S = i;
    ListBox1->Items->Add(S);
    ListBox2->Items->Add(S);
  }
  ListBox1->ItemIndex = 0;
  ListBox2->ItemIndex = 0;
}
//-------------------------------------------------------------------
void __fastcall TForm1::ListBox1Click(TObject *Sender)
{
  DMod->RunQuery(ListBox1->Items->Strings[ListBox1->ItemIndex].ToInt(),
                 ListBox1->Items->Strings[ListBox2->ItemIndex].ToInt());
}
//-------------------------------------------------------------------
void __fastcall TForm1::FormShow(TObject *Sender)
{
  DMod->RunQuery(0, 0);
}
//-------------------------------------------------------------------
```

Listing 10.2. The data module for the PARAMS2 program.

```
//-------------------------------------------------------------------
#include <vcl\vcl.h>
#pragma hdrstop
#include "DMod1.h"
//-------------------------------------------------------------------
#pragma resource "*.dfm"
TDMod *DMod;
//-------------------------------------------------------------------
__fastcall TDMod::TDMod(TComponent* Owner)
    : TDataModule(Owner)
{
}
//-------------------------------------------------------------------
void TDMod::RunQuery(int Box1, int Box2)
{
  AnimalsQuery->Close();
  AnimalsQuery->Prepare();
  AnimalsQuery->Params->Items[0]->AsInteger = Box1;
  AnimalsQuery->Params->Items[1]->AsInteger = Box2;
  AnimalsQuery->Open();
}
```

The interesting thing about the PARAMS2 program is that it lets inexperienced database users ask a relatively complex question of a table. In particular, it lets users ask for a list of all the animals that are larger than a certain size or weight. Users can ask this question of the program without having to understand anything about SQL.

The SQL Property and the Format Function

I stated earlier that normally you can use parameterized variables only in cases in which there is a where clause or an insert clause. There are times, however, when these guidelines can be a bit limiting. If you find that you need more flexibility, you can use BCB's Format function to create your own special version of parameterized variables. Alternatively, you can use sprintf to achieve the same ends through a similar method.

Consider the following SQL statement:

```
Select * from Country
```

There are definitely times when you might want to parameterize the last word in this statement so that it could vary over the life of a program:

```
Select * from :ACountry
```

Unfortunately, most SQL servers won't support this syntax, so you're forced to find another solution.

At times like these, the Format function can come to the rescue. The VCL Format function works a lot like sprintf, except that it is focused on AnsiStrings rather than C strings. All you really need to know about it is that it enables you to substitute variables of almost any type for certain words in a string. More specifically, you can compose a string that looks like this:

```
S = "Select * from %s";
```

In this string, the syntax %s performs the same role that the :FileName syntax does in a parameterized query. The one difference, of course, is that you should use %s only when you're working with a string. If you're working with an Integer, use %d. In other words, it works exactly as you'd expect it to work from your experience with sprintf.

The second parameter passed to Format is an OpenArray. When you've declared two strings like this:

```
AnsiString ParamString("COUNTRY");
AnsiString SQLStatement;
```

you can plug them into a Format statement:

```
SQLStatement = Format("Select * from %s", OPENARRAY(TVarRec, (S)));
```

Given the preceding code, after the Format function executed you would end up with the following string in the variable SQLStatement:

```
"Select * from COUNTRY"
```

Needless to say, this was exactly what you hoped to achieve, and the Format function enables you to reach your goal without any of the restrictions placed on parameterized variables.

Of course, this example was fairly simplistic, but if you wanted, you could create a string that looks like this:

```
"Select * from %s where %s = %d";
```

This string contains three variables that can be changed at runtime, and it should give you some hints as to the kind of flexibility you can achieve using this system. For instance, you could write code that looks like this:

```
AnsiString GetQuery(AnsiString S1, AnsiString S2, int Value)
{
  return Format("Select * from %s where %s = %d", OPENARRAY(TVarRec, (S1, S2,
             Value)));
}
void __fastcall TForm1::StringTrick1Click(TObject *Sender)
{
  Caption = GetQuery("Customer", "CustNo", 42);
}
```

After substitutions are made, this sets the Caption of Form1 to the following string:

```
select * from Customer where CustNo = 42
```

To see this entire process in action, refer to the PARAMS1 program in the CHAP08 subdirectory. This program, shown in Listings 10.3 and 10.4, lets you pick from a list of tables and display the contents of each table in a data grid.

Listing 10.3. The header for the PARAMS1 program.

```
//---------------------------------------------------------------
#ifndef MainH
#define MainH
//---------------------------------------------------------------
#include <vcl\Classes.hpp>
#include <vcl\Controls.hpp>
#include <vcl\StdCtrls.hpp>
#include <vcl\Forms.hpp>
#include <vcl\DBTables.hpp>
#include <vcl\DB.hpp>
#include <vcl\DBGrids.hpp>
#include <vcl\Grids.hpp>
#include <vcl\Menus.hpp>
//---------------------------------------------------------------
class TForm1 : public TForm
{
__published:    // IDE-managed Components
    TListBox *ListBox1;
    TQuery *FormatQuery;
    TDataSource *dsFormat;
    TDBGrid *DBGrid1;
    TMainMenu *MainMenu1;
    TMenuItem *StringTrick1;
    void __fastcall FormCreate(TObject *Sender);
    void __fastcall ListBox1Click(TObject *Sender);
    void __fastcall StringTrick1Click(TObject *Sender);
```

continues

Listing 10.3. continued

```
private:          // User declarations
public:           // User declarations
    virtual __fastcall TForm1(TComponent* Owner);
};
//---------------------------------------------------------------
extern TForm1 *Form1;
//---------------------------------------------------------------
#endif
```

Listing 10.4. The PARAMS1 program shows how to use the Format function with a SQL query.

```
//---------------------------------------------------------------
#include <vcl\vcl.h>
#pragma hdrstop
#include "Main.h"
//---------------------------------------------------------------
#pragma resource "*.dfm"
TForm1 *Form1;
//---------------------------------------------------------------
__fastcall TForm1::TForm1(TComponent* Owner)
  : TForm(Owner)
{
}
//---------------------------------------------------------------
void __fastcall TForm1::FormCreate(TObject *Sender)
{
  Session->GetTableNames(FormatQuery->DatabaseName, "", False, False, ListBox1-
                      >Items);
}
//---------------------------------------------------------------
void __fastcall TForm1::ListBox1Click(TObject *Sender)
{
  AnsiString S = ListBox1->Items->Strings[ListBox1->ItemIndex];
  S = Format("Select * from %s", OPENARRAY(TVarRec, (S)));
  Caption = S;
  FormatQuery->Close();
  FormatQuery->SQL->Clear();
  FormatQuery->SQL->Add(S);
  FormatQuery->Open();
}
//---------------------------------------------------------------
AnsiString GetQuery(AnsiString S1, AnsiString S2, int Value)
{
  return Format("Select * from %s where %s = %d", OPENARRAY(TVarRec, (S1, S2,
             Value)));
}
void __fastcall TForm1::StringTrick1Click(TObject *Sender)
{
  Caption = GetQuery("Customer", "CustNo", 42);
}
//---------------------------------------------------------------
```

To create the PARAMS1 program, place a query on the form and set its DatabaseName property to DBDEMOS. To create the list of tables, place a TListBox object on the form and create the following FormCreate method:

```
void __fastcall TForm1::FormCreate(TObject *Sender)
{
  Session->GetTableNames(FormatQuery->DatabaseName, "", False, False, ListBox1-
  >Items);
}
```

The call to the TSession object's GetTableNames routine returns a complete list of valid table names from the database specified in the first parameter. The second parameter is a string that can contain a file mask, if you so desire. For instance, you can enter c*.* to get a list of all tables beginning with the letter C. Just pass in an empty string if you want a list of all tables. The fourth parameter is a Boolean value that specifies whether you want to work with system tables, and the final parameter is a value of type TStrings that holds the output from the function.

NOTE

Depending on your point of view, the TSession object is either one of the most interesting, or least interesting, BCB database objects. The argument in favor of its not being important is simply that you don't have to know about it in order to do most kinds of database programming. The argument in favor of its importance rests on the fact that the TSession object is a vast repository of information similar to the kind retrieved by the GetTableNames method.

In general, the TSession object specializes in lists. Here are some of the lists you can retrieve with the TSession object:

- Available databases
- Available tables
- Available aliases
- Available drivers
- Available stored procedures

You can also use the TSession object to create Aliases, to Modify Aliases, and to save these Aliases into the IDAPI.CFG file.

Because the subject of the TSession object is so powerful, I will give this subject almost the whole of Chapter 11, "Working with Field Objects."

To enable the user to view the contents of the tables listed in the FormCreate method, you should add a TDataSource and TDBGrid to the form, and then wire them up.

Next, create a response method for the ListBox1.OnClick event:

```
void __fastcall TForm1::ListBox1Click(TObject *Sender)
{
  AnsiString S = ListBox1->Items->Strings[ListBox1->ItemIndex];
  S = Format("Select * from %s", OPENARRAY(TVarRec, (S)));
  Caption = S;
  FormatQuery->Close();
  FormatQuery->SQL->Clear();
  FormatQuery->SQL->Add(S);
  FormatQuery->Open();
}
```

The first line of the code shown here assigns a string the value from the currently selected item from a list box.

The next line in the program creates a new SQL statement. To do this, it calls on the Format function, and uses the string selected from the list box. The result is a new SQL statement that requests a dataset containing the contents of a table. For example, the string might look like this:

```
select * from ORDERS
```

The next line of code checks to make sure that the query is closed:

```
Query1->Close()
```

The next line then clears out any strings currently sitting in the SQL property:

```
Query1->SQL->Clear();
```

That's the end of the discussion of using parameterized queries from inside the code of your program. The next section shows how to use them without having to write any C++ code.

Passing Parameters Through TDataSource

In the last chapter, you learned about a technique for creating a one-to-many relationship between two tables. Now, you'll learn about a second technique for performing the same action, but this time using a TQuery object.

The TQuery object has a DataSource property that can be used to create a link between itself and another dataset. It doesn't matter whether the other dataset is a TTable object, TQuery object, or some other descendant of TDataSet that you or another programmer might create. All you have to do is ensure that the dataset is connected to a data source, and then you're free to make the link.

In the following explanation, assume that you want to create a link between the ORDERS table and the CUSTOMERS table, so that whenever you view a particular customer record, only the orders associated with that customer will be visible.

Consider the following parameterized query:

```
Select * from Orders where CustNo = :CustNo
```

In this statement, :CustNo is a bind variable that needs to be supplied a value from some source. BCB enables you to use the TQuery DataSource field to point at another dataset, which can supply that information to you automatically. In other words, instead of being forced to use the Params property to manually supply a variable, the appropriate variable can simply be plucked from another table. Furthermore, BCB always first tries to satisfy a parameterized query by using the DataSource property. Only if that fails does it expect to get the variable from the Params property.

Take a moment to consider exactly what happens in these situations. As you saw in the last chapter, the CustNo field forms a link between the ORDERS table and the CUSTOMER table. (It's the Primary Key in the CUSTOMER table, and a Foreign Key in the Orders table.) Therefore, if both tables are visible on a form, the appropriate CustNo value is always available in the current record of the CUSTOMER table. All you need to do is point the Query object in the appropriate direction.

To obtain the bind value, just set the DataSource for the Query object to the TDataSource object that's associated with the CUSTOMER table. That's all there is to it! Just enter a short SQL statement, link up the DataSource property, and Bingo! You've established a one-to-many relationship like the linked cursors example from the last chapter!

On the CD-ROM that accompanies this book, you'll find an example called QuickLinks that demonstrates how this technique works. To create the QuickLinks program, place two TQuery, two TDataSource, and two TDBGrids on a form, as shown in Figure 10.5.

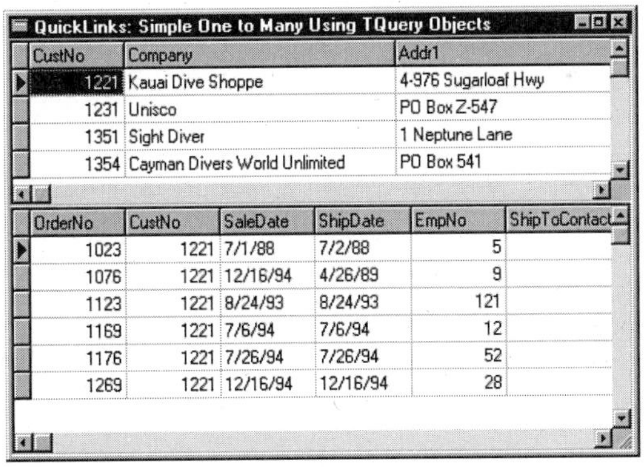

FIGURE 10.5.

The QuickLinks program shows how to create a one-to-many relationship using the TQuery *object.*

In the SQL property for the first TQuery component, enter the following:

```
select * from Customer
```

In the second TQuery component, enter the following:

```
select * from Orders where CustNo = :CustNo
```

To complete the program, all you have to do is wire up the controls by attaching `DBGrid1` to `DataSource1`, and `DataSource1` to `Query1`. Perform the same action for the second set of controls, and then set the `Query2.DataSource` property to `DataSource1`. This last step is the main action that forms the link between the two tables. If you now run the program, you'll see that the two tables work together in the desired manner.

If you want to create a link between two tables using multiple fields, you can simply specify the relevant fields in your query:

```
select * from Orders
   where CustNo = :CustNo and
   CustCountry = :CustCountry
```

The important point to understand is that this one-to-many example works simply because BCB supports parameterized variables. There is no other hand-waving going on in the background. All that's happening is that you're using a basic SQL statement to view the members of the `ORDERS` table that happen to have a particular customer number. The customer number in question was passed to you through the `DataSource` property and the bind variable you created.

The examples you've seen so far in this chapter should give you some feeling for the extreme power and flexibility inherent in the `TQuery` object. If you're looking for a lever powerful enough to move the roadblocks in your client/server programming world, `TQuery` is likely to be the tool you require.

In the next section, you'll learn more about the `TQuery` object when you see how to join two tables together so that you can view them both in a single dataset.

Performing Joins Between Multiple Tables

You've seen that the `CUSTOMERS` and `ORDERS` tables are related in a one-to-many relationship based on the `CustNo` field. The `ORDERS` table and `ITEMS` tables are also bound in a one-to-many relationship, only this time the field that connects them is called `OrderNo`.

More specifically, each order that exists in the `ORDERS` table will have one or more records from the `ITEMS` table associated with it. The records from the `ITEMS` table specify characteristics, such as price and part number, of the items associated with a particular sale.

Consider what happens when you go to a restaurant and order steamed shrimp, steamed artichoke, Caesar salad, and mineral water. The result of this pleasurable exercise is that you've made one order that has four different line items associated with it:

```
ORDERS1: Suzie Customer (Oct 1, 1994):
   ITEMS1: Shrimp          $12.95
   ITEMS2: Artichoke        $6.25
   ITEMS3: Caesar salad     $3.25
   ITEMS4: Mineral water    $2.50
```

In a situation like this, it's sometimes simplest to join the data from the ORDERS table and the ITEMS table, so that the resulting dataset contains information from both tables:

```
Suzie     Oct 1, 1994    Shrimp        $12.95
Suzie     Oct 1, 1994    Artichoke      $6.25
etc...
```

The act of merging these two tables is called a join, and it is one of the fundamental operations you can perform on a set of two or more tables.

Given the ORDERS and ITEMS tables from the demos subdirectory, you can join them in such a way that the CustNo, OrderNo, and SaleDate fields from the ORDERS table are merged with the StockNo, Price, and Qty fields from the ITEMS table to form a new dataset containing all six fields. A grid containing the resulting dataset is shown in Figure 10.6.

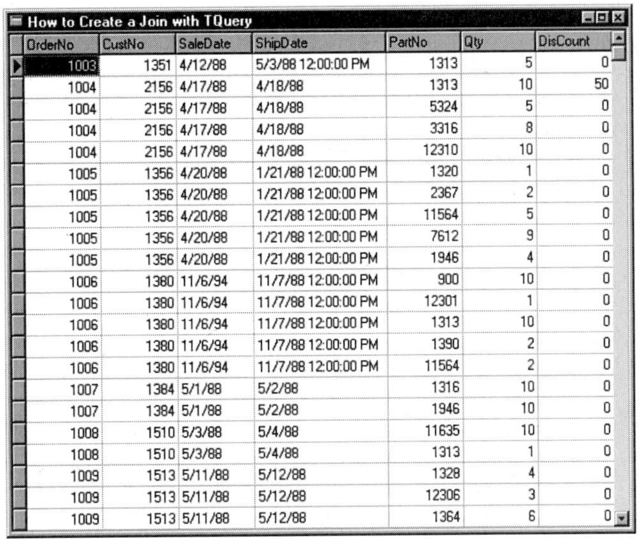

FIGURE 10.6.

The QJOIN program joins the ORDERS *and* ITEMS *table producing a dataset with fields from each table.*

OrderNo	CustNo	SaleDate	ShipDate	PartNo	Qty	DisCount
1003	1351	4/12/88	5/3/88 12:00:00 PM	1313	5	0
1004	2156	4/17/88	4/18/88	1313	10	50
1004	2156	4/17/88	4/18/88	5324	5	0
1004	2156	4/17/88	4/18/88	3316	8	0
1004	2156	4/17/88	4/18/88	12310	10	0
1005	1356	4/20/88	1/21/88 12:00:00 PM	1320	1	0
1005	1356	4/20/88	1/21/88 12:00:00 PM	2367	2	0
1005	1356	4/20/88	1/21/88 12:00:00 PM	11564	5	0
1005	1356	4/20/88	1/21/88 12:00:00 PM	7612	9	0
1005	1356	4/20/88	1/21/88 12:00:00 PM	1946	4	0
1006	1380	11/6/94	11/7/88 12:00:00 PM	900	10	0
1006	1380	11/6/94	11/7/88 12:00:00 PM	12301	1	0
1006	1380	11/6/94	11/7/88 12:00:00 PM	1313	10	0
1006	1380	11/6/94	11/7/88 12:00:00 PM	1390	2	0
1006	1380	11/6/94	11/7/88 12:00:00 PM	11564	2	0
1007	1384	5/1/88	5/2/88	1316	10	0
1007	1384	5/1/88	5/2/88	1946	10	0
1008	1510	5/3/88	5/4/88	11635	10	0
1008	1510	5/3/88	5/4/88	1313	1	0
1009	1513	5/11/88	5/12/88	1328	4	0
1009	1513	5/11/88	5/12/88	12306	3	0
1009	1513	5/11/88	5/12/88	1364	6	0

Title: How to Create a Join with TQuery

There's a substantial difference between linking cursors and joining tables. However, they both have two things in common:

- They involve two or more tables.
- Each table is linked to the other by one or more shared fields.

The act of joining the ORDERS and ITEMS tables can be accomplished by a single SQL statement that looks like this:

```
select
  O."OrderNo", O."CustNo",
  O."SaleDate", O."ShipDate",
  I."PartNo ", I."Qty",  I."Discount "
from
  Orders O, Items I
where
  O.OrderNo = I.OrderNo
```

This statement consists of four parts:

- The select statement specifies that you expect a cursor to be returned containing some form of dataset.

- Next, there is a list of the fields that you want included in the dataset you are requesting. This list includes the OrderNo, CustNo, SaleDate, ShipDate, PartNo, Qty, and Discount fields. The first four fields originate in the ORDERS table, and the next three fields originate in the ITEMS table.

- The from clause states that you're working with two tables, one called ORDERS and the other called ITEMS. For the sake of brevity, the statement uses an optional SQL feature that lets you specify the ORDERS table with the letter O, and the ITEMS table with the letter I.

- The where clause is vitally important, because it specifies which field will link the two tables. Some servers are capable of returning valid datasets even if you don't include a where clause in your join, but the resulting set of records will almost surely not be what you want. To get the results you're looking for, be sure to include a where clause.

When you've created the SQL statement that you want to use, there is nothing at all difficult about performing a join. The QJOIN example that ships with BCB demonstrates exactly how to proceed. All you need do is drop a TQuery, TDataSource, and TDBGrid onto a form and then wire them up in the standard way. When you're hooked up, you can paste the query statement in the SQL property of the query, fill in the DatabaseName property, and then set Active to True. Now, compile and run the program and take a moment to scroll through the new dataset you've created from the raw materials in the ORDERS and ITEMS tables.

> **NOTE**
>
> When you are composing SQL statements in the SQL field of the TQuery object, you may find that the space you are working in is a little cramped. To open up your horizons, click the Code Editor button in the String List Editor dialog. Your code will then be transferred from the String List Editor to BCB's main editor. The main editor gives you more room to work and provides syntax highlighting for your SQL statements.

There is not much point to showing you the actual source code for the QJOIN program, because all the magic occurs in the SQL statement quoted previously.

The RequestLive Property

The RequestLive field of the TQuery object can play an important role in SQL programming. By default, any query you make with the TQuery object will return a read-only dataset. However, you can attempt to get a live query by setting the TQuery RequestLive property to True. As a rule, if your query involves only one table, then you can set RequestLive to True. If your query involves multiple tables, setting RequestLive to True might not produce the desired result. You can check the CanModify property to see if your request has succeeded.

In general, I use the TTable object rather than the TQuery object when I want to edit the results of a direct link between one or more tables. This has some limitations, but it is the simplest way to proceed in some cases. If you want to let the user edit tables at will, then you should use the TTable object. Of course, there are some things you can't do with TTable objects, such as produce a true join.

If you want to update a table with a SQL query, then you should use the SQL Update or Insert commands. That's the way SQL is supposed to work. It's a conservative language. (Update, Insert, Delete, and other SQL statements will be discussed later in this chapter.)

There is also an UpdateSQL component that can be useful in these circumstances, but I often find it simplest to place one or more TQuery objects on a form or data module, and then use them to issue statements that will update a table. In particular, if you have created a join between three tables, you might not be able to set RequestLive to True. If that is the case, then you will have to pop up a separate dialog with a series of simple TEdit controls in it. Use this dialog to get input from the user, and then simply use the TQuery component to issue three Update commands, one for each table in your join. When you are done, Refresh your join. This is a good system, with a natural, intuitive rhythm that's easy to follow. Furthermore, it helps prevent anyone from accidentally editing a live dataset when he or she only means to be scrolling around in it.

Whatever limitations the RequestLive property may have are not unique to BCB. If you want to edit tables quickly with a high-performance system, use the TTable object. Of course, you can try to use the TQuery object first, and see how these requests are handled with your particular server. Your ability to set RequestLive to True is somewhat server-dependent. If you can't set RequestLive to True, and you don't want to use TTable, just start writing some SQL statements to perform the update for you. Part of the purpose of this chapter is to outline enough about TQuery and SQL so that you will know how to write these kinds of statements by the time you finish this chapter.

Parameterized Queries and join Statements

You can mix parameterized queries and join statements. This is useful if you want to show the CUSTOMER table at the top of a form, and then beneath it, show another dataset that contains records with information from both the ORDERS and ITEMS table. The result is a program that enables you to iterate through a list of customers in the top half of a form, while the bottom half of the form shows only the purchases associated with any particular customer, including a list of the line items that were bought. This is the type of form you'd produce if you wanted to create an electronic invoice.

The QJOIN2 program on your system shows how a program of this type looks in practice. The main form for the QJOIN2 program is shown in Figure 10.7.

FIGURE 10.7.

The QJOIN2 program shows three tables linked together in a logical and coherent fashion.

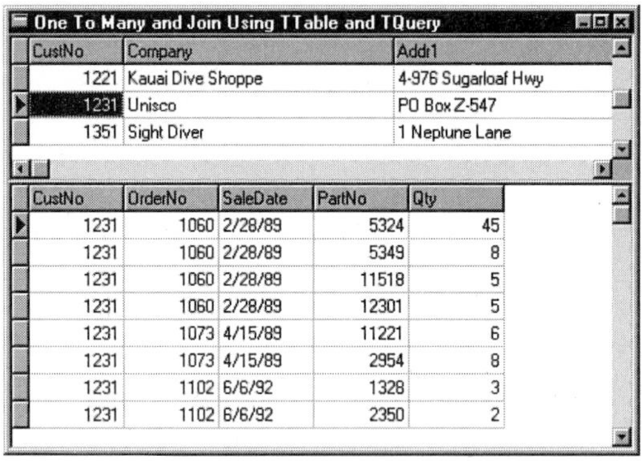

To create this program, drop down a TTable, a TQuery, two data sources, and two data grids. Hook up the TTable, the first data source, and the first grid to the CUSTOMER table. Wire up the remaining controls and specify DataSource1 in the Query1.DataSource property. Now add the following SQL statement in the Query1.SQL property:

```
select
  O.CustNo, O.OrderNo, O.SaleDate,
  L.PartNo, L.Discount, L.Qty
from
  Orders O, Items L
where
  O.CustNo = :CustNo and
  O.OrderNo = L.OrderNo
```

The statement pictured here is very much like the one you saw in the last section, except that the where clause has been expanded to include a bind variable:

```
where
  O.CustNo = :CustNo and
  O.OrderNo = L.OrderNo
```

This clause now specifies two different relationships: one between the CUSTOMER table and the ORDERS table, and the second between the ORDERS table and the ITEMS table. More specifically, the value for the CustNo variable will be supplied by the current record of the CUSTOMER table through the link on the Query1.DataSource property. The link between the ORDERS table and ITEMS table will be the OrderNo field.

Conceptually, the QJOIN2 program forces you to wrestle with some fairly complex ideas. This complexity is inherent in the task being performed. BCB, however, enables you to encapsulate these complex ideas in a few simple mechanical steps. In short, once you understand the goal you want to achieve, BCB enables you to perform even complex data operations with just a few minutes of work.

ExecSQL and the Delete and Insert Statements

After you've composed a SQL statement, there are two different ways to process it. If you need to get a cursor back from the Query, you should always call Open. If you don't need to return a cursor, you should call ExecSQL. For instance, if you're inserting, deleting, or updating data, you should call ExecSQL. To state the same matter in slightly different terms, you should use Open whenever you compose a select statement, and you should use ExecSQL whenever you write any other kind of statement.

Here's a typical SQL statement that you might use to delete a record from a table:

```
delete from Country where Name = 'Argentina';
```

This statement deletes any record from the COUNTRY database that has Argentina in the Name field.

It doesn't take long to see that this is a case in which you might want to use a parameterized query. For instance, it would be nice to be able to vary the name of the country you want to delete:

```
delete from Country where Name = :CountryName
```

In this case, CountryName is a variable that can be changed at runtime by writing code that looks like this:

```
Query2->Prepare;
Query2->Params->Items[0]->AsString = "Argentina";
Query2->ExecSQL;
Query1->Refresh;
```

The code shown here first calls Prepare to inform BCB that it should parse the SQL statement you gave it and ready the Params property. The next step is to insert a value into the Params property, and then to execute the newly prepared SQL statement. Note that you execute the statement not by calling Open, but by calling ExecSQL. Call ExecSQL when you don't need to return a dataset. Finally, you display the results of your actions to the user by asking the first query to refresh itself.

The INSERT2 program from the Examples subdirectory demonstrates this technique. That program uses three different TQuery objects. The first TQuery object works with a TDataSource and a TDBGridid object to display the COUNTRY database on screen. In Figure 10.8, you can see that the program has two buttons: one for deleting records, and the other for inserting records.

The second TQuery object in the SQLInsert program is used to insert a record into the COUNTRY table, as explained next. The third TQuery object is used for deleting records. It has the following statement in its SQL property:

```
delete from Country where Name = :Name;
```

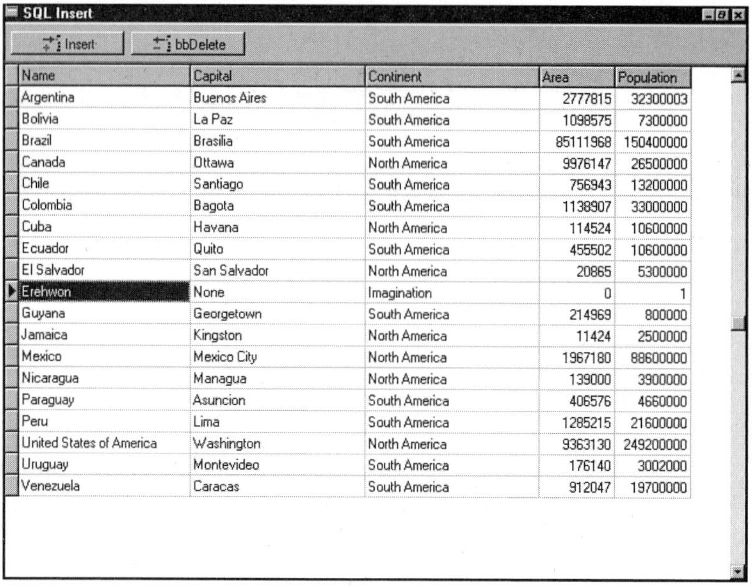

FIGURE 10.8.

The SQLInsert program uses three TQuery *components and one* TDataSource *component.*

The code associated with the Delete button looks like this:

```
void TDMod::Delete(void)
{
  AnsiString S("Delete " + CountryQuery->Fields[0]->AsString + "?");
  if (MessageDlg(S, mtConfirmation,
      TMsgDlgButtons() << mbYes << mbNo, 0) != ID_YES)
    return;
  DeleteQuery->Prepare();
  DeleteQuery->Params->Items[0]->AsString = CountryQuery->Fields[0]->AsString;
  DeleteQuery->ExecSQL();
  CountryQuery->Refresh();
}
```

DeleteQuery snags the name of the record to delete from the currently selected record in the first query. This enables the user to scroll through the list of records using the TDBGrid tool, and then delete whatever record is current. After the deletion, CountryQuery.Refresh is called. A call to Refresh forces the Query to go and obtain the most recent data from the disk, thereby allowing the program to reflect the deletion at almost the same moment it is made. (Note that a real-world program meant to be used with a typical set of users would query the user before performing a deletion of this sort.)

Here is a typical SQL statement for inserting data into a table:

```
insert into
  Country
  (Name, Capital, Continent, Area, Population)
```

```
values
  ('Argentina', 'Buenos Ares',
   'South America', 2777815, 32300003)
```

This is a convenient system, but it has the disadvantage of forcing you to hard-code values into the statement. To avoid this problem, the Query2 object has the following code in its SQL property:

```
insert
  into Country (Name, Capital, Continent, Area,  Population)
  values (:Name, :Capital, :Continent, :Area, :Population)
```

Note that in this code, all the actual values intended for insertion are specified by bind variables. These bind variables are convenient because they enable you to write code that looks like this:

```
void TDMod::AutoInsert(void)
{
  InsertQuery->Prepare();
  InsertQuery->Params->Items[0]->AsString = "Erehwon";
  InsertQuery->Params->Items[1]->AsString = "None";
  InsertQuery->Params->Items[2]->AsString = "Imagination";
  InsertQuery->Params->Items[3]->AsFloat = 0.0;
  InsertQuery->Params->Items[4]->AsFloat = 1.0;
  InsertQuery->ExecSQL();
  CountryQuery->Refresh();
}
```

In the code shown here, you can use edit controls to dynamically specify the values that you want to insert at runtime. Notice that once again, the program calls ExecSQL rather than Open. This is because there's no need to return a cursor from a SQL insert statement. The function ends with a call to Refresh, which assures that InsertQuery goes out to the disk and gets the most recent data.

> **NOTE**
>
> You might want to compare this version of the INSERT program with the INSERT1 application that uses the TTable object. There are advantages to both techniques, but you should remember that keeping code as simple as possible is one way to construct applications that are robust and easy to maintain.

In this section, you've learned about the differences between ExecSQL and Open. The major point to remember is that select statements return a cursor and therefore require a call to Open. delete, insert, and update don't return a cursor, and should therefore be accompanied by calls to ExecSQL. All of this is demonstrated on disk in the INSERT2 program. The call to Refresh ensures that the data displayed to the user reflects the changes made by the delete statement.

Specialized TQuery Properties

By this time, you should have a good feeling for how to use BCB to create and execute SQL statements. There are, however, a few properties belonging to, or inherited by, TQuery that have not yet been mentioned:

```
__property System::Boolean UniDirectional;
__property Bde::hDBIStmt StmtHandle;
__property Bde::hDBIDb DBHandle; // From TDBDataSet
__property Bde::hDBIDb Handle;   // From TDBDataSet
```

The UniDirectional property is used to optimize your access to a table. If you set UniDirectional to True, you can iterate through a table more quickly, but you'll be able to move only in a forward direction.

The StmtHandle property is related to the Handle property from TDBDataSet; it's included solely so you can make your own calls directly to the Borland Database Engine. Under normal circumstances, there would be no need for you to use this property, because BCB's components can handle the needs of most programmers. However, if you're familiar with the Borland Database Engine, and if you know that it has some particular capability that isn't encapsulated in the VCL, you can use TQuery .StmtHandle or TQuery .Handle to make calls directly to the engine.

The following short code fragment shows two calls being made directly to the BDE:

```
void __fastcall TForm1::bGetRecordCountClick(TObject *Sender)
{
  int Records;
  DbiGetRecordCount(Query1->Handle, Records);
  Edit1->Text = (AnsiString)Records;
}
//----------------------------------------------------------------
void __fastcall TForm1::bbGetNetUserNameClick(TObject *Sender)
{
  char Name[100];
  DbiGetNetUserName(Name);
  Edit2->Text = (String)Name;
}
```

The BDE.HPP unit contains a list of all the possible calls made to the Borland Database Engine. This file may appear on your system in the INCLUDE\VCL directory.

Having a Little Fun with SQL

The last two chapters have been chock-full of information, perhaps even more information than you would want to absorb all at once. As a result, it might be a good idea to end this chapter by learning a few simple things you can do with SQL that produce interesting results.

To get started, you will need a place where you can interactively enter some SQL, just to see what it does. One simple way to do this is to place a TQuery, TDataSource, TDBGrid, TButton and TMemo objects on a form, as shown in Figure 10.9. Wire up the data components and set the TQuery to the DBDEMOS alias.

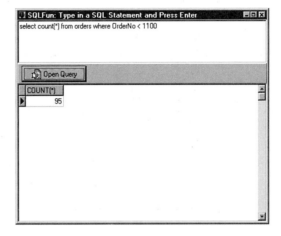

If the user selects the button, the following code will be executed:

```
void __fastcall TForm1::OpenQueryBtnClick(TObject *Sender)
{
  Query1->Close();
  Query1->SQL->Clear();
  Query1->SQL = Memo1->Lines;
  Query1->Open();
}
```

This code does nothing more than attempt to execute as a SQL statement whatever text the user types into the memo control.

To make the program somewhat easier to use, you can add the following code to the OnKeyPress event for the TMemo object:

```
void __fastcall TForm1::Memo1KeyPress(TObject *Sender, char &Key)
{
  if (Key == '\r')
    OpenQueryBtnClick(NULL);
}
```

This code traps presses on the Enter key and delegates them to the same routine that handles clicks on the form's button. This enables the user to enter a SQL statement, and then press the Enter key to see the results of the statement. This means the user never has to lift up his or her hands from the keyboard while playing with the program.

To get started with the program, you might enter the following:

```
select * from customer
```

This statement selects all the records from the CUSTOMER table.

To find out how many records are in the table, enter the following:

```
select Count(*) from customer
```

To see just the Company field from the table, enter this:

```
select company from customer
```

To see only the Company field from the CUSTOMER table and to have the data arranged in alphabetical order, write this:

```
select company from customer order by company
```

To see the Company field all in caps, enter this:

```
select upper(company) from customer
```

To see the Company field all in caps, and next to it the company field in normal letters, and to arrange the result alphabetically, write this:

```
select upper(company), company from customer order by company
```

Note that you could not order the table by the Company field in the first of the last two examples. This is because the Company field must be present in the dataset to sort on it, and it is not considered present in the dataset if it is only used in an upper clause.

To group the data from the table by state, enter the following:

```
select Company, State from customer order by State
```

This statement shows the Company and State fields from the table, and orders them by state. Many of the fields in the table do not have a value for the state field, and you will have to scroll past these blank fields before you can properly see the results of this query.

The following statement selects the OrderNo and ItemsTotal fields from the Orders table:

```
select OrderNo, ItemsTotal from orders
```

To find the largest value in the ItemsTotal field, enter the following:

```
select Max(ItemsTotal) from orders
```

And finally, here is how to get the sum of all the values in the ItemsTotal field of the Orders table:

```
select Sum(ItemsTotal) from orders
```

Just to spice things up a bit, you can try the following slightly more complex query that returns all the companies from the CUSTOMER table that had orders with an ItemTotal larger than 100,000:

```
select Company, State from customer
where CustNo in (select CustNo from Orders where ItemsTotal > 100000)
```

Statements like this that contain one query embedded in another query are called, naturally enough, subqueries.

All these queries are not only fun to play with, but they also show that the local SQL that ships with the BDE is a fairly powerful tool. Indeed, SQL is a flexible and powerful language for manipulating databases. This brief taste of it should give you some sense of the tool's possibilities, and some sense of how much work SQL can save you if you know how to use it. Don't spend hours trying to do something in C++ if it can be done in two short lines of SQL!

Summary

In this chapter, you have learned the main features of the TQuery component. You have seen that you can use this component to create SQL statements that enable you to manipulate tables in a wide variety of useful ways.

One of the keys to understanding TQuery's SQL property is the ability to manipulate it at runtime. In this chapter, you saw three different methods of manipulating this property. The first, and conceptually simplest, is to merely use the Query1->SQL->Add function whenever you need to change a query at runtime. Parameterized queries are less wasteful than using the Add property, but there are some limits on what you can do with parameterized queries. To get beyond these limits, you can use the Format function, which enables you to create almost any kind of SQL statement you could want at runtime.

Regardless of how you treat the SQL property, there is no doubt that it is one of the power centers in the BCB environment. Programmers who want to write powerful SQL applications need to know almost everything they can about the SQL property.

In the next chapter, you will learn how to use the Fields Editor, as well as other tools to automate some of the database tasks you have been performing in the last two chapters.

Working with Field Objects

CHAPTER 11

IN THIS CHAPTER

This chapter covers a set of visual tools you can use to simplify database development. The major areas covered are as follows:

- The Fields Editor
- TField descendant objects
- Calculated fields
- The TDBGrid component
- Lookup fields
- MultiRecord objects—TDBCtrlGrid

These subjects are all related to databases, and to the TField and TDBGrid objects in particular. BCB is a very sophisticated database tool, and it takes time to get a feeling for the breadth and depth of the tools it provides for client/server developers. One of the goals of this chapter is to give you some sense of the powerful TField object and its impact on designing database applications.

One of the most frequently mentioned tools in this chapter is the Fields Editor. By using the Fields Editor, you can create objects that influence the appearance of data shown in visual controls such as TDBEdit and TDBGrid. For instance, you can use the objects made in the Fields Editor to format data so that it appears as currency or as a floating-point number with a defined precision. These same changes can be accomplished through the Data Dictionary in the Database Explorer or through the Database Desktop. These latter tools, however, have a global impact on the field's potential values, whereas the changes made in the Object Inspector affect only the current application.

If you want to dynamically emphasize a particular column or row in a table, this is the chapter you should read to get the information you need. For instance, this chapter covers the Columns property of the TDBGrid control. The Columns property can be used to change the appearance of a grid so that its columns are arranged in a new order or are hidden. You can also use the Columns property to change the color of columns in a grid, or to insert drop-down combo boxes into a grid.

The lessons you learn in this chapter will arm you with key techniques used by most programmers when they present database tables to their users. Much of the material involves manipulating visual tools, but the basic subject matter is fairly technical and assumes a basic understanding of the BCB environment and language. Note that third parties such as TurboPower (www.turbopower.com) and Woll2Woll (www.woll2woll.com) have grid objects that go beyond the capability of the native grids that ship with BCB.

The Fields Editor

To get things rolling, it might be a good idea to take a close look at the invaluable Fields Editor. This tool lies very much at the heart of BCB database programming. To access it, you double-click or right-click on a TTable or TQuery object.

The Fields Editor helps you associate custom objects with some or all of the fields from a table. By associating a custom object with a field, you can control the way a field displays, formats, validates, and inputs data. The Fields Editor also enables you to add new fields to a table at runtime and then to calculate the values that will be shown in the new fields. This latter procedure is referred to as *calculated fields*. Another benefit of the Fields Editor is that it helps you create lookup fields. Lookup fields perform a lookup from one table into another based on a foreign key.

It's important to understand that the Fields Editor is just a utility. Everything done inside the Fields Editor could be done in code, although in this particular case the code in question becomes a little complicated, or at least time consuming.

In this section and the next, you will be building a program called MASS, which illustrates both the Fields Editor and calculated fields. This is an important program, so you should try to use your copy of BCB to follow the steps described.

Getting Started with the Fields Editor

You can access the Fields Editor from either a TTable or TQuery object. To get started, drop a TQuery object on a data module, set up the BCDEMOS alias, enter the SQL statement select * from animals, and make the table active. (The BCDEMOS alias is created automatically when you install BCB. It points at the data in the CBuilder/Examples/Data directory. If you are having trouble with aliases, see the readme file on the CD or visit my Web site.)

Drop down the Object Selector at the top of the Object Inspector. Notice that you currently have two components in use: TDataModule and TQuery.

Right-click the TQuery object and select the Fields Editor menu choice to bring up the Fields Editor. Right-click the Fields Editor and select Add Fields from the menu to pop up the Add Fields dialog, as shown in Figure 11.1.

FIGURE 11.1.
The Add Fields dialog box from the Fields Editor.

By default, all of the fields in the dialog box are selected. Click the OK button to select all five fields, and then close the Fields Editor.

Open the Object Selector a second time; notice that there are now five new objects on your form, as shown in Figure 11.2.

FIGURE 11.2.

The Object Selector lists the objects created in the Fields Editor. You also can find this list in the TForm1 class definition.

These objects help you hone and define your presentation of the Animals table to the user.

Here's a complete list of the objects you just created, as they appear in your header file:

```
TStringField *AnimalsQueryNAME;
TSmallintField *AnimalsQuerySIZE;
TSmallintField *AnimalsQueryWEIGHT;
TStringField *AnimalsQueryAREA;
TBlobField *AnimalsQueryBMP;
```

The origins of the names shown here should be fairly obvious. The string AnimalsQuery comes from the name I've given to the TQuery object, and the second half of the name comes from the fields in the Animals table. This naming convention I've adopted here can be very useful if you are working with several tables and want to know at a glance which table and field are being referenced by a particular variable.

NOTE

The names of the fields in the example shown here are capitalized only because the table in question is a dBASE table. dBASE tables automatically capitalize all letters in field names. If I had chosen to work with some other type of table, the capitalization of the letters in the field name would have followed the rules defined by the current database software.

This principle appears again and again in BCB database programming. Whenever possible, the actual naming conventions and other traits of a server are surfaced inside of BCB. The developers of C++Builder did not aim to make all servers appear the same to you, but rather to give you access to their features as transparently as possible. Of course, generic tools such as the TTable object are also common in BCB. The VCL team, however, strove to find the right balance between expediting access to the database and unintentionally crippling the database by wrapping too many of its features inside objects. As a rule,

> the developers did whatever they could to ease the path, without ever going so far as to actually cut you off from a feature of the server you are accessing.
>
> This same principle applies to the VCL. The developers tried to do everything they could to make Windows programming simple, but they drew the line if a particular feature was so warm and fuzzy that it cut you off from direct access to the OS when and if you needed it.

Each of the objects created in the Fields Editor is a descendant of TField. The exact type of descendant depends on the type of data in a particular field. For instance, the AnimalsQueryWEIGHT field is of type TSmallIntField, whereas the AnimalsQueryNAME field is of type TStringField. These are the two field types you will see most often. Other common types include TDateField and TCurrencyField, neither of which are used in this particular table. Remember that these types were selected to correspond with the field types in the table itself.

TStringField, TSmallIntField, and the other objects shown here are all descendants of TField and share its traits. If you want, you can treat these objects exactly as you did the TField objects that you learned about in Chapter 9, "Using TTable and TDataSet." For instance, you can write this:

```
S = MyIntegerField->AsString;
```

and this:

```
S = MyIntegerField->Name;
```

However, these descendants of TField are very smart objects and have several traits that go beyond the functionality of their common ancestor.

The most important property you will see is called Value. You can access it like this:

```
void __fastcall TForm1::Button1Click(TObject *Sender)
{
  int i;
  AnsiString S;
  DMod->AnimalsQuery->Edit();
  i = DMod->AnimalsQuerySIZE->Value;
  S = DMod->AnimalsQueryNAME->Value;
  i += 1;
  S = "Foo";
  DMod->AnimalsQuerySIZE->Value = i;
  DMod->AnimalsQueryNAME->Value = S;
}
```

The code shown here first assigns values to the variables i and S. The next two lines change these values, and the last two lines reassign the new values to the objects. It usually wouldn't make much sense to write code exactly like this in a program, but it serves to illustrate the syntax used by TField descendants. (If you bother to try to write code like this as a test, remember that the RequestLive property for a TQuery object is set to False by default. You would have to set it to True before the code would work.)

The `Value` property always conforms to the type of field you have instantiated. For instance, `TStringFields` are strings, whereas `TCurrencyFields` always return floating-point double values. However, if you show a `TCurrencyField` in a data-aware control, it will return a string that looks like this: `"$5.00"`. The dollar sign and the rounding to decimal places are simply part and parcel of what a `TCurrencyField` is all about.

The preceding example might make you think that these variables are declared as `Variants`, which indeed is the case for the `TField` object itself. In the actual implementation, however, the `TCurrencyField->Value` is declared as a `Double`. If you tried to assign a string to it, you would get a type mismatch. Likewise, `TIntegerField.Value` is declared as a `LongInt`, and so on. `TSmallIntField` and `TWordField` are both descendants of `TIntegerField` and inherit the `Value` declaration as a `LongInt`. However, they have other internal code that affects the `Value` field, just as `TCurrencyField` rings some changes on its `Value` field to make it look like a monetary value. If you have the source, look up `DBTABLES.PAS` and `DB.PAS` to find the details of these constructions. (The Pascal source ships with some versions of BCB.) At any rate, the point here is that the preceding code is an example of polymorphism; it is not an example of relaxed type-checking. The `Value` field has a specific type—it's just that it undergoes polymorphic changes.

If you want the names of each field in the current dataset, you should reference the `FieldName` property through one of the following two methods:

```
S = AnimalsQuery->Fields[0]->FieldName;
S = AnimalsQueryNAME.FieldName;
```

If you want the name of an object associated with a field, you should use the `Name` property:

```
S = AnimalsQuery->Fields[0]->Name;
S = AnimalsQueryNAME->Name;
```

When using the `ANIMALS` table, the first two examples shown previously yield the string `"Name"`, while the second two lines yield `"Query1NAME"`.

Special properties are associated with most of the major field types. For instance, `TIntegerFields` have `DisplayFormat` and `DisplayEdit` properties, as well as `MinValue` and `MaxValue` properties. `TStringFields`, on the other hand, have none of these properties, but they do have an `EditMask` property, which works just like the `TEditMask` component found on the Additional page of the Component Palette. All these properties are used to control the way data is displayed to the user, or the way that input from the user should be handled.

> **NOTE**
>
> I don't want to get ahead of myself, but properties such as `MinValue` and `MaxValue` are also used in the Data Dictionary, as will be explained later in this chapter. Changes made in the Data Dictionary will affect these values as seen in the Object Inspector, but changes in the Object Inspector will not affect the Data Dictionary. Don't worry if this doesn't make the slightest bit of sense yet, as I will get to the Data Dictionary in just a little while.

Calculated Fields

You should be aware of one more thing about the Fields Editor. You can use this tool not only to build objects that encapsulate existing fields, but also to build objects that represent new fields. For instance, suppose you wanted to create a sixth field, Mass, which contains the product of the SIZE and WEIGHT fields, in the Animals table.

To create the Mass field, open the Fields Editor again, right-click it, and select the New Field menu choice. In the top part of the New Field dialog, enter the word Mass. Now set its type to Integer, and leave its field type as Calculated, as shown in Figure 11.3.

FIGURE 11.3.

Creating the Mass *field in the Fields Editor.*

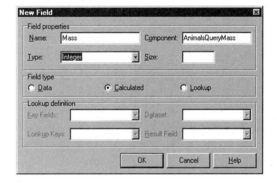

If you close the Fields Editor and add a TDataSource and TDBGrid to your project, you will see that the Animals table now appears to have six fields, the last of which is called MASS.

Of course, it's one thing to create a field, and another to fill it in at runtime with an appropriate value. The act of placing a value in the new field you have created involves a concept called calculated fields.

Calculated fields are one of the most valuable features of the TField object and its related architecture. You can use these calculated fields for several different purposes, but two stand out:

- If you need to perform calculations on two or more of the fields in a dataset and want to show the results of the calculations in a third field, you can use calculated fields. A scenario describing this type of situation was set up at the beginning of this section.

- If you are viewing one dataset and want to perform calculations or display data that involve lookups in at least one additional dataset, you can use the Fields Editor and calculated fields to show the results of these calculations in a new field of the first dataset. There is also a second, much better method for doing lookups. I will talk about that method later in this chapter. As a rule, you should do calculations in calculated fields, and lookups in lookup fields, though calculated fields are powerful enough to fill a number of different roles in your programs.

The MASS program illustrates one example of the first of the two uses for calculated fields. You got this program started in the last section when you created the field called MASS and displayed it in a grid.

To continue working with the MASS program, highlight the `AnimalsQuery` object and set the Object Inspector to the Events page. Now create an `OnCalcFields` event that looks like this:

```
void __fastcall TDMod::AnimalsQueryCalcFields(TDataSet *DataSet)
{
  AnimalsQueryMass->AsInteger =
    AnimalsQuerySIZE->AsInteger * AnimalsQueryWEIGHT->AsInteger;
}
```

The code shown here assigns the value of the `AnimalsQueryMass` object to the product of the `AnimalsQuerySIZE` and `sqlWeightWEIGHT` fields. This kind of multiplication is legal to do because all of the fields are of the same type. Furthermore, you could have used the `Value` property instead of `AsInteger`. I explicitly declared the type in this example to help illustrate precisely what is going on.

`OnCalcField` methods are called each time a record is displayed to the user. As a result, all of the `Mass` fields displayed in the grid are properly filled in, as shown in Figure 11.4.

FIGURE 11.4.

The MASS *field contains the product of the* WEIGHT *and* SIZE *fields. A* TDBImage *control contains a bitmap from the* BMP *field of the table.*

To get the screen shot shown in Figure 11.4, I opened the `Column` property in the `TDBGrid` object and selected Add All Fields. I then deleted the Area and BMP fields and closed the `Column` property editor. I will talk more about the grid object later in this chapter.

If you choose to never instantiate a particular field in the Fields Editor, the current dataset you are working with no longer contains that field. It can't be accessed programmatically or visually at runtime. Usually, this is exactly the effect you want to achieve, and so this trait will generally be perceived as a strong benefit. However, there are times when it might not serve your purposes, and in those cases you should either create an object for all the fields in a table or stay away from the Fields Editor altogether. Remember that you can hide fields inside a grid by using the Column property, as shown previously. That way, you create objects for all fields, but show only certain ones to the user.

Lookup Fields

You can use lookup fields to look up a value in one table that you want to use in a second table. For instance, suppose you had two tables, one of which contained a list of books, and the other contained a list of authors. It would be nice if you could automatically view a list of the existing authors whenever you needed to add a new book to the Books table. That way, you could enter the book's name, look up the author in a drop-down list, and presto, you would be done. The Books table would then automatically contain a reference to the appropriate author in the Authors table. That is, the author number from the Authors table would automatically be inserted in the Books table.

Another way to think about lookup fields is that they provide the ability to perform a powerful kind of pseudo-join using the TTable object. Suppose two tables called Authors and Books are related on a field called AuthNo. AuthNo is the primary key of the Authors table, and it is a foreign key in the Books table. When you are looking at the Books table, sometimes you would like to be able to include the name of the author of each book inside the book table. That is, you would like to perform a join on the book and author table. You can't actually perform a join, however, because you are using the TTable object, and not TQuery. The solution to this dilemma is the lookup field. It will use the foreign key in the Books table to reference the name of the author from the Author table. This technique does join one better, however, because it will let you not only view a field from the Authors table as if it were part of the Books table, but also enables you to drop down a list of all the authors in the Authors table while you are still viewing the Books table, as shown in Figure 11.5.

In short, lookup fields give you the same type of benefits you derive from performing a join between two tables. In particular, they let you combine the fields of two tables so that you can create one dataset with fields from multiple tables.

> **NOTE**
>
> Lookup fields are a bit like a combination of a one-to-many relationship and a calculated field. The techniques used to actually implement them, however, have more in common with calculated fields than they do with one-to-many relationships. There are significant differences between the three technologies, but I still tend to think of calculated fields, lookup fields, and one-to-many relationships as being interrelated concepts.
>
> Because lookup fields are so much like one-to-many relationships, it is usually not a good idea to use both techniques simultaneously with the same two TTable objects. For instance, if you have the Authors table related to the books table in a one-to-many, you wouldn't want to simultaneously do a lookup from the Books table to the author table. This problem, and its solution, are addressed in the Lookup example on the CD-ROM that accompanies this book. That program will be discussed throughout the rest of this section of the chapter.
>
> I should perhaps add that lookup fields are a great technique to use with relatively small datasets. If you are from the world of big iron, and work with tables that contain tens of thousands of records or more, you will probably find lookup fields are of only limited use to you.

Needless to say, BCB gives good support for using lookup fields. You can now perform automatic lookups inside grids, list boxes, and combo boxes. In particular, the following controls support lookups: TDBGrid, TDBCtrlGrid, TDBLookupListBox, and TDBLookupComboBox.

The Lookup program shows how to proceed. The code for this application is shown in Listings 11.1 through 11.3. Two views of the program are shown in Figures 11.5 and 11.6.

FIGURE 11.5.

The main form for the Lookup program.

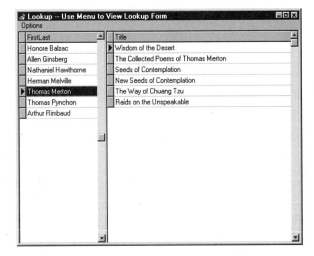

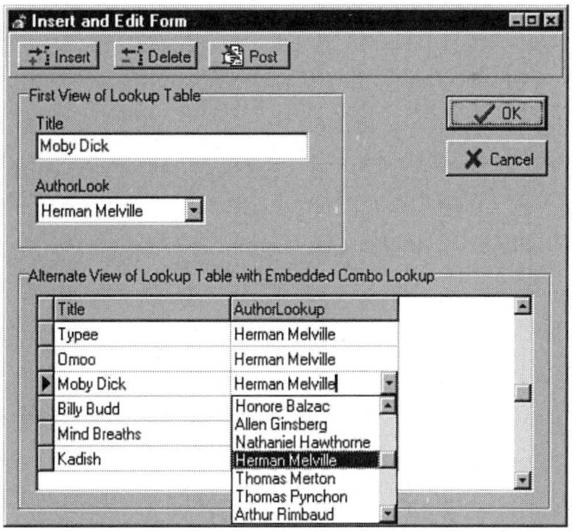

FIGURE 11.6.

This form features a combo box that lets you perform lookups from the Books *table into the* Authors *table.*

NOTE

The first version of Delphi had a `TDBLookupCombo` control and a `TDBLookupList` control that had certain limited capabilities. Both of these controls are still present in some versions of BCB, but they have been moved off the Data Controls page onto the Win 3.1 page. They are being kept around solely for compatibility with legacy Pascal code, and you should not use them in new programs.

The `TDBLookupComboBox` control and the `TDBLookupListBox` control now replace the old 16-bit controls, and they outperform them on several fronts. In particular, the `TDBLookupComboBox` and `TDBLookupListBox` will be filled up automatically with the data from the lookup table. Don't confuse the old control with the new ones! `TDBLookupComboBox` is the fancy one; the `TDBLookupCombo` is the old-fashioned one. You might use the following somewhat whimsical mnemonic: The `TDBLookupListBox` has a bigger name than the `TDBLookupList` because it has "bigger" capabilities.

By the way, this is a classic example of why it is important to get things right the first time. In particular, it shows why it is sometimes better to cut a feature rather than trying to put in a hack that you will want to improve in later versions. In particular, the `TDBLookupCombo` was poorly implemented in the first version of Delphi, which was a 16-bit program. Because Delphi 2.0 promised to compile all your 16-bit programs, this component had to be left in the product even though it was replaced with a far superior tool. Now, this old nemesis lives on even in the C++ version of the product, because BCB advertises the fact that it supports all the legacy Pascal code you might want to bring into a project.

Here's the summary: The original error was made back in Delphi 1.0, but the repercussions still echo even when the 32-bit version of the Delphi is ported to C++! Clearly, it is worthwhile making sure that things are designed right the first time, or else they should be left out of the product altogether. Of course, this is a rule that can be stated fairly easily, but is difficult to live up to.

Listing 11.1. The core functionality for the Lookup program is done in the Object Inspector for the TDMod object and not here in the code for Dmod1.cpp.

```cpp
//////////////////////////////////////
// File: DMod1.cpp
// Project: Lookup
// Copyright (c) 1997 by Charlie Calvert
#include <vcl\vcl.h>
#pragma hdrstop
#include "DMod1.h"
#pragma resource "*.dfm"
TDMod *DMod;
__fastcall TDMod::TDMod(TComponent* Owner)
  : TDataModule(Owner)
{
  AuthorTable->Open();
  BookDetailTable->Open();
  BookLookupTable->Open();
}
void __fastcall TDMod::AuthorTableCalcFields(TDataSet *DataSet)
{
  AuthorTableFirstLast->AsString =
    AuthorTableFirst->AsString + " " + AuthorTableLast->AsString;
}
void TDMod::RefreshBookDetail()
{
  BookDetailTable->Refresh();
}
AnsiString TDMod::GetCurBook()
{
  return BookDetailTable->FieldByName("Title")->AsString;
}
AnsiString TDMod::GetCurAuthor(void)
{
  return AuthorTable->FieldByName("FirstLast")->AsString;
}
void TDMod::FindAuthor(AnsiString S)
{
  AuthorTable->FindNearest(OPENARRAY(TVarRec, (S)));
}
void TDMod::FindTitle(AnsiString S)
{
  AnsiString Temp(BookLookupTable->IndexName);
  BookLookupTable->IndexName = "idxTitle";
  BookLookupTable->FindNearest(OPENARRAY(TVarRec, (S)));
  BookLookupTable->IndexName = Temp;
}
void TDMod::BookLookupInsert()
{
  BookLookupTable->Insert();
}
void TDMod::BookLookupPost()
{
  if ((BookLookupTable->State == dsEdit)||(BookLookupTable->State == dsInsert))
    BookLookupTable->Post();
}
void TDMod::BookLookupCancel()
{
```

```
    if ((BookLookupTable->State == dsEdit)¦¦(BookLookupTable->State == dsInsert))
        BookLookupTable->Cancel();
}
void TDMod::BookLookupDelete()
{
    BookLookupTable->Delete();
}
```

Listing 11.2. Form1 **gives you a look at both the** Authors **table and the** Books **table. A drop-down in** dbGrid2 **lets you view the lookup field.**

```
/////////////////////////////////////
// File: InsertEdit.cpp
// Project: Lookup
// Copyright (c) 1997 by Charlie Calvert
#include <vcl\vcl.h>
#pragma hdrstop
#include "Main.h"
#include "DMod1.h"
#include "InsertEdit.h"
#pragma resource "*.dfm"
TForm1 *Form1;
__fastcall TForm1::TForm1(TComponent* Owner)
    : TForm(Owner)
{
}
void __fastcall TForm1::Exit1Click(TObject *Sender)
{
    Close();
}
void __fastcall TForm1::EditBook1Click(TObject *Sender)
{
    InsertEditForm->ShowEdit(DMod->CurBook);
    DMod->RefreshBookDetail();
}
void __fastcall TForm1::NewBook1Click(TObject *Sender)
{
    InsertEditForm->ShowInsert();
    DMod->RefreshBookDetail();
}
```

Listing 11.3. The InsertEditForm **shows how to use** DBLookupComboBoxes**.**

```
/////////////////////////////////////
// File: InsertEdit.cpp
// Project: Lookup
// Copyright (c) 1997 by Charlie Calvert
#include <vcl\vcl.h>
#pragma hdrstop
#include "InsertEdit.h"
```

continues

Listing 11.3. continued

```
#include "DMod1.h"
#pragma resource "*.dfm"
TInsertEditForm *InsertEditForm;
__fastcall TInsertEditForm::TInsertEditForm(TComponent* Owner)
  : TForm(Owner)
{
}
void __fastcall TInsertEditForm::bbInsertClick(TObject *Sender)
{
  DMod->BookLookupTable->Insert();
}
void __fastcall TInsertEditForm::bbPostClick(TObject *Sender)
{
  DMod->BookLookupPost();
}
void TInsertEditForm::ShowEdit(AnsiString S)
{
  DMod->FindTitle(S);
  ShowModal();
  DMod->BookLookupPost();
}
void TInsertEditForm::ShowInsert()
{
  DMod->BookLookupInsert();
  DMod->BookLookupTableTitle->AsString = "My New Book";
  ShowModal();
  DMod->BookLookupPost();
}
void __fastcall TInsertEditForm::CancelBtnClick(TObject *Sender)
{
  DMod->BookLookupCancel();
}
void __fastcall TInsertEditForm::DeleteBtnClick(TObject *Sender)
{
  if (MessageBox(Handle, "Delete?" , "Delete Dialog", MB_YESNO) == ID_YES)
    DMod->BookLookupDelete();
}
void __fastcall TInsertEditForm::FormShow(TObject *Sender)
{
  TitleEdit->SetFocus();
}
```

The Lookup program enables you to easily fill in the key fields of the Books table by looking them up in the Authors table. To understand why this capability is important, notice that the only way to tell which author is associated with which book is by placing the appropriate author number in the AuthNo field of the Book table. This is convenient from the point of view of the programmer who wants to construct a well-made relational database. In particular, it saves space by allowing the construction of one-to-many relationships. However, the user isn't going to want to have to remember that Herman Melville is associated with the number 2, Jack Kerouac with the number x, and so on. The point of a lookup field is that it lets you look up a list of authors in the author table, and then automatically assigns the chosen author number to the AuthNo field in the Books table.

This program uses two tables called, not surprisingly, `Author.db` and `Book.db`. Both of these tables are found on the CD-ROM that accompanies this book. Tables 11.1 and 11.2 show the schema for the tables.

Table 11.1. `Author.db` table structure.

Name	Type	Keyed
AuthNo	AutoInc	Key
First	Character(25)	N/A
Last	Character(25)	N/A
Dates	Character(25)	N/A
BirthPlace	Character(25)	N/A

Table 11.2. `Book.db` table structure.

Name	Type	Keyed
BookNo	AutoInc	Key
AuthNo	LongInt	Foreign Key
Title	Character (35)	N/A

NOTE

Notice the use of the `AutoIncrement` fields in the table definitions shown in Tables 11.1 and 11.2. These fields will automatically be filled in when the user adds a new record at runtime. For instance, when you add the first record to the `Books` table, it will automatically be given a `BookNo` of 1. The second record will automatically be given a `BookNo` of 2, and so on. `AutoIncrement` fields are read-only, and frequently there is no need to show them to the user at runtime.

Furthermore, I use Referential Integrity to ensure that the `AuthNo` field properly binds to the `Author` table. In particular, it ensures that you cannot insert records into the `Book` table that are not properly related to the `Authors` table through the `AuthNo` field. Referential Integrity also ensures that the value of the `AuthNo` field is filled in automatically when you insert a new record into the `Books` table. To view the Referential Integrity, load the book table into the Database Desktop, choose Table | Info Structure, select Referential Integrity in the Table Properties, highlight the `AuthNoRI` rule, and press the Detail Info button. There is more on this subject in the next chapter, called "Understanding Relational Databases."

There is little actual work required to construct this program. In particular, look over the source code shown earlier, and you will see that the only significant line of code in the whole program is the one for the OnCalcFields event. Other than that, it's just a matter of manipulating the visual tools.

To get started, create a new application and add a data module to it. Set up the Authors and Books tables on the data module. Bring up the Fields Editor for both tables and create objects for all of their fields. Give the tables and data sources appropriate names, such as AuthorTable and BookLookupTable, as shown in Figure 11.7. Note that later on I will add a second instance of the Book table to the program so that I can simultaneously perform a lookup and a one-to-many.

FIGURE 11.7.

The TDataModule *for the Lookup program.*

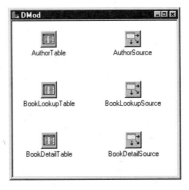

Inside the Author table, create a calculated field called LastFirst. To create the calculated field, first right-click the TTable object, and then right-click the Fields Editor and select New from the menu. After creating the calculated field, assign the following method to the OnCalcFields event:

```
void __fastcall TDMod::AuthorTableCalcFields(TDataSet *DataSet)
{
  AuthorTableFirstLast->AsString =
    AuthorTableFirst->AsString + " " + AuthorTableLast->AsString;
}
```

This field will be the one that is looked up in the second table. The issue here is that just looking up the last name of an author is not sufficient—you need to look up both first and last names in order to be sure you are finding a unique author. In other words, you can't tell Henry James from William James or Tom Wolfe from Thomas Wolfe unless you have both the first and last name present. It would be wasteful of disk space to permanently add a field to the table that combined the first and last names, but you can create a temporary copy of that field with a calculated field.

Now that you have a calculated field in place, it is time to create a lookup field. To get started, bring up the Fields Editor for the Book table. Right-click it and create a new field called AuthorLookup. Set its Type to String and its Field Type to Lookup. The KeyField should be set to AuthNo, the Dataset to AuthorTable, the Lookup Key to AuthNo, and the Result field to LastFirst. Figure 11.8 shows how the New Field dialog should look when you are done. Notice that you can also fill in this same information in the Object Inspector if you first select the BookLookupTable object. (In other words, you could create a new object and then close the Fields Editor without specifying any of its properties. Later, you could select the object and designate its type, its lookup fields, and so on.)

FIGURE 11.8.

*Filling in the New
Field dialog.*

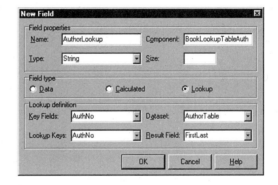

Go back to Form1 and make sure the two TDBGrids are arranged one above the other and are hooked up properly to the tables on the TDataModule. Run the application.

The AuthorLookup field in the TDBGrid object associated with the Books table is now a drop-down combo box. If you click it once, and then drop down its list, you can then perform a lookup into the LastFirst field of the Author table. This lookup will automatically fill in the AuthNo field of the book table. You can use this lookup to insert a new author into a new record or to change the author of an existing record.

Note that lookup fields give you two distinct benefits. They enable you to perform a "join" between the Books table and the Authors table, and they allow you to look up a reference in a drop-down list.

The implementation of this program found on the CD-ROM that accompanies this book actually enables the user to perform the lookup on a second form. I implement things that way because it is probably easiest from the user's perspective, and because I want to support both a one-to-many relationship and a lookup between the Authors and Books tables. However, if you just want to see how lookups work, then you should follow the technique described previously.

> **NOTE**
>
> The capability of having a drop-down list in a grid object comes for free in BCB, even when you are not doing lookups. Go back in design mode and open up the Columns property of a grid object. Add all the fields to the Columns list box. You can now select one of the fields, such as Title, and choose the PickList button in order to create a set of default values available for the field. The user can access these values at runtime by clicking the field and dropping down the combo box, per the lookup example discussed previously. This is the capability supported by the old TDBLookupList and TDBLookupCombo from the old Windows 3.1 days.

Besides the TDBGrid object, there are two other controls in BCB that understand lookup fields. The first of these controls is shown on Form2 of the Lookup program found on the CD-ROM that accompanies this book. The TDBLookupComboBox is the default control you will get if you drag and drop the AuthorLookup field from the Fields Editor onto a form. If you perform the drag-and-drop operation, the control will be hooked up automatically. If you want to hook it up manually, just connect its DataSource to the dsBook object and its DataField to the AuthorLookup field. There is also a TDBLookupListBox, which works exactly the same way as the TDBLookupComboBox.

> **NOTE**
>
> Both the TDBLookupListBox and TDBLookupComboBox have fields that correspond to the ones you filled in with the New Field dialog shown in Figure 11.7. However, there is no need to fill in these fields a second time. Just hook up the DataSource and DataFields properties, and you are ready to go.

When you are working with the Lookup program found on the book's CD-ROM, you should note that Form1 does not contain a lookup. It's meant to help you scan through all the available data so you can grok the significance of the lookup process. The top part of the second form, called the InsertEditForm, is somewhat closer to the type of display you would want to present to the user in a real program. However, I have extended this form to include a TDBGrid object, just so you can see how the lookup combo box is inserted automatically into the grid.

When working with the InsertEditForm, notice how easy it is to simply type in a new book name, select an author in the combo box, and then perform a Post by clicking the OK button. The process is very simple from the user's point of view. In particular, a new BookNo is being assigned automatically by the AutoIncrement field, and the new AuthNo is being filled in automatically by the lookup process.

Here are the two ways to handle the data in `InsertEditForm`:

- **`InsertMode`:** A temporary book name appears in the `TitleEdit` control when you bring up the form in this mode. Type in the name of the book you want to record in the `Title` field, and then drop down the `AuthorLookup` combo to select an author.

- **`EditMode`:** There is usually data in both the `Title` and `AuthorLookup` fields when you bring up the mode in this form. The user can either edit the `Title` field, or associate the book with a new author. I call a method called `FindTitle` in the `DMod` module to make sure that the form shows the record the user wants to edit.

It's important to note that lookup controls probably would not be appropriate for use with big datasets because drop-down controls aren't very handy for displaying thousands of items. Even list boxes are fairly limited in these circumstances. You would therefore use lookups mostly with smaller datasets.

It should also be pointed out that not being able to use both one-to-many relationships and lookups between the same two tables is a significant inconvenience. However, the Lookup example discussed in these sections and implemented on the book's CD-ROM shows that the workaround is not that complex.

NOTE

If you are concerned that the solution to the problem in the last paragraph requires using three `TTable` objects instead of only two, I would ask you to recall that the goal of this book is to show how to get things done, not how to do things in the smallest possible space.

If you can get things done in five minutes through a technique that you know is bug free, that is something you should give up only reluctantly, particularly if the alternative is working for days or weeks to implement a solution that is likely to have bugs that will take another week or two to squash. At the very least, you should implement the quick solution for the first draft of your application, and then come back and look for optimizations once you have a working version of the product.

Don't ever try to optimize during your first draft of an application! There is no such thing as getting things right the first time in programming. Instead, you should implement a reasonable solution, critique it, come back and make improvements, critique the improvements, make another pass over the application, and so on. This kind of cycle demands that you not get too hung up on optimizations during early drafts, because you are likely to find that any one part of the application will change in future revisions. If you have the thing implemented correctly, and there is still time left in the project cycle, *then* you can come back and seek to optimize the code!

The final kicker in this analysis is that contemporary application programmers rarely have time to optimize. Given the success rate of most projects, your customers or managers will

continues

continued

usually be ecstatic if you just turn in a working solution to the problem on time. If you release the same application 10 percent faster and 20 percent smaller, but six months later, it's unlikely you will win quite the same number of kudos you think you deserve. I usually leave the minute optimizations up to the development teams at Borland. They know how to reach into the fire without getting burned.

If you want to change the author associated with a particular record, you just click a new item in the list box. The author number will be changed automatically for you by the lookup. It's all very simple and intuitive when viewed from the user's perspective.

TDBGrid at Runtime

TDBGrid objects can be completely reconfigured at runtime. You can hide and show columns, change the order of columns, the color of columns, the color of rows, the color of fields, and the width of columns.

The GridTricks program, shown in Figure 11.9, demonstrates how to take a TDBGrid through its paces at runtime. The program is fairly straightforward except for two brief passages. The first passage involves creating checkbox controls on-the-fly, and the second shows how to change the traits of columns.

Figure 11.9.

The main GridTricks program enables you to change the appearance of a grid at runtime. You need a color monitor to really see what is happening.

OrderNo	CustNo	SaleDate	ShipDate	EmpNo	
#1030	CN 3615	7/25/88	7/26/88	Emp# 0107	
#1031	CN 2118	7/28/88	8/1/88	Emp# 0127	
#1032	CN 2163	7/28/88	8/1/88	Emp# 0144	
#1033	CN 1384	8/1/88	8/2/88	Emp# 0138	
#1034	CN 1680	8/13/88	8/14/88	Emp# 0024	
#1035	CN 1560	8/16/88	8/17/88	Emp# 0015	
#1036	CN 5384	8/25/88	8/26/88	Emp# 0004	
#1037	CN 1984	8/26/88	8/27/88	Emp# 0012	
#1038	CN 1645	8/26/88	8/27/88	Emp# 0072	
#1039	CN 3158	8/29/88	9/1/88	Emp# 0061	
#1040	CN 6812	9/4/88	9/5/88	Emp# 0052	
#1041	CN 4652	9/16/88	9/17/88	Emp# 0109	
#1042	CN 3984	9/24/88	9/25/88	Emp# 0009	

Column 4 is Marked — File Names Options

When the user wants to decide which fields are visible, GridTricks pops up a second form and displays the names of all the fields from the ORDERS table in a series of checkboxes. The user can then select the fields that he or she wants to make visible. The selected checkboxes designate fields that are visible, whereas the nonselected ones represent invisible fields. The program also enables you to set the order and width of fields, as well as to hide and show the titles at the top of the grid. (See Listings 11.1 and 11.2.) The code for the GridTricks program is in the CHAP17 directory on this book's CD-ROM. (See Listings 11.4–11.8.)

Listing 11.4. The main unit for the GridTricks Program.

```
/////////////////////////////////////
// File: Main.cpp
// Project: GridTricks
// Copyright (c) 1997 by Charlie Calvert
#include <vcl\vcl.h>
#pragma hdrstop
#include "Main.h"
#include "DMod1.h"
#include "NamesDlg.h"
#include "ColumnEditor1.h"
#include "ShowOptions1.h"
#define NEWCOLOR clGreen
#pragma resource "*.dfm"
TForm1 *Form1;
__fastcall TForm1::TForm1(TComponent* Owner)
  : TForm(Owner)
{
}
void __fastcall TForm1::Exit1Click(TObject *Sender)
{
  Close();
}
void __fastcall TForm1::FieldNames1Click(TObject *Sender)
{
  NamesDialog->ShowNames(fdFieldNames);
}
void __fastcall TForm1::FieldObjectNames1Click(TObject *Sender)
{
  NamesDialog->ShowNames(fdObjectNames);
}
/////////////////////////////////////
// DBGrid1DrawColumnCell
// Paints ROW different color depending on value of ItemsTotal field
/////////////////////////////////////
void __fastcall TForm1::DBGrid1DrawColumnCell(TObject *Sender,
      const TRect &Rect, Integer DataCol, TColumn *Column,
      TGridDrawState State)
{
    if (ColorRows1->Checked)
    {
      if (DMod->OrdersTableItemsTotal->Value < 1000)
        DBGrid1->Canvas->Font->Color = clRed;
      else if (DMod->OrdersTableItemsTotal->Value < 10000)
        DBGrid1->Canvas->Font->Color = clBlue;
      else
        DBGrid1->Canvas->Font->Color = clGreen;
    }
    DBGrid1->DefaultDrawColumnCell(Rect, DataCol, Column, State);
}
```

continues

Listing 11.4. continued

```cpp
void TForm1::ColorTitles(BOOL UseDefaultColor)
{
  TColor Colors[] = {clRed, clBlue, clGreen, clLime, clWhite, clFuchsia};
  int i;
  for (i = 0; i < DBGrid1->Columns->Count; i++)
  {
    TColumn *Column = DBGrid1->Columns->Items[i];
    TColumnTitle *ColumnTitle = Column->Title;
    if (UseDefaultColor)
      ColumnTitle->Font->Color = FDefaultColor;
    else
      ColumnTitle->Font->Color = Colors[random(7)];
  }
}
void __fastcall TForm1::AnimateTitles1Click(TObject *Sender)
{
  Timer1->Enabled = (!Timer1->Enabled);
  AnimateTitles1->Checked = Timer1->Enabled;
  if (!AnimateTitles1->Checked)
    ColorTitles(True);
}
void __fastcall TForm1::ColorRows1Click(TObject *Sender)
{
  ColorRows1->Checked = (!ColorRows1->Checked);
  DBGrid1->Repaint();
}
void __fastcall TForm1::MarkColumnClick(TObject *Sender)
{
  MarkColumn->Checked = (!MarkColumn->Checked);
  TColumn *Column = DBGrid1->Columns->Items[DBGrid1->SelectedIndex];
  if (MarkColumn->Checked)
  {
    Column->Font->Color = NEWCOLOR;
    Column->Font->Style = TFontStyles() << fsBold;
  }
  else
  {
    Column->Font->Color = FDefaultColor;
    Column->Font->Style = TFontStyles();
  }
  HandleCaption();
}
//////////////////////////////////////
// Handle Caption
//////////////////////////////////////
void TForm1::HandleCaption()
{
  TColumn *Column = DBGrid1->Columns->Items[DBGrid1->SelectedIndex];

  AnsiString S(DBGrid1->SelectedIndex);
  Caption = S;
  if (Column->Font->Color == FDefaultColor)
    Caption = "Column " + S + " is Default";
  else
    Caption = "Column " + S + " is Marked";
}
```

```cpp
void __fastcall TForm1::DBGrid1ColEnter(TObject *Sender)
{
  TColumn *Column = DBGrid1->Columns->Items[DBGrid1->SelectedIndex];
  MarkColumn->Checked = (Column->Font->Color == NEWCOLOR);
  HandleCaption();
}
void __fastcall TForm1::FormCreate(TObject *Sender)
{
  FDefaultColor = DBGrid1->Font->Color;
  HandleCaption();
}
void __fastcall TForm1::Timer1Timer(TObject *Sender)
{
  ColorTitles(False);
}
void __fastcall TForm1::ShowFieldEditor1Click(TObject *Sender)
{
  ColumnEditor->ShowColumns();
}
void __fastcall TForm1::ToggleTitles1Click(TObject *Sender)
{
  if (DBGrid1->Options.Contains(dgTitles))
    DBGrid1->Options = TDBGridOptions(DBGrid1->Options) >> dgTitles;
  else
    DBGrid1->Options = TDBGridOptions(DBGrid1->Options) << dgTitles;
}
void __fastcall TForm1::ToggleIndicator1Click(TObject *Sender)
{
  if (DBGrid1->Options.Contains(dgIndicator))
    DBGrid1->Options = TDBGridOptions(DBGrid1->Options) >> dgIndicator;
  else
    DBGrid1->Options = TDBGridOptions(DBGrid1->Options) << dgIndicator;
}
void __fastcall TForm1::ShowTitlesIndicator1Click(TObject *Sender)
{
  ShowTitlesIndicator1->Checked =
    !(TDBGridOptions(DBGrid1->Options).Contains(dgIndicator) &&
    TDBGridOptions(DBGrid1->Options).Contains(dgTitles));
  if (ShowTitlesIndicator1->Checked)
    DBGrid1->Options = TDBGridOptions(DBGrid1->Options) << dgIndicator << dgTitles;
  else
    DBGrid1->Options = TDBGridOptions(DBGrid1->Options) >> dgIndicator >> dgTitles;
  DBGrid1->Refresh();
}
void __fastcall TForm1::ColLines1Click(TObject *Sender)
{
  if (DBGrid1->Options.Contains(dgColLines))
    DBGrid1->Options = TDBGridOptions(DBGrid1->Options) >> dgColLines;
  else
    DBGrid1->Options = TDBGridOptions(DBGrid1->Options) << dgColLines;
  ColLines1->Checked = DBGrid1->Options.Contains(dgColLines);
}
void __fastcall TForm1::RowLines1Click(TObject *Sender)
{
  if (DBGrid1->Options.Contains(dgRowLines))
    DBGrid1->Options = TDBGridOptions(DBGrid1->Options) >> dgRowLines;
```

continues

Listing 11.4. continued

```
    else
      DBGrid1->Options = TDBGridOptions(DBGrid1->Options) << dgRowLines;
    RowLines1->Checked = DBGrid1->Options.Contains(dgRowLines);
}
void __fastcall TForm1::ShowAllOptions1Click(TObject *Sender)
{
  ShowOptionsForm->ShowOptions(DBGrid1->Options);
}
void __fastcall TForm1::MustPressF2orEntertoEdit1Click(TObject *Sender)
{
  DBGrid1->Options = TDBGridOptions(DBGrid1->Options) >> dgAlwaysShowEditor;
  MustPressF2orEntertoEdit1->Checked =
    !TDBGridOptions(DBGrid1->Options).Contains(dgAlwaysShowEditor);
}
void __fastcall TForm1::ChangeWidthofField1Click(TObject *Sender)
{
  AnsiString S("");
  TColumn *Column = DBGrid1->Columns->Items[DBGrid1->SelectedIndex];
  if (InputQuery("Data Needed", "New Width of Selected Field", S))
    Column->Width = S.ToInt();
}
void __fastcall TForm1::HideCurrentColumn1Click(TObject *Sender)
{
  if (MessageBox(Handle, "Hide Column?",
       "Hide Info?", MB_YESNO | MB_ICONQUESTION) == ID_YES)
  {
    TColumn *Column = DBGrid1->Columns->Items[DBGrid1->SelectedIndex];
    Column->Free();
  }
}
void __fastcall TForm1::MoveCurrentColumn1Click(TObject *Sender)
{
  AnsiString S("");
  if (InputQuery("Data Needed", "Enter new position of column", S))
  {
    DMod->OrdersTable->Fields[DBGrid1->SelectedIndex]->Index = S.ToInt();
  }
}
```

Listing 11.5. The data module for the GridTricks program.

```
////////////////////////////////////
// File: ColumnEditor1.cpp
// Project: GridTricks
// Copyright (c) 1997 by Charlie Calvert
#include <vcl\vcl.h>
#pragma hdrstop
#include "DMod1.h"
#pragma resource "*.dfm"
TDMod *DMod;
__fastcall TDMod::TDMod(TComponent* Owner)
  : TDataModule(Owner)
{
}
```

```cpp
void TDMod::GetFieldNames(TStringList *Items)
{
  int i;
  Items->Clear();
  for (i = 0; i < OrdersTable->FieldCount - 1; i++)
    Items->Add(OrdersTable->Fields[i]->FieldName);
}
void TDMod::GetObjectNames(TStringList *Items)
{
  int i;
  Items->Clear();
  for (i = 0; i < OrdersTable->FieldCount - 1; i++)
    Items->Add(OrdersTable->Fields[i]->Name);
}
```

Listing 11.6. The Column Editor for the GridTricks program.

```cpp
/////////////////////////////////////
// File: ColumnEditor1.cpp
// Project: GridTricks
// Copyright (c) 1997 by Charlie Calvert

// The last build of BCB I checked this on before shipping
// was still broken. BCB was not properly updating the
// data on the grids. Hopefully this program will start
// working properly once there is an update for BCB 1.0.
// The code I have here works fine in Delphi. In short, the
// problem is not in my code, and its not in the VCL. Its a
// BCB problem.
//
// Check my website for updates: users.aol.com/charliecal
//
#include <vcl\vcl.h>
#pragma hdrstop
#include "ColumnEditor1.h"
#include "DMod1.h"
#include "Main.h"
#pragma resource "*.dfm"
#define GAP 2

TColumnEditor *ColumnEditor;
//---------------------------------------------------------------------------
__fastcall TColumnEditor::TColumnEditor(TComponent* Owner)
  : TForm(Owner)
{
}

void TColumnEditor::CreateCheckBox(int Index, AnsiString Name, BOOL Visible)
{
  CheckBoxAry[Index] = (TCheckBox*) new TCustomCheckBox(this);
  CheckBoxAry[Index]->Parent = ColumnEditor;
  CheckBoxAry[Index]->Caption = Name;
  CheckBoxAry[Index]->Left = 10;
```

continues

Listing 11.6. continued

```
    CheckBoxAry[Index]->Top = Index * (CheckBoxAry[Index]->Height + GAP);
    CheckBoxAry[Index]->Width = 200;
    CheckBoxAry[Index]->Checked = Visible;
}

void TColumnEditor::ShowColumns(void)
{
  int i;
  TColumn *Column;

  for (i = 0; i < DMod->OrdersTable->FieldCount; i++)
    CreateCheckBox(i, DMod->OrdersTable->Fields[i]->Name,
      DMod->OrdersTable->Fields[i]->Visible);
  Height = (DMod->OrdersTable->FieldCount - 1) * (CheckBoxAry[0]->Height + GAP);
  if (Height > 470)
    Height = 470;
  ShowModal();
  for (i = 0; i < DMod->OrdersTable->FieldCount; i++)
    DMod->OrdersTable->Fields[i]->Visible = CheckBoxAry[i]->Checked;
}
```

Listing 11.7. The `NamesDlg` for the GridTricks program.

```
/////////////////////////////////////
// File: NamesDlg.cpp
// Project: GridTricks
// Copyright (c) 1997 by Charlie Calvert
#include <vcl\vcl.h>
#pragma hdrstop
#include "NamesDlg.h"
#include "DMod1.h"
#pragma resource "*.dfm"
TNamesDialog *NamesDialog;
__fastcall TNamesDialog::TNamesDialog(TComponent* Owner)
  : TForm(Owner)
{
}
void TNamesDialog::ShowNames(TFieldData FieldData)
{
  switch(FieldData)
  {
    case fdFieldNames:
      DMod->GetFieldNames((TStringList *)ListBox1->Items);
      break;
    case fdObjectNames:
      DMod->GetObjectNames((TStringList *)ListBox1->Items);
      break;
  }
```

```
  Show();
}
void __fastcall TNamesDialog::BitBtn1Click(TObject *Sender)
{
  Close();
}
```

Listing 11.8. The ShowOptions module shows which DBGrid options are currently active.

```
#include <vcl\vcl.h>
#pragma hdrstop
#include "ShowOptions1.h"
#pragma resource "*.dfm"
TShowOptionsForm *ShowOptionsForm;
__fastcall TShowOptionsForm::TShowOptionsForm(TComponent* Owner)
  : TForm(Owner)
{
  int i;
  int j = 0;
  for (i = 0; i < ComponentCount; i++)
    if (dynamic_cast<TCheckBox*>(Components[i]))
    {
      CheckBox[j] = (TCheckBox*)Components[i];
      j++;
    }
}
void TShowOptionsForm::ShowOptions(TDBGridOptions Options)
{
  int i;
  for (i = 0; i < 12; i++)
    if (Options.Contains(i))
      CheckBox[i]->Checked = True;
    else
      CheckBox[i]->Checked = False;
  ShowModal();
}
```

In the next few paragraphs you will find descriptions of the key parts of the GridTricks program. Understanding its constituent parts will help you to take control over the grids you display in your programs.

Most of the code in the GridTricks program is fairly simple. However, the program performs a number of separate tasks. To grasp the program, it's necessary to divide and conquer; that is, to take the tasks performed by the program one at a time. Find out how each one works, and then move on to the next one. If you proceed in this fashion, you will find the program easy to understand.

Controlling the Options Property of a DBGrid at Runtime

You can use the Options field of a TDBGrid to change its appearance. The Options property has the following possible values:

dgEditing	Set to True by default, it enables the user to edit a grid. You can also set the grid's ReadOnly property to True or False.
dgTitles	Designates whether titles can be seen.
dgIndicator	Determines whether to show the small icons on the left of the grid.
dgColumnResize	Designates whether or not the user can resize columns.
dgColLines	Determines whether or not to show the lines between columns.
dgRowLines	Designates whether or not to show the lines between rows.
dgTabs	Enables the user to tab and Shift+tab between columns.
dgAlwaysShowEditor	If you select a field will you be in Edit mode automatically?
dgRowSelect	Can select rows, mutually exclusive with dgAlwaysShowEditor.
dgAlwaysShowSelection	Selection remains even when grid loses focus.
dgConfirmDelete	Shows message box when user presses Ctrl+Delete.
dgCancelOnExit	Cancels Inserts on exit if no changes were made to row.
dgMultiSelect	Can select multiple noncontiguous rows with Ctrl+Click.

Here is the declaration for the enumerated type where these values are declared:

```
enum TDBGridOption { dgEditing, dgAlwaysShowEditor, dgTitles, dgIndicator,
                     dgColumnResize, dgColLines, dgRowLines, dgTabs, dgRowSelect,
                     dgAlwaysShowSelection, dgConfirmDelete, dgCancelOnExit,
                     dgMultiSelect };
```

For instance, you can set the options at runtime by writing code that looks like this:

```
DBGrid1->Options = TDBGridOptions() << dgTitles;
```

This code in effect turns all the options to False except dgTitles. This code turns off all options but dgTitles and dgIndicator.

```
DBGrid1->Options = TDBGridOptions() << dgTitles << dgIndicator;
```

More specifically, the code sets the DBGrid1 Options property to a set that contains only dgTitles and dgIndicator. This code toggles dgTitles and dgIndicator off and on each time it is called:

```
void __fastcall TForm1::ToggleTitles1Click(TObject *Sender)
{
  if (DBGrid1->Options.Contains(dgTitles))
    DBGrid1->Options = TDBGridOptions(DBGrid1->Options) >> dgTitles;
  else
    DBGrid1->Options = TDBGridOptions(DBGrid1->Options) << dgTitles;
}
```

The set operators shown in ToggleTitles1Click move the dgTitles option in and out of DBGrid->Options.

The following code shows how to toggle back and forth between showing both indicators and titles and hiding both indicators and titles:

```
void __fastcall TForm1::ShowTitlesIndicator1Click(TObject *Sender)
{
  ShowTitlesIndicator1->Checked =
    !(TDBGridOptions(DBGrid1->Options).Contains(dgIndicator) &&
    TDBGridOptions(DBGrid1->Options).Contains(dgTitles));
  if (ShowTitlesIndicator1->Checked)
    DBGrid1->Options = TDBGridOptions(DBGrid1->Options) << dgIndicator << dgTitles;
  else
    DBGrid1->Options = TDBGridOptions(DBGrid1->Options) >> dgIndicator >> dgTitles;
  DBGrid1->Refresh();
}
```

This code moves both the dgIndicator and dgTitles elements in and out of the Options array as needed. The << operator adds elements to a set, while the >> operator moves things out of the set. If you need to move multiple elements in and out of the set, just use the operator multiple times as shown in the ShowTitlesIndicator1Click method.

> **NOTE**
>
> The following standard set operations will not work with the Options property because the += and -= operators do not work with sets that are properties because of the extra work involved in calling get and set methods:
>
> ```
> TDBGridOptions Options;
> Options << dgTitles << dgIndicator;
> DBGrid1->Options += Options;
> DBGrid1->Options -= Options;
> ```

Here is an example of code showing how to toggle the dgRowLines element of the Options property on and off at runtime.

```
void __fastcall TForm1::RowLines1Click(TObject *Sender)
{
  if (DBGrid1->Options.Contains(dgRowLines))
    DBGrid1->Options = TDBGridOptions(DBGrid1->Options) >> dgRowLines;
```

```
  else
    DBGrid1->Options = TDBGridOptions(DBGrid1->Options) << dgRowLines;
    RowLines1->Checked = DBGrid1->Options.Contains(dgRowLines);
}
```

The last line of code in the routine toggles the check mark before the RowLines menu item so that it reflects the current state of the grid. In other words, if dgRowLines is part of the set, the menu item will be checked; if it is not part of the set, the menu item will not be checked:

```
RowLines1->Checked = DBGrid1->Options.Contains(dgRowLines);
```

In this section you have seen how to toggle the elements of the Options set back and forth at runtime. Most of the code for doing this is fairly simple, although you need to have a basic grasp of BCB set operations to understand how it works. If you need to brush up on this material, sets were covered in more depth in Chapter 2, "Basic Facts About C++Builder."

Displaying the DBGrid Options at Runtime

Now that you know how to toggle the Options of a DBGrid, it might be worthwhile spending a few moments learning how to display the Options to the user at runtime. As shown in Figure 11.10, I use a set of 12 CheckBoxes to depict the current state of 12 DBGrid options. In the next few paragraphs I will explain how the code that drives this form works.

FIGURE 11.10.

Using checkboxes to depict the available DBGrid *options to the user at runtime.*

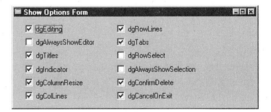

In the header file for the unit, I declare an array of checkboxes:

```
TCheckBox *CheckBox[12];
```

I initialize these checkboxes in the constructor for the form:

```
__fastcall TShowOptionsForm::TShowOptionsForm(TComponent* Owner)
  : TForm(Owner)
{
  int i;
  int j = 0;
  for (i = 0; i < ComponentCount; i++)
    if (dynamic_cast<TCheckBox*>(Components[i]))
    {
      CheckBox[j] = (TCheckBox*)Components[i];
      j++;
    }
}
```

This code iterates over all the components on the form checking for ones that are of type TCheckBox. When it finds one, it adds it to the array of CheckBoxes. The code uses dynamic_cast to check whether each item in the Components array is of type TCheckBox.

> **NOTE**
>
> A Components array is implemented in TComponent and is maintained automatically for all components that descend from TComponent. The concept of ownership is what governs which items are put in the Components array. All components that are owned by the form are automatically, and by definition, included in the Components array for the form. In other words, if you drop a component on a form, it will be listed in the Components array for the form. You can use the ComponentCount property of the form to determine how many items are in the Components array.

After filling in the array of checkboxes, it is a simple matter to toggle the Checked property of each checkbox depending on the current state of each DBGrid option:

```
void TShowOptionsForm::ShowOptions(TDBGridOptions Options)
{
  int i;
  for (i = 0; i < 12; i++)
    if (Options.Contains(TDBGridOption(i)))
      CheckBox[i]->Checked = True;
    else
      CheckBox[i]->Checked = False;
  ShowModal();
}
```

This code determines which items in the DBGridOptions set are turned on, and then toggles the appropriate checkbox. The code depends, of course, on the fact that the DBGridOptions set is a list of items with values ranging from 0 to 11.

To understand this code, you must grasp that DBGridOption is an enumerated type, and DBGridOptions is a set ranging over the values in that enumerated type, with dgEditing being the minimum value and dgMultiSelect being the maximum value:

```
enum TDBGridOption {dgEditing, dgAlwaysShowEditor, dgTitles, dgIndicator,
                    dgColumnResize, dgColLines, dgRowLines, dgTabs, dgRowSelect,
                    dgAlwaysShowSelection, dgConfirmDelete, dgCancelOnExit,
                    dgMultiSelect};
typedef Set<TDBGridOption, dgEditing, dgMultiSelect>  TDBGridOptions;
```

Changing the Colors and Fonts in a Grid

The next three sections of the chapter cover changing the colors of all the titles, columns, rows, and even individual cells in a TDBGrid. This is not something you have to do all that often, but when the need comes around it is fairly pressing. Before reading these sections, you should be sure to run the GridTricks program, because it will be hard to read the code without some understanding of what it does.

Changing the Titles in a TDBGrid Object

Here is how to color the titles in a TDBGrid:

```
void TForm1::ColorTitles(BOOL UseDefaultColor)
{
  TColor Colors[] = {clRed, clBlue, clGreen, clLime, clWhite, clFuchsia};
  int i;
  for (i = 0; i < DBGrid1->Columns->Count; i++)
  {
    TColumn *Column = DBGrid1->Columns->Items[i];
    TColumnTitle *ColumnTitle = Column->Title;
    if (UseDefaultColor)
      ColumnTitle->Font->Color = FDefaultColor;
    else
      ColumnTitle->Font->Color = Colors[random(7)];
  }
}
```

This code first declares an array of colors. The constants seen here are pre-declared colors of type TColor.

The actual number of colors in the array was chosen at random. I could have added or subtracted colors from the array without changing the rest of code in the routine, with the exception of the number 7, which is passed to random in the routine's last line of code.

The TColumn object defines how a column in a TDBGrid should look. That is, it defines the font, color, and width of the column. The Columns property of a TDBGrid is of type TDBGridColumns, which is a collection of TColumn objects. Each TColumn object has a title. This title is defined in an object of type TColumnTitle. Finally, a TColumnTitle has color, font, and caption properties:

```
TDBGrid Object
  Columns Property
    TColumn Object
      TColumnTitle
        Font, Color, Caption
```

The preceding list is not an object hierarchy, but just a way of illustrating the relationship between these different entities. In other words, the grid object contains a Columns property, and the Columns property contains TColumn objects, and the TColumn object contains a TColumnTitle, which in turn contains a Font, Color, and Caption.

To get hold of a TColumn object, you can use the Items property of TDBGridColumns:

```
TColumn *Column = DBGrid1->Columns->Items[i];
```

To move from there to a `TColumnTitle` object, you can use the `Title` property of a `TColumn` object:

```
TColumnTitle *ColumnTitle = Column->Title;
```

Once the preceding `ColorTitles` method has the `ColumnTitle` in its hands, it can set it to whatever color it wants:

```
if (UseDefaultColor)
  ColumnTitle->Font->Color = FDefaultColor;
else
  ColumnTitle->Font->Color = Colors[random(7)];
```

The `FDefaultColor` variable is of type `TColor`. In the `OnCreate` event for the form, I set it to the default color for the grid's font:

```
FDefaultColor = DBGrid1->Font->Color;
```

Phew! That was the hard one. If you understand what has happened here, you will have no trouble with the next two sections, which cover changing the color of columns and rows in a grid.

Changing an Entire Column in a Grid

If you understand the code in the last section, it will be easy to understand how to change the look of a single column. Writing this kind of code will enable you to emphasize a certain part of a dataset or to bring the users eye to certain part of your form.

Here is the method that changes the appearance of a column in a `TDBGrid`:

```
void __fastcall TForm1::MarkColumnClick(TObject *Sender)
{
  MarkColumn->Checked = (!MarkColumn->Checked);
  TColumn *Column = DBGrid1->Columns->Items[DBGrid1->SelectedIndex];
  if (MarkColumn->Checked)
  {
    Column->Font->Color = NEWCOLOR;
    Column->Font->Style = TFontStyles() << fsBold;
  }
  else
  {
    Column->Font->Color = FDefaultColor;
    Column->Font->Style = TFontStyles();
  }
  HandleCaption();
}
```

This code first grabs hold of a selected column in a grid:

```
TColumn *Column = DBGrid1->Columns->Items[DBGrid1->SelectedIndex];
```

If the user has indicated that he wants this column to stand out, it is a simple matter to change its color and set its font to bold:

```
Column->Font->Color = NEWCOLOR;
Column->Font->Style = TFontStyles() << fsBold;
```

Notice that the Style property is a set, and so you use a template class to manipulate its members. Here, as found in GRAPHICS.HPP, are the different styles you can associate with a font:

```
enum TFontStyle { fsBold, fsItalic, fsUnderline, fsStrikeOut };
```

There are some parts of the code, such as MarkColumn and HandleCaption, that I don't mention. I ignore these elements because they are merely part of the logic of this program and are not germane to the subject of changing an individual column.

Changing the Color of a Row in a Grid

In the last two sections on columns and column titles, you have been working with the TColumn object. You can also change the color of the text in a TDBGrid by working with the font associated with the grid's TCanvas object:

```
void __fastcall TForm1::DBGrid1DrawColumnCell(TObject *Sender,
    const TRect &Rect, Integer DataCol, TColumn *Column,
    TGridDrawState State)
{
  if (ColorRows1->Checked)
  {
    if (DMod->tblOrdersItemsTotal->Value < 1000)
      DBGrid1->Canvas->Font->Color = clRed;
    else if (DMod->tblOrdersItemsTotal->Value < 10000)
      DBGrid1->Canvas->Font->Color = clBlue;
    else
      DBGrid1->Canvas->Font->Color = clGreen;
  }
  DBGrid1->DefaultDrawColumnCell(Rect, DataCol, Column, State);
}
```

If you run the GridTricks program, you can see the effect of this code by choosing Color Rows from the Options menu of that program. Be sure that none of the other special effects are turned on when you choose this option, because they can interfere with your ability to see its results. Be sure to scroll the grid up and down after turning the effect on, because the data at the top of the grid is fairly homogenous.

The data shown in the grid is from the Orders table in the BCDEMOS database. The code shown here colors each row in the grid according to the amount of money reported in the ItemsTotal field of the Orders table. For instance, if the ItemsTotal field contains a sum less than $1,000 dollars, that row is painted Red:

```
DBGrid1->Canvas->Font->Color = clRed;
```

Here the code sets the font of the TCanvas object for the grid to clRed. Nothing could be simpler.

Changing the Width of a Column

The user can change the width of a column at runtime with the mouse. But how can you do the same thing programmatically without any input from the user?

If you want to change the width of a column at runtime, just change the DisplayWidth property of the appropriate TField object:

```
TblOrders->FieldByName("CustNo")->DisplayWidth = 12;
TblOrdersCustNo->DisplayWidth = 12;
```

The value 12 refers to the approximate number of characters that can be displayed in the control. Various factors, such as whether or not you are using a fixed-pitch font, affect the interpretation of this value. See the online help for additional information.

Here is how you can change the width of the column in the grid without affecting the properties of the underlying field:

```
void __fastcall TForm1::ChangeWidthofField1Click(TObject *Sender)
{
  AnsiString S("");
  TColumn *Column = DBGrid1->Columns->Items[DBGrid1->SelectedIndex];
  if (InputQuery("Data Needed", "New Width of Selected Field", S))
    Column->Width = S.ToInt();
}
```

This code asks the user for the width he or she wants to assign to the currently selected column. The code then makes the change by retrieving the column and changing its Width property.

Hiding or Moving Columns in a TDBGrid

The user can change the order of columns in a TDBGrid simply by clicking them and dragging them with a mouse. But how do you proceed if you want to do the same thing at runtime without the user's direct input?

If you want to hide a field at runtime, you can set its Visible property to False:

```
OrdersTable->FieldByName("CustNo")->Visible = False;
OrdersTableCustNo->Visible = False;
```

NOTE

This code will not work in the first version of BCB. See the top of the ColumnEditor1.cpp file for late-breaking information on this process.

Both lines of code perform identical tasks. To show the fields again, simply set Visible to True.

Alternatively, you can retrieve a TColumn object from the grid, and then quietly dispose of it:

```
void __fastcall TForm1::HideCurrentColumn1Click(TObject *Sender)
{
  if (MessageBox(Handle, "Hide Column?",
      "Hide Info?", MB_YESNO | MB_ICONQUESTION) == ID_YES)
  {
    TColumn *Column = DBGrid1->Columns->Items[DBGrid1->SelectedIndex];
    Column->Free();
  }
}
```

That'll do it! The column disappears from the grid once it has been freed. Alternatively, you can set the width of a column to 0, which makes the column itself go away, but not the lines between columns.

In order to allow the user to decide which fields are visible, GridTricks pops up a second form with a series of checkboxes on it. The program actually creates each of these checkboxes at runtime. In other words, it doesn't just pop up a form with the correct number of checkboxes on it, but instead iterates through the TblOrders object, finds out how many checkboxes are needed, and then creates them dynamically at runtime.

To perform these tasks, GridTricks calls on a form that is specially designed to display the checkboxes:

```
void __fastcall TForm1::ShowFieldEditor1Click(TObject *Sender)
{
  ColumnEditor->ShowColumns();
  DMod->tblOrders->Refresh();
}
```

The ShowColumns method of the VisiForm first calls a routine called CreateCheckBox that creates the checkboxes, displays the form, and finally sets the state of the checkboxes:

```
void TColumnEditor::ShowColumns(void)
{
  int i;
  TColumn *Column;


  for (i = 0; i < DMod->OrdersTable->FieldCount; i++)
    CreateCheckBox(i, DMod->OrdersTable->Fields[i]->Name,
      DMod->OrdersTable->Fields[i]->Visible);
  Height = (DMod->OrdersTable->FieldCount - 1) * (CheckBoxAry[0]->Height + GAP);
  if (Height > 470)
    Height = 470;
  ShowModal();

  // This is the code that does not work in BCB 1.0
  for (i = 0; i < DMod->OrdersTable->FieldCount; i++)
    DMod->OrdersTable->Fields[i]->Visible = CheckBoxAry[i]->Checked;
}
```

The ShowColumns method iterates through the Query1 object and assigns one checkbox to each field. It also asks TQuery for the names of the fields, and determines whether or not each field is currently hidden or visible. Here is the code that creates a checkbox on-the-fly:

```
void TColumnEditor::CreateCheckBox(int Index, AnsiString Name, BOOL Visible)
{
  CheckBoxAry[Index] = (TCheckBox*) new TCustomCheckBox(this);
  CheckBoxAry[Index]->Parent = ColumnEditor;
  CheckBoxAry[Index]->Caption = Name;
  CheckBoxAry[Index]->Left = 10;
  CheckBoxAry[Index]->Top = Index * (CheckBoxAry[Index]->Height + GAP);
  CheckBoxAry[Index]->Width = 200;
  CheckBoxAry[Index]->Checked = Visible;
}
```

Most of the code in this example is performing relatively mundane tasks such as assigning names and locations to the checkboxes. These are the two key lines:

```
CheckBoxAry[Index] = (TCheckBox*) new TCustomCheckBox(this);
CheckBoxAry[Index]->Parent = ColumnEditor;
```

The first line actually creates the checkbox and gives it an owner. The second line assigns a parent to the checkbox.

NOTE

The difference between a parent and an owner can be confusing at times. A form is always the owner of the components that reside inside it. As such, it is responsible for allocating and deallocating memory for these components. A form might also be the parent of a particular component, which means that Windows will ensure the component will be displayed directly on the form. However, one component might also find that another component is its parent, even though both components are owned by the form. For instance, if you place a TPanel on a form and then two TButtons on the TPanel, all three components will be owned by the form; however, the buttons will have the panel as a parent, whereas the TPanel will have the form as a parent. Ownership has to do with memory allocation. Parenthood usually describes what surface a component will be displayed on. Ownership is a BCB issue—parenthood is mostly a Windows API issue. In particular, it's Windows that cares about parenting, and it's Windows that handles that actual drawing of the controls. If you get confused about this while in the midst of a lengthy programming session, you can look it up in the online help by searching on the topic *Parent*.

The grids supplied with the first version of BCB are reasonably flexible objects that perform most of the tasks required of them. If you feel you need some additional functionality, check with third-party tool makers such as TurboPower software. A number of third-party grids with extended capabilities are available on the market, and some of them are well worth the purchase price.

New features of the TDuBGrid object not found in BCB 1.0 include the capability to add combo boxes to the grid, and to color the columns of your grids.

Moving Columns at Runtime

To move the location of a column at runtime, you can simply change its index, which is a zero-based number:

```
DMod->OrdersTable->FieldByName("CustNo")->Index = 0;
DMod->OrdersTable->FieldByName("CustNo")->Index = 2;
```

By default, the CustNo field in the Orders table is at the second position, which means its index is 1. The code in the first example moves it to the first position, whereas the code that reads Query1CustNo.Index = 2; moves it to the third position. Remember, the Index field is zero-based, so moving a field to Index 1 moves it to the second field in a record. The first field is at Index 0.

When you change the index of a field, you do not need to worry about the indexes of the other fields in a record; they will be changed automatically at runtime.

That is all I'm going to say about DBGrid objects. I've gone on at considerable length about this one component, but this is one of the tools that lie at the heart of many database programs, and it's therefore worthy of a fairly serious look.

Multirecord Objects

Another object that deserves mention is the TDBCtrlGrid, shown in Figure 11.11. You can use this object to view multiple records from a single table at one time without using the TDBGrid component. In other words, you can drop down TDBEdit controls onto a TDBCtrlGrid, and these edit controls will automatically be duplicated in a series of rows, where the first set of controls shows the first record, the second set the second record, and so on. You only have to drop down one set of controls—the extra sets are duplicated for you automatically by the DBCtrlGrid.

To get started with this object, drag and drop the Country table off the Explorer. Delete the TDBGrid object created for you automatically by BCB, and add the TDBCtrlGrid object off the Data Controls page of the Component Palette. Use the Fields Editor to drag and drop all the fields from Country table onto the top section of the TDBCtrlGrid. Arrange them as shown in Figure 11.11. If you need help getting everything arranged properly, notice that TDBCtrlGrids have RowCount and ColCount properties that enable you to define the number of rows and columns in the object. In this case, I have set the RowCount to 7.

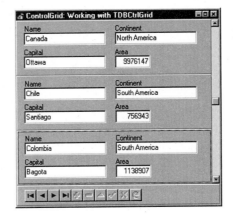

When displaying a grid on a form, it often helps to add a DBNavigator control to the form so the user can easily iterate through records without using the scrollbar. I like to place the DBNavigator on a panel at the bottom of the form.

When arranging the grid and other components on the form at runtime, it sometimes helps to respond to the OnResize event for the form:

```
void __fastcall TForm1::FormResize(TObject *Sender)
{
  Grid->Left = 0;
  Grid->Top = 0;
  Grid->Width = ClientWidth;
  Grid->Height = ClientHeight - Panel1->Height;
}
```

The code shown here arranges the grid so that it reaches from the top left of the form, all the way to the right of the form and down to the top of the panel on which the DBNavigator resides. The preceding few simple lines of code will automatically be called whenever the form is resized by the user, thereby guaranteeing that all the components stay properly arranged.

The DBCtrlGrid component doesn't bring any new functionality to BCB. It's useful, however, because it eliminates the need to have the user slide the scrollbar back and forth on a TDBGrid object. In other words, the TDBGrid object sometimes forces you to use the scrollbar in order to view all the fields of a record. That can be inconvenient, but the ability to view multiple records at once is so valuable that users are willing to put up with the minor annoyance of the scrollbar. The point of the TDBCtrlGrid object is that it lets you view multiple records at one time, while eliminating the need to scroll back and forth when viewing the data. It's hardly earth-shattering in its importance, but it can be very useful under some circumstances. It's a way to make the presentation of your data potentially more viable to the user.

Summary

In this chapter you learned some fairly sophisticated methods for displaying the data from multiple tables. In particular, you saw how BCB handles the key features of a relational database.

The tools discussed in this chapter include the following:

- The Fields Editor
- The Query by Example tool in the DBD

The components discussed in this chapter include the following:

- TField descendant objects
- The TDBCtrlGrid, TDBLookupComboBox, and TDBLookupListBox objects
- The DBGrid and DBCtrlGrid components

The properties discussed in this chapter include the following:

- Calculated fields
- Lookup fields

Good database programmers will find that there is a considerable amount of hidden power in the TField object and in the Fields Editor, as well as the other tools and components mentioned in this chapter.

Understanding
Relational Databases

CHAPTER

12

In order to make sure everyone is following the discussion in the next few chapters, I'm going to spend a few pages giving a quick-and-dirty introduction to relational databases. This discussion will also include a brief overview of the Database Desktop.

My purpose here is to give a relatively concise explanation of what it means to use a relational, as opposed to a flat-file, database. Naturally, this will be a very broad overview of a complex and highly detailed subject. I am not attempting an academic analysis of this field of study, but instead want to provide a practical guide for everyday use.

In this chapter, I will be working with Paradox tables and InterBase tables. Each database has its own unique set of rules. There is no definitive example of a relational database, any more than there is a definitive operating system or a definitive compiler. All databases have things in common, just as all compilers and all operating systems have things in common. As much as possible, I try to stress these common traits throughout this chapter. However, the specific implementation that I am referencing here is for Paradox and InterBase databases, and not everything I say will apply to Oracle or dBASE tables.

In particular, this chapter is about the following:

- Indices
- Primary keys
- Foreign keys
- Referential integrity

If you already understand these subjects, you probably won't have much use for this chapter. If you need to review these subjects, or need to be introduced to them, you should read this chapter.

Getting Started with Relational Databases

There are many different kinds of possible databases, but in today's world, there are only two kinds that have any significant market share for the PC:

1. Flat-file databases
2. Relational databases

> **NOTE**
>
> Emerging in recent years has a been a new system called *object-oriented databases*. These databases represent an interesting form of technology, but I will omit discussion of them here because they have a small user base at this time.
>
> The subject of object-oriented databases will come up again briefly in the chapters on OOP called "Inheritance," "Encapsulation," and "Polymorphism." In those chapters you will see that OOP has some powerful features that it can bring to the database world.

Flat-file databases consist of a single file. The classic example would be an address book that contains a single table with six fields in it: Name, Address, City, State, Zip, and Phone. If that is your entire database, what you have is a flat-file database. In a flat-file database, the words table and database are synonymous.

In general, relational databases consist of a series of tables related to each other by one or more fields in each table. In Chapter 9, "Using `TTable` and `TDataSet`," and Chapter 10, "SQL and the `TQuery` Object," you saw how to use the `TTable` and `TQuery` objects to relate the `Customer` and `Orders` tables together in a one-to-many relationship. As you recall, the two tables were joined on the `CustNo` field. The relationship established between these two tables on the `CustNo` field is very much at the heart of all relational databases.

The Address program shown in Chapter 13, "Flat-File, Real-World Databases," is an example of a flat-file database. In Chapter 14, "Sessions and Relational Real-World Databases," you will see a second program, called KDAdd, which is a relational database.

Here are three key differences between relational and flat-file databases:

1. A flat-file database, like the address book example outlined previously, consists of one single table. That's the whole database. There is nothing more to say about it. Each table stands alone, isolated in its own little solipsistic world.

2. Relational databases always contain multiple tables. For instance, the `Customer` and `Orders` tables are both part of the `BCDEMOS` database. As you will see, there are many other tables in this database, but for now just concentrate on the `Customer` and `Orders` tables.

3. Tables in relational databases are tied together in special fields. These fields are called primary and foreign keys. They are usually indexes, and they usually consist of a simple integer value. For instance, the `Customer` and `Orders` tables are related to one another by the `CustNo` field. The `CustNo` field is a primary key in the `Customer` table, and a foreign key in the `Orders` table. There are also indexes on both fields.

NOTE

Indices are about searching and sorting. Keys, on the other hand, are about relating tables, and particularly about something called referential integrity.

In practice, these concepts get mixed together in some pretty ugly ways, but the underlying theory relies on the kind of distinctions I am drawing in this note. For instance, keys are usually indexed, and so people often talk about keys and indexes as if they were the same thing. However, they are distinct concepts.

One way to start to draw the distinction is to understand that keys are part of the theory of relational databases, while indexes are part of the implementation of relational databases. More on this as the chapter evolves.

Clearly relational databases are radically different from flat-file databases. Relational databases typically consist of multiple tables, at least some of which are related together by one or more fields. Flat-file databases, on the other hand, consist of only one single table, which is not related to any other table.

Advantages of the Relational Database Model

What advantages do relational databases have over flat-file databases? Well, there are many strengths to this system; here are a few of the highlights:

- Relational databases enforce something called referential integrity. These constraints help you enter data in a logical, systematic, and error-free manner.

- Relational databases save disk space. For instance, the Customer table holds information about customers, including their address, phone, and contact information. The Orders table holds information about orders, including their date, cost, and payment method. If you were forced to keep all this information in a single table, each order would also have to list the customer information, which would mean that some customers' addresses would be repeated dozens of times in the database. In a big database, that kind of duplication can easily burn up megabytes of disk space. It's better to use a relational database because each customer's address would be entered only once. You could also have two flat-file databases, one holding the customer information and the other holding the orders information. The problem with this second scenario is that flat-file databases provide no means of relating the two tables so that you can easily see which orders belong to which customer.

- Relational databases enable you to create one-to-many relationships. For instance, you can have one name that is related to multiple addresses. There is no simple way to capture that kind of relationship in a flat-file database. In the KDAdd program, you will see that it is possible to easily relate multiple addresses, phone numbers, and so on with each name. The flexible structure of relational databases enables programmers to adopt to these kinds of real-world situations. For many entries in a database, you will want to keep track of two addresses: one for a person's home, and the other for his or her work. If someone you know has a summer home or an apartment in the city, you need to add yet more addresses to the listing. There is no convenient way to do that in flat-file databases. Relational databases handle this kind of problem with ease. In the last paragraph I emphasized that this kind of feature saves space; in this paragraph I'm emphasizing that it allows for a more logical, flexible, and easy-to-use arrangement of your data.

To summarize, a relational database offers these possibilities:

- You can view the Customer table alone, or you can view the Orders table alone.

- You can place the two tables in a one-to-many relationship, so that you can see them side-by-side, but only see the orders relating to the currently highlighted customer.

■ You can perform a join between the two tables, so that you see them as one combined table, much like the combined table you would be forced to use if you wanted to "join" the Customer and Orders tables in a single flat-file database. However, you can decide which fields from both tables will be part of the join, leaving out any you don't want to view. The joined table is also temporary, and does not take up unnecessary disk space. In short, relational databases can use joins to provide some of the benefits of flat-file databases, whereas flat-file databases cannot emulate the virtues of relational databases.

As you can see, the three concepts that stand out when talking about relational databases are referential integrity, flexibility, and conservation of disk space. In this case, the word "flexibility" covers a wide range of broad features that can only be fully appreciated over time.

The one disadvantage that relational databases have when compared to flat-file databases is that they are more complicated to use. This is not just a minor sticking point. Neophytes are often completely baffled by relational databases. They don't have a clue as to what to do with them. Even if you have a relative degree of expertise, anyone can still become overwhelmed by a relational database that consists of three dozen tables related to one another in some hundred different ways. (And yes, complexity on that scale is not uncommon in corporate America!) As you will see later in the book, almost the only way to work with big systems of that type is through case tools.

Simple Set Logic: The Basis of Relational Databases

The basis for relational databases is a very simple form of mathematics. Each table represents a simple set that can be related to other tables through very fundamental mathematics. Because computers are so good at math, and particularly at integer math, they find relational databases easy to manipulate.

One common feature of relational databases is that most records will have a unique number associated with them, and these numbers will be used as the keys that relate one table to another. This enables you to group tables together using simple mathematical relationships. In particular, you can group them using simple integer-based set arithmetic.

For instance, in the Customers table from BCDEMOS, there is a unique CustNo field in each record. Furthermore, the Orders table has a unique OrderNo field associated with it. The Orders table also has a CustNo field that will relate it to the Customer table. The terminology of relational databases expresses these ideas by saying that the Customer table has a primary key called CustNo, and the Orders table has a primary key called OrderNo and a foreign key called CustNo:

Table name	Primary key	Foreign key (secondary index)
Customer	CustNo	
Orders	OrderNo	CustNo

Given this scenario, you can say "Show me the set of all orders such that their CustNo field is equal to X or within the range of X - Y." Computers love these kinds of simple mathematical relationships. It's their bread and butter. In essence, you are just asking for the intersection of two sets: "Show me the intersection of this record from the Customer table with all the records from the Orders table." This intersection will consist of one record from the Customer table with a particular CustNo plus all the records from the Orders table that have the same CustNo in their foreign key.

These CustNo, OrderNo, AuthorNo, BookNo, and similar fields might also be used in flat-file databases as indexes, but they play a unique role in relational databases because they are the keys used to relate different tables. They make it possible to reduce the relationship between tables to nothing more than a simple series of mathematical formulas. These formulas are based on keys rather than on indexes. It is merely a coincidence that most keys also happen to be indexed.

Viewing Indices and Keys in DBD or the Explorer

In the next few sections I define primary and secondary keys, and describe how to use them. It might be helpful if I preface this discussion with a brief description of how to view keys using some of the tools that ship with BCB. This is just a preliminary look at this material. I cover it again in greater depth later in this chapter in a section called "Exploring the Indices in the BCDEMOS Database."

> **NOTE**
>
> Right now it is not so important that you understand what primary and foreign keys do, but only that you know how to view them using the tools that ship with the product. The theory will become clear as the chapter progresses.

There are two ways to view the indexes and keys on a table. The best way is in the Database Explorer. Open up the Explorer and view the BCDEMOS database as shown in Figure 12.1.

Click the Orders table and open up the Referential Constraints branch as shown in Figure 12.2. Notice that there are two constraints on this table, one called RefCustInOrders and the second called RefOrders. The RefCustInOrders field defined CustNo as a foreign key that relates to the CustNo field in the Customer table.

A second way to view this key is in the Database Desktop. Set the Working Directory from the File menu to BCDEMOS. Open up the Orders table in the Database Desktop and select Table | Info structure from the menu. Drop down the Table Properties and select Referential Integrity, as shown in Figure 12.3.

FIGURE 12.1.

Viewing the BCDEMOS *database in the Database Explorer.*

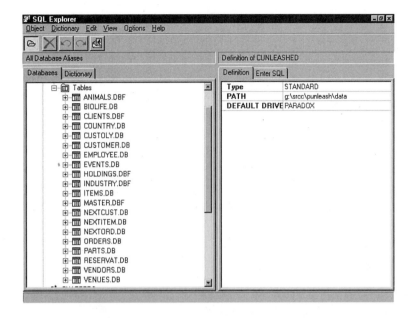

FIGURE 12.2.

The primary and foreign fields of the Orders *table.*

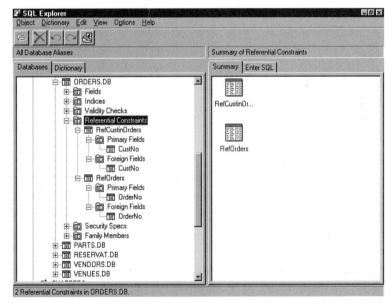

FIGURE 12.3.

*Selecting Referential
Integrity in the
Database Desktop.*

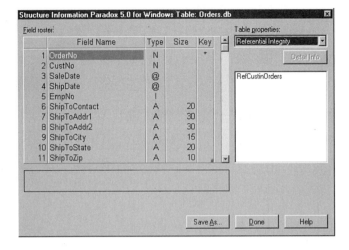

Double-click RefCustInOrders to bring up the Referential Integrity dialog shown in Figure 12.4.

FIGURE 12.4.

The CustNo *field in the*
Orders *table relates to
the* CustNo *field in the*
Customer *table.*

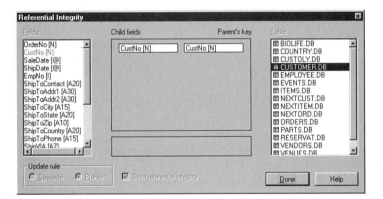

The fields in the left side of this dialog belong to the Orders table. On the right is a list of all the tables in the database. In the center, you can see that the CustNo field has been selected from the Orders table and the CustNo field has been selected from the Customer table. The primary key of the Customer table is related to the foreign key of the Orders table.

Now go back to the Database Explorer and open up the Indices branch of the Orders table, as shown in Figure 12.5.

Note that you can see the names of the indexes, here labeled as <primary> and as CustNo. The fields found in the indexes are also displayed. For instance, you can see that the primary index consists of the OrderNo field and the secondary index consists of the CustNo field.

FIGURE 12.5.

The primary and CustNo *indexes on the* Orders *table.*

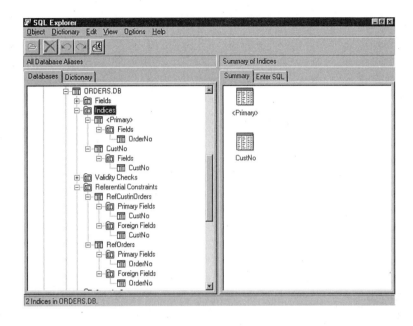

I am showing these to you so that you will begin to see the distinction between keys and indexes. The two concepts are distinct. For further proof of this, open up the IBLOCAL database in the Database Explorer. Use SYSDBA as the user name, and masterkey as the password. Now open up the Employee project table as shown in Figure 12.6. Note that there are separate listings for the index, primary key, and foreign keys.

FIGURE 12.6.

The Employee_Project *table has three indexes, one primary key, and two foreign keys.*

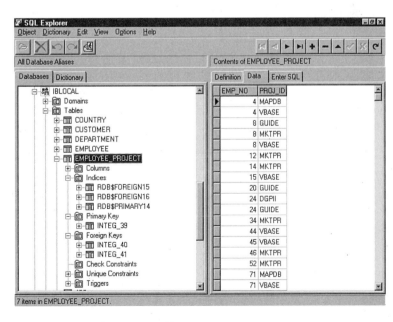

In practice, almost all keyed fields will also have indexes. This leads people to think the two concepts are the same. However, indexes are about searching and sorting, and keys are about referential integrity. These distinctions will become blurred at times, but it helps if you can keep it in your mind that they are different ideas. The actual details concerning these distinctions will become clear in the next few pages.

You can also see the indexes for a table inside the Database Desktop. To get started, open up the Orders table and select Table | Info Structure from the menu. The fields with the stars beside them are part of the primary index. Drop down the Table Properties combo box to view the secondary indexes. Double-click the indexes you see to view the details of their design. If you want to change the structure of a table, choose Table | Restructure from the menu, rather than Table | Info Structure.

Most of the time, I find the Database Desktop is the right tool to use when I want to create or modify a table, and the Database Explorer is the right tool to use when I want to view the structure of a table. However, I often find myself jumping back and forth between the two tools, to get the best features of each. Later in the book I will talk about case tools, which are generally superior to either of the products discussed in this section. However, there are no case tools that ship with BCB, so I emphasize the universally available tools in this text.

Throughout the ensuing discussion, you might have occasion to use the Database Explorer to examine the structure of the Customer, Orders, Items, and Parts tables. These are the tables I use when defining what relational databases are all about.

Rule Numero Uno: Create a Primary Key for Each Table!

The last two sections have introduced you to some of the key concepts in relational databases. If there is one lesson to take out of this chapter, it is the importance of creating a unique numerical key in the first field of most tables you create. This field is called a primary key. In both Paradox and InterBase, it is impossible to create a primary key without also simultaneously creating an index.

If you want to have a list of addresses in a table, don't just list the Address, City, State, and Zip. Be sure to also include an integer-based CustNo, AddressNo, or Code field. This field will usually be both an index and the first field of the database. It is the primary key for your table, and must be, by definition, unique. That is, each record should have a unique Code field associated with it.

The primary key

- Serves as the means of differentiating one record from another
- Is also in referential integrity
- Can also help with fast searches and sorts

As I said earlier, the distinction between indexes and keys becomes blurred at times. However, they are distinct concepts and you should endeavor to discover the differences.

> **NOTE**
>
> In this discussion I am taking a liberty in saying that you have to create a primary key for a table in a relational database. In fact, you can simply create a field that contains a unique integer value. It doesn't have to be an index. However, making a unique index for the field will speed up the operation of your database, and it will help enforce rules that make it easy to create robust relational databases. In particular, the restraints on a primary key make it impossible for you to create two fields in one table with the same primary key.

Just to make sure this is clear, I'll go ahead and list out the right and wrong way to create a table.

Right Method

CustNo: Integer

LastName, FirstName, Address, City, State, Zip: string

Wrong Method

LastName, FirstName, Address, City, State, Zip: string

The first example is "correct" because it has a primary index called CustNo. It is declared as a unique Integer value. The second example is "wrong" because it omits a simple numerical field as the primary index.

> **NOTE**
>
> I put the words "correct" and "wrong" in quotes because there really are no hard-and-fast rules in this discipline. There are occasions when you might not want to create a table that has a simple integer as a primary index. However, ninety-nine percent of the time, that's exactly what you want to do.
>
> At the height of a warm May spring day, there is such a thing as a rose bush that has no buds or flowers. However, the whole point of rose bushes in May is that they flower. I doubt we would feel quite the same way about roses if they did not have beautiful blooms. In the same way, relational databases without primary indexes wouldn't garner quite so much attention as they do now.
>
> I should add that not all primary indexes are numeric fields. For instance, many tables might use alpha fields containing values such as HDA1320WW35180. I'm stressing simple numeric fields in this chapter because they are easy to work with and easy to understand.

Even if you don't yet understand how databases work, for now I would suggest automatically adding a simple numerical value in a primary index to all your tables. Do so even if you are not using the field at this time. Believe me, as you come to understand relational databases, you will see why I recommend doing this in most, though not all, cases. At this point, however, you will probably be better off creating the extra field and letting it go to waste, even if you don't understand why you are doing it. After you get a better feeling for relational databases, you will understand intuitively when the field is needed, and when you are encountering one of those rare occasions when it is going to be useless.

When people first work with relational databases, they can get a little hung up about the overhead involved in creating all these extra key fields. The point to remember is that these fields allow the database to be treated as nothing more than sets of simple integers related together in various combinations. Computers fly through integer math. Adding these extra index fields to your tables makes your data become computer-friendly. Computers love those simple integer fields; your computer will show its thanks by running faster if you add them to your tables!

Computers don't feel weighed down by the extra field any more than a car feels weighed down by a steering wheel, people feel weighed down by their hands, or a rose bush feels weighed down by a rose. Relational databases want you to add an extra integer field as a primary index to your tables!

Remember, people like beautiful paintings, eloquent words, and lovely members of the opposite sex. Computers like logic. They like numbers, they like nice, clean, easily defined relationships! They like simple, integer-based primary keys in the first field of a table!

One-to-Many Relationships: The Data and the Index

One good way to start to understand relational databases is by working with the `Customer`, `Orders`, `Items`, and `Parts` tables from the `BCDEMOS` database. All four of these tables are related in one-to-many relationships, each-to-each. That is, the `Customer` table is related to the `Orders` table, the `Orders` table to the `Items` table, and the `Items` table to the `Parts` table. (The relationship also works in the opposite direction, but it may be simpler at first to think of it as going in only one direction.)

Master	*Detail*	*Connector (primary key and foreign key)*
Customer	Orders	CustNo
Orders	Items	OrderNo
Items	Parts	PartNo

Read the preceding table as a series of rows, starting left and moving to the right, as if they were sentences. The preceding list shows that the `Customer` and `Orders` tables are related in a one-to-many relationship, with `Customer` being the master table and `Orders` being the detail table. The connector between them is the `CustNo` field. That is, they both have a `CustNo` field.

The `CustNo` field is the primary key of the `Customer` table and the foreign key of the `Orders` table. The `OrderNo` field is the primary key of the `Orders` table and a foreign key of the `Items` table. The `PartNo` field is the primary key of the `Parts` table and a foreign key of the `Items` table.

The relationship between these tables can be reversed. For instance, the `Parts` table could become the master table and the `Items` table the detail table, and so on, back down the line. The reason you can reverse the relationship becomes clear when you think in purely mathematical terms. The `Customer` table has a series of `CustNo` fields. Say the `CustNo` for the first record is `1000`. To get the `Orders` associated with that customer, you ask this question: "What are all the rows from the `Orders` table that have a `CustNo` of `1000`?" That is:

```
Select * from Orders where CustNo = 1000
```

Clearly, you could reverse this question. If you select a particular row from the `Orders` table, you could find which item from the `Customer` table it is related to by asking for the set of all `Customer` records with a `CustNo` of `1000`. Because the `CustNo` field for the `Customer` table is a unique index, you will get only one record back. However, the way you relate the tables is still the same:

```
Select * from Customer where CustNo = 1000
```

Working with Primary Keys

The `Parts`, `Orders`, `Items`, and `Customer` tables have various keys. As it happens, these keys are also indexes. An index enables you to sort tables on a particular field. A key helps you define the relationship between two tables, or otherwise group related bits of information by a set of predefined and automatically enforced rules.

Unfortunately, sadly, and confusingly, you can still relate tables even without the presence of any keys or indexes. For instance, if there were no `CustNo` primary and foreign keys in the `Customer` and `Orders` tables, Paradox would still let you use SQL to relate the tables in a one-to-many relationship. However, in this scenario, performance would be slow because there is no index, and there would be no constraints on the data you could enter in the two tables because there would be no primary and foreign keys that define referential integrity. In this scenario you are back to the rosebush-without-a-rose phenomena. Yes, the tables are still part of a relational database, but they lack the features that make a relational database appealing. You need both the keys and the indexes to make a relational database appealing.

I'll draw a distinction between only two different kinds of keys. The first kind I will discuss is called a primary key. The second is called a foreign key.

■ A primary *key* is a unique value used to identify a record in a table. It is usually numerical, and it is usually indexed. It can be combined with a foreign key to define referential integrity. I will talk more about referential integrity later in this chapter.

- Because it is indexed, the primary key defines the default sort order for the table. When you first open up a table, it will be automatically sorted on this field. If a table does not have a primary index, records will appear in the order in which they were added to the table. For all practical purposes, a table without an index has no defined order in which records will appear.

- With Paradox tables, each entry in the primary index must be unique. That is, you can't have two `CustNos` in the `Customer` table that are the same. You can, however, have multiple foreign keys that are not unique.

- It is legal to have multiple fields in the primary index of a Paradox table. This is called a composite index. These fields must be sequential, starting with the first field in the table. You can't have the primary index consist of the first, third, and fourth fields of a table. A composite index with three fields must consist of the first, second, and third fields. If you have a `FirstName` and a `LastName` field in your database, they can both be part of the primary index. You should, however, declare the `LastName` before the `FirstName`, so that your index will list people alphabetically by last name: `CustNo`, `LastName`, `FirstName`.

- The primary and foreign keys are never composite. They always consist of one field.

Creating a primary key enables you to have two people with the same name, but with different addresses. For instance, you can list a John Doe on Maple Street who has a `CustNo` of 25, and a John Doe on Henry Street who has a `CustNo` of 2000. The names may be the same, but the database can distinguish them by their `CustNo`. Once again, this shows why databases love those simple integer indexes. If the database had to sort on the address fields every time it tried to distinguish these two John Does, it would take a long time for the sort to finish.

Computers can easily distinguish the number 25 from the number 2000, but it takes them longer to do a string compare on `"Maple Street"` and `"Henry Street"`. Furthermore, just comparing the streets wouldn't be enough; you would also have to compare cities, states, and so on. If two entries with the same name were both missing addresses, the whole system would be in danger of falling apart altogether. The same thing would happen if two people named John Doe lived at the same address. Use those integer indexes; they make your life simpler!

Working with Secondary Indices and Foreign Keys

It's now time to move on to a consideration of foreign keys. The `CustNo` field of the `Orders` table is a foreign key because it relates the `Orders` table to the primary key of the `Customer` table. It is also a secondary index which aids in sorting and searching through data. Indices also speed up operations such as joins and other master-detail relationships.

When writing this section, I have found it difficult to totally divorce the idea of foreign key and secondary indexes. However, I will try to split them up into two categories, taking foreign keys first:

- A foreign key provides a means for relating two tables according to a set of predefined rules called referential integrity.

- In Paradox, you use the Referential Integrity tools from the Database Desktop to define foreign keys. There is no such thing as a composite foreign key.

- Using SQL you can relate two tables in a one-to-many relationship even if there is no index or key in either table. However, your performance will be better if you have indexes. There will be no way to enforce referential integrity if you don't define foreign and primary keys.

- Using the `TTable` object, it is impossible to relate two tables in a one-to-many relationship without indexes. (This is one of the points that doesn't clearly belong in either the section on keys, or the one on indexes. It relates to both subjects.)

Here are some facts about secondary indexes:

- A secondary index provides an alternative sort order to the one provided by the primary key.

- You need to explicitly change the index if you want to switch away from the primary index to a secondary index. Remember that the default sort order for a Paradox table is provided by the primary index. If you want to switch from the primary index to a secondary index, you need to change the `IndexName` or `IndexFieldName` property of your table. If you want to use the primary index, you don't have to do anything; the table will sort on that field automatically.

- An index that contains more than one field is called a composite index. You can create composite secondary indexes, which means the indexes will contain multiple fields. In practice, fields such as `FirstName` and `LastName` can often be part of a secondary index, because your primary index is usually a unique numerical value. Sometimes a primary index will consist of three fields, such as the `CustNo`, `FirstName`, and `LastName` fields.

- In Paradox tables all primary and foreign keys must be indexed. You can't define referential integrity without indexes, and in particular, you must have a primary key. Furthermore, in InterBase tables, the act of defining a primary or foreign key will automatically generate an index. (Once again, this is an item that doesn't clearly belong in either the discussion of keys or of indexes, but rather it relates to both. As I said earlier, there are times when the distinction between the two subjects becomes blurred.)

If you are new to databases, you will undoubtedly be frustrated to discover that different databases have varying rules for setting up indexes, keys, and so on. In this book, I tend to use Paradox tables as the default, but I also spend considerable time describing InterBase tables. If you use some other database, such as dBASE, Oracle, or Sybase, you should be sure to read up on the basic rules for using those tools. For instance, some databases let you set up a foreign key that is not an index. In the Paradox and InterBase world, however, foreign keys are always accompanied by an index, so the two words become synonymous, particularly in the hands of people who don't really understand how relational databases work.

The good news is that you will find that overall there are certain basic principles that define how databases work. The details may vary from implementation to implementation, but the fundamental ideas stay the same.

Keys Are the Keys to the Kingdom!

Let me take this whole paradigm even one step further. When I first looked at a database, I thought of it as a place to store information. After spending a lot of time with relational databases, I now think of them primarily as a way to relate bits of information through keys and indexes.

I know this is putting the cart before the horse, but what really interests me about databases now is not the fact that they contain information per se, but that I can query them to retrieve related bits of information. In other words, I'm more interested in the logic that defines how tables relate to one another than I am in the information itself.

No one can get excited about a list of addresses or a list of books. The lists themselves are very boring. What's interesting is the system of keys and indexes that relate tables together, and the various SQL statements you can use to ask questions against various sets of tables.

When I picture a table, I see its primary and foreign keys as great big pillars, and I envision all the rest of the data as a little stone altar that is dwarfed by the pillars. Like a pagan temple, it's the pillars that you notice first; the altar is just a small stone structure you might overlook until someone points it out. Of course the temple is built around the altar, and databases are built around their data. But in practice it is easy to overlook the data. You care about the pillars, and you care about the primary and foreign keys. The rest tends to fade into the background.

Give me a well-designed database with lots of interrelated tables and I can have fun asking it all sorts of interesting questions. It's not the data per se that is important, but the way the data is related!

The act of properly relating a set of tables in a database is called, tragically enough, "normalizing" the data. Where this dreadful term came from I have no idea, but "normalizing" a database is the fun part of creating a database application.

Exploring the Keys and Indices in the BCDEMOS Database

I am now going to look again at the tools that ship with BCB, and show how to use them to view and create indexes and keys. This examination of the subject will have greater depth than the quick overview presented earlier in this chapter.

Here is a list of the indexes on the `Customers`, `Orders`, `Items`, and `Parts` tables:

Table name	Primary indexes	Secondary indexes
Customer	CustNo	Company
Orders	OrderNo	CustNo
Items	OrderNo, ItemNo	OrderNo, PartNo
Parts	PartNo	VendorNo, Description

Notice that the `Items` table has a composite primary index consisting of the `OrderNo` and `ItemNo` fields. It also has two secondary indexes, one on the `OrderNo` field and one on the `PartNo` field. The `Parts` table has two secondary indexes, one on the `VenderNo`, and one on the `Description` field.

If you do not have a pre-made list like this one, you could find this information in at least four ways:

- ■ The Object Inspector
- ■ The Database Explorer
- ■ The Database Desktop
- ■ By creating a program that leverages the methods of the `TSession` object. Such a program will be shown in Chapter 14.

I will explain all these methods and then discuss some possible alternative techniques.

If you drag the `Customer` table off the Explorer and onto a form, you will be able to view its Indices in the Object Inspector. If you drop down the `IndexName` property editor, you will see that there is one index listed there. This is the secondary index, called `ByCompany`. If you select this index, the table will sort on the `Company` field.

If you set the `IndexName` property back to blank, the table will sort automatically on the primary index, which is the `CustNo` field. In other words, BCB never explicitly lists the primary index in the `IndexName` property editor. I suppose that the architects of the VCL assumed that all tables have a primary index, and that if you don't specify a particular index name, you want to sort on that index. Of course, it is not an error to create a table that has no primary index, and BCB can still work with that kind of table.

You can also drop down the `IndexFieldNames` property, which gives you a list of the fields that are indexed, in this case the `CustNo` and `Company` fields. Here you can see the fields included in the primary index, but they are not marked as belonging to any particular index.

> **NOTE**
>
> To study an interesting case, drop down the `Items` table on a form. Recall that it has a primary index on the `OrderNo` and `ItemNo` fields, and secondary indexes on the `OrderNo` and `PartNo` fields. If you drop down the index field names, you see the following list:
>
> ```
> OrderNo
> OrderNo; ItemNo
> PartNo
> ```
>
> The first item is the `ByOrderNo` index—the second the primary index—and the third, the `PartNo` index.

The `IndexName` and `IndexFieldNames` properties give you a handy way of tracking `Indices` at design time. They don't, however, give you all the information you might need, such as exactly what fields make up which parts of the primary and secondary `Indices`. In this case, you could probably guess, but it would still be nice to get a more definitive answer.

 If you open up the Database Explorer, expand the `BCDEMOS` node, the `Tables` node, the `Customer` node, and finally the `Indices` node, you get (naturally enough) a list of the `Indices` on the `Customer` table! This is a great feature, and you should use it whenever possible. Figure 12.7 shows the expanded nodes of the `Indices` for the `Customer` table. (The program kdAddExplore in the `Chap14` subdirectory on the CD-ROM that accompanies this book uses the `TSession` object to do the same thing in a BCB program.)

While you have the Explorer open, you should also expand the `Fields` node, as shown in Figure 12.8. This gives a quick list of all the fields and their types. Notice that you can drag and drop individual fields onto a form.

A third way to get a look at the structure of a table is through the Database Desktop (DBD). You can open this program from the Tools menu in C++Builder. Use the File menu in the DBD to set the Working Directory to the `BCDEMOS` `Alias`. Open up the `Customer` table and choose the Table | Info Structure menu choice. Drop down the Table Properties combo box and look up the secondary `Indices`, as shown in Figure 12.9. The primary index is designated by the asterisks after the keyed fields in the Key Roster. In this case, only the `CustNo` field is starred, because it is the sole keyed field.

FIGURE 12.7.

The Indices *of the* Customer *table viewed in the Database Explorer.*

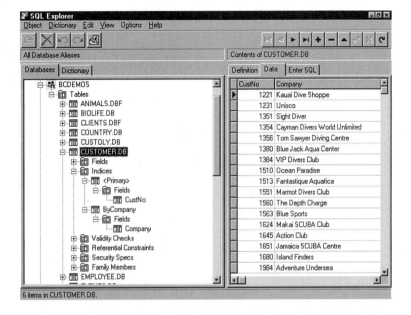

FIGURE 12.8.

The Fields view of the Customer *table from the Database Explorer.*

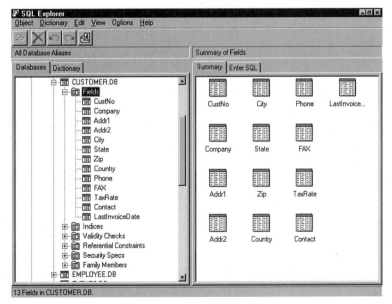

FIGURE 12.9.

The Database Desktop struts its venerable features by displaying the Indices *on the* Customer *table.*

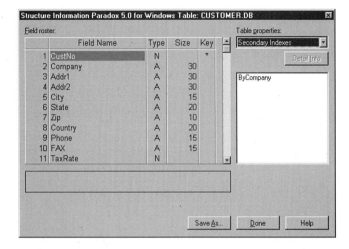

> **NOTE**
>
> Over time, the Database Desktop will probably be replaced entirely by the Explorer. However, there are still some things that the DBD does better than the Explorer, so both products are shipped with C++Builder.

Notice the Save As button on the Info Structure dialog. You can use this to save a table that contains the structure of the Customer table. You can then print this out on a printer using TQuickReports. Be sure to use a fixed-size font, not a proportional font:

```
Field Name        Type   Size Key
CustNo            N            *
Company           A      30
Addr1             A      30
Addr2             A      30
City              A      15
State             A      20
Zip               A      10
Country           A      20
Phone             A      15
FAX               A      15
TaxRate           N
Contact           A      20
LastInvoiceDate   @
```

In the example shown here, I have printed out only the first four fields of the table because of space considerations. (The fields are Field Name, Type, Size, and Key.) If I then recursively print out the structure of the table used to house the structure of the `Customer` table, I get the following report:

```
Field Name           Type  Size  Key
Field Name           A     25
Type                 A     1
Size                 S
Key                  A     1
_Invariant Field ID  S
_Required Value      A     1
_Min Value           A     255
_Max Value           A     255
_Default Value       A     255
_Picture Value       A     176
_Table Lookup        A     255
_Table Lookup Type   A     1
```

This is the same information found in the Data Dictionary, and it should prove sufficient under most circumstances.

Using the Database Desktop to Create Indexes

To create a unique primary key in a Paradox table, open up the Database Desktop, and create a table with the first field declared as an Integer or autoincrement value. Place a star next to the first field, which tells Paradox to create a primary index on it, as shown in Figure 12.10.

FIGURE 12.10.

Place asterisks next to the first field or fields of a table to designate the primary index.

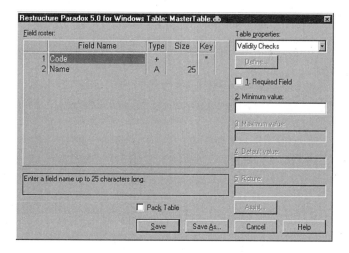

To create a secondary index, drop down the table properties list and choose Secondary Indices. (See Figure 12.11.) Click the Define button. Select the fields from your table that you want to be part of your index. Click OK. A simple dialog will then pop up asking you to name the index. I usually give the index a name based on the fields being indexed. For instance, if I want to create an index on the `CustNo` field, I would call the index `CustNo`, `CustNoIndex`, or `ByCustNo`. If I wanted to create one on a field called `Name`, I would call the index `Name`, `NameIndex`, or `ByName`.

FIGURE 12.11.

Creating a secondary index in a Paradox table.

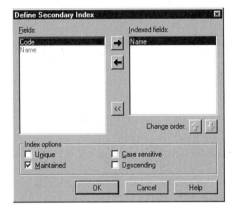

Using the Database Desktop to Create Primary and Foreign Keys

To create a primary or foreign key on a Paradox table you need to define something called referential integrity. You cannot define referential integrity without first defining primary keys on both tables involved. There also must be an index on the foreign key, but this index will be created automatically for you when you create the foreign key.

In InterBase, the situation is somewhat different. The act of creating primary or foreign keys will automatically define indexes. As I said earlier, there are little variations on the main themes of relational databases, depending on what kind of database you use.

In the `Data` subdirectory from the CD that ships with this book you will find two tables called `MasterTable` and `DetailTable`. Figure 12.10 shows how to use the Database desktop to create the `MasterTable`. These tables look like this, with the `MasterTable` listed first and the `DetailTable` listed second:

Field name	Type	Size	Primary index?
Code	+		*
Name	A	25	

Field name	Type	Size	Primary index?
Code	+		*
MasterCode	I		
SubName	A	25	

To create referential integrity between these two tables, you should open up the `DetailTable` in the Database Desktop. Open the Table | Restructure menu item. Select Referential Integrity from the Table Properties combo box. Click the Define button, and set things up so they look like they do in Figure 12.12. Click the OK button and give this relationship a name, such as `RefMasterDetail`.

FIGURE 12.12.

Defining referential integrity between the `DetailTable` *and* `MasterTable`.

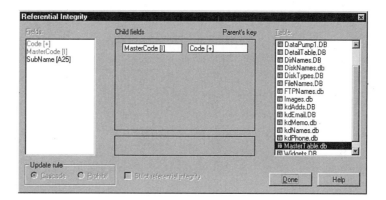

When you are done, you will have created primary keys and foreign keys on the `MasterTable` and `DetailTable`. The best way to see these keys is in the Database Explorer. On my system I used the BDE Configuration Utility to create an alias called `CUnleashed` that points at the `Data` subdirectory. If you open this alias in the Database Explorer and go to `MasterTable`, you can see the primary and foreign keys, which Paradox calls Primary and Foreign Fields.

Why Use Referential Integrity?

Referential integrity is one of the most valuable tools in a database programmer's arsenal. In particular, referential integrity will help guide the user so that they do not accidentally enter invalid data, or accidentally delete needed records.

To see referential integrity in action, use the Database Desktop to enter two records in the `MasterTable`. The first should have the word `Day` in the `Name` field and the second should have the word `Month` in the `Name` field. You do not have to fill in the `Code` field, because it is an autoincrement field (+) and will be updated automatically.

Code	Name
1	Days
2	Months

In the `DetailTable`, enter in a few names of days of the week or months of the year in the `SubName` field. Give the `MasterCode` field a 1 if you are entering a day, and 2 if you are entering a month.

Code	MasterCode	SubName
1	1	Monday
2	1	Tuesday
3	2	January
4	2	February
5	2	March

With this data in the tables, you could define a one-to-many relationship such that if you viewed the `MasterTable` record with `Days` in the `Name` field you would see only the days in the `DetailTable`, and if you selected `Months`, you would see only the month names from the `DetailRecord`.

Referential integrity will do two things to help make sure that these tables stay in good shape. It will prevent you from deleting a record in the `MasterTable` that has detail records associated with it in the `DetailTable`. For instance, if you select the `MasterTable`, set the Database Desktop in Edit mode and press Control+Delete, you will not be able to delete a record from the `MasterTable`. Referential integrity will prevent you from entering a value in the `MasterCode` field of the `DetailTable` that is not in the primary key of the `MasterTable`. For instance, if you tried to enter the number 3 in the `DetailTable`'s `MasterCode` field, you would get the error message `"Master field missing"`. This is because there is no record in the `MasterTable` with a `Code` field of 3. Of course, if you added a record to the `MasterTable` with a `Code` field that had 3 in it, the database would let you enter the data.

Needless to say, these rules are also enforced inside BCB. In your own programs, you might want to create exception handlers that would pop up messages that explained to the user exactly what was wrong, and why they could not perform a particular operation. Most users would not respond well to an exception that said no more than "Master field missing!"

That is the end of my explanation of relational databases. In the last few pages you have learned about primary keys, foreign keys, indexes, referential integrity, and how all these pieces fit together to help you create robust applications. In the next few pages I will step you through some simple examples that illustrate these points.

One-to-Many Relationships: The Code

Now that you know something about the data in the `Customer`, `Orders`, `Items`, and `Parts` tables, it's time to link them together in a single program called `Relate`. To get started, begin a new project and add a data module to it. Place four `TTable` objects and four `TDataSource` objects on the data module, wire each data source to a `TTable` object, and then wire each of the `TTable` objects to one of the four tables mentioned earlier. You can also rename the `TTable` and `TDataSource` objects so that they correspond with their respective tables, as shown in Figure 12.13.

FIGURE 12.13.

The data module for the Relate *project.*

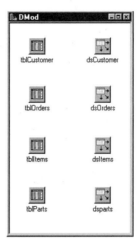

Drop four TDBGrid objects on the main form for the project. Use the File | Include Unit Header menu option to link Form1 to DataModule1. Wire the grids to the datasources on the datamodule, making sure that each grid has its DataSource property assigned to a unique object. For instance, link the first grid to the Customer table, the second to the Orders table, and so on.

Using the names visible in Figure 12.4, click the OrdersTable component and set its MasterSource property equal to CustomerSource, that is, set its MasterSource equal to the TDataSource object that is linked to the TTable object that hosts the Customer table. Set the ItemsTable MasterSource property equal to OrdersSource and the PartsTable MasterSource equal to ItemsSource.

Click the OrdersTable MasterFields property and link up the Orders and Items tables on the CustNo field, as described in Chapter 9, "Using TTable and TDataSet." In the same way, hook up the TblItems to OrdersTable on the OrderNo field, and PartsTable to ItemsTable on the PartNo field. If you set all the tables to active and then run the program, the result should look like what you see in Figure 12.14.

Spend a little time mucking about with this program. Notice, for instance, that if you change the selected item in the Customer table, the contents of the grids showing the Orders, Items, and Parts tables will change. In particular, notice that the CustNo in all the items in the Orders table is always equal to the CustNo in the currently selected item in the Customer table. The same thing can be said about the OrderNo field in the Orders and Items tables, and the PartNo field in the Items and Parts tables.

In general, selecting one item at any level but the lowest in the hierarchy will force many detail records to change. That is why these are called *one-to-many* relationships. One record in the Orders table points to many records in the Items and Parts tables.

FIGURE 12.14.

The Relate program at runtime.

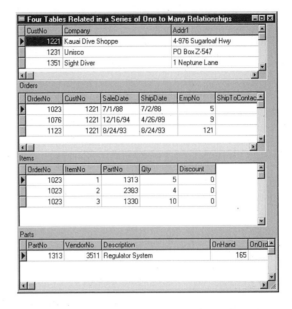

In this particular example, you might notice that the Parts table is always arranged in a one-to-one relationship with the Items table. However, if you reverse the order of these tables and make the Parts table the master, the arrangement will look more like a proper one-to-many relationship. However, it is not wrong to make either table the master. The point is simply to arrange the tables so that you get the information from them that you want to obtain.

This discussion of the Relate program has given you a look at some of the important features in the Database Explorer and Database Desktop. It has also given you a quick run-down on some of the key ideas behind the construction of relational databases. The point here is that C++Builder has lots of built-in tools that help you construct relational databases. There is more that I want to say about these topics, even in this rather sketchy overview of a complicated subject. In particular, I have not yet talked about joins.

Relational Databases and Joins

In the last section, you saw how to relate the Customers, Orders, Items, and Parts tables in a one-to-many relationship that is sometimes called a master-detail relationship. In this section, you will again relate all four tables, but in a different kind of relationship, called a *join*.

You had a look at joins in the last chapter, "Working with Field Objects." This time the query that you need to build is a bit longer:

```
SELECT DISTINCT d.Company, d1.AmountPaid, d2.Qty,
                d3.Description, d3.Cost, d3.ListPrice
FROM "Customer.db" d, "Orders.db" d1,
     "Items.db" d2, "Parts.db" d3
WHERE (d1.CustNo = d.CustNo)
      AND (d2.OrderNo = d1.OrderNo)
      AND (d3.PartNo = d2.PartNo)
ORDER BY d.Company, d1.AmountPaid, d2.Qty,
         d3.Description, d3.Cost, d3.ListPrice
```

Though not horrendously complicated, the syntax shown here is still ugly enough to give some people pause.

The basic principles involved in this kind of statement are simple enough to describe. All that's happening is that the Customer, Orders, Items, and Parts tables are being joined together into one large table of the type you would have to create if you were trying to track all this information in a single flat-file database. The one proviso, of course, is that not all the fields from the four tables are being used. In fact, the only ones mentioned are

```
d.Company, d1.AmountPaid, d2.Qty,
d3.Description, d3.Cost, d3.ListPrice
```

Here the d, d1, d2, and d3 are described in the following From clause:

```
"Customer.db" d, "Orders.db" d1,
"Items.db" d2, "Parts.db" d3
```

The Order By clause, of course, simply defines the sort order to be used on the table created by this join. I am guilty here of using meaningless variable names. In general, you should choose identifiers more informative than d1 or d2.

You can create a program that performs this join by dropping a TQuery, TDataSource, and TDBGrid on a form. Wire the objects together, wire the TQuery to the BCDEMOS database, and set its SQL property to the query shown previously. A sample program called FourWayJoin demonstrates this process. The output from the program is shown in Figure 12.15.

If you are not familiar with this kind of join, you might want to bring up the Relate and FourWayJoin tables side by side and compare them. Look, for instance, at the Action Club entries in the FourWayJoin program and trace them through so that you see how they correspond to the entries in the Relate program. Both programs describe an identical set of relationships; they just show the outcome in a different manner.

Notice that the AmountPaid column in the FourWayJoin program has the same number repeated twice in the Action Club section, as shown in Figure 12.15. In particular, the numbers $1,004.80 and $20,108 both appear twice. This is because there are two different items associated with these orders, as you can tell from glancing at the Parts table in the Relate program.

Company	AmountPaid	Qty	Description	Cost	ListPrice
Action Club	$134.85	3	Krypton Flashlight	$20.68	$44
Action Club	$1,004.80	1	95.1 cu ft Tank	$130.00	$325
Action Club	$1,004.80	4	Flashlight (Rechargeable)	$50.99	$169
Action Club	$10,152.00	54	Depth/Pressure Gauge Console	$73.32	$188
Action Club	$20,108.00	8	Safety Knife	$13.12	$41
Action Club	$20,108.00	46	Regulator System	$154.80	$430
Action Diver Supply	$536.80	1	Second Stage Regulator	$95.79	$309
Action Diver Supply	$536.80	4	Medium Titanium Knife	$26.77	$56
Adventure Undersea	$0.00	1	Navigation Compass	$9.18	$19
Adventure Undersea	$0.00	2	Depth/Pressure Gauge	$48.30	$105
Adventure Undersea	$0.00	3	Electronic Console	$120.90	$390
Adventure Undersea	$0.00	3	Flashlight (Rechargeable)	$50.99	$169
Adventure Undersea	$0.00	3	Underwater Diver Vehicle	$504.00	$1,680
Adventure Undersea	$0.00	3	Welded Seam Stabilizing Vest	$109.20	$280
Adventure Undersea	$0.00	4	Depth/Pressure Gauge	$48.30	$105
Adventure Undersea	$0.00	5	Compass Console Mount	$10.15	$29
Adventure Undersea	$0.00	15	Flashlight	$29.25	$65
Adventure Undersea	$0.00	45	Depth/Pressure Gauge Console	$73.32	$188
Adventure Undersea	$2,195.00	5	Sonar System	$215.11	$439
Adventure Undersea	$3,117.00	3	60.6 cu ft Tank	$57.28	$179
Adventure Undersea	$3,117.00	6	Stabilizing Vest	$146.20	$430
Adventure Undersea	$3,304.85	1	Medium Titanium Knife	$26.77	$56
Adventure Undersea	$3,304.85	1	Wrist Band Thermometer (C)	$6.48	$18

NOTE

Unless you are already familiar with this material, be sure to run the FourWayJoin and Relate programs and switch back and forth between them until you understand why the FourWayJoin program works as it does. I find it easy to understand the Relate program at a glance, but the FourWayJoin program is a bit more subtle.

Joins and QBE

The FourWayJoin program is a good advertisement for the power of SQL. Once you had the SQL statement composed, it was simple to put the program together. All the work is embodied in just a few lines of code, and everything else was trivial to construct. SQL can help concentrate the intelligence of a program in one small area—or at least it does in this one example.

The sticking point, of course, is that not everyone is a whiz at composing SQL statements. Even if you understand SQL thoroughly, it can still be confusing to try to string together all those interrelated Select, Order By, From, and Where clauses. What is needed here is a way to automate this process.

Most of the versions of C++Builder ship with a very useful tool that makes it easy to compose even relatively complex SQL statements. In particular, I'm talking about the QBE tool in the Database Desktop. If you want, you can use the Query Builder instead, or some other third-party tool that you might favor. However, in this section of the book, I will concentrate on the

QBE tool, because it will be available to nearly all readers of this book. (QBE is also built into Paradox. Furthermore, there are some third-party QBE components on the market. The Query Builder only ships with the client/server version of C++Builder or Delphi.)

Start the DBD and set the Working Directory to the BCDEMOS alias. Choose File | New | QBE Query from the menu. A dialog will appear listing the tables in the BCDEMOS database. Select the Customer table. Reopen the Select File dialog by clicking the Add Table icon in the Toolbar. You can find the Add Table icon by holding the mouse over each icon until the fly-by help comes up or until you see the hint on the status bar. You can also simply look for the icon with the plus sign on it. Continue until you have added the Customer, Orders, Items, and Parts tables to the query. You can multiselect from inside the FileOpenDialog. Resize the query window until all four tables are visible, as shown in Figure 12.16.

FIGURE 12.16.

Four tables used in a single QBE example.

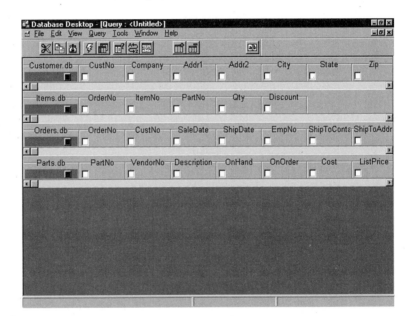

To join these tables together, select the Join Tables icon, located just to the right of the lightning bolt. Click once on the Join Tables icon, and then click the CustNo fields for the Customer and Orders tables. The symbol "join1" will appear in each field. Click the Join Tables icon again, and link the Orders and Items tables on the OrderNo field. Join the Parts and Items tables on the PartNo field.

After joining the tables, select the fields you want to show by clicking once in the check box associated with the fields you want to view. When you are done, the result should look like Figure 12.17.

FIGURE 12.17.

The complete QBE query for joining the Customer, Orders, Items, *and* Parts *tables.*

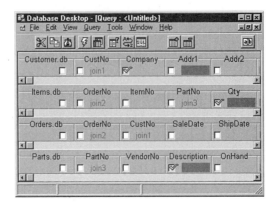

 To test your work, click the lightning bolt icon once. You should get a table that looks just like the one in the FourWayJoin program. You will find a copy of this QBE query in the Chap12 directory on the CD-ROM that accompanies this book.

To translate the QBE statement into SQL, first close the result table so you can view the query shown in Figure 12.17. Click once on the SQL icon to perform the translation. You can save this SQL to disk, or just block-copy it and deposit it in the SQL property of a TQuery object.

On paper, this process takes a few minutes to explain. However, once you understand the QBE tool, you can use it to relate multiple tables in just a very few seconds. For most people, QBE is probably the simplest and fastest way to compose all your SQL Select statements. Don't neglect learning to use this tool. It's a simple, easy-to-use tool that can save you hours of time.

NOTE

The only peculiarity of the QBE tool is that by default it saves its output in a text-based language called QBE, rather than in SQL. However, once you press the SQL button, it converts the QBE code to SQL, thereby rendering the exact same results produced by standard SQL query builders. Once again, the great advantage of the QBE tool over other SQL tools is that it ships with the DBD product that accompanies nearly all versions of C++Builder. If you have access to a more powerful SQL builder, you might want to use it instead of the QBE tool. However, QBE works fine in most circumstances, even when running against SQL data in an InterBase table.

What I have said here, is, of course, heresy to many members of the hard-core client server crowd. They tend to have a natural aversion to QBE, just as C++ and Object Pascal programmers shy away from BASIC. However, QBE ships for free with both Paradox and the Database Desktop, and it will meet the needs of ninety percent, but not all, of the programmers out there. So it's worth a look, yes?

That's it for the discussion of the basic principles of relational databases. You've seen how to build master-detail relationships, and how to construct joins. More importantly, you've seen how C++Builder encapsulates these key aspects of relational database design. There is, of course, much more to the theory of relational databases. There are whole books on this subject, particularly on the best way to design relational databases.

Which Database Should I Use?

If you are not sure of which database to use, I would tentatively suggest using Paradox to get started. It has a robust set of rules for enforcing data integrity, a rich set of types, and some nice features such as autoincrement fields. It works fine on a network, as long as everyone can attach their PCs to one centralized server and you aren't expecting a large number of simultaneous users.

If you are expecting 30 or more simultaneous users, I would bite the bullet financially and switch to InterBase or to another standard SQL server such as Oracle, Sybase, or MS SQL Server. You could have a hundred or even two hundred users hitting a Paradox table at the same time, but I wouldn't recommend it. If you have a hundred users, but only ten or fifteen are likely to be after a table at one time, I would still feel comfortable with Paradox, though I would start leaning in the direction of a real client/server database.

Client/server databases such as InterBase will

- Let you talk to the server over TCP/IP, or some other network protocol
- Put much of the computational burden on the server rather than the client machine
- Prove to be much more robust
- Enable you to use stored procedures, triggers, views, and other advanced server-side technologies

Remember that when I make suggestions about databases or about anything else, I am usually not so much trying to establish a definitive standard as I am trying to give reasonable advice to those readers who are not sure which way to turn.

Summary

My suggestion at this point is to dig into relational databases and learn as much about them as you can. Raw data sitting on a disk is boring. Rows of data in a grid are boring. Relational databases, however, are innately interesting. This is the fun part of database programming. Play around with indexes, or play around with joins and one-to-many relationships. The name of the game here is to find ways to arrange data in relational tables so that you can get at it easily. When you arrange data correctly, it's amazing to see how quickly you can locate very obscure pieces of information. In fact, a number of very fun games, such as Civilization or the Ultima series, rely heavily on databases in order to further the game play. Take some time to dig into this stuff. It's more interesting than you might think.

If you are wishing that I had spent more time on InterBase tables, don't worry, because I cover that topic heavily later in the book. Much of the material covered in this chapter will be reviewed again, in much shorter form, in the light of the InterBase server.

Flat-File, Real-World Databases

## CHAPTER 13

Overview

This chapter is the first of a "two-part series" on constructing real-world databases. The goal is to move from the largely theoretical information you got in the preceding chapter into a few examples of how to make programs that someone could actually use for a practical purpose in the real world.

In several sections of this chapter, I go into considerable depth about design-related issues. One of the burdens of this chapter is not merely to show how database code works, but to talk about how to create programs that have some viable use in the real world. These design-related issues are among the most important that any programmer will ever face.

In this chapter, you will get a look at a simple, nearly pure, flat-file address book program called Address2. This program is designed to represent the simplest possible database program that is still usable in a real-world situation. In the next chapter, I will create a second address program, designed to be a "killer" relational database with much more power than the one you see in this chapter.

One of my primary goals in these two chapters is to lay out in the starkest possible terms the key differences between flat-file and relational databases. The point is for you to examine two database tools that perform the same task and see exactly what the relational tool brings to the table. I found, however, that it was simply impossible for me to create a completely flat-file database design. As a result, I had to content myself with a design that was nearly a pure example of a flat-file database. It does, however, contain one smaller helper table that is linked in using relational database design principles. My simple inability to omit this table does more than anything else I can say to stress the weaknesses of the flat-file model, and to show why relational databases are essential.

The second database program you see will contain a very powerful set of relational features that could, with the aid of a polished interface, stand up under the strain of heavy and complex demands. You could give this second program to a corporate secretary or executive, and that person could make some real use of it. The database shown in this chapter, on the other hand, is meant to be a quick solution to a simple problem. One of the points you shouldn't miss, however, is that the database from this chapter more than suits the needs of most people.

One of the classic and most commonly made mistakes is to give people too many features, or to concentrate on the wrong set of features. Those of us who work in the industry forget how little experience most users have with computers. Even the simple database program outlined in this chapter might be too much for some people. Any attempt to sell them on the merits of the database from the next chapter would simply be an exercise in futility. They would never be willing to take the time to figure out what to do with it. As a result, I suggest that you not turn your nose up at the database shown in this chapter just because it is not as powerful as the one in the next chapter. Just because your typical Volkswagen is not as powerful as an Alpha Romeo does not mean that the Volkswagen people are in a small business niche, or even that there is less money in VWs than in Alpha Romeos.

Here is a quick look at the terrain covered in this chapter:

- Sorting data.
- Filtering data.
- Searching for data.
- Dynamically moving a table in and out of a read-only state.
- Forcing the user to select a field's value from a list of valid responses.
- Allowing the user to choose the colors of a form at runtime.
- Saving information to the Registry. In particular, you see how to use the Registry to replace an INI file, and how to save and restore information from and to the Registry at program startup.
- Using events that occur in a `TDataModule` inside the main form of your program. That is, the chapter shows how to respond to events specific to one form from inside a second form. Or, more generally, it shows how to handle events manually rather than let BCB set up the event handler for you.

After finishing this chapter, you will have learned something about the kinds of problems experienced when writing even a very basic database program that serves a real-world purpose. The final product, though not quite up to professional standards, provides solutions to many of the major problems faced by programmers who want to create tools that can be used by the typical user. In particular, the program explores how to use BCB to create a reasonably usable interface.

You will find that the final program is relatively long when compared to most of the programs you have seen so far in this book. The length of the program is a result of my aspiration to make it useful in a real-world setting, while simultaneously providing at least a minimum degree of robustness. The act of adding a few niceties to the interface for a program gives you a chance to see how RAD programming can help solve some fairly difficult problems.

Before closing this overview, I should perhaps explicitly mention that this chapter does not cover printing, which is certainly one of the most essential real-world needs for a database program. I will, however, add printing capabilities to this program in Chapter 17, "Printing: QuickReport and Related Technologies." In fact, that chapter will show how to add printing to all the useful database programs that will be created in the next few chapters of this book. My plan is to isolate the important, even crucial, subject of printing in its own chapter where it can be properly addressed.

You should also be sure you have read the readme files on the CD that accompanies this book for information about the alias used in the Address2 program and in other programs in this book. If you have trouble getting any of these programs running, be sure to check my Web site (`users.aol.com/charliecal`) for possible updates.

Defining the Data

When you're considering an address program, you can easily come up with a preliminary list of needed fields:

```
First Name
Last Name
Address
City
State
Zip
Phone
```

After making this list and contemplating it for a moment, you might ask the following questions:

- What about complex addresses that can't be written on one line?
- Is one phone number enough? What about times when I need a home phone and a work phone?
- Speaking of work, what about specifying the name of the company that employs someone on the list?
- What about faxes?
- This is the 1990s, so what about an e-mail address?
- What about generic information that doesn't fit into any of these categories?

This list of questions emerges only after a period of gestation. In a real-world situation, you might come up with a list of questions like this only after you talk with potential users of your program, after viewing similar programs that are on the market, and after experimenting with a prototype of the proposed program. Further information might be culled from your own experience using or writing similar programs. Whatever way you come up with the proper questions, the key point is that you spend the time to really think about the kind of data you need.

> **NOTE**
>
> Many books tell you to complete your plan before you begin programming. The only thing wrong with this theory is that I have never seen it work out as expected in practice.
>
> Nearly all the real-world programs that I have seen, both my own and others, whether produced by individuals or huge companies, always seem to go through initial phases that are later abandoned in favor of more sophisticated designs. This is part of what Delphi and RAD programs in general are all about. They make it possible for you to create a draft of your program and then rewrite it.
>
> Think hard about what you want to do. Then get up a prototype in fairly short order, critique it, and then rethink your design. Totally abandoning the first draft is rarely necessary,

but you are almost certainly going to have to rewrite. For this reason, concentrating on details at first is not a good idea. Get things up and running; then if they look okay, go back and optimize.

The point is that the process is iterative. You keep rewriting, over and over, the same way authors keep rewriting the chapters in their books. RAD programming tools help make this kind of cycle possible. The interesting thing about Delphi is that the same tool that lets you prototype quickly is also the tool that lets you optimize down to the last clock cycle.

I don't, however, think most contemporary application programming is really about optimization any more than it's about attempting to design a program correctly on paper before writing it. My experience leads me to believe that the practical plan that really works is iterative programming. Think for a little bit and then write some code. Review it, then rewrite it, then review it, and then rewrite it, and so on. Another, somewhat more old-fashioned name for this process is simply: One heck of a lot of hard work!

After considering the preceding questions, you might come up with a revised list of fields for your program:

```
First Name
Last Name
Company
Address1
Address2
City
State
Zip
Home Phone
Work Phone
Fax
EMail1
EMail2
Comment
```

This list might actually stand up to the needs of a real-world user. Certainly, it doesn't cover all possible situations, but it does represent a reasonable compromise between the desire to make the program easy to use and the desire to handle a variety of potential user demands.

At this stage, you might start thinking about some of the basic functionality you want to associate with the program. For example, you might decide that a user of the program should be able to search, sort, filter, and print the data. After stating these needs, you'll find that the user will need to break up the data into various categories so that it can be filtered. The question, of course, is how these categories can be defined.

After considering the matter for some time, you might decide that two more fields should be added to the list. The first field can be called `Category`; it holds a name that describes the type of record currently being viewed. For example, some entries in an address book might consist of family members, whereas other entries might reference friends, associates from work, companies where you shop, or other types of data. A second field can be called `Marked`; it designates whether a particular field is marked for some special processing.

Here is the revised list, with one additional field called `Category`, that is used to help the user filter the data he or she might be viewing:

```
First Name
Last Name
Company
Address1
Address2
City
State
Zip
Home Phone
Work Phone
Fax
EMail1
EMail2
Comment
Category
Marked
```

After you carefully consider the fields that might be used in the Address2 program, the next step is to decide how large and what type the fields should be. Table 13.1 shows proposed types and sizes.

Table 13.1. The lengths and types of fields used by the Address2 program.

Name	Type	Size
FName	Character	40
LName	Character	40
Company	Character	40
Address1	Character	40
Address2	Character	40
City	Character	40
State	Character	5
Zip	Character	15
HPhone	Character	15
WPhone	Character	15
Fax	Character	15
EMail1	Character	45

EMail2	Character	45
Comment	Memo	20
Category	Character	15
Marked	Logical	

As you can see, I prefer to give myself plenty of room in all the fields I declare. In particular, notice that I have opted for wide EMail fields to hold long Internet addresses, and I have decided to make the Comment field into a memo field so that it can contain long entries, if necessary. The names of some of the fields have also been altered so that they don't contain any spaces. This feature might prove useful if the data is ever ported to another database.

Now that you have decided on the basic structure of the table, the next task is to work out some of the major design issues. In particular, the following considerations are important:

- The program should run off local tables, because this is the kind of tool likely to be used on individual PCs rather than on a network. The choice of whether to use Paradox or dBASE tables is a toss-up, but I'll opt to use Paradox tables because they provide more features.
- The user should be able to sort the table on the FName, LName, and Company fields.
- Searching on the FName, LName, and Company fields should be possible.
- The user should be able to set up filters based on the Category field.
- The times when the table is editable should be absolutely clear, and the user should be able to easily move in and out of read-only mode.
- Printing the contents of the table based on the filters set up by the Category field should be possible.
- Choosing a set of colors that will satisfy all tastes is very difficult, so the user should be able to set the colors of the main features in the program.

A brief consideration of the design decisions makes it clear that the table should have a primary index on the first three fields and secondary indexes on the FName, LName, Company, and Category fields. The primary index can be used in place of a secondary index on the FName field, but the intent of the program's code will be clearer if a secondary index is used for this purpose. In other words, the code will be easier to read if it explicitly sets the IndexName to something called FNameIndex instead of simply defaulting to the primary index. Table 13.2 shows the final structure of the table. The three asterisks in the fourth column of the table show the fields that are part of the primary index.

> **NOTE**
>
> This table does not have a code field—that is, it does not have a simple numerical number in the first field of the primary index. Most tables will have such a value, but it is not necessary here, because this database is, at least in theory, a flat-file database. I say, "at least in theory," because I am going to make one small cheat in the structure of this database. In short, there will be a second table involved, simply because I could see no reasonable way to omit it from the design of this program.

Table 13.2. The fields used by the Address2 program.

Name	Type	Size	PIdx	Index
FName	Character	40	*	FNameIndex
LName	Character	40	*	LNameIndex
Company	Character	40	*	CompanyIndex
Address1	Character	40		
Address2	Character	40		
City	Character	40		
State	Character	5		
Zip	Character	15		
HPhone	Character	15		
WPhone	Character	15		
Fax	Character	15		
EMail1	Character	45		
EMail2	Character	45		
Comment	Memo	20		
Category	Character	15		CategoryIndex
Marked	Logical			

Now that you have a clear picture of the type of table that you need to create, you can open the Database Desktop and create the table, its primary index, and its four secondary indexes. When you're done, the structure of the table should look like that in Figure 13.1. You can save the table under the name ADDRESS.DB.

FIGURE 13.1.

Designing the main table for the Address2 program. Portions of the table are not visible in this picture.

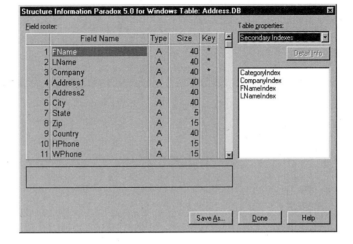

Here is another way of looking at the indexes for this table:

```
Primary Index
LName
FName
Company

Category Index
Category

Company Index
Company
FName
LName

LName Index
LName
FName
Company
```

In this particular case, I will actually end up using these fields and indexes as designed. However, in a real-world situation, you should expect to come up with a carefully thought-out draft like this, and then know in your heart that after you get the program up and running, some things will have to change. Don't tell someone: "Oh, I can complete this program in two weeks; this is going to be easy!" Instead, say: "In two weeks, I can get you a prototype, and then we can sit down and decide what changes need to be made."

You should, however, have some clearly defined boundaries. For example, this program is designed to be a flat-file database. If someone (yourself most especially included!) tries to talk you into believing that this program should really be a relational database of the kind planned for the next chapter, then you have to slam your foot down and say: "No way!" After you've started on a project, you should expect revisions, but you must not allow the goal of the project to be redefined. That way leads to madness!

Defining the Program's Appearance

Before beginning the real programming chores, you need to create a main form and at least one of the several utility forms that will be used by the program. You can let the Database Expert perform at least part of this task for you, but I prefer to do the chore myself to give my program some individuality.

The main form of the Address2 program, shown in Figure 13.2, contains two panels. On the top panel are all the labels and data-aware controls necessary to handle basic input and output chores. All the main fields in the program can be encapsulated in TDBEdit controls, except for the Comment field, which needs a TDBMemo, and the Category field, which needs a TDBLookupComboBox. The names of the data-aware controls should match the field with which they are associated, so the first TDBEdit control is called FNameEdit; the second, LNameEdit; and so on. The TDBLookupComboBox is therefore called CategoryCombo—and the memo field, CommentMemo.

FIGURE 13.2.

The main form for the Address2 program.

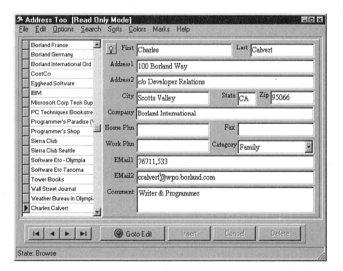

> Then there came a day when I was squinting at some egregious variable name dreamed up by an undoubtedly besotted Microsoft employee, and I just knew that I had had enough of abbreviations, and especially of prefixing them to a variable name.
>
> One of my original goals was to keep variable names short. I went to great lengths to achieve this end. Then I watched C++ linkers mangle my short variable names into behemoths that consumed memory like sharks possessed by a feeding frenzy. After contemplating this situation for a while, I decided that the one thing I could bring to the table that I really cared about was clarity. As a result, I dropped Hungarian notation from all my new code and began using whole words whenever possible.

The bottom panel should contain four buttons for navigating through the table's records, as well as Edit, Insert, and Cancel buttons. A status bar at the bottom of the main form provides room for optionally reporting on the current status of the program.

The top of the program contains a menu with the following format:

```
Caption = 'File'
  Caption = 'Print'
  Caption = '-'
  Caption = 'Exit'
Caption = 'Edit'
  Caption = 'Copy'
  Caption = 'Cut'
  Caption = 'Paste'
Caption = 'Options'
  Caption = 'Filter'
  Caption = 'Set Category'
Caption = 'Search'
  Caption = 'First Name'
  Caption = 'Last Name'
  Caption = 'Company'
Caption = 'Sorts'
  Caption = 'First Name'
  Caption = 'Last Name'
  Caption = 'Company'
Caption = 'Colors'
  Caption = 'Form'
  Caption = 'Edits'
  Caption = 'Edit Text'
  Caption = 'Labels'
  Caption = '------'
  Caption = 'Panels'
  Caption = 'System'
  Caption = 'Default'
  Caption = '------'
  Caption = 'The Blues'
  Caption = 'Save Colors'
  Caption = 'Read Colors'
Caption = 'Marks'
  Caption = 'Mark All'
```

```
   Caption = 'Clear All Marks'
   Caption = 'Print Marked to File'
   Caption = 'Show Only Marked'
Caption = 'Help'
   Caption = 'About'
```

Each line represents the caption for one entry in the program's main menu. The indented portions are the contents of the drop-down menus that appear when you select one of the menu items visible in Figure 13.2.

 After you create the program's interface, drop down a TTable and TDataSource on a data module, wire them up to ADDRESS.DB, and hook up the fields to the appropriate data-aware control. Name the TTable object AddressTable and name the TDataSource object AddressSource. To make this work correctly, you should create an alias, called Address, that points to the location of ADDRESS.DB. Alternatively, you can create a single alias called CUnleashed that points to the tables that ship on the CD that accompanies this book. Take a look at the readme files on the CD that accompanies this book for further information on aliases.

Now switch back to the main form, use the File | Include Unit Header option to connect the main form and the TDataModule, and hook up the data-aware controls shown in Figure 13.2 to the fields in the address table. The only tricky part of this process involves the Category field, which is connected to the TDBLookupComboBox. I will explain how to use this field over the course of the next few paragraphs.

If you run the program you have created so far, you will find that the TDBLookupComboBox for the Category field does not contain any entries; that is, you can't drop down its list. The purpose of this control is to enable the user to select categories from a prepared list rather than force the user to make up categories on the fly. The list is needed to prevent users from accidentally creating a whole series of different names for the same general purpose.

Consider a case in which you want to set a filter for the program that shows only a list of your friends. To get started, you should create a category called Friend and assign it to all the members of the list that fit that description. If you always choose this category from a drop-down list, it will presumably always be spelled the same. However, if you rely on users to type this word, you might get a series of related entries that look like this:

```
Friend
Friends
Frends
Acquaintances
Buddies
Buds
Homies
HomeBoys
Amigos
Chums
Cronies
Companions
```

This mishmash of spellings and synonyms won't do you any good when you want to search for the group of records that fits into the category called Friend.

The simplest way to make this happen is to use not a TDBLookupComboBox, but a TDBLookupCombo. To use this control, simply pop open the Property Editor for the Items property and type in a list of categories such as the following:

```
Home
Work
Family
Local Business
Friend
```

Now when you run the program and drop down the Category combo box, you will find that it contains the preceding list.

The only problem with typing names directly into the Items property for the TDBLookupCombo is that changing this list at runtime is impractical. To do away with this difficulty, the program stores the list in a separate table, called CATS.DB. This table has a single character field that is 20 characters wide. After creating the table in the Database Desktop, you can enter the following five strings into five separate records:

```
Home
Work
Family
Local Business
Friend
```

Now that you have two tables, it's best to switch away from the TDBLookupCombo and go instead with the TDBLookupComboBox. You make the basic connection to the TDBLookupComboBox by setting its DataSource field to AddressSource and its DataField to Category. Then set the ListSource for the control to CatSource, and set ListField and KeyField to Category.

> **NOTE**
>
> The addition of the TDBLookupComboBox into the program begs the question of whether Address2 is really a flat-file database because lookups at least give the feel commonly associated with relational databases. The lookup described in the preceding few paragraphs is not, however, a pure relational technique, in that the CATS and Address tables are not bound by a primary and a foreign key.
>
> It is, however, a cheat in the design of the program, since my goal was to create a pure flat-file database. The facts here are simple: I want the database to be as simple as possible, but I also want it to be useful. Without this one feature, I saw the program as hopelessly crippled. As stated earlier, this shows the importance of relational database concepts in even the simplest programs. In short, I don't think I can get any work done without using relational techniques. Relational database design is not a nicety; it's a necessity.

To allow the user to change the contents of the CATS table, you can create a form like the one shown in Figure 13.3. This form needs only minimal functionality because discouraging the user from changing the list except when absolutely necessary is best. Note that you need to add the `CategoryDlg` module's header to the list of files included in the main form. You can do so simply by choosing File | Include Unit Header.

FIGURE 13.3.

The Category form enables the user to alter the contents of `CATS.DB`.

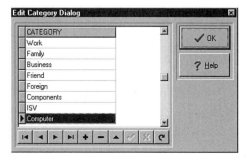

At program startup, the Category dialog, and the memory associated with it, does not need to be created and allocated. As a result, you should choose Options | Project, select the Forms page, and move the Category dialog into the Available Forms column. In response to a selection of the Set Category menu item from the main form of the Address2 program, you can write the following code:

```
void __fastcall TForm1::Category1Click(TObject *Sender)
{
  CategoryDlg = new TCategoryDlg(this);
  CategoryDlg->ShowModal();
  CategoryDlg->Free();
}
```

This code creates the Category dialog, shows it to the user, and finally deallocates its memory after the user is done. You can take this approach because it assures that the Category dialog is in memory only when absolutely necessary.

Setting Up the Command Structure for the Program

The skeletal structure of the Address2 program is starting to come together. However, you must complete one remaining task before the core of the program is complete. A number of basic commands are issued by the program, and they can be defined in a single enumerated type:

```
enum TCommandType {ctClose, ctInsert, ctPrior,
                   ctEdit, ctNext, ctCancel,
                   ctPrint, ctFirst, ctLast,
                   ctPrintPhone, ctPrintAddress,
                   ctPrintAll, ctDelete};
```

This type enables you to associate each of the program's commands with the Tag field of the appropriate button or menu item, and then to associate all these buttons or menu items with a single method that looks like this:

```
void __fastcall TForm1::CommandClick(TObject *Sender)
{
  switch (dynamic_cast<TComponent*>(Sender)->Tag)
  {
    case ctClose: Close(); break;
    case ctInsert: DMod->AddressTable->Insert(); break;
    case ctPrior: DMod->AddressTable->Prior(); break;
    case ctEdit: HandleEditMode(); break;
    case ctNext: DMod->AddressTable->Next(); break;
    case ctCancel: DMod->AddressTable->Cancel(); break;
    case ctPrint: PrintData(ctPrint); break;
    case ctFirst: DMod->AddressTable->First(); break;
    case ctLast: DMod->AddressTable->Last(); break;
    case ctPrintPhone: PrintData(ctPrintPhone); break;
    case ctPrintAddress: PrintData(ctPrintAddress); break;
    case ctPrintAll: PrintData(ctPrintAll); break;
    case ctDelete:
      AnsiString S = DMod->AddressTableLName->AsString;
      if (MessageBox(Handle, "Delete?", S.c_str(), MB_YESNO) == ID_YES)
        DMod->AddressTable->Delete();
      break;
  }
}
```

This code performs a simple typecast to allow you to access the Tag field of the component that generated the command. This kind of typecast was explained in depth in Chapter 4, "Events."

There is no reason why you can't have a different method associated with each of the buttons and menu items in the program. However, handling things this way is neater and simpler, and the code you create is much easier to read. The key point here is to be sure that the Tag property of the appropriate control gets the correct value and that all the controls listed here have the OnClick method manually set to the CommandClick method. I took all these steps while in design mode, being careful to associate the proper value with the Tag property of each control.

Table 13.3 gives a brief summary of the commands passed to the CommandClick method.

Table 13.3. Commands passed to CommandClick.

Command	Type	Name	Tag
Exit	TMenuItem	btClose	0
Insert	TButton	btInsert	1
Prior	TButton	btPrior	2
Edit	TButton	btEdit	3
Next	TButton	btNext	4

continues

13

FLAT-FILE,
REAL-WORLD
DATABASES

Table 13.3. continued

Command	Type	Name	Tag
Cancel	TButton	btCancel	5
Print	TMenuItem	btPrint	6
First	TButton	btFirst	7
Last	TButton	btLast	8

The task of filling in the Tag properties and setting the OnClick events for all these controls is a bit tedious, but I like the easy-to-read code produced by following this technique. In particular, I like having all the major commands send to one method, thereby giving me a single point from which to moderate the flow of the program. This is particularly useful when you can handle most of the commands with a single line of code. Look, for example, at the ctNext and ctCancel portions of the case statement in the CommandClick method.

All the code in this program will compile at this stage except for the references in CommandClick to HandleEditMode and PrintData. For now, you can simply create dummy HandleEditMode and PrintData private methods and leave their contents blank.

At this stage, you're ready to run the Address2 program. You can now insert new data, iterate through the records you create, cancel accidental changes, and shut down the program from the menu. These capabilities create the bare functionality needed to run the program.

Examining the "Rough Draft" of an Application

The program as it exists now is what I mean by creating a "rough draft" of a program. The rough draft gets the raw functionality of the program up and running with minimum fuss, and it lets you take a look at the program to see if it passes muster.

If you were working for a third-party client, or for a demanding boss, now would be the time to call the person or persons in question and have them critique your work.

"Is this what you're looking for?" you might ask. "Do you think any fields need to be there that aren't yet visible? Do you feel that the project is headed in the right direction?"

Nine times out of ten, these people will come back to you with a slew of suggestions, most of which have never occurred to you. If they have irreconcilable differences of opinion about the project, now is the time to find out. If they have some good ideas you never considered, now is the time to add them.

Now you also have your chance to let everyone know that after this point making major design changes may become impossible. Let everyone know that you're about to start doing the kind of detail work that is very hard to undo. If people need a day or two to think about your proposed design, give it to them. Making changes now, at the start, is better than after you have

```
TButton *EditBtn;
TButton *CancelBtn;
TMainMenu *MainMenu1;
TMenuItem *File1;
TMenuItem *PrintAddresses1;
TMenuItem *PrintPhoneOnly1;
TMenuItem *PrintEverything1;
TMenuItem *Print1;
TMenuItem *N1;
TMenuItem *Exit1;
TMenuItem *Edit1;
TMenuItem *Copy1;
TMenuItem *Cut1;
TMenuItem *Paste1;
TMenuItem *Options1;
TMenuItem *Search1;
TMenuItem *Filter1;
TMenuItem *Category1;
TMenuItem *Sorts1;
TMenuItem *FirstName1;
TMenuItem *LastName1;
TMenuItem *Company1;
TMenuItem *Colors1;
TMenuItem *FormColor1;
TMenuItem *EditColor1;
TMenuItem *EditText1;
TMenuItem *Labels1;
TMenuItem *Panels1;
TMenuItem *Marks1;
TMenuItem *MarkAll1;
TMenuItem *ClearAllMarks1;
TMenuItem *PrintMarkedtoFile1;
TMenuItem *Help1;
TMenuItem *About1;
TColorDialog *ColorDialog1;
TDBNavigator *DBNavigator1;
TStatusBar *StatusBar1;
TBevel *Bevel1;
TPanel *Panel1;
TLabel *Label2;
TLabel *Label3;
TLabel *Address1;
TLabel *Address2;
TLabel *City;
TLabel *State;
TLabel *Zip;
TLabel *Company;
TLabel *HPhone;
TLabel *WPhone;
TLabel *Fax;
TLabel *Comment;
TLabel *EMail1;
TLabel *Category;
TLabel *EMail2;
TSpeedButton *SpeedButton1;
TDBEdit *LNameEdit;
TDBEdit *FNameEdit;
```

continues

Listing 13.1. continued

```cpp
TDBEdit *Address1Edit;
TDBEdit *Address2Edit;
TDBEdit *CityEdit;
TDBEdit *StateEdit;
TDBEdit *ZipEdit;
TDBEdit *CompanyEdit;
TDBEdit *HomePhoneEdit;
TDBEdit *WorkPhoneEdit;
TDBEdit *FaxEdit;
TDBEdit *EMail1Edit;
TDBEdit *EMail2Edit;
TDBMemo *CommentMemo;
TDBLookupComboBox *CategoryCombo;
TButton *DeleteBtn;
TDBGrid *DBGrid1;
TMenuItem *FNameSearch;
TMenuItem *LNameSearch;
TMenuItem *CompanySearch;
TMenuItem *N3;
TMenuItem *System1;
TMenuItem *Defaults1;
TMenuItem *Blues1;
TMenuItem *N4;
TMenuItem *SaveCustom1;
TMenuItem *ReadCustom1;
TMenuItem *N2;
TMenuItem *ShowOnlyMarked1;
void __fastcall Copy1Click(TObject *Sender);
void __fastcall CommandClick(TObject *Sender);
void __fastcall AddressSourceStateChange(TObject *Sender);
void __fastcall FormShow(TObject *Sender);
void __fastcall About1Click(TObject *Sender);
void __fastcall CommandSortClick(TObject *Sender);
void __fastcall CommandSearchClick(TObject *Sender);
void __fastcall CommandColorClick(TObject *Sender);
void __fastcall System1Click(TObject *Sender);
void __fastcall Defaults1Click(TObject *Sender);
void __fastcall Blues1Click(TObject *Sender);
void __fastcall SaveCustom1Click(TObject *Sender);
void __fastcall ReadCustom1Click(TObject *Sender);
void __fastcall Filter1Click(TObject *Sender);
void __fastcall AddressSourceDataChange(TObject *Sender, TField *Field);
void __fastcall Category1Click(TObject *Sender);
void __fastcall MarkAll1Click(TObject *Sender);
void __fastcall ClearAllMarks1Click(TObject *Sender);
void __fastcall SpeedButton1Click(TObject *Sender);
void __fastcall FormDestroy(TObject *Sender);
void __fastcall ShowOnlyMarked1Click(TObject *Sender);
private:        // User declarations
AnsiString FCaptionString;
void DoSort(TObject *Sender);
void HandleEditMode();
void SetReadOnly(BOOL NewState);
void PrintData(TCommandType Command);
void SetEdits(TColor Color);
void SetEditText(TColor Color);
```

```
  void SetLabels(TColor Color);
  void SetPanels(TColor Color);
  TColor GetColor(TObject *Sender);
public:          // User declarations
  virtual __fastcall TForm1(TComponent* Owner);
};
//------------------------------------------------------------------------
extern TForm1 *Form1;
//------------------------------------------------------------------------
#endif
```

Listing 13.2. The main form for the Address2 program.

```
//////////////////////////////////////////
// File: Main.cpp
// Project: Address2
// Copyright (c) 1997 by Charlie Calvert
#include <vcl\vcl.h>
#include <vcl\clipbrd.hpp>
#include <vcl\registry.hpp>
#pragma hdrstop
#include "Main.h"
#include "DMod1.h"
#include "AboutBox1.h"
#include "FileDlg1.h"
#include "Category1.h"
#pragma resource "*.dfm"
TForm1 *Form1;
__fastcall TForm1::TForm1(TComponent* Owner)
  : TForm(Owner)
{
  FCaptionString = Caption;
  ReadCustom1Click(NULL);
}
void __fastcall TForm1::FormDestroy(TObject *Sender)
{
  SaveCustom1Click(NULL);
}
void TForm1::DoSort(TObject *Sender)
{
  switch (dynamic_cast<TComponent *>(Sender)->Tag)
  {
    case stFirst:
      DMod->AddressTable->IndexName = "FNameIndex";
      break;
    case stLast:
      DMod->AddressTable->IndexName = "LNameIndex";
      break;
    case stCompany:
      DMod->AddressTable->IndexName = "CompanyIndex";
      break;
  }
}
```

continues

Listing 13.2. continued

```cpp
void __fastcall TForm1::Copy1Click(TObject *Sender)
{
  if (dynamic_cast<TDBEdit*>(ActiveControl))
    (dynamic_cast<TDBEdit*>(ActiveControl))->CopyToClipboard();
  if (dynamic_cast<TDBMemo*>(ActiveControl))
    dynamic_cast<TDBMemo*>(ActiveControl)->CopyToClipboard();
  if (dynamic_cast<TDBComboBox*>(ActiveControl))
    Clipboard()->AsText = dynamic_cast<TDBComboBox*>(ActiveControl)->Text;
}
void __fastcall TForm1::CommandClick(TObject *Sender)
{
  switch (dynamic_cast<TComponent*>(Sender)->Tag)
  {
    case ctClose: Close(); break;
    case ctInsert: DMod->AddressTable->Insert(); break;
    case ctPrior: DMod->AddressTable->Prior(); break;
    case ctEdit: HandleEditMode(); break;
    case ctNext: DMod->AddressTable->Next(); break;
    case ctCancel: DMod->AddressTable->Cancel(); break;
    case ctPrint: PrintData(ctPrint); break;
    case ctFirst: DMod->AddressTable->First(); break;
    case ctLast: DMod->AddressTable->Last(); break;
    case ctPrintPhone: PrintData(ctPrintPhone); break;
    case ctPrintAddress: PrintData(ctPrintAddress); break;
    case ctPrintAll: PrintData(ctPrintAll); break;
    case ctDelete:
      AnsiString S = DMod->AddressTableLName->AsString;
      if (MessageBox(Handle, "Delete?", S.c_str(), MB_YESNO) == ID_YES)
        DMod->AddressTable->Delete();
      break;
  }
}
void TForm1::HandleEditMode()
{
  InsertBtn->Enabled = !DMod->AddressSource->AutoEdit;
  CancelBtn->Enabled = !DMod->AddressSource->AutoEdit;
  DeleteBtn->Enabled = !DMod->AddressSource->AutoEdit;
  if (!DMod->AddressSource->AutoEdit)
  {
    SetReadOnly(True);
    EditBtn->Caption = "Stop Edit";
    Caption = FCaptionString + EDIT_MODE_STRING;
  }
  else
  {
    if (DMod->AddressTable->State != dsBrowse)
      DMod->AddressTable->Post();
    SetReadOnly(False);
    EditBtn->Caption = "Goto Edit";
    Caption = FCaptionString + READ_ONLY_STRING;
  }
}
void TForm1::PrintData(TCommandType Command)
{

}
```

```
void TForm1::SetReadOnly(BOOL NewState)
{
  DMod->AddressSource->AutoEdit = NewState;
}
void __fastcall TForm1::AddressSourceStateChange(TObject *Sender)
{
  AnsiString S;
  switch (DMod->AddressTable->State)
  {
    case dsInactive:
      S = "Inactive";
      break;
    case dsBrowse:
      S = "Browse";
      break;
    case dsEdit:
      S = "Edit";
      break;
    case dsInsert:
      S = "Insert";
      break;
    case dsSetKey:
      S = "SetKey";
      break;
  }
  StatusBar1->SimpleText = "State: " + S;
}
void __fastcall TForm1::AddressSourceDataChange(TObject *Sender,
  TField *Field)
{
  HBITMAP BulbOn, BulbOff;
  Caption = DMod->AddressTable->FieldByName("Marked")->AsString;
  if (DMod->AddressTable->FieldByName("Marked")->AsBoolean)
  {
    BulbOn = LoadBitmap((HINSTANCE)HInstance, "BulbOn");
    SpeedButton1->Glyph->Handle = BulbOn;
  }
  else
  {
    BulbOff = LoadBitmap((HINSTANCE)HInstance, "BulbOff");
    SpeedButton1->Glyph->Handle = BulbOff;
  }
}
void __fastcall TForm1::SpeedButton1Click(TObject *Sender)
{
  DMod->AddressTable->Edit();
  DMod->AddressTableMarked->AsBoolean = !DMod->AddressTableMarked->AsBoolean;
  DMod->AddressTable->Post();
}
void __fastcall TForm1::FormShow(TObject *Sender)
{
  DMod->AddressSource->OnStateChange = AddressSourceStateChange;
  AddressSourceStateChange(NULL);
  DMod->AddressSource->OnDataChange = AddressSourceDataChange;
  AddressSourceDataChange(NULL, NULL);
}
```

continues

Listing 13.2. continued

```
void __fastcall TForm1::About1Click(TObject *Sender)
{
  AboutBox->ShowModal();
}
void __fastcall TForm1::CommandSortClick(TObject *Sender)
{
  DoSort(Sender);
  DMod->AddressTable->FindNearest(OPENARRAY(TVarRec, ("AAAA")));
}
void __fastcall TForm1::CommandSearchClick(TObject *Sender)
{
  AnsiString S;
  if (InputQuery("Search Dialog", "Enter Name", S))
  {
    DoSort(Sender);
    DMod->AddressTable->FindNearest(OPENARRAY(TVarRec, (S)));
  }
}
TColor TForm1::GetColor(TObject *Sender)
{
  switch (dynamic_cast<TComponent *>(Sender)->Tag)
  {
    case ccForm:
      return Form1->Color;
      break;
    case ccEdit:
      return FNameEdit->Color;
      break;
    case ccEditText:
      return FNameEdit->Font->Color;
      break;
    case ccLabel:
      return Label2->Color;
      break;
    case ccPanel:
      return Panel1->Color;
      break;
  }
}
void __fastcall TForm1::CommandColorClick(TObject *Sender)
{
  ColorDialog1->Color = GetColor(Sender);
  if (!ColorDialog1->Execute())
    return;
  switch (dynamic_cast<TComponent *>(Sender)->Tag)
  {
    case ccForm:
      Form1->Color = ColorDialog1->Color;
      break;
    case ccEdit:
      SetEdits(ColorDialog1->Color);
      break;
    case ccEditText:
      SetEditText(ColorDialog1->Color);
      break;
    case ccLabel:
```

```
          SetLabels(ColorDialog1->Color);
          break;
        case ccPanel:
          SetPanels(ColorDialog1->Color);
          break;
  }
}
void TForm1::SetEdits(TColor Color)
{
  int i;
  for (i = 0; i < ComponentCount; i++)
  {
    if (dynamic_cast<TDBEdit *>(Components[i]))
     dynamic_cast<TDBEdit *>(Components[i])->Color = Color;
    else if (dynamic_cast<TDBGrid *>(Components[i]))
      dynamic_cast<TDBGrid *>(Components[i])->Color = Color;
    else if (dynamic_cast<TDBMemo *>(Components[i]))
      dynamic_cast<TDBMemo *>(Components[i])->Color = Color;
    else if (dynamic_cast<TDBLookupComboBox *>(Components[i]))
      dynamic_cast<TDBLookupComboBox *>(Components[i])->Color = Color;
  }
}
void TForm1::SetEditText(TColor Color)
{
  int i;
  for (i = 0; i < ComponentCount; i++)
  {
    if (dynamic_cast<TDBEdit *>(Components[i]))
      dynamic_cast<TDBEdit *>(Components[i])->Font->Color = Color;
    else if (dynamic_cast<TDBGrid *>(Components[i]))
      dynamic_cast<TDBGrid *>(Components[i])->Font->Color = Color;
    else if (dynamic_cast<TDBMemo *>(Components[i]))
      dynamic_cast<TDBMemo *>(Components[i])->Font->Color = Color;
    else if (dynamic_cast<TDBLookupComboBox *>(Components[i]))
      dynamic_cast<TDBLookupComboBox *>(Components[i])->Font->Color = Color;
  }
}
void TForm1::SetLabels(TColor Color)
{
  int i;
  for (i = 0; i < ComponentCount; i++)
   if (dynamic_cast<TLabel *>(Components[i]))
     dynamic_cast<TLabel *>(Components[i])->Font->Color = Color;
}
void TForm1::SetPanels(TColor Color)
{
  int i;
  for (i = 0; i < ComponentCount; i++)
   if (dynamic_cast<TPanel *>(Components[i]))
     dynamic_cast<TPanel *>(Components[i])->Color = Color;
}
void __fastcall TForm1::System1Click(TObject *Sender)
{
  SetEdits(clWindow);
  SetEditText(clBlack);
```

continues

Listing 13.2. continued

```cpp
  SetLabels(clBlack);
  SetPanels(clBtnFace);
  Form1->Color = clBtnFace;
}
void __fastcall TForm1::Defaults1Click(TObject *Sender)
{
  SetEdits(clNavy);
  SetEditText(clYellow);
  SetLabels(clBlack);
  SetPanels(clBtnFace);
  Form1->Color = clBtnFace;
}
void __fastcall TForm1::Blues1Click(TObject *Sender)
{
  SetEdits(0x00FF8080);
  SetEditText(clBlack);
  SetLabels(clBlack);
  SetPanels(0x00FF0080);
  Form1->Color = clBlue;
}
void __fastcall TForm1::SaveCustom1Click(TObject *Sender)
{
  TRegIniFile *RegFile = new TRegIniFile("SOFTWARE\\Charlie's Stuff\\Address2");
  RegFile->WriteInteger("Colors", "Form", Form1->Color);
  RegFile->WriteInteger("Colors", "Edit Text", FNameEdit->Font->Color);
  RegFile->WriteInteger("Colors", "Panels", Panel1->Color);
  RegFile->WriteInteger("Colors", "Labels", Label2->Font->Color);
  RegFile->WriteInteger("Colors", "Edits", FNameEdit->Color);
  RegFile->Free();
}
void __fastcall TForm1::ReadCustom1Click(TObject *Sender)
{
  TColor Color = RGB(0,0,255);
  TRegIniFile *RegFile = new TRegIniFile("SOFTWARE\\Charlie's Stuff\\Address2");
  Form1->Color = RegFile->ReadInteger("Colors", "Form", Color);
  Color = RegFile->ReadInteger("Colors", "Edit Text", Color);
  SetEditText(Color);
  Color = RegFile->ReadInteger("Colors", "Panels", Color);
  SetPanels(Color);
  Color = RegFile->ReadInteger("Colors", "Labels", Color);
  SetLabels(Color);
  Color = RegFile->ReadInteger("Colors", "Edits", Color);
  SetEdits(Color);
  RegFile->Free();
}
void __fastcall TForm1::Filter1Click(TObject *Sender)
{
  AnsiString S;
  if (Filter1->Caption == "Filter")
  {
    if (FilterDlg->ShowModal() == mrOk)
    {
      S = DMod->CatsTableCATEGORY->Value;
      if (S.Length() == 0)
        return;
      Filter1->Caption = "Cancel Filter";
```

```
                DMod->AddressTable->IndexName = "CategoryIndex";
                DMod->AddressTable->SetRange(OPENARRAY(TVarRec, (S)), OPENARRAY(TVarRec,
                                     (S)));
    }
  }
  else
  {
     Filter1->Caption = "Filter";
     DMod->AddressTable->CancelRange();
  }
}
void __fastcall TForm1::Category1Click(TObject *Sender)
{
  CategoryDlg = new TCategoryDlg(this);
  CategoryDlg->ShowModal();
  CategoryDlg->Free();
}
void __fastcall TForm1::MarkAll1Click(TObject *Sender)
{
  DMod->ChangeMarked(True);
}
void __fastcall TForm1::ClearAllMarks1Click(TObject *Sender)
{
  DMod->ChangeMarked(False);
}
void __fastcall TForm1::ShowOnlyMarked1Click(TObject *Sender)
{
  ShowOnlyMarked1->Checked = !ShowOnlyMarked1->Checked;
  DMod->AddressTable->Filtered = ShowOnlyMarked1->Checked;
}
```

Listing 13.3. The header for the TDataModule for the Address2 program.

```
////////////////////////////////////
// File: DMod1.h
// Project: Address2
// Copyright (c) 1997 by Charlie Calvert
#ifndef DMod1H
#define DMod1H
#include <vcl\Classes.hpp>
#include <vcl\Controls.hpp>
#include <vcl\StdCtrls.hpp>
#include <vcl\Forms.hpp>
#include <vcl\DBTables.hpp>
#include <vcl\DB.hpp>
class TDMod : public TDataModule
{
__published:    // IDE-managed Components
  TTable *AddressTable;
  TStringField *AddressTableFName;
  TStringField *AddressTableLName;
  TStringField *AddressTableCompany;
  TStringField *AddressTableAddress1;
```

continues

Listing 13.3. continued

```
  TStringField *AddressTableAddress2;
  TStringField *AddressTableCity;
  TStringField *AddressTableState;
  TStringField *AddressTableZip;
  TStringField *AddressTableCountry;
  TStringField *AddressTableHPhone;
  TStringField *AddressTableWPhone;
  TStringField *AddressTableFax;
  TStringField *AddressTableEMail1;
  TStringField *AddressTableEMail2;
  TStringField *AddressTableCategory;
  TBooleanField *AddressTableMarked;
  TStringField *AddressTableFirstLast;
  TStringField *AddressTableCityStateZip;
  TMemoField *AddressTableComment;
  TDataSource *AddressSource;
  TTable *CatsTable;
  TDataSource *CatsSource;
  TStringField *CatsTableCATEGORY;
  TQuery *ChangeMarkedQuery;
  void __fastcall AddressTableCalcFields(TDataSet *DataSet);
  void __fastcall AddressTableFilterRecord(TDataSet *DataSet, bool &Accept);
private:        // User declarations
public:         // User declarations
  virtual __fastcall TDMod(TComponent* Owner);
  void ChangeMarked(BOOL NewValue);
};
extern TDMod *DMod;
#endif
```

Listing 13.4. The code for the data module of the Address2 program.

```
///////////////////////////////////////
// File: DMod1.cpp
// Project: Address2
// Copyright (c) 1997 by Charlie Calvert
#include <vcl\vcl.h>
#pragma hdrstop
#include "DMod1.h"
#pragma resource "*.dfm"
TDMod *DMod;
__fastcall TDMod::TDMod(TComponent* Owner)
  : TDataModule(Owner)
{
  AddressTable->Open();
  CatsTable->Open();
}
void __fastcall TDMod::AddressTableCalcFields(TDataSet *DataSet)
{
  if ((!AddressTableFName->IsNull) || (!AddressTableLName->IsNull))
    AddressTableFirstLast->Value =
      AddressTableFName->Value + " " + AddressTableLName->Value;
```

```
  else if (!AddressTableCompany->IsNull)
    AddressTableFirstLast->Value = AddressTableCompany->Value;
  else
    AddressTableFirstLast->Value = "Blank Record";
}
void TDMod::ChangeMarked(BOOL NewValue)
{
  ChangeMarkedQuery->Close();
  if (NewValue)
    ChangeMarkedQuery->ParamByName("NewValue")->AsString = "T";
  else
    ChangeMarkedQuery->ParamByName("NewValue")->AsString = "F";
  ChangeMarkedQuery->ExecSQL();
  AddressTable->Refresh();
}
void __fastcall TDMod::AddressTableFilterRecord(TDataSet *DataSet,
  bool &Accept)
{
  Accept = (AddressTableMarked->AsBoolean == True);
}
```

Listing 13.5. The `FilterDialog` has very little code in it.

```
/////////////////////////////////////////
// File: FileDlg1.cpp
// Project: Address2
// Copyright (c) 1997 by Charlie Calvert
//
#include <vcl\vcl.h>
#pragma hdrstop
#include "FileDlg1.h"
#include "DMod1.h"
#pragma resource "*.dfm"
TFilterDlg *FilterDlg;

__fastcall TFilterDlg::TFilterDlg(TComponent* Owner)
  : TForm(Owner)
{
}
```

Listing 13.6. The Category dialog allows the user to edit the list of categories.

```
#include <vcl\vcl.h>
#pragma hdrstop
#include "Category1.h"
#include "DMod1.h"
#pragma resource "*.dfm"
TCategoryDlg *CategoryDlg;
__fastcall TCategoryDlg::TCategoryDlg(TComponent* Owner)
  : TForm(Owner)
{
}
```

continues

Listing 13.6. continued

```cpp
void __fastcall TCategoryDlg::HelpBtnClick(TObject *Sender)
{
  AnsiString S =
    "'Twas brillig, and the slithy toves\r"
    "Did gyre and gimble in the wabe;\r"
    "All mimsy were the borogoves,\r"
    "And the mome raths outgabe.\r"
    "Beware the Jabberwock, my son!\r"
    "The jaws that bite, the claws that catch!\r"
    "Beware the Jubjub bird, and shun\r"
    "The frumious Bandersnatch!\r"
    "He took his vorpal sword in hand:\r"
    "Long time the manxome foe he sought--\r"
    "So rested he by the Tumtum tree,\r"
    "And stood a while in thought\r"
    "And as in uffish though he stood,\r"
    "The Jabberwock, with eyes of flame,\r"
    "Came whiffling through the tulgey wood,\r"
    "And burbled as he came!\r"
    "One, two!, One, two! And through and through\r"
    "The vorpal blade went snicker-snack!\r"
    "He left it dead, and with its head\r"
    "He went galumphing back.\r"
    "And hast thou slain the Jabberwock!\r"
    "Come to my arms, my beamish boy!\r"
    "Oh frabjous day! Callooh! Callay!\r"
    "He chortled in his joy.\r"
    "'Twas brillig, and the slithy toves\r"
    "Did gyre and gimble in the wabe;\r"
    "All mimsy were the borogoves,\r"
    "And the mome raths outgabe.\r"
    "-- Lewis Carroll (1832-98)";
  ShowMessage(S);
}
```

Listing 13.7. The AboutDlg is a no-brainer. You don't need to add any code to the default output generated by BCB.

```cpp
//////////////////////////////////////
// File: AboutBox1.cpp
// Project: Address2
// Copyright (c) 1997 by Charlie Calvert
#include <vcl.h>
#pragma hdrstop
#include "AboutBox1.h"
#pragma resource "*.dfm"
TAboutBox *AboutBox;
__fastcall TAboutBox::TAboutBox(TComponent* AOwner)
: TForm(AOwner)
{
}
```

The special forms included in Listings 13.1 through 13.7 are the `FilterDlg` and `AboutBox`. My feeling is that you can readily grasp the concepts of these forms from just looking at the screen shots of them, shown in Figures 13.4, 13.5, and 13.6.

FIGURE 13.4.

The FilterDlg from the Address2 program.

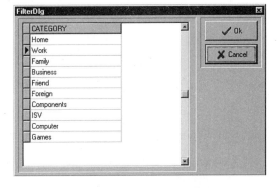

FIGURE 13.5.

The help screen from the Category dialog.

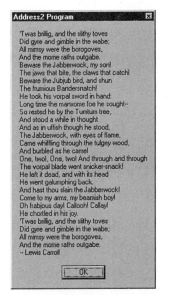

FIGURE 13.6.

The About box from the Address2 program.

The complete sample program, including all the forms shown here, is included on the CD that accompanies this book. You will probably find it helpful to load that program into BCB and refer to it from time to time while reading the various technical discussions in the last half of this chapter.

Moving In and Out of Read-Only Mode

Perhaps the most important single function of the Address2 program is its capability to move in and out of read-only mode. This capability is valuable because it enables the user to open the program and browse through data without ever having to worry about accidentally altering a record. In fact, when the user first opens the program, typing into any of the data-aware controls should be impossible. The only way for the program to get into edit mode is for the user to click the Goto Edit button, which then automatically makes the data live.

When the program is in read-only mode, the Insert and Cancel buttons are grayed, and the Delete button is also dimmed. When the user switches into edit mode, all these controls become live, and the text in the Goto Edit button is changed so that it reads "Stop Edit". In other words, the caption for the Edit button says either Goto Edit or Stop Edit, depending on whether you are in read-only mode. I also use red and green colored bitmaps to help emphasize the current mode and its capabilities. All these visual clues help make the current mode of the program obvious to the user.

The functionality described is quite simple to implement. The key methods to trace are the HandleEditMode and SetReadOnly methods.

The HandleEditMode routine is called from the CommandClick method described in the preceding section:

```
void TForm1::HandleEditMode()
{
  InsertBtn->Enabled = !DMod->AddressSource->AutoEdit;
  CancelBtn->Enabled = !DMod->AddressSource->AutoEdit;
  DeleteBtn->Enabled = !DMod->AddressSource->AutoEdit;
  if (!DMod->AddressSource->AutoEdit)
  {
    SetReadOnly(True);
    EditBtn->Caption = "Stop Edit";
    Caption = FCaptionString + EDIT_MODE_STRING;
  }
  else
  {
    if (DMod->AddressTable->State != dsBrowse)
      DMod->AddressTable->Post();
    SetReadOnly(False);
    EditBtn->Caption = "Goto Edit";
    Caption = FCaptionString + READ_ONLY_STRING;
  }
}
```

The primary purpose of this code is to ensure that the proper components are enabled or disabled, depending on the current state of the program. After you alter the appearance of the program, the code calls SetReadOnly:

```
void TForm1::SetReadOnly(BOOL NewState)
{
  DMod->AddressSource->AutoEdit = NewState;
}
```

The center around which this routine revolves is the AddressSource->AutoEdit property. When this property is set to False, all the data-aware controls on the form are disabled, as shown in Figure 13.7, and the user cannot type in them. When the property is set to True, the data becomes live, as shown in Figure 13.8, and the user can edit or insert records.

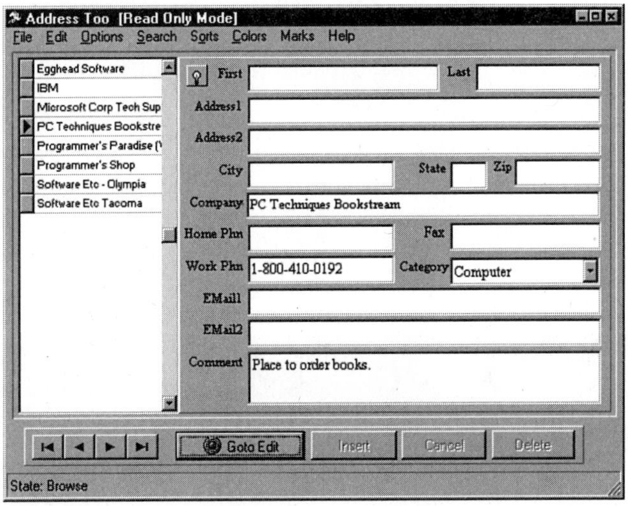

FIGURE 13.7.

Address2 as it appears in read-only mode.

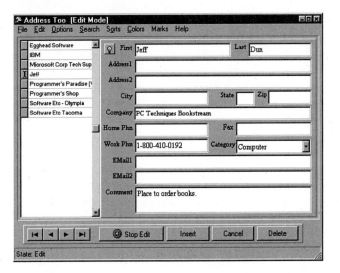

FIGURE 13.8.

The Address2 program as it appears in edit mode.

The purpose of the AutoEdit property is to determine whether a keystroke from the user can put a table directly into edit mode. When AutoEdit is set to False, the user can't type information into a data-aware control. When AutoEdit is set to True, the user can switch the table into edit mode simply by typing a letter in a control. Note that even when AutoEdit is set to False, you can set a table into edit mode by calling AddressTable->Edit or AddressTable->Insert. As a result, the technique shown here won't work unless you gray out the controls that give the user the power to set the table into edit mode. You should also be sure to set the dgEditing element of the TDBGrids option property to False so that the user can never type anything in this control. The grid is simply not meant for allowing the user to modify records.

The code in the HandleEditMode method is concerned entirely with interface issues. For instance, it enables or disables the Insert, Cancel, and Delete controls, depending on whether the table is about to go in or out of read-only mode. The code also ensures that the caption for the Edit button provides the user with a clue about the button's current function. In other words, the button doesn't report on the state of the program, but on the functionality associated with the button.

The HandleEditMode method is written so that the program is always moved into the opposite of its current state. At start-up time, the table should be set to read-only mode (AutoEdit = False), and the appropriate controls should be disabled. Thereafter, every time you click the Edit button, the program will switch from its current state to the opposite state, from read-only mode to edit mode, and then back again.

NOTE

In addition to the TDataSource AutoEdit property, you can also take a table in and out of read-only mode in a second way. This second method is really more powerful than the first because it makes the table itself completely resistant to change. However, this second method is more costly in terms of time and system resources. The trick, naturally enough, is to change the ReadOnly property of a TTable component.

You cannot set a table in or out of read-only mode while it is open. Therefore, you have to close the table every time you change the ReadOnly property. Unfortunately, every time you close and open a table, you are moved back to the first record. As a result, you need to set a bookmark identifying your current location in the table, close the table, and then move the table in or out of read-only mode. When you are done, you can open the table and jet back to the bookmark. This process sounds like quite a bit of activity, but in fact it can usually be accomplished without the user being aware that anything untoward has occurred.

With the Address2 program, clearly the first technique for moving a program in and out of read-only mode is best. In other words, switching DataSource1 in and out of AutoEdit mode is much faster and much easier than switching AddressTable in and out of read-only mode.

On the whole, the act of moving Address2 in and out of read-only mode is fairly trivial. The key point to grasp is the power of the TDataSource AutoEdit method. If you understand how it works, you can provide this same functionality in all your programs.

Sorting Data

At various times, you might want the records stored in the program to be sorted by first name, last name, or company. These three possible options are encapsulated in the program's menu, as depicted in Figure 13.9, and also in an enumerated type declared in Main.h:

```
enum TSearchSortType {stFirst, stLast, stCompany};
```

FIGURE 13.9.

The Sorts menu has three different options.

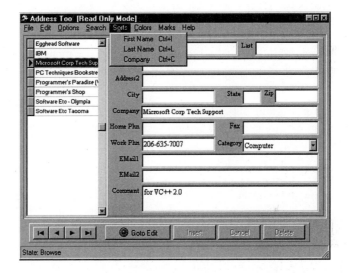

Once again, the Tag field from the Sorts drop-down menu makes it possible to detect which option the user wants to select:

```
void TForm1::DoSort(TObject *Sender)
{
  switch (dynamic_cast<TComponent *>(Sender)->Tag)
  {
    case stFirst:
      DMod->AddressTable->IndexName = "FNameIndex";
      break;
    case stLast:
      DMod->AddressTable->IndexName = "LNameIndex";
      break;
    case stCompany:
      DMod->AddressTable->IndexName = "CompanyIndex";
      break;
  }
}
```

13

FLAT-FILE, REAL-WORLD DATABASES

If the user selects the menu option for sorting on the first name, then the first element in the switch statement is selected; if the user opts to sort on the last name, then the second element is selected, and so on.

Here is another way to state the same process: If the Tag property for a menu item is zero, it is translated into stFirst; if the property is one, it goes to stLast, and two goes to stCompany. Everything depends on the order in which the elements of the enumerated type are declared in the declaration for TSearchSortType. Of course, you must associate a different value between 0 and 2 for the Tag property of each menu item and then associate the following method with the OnClick event for each menu item:

```
void __fastcall TForm1::CommandSortClick(TObject *Sender)
{
  DoSort(Sender);
  DMod->AddressTable->FindNearest(OPENARRAY(TVarRec, ("A")));
}
```

The CommandSortClick method receives input from the menus. After finding out whether the user wants to sort by first name, last name, or company, CommandSortClick asks DoSort to straighten out the indexes.

After sorting, a group of blank records might appear at the beginning of the table. For example, if you choose to sort by the Company field, many of the records in the Address table are not likely to have anything in the Company field. As a result, several hundred, or even several thousand, records at the beginning of the table might be of no interest to someone who wants to view only companies. The solution, of course, is to search for the first record that has a non-blank value in the Company field. You can do so by using FindNearest to search for the record that has a Company field that is nearest to matching the string "A". The actual details of searching for a record are covered in the next section. The downside of this process is that the cursor moves off the currently selected record whenever you sort.

That's all there is to sorting the records in the Address2 program. Clearly, this subject is not difficult. The key points to grasp are that you must create secondary indexes for all the fields on which you want to sort, and then performing the sort becomes as simple as swapping indexes.

Searching for Data

Searching for data in a table is a straightforward process. If you want to search on the Company field, simply declaring a secondary index called CompanyIndex is not enough. To perform an actual search, you must make the CompanyIndex the active index and then perform the search. As a result, before you can make a search, you must do three things:

1. Ask the user for the string he or she wants to find.
2. Ask the user for the field where the string resides.
3. Set the index to the proper field.

Only after jumping through each of these hoops are you free to perform the actual search.

I use the same basic algorithm in the Search portion of the program as I do in the infrastructure for the sort procedure. The search method itself is simple enough:

```
void __fastcall TForm1::CommandSearchClick(TObject *Sender)
{
  AnsiString S;
  if (InputQuery("Search Dialog", "Enter Name", S))
  {
    DoSort(Sender);
    DMod->AddressTable->FindNearest(OPENARRAY(TVarRec, (S)));
  }
}
```

This code retrieves the relevant string to search on from a simple `InputQuery` dialog. `InputQuery` is a built-in VCL function that pops up a dialog with an edit field in it. The first field of the call to `InputQuery` defines the title of the dialog, the second contains the prompt string, and the third contains the string you want the user to edit.

After you get the search string from the user, the `DoSort` method is called to set up the indexes, and then the search is performed using `FindNearest`. The assumption, of course, is that the menu items appear in the same order as those for the sort process, and they have the same tags associated with them.

Once again, the actual code for searching for data is fairly straightforward. The key to making this process as simple as possible is setting up the `DoSort` routine so that it can be used by both the Sorting and Searching portions of the program.

Filtering Data

The Address2 program performs two different filtering chores. The first involves allowing the user to see the set of records that fits in a particular category. For example, if you have set the `Category` field in 20 records to the string `"Friend"`, then you can reasonably expect to be able to filter out all other records that do not contain the word `"Friend"` in the `Category` field. After you have this process in place, you can ask the database to show you all the records that contain information about computers or work or local business, and so on.

The second technique for filtering in the Address2 program involves the Marked field. You might, for example, first use the Filter Category technique to show only the records of your friends. Let's pretend you're popular, so this list contains 50 people. You can then use the Marked field to single out 10 of these records as containing the names of people you want to invite to a party. After marking the appropriate records, you can then filter on them so that the database now contains only the lists of your friends who have been "marked" as invited to the party. In the chapter on printing, you will see how to print this list on a set of labels. (If the "Friends" example is too unbearably warm and cozy for you, you can think instead of sorting on the list of clients who use a particular product and then marking only those you want to receive a special mailing.)

In the next few paragraphs, I will tackle the Category filter first and then explain how to filter on the Boolean Marked field.

Setting up a filter and performing a search are similar tasks. The first step is to find out the category the user wants to use as a filter. To do so, you can pop up a dialog that displays the CATS table to the user. The user can then select a category and click the OK button. You don't need to write any custom code for this dialog. Everything can be taken care of by the visual tools.

Here is how to handle the process back in the main form:

```
void __fastcall TForm1::Filter1Click(TObject *Sender)
{
  AnsiString S;
  if (Filter1->Caption == "Filter")
  {
    if (FilterDlg->ShowModal() == mrOk)
    {
      S = DMod->CatsTableCATEGORY->Value;
      if (S.Length() == 0)
        return;
      Filter1->Caption = "Cancel Filter";
      DMod->AddressTable->IndexName = "CategoryIndex";
      DMod->AddressTable->SetRange(OPENARRAY(TVarRec, (S)), OPENARRAY(TVarRec,
```

```
    (S)));
    }
  }
  else
  {
    Filter1->Caption = "Filter";
    DMod->AddressTable->CancelRange();
  }
}
```

This code changes the Caption of the menu item associated with filtering the Category field. If the Address table is not currently filtered, then the menu reads "Filter". If the table is filtered, then the menu reads "Cancel Filter". Therefore, the preceding code has two sections: one for starting the filter and the second for canceling the filter. The second part is too simple to merit further discussion, as you can see from a glance at the last two lines of written code in the method.

After allowing the user to select a category on which to search, the Address2 program sets up the CategoryIndex and then performs a normal filter operation:

```
DMod->AddressTable->IndexName = "CategoryIndex";
DMod->AddressTable->SetRange(OPENARRAY(TVarRec, (S)), OPENARRAY(TVarRec, (S)));
```

This simple process lets you narrow the number of records displayed at any one time. The key point to remember is that this whole process works only because the user enters data in the Category field by selecting strings from a drop-down combo box. Without the TDBComboBox, the number of options in the Category field would likely become unmanageable.

Marking Files

The Marked field in this table is declared to be of type Boolean. (Remember that one of the fields of ADDRESS.DB is actually called Marked. In the first sentence, therefore, I'm not referring to an attribute of a field, but to its name.)

On the main form for the program is a TSpeedButton component that shows a switched-on light bulb if a field is marked and a switched-off light bulb if a field is not marked. When the user scrolls up and down through the dataset, the light bulb switches on and off depending on whether a field is marked.

Here is a method for showing the user whether the Boolean Marked field is set to True or False:

```
void __fastcall TForm1::AddressSourceDataChange(TObject *Sender,
  TField *Field)
{
  HBITMAP BulbOn, BulbOff;
  if (DMod->AddressTable->FieldByName("Marked")->AsBoolean)
  {
    BulbOn = LoadBitmap((HINSTANCE)HInstance, "BulbOn");
    SpeedButton1->Glyph->Handle = BulbOn;
  }
  else
  {
```

```
    BulbOff = LoadBitmap((HINSTANCE)HInstance, "BulbOff");
    SpeedButton1->Glyph->Handle = BulbOff;
  }
}
```

If the field is marked, a bitmap called BulbOn is loaded from one of the program's two resource files. This bitmap is then assigned to the Glyph field of a TSpeedButton. If the Marked field is set to False, a second bitmap is loaded and shown in the TSpeedButton. The bitmaps give a visual signal to the user as to whether the record is marked.

As I hinted in the preceding paragraph, the Address2 program has two resource files. The first is the standard resource file, which holds the program's icon. The second is a custom resource build from the following RC file:

```
BulbOn BITMAP "BULBON.BMP"
BulbOff BITMAP "BULBOFF.BMP"
```

This file is called BITS.RC, and it compiles to BITS.RES. You should add BITS.RC to your project to make sure that the file is compiled automatically and that it is linked into your program. Delphi programmers take note: The automating of this process is a feature added to BCB that is not present in Delphi!

Here are the changes the IDE makes to the Project Source file for your application:

```
//---------------------------------------------------------------
#include <vcl\vcl.h>
#pragma hdrstop
//---------------------------------------------------------------
USEFORM("Main.cpp", Form1);
USEDATAMODULE("DMod1.cpp", DMod);
USERES("Address2.res");
USEFORM("AboutBox1.cpp", AboutBox);
USEFORM("FileDlg1.cpp", FilterDlg);
USEFORM("Category1.cpp", CategoryDlg);
USERC("glyphs.rc");
```

The relevant line here is the last one. Note that you can get to the Project Source by choosing View | Project Source from the BCB menu.

The AddressSourceDataChanged method shown previously in this section is a delegated event handler for the AddressSource component in the data module. The interesting point here, of course, is that AddressSource is located in Form1, not in DMod1.

To associate a method from Form1 with an event located in DMod1, you can write the following code in response to the OnShow event for Form1:

```
void __fastcall TForm1::FormShow(TObject *Sender)
{
  DMod->AddressSource->OnStateChange = AddressSourceStateChange;
  AddressSourceStateChange(NULL);
  DMod->AddressSource->OnDataChange = AddressSourceDataChange;
  AddressSourceDataChange(NULL, NULL);
}
```

As you can see, I set up two event handlers, one for the OnStateChange event and the other for the OnDataChange event. Now these methods will be called automatically when changes occur in the data module.

> **NOTE**
>
> I suppose you could argue whether the code from the FormShow event handler is an example of good or bad coding practices. On the one hand, it seems to tie TForm1 and TDMod together with rather unseemly intimacy, but on the other hand, it does so by working with a published interface of TDMod. The key points in favor of it being good code are that you can safely decouple TDMod from TForm1 without impairing the integrity or virtue of TDMod. Furthermore, TForm1 uses only the published interface of TDMod and does not require carnal knowledge of the most intimate parts of TDMod. (Perhaps if I push this metaphor just a little further, I can be the first technical writer to get involved in a censorship dispute. On the other hand, that's probably not such a worthy goal, so I'll discreetly end the note here.)

Whenever the user toggles the TSpeedButton on which the BulbOn and BulbOff bitmaps are displayed, then the logical Marked field in the database is toggled:

```
void __fastcall TForm1::SpeedButton1Click(TObject *Sender)
{
  DMod->AddressTable->Edit();
  DMod->AddressTableMarked->AsBoolean = !DMod->AddressTableMarked->AsBoolean;
  DMod->AddressTable->Post();
}
```

Note that this code never checks the value of the Marked field—it just sets that value to the opposite of its current state.

The program allows the user to show only the records that are currently marked. This filter can be applied on top of the Category filter or can be applied on a dataset that it is not filtered at all:

```
void __fastcall TForm1::ShowOnlyMarked1Click(TObject *Sender)
{
  ShowOnlyMarked1->Checked = !ShowOnlyMarked1->Checked;
  DMod->AddressTable->Filtered = ShowOnlyMarked1->Checked;
}
```

The preceding code sets the AddressTable into Filtered mode. The OnFilterRecordEvent for the table, which is in the DMod1 unit, looks like this:

```
void __fastcall TDMod::AddressTableFilterRecord(TDataSet *DataSet,
  bool &Accept)
{
  Accept = (AddressTableMarked->AsBoolean == True);
}
```

Only the records that have the Marked field set to be True will pass through this filter. If the table is filtered, therefore, only those records that are marked are visible to the user.

If you give the user the ability to mark records, then you also probably should give him or her the ability to clear all the marks in the program, or to mark all the records in the current dataset and then possibly unmark a few key records. For example, you might want to send a notice to all your friends, except those who live out of town. To do so, you can first mark the names of all your friends and then unmark the names of those who live in distant places.

The data module for the Address2 program contains a query with the following SQL statement:

```
Update Address
  Set Marked = :NewValue
```

This statement does not have a where clause to specify which records in the Marked field you want to toggle. As a result, the code will change all the records in the database with one stroke. Note how much more efficient this method is than iterating through all the records of a table with a while (!Table1->Eof) loop.

To use this SQL statement, you can write the following code:

```
void TDMod::ChangeMarked(BOOL NewValue)
{
  ChangeMarkedQuery->Close();
  if (NewValue)
    ChangeMarkedQuery->ParamByName("NewValue")->AsString = "T";
  else
    ChangeMarkedQuery->ParamByName("NewValue")->AsString = "F";
  ChangeMarkedQuery->ExecSQL();
  AddressTable->Refresh();
}
```

This method sets the "NewValue" field of the query to T or F, depending on how the method is called.

The following self-explanatory method responds to a menu click and uses the ChangeMarked method:

```
void __fastcall TForm1::ClearAllMarks1Click(TObject *Sender)
{
  DMod->ChangeMarked(False);
}
```

That's all I'm going to say about the filters in this program. This subject, like the searching and sorting topics, is extremely easy to master. One of the points of this chapter is how easily you can harness the power of BCB to write great code that produces small, easy-to-use, robust applications.

Setting Colors

Using the Colors menu, shown in Figure 13.10, you can set the colors for most of the major objects in the program. The goal is not to give the user complete control over every last detail in the program, but to let him or her customize the most important features. Even if you're not interested in giving the user the ability to customize colors in your application, you may still be interested in this section because I discuss Run Time Type Information (RTTI), as well as a method for iterating over all the components on a form.

FIGURE 13.10.

The options under the Colors menu enable you to change the appearance of the Address2 program.

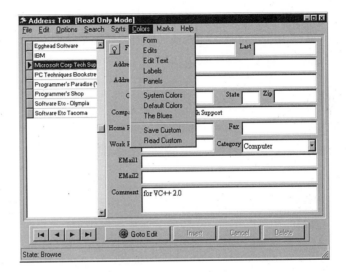

The `ColorClick` method uses the time-honored method of declaring an enumerated type and then sets up the `Tag` property from a menu item to specify the selection of a particular option. Here is the enumerated type in question:

```
enum TColorType {ccForm, ccEdit, ccEditText, ccLabel, ccPanel};
```

The routine begins by enabling the user to select a color from the Colors dialog and then assigns that color to the appropriate controls:

```
void __fastcall TForm1::CommandColorClick(TObject *Sender)
{
  ColorDialog1->Color = GetColor(Sender);
  if (!ColorDialog1->Execute())
    return;
  switch (dynamic_cast<TComponent *>(Sender)->Tag)
  {
    case ccForm:
      Form1->Color = ColorDialog1->Color;
      break;
```

```
      case ccEdit:
        SetEdits(ColorDialog1->Color);
        break;
      case ccEditText:
        SetEditText(ColorDialog1->Color);
        break;
      case ccLabel:
        SetLabels(ColorDialog1->Color);
        break;
      case ccPanel:
        SetPanels(ColorDialog1->Color);
        break;
    }
}
```

If the user wants to change the form's color, the code to do so is simple enough:

```
Form1->Color = ColorDialog1->Color;
```

However, changing the color of all the data-aware controls is a more complicated process. To accomplish this goal, the ColorClick method calls the SetEdits routine:

```
void TForm1::SetEdits(TColor Color)
{
  int i;
  for (i = 0; i < ComponentCount; i++)
  {
    if (dynamic_cast<TDBEdit *>(Components[i]))
      dynamic_cast<TDBEdit *>(Components[i])->Color = Color;
    else if (dynamic_cast<TDBGrid *>(Components[i]))
      dynamic_cast<TDBGrid *>(Components[i])->Color = Color;
    else if (dynamic_cast<TDBMemo *>(Components[i]))
      dynamic_cast<TDBMemo *>(Components[i])->Color = Color;
    else if (dynamic_cast<TDBLookupComboBox *>(Components[i]))
      dynamic_cast<TDBLookupComboBox *>(Components[i])->Color = Color;
  }
}
```

This code iterates though all the components belonging to the main form of the program and checks to see if any of them are TDBEdits, TDBComboBoxes, or TDBMemos. When it finds a hit, the code casts the control as a TDBEdit and sets its color to the new value selected by the user:

```
dynamic_cast<TDBEdit *>(Components[i])->Color = Color;
```

Because this code searches for TDBEdits, TDBMemos, and TDBGrids, it will very quickly change all the data-aware controls on the form to a new color. Note that you need to check whether the dynamic cast will succeed before attempting to change the features of the controls. If you try to do it all in one step, an access violation will occur.

The code for setting labels and panels works exactly the same way as the code for the data-aware controls. The only difference is that you don't need to worry about looking for multiple types of components:

```
void TForm1::SetLabels(TColor Color)
{
```

```
    int i;
    for (i = 0; i < ComponentCount; i++)
     if (dynamic_cast<TLabel *>(Components[i]))
       dynamic_cast<TLabel *>(Components[i])->Font->Color = Color;
}
void TForm1::SetPanels(TColor Color)
{
    int i;
    for (i = 0; i < ComponentCount; i++)
     if (dynamic_cast<TPanel *>(Components[i]))
       dynamic_cast<TPanel *>(Components[i])->Color = Color;
}
```

After you set up a set of routines like this, you can write a few custom routines that quickly set all the colors in the program to certain predefined values:

```
void __fastcall TForm1::System1Click(TObject *Sender)
{
  SetEdits(clWindow);
  SetEditText(clBlack);
  SetLabels(clBlack);
  SetPanels(clBtnFace);
  Form1->Color = clBtnFace;
}
void __fastcall TForm1::Defaults1Click(TObject *Sender)
{
  SetEdits(clNavy);
  SetEditText(clYellow);
  SetLabels(clBlack);
  SetPanels(clBtnFace);
  Form1->Color = clBtnFace;
}
void __fastcall TForm1::Blues1Click(TObject *Sender)
{
  SetEdits(0x00FF8080);
  SetEditText(clBlack);
  SetLabels(clBlack);
  SetPanels(0x00FF0080);
  Form1->Color = clBlue;
}
```

The System1Click method sets all the colors to the default system colors as defined by the current user. The Default1Click method sets colors to values that I think most users will find appealing. The Blues1Click method has a little fun by setting the colors of the form to something a bit unusual. The important point here is that the methods shown in this section of the chapter show how to perform global actions that affect all the controls on a form.

Clearly, taking control over the colors of the components on a form is a simple matter. The matter of saving the settings between runs of the program is a bit more complicated. The following section, which deals with the Registry, focuses on the matter of creating persistent data for the user-configurable parts of a program.

Working with the Registry

The simplest way to work with the Registry is with the `TRegIniFile` class that ships with BCB. This object is a descendent of `TRegistry`. `TRegistry` is meant exclusively for use with the Windows Registry, but `TRegIniFile` also works only with the Registry; however, it uses methods similar to those used with an INI file. In other words, `TRegIniFile` is designed to smooth the transition from INI files to the Registry and to make it easy to switch back if you want.

I am not, however, interested in the capability of `TRegIniFile` to provide compatibility with INI files. This book works only with the Registry. I use `TRegIniFile` rather than `TRegistry` simply because the former object works at a higher level of abstraction than the latter object. Using `TRegIniFile` is easier than using `TRegistry`; therefore, I like it more. I can get my work done faster with it, and I am less likely to introduce a bug. The fact that knowing it well means that I also know how to work with INI files is just an added bonus, not a deciding factor.

> **NOTE**
>
> Again, I find myself wrestling against my tendency to use `TRegistry` because it is a parent of `TRegIniFile`. It is therefore smaller and perhaps somewhat faster. However, I have to remember that my primary goal is to actually finish applications that are as bug free as possible. If I find that the completed application is too slow, and I have time left in my schedule, then I can worry about optimizations. The key is just to get things done.
>
> Furthermore, entering code in the Registry is an extremely bad candidate for speed or size optimizations. This just is not a major bottleneck in most programs, and the difference in size between `TRegIniFile` and `TRegistry` is too small to have a significant impact on my program. Therefore, I go with the simplest possible solution, unless I have a good reason for creating extra work for myself. The worst crime is spending hours, days, or even weeks optimizing a part of a program that doesn't have much impact on code size or program performance.

The Registry is a fairly complex topic, so I have created a separate program called `RegistryDemo` that shows how to get around in it. Once you are clear on the basics, I can come back to the Address2 program and add Registry support.

> **NOTE**
>
> When you're working with the Registry, damaging it is always possible. Of course, I don't think any of the code I show you in this book is likely to damage the Registry; it's just that being careful is always a good idea. Even if you're not writing code that alters the Registry, and even if you're not a programmer, you should still back up the Registry, just to be safe.

I've never found a way to recover a badly damaged Registry. Whenever my Registry has been mangled by a program, I've always had to reinstall Windows from scratch.

Each time Windows starts, it saves a previous copy of the Registry in the Windows directory under the name SYSTEM.DA0. The current working version of the Registry is in SYSTEM.DAT. The Registry is made up of read-only, hidden system files, so you need to make sure you go to View | Options in the Explorer and turn off that silly business about hiding files of certain types.

You should probably back up your current copy of SYSTEM.DAT from time to time, and you should always remember that if the worst happens, SYSTEM.DA0 holds a good copy of the Registry for you, at least until the next time you successfully restart Windows.

If you right-click a filename in the Explorer, you can pop up the Properties dialog, which lets you change the attributes of the file, such as whether it is hidden. More information is available from the Microsoft MSDN in the document called "Backing Up the Registry or Other Critical Files."

 The RegistryDemo application, found on the CD that accompanies this book, exists only to show you how to work with the Registry. The code for this application is shown in Listings 13.8 and 13.9.

Listing 13.8. The header file for the RegistryDemo application.

```
#ifndef MainH
#define MainH
#include <vcl\Classes.hpp>
#include <vcl\Controls.hpp>
#include <vcl\StdCtrls.hpp>
#include <vcl\Forms.hpp>
#include <vcl\Menus.hpp>
#include <vcl\ExtCtrls.hpp>
class TForm1 : public TForm
{
__published: // IDE-managed Components
  TListBox *ListBox1;
  TMainMenu *MainMenu1;
  TMenuItem *File1;
  TMenuItem *OpenRegistry1;
  TMenuItem *N1;
  TMenuItem *MakeHomeinTheRegistry1;
  TMenuItem *N2;
  TMenuItem *Exit1;
  TPanel *Panel1;
  TListBox *ListBox2;
  TMenuItem *BackOneLevel1;
  TMenuItem *RegisterEXE1;
  void __fastcall MakeHomeInRegistryClick(TObject *Sender);
  void __fastcall OpenRegistry1Click(TObject *Sender);
  void __fastcall Exit1Click(TObject *Sender);
```

continues

Listing 13.8. continued

```cpp
  void __fastcall FormDestroy(TObject *Sender);
  void __fastcall ListBox1DblClick(TObject *Sender);

  void __fastcall BackOneLevel1Click(TObject *Sender);
  void __fastcall ListBox1Click(TObject *Sender);

  void __fastcall RegisterEXE1Click(TObject *Sender);
private:    // User declarations
  TRegIniFile *FViewReg;
public:         // User declarations
  virtual __fastcall TForm1(TComponent* Owner);
};
extern TForm1 *Form1;
#endif
```

Listing 13.9. The main module for the RegistryDemo application.

```cpp
////////////////////////////////////////
// File: Main.cpp
// Project: RegistryDemo
// Copyright (c) 1997 Charlie Calvert
#include <vcl\vcl.h>
#include <regstr.h>
#include <vcl\registry.hpp>
#pragma hdrstop
#include "Main.h"
#include "codebox.h"
//-------------------------------------------------------------------------
#pragma resource "*.dfm"
TForm1 *Form1;
//-------------------------------------------------------------------------
__fastcall TForm1::TForm1(TComponent* Owner)
  : TForm(Owner)
{
  FViewReg = new TRegIniFile("");
}
void __fastcall TForm1::FormDestroy(TObject *Sender)
{
  FViewReg->Free();
}
void __fastcall TForm1::Exit1Click(TObject *Sender)
{
  Close();
}
void __fastcall TForm1::ViewRegistry1Click(TObject *Sender)
{
  Panel1->Caption = FViewReg->CurrentPath;
  if (FViewReg->HasSubKeys())
    FViewReg->GetKeyNames(ListBox1->Items);
  ListBox1Click(NULL);
}
void __fastcall TForm1::ListBox1Click(TObject *Sender)
{
```

```
  int i = ListBox1->ItemIndex;
  if (i < 0)
    i = 0;
  AnsiString S = ListBox1->Items->Strings[i];
  TRegIniFile *RegFile = new TRegIniFile(FViewReg->CurrentPath + "\\" + S);
  if (RegFile->HasSubKeys())
    RegFile->GetKeyNames(ListBox2->Items);
  else
    RegFile->GetValueNames(ListBox2->Items);
  RegFile->Free();
}
void __fastcall TForm1::ListBox1DblClick(TObject *Sender)
{
  AnsiString S = ListBox1->Items->Strings[ListBox1->ItemIndex];
  FViewReg->OpenKey(S, False);
  ViewRegistry1Click(NULL);
}
void __fastcall TForm1::BackOneLevel1Click(TObject *Sender)
{
  AnsiString S = FViewReg->CurrentPath;
  AnsiString Temp;
  Caption = S;
  if (S.Length() != 0)
  {
    if (S[1] != '\\')
      S = "\\" + S;
    Temp = StripLastToken(S, '\\', Temp);
    if (Temp.Length() == 0)
      Temp = "\\";
    FViewReg->OpenKey(Temp, False);
    ViewRegistry1Click(NULL);
  }
}
void __fastcall TForm1::MakeHomeInRegistryClick(TObject *Sender)
{
  TRegIniFile *RegFile = new TRegIniFile("SOFTWARE\\Charlie's Stuff");
  RegFile->WriteString("Colors", "Form", "1");
  RegFile->WriteString("Colors", "Edit Text", "1");
  RegFile->WriteString("Colors", "Panels", "1");
  RegFile->WriteString("Colors", "Labels", "1");
  RegFile->WriteString("Colors", "Edits", "1");
  RegFile->Free();
}
void __fastcall TForm1::RegisterEXE1Click(TObject *Sender)
{
  AnsiString Path(ParamStr(0));
  Path = ExtractFilePath(Path);
  TRegIniFile *Registry = new TRegIniFile("");
  Registry->RootKey = HKEY_LOCAL_MACHINE;
  Registry->OpenKey(REGSTR_PATH_APPPATHS, false);
  Registry->WriteString("RegistryDemo.exe", "", Path + "registrydemo.exe");
  Registry->WriteString("RegistryDemo.exe", "Path", Path);
//  ShowMessage(REGSTR_PATH_APPPATHS);
  Registry->Free();
}
```

This rather loosely put-together demo shows off several features of the Registry, with only a minimum of error checking. In particular, the preceding code shows how to save the settings for a program in the Registry, to register an application in the Registry, and to iterate back and forth through one major branch of the Registry.

The purpose of this program is simply to illustrate in one place most of the key tasks you can perform with the Registry. Parts of the program give you some of the features of the Windows utility called RegEdit.exe, but it does not attempt to duplicate this technology because RegEdit works well enough on its own. However, if your heart is set on creating an advanced editor for the Registry, the RegistryDemo program would at least get some of the basic grunt work out of the way for you.

Here's the simplest thing you can do with the TRegIniFile object:

```
TRegIniFile *RegFile = new TRegIniFile("SammysEntry");
RegFile->Free();
```

These two lines of code add a key called "SammysEntry" to the Registry. If you've ever tried the tiresome task of manipulating the Registry using raw Windows API calls, then these two simple lines of code may suggest to you how much time the TRegIniFile can save programmers.

By default, TRegIniFile starts working in HKEY_CURRENT_USER. Therefore, after running the two lines shown here, you can go to the Run menu, type REGEDIT, click OK, and launch the Windows program that lets you explore the Registry. If you open the HKEY_CURRENT_USER branch of the program, you will see the Registry entry shown in Figure 13.11.

Figure 13.11.

The Registry after passing the string "SammysEntry" *to the* TRegIniFile *constructor.*

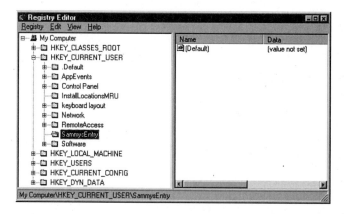

If you're not concerned about OLE and you are working with the Registry, you care about two major keys:

- HKEY_LOCAL_MACHINE\Software: Here you register your application with the system. Typical programs place only a few general pieces of information in this key.

- HKEY_CURRENT_USER\Software: Here you define the current settings for your program. This part of the Registry replaces the old INI files used in Windows 3.1. For example, if you want to save the location of a window or the size of a font, then you save them here. Many entries in this section are extremely detailed and prolix. For example, check out the entries beneath Borland C++Builder in the Registry. You will find a long, unfriendly list of the many changes you can make to the IDE via the menus and dialogs of BCB.

After you consider the information laid out in the preceding bullet points, you should clearly see you would rarely want to store any information directly off HKEY_CURRENT_USER. A more likely place to store information would be off the Software key beneath HKEY_CURRENT_USER.

> **NOTE**
>
> If you've never worked with the Registry before, it can appear a bit daunting at first. Indeed, I am not convinced that it was the simplest way to solve the problems it handles. However, if you spend time with the Registry, little by little you will unravel its secrets. Certainly, it's much more complex than the old Autoexec.bat and Config.sys files that Intel-based programmers have wrestled with for years. However, just as we all slowly became familiar with the intricacies of the DOS start-up files, so do we learn how to become familiar with the Registry.

If you want to write into HKEY_CURRENT_USER\Software rather than into the root of HKEY_CURRENT_USER, you could write the following lines of code:

```
TRegIniFile *RegFile = new TRegIniFile("SOFTWARE\\Charlie's Stuff");
RegFile->Free();
```

These lines create a new key in the Registry, as shown in Figure 13.12. If you want to change the base key from which you start writing code, then you can write the following:

```
Registry->RootKey = HKEY_LOCAL_MACHINE;
```

Now the code you write will go under HKEY_LOCAL_MACHINE rather than under HKEY_CURRENT_USER.

The settings shown in Figure 13.12 are probably closer to what most programmers want to achieve than the results of the first effort. Now your code is listed right up there next to Borland's, Microsoft's, Netscape's, and all the others who will futilely attempt to compete with you for market share.

> **NOTE**
>
> If I were conducting a study exploring which companies have the largest shares of the Windows market, a cross section of the HKEY_CURRENT_USER\Software portion of the Registry from a large number of machines might provide some valuable clues!

13

FLAT-FILE, REAL-WORLD DATABASES

FIGURE 13.12.

Setting up a home for your program's settings under HKEY_CURRENT_USER \Software.

Now that you have set up everything properly, you can start storing information in the Registry. In particular, our current goal is to save the colors for the key features of the Address2 program after the user has set them at runtime. Back in the old days, when INI files were in fashion, you might have created an INI file with this information in it:

```
[Colors]
Form=8421440
Edits=8421376
EditText=0
Labels=0
Panels=12639424
```

This cryptic information might be stored in a text file called Address2.ini and read at runtime by using calls such as ReadPrivateProfileString or by using the TIniFile object that ships with BCB. This INI file has a single section in it called Colors, and under the Colors section are five entries specifying the colors for each of the major elements in the program. Translated into the language of the Registry, this same information looks like the Registry Editor window captured in Figure 13.13.

Here is how to use the TRegIniFile class to write code that enters the pertinent information into the Registry:

```
TRegIniFile *RegFile = new TRegIniFile("SOFTWARE\\Charlie's Stuff");
RegFile->WriteString("Colors", "Form", "1");
RegFile->WriteString("Colors", "Edit Text", "1");
RegFile->WriteString("Colors", "Panels", "1");
RegFile->WriteString("Colors", "Labels", "1");
RegFile->WriteString("Colors", "Edits", "1");
RegFile->Free();
```

FIGURE 13.13.

The Registry set up to hold the key information for the current colors of the Address2 application.

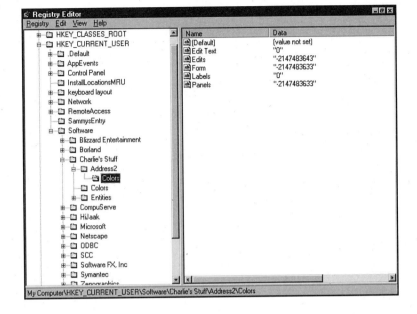

The WriteString method takes three parameters:

- The first is the name of the section (key) under which you want to enter information. I use the word "section" because it corresponds to the Colors section in the INI file shown right after Figure 13.12.

- The second is the key under which the information will be stored. This corresponds to the place where words like Form, Edits, and so on were stored in the INI file.

- The third parameter is the actual value of the key that initially compelled you to store information in the Registry.

If the section or key that you want to use is not already in the Registry, then the preceding code will create the section automatically. If the section or key is already present, then the preceding code can be used to update the values of the keys. In other words, you can use the same code to create or update the sections, keys, and values.

> **NOTE**
>
> Clearly, the TRegIniFile object makes it simple for you to begin adding entries to the Registry. If you know the bothersome Windows API code for doing the same thing, then you can perhaps understand why I think TRegIniFile is a textbook case of how to use objects to hide complexity and to promote code reuse. Here is an object that makes a common task easy to perform. Furthermore, now that this object has been written once correctly, you can use it over and over again to resolve Registry-related problems.

Before going any further with the discussion of the `TRegIniFile`, I should mention that after you are through with the object, you must deallocate the memory you created for it:

```
RegIniFile->Free();
```

You might want to call a number of methods between the time you create a `TRegIniFile` object and the time you free it. However, you cannot call these methods successfully without first allocating memory for the object, and you must free that memory when you are through with the object.

The `TRegIniFile` object allows you to both read and write values, and it allows you to work with a variety of types, including integers:

```
Color = RegFile->ReadInteger("Colors", "Edit Text", Color);
```

Here the `ReadInteger` method looks a good deal like the `WriteString` method, except that the third parameter is a default `Integer` value, and the method itself returns an integer. You should note, however, that the third parameter is a default value that will be returned from the function if it is unable to retrieve a value from the Registry. In other words, if the function fails to find the specified entry in the Registry, it will return the value specified in the third parameter; otherwise, it returns the item you sought. Further examples of reading from the Registry appear in the section "Using the Registry in the Address2 Program."

Navigating Through the Registry

The only question left is how to move around inside the Registry. The `RegistryDemo` program's constructor for the main form opens a `TRegIniFile` in the root of the `HKEY_CURRENT_USER` key:

```
__fastcall TForm1::TForm1(TComponent* Owner)
  : TForm(Owner)
{
  FViewReg = new TRegIniFile("");
}
```

If you select a menu item, you can begin browsing the Registry:

```
void __fastcall TForm1::ViewRegistry1Click(TObject *Sender)
{
  Panel1->Caption = FViewReg->CurrentPath;
  if (FViewReg->HasSubKeys())
    FViewReg->GetKeyNames(ListBox1->Items);
  ListBox1Click(NULL);
}
void __fastcall TForm1::ListBox1Click(TObject *Sender)
{
  int i = ListBox1->ItemIndex;
  if (i < 0)
    i = 0;
  AnsiString S = ListBox1->Items->Strings[i];
  TRegIniFile *RegFile = new TRegIniFile(FViewReg->CurrentPath + "\\" + S);
```

```
  if (RegFile->HasSubKeys())
    RegFile->GetKeyNames(ListBox2->Items);
  else
    RegFile->GetValueNames(ListBox2->Items);
  RegFile->Free();
}
```

These two methods work together to show you the current level of the Registry, plus the values associated with any selected key. This is similar to showing someone the root directory of a drive, plus any files or directories inside the currently selected directory. This task, of course, is the same one undertaken by the RegEdit program, though RegEdit uses a TTreeView object rather than list boxes. The form for the program is shown in Figure 13.14.

FIGURE 13.14.

The main form for the RegistryDemo program features two list boxes that show values from the Registry.

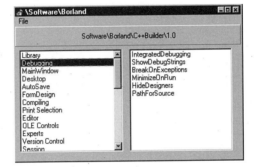

The important calls here are the GetKeyNames and GetValueNames methods of TRegIniFile. These routines take a TStrings object as their sole parameter. Because a list box has a built-in TStrings object, you can just pass it to these methods and get back a list of keys from the system.

> **NOTE**
>
> It is vitally important that you understand the role the abstract TStrings class plays in BCB programming. For example, TListBox, TComboBox, and TMemo, along with their data-aware descendants, all use descendants of the TStrings object. You can create your own stand-alone to TStrings objects with the TStringList class. All these objects can swap their lists back and forth at will, because they all descend from the abstract TStrings class. This subject is covered in some depth in Chapter 2, "Basic Facts About C++Builder."

Note that the program has both a ListBox1Click and a ListBox1DblClick method. A single click displays information in a subkey, and a double-click navigates through the Registry. You can find this same behavior in the Windows Explorer and in RegEdit.

The following two methods allow you to move back and forth through the Registry:

```
void __fastcall TForm1::ListBox1DblClick(TObject *Sender)
{
  AnsiString S = ListBox1->Items->Strings[ListBox1->ItemIndex];
  FViewReg->OpenKey(S, False);
  ViewRegistry1Click(NULL);
}
void __fastcall TForm1::BackOneLevel1Click(TObject *Sender)
{
  AnsiString S = FViewReg->CurrentPath;
  AnsiString Temp;
  Caption = S;
  if (S.Length() != 0)
  {
    if (S[1] != '\\')
      S = "\\" + S;
    Temp = StripLastToken(S, '\\', Temp);
    if (Temp.Length() == 0)
      Temp = "\\";
    FViewReg->OpenKey(Temp, False);
    ViewRegistry1Click(NULL);
  }
}
```

The most important routine shown here is called OpenKey. It takes the name of the key you want to open in the first parameter and a Boolean value specifying whether you want to create a key if it does not exist. I prefer to create keys with the WriteString or WriteInteger methods shown previously, so I always pass False in the second parameter of this method and use it only for iterating through the Registry.

The first of the two methods shown here is called when the user double-clicks an item in the first list box. The string selected by the user is retrieved, and OpenKey is called to move to that location. The two routines discussed previously that are used to display the Registry are then called to show the new values to the user.

The BackOneLevel1Click method moves you back through the Registry. For example, if you are viewing the HKEY_CURRENT_USER\Software key and you select Back One Level from the menu, you are moved to HKEY_CURRENT_USER. You can find the StripLastToken method in the CodeBox unit that ships with this book. The rest of the code ensures that a backslash is included in the correct location when you pass the new key to the system. If you have trouble using OpenKey, check to make sure that you are placing backslashes in the right location, because it is easy to omit them.

I hope that the simple methods shown in this section give you some sense of how to move about in the Registry. This subject is not difficult, but I find I need to stay alert and be careful to avoid careless errors, particularly when working with OpenKey.

Starting Your Program from the Run Menu

I often find myself in a DOS window and am therefore fond of the Start command that allows me to run applications from the command prompt. For example, if I am in a DOS window, and want to run Word for Windows, I frequently type a command like this:

```
Start Chap13.doc
```

As long as I have DOC files associated with Word, this command will open Word and load the file called Chap11.doc. I also use the Start command to begin applications that do not reside on the current path. For example, I can be in a DOS window and type the following:

```
start dbd32.exe
```

This command loads the Database Desktop, even though dbd32.exe is not on the current path. This command depends on the presence of certain values in the following extremely obscure key:

```
HKEY_LOCAL_MACHINE\Softare\Microsoft\Windows\CurrentVersion\AppPaths
```

To help manage the use of this absurdly remote location, you can use the following macro from the REGSTR.H header file:

```
REGSTR_PATH_APPPATHS \
  TEXT("Software\\Microsoft\\Windows\\CurrentVersion\\App Paths")
```

Here, for example, is a method that registers the RegistryDemo program with the system:

```
void __fastcall TForm1::RegisterEXE1Click(TObject *Sender)
{
  AnsiString Path(ParamStr(0));
  Path = ExtractFilePath(Path);
  TRegIniFile *Registry = new TRegIniFile("");
  Registry->RootKey = HKEY_LOCAL_MACHINE;
  Registry->OpenKey(REGSTR_PATH_APPPATHS, false);
  Registry->WriteString("RegistryDemo.exe", "", Path + "registrydemo.exe");
  Registry->WriteString("RegistryDemo.exe", "Path", Path);
  Registry->Free();
}
```

This code opens up the TRegIniFile object, switches to HKEY_LOCAL_MACHINE, uses the REGSTR_PATH_APPPATHS macro to find the desired directory, adds some entries to the Registry, and retires into obscurity. Note the use of the VCL ParamStr function to locate the home directory of the RegistryDemo program.

Using the Registry in the Address2 Program

Now that you understand something about how to use the Registry, you can view simple examples of how to add Registry support to the Address2 program.

Code in the constructor for the Address2 program calls a method that loads the user's currently selected color choices from the Registry:

```
__fastcall TForm1::TForm1(TComponent* Owner)
  : TForm(Owner)
{
  FCaptionString = Caption;
  TColor Color = RGB(254,50,223);
  TColor TestColor;
  TRegIniFile *RegFile = new TRegIniFile("SOFTWARE\\Charlie's Stuff\\Address2");
  TestColor = RegFile->ReadInteger("Colors", "Form", Color);
  RegFile->Free();
  if (TestColor == Color)
    Defaults1Click(NULL);
  else
    ReadCustom1Click(NULL);
}
void __fastcall TForm1::ReadCustom1Click(TObject *Sender)
{
  TColor Color = RGB(0,0,255);
  TRegIniFile *RegFile = new TRegIniFile("SOFTWARE\\Charlie's Stuff\\Address2");
  Form1->Color = RegFile->ReadInteger("Colors", "Form", Color);
  Color = RegFile->ReadInteger("Colors", "Edit Text", Color);
  SetEditText(Color);
  Color = RegFile->ReadInteger("Colors", "Panels", Color);
  SetPanels(Color);
  Color = RegFile->ReadInteger("Colors", "Labels", Color);
  SetLabels(Color);
  Color = RegFile->ReadInteger("Colors", "Edits", Color);
  SetEdits(Color);
  RegFile->Free();
}
```

Though the code itself is somewhat complex, you should find it fairly easy to understand at this stage because you have already seen all the various routines called in this loop. It's just a question of bringing all the routines together so the program can read the Registry and set the appropriate controls to the appropriate colors.

The only tricky part involves finding out what to do if the program does not currently have entries in the Registry. I cheat here by singling out a deplorable color:

```
TColor Color = RGB(254,50,223);
```

I then use this color as a test case for checking whether any valid entries exist in the Registry. My theory is that most reasonable people would agree that a user deserves punishment if he or she selects it as the shade of his or her main form. At any rate, the worst case scenario is that a user who chooses this color for a main form will merely be reminded that he or she has gone too far, and will find that the colors are reset to the defaults:

```
TColor TestColor;
TRegIniFile *RegFile = new TRegIniFile("SOFTWARE\\Charlie's Stuff\\Address2");
TestColor = RegFile->ReadInteger("Colors", "Form", Color);
RegFile->Free();
```

```
if (TestColor == Color)
  Defaults1Click(NULL);
else
  ReadCustom1Click(NULL);
```

If good colors are found in the Registry, then they are used, and the program appears in the state it was in when the program last closed. The `Defaults1Click` method simply gives the form a reasonable set of colors that should please most users.

As I implied previously, the destructor for the program saves the current colors to the Registry:

```
void __fastcall TForm1::FormDestroy(TObject *Sender)
{
  SaveCustom1Click(NULL);
}
void __fastcall TForm1::SaveCustom1Click(TObject *Sender)
{
  TRegIniFile *RegFile = new TRegIniFile("SOFTWARE\\Charlie's Stuff\\Address2");
  RegFile->WriteInteger("Colors", "Form", Form1->Color);
  RegFile->WriteInteger("Colors", "Edit Text", FNameEdit->Font->Color);
  RegFile->WriteInteger("Colors", "Panels", Panel1->Color);
  RegFile->WriteInteger("Colors", "Labels", Label2->Font->Color);
  RegFile->WriteInteger("Colors", "Edits", FNameEdit->Color);
  RegFile->Free();
}
```

The `SaveCustom1Click` method can also be called from the menu of the program. I described the logic for this method in the section "Working with the Registry."

You're now at the end of the discussion of colors and the Registry. I've devoted considerable space to this subject because it is so important for developers who want to present finished applications to users. If you program for Windows 95 or Windows NT, you have to understand the Registry and how to get values in and out of it easily. I hope that the preceding few sections of this chapter have given you the knowledge you need to get this part of your application done quickly.

The Clipboard: Cut, Copy, and Paste

Using BCB, you can easily cut information from a database to the Clipboard. The key point to understand here is that the currently selected control will always be accessible from the `ActiveControl` property of the main form:

```
void __fastcall TForm1::Copy1Click(TObject *Sender)
{
  if (dynamic_cast<TDBEdit*>(ActiveControl))
    (dynamic_cast<TDBEdit*>(ActiveControl))->CopyToClipboard();
  if (dynamic_cast<TDBMemo*>(ActiveControl))
    dynamic_cast<TDBMemo*>(ActiveControl)->CopyToClipboard();
  if (dynamic_cast<TDBComboBox*>(ActiveControl))
    Clipboard()->AsText = dynamic_cast<TDBComboBox*>(ActiveControl)->Text;
}
```

This method is called when the user chooses Edit | Copy. The code first checks to see if the currently selected control is one that contains data from the `Address` table; that is, the code checks to see if the control is a `TDBEdit`, `TDBMemo`, or `TDBComboBox`. If it is, the control is typecast so that its properties and methods can be accessed.

The `TDBEdit` and `TDBLookupComboBox` controls have `CopyToClipBoard`, `PasteFromClipBoard`, and `CutToClipBoard` commands. Each of these commands simply copies, cuts, or pastes data from the live database control to or from the clipboard. The `TDBLookupComboBox` does not have quite as rich a set of built-in functions, so it is handled as a special case. In particular, note that you have to use the built-in `ClipBoard` object, which can easily be a part of every BCB project. To access a fully allocated instance of this object, simply include the `ClipBrd` unit in your current module:

```
#include <vcl\clipbrd.hpp>
```

You can see that working with the clipboard is a trivial operation in BCB. The `Paste1Click` and `Cut1Click` methods from the Address2 program demonstrate a specific technique you can use when pasting and cutting from or to the clipboard.

Summary

In this chapter, you have had a chance to look at all the major portions of the Address2 program. The only items not mentioned in this chapter were the construction of the About dialog and few other similar trivial details.

I went into such detail about the Address2 program because it contains many of the features that need to be included in real-world programs. As I stated earlier, the Address2 program isn't quite up to the standards expected from a professional program, but it does answer some questions about how you can take the raw database tools described in the preceding chapters and use them to create a useful program.

The code shown in this chapter should also serve as a review of some key concepts introduced in the preceding chapters. My plan has been to first show you a wide range of techniques and then to bring them together in the Address2 program so that you can see how they fit into the proverbial "big picture."

Remember, however, that an essentially flat-file database of the type shown in this chapter has a number of limitations in terms of its capability. The relational database shown in the next chapter is considerably more powerful, but also considerably more difficult for most users to master. In the future, it is likely that object oriented databases will play an increasingly important role in programming, though at this time their use is still limited to only a very few sites.

CHAPTER 14

Sessions and Relational Real-World Databases

IN THIS CHAPTER

Overview

Now you can take a look at a real relational database in action. The preceding six chapters have really been nothing but a long prelude to this chapter, where all the pieces finally come together.

This chapter features another address book program, but this time it will be based on a relational database. This second database will allow you to add multiple addresses, phone numbers, and e-mail addresses to each name in the address book.

Subjects covered in this chapter include the following:

- Creating the tables for a relational database
- Cascading deletes
- At runtime, iterating through the controls on a form or a data module and performing certain actions on selected components. For instance, the code shows how to iterate through all the tables on TDataModule to make sure that they are all posted.
- Working with the TPageControl and TTabSheet objects
- Working with TTreeView, TImageList, and TTreeNode
- Retrieving error strings from a resource
- Using the TSession object

After you get a look at the address book program, I start a second program called kdAddExplore. This program looks and feels a lot like a miniature version of the Database Explorer. You can use this program to explore the structure of the five tables used in the address book program found in the first half of this chapter.

The main purpose of the kdAddExplore program is to let you see some of the functionality of the global TSession object that is automatically available in all BCB database applications. The Session object is created automatically when you call Application->Initialize at the startup of a database program. This call is found in the program source generated for you by BCB. To view the program source, choose View | Program Source from the main BCB menu. Don't forget to check the readme file on the CD that comes with this book for additional information about the aliases used in this book.

Data in the Real World

The code in this chapter addresses the kinds of problems you find in real-world situations. In particular, the conflict that needs to be resolved is between the rigid, inflexible nature of simple tables and the fluid, kaleidoscope-like nature of information in the real world.

When most people first try to build database programs, they tend to create one simple table, like the one shown in the Address2 program from the preceding chapter. The limitations with that kind of system might well emerge on the first day of use. For example, you might start transferring handwritten addresses into the database. At first, this process might go fairly well, but then you are likely to encounter a situation in which one person has multiple phone numbers or multiple addresses. It's not at all unusual for one person to have three or more e-mail addresses. The Address2 program does not have a good solution for that kind of problem.

In professional settings, this problem can be multiplied many times. For example, I need to track all the Borland offices in the world. This task involves tracking addresses in Germany, England, France, Australia, Hong Kong, Japan, and various other locations throughout the world.

My job puts me in contact with a number of software vendors (ISVs) that use or create Borland tools. Many of these people maintain offices both at home and at their businesses. Some of them frequent certain sites, and others have complex relationships with their companies that I can track only via freehand notes.

As you can see, information in the real world is messy and complex. The Address2 program is simple and straightforward. Many people can make do with simple tools, but others need to have a more sophisticated system.

The kdAdd program found in this chapter is an attempt to resolve the kinds of problems you find in real-world situations. In the form you see it here, it is not quite as polished as the Address2 program. It is, however, much more sophisticated and much more powerful. With some work, it could easily form the basis for a professional-level database used in an office.

Examining the Relational Address Program

The kdAdd program uses five tables called `kdNames`, `kdAddress`, `kdPhone`, `kdMemo`, and `kdEmail`. The `kdNames` table is the master table that "owns" the other four tables. The other tables are detail tables.

When the program first appears, it looks like the image shown in Figure 14.1. As you can see, the program uses a `TPageControl` with five pages, one for each of the tables. The Address and Phone tables are also shown on the first page so that the user can see them easily. If you want to delete items from either an address or phone number, then you should turn to the respective pages for those items.

The data for the program is kept in the `Data` directory on the CD that comes with this book. You should create a Standard Paradox alias called `CUNLEASHED` that points to a copy of this directory, which resides on your hard drive. Refer to the readme file on the CD that comes with this book if you need additional information setting up the alias. The fields for the tables in the database are shown in Table 14.1 through Table 14.5.

FIGURE 14.1.

The main screen for the kdAdd program.

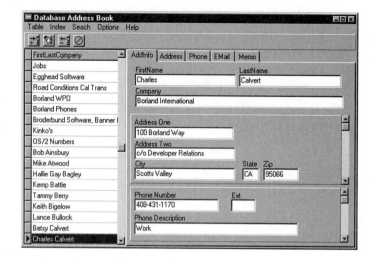

Table 14.1. The format for the kdName table.

Table name	Type	Size	Primary index
NameCode	+		*
FirstName	A	30	
LastName	A	30	
Company	A	30	

Table 14.2. The structure for the kdAdd table.

Table name	Type	Size	Primary index
AddCode	+		*
Address1	A	30	
Address2	A	30	
City	A	30	
State	A	3	
Zip	A	10	
NameCode	I		

Table 14.3. The structure for the kdPhone table.

Table name	Type	Size	Primary index
PhoneCode	+		*
Description	A	15	
Number	A	25	
Ext	A	5	
NameCode	I		

Table 14.4. The structure for the kdEMail table.

Table name	Type	Size	Primary index
EMailCode	+		*
Address	A	50	
Description	A	65	
Service	A	25	
NameCode	I		

Table 14.5. The structure for the kdMemo table.

Table name	Type	Size	Primary index
MemoCode	+		*
Description	A	25	
MemoData	M	15	
NameCode	I		

Four constraints are placed on the table in the form of foreign keys called NameCode. They are placed in each of the program's tables except for the master table. These constraints are shown in Figure 14.2.

When you're viewing this information in the Database Explorer (DBX), you should highlight the name of each constraint and then look at the definition page to read the Reference Type and Reference To fields. As you can see from Figure 14.2, these fields show which table the constraint references. The view shown here is of the kdNames table, and it is the master table in these relationships. The riAddNameCode constraint references the kdAdds table.

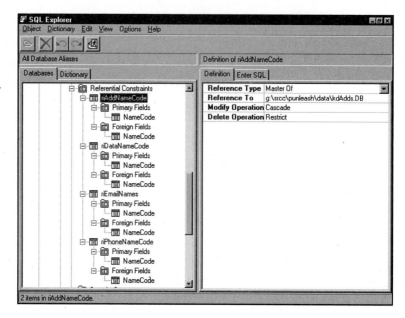

Table 14.6 shows another way to think about the referential integrity in this database.

Table 14.6. The keys in the database shown in table format.

Table	Primary key	Foreign key
kdName	NameCode	
kdAdd	AddCode	NameCode references kdName.NameCode
kdPhone	PhoneCode	NameCode references kdName.NameCode
kdEMail	EMailCode	NameCode references kdName.NameCode
kdMemo	MemoCode	NameCode references kdName.NameCode

As you can see, kdAdd, kdPhone, kdEmail, and kdMemo all have a single foreign key called NameCode that references the NameCode primary key in kdNames. The number in the foreign keys therefore must be a number found in the primary key of the kdNames table. Furthermore, you cannot delete a row from the kdNames table unless all its related fields in the other tables have been deleted first. You also cannot change the value in the NameCode field of kdNames if it will leave records in the other tables "stranded."

NOTE

If you are new to referential integrity, take the time to play with the database and test these constraints. Referential integrity exists to prevent the user from accidentally deleting needed data, and from accidentally entering erroneous data. During the course of this chapter, you should test the restraints on this database so you can see how it establishes rules that help both the programmer and the user maintain a valid set of data.

The referential integrity relationships you see here represent the classic simplest case for constructing a real relational database. Most databases in the real world have more tables and more foreign keys. However, this one has all the elements of a real relational database, and the complexity level is sufficient for programmers who are new to this kind of programming.

Several secondary indexes are used in this program, as shown in Table 14.7 through Table 14.11. Most of these indexes are the result of the foreign keys on the NameCode fields of kdAdds, kdPhone, kdEMail, and kdMemo. However, indexes are also set up on the Company, FirstName, and LastName fields of the kdNames table. Note that idxLastName consists of both the last name and first name of each entry in the kdNames table. This convention is helpful when sorting lists wherein you have more than one entry with a particular last name. For instance, if you have two people with the last name of Jones, creating a key on the last and first names will ensure that Able Jones is listed before Betty Jones. If you further study the tables shown here, you will see that the kdPhone and kdMemo tables also have indexes on their description fields.

Table 14.7. The indexes on the kdNames table.

Table	Index fields
idxCompany	Company
idxFirstName	FirstName
idxLastName	LastName, FirstName

Table 14.8. The index on the kdAdds table.

Table	Index fields
NameCode	NameCode

Table 14.9. The indexes on the kdPhone table.

Index	Index fields
idxDescription	Description
NameCode	NameCode

Table 14.10. The index on the kdEmail table.

Index	Index fields
NameCode	NameCode

Table 14.11. The indexes on the kdMemo table.

Index	Index fields
NameCode	NameCode
idxDescription	Description

You now know all the core facts about the kdAdds program. After you have laid out the tables as shown here, all the really heavy work in constructing the program is completed. You still have considerable work to do in creating a front end for the program, but the core work for the project is done after you have created the tables and defined the ways in which they interrelate.

The Code for kdAdds

The code for the kdAdds program is shown in Listings 14.1 through 14.8. Notice the custom RC file and the include file for the project. These two tiny files store error strings. In later versions of the program, these files will become larger as more error strings are added to the code. For this release, all I have done is stub out these files so that they can easily be expanded later.

Listing 14.1. The header for the main module in the kdAdds program.

```
/////////////////////////////////////
// File: Main.h
// Project: kdAdd
// Copyright (c) 1997 by Charlie Calvert
//
#ifndef MainH
#define MainH
#include <Forms.hpp>
```

```cpp
#include <StdCtrls.hpp>
#include <Controls.hpp>
#include <Classes.hpp>
#include <DBCtrls.hpp>
#include <Mask.hpp>
#include <DBGrids.hpp>
#include <Grids.hpp>
#include <Menus.hpp>
#include <ExtCtrls.hpp>
#include <ComCtrls.hpp>
#include <DBCGrids.hpp>
#include <vcl\Buttons.hpp>
class TForm1 : public TForm
{
__published:
  TMainMenu *MainMenu1;
  TMenuItem *Sorts1;
  TMenuItem *Last1;
  TMenuItem *First1;
  TMenuItem *Company1;
  TPanel *Panel1;
  TDBGrid *FirstLastGrid;
  TPageControl *PageControl1;
  TTabSheet *tsAddress;
  TTabSheet *tsPhone;
  TTabSheet *tsMemo;
  TDBGrid *DBGrid2;
  TDBMemo *DBMemo1;
  TDBCtrlGrid *DBCtrlGrid2;
  TLabel *Label1;
  TLabel *Label2;
  TLabel *Label3;
  TLabel *Label4;
  TLabel *Label5;
  TDBEdit *DBEdit1;
  TDBEdit *DBEdit2;
  TDBEdit *City;
  TDBEdit *DBEdit4;
  TDBEdit *Zip;
  TTabSheet *tsEMail;
  TDBCtrlGrid *DBCtrlGrid3;
  TLabel *Label12;
  TDBEdit *DBEdit10;
  TLabel *Label13;
  TDBEdit *DBEdit11;
  TLabel *Label14;
  TDBEdit *DBEdit12;
  TMenuItem *Table1;
  TMenuItem *Insert1;
  TMenuItem *Delete1;
  TMenuItem *Post1;
  TSpeedButton *InsertBtn;
  TSpeedButton *PostBtn;
  TSpeedButton *DeleteBtn;
  TSpeedButton *CancelBtn;
  TMenuItem *Cancel1;
```

14

SESSIONS AND
RELATIONAL REAL-
WORLD DATABASES

continues

Listing 14.1. continued

```
    TMenuItem *Seach1;
    TMenuItem *First2;
    TMenuItem *Last2;
    TMenuItem *Company2;
    TMenuItem *Help1;
    TMenuItem *Contents1;
    TMenuItem *N1;
    TMenuItem *About1;
    TTabSheet *AddInfo1;
    TLabel *Label15;
    TLabel *Label16;
    TLabel *Label17;
    TDBEdit *DBEdit13;
    TDBEdit *DBEdit14;
    TDBEdit *DBEdit15;
    TDBCtrlGrid *DBCtrlGrid4;
    TLabel *Label18;
    TLabel *Label19;
    TLabel *Label20;
    TLabel *Label21;
    TLabel *Label22;
    TDBEdit *DBEdit17;
    TDBEdit *DBEdit18;
    TDBEdit *DBEdit19;
    TDBEdit *DBEdit20;
    TDBCtrlGrid *DBCtrlGrid5;
    TLabel *Label23;
    TLabel *Label24;
    TLabel *Label25;
    TDBEdit *DBEdit21;
    TDBEdit *DBEdit22;
    TDBEdit *DBEdit23;
    TDBEdit *DBEdit6;
    TDBCtrlGrid *DBCtrlGrid1;
    TLabel *Label6;
    TLabel *Label7;
    TLabel *Label8;
    TDBEdit *DBEdit7;
    TDBEdit *DBEdit8;
    TDBEdit *DBEdit16;
    void __fastcall Last1Click(TObject *Sender);
    void __fastcall Insert1Click(TObject *Sender);
    void __fastcall Cancel1Click(TObject *Sender);
    void __fastcall Delete1Click(TObject *Sender);
    void __fastcall Last2Click(TObject *Sender);
    void __fastcall About1Click(TObject *Sender);
    void __fastcall PostBtnClick(TObject *Sender);
private:
public:
    virtual __fastcall TForm1(TComponent* Owner);
};
extern TForm1 *Form1;
#endif
```

Listing 14.2. The main module for the kdAdds program.

```cpp
////////////////////////////////////////
// File: Main.cpp
// Project: KdAdd
// Copyright (c) 1997 by Charlie Calvert
//
#include <vcl.h>
#pragma hdrstop
#include "Main.h"
#include "DMod1.h"
#include "Globals.h"
#include "AboutBox1.h"
#pragma resource "*.dfm"
TForm1 *Form1;
__fastcall TForm1::TForm1(TComponent* Owner)
  : TForm(Owner)
{
  PageControl1->ActivePage = AddInfo1;
}
void __fastcall TForm1::SetupIndex(TObject *Sender)
{
  switch (dynamic_cast<TComponent *>(Sender)->Tag)
  {
    case 100:
      DMod->NamesTable->IndexName = "idxLastName";
      break;
    case 101:
      DMod->NamesTable->IndexName = "idxFirstName";
      break;
    case 102:
      DMod->NamesTable->IndexName = "idxCompany";
      break;
    case 103:
      DMod->NamesTable->IndexName = "";
      break;
  }
}
void __fastcall TForm1::IndexClick(TObject *Sender)
{
  SetupIndex(Sender);
  DMod->NamesTable->FindNearest(OPENARRAY(TVarRec, ("AAAA")));
}
void __fastcall TForm1::Insert1Click(TObject *Sender)
{
  switch (dynamic_cast<TComponent&>(*PageControl1->ActivePage).Tag)
  {
    case 1:
      DMod->NamesTable->Insert();
      break;
    case 2:
      DMod->AddressTable->Insert();
      break;
```

14

SESSIONS AND
RELATIONAL REAL-
WORLD DATABASES

continues

Listing 14.2. continued

```cpp
    case 3:
      DMod->PhoneTable->Insert();
      break;
    case 4:
      DMod->EMailTable->Insert();
      break;
  }
}
void __fastcall TForm1::Cancel1Click(TObject *Sender)
{
  AnsiString S;
  switch (dynamic_cast<TComponent&>(*PageControl1->ActivePage).Tag)
  {
    case 1:
      DMod->NamesTable->Cancel();
      break;
    case 2:
      DMod->AddressTable->Cancel();
      break;
    case 3:
      DMod->PhoneTable->Cancel();
      break;
    case 4:
      DMod->EMailTable->Cancel();
      break;
    default:
      ShowMessage(GetError(1, S));
  }
}
void __fastcall TForm1::Delete1Click(TObject *Sender)
{
  AnsiString S;
  AnsiString Msg("Are you sure you want to delete \r %s?");
  Set<TMsgDlgBtn, 0, 8> Btns;
  Btns << mbYes << mbNo;
  switch (dynamic_cast<TComponent&>(*PageControl1->ActivePage).Tag)
  {
    case 1:
      Msg = Format(Msg, OPENARRAY(TVarRec,
        (DMod->NamesTableFirstLastCompany->AsString)));
      if (MessageDlg(Msg, mtInformation, Btns, 0) == ID_YES)
        DMod->CascadingDelete();
      break;
    case 2:
      Msg = Format(Msg, OPENARRAY(TVarRec, (DMod->Address)));
      if (MessageDlg(Msg, mtInformation, Btns, 0) == ID_YES)
        DMod->AddressTable->Delete();
      break;
    case 3:
      Msg = Format(Msg, OPENARRAY(TVarRec, (DMod->Phone)));
      if (MessageDlg(Msg, mtInformation, Btns, 0) == ID_YES)
        DMod->PhoneTable->Delete();
      break;
```

```
    case 4:
      Msg = Format(Msg, OPENARRAY(TVarRec, (DMod->EMail)));
      if (MessageDlg(Msg, mtInformation, Btns, 0) == ID_YES)
        DMod->EMailTable->Delete();
      break;

    default:
      ShowMessage(GetError(1, S));
  }
}
void __fastcall TForm1::SearchClick(TObject *Sender)
{
  AnsiString S, IndexName;
  if (InputQuery("Search for Name", "Enter Name: ", S))
  {
    IndexName = DMod->NamesTable->IndexName;
    SetupIndex(Sender);
    DMod->NamesTable->FindNearest(OPENARRAY(TVarRec, (S)));
    DMod->NamesTable->IndexName = IndexName;
  }
}
void __fastcall TForm1::About1Click(TObject *Sender)
{
  AboutBox->ShowModal();
}
void __fastcall TForm1::PostBtnClick(TObject *Sender)
{
  DMod->PostAll();
}
```

Listing 14.3. The header for the data module.

```
//////////////////////////////////////
// File: DMod1.h
// Project: KdAdd
// Copyright (c) 1997 by Charlie Calvert
//
#ifndef DMod1H
#define DMod1H
#include <Forms.hpp>
#include <DBTables.hpp>
#include <DB.hpp>
#include <Classes.hpp>
class TDMod : public TDataModule
{
__published:
  TTable *NamesTable;
  TDataSource *dsNames;
  TTable *AddressTable;
  TTable *PhoneTable;
  TTable *MemoTable;
  TDataSource *dsAddress;
```

14

SESSIONS AND
RELATIONAL REAL-
WORLD DATABASES

continues

Listing 14.3. continued

```cpp
    TDataSource *dsPhone;
    TDataSource *dsMemo;
    TAutoIncField *PhoneTablePhoneCode;
    TStringField *PhoneTableDescription;
    TStringField *PhoneTableNumber;
    TStringField *PhoneTableExt;
    TIntegerField *PhoneTableNameCode;
    TTable *EMailTable;
    TDataSource *dsEmail;
    TAutoIncField *EMailTableEMailCode;
    TStringField *EMailTableAddress;
    TStringField *EMailTableDescription;
    TStringField *EMailTableService;
    TIntegerField *EMailTableNameCode;
    TQuery *EMailDeleteQuery;
    TQuery *MemoDeleteQuery;
    TQuery *PhoneDeleteQuery;
    TQuery *AddressDeleteQuery;
    TQuery *NamesDeleteQuery;
    TAutoIncField *MemoTableMemoCode;
    TStringField *MemoTableDescription;
    TMemoField *MemoTableMemoData;
    TIntegerField *MemoTableNameCode;
    TAutoIncField *NamesTableNameCode;
    TStringField *NamesTableFirstName;
    TStringField *NamesTableLastName;
    TStringField *NamesTableCompany;
    TAutoIncField *AddressTableAddCode;
    TStringField *AddressTableAddress1;
    TStringField *AddressTableAddress2;
    TStringField *AddressTableCity;
    TStringField *AddressTableState;
    TStringField *AddressTableZip;
    TIntegerField *AddressTableNameCode;
    TStringField *NamesTableFirstLastCompany;
    void __fastcall NamesTableCalcFields(TDataSet *DataSet);
private:
    AnsiString __fastcall GetAddress();
    AnsiString __fastcall GetPhone();
    AnsiString __fastcall GetEMail();
public:
    virtual __fastcall TDMod(TComponent* Owner);
    void PostAll(void);
    void CascadingDelete(void);
    __property AnsiString Address={read=GetAddress};
    __property AnsiString Phone={read=GetPhone};
    __property AnsiString EMail={read=GetEMail};
};
extern TDMod *DMod;
#endif
```

Listing 14.4. The code for the data module.

```cpp
/////////////////////////////////////
// File: DMod1.cpp
// Project: KdAdd
// Copyright (c) 1997 by Charlie Calvert
//
#include <vcl.h>
#pragma hdrstop
#include "DMod1.h"
#pragma resource "*.dfm"
TDMod *DMod;
__fastcall TDMod::TDMod(TComponent* Owner)
  : TDataModule(Owner)
{
  NamesTable->Open();
  AddressTable->Open();
  PhoneTable->Open();
  MemoTable->Open();
  EMailTable->Open();
}
void __fastcall TDMod::NamesTableCalcFields(TDataSet *DataSet)
{
  AnsiString Temp = NamesTableFirstName->Value+ " " +NamesTableLastName->Value;
  if (Temp == " ")
    NamesTableFirstLastCompany->Value = NamesTableCompany->Value;
  else
    NamesTableFirstLastCompany->Value = Temp;
}
void DoPost(TDataSet *Data)
{
  if ((Data->State == dsInsert) || (Data->State == dsEdit))
    Data->Post();
}
void TDMod::PostAll(void)
{
  int i;
  for (i = 0; i < ComponentCount; i++)
    if (dynamic_cast<TTable*>(Components[i]))
      DoPost((TDataSet*)(Components[i]));
}
void TDMod::CascadingDelete(void)
{
  EMailDeleteQuery->ParamByName("NameCode")->AsInteger =
    EMailTableNameCode->Value;
  EMailDeleteQuery->ExecSQL();
  MemoDeleteQuery->ParamByName("NameCode")->AsInteger =
    MemoTableNameCode->Value;
  MemoDeleteQuery->ExecSQL();
  PhoneDeleteQuery->ParamByName("NameCode")->AsInteger =
    PhoneTableNameCode->Value;
```

continues

14

SESSIONS AND
RELATIONAL REAL-
WORLD DATABASES

Listing 14.4. continued

```
    PhoneDeleteQuery->ExecSQL();
    AddressDeleteQuery->ParamByName("NameCode")->AsInteger =
      AddressTableNameCode->Value;
    AddressDeleteQuery->ExecSQL();
    NamesDeleteQuery->ParamByName("NameCode")->AsInteger =
      NamesTableNameCode->Value;
    NamesDeleteQuery->ExecSQL();
    NamesTable->Refresh();
}
AnsiString __fastcall TDMod::GetAddress()
{
  return DMod->AddressTableAddress1->AsString + '\r' +
    DMod->AddressTableAddress2->AsString + '\r' +
    DMod->AddressTableCity->AsString + '\r' +
    DMod->AddressTableState->AsString + '\r' +
    DMod->AddressTableZip->AsString;
}
AnsiString __fastcall TDMod::GetPhone()
{
  return DMod->PhoneTableDescription->AsString + '\r' +
    DMod->PhoneTableNumber->AsString + '\r' +
    DMod->PhoneTableExt->AsString;
}
AnsiString __fastcall TDMod::GetEMail()
{
  return DMod->EMailTableAddress->AsString + '\r' +
    DMod->EMailTableDescription->AsString + '\r' +
    DMod->EMailTableService->AsString;
}
```

Listing 14.5. The header for the Globals unit.

```
/////////////////////////////////////
// File: Globals.h
// Project: KdAdd
// Copyright (c) 1997 by Charlie Calvert
//
#ifndef GlobalsH
#define GlobalsH
AnsiString GetError(int ErrNo, AnsiString &S);
#endif
```

Listing 14.6. The main module for the Globals unit.

```
/////////////////////////////////////
// File: Globals.cpp
// Project: KdAdd
// Copyright (c) 1997 by Charlie Calvert
//
```

```
#include <vcl\vcl.h>
#pragma hdrstop
#include "Globals.h"
#define ERR_STRING_SIZE 255
AnsiString GetError(int ErrNo, AnsiString &S)
{
  S.SetLength(ERR_STRING_SIZE);
  LoadString(HINSTANCE(HInstance), 1, S.c_str(), ERR_STRING_SIZE);
  return S;
}
```

Listing 14.7. The custom RC file for the project. This is a stub to be filled out later.

```
#include "kderrs.inc"
STRINGTABLE
{
  KDERR_CASESTATEMENT, "Command fell through case statement"
}
```

Listing 14.8. The `include` file for the project has only one entry. This is a stub to be filled out later.

```
#define KDERR_CASESTATEMENT 1
```

The pages in the TPageControl are hidden from view in Figure 14.1. In Figure 14.3 through Figure 14.6, you can see the remaining TTabSheet objects.

FIGURE 14.3.

The tab sheet for the Address table.

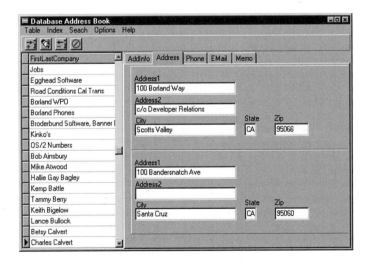

FIGURE 14.4.

The tab sheet for the Phone table.

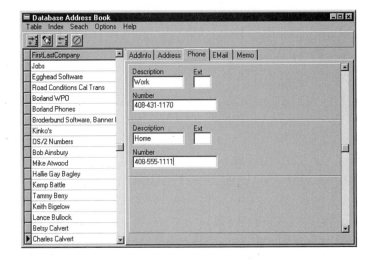

FIGURE 14.5.

The tab sheet for the E-mail table.

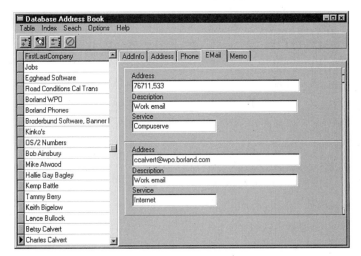

Using the kdAdd Program

The kdAdd program has the minimal functionality needed to support the user's needs. For example, you can perform Insert, Post, Delete, and Cancel operations on all the tables. Access to these features is provided through both the menus and a speedbar. You can also set the index to the Company, First, or Last fields of the kdNames table. Finally, you can search on either the Company, First, or Last fields.

FIGURE 14.6.

The tab sheet for Memo.

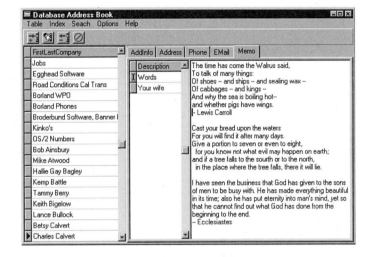

Setting Up the Index for kdAdd

One of the hubs around which the kdAdd program revolves involves the code that controls the index for the program. This code is called from several different places in the program. The obvious place to start studying it, however, is in the response method for the menu items that let the user change the index:

```
void __fastcall TForm1::SetupIndex(TObject *Sender)
{
  switch (dynamic_cast<TComponent *>(Sender)->Tag)
  {
    case 100:
      DMod->NamesTable->IndexName = "idxLastName";
      break;
    case 101:
      DMod->NamesTable->IndexName = "idxFirstName";
      break;
    case 102:
      DMod->NamesTable->IndexName = "idxCompany";
      break;
    case 103:
      DMod->NamesTable->IndexName = "";
      break;
  }
}
void __fastcall TForm1::IndexClick(TObject *Sender)
{
  SetupIndex(Sender);
  DMod->NamesTable->FindNearest(OPENARRAY(TVarRec, ("AAAA")));
}
```

The code has three menu choices for changing the index. The first lets the user set the index to the last name; the second, to the first name; and the third, to the company name. All three menu items are attached to the `IndexClick` method shown here.

`IndexClick` calls `SetupIndex` to do the real work. You use the tag property of the `TMenuItem` that is clicked to decide which index to choose:

```
switch (dynamic_cast<TComponent *>(Sender)->Tag)
```

This way, you can call the function with a simple one-line command:

```
SetupIndex(Sender);
```

After the index has been set up properly, you can search for the first relevant record in the database:

```
DMod->NamesTable->FindNearest(OPENARRAY(TVarRec, ("AAAA")));
```

The goal of this line is to skip over all the records that contain blanks in the field on which you're searching. For example, if you switch to the company index, you might find 20, 100, or even 5,000 records in the table that have no information in the `Company` field. To skip over these records, you can search for the first row that begins with the letter *A*.

Searching for Records

The program also uses the `SetupIndex` method when it is conducting searches. As I stated previously, you can use three possible menu items to start a search. The first searches on last names; the second, on first names; and the third, on a company name. I have assigned the same values to the `Tag` fields of these `TMenuItems` that I did to the `Tag` fields of the `TMenuItems` concerned with switching indexes. That way, I can set up the index properly with a simple call to `SetupIndex`:

```
AnsiString IndexName, S;
if (InputQuery("Search for Name", "Enter Name: ", S))
{
  IndexName = DMod->NamesTable->IndexName;
  SetupIndex(Sender);
  DMod->NamesTable->FindNearest(OPENARRAY(TVarRec, (S)));
  DMod->NamesTable->IndexName = IndexName;
}
```

As you can see, the code also saves the current index so that the current state of the index can be restored after the search:

```
AnsiString IndexName;
IndexName = DMod->NamesTable->IndexName;
... // Code omitted here
DMod->NamesTable->IndexName = IndexName;
```

The big point to notice here is how easily you can take care of these chores by using the VCL. BCB makes database programming easy, even when you're working with a fairly complex program.

Inserting Data, Canceling Operations

Because this database has five tables, you have to devise a technique for specifying the name of the table on which you want to perform an insertion, deletion, or post. I use the TPageControl to handle these chores. In particular, I assume that if the user is looking at the Address page, then he or she wants to perform an action on the kdAdds table, and if the user is looking at the first page, then he or she wants to perform an operation on the kdNames table, and so on:

```
void __fastcall TForm1::Insert1Click(TObject *Sender)
{
  switch (dynamic_cast<TComponent&>(*PageControl1->ActivePage).Tag)
  {
    case 1:
      DMod->NamesTable->Insert();
      break;
    case 2:
      DMod->AddressTable->Insert();
      break;
    case 3:
      DMod->PhoneTable->Insert();
      break;
    case 4:
      DMod->EMailTable->Insert();
      break;
  }
}
```

As you can see, I have set the Tag field for each of the pages to a unique value so that I can easily determine the current page:

```
switch (dynamic_cast<TComponent&>(*PageControl1->ActivePage).Tag)
```

If the user accidentally makes a wrong decision, he or she can undo the most recent operation on the currently selected table by clicking Cancel:

```
void __fastcall TForm1::Cancel1Click(TObject *Sender)
{
  AnsiString S;
  switch (dynamic_cast<TComponent&>(*PageControl1->ActivePage).Tag)
  {
    case 1: DMod->NamesTable->Cancel(); break;
    case 2: DMod->AddressTable->Cancel(); break;
    case 3: DMod->PhoneTable->Cancel(); break;
    case 4: DMod->EMailTable->Cancel(); break;
    default:
      ShowMessage(GetError(1, S));
  }
}
```

This system is easy to implement, but it can be a bit confusing to the user when he or she is looking at the first page, which holds information about not only the kdNames table, but also the kdAdds and kdPhone tables. The issue here is that the database itself won't be much fun if you have to flip pages to get even the most basic information about a name. To remedy this problem, I put the Name, Address, and Phone information on the first page but really expect the user to perform edits on these fields by turning to the Address or Phone page.

To enforce this rule, you can set up an options menu that can be turned on and off:

```
void __fastcall TForm1::SetAddressPhoneClick(TObject *Sender)
{
  SetAddressPhone->Checked = !SetAddressPhone->Checked;
  DBEdit6->ReadOnly = SetAddressPhone->Checked;
  DBEdit17->ReadOnly = SetAddressPhone->Checked;
  DBEdit18->ReadOnly = SetAddressPhone->Checked;
  DBEdit19->ReadOnly = SetAddressPhone->Checked;
  DBEdit20->ReadOnly = SetAddressPhone->Checked;
  DBEdit8->ReadOnly = SetAddressPhone->Checked;
  DBEdit17->ReadOnly = SetAddressPhone->Checked;
  DBEdit7->ReadOnly = SetAddressPhone->Checked;
}
```

If you include this code in the program as a response to a TMenuItem called SetAddressPhone, then the user can decide whether the views on the kdAdds and kdPhones table will be editable. By default, this function should be turned off, because it really is better that the user does not input information in these fields.

I should perhaps add that the user does not have to understand that he or she is entering data in separate tables. For example, the user doesn't have to know that the kdAdds and kdPhones tables exist. All he or she has to understand is that inputting information about phones is a separate operation from entering data about addresses or names. This much conceptual background the user must have; otherwise, he or she will not be able to use the tool at all.

The design of the program helps the user by putting each table on a separate page. That way, the user can rely on the page metaphor when thinking about the underlying structure of the database. Providing metaphors for the user is a useful way to simplify the operation of an application.

NOTE

As you might recall, when I first talked about the Address2 program, I said that for many users, a simple flat-file database is best. When I said that, I was thinking particularly about the kinds of problems currently under discussion. Using a relational database takes a certain amount of conceptual ability that some users may not have the patience to master. The actual ideas involved are simple, but many users are still so overwhelmed by the very idea of computers that they can't clear their heads sufficiently to grasp concepts that would be easy for them to assimilate in some other field with which they are more familiar.

It may sound as though I am being overly polite in this note, but I'm trying to state the facts as I see them. Many intelligent people's minds really do become inexplicably opaque when it comes to thinking about computers. This problem will disappear as more and more children grow up using these machines, but for now programmers have to think seriously every time they add any level of complexity to their programs. Programmers will understand relational databases, and so will the small subset of users that are targeted by a program of this type; but it is important to understand that at this point in history, many users will find relational databases perhaps too difficult to understand.

My point is simply that not everyone is ready to work with relational databases. Some people need them, but others will be confused by them. It is good to use relational databases when necessary, but programmers should also be aware that some users might not properly understand them.

Deleting Data: A First Look at the Program's Data Module

Deleting data is the last topic to be covered before moving over to examination of the TDataModule for the application. In fact, you will find that this subject touches on matters that are specific to the program's data module, so it serves as a good segue into new territory.

Here is the method the main form uses to delete data:

```
void __fastcall TForm1::Delete1Click(TObject *Sender)
{
  AnsiString S;
  AnsiString Msg("Are you sure you want to delete \r %s?");
  Set<TMsgDlgBtn, 0, 8> Btns;
  Btns << mbYes << mbNo;
  switch (dynamic_cast<TComponent&>(*PageControl1->ActivePage).Tag)
  {
    case 1:
      Msg = Format(Msg, OPENARRAY(TVarRec,
        (DMod->NamesTableFirstLastCompany->AsString)));
      if (MessageDlg(Msg, mtInformation, Btns, 0) == ID_YES)
        DMod->CascadingDelete();
      break;
    case 2:
      Msg = Format(Msg, OPENARRAY(TVarRec, (DMod->Address)));
      if (MessageDlg(Msg, mtInformation, Btns, 0) == ID_YES)
        DMod->AddressTable->Delete();
      break;
    case 3:
      Msg = Format(Msg, OPENARRAY(TVarRec, (DMod->Phone)));
      if (MessageDlg(Msg, mtInformation, Btns, 0) == ID_YES)
        DMod->PhoneTable->Delete();
      break;
    case 4:
      Msg = Format(Msg, OPENARRAY(TVarRec, (DMod->EMail)));
      if (MessageDlg(Msg, mtInformation, Btns, 0) == ID_YES)
        DMod->EMailTable->Delete();
      break;
    default:
      ShowMessage(GetError(1, S));
  }
}
```

14

SESSIONS AND RELATIONAL REAL-WORLD DATABASES

As you can see, this code uses the `Tag` field of the `TTabSheet` to determine which table is focused.

The code then pops up a message box asking the user if he or she is sure about continuing with the deletion. In some cases, you can easily give the user an intelligent prompt about the contents of the current field:

```
Msg = Format(Msg, OPENARRAY(TVarRec,
  (DMod->NamesTableFirstLastCompany->AsString)));
```

In this case, the string garnered from one of the fields of the `NamesTable` provides all the information the user needs. In fact, the `FirstLast` field of the database is a calculated field. This calculated field consists of combined information from the `First`, `Last`, and `Company` fields of the `kdNames`. This combined information uniquely identifies a record so the user can feel secure when deleting it:

```
void __fastcall TDMod::NamesTableCalcFields(TDataSet *DataSet)
{
  AnsiString Temp = NamesTableFirstName->Value + " " +NamesTableLastName->Value;
  if (Temp == " ")
    NamesTableFirstLastCompany->Value = NamesTableCompany->Value;
  else
    NamesTableFirstLastCompany->Value = Temp;
}
```

As you can see, this code combines the first and last names into a single string. If the string is not empty, it is shown to the user as if it were a standard field of the database. If the current record has no information in either the first or last field, then the program assumes that the record must contain only company information:

```
NamesTableFirstLastCompany->Value = NamesTableCompany->Value;
```

The end result of this system is to show the user records that contain either someone's first or last name or just a company name. This way, you can ask the database to perform double duty as both a way of tracking company names and as a means of tracking the names of people.

This calculated field can be used not only to help with deletions, but also as an index appearing on the extreme left of the main form, as shown in Figure 14.1. The user will never edit this field directly but will use it as a guide to all the nearby records in the database. This kind of index is useful if you're searching for a particular name. For example, I use the database to track the members of my family. As a result, it has lots of Calverts in it. I can use the Last Name search to find the section where the Calverts are stored and then use the index to move back and forth between members of the family.

> **NOTE**
>
> You actually have no guarantee that the string generated by this calculated field will be unique. The program is designed to make sure the NameCode in the kdNames table is unique, but nothing in the program prevents you from entering two identical names, addresses, phone numbers, and so on.

If the user wants to delete an address, you once again need to provide information from several different fields to identify a record uniquely, as you can see in Figure 14.7.

FIGURE 14.7.

A prompt that uniquely identifies the address shown in a particular row.

This time, I found it more convenient simply to add to the data module a method that would return a string uniquely identifying a record:

```
AnsiString __fastcall TDMod::GetAddress()
{
  return DMod->AddressTableAddress1->AsString + '\r' +
    DMod->AddressTableAddress2->AsString + '\r' +
    DMod->AddressTableCity->AsString + '\r' +
    DMod->AddressTableState->AsString + '\r' +
    DMod->AddressTableZip->AsString;
}
```

I thought the most sensible approach was to add a read-only property to the data module to aid in retrieving this information:

```
__property AnsiString Address={read=GetAddress};
```

You can access this property by writing code that looks like this:

```
AnsiString S = DMod->Address;
```

In this particular case, it is arguable that a property doesn't do much for you other than cover the remote contingency that you might change the parameters of the GetAddress method. On the other hand, the property doesn't cost you anything either because the compiler will obviously map any calls to the Address property directly to the GetAddress method. In other words, this programming is very cautious because it is unlikely that the GetAddress method will ever change its spots. However, being conservative when writing code is almost always best, as long as you're not doing serious damage to the performance of your program.

I won't bother discussing any of the means for deleting from the other tables in this program, as they follow the same pattern already established. The key point to grasp is that you have to show several fields to the user to identify a record uniquely. Furthermore, placing the burden of generating these strings on the program's data module is probably best. The reason for doing so is simply that the generation of these strings is dependent on the structure of the tables underlying the program. Isolating all code dependent on these structures inside one object is best so that you won't have to hunt all over your program to find code that might need to be modified because of a change in the program's database.

The Data Module: Cascading Deletes

You have already seen that the data module contains special properties that retrieve strings uniquely identifying certain records. You have also seen the calculated field that generates a string "uniquely" identifying records from the kdNames table. What's left to explore are methods that aid in posting and deleting records.

The issue here is simply that the database contains a number of tables. If the user wants to delete a name from the database, then he or she is really asking to not just delete the name, but also the addresses, phone numbers, and other information associated with that name. This process is known as a *cascading delete.*

Delphi provides support for cascading deletes via the referential integrity dialog found in the Database Desktop. You can see this option in Figure 14.8.

Many databases do not support cascading deletes, so you can implement it on the client side with just a few lines of code:

```
void TDMod::CascadingDelete(void)
{
  EMailDeleteQuery->ParamByName("NameCode")->AsInteger =
    EMailTableNameCode->Value;
  EMailDeleteQuery->ExecSQL();
  MemoDeleteQuery->ParamByName("NameCode")->AsInteger =
    MemoTableNameCode->Value;
  MemoDeleteQuery->ExecSQL();
  PhoneDeleteQuery->ParamByName("NameCode")->AsInteger =
    PhoneTableNameCode->Value;
  PhoneDeleteQuery->ExecSQL();
  AddressDeleteQuery->ParamByName("NameCode")->AsInteger =
    AddressTableNameCode->Value;
  AddressDeleteQuery->ExecSQL();
  NamesDeleteQuery->ParamByName("NameCode")->AsInteger =
    NamesTableNameCode->Value;
  NamesDeleteQuery->ExecSQL();
  NamesTable->Refresh();
}
```

FIGURE 14.8.

Choose Cascade or Restrict to get support for cascading deletes in databases that support this feature.

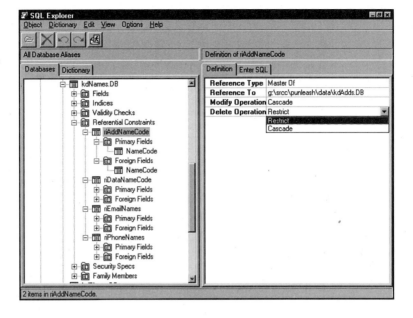

This code looks a bit complicated, in part because some of the lines are long and need to be wrapped. Underneath, however, its structure is very simple. I simply walk down the list of tables in the database, accessing the `kdNames` table last. I have created a SQL statement for each table that will delete all the records in the table that have a particular `NameCode`. For example, here are the SQL statements for deleting records in the `kdNames` or `kdAdds` tables:

```
Delete from kdNames where NameCode = :NameCode
Delete from KDAdds where NameCode = :NameCode
```

As I said, this technology is very simple, and the act implementing cascading deletes in your application is trivial. The key to the whole process is simply recognizing that this act is the responsibility of the program's data module. Then you can create a simple method in the data module to handle the logic of the operation, and after about five minutes work, you have a method that can be called from anywhere in your application with a single line of code. (You should, however, take more than five minutes to test your code against sample data to make sure that it is working properly.)

14

SESSIONS AND RELATIONAL REAL-WORLD DATABASES

NOTE

You should use the alias system built into the BDE to aid in the process of creating sample data against which you can run tests. In particular, the ideal way to set up this situation is to include a `TDatabase` object in your database and then attach each of your tables and queries to that single `TDatabase` object. That way, you can change the alias for the

continues

> *continued*
>
> TDatabase object and thereby globally change the data all your tables are accessing. Needless to say, you should also make a dummy copy of your data and place it in a separate database (directory, in Paradox).
>
> I don't use this structure in the current program, but I will in the sections on InterBase programs that are coming up in the next few chapters. For example, the Music program from Chapter 16, "Advanced InterBase Concepts," uses this structure.

The Data Module: Mass Posts

The opposite problem from deleting records occurs when you have to post the data in your program. In these cases, you want to be sure that all the data in all the tables is posted. You wouldn't want to post just the data in the kdNames table and then leave updates to the kdAddress or kdPhones tables stranded.

The methods that handle posting the data look like this:

```
void DoPost(TDataSet *Data)
{
  if ((Data->State == dsInsert) || (Data->State == dsEdit))
    Data->Post();
}
void TDMod::PostAll(void)
{
  int i;
  for (i = 0; i < ComponentCount; i++)
    if (dynamic_cast<TTable*>(Components[i]))
      DoPost(dynamic_cast<TDataSet*>(Components[i]));
}
```

This code iterates through all the components on the program's data module looking for TTable objects. When the code finds one, it passes the object to a method called DoPost that calls the Post method for the table. The code in DoPost first checks to make sure the table is in dsInsert or dsEdit mode, as it is an error to call Post on a table that is in dsBrowse or some other mode where a Post can't occur.

Notice that I use the ComponentCount property of TDataModule to determine how many components I need to check. I then call dynamic_cast to check whether it is safe to assume the current component is a TTable. The preceding code is actually a bit wasteful of clock cycles, in that it is not necessary to support the overhead of a dynamic_cast after you're sure the cast will succeed:

```
void TDMod::PostAll(void)
{
  int i;
  for (i = 0; i < ComponentCount; i++)
    if (dynamic_cast<TTable*>(Components[i]))
      DoPost((TDataSet*)(Components[i]));
}
```

In this case, the first cast has additional overhead but is safe, in that no exceptions will be raised if it fails. The second cast is then guaranteed to succeed, so you can ask the compiler to do it at compile time rather than generate runtime code:

```
DoPost((TDataSet*)(Components[i]));
```

Putting Error Strings in String Resources

The other subject worth touching on briefly in regard to this program involves the matter of using string resources to handle error strings. The program has a very small string resource that contains only one string:

```
#include "kderrs.inc"
STRINGTABLE
{
  KDERR_CASESTATEMENT, "Command fell through case statement"
}
```

In a program used in the real world, you would probably want to generate many more error strings.

You can use the following method to retrieve error strings from the program's resource:

```
#define ERR_STRING_SIZE 255
AnsiString GetError(int ErrNo, AnsiString &S)
{
  S.SetLength(ERR_STRING_SIZE);
  LoadString(HINSTANCE(HInstance), 1, S.c_str(), ERR_STRING_SIZE);
  return S;
}
```

This code calls the Windows API routine called LoadString to do the actual grunt work. Several built-in VCL routines also provide this same functionality. Notice that an include file defines the KDERR_CASESTEMENT constant:

```
#define KDERR_CASESTATEMENT 1
```

That's all I'm going to say about this error-handling code. If you want more information, you can refer to the discussion of string resources at the end of Chapter 5, "Exceptions."

The About Box

For the sake of completeness, I will wrap up the examination of this program by showing you the About box for the program, shown in Figure 14.9. You can generate About boxes automatically in BCB by choosing File | New, turning to the Forms page of the Object Repository, and choosing About Box, as shown in Figure 14.10. I choose to Copy the code rather than to Inherit or Use it, as you can see in the bottom left of Figure 14.10. Proceeding this way is usually the best and simplest method unless you're sure you have mastered the technology involved with form inheritance.

14

SESSIONS AND RELATIONAL REAL-WORLD DATABASES

FIGURE 14.9.

The About box for the kdAdds program.

FIGURE 14.10.

Creating an About box from the Object Repository.

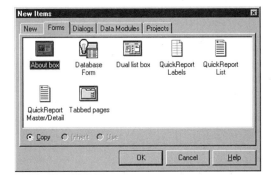

You've now come to the end of the discussion of the kdAdds program. The rest of the chapter consists of a discussion of two utilities associated with this program. One will transfer data from the Address2 program to the kdAdds program, and the second will show how to use the TSession object to explore the structure of the tables used in the kdAdds program.

Using the kdAddExplore Program

The kdAddExplore program uses the TSession object to explore the tables used in the kdAdds program. The TSession object is often overlooked by VCL programmers because its operation is usually handled behind the scenes without need for intervention. However, if you want to explore the structure of a database at runtime, this is the object to use. In fact, this object might have been more usefully called the TDataExplorer object rather than TSession.

> **NOTE**
>
> The TSession is created automatically by an application on startup. If you're working inside a DLL or in a console mode application, then no default TApplication object exists to start up a session. As a result, you may have to create your own TSession object or else call the Initialize method of a TApplication object. Otherwise, you will not be able to use databases inside your program.

Before you begin the technical part of this chapter, spending a few moments running the kdAddExplore program found on disk might be helpful. This program demonstrates techniques of examining the structure of an existing database.

> **NOTE**
>
> The kdAddExplore program bears a close resemblance to a cut-down version of the Database Explorer (DBX). There is nothing coincidental about this similarity. However, I have never seen the source to DBX nor discussed its structure with its author. My intention here is not to create a substitute for the DBX, but only to provide a simple means of showing the reader how to explore database objects at runtime.
>
> You can use this kind of information to provide utilities for your users or merely to extend your own knowledge of the BDE and VCL. The code also provides an example of how to use the `TTreeView` object.

Throughout the rest of this chapter, I will use a global `TSession` object created automatically whenever you include database code in your programs. However, you also can drop down a `TSession` component on your forms if you would like to look at a visual object. I do not use it here because it would bring no additional functionality to my program. However, you might want to at least view the `TSession` component and take a look at its password-related properties.

Working with TSession

`TSession` is used to manage all the database connections within a session. It is a global object that wraps up not only `TTable` and `TQuery`, but also `TDatabase`. A single `TSession` object might manage many tables, queries, and databases.

The `TSession` object has two sets of methods. The first has to do with managing a session. The methods encompassing this set of functionality are shown in Table 14.12.

Table 14.12. The session management routines from the TSession object.

Routine	Description
Close	Closes all databases
CloseDatabase	Closes a particular database
Open	Opens the session: `Active = True;`
OpenDatabase	Opens a specific database
AddPassword	Creates a password for the session

continues

Table 14.12. continued

Routine	Description
RemovePassword	Deletes a password
RemoveAllPasswords	Clears the password list
DropConnections	Closes all currently inactive databases and datasets

The second set of routines found in TSession are the methods that are of interest in the current context of this book. These routines are shown in Table 14.13.

Table 14.13. Routines for querying a session regarding the available databases, tables, drivers, and stored procedures.

Routine	Description
GetAliasNames	Gets the list of BDE aliases for a database
GetAliasParams	Gets the list of parameters for a BDE alias
GetAliasDriverName	Gets the BDE driver for an alias of a database
GetDatabaseNames	Gets a list of BDE aliases and TDatabase objects
GetDriverNames	Gets the names of installed BDE drivers
GetDriverParams	Gets parameters for a BDE driver
GetTableNames	Gets tables associated with a database
GetStoredProcNames	Gets stored procedures for a database

Routines such as GetDatabaseNames and GetTableNames can retrieve a list of all the available databases and tables on the current system. You can see this data on display inside the kdAddExplore program. For example, all the databases in my system at the time of this writing are visible in the main screen of the kdAddExplore program, as shown in Figure 14.11.

You can open up the nodes of the kdAddExplore program to see a list of all the tables in a particular database, as shown in Figure 14.12. You can then drill down even further to the names of the fields and indexes in a particular table. Finally, you can even see the names of the fields involved in a particular index, as shown in Figure 14.13.

Another set of TSession functionality tapped into by the kdAddExplore program involves looking at the alias found on a system. You can drill down in this dialog to see the parameters passed to a particular alias, as shown in Figure 14.14.

FIGURE 14.11.

The kdAddExplore program displays all the available databases on my system.

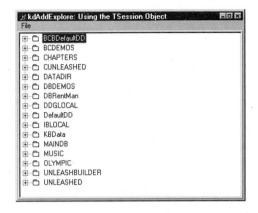

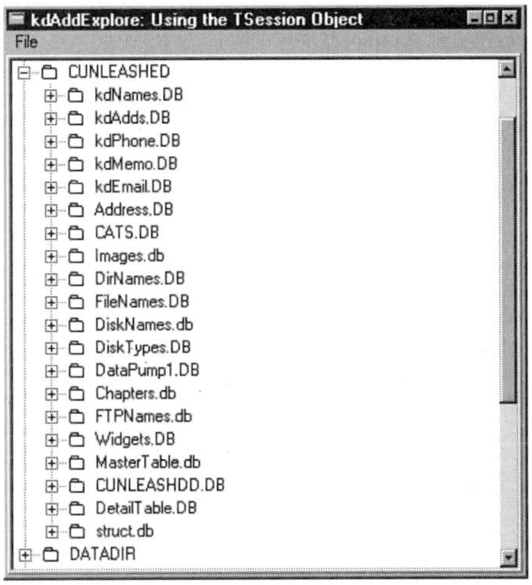

FIGURE 14.12.

The tables in the CUnleashed database, which holds most of the data used in this book.

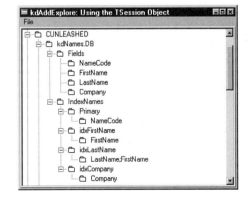

FIGURE 14.13.

The fields and indexes on the kdNames table. Notice that you can drill down to see the fields in each index.

FIGURE 14.14.

The kdAddExplore
program shows all the
aliases on the system.
The open branch is
from an InterBase
database.

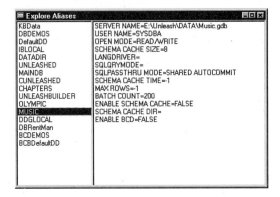

The Code for the kdAddExplore Program

Most of the complexity in the kdAddExplore program comes from manipulating the TTreeView object. The code for querying the TSession object is fairly straightforward in most cases; the TTreeView makes the code a bit tricky in places. The source for this program is shown in Listings 14.9 through 14.15.

Listing 14.9. The header file for the main module in the kdAddExplore program.

```
///////////////////////////////////////
// FILE: Main.h
// PROJECT: KdAddExplore
// Copyright (c) 1997 Charlie Calvert
//
#ifndef MainH
#define MainH
#include <vcl\Classes.hpp>
#include <vcl\Controls.hpp>
#include <vcl\StdCtrls.hpp>
#include <vcl\Forms.hpp>
#include <vcl\ExtCtrls.hpp>
#include <vcl\ComCtrls.hpp>
#include <vcl\Menus.hpp>
class TDBNames : public TForm
{
__published:    // IDE-managed Components
  TPanel *Panel1;
  TTreeView *TView;
  TImageList *ImageList1;
  TMainMenu *MainMenu1;
  TMenuItem *File1;
  TMenuItem *AliasView1;
  TMenuItem *N1;
  TMenuItem *Exit1;
  void __fastcall FormShow(TObject *Sender);
  void __fastcall TViewExpanding(TObject *Sender, TTreeNode *Node,
    Boolean &AllowExpansion);
```

```
  void __fastcall Exit1Click(TObject *Sender);
  void __fastcall AliasView1Click(TObject *Sender);
private:          // User declarations
  void DeleteTemp(TTreeNode *Node);
  void AddTables(TTreeNode *Node);
  void FindFieldsAndIndices(TTreeNode *Node);
  void FindFields(TTreeNode *Node, TTable *Table);
  void FindIndices(TTreeNode *Node, TTable *Table);
public:          // User declarations
  virtual __fastcall TDBNames(TComponent* Owner);
};
extern TDBNames *DBNames;
#endif
```

Listing 14.10. The main module in the kdAddExplore program.

```
/////////////////////////////////////
// FILE: MAIN.CPP
// PROJECT: KDADDEXPLORER
// Copyright (c) 1997 Charlie Calvert
//
#include <vcl\vcl.h>
#pragma hdrstop
#include "Main.h"
#include "AliasView.h"
#pragma resource "*.dfm"
#pragma resource "image.res"
TDBNames *DBNames;
__fastcall TDBNames::TDBNames(TComponent* Owner)
  : TForm(Owner)
{
}
void __fastcall TDBNames::FormShow(TObject *Sender)
{
  int i;
  AnsiString S;
  TStringList *DBNamesList = new TStringList;
  TTreeNode *Node;
  ImageList1->ResourceLoad(rtBitmap, "FolderShut", clPurple);
  Session->GetDatabaseNames(DBNamesList);
  for (i = 0; i < DBNamesList->Count; i++)
  {
    S = DBNamesList->Strings[i];
    Node = TView->Items->Add(TView->Selected, S);
    TView->Items->AddChild(Node, "TEMP");
  }
  DBNamesList->Free();
}
void TDBNames::DeleteTemp(TTreeNode *Node)
{
  TTreeNode *TempNode;

  if (Node->Count == 1)
  {
```

continues

Listing 14.10. continued

```cpp
    TempNode = Node->getFirstChild();
    if (TempNode->Text == "TEMP")
      TempNode->Delete();
  }
}
void TDBNames::AddTables(TTreeNode *Node)
{
  int j;
  AnsiString S(Node->Text);
  TTreeNode *TempNode, *ChildNode;
  TStringList *List = new TStringList;
  DeleteTemp(Node);
  Session->GetTableNames(S, "*.*", True, False, List);
  for (j = 0; j < List->Count; j++)
  {
    TempNode = TView->Items->AddChild(Node, List->Strings[j]);
    ChildNode = TView->Items->AddChild(TempNode, "Fields");
    TView->Items->AddChild(ChildNode, "TEMP");
    ChildNode = TView->Items->AddChild(TempNode, "IndexNames");
    TView->Items->AddChild(ChildNode, "TEMP");
  }
  List->Free();
}
void TDBNames::FindFields(TTreeNode *Node, TTable *Table)
{
  int i;
  for (i = 0; i < Table->FieldCount; i++)
    TView->Items->AddChild(Node, Table->Fields[i]->FieldName);
}
void TDBNames::FindIndices(TTreeNode *Node, TTable *Table)
{
  int i;
  TStringList *List = new TStringList;
  TTreeNode *ChildNode;
  AnsiString S;
  Table->GetIndexNames(List);
  TIndexDefs *IndexDefs = Table->IndexDefs;
  for (i = 0; i < IndexDefs->Count; i++)
  {
    S = IndexDefs->Items[i]->Name;
    if (S.Length() == 0)
      S = "Primary";
    ChildNode = TView->Items->AddChild(Node, S);
    S = IndexDefs->Items[i]->Fields;
    TView->Items->AddChild(ChildNode, S);
  }
  List->Free();
}
void TDBNames::FindFieldsAndIndices(TTreeNode *Node)
{
  TTable *Table = new TTable(this);
  Table->DatabaseName = Node->Parent->Parent->Text;
  Table->TableName = Node->Parent->Text;
  Table->Open();

  DeleteTemp(Node);
  if (Node->Count < 1)
```

```
    switch (Node->Index)
    {
      case 0:
        FindFields(Node, Table);
        break;
      case 1:
        FindIndices(Node, Table);
        break;
    }
  Table->Free();
}
void __fastcall TDBNames::TViewExpanding(TObject *Sender, TTreeNode *Node,
    Boolean &AllowExpansion)
{
  switch (Node->Level)
  {
    case 0:
      if (Node->Count <= 1)
        AddTables(Node);
      break;
    case 2:
      FindFieldsAndIndices(Node);
      break;
  }
}
void __fastcall TDBNames::Exit1Click(TObject *Sender)
{
  Close();
}
void __fastcall TDBNames::AliasView1Click(TObject *Sender)
{
  AliasForm->Show();
}
```

Listing 14.11. The header for the unit that displays information on aliases.

```
//////////////////////////////////////
// FILE: AliasView.h
// PROJECT: KDADDEXPLORER
// Copyright (c) 1997 Charlie Calvert
//
#ifndef AliasViewH
#define AliasViewH
#include <vcl\Classes.hpp>
#include <vcl\Controls.hpp>
#include <vcl\StdCtrls.hpp>
#include <vcl\Forms.hpp>
#include <vcl\DBTables.hpp>
#include <vcl\DB.hpp>
#include <vcl\Menus.hpp>
class TAliasForm : public TForm
{
__published:
  TListBox *ListBox1;
```

continues

Listing 14.11. continued

```
  TListBox *ListBox2;
  void __fastcall ListBox1Click(TObject *Sender);
  void __fastcall FormShow(TObject *Sender);
private:
public:
  virtual __fastcall TAliasForm(TComponent* Owner);
};
extern TAliasForm *AliasForm;
#endif
```

Listing 14.12. The main source file of the unit that displays information about the aliases on the system.

```
/////////////////////////////////////
// FILE: AliasView.cpp
// PROJECT: KDADDEXPLORER
// Copyright (c) 1997 Charlie Calvert
//
#include <vcl\vcl.h>
#pragma hdrstop
#include "AliasView.h"
#pragma resource "*.dfm"
TAliasForm *AliasForm;
__fastcall TAliasForm::TAliasForm(TComponent* Owner)
  : TForm(Owner)
{
}
void __fastcall TAliasForm::ListBox1Click(TObject *Sender)
{
  AnsiString S(ListBox1->Items->Strings[ListBox1->ItemIndex]);
  Session->GetAliasParams(S, ListBox2->Items);
}
void __fastcall TAliasForm::FormShow(TObject *Sender)
{
  Session->GetAliasNames(ListBox1->Items);
}
```

Listing 14.13. The header file for the program's data module.

```
/////////////////////////////////////
// FILE: DMOD1.h
// PROJECT: KDADDEXPLORER
// Copyright (c) 1997 Charlie Calvert
//
#ifndef DMod1H
#define DMod1H
#include <vcl\Classes.hpp>
#include <vcl\Controls.hpp>
#include <vcl\StdCtrls.hpp>
#include <vcl\Forms.hpp>
```

```
#include <vcl\DB.hpp>
#include <vcl\DBTables.hpp>
class TDMod : public TDataModule
{
__published:
    TDatabase *Database1;
private:
public:
    virtual __fastcall TDMod(TComponent* Owner);
};
extern TDMod *DMod;
//-----------------------------------------------------------------------
#endif
```

Listing 14.14. The data module for the main program contains a TDatabase object but no custom code.

```
//////////////////////////////////////////
// FILE: DMOD1.CPP
// PROJECT: KDADDEXPLORER
// Copyright (c) 1997 Charlie Calvert
//
#include <vcl\vcl.h>
#pragma hdrstop
#include "DMod1.h"
#pragma resource "*.dfm"
TDMod *DMod;
__fastcall TDMod::TDMod(TComponent* Owner)
    : TDataModule(Owner)
{
}
```

Listing 14.15. The custom resource file holding the bitmap displayed in the TTreeView.

```
FolderShut BITMAP "FLDRSHUT.BMP"
```

Using a TTreeView to Display the Databases on a System

When the kdAddExplore program is launched, it first iterates through the available databases on the system and displays to the user in a TTreeView:

```
void __fastcall TDBNames::FormShow(TObject *Sender)
{
  int i;
  AnsiString S;
  TStringList *DBNamesList = new TStringList;
  TTreeNode *Node;
  ImageList1->ResourceLoad(rtBitmap, "FolderShut", clPurple);
```

```
Session->GetDatabaseNames(DBNamesList);
for (i = 0; i < DBNamesList->Count; i++)
{
  S = DBNamesList->Strings[i];
  Node = TView->Items->Add(TView->Selected, S);
  TView->Items->AddChild(Node, "TEMP");
}
DBNamesList->Free();
}
```

This code needs to have an icon that it can use to spruce up the nodes of the TTreeView. It stores the bitmap used as an icon in a resource file that looks like this:

```
FolderShut BITMAP "FLDRSHUT.BMP"
```

FLDRSHUT.BMP is one of the files that ships in the Images subdirectory that is created when you install BCB.

The code loads the bitmap into a TImageList object, which is associated with the TTreeView object via the Images property. You can view the Images property of the TTreeView object in the Object Inspector, and you can use a drop-down list to select the TImageList you want to use with this component. Because only one image appears in this image list, it will automatically be associated with all the nodes of the TTreeView object. In this particular case, that is a satisfactory solution to the problem of how to give some visual interest to the object.

After getting the icon set up, the program retrieves the list of available aliases from the TSession object and stores them inside a TStringList:

```
TStringList *DBNamesList = new TStringList;
Session->GetDatabaseNames(DBNamesList);
```

After you have the list of items, you can easily store each one inside a TTreeNode object that can be hung on the TTreeView for display to the user:

```
TTreeNode *Node;
for (i = 0; i < DBNamesList->Count; i++)
{
  S = DBNamesList->Strings[i];
  Node = TView->Items->Add(TView->Selected, S);
  TView->Items->AddChild(Node, "TEMP");
}
```

Clearly, the TTreeNode object is the key to working with TTreeViews. This object represents an individual node on a TTreeView. It encapsulates a bitmap and a caption, and can be identified by a unique index number.

Notice that I call two methods of the Items property of the TTreeView object, which in this program is called TView; it is not a type, but an abbreviation for TreeView. The first call adds the name of the database as a node. The next call adds a child to that database node containing a string consisting of the word "Temp". The "Temp" node is never shown to the user but exists only to force the TTreeView to display a plus sign indicating to the user that the node can be expanded further. When it comes time to expand the node, I delete the word Temp and substitute a word that actually displays the name of the one of tables in the database.

The use of the "Temp" node may seem like a nasty kluge at first, but it really is more intelligent to do things this way rather than force the user to sit still while I open all the databases, including those that might need a password, and find all the tables inside them. When you think of things from this perspective, adding a temporary node to each item in the tree suddenly seems very logical. If the user wants to expand a particular node, then you can retrieve detailed information about that particular database. This approach is much better than trying to retrieve information about every table on the system.

Expanding the Nodes of the TTreeView

The program must respond appropriately when the user clicks on a node of the TTreeView object. In particular, if the user is first opening a particular database node, then the code needs to retrieve the list of tables in that database and display them to the user. If the user clicks one of the tables, then a list of fields and indexes must be retrieved, and so on.

An OnExpanding event gets called automatically when the user wants to open a node. Here is how the kdAddExplore program responds to this event:

```
void __fastcall TDBNames::TViewExpanding(TObject *Sender, TTreeNode *Node,
        Boolean &AllowExpansion)
{
  switch (Node->Level)
  {
    case 0:
      if (Node->Count <= 1)
        AddTables(Node);
      break;
    case 2:
      FindFieldsAndIndices(Node);
      break;
  }
}
```

As you can see, the program calls a method named AddTables if the user is working at the first level of the tree, and it calls a method called FindFieldsAndIndices if the user is working at the second level of the tree. The level the user is currently exploring appears in the Level field of the TTreeNode passed to the OnExpanding event handler.

Before calling AddTables, I check to see if more than one child node already appears on this particular node of the TTreeView. If more than one node exists, then I assume that the database has already been explored and that the node can be opened without any further querying of the system. If only one node exists, then I assume that this is the "Temp" node created in the program's OnShow event, and I call AddTables so that the node can be updated.

Adding a List of Available Tables to the `TTreeView`

Here is the code that is called when it's time to explore the tables on the system:

```cpp
void TDBNames::DeleteTemp(TTreeNode *Node)
{
  TTreeNode *TempNode;

  if (Node->Count == 1)
  {
    TempNode = Node->getFirstChild();
    if (TempNode->Text == "TEMP")
      TempNode->Delete();
  }
}
void TDBNames::AddTables(TTreeNode *Node)
{
  int j;
  AnsiString S(Node->Text);
  TTreeNode *TempNode, *ChildNode;
  TStringList *List = new TStringList;
  DeleteTemp(Node);
  Session->GetTableNames(S, "*.*", True, False, List);
  for (j = 0; j < List->Count; j++)
  {
    TempNode = TView->Items->AddChild(Node, List->Strings[j]);
    ChildNode = TView->Items->AddChild(TempNode, "Fields");
    TView->Items->AddChild(ChildNode, "TEMP");
    ChildNode = TView->Items->AddChild(TempNode, "IndexNames");
    TView->Items->AddChild(ChildNode, "TEMP");
  }
  List->Free();
}
```

The first method shown here, called `DeleteTemp`, is used to delete the `"Temp"` nodes created in the `OnShow` event. The code checks to make sure the string is actually set to `"Temp"` just to be sure that I haven't stumbled across a database that has only one table in it. The program would, of course, behave badly if it encountered a database with a single table in it called `"Temp"`!

The next step is for the program to retrieve the list of tables in a database from the `Session` object:

```cpp
Session->GetTableNames(S, "*.*", True, False, List);
```

The code uses the string name from the node passed to the `OnExpanded` event to query `TSession` for the proper set of tables. You can look up `GetTableNames` in the online help for detailed explanation of this call, but most readers should be able to figure out what is going on from this declaration:

```cpp
void __fastcall GetTableNames(
  const System::AnsiString DatabaseName,
  const System::AnsiString Pattern,
  bool Extensions,
```

```
    bool SystemTables,
    Classes::TStrings* List);
```

Set `Extensions` to `True` if you want to retrieve the extension for a dBASE or Paradox table. Also set `Extensions` to `True` if you want to retrieve system tables for SQL databases such as InterBase.

The program is at last ready to add the tables to the `TTreeView`:

```
TempNode = TView->Items->AddChild(Node, List->Strings[j]);
ChildNode = TView->Items->AddChild(TempNode, "Fields");
TView->Items->AddChild(ChildNode, "TEMP");
ChildNode = TView->Items->AddChild(TempNode, "IndexNames");
TView->Items->AddChild(ChildNode, "TEMP");
```

This code first adds a table name to the `TTreeView`:

```
TempNode = TView->Items->AddChild(Node, List->Strings[j]);
```

It then adds two child nodes labeled `Fields` and `IndexNames` to the Table Name. Once again, I resort to the trick of placing a `"Temp"` node under these two fields to indicate to the user that the nodes can be expanded further. However, I do not actually expand the nodes at this time because the user may not ever want to see the data in question.

Finding Out About Indexes and Fields

To find out about indexes and fields, I abandon the `TSession` object and instead create a `TTable` object, since that is the object that can give me the information I need:

```
void TDBNames::FindFieldsAndIndices(TTreeNode *Node)
{
  TTable *Table = new TTable(this);
  Table->DatabaseName = Node->Parent->Parent->Text;
  Table->TableName = Node->Parent->Text;
  Table->Open();

  DeleteTemp(Node);
  if (Node->Count < 1)
    switch (Node->Index)
    {
      case 0:
        FindFields(Node, Table);
        break;
      case 1:
        FindIndices(Node, Table);
        break;
    }
  Table->Free();
}
```

The program first queries `TTreeView` to retrieve the name of the database the user wants to explore and the name of the particular table under examination:

```
Table->DatabaseName = Node->Parent->Parent->Text;
Table->TableName = Node->Parent->Text;
```

14

SESSIONS AND
RELATIONAL REAL-
WORLD DATABASES

The table is then opened, and the `"Temp"` node associated with it is deleted:

```
Table->Open();
DeleteTemp(Node);
```

I hung the nodes with the labels `Fields` and `IndexNames` in a particular order, so I can use the `Index` field of the current `Node` to know when to retrieve information on fields and when to retrieve information on indexes:

```
switch (Node->Index)
{
  case 0:
    FindFields(Node, Table);
    break;
  case 1:
    FindIndices(Node, Table);
    break;
}
```

The `FindFields` method is very simple, in large part because it is a leaf node on the tree and does not need to be expanded further:

```
void TDBNames::FindFields(TTreeNode *Node, TTable *Table)
{
  int i;
  for (i = 0; i < Table->FieldCount; i++)
    TView->Items->AddChild(Node, Table->Fields[i]->FieldName);
}
```

I have to do a little coaxing to get the system to give up information on indexes:

```
void TDBNames::FindIndices(TTreeNode *Node, TTable *Table)
{
  int i;
  TStringList *List = new TStringList;
  TTreeNode *ChildNode;
  AnsiString S;
  Table->GetIndexNames(List);
  TIndexDefs *IndexDefs = Table->IndexDefs;
  for (i = 0; i < IndexDefs->Count; i++)
  {
    S = IndexDefs->Items[i]->Name;
    if (S.Length() == 0)
      S = "Primary";
    ChildNode = TView->Items->AddChild(Node, S);
    S = IndexDefs->Items[i]->Fields;
    TView->Items->AddChild(ChildNode, S);
  }
  List->Free();
}
```

I first get the list of index names from the `TTable` object and then retrieve the relevant `TIndexDefs` object. This object contains information on a particular index. I iterated through the `Items` in the `IndexDefs` and displayed the information to the user.

You might think that I would have to have a second loop inside the first loop to handle the case in which an index consists of more than one field. However, a second loop is not necessary, because the list is sent to me in the form of a single string, with each index delimited by a semicolon. For example, the primary index of the Items table from BCDEMOS consists of two fields. This information is displayed by TIndexDefs as follows:

```
OrderNo;ItemNo
```

Displaying Aliases and Alias Parameters

After all the work involved with displaying information about databases, tables, indexes, and fields, you will find that querying the system about aliases is relatively trivial. One of the main reasons this process is so much simpler is that I use list boxes rather than a TTreeView to display information. TTreeViews are great for the user, but not much fun for the programmer!

Here is the custom code from the unit that displays the alias to the user. All the other code in the unit is generated by the system:

```
void __fastcall TAliasForm::ListBox1Click(TObject *Sender)
{
  AnsiString S(ListBox1->Items->Strings[ListBox1->ItemIndex]);
  Session->GetAliasParams(S, ListBox2->Items);
}

void __fastcall TAliasForm::FormShow(TObject *Sender)
{
  Session->GetAliasNames(ListBox1->Items);
}
```

The program opts to display this information in a separate form, rather than overlaying it on top of the information about databases. This form has two list boxes in it. The first list box holds the various aliases available on the system, and the second list box holds the parameters for the currently selected alias.

When the form is first shown, I call the GetAliasNames method of the global Session object and then pass it the TStrings-based property of TListBox. That's all I need to do to show the user the aliases!

If the user selects a particular item in the first list box, then the ListBox1Click event handler is called. This code initializes a string to the name of the currently selected alias:

```
AnsiString S(ListBox1->Items->Strings[ListBox1->ItemIndex]);
```

Then it queries the Session object for the list of parameters associated with that object:

```
Session->GetAliasParams(S, ListBox2->Items);
```

As you can see, this second list is displayed in the second list box, as shown in Figure 14.14.

Data Migration, Temporary Tables, NULL Fields

On the CD that comes with this book, in the Chapter 14 directory, you will find a program that transfers the data from the Address2 program to the kdAdds program. By and large, this code is too mundane to bother including in the text of this book. However, migration poses a common problem, and one that you may need to tackle. If so, you can examine the program.

A TBatchMove component is on the Data Access page of the Component Palette. This object can be used to move data quickly between two tables. For example, it can be very helpful when you want to move data from an abstract dataset to a temporary table that is saved to disk. For example, Paradox is always creating temporary tables called Answer.db. If you want to create tables of that type, then use the TBatchMove component.

Another powerful tool that ships with BCB is the Data Migration Expert. This tool can help you migrate data from one database to another. For example, if you want to move a database from Paradox to InterBase, then you can use the Data Migration Expert. This tool will re-create all the fields, the aliases, and even the referential integrity that you have built into your first database. Needless to say, no tool of this type is going to be perfect, due the nature of the wide variety of databases available. However, I have had surprisingly good luck with it and have found that it can save me hours, if not days, of work.

The particular problem I deal with in this case cannot be aided much by the kinds of tools mentioned in the preceding few paragraphs. The reason for this failure is simply that I need to completely restructure the database used in Address2 before it can be used in kdAdds. In particular, I need to break up the one table used in Address2 into five tables used in the relational model that underlies kdAdds. I cannot automate that kind of process using any tools that ship with BCB, so I do it by hand in the program called AddressToKd (also found on the CD).

The only code from the AddressToKd program that I want to show you in this text is the code that checks to see whether a field is set to NULL:

```
void TDMod::TransferEMail()
{
  if (!AddressTableEMail1->IsNull)
  {
    KDEMailTable->Insert();
    KDEMailTableAddress->AsString = AddressTableEMail1->AsString;
    KDEMailTable->Post();
  }

  if (!AddressTableEMail2->IsNull)
  {
    KDEMailTable->Insert();
    KDEMailTableAddress->AsString = AddressTableEMail2->AsString;
    KDEMailTable->Post();
  }
}
```

This code checks to see whether the `Email1` and `Email2` fields of the Address table from the Address2 program are set to `NULL`. This process is necessary because trying to access a field that has no data in it whatsoever is sometimes not a good idea. Because you, too, might run across a situation in which you need to do this, I have included the code here. As you can see, all you need to do is call the `IsNull` method of the `TField` object. This method returns `True` if the field is set to `NULL`, and it returns `False` otherwise. A `NULL` field is a blank or empty field that contains no data.

After I'm sure that it's safe to work with the field, I insert a record into the `kdEMail` table, add the e-mail information to it, and post the record. That's all I'm going to say about the program here in the text of this book, but you can open it up in BCB and explore it at your leisure if you are interested in it.

Summary

In this chapter, you have had a look at relational databases. The core material was divided into two sections. The first section looked at a simple relational database program consisting of five interrelated tables. You saw how these tables are tied together and how to add, delete, insert, and edit records in these tables. Also included is a relatively lengthy discussion of the indexes and keys in the table and of why they were created. Other subjects include searching and storing strings in a string table.

The second half of the chapter was dedicated to an examination of the global `TSession` object that is created automatically whenever you use the BDE database tools in your program. You saw that you can use this object to query the system about the aliases, databases, and tables it is using. You also saw how to query a `TTable` object about its fields and indexes.

Other information included in this chapter relates mostly to using standard BCB components such as the `TTreeView`. You saw that the `TTreeView` object is very powerful, and it allows you to display information in a way that the user can easily comprehend. Several portions of the chapter focus on the `TTreeNode` object used to fill in the nodes of a `TTreeView`. In particular, you saw how to add child nodes to a `TTreeView`.

IN THIS PART

PART

III

Client/Server Databases

Working with the Local InterBase Server

CHAPTER 15

Overview

BCB ships with the Local InterBase Server, which is sometimes simply called LIBS. This tool provides all the capabilities of the full InterBase server, but it runs on a local machine. You do not need to be connected to a network to be able to run the Local InterBase Server.

The client software you get with BCB will talk to either LIBS or the standard version of the InterBase Server. From your point of view as a programmer, you will find no difference at all between talking to LIBS and talking to an InterBase server across a network. The only way to tell which server you're connected to is by examining the path in your current alias. In short, LIBS is the perfect tool for learning or practicing real client/server database programming even if you're not connected to a LAN.

The goal of this chapter is to provide you with a useful introduction to LIBS and also a brief overview of transactions. In particular, you will see how to do the following:

- Connect to local InterBase tables
- Connect without having to specify a password
- Create databases
- Work with TDatabase objects
- Create tables
- Commit and roll back transactions in both local and InterBase tables
- Maintain the data you have created
- Work with cached updates
- Create many-to-many relationships

Everything that is said about the local InterBase in this chapter applies equally to the full server version of InterBase. As a result, this chapter will also be of interest to people who use InterBase on a network. In particular, this chapter shows how you can use a local system to create a database that is fully compatible with the network version of InterBase. To convert a LIBS database to a real client/server application on a network, you just have to copy your database onto another machine:

```
copy MyDatabase.gdb p:\remote\nt\drive
```

You just copy the one file onto the network. No other steps are necessary, other than changing the path in your alias. Of course, you will also need a real copy of the InterBase server.

Note that some versions of BCB ship with at least two licenses for the InterBase server. The real InterBase server runs on most platforms, including Windows 95, Windows NT, and a wide range of UNIX platforms.

Many readers of this book will come from the world of "big iron," where the only kinds of databases that exist are servers such as Oracle, Sybase, InterBase, AS400, or DB2. Other readers come from the world of PCs, where tools such as dBASE, Paradox, Access, or FoxPro are considered to be the standard database tools. Overemphasizing the huge gap that exists between these two worlds is almost impossible.

Readers who are familiar with "big iron" and large network-based servers are likely to find the Local InterBase Server very familiar. Readers who come from the world of PCs are likely to find InterBase very strange indeed, especially at first.

InterBase is meant to handle huge numbers of records, which are stored on servers. It does not come equipped with many of the amenities of a tool such as dBASE or Paradox. In fact, InterBase supplies users with only the most minimal interface and instead expects you to create programs with a client-side tool such as BCB. However, you will find that InterBase is not a particularly difficult challenge, after you get some of the basics under your belt.

Databases and the Job Market

Having been in this business for a while, I know that most of the readers of this book probably work inside a corporation or at a small company. However, if you are a student or someone who wants to enter the computer programming world, you should pay special attention to the material in this, and other, chapters on InterBase.

Perhaps 80 percent of the applications built in America today use databases in one form or another. Indeed, most of these applications revolve around, and are focused on, manipulating databases. Furthermore, client/server databases such as InterBase, Oracle, or MS SQL Server form the core of this application development.

If you want to enter the programming world, getting a good knowledge of databases is one of the best ways to get started. Right now, there is virtually an endless need for good database programmers.

One note of caution should perhaps be added here. I happen to enjoy database programming. However, it is not the most romantic end of the computer business. If you're primarily interested in systems programming or games programming, then you should hold out for jobs in those fields rather than focus your career in an area of only minor interest to you.

Databases, however, offer the greatest opportunity for employment. In particular, client/server database programmers are almost always in demand. Because LIBS ships with your copy of BCB, you have a great chance to learn the ins and outs of this lucrative field.

Setting Up the Local InterBase

LIBS is installed for you automatically when you install BCB. In most cases, InterBase will run smoothly without any need for you to worry about setup. However, you should take several key steps to ensure that all is as it should be.

First, find out if LIBS is running. By default, it will load into memory every time you boot up the system. If you're running Windows 95 or NT 4.0, you should see LIBS as a little splash of green on the system tray to the right of the toolbar. On Windows NT 3.51, an icon appears at the bottom of your screen. Whatever shape it takes on your system, just click this green object, and you will see a report on the Local InterBase Server configuration.

You need to know where your copy of LIBS is installed. Most likely, it is in the ..\PROGRAM FILES\BORLAND\INTRBASE subdirectory on the boot drive of your computer. For example, my copy of the local InterBase is in C:\PROGRAM FILES\BORLAND\INTRBASE. To find out for sure, open the InterBase Configuration applet that ships with BCB. It will report on the InterBase root subdirectory and enable you to change that directory if need be.

To find this same information in the Registry, run REGEDIT.EXE and open HKEY_LOCAL_MACHINE/ SOFTWARE/BORLAND/INTERBASE. Several nodes report on the location of your server and other related information.

In the INTRBASE subdirectory, you will find a copy of a file called INTERBAS.MSG. You should also be able to locate a copy of GDS32.DLL somewhere on your system, most likely in the ..\WINDOWS\SYSTEM subdirectory, but possibly in either your BDE or INTRBASE subdirectory.

A common problem occurs when InterBase users end up with more than one copy of GDS32.DLL. If you work with the networked version of InterBase, you probably already have a copy of the InterBase Client on your system. If this is the case, you should make sure that you don't have two sets of the file GDS32.DLL on your path. On my system, I use the copy of GDS32.DLL that comes with the local InterBase. These tools communicate with both LIBS and the full networked version of InterBase. This setup works fine for me. However, the point is not which version you use, but only that you know which version is on your path and that you have only one version on your system at a time.

To find out which version you are currently using, run the InterBase Communications Diagnostics Tool that ships with BCB. Use the Browse button to find the EMPLOYEE.GDB file, which is probably located in the ..PROGRAM FILES\BORLAND\INTRBASE\EXAMPLES subdirectory. Enter SYSDBA as the user name and masterkey as the password, all lowercase. (This example assumes that you have not changed the password from its default value.) You should get the following readout, or something like it:

```
Path Name       = C:\WINDOWS\SYSTEM\gds32.dll
Size            = 348672 Bytes
File Time       = 04:10:00
File Date       = 12/18/1995
Version         = 4.1.0.6
This module has passed the version check.
Attempting to attach to C:\Borland\Intrbase\EXAMPLES\Employee.gdb
     Attaching      ...Passed!
     Detaching      ...Passed!
InterBase versions for this connection:
InterBase/Windows NT (access method), version "WI-B4.1.0"
on disk structure version 8.0
InterBase Communication Test Passed!
```

The key piece of information you're getting here is the location of GDS32.DLL.

> **NOTE**
>
> Readers who want to connect to the full server version of InterBase will find that the procedure I have just outlined works fine, except that you must have a network protocol such as TCP/IP loaded first. This book includes a description of the wizardry needed to set up a TCP/IP network protocol successfully in Chapter 8, "Database Basics and Database Tools." As I explained in that chapter, this task is usually handled automatically by either Windows 95 or Windows NT, though it helps to have a few extra tips to guide you through the process. I should add that setting up an InterBase connection is usually a fairly straightforward process when compared to setting up other servers.

The most obvious thing that can go wrong with an InterBase connection is simply that it is not being started automatically when you start Windows. If you are having trouble, try simply pointing the Explorer to the IntrBase/bin subdirectory and clicking the IBServer.exe icon. The trouble could be that all is set up correctly, but for some reason the server is not currently running on your machine!

Setting Up an InterBase Alias

In the preceding section, you learned how to run a diagnostic tool to be sure you are connected to InterBase. This section deals with the issue of making sure that the BDE is connected to InterBase. In other words, that section dealt with making sure that InterBase was running correctly on your machine; this section deals with making sure BCB is connected to InterBase. You should also check the readme file on the CD that accompanies this book for general information about setting up aliases for the programs supplied in this book.

After you have the local InterBase set up, you should take a few minutes to make sure the connection to the BDE is working correctly. In particular, you should make sure an alias points to one of the sample tables that ship with LIBS. For example, after a normal full installation of BCB, you should have an alias called IBLOCAL that points to the EMPLOYEE.GDB file.

In the next few paragraphs, I describe how to set up an alias identical to the IBLOCAL alias, except you can give it a different name. To begin, open the Database Explorer and turn to the Databases page. Select the first node in the tree, the one that's called Databases. Choose Database | New, and then select IntrBase as the Database Driver Name in the New Database Alias page dialog. Click OK.

Name the new alias TESTGDB, or give it whatever name you prefer. The ServerName property for this alias should be set to

```
c:\program files\borland\intrbase\examples\employee.gdb
```

You can adjust the drive letter and path to reflect the way you have set up the files on your machine.

The user name should be set to SYSDBA, and the default password you will use is masterkey. (If someone has changed the password on your system, then use the new password.) All the other settings in the Database Explorer can have their default values, as shown in Figure 15.1. After you have everything set up correctly, choose Database | Apply.

FIGURE 15.1.

A sample InterBase alias as it appears in the Database Explorer.

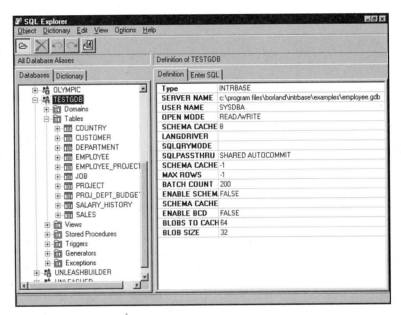

After you have set up and saved your alias, you can connect to the TESTGDB alias exactly as you would with any other set of data. From inside the Explorer, just click the plus symbol before the TESTGDB node. A dialog will pop up prompting you for a password. Make sure the user name is set to SYSDBA, and then enter masterkey as the password. Everything else will then be the same as when working with a Paradox table, except that you will find many new features such as stored procedures and triggers. Most of these new features will be described in this chapter and the next.

To connect to the database from inside BCB proper, first drop a table onto a form, and set its DatabaseName property to TESTGDB. When you try to drop down the list of TableNames, you will be prompted for a password. You should enter masterkey at this point, all in lowercase. Now drop down the list again and select a table. After taking these steps, you can set the Active property for Table1 to True. If this call succeeds, everything is set up correctly, and you can begin using the local InterBase to create BCB database programs. If you can't set Active to True, you should go over the steps outlined previously and see whether you can correct the problem.

> **NOTE**
>
> I usually use SYSDBA and masterkey as the user name and password combination for the InterBase databases in this book. However, I sometimes work with USER1 and USER1 instead, simply because typing USER1 is easier than typing masterkey. One way to change the sign on criteria for InterBase is via the InterBase Server Manager. This, and other tools, will be discussed in Chapter 16, "Advanced InterBase Concepts."

In the preceding two sections, you have learned the basic facts about using LIBS. The next step is to learn how to create your own databases and tables.

Creating Databases

Unlike local Paradox or dBASE files, InterBase tables are not stored in separate files located within a directory. Instead, InterBase tables are stored in one large file called a database. Therefore, you need to first go out and create a database, and then you can create a series of tables inside this larger database.

> **NOTE**
>
> The single file system is, in my opinion, vastly superior to having a series of separate files. I'm sure you've noticed what happens after you have placed a few indexes on a typical Paradox table. The end result is that your table is associated with six or seven other files, some of which have to be present or you can't get at your data! A big Paradox database might consist of a hundred or more files, all of which have to be backed up, moved from place to place, and maintained. Life is much simpler when your whole database is stored in a single file!

The simplest way to create a database is with a CASE tool such as SDesigner or Cadet. However, these tools do not ship with BCB, so you must instead choose between the Database Desktop, BCB itself, and the WISQL program that ships with the Local InterBase Server. Absent the presence of a CASE tool, I find that my weapon of choice is WISQL, though this is certainly a debatable decision. (Cadet will be discussed briefly, along with SDesigner, in Chapter 18, "Working with CASE Tools: Cadet, ER1, and SDesigner.")

WISQL stands for Windows Interactive Standard Query Language, or simply the Interactive SQL tool. WISQL is fundamentally a tool for entering SQL statements, with a few other simple features thrown in for good measure. One advantage of relying on WISQL is that it allows you to work directly in the mother tongue of databases, which is SQL. I find that defining databases directly in SQL helps me understand their structure, though of course, there is little reason for resorting to these measures if you have a copy of SDesigner or ERWin available.

You should also remember that WISQL bypasses the BDE altogether. You can therefore use it to test your connections to InterBase even if you are not sure that you have the BDE set up correctly. For example, if you're having trouble connecting to InterBase and you're not sure where the problem lies, start by trying to connect with WISQL. If that works but you can't connect from inside BCB, the problem might lie not with your InterBase setup, but with the way you have deployed the BDE.

NOTE

In addition to WISQL, the other important tool that ships with InterBase is the InterBase Server Manager, IBMGR.EXE. It enables you to test connections to servers and perform simple maintenance tasks such as backing up and restoring databases and setting passwords. You can use IBMGR to back up your data so that you can recover if disaster strikes. What little information you need for this easy-to-use tool is available in the InterBase documentation and in the short section on this tool that appears later in this chapter.

After starting WISQL, choose File | Create Database. A dialog like the one shown in Figure 15.2 appears. Set the Location Info to Local Engine, because you are in fact working with local InterBase. (Actually, there is no reason that you have to use Local InterBase rather than the full server version when working through these examples. However, I will reference LIBS throughout this chapter because it will be the tool of choice for most readers.)

Figure 15.2.

The dialog used for creating databases inside WISQL.

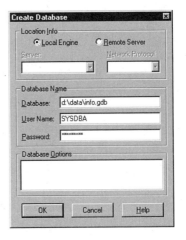

In the Database field, enter the name of the table you want to create. If the table is to be located inside a particular directory, include that directory in the database name. For practice, you should create a database called INFO.GDB that is located in a subdirectory called DATA. If it does not already exist on your system, you should first go to DOS or the Windows Explorer and create the DATA subdirectory. After you set up the subdirectory, enter the following in the Database field:

```
E:\DATA\INFO.GDB
```

You can replace E: with the letter for the appropriate drive on your system. The extension .GDB is traditional, though not mandatory. However, I suggest always using this extension so that you can recognize your databases instantly when you see them. Accidentally deleting even a recently backed up database can be a tragedy.

You can set the user name to anything you want, although the traditional entry is SYSDBA, and the traditional password is masterkey. When you first start out with InterBase, sticking with this user name and password combination is probably best. Even if you assign new passwords to your database, the SYSDBA/masterkey combination will still work unless you explicitly remove it using the IBMGR.

After you have entered a user name and password, you can create the database by clicking the OK button. If all goes well, you are then placed back inside WISQL proper. At this stage, you can either quit WISQL or add a table to your database. If something goes wrong, an error message will appear. Click the Details button to try to track down the problem.

Assuming all goes well, the following SQL statement can be run inside WISQL if you want to create a very simple table with two fields:

```
CREATE TABLE TEST1 (FIRST VARCHAR(20), LAST INTEGER);
```

Enter this line in the SQL Statement field at the top of WISQL, and then click the Run button. If all goes smoothly, your statement will be echoed in the ISQL output window without being accompanied by an error dialog. The lack of an error dialog signals that the table has been created successfully.

The preceding CREATE TABLE command creates a table with two fields. The first is a character field containing 20 characters, and the second is an integer field.

NOTE

The table-creation code shown here is used to describe or create a table in terms that WISQL understands. In fact, you can use this same code inside a TQuery object in a BCB program.

Throughout most of this chapter and the next, I work with WISQL rather than with the DBD. In describing how to perform these actions in WISQL, I do not mean to imply that you can't use the Database Desktop to create or alter InterBase tables. In fact, the 32-bit version of DBD provides pretty good support for InterBase tables. Still, I have found WISQL to be considerably more powerful than I suspected when I first started using it. Once again, I should add that neither of these tools is as easy to use as a good CASE tool.

15

WORKING WITH THE LOCAL INTERBASE SERVER

After creating a database and table, you should choose File | Commit Work. This command causes WISQL to actually carry out the commands you have issued. At this stage, you should choose File | Disconnect from Database.

In this section, you have learned the basic steps required to use InterBase to create a database and table. The steps involved are not particularly complicated, although they can take a bit of getting used to if you're new to the world of SQL.

Exploring a Database with WISQL

WISQL provides a number of tools that can help you explore a database and its contents. In the preceding section, you created a database with a single table. In this section, you will learn how to connect to the database and table from inside WISQL. You will also see how to examine the main features of the entities you have created.

To connect to `INFO.GDB`, choose File | Connect to Database, which brings up the dialog shown in Figure 15.3. Enter the drive and the database as `e:\data\info.gdb`, where `e:` represents the appropriate drive on your machine. Enter the user as `SYSDBA`, and the password as `masterkey`. If all goes well, you should be able to connect to the database by clicking the OK button. Once again, success is signaled by the lack of an error message.

FIGURE 15.3.

Connecting to the
`INFO.GDB` *database*
using WISQL.

Choose View | Metadata Information and set View Information On to Database, as shown in Figure 15.4. After you click OK, the information displayed in the ISQL output window should look something like this:

```
SHOW DB
Database: c:\data\info.gdb
        Owner: SYSDBA
PAGE_SIZE 1024
Number of DB pages allocated = 210
Sweep interval = 20000
```

FIGURE 15.4.

*Preparing to view
information on the
INFO.GDB database.*

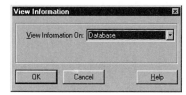

To see the tables available in a database, choose View | Metadata Information, and set View Information On to Table. You can leave the edit control labeled Object Name blank. If you fill it in with a table name, you will get detailed information on a specific table—but in this case we want general information on all tables. Click the OK button and view the information, which should look like the following, in the ISQL output window:

```
SHOW TABLES
     TEST1
```

Browsing through the Metadata Information menu choice, you can see that InterBase supports triggers, stored procedures, views, and a host of other advanced server features.

The Extract menu choice enables you to find out more detailed information about the database and its tables. For example, if you choose Extract | SQL Metadata for a Database, you get output similar to the following:

```
/* Extract Database e:\data\info.gdb */
CREATE DATABASE "e:\data\info.gdb" PAGE_SIZE 1024
;
/* Table: TEST1, Owner: SYSDBA */
CREATE TABLE TEST1 (FIRST VARCHAR(20),
       LAST INTEGER);
/* Grant permissions for this database */
```

If you choose Extract | SQL Metadata for Table, you get the following output:

```
/* Extract Table TEST1 */
/* Table: TEST1, Owner: SYSDBA */
CREATE TABLE TEST1 (FIRST VARCHAR(20),
       LAST INTEGER);
```

You should note that WISQL often asks whether you want to save the output from a command to a text file, and the File menu gives you some further options for saving information to files. You can take advantage of these options when necessary, but 90 percent of the time, I pass them by with barely a nod. (Some CASE tools use the output from Extract | SQL Metadata to reverse-engineer a database. If your CASE tool asks you for a script file, you can produce one this way.)

> **NOTE**
>
> The WISQL program accepts most SQL statements. For example, you can perform Insert, Select, Update, and Delete statements from inside WISQL. Just enter the statement you want to perform in the SQL Statement area, and then click the Run button.
>
> WISQL also comes equipped with a handy online reference to SQL. If you have questions about how to format an Alter, Drop, Insert, Create Index, or other SQL statement, you can look it up in the help for WISQL. (For better or worse, this is my number-one reference for SQL statements. Another book I have found useful is called *The Practical SQL Handbook*, by Bowman, Emerson, and Darnovsky, Addison Wesley, ISBN 0-201-62623-3.)

After reading the preceding three sections, you should have a fair understanding of how WISQL works and how you can use it to manage a database. The information provided in this chapter is nothing more than an introduction to a complex and very sophisticated topic. However, you now know enough to begin using the local InterBase. This accomplishment is not insignificant. Tools such as InterBase, Oracle, and Sybase lie at the heart of the client/server activity that is currently so volatile and lucrative. If you become proficient at talking to servers such as InterBase, you might find yourself at an important turning point in your career.

Transactions

Now you can break out of the abstract theory rut and start writing some code that actually does something. In this section, you will look at transactions, followed by a discussion of cached updates and many-to-many relationships. In the next chapter, you will see another "real-world" database, when you take a look at a sample program that tracks the albums, tapes, and CDs in a music collection.

The TRANSACT program, found on the CD that accompanies this book, gives a brief introduction to transactions. To use transactions, you must have a TDataBase component on your form. Transactions work not only with real servers such as Sybase, Informix, InterBase, or the local InterBase, but also with the 32-bit BDE drivers for Paradox or dBASE files. In other words, transactions can be part of most of the database work you will do with BCB. Using transactions is, however, a technique most frequently associated with client/server databases.

To begin, drop down a TDatabase component on a TDataModule. Set the AliasName property of the TDataBase object to a valid alias such as IBLOCAL. Create your own string, such as TransactionDemo, to fill in the DatabaseName property of the TDatabase object. In other words, when you're using a TDatabase component, you make up the DatabaseName rather than pick it from a list of available aliases.

Drop down a TQuery object, and hook it up to the EMPLOYEE.GDB file that ships with BCB. In particular, set the DatabaseName property of the TQuery object to TransactionDemo, not to IBLOCAL. In other words, set the DatabaseName property to the string you made up when filling in the DatabaseName property of the TDatabase component. You will find that TransactionDemo, or whatever string you chose, has been added to the list of aliases you can view from the Query1.DatabaseName Property Editor. Now rename Query1 to EmployeeQuery and attach a TDataSource object called EmployeeSource to it.

Finally, set the EmployeeQuery->SQL property to the following string:

```
select * from employee
```

Then set the Active property to True and set RequestLive to True.

Add a TTable object to the project, hook it up to the SALARY_HISTORY table, and call it SalaryHistoryTable. Relate the SalaryHistoryTable to the EmployeeQueryTable via the EMP_NO fields of both tables. In particular, you should set the MasterSource property for the SalaryHistoryTable to EmployeeSource. Then click the MasterFields property of the TTable object, and relate the EMP_NO fields of both tables. This way, you can establish a one-to-many relationship between the EmployeeQueryTable and the SalaryHistoryTable.

After you're connected to the database, you can add two grids to your main form so that you can view the data. Remember that you should use the File | Include Unit Header option to link the TDataModule to the main form.

On the surface of the main form, add four buttons, and give them the following captions:

```
Start Transaction
Rollback
Commit
Refresh
```

The code associated with these buttons should look like this:

```
void __fastcall TForm1::StartTransactionBtnClick(TObject *Sender)
{
  DMod->TransDemo->StartTransaction();
}
void __fastcall TForm1::RollbackBtnClick(TObject *Sender)
{
  DMod->TransDemo->Rollback();
}
void __fastcall TForm1::CommitBtnClick(TObject *Sender)
{
  DMod->TransDemo->Commit();
}
void __fastcall TForm1::RefreshBtnClick(TObject *Sender)
{
  DMod->SalaryHistoryTable->Refresh();
}
```

Run the program, click Start Transaction and edit a record of the `SalaryHistoryTable`. When you do so, be sure to fill in all the fields of the table except for the first and last, which are called `EMP_NO` and `NEW_SALARY`. Be sure not to touch either of those fields, as they will be filled in for you automatically. In particular, you might enter the following values:

```
CHANGE_DATE: 12/12/12
UPDATER_ID: admin2
OLD_SALARY: 105900
PERCENT_CHANGE: 3
```

These values are not randomly chosen. For example, you have to enter `admin2`, or some other valid `UPDATE_ID`, in the `UPDATER_ID` field. You can, of course, enter whatever values you want for the date, old salary, and percent change fields. Still, you need to be careful when working with the Employee tables. This database has referential integrity with a vengeance!

After entering the preceding values, you can post the record by moving off it. When you do, the `NEW_SALARY` field will be filled in automatically by something called a *trigger*. Go ahead and experiment with these tables some if you want. For example, you might leave some of the fields blank, or enter invalid data in the `UPDATER_ID` field, just to see how complex the rules that govern this database are. This data is locked up tighter than Fort Knox, and you can't change it unless you are very careful about what you're doing. (It's worth noting, however, that the developers of this database probably never planned to have anyone use these two tables exactly as I do here. Defining rules that limit how you work with a database is easy, but finding ways to break them is easier still. For all of its rigor, database programming is still not an exact science.)

If you started your session by clicking the Start Transaction button, you can now click RollBack and then Refresh. You will find that all your work is undone, as if none of the editing occurred. If you edit three or four records and then click Commit, you will find that your work is preserved.

> **NOTE**
>
> Though you are safe in this particular case, in some instances like this you can't call `Refresh` directly because the table you're using is not uniquely indexed. In lieu of this call, you can close the table and then reopen it. You could use bookmarks to preserve your location in the table during this operation, or if you're working with a relatively small dataset, as in this example, you can just let the user fend for himself or herself.

Note that when you run the TRANSACT program included on the CD, you don't have to specify a password because the `LoginPrompt` property of the `TDatabase` object is set to `False`, and the `Params` property contains the following string:

```
password=masterkey
```

Now that you have seen transactions in action, you probably want a brief explanation of what they are all about. Here are some reasons for using transactions:

1. *To ensure the integrity of your data.* Sometimes you need to perform a transaction that effects several different interrelated tables. In these cases, it might not be a good idea to alter two tables and then find the session is interrupted for some reason before you can alter the next two tables. For example, you might find that a data entry clerk posts data to two records, but the system crashes before he can finish updating two more records in a different table. As a result, the data in your database may be out of sync. To avoid this situation, you can start a transaction, edit all the rows and tables that need to be edited, and then commit the work in one swift movement. This way, an error is far less likely to occur because of a system crash or power failure.

2. *To handle concurrency issues in which two or more people are accessing the same data at the same time.* You can use a transactions feature called `TransIsolation` levels to fine-tune exactly how and when updates are made. This way, you can decide how you will react if another user is updating records exactly on or near the record you're currently editing.

Now that you have read something about the theory behind transactions, you might want to think for a moment about the `TransIsolation` property of the `TDatabase` object, which affects the way transactions are handled. Here are some quotes from the very important online help entry called "Transaction Isolation Levels."

`tiDirtyRead`	Permits reading of uncommitted changes made to the database by other simultaneous transactions. Uncommitted changes are not permanent, and might be rolled back (undone) at any time. At this level a transaction is least isolated from the effects of other transactions.
`tiReadCommitted`	Permits reading of committed (permanent) changes made to the database by other simultaneous transactions. This is the default `TransIsolation` property value.
`tiRepeatableRead`	Permits a single, one-time reading of the database. The transaction cannot see any subsequent changes made by other simultaneous transactions. This isolation level guarantees that after a transaction reads a record, its view of that record does not change unless it makes a modification to the record itself. At this level, a transaction is most isolated from other transactions.

Most of the time, you can simply leave this field set to `tiReadCommitted`. However, it is important to understand that you have several options regarding how the data in your database is affected by a transaction. The whole subject of how one user of a database might alter records in a table while they are being used by another user is quite complicated, and it poses several paradoxes for which no simple solution exists. The preceding `TransIsolation` levels allow you to choose your poison when dealing with this nasty subject.

15

WORKING WITH THE LOCAL INTERBASE SERVER

You must consider other issues when you're working with transactions, but I have tried to cover some of the most important here. In general, I find that transactions are extremely easy to use. However, they become more complex when you consider the delicate subject of concurrency problems, which are frequently addressed through setting the `TransIsolation` levels of your transactions.

Cached Updates

Cached updates are like the transactions just described, except that they enable you to edit a series of records without causing any network traffic. When you are ready to commit your work, cached updates enable you to do so on a record-by-record basis, where any records that violate system integrity can be repaired or rolled back on a case-by-case basis.

> **NOTE**
>
> Some users have reported remarkable increases in performance on some operations when they use cached updates.

The key feature of cached updates is that they let you work with data without allowing any network traffic to occur until you are ready for it to begin. This relatively complex mechanism also enables you to keep track of the status of each record on a field-by-field basis. In particular, when cached updates are turned on, you can query your records one at a time and ask them whether they have been updated. Furthermore, if they have been updated, you can ask the current value of each field in the updated record, and you can also retrieve the old, or original, value of the field.

You can do three things with the records in a dataset after the `CachedUpdates` property for the dataset has been set to `True`:

1. You can call `ApplyUpdates` on the dataset, which means that you will try to commit all the other records updated since `CachedUpdates` was set to `True` or since the last attempt to update the records. This is analogous to committing a transaction.

2. You can call `CancelUpdates`, which means that all the updates made so far will be canceled. This is analogous to rolling back a transaction.

3. You can call `RevertRecord`, which will roll back the current record, but not any of the other records in the dataset.

An excellent sample program in the BCB DEMOS subdirectory shows how to use cached updates. This program is a bit complex in its particulars, however, and therefore can be hard to understand. So, instead of trying to go it one better, I will create a sample program that takes the basic elements of cached updates and presents them in the simplest possible terms.

The CacheUp program, shown in Figure 15.5, has one form. On the form is a copy of the OrdersTable. The OrdersTable, as you recall, is related to both the Customer table and the Items table. As a result, changing either the OrderNo or CustNo fields without violating system integrity in one way or another is difficult. When working with this program, you should change these fields to values like 1 or 2, which will almost surely be invalid. You can then watch what happens when you try to commit the records you have changed.

The code for the CachedUpdates program is shown in Listing 15.1. Go ahead and get this program up and running, and then come back for a discussion of how it works. When you're implementing the code shown here, the key point to remember is that none of it will work unless the CachedUpdates property of the OrdersTable is set to True.

Listing 15.1. The form for the CachedUpdates program.

```
/////////////////////////////////////////
// File: Main.cpp
// Project: CachedUpdates
// Copyright (c) 1997 Charlie Calvert
#include <vcl\vcl.h>
#include <typinfo.hpp>
#include <sysutils.hpp>
#pragma hdrstop
#include "Main.h"
#pragma resource "*.dfm"
TForm1 *Form1;
__fastcall TForm1::TForm1(TComponent* Owner)
  : TForm(Owner)
{
}
void __fastcall TForm1::ApplyBtnClick(TObject *Sender)
{
  OrdersTable->ApplyUpdates();
}
void __fastcall TForm1::RevertBtnClick(TObject *Sender)
{
  OrdersTable->RevertRecord();
}

void __fastcall TForm1::CancelClick(TObject *Sender)
{
  OrdersTable->CancelUpdates();
}
void __fastcall TForm1::OkBtnClick(TObject *Sender)
{
  Close();
}
void __fastcall TForm1::OrdersTableUpdateError(TDataSet *DataSet,
  EDatabaseError *E, TUpdateKind UpdateKind, TUpdateAction &UpdateAction)
{
  TTypeInfo TypeInfo;
  AnsiString UpdateKindStr[] = {"Modified", "Inserted", "Deleted"};
  AnsiString S(UpdateKindStr[UpdateKind]);
  S += ": " + E->Message;
```

continues

Listing 15.1. continued

```
  AnsiString Temp = DataSet->Fields[0]->OldValue;
  Temp = + ": " + S;
  ListBox1->Items->Add(Temp);
  UpdateAction = uaSkip;
}
void __fastcall TForm1::DataSource1DataChange(TObject *Sender,
  TField *Field)
{
  AnsiString UpdateStat[] = {"Unmodified", "Modified", "Inserted", "usDeleted"};
  Panel1->Caption = UpdateStat[OrdersTable->UpdateStatus()];
  if (OrdersTable->UpdateStatus() == usModified)
  {
    Edit1->Text = OrdersTable->Fields[0]->OldValue;
    Edit2->Text = OrdersTable->Fields[0]->NewValue;
  }
  else
  {
    Edit1->Text = "Unmodified";
    Edit2->Text = "Unmodified";
  };
}
void __fastcall TForm1::ListBox1DblClick(TObject *Sender)
{
  AnsiString S(ListBox1->Items->Strings[ListBox1->ItemIndex]);
  if (S.Length() > 0)
    ShowMessage(S);
}
```

The first thing to notice about the CachedUpdates program is that it tracks which records have been modified. For example, change the OrderNo field of the first two records to the values 1 and 2. If you now select one of these records, you will see that the small panel in the lower left corner of the screen gets set to Modified. This means that the update status for this field has been set to modified.

Here is the TUpdateStatus type:

```
TUpdateStatus = (usUnmodified, usModified, usInserted, usDeleted);
```

Any particular record in a database is going to be set to one of these values.

Here is the code that sets the value in the TPanel object:

```
void __fastcall TForm1::DataSource1DataChange(TObject *Sender,
  TField *Field)
{
  AnsiString UpdateStat[] = {"Unmodified", "Modified", "Inserted", "usDeleted"};
  Panel1->Caption = UpdateStat[OrdersTable->UpdateStatus()];
  if (OrdersTable->UpdateStatus() == usModified)
  {
    Edit1->Text = OrdersTable->Fields[0]->OldValue;
    Edit2->Text = OrdersTable->Fields[0]->NewValue;
  }
  else
  {
```

```
    Edit1->Text = "Unmodified";
    Edit2->Text = "Unmodified";
  };
}
```

The relevant line in this case is the second in the body of the function. In particular, notice that it reports on the value of `OrdersTable->UpdateStatus`. This value will change to reflect the update status of the currently selected record.

NOTE

Notice that in this case, I explicitly type out the names associated with the elements of the `TUpdateStatus` type. In some cases, you can use an alternative means to accomplish the same end without explicitly typing out the strings. This second technique involves using the advanced RTTI supported by BCB. To show this value to the user, the code could call the `GetEnumName` routine from the `TypInfo` unit. This routine retrieves the name of an enumerated value. To use this routine, pass in the type that you want to examine, as well as the ordinal value of the element in that type whose name you want to see:

```
PPropInfo PropInfo =
  GetPropInfo(PTypeInfo(ClassInfo(__classid(TForm1))), "Borderstyle");
ShowMessage(GetEnumName(PropInfo->PropType, int(bsDisabled)));
```

Unfortunately, this type of code will work only for VCL-style classes and for properties of VCL-style classes. Because a `TDataSet` does not have an `UpdateStatus` property, the code in the `DataSource1DataChange` method must use the more pedantic method outlined previously.

At the same time that the CachedUpdates program reports that a record has been modified, it also reports on the old and new value of the `OrderNo` field for that record. In particular, if you change the first record's `OrderNo` field to 1, it will report that the old value for the field was 1003, and the new value is 1. (This assumes that you have the original data as it shipped with BCB. Remember that if you end up ruining one of these tables performing these kinds of experiments, you can always copy the table over again from the CD.)

In the code that reports on the old and new value of the `OrderNo` field, you should examine these lines in particular:

```
Edit1->Text = OrdersTable->Fields[0]->OldValue;
Edit2->Text = OrdersTable->Fields[0]->NewValue;
```

As you can see, this information is easy enough to come by—you just have to know where to look.

If you enter the values 1 and 2 into the `OrderNo` fields for the first two records, you will encounter errors when you try to commit the data. In particular, if you try to apply the data, the built-in referential integrity will complain that there is no way to link the `Orders` and `Items` table on the new `OrderNo` you have created. As a result, committing the records is not possible. The code then rolls back the erroneous records to their original state.

When viewing these kinds of errors, choose Options | Environment | Preferences and then turn off the Break on Exception option. The issue here is that you want the exception to occur, but you don't want to be taken to the line in your program where the exception surfaced. You don't need to view the actual source code because these exceptions are not the result of errors in your code. In fact, these exceptions are of the kind you want and need to produce and which appear to the user in an orderly fashion via the program's list box.

NOTE

Referential integrity is a means of enforcing the rules in a database. This subject is discussed in some detail in Chapter 16 and also in Chapter 12, "Understanding Relational Databases." For now, you should not be concerned with the details of how referential integrity works. The key point is simply that some tables have to obey rules, and the BDE will not let users enter invalid data that violates these rules.

Here is the code that reports on the errors in the `OrderNo` field and rolls back the data to its original state:

```
void __fastcall TForm1::OrdersTableUpdateError(TDataSet *DataSet,
  EDatabaseError *E, TUpdateKind UpdateKind, TUpdateAction &UpdateAction)
{
  TTypeInfo TypeInfo;
  AnsiString UpdateKindStr[] = {"Modified", "Inserted", "Deleted"};
  AnsiString S(UpdateKindStr[UpdateKind]);
  S += ": " + E->Message;
  AnsiString Temp = DataSet->Fields[0]->OldValue;
  Temp = + ": " + S;
  ListBox1->Items->Add(Temp);
  UpdateAction = uaSkip;
}
```

This particular routine is an event handler for the `OnUpdateError` event for the `Table1` object. To create the routine, click once on the `Table1` object, select its Events page in the Object Inspector, and then double-click the `OnUpdateError` entry.

The `OrdersTableUpdateError` method will get called only if an error occurs in attempting to update records. It will get called at the time the error is detected and before BCB tries to commit the next record.

`OrdersTableUpdateError` gets passed four parameters. The most important is the last, which is a var parameter. You can set this parameter to one of the following values:

```
TUpdateAction = (uaAbort, uaSkip, uaRetry, uaApplied);
```

If you set the `UpdateAction` variable to `uaAbort`, the entire attempt to commit the updated data will be aborted. None of your changes will take place, and you will return to edit mode as if you had never attempted to commit the data. The changes you have made so far will not be undone, but neither will they be committed. You are aborting the attempt to commit the data, but you are not rolling it back to its previous state.

If you choose `uaSkip`, the data for the whole table will still be committed, but the record that is currently in error will be left alone. That is, it will be left at the invalid value assigned to it by the user.

If you set `UpdateAction` to `uaRetry`, that means you have attempted to update the information in the current record and that you want to retry committing it. The record you should update is the current record in the dataset passed as the first parameter to `OrdersTableUpdateError`.

In the `OrdersTableUpdateError` method, I always choose `uaSkip` as the value to assign to `UpdateAction`. Of course, you could pop up a dialog and show the user the old value and the new value of the current record. The user would then have a chance to retry committing the data. Once again, you retrieve the data containing the current "problem child" record from the dataset passed in the first parameter of `OrdersTableUpdateError`. I show an example of accessing this data when I retrieve the old value of the `OrderNo` field for the record:

```
AnsiString Temp = DataSet->Fields[0]->OldValue;
Temp = + ": " + S;
ListBox1->Items->Add(Temp);
```

Needless to say, the `OldValue` field is declared as a `Variant` in the source code to `DB.HPP`, which is the place where the `TDataSet` declaration is located:

```
System::Variant __fastcall GetOldValue(void);
...
__property System::Variant OldValue = {read=GetOldValue};
```

Two other values are passed to the `TableUpdateError` method. The first is an exception reporting on the current error, and the second is a variable of type `TUpdateKind`:

```
enum TUpdateKind { ukModify, ukInsert, ukDelete };
```

The variable of type `TUpdateKind` just tells you how the current record was changed. Was it updated, inserted, or deleted? The exception information is passed to you primarily so that you can get at the message associated with the current error:

```
E->Message;
```

If you handle the function by setting `UpdateAction` to a particular value, say `uaSkip`, then BCB will not pop up a dialog reporting the error to the user. Instead, it assumes that you are handling the error explicitly, and it leaves it up to you to report the error or not, as you see fit. In this case, I just dump the error into the program's list box, along with some other information.

15

WORKING WITH THE LOCAL INTERBASE SERVER

That's all I'm going to say about cached updates. At this point, you should go back and run the Cache program that ships with BCB. It covers all the same ground covered in the preceding few pages, but it does so in a slightly different form. In particular, it shows how to pop up a dialog so that you can handle each OnUpdateError event in an intelligent and sensible manner.

In general, cached updates give you a great deal of power you can tap into when updating the data in a dataset. If necessary, go back and play with the CachedUpdates program until it starts to make sense to you. This subject isn't prohibitively difficult, but it does take a few moments' thought to absorb the basic principles involved.

Many-to-Many Relationships

Many-to-many relationships are necessities in most relational database projects. Suppose, for example, that you have a set of software routines that you want to store in a database. Some of the routines you can use in DOS, some in UNIX, some in Windows NT, and some in Windows 95. Some routines, however, apply to two or more of the operating systems.

To track this information, you might try adding an OS field to your Routines table, where OS stands for Operating System. This solution sounds simple enough. However, there is one problem. The issue, of course, is that some routines will work with more than one OS. For example, you may have a routine that works in Windows NT and Windows 95, but not in UNIX or DOS. As a result, the fairly simple one-to-many relationship you try to establish with the OS fields really needs to be converted into a many-to-many relationship.

Here, for example, is a list of operating systems:

CODE	*OS*
1	DOS
2	UNIX
3	Windows

Here is a list of routines:

CODE	FUNCTION_NAME	*OSCODE*
1	FormatDriveC	1
2	AssignAllIRQsToTheMouse	2

As you can see, the format shown here allows you to assign only one OSCODE to each routine. The goal is to find a way to specify that a routine works in more than one OS. As you will see, one good solution involves creating a third table that stands in the middle, between the OS and FUNCTION tables shown here.

The rest of this section describes how to actually go about creating many-to-many relationships. This subject is annoyingly complex, but one that you can master if you take a little time to think things through. My basic goal is to break down this process into a series of steps that you can follow whenever you have to create one of these many-to-many relationships. I might be going too far to say that these steps make the process simple. They do make it manageable, however.

In Listing 15.2, you will find the database definition for a simple set of InterBase tables. You can run this definition through WISQL by choosing File | Run ISQL Script. Alternatively, you can create a new database and pass through the key statements shown here one at a time.

Beneath the data definition for the database, you will find the code to a program called ManyToMany. This code, in Listings 15.3 through 15.5, shows how to handle a many-to-many relationship in a BCB program.

Listing 15.2. The schema for a simple database that can capture a many-to-many relationship.

```
/* Extract Database c:\src\unleash2\data\man2man.gdb */
CREATE DATABASE "c:\src\unleash2\data\man2man.gdb" PAGE_SIZE 1024;
/* Table: ATTRIBS, Owner: SYSDBA */
CREATE TABLE ATTRIBS (ATTRIBNO INTEGER NOT NULL,
        ATTRIB VARCHAR(34),
PRIMARY KEY (ATTRIBNO));
/* Table: CUSTOMERS, Owner: SYSDBA */
CREATE TABLE CUSTOMERS (CUSTNO INTEGER NOT NULL,
        NAME VARCHAR(35),
PRIMARY KEY (CUSTNO));
/* Table: MIDDLE, Owner: SYSDBA */
CREATE TABLE MIDDLE (CUSTNO INTEGER,
        ATTRIBNO INTEGER);
/* Grant permissions for this database */
```

Listing 15.3. The main form for the ManyToMany program.

```
#include <vcl\vcl.h>
#pragma hdrstop
#include "Main.h"
#include "DMod1.h"
#include "Relater.h"
#pragma resource "*.dfm"
TForm1 *Form1;
__fastcall TForm1::TForm1(TComponent* Owner)
: TForm(Owner)
{
}
void __fastcall TForm1::ChangeAttrBtnClick(TObject *Sender)
{
  RelateForm->RunDialogModal();
}
```

Listing 15.4. The Relater form from the ManyToMany program.

```cpp
#include <vcl\vcl.h>
#pragma hdrstop
#include "Relater.h"
#include "DMod1.h"
#pragma resource "*.dfm"
TRelateForm *RelateForm;
__fastcall TRelateForm::TRelateForm(TComponent* Owner)
: TForm(Owner)
{
}
void __fastcall TRelateForm::RunDialogModal()
{
  FCustNo = DMod->CustomerTable->FieldByName("CustNo")->AsInteger;
  Caption = "Attributes for " + DMod->CustomerTable->FieldByName("Name")->AsString;
  ShowModal();
}
void __fastcall TRelateForm::bbInsertClick(TObject *Sender)
{
  InsertQuery->Params->Items[0]->AsInteger = FCustNo;
  InsertQuery->Params->Items[1]->AsInteger =
    DMod->AttributeTable->FieldByName("AttribNo")->AsInteger;
  InsertQuery->ExecSQL();
  ViewAttribs();
}
void __fastcall TRelateForm::ViewAttribs()
{
  DMod->ViewAttributes(FCustNo);
}
void __fastcall TRelateForm::bbDeleteClick(TObject *Sender)
{
  DeleteQuery->Params->Items[0]->AsInteger = FCustNo;
  DeleteQuery->Params->Items[1]->AsInteger =
    DMod->ViewAttributesQuery->FieldByName("AttribNo")->AsInteger;
  DeleteQuery->ExecSQL();
  ViewAttribs();
}
void __fastcall TRelateForm::FormShow(TObject *Sender)
{
  ViewAttribs();
}
```

Listing 15.5. The data module for the ManyToMany program.

```cpp
#include <vcl\vcl.h>
#pragma hdrstop
#include "DMod1.h"
#pragma resource "*.dfm"
TDMod *DMod;
__fastcall TDMod::TDMod(TComponent* Owner)
: TDataModule(Owner)
{
  ManyToMany->Connected = True;
  CustomerTable->Open();
  AttributeTable->Open();
```

```
}
void TDMod::ViewAttributes(int CustNo)
{
  ViewAttributesQuery->Close();
  ViewAttributesQuery->Params->Items[0]->AsInteger = CustNo;
  ViewAttributesQuery->Open();
}
void __fastcall TDMod::CustomerSourceDataChange(TObject *Sender,
    TField *Field)
{
  ViewAttributes(CustomerTable->FieldByName("CustNo")->AsInteger);
}
```

The ManyToMany program enables you to pop up a dialog that contains two lists of attributes. The left-hand list shows all the possible attributes that can be associated with a record in the main table for this program. The right-hand list shows the currently selected attributes for the current record in the main table. Buttons are supplied so that you can add items from the left-hand column to the column on the right. The dialog in question is shown in Figure 15.5.

FIGURE 15.5.
The Relater dialog relates the Customers *table to the* Attributes *table.*

The basic idea behind a many-to-many relationship is that you need to have an intermediate table between the main table and the list of attributes that you assign to it. For example, if you have the Routines and the OS tables described, you need a middle table that relates the Routine ID from the Routines table to the OS ID from the OS table.

In the database just shown, the Middle table serves as the intermediary between the Customers table and the Attribs table. Here's how it works.

The Customers table has a series of records in it like this:

```
select * from Customers
    CUSTNO NAME
=========== ================================
          1 SAM
          2 MIKE
          3 FREDDY FREELOADER
          4 SUNNY SUZY
          5 LOU
```

```
 6  TYPHOID MARY
 7  SANDRA
 8  MICHELLE
 9  NICK
10  NANCY
```

The `Attribs` table also has a set of attributes that can be assigned to these customers:

```
select * from Attribs
   ATTRIBNO ATTRIB
=========== ===================================
         1 Nice
         2 Naughty
         3 Generous
         4 Guilty
         5 Onerous
         6 Criminal
         7 Hostile
         8 Beautiful
         9 Bodacious
        10 Endearing
```

Suppose that Sunny Suzy is both Nice and Bodacious. To connect her to these two attributes, you could add two fields to the `Middle` table:

```
CustNo AttribNo
4      1
4      9
```

Now when you open the `Middle` table, you will find two entries in it. The first entry has a `CustNo` of 4, which stands for Sunny Suzy, and an `AttribNo` of 1, which stands for Nice. Likewise, the second line translates into Sunny Suzy, Bodacious. Here is the key to decoding the table:

```
4 in CustNo field       = Sunny Suzy
1 in the AttribNo field = Nice
9 in the AttribNo field = Bodacious
```

Of course, you need to make sure that you're doing the right lookups on these numbers. For example, 9 in the `AttribNo` field equals `Bodacious`, but 9 in the `CustNo` field equals `Nick`!

Now that you understand the principle behind creating a many-to-many relationship, the next step is to create a dialog that can capture this relationship in terms that the user can understand. The ManyToMany program has a main form that contains a grid showing the fields of the `Customers` table. You can find a button called Attribute on the main form. If you click this button, a dialog like the one shown in Figure 15.5 appears.

On the left-hand side of the Relater dialog is a list of possible attributes that can be assigned to a customer. On the right-hand side of the dialog is a list of the attributes that have in fact been assigned to the current customer. In between the two lists are two buttons. If you click the button with the arrows pointing to the right, the word selected on the left will be added to the list on the right. That is, the attribute will be assigned to the currently selected customer. (The customer list, remember, is back on the main form.) The button with the arrows pointing left will delete the current selected attribute in the right-hand list. This, in effect, removes that attribute from the current customer's list of traits.

At this stage, you are ready to prepare a list of things that you must do to complete the many-to-many relationship:

1. Create a way to insert a new item into the Middle table.
2. Assuming you know the CustNo of the currently selected record, you need a way to view the attributes associated with the current customer.
3. Find a way to delete an item from the Middle table.

Some other tasks are associated with creating the Relater dialog. For example, you must put up the table showing the list of possible attributes, and you must add buttons and grids to the dialog. However, I am assuming that all these tasks are too trivial to be worth describing. The key tasks are the three just listed. Keep your mind focused on them, and the rest will be easy.

To begin, drop down a table, data source, and grid, and then set up the list of possible attributes as shown in the left-hand side grid in Figure 15.5. Name the TTable object containing this dataset AttributeTable.

Now drop down a button that will move things from the left-hand grid to the right-hand grid. Put two arrows on it, as shown in Figure 15.5. Drop down a TQuery object, call it InsertQuery, and place the following line of code in its SQL property:

```
insert into middle (CustNo, AttribNo)
 values (:CustNo, :AttribNo);
```

Here is the code you can create to fill in the two bind variables called :CustNo and :AttribNo. This code should be associated with the button that points to the right:

```
void __fastcall TRelateForm::bbInsertClick(TObject *Sender)
{
  InsertQuery->Params->Items[0]->AsInteger = FCustNo;
  InsertQuery->Params->Items[1]->AsInteger =
    DMod->AttributeTable->FieldByName("AttribNo")->AsInteger;
  InsertQuery->ExecSQL();
  ViewAttribs();
}
```

The FCustNo variable is assigned a value when the dialog is launched. It's the CustNo of the currently selected customer, and it is retrieved when the dialog is first called by the main form. The AttribNo value is retrieved from the currently selected record in the grid on the left. To actually insert the data into the database, you call ExecSQL.

The ViewAttribs routine shows the attributes associated with the current customer. That is, this routine fills in the grid on the right-hand side of the Relater dialog. The ViewAttribs routine is very simple:

```
void TDMod::ViewAttributes(int CustNo)
{
```

```
    ViewAttributesQuery->Close();
    ViewAttributesQuery->Params->Items[0]->AsInteger = CustNo;
    ViewAttributesQuery->Open();
}
```

This code does nothing more than resolve a single bind variable and then open the
ViewAttributesQuery object. The SQL property of the ViewAttributesQuery object should look
like this:

```
SELECT DISTINCT A.ATTRIB, A.ATTRIBNO
FROM MIDDLE M, ATTRIBS A
WHERE
    (M.CUSTNO = :CustNo)
    AND (A.ATTRIBNO = M.ATTRIBNO)
ORDER BY A.ATTRIB
```

This code selects the Attribute and AttribNo from the Attribs table in all the cases in which
the AttribNo in the Attribs table is also found in a record from the Middle table that has the
CustNo of the currently selected customer. (Phew!) The resulting set of data is shown in the
grid on the right-hand side of the dialog shown in Figure 15.5.

To help make this process intelligible, consider the case I outlined, where Sunny Suzy was both
Nice and Bodacious:

```
CustNo AttribNo
4      1
4      9
```

This SQL code searches through the Middle table and finds all the cases where Sunny Suzy is
mentioned in it. In other words, it finds the two records shown. The code then performs a
lookup in the Attribs table, finding the words that are associated with the two AttribNos shown
in the preceding code. Whenever it finds a match, it displays the match in the right-hand grid.
When you have only two records in the Middle table, this does not seem like much of a trick,
but the SQL shown here seems a bit smarter if thousands of records appear in the Middle table,
only two of which relate to Sunny Suzy.

NOTE

Notice that I call ViewAttributesQuery from both the RelateForm and from the main form.
The call from the main form is made each time the user selects a new record to view in the
CustomerTable:

```
void __fastcall TDMod::CustomerSourceDataChange(TObject *Sender,
    TField *Field)
{
    ViewAttributes(CustomerTable->FieldByName("CustNo")->AsInteger);
}
```

At this stage, you are two-thirds of the way through completing the many-to-many relationship. You have found out how to insert records and how to show the list of currently selected

items associated with a particular customer. The only step left is to come up with a technique for deleting records.

The SQL to perform a delete from the `Middle` table looks like this:

```
delete from Middle where
  CustNo = :CustNo and
  AttribNo = :AttribNo;
```

Here is the code, associated with the leftward-pointing button, that fills in the bind variables in the SQL `delete` code shown in the preceding paragraph:

```
void __fastcall TRelateForm::bbDeleteClick(TObject *Sender)
{
  DeleteQuery->Params->Items[0]->AsInteger = FCustNo;
  DeleteQuery->Params->Items[1]->AsInteger =
    DMod->ViewAttributesQuery->FieldByName("AttribNo")->AsInteger;
  DeleteQuery->ExecSQL();
  ViewAttribs();
}
```

The `CustNo` bind variable is resolved easily enough, because you had the appropriate `CustNo` passed in from the main form when the dialog was first created. The `ViewAttributesQuery` holds a list of the currently selected attributes and their `AttribNo`. Therefore, you can simply ask the `ViewAttributesQuery` object for the `AttribNo` of the currently selected record to find out what item the user wants to delete. Now both bind variables are satisfied, and you can perform the deletion by calling `ExecSQL`!

All in all, creating a many-to-many relationship is not so bad as long as you are methodical about the process. Remember that four key steps are involved:

- First, you have to add to the `Middle` table.
- Then you have to show the attributes associated with the current customer. This part is tricky because it involves writing a fairly complex SQL statement. Try using the QueryBuilder or QBE to help you create these SQL statements.
- You have to write SQL to make inserts into the `Middle` table.
- Finally, you have to delete from the `Middle` table.

Tackle these tasks one at a time, and the process will not prove to be terribly difficult.

Summary

This chapter gave you a basic introduction to the local InterBase and to several related subjects. In particular, you saw how to create and open InterBase databases, how to set up aliases, and how to perform fundamental database tasks such as transactions.

I should stress that InterBase is a very complex and powerful product, and what you have seen in this chapter should serve as little more than a brief introduction that will whet your appetite. In the next chapter, you will look at stored procedures, triggers, InterBase calls, and a few other tricks that should help you grasp the extent of the power in both the local and server-based versions of InterBase.

BCB protects you from the details of how a server handles basic database chores. However, BCB also enables you to tap into the power associated with a particular server. This was one of the most delicate balances that the developers had to consider when they created BCB: How can you make a database tool as generic as possible, without cutting off a programmer's access to the special capabilities of a particular server? The same type of question drove the developers' successful quest to make BCB's language as simple and elegant as possible without cutting off access to the full power of the Windows API.

Now you can forge on to the next chapter. By this time, we are deep into the subject of databases. In fact, the stage is now set to open a view onto the most powerful tools in a database programmer's arsenal. After you master the stored procedures, generators, and triggers shown in the next chapter, you will be entering into the world of real client/server programming as it is done on the professional level. These tools drive the big databases used by corporations, governments, and educational institutions around the world.

Advanced InterBase Concepts

CHAPTER 16

IN THIS CHAPTER

In this chapter, you get a look at the Music program, which shows a good deal about working with relational databases in general and about working with InterBase in particular. This chapter is also meant to sum up much of what has been said so far about databases and push the whole subject on to another level. It should help advance your knowledge of SQL, database design, and client/server programming. This is not, however, a review chapter. There is a lot of important new material in this chapter.

This chapter features overviews of

- InterBase and Security: granting rights on a table
- The InterBase Server Manager: backing up a database
- Relational database design
- Referential integrity
- Stored procedures and the `TStoredProc` components
- Triggers
- Generators
- Domains
- Querying data with SQL. These techniques help you prepare reports on the information in a database, as well as answer the user's questions about how much data they have and what kind.
- Using SQL to extract facts from a database. How many of this type of item do I have? How can I write a stored procedure that retrieves information from several tables at once while still answering a real-world question about the amount of a particular kind of data?
- Placing forms on a `TabControl`. The kdAdd program had a huge number of fields in the main form for the application. In this chapter, you will see how to create separate forms for each page in an application that uses a tabbed notebook metaphor. This way, each page exists inside its own discrete object, which helps you create well-organized, robust applications.
- Create the illusion of dynamically changing the shape of a form at runtime. It turns out that placing forms on a `TabControl` gives you a remarkable amount of flexibility. In particular, you can show one form on a particular page under one set of circumstances and another form on the same page under slightly different circumstances. This gives the user the impression that you know how to dynamically change the shape of a form at runtime.

- Storing multiple types of data in a database and displaying it with one program. This database shows information on both a table that contains books and a table that contains albums and CDs. The TabControl technique described in the last section allows you to seamlessly integrate different types of data in one program. From your user's point of view, it appears that the program morphs to accommodate the type of data currently being displayed.

- Using SQL to alter a table

The burden of the argument for this chapter is again carried by a sample database application. This one is designed to track household items such as books, CDs, or records. However, you can easily expand it to hold many different types of data. The core strength of this program is its flexible, extensible design.

One of the interesting features of the Music database is the way it uses stored procedures to report on the information in the database. For instance, it lets you store CDs, tapes, and records and rate them according to four different extensible criteria:

- What type of music is it? Classical? Jazz? Rock? Do you have categories of your own you want to add?

- How loud is the music? Is it peaceful, moderate, or loud? You can add other categories if you want.

- How good is the music? On a scale of one to ten, how do you rate it?

- Finally, what medium is it on? CD? Tape? Record?

You can easily expand most of these lists to create as many categories as you want. Furthermore, you can query the database to ask questions such as

- How many records do I have?

- How many different artists are listed here?

- How many albums do I have that I rated in a certain range? For instance, which records did I rate as a complete ten? Which ones did I rate as only one or two?

- Which albums did I rate as loud?

- What albums are listed under the category called Jazz or Folk?

By the time you finish this chapter, you should have a pretty good feel for how to tap into the power of InterBase. This chapter is not meant to appeal only to InterBase developers, however. It also contains many general comments about working with relational databases in general and SQL databases in particular. In other words, this chapter is about real client/server database programming.

The Music program uses several advanced database features of Borland C++Builder (BCB). For instance, there are examples of calculated fields, data modules, lookups, filters, and searching a database with `FindFirst` and `FindNearest`. This program uses many other standard database techniques, such as calculated fields and working with ranges. There are numerous examples of how to use stored procedures and also an example of how to search on records in the detail table of a master-detail relationship.

My favorite feature of this program is the way it leverages form inheritance to give the user the ability to switch back and forth between the `Album` and `Book` tables. I like the idea of having one program that can deal with multiple types of data. The program was designed so you can add new modules to it, such as forms for handling addresses or inventory items and so on.

When working with this chapter, you should remember that a complete copy of the Music database is available on the CD that accompanies this book. Throughout the first half of this chapter, I talk about the incremental steps involved in creating this database, but if you feel the need to see the complete database at any time, then you can retrieve it from the CD. I quote the entire data definition for the database about two thirds of the way through this chapter, and it is available on the CD in the `Data` directory in the file called `Music.ddl`.

If you need to set up the alias for the database on the CD, a full description of how to do so is provided in the readme file on the CD that accompanies this book. I also talk about the alias at several points in this chapter.

Music is a fairly complex program, but I assure you that the version on the CD works correctly. If you are having trouble with it, check my Web sites for tips or hints on using the program.

Overall, this chapter aims at taking the discussion of databases to a new level. After you read the text, you will be prepared to write professional-level client/server applications. All the information in this chapter applies to common professional database tasks such as creating an inventory system or even a point of sales application.

Security and the InterBase Server Manager

Before beginning the discussion of the Music program, it might be a good idea to cover a few basic issues regarding security. I included enough information so far to make any BCB programmer dangerous, so I might as well also equip you with some of the tools you need to defend your work against prying eyes. If you have the skill to create programs that others can use, then you have to know how to manage those clients.

When working with passwords, it's important to make a distinction between user security for a whole server and access rights for a particular table. If you open the InterBase Server Manager, log on, and select Tasks | User Security, you will find menu options that let you create new users for the system. By default, these users have access to very little. All you do is let them in the front door. You haven't yet given them a pass to visit any particular rooms in the house.

Advanced InterBase Concepts

CHAPTER 16

633

16

**ADVANCED
INTERBASE
CONCEPTS**

As this discussion matures, I discuss how to grant particular rights to a user after he or she has been admitted into the "building."

If you are interested in setting up real security for your database, then the first thing you should do is change the SYSDBA password. To change the password, sign on to the InterBase Server Manager as SYSDBA using the password masterkey. Select Tasks and then User Security from the menu. Select the username SYSDBA, and choose Modify User. Now enter a new password. Once you do this much, the system is truly under your control. No one else can get at your data unless you decide they should have the right to do so. Even then, you can severely proscribe their activities with a remarkable degree of detail. (If you are a control freak, this is paradise!)

After establishing your sovereignty, the next step is to go out and recruit the peons who will inhabit your domain. Once you find a new user, select Tasks | User Security and choose Add User and give him or her a password. The person who creates users is the one who signs on as SYSDBA. SYSDBA has all the power, which is why it is important to change the SYSDBA password if you are really serious about security.

If you create a new user, this newcomer has no rights on the system by default. To give a user rights, you must use the SQL Grant command, which is discussed in the next section.

Defining Access Rights to a Table

After you create a user in the InterBase Server Manager, you grant them rights to access a table. SQL databases give you extraordinary control over exactly how much access a user can have to a table. For instance, you can give a user only the right to query one or more tables in your database:

```
grant select on Test1 to user1
```

Conversely, you may, if you want, give a user complete control over a table, including the right to grant other people access to the table:

```
grant all on album to Sue with grant option
```

The with grant option clause shown here specifies that Sue not only has her way with the album table, but also can give access to the table to others.

You can give a user six distinct types of privileges:

All	Has select, delete, insert, update, and execute privileges
Select	Can view a table or view
Delete	Can delete from a table or view
Insert	Can add data to a table or view
Update	Can edit a table or view
Execute	Can execute a stored procedure

Using these keys to the kingdom, you can quickly start handing out passes to particular rooms in the palace. For instance, you can write

```
grant insert on Test1 to Sue
grant delete on Test1 to Mary with grant option
grant select on Test1 to Tom, Mary, Sue, User1
grant select, insert, delete, update on Test1 to Mary
grant delete, insert, update, references on country to public with grant option;
```

The last statement in this list comes from the Employee.gdb example that ships with BCB. Notice that it grants rights to the public, which means all users have absurdly liberal rights on the table.

The opposite of the Grant command is Revoke. Revoke removes privileges given with Grant. Here is an example of using Revoke:

```
revoke select on Test1 from Sue
```

This brief overview of the Server Manager and some related issues involving the grant command should give you a sense of how to limit access to your database. None of this material is particularly difficult, but you should be sure you understand it because SQL databases can be mysterious and frustrating if you don't know the basics about how to control them. If you need more information than what I presented here, you will probably find all you need to know to cover this small domain of knowledge in the online help.

Backing Up Tables with the Server Manager

Another important feature of the InterBase Server Manager is backing up tables. This task can be especially important if you need to move a table from Windows 95 or Windows NT to UNIX. The highly compressed backup format for InterBase tables is completely version-independent, so you can back up an NT table and then restore it on a UNIX system.

To get started backing up a database, sign on to the InterBase Server Manager. To sign on, all you need to do is specify the masterkey password; everything else is automatic when signing on to the local version of InterBase. Of course, if you changed the SYSDBA password from masterkey to something else, then you need to use the new password you created.

Go to the Tasks menu and select Backup. Enter the path to the local database you want to back up. For instance, you might type e:\data\info.gdb in the edit control labeled Database Path. This means you want to back up the database called info.gdb.

Enter the name of the backup table you want to create in the Backup File or Device field. For instance, you might type e:\data\info.gbk. Use the GDB extension for live tables and GBK for backed-up tables. These are just conventions, but they are good ones.

Select Transportable Format from the Options group box and set any other flags you want to use. Click OK, and then be prepared for a short delay while InterBase contemplates certain

Advanced InterBase Concepts

CHAPTER 16

635

16

ADVANCED
INTERBASE
CONCEPTS

knotty passages from the works of the philosopher Immanuel Kant. If all goes well, the results of your work might look something like this:

```
Backup started on Tue Dec 24 15:26:42 1996...
gbak: gbak version WI-V4.1.0.194
gbak:     Version(s) for database "e:\data\info.gdb"
    InterBase/x86/Windows NT (access method), version "WI-V4.2.1.328"
    on disk structure version 8.0
Request completed on Tue Dec 24 15:26:45 1996
```

You can now close the InterBase Server Manager and copy your backed-up file to a floppy disk, zip drive, or other storage medium. Remember, the great thing about these files is that they are small, highly compressed, and can be moved from one operating system to another.

> **NOTE**
>
> I exist so completely within the Windows world that I neglected to point out that InterBase runs on a wide variety of UNIX platforms.

The Music Program

It's now time to begin work on the Music program. This program enables you to keep track of CDs, records, tapes, and books. The main goal of the program is to enable you to enter the name of an artist (a musician or a writer) and add one or more titles associated with that artist.

> **NOTE**
>
> The main table of this program is called Artist for historical reasons. The database was originally intended to hold only CDs, records, and tapes. I expanded the program's scope later when I suddenly saw a way to add the Book table to the project. You can now regard the Artist table as featuring a somewhat quaint conceit for a naming convention. Of course, it is difficult to undo the naming convention at this stage because the names of the Artist table and its fields are already spread throughout the program's code as well as the 12 stored procedures that support the code.

The Music program uses eight tables, but three of them, called Artist, Book, and Album, dominate the application. The Artist table is the master table, and the Book and Album tables are detail tables.

Besides the three main tables, several lookup tables are used to store the various lists of possible categories to which the albums and books can belong. For instance, a record can be type Jazz,

Rock, Folk, Blues, and so on, and a book can be type Fiction, Computer, Mystery, Science Fiction, Reference, and so on. These words are stored in the lookup tables. In some cases, I can store information used by both the Album and Book tables in one lookup, using a filter and the range of the table's primary key to distinguish between the different groups of information. More on this technique later in the chapter.

Even with this relatively simple structure, however, there are still enough tables to provide some food for thought. In particular, how are these tables related, and how can you put constraints on them so that it's difficult for the user to accidentally break a dependency? For instance, if there are six albums associated with an artist, a user should not be able to delete the artist without first deleting or reassigning the albums. How about generating the IDs for each artist and each album? This is not Paradox, so there is no autoincrement field. This means that you must create generators and employ some means of accessing the generators.

Clearly, there are enough questions to keep someone busy for an hour or two. To resolve these issues, you need to generate a specific database schema.

Creating the Database Schema

It's probably best to start your work at the top with the Artist table:

```
/* Table: ARTIST, Owner: SYSDBA */
CREATE TABLE ARTIST (CODE CODE_DOM NOT NULL,
        LAST VARCHAR(30),
        FIRST VARCHAR(30),
        BORN DATE,
        DIED DATE,
        BIRTHPLACE VARCHAR(35),
        COMMENT BLOB SUB_TYPE TEXT SEGMENT SIZE 80,
        ARTISTTYPE INTEGER NOT NULL,
        PRIMARY KEY (CODE));
```

The definition for this table assumes the presence of a domain called CODE_DOM. You can create a domain in WISQL with the following code:

```
CREATE DOMAIN CODE_DOM AS INTEGER;
```

This code states that CODE_DOM is a domain of type Integer.

A *domain* is an alias for a type that is used more than once in the program. For instance, the Code field used in the Album table is referenced in the Album table in the GroupCode field:

```
CREATE TABLE ALBUM (CODE CODE_DOM NOT NULL,
        ALBUM VARCHAR(25) NOT NULL,
        TYPES SMALLINT,
        LOUDNESS SMALLINT,
        MEDIUM SMALLINT,
        RATING SMALLINT,
        GROUPCODE CODE_DOM NOT NULL,
        PRIMARY KEY (CODE));
```

Advanced InterBase Concepts

CHAPTER 16

637

16

ADVANCED
INTERBASE
CONCEPTS

Make sure you understand what is happening here. The GroupCode field in the Album table references the Group, or Artist, associated with this particular album. For instance, if Bob Dylan's code is 57, and the name of the current album is *Blonde on Blonde*, the GroupCode field in the Album table is set to 57. This ties the album *Blonde on Blonde* to the artist Bob Dylan. (Properly speaking, this is a foreign key, but I get to that subject as it applies to InterBase later in the chapter.)

Creating a domain called CODE_DOM allows you to easily assign the same type to the Code field in the Artist table and the GroupCode field in the Album table. It's not earth-shattering in importance, but it can be helpful.

Altering Tables: To Null or Not to Null

Notice that the Code field is declared as Not Null. This means that the user cannot leave this field blank. This rule is implemented by the server and is enforced regardless of which front end you use to access the data. By definition, all primary keys must be declared Not Null.

The ArtistType field in the Artist table is declared as Not Null. All artists must be distinguished by type; that is, they have to be labeled as either Authors or Musicians. If they don't fit into one of these two categories, then they are never seen by the user because I set up a filter on this field, excluding all but the one type that the user currently wants to see. In short, the table is filtered to show either only musicians or only authors. If an entry in the Artist table does not fit into one of these two categories, then it is never seen by the user. As a result, I declare this field as Not Null and then use a lookup table to give the user only two choices when filling it in. This way, I am sure that no records are lost.

Deciding which fields should get the value Not Null is one of the more difficult chores in creating a database. This is one of those designations that I almost never call right in design mode. Instead, I am forced to go back and massage my data after creating a first draft of the data definition.

To change a table using WISQL, you must call an SQL command called Alter Table:

```
ALTER TABLE MYTABLE
ADD NAME VARCHAR(25),
DROP NAMES;
```

This code adds a field called NAME to a table and drops a field called NAMES. You don't have to add and drop fields at the same time; for instance, you can write

```
ALTER TABLE MYTABLE
ADD NAME VARCHAR(25)
```

You can also write

```
ALTER TABLE MYTABLE
  DROP NAMES
```

Because you often alter the structure of an existing table, make sure you run many tests on your program before entrusting a large amount of data to your tables.

You cannot alter a field that is part of a unique index, primary key, or foreign key, nor can you drop a unique index, primary key, or foreign key. You can, however, drop a standard index:

```
drop index myindex
```

When you start altering tables, you soon need to transfer the values from one field to a new field. In other words, you want to slightly alter the traits of one field. The rest of this section outlines a simple technique for altering a table.

To get started, I will create a simple table that can serve as a scratch pad. All the work shown here was done with the WISQL32 utility that ships with InterBase in the BIN directory. I always keep WISQL on the Tools menu of my copy of BCB:

```
create table foo (sam Integer not null, Name VarChar(30), primary key (Sam));
insert into foo (Sam, Name) values (1, "Fred");
insert into foo (Sam, Name) values (2, "Sam");
insert into foo (Sam, Name) values (3, "Joe");
```

The four lines shown here create a table called Foo and place some simple values in it. WISQL lets you use the Previous and Next commands so you can easily alter the insert command without retyping it each time.

After creating the table, I can easily test the data:

```
select * from foo
         SAM NAME
=========== ===============================
          1 Fred
          2 Sam
          3 Joe
```

Suppose that I now decide I want to change the Name field to be Not Null and somewhat longer. How do I proceed?

The first step is to create a new field with all the traits in it that I want:

```
alter table foo
  add AName Varchar(50) Not Null;
```

Now the table has a field called AName that is longer than the Name field and declared Not Null.

To copy the data from the Name field to AName, issue the following command in WISQL:

```
update foo
  set Aname = Name;
```

Advanced InterBase Concepts

CHAPTER 16

639

16

ADVANCED
INTERBASE
CONCEPTS

Here is how things stand at this point:

```
select * from Foo;
         SAM NAME                               ANAME
========== ============================= =========
          1 Fred                                Fred
          2 Sam                                 Sam
          3 Joe                                 Joe
```

You can simply delete the Name column:

```
alter table foo
  drop name;
```

Now you have a table that looks like what you want:

```
select * from foo;
         SAM ANAME
========== =================================================
          1 Fred
          2 Sam
          3 Joe
```

If necessary, you can then repeat the process to copy ANname to a field called Name, or else you can just keep the new name for your table.

This whole technique is a bit laborious. However, if you play with SQL for a while, all this work starts to become second nature. For instance, I can copy the ANName field back to a new field called name in well under a minute just by rapidly typing the following:

```
alter table foo add Name varchar(50) not null;
update Foo
   set Name = AName;
alter table foo drop Aname
```

Once you know SQL, and assuming you can type well, you can usually invoke WISQL, enter the commands, and get out faster than you can load the weighty Database Desktop application. Certainly by the time I open Database Desktop, open the Restructure window, and start making changes, I've usually spent more time than it takes to do the whole procedure in WISQL. This argument is a bit like the command line versus the Windows Explorer. The Windows Explorer is considerably more intuitive to use, but it is not necessarily faster than using the command line. Another nice thing about WISQL is that it has a small footprint and can be left in memory without slowing down the system.

Creating Blob Fields

After the discussion of Code fields and the related Null versus Not Null issues, the other fields in the Artist table are pretty straightforward:

```
CREATE TABLE ARTIST (CODE CODE_DOM NOT NULL,
        LAST VARCHAR(30),
        FIRST VARCHAR(30),
```

```
BORN DATE,
DIED DATE,
BIRTHPLACE VARCHAR(35),
COMMENT BLOB SUB_TYPE TEXT SEGMENT SIZE 80,
ARTISTTYPE INTEGER NOT NULL,
PRIMARY KEY (CODE));
```

The code for creating a blob field looks a bit tricky, but basically, you can just repeat this code any time you need to create a text blob in InterBase. If you create a blob field as shown previously, then you can use it with the TDBMemo data-aware control that ships with BCB.

BCB offers two objects for working with blobs, TBlobField and TBlobStream. TBlobField has methods called LoadFromFile, SaveToFile, LoadFromStream, and SaveToStream that can be used to read and write blob data in and out of a database. You can also usually cut and paste data directly into a TDBMemo or TDBImage control by copying it to the clipboard and then pasting it into the control using Ctrl+V. To copy an image from a blob field to the clipboard, use Ctrl+C or Ctrl+X or else use the built-in CopyToClipBoard feature of both TDBMemo or TDBImage.

You can use blob fields to store bitmapped images, sounds, video segments, and text.

Primary Keys and Foreign Keys

The final line in the definition for the Artist table defines the primary key:

```
PRIMARY KEY (CODE));
```

This states that the primary key is the Code field. It's important that Code is a keyed field because it is referenced by a foreign key in the Album table. Furthermore, you want to be sure that no two rows have the same code in it, and the primary key syntax enforces this rule. Remember that all primary keys must be Not Null by definition.

Here, once again in slightly different form, is the definition for the Album table:

```
CREATE TABLE ALBUM (CODE CODE_DOM NOT NULL,
      ALBUM VARCHAR(25) NOT NULL,
      TYPES SMALLINT,
      LOUDNESS SMALLINT,
      MEDIUM SMALLINT,
      RATING SMALLINT,
      GROUPCODE CODE_DOM NOT NULL,
      PRIMARY KEY (CODE),
      FOREIGN KEY (TYPES) REFERENCES TYPES(CODE),
      FOREIGN KEY (LOUDNESS) REFERENCES LOUDNESS(CODE),
      FOREIGN KEY (MEDIUM) REFERENCES MEDIUM(CODE),
      FOREIGN KEY (GROUPCODE) REFERENCES ARTIST(CODE)
      );
```

This time through, I modified the table to include foreign keys. These keys show the dependencies that this table has on the fields of other tables.

Once again, the Code field is the primary key. This field contains a unique number for each new Album record entered by the user. A character field designates the name of the album or book, and the GroupCode field relates each record to the Artist table.

Notice that the GroupCode field is a foreign key referencing the Code field of the Artist table. A foreign key provides *referential integrity*. The foreign key asserts that

- Every GroupCode entry must have a corresponding Code field in the Artist table.
- You can't delete an Artist record if there is a corresponding record in the Album table with a GroupCode the same as the Code field of the record you want to delete.

These two rules go a long way toward describing what foreign keys are all about. They also help to explain what referential integrity is all about. In particular, note that these rules are enforced by the server, and they are implemented regardless of what type of front end attempts to alter the table.

You rarely want to make a foreign key unique because the whole point of this exercise is to relate multiple albums with one artist. The artist is the master in the master-detail relationship because there is only one artist for each set of albums. The artist has a primary key, which means there is only one of each artist entered in the database. The album is a foreign key, and there are usually multiple GroupCode foreign keys for each single Code primary key.

> **NOTE**
>
> As you saw earlier, referential integrity is not unique to InterBase. In fact, Paradox supplies good tools for supporting referential integrity. It's built right into the Database Desktop, and every Paradox table that you create can have referential integrity if you want it. In most cases, you do indeed want it!

To see referential integrity in action, run the Music program that comes with this book and try to delete one of the Artist records that has an Album associated with it. For instance, try to delete Bob Dylan, Miles Davis, or Philip Glass. Your efforts are stymied because there are albums associated with all these artists. In particular, you get the lovely message that reads

```
General SQL Error: Violates FOREIGN KEY constraint "INTEG_19" on table "Album"
```

You might as well savor this one because it is as close to poetry as you can get in the SQL database world.

Go into the Database Desktop, enter a new album, and try to give it a GroupCode that does not have a corresponding entry in the Code field of the Artist table. The Database Desktop doesn't let you do it. (Note that there are other fields that have foreign keys in this table, so you have to give valid values all the way around, or you aren't able to enter a record. You can, however, leave the other fields blank if you want.)

The key point here is that referential integrity is enforced automatically in BCB and the Database Desktop. In fact, the rules are enforced on the server side, so no matter how you try to get at the data, you must obey the rules. It's not just some client-side code in BCB; the rule is built into the database itself, which is what you want.

This concept is so important that I will repeat it once more: These rules are enforced automatically no matter what front end the user attempts to use on the table!

The `Types`, `Loudness`, `Medium`, and `Rating` fields are all integers. `Types`, `Loudness`, and `Medium` are all foreign keys that reference one of three small tables called, logically enough, Types, Loudness, and Medium:

```
/* Table: LOUDNESS, Owner: SYSDBA */
CREATE TABLE LOUDNESS (LOUDNESS VARCHAR(15) NOT NULL,
        CODE INTEGER NOT NULL,
        PRIMARY KEY (CODE));
/* Table: MEDIUM, Owner: SYSDBA */
CREATE TABLE MEDIUM (MEDIUM VARCHAR(15) NOT NULL,
        CODE INTEGER NOT NULL,
        PRIMARY KEY (CODE));
/* Table: TYPES, Owner: SYSDBA */
CREATE TABLE TYPES (TYPES VARCHAR(15) NOT NULL,
        CODE INTEGER NOT NULL,
        PRIMARY KEY (CODE));
```

The structure of these tables ought to be intuitively obvious. The Types table, for instance, is designed to hold the following records:

```
select * from types
TYPES                 CODE
================ ============
JAZZ                     1
ROCK                     2
CLASSICAL                3
NEW AGE                  4
FOLK                     5
BLUES                    6
COMPUTER              1000
FICTION               1001
SCIFI                 1002
MYSTERY               1003
REFERENCE             1004
```

What you have here are six types for albums and five types for books. I separate the two types of types by a large range so that you can add a virtually unlimited number of additional types of either kind. (If you want to work with more that 999 different types of music, you have a problem! Of course, I could have made the split at 10,000 or 100,000 instead of at 1,000, but it's unlikely you want to have more than 999 distinct types of music in this, or any other, database.)

The key point to grasp here is that you cannot add a number to the `Types` field of the Album table unless it has a corresponding entry in the Types table. The foreign key on the `Types` field is placed there explicitly to enforce this rule. Furthermore, you can't delete an entry from the Types table if it has a corresponding element in the `Types` field of the Album table. You can, however, change the content of one of the strings in the Types table and thereby either enhance, or totally trash, your data.

Astute readers probably notice that I designed the relationship between the Types field of the Album table and the Types table itself so that it is easy to perform lookups on the Types table when necessary. You will hear more about this topic later in the chapter, or you can refer to the discussion of lookup fields in Chapter 11, "Working with Field Objects."

Here is the definition for the Book table, which plays the same role in this program as the Album table. The key point to notice, however, is that the two tables differ in several particulars. The interesting thing about the Music program is that it can handle both kinds of tables seamlessly. To the user, the forms involved with displaying this data just seem to morph as needed to accommodate the data.

```
CREATE TABLE BOOK (CODE CODE_DOM NOT NULL,
        ALBUM VARCHAR(25) NOT NULL,
        TYPES SMALLINT,
        MEDIUM SMALLINT,
        RATING SMALLINT,
        COMMENT BLOB SUB_TYPE TEXT SEGMENT SIZE 80,
        GROUPCODE CODE_DOM NOT NULL,
        PRIMARY KEY (CODE),
        Foreign key(GroupCode) references Artist(Code),
        Foreign key(Types) references Types(Code),
        Foreign key(Medium) references Medium(Code)
    );
```

Creating Indexes on the Music Table

By now, you have seen most of the data definition for MUSIC.GDB. However, I want to discuss a few more details before moving on to take a look at the interface for the program.

The indexes on the Music database are all defined to enhance your access to the data and provide automatic sorting of the data. Indexes have no other purpose than to speed your access to data and help with sorting. They allow you to search for data very quickly. If any of your searches takes too long, one of the best ways to address the problem is through enhancing your indexes.

It's important to see the difference between the primary and foreign keys that create referential integrity and add constraints to a table and the ordinary indexes, which speed up access to a particular record. A primary key is an index on speed. It gives you everything an index gives you and then a little more.

In particular, when you create a primary key or foreign key in InterBase (or in Paradox), then a unique index is automatically created on that key. For instance, the Artist and Album tables both have unique indexes on the Code field. The Foo table, created in the last section, has a unique index on the field called Sam.

One simple way to see these indexes is to open the Database Explorer and examine the indexes listed under the Album or Artist tables. The Artist table, for instance, has two indexes. One is called Artist_LastFirst_Ndx, and I will describe it later in this chapter. The other index has the strange name RDB$PRIMARY1. This is the index that was created when the code field was designated as a primary key. The only really important part of the name is the word primary, which helps you to understand that this is part of a primary key. The rest is just syntactical sugar used internally by InterBase.

NOTE

You can add a primary or foreign key after a table is created, as long as doing so does not violate any other database rules. You should make sure that the tables involved are not in use by another program when you make these kinds of modifications.

Here is an example of adding a primary key:

```
ALTER TABLE FOO ADD PRIMARY KEY (Sam);
```

Here is an example of adding a foreign key:

```
ALTER TABLE FOO ADD FOREIGN KEY (Foreigner) REFERENCES Book(CODE);
```

The foreign key example shown here assumes that you added an Integer field to the Foo table called Foreigner.

Besides the primary keys and foreign keys, the following indexes are also defined on the Artist and Album tables:

```
CREATE INDEX GROUPALBUM_IDX ON ALBUM(GROUPCODE, ALBUM);
CREATE INDEX ARTIST_LASTFIRST_NDX ON ARTIST(LAST, FIRST);
```

If you want to create a new index in WISQL, you can do so with the SQL Create Index command, as shown in the preceding code. The command takes the name of the index, the name of the table on which the index is enforced, and finally, in parentheses, the names of the fields in the index. For more information on this and other commands, see the *InterBase Workgroup Server Language Reference,* or, more practicable, the online help for WISQL. Also helpful are third-party books such as the *Practical SQL Handbook* (ISBN: 0-201-62623-3).

I created these two indexes for different reasons. The Artist_LastFirst_Ndx is meant primarily to speed up searches and sorts in the Artist table.

The GroupAlbum_idx is created for a more specific reason. Many of the artists have numerous albums associated with them. I relate the Album table to the Artist table using the standard MasterSource, MasterField, and IndexFieldName gambit you saw in Chapter 9, "Using TTable and TDataSet." To set up this relationship inside BCB, I need an index on the Code field from the Artist table and the GroupCode field from the Album table. Both of those are provided for me automatically by my primary and foreign keys. However, I try to relate the two tables and also make sure the records from the Album table are sorted correctly. To do this, I need to create a new index that both relates the Album table to the Artist table and also makes sure that the Album table is sorted correctly. The GroupAlbum_Idx serves this purpose. (I had a little trouble getting the GroupAlbum_Idx to work properly at first, but things cleared up when I closed the Album table and then reopened it.)

Advanced InterBase Concepts
CHAPTER 16

645

16

ADVANCED
INTERBASE
CONCEPTS

Generators, Triggers, and Stored Procedures

The next few sections of this chapter deal with triggers and generators. You will read a good deal about automatically generating values for primary keys and a little about the relative merits of triggers and generators.

Three generators provide unique numbers to use in the Code fields of the Artist, Book, and Album tables. Generators provide almost the same functionality in InterBase tables that autoincrement fields provide in Paradox tables. That is, they provide numbers to use in the keyed fields that bind tables together.

Autoincrement fields are filled in automatically at runtime. Generators, however, merely generate random numbers in sequence, where the first number generated might be one, the second two, and so on. You can tell a generator to start generating numbers at a particular starting value, where the first number might be x, the next x + 1, and so on.

Here is how you create a generator in WISQL and set it to a particular value:

```
CREATE GENERATOR MUSIC_GEN;
SET GENERATOR MUSIC_GEN TO 300;
```

As a result of this code, the first number generated is 300, the next is 301, and so on.

I will now show how to write a trigger. The Music program uses triggers on the Artist table but not on the Album table. The reason for splitting things up this way is explained in this section and in the upcoming section of this chapter called "Deciding When to Use Triggers."

Here is how you write a trigger that automatically puts this value into the Code field of the Artist table whenever an Insert occurs:

```
CREATE TRIGGER SETMUSICGEN FOR ARTIST
BEFORE INSERT AS
BEGIN
  NEW.CODE = GEN_ID(MUSIC_GEN, 1);
END
```

This code appears on the server side. It's not BCB code. You enter it exactly as shown in WISQL. The procedure runs on the server end; it is not processed by BCB. There is never any need to call this procedure explicitly. The whole point of triggers is that they run automatically when certain events occur. This one is designed to run right before an Insert occurs. In other words, the way to call this procedure from BCB is to perform an Insert.

This code states that you want to create a trigger called SetMusicGen to run on the Artist table. The generator is called before an insert operation:

```
BEFORE INSERT AS
```

The actual body of the code is simple:

```
NEW.CODE = GEN_ID(MUSIC_GEN, 1);
```

The NEW statement says that you are going to define the new value for the CODE field of the record that is about to be inserted into a table. In this case, you reference the new value for the CODE field of the Artist table.

GEN_ID is a function built into InterBase that produces an integer value. It takes a generator as its first parameter and a step value as its second parameter. The step value increases or decreases the value produced by the generator. For instance, the preceding code increments the value by 1.

NOTE

You can get a generator to fill in a field automatically with the trigger shown previously. Unfortunately, BCB does not provide particularly good support for triggers, in part because each server generates a different kind of trigger. The developers of BCB didn't want to run around finding out how to handle triggers for 30 different kinds of servers and neither did the developers of the BDE.

Some third-party solutions to this problem include a good one that works with InterBase called the IBEventAlerter. This solution ships with BCB but is found on the samples page. Its presence on the samples page means it lives in a never-never land between the hard code made by the IDE team and the sample code, written by me and many others like me, which appears in the Examples directory of a standard BCB install.

In the example under discussion, BCB's poor support for triggers is not crucial because the table is not sorted on the Code field. If it were, this trigger might cause BCB to lose track of the current record after the insert operation. BCB would not know that the Code value was inserted because it would not know that the trigger fired. As a result, the current record might be lost because it was sorted on a value of which BCB was not aware. In other words, the index would cause the record to be moved to a particular place in the dataset, but BCB would not know how to follow it. As far as BCB is concerned, the Code field is still blank!

There may be a problem with BCB reporting a referential integrity error because the field appears to be blank and yet the field is defined as Not Null. Underneath, the field is not really blank, but it appears that way to BCB. If this problem occurs, you can fix it by filling in the field with any randomly chosen value in an OnAfterInsert response method:

```
void __fastcall TDMod::ArtistTableAfterInsert(TDataSet *DataSet)
{
  ArtistTableCODE->AsInteger = 0;
}
```

Here it doesn't matter what you set for the CODE field, as long as some value is there so that the Not Null constraint is satisfied. The correct value is filled in later by the trigger.

Unfortunately, that is not yet the end of the story. The grid that most programmers use to view a table depends on the current image of a table reported by the VCL. As a result, having a field updated by a trigger can confuse the grid and cause it to show more than one copy of a record. This leads to all kinds of confusion. The best solution is to either call Refresh after posting an insert or else to close and then reopen the table. This latter step is not quite as drastic as it may seem because the TDatabase object keeps you connected to the database even if you close a table.

The key point to grasp is that this is one of the cases where it is possible to use a trigger to update an index inside BCB. It works because the table is sorted on the Last and First fields, not on the CODE field. Therefore, you can use a trigger to fill in the CODE field. If you tried to fill in the Last field with a trigger, then there would be trouble!

NOTE

Here is another example of how to create a trigger using WISQL:

```
CREATE TRIGGER SET_COMPANY_UPPER FOR COMPANY
ACTIVE BEFORE INSERT POSITION 1
AS
BEGIN
  NEW.COMPANY_UPPER = UPPER(NEW.COMPANY);
END
```

This code is called just before an insert operation on a table called Company. This table contains a string field also called Company and a second field called Company_Upper. The second field is meant to mirror the Company field but with all its characters in uppercase. Having this second field takes up a lot of space, but it allows you to conduct searches and sorts on the Company field without taking into account character case. The goal of the trigger shown previously is to take the new value for the Company field and convert it into an uppercase version of the string for use in the COMPANY_UPPER field. The Upper macro shown here is built into InterBase.

Notice the line that states when this trigger is fired:

```
ACTIVE BEFORE INSERT POSITION 1
```

For a detailed understanding of how to create triggers, turn to the *Language Reference* for the InterBase server.

I show you this trigger because it works fine under most circumstances when used with BCB. BCB does not need to know that the Set_Company_Upper trigger occurred. The trigger can take place in the background without impacting BCB's inner workings.

If you find yourself in a situation where you can't use a trigger, there is no great need for alarm. The absence of trigger support is not a big concern under most circumstances. Instead of using a trigger, you can use a stored procedure to retrieve the next number from a generator. In my opinion, it is simpler and easier to use a stored procedure rather than a trigger if you want to fill in the primary key of a table.

Working with Stored Procedures

In this section, you will see a discussion of the stored procedures used by the Music program to enforce or support referential integrity. These simple stored procedures use a generator to fill in the value of a primary key. Near the end of the chapter, I discuss a series of more complicated stored procedures used to query the data in the database.

A *stored procedure* is simply a routine that is stored on the server side rather than listed in your Object Pascal source code. Like the language for writing triggers, there is a unique language for writing stored procedures that has nothing to do with Object Pascal or SQL. In fact, you need to keep in mind that there is no particular relationship between BCB and InterBase. They are made by two different teams, using two different languages, with two different goals in mind. The stored procedure language was made up long before anyone thought of creating BCB, and in general, the two languages have absolutely nothing to do with one another.

One key difference between BCB code and InterBase code is that the language of stored procedures is completely platform independent. If you want to move your database back and forth between Windows and UNIX, then you might find it helpful to create many stored procedures that handle the majority of work for your databases. Then you can write very thin clients that simply ask the stored procedures to do all the work.

Stored procedures are not difficult to create. Here, for instance, is a stored procedure that returns the next number generated by the Music_Gen generator:

```
CREATE PROCEDURE GETALBUMGEN
RETURNS (NUM INTEGER)
AS
BEGIN  NUM = GEN_ID(ALBUM_GEN, 1);
END
```

The first line tells WISQL that you are going to create a procedure called GetMusicGen. The next line states that it is going to return a value called Num, which is an integer. The AS statement tells InterBase that you are now ready to define the body of the procedure. The procedure itself appears between a BEGIN..END pair and consists of a call to the GEN_ID function, which returns the next number from the MUSIC_GEN generator. When it retrieves the number, it asks InterBase to increment its value by one.

> **NOTE**
>
> Stored procedures are handled on the BCB end with either a TStoredProc component or by returning an answer set by way of a SQL statement. In general, if the stored procedure returns several rows of data, you access it by way of a SQL statement in a TQuery component. The SQL statement to use in such a case is Select * from GetAlbumGen, where GetAlbumGen is the name of the procedure that returns one or more rows of data. If the

stored procedure returns only a single item of data, you can call it with a TStoredProc
component. Examples of both methods for calling stored procedures from BCB appear in
the next section, in the form of excerpts from the Music program.

Stored Procedures from BCB's End

The Album and Book tables of the Music program use stored procedures to fill in their primary index. Because both procedures are identical, I describe only the one on the Album page.

To get started, you need to be sure the stored procedure is set up on the server side. Here is the
code you should enter into WISQL to create the procedure:

```
CREATE PROCEDURE GETALBUMGEN RETURNS (NUM INTEGER)
AS
BEGIN
  NUM = GEN_ID(ALBUM_GEN, 1);
END
```

As you can see, this is a simple stored procedure that does nothing more than return a single
value.

NOTE

If you are having trouble setting up the procedure, the entire data definition for the database is supplied later in this chapter, or you can just use the version of the database that is found on disk. You can add the code shown in this section to your current version of the music program. Or, if you want, you can just start a new project, create a data module, drop a TDatabase object on it, and connect it to the Music database that ships on the CD that accompanies this book. Setting up the alias for the database is described in depth in the readme file from the CD. Once you have the TDatabase object connected to Music.gdb, you can drop down the TStoredProc and start working with it, as described in the rest of this section.

To get started using a TStoredProc, drop it onto the Album page or onto a data module. Set
the StoredProcName alias to the GetAlbumGen stored procedure.

After selecting the procedure to use with the TStoredProc, you can pop up the Params field to
see the parameters passed to or returned by the function. In this case, only one parameter returned as the result of the function.

Whenever the user wants to insert a record into the Album table, the following procedure is called:

```
void __fastcall TAlbumForm::sbInsertClick(TObject *Sender)
{
  AnsiString S;
  if (!InputQuery("Insert New Album Dialog", "Enter album name", S))
    return;
  DMod->AlbumTable->Insert();
  DMod->AlbumTable->FieldByName("Album")->AsString = S;
  DMod->AlbumTable->FieldByName("Types")->AsString = "";
  DMod->AlbumTable->FieldByName("Loudness")->AsString = "";
  DMod->AlbumTable->FieldByName("Medium")->AsString = "";
  DMod->AlbumTable->Post();
  TypeCombo->SetFocus();
}
```

As you can see, there is no reference to a stored procedure in these lines of code. Instead, I reference the stored procedure in the `BeforePost` event for the `AlbumTable`:

```
void __fastcall TDMod::AlbumTableBeforePost(TDataSet *DataSet)
{
  if (AlbumSource->State == dsInsert)
  {
    GetAlbumGen->Prepare();
    GetAlbumGen->ExecProc();
    AlbumTableCODE->AsInteger = GetAlbumGen->ParamByName("Num")->AsInteger;
  }
}
```

The key lines of this procedure are the ones involving the stored procedure:

```
GetAlbumGen->Prepare();
GetAlbumGen->ExecProc();
AlbumTableCODE->AsInteger = GetAlbumGen->ParamByName("Num")->AsInteger;
```

This code first executes the stored procedure and then snags its return value from the `Params` field of the `TStoredProc`. The `Params` field for stored procedures works the same way as the `Params` field for `TQuery` objects.

As you can see, BCB makes it easy for you to use stored procedures in your programs. In this particular case, you could have used a stored procedure rather than a trigger. However, it is not a great crisis if you have to use a stored procedure rather than a trigger. The one advantage triggers have over stored procedures is that they are called automatically, thereby helping you to ensure data integrity.

Near the end of this chapter, I return to the subject of stored procedures when I discuss techniques for querying the data in a database in the section "Asking the Database a Question."

Deciding When to Use Triggers

When working with triggers, you should keep the following ideas in mind:

- BCB has no support for InterBase events. As a result, it does not know when a trigger occurs. This means you should never use a trigger to alter a field that your program is indexed on. It's okay to use a trigger to alter a field that is indexed; just don't let it fire while your program is actively using that index.

- C++Builder's lack of support for InterBase events usually is not a problem. Trouble only occurs if you index on the field that is updated by a trigger or if you rely on a grid to perform certain operations. If you index on a field that is updated by a trigger, the record disappears out from under the user. It doesn't matter if some index you are not currently using is updated; it must be a live index currently in use by your program to cause this kind of trouble. For instance, if there is a CODE or CUSTNO field on a table, and you currently index on that field, you will have trouble after an insert because the record seems to disappear beneath you. In other words, Builder won't know about the new CUSTNO or CODE number and will not be able to find the record after the insert.

- The best solution to the problem outlined previously is to never have the current index be the same field that is updated by a trigger. If you use this solution, be sure not to show the user the field that is updated by the trigger because it might not be updated automatically by Builder when displayed in a visual control. In other words, Builder doesn't know the trigger was fired, so it doesn't know to update a TDBGrid or TDBEdit control. However, it won't matter if the data is out of date, as long as you do not index on it and the user can't see the field in your grid.

- If you must index on a field that is updated, then the solution is to delete the trigger and insert a stored procedure instead. The stored procedure returns the new number created by a generator. You can then call this stored procedure inside a BeforePost event and use the number returned to fill in the CUSTNO or CODE field. You should do all this inside a TDataModule and then insist that all members of your team use that TDataModule whenever they access the table in question. This is the solution used throughout the Music program and the one that I prefer to use in most cases.

- A third alternative is to use triggers in combination with the IBEventAlerter component from the samples page in the Examples directory that ships with BCB. There is no description of the IBEventAlerter in this book, and you will have to explicitly add the Samples page to the Component Palette before you can use it. A description of how to add it to the IDE is found in the Examples directory set up by BCB during the default installation.

Following is the code for generating both the trigger and the stored procedure described previously. You do not ever want to include both the trigger and the stored procedure in the same database. You have to choose between the two techniques:

```
CREATE GENERATOR IMAGECODE;
CREATE PROCEDURE GETIMAGECODE RETURNS (NUM INTEGER)
AS
BEGIN  NUM = GEN_ID(IMAGECODE, 1);END
CREATE TRIGGER GENERATE_IMAGECODE FOR IMAGES
ACTIVE BEFORE INSERT POSITION 0
AS BEGIN  New.Code = Gen_ID(ImageCode, 1);END
```

When checking for referential integrity, your program may raise an exception because you failed to fill in a field specified as NOT NULL before the BeforePost event is fired. In other words, you might need to fill in the field even before the code reaches the BeforePost event. One way to solve this problem is to simply put in a dummy number at the time the user first decides to do an Insert:

```
void __fastcall TDMod::AlbumTableAfterInsert(TDataSet *DataSet)
{
   AlbumTableCODE->AsInteger = 0; // Temp value, real value in BeforePost
}
```

The value 0 shown in this code serves as a placeholder. It is replaced during the BeforePost event or during the execution of a trigger. All the value 0 does is satisfy the referential integrity code that insists the field not be null. The actual value, of course, is supplied later by the OnBeforePost event handler.

The Complete Data Definition for MUSIC.GDB

Here is the complete data definition for MUSIC.GDB:

```
/* Extract Database e:\unleash\data\music.gdb */
CREATE DATABASE "e:\unleash\data\music.gdb" PAGE_SIZE 1024
;

/* Domain definitions */
CREATE DOMAIN CODE_DOM AS INTEGER;

/* Table: ALBUM, Owner: SYSDBA */
CREATE TABLE ALBUM (CODE CODE_DOM NOT NULL,
        ALBUM VARCHAR(25) NOT NULL,
        TYPES SMALLINT,
        LOUDNESS SMALLINT,
        MEDIUM SMALLINT,
        RATING SMALLINT,
        GROUPCODE CODE_DOM NOT NULL,
PRIMARY KEY (CODE));

/* Table: ARTIST, Owner: SYSDBA */
CREATE TABLE ARTIST (CODE CODE_DOM NOT NULL,
        LAST VARCHAR(30),
        FIRST VARCHAR(30),
```

```
        BORN DATE,
        DIED DATE,
        BIRTHPLACE VARCHAR(35),
        COMMENT BLOB SUB_TYPE TEXT SEGMENT SIZE 80,
        ARTISTTYPE INTEGER NOT NULL,
PRIMARY KEY (CODE));

/* Table: ARTISTTYPE, Owner: SYSDBA */
CREATE TABLE ARTISTTYPE (ARTISTTYPE VARCHAR(15) NOT NULL,
        CODE INTEGER NOT NULL,
PRIMARY KEY (CODE));

/* Table: BOOK, Owner: SYSDBA */
CREATE TABLE BOOK (CODE CODE_DOM NOT NULL,
        BOOK VARCHAR(25) NOT NULL,
        TYPES SMALLINT,
        MEDIUM SMALLINT,
        RATING SMALLINT,
        COMMENT BLOB SUB_TYPE TEXT SEGMENT SIZE 80,
        GROUPCODE CODE_DOM NOT NULL,
PRIMARY KEY (CODE));

/* Table: CDROM, Owner: SYSDBA */
CREATE TABLE CDROM (CODE CODE_DOM NOT NULL,
        NAME VARCHAR(25) NOT NULL,
        TYPES SMALLINT,
        LOCATIONCODE INTEGER,
PRIMARY KEY (CODE));

/* Table: FOO, Owner: SYSDBA */
CREATE TABLE FOO (SAM INTEGER NOT NULL,
        NAME VARCHAR(50) NOT NULL,
        FOREIGNER INTEGER NOT NULL,
PRIMARY KEY (SAM));

/* Table: LOCATION, Owner: SYSDBA */
CREATE TABLE LOCATION (CODE INTEGER,
        LOCATION VARCHAR(25));

/* Table: LOUDNESS, Owner: SYSDBA */
CREATE TABLE LOUDNESS (LOUDNESS VARCHAR(15) NOT NULL,
        CODE INTEGER NOT NULL,
PRIMARY KEY (CODE));

/* Table: MEDIUM, Owner: SYSDBA */
CREATE TABLE MEDIUM (MEDIUM VARCHAR(15) NOT NULL,
        CODE INTEGER NOT NULL,
PRIMARY KEY (CODE));

/* Table: TYPES, Owner: SYSDBA */
CREATE TABLE TYPES (TYPES VARCHAR(15) NOT NULL,
        CODE INTEGER NOT NULL,
PRIMARY KEY (CODE));

/*  Index definitions for all user tables */
CREATE INDEX GROUPALBUM_IDX ON ALBUM(GROUPCODE, ALBUM);
CREATE INDEX ARTIST_LASTFIRST_NDX ON ARTIST(LAST, FIRST);
```

```
CREATE UNIQUE INDEX IDXLOCATION ON LOCATION(CODE);
CREATE UNIQUE INDEX LOUDNESS_IDX ON LOUDNESS(LOUDNESS);
CREATE UNIQUE INDEX MEDIUM_IDX ON MEDIUM(MEDIUM);
CREATE UNIQUE INDEX TYPE_IDX ON TYPES(TYPES);
ALTER TABLE ALBUM ADD FOREIGN KEY (TYPES) REFERENCES TYPES(CODE);
ALTER TABLE ALBUM ADD FOREIGN KEY (LOUDNESS) REFERENCES LOUDNESS(CODE);
ALTER TABLE ALBUM ADD FOREIGN KEY (MEDIUM) REFERENCES MEDIUM(CODE);
ALTER TABLE ALBUM ADD FOREIGN KEY (GROUPCODE) REFERENCES ARTIST(CODE);
ALTER TABLE FOO ADD FOREIGN KEY (FOREIGNER) REFERENCES BOOK(CODE);
ALTER TABLE BOOK ADD FOREIGN KEY (GROUPCODE) REFERENCES ARTIST(CODE);
ALTER TABLE BOOK ADD FOREIGN KEY (TYPES) REFERENCES TYPES(CODE);
ALTER TABLE BOOK ADD FOREIGN KEY (MEDIUM) REFERENCES MEDIUM(CODE);

CREATE GENERATOR MUSIC_GEN;
CREATE GENERATOR ALBUM_GEN;
CREATE GENERATOR CDROM_GEN;
CREATE GENERATOR ARTIST_GEN;
CREATE GENERATOR BOOK_GEN;

COMMIT WORK;
SET AUTODDL OFF;
SET TERM ^ ;

/* Stored procedures */
CREATE PROCEDURE GETCDROMGEN AS BEGIN EXIT; END ^
CREATE PROCEDURE GETBOOKGEN AS BEGIN EXIT; END ^
CREATE PROCEDURE ALBUMSPERARTIST AS BEGIN EXIT; END ^
CREATE PROCEDURE GETALBUMCOUNTS AS BEGIN EXIT; END ^
CREATE PROCEDURE RATINGRANGE AS BEGIN EXIT; END ^
CREATE PROCEDURE NINEORBETTER AS BEGIN EXIT; END ^
CREATE PROCEDURE GETRATINGS AS BEGIN EXIT; END ^
CREATE PROCEDURE GETALBUMGEN AS BEGIN EXIT; END ^
CREATE PROCEDURE ALBUMCOUNT AS BEGIN EXIT; END ^
CREATE PROCEDURE GETLOUDNESS AS BEGIN EXIT; END ^
CREATE PROCEDURE GETTYPE AS BEGIN EXIT; END ^
CREATE PROCEDURE GETMEDIA AS BEGIN EXIT; END ^
CREATE PROCEDURE ALBUMSEARCH AS BEGIN EXIT; END ^

ALTER PROCEDURE GETCDROMGEN RETURNS (NUM INTEGER)
AS

BEGIN
  NUM = GEN_ID(CDROM_GEN, 1);
END
  ^

ALTER PROCEDURE GETBOOKGEN RETURNS (NUM INTEGER)
AS

 BEGIN
  NUM = GEN_ID(BOOK_GEN, 1);
END
  ^

ALTER PROCEDURE ALBUMSPERARTIST (ARTISTCODE INTEGER)
RETURNS (NUMALBUMS INTEGER)
AS
```

```
begin
  select Count(*) Num_Albums
  from Album where GroupCode = :ArtistCode
  into :NumAlbums;
  exit;
end
^

ALTER PROCEDURE GETALBUMCOUNTS RETURNS (FIRST VARCHAR(30),
LAST VARCHAR(30),
ACOUNT INTEGER)
AS

begin
  select Artist.First, Artist.Last, Count(Album.Album)
  from Album, Artist
  where Album.GroupCode = Artist.Code
  Group By Artist.First, Artist.Last
  order by Artist.last
  into :First, :Last, :ACount;
  suspend;
end
^

ALTER PROCEDURE RATINGRANGE (LOWRATING INTEGER,
HIGHRATING INTEGER)
RETURNS (LAST VARCHAR(30),
ALBUM VARCHAR(30),
RATING INTEGER)
AS


begin
  for
  select Artist.Last, Album.Album, Album.Rating
  from Album, Artist
  where Album.GroupCode = Artist.Code and
  Album.Rating >= :LowRating and
  Album.Rating <= :HighRating
  Order By Album.Rating Desc
  into :Last, :Album, :Rating
  do
    suspend;
end
^

ALTER PROCEDURE NINEORBETTER RETURNS (LAST VARCHAR(30),
ALBUM VARCHAR(30),
RATING INTEGER)
AS

begin
  for
  select Artist.Last, Album.Album, Album.Rating
  from Album, Artist
  where Album.GroupCode = Artist.Code and Album.Rating >= 9
```

```
    Order By Album.Rating Desc
    into :Last, :Album, :Rating
    do
        suspend;
end
    ^


ALTER PROCEDURE GETRATINGS (STARTRATING INTEGER)
RETURNS (LAST VARCHAR(30),
ALBUM VARCHAR(30),
RATING INTEGER)
AS

begin
    for
    select Artist.Last, Album.Album, Album.Rating
    from Album, Artist
    where Album.GroupCode = Artist.Code and Album.Rating >= :StartRating
    Order By Album.Rating Desc
    into :Last, :Album, :Rating
    do
        suspend;
end
    ^


ALTER PROCEDURE GETALBUMGEN RETURNS (NUM INTEGER)
AS

BEGIN
    NUM = GEN_ID(ALBUM_GEN, 1);
END
    ^


ALTER PROCEDURE ALBUMCOUNT RETURNS (NUM INTEGER)
AS

begin
    for
        select Count(*) from Album
            into :Num
    do
        exit;
end
    ^


ALTER PROCEDURE GETLOUDNESS (LOUDNESSVALUE INTEGER)
RETURNS (LAST VARCHAR(30),
ALBUM VARCHAR(30),
RATING INTEGER,
LOUDNESSSTR VARCHAR(30))
AS


begin
    for
    select Artist.Last, Album.Album, Album.Rating, Loudness.Loudness
    from Album, Artist, Loudness
    where Album.GroupCode = Artist.Code and
```

```
      Album.Loudness = :LoudnessValue and
      Loudness.Code = :LoudnessValue
      Order By Album.Album Desc
      into :Last, :Album, :Rating, :LoudnessStr
      do
         suspend;
   end
      ^


ALTER PROCEDURE GETTYPE (TYPEVALUE INTEGER)
RETURNS (LAST VARCHAR(30),
ALBUM VARCHAR(30),
RATING INTEGER,
TYPESTR VARCHAR(30),
MEDIUMSTR VARCHAR(30))
AS

begin
   for
   select Artist.Last, Album.Album, Album.Rating, Types.Types, Medium.Medium
   from Album, Artist, Types, Medium
   where Album.GroupCode = Artist.Code and
   Album.Types = :TypeValue and
   Types.Code = :TypeValue and
   Medium.Code = Album.Medium
   Order By Album.Album Desc
   into :Last, :Album, :Rating, :TypeStr, :MediumStr
   do
      suspend;
   end
      ^


ALTER PROCEDURE GETMEDIA (MEDIAVALUE INTEGER)
RETURNS (LAST VARCHAR(30),
ALBUM VARCHAR(30),
RATING INTEGER,
TYPESTR VARCHAR(30),
MEDIUMSTR VARCHAR(30))
AS

begin
   for
   select Artist.Last, Album.Album, Album.Rating, Types.Types, Medium.Medium
   from Album, Artist, Types, Medium
   where Album.GroupCode = Artist.Code and
   Album.Medium = :MediaValue and
   Types.Code = Album.Types and
   Medium.Code = :MediaValue
   Order By Album.Album Desc
   into :Last, :Album, :Rating, :TypeStr, :MediumStr
   do
      suspend;
   end
      ^


ALTER PROCEDURE ALBUMSEARCH (ANALBUMNAME VARCHAR(75))
RETURNS (ARTISTNAME VARCHAR(30),
ALBUMNAME VARCHAR(30),
```

```
RATINGVALUE VARCHAR(30),
TYPENAME VARCHAR(30),
MEDIUMNAME VARCHAR(30))
AS

begin
  for
  select Artist.Last, Album.Album, Album.Rating, Types.Types, Medium.Medium
    from  Album, Artist, Types, Medium
  where artist.code = album.groupcode and
  Album.Album like :AnAlbumName and
  Types.Code = Album.Types and
  Medium.Code = Album.Medium
  order by Artist.Last
  into :ArtistName, :AlbumName, :RatingValue, :TypeName, MediumName
  do
  suspend;
end
  ^
SET TERM ; ^
COMMIT WORK ;
SET AUTODDL ON;
SET TERM ^ ;

/* Triggers only will work for SQL triggers */
CREATE TRIGGER SETMUSICGEN FOR ARTIST
ACTIVE BEFORE INSERT POSITION 0
AS
BEGIN
  NEW.CODE = GEN_ID(MUSIC_GEN, 1);
END
  ^
COMMIT WORK ^
SET TERM ; ^

/* Grant permissions for this database */
GRANT SELECT ON ALBUM TO SAM;
GRANT DELETE, INSERT, SELECT, UPDATE, REFERENCES ON ALBUM
  TO SAM WITH GRANT OPTION;
GRANT DELETE, INSERT, SELECT, UPDATE, REFERENCES ON ALBUM
  TO USER1 WITH GRANT OPTION;
```

If you want to create this database from scratch, you can run this entire statement through WISQL from the File menu. Otherwise, you can create the database and pass the statements through one at a time. A third use for the code is simply to give you one place to look when you need a reference for MUSIC.GDB. If you already have a copy of the database, you can create the output shown here; select Extract | SQL Data from Database from the WISQL menu.

Server-Side Rules Versus Client-Side Rules

A few more words about database design: In many people's minds, the holy grail of contemporary client/server development is to place as many rules as possible on the server side of the equation. This means that no matter how the user accesses the data, and no matter how many front ends are written to access the data, the basic rules of the database are enforced.

This means that you must create referential integrity on the server side using foreign keys or whatever tools are at your disposal. Furthermore, you should use triggers whenever possible to enforce additional rules. For instance, some people view it as an error to insert the Code field of the Album table using a stored procedure rather than a trigger. I do things this way simply because it makes it easier for me to create the kind of front end I want for the Music table.

Even using triggers and referential integrity is not enough for many hard-core adherents of the server-side philosophy. This book, however, is written about a client-side tool, so I generally promote just placing the referential integrity on the server side and maybe adding a few more triggers or stored procedures where necessary.

If you can use QBE, or some other SQL builder, to create powerful SQL statements that you use in your programs, you probably should place those SQL statements in stored procedures, as shown previously and discussed in more depth later in this chapter, in the section called "Asking the Database a Question."

I find that most other database chores are easier to perform on the BCB side. BCB is a powerful language with powerful debuggers to back it up. Most servers have neither a powerful language nor a powerful debugger. As a result, I feel it's often wisest to keep certain kinds of database logic on your client side, as long as it does not exact a huge penalty in terms of performance. Obviously, if you need to fetch a lot of rows and then process them, it's best to do that on the server side where the data itself is stored.

The emergence of Distributed OLE and other tools that support Remote Procedure Calls (RPCs) is likely to have a powerful impact on the future of this issue. If PC-based developers can use Distributed OLE to place rules easily on remote servers, the whole way databases are constructed is likely to change. In other words, if I could use BCB to enforce a bunch of rules and then encapsulate those rules in an object that resides on the same machine as the InterBase server, I would do it. I would put all my database logic out there and just provide a few entry points for my front-end program to call.

An Overview of the Interface for the Music Program

The interface for MUSIC.DPR presents the user with a main screen with three pages embedded inside it. One page (shown in Figure 16.1) is meant only for performing searches. It gives you a view of both the Artist table and either the Book table or the Album table. You can't alter the Artist table from this screen, but you can change the Album or Book table.

FIGURE 16.1.

The Index page from
MUSIC.DPR *enables you
to view artists and their
related productions.*

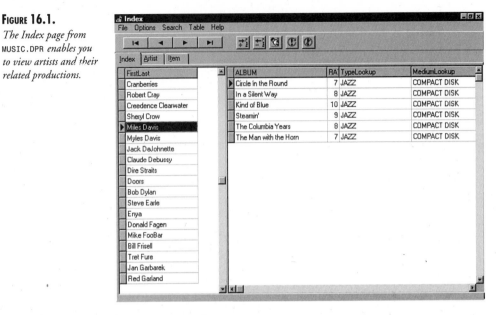

NOTE

I use the following code to prevent the user from using the Insert key to insert a record into either of the grids on the Index page:

```
void __fastcall TIndexForm::ArtistGridKeyPress(TObject *Sender,
  char &Key)
{
  if ((Key == VK_INSERT) || (Key == VK_DELETE))
    Key = 0;
}
```

This code disarms Insert and Delete keystrokes. Users never know the method is called but find that they can't use the Insert or Delete keys. The code is called in response to OnKeyDown events.

The second page in the Music program allows you to see one record from the Artist table, as shown in Figure 16.2. Users can browse or search through the data using the Index page shown in Figure 16.1. If they want to look at a particular record, they can switch to the Artist, Album, or Book pages. Figures 16.3 and 16.4 show the latter two of these three pages.

FIGURE 16.2.

The Artist page from the Music program.

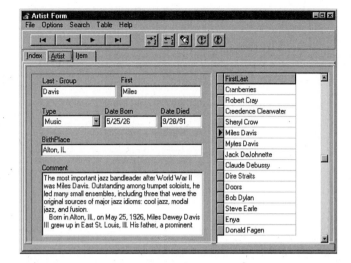

FIGURE 16.3.

The Album page from the Music program.

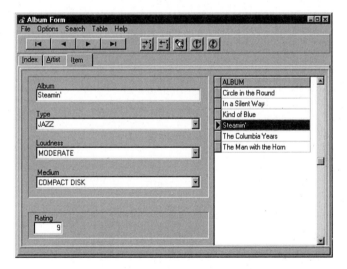

The Book or Album page is always the third page in the program. There is no fourth page. If the current record is an album, then the Album form is shown; if it is a book, then the Book form is shown.

FIGURE 16.4.

The Book page from the Music program.

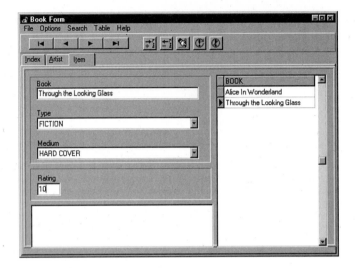

Working with Paged Forms

BCB provides a number of paged dialogs or notebooks that you can use to present data to the user. In this particular program, I use the TTabControl tool in conjunction with a series of forms. My primary concern is allowing the programmer to place each major object in a separate unit, rather than forcing the combination of various different sets of functionality into one paged notebook. In other words, the Album page is a separate object, not a part of the TNotebook object.

The Music program really has five major forms in it, the first representing the frame for the entire program, and the rest representing the Index, Artist, Album, and Book pages. The next few paragraphs describe how to make a form become a child of a second form, which is what is really happening inside the Music program.

The key point to grasp is that you need to convert the standard BCB pop-up form to a child form that has Form1 as its parent. Here is how to proceed:

```
#include <vcl\vcl.h>
#pragma hdrstop
#include "ChildForm1.h"
#pragma resource "*.dfm"
TChildForm *ChildForm;
__fastcall TChildForm::TChildForm(TComponent* Owner)
   : TForm(Owner)
{
}
void __fastcall TChildForm::Loaded(void)
{
  TForm::Loaded();
  Visible = False;
  Position = poDefault;
```

Advanced InterBase Concepts

CHAPTER 16

663

16

ADVANCED
INTERBASE
CONCEPTS

```
    BorderIcons = TBorderIcons();
    BorderStyle = bsNone;
    HandleNeeded();
    SetBounds(0, 0, Width, Height);
}
void __fastcall TChildForm::CreateParams(Controls::TCreateParams &Params)
{
    TForm::CreateParams(Params);
    if (dynamic_cast<TForm*>(Owner))
      Params.WndParent = dynamic_cast<TForm*>(Owner)->Handle;
    else
      ShowMessage("No Cast in ChildForm CreateParams");
    Params.Style = WS_CHILD | WS_CLIPSIBLINGS;
    Params.X = 0;
    Params.Y = 0;
}
```

The logic for the code shown here was based on work done by Pat Ritchey.

In the Music program, all the main forms descend from the ChildForm shown previously. As a result, they inherit the capability to live as a child form pasted on top of another form:

```
class TAlbumForm : public TChildForm
{
__published: // IDE-managed Components
    ... // Code omitted here.
}
```

When using this technique, you want the parent form to explicitly create the child forms. To do this, do not autocreate the forms but choose Options | Project | Forms and move the forms from the Auto-Create list box into the Available Forms list box. Then you can create the forms as needed inside of Form1 with code that looks like this:

```
__fastcall TForm1::TForm1(TComponent* Owner)
 : TForm(Owner)
{
    ArtistForm = new TArtistForm(this);
    AlbumForm = new TAlbumForm(this);
    IndexForm = new TIndexForm(this);
    BookForm = new TBookForm(this);
    ChildForms[0] = IndexForm;
    ChildForms[1] = ArtistForm;
    ChildForms[2] = AlbumForm;
    ChildForms[3] = BookForm;
}
```

I describe this process in more depth later in this chapter in the section that examines the FormCreate event for the main module.

To make sure the form adheres to the dimensions of its parent, you can respond to OnResize events:

```
void __fastcall TForm1::FormResize(TObject *Sender)
{
    int i;
    RECT R = TabControl1->DisplayRect;
```

```
R.top += Panel2->Height;
R.bottom -= Panel2->Height;
for (i = 0; i < MAXFORMS; i++)
{
    MoveWindow(ChildForms[i]->Handle, R.left, R.top, R.right, R.bottom, True);
}
}
```

This code uses the `TabControl1->DisplayRect` function call to get the size of the window to draw in, excluding the location where the tabs reside. It then resizes the child form so that it fits in this space.

The Code for the Music Program

Now that you understand the basic structure of the Music program, the next step is to take a look at the code and analyze any sections that need explanation. The code appears in Listings 16.1 through 16.12.

Listing 16.1. The Main header form for the Music program.

```
/////////////////////////////////////
// File Main.h
// Project Music
// Copyright (c) 1997 by Charlie Calvert
/////////////////////////////////////
//-------------------------------------------------------------
#ifndef MainH
#define MainH
//-------------------------------------------------------------
#include <vcl\Classes.hpp>
#include <vcl\Controls.hpp>
#include <vcl\StdCtrls.hpp>
#include <vcl\Forms.hpp>
#include <vcl\ComCtrls.hpp>
#include <vcl\ExtCtrls.hpp>
#include <vcl\DBGrids.hpp>
#include <vcl\Grids.hpp>
#include <vcl\Menus.hpp>
#include <vcl\Buttons.hpp>
#include <vcl\DBCtrls.hpp>
//-------------------------------------------------------------
#define MAXFORMS 4
class TForm1 : public TForm
{
__published:
    TTabControl *TabControl1;
    TMainMenu *MainMenu1;
    TMenuItem *File1;
    TMenuItem *Go1;
    TMenuItem *N1;
    TMenuItem *Exit1;
    TPanel *Panel2;
    TSpeedButton *InsertBtn;
    TSpeedButton *DeleteBtn;
```

```cpp
    TDBNavigator *DBNavigator1;
    TMenuItem *Options1;
    TMenuItem *AlbumsCount1;
    TMenuItem *AlbumsPerArtist1;
    TMenuItem *RatedNineorBetter1;
    TMenuItem *Ratings1;
    TSpeedButton *CancelBtn;
    TSpeedButton *RefreshBtn;
    TSpeedButton *PostBtn;
    TMenuItem *Search1;
    TMenuItem *LastGroup1;
    TMenuItem *First1;
    TMenuItem *N2;
    TMenuItem *IndexPage1;
    TMenuItem *ArtistPage1;
    TMenuItem *ItemPage1;
    TMenuItem *About1;
    TMenuItem *About2;
    TMenuItem *Table1;
    TMenuItem *Insert1;
    TMenuItem *Delete1;
    TMenuItem *Post1;
    TMenuItem *Refresh1;
    TMenuItem *Cancel1;
    TMenuItem *N3;
    TMenuItem *MusiciansOnly1;
    TMenuItem *WritersOnly1;
    TMenuItem *N4;
    TMenuItem *LoudnessRatings1;
    TMenuItem *SelectbyType1;
    TMenuItem *SelectbyMedia1;
    TMenuItem *TotalAlbumsCount1;
    void __fastcall AlbumsforthisArtist1Click(TObject *Sender);
    void __fastcall AlbumCountForAll1Click(TObject *Sender);
    void __fastcall AlbumsRatedNineorBetter1Click(TObject *Sender);
    void __fastcall AlbumsRatedinaRange1Click(TObject *Sender);
    void __fastcall TabControl1Change(TObject *Sender);
    void __fastcall Exit1Click(TObject *Sender);
    void __fastcall FormResize(TObject *Sender);
    void __fastcall FormShow(TObject *Sender);
    void __fastcall LastGroup1Click(TObject *Sender);
    void __fastcall IndexPage1Click(TObject *Sender);
    void __fastcall About2Click(TObject *Sender);
    void __fastcall FilterOptionsClick(TObject *Sender);
    void __fastcall LoudnessRatings1Click(TObject *Sender);
    void __fastcall SelectbyType1Click(TObject *Sender);
    void __fastcall SelectbyMedia1Click(TObject *Sender);
    void __fastcall TotalAlbumsCount1Click(TObject *Sender);
private:
    TForm *ChildForms[MAXFORMS];
public:
    virtual __fastcall TForm1(TComponent* Owner);
};
//---------------------------------------------------------------------------
extern TForm1 *Form1;
//---------------------------------------------------------------------------
#endif
```

Listing 16.2. The Main form for the Music program.

```cpp
///////////////////////////////////////
// File Main.cpp
// Project Music
// Copyright (c) 1997 by Charlie Calvert
///////////////////////////////////////
#include <vcl\vcl.h>
#pragma hdrstop
#include "Main.h"
#include "DMod1.h"
#include "QueryReport1.h"
#include "AlbumForm1.h"
#include "ArtistForm1.h"
#include "BookForm1.h"
#include "IndexForm1.h"
#include "AboutBox1.h"
#pragma resource "*.dfm"
TForm1 *Form1;
//---------------------------------------------------------------------
__fastcall TForm1::TForm1(TComponent* Owner)
: TForm(Owner)
{
  ArtistForm = new TArtistForm(this);
  AlbumForm = new TAlbumForm(this);
  IndexForm = new TIndexForm(this);
  BookForm = new TBookForm(this);
  ChildForms[0] = IndexForm;
  ChildForms[1] = ArtistForm;
  ChildForms[2] = AlbumForm;
  ChildForms[3] = BookForm;
}
void __fastcall TForm1::TabControl1Change(TObject *Sender)
{
  DMod->PostAll();
  switch (TabControl1->TabIndex)
  {
    case 0:
      ChildForms[TabControl1->TabIndex]->BringToFront();
      Caption = "Index";
      DBNavigator1->DataSource = DMod->ArtistSource;
      DMod->TypesTable->Filtered = False;
      break;
    case 1:
      ChildForms[TabControl1->TabIndex]->BringToFront();
      Caption = "Artist Form";
      DBNavigator1->DataSource = DMod->ArtistSource;
      InsertBtn->OnClick = ArtistForm->sbInsertClick;
      // Insert1->OnClick = ArtistForm->sbInsertClick;
      DeleteBtn->OnClick = ArtistForm->sbDeleteClick;
      PostBtn->OnClick = ArtistForm->PostBtnClick;
      CancelBtn->OnClick = ArtistForm->CancelBtnClick;
      break;
    case 2:
      if (DMod->ArtistTable->FieldByName("ArtistType")->AsInteger == 1)
      {
        ChildForms[2]->BringToFront();
        Caption = "Album Form";
```

```
            DBNavigator1->DataSource = DMod->AlbumSource;
            InsertBtn->OnClick = AlbumForm->sbInsertClick;
//          Insert1->OnClick = AlbumForm->sbInsertClick;
            DeleteBtn->OnClick = AlbumForm->sbDeleteClick;
            CancelBtn->OnClick = AlbumForm->CancelBtnClick;
            PostBtn->OnClick = AlbumForm->PostBtnClick;
            DMod->TypesTable->Filtered = False;
            DMod->MaxTypes = 999;
            DMod->MinTypes = 0;
            DMod->TypesTable->Filtered = True;
        }
        else
        {
            ChildForms[3]->BringToFront();
            Caption = "Book Form";
            DBNavigator1->DataSource = DMod->BookSource;
            Insert1->OnClick = InsertBtn->OnClick = BookForm->sbInsertClick;
            DeleteBtn->OnClick = BookForm->sbDeleteClick;
            CancelBtn->OnClick = BookForm->CancelBtnClick;
            PostBtn->OnClick = BookForm->PostBtnClick;
            DMod->TypesTable->Filtered = False;
            DMod->MaxTypes = 1999;
            DMod->MinTypes = 1000;
            DMod->TypesTable->Filtered = True;
            BookForm->TypesCombo->Update();
        }
        break;
    }
}
void __fastcall TForm1::Exit1Click(TObject *Sender)
{
    DMod->PostAll();
    Close();
}
void __fastcall TForm1::FormResize(TObject *Sender)
{
    int i;
    RECT R = TabControl1->DisplayRect;
    R.top += Panel2->Height;
    R.bottom -= Panel2->Height;
    for (i = 0; i < MAXFORMS; i++)
    {
        MoveWindow(ChildForms[i]->Handle, R.left, R.top, R.right, R.bottom, True);
    }
}
void __fastcall TForm1::FormShow(TObject *Sender)
{
    int i;
    for (i = MAXFORMS-1; i >= 0; i--)
        ChildForms[i]->Show();
    FilterOptionsClick(MusiciansOnly1);
    TabControl1Change(NULL);
}
void __fastcall TForm1::LastGroup1Click(TObject *Sender)
{
    AnsiString S;
```

continues

Listing 16.2. continued

```
  if (InputQuery("Search Dialog", "Enter Name", S))
  {
    DMod->ArtistTable->FindNearest(OPENARRAY(TVarRec, (S)));
    TabControl1Change(NULL);
  }
}
void __fastcall TForm1::IndexPage1Click(TObject *Sender)
{
  TabControl1->TabIndex = dynamic_cast<TComponent *>(Sender)->Tag;
  TabControl1Change(NULL);
}
void __fastcall TForm1::About2Click(TObject *Sender)
{
  AboutBox->ShowModal();
}
void __fastcall TForm1::FilterOptionsClick(TObject *Sender)
{
  DMod->ArtistTable->Filtered = False;
  switch (dynamic_cast<TComponent *>(Sender)->Tag)
  {
    case fiAlbumFilter:
      IndexForm->BookGrid->Align = alNone;
      IndexForm->BookGrid->Visible = False;
      DMod->FilterType = fiAlbumFilter;
      IndexForm->AlbumGrid->Align = alClient;
      IndexForm->AlbumGrid->Visible = True;
    break;
    case fiBookFilter:
      IndexForm->AlbumGrid->Align = alNone;
      IndexForm->AlbumGrid->Visible = False;
      DMod->FilterType = fiBookFilter;
      IndexForm->BookGrid->Align = alClient;
      IndexForm->BookGrid->Visible = True;
    break;
  }
  DMod->ArtistTable->Filtered = True;
}
void __fastcall TForm1::AlbumsforthisArtist1Click(TObject *Sender)
{
  ShowMessage(DMod->AlbumsPerArtist());
}
void __fastcall TForm1::AlbumCountForAll1Click(TObject *Sender)
{
  QueryReportForm->ShowQueryResults(qrAlbumCount);
}
void __fastcall TForm1::AlbumsRatedNineorBetter1Click(TObject *Sender)
{
  QueryReportForm->ShowQueryResults(qrNineOrBetter);
}
void __fastcall TForm1::AlbumsRatedinaRange1Click(TObject *Sender)
{
  QueryReportForm->ShowQueryResults(qrRatingRange);
}
void __fastcall TForm1::LoudnessRatings1Click(TObject *Sender)
{
```

```
  QueryReportForm->ShowQueryResults(qrLoudness);
}
void __fastcall TForm1::SelectbyType1Click(TObject *Sender)
{
  QueryReportForm->ShowQueryResults(qrTypes);
}
void __fastcall TForm1::SelectbyMedia1Click(TObject *Sender)
{
  QueryReportForm->ShowQueryResults(qrMedia);
}
void __fastcall TForm1::TotalAlbumsCount1Click(TObject *Sender)
{
  ShowMessage(DMod->GetTotalAlbumCount());
}
```

Listing 16.3. The Index header for the Music program.

```
#ifndef IndexForm1H
#define IndexForm1H
#include <vcl\Classes.hpp>
#include <vcl\Controls.hpp>
#include <vcl\StdCtrls.hpp>
#include <vcl\Forms.hpp>
#include <vcl\DBGrids.hpp>
#include <vcl\Grids.hpp>
#include "childform1.h"
class TIndexForm : public TChildForm
{
__published: // IDE-managed Components
  TDBGrid *ArtistGrid;
  TDBGrid *AlbumGrid;
  TDBGrid *BookGrid;
  void __fastcall ArtistGridKeyPress(TObject *Sender, char &Key);
private:// User declarations
public: // User declarations
  virtual __fastcall TIndexForm(TComponent* Owner);
};
extern TIndexForm *IndexForm;
#endif
```

Listing 16.4. The Index form for the Music program.

```
#include <vcl\vcl.h>
#pragma hdrstop
#include "IndexForm1.h"
#include "DMod1.h"
#pragma resource "*.dfm"
TIndexForm *IndexForm;
__fastcall TIndexForm::TIndexForm(TComponent* Owner)
```

continues

Listing 16.4. continued

```
  : TChildForm(Owner)
{
}
void __fastcall TIndexForm::ArtistGridKeyPress(TObject *Sender, char &Key)
{
  if ((Key == VK_INSERT) || (Key == VK_DELETE))
    Key = 0;
}
```

Listing 16.5. The header from the `Artist` form for the `Music` program.

```
//-----------------------------------------------------------------
#ifndef ArtistForm1H
#define ArtistForm1H
//-----------------------------------------------------------------
#include <vcl\Classes.hpp>
#include <vcl\Controls.hpp>
#include <vcl\StdCtrls.hpp>
#include <vcl\Forms.hpp>
#include <vcl\ExtCtrls.hpp>
#include <vcl\Buttons.hpp>
#include <vcl\DBCtrls.hpp>
#include <vcl\Mask.hpp>
#include "childform1.h"
#include <vcl\DBGrids.hpp>
#include <vcl\Grids.hpp>
//-----------------------------------------------------------------
class TArtistForm : public TChildForm
{
__published:  // IDE-managed Components
  TPanel *Panel2;
  TLabel *Label1;
  TLabel *Label2;
  TLabel *Label3;
  TLabel *Label4;
  TLabel *Label5;
  TLabel *Label6;
  TLabel *Label7;
  TDBEdit *LastEdit;
  TDBEdit *dbeFirst;
  TDBEdit *DBEdit2;
  TDBEdit *dbeDied;
  TDBEdit *dbeBirthPlace;
  TDBMemo *dbeComment;
  TDBLookupComboBox *DBLookupComboBox1;
  TBevel *Bevel1;
  TDBGrid *DBGrid1;
  void __fastcall sbInsertClick(TObject *Sender);
  void __fastcall sbDeleteClick(TObject *Sender);
```

```
  void __fastcall PostBtnClick(TObject *Sender);
  void __fastcall CancelBtnClick(TObject *Sender);
private: // User declarations
public: // User declarations
  virtual __fastcall TArtistForm(TComponent* Owner);
};
//--------------------------------------------------------------------------
extern TArtistForm *ArtistForm;
//--------------------------------------------------------------------------
#endif
```

Listing 16.6. The Artist form for the Music program.

```cpp
/////////////////////////////////////////
// File ArtistForm1.cpp
// Project Music
// Copyright (c) 1997 by Charlie Calvert
/////////////////////////////////////////
#include <vcl\vcl.h>
#pragma hdrstop
#include "ArtistForm1.h"
#include "DMod1.h"
#pragma resource "*.dfm"
TArtistForm *ArtistForm;
__fastcall TArtistForm::TArtistForm(TComponent* Owner)
  : TChildForm(Owner)
{
}
void __fastcall TArtistForm::sbInsertClick(TObject *Sender)
{
  DMod->ArtistTable->Insert();
  LastEdit->SetFocus();
}
void __fastcall TArtistForm::sbDeleteClick(TObject *Sender)
{
  AnsiString S = DMod->ArtistTable->FieldByName("FirstLast")->AsString;
  if (MessageDlg("Delete " + S + " from Artist Table?",
    mtConfirmation, TMsgDlgButtons() << mbYes << mbNo, 0) == ID_YES)
  {
    DMod->ArtistTable->Delete();
    DMod->ArtistTable->Refresh();
  }
}
void __fastcall TArtistForm::PostBtnClick(TObject *Sender)
{
  DMod->PostAll();
}
void __fastcall TArtistForm::CancelBtnClick(TObject *Sender)
{
  DMod->ArtistTable->Cancel();
}
```

Listing 16.7. The header from the Album form from the Music program.

```c
/////////////////////////////////////
// File AlbumForm1.h
// Project Music
// Copyright (c) 1997 by Charlie Calvert
//
#ifndef AlbumForm1H
#define AlbumForm1H
#include <vcl\Classes.hpp>
#include <vcl\Controls.hpp>
#include <vcl\StdCtrls.hpp>
#include <vcl\Forms.hpp>
#include <vcl\ExtCtrls.hpp>
#include <vcl\Buttons.hpp>
#include <vcl\DBCtrls.hpp>
#include <vcl\Mask.hpp>
//#include <vcl\Spin.hpp>
#include "ChildForm1.h"
#include <vcl\DBGrids.hpp>
#include <vcl\Grids.hpp>
class TAlbumForm : public TChildForm
{
__published:
  TPanel *Panel1;
  TBevel *Bevel2;
  TLabel *Label1;
  TLabel *Label2;
  TLabel *Label4;
  TLabel *Label5;
  TBevel *Bevel1;
  TLabel *Label3;
  TDBEdit *AlbumEdit;
  TDBLookupComboBox *TypeCombo;
  TDBLookupComboBox *lcbLoud;
  TDBLookupComboBox *lcbMedium;
  TDBGrid *DBGrid1;
  TDBEdit *DBEdit1;
  void __fastcall sbInsertClick(TObject *Sender);
  void __fastcall sbDeleteClick(TObject *Sender);
  void __fastcall Spin1UpClick(TObject *Sender);
  void __fastcall Spin1DownClick(TObject *Sender);
  void __fastcall CancelBtnClick(TObject *Sender);
  void __fastcall PostBtnClick(TObject *Sender);
  void __fastcall FormActivate(TObject *Sender);
private:
protected:
public:
  virtual __fastcall TAlbumForm(TComponent* Owner);
};
extern TAlbumForm *AlbumForm;
#endif
```

Advanced InterBase Concepts

CHAPTER 16

673

16

ADVANCED
INTERBASE
CONCEPTS

Listing 16.8. The Album form from the Music program.

```cpp
/////////////////////////////////////
// File AlbumForm1.cpp
// Project Music
// Copyright (c) 1997 by Charlie Calvert
/////////////////////////////////////
//----------------------------------------------------------------------
#include <vcl\vcl.h>
#pragma hdrstop

#include "AlbumForm1.h"
#include "ChildForm1.h"
#include "DMod1.h"
//----------------------------------------------------------------------
#pragma resource "*.dfm"
TAlbumForm *AlbumForm;
//----------------------------------------------------------------------
__fastcall TAlbumForm::TAlbumForm(TComponent* Owner)
  : TChildForm(Owner)
{
}
void __fastcall TAlbumForm::sbInsertClick(TObject *Sender)
{
  AnsiString S;
  if (!InputQuery("Insert New Album Dialog", "Enter album name", S))
    return;
  DMod->AlbumTable->Insert();
  DMod->AlbumTable->FieldByName("Album")->AsString = S;
  DMod->AlbumTable->FieldByName("Types")->AsString = "";
  DMod->AlbumTable->FieldByName("Loudness")->AsString = "";
  DMod->AlbumTable->FieldByName("Medium")->AsString = "";
  DMod->PostAll();
  TypeCombo->SetFocus();
}
void __fastcall TAlbumForm::sbDeleteClick(TObject *Sender)
{
  AnsiString S = DMod->AlbumTable->FieldByName("Album")->AsString;
  if (MessageDlg("Delete " + S + " from Album Table?",
    mtConfirmation, TMsgDlgButtons() << mbYes << mbNo, 0) == ID_YES)
  {
    DMod->AlbumTable->Delete();
  }
}
void __fastcall TAlbumForm::Spin1UpClick(TObject *Sender)
{
  int i;
  i = DMod->AlbumTable->FieldByName("Rating")->AsInteger;
  if (i < 1)
    i = 1;
  if (i < 10)
    i++;
  if ((DMod->BookTable->State != dsEdit)||(DMod->BookTable->State != dsInsert))
    DMod->AlbumTable->Edit();
```

continues

Listing 16.8. continued

```cpp
  DMod->AlbumTable->FieldByName("Rating")->AsInteger = i;
}
void __fastcall TAlbumForm::Spin1DownClick(TObject *Sender)
{
  int i;
  i = DMod->AlbumTable->FieldByName("Rating")->AsInteger;
  if (i < 1)
    i = 1;
  if (i > 1)
    i--;
  if ((DMod->BookTable->State != dsEdit)||(DMod->BookTable->State != dsInsert))
    DMod->AlbumTable->Edit();
  DMod->AlbumTable->FieldByName("Rating")->AsInteger = i;
}
void __fastcall TAlbumForm::CancelBtnClick(TObject *Sender)
{
  DMod->AlbumTable->Cancel();
}
void __fastcall TAlbumForm::PostBtnClick(TObject *Sender)
{
  DMod->PostAll();
}
void __fastcall TAlbumForm::FormActivate(TObject *Sender)
{
  AlbumEdit->SetFocus();
}
```

Listing 16.9. The header for the Book form from the Music program.

```cpp
////////////////////////////////////////
// File BookForm1.h
// Project Music
// Copyright (c) 1997 by Charlie Calvert
//
#ifndef BookForm1H
#define BookForm1H
#include <vcl\Classes.hpp>
#include <vcl\Controls.hpp>
#include <vcl\StdCtrls.hpp>
#include <vcl\Forms.hpp>
#include <vcl\ExtCtrls.hpp>
#include <vcl\Buttons.hpp>
#include <vcl\DBCtrls.hpp>
#include <vcl\Mask.hpp>
//#include <vcl\Spin.hpp>
#include "ChildForm1.h"
#include <vcl\DBGrids.hpp>
#include <vcl\Grids.hpp>
class TBookForm : public TChildForm
{
__published:
  TPanel *Panel1;
  TBevel *Bevel2;
  TBevel *Bevel1;
```

```
    TLabel *Book;
    TLabel *Label2;
    TLabel *Label3;
    TLabel *Label1;
    TDBEdit *BookEdit;
    TDBLookupComboBox *TypesCombo;
    TDBLookupComboBox *DBLookupComboBox2;
    TDBGrid *DBGrid1;
    TDBMemo *DBMemo1;
    TDBEdit *DBEdit1;
    void __fastcall sbDeleteClick(TObject *Sender);
    void __fastcall sbInsertClick(TObject *Sender);
    void __fastcall CancelBtnClick(TObject *Sender);
    void __fastcall PostBtnClick(TObject *Sender);
    void __fastcall Spin1DownClick(TObject *Sender);
    void __fastcall Spin1UpClick(TObject *Sender);
private:
public:
    virtual __fastcall TBookForm(TComponent* Owner);
};
extern TBookForm *BookForm;
#endif
```

Listing 16.10. The Book form from the Music program.

```
/////////////////////////////////////
// File BookForm1.cpp
// Project Music
// Copyright (c) 1997 by Charlie Calvert
//
#include <vcl\vcl.h>
#pragma hdrstop
#include "BookForm1.h"
#include "DMod1.h"
#pragma resource "*.dfm"
TBookForm *BookForm;
__fastcall TBookForm::TBookForm(TComponent* Owner)
  : TChildForm(Owner)
{
}
void __fastcall TBookForm::sbInsertClick(TObject *Sender)
{
  AnsiString S;
  if (!InputQuery("Insert New Book Dialog", "Enter book name", S))
    return;
  DMod->BookTable->Insert();
  DMod->BookTable->FieldByName("Book")->AsString = S;
  DMod->BookTable->FieldByName("Types")->AsString = "";
  DMod->BookTable->FieldByName("Medium")->AsString = "";
  DMod->PostAll();
  BookEdit->SetFocus();
}
void __fastcall TBookForm::sbDeleteClick(TObject *Sender)
{
```

continues

Listing 16.10. continued

```cpp
  AnsiString S = DMod->BookTable->FieldByName("Book")->AsString;
  if (MessageDlg("Delete " + S + " from Book Table?",
    mtConfirmation, TMsgDlgButtons() << mbYes << mbNo, 0) == ID_YES)
  {
    DMod->BookTable->Delete();
  }
}
void __fastcall TBookForm::CancelBtnClick(TObject *Sender)
{
  DMod->BookTable->Cancel();
}
void __fastcall TBookForm::PostBtnClick(TObject *Sender)
{
  DMod->PostAll();
}
void __fastcall TBookForm::Spin1DownClick(TObject *Sender)
{
  int i;
  i = DMod->BookTable->FieldByName("Rating")->AsInteger;
  if (i < 1)
    i = 1;
  if (i > 1)
    i--;
  if ((DMod->BookTable->State != dsEdit)||(DMod->BookTable->State != dsInsert))
    DMod->BookTable->Edit();
  DMod->BookTable->FieldByName("Rating")->AsInteger = i;
}
void __fastcall TBookForm::Spin1UpClick(TObject *Sender)
{
  int i;
  i = DMod->BookTable->FieldByName("Rating")->AsInteger;
  if (i < 1)
    i = 1;
  if (i < 10)
    i++;
  if ((DMod->BookTable->State != dsEdit)||(DMod->BookTable->State != dsInsert))
    DMod->BookTable->Edit();
  DMod->BookTable->FieldByName("Rating")->AsInteger = i;
}
```

Listing 16.11. The header for the TDataModule for the Music program.

```cpp
////////////////////////////////////
// File DMod1.h
// Project Music
// Copyright (c) 1997 by Charlie Calvert
//
//
#ifndef DMod1H
#define DMod1H
#include <vcl\Classes.hpp>
#include <vcl\Controls.hpp>
```

```cpp
#include <vcl\StdCtrls.hpp>
#include <vcl\Forms.hpp>
#include <vcl\DB.hpp>
#include <vcl\DBTables.hpp>

enum TFilterIndex {fiAlbumFilter, fiBookFilter};

class TDMod : public TDataModule
{
__published:
  TTable *ArtistTable;
  TDataSource *ArtistSource;
  TIntegerField *ArtistTableCODE;
  TStringField *ArtistTableLAST;
  TStringField *ArtistTableFIRST;
  TDateTimeField *ArtistTableBORN;
  TDateTimeField *ArtistTableDIED;
  TStringField *ArtistTableBIRTHPLACE;
  TMemoField *ArtistTableCOMMENT;
  TStringField *ArtistTableFirstLast;
  TStoredProc *GetAlbumGen;
  TStoredProc *AlbumsPerArtistProc;
  TQuery *AlbumCountQuery;
  TDataSource *AlbumCountSource;
  TDataSource *RatingRangeSource;
  TDataSource *NineOrBetterSource;
  TQuery *RatingRangeQuery;
  TQuery *NineOrBetterQuery;
  TTable *LoudnessTable;
  TDataSource *LoudnessSource;
  TTable *TypesTable;
  TDataSource *TypesSource;
  TTable *MediumTable;
  TDataSource *MediumSource;
  TStoredProc *GetArtistGen;
  TTable *ArtistTypeTable;
  TDataSource *ArtistTypeSource;
  TIntegerField *ArtistTableARTISTTYPE;
  TStringField *ArtistTableArtistTypeLookup;
  TTable *AlbumTable;
  TDataSource *AlbumSource;
  TIntegerField *AlbumTableCODE;
  TStringField *AlbumTableALBUM;
  TSmallintField *AlbumTableTYPES;
  TSmallintField *AlbumTableLOUDNESS;
  TSmallintField *AlbumTableMEDIUM;
  TSmallintField *AlbumTableRATING;
  TIntegerField *AlbumTableGROUPCODE;
  TStringField *AlbumTableLoudLookup;
  TStringField *AlbumTableMediumLookup;
  TStringField *AlbumTableTypeLookup;
  TQuery *GetLoudnessQuery;
  TDataSource *GetLoudnessSource;
  TQuery *GetTypesQuery;
  TQuery *GetMediaQuery;
  TDataSource *GetMediaSource;
```

continues

Listing 16.11. continued

```
TDataSource *GetTypesSource;
TTable *BookTable;
TDataSource *BookSource;
TIntegerField *BookTableCODE;
TStringField *BookTableBOOK;
TSmallintField *BookTableTYPES;
TSmallintField *BookTableMEDIUM;
TSmallintField *BookTableRATING;
TMemoField *BookTableCOMMENT;
TIntegerField *BookTableGROUPCODE;
TStringField *BookTableTypesLookup;
TStoredProc *GetBookGen;
TStringField *BookTableMediumLookup;
TStoredProc *GetAlbumCount;
TQuery *AlbumSearchQuery;
TDataSource *AlbumSearchSource;
TDatabase *Music;
void __fastcall ArtistTableCalcFields(TDataSet *DataSet);
void __fastcall ArtistTableAfterInsert(TDataSet *DataSet);
void __fastcall AlbumTableBeforePost(TDataSet *DataSet);
void __fastcall AlbumTableAfterInsert(TDataSet *DataSet);
void __fastcall ArtistTableFilterRecord(TDataSet *DataSet, bool &Accept);
void __fastcall TypesTableFilterRecord(TDataSet *DataSet, bool &Accept);
void __fastcall BookTableBeforePost(TDataSet *DataSet);
void __fastcall BookTableAfterInsert(TDataSet *DataSet);
void __fastcall DModDestroy(TObject *Sender);
private:
  int FFilterType;
  int FMaxTypes;
  int FMinTypes;
public:
  virtual __fastcall TDMod(TComponent* Owner);
  int AlbumsPerArtist();
  void NineOrBetter(void);
  void RatingRange(int Low, int High);
  void ArtistRefresh();
  void AlbumRefresh();
  void PostAll(void);
  void GetLoudness(int LoudnessValue);
  void GetMedia(int MediaValue);
  void GetTypes(int TypesValue);
  int GetTotalAlbumCount(void);
  void AlbumSearch(AnsiString SearchValue);
__property int MaxTypes={read=FMaxTypes, write=FMaxTypes, nodefault};
__property int MinTypes={read=FMinTypes, write=FMinTypes, nodefault};
__property int FilterType={read=FFilterType, write=FFilterType, nodefault};
};

extern TDMod *DMod;

#endif
```

Advanced InterBase Concepts

CHAPTER 16

679

16

ADVANCED
INTERBASE
CONCEPTS

Listing 16.12. The data module for the Music program.

```cpp
/////////////////////////////////////
// File DMod1.cpp
// Project Music
// Copyright (c) 1997 by Charlie Calvert
//

#include <vcl\vcl.h>
#pragma hdrstop

#include "DMod1.h"
//---------------------------------------------------------------------------
#pragma resource "*.dfm"
TDMod *DMod;

__fastcall TDMod::TDMod(TComponent* Owner)
: TDataModule(Owner)
{
  FilterType = fiAlbumFilter;
  ArtistTable->Open();
  AlbumTable->Open();
  BookTable->Open();
  LoudnessTable->Open();
  TypesTable->Open();
  MediumTable->Open();
}

void TDMod::PostAll(void)
{
  if (ArtistTable->State == dsInsert)
  {
    ArtistTable->Post();
    ArtistRefresh();
  }
  else if (ArtistTable->State == dsEdit)
  {
    ArtistTable->Post();
  }

  if ((AlbumTable->State == dsInsert) || (AlbumTable->State == dsEdit))
  {
    AlbumTable->Post();
//    AlbumRefresh();
  }

  if ((BookTable->State == dsInsert) || (BookTable->State == dsEdit))
  {
    BookTable->Post();
//    BookRefresh();
  }

}

void __fastcall TDMod::ArtistTableCalcFields(TDataSet *DataSet)
{
```

continues

Listing 16.12. continued

```
  if (ArtistTableFIRST->IsNull)
    ArtistTableFirstLast->Value = ArtistTableLAST->Value;
  else
    ArtistTableFirstLast->Value =
      ArtistTableFIRST->Value + " " + ArtistTableLAST->Value;
}

int TDMod::AlbumsPerArtist()
{
  AlbumsPerArtistProc->Prepare();
  AlbumsPerArtistProc->ParamByName("ArtistCode")->AsInteger =
    ArtistTableCODE->AsInteger;
  AlbumsPerArtistProc->ExecProc();
  return AlbumsPerArtistProc->ParamByName("NumAlbums")->AsInteger;
}

void TDMod::NineOrBetter(void)
{
  NineOrBetterQuery->Close();
  NineOrBetterQuery->Prepare();
  NineOrBetterQuery->Open();
}

void TDMod::RatingRange(int Low, int High)
{
  RatingRangeQuery->Prepare();
  RatingRangeQuery->ParamByName("LowRating")->AsInteger = Low;
  RatingRangeQuery->ParamByName("HighRating")->AsInteger = High;
  RatingRangeQuery->Open();
}

void TDMod::ArtistRefresh()
{
  AnsiString Last = ArtistTableLAST->Value;
  AnsiString First = ArtistTableFIRST->Value;
  ArtistTable->Close();
  ArtistTable->Open();
  ArtistTable->FindNearest(OPENARRAY(TVarRec, (Last, First)));
}

void TDMod::AlbumRefresh()
{
  AlbumTable->Refresh();
}

void __fastcall TDMod::ArtistTableAfterInsert(TDataSet *DataSet)
{
  ArtistTableCODE->AsInteger = 0;
}

void __fastcall TDMod::AlbumTableBeforePost(TDataSet *DataSet)
{
  if (AlbumSource->State == dsInsert)
  {
    GetAlbumGen->Prepare();
    GetAlbumGen->ExecProc();
```

```cpp
      AlbumTableCODE->AsInteger = GetAlbumGen->ParamByName("Num")->AsInteger;
  }
}

void __fastcall TDMod::AlbumTableAfterInsert(TDataSet *DataSet)
{
  AlbumTableCODE->Value = 0;
  AlbumTableGROUPCODE = 0;
}

void __fastcall TDMod::ArtistTableFilterRecord(TDataSet *DataSet,
  bool &Accept)
{
  Accept = ArtistTable->FieldByName("ArtistType")->AsInteger == FilterType + 1;
}

void TDMod::GetLoudness(int LoudnessValue)
{
  GetLoudnessQuery->Close();
  GetLoudnessQuery->Prepare();
  GetLoudnessQuery->ParamByName("LoudnessValue")->AsInteger = LoudnessValue;
  GetLoudnessQuery->Open();
}

void TDMod::GetTypes(int TypesValue)
{
  GetTypesQuery->Close();
  GetTypesQuery->Prepare();
  GetTypesQuery->ParamByName("TypeValue")->AsInteger = TypesValue;
  GetTypesQuery->Open();
}

void TDMod::GetMedia(int MediaValue)
{
  GetMediaQuery->Close();
  GetMediaQuery->Prepare();
  GetMediaQuery->ParamByName("MediaValue")->AsInteger = MediaValue;
  GetMediaQuery->Open();
}

void __fastcall TDMod::TypesTableFilterRecord(TDataSet *DataSet,
  bool &Accept)
{
  Accept = ((TypesTable->FieldByName("CODE")->Value >= MinTypes) &&
           (TypesTable->FieldByName("CODE")->Value <= MaxTypes));
}

void __fastcall TDMod::BookTableBeforePost(TDataSet *DataSet)
{
  if (BookSource->State == dsInsert)
  {
    GetBookGen->Prepare();
    GetBookGen->ExecProc();
    BookTableCODE->AsInteger = GetBookGen->ParamByName("Num")->AsInteger;
```

continues

Listing 16.12. continued

```cpp
    BookTableGROUPCODE->AsInteger = ArtistTableCODE->AsInteger;
  }
}

int TDMod::GetTotalAlbumCount(void)
{
  GetAlbumCount->Prepare();
  GetAlbumCount->ExecProc();
  return GetAlbumCount->ParamByName("Num")->AsInteger;
}

void __fastcall TDMod::BookTableAfterInsert(TDataSet *DataSet)
{
  BookTableCODE->AsInteger = 0;
}

void __fastcall TDMod::DModDestroy(TObject *Sender)
{
  PostAll();
}

void TDMod::AlbumSearch(AnsiString SearchValue)
{
  AlbumSearchQuery->Close();
  AlbumSearchQuery->ParamByName("SearchValue")->Value = SearchValue;
  AlbumSearchQuery->Open();
}
```

Several other utility forms from the Music program are not shown here. I do not include them because they are mostly empty of code and are used primarily as a place to display data or else to retrieve simple input from the user.

Using the Music Program

There are many interrelated tables in the Music program all working together to produce a particular result. The thing to understand when studying this program is how you can make the tables in a relational database work together seamlessly toward a particular end.

Because this program uses InterBase, you can use it in a rigorous multi-user environment without fear that it would collapse under the load. For instance, there is no reason why this program, as is, cannot handle 200–300 simultaneous users.

Suppressing the Password: The TDatabase Object

The TDatabase object on the main form has its AliasName property set to the Music alias. This alias was defined in the Database Explorer, and it points to the tables that make up the music database. The alias is shown in Figure 16.5.

FIGURE 16.5.

The alias for MUSIC.GDB *as it appears in the Database Explorer.*

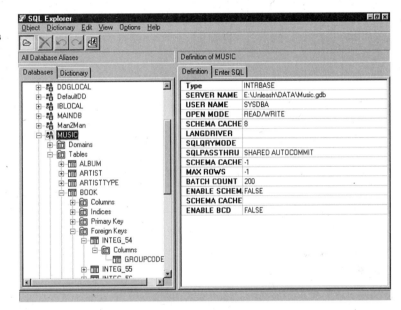

The DatabaseName property of the TDatabase object is set to the string MusicData, which is the alias attached to by all the other TTable, TStoredProc, and TQuery objects in the program. Remember: Only the TDatabase object attaches directly to the Music alias. This allows you to point the entire program at a second database by changing only one variable: the AliasName property. This feature can be handy if you need to experiment without touching your primary data.

The Params property for the TDatabase object contains the following information:

```
USER NAME=SYSDBA
PASSWORD=masterkey
```

The LoginPrompt property is then set to False, which makes it possible to launch the program without entering a password. This is pretty much a necessity during development, and it's a useful trait in a program such as this that probably has little fear of hostile attacks on its data.

The FormCreate Event

It's up to the constructor for the main form to create the child windows that hold all the main controls used in the program:

```
__fastcall TForm1::TForm1(TComponent* Owner)
 : TForm(Owner)
{
  ArtistForm = new TArtistForm(this);
  AlbumForm = new TAlbumForm(this);
  IndexForm = new TIndexForm(this);
  BookForm = new TBookForm(this);
  ChildForms[0] = IndexForm;
  ChildForms[1] = ArtistForm;
  ChildForms[2] = AlbumForm;
  ChildForms[3] = BookForm;
}
```

The first four lines of the routine create the forms. The next four lines assign them to an array of TForm objects. You can then use this array to iterate through all the main forms for the program, as shown in the last two lines of the routine, and in the OnResize response method shown previously.

As you can see, an ordinal value of 0 gives you immediate access to the Index form if you write code that looks like this:

```
ChildForms[0]->Width = X;
```

One of the most important methods in the program is the TabControl1Change event handler:

```
void __fastcall TForm1::TabControl1Change(TObject *Sender)
{
  DMod->PostAll();
  switch (TabControl1->TabIndex)
  {
    case 0:
      ChildForms[TabControl1->TabIndex]->BringToFront();
      Caption = "Index";
      DBNavigator1->DataSource = DMod->ArtistSource;
      InsertBtn->OnClick = NULL;
      DeleteBtn->OnClick = NULL;
      PostBtn->OnClick = NULL;
      CancelBtn->OnClick = NULL;
      DMod->TypesTable->Filtered = False;
      break;
    case 1:
      ChildForms[TabControl1->TabIndex]->BringToFront();
      Caption = "Artist Form";
      DBNavigator1->DataSource = DMod->ArtistSource;
      InsertBtn->OnClick = ArtistForm->sbInsertClick;
```

Advanced InterBase Concepts

CHAPTER 16

685

16

ADVANCED
INTERBASE
CONCEPTS

```
        DeleteBtn->OnClick = ArtistForm->sbDeleteClick;
        PostBtn->OnClick = ArtistForm->PostBtnClick;
        CancelBtn->OnClick = ArtistForm->CancelBtnClick;
        break;
    case 2:
        if (DMod->ArtistTable->FieldByName("ArtistType")->AsInteger == 1)
        {
            ChildForms[2]->BringToFront();
            Caption = "Album Form";
            DBNavigator1->DataSource = DMod->AlbumSource;
            InsertBtn->OnClick = AlbumForm->sbInsertClick;
            DeleteBtn->OnClick = AlbumForm->sbDeleteClick;
            CancelBtn->OnClick = AlbumForm->CancelBtnClick;
            PostBtn->OnClick = AlbumForm->PostBtnClick;
            DMod->TypesTable->Filtered = False;
            DMod->MaxTypes = 999;
            DMod->MinTypes = 0;
            DMod->TypesTable->Filtered = True;
        }
        else
        {
            ChildForms[3]->BringToFront();
            Caption = "Book Form";
            DBNavigator1->DataSource = DMod->BookSource;
            InsertBtn->OnClick = BookForm->sbInsertClick;
            DeleteBtn->OnClick = BookForm->sbDeleteClick;
            CancelBtn->OnClick = BookForm->CancelBtnClick;
            PostBtn->OnClick = BookForm->PostBtnClick;
            DMod->TypesTable->Filtered = False;
            DMod->MaxTypes = 1999;
            DMod->MinTypes = 1000;
            DMod->TypesTable->Filtered = True;
            BookForm->TypesCombo->Update();
        }
        break;
    }
}
```

The primary burden of this code is to move the appropriate form to the front when requested by the user:

```
ChildForms[2]->BringToFront();
```

This code brings the AlbumForm to the front. To the user, this looks as though a hit on the TabControl caused the "page to be turned" inside the control. Of course, what really happens is that you simply push one form down in the Z order and bring another to the top. In short, you create your own page control out of separate forms. The beauty of this arrangement is that it ensures that each page of the TabControl exists as a separate object in its own module. This is much better than the system used in the kdAdd program.

Another key chore of the TabControlOnChange handler is to set the OnClick event for the buttons at the top of the form so that they reflect what happens inside the current page. For instance, if the BookForm is selected, a click on the Post button should call the Post method of the

Book table, not the Album or Artist table. To ensure that all works correctly, this method simply sets the OnClick method to the appropriate routine whenever the TabControl is moved:

```
InsertBtn->OnClick = BookForm->sbInsertClick;
DeleteBtn->OnClick = BookForm->sbDeleteClick;
PostBtn->OnClick = BookForm->PostBtnClick;
CancelBtn->OnClick = BookForm->CancelBtnClick;
```

In this case, the methods associated with the InsertBtn and so on are the methods from the BookForm. This technique helps you to see how dynamic the delegation model can be if you need to push the envelope a bit.

I'd mentioned earlier that the Types table holds a series of types that can apply to either musical or written works. For instance, the table might look like this:

```
TYPES               CODE
================ ===========
JAZZ                1
ROCK                2
CLASSICAL           3
NEW AGE             4
FOLK                5
BLUES               6
COMPUTER            1000
FICTION             1001
SCIFI               1002
MYSTERY             1003
REFERENCE           1004
```

When the application is in Music mode, then the first half of the table is used; otherwise the second half of the table is used. Here is code from the TabControlOnChange event that ensures that the proper part of the code is operative when the program is in Book mode:

```
DMod->TypesTable->Filtered = False;
DMod->MaxTypes = 1999;
DMod->MinTypes = 1000;
DMod->TypesTable->Filtered = True;
```

The following lines are executed when the user switches the program into Music mode:

```
DMod->TypesTable->Filtered = False;
DMod->MaxTypes = 999;
DMod->MinTypes = 0;
DMod->TypesTable->Filtered = True;
```

After looking at the code, it should come as no surprise to learn that the Types table has an OnFilterRecord event handler:

```
void __fastcall TDMod::TypesTableFilterRecord(TDataSet *DataSet,
  bool &Accept)
{
  Accept = ((TypesTable->FieldByName("CODE")->Value >= MinTypes) &&
           (TypesTable->FieldByName("CODE")->Value <= MaxTypes));
}
```

Advanced InterBase Concepts

CHAPTER 16

687

16

ADVANCED
INTERBASE
CONCEPTS

Once this method is defined, all you have to do is set the `TypesTable filtered` property to `true`, and only the selected half of the types table is visible. By the time the Album or Book form gets at this table, it appears that it only contains value pertinent to the relevant form.

Of course, I defined a property so that the code in the main form never directly touches the privates of the `TDataModule` object:

```
__property int MaxTypes={read=FMaxTypes, write=FMaxTypes, nodefault};
__property int MinTypes={read=FMinTypes, write=FMinTypes, nodefault};
```

`FMinTypes` and `FMaxTypes` are private data for the program.

The following code from the main module of the program gets executed whenever the user switches between Music and Book mode:

```
void __fastcall TForm1::FilterOptionsClick(TObject *Sender)
{
  DMod->ArtistTable->Filtered = False;
  switch (dynamic_cast<TComponent *>(Sender)->Tag)
  {
    case fiAlbumFilter:
      IndexForm->BookGrid->Align = alNone;
      IndexForm->BookGrid->Visible = False;
      DMod->FilterType = fiAlbumFilter;
      IndexForm->AlbumGrid->Align = alClient;
      IndexForm->AlbumGrid->Visible = True;
    break;
    case fiBookFilter:
      IndexForm->AlbumGrid->Align = alNone;
      IndexForm->AlbumGrid->Visible = False;
      DMod->FilterType = fiBookFilter;
      IndexForm->BookGrid->Align = alClient;
      IndexForm->BookGrid->Visible = True;
    break;
  }
  DMod->ArtistTable->Filtered = True;
}
```

The purpose of this code is to properly set up the two grids on the index page. When the program is in Music mode, you want the right-hand grid on the Music page to show the Music table, and when you are in Book mode, you want it to show the Book table. I could have simply switched the `DataSource` for one form as needed, but that does not take care of the issue of defining the fields to be shown in the grid. Rather than try to create the columns on-the-fly, I decided instead to use the code shown here.

Lookups

This program uses a large number of lookups. All of them are defined on the `TDataModule` itself, although some are used in the grids on the Index form, others on the Book and Album pages, and some in both locations.

The primary purpose of the lookups is to ensure that the user always chooses from preselected lists of values and does not start typing in her own values on-the-fly. For instance, you want the user to choose a type from the Types table and not make up new types at random.

Both the Book and Album tables have lookups into the Types and Medium tables, whereas the Album table also has a lookup into the Loudness table. These lookups are visible to the user both on the grids from the index page and also on the Book and Album forms.

Because these lookups are so readily available, the user rarely has to type anything into a control. Instead, he can quickly select options from a lookup list. It is not currently available, but it is a nice gesture to the user to provide a means of editing the lookup tables, as shown in the Address program from Chapter 13, "Flat-File, Real-World Databases."

Asking the Database a Question

By this time, you know most of what you need to know to construct a reasonably powerful database. This is a good feeling, and it's nice to know that you can get this kind of control over an important domain of information.

Nevertheless, despite this sense of accomplishment, there may still be a nagging feeling that something is missing. After all, it's work to construct the database and work to enter data into it, so where is the fun part? Where is the part that makes you say in the inimitable words of the fearless leader from Redmond, "Hey, that's cool!"

Once you have a database up and running, the way to get joy from it is to ask it questions. At first, you might just want to ask simple questions. For instance, you might remember the beginning of the name of an album, but you can't remember the whole thing.

Suppose that you remember that an album begins with the letter L. If you bring up WISQL, you can ask the following question:

```
select Album from album where album like "L%"
ALBUM
===========================
Letter From Home
La Mer
Life
Landing on Water
Live at the BBC
Longing in their Hearts
Live at the Royal Festival
Love Deluxe
Live at Memory Lane
Lookout Farm
Living
Lives in the Balance
Lawyers in Love
```

As you can see, the results returned from this question are a list of the albums and books that start with the letter L.

This is fairly useful, but you really want to know not only the name of the album, but also the artist behind the album. You could, of course, ask the following question:

```
select Album, GroupCode from album where album like "L%"
ALBUM                       GROUPCODE
=========================== ===========
Letter From Home                 11
La Mer                           50
Life                              9
Landing on Water                  9
Live at the BBC                  13
Longing in their Hearts          28
Live at the Royal Festiva        92
Love Deluxe                      61
Live at Memory Lane             116
Lookout Farm                    130
Living                          161
Lives in the Balance            142
Lawyers in Love                 142
```

This gives you the name of an album plus the GroupCode associated with the album. Then, all you have to do is run one more query to get the answer you need:

```
select First,Last from Artist where Code = 11
FIRST                         LAST
============================= =============================
Pat                           Metheny
```

Of course, it would be nice if you didn't have to ask this question in two stages. Instead, you might want to ask the following question, which performs a join between the Album and Artist tables:

```
select Artist.Last, Album.Album
   from  Album, Artist
where artist.code = album.groupcode and
Album.Album like "L%"
order by Artist.last
LAST                          ALBUM
============================= ===========================
Adderley                      Live at Memory Lane
Beatles                       Live at the BBC
Browne                        Lawyers in Love
Browne                        Lives in the Balance
Collins                       Living
Debussy                       La Mer
Liebman                       Lookout Farm
McLaughlin                    Live at the Royal Festiva
Metheny                       Letter From Home
Raitt                         Longing in their Hearts
Sade                          Love Deluxe
Young                         Landing on Water
Young                         Life
```

Now you are starting to get somewhere. This information is fairly valuable to you. When composing the preceding query, you should be careful to include where clauses that both specify the letters you want to search on and the relationship between the Artist and Album tables:

```
where artist.code = album.groupcode
```

If you don't qualify the question in this way, then you end up getting a much larger result set than you want. In particular, you indicate that the query shouldn't link the resulting albums to all the names in the Artist table but just link them to the names of the artists that have the same code as the groupcode of a particular album.

Now that you have seen this much, most people also want to get information about the rating for the album, as well as its type. One way to ask that question looks like this:

```
select Artist.Last, Album.Album, Album.Rating, Album.Types
  from  Album, Artist
  where artist.code = album.groupcode and
     Album.Album like "L%"
  order by Artist.last
```

LAST	ALBUM	RATING	TYPES
===	===	===	===
Adderley	Live at Memory Lane	\<null\>	1
Beatles	Live at the BBC	6	2
Browne	Lawyers in Love	6	2
Browne	Lives in the Balance	6	2
Collins	Living	6	5
Debussy	La Mer	7	3
Liebman	Lookout Farm	6	1
McLaughlin	Live at the Royal Festiva	\<null\>	1
Metheny	Letter From Home	9	1
Raitt	Longing in their Hearts	\<null\>	\<null\>
Sade	Love Deluxe	8	1
Young	Landing on Water	7	2
Young	Life	7	2

When reviewing this data, it's hard not to feel that there is something missing from the Types field. After all, what does the number 1 mean? What type is that?

Once again, you can get the question answered by going to the well a second time and querying the Types table. However, it should come as no surprise to learn that there is a second solution:

```
select Artist.Last, Album.Album, Album.Rating, Types.Types
  from  Album, Artist, Types
where artist.code = album.groupcode and
Album.Album like "L%" and
Types.Code = Album.Types
order by Artist.last
```

LAST	ALBUM	RATING	TYPES
===	===	===	===
Adderley	Live at Memory Lane	\<null\>	JAZZ
Beatles	Live at the BBC	6	ROCK
Browne	Lawyers in Love	6	ROCK

```
Browne          Lives in the Balance        6 ROCK
Collins         Living                      6 FOLK
Debussy         La Mer                      7 CLASSICAL
Liebman         Lookout Farm                6 JAZZ
McLaughlin      Live at the Royal Festiva <null> JAZZ
Metheny         Letter From Home            9 JAZZ
Sade            Love Deluxe                 8 JAZZ
Young           Landing on Water            7 ROCK
Young           Life                        7 ROCK
```

Here you broadened the question by specifying that you want to bring in the Types table:

```
from  Album, Artist, Types
```

Include one of its fields in the result set:

```
select Artist.Last, Album.Album, Album.Rating, Types.Types
```

Link the Album table and Types table on the primary and foreign keys of the two tables:

```
where ... Types.Code = Album.Types
```

You get all the things you need; the only problem is that you can't ask the user to open up WISQL—of all applications!—just to get the answer to a simple question.

You can take a number of courses at this point, but one of the best is to simply wrap your query in a stored procedure:

```
CREATE PROCEDURE ALBUMSEARCH (ANALBUMNAME VARCHAR(75))
RETURNS (ARTISTNAME VARCHAR(30),
ALBUMNAME VARCHAR(30),
RATINGVALUE VARCHAR(30),
TYPENAME VARCHAR(30),
MEDIUMNAME VARCHAR(30))
AS
begin
  for
    select Artist.Last, Album.Album, Album.Rating, Types.Types, Medium.Medium
    from Album, Artist, Types, Medium
    where artist.code = album.groupcode
      and Album.Album like :AnAlbumName
      and Types.Code = Album.Types and  Medium.Code = Album.Medium
    order by Artist.Last
    into :ArtistName, :AlbumName, :RatingValue, :TypeName, MediumName
  do  suspend;
end
```

You can break this procedure down into several sections in order to make some sense of it. First, notice the header:

```
CREATE PROCEDURE ALBUMSEARCH (ANALBUMNAME VARCHAR(75))
```

This says that you are creating a stored procedure named AlbumSearch that takes a string as a parameter. You supply the name of the album you want to search in this string.

The next part of the procedure declares what is returned to the user:

```
RETURNS (ARTISTNAME VARCHAR(30),
ALBUMNAME VARCHAR(30),
RATINGVALUE VARCHAR(30),
TYPENAME VARCHAR(30),
MEDIUMNAME VARCHAR(30))
```

These rows set up what you want returned from the procedure. At the very bottom of the procedure, you state these names again, saying that you want the query to be returned in these variables:

```
into :ArtistName, :AlbumName, :RatingValue, :TypeName, MediumName
```

The query itself sits in between a `begin..end` pair, which nests around a `for...do` statement:

```
as
begin  for      // Query goes here
  do   suspend;
end
```

If you forget to wrap your query in this faintly ridiculous-looking syntactical sugar, InterBase complains about a singleton query not being able to return multiple rows.

Now that you have your stored procedure all set up, the next thing to do is call it from BCB. The syntax for doing this could not be simpler:

```
select * from AlbumSearch(:SearchValue);
```

This simple SQL statement should reside inside the SQL property of a BCB `TQuery` component. You can then call this procedure with code that looks like this:

```
void TDMod::AlbumSearch(AnsiString SearchValue)
{
  AlbumSearchQuery->Close();
  AlbumSearchQuery->ParamByName("SearchValue")->Value = SearchValue;
  AlbumSearchQuery->Open();
}
```

That's all there is to it. Now you can hook up a `TDataSource` to the `TQuery` and a `TDBGrid` to the `TDataSource`, and after calling the `AlbumSearch` function, you see the results of your query inside a BCB application.

You can access a number of interesting stored procedures in this manner from the menus of the BCB program. Some of the most interesting ones involve asking about the ratings you assign to albums. For instance, you can ask to see all the albums that have a rating between five and seven or a rating higher than nine. This is such an important set of queries that I review them in the last section of this chapter, "Viewing a Range of Data."

Asking Questions That Do Not Return Datasets

In the preceding section, you saw how to ask a question that returns a dataset. A different kind of stored procedure asks how to return a particular value such as a single number or string. For instance, you might want to ask the answer man how many albums are in the database:

```
select Count(*) from album;
      COUNT
===========
        290
```

To create a stored procedure that returns this kind of information, you should write

```
CREATE PROCEDURE ALBUMCOUNT
RETURNS (NUM INTEGER)
AS
begin
  for
    select Count(*) from Album
    into :Num
  do    exit;
end
```

This procedure doesn't take any parameters:

```
CREATE PROCEDURE ALBUMCOUNT
```

It does, however, return a value:

```
RETURNS (NUM INTEGER)
```

Because you ask for a single answer and not a series of rows, you can use `exit` instead of `suspend`:

```
for    // Query goes here
do     exit;
```

Once you compose the query, you can use a stored procedure on the BCB end to get data from it. To set up the stored procedure, all you have to do is drag it off the Component Palette, set its `DataBaseName` to the `Music` alias, and drop down the list from its `StoredProcName` property so you can choose the appropriate stored procedure.

The following code shows how to call the stored procedure from BCB:

```
int TDMod::GetTotalAlbumCount(void)
{
  GetAlbumCount->Prepare();
  GetAlbumCount->ExecProc();
  return GetAlbumCount->ParamByName("Num")->AsInteger;
}
```

This method returns an integer, which you can display to the user in any manner you think appropriate.

Viewing a Range of Data

Two interesting stored procedures allow you to ask questions such as, "What albums have a particular rating?" and "What albums have a rating of nine or better?"

```
CREATE PROCEDURE NINEORBETTER
RETURNS (LAST VARCHAR(30),
ALBUM VARCHAR(30),
RATING INTEGER)
AS
begin
  for
    select Artist.Last, Album.Album, Album.Rating
    from Album, Artist
    where Album.GroupCode = Artist.Code
      and Album.Rating >= 9
    Order By Album.Rating Desc
    into :Last, :Album, :Rating
  do suspend;
end
```

The query at the heart of this procedure asks to see albums that have a rating larger than or equal to nine. To properly qualify the query, the code also asks to see only the entries from the Artist table that are associated with the albums that make it into the result set. The last line of the query asks to order the result set on the `album.rating` field with the highest ratings first.

The stored procedure shown here lets you ask for data from the table that falls into a particular range:

```
CREATE PROCEDURE RATINGRANGE (LOWRATING INTEGER,
HIGHRATING INTEGER)
RETURNS (LAST VARCHAR(30),
ALBUM VARCHAR(30),
RATING INTEGER)
AS
begin
  for
    select Artist.Last, Album.Album, Album.Rating
    from Album, Artist  where Album.GroupCode = Artist.Code
      and  Album.Rating >= :LowRating
      and  Album.Rating <= :HighRating
    Order By Album.Rating Desc
    into :Last, :Album, :Rating
  do      suspend;
end
```

This procedure is very much like the last one, but it takes parameters that allow you to specify the range you want to see, and it uses those parameters to customize the result set to your needs:

```
Album.Rating >= :LowRating andAlbum.Rating <= :HighRating
```

NOTE

Here is another example of a stored procedure that uses SQL:

```
CREATE PROCEDURE CONTACTBYPRODUCT (PRODNAME VARCHAR(20))
RETURNS (SFIRST VARCHAR(30),
         SLAST VARCHAR(30),
         STITLE VARCHAR(30))
AS
BEGIN
  SELECT DISTINCT C.LAST, C.FIRST, C.TITLE
  FROM CONTACTS C, CONT2PROD C1, BORPRODS B
  WHERE
    (C1.CONTACTNO = C.CONTACTNO)
     AND (B.BORPRODID = C1.BORPRODID)
     AND (B.PRODUCT = :ProdName)
  ORDER BY C.LAST, C.FIRST, C.TITLE
  INTO : SLAST, SFIRST, STITLE;
  SUSPEND;
END
```

This code is part of the expression of a many-to-many relationship. The BorProds table contains a list of products that might be associated with the people listed in the Contacts table. This situation calls for a many-to-many relationship because there can be more than one product associated with each of the records listed in the Contacts table, and there can be more than one contact associated with each of the records in the BorProds table. As a result, there is an intermediate table that lists a series of IDs from the Contacts and BorProds tables.

The query shown previously fulfills the request: Show me a list of contacts associated with one particular product. You pass in a product name, and you get back all the Contacts associated with that product. The product name passed in is bound to the query as a parameter:

```
AND (B.PRODUCT = :ProdName)
```

Notice that you will get back a dataset, not just three variables, when you call this function. In other words, you get back a series of records, each containing the SLAST, SFIRST, and STITLE fields. The results of the query are placed in the dataset via the syntax that reads

```
INTO : SLAST, SFIRST, STITLE;
```

The SUSPEND statement temporarily delays the execution of the procedure while a Fetch statement is carried out. Imagine the moment after the first row is calculated, while it is returned via the calling procedure. The loop is temporarily put on hold while this is going on; that is, it is SUSPENDed. After the fetch is complete, the next row is calculated, and so on. You use SUSPEND statements in procedures that return rows of values, not in simple procedures that return only one value.

The point here is that you can store a particular query in a stored procedure and then call it from a TQuery or TStoredProc component. This approach can eliminate considerable

continues

> *continued*
>
> complexity in programs that need to perform complex operations such as creating many-to-many relationships. This process allows you to keep a SQL statement on the server side rather than in the SQL property of a TQuery component.

I've shown you several examples of stored procedures so that you might understand how much power there is in a simple query. To me, the most interesting thing about database programming is the ability to ask questions of the data you have collected. The key to that process is to write a query and then place it in a stored procedure so you can call it from your applications. You can also place the query directly in a TQuery component, but then the query takes longer to execute, and you have the bother of managing it on the client side. Everything is easier if you just leave the query on the server where it belongs.

Summary

That's all I'm going to say about the Music program. A few lines of code in the program were never mentioned, but most of the application was reviewed in this chapter.

Once again, this program contains a lot of the basic code that anyone uses when constructing a relational database with BCB. The particular example shown is not robust enough to use in a professional setting, but it gives you a good feeling for how to proceed if you want to construct such an application.

In particular, you got a good look at the techniques used to create a robust database with referential integrity. You also saw how to use generators, triggers, and stored procedures and how to perform filters and lookups on relational data. In general, this chapter is the one that sums up the core information necessary to produce a professional database program. If you understand all this material, you are not yet necessarily an expert, but you are ready to start building relational databases in a professional setting.

CHAPTER 17

Printing: QuickReport and Related Technologies

IN THIS CHAPTER

Overview

In this chapter you will get a look at seven ways to print data:

- Printing data from databases via QuickReport
- Printing QuickReport data in multiple columns and rows
- Printing QuickReport data by group
- Printing QuickReport data in one-to-many relationships
- Using the TPrinter object to print a graphic image of a form exactly as the form appears to the user at runtime
- Printing via the GDI, so that you can duplicate, fonts, pictures, and shapes drawn through the GDI
- Using ReportSmith

I am going to explain QuickReport first, since it is by far the most important technique. However, you should be sure to glance down at the other techniques, because they are valuable and can be absorbed fairly quickly.

Printing has traditionally been a complicated subject in Windows. In DOS, it was easier, but still very time-consuming. In BCB, all forms of printing are easy to master, and QuickReport is a subject most programmers can learn in a few hours and master in a few days. After you understand the basics of how to use QuickReport, you should be able to prepare many reports in well under an hour. Even if you were a perfectionist struggling to put together a complicated report, it is unlikely that you would spend more than a few hours on a report.

If you are familiar with ReportSmith or Crystal Reports, you might be inclined to use them first without examining QuickReport. I would, however, spend the time it takes to get up to speed on QuickReport. You might be surprised to find how powerful this tool can be. Certainly, QuickReport is almost preternaturally easy to use, especially when considering how much quicker it makes a traditionally long, complex and frustrating task.

Having said all this, I have to confess that printing is still a task I don't enjoy much. I personally don't have much need for printed reports, because they take up space, become outdated quickly, and are very difficult to track. As a result, I prefer to keep information in electronic form. However, I recognize the importance of printing, and will deal with it in this chapter in considerable depth.

One hint that can help you ease the burden of creating reports is to let SQL statements carry the burden of the work. If you need to create a particular report, write a SQL statement that will generate it as nearly as possible, and then let the statement do double duty as a way of preparing an electronic report, and as a way of preparing a paper-based report. This technique makes the task less onerous to me, and it is usually the quickest way to complete the chore. In this chapter, I examine this technique in my analysis of making a grouped report for the Music program.

QuickReport Basics

QuickReport was originally a third-party tool written in Object Pascal that the VCL team decided to incorporate into the product. This unusual move came about as a result of the high quality of this product, along with its relatively close conformance to the VCL programming paradigm. You will, however, notice a few rough edges because some of the conventions in this product do not exactly match the conventions used elsewhere in the VCL.

> **NOTE**
>
> The rough edges between the VCL and QuickReport will probably be smoothed over in later releases. As a result, you should be prepared for the possibility that your code in this one area might break in future releases of BCB. However, QuickReport is easy to use, and the code associated with it is by definition isolated from the rest of the code in your application. As a result, you should be able to adapt to the change fairly easily.
>
> Because QuickReport is made by a third party, you should look on the Web to see if you can find updates to this product. For instance, Delphi 3 will ship with a version of QuickReport that is much more sophisticated than the version included with BCB 1.0.

The basic idea behind QuickReport is to provide a set of components that are as closely parellel as possible to the tools you use when creating a standard BCB form. For instance, Table 17.1 gives a list of standard visual controls and visual database controls with their QuickReport equivalents.

Table 17.1. Standard VCL controls on the left and QuickReport equivalents on the right.

VCL controls	QuickReport controls
TLabel	TQRLabel
TDBEdit	TQRDBText
TDBLabel	TQRDBText
TDBMemo	TQRMemo
TShape	TQRShape

As you can see, there is no difference between a QuickReport label and a QuickReport edit control. Needless to say, this makes sense when you consider the fact that you can't edit a field in a report!

Each of the data-aware controls has a `DataSource` and `DataField` property. The `TQRLabel` and `TQRShape` controls do not have a these properties, because they are not data-aware.

Each report that you generate appears on its own form. The act of creating the form is a simple matter of laying out `TQRMemo` and `TQRDBText` controls on a series of bands called `TQRBand` controls.

One visual QuickReport component that does not fit into any predefined category is called `TQRSysData`. This component can display the current project title, page number, date, time, or record count. The particular function adopted by the component is controlled by its `Data` property. I will explain how to use the component in more depth later in the chapter.

Each time you create a new QuickReport form, you should also drop down a `TQuickReport` component and at least one `TQRBand` component. (Don't confuse the `TQuickReport` component with the product itself, which is called QuickReport.) The `TQuickReport` component is a "magic" component that converts a regular form into a QuickReport form. All you need to do is drop the component on the form and set its `DataSource` property to a `TDataSource`, just as you would when using a `TDBGrid`. The `TQRBand` component is the surface on which you should place the QuickReport visual controls.

> **NOTE**
>
> In most reports you want to print multiple rows, as you would when showing data in a grid. To do this, set the `BandType` property of a `TQRBand` report to `rbDetail`. If you want to have multiple columns in your report, set the `Columns` property of `TQuickReport` to the number of columns you want to use. I will explain all this in more depth later in this chapter.

After you finish designing a form, you can run the program and call the `Preview` method of `TQuickReport` to view the output. The preview form has a print button on it so you can print the report. If you want, you can skip the preview screen and directly call the `Print` method of `TQuickReport`.

The great thing about QuickReport is that it lets you use existing datasets, including calculated fields and lookup fields, that are already part of your project. Rather than concerning yourself with creating custom queries or with setting up sort orders, you can just plug your QuickReport components directly into your existing datasets. If you sort the data in some particular way on a form, that is the same sort order you see when you pop up a QuickReport based on the tables used by that form.

Using TQRBand: Creating Rows and Columns in QuickReport

Most people can figure out how to use QuickReport without help from a book like this. However, there are a few things that people sometimes can't figure out on their own:

- How to print rows of data
- How to print columns of data

■ How to group data

■ How to create a one-to-many report

All four of these subjects will be covered in this chapter. I've already described how to perform the first two chores earlier, but I will repeat the information here, just so these key bits of information will be as easy as possible to find.

To create multiple rows of data, set the `BandType` property of a `TQRBand` report to `rbDetail`. If you want to have multiple columns in your report, set the `Columns` property of `TQuickReport` to the number of columns you want to use. That's all you have to do.

If you dig into the QuickReport controls a bit, you will find the `TQRBand` component has a `BandType` property that can be set to one of the values in Table 17.2.

Table 17.2. BandType property values and purposes.

Value	*Purpose*
`rbTitle`	A title printed once at the start of the report.
`rbPageHeader`	Appears at the top of each page.
`rbDetail`	Use this type if you want to repeat many rows of data, or for use with one-to-many reports.
`rbSubDetail`	The detail band in a one-to-many report. This connects the `DetailGroup` band to the `DetailLink` component using the `QRDetailLink.DetailBand` property.
`rbPageFooter`	Creates a footer at the bottom of the page.
`rbSummary`	Creates a summary at the end of the report.
`rbGroupHeader`	Creates group headers for use with `QRGroup` and `QRDetailLink` components.
`rbGroupFooter`	Creates footers for use with `QRGroup` and `QRDetailLink` components.
`rbColumnHeader`	Labels each column in a column-based report.
`rbOverlay`	Floats on top of all other text and graphics printed on the page.

The best way to learn about these properties is through experience. In particular, you will find that the `BandType` property should be set to reflect the types of components being used in a particular context. For instance, the `TQRSysData` component, which is often used to display the date, time, or page count will generally go on `TQRBand` components set to `rbPageHeader` or `rbPageFooter`. This is only logical, because page count, date, and time information usually appears on the header or footer of a report.

The easiest way to learn how to use `TQRBands` and their related components is through experience. The next several sections of this chapter give working examples of using these components.

Working with the Sample Programs

In the next few pages I describe the reports from all three major database programs found in this book:

- The reports for the flat file Address2 program illustrate the basic facts about using QuickReport, including grouping.
- The reports for the relational kdAdds and Music program show how to create master detail reports, and how to write custom queries that make it easy to create reports.

Many people could probably learn how to use QuickReport by running these programs and popping up the various preview pages. After they are familiar with the different styles I use in my preview pages, they can just go back to design mode and study my QuickReport forms to see how I achieved a particular effect. In other words, I expect many people will learn by example.

The text that follows is therefore a bit sketchier than what you find elsewhere in the book. The issue here is simply that this is primarily a mechanical task that takes only a minimal amount of understanding. As a result, I will try to point you in the right direction wherever possible, and then step out of the way so you can experiment on your own computer.

The Address2 Program

I add five reports to the Address2 program from Chapter 13, "Flat-File, Real-World Databases." The first prints only addresses, the second prints only phone numbers, the third prints all the data in the report, and the fourth prints reports by grouping them on the `Category` field. Later in the chapter, I will also include a section that describes how to print a report from inside of ReportSmith.

Address2: Printing Address

This report has the task of printing out addresses. I do not include phone numbers, just addresses—as if I were making labels. A copy of the finished report as it appears in preview mode is shown in Figure 17.1. Figure 17.2 shows the same report in design mode.

To create the report, start by laying down a `TQuickReport` component. Connect it to the `AddressSource` on the program's data module. To do this, you will need to include `DMod1` in your project by pulling down the File menu and selecting Include Unit Header.

FIGURE 17.1.

The Address Report from the Address2 program.

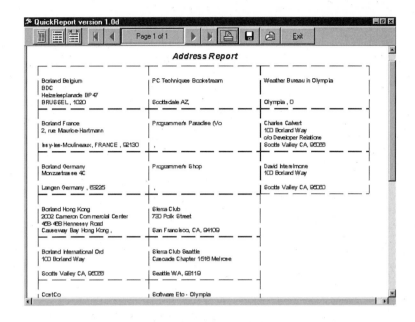

FIGURE 17.2.

The Address Report in design mode.

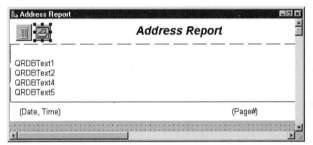

> ## NOTE
>
> I don't think you can make it through this chapter without at least a minimal understanding of the Address2 program. This program was discussed in depth in Chapter 13. The source for that program, including the reports it uses, are found in the Chap13 directory on the CD that accompanies this book.
>
> If you want to work along with me by creating the forms on your machine as I describe them in this book, open up the Address2 program, and add a new form to it. There is no harm in having two forms in the program that perform the same task; that way, you can easily open up my sample form if you get stuck.
>
> Remember, this material does not cause brain strain. You just need to understand how these components work, and then you will be able to write your own reports.

Now drop down three TQRBand components. Don't place them one on top of the other; lay one down, click on the main form, lay the next one down, and so on. That way, they are positioned one above the other on the main form. The final position of the controls at runtime is determined by the BandType property of each TQRBand. If you want to change the order of the controls on the form, drag them around with the mouse, the same way you move items in the Tab Order list box from the Edit menu. The Align property for these forms can be left at the default position of alTop. Remember, it usually doesn't really matter what order these controls have on your form; what matters is the BandType property.

The BandType for the top QRBand control should be set to rbTitle, the next one should be set to rbDetail, and the last one should be set to rbPageFooter. Drop down the Frame property of the detail band and set its DrawLeft, DrawRight, DrawTop, and DrawBottom properties to True.

The title band should have a TQRLabel component placed on it. Set its alignment to taCenter and set AlignToBand to True. Use the Font property to select a large bold font. Set the Caption property to the title of the report.

Another way to create a title involves using the TQRSysData component. Drop one down on the title band and set its alignment and font as you did the TQRLabel. Instead of changing the Caption property of this component, set its Data property to qrsReportTitle. Click on the TQuickReport component and set its ReportTitle property to the name of the report. For instance, you might set it to Address Report. Now when you run the report, the title will show up automatically at the top of the first page.

On the detail band, drop down four TQRDBText controls and set their DataSource property to the AddressSource from the program's data module and their fields to FirstLast, Address1, Address2, and CityStateZip. The first and last fields are calculated fields. The code for creating the calculated fields looks like this:

```
void __fastcall TDMod::AddressTableCalcFields(TDataSet *DataSet)
{
  if ((!AddressTableFName->IsNull) || (!AddressTableLName->IsNull))
    AddressTableFirstLast->Value =
      AddressTableFName->Value + " " + AddressTableLName->Value;
  else if (!AddressTableCompany->IsNull)
    AddressTableFirstLast->Value = AddressTableCompany->Value;
  else
    AddressTableFirstLast->Value = "Blank Record";
  AddressTableCityStateZip->Value = AddressTableCity->Value + " " +
    AddressTableState->Value + ", " + AddressTableZip->Value;
}
```

The code for creating the AddressTableFirstLast field was described during the initial discussion of the Address2 program in Chapter 13. The code for creating the AddressTableCityStateZip field involves nothing more than concatenating the three fields, and adding spaces and commas where appropriate. In a professional program, you might want to add more code to eliminate the possibility that a blank set of fields would generate a string that consists of nothing but a comma. I will omit such code here so that you can more easily decipher the code I do include.

To display more than one column in a report, turn to the `TQuickReport` component and set its `Column` property to the value you desire, such as `2` or `3`.

The final band in the report cover appears as a footer with the current date and time on it, as well as the page number. You can use the `TQRSysData` component to retrieve this data. Set one component's `Data` property to `qrsDateTime` and the other to `qrsPageNumber`.

If you want to show a print dialog to the user, you can do so in the `BeforePrint` event of the `TQuickReport` component:

```
void __fastcall TAddressReport::QuickReport1BeforePrint(bool &PrintReport)
{
  if (PrintDialog1->Execute())
  {
    PrintReport = True;
  }
  else
  {
    PrintReport = False;
  }
}
```

This code pops up a print dialog, as shown in Figure 17.3. The `TPrintDialog` component is found on the Dialogs page of the Component Palette. The settings selected by the user in the print dialog are sometimes passed on to the system without intervention on your part. However, if you need to access the settings, you can do so via the fields of the component. You can then pass this information on to QuickReport if necessary.

FIGURE 17.3.

Showing a print dialog so the user can select a printer.

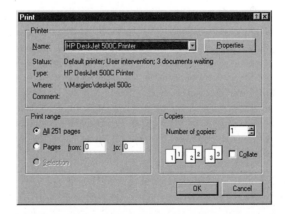

NOTE

There is a button on the `TPrintDialog` control that will pop up a setup dialog for the printer. As a result, there is rarely any reason for you to include a `TPrinterSetupDialog` in your program. The act of including a `TPrintDialog` covers both bases automatically.

To show the report to the user, you can set up a menu item on the main form of the program with its caption set to the string "Address Report". This is what the response to a click on this control should look like:

```
void __fastcall TForm1::PrintAddresses1Click(TObject *Sender)
{
  AddressReport->QuickReport1->Preview();
}
```

This assumes the name of the form on which the report is stored is called AddressReport, and the unit containing this form has been included in the main form:

```
#include "QRAddress1.h"
```

The Preview screen has a button on it that allows the user to print the report. If you didn't want to show the preview first, you can call PRINT directly:

```
AddressReport->QuickReport1->Print();
```

As you can see, creating reports using TQuickReport is trivial in the extreme. This is the kind of operation you can usually roll out in about 30 minutes, or less. If you find things getting complicated, you can usually clean up the mess by writing a query. On the rare occasions when you need more power than QuickReport offers, you should use another printing tool, such as ReportSmith or Crystal Reports. These third-party products ship with VCL links for both high-quality tools.

> **NOTE**
>
> ReportSmith is still officially part of the Borland suite of products, but most of its day-to-day operations are now being handled by a third party. As a result, it does not ship with the new versions of BCB or Delphi, though it did ship with Delphi 1.0 and Delphi 2.0.

Address2: Grouping Data in a Report

Reports often have to be presented in groups. For instance, the Address2 program has a Category field that allows the user to put each record in a separate category, such as Work, Home, Family, Fun, or Entertainment. The user wants to be able to generate reports by groups, as shown in Figure 17.4.

QuickReport makes it easy to create a report of this kind. To get started, drop down three TQRBand components, setting the BandType property from the first to rbGroupHeader, the second to rbDetail, and the third to rbGroupFooter. Also drop down a TQuickReport control and set its DataSource property to the AddressSource control from the program's data module.

You now need to drop down a TQRGroup component and set its DataSource to AddressSource and its DataField to Category. Set the HeaderBand property to the first TQRBand control and the FooterBand property to the third TQRBand control.

FIGURE 17.4.

A report from the Address2 program grouped on the Category *field.*

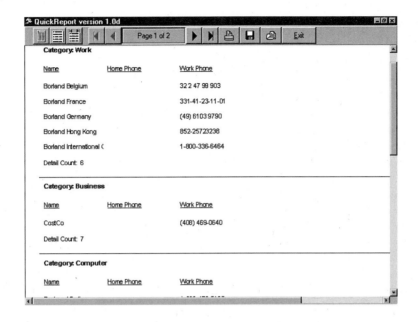

You can now drop down and hook up some TQRSysData and TQRDBText controls so that you can display information to the user. The final report should look like the screen shot shown in Figure 17.5.

FIGURE 17.5.

The GroupReport as it appears at design time.

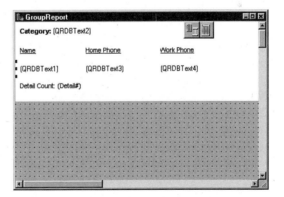

Troubleshooting Tips

Generating reports with TQuickReport is very simple, but occasionally things will go wrong. Here are some troubleshooting tips:

- If you see only one record when you are expecting to see many, check to see if you have set the DataSource field of the TQuickReport control to the correct data set.
- If one of the fields is blank, check its DataSource and DataField properties.

Reports in the Music Program

The Music program appeared in Chapter 16, "Advanced InterBase Concepts." There are two types of reports in the music program:

1. A one-to-many report that shows all the albums associated with each artist.
2. A group-by report that groups each album under its associated type, such as jazz or rock.

The next few pages cover both types of reports. Again, my text will be a bit abrupt at times. The material here is so simple that the best approach is just to give you a few hints about how to proceed, and then let you hammer out the details by working live with the tools.

One-to-Many Reports

The one-to-many report from the Music program shows how to use the TQRDetailLink component. See Figure 17.6.

FIGURE 17.6.

The one-to-many Album report as it appears in print preview mode.

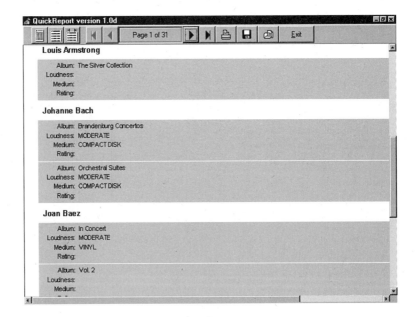

To get started, drop down four TQRBand components. Set the BandType for the first component to rbPageHeader, the second one to rbGroupHeader, the third one to rbSubDetail, and the last one to rbPageFooter. You might find it useful to name each component after its type:

Component name	BandType
PageHeaderBand	rbPageHeader
GroupHeaderBand	rbGroupHeader
SubDetailBand	rbSubDetail
PageFooterBand	rbPageFooter

The header and footer bands should use TQRSysData components to display standard information such as the report title, page number, and the time and date the report is printed.

Drop down a TQuickReport component and connect it to the ArtistSource on the data module. Now drop down a TQRDetailLink component, which is designed to help you set up one-to-many reports. The TQRDetailLink component should have its DataSource property set to the ArtistSource from the data module and its Master property set to QuickReport1. The DetailBand property should be set to the SubDetailBand and the HeaderBand property to the GroupHeaderBand.

After you have everything in place, drop down TQRDBText controls to display the fields of your data. In particular, place one TQRDBText control on the GroupHeaderBand, set the DataSource property equal to ArtistSource from the program's data module, and set its DataField property equal to its FirstLast calculated field.

On the SubDetailBand, drop down four TQRDBText components and set the DataSource property equal to DMod->AlbumSource. Set the DataField property for these controls to the Album and Rating fields, and to the LoudLookup and MediumLookup calculated fields. The result should look like the image shown in Figure 17.7.

FIGURE 17.7.

The one-to-many Album report as it appears at design time.

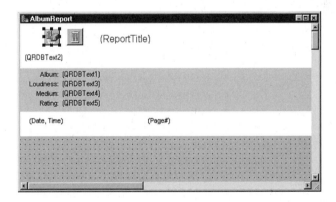

You can now set up a menu item on the program's main page that will launch the form. When you run the program, the form you have created should make a report like that shown in Figure 17.7.

Using Queries to Help with Grouped Reports

The second report from the Music program groups all the records in the report according to their type. For instance, it groups all the jazz albums together and all the rock albums together.

I've already shown you one grouped report in this chapter. I'm showing you another because this one uses queries to easily resolve what appears to be a rather complicated problem. The difficulty here is that you want the report to group according to the type of album, but to also organize the report so that each album is grouped under a particular artist. This is a bit tricky to do, given the design of the database. To remedy the problem, I created a query that generates most of my report for me:

```
select Types.Types, Artist.First,
  Artist.Last, Album.Album, Album.Rating, Loudness.Loudness
  from Artist, Album, Types, Loudness
  where Artist.Code = Album.GroupCode and
    Types.Code=Album.Types and
    Loudness.Code = Album.Loudness
  group by Types.Types, Artist.Last,
    Artist.First, Album.Album, Album.Rating, Loudness.Loudness
```

This is a fairly straightforward query that gives me all the records in the table sorted first by record type, and secondly by artist. That way, all the Bob Dylan albums that I consider to be folk records appear together, and all the Dylan albums that I think are rock albums are grouped together. Inside of each type, I group the albums alphabetically. The query also does lookups into the Types and Loudness tables so I can substitute human-readable strings for the numeric codes found in the Albums table.

NOTE

Queries not only have the power to solve complicated problems, but they are also fun to use and can therefore spice up the mundane task of creating a report. They can also be reused in the main body of your program. Often, it makes sense to place queries like this inside a stored procedure.

After creating the query, I need to create a calculated field called FirstLast that gives me a single string containing the first and last names:

```
void __fastcall TAlbumGroupForm::AlbumQueryCalcFields(TDataSet *DataSet)
{
  AlbumQueryFirstLast->Value =
    AlbumQueryFIRST->Value + " " + AlbumQueryLAST->Value;
}
```

There is no need to create lookup fields for the Loudness and Types values because I retrieved the strings associated with these fields from the Loudness and Types tables in the original query.

After writing the query, most of the work I need to do for the report is done. Now I can simply drop down some TQRBand components, a TQuickReport component, and a TQRGroup component, and link them together as explained earlier in the chapter. I perform the grouping on the `Types` field from the query.

On the `rbGroupHeader` band I drop down a `TQRDBText` control that is set equal to the `Types` field. I then add fields `rbDetail` band that will display each artist's name, each album's name, and each's loudness and type. The final report looks like the image shown in Figure 17.8, and the design time shape of the form is shown in Figure 17.9.

FIGURE 17.8.

The Album Group report as it appears in print preview mode.

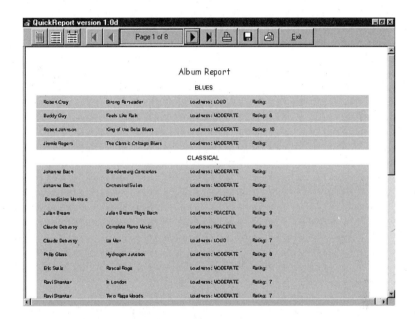

FIGURE 17.9.

The Album Group report as it appears at design time.

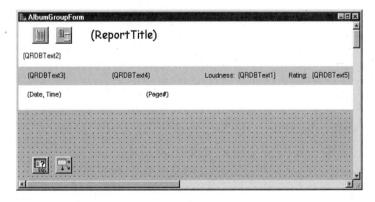

That is all I want to say about QuickReport in this book. If you want additional examples of using QuickReport, you should view the kdAdd program.

Printing Forms

One of the easiest ways to print information in BCB is to simply send the image of a form to a printer. The code for doing this is trivial in the extreme:

```
void __fastcall TForm1::Print1Click(TObject *Sender)
{
  Form1->Print();
}
```

It doesn't get any easier than this.

 On the CD that accompanies this book, you will find a program called PrintForm that contains a menu item that will print the contents of the current form. This option will not help you print a dataset, but it will print whatever you can see on the current form. For instance, the PrintForm program prints the current form as shown in Figure 17.10, minus the menu, border, and caption areas. The quality of the picture in the printed output can differ depending on a number of factors.

FIGURE 17.10.

The main form of the PrintForm application just as the user selects the Print option from the menu.

The Address2 program gives you the option of printing a series of forms. In particular, it iterates through the database, printing one form, on one page, for each record in the database. This is a waste of resources, but it does produce clean-looking, easy-to-read reports. However, the user would have to turn the page each time he or she views a new record. This task is so onerous that it leaves this solution virtually useless for all but a few, unusual tasks.

Here is the code that prints all the forms in the Address2 program:

```
void __fastcall TForm1::PrintForms1Click(TObject *Sender)
{
```

```
    if (ScalingForm->ShowModal() == mrOk)
    {
      switch (ScalingForm->ScalingOptions->ItemIndex)
      {
       case 0: PrintScale = poNone; break;
       case 1: PrintScale = poProportional; break;
       case 2: PrintScale = poPrintToFit; break;
      }
      Panel2->Visible = False;
      DBGrid1->Visible = False;
      DMod->AddressTable->First();
      while (!DMod->AddressTable->Eof)
      {
        Print();
        DMod->AddressTable->Next();
      }
      DBGrid1->Visible = True;
      Panel2->Visible = True;
    }
}
```

This code first pops up a custom dialog like the one shown in Figure 17.11. This dialog lets you choose three printing options provided by the TForm object in a property called PrintScale. The print options (poNone, poProportional, poPrintToFit) are declared in Forms.hpp.

If you choose PrintToFit, your form will take up the maximum amount of space it can on the pages you are printing. In short, it will expand to fill the available space but will continue to remain in proportion. That is, it won't be stretched but will expand as far as it can in both the horizontal and vertical directions. When it reaches the limit in either direction, it will stop expanding in both directions, so that the view you have of the form remains proportional.

The code for this routine also makes invisible all the controls on the form that are not needed when printing. For instance, the buttons on the form serve no purpose on the printed form, so I make them invisible. A second solution is to create a custom form featuring only the portions of this view that need to be printed.

The code then iterates through the database, printing each form:

```
DMod->AddressTable->First();
while (!DMod->AddressTable->Eof)
{
  Print();
  DMod->AddressTable->Next();
}
```

FIGURE 17.11.

The Scaling form dialog gives you a chance to choose how the reports will look when printed.

Be careful, because with this kind of code, it's easy to get stuck in an endless loop by forgetting to call Next(). This is a no-brainer error that everyone can see why it is a mistake, but people still tend to make it when they are rushed or tired.

TPrinter: Printing Text, Shapes, and Bitmaps

There are two easy ways to send output directly to the printer from a VCL program. One is to open up the printer as a device and send output to it, and the second is to use the VCL TPrinter object. The program shown in this section uses the latter method.

TPrinter provides a TCanvas object initialized to the DC for the printer. As a result, you can send text or graphics objects to the printer just as easily as you can send them to the screen.

The PrintGDI program found on the CD that accompanies this book shows how to print text, shapes, and bitmaps using the TPrinter object. It consists of three forms, shown in Figures 17.12, 17.13, and 17.14. The source for the program is shown in Listings 17.1. through 17.6.

FIGURE 17.12.

The text from a Shakespearean sonnet shown in a form. You can use the program to print the text.

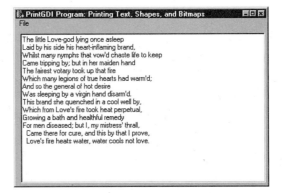

FIGURE 17.13.

The form shown here has a TPaintBox component with some shapes drawn in it. You can print the contents of the paint box.

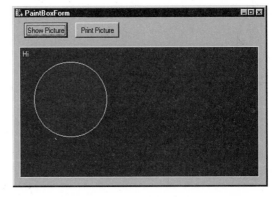

FIGURE 17.14.

This form can display bitmaps and also send their contents to the printer.

Listing 17.1. The header for the main module of the PrintGDI program.

```
//////////////////////////////////////
// File: Main.h
// Project: PrintText
// Copyright (c) 1997 by Charlie Calvert
//
#ifndef MainH
#define MainH
#include <vcl\Classes.hpp>
#include <vcl\Controls.hpp>
#include <vcl\StdCtrls.hpp>
#include <vcl\Forms.hpp>
#include <vcl\Buttons.hpp>
#include <vcl\ExtCtrls.hpp>
#include <vcl\Menus.hpp>
#include <vcl\Dialogs.hpp>
class TForm1 : public TForm
{
__published:
  TMainMenu *MainMenu1;
  TMenuItem *File1;
  TMenuItem *ShapeForm1;
  TMenuItem *Print1;
  TMenuItem *N1;
  TMenuItem *Exit1;
  TPrintDialog *PrintDialog1;
  TMemo *Memo1;
  TMenuItem *Open1;
  TOpenDialog *OpenDialog1;
  TMenuItem *N2;
  TMenuItem *BitmapForm1;
  void __fastcall Print1Click(TObject *Sender);
  void __fastcall Open1Click(TObject *Sender);
  void __fastcall ShapeForm1Click(TObject *Sender);
  void __fastcall BitmapForm1Click(TObject *Sender);
private:
  void SendToPrinter();
  void PrintText(TCanvas *Canvas);
public:
  __fastcall TForm1(TComponent* Owner);
```

continues

Listing 17.1. continued

```
};
extern TForm1 *Form1;
#endif
```

Listing 17.2. The main module for the PrintGDI program.

```cpp
//////////////////////////////////////////
// File: Main.cpp
// Project: PrintText
// Copyright (c) 1997 by Charlie Calvert
//
#include <vcl\vcl.h>
#include <vcl\printers.hpp>
#pragma hdrstop
#include "Main.h"
#include "PaintBoxPrint.h"
#include "PrintBmp1.h"
#pragma resource "*.dfm"
TForm1 *Form1;
__fastcall TForm1::TForm1(TComponent* Owner)
: TForm(Owner)
{
}
void TForm1::PrintText(TCanvas *Canvas)
{
  int i, x;
  AnsiString S("Test String");
  x = Canvas->TextHeight(S);
  for (i = 0; i < Memo1->Lines->Count; i++)
  {
    S = Memo1->Lines->Strings[i];
    Canvas->TextOut(1, x * i, S);
  }
}
void TForm1::SendToPrinter()
{
  TPrinter *APrinter = Printer();
  APrinter->BeginDoc();
  PrintText(APrinter->Canvas);
  APrinter->EndDoc();
}
void __fastcall TForm1::Print1Click(TObject *Sender)
{
  if (PrintDialog1->Execute())
  {
    SendToPrinter();
  }
}
void __fastcall TForm1::Open1Click(TObject *Sender)
{
  if (OpenDialog1->Execute())
  {
    Memo1->Lines->LoadFromFile(OpenDialog1->FileName);
void __fastcall TForm1::ShapeForm1Click(TObject *Sender)
{
```

```
  PaintBoxForm->ShowModal();
}
void __fastcall TForm1::BitmapForm1Click(TObject *Sender)
{
  PrintBitmapForm->ShowModal();
}
```

Listing 17.3. The header for the PaintBoxPrint module.

```
////////////////////////////////////////
// File: PaintBoxPrint.h
// Project: PrintText
// Copyright (c) 1997 by Charlie Calvert
//
#ifndef PaintBoxPrintH
#define PaintBoxPrintH
#include <vcl\Classes.hpp>
#include <vcl\Controls.hpp>
#include <vcl\StdCtrls.hpp>
#include <vcl\Forms.hpp>
#include <vcl\ExtCtrls.hpp>
#include <vcl\Buttons.hpp>
#include <vcl\Dialogs.hpp>
class TPaintBoxForm : public TForm
{
__published:
  TPaintBox *PaintBox1;
  TBitBtn *PrintPictureBtn;
  TBitBtn *ShowPictureBtn;
  TPrintDialog *PrintDialog1;
  void __fastcall PrintPictureBtnClick(TObject *Sender);
private:
  void __fastcall ShowData(TCanvas *Canvas);
  void SendToPrinter();
public:
  __fastcall TPaintBoxForm(TComponent* Owner);
};
extern TPaintBoxForm *PaintBoxForm;
#endif
```

Listing 17.4. The main module for the PaintBoxPrint module.

```
////////////////////////////////////////
// File: PaintBoxPrint.cpp
// Project: PrintText
// Copyright (c) 1997 by Charlie Calvert
//
#include <vcl\vcl.h>
#include <vcl\printers.hpp>
#pragma hdrstop
#include "PaintBoxPrint.h"
#pragma resource "*.dfm"
```

continues

17

PRINTING:
QUICKREPORT

Listing 17.4. continued

```cpp
TPaintBoxForm *PaintBoxForm;
__fastcall TPaintBoxForm::TPaintBoxForm(TComponent* Owner)
: TForm(Owner)
{
}
void __fastcall TPaintBoxForm::ShowData(TCanvas *Canvas)
{
  Canvas->Brush->Color = clBlue;
  Canvas->Pen->Color = clYellow;
  Canvas->Rectangle(0, 0, PaintBox1->Width, PaintBox1->Height);
  Canvas->Font->Color = clYellow;
  Canvas->TextOut(5, 5, "Hi");
  Canvas->Brush->Color = clPurple;
  Canvas->Ellipse(25, 25, 150, 150);
}
void TPaintBoxForm::SendToPrinter()
{
  if (PrintDialog1->Execute())
  {
    TPrinter *APrinter = Printer();
    APrinter->BeginDoc();
    ShowData(APrinter->Canvas);
    APrinter->EndDoc();
  }
}
void __fastcall TPaintBoxForm::PrintPictureBtnClick(TObject *Sender)
{
  switch(dynamic_cast<TButton *>(Sender)->Tag)
  {
    case 0:
    {
      SendToPrinter();
      break;
    }
    case 1:
    {
      ShowData(PaintBox1->Canvas);
      break;
    }
  }

}
```

Listing 17.5. The header for the `PrintBitmap` module.

```cpp
/////////////////////////////////////
// File: PrintBmp.h
// Project: PrintText
// Copyright (c) 1997 by Charlie Calvert
//
#ifndef PrintBmp1H
#define PrintBmp1H
#include <vcl\Classes.hpp>
#include <vcl\Controls.hpp>
#include <vcl\StdCtrls.hpp>
```

```
#include <vcl\Forms.hpp>
#include <vcl\ExtCtrls.hpp>
#include <vcl\Menus.hpp>
#include <vcl\Dialogs.hpp>
class TPrintBitmapForm : public TForm
{
__published:
  TImage *Image1;
  TMainMenu *MainMenu1;
  TMenuItem *File1;
  TMenuItem *Open1;
  TMenuItem *Print1;
  TMenuItem *N1;
  TMenuItem *Exit1;
  TOpenDialog *OpenDialog1;
  TPrintDialog *PrintDialog1;
  TMenuItem *Options1;
  TMenuItem *Stretch1;
  void __fastcall Open1Click(TObject *Sender);
  void __fastcall Print1Click(TObject *Sender);
  void __fastcall Exit1Click(TObject *Sender);
  void __fastcall Stretch1Click(TObject *Sender);
private:
public:
  __fastcall TPrintBitmapForm(TComponent* Owner);
};
extern TPrintBitmapForm *PrintBitmapForm;
#endif
```

Listing 17.6. The main form for the `PrintBitmap` module.

```
//////////////////////////////////////
// File: PrintBmp.cpp
// Project: PrintText
// Copyright (c) 1997 by Charlie Calvert
//
#include <vcl\vcl.h>
#include <vcl\printers.hpp>
#pragma hdrstop
#include "PrintBmp1.h"
#pragma resource "*.dfm"
TPrintBitmapForm *PrintBitmapForm;
__fastcall TPrintBitmapForm::TPrintBitmapForm(TComponent* Owner)
    : TForm(Owner)
{
}
void __fastcall TPrintBitmapForm::Open1Click(TObject *Sender)
{
  if (OpenDialog1->Execute())
  {
    Image1->Picture->LoadFromFile(OpenDialog1->FileName);
  }
}
void __fastcall TPrintBitmapForm::Print1Click(TObject *Sender)
{
```

continues

Listing 17.6. continued

```
  if (PrintDialog1->Execute())
  {
    TPrinter *APrinter = Printer();
    APrinter->BeginDoc();
    APrinter->Canvas->Draw(1, 1, Image1->Picture->Bitmap);
    APrinter->EndDoc();
  }
}
void __fastcall TPrintBitmapForm::Exit1Click(TObject *Sender)
{
  Close();
}
void __fastcall TPrintBitmapForm::Stretch1Click(TObject *Sender)
{
  Stretch1->Checked = !Stretch1->Checked;
  Image1->Stretch = Stretch1->Checked;
}
```

The main form of the program can print text, such as that shown in Figure 17.12, where you can see one of Shakespeare's sonnets. To send this text to the printer, you need to retrieve the printer object from the VCL. This object is declared in the Printers unit, so you must include that unit in your form. You can the write the following code:

```
void TForm1::SendToPrinter()
{
  TPrinter *APrinter = Printer();
  APrinter->BeginDoc();
  PrintText(APrinter->Canvas);
  APrinter->EndDoc();
}
```

This code first calls the Printer method to retrieve an object of type TPrinter. It then calls the BeginDoc method of the TPrinter object to start a document. When the printing task is done, you should call EndDoc.

The following method handles the actual printing chores:

```
void TForm1::PrintText(TCanvas *Canvas)
{
  int i, x;
  AnsiString S("Test String");
  x = Canvas->TextHeight(S);
  for (i = 0; i < Memo1->Lines->Count; i++)
  {
    S = Memo1->Lines->Strings[i];
    Canvas->TextOut(1, x * i, S);
  }
}
```

As you can see, this code starts at the beginning of the list of strings and iterates through them all, using the TPrinter Canvas object to print the current information. You can change the font, colors, and other aspects of the canvas in any way you like. Recall that in Chapter 7, "Graphics," I described how to use the Canvas object.

Printing Shapes to the Printer

One of the great advantages of the code shown in the `PrintText` method is that you can use it with any `Canvas` object. For instance, I could pass in the `Canvas` of the main form and then print the output to the main form, rather than to the printer.

The technique described in the last paragraph is what goes on in the form shown in Figure 17.13. This form provides the user with two buttons, one for printing information to a control on the current form and the other for printing information to a printer:

```
void __fastcall TPaintBoxForm::PrintPictureBtnClick(TObject *Sender)
{
  switch(dynamic_cast<TButton *>(Sender)->Tag)
  {
    case 0:
    {
      SendToPrinter();
      break;
    }
    case 1:
    {
      ShowData(PaintBox1->Canvas);
      break;
    }
  }

}
```

If you opt to send information to the printer, the following code is called:

```
void TPaintBoxForm::SendToPrinter()
{
  if (PrintDialog1->Execute())
  {
    TPrinter *APrinter = Printer();
    APrinter->BeginDoc();
    ShowData(APrinter->Canvas);
    APrinter->EndDoc();
  }
}
```

This code first pops up a `TPrintDialog` and lets the user set up the printer, and switch into color printing mode, if necessary. A document is started, and the `ShowData` method is called:

```
void __fastcall TPaintBoxForm::ShowData(TCanvas *Canvas)
{
  Canvas->Brush->Color = clBlue;
  Canvas->Pen->Color = clYellow;
  Canvas->Rectangle(0, 0, PaintBox1->Width, PaintBox1->Height);
  Canvas->Font->Color = clYellow;
  Canvas->TextOut(5, 5, "Hi");
  Canvas->Brush->Color = clPurple;
  Canvas->Ellipse(25, 25, 150, 150);
}
```

As you can see, this method draws some text and a series of shapes into a canvas. If the canvas you pass to this program is for the main form or for a control placed on the main form, the output will appear there. If the canvas you pass in belongs to the printer, the output will be sent to the printer.

> **NOTE**
>
> One problem that I do not address in this code involves selecting the proper size and proportions for the current printer. As a rule, you will find that text or shapes that look okay on the screen will be far too small when shown on a printer. For hints on how to remedy the situation, view the code in Forms.pas that shows how to implement the poProportional and poPrintToFit options discussed earlier in this chapter. This code is almost all straight Windows API code, and will look virtually identical in C++ and Object Pascal.

Print Bitmaps

The final portion of the PrintGDI program that might be of interest to some users involves printing bitmaps. This sounds like it must be a complicated subject, but the VCL makes it easy.

The key to this process is using a TImage control on the form from which you want to print a bitmap. The following code can be used to load an image into that TImage control.

```
void __fastcall TPrintBitmapForm::Open1Click(TObject *Sender)
{
  if (OpenDialog1->Execute())
  {
    Image1->Picture->LoadFromFile(OpenDialog1->FileName);
  }
}
```

To print the image, just write the following code:

```
void __fastcall TPrintBitmapForm::Print1Click(TObject *Sender)
{
  if (PrintDialog1->Execute())
  {
    TPrinter *APrinter = Printer();
    APrinter->BeginDoc();
    APrinter->Canvas->Draw(1, 1, Image1->Picture->Bitmap);
    APrinter->EndDoc();
  }
}
```

This code pops up a TPrintDialog, grabs the printer, and begins a document. You can draw a bitmap on the TPrinter canvas by calling Draw and passing in the bitmap already loaded into the TImage component. The first two parameters passed to draw specify where you want the printing to begin as expressed in X, Y coordinates. The final step is to call EndDoc, which sends a form-feed to the printer.

That is all I'm going to say about the TPrinter class. There are more features of this object that you can explore via the online help or by opening up Printers.hpp. However, the basic facts outlined here should give you most of the information you need to get started with this object.

Printing Records in ReportSmith

ReportSmith is no longer an integrated part of the VCL family of products. However, I will touch on this subject briefly, just to give you a few clues about how to proceed with the tool if you need it. In particular, I will show how to create a report for the Address2 program.

> **NOTE**
>
> In the current shipping version of BCB, there aren't any TReportSmith or TReport components. However, I am sure that the people now making ReportSmith supply this component with the product. In the worst-case scenario, you can just use the Windows API command called WinExec to start ReportSmith and pass as a parameter the name of the report you want to run. There are also ways to pass macros to ReportSmith, and you can talk to the product using DDE.

To start creating a report, bring up ReportSmith using the Explorer and select the type of report you want to make, which is probably a label-based report. Go to the Tables page in the Report Query dialog, choose Add Table, and select ADDRESS.DB. ReportSmith understands BDE aliases, so you can use those to help you select a table.

Next, go to the Report Variables page and create a new variable called Filter. Set its type to String, its title to Filter List, and the prompt to "What filter do you want to use?". Set the entry to Type-in, as shown in Figure 17.15. When you are done, choose Add.

> **NOTE**
>
> You do not have to choose Type-in as the entry method. In fact, the Address2 program is ideally suited for using the Choose from a Table method. After you select this method, a work space will appear in the bottom-right corner of the Report Variables page that enables you to choose a table and field that contain a list of available entries. In this case, you can choose the CATS.DB table and the Category field. Now when the user wants to run the report, he or she will be prompted with a list of valid categories and can choose the appropriate one, without the likelihood of an error being introduced. The copy of the ReportSmith report that ships with the CD for this book uses this method.

FIGURE 17.15.

Creating report variables in ReportSmith.

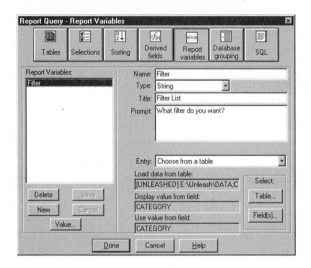

Turn to the Selections page, click on the yellow number 1 in the center of the page, and choose Select SQL selection criteria from the drop-down list. Select the Category field from the DataFields list box on the left and choose x=y from the Comparison Operators in the middle list box. Go back to the left-hand list box and change the combo box at the top so it reads Report Variables rather than Data Fields. Choose Filter and then set this variable in quotes:

```
'ADDRESSxDB'.'CATEGORY' = '<<Filter>>'
```

When you are done, the dialog should look like that in Figure 17.16. Now click the OK button at the bottom of the dialog.

FIGURE 17.16.

Creating SQL selection criteria in ReportSmith.

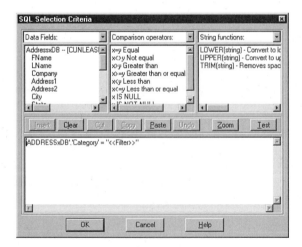

The final step in this process is to create derived fields in the Derived Fields page of the Report Query dialog. The first derived field should combine the FName and LName fields, so you might want to call this field FirstLast. After typing in the name, select Add, and the Edit Derived Fields dialog box will appear. Select FName from the left column:

```
'ADDRESSxDB'.'FName'
```

Choose Addition from the middle column:

```
'ADDRESSxDB'.'FName' +
```

Add a space by writing the string ' ':

```
'ADDRESSxDB'.'FName' + ' '
```

Choose Addition again from the middle column:

```
'ADDRESSxDB'.'FName' + ' ' +
```

End by adding the LName field. The string you create should look like this:

```
'ADDRESSxDB'.'FName' + ' ' + 'ADDRESSxDB'.'LName'
```

This statement combines the FName and LName fields so that they produce a single string out of a first and last name:

```
Kurt Weill
```

You should then create a second derived field called CityStateZip, which combines the City, State, and Zip fields:

```
'ADDRESSxDB'.'CITY' + ', ' + 'ADDRESSxDB'.'STATE' + ' '  +
  'ADDRESSxDB'.'ZIP'
```

You have now created the logic behind a report, so choose Done from the bottom of the Report Query dialog. ReportSmith will then pop up a dialog to fill in the report variable you created. In other words, it's time for you to fill in the Filter portion of the following statement:

```
'ADDRESSxDB'.'CATEGORY' = '<<Filter>>'
```

You can type the word Family, Work, or whatever value you feel will return a reasonably sized dataset.

The Insert Field dialog now appears, and you can enter the fields and derived fields that you have created. The combo box at the top of the dialog enables you to switch back and forth between data fields and derived fields; you should do so when you think it's appropriate. For instance, the first field you select will probably be the derived field called FirstLast, whereas the second will probably be the data field called Address1. When you are done, the report you create should look something like the image shown in Figure 17.17.

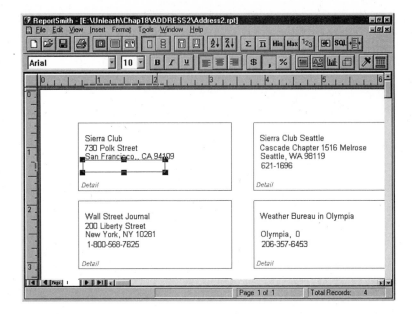

Even the report shown here is probably not totally complete; you might want to rearrange the location of the fields inside each label and change the size and location of each individual label. You will find that you can move individual fields around by simply dragging them with the mouse. The actual decisions you make will be based on your personal tastes and on the type of labels you have in your office or home. When you are performing these tasks, you will probably find it easiest to do so by choosing the File | Page Setup menu option from the ReportSmith main menu.

If you want to change the fonts used in your report, select one of the fields in a label, right-click on the page, and choose Character from the pop-up menu. Other options, such as adjusting borders and field height and inserting pictures are available when you right-click a report.

When you are completely finished preparing a report, choose File | Save to save the report you have created under the name Address, in the same directory where the Address2 program resides.

As I stated previously, this brief tutorial on ReportSmith is not meant to be anything more than a very loosely structured primer. ReportSmith is very easy to use, and most of the actions you will perform are intuitive variations on the simple steps already outlined. However, you will probably also want to study the ReportSmith manuals, online help, and perhaps a third-party book dedicated to this subject.

> **NOTE**
>
> ReportSmith has a fairly sophisticated query builder in the Selections page of the Report Query dialog. On several occasions, I have actually abandoned BCB's query builder and opened up ReportSmith to construct a SQL statement. When I'm done, I just block-copy the SQL code from ReportSmith into the SQL property of my current Delphi TQuery object. This is a major kludge, but under some circumstances you might want to consider it as an option.

ReportSmith is a good tool that has the enormous advantage of being easy to use. In fact, ReportSmith is so easy to use that it turns the task of generating reports into something very similar to playing. As a result, you can quickly generate elegant-looking reports and then get back to the more interesting task of writing code.

Summary

In this chapter you have had an overview of printing in BCB. In particular, you have seen how to use QuickReport, the TPrinter object, and ReportSmith. You should remember that there might be updates available for QuickReport, and that another important third-party tool in the printing world is Seagate's Crystal Reports.

The point to grasp when reading this chapter is that BCB makes printing easy. Whether you are using TPrinter or QuickReport, you can output most information on a printer with only a few short minutes of work. If the printing task begins to look complicated, use a SQL query to get the information you need and then print the output of the query. This is the best course of action in terms of ease of use, and also in terms of creating an easy to maintain program.

As I said in the beginning, most people regard printing as a fairly boring chore. There is little in this chapter likely to change anyone's mind on this subject, but by now you should see that you have the tools necessary to quickly and easily generate powerful reports that users will love. If you take the time to learn how to use these tools, you can generate lots of reports easily. This is a skill you simply must have if you want to work in the client/server database world.

Working with CASE Tools: Cadet, ER1, and SDesigner

IN THIS CHAPTER

Overview

In this chapter, I will give a very superficial overview of three CASE tools. The purpose of this chapter is merely to introduce you to these tools so that you know that they exist and to tell you something about what they can do for you.

In particular, this chapter focuses on the following products:

- The Data Module Designer from Paradox 7.0: This tool can help you design Paradox databases. It gives you a visual overview of your database and gives you a handy visual method for establishing referential integrity.
- SDesigner: This full-featured, powerful, and very complex tool is meant for professional database designers.
- ER1: Embarcadero makes one of the hottest data modeling tools on the market. Like SDesigner, this full-featured database tool is meant for professionals. ER1 is known for its advanced technology and easy-to-use tools.
- Cadet: This shareware tool is developed in Delphi. It provides an inexpensive yet very powerful means of working with Paradox, dBASE, and InterBase tables.

Before going any further, I want to stress that this subject is starting to wander fairly far afield from the main topics of this book. In particular, my goal is to describe BCB, not third-party tools such as SDesigner or Cadet.

The main purpose of this chapter is to alert you to the existence of these tools and of others like them. My intention is not to recommend these tools above competing products, nor am I interested in describing these tools in any depth.

I have gone into considerable depth about database programming in this book. I feel that I would be remiss at this point if I did not at least point you toward these kinds of tools. If you earn your living creating databases, then you already know how important data modeling tools can be. In that case, your only interest in this chapter will be simply to see highly abstracted database tools working with BCB. On the other hand, if you're interested in entering the database field, then this is a subject you should master, and hopefully this chapter will inspire you to explore this field in more depth.

Once again, I want to stress that this subject is too wide of the main interests of this book to merit an in-depth examination. Instead, I want to give a quick overview of the subject to alert you to its importance and to the availability of some valuable tools. Unlike all the other chapters in this book, this one is designed to be completed in only a few minutes.

What Are CASE and Data Modeling Tools?

The primary problem solved by CASE and data modeling tools is managing complexity. Most of the databases in this book are fairly simple. Even the more complex databases I've presented, such as the ones for kdAdds or Music, are fairly easy to grasp.

Problems arise, however, when you have huge databases consisting of 30 or more tables that are related in a maze of complex links. If you're wrestling with that kind of complexity, or if you're considering taking on a project of that size, then you will find some kind of data modeling tool to be a necessity.

Good tools of this kind will reverse-engineer a database and show you a diagram depicting the relationship between tables. An example of this kind of diagram, as drawn by SDesigner, is shown in Figure 18.1. While you're studying this screen shot, understand that sometimes pictures shown in books look best when shot in 640×480 screen mode but that tools such as SDesigner were made to be run in much higher resolutions. If you increase the resolution to 1024×768, for example, then you can get a clear view of a larger number of tables.

FIGURE 18.1.

A portion of a physical data model displayed in SDesigner.

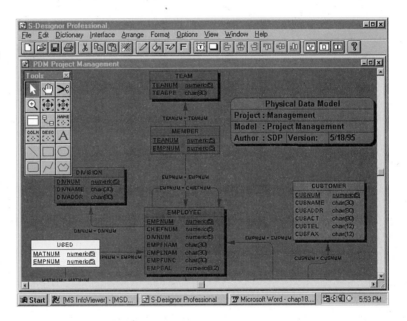

Powerful data modeling tools will also let you add tables, fields, indexes, and referential integrity to your database. The goal is to allow you to use the mouse to drag lines between the tables to designate how they interrelate. At the appropriate times, dialogs should pop up automatically asking you to specify the details of your links. After you're done, you can save the data model, at which time SQL or some other code that will automatically update the database is generated.

A number of sophisticated CASE tools will also automatically generate code for you. For example, Delphi has CASE tools available from third parties that will automatically generate forms and code for projects after you're through designing the tables and their relationships. At the time of this writing, I do not know of any CASE tools that perform this task for BCB, but I assume that they will appear over the next few months.

The Paradox Data Model Designer

If you have Paradox 7.0, you have a data modeling tool that you can use with BCB. To get started, launch Paradox and select the CUNLEASHED alias. This alias points to most of the Paradox tables that ship with this book. A description of the way to create this alias is provided or referenced in the readme file on the CD that ships with this book.

After you set up the alias, choose Tools | Data Model Designer from the Paradox menu. A window like the one shown in Figure 18.2 appears.

FIGURE 18.2.

The Data Model Designer as it appears when first selected from the Tools menu of Paradox 7.0.

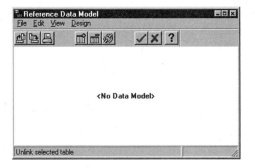

The goal of this exercise will be to get an overview of the tables in the kdAdds program from Chapter 14, "Sessions and Relational Real-World Databases." To get started, add all the tables from the database to the Data Model Designer, as shown in Figure 18.3.

FIGURE 18.3.

The Data Model Designer after you have added all the tables used in the kdAdds program.

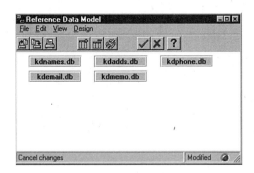

Now that the tables are in place, the next step is to show the relationships between these tables. Click once on the kdNames table, drag the mouse cursor on top of the kdAdds table, and let go. Afterward, you will see the image shown in Figure 18.4.

FIGURE 18.4.

The relationship between the kdAdds *and* kdNames *tables as shown in the Paradox Data Model Designer.*

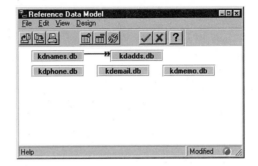

At this stage, you might try connecting the kdNames table to the other tables in the database, as shown in Figure 18.5.

FIGURE 18.5.

The kdNames *table is the controlling table in the relationship between it and* kdAdds, kdPhone, kdEmail, *and* kdMemo.

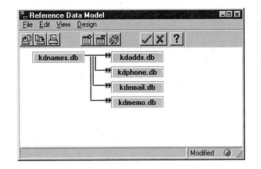

When you're defining these relationships, be sure you drag from the kdNames table to the tables that are subordinate to it. If you define the relationship in the opposite direction, you end up with a different depiction of the relationship between the tables, as shown in Figure 18.6. This view of the table is not incorrect, but it gives you a different perspective.

If you try to define a relationship between two tables that have no links, a dialog pops up explaining what has happened, as shown in Figure 18.7.

If you drag the mouse cursor between two indexed tables, a dialog that lets you define the relationship between the tables will pop up. You can use this tool to actually design the elements of your database, as shown in Figure 18.8.

That's all I'm going to say about the Paradox Data Model Designer. As I said in the beginning of this chapter, dwelling on Paradox in a book about BCB would make no sense. However, I wanted to give you a brief introduction to this subject so that you can understand something about the tools available on the market.

18

WORKING WITH CASE TOOLS

FIGURE 18.6.

The relationship between the kdMemo *and* kdNames *table from the point of view of the* kdMemo *table.*

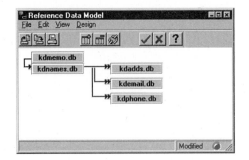

FIGURE 18.7.

The dialog you get when you try to relate two tables that have no links on which a relationship can be defined.

FIGURE 18.8.

Establishing a relationship between two tables in the Paradox Data Model Designer.

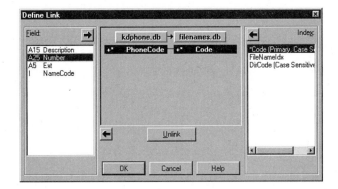

SDesigner

SDesigner is a much more powerful and much more complex tool than Paradox. To get started with it, you should have ODBC drivers installed on your system. In Chapter 8, "Database Basics and Database Tools," I described how to set up an ODBC connection to an InterBase table.

Assuming you have SDesigner, InterBase, and ODBC installed on your system, you can get started by launching SDesigner. Close all the windows and open the File menu, as shown in Figure 18.9.

FIGURE 18.9.

The File menu in SDesigner gives you the option of reverse-engineering a database.

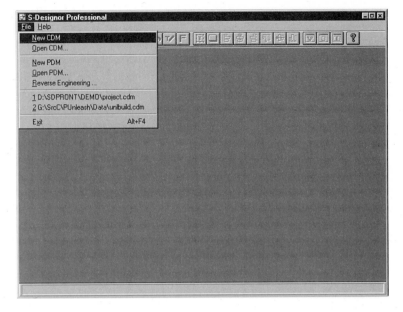

If you select Reverse Engineering from the menu, you can choose the name of the database you want to use from the list of available drivers, as shown in Figure 18.10. If you don't see InterBase in this list, then you probably don't have the ODBC drivers for InterBase installed. In this case, you still have a course of action open to you since SDesigner can reverse-engineer the schematic SQL code produced when you choose Extract | SQL Metadata for Database from the WISQL menu. In particular, you should choose the menu item in WISQL and then save the output to a text file. Then point SDesigner at the text file, and it will reverse-engineer it. The Music.ddl files in the Data directory on the CD that accompanies this book are examples of the type of file that SDesigner can reverse-engineer.

After clicking OK, you are presented with a dialog that lets you select the InterBase database to which you want to connect. I described how to set up these database links in Chapter 8. In this case, I signed into the link to the Music database, filling in my username of SYSDBA and the default password of masterkey. The password might be different on your system.

You can then select which tables you want to examine, as well as which parts of the tables, such as indexes, primary keys, and foreign keys. The selections I made are shown in Figure 18.11.

18

WORKING WITH CASE TOOLS

FIGURE 18.10.

Selecting a database name.

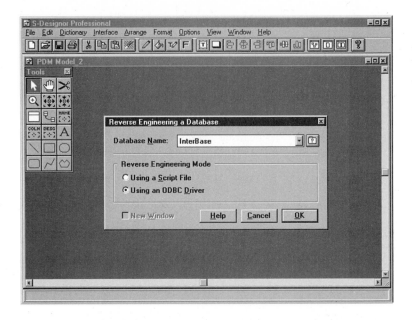

FIGURE 18.11.

Selecting the tables that I want to import from the Music database. Notice that you can choose to view the primary keys, foreign keys, and other pieces of metadata.

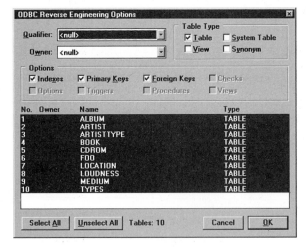

In Figure 18.12, you can see what the diagram of the database looks like after SDesigner has finished the reverse-engineering process. Notice that the links between the tables are visible.

FIGURE 18.12.

The Music database after it has been imported into SDesigner.

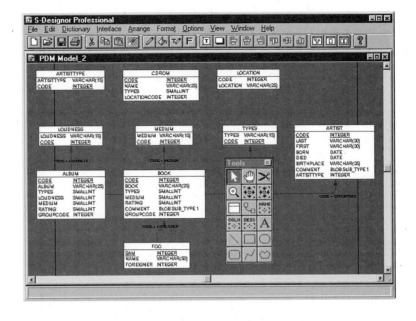

From the view shown in Figure 18.12, you can perform almost any action you want on the databases. You can physically move around the relative positions of the tables, and you can examine or redefine the metadata in any manner you choose. For example, if you look at Figure 18.13, you can see part of a list of all the indexes in the music database. The columns on the far right designate whether a particular index is primary, foreign, or unique, as designated by the columns headed by P, F, and U.

FIGURE 18.13.

Examining the indexes from the Music database.

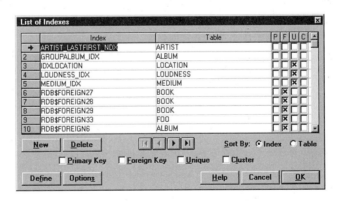

If you click the Define button at the bottom left of the dialog, you can edit an index. If you click the New button, you can create a New index, and—well, I'll leave it up to you to figure out what the Delete button does!

That's all I'm going to say about SDesigner. I'm sure you can tell from this brief introduction that this tool is very powerful. I have not touched on even one-tenth of the capabilities of this tool. For example, if you drop down the Dictionary menu, as in Figure 18.14, you can see some of the many features of this product.

FIGURE 18.14.

The Dictionary menu gives some hint to the capabilities to be found in SDesigner.

Of all the traits of a tool like SDesigner, perhaps the most important is the capability to give a visual overview of your database. You can often spot flaws in your database design after just a glance at one of these views.

ER1

ER1, a tool from Embarcadero Technologies Inc. (www.embarcadero.com, 415-834-3131), is comparable to SDesigner in terms of its scope and capabilities. It does not, however, have as large a presence in the market.

You can reverse-engineer a database in ER1 exactly as you did in SDesigner. Once again, the key to the process is having the ODBC drivers in place. The result of importing the Music database is shown in Figure 18.15. Notice the fancy zoom window in the bottom right of the screen; it shows the currently selected database in a mode that is easier to read. Both SDesigner and ER1 let you zoom in as much as you want on the view of a table, but this handy zoom window is particularly easy to use.

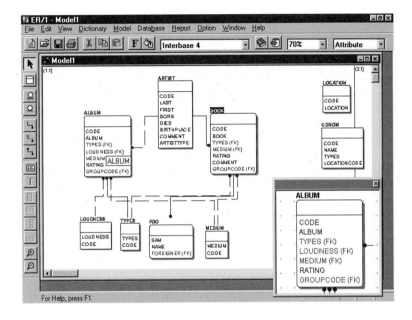

If you click any one table, you can pop up an Entity Editor window that lets you examine the attributes, columns, indexes, relationships, and other aspects of the table. Sample views of the Entity Editor are shown in Figure 18.16 and Figure 18.17.

FIGURE 18.16.

The Columns page in the Entity Editor from ER1.

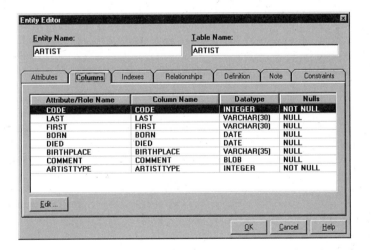

FIGURE 18.17.

*The Relationships page
in the Entity Editor
from ER1.*

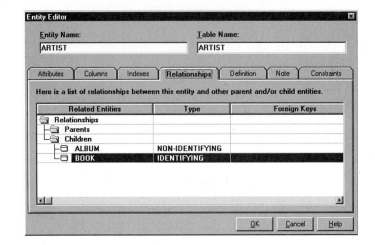

Some of the pages in the Entity Editor are designed to let you enter notes so that you can add comments about a particular table. Your comments, of course, will be attached specifically to a particular table, and they can be viewed by others who want to be apprised of your work or design.

SDesigner also gives you at least this much functionality, if not more. However, I do find that ER1 has a particularly clear view of the tables in a database, as well as a very cleverly designed interface. Remember that this description is not meant to be a comparative review of the two products, and you should definitely examine other sources of information before spending money on any of these tools.

These products all enable you to print out the diagrams they make of a database. You can then hang this printout on a communal bulletin board where it can be referenced or reviewed by others working on your team. In general, both SDesigner and ER1 have numerous features designed to aid a team of programmers in database design.

Cadet

I don't think the talented creator of Cadet would mind if I preface my overview of his product by stating that it is not as powerful as either SDesigner or ER1. It is a much cheaper product to buy, and you can get trial shareware versions for free from the Net. I should add, however, that Cadet has more to offer than the Data Model Designer from Paradox.

18

WORKING WITH
CASE TOOLS

NOTE

I should perhaps add here that price is a big issue on these products. The big professional database tools like ER1 and SDesigner can be very pricey. Finding a relatively affordable product like Cadet can be a boon to programmers. In fact, you should check the CD that accompanies this book to see whether it includes a trial version of Cadet.

Cadet can reverse-engineer an InterBase table via ODBC. Note, however, that you do not have as much detailed information available after you import. For example, no lines designate the links between the tables.

Cadet does, however, allow you to draw the relationships yourself using a few easy-to-master visual tools. If you take a few minutes to do this work, you can get a neat, easy-to-read diagram showing the relationship between the tables.

Finally, you can use Cadet to edit the metadata of your database. For example, you can create tables, edit the fields of the tables, or set up indexes.

That's all I'm going to say about Cadet in this book. Before closing this section, however, I want to point out what a great bargain Cadet can be for small programming houses or independent programmers. It does not pack the power of a tool such as ER1 or SDesigner, but it is still a very powerful tool that can dramatically improve your ability to manipulate and maintain a database. For example, take a look at a view from WISQL, as shown in Figure 18.18. When you get down to it, wouldn't you rather use Cadet than a tool like WISQL?

FIGURE 18.18.

WISQL provides a very primitive view of a database compared to what you see in a product like Cadet.

Summary

In this brief chapter, I have given you an overview of some of the CASE tools you can use with BCB. I have made no attempt to cover all the products in the field. I have also made no attempt to explore these products in depth, in large part because this book is about BCB, not about any third-party CASE tool, regardless of its merits.

I want to stress that the information shown in this chapter is not a form of review, nor have I tried to compare or rate these tools. On the contrary, my goal has been merely to make sure you are aware of the presence of these tools and of the fact that you can use them with BCB.

CASE and data modeling tools can provide an enormous boost to difficult database projects. If you work with databases all day long, then you probably ought to be using one of these tools. Certainly, they are worth careful consideration for anyone who works full-time in the field. As a rule, after you have spent a day or two with any one of them, you will find it difficult to consider programming without it.

Another great benefit of data modeling tools is that they can teach you a good deal about database design, and they can help steer you in the right direction when creating your data model. Just wandering through the menus of a product like SDesigner is an education in itself, and no one who has mastered the tool could ever be said to be less than a solid intermediate-level database programmer. Becoming an expert at using these tools is likely to improve the skills of most programmers and to add considerably to your knowledge of database design.

IV PART

Creating Components

Inheritance

IN THIS CHAPTER

This chapter focuses on object-oriented programming (OOP) as it applies to the VCL. Specifically, it takes a close look at *inheritance*, one of the big-three topics in object-oriented code. The other two key topics are *encapsulation* and *polymorphism*, which you learn about in the next two chapters. Even if you already know all about OOP, you should still at least skim this chapter so you can learn about the difference between VCL objects and standard C++ objects.

In particular, this chapter covers the following topics:

- OOP theory and basics
- VCL object construction
- Inheritance
- Virtual methods
- Aggregation
- Form inheritance

The text focuses on several programs designed to show how objects are constructed. One of the programs is developed in several stages so that you can see how an object hierarchy emerges out of a set of raw ideas.

After you read the next three chapters on inheritance, encapsulation, and polymorphism, the next big step is to learn how to build components. In fact, the real justification for learning this material is that it gives you the ability to start creating your own components. Building your own components is one of the most important tasks you can tackle in BCB, so I will lay the groundwork for it carefully.

It is important to understand that the next three chapters are aimed at programmers who want to work inside the VCL. I make no attempt to do justice to all the complex features of the C++ object model. Instead, I try to present you with a subset of those features as they apply to the VCL. This means that I make short shrift of interesting topics such as function and operator overloading. My intent, however, is to show you how to create components. You do not have to be an expert in C++ OOP theory to achieve that goal.

For all its wonders, I don't think there is anything in C++Builder that even approaches the significance of components. VCL components are the most amazing technological achievement I have seen in contemporary programming. If you want to do something really fantastic with your computer, then pay attention to the next few chapters so that you can learn how to build great components.

When reading this chapter, you might want to make use of the ClassBrowser sample program that ships with BCB. It allows you to explore the hierarchy of the VCL. This program is found in the Examples/ClassBrw directory. It is far from perfect, but it will serve to give you an overview of the VCL classes. You should also go to www.object-domain.com and see whether they have a version of Snorkle for C++Builder available. The versions of Snorkle for Delphi that I have seen are very nice indeed, and if they can duplicate their efforts in the world of C++, then most readers of this book will want to test their technology.

About Objects

It might seem a little strange to start focusing on objects this late in the book. After all, almost every program I have shown so far uses object-oriented code. So how could I wait this long to begin talking seriously about objects? To answer this question, I need to discuss two different issues:

- ■ How does BCB treat objects?
- ■ Why do people write object-oriented code?

The developers wanted BCB to be very easy to use. By its very nature, OOP is not always a simple topic. As a result, BCB goes to considerable lengths to hide some of the difficulties of object-oriented programming from the user. The biggest steps in this direction include the automatic construction of Form1 as an object and the existence of the delegation model. The fact that the scaffolding for most methods is produced automatically by the IDE is one of the key ways the product saves time—and one of the key ways it eases the process of producing applications.

The simple fact is that some people would never be able to approach BCB if they had to go through the process of writing all this every time they created a form:

```
//--------------------------------------------------------------
#ifndef Unit1H
#define Unit1H
//--------------------------------------------------------------
#include <vcl\Classes.hpp>
#include <vcl\Controls.hpp>
#include <vcl\StdCtrls.hpp>
#include <vcl\Forms.hpp>
//--------------------------------------------------------------
class TForm1 : public TForm
{
__published:
private:
public:          // User declarations
  virtual __fastcall TForm1(TComponent* Owner);
};
//--------------------------------------------------------------
extern TForm1 *Form1;
//--------------------------------------------------------------
#endif
```

I'm leaving out the implementation of the constructor, and a few other features, but in a stripped-down form, this code is indeed the basis for most BCB units. It's simple enough to write; none-theless, it could form a barrier between the product and certain types of programmers.

The next obvious question is, "Why did the developers choose to write object-oriented code if the subject itself can at times become somewhat complex? Why not just use the relatively simpler framework provided by structured programming?" The answer is that although it is simpler to create small structured programs than small object-oriented programs, it's easier to write large object-oriented programs than it is to write large structured programs.

19

OOP brings discipline and structure to a project. In the long run, this makes coding easier. The problem is the learning curve associated with understanding OOP.

Almost everyone agrees that it's easier to finish a group project if you appoint a leader for the group; it's easier to win at sports if you practice regularly; and, ultimately, it's easier to become a good musician if you sit through some boring lessons with a professional. It also might seem at first as if structured programs are simpler to learn how to write and, therefore, are simpler to write, but this isn't true. Just as it helps to take lessons, practice, and learn discipline if you want to become good at playing a sport or a musical instrument, it helps to learn object-oriented code if you want to write good programs.

Here's another way of stating the same matter. There is nothing you can do with object-oriented code that you can't also do with structured programming. It's just that OOP makes it relatively easy to construct programs that are fundamentally sound and easily maintained. This doesn't mean you can't write structured programs that are every bit as architecturally sound as object-oriented programs. The problem, however, is that it is very difficult to design a structured program that is truly modularized and truly easy to maintain. Object-oriented code, on the other hand, has a natural tendency to move you in the direction of a sound, well-structured design.

The thesis of this chapter is that object-oriented code is basically a technique for designing robust, well-planned programs. The syntax of OOP emerged out of the desire to help programmers design applications that work. It is perhaps arguable as to whether or not OOP by itself succeeded in achieving its goal, though certainly I personally believe that it is a success. However, I think it is undeniable that OOP in conjunction with components is the answer to many core programming problems. If your only experience with components is in creating ActiveX controls, then you haven't yet seen what this technology can do. The combination of OOP and components is something that can make programmers many times more productive than they had ever imagined possible when writing structured code, or when working with either objects or components alone.

> **NOTE**
>
> It's probably worth pointing out that OOP is not a separate subject from structured programming but its natural child. OOP emerged out of the same types of thinking that generated structured code. Much of what is true in structured programs is also true in object-oriented programs, except OOP takes these theories much further. Object-based programmers should know nearly everything that structured programmers know and should then add another layer of information on top of it.

OOP is certainly not the end-all and be-all of programming. Rather, it is an intermediate step in an ongoing process that might never have an end. BCB, with its heavy use of components, already shows part of what the future holds. In particular, the future is about components and visual manipulation of objects.

The Object Inspector enables you to see inside objects and to start to manipulate them visually. You can do this without having to write code. It is quite likely that this trend will continue in the future, and you will start to see programs not as code but as a series of objects depicted as a hierarchy. If programmers want to manipulate these objects, they will be able to do so through tools such as the Object Inspector or through other means currently being used only in experimental languages.

To take this out of the clouds for a moment, here is my list of what's best about BCB:

- Visual design tools
- A component architecture replete with a delegation model
- A real object-oriented language

Here are the same ideas looked at again from a slightly more in-depth perspective:

- Visual Tools: You can easily design a form using visual tools. To create a useful form, you want to be able to arrange and rearrange the elements of the visual design quickly and easily. BCB excels at this.

- Components: You want to be able to manipulate objects not only as code, but as seemingly physical entities you can handle with the mouse. Components provide an ideal solution to this problem. For example, the plastic Lego sets you played with as a child were fascinating because they enabled you to build complex structures out of simple, easy-to-manipulate pieces. In other words, Legos let you concentrate on the design of structures, making the actual construction of a robust and easy-to-maintain building relatively trivial. Components give the same kind of flexibility.

- OOP: Objects, and particularly the ability to view object hierarchies in a browser, make it easy to see the overall design of a program. It's possible to see how a program is constructed not only by looking at the code, but also by looking at an object hierarchy made up of reusable classes. Use the ClassBrowser example or a copy of Snorkle to view these hierarchies as they appear in your own programs. These kinds of abstract, visual representations of a code base aid in the process of designing and maintaining a program. A key word here is *reuse.* You can write an object once and then use it over and over again. Reusability is what OOP is all about.

OOP, then, is part of a theory of design that is moving increasingly in the direction of reusable, visual components that can be manipulated with the mouse. Undoubtedly, this means that some types of programs that are difficult to construct today will become trivial to build in the future. BCB has already performed this magic with databases. A 10-year-old child could use BCB to construct a simple database application. However, creating complex programs will probably always be difficult, simply because it is so hard to design a good program that performs anything more than trivial tasks. First printing presses, then typewriters, and finally word processors have made writing much easier than it used to be, but they have not succeeded in making us all into a race of Shakespeares.

NOTE

One thing that is not built into BCB that can help you create robust programs is a good object-modeling tool. There are some tools, such as the products called *WithClass and Snorkle*, that are designed to work with the Delphi VCL and should soon appear in a BCB-based format.

It is worth pointing out that it is easy to draw object hierarchies using some form of custom or agreed upon notation. Programs such as Visio or Playground can help with this process. Even if there is no direct code generation involved, there is still an enormous benefit to be derived from this process.

I have worked on projects I thought had gone hopelessly astray and could not ever be salvaged. These "lost causes" were saved by simply drawing out my object hierarchy with a tool that would let me rearrange its elements in several different patterns. C++ is a great language, but it offers no means for providing an overview of your object hierarchy. Drawing the object hierarchy with a simple object notation can help enormously when it is not clear how to design a particular feature or when you need to try to salvage a product that has gone astray.

BCB's object-oriented, component-based architecture makes programming easier than it used to be. That doesn't mean that now everyone will be able to program. It just means that now the best programmers can make better applications. The key terms are *reuse, visual design tools, components,* and *objects.* If you can find an object-modeling tool that can aid in program development, you will be even further ahead.

Creating Simple Objects

To start a discussion of objects, it might be a good idea to cut the VCL out of the picture as much as possible. This will eliminate the complex object hierarchy associated with the VCL. In its place, you can construct some very simple objects with a known hierarchy that is easy to define. As the discussion progresses, the VCL can be introduced into the programs in a planned and sensible manner.

1. Start a new project.
2. Bring up the Project Manager from the View menu and remove `Form1.cpp` and the project resource file.
3. Go to the View menu again and choose Project Source.
4. Go to Options | Project | Linker and choose Console application, as shown in Figure 19.1.

FIGURE 19.1.

Creating a console application in BCB.

Edit the main source file for the project so it looks like this:

```c
#include <stdio.h>
int main(void)
{
  printf("Daughters of Time, the hypocritic Days,\n");
  printf("Muffled and dumb like barefoot dervishes\n");
  printf("-- Ralph Waldo Emerson");
  return 0;
}
```

Save this file as `Object1.mak`. It is now a complete application that circumvents the VCL. If you open up a DOS window and run the program from the DOS prompt, the output looks like Figure 19.2.

FIGURE 19.2.

The output from the first take of the OBJECT1 program as it appears when run from the DOS prompt.

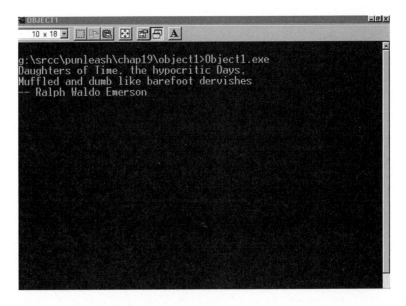

It might seem strange to you that I have gone out of my way to eliminate so much of the object hierarchy in a chapter that is about objects. My goal, however, is to clear the boards so that you can view objects in a simplified state, thereby clearly delineating their most salient points.

The program that unfolds through the next few pages is called OBJECT1. This is a very simple object-oriented program that you will build on the console application framework established earlier. I'm not going to start by showing you the code for the whole program, because I want you to build it one step at a time so that its structure emerges little by little.

To begin, you should create a small object at the top of the program:

```
class TMyObject
{
};

int main(void)
{
   return 0;
}
```

All I have done here is added a simple class definition and removed the `printf()`statements.

Delphi programmers should note that this class is not a descendant of TObject, even though it would have been in Object Pascal. One of the fundamental rules of Object Pascal programming is that it is impossible to build an object that is not a descendant of TObject or one of TObject's children. The reason for this rule is that TObject contains some RTTI-based intelligence that is needed by all BCB objects. This same intelligence is present in the metaclass that is part of the BCB version of TObject. However, you can create C++ objects that do not descend from TObject and thus do not include this intelligence.

> **NOTE**
>
> You will find that I use the words *class* and *object* almost completely interchangeably. This is technically correct, although there is some merit in using the word *class* to describe the written declarations that appear in a text file and *object* to refer to a compiled class that is part of a binary file. In other words, programs are made up of objects, whereas source files show class definitions. However, this distinction is not one that I spend a great deal of time stressing in this book.

To create a true VCL object, you should change TMyObject's definition so that it reads as follows:

```
#include <vcl\vcl.h>

class TMyObject : public TObject
{
public:
   __fastcall TMyObject(void) : TObject() {};
```

```
}

int main(void)
{
  return 0;
}
```

Logically, there is now a considerable difference between this declaration and the one you created earlier. In particular, this is now a VCL object and must be created on the heap. It also supports VCL specific syntax such as the __published directive.

All VCL objects must have a constructor, and it should be declared __fastcall. Methods or functions declared __fastcall can have some of their parameters passed in registers, rather than always being pushed on the stack. This is the calling convention used by VCL constructors, so you should conform to it.

All VCL objects that are descendants of TComponent must have destructors declared __fastcall virtual:

```
__fastcall virtual TComponent(TComponent* Aowner);
```

The reason for the __fastcall and virtual restrictions has to do with conformance to the VCL programming model. In particular, the VCL declares the constructor for TComponent as virtual, so C++ objects that descend from TComponent must follow along. This means that all components you create must be declared with virtual constructors, because all components are, at least in practice, descendants of TComponent. I comment on this fact simply because it is very unusual for C++ constructors to be declared virtual.

> **NOTE**
>
> Actually, it is theoretically possible for you to create your own class that performs the same chores that TComponent performs. There is nothing magical about TComponent; it simply contains standard VCL code that makes it possible for an object to live on the Component Palette. It is not practical to duplicate this effort in your own code, and so one could perhaps go so far as to say that "by definition" all components are descendants of TComponent. However, this is not strictly true, as you could create your own class that appears on the Component Palette without descending from TComponent. I personally cannot imagine any set of circumstances that would justify the effort involved in duplicating the work done in TComponent.

The declaration and implementation for a C++ constructor can have two forms. They can appear entirely inside a class declaration, or you can split them up, with the declaration inside the class and the implementation outside:

```
#include <vcl\vcl.h>

class TMyObject : public TObject
```

19

INHERITANCE

```
{
public:
    __fastcall TMyObject(void);
};

__fastcall TMyObject::TMyObject(void) : TObject()
{
}

int main(void)
{
   return 0;
}
```

When you implement a constructor, you should follow the header with a colon and a call to the ancestor's constructor:

```
_fastcall TMyObject::TMyObject(void) : TObject()
```

Now that you have an overview of a basic VCL object declaration, the next step is to declare a variable of type TMyObject and then instantiate it and dispose of it:

```
class TMyObject : public TObject
{
public:
    __fastcall TMyObject() : TObject()  {}
};

int main(void)
{
   TMyObject *MyObject = new TMyObject;
   delete MyObject;
   return 0;
}
```

The code shown here doesn't do anything functional. Its only purpose is to teach you how objects work. Specifically, it declares a variable of type TMyObject:

```
TMyObject *MyObject
```

Next, it allocates the memory for the object:

```
new TMyObject;
```

Put together on one line, the statement looks like this:

```
TMyObject *MyObject = new TMyObject;
```

This statement actually creates a pointer variable of type TMyObject. In VCL programming, you have to take this step if you want to use MyObject, and, furthermore, you must dispose of this memory when you are finished with it.

There are two ways to destroy an object. One is to call Free, and the other is to use the delete operator:

```
MyObject->Free();
delete MyObject;
```

Both techniques have the same outcome. I believe the majority of people prefer `delete`, and it is what I use most often in the code found in this book. However, there are reasons you might want to call `Free`, so I will discuss it in the next few paragraphs.

When you free an object, what you are really doing is calling the object's destructor. The following code shows approximately what takes place in the `Free` method of `TObject`:

```
procedure TObject.Free;
begin
  if Self <> nil then
    Destroy;
end;
```

The variable `Self` always points to the current object. It plays the same role in Object Pascal that `this` plays in C++. If you are inside one of the methods of an object, you can refer to that object by using `Self`. (`Self` is passed as an implicit parameter to all BCB methods.) Here is how the VCL `Free` method would look in C++:

```
void __fastcall TObject::Free()
{
  if (this != NULL)
    ~TObject();
}
```

> **NOTE**
>
> Programmers use the words *descendant*, *child object*, *derived class*, and *subclass* as synonyms. I prefer to use either *descendant* or *child object*, because *subclass* is also used in another context and *derived class* seems unnecessarily obscure. My feeling is that it's best to stick to one metaphor: parent, child, ancestor, and descendant, where *child* and *descendant* are synonymous, and *parent* and *ancestor* are synonymous.

Standard C++ does not define a `Free` method. This is something specific to the VCL. It is added to the VCL to make objects easier to use. It is very bad to call the destructor of an object that no longer exists. As a result, the `Free` method is there to provide a check that gives you some measure of protection against this error. Despite this, the general consensus is that it is best to call delete. The great virtue of delete is that it looks like standard C++ code, and C++ programmers care a lot about standards.

Now that you know how to declare, allocate, and deallocate a simple object, it's time to narrow the focus and tackle the subject of inheritance. The next two sections are dedicated to this chore—specifically, to explaining the relationship between a parent and child object.

Understanding Inheritance

In general, a child object can use any of its parent's methods. A descendant of an object gets the benefit of its parent's capabilities, plus any new capabilities it might bring to the table. I say that this is true in general, because the private directive can limit the capability of a child to call some of its parent's routines. The private directive is explained in depth later in this chapter.

Except for its constructor, all of TMyObject's methods and fields are inherited:

```
class TMyObject : public TObject
{
public:
   __fastcall TMyObject() : TObject()  {}
};
```

This declaration is somewhat deceiving because TObject contains many methods that are available to instances of TMyObject. In other words, TMyObject is not quite as simple an object as it appears at first.

So, what are all these methods associated with TObject? Well, you can see their definitions, as well as their implementations, if you open up the SysDefs.h file from the \BCB\Include\VCL subdirectory:

```
class   __declspec(delphiclass) TObject
{
  public:
    __fastcall TObject() {}
    __fastcall Free();
    TClass __fastcall ClassType();
    void __fastcall CleanupInstance();
    void * __fastcall FieldAddress(const ShortString &Name);
    static TObject * __fastcall InitInstance(TClass cls, void *instance);
    static ShortString __fastcall ClassName(TClass cls);
    static bool __fastcall ClassNameIs(TClass cls, const AnsiString string);
    static TClass __fastcall ClassParent(TClass cls);
    static void * __fastcall ClassInfo(TClass cls);
    static long __fastcall InstanceSize(TClass cls);
    static bool __fastcall InheritsFrom(TClass cls, TClass aClass);
    static void * __fastcall MethodAddress(TClass cls, const ShortString &Name);
    static ShortString __fastcall MethodName(TClass cls, void *Address);
    ...// Code omitted here
    virtual void __fastcall Dispatch(void *Message);
    virtual void __fastcall DefaultHandler(void* Message);
  private:
    virtual TObject* __fastcall NewInstance(TClass cls);
  public:
    virtual void __fastcall FreeInstance();
    virtual __fastcall ~TObject() {}
};
```

You can find the entire implementation of TObject in the Object Pascal System.pas unit that ships with BCB. Much of it is actually in assembler, but the source is there if you want to study it. You should, of course, also examine the declaration for TObject in SysDefs.h. The calls in

SysDefs.h, however, ultimately resolve into calls to the Pascal implementation in System.pas. I should perhaps add that the TObject declaration in SysDefs.h is very hard to understand, but I promise you that it does end up resolving into calls that access the System.pas version of TObject.

> **NOTE**
>
> Although I have mentioned this subject before, it's probably once again time to stress the importance of viewing the Pascal source code to the VCL. Your version of BCB might or might not ship with the source, but if you don't have it and can possibly afford to buy it, you should think seriously about obtaining it. You should peruse the BCB\Include\VCL subdirectory that contains the header files for the imported VCL Pascal units. These files provide the interface for key BCB units. They are not as good as having the source, but they are very valuable. I refer to both the header files and the Pascal source continuously.

You can see that TObject has a few basic functions declared right at the top:

```
__fastcall TObject() {}
__fastcall Free();
virtual __fastcall ~TObject() {}
```

The point to grasp here is that TMyObject has a destructor and Free method because it inherits them from TObject.

To understand this point, you can add a line of code to the nascent OBJECT1 program:

```
#include <conio.h>
#include <stdio.h>
int main(void)
{
  TMyObject *MyObject = new TMyObject;
  AnsiString S = MyObject->ClassName();
  printf(S.c_str());
  delete MyObject;
  getch();
  return 0;
}
```

This code enables the object to write its name to the screen. The output from this program is a single string:

TMyObject

When you run the program, this string might flash by too quickly for leisurely perusal. To remedy the situation, add a getch() at the very end of the code, right before the return statement. To end this program, press Enter. (That's the way it used to be done back in the DOS world.)

If you want to, you can even get this object to say its parent's name:

```
int main(void)
{
  TMyObject *MyObject = new TMyObject;
  printf(Format("ClassName: %s\nParent's ClassName: %s",
    OPENARRAY(TVarRec, (
      MyObject->ClassName(),
      MyObject->ClassParent()->ClassName())))).c_str());

  delete MyObject;
  getch();
  return 0;
}
```

The output from this code is the following:

```
ClassName: TMyObject
Parent's ClassName: TObject
```

The point, of course, is that TMyObject inherits quite a bit of functionality from its parent, and, as a result, it has numerous capabilities that might not be obvious from merely viewing its declaration.

The ability to trace an object's ancestry is relatively appealing, so it might be nice to add it to TMyObject as a method:

```
#include <vcl/vcl.h>
#include <stdio.h>
#include <conio.h>
#include "classrefs.h"
USEUNIT("ClassRefs.cpp");

class TMyObject : public TObject
{
public:
  TMyObject() : TObject()  {}
  void PrintString(AnsiString S);
  void ShowHierarchy();
};

void TMyObject::PrintString(AnsiString S)
{
  printf("%s\n", S.c_str());
}

void TMyObject::ShowHierarchy()
{
  TClass AClass;

  AnsiString AClassName = AnsiString(ClassName()).c_str();
  PrintString(AClassName);
  AClass = ClassParent();
  while (AClass)
  {
    AClassName = AnsiString(AClass->ClassName());
    PrintString(AClassName);
```

```
        AClass = AClass->ClassParent();
    }
}

int main(void)
{
    ShowClassReferences();
    TMyObject *MyObject = new TMyObject;
    MyObject->ShowHierarchy();
delete MyObject;
    getch();
    return 0;
}
```

This version of the OBJECT1 program includes two methods, listed in the TMyObject class declaration:

```
class TMyObject : public TObject
{
public:
    TMyObject() : TObject()  {}
    void PrintString(AnsiString S);
    void ShowHierarchy();
};
```

Take a look at the implementation for ShowHierarchy. Perhaps the first thing you notice in it is the class reference in the first line, which uses the TClass type.

The type TClass is an object reference and is declared in Sysdefs.h as follows:

```
typedef TMetaClass* TClass;
```

Because ClassParent returns a variable of type TClass, it is obviously what needs to be used here.

NOTE

An *object reference* is a special metaclass that can be assigned to an object. Here is a unit that shows some legal uses of an object reference:

```
//////////////////////////////////////
// ClassRefs.cpp
// Object1
// copyright (c) 1997 by Charlie Calvert
//
#include <vcl\vcl.h>
#include <forms.hpp>
#pragma hdrstop
#include "ClassRefs.h"
TClass AClass;
  class TDescendant: public TObject
  {
  public:
    TDescendant(): TObject() {}
```

continues

19

INHERITANCE

continued

```
  };
void ShowClassReferences()
{
  printf("** Start object references **\n");
  AClass = __classid(TObject);
  printf("%s\n", AnsiString(AClass->ClassName()).c_str());
  AClass = __classid(TDescendant);
  printf("%s\n", AnsiString(AClass->ClassName()).c_str());
  AClass = __classid(TForm);
  printf("%s\n", AnsiString(AClass->ClassName()).c_str());
  printf("** End object references **\n\n");
}
```

Notice that you do not have to create an object before you can use it with an `object reference`. In general, you can call any of the static methods of `TObject` with a class reference.

You cannot use an object reference to refer to a field that belongs only to the child of the `object reference` type. For instance, this code does not compile because `Caption` is not a property of `TObject`:

```
ObjectRef = __classid(TForm)
ObjectRef.Caption := 'Sam';
WriteLn(ObjectRef.Caption);
```

You will find a version of the `CLSREF` unit in the same subdirectory as OBJECT1. You can use the Project Manager to add this file to the project, and you can then call it in the second line of the body of the OBJECT1 program. However, you should not leave this unit as part of the project, because it will muddy the view of the object hierarchy that you get in the Browser.

There are not that many times in which you need to use an object reference in day-to-day programming. If you are not totally clear on what they do, you can probably afford to skip the subject. If you really want to know more, you should examine `Sysdefs.h`; recognize that the `TMetaClass` you see there is the C++ way of creating a feature that exists in the VCL. The reason the VCL supports this feature is that it needs fairly extensive Run Time Type Information (RTTI) in order to run, and it gets a good portion of that information from the methods in `TObject` that are part of `TMetaClass` and are in turn used in an object reference.

When you get past the object reference, the remaining portions of the `ShowHierarchy` method are fairly straightforward:

```
void TMyObject::ShowHierarchy()
{
  TClass AClass;
  AnsiString AClassName = AnsiString(ClassName()).c_str();
  PrintString(AClassName);
  AClass = ClassParent();
  while (AClass)
  {
```

```
    AClassName = AnsiString(AClass->ClassName());
    PrintString(AClassName);
    AClass = AClass->ClassParent();
  }
}
```

This code first writes the `ClassName` of the current object, which is `TMyObject`. Then it gets the `ClassParent`, which is `TObject`, and writes its name to the screen. The code then tries to get `TObject`'s parent and fails, because `TObject` has no parent. At this point, `AClass` is set to `NULL` and the code exits the `while` loop. The output for the program is shown in Figure 19.3.

FIGURE 19.3.

The output from the OBJECT1 program.

In this section, you have learned about the `Create`, `Destroy`, `Free`, `ClassParent`, and `ClassName` methods of `TObject`. The declaration of `TObject` shows that several other methods are available to BCB programmers. However, I do not discuss these methods in depth because they are either self-explanatory (`InheritsFrom`) or beyond the scope of this book. I should mention, however, that some of these routines are used by the compiler itself when dispatching routines or performing other complex tasks that usually require RTTI support. These are advanced programming issues that impact only a very small percentage of BCB programmers.

Virtual Methods

Inheritance, in itself, is an interesting feature, but it would not take on much significance were it not for the presence of *virtual methods*. Virtual methods can be overridden in a descendant class. As such, they provide the key to polymorphism, which is a trait of OOP programs that enables you to give the same command to two different objects but have them respond in different ways. This chapter introduces polymorphism, but I will leave the more complex aspects of this subject for Chapter 21, titled, appropriately enough, "Polymorphism." Polymorphism is a relatively difficult subject to grasp; therefore, I have stretched out a full explanation of it over several chapters.

Unlike Object Pascal, BCB has only one type of virtual method. This directive tells the compiler to store the address of the function in a virtual method table.

> **NOTE**
>
> Delphi programmers should note that C++ does not support either the dynamic or message directives. In their place, you can use the MESSAGE_MAP macro.

The OBJECT2 program (shown in Listing 19.2) has one `virtual` method. The `virtual` method is overridden in a child object. When you are creating the OBJECT2 program, you should start with the source code for the OBJECT1 program. Modify the code by declaring `PrintString` as `virtual` and by creating a descendant of `TMyObject` called `THierarchy`. Also, don't forget to make sure the program is set to work as a console application. If you don't have this option checked, you can get an `EInOutError` exception. After changing the setting, you should also rebuild your project so the new option takes effect.

> **NOTE**
>
> When creating one project based on another, you can often copy the code from the directory where the first project is stored into a separate directory made for the second project. After copying the project, it is probably simplest to delete everything but the actual source files from the new directory. For instance, delete the DSK file, the MAK file, and any other extraneous files you will not need. Then create a new project, delete its main form, and add copies of the source files you want to reuse from the previous project. Otherwise, you might find paths hard-coded into your DSK or MAK files that address files stored in the first program's directory. In this particular case, it is probably easiest just to re-create the project entirely from scratch, but the information in this note can be used as a general set of guidelines for use when copying projects from one directory to another.

Listing 19.2. The source code for the main unit in the OBJECT2 program.

```
////////////////////////////////////////
// Object2.cpp
// Project: Object2
// Copyright (c) 1997 by Charlie Calvert
//
#include <vcl/vcl.h>
#include <stdio.h>
#include <conio.h>

class TMyObject :public TObject
{
```

```
public:
  TMyObject() : TObject()  {}
  void ShowHierarchy();
  virtual void PrintString(AnsiString S);
};


class THierarchy: public TMyObject
{
  int FColor;
public:
  THierarchy() : TMyObject() {}
  virtual void PrintString(AnsiString S);
  __property int Color={read=FColor,write=FColor};
};

void TMyObject::PrintString(AnsiString S)
{
  printf("%s\n", S.c_str());
}

void TMyObject::ShowHierarchy()
{
  TClass AClass;

  AnsiString AClassName = AnsiString(ClassName()).c_str();
  PrintString(AClassName);

  AClass = ClassParent();
  while (AClass)
  {
    AClassName = AnsiString(AClass->ClassName());
    PrintString(AClassName);
    AClass = AClass->ClassParent();
  }
}

void THierarchy::PrintString(AnsiString S)
{
  char Temp[250];

  textcolor(FColor);
  sprintf(Temp, "%s\n\r", S.c_str());
  cputs(Temp);
}

int main(void)
{
  TMyObject *MyObject = new TMyObject();
  MyObject->ShowHierarchy();
  MyObject->Free();

  THierarchy *Hierarchy = new THierarchy();
  Hierarchy->Color = YELLOW;
  Hierarchy->ShowHierarchy();
  Hierarchy->Free();

  getch();
  return 0;
}
```

In OBJECT1, the ShowHierarchy method wrote its output to the screen. Suppose that you found this object somewhere and liked the way it worked but wanted to change its behavior so it could also write its output in color. The OBJECT2 program shows a preliminary version of how you might proceed. After completing this first take on creating a descendant of TMyObject, I will revisit the subject and show ways to improve the model shown here. The output from the program is shown in Figure 19.4.

FIGURE 19.4.

The output from the OBJECT2 program.

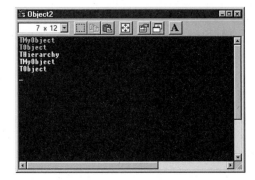

In the old world of structured programming, the most likely step would be to rewrite the original ShowHierarchy method. However, rewriting an existing method can be a problem for two reasons:

■ You might not have the source code to the routine, so you can't rewrite it. This is a common problem because most programming tools are delivered in binary libraries.

■ You might have the source code but also know that this particular method is already being called by several different programmers. You, therefore, might be afraid to rewrite it because you might break the other programmers' code. Furthermore, making changes like this cuts you off from the upgrade path provided by the maker of the library. You can't just use the maker's next version of the product out of the box, because you now have a customized version of his or her library.

A combination of design and maintenance issues might deter the impulse to rewrite the original method. Many projects have been delayed or mothballed because changes in their designs have broken existing code and thrown the entire project into chaos.

OOP has a simple solution to this whole problem. Instead of declaring TMyObject as

```
class TMyObject :public TObject
{
public:
  TMyObject() : TObject()  {}
  void ShowHierarchy();
  void PrintString(AnsiString S);
};
```

thoughtful programmers declare it like this:

```
class TMyObject :public TObject
{
public:
  TMyObject() : TObject()  {}
  void ShowHierarchy();
  virtual void PrintString(AnsiString S);
};
```

The difference is that in the second example, the PrintString method is declared as virtual.

If PrintString is declared as virtual, you can override it in a descendant object, thereby changing the way the method works without ever changing the original version of the method. This means that all the other code that relies on the first version of the program continues to work, and yet you can rewrite the function for your own purposes. Furthermore, this technique would work even if you didn't have the source code for TMyObject! I will show you how this works in just a moment.

Some readers might have asked themselves earlier why I created the PrintString method in the first place. The answer hinges on the fact that iterating through a hierarchy of VCL objects can always be accomplished by the same algorithm. The same technique works for all VCL objects. But the act of printing information to the screen changes depending on your current circumstances. Are you in DOS? Are you in Windows? Do you want to use colors? Each of these circumstances calls for a different way of printing information to the screen. As a result, I separated the screen IO portion of TMyObject from the portion of the object that iterates through a hierarchy. Furthermore, there is no need to declare ShowHierarchy as virtual, but I must declare PrintString as virtual. The reasoning here is simply that ShowHierarchy does not need to change in descendants of the object, but PrintString will need to change. In particular, it will need to change so that it can write output in color. These types of considerations are part of a subject known as *object design*.

At this point, you might think that using virtual methods seems like an unnecessarily opaque solution to this problem. Wouldn't it have been simpler to add new methods to the inherited class? Then the user of this second class could call these new methods rather than the ones from the first instance of the class. There are three problems with this technique:

■ It requires the user to memorize a whole slew of different method names that perform related but slightly different tasks. This is precisely what you have to do in structured programming, and it is exactly what you want to avoid. Instead, you want to have one name that applies to all similar methods of this family. For instance, if you have an animal object, you are going to have to make the Walk method virtual because a bird walks on two legs, and a cat walks on four. The implementation of Walk is different for each animal, so you need to declare the method virtual. When you are done, you can use Cat->Walk(), and the cat will walk properly. Conversely, you can use Bird->Walk(), and the bird will walk properly. It would be a mess if you had to use Bird->WalkOnTwoLegs() and Cat->WalkOnFourLegs(). This proliferation of similar but

19

INHERITANCE

slightly different method names is exactly the kind of structured programming fiasco that OOP was designed to avoid. Instead of a bunch of similar names like `WalkOnTwoLegs`, `CrawlOnYourBelly`, `WalkOnFourLegs`, and `WalkOnOneHundredLegs`, you want to have just one word, such as `Walk`, that applies to a whole family of objects. In other words, each object in the family will implement the `walk` method differently.

■ The second problem is that these objects call the `PrintString` method internally. If you did not declare the method as `virtual`, you would have to figure out some way for the `ShowHierarchy` method to know whether it should call the implementation of `PrintString` that is part of `TMyObject`, or whether it should call the implementation that is part of `THierarchy`. By declaring a method as `virtual`, this chore will be handled for you automatically. If you create an instance of `THierarchy`, `ShowHierarchy` will call `THierarchy->PrintString` automatically; and if you create an instance of `TMyObject`, it will call `TMyObject->PrintString`. This is the way OOP handles virtual methods, and it is one of the key concepts that makes this system work.

■ The final, and best, reason for doing things this way has to do with polymorphism. As such, it may not be clear to all readers at this time, but I promise that it will make sense after you have read the polymorphism chapter. You can declare a pointer of type `TMyObject` that can be assigned to a pointer of type `THierarchy`. When you then call `TMyObject->PrintString()`, the `PrintString` method of `THierarchy` will be called even though the object instance is of type `TMyObject`. This would not occur if `PrintString` were not declared `virtual`. In fact, this behavior is what polymorphism is all about, and indeed, it is one of the cornerstones of OOP programming.

The word *virtual* is inherited from one class to the next. If a base class declares a method `virtual`, the descendants need not do so, because they will inherit the `virtual` declaration for a particular method from the base class. Delphi users take note, as this is the exact opposite of what happens in Object Pascal. I should add that it is generally considered bad form not to repeat the declaration in child objects, as you want to be sure the reader of your code can see at a glance how it is structured.

Here is a look at a stripped-down descendant of `TMyObject` that overrides the `PrintString` method:

```
class THierarchy: public TMyObject
{
  int FColor;
public:
  THierarchy() : TMyObject() {}
  virtual void PrintString(AnsiString S);
  __property int Color={read=FColor,write=FColor};
};
```

This declaration states that class `THierarchy` is a descendant of class `TMyObject` and that it over-rides `PrintString`.

A first take on the new version of the PrintString method looks like this:

```
void THierarchy::PrintString(AnsiString S)
{
  char Temp[250];
  textcolor(FColor);
  sprintf(Temp, "%s\n\r", S.c_str());
  cputs(Temp);
}
```

This code depends on functionality from Conio.h that allows you to print strings to the screen in color.

You can see that a field called FColor has been added to this object: THierarchy now contains not only procedures but also data. One of the key aspects of class declarations is that they can contain both methods and data, so that you can bring all the code related to the THierarchy object together in one place. This is part of a concept called *encapsulation*, explained in the next chapter.

When you run the OBJECT2 program, the following code is executed in its main body:

```
int main(void)
{
  TMyObject *MyObject = new TMyObject();
  MyObject->ShowHierarchy();
  MyObject->Free();
  THierarchy *Hierarchy = new THierarchy();
  Hierarchy->Color = GREEN;
  Hierarchy->ShowHierarchy();
  Hierarchy->Free();
  getch();
  return 0;
}
```

This code creates an object of type THierarchy and then shows you how to use the new functionality of the ShowHierarchy method. I also create an instance of TMyObject so that you can compare the two classes demonstrated so far in this chapter.

> **NOTE**
>
> I should perhaps mention that it is more expensive to declare or call virtual methods than it is to call a static method. As a result, you need to weigh the whole issue of whether you want to declare a method to be virtual.
>
> In my opinion, you should usually create objects that have the best possible design, regardless of the amount of overhead they entail. Of course, it is possible to take this theory too far, but the mere fact of adding a few virtual methods is usually not the problem in bloated object hierarchies.
>
> Besides space and performance, a second reason for not declaring an object virtual is a desire to hide its implementation so you can change it later. There is usually no point in declaring a private method virtual, because it can't be seen by other objects, unless they are friends of the original object. (I will talk about *friend objects* later in this chapter.) The great advantage of private methods is that they can always be changed later to whatever degree you want, because other objects usually cannot see them and cannot access them directly. As a result, you may want to declare methods private, and non-virtual, so you can change their implementation later on. Needless to say, I am referring specifically to the act of changing the number of parameters these methods take.
>
> Your users will, of course, complain if you take a method they occasionally want to override and make it private and non-virtual. However, it is sometimes better to listen to their complaints than to saddle them with a broken object that cannot be fixed without breaking existing code.

In this section, you have learned about the virtual directive. This subject's true significance won't be clear until you read about polymorphism. However, before you tackle that subject, it's best to learn more about inheritance and encapsulation. In particular, the next section of the chapter looks at more issues involving object design.

Searching for the Right Design

It is almost impossible to find the right design for an object the first time you write it. As a rule, the only way you can figure out the design for an object is by creating it, discovering its limitations, and then making improvements to its design. In short, object design is an iterative process.

There is no good way to step you through the process of discovering the correct object design in a book, because the written word is by its nature static, and the process I'm describing is dynamic. Furthermore, it's confusing to the reader to show a series of poorly designed objects that are successively improved in each iteration. The problem with this technique is that the reader keeps seeing the *wrong* way to create an object and can easily pick up bad habits or fundamental misconceptions about object design. Even worse, the reader tends to get frustrated with having to unlearn the techniques they just acquired in the previous example that are now revealed as being flawed.

To avoid the problems outlined in the preceding paragraph, I will simply show you a second version of the THierarchy object and explain why it contains changes to the original version of the object you saw in the last section. This process does not tell you much about how I discovered the flaws in the object, but it will show you what the flaws are and how I got around them. The main point to grasp is that object design is an iterative process, and that the correct way to find the flaws in an object is to implement them once as best you can, and then look for problems.

> **NOTE**
>
> There is a second school of thought that states that you can find the correct design for an object before implementing it. Proponents of this technique often suggest that a team be split in two, with part of the members designing objects and the other part implementing them. I have to confess that I've never actually discussed the results of this technique with someone who has used it successfully, as all my experience has been with programmers who use the iterative technique I discuss here. (Some of these programmers have also tried the second school of programming, but it did not work for them.)
>
> Of course, you should try to get an object right the first time, and you should use high-level tools that help with design. However, you should also expect to have to refine the objects you create through a perhaps lengthy, iterative process.
>
> Furthermore, you should design your object defensively. That is, you should carefully hide your implementation inside private methods and data because you will surely have to change its design at a later time.

The first problem with the original version of the THierarchy object became clear when I wanted to find a method to clear the screen. When doing so, I needed to first set the text and background color to which I wanted the screen to be cleared. As a result, I added new properties and new set methods to the object. The new property let me add a background color, and the set methods let me change the text and background colors at the same time I assigned them to the private data:

```
class THierarchy: public TMyObject
{
  int FTextColor;
  int FBackColor;
protected:
  virtual void SetTextColor(int Color)
    { FTextColor = Color; textcolor(FTextColor); }
```

```
   virtual void SetBackColor(int Color)
     { FBackColor = Color; textbackground(FBackColor); }
public:
  THierarchy() : TMyObject() {}
  virtual void PrintString(AnsiString S);
  virtual void ClrScr();
  __property int TextColor={read=FTextColor,write=SetTextColor};
  __property int BackColor={read=FBackColor,write=SetBackColor};
};
```

The implementation of PrintString now looks like this:

```
void THierarchy::PrintString(AnsiString S)
{
  char Temp[250];
  sprintf(Temp, "%s\n\r", S.c_str());
  cputs(Temp);
}
```

Note that I have removed the code that changed the color of the text. This code is no longer necessary as the color gets changed in the SetTextColor method.

The extremely straightforward implementation of ClrScr looks like this:

```
void THierarchy::ClrScr()
{
  clrscr();
}
```

> **NOTE**
>
> C++ allows you to declare methods inline, as shown by the SetTextColor and SetBackColor method declarations. Conversely, you can also declare a method outside of the object, as I do in the case of ClrScr. This latter technique is called an out_of_line declaration, but that has such a ghastly ring in my ear that I refuse to use it.
>
> You can, in fact, implement a method outside an object and make it inline by using the inline directive:
>
> ```
> inline void SetTextColor(int Color)
> {
>   FTextColor = Color;
>   textcolor(FTextColor);
> }
> ```
>
> Inline methods usually execute faster than regular methods because they are placed directly in your code and do not require the overhead associated with a function call. Whether you implement them inside or outside of a class declaration, you should declare only very small methods as inline, and they should not contain any loops.
>
> Inline methods are great, and I use them regularly. The only drawback I see to them is that they can make object declarations difficult to read. In particular, the great thing about an object declaration is that it can provide a summary of the functionality of an object without asking you to wade through its implementation. Inline methods implemented inside a class declaration detract from this feature because they clutter up the landscape.

> One possible workaround is to declare inline functions separately from the object declaration by using the `inline` keyword. In fact, this is probably the ideal solution, and it is only laziness that keeps me from using it at all times. I, for one, would have been glad if the compiler enforced this rule.

The next change I made to THierarchy involved a desire to increase the flexibility of the object. In particular, it would be great to be able to use this object even if you do not descend from it directly. One way to do this is via multiple inheritance, but that technology is not supported by VCL objects. I should perhaps add that I am not particularly partial to multiple inheritance as a technology for use in real-world applications.

A much simpler way to make the object more flexible is to pass the ShowHierarchy method a copy of the object whose hierarchy you want to explore:

```
void TMyObject::ShowHierarchy(TObject *AnObject)
{
  TClass AClass;

  AnsiString AClassName = AnsiString(AnObject->ClassName()).c_str();
  PrintString(AClassName);
  AClass = AnObject->ClassParent();
  while (AClass)
  {
    AClassName = AnsiString(AClass->ClassName());
    PrintString(AClassName);
    AClass = AClass->ClassParent();
  }
}
```

The interesting thing about this change is that it occurs at the level of the TMyObject implementation and declaration. In other words, it represents changes not to THierarchy but to TMyObject. If this object were of more earth-shaking import and if I had released TMyObject to the public, I could not have made this sort of change because I would be breaking the code of those who already called the ShowHierarchy method. There are, I suppose, three things you can learn from this example:

1. Try not to publish any part of an object hierarchy until you are sure you can live with its current public interface.

2. Hide your implementation. Avoid letting consumers of your objects directly call one of the methods that involves a significant part of your implementation.

3. Object design is an art, not a science. There is no such thing as a perfect object. All objects have flaws. Plan them out carefully ahead of time, bring them to fruition by a lengthy iterative process, and then send them out into the world with the understanding that your design is flawed by definition. Recognize that you are going to have to support the objects you send into the world, because your users are going to find flaws in them. It is the mark of an amateur to stonewall the consumer of an object when he or she offers intelligent criticism of an object implementation. Likewise, it is naïve for

19

INHERITANCE

the consumer of an object to expect it to be perfect. Perfection is too high a goal. Instead, shoot for high quality, and then demand that object producers provide fixes when flaws are discovered. Fixes need not arrive immediately, but they should appear in the next version of the product.

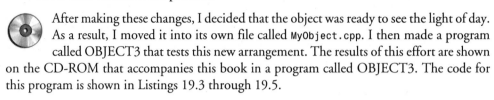 After making these changes, I decided that the object was ready to see the light of day. As a result, I moved it into its own file called MyObject.cpp. I then made a program called OBJECT3 that tests this new arrangement. The results of this effort are shown on the CD-ROM that accompanies this book in a program called OBJECT3. The code for this program is shown in Listings 19.3 through 19.5.

Listing 19.3. `TMyObject` and `THierarchy` now reside in their own file, called `MyObject`.

```
/////////////////////////////////////
// MyObject.h
// Learning how to use objects
// Copyright (c) 1997 by Charlie Calvert
//
#ifndef MyObjectH
#define MyObjectH
#include <conio.h>
#include <vcl\stdctrls.hpp>

class TMyObject :public TObject
{
public:
  TMyObject() : TObject()  {}
  void ShowHierarchy(TObject *AnObject);
  virtual void PrintString(AnsiString S);
};

class THierarchy: public TMyObject
{
  int FTextColor;
  int FBackColor;
protected:
  virtual void SetTextColor(int Color)
    { FTextColor = Color; textcolor(FTextColor); }
  virtual void SetBackColor(int Color)
    { FBackColor = Color; textbackground(FBackColor); }
public:
  THierarchy() : TMyObject() {}
  virtual void PrintString(AnsiString S);
  virtual void ClrScr();
  __property int TextColor={read=FTextColor,write=SetTextColor};
  __property int BackColor={read=FBackColor,write=SetBackColor};
};

#endif
```

Listing 19.4. The implementation for TMyObject and THierarchy are shown here in MyObject.cpp.

```
//////////////////////////////////////
// MyObject.cpp
// Learning how to use objects
// Copyright (c) 1997 by Charlie Calvert
//
#include <vcl\vcl.h>
#include <conio.h>
#pragma hdrstop
#include "myobject.h"

void TMyObject::PrintString(AnsiString S)
{
  printf("%s\n", S.c_str());
}

void TMyObject::ShowHierarchy(TObject *AnObject)
{
  TClass AClass;

  AnsiString AClassName = AnsiString(AnObject->ClassName()).c_str();
  PrintString(AClassName);

  AClass = AnObject->ClassParent();
  while (AClass)
  {
    AClassName = AnsiString(AClass->ClassName());
    PrintString(AClassName);
    AClass = AClass->ClassParent();
  }
}

void THierarchy::PrintString(AnsiString S)
{
  char Temp[250];

  sprintf(Temp, "%s\n\r", S.c_str());
  cputs(Temp);
}

void THierarchy::ClrScr()
{
  clrscr();
}
```

Listing 19.5. The test program for the MyObject unit.

```
#include <vcl\vcl.h>
#include <conio.h>
#pragma hdrstop
#include "myobject.h"
USEUNIT("MyObject.cpp");
void main()
{
```

continues

Listing 19.5. continued

```
THierarchy *H = new THierarchy();
H->TextColor = YELLOW;
H->BackColor = BLUE;
H->ClrScr();
H->ShowHierarchy(H);
delete H;
getch();
}
```

Notice that I include code in the test program that "uses" the MyObject unit. I did not insert this code manually but instead used the program manager to add the MyObject module to the project. This is the best way to proceed, as it allows you to avoid editing the make file.

The program itself simply sets a background and text color for the output, then clears the screen to those colors and shows the hierarchy to the user. The next-to-last line in the program calls delete rather than Free. You can use either technique, depending on the dictates of your taste and background.

Showing the Hierarchy of a VCL Program

To really appreciate the new objects developed in the last section, you need to add them to a regular BCB application. For instance, if you use them in a standard Form1 class, here is the output you get:

```
TForm1
TForm
TScrollingWinControl
TWinControl
TControl
TComponent
TPersistent
TObject
```

This shows the whole hierarchy of class TForm1, starting with this, moving to TForm, back to TScrollingWinControl, and so on, all the way back to TObject.

As you know, VCL objects do not support multiple inheritance. As a result, I could not add the functionality of THierarchy to TForm by letting the object inherit it. This is fine with me, because I use multiple inheritance only very reluctantly.

Instead of multiple inheritance, I prefer to use a technique called *aggregation*. In aggregation, you add the object you want to use as a field of your current object and then expose its methods either by publishing the whole object as a property, or by wrapping the methods of the object inside methods of your current object. This technique allows you to easily take precise control of the functionality from the new object, and it tends to support clean, bug-free programming.

Before I show you how to use aggregation, I need to point out that it is not possible to use THierarchy directly in a Windows program because THierarchy uses Conio.h. The question then becomes, "Is THierarchy designed in such a way that I can descend from it and change its functionality so that it works with a Windows program?"

Well, part of the answer should be obvious. The key method that had to be virtual, the one that had to be overridden to make this work, is PrintString. And indeed, PrintString is declared virtual, so it is possible to change THierarchy's stripes. In fact, you will find that I also override the setters and the ClrScr method.

> **NOTE**
>
> You might feel that having to override so many methods in order to change the output of this program is an excessive amount of work when compared to the relatively simple task of rewriting the ShowHierarchy method from scratch. Indeed, when looked at from this perspective, the whole task of creating an object in this case seems fruitless. I readily confess that it would indeed have been simpler to write three versions of a non-OOP method called ShowHierarchyBlackandWhite, ShowHierarchyColor, and ShowHierarchyWindows. Here is a ShowHierarchy method tailored for use with a VCL form-based program:
>
> ```
> void TForm1::ShowHierarchy()
> {
>   TClass AClass;
>   Memo1->Clear();
>   Memo1->Lines->Add(AnsiString(ClassName()));
>   AClass = ClassParent();
>   while (True)
>   {
>     AnsiString S = AnsiString(AClass->ClassName());
>     Memo1->Lines->Add(S);
>     if (AnsiString(AClass->ClassName()) == "TObject")
>       break;
>     AClass = AClass->ClassParent();
>   }
> }
> ```
>
> Clearly, this object is easier to write than the objects I have produced here. The key reason I created an object like THierarchy is simply that it illustrates how OOP works. In real life, objects often contain 20, 30, or even 50 methods. When seen in that light, having to override three or four methods does not seem like such a big chore. Furthermore, you can often use delegation to solve these kinds of problems.
>
> Of course, this isn't real life but a book on programming. I have therefore intentionally created a small object with few methods so that I can focus your attention solely on virtual methods that need to be overridden. If I had cluttered up this chapter with a big object, you never could have seen the trees for the forest, because at least half the chapter would have involved an explanation of a huge object.
>
> *continues*

19

INHERITANCE

continued

Furthermore, the ShowHierarchy method is the difficult method in this program. It's easy to write the methods that need to be overridden, while some programmers might have trouble creating ShowHierarchy. In this sense, even the rather simple object I have created here does a good job of hiding complexity and promoting bug-free reuse.

A final point about this subject is that OOP's main strength is not in producing small code, nor is it true that objects are necessarily easier to create than equivalent structured code. Rather, the strength of OOP is in letting you easily and safely reuse premade objects. Now that these objects are completed, they can be reused easily in any WinTel-based C++ program, whether it runs in Windows or from the command line. OOP never makes sense if you think in terms of writing your whole program from scratch. Instead, the advantage of OOP comes when you want to create programs by reusing premade objects. OOP is about code reuse and about writing bug-free programs; it is not about finding the smallest possible implementation of an algorithm. When you add components to OOP, you can also get RAD, which is another major boost in productivity.

In Listings 19.6 through 19.9, you will find the code for the new version of the Object1.cpp module, as well as the code for a standard VCL form-based program called HIERARCHY that uses the object. The output from the program is shown in Figure 19.5.

Figure 19.5.

The HIERARCHY form sports a TButton and a TMemo component.

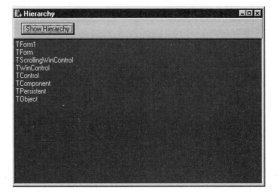

Listing 19.6. The new code for the MyObject header file.

```
///////////////////////////////////////
// MyObject.h
// Learning how to use objects
// Copyright (c) 1997 by Charlie Calvert
//
#ifndef MyObjectH
#define MyObjectH
#include <conio.h>
#include <vcl\stdctrls.hpp>
```

```
class TMyObject :public TObject
{
protected:
  virtual void PrintString(AnsiString S);
public:
  TMyObject() : TObject()  {}
  void ShowHierarchy(TObject *AnObject);
};

class TListHierarchy: public TMyObject
{
private:
  TStringList *FList;
protected:
  virtual void PrintString(AnsiString S)
    { FList->Add(S); }
public:
  TListHierarchy() { FList = new TStringList(); }
  __fastcall virtual ~TListHierarchy() { delete FList; }
  TStringList *GetHierarchy(TObject *AnObject)
    { FList->Clear(); ShowHierarchy(AnObject); return FList; }
};

class __declspec(delphiclass) TVCLHierarchy;

class THierarchy: public TMyObject
{
  friend TVCLHierarchy;
  int FTextColor;
  int FBackColor;
protected:
  virtual __fastcall void SetTextColor(int Color)
    { FTextColor = Color; textcolor(FTextColor); }
  virtual __fastcall void SetBackColor(int Color)
    { FBackColor = Color; textbackground(FBackColor); }
public:
  THierarchy() : TMyObject() {}
  virtual void PrintString(AnsiString S);
  virtual void ClrScr();
  __property int TextColor={read=FTextColor,write=SetTextColor};
  __property int BackColor={read=FBackColor,write=SetBackColor};
};

class TVCLHierarchy : public THierarchy
{
  TMemo *FMemo;
protected:
  virtual __fastcall void SetTextColor(int Color)
    { FTextColor = Color; FMemo->Font->Color = TColor(FTextColor); }
  virtual __fastcall void SetBackColor(int Color);

public:
  TVCLHierarchy(TMemo *AMemo): THierarchy() { FMemo = AMemo; }
  virtual void PrintString(AnsiString S)
    { FMemo->Lines->Add(S); }
  virtual void ClrScr() { FMemo->Clear(); }
};

#endif
```

Listing 19.7. The new code for the MyObject implementation.

```cpp
///////////////////////////////////////
// MyObject.cpp
// Learning how to use objects
// Copyright (c) 1997 by Charlie Calvert
//
#include <vcl\vcl.h>
#include <conio.h>
#pragma hdrstop
#include "myobject.h"

void TMyObject::PrintString(AnsiString S)
{
  printf("%s\n", S.c_str());
}

void TMyObject::ShowHierarchy(TObject *AnObject)
{
  TClass AClass;

  AnsiString AClassName = AnsiString(AnObject->ClassName()).c_str();
  PrintString(AClassName);

  AClass = AnObject->ClassParent();
  while (True)
  {
    AClassName = AnsiString(AClass->ClassName());
    PrintString(AClassName);
    if (AClassName == "TObject")
      break;
    AClass = AClass->ClassParent();
  }
}

void THierarchy::PrintString(AnsiString S)
{
  char Temp[250];

  sprintf(Temp, "%s\n\r", S.c_str());
  cputs(Temp);
}

void THierarchy::ClrScr()
{
  clrscr();
}

void __fastcall TVCLHierarchy::SetBackColor(int Color)
{
  FBackColor = Color;
  FMemo->Color = TColor(FBackColor);
}
```

Listing 19.8. The code for the HIERARCHY header file.

```cpp
/////////////////////////////////////
// Main.h
// Copyright (c) 1997 by Charlie Calvert
//

#ifndef MainH
#define MainH

#include <vcl\Classes.hpp>
#include <vcl\Controls.hpp>
#include <vcl\StdCtrls.hpp>
#include <vcl\Forms.hpp>
#include <vcl\ExtCtrls.hpp>
#include "MyObject.h"


class TForm1 : public TForm
{
__published:
  TButton *ShowHierarchyBtn;
  TMemo *Memo1;
  TPanel *Panel1;
  void __fastcall ShowHierarchyBtnClick(TObject *Sender);
  void __fastcall FormDestroy(TObject *Sender);
private:
  TVCLHierarchy *FHierarchy;
  void ShowHierarchy(TObject *Object);
public:
  virtual __fastcall TForm1(TComponent* Owner);
  __property TVCLHierarchy *Hierarchy=
    {read=FHierarchy, write=FHierarchy};
};

extern TForm1 *Form1;

#endif
```

Listing 19.9. The code for the HIERARCHY program.

```cpp
/////////////////////////////////////
// Main.cpp
// Copyright (c) 1997 by Charlie Calvert
//
#include <vcl\vcl.h>
#pragma hdrstop
#include "Main.h"
#pragma resource "*.dfm"
TForm1 *Form1;

__fastcall TForm1::TForm1(TComponent* Owner)
  : TForm(Owner)
{
  FHierarchy = new TVCLHierarchy(Memo1);
```

continues

Listing 19.9. continued

```
  Hierarchy->BackColor = clBlue;
  Hierarchy->TextColor = clYellow;
}

void __fastcall TForm1::FormDestroy(TObject *Sender)
{
  delete Hierarchy;
}

void TForm1::ShowHierarchy(TObject *Object)
{
  Hierarchy->ShowHierarchy(Object);
}

void __fastcall TForm1::ShowHierarchyBtnClick(TObject *Sender)
{
  ShowHierarchy(this);
}
```

When you run this program, it will display the hierarchy of the TForm object in a memo control. It does so by creating an aggregate of the THierarchy object and the TForm1 object.

Creating Friend Objects

Here is the declaration for the descendant of THierarchy that works in Windows:

```
class TVCLHierarchy : public THierarchy
{
  TMemo *FMemo;
protected:
  virtual void SetTextColor(int Color)
    { FTextColor = Color; FMemo->Font->Color = TColor(FTextColor); }
  virtual void SetBackColor(int Color)
    { FBackColor = Color; FMemo->Color = TColor(FBackColor); }
public:
  TVCLHierarchy(TMemo *AMemo): THierarchy() { FMemo = AMemo; }
  virtual void PrintString(AnsiString S)
    { FMemo->Lines->Add(S); }
  virtual void ClrScr() { FMemo->Clear(); }
};
```

Several changes to this program should jump right out at you. First, notice that the constructor now takes a parameter. This parameter is the memo control that will be used to display text to the user. The SetTextColor, SetBackColor, PrintString, and ClrScr methods have all been rewritten to take advantage of this new control.

As a result, the only parts of the original object that have come through unchanged are as shown in the following pseudocode:

```
class THierarchy: public TMyObject}
{
  int FTextColor;
  int FBackColor;
public:
  void ShowHierarchy(TObject *AnObject); // inherited from TMyObject
  __property int TextColor={read=FTextColor,write=SetTextColor};
  __property int BackColor={read=FBackColor,write=SetBackColor};
};
```

In this particular case, it is not possible to use the TextColor and BackColor properties to access the private FTextColor and FBackColor data stores. Instead, I declare TVCLHierarchy to be a friend of THierarchy:

```
class TVCLHierarchy;
class THierarchy: public TMyObject
{
  friend TVCLHierarchy;

  int FTextColor;
  int FBackColor;
  ... // Code omitted here
}
```

Notice that TVCLHierarchy is declared as a friend in the first line of the THierarchy declaration. This means that TVCLHierarchy has access to the private data of THierarchy. Descendants of TVCLHierarchy will not inherit this trait.

Using Aggregation

Rather than use multiple inheritance to access TVCLHierarchy, TForm1 declares a field of this type:

```
class TForm1 : public TForm
{
  ... // Code omitted here
  TVCLHierarchy *Hierarchy;
  void ShowHierarchy();
public:
  virtual __fastcall TForm1(TComponent* Owner);
  __property TVCLHierarchy *Hierarchy=
    {read=FHierarchy, write=FHierarchy};
};
```

I have also added a method called ShowHierarchy and a new property called Hierarchy so that descendants of TForm1 can have access to the BackColor and TextColor properties of TVCLHierarchy.

A fine point of object design could be debated here. In this particular case, I have created a property of type TVCLHierarchy that is exposed to consumers of TForm1. Alternatively, I could have completely hidden TVCLHierarchy behind a set of properties that provided access to the FTextColor and FBackColor fields of THierarchy:

```
class TForm1 : public TForm
{
  ... // Code omitted here
  TVCLHierarchy *Hierarchy;
  void ShowHierarchy(TObject *Object);
  int GetHierarchyBackColor();
  void SetHierarchyBackColor(int Color);
  int GetHierarchyTextColor();
  void SetHierarchyTextColor(int Color);
public:
  virtual __fastcall TForm1(TComponent* Owner);
  __property int HierarchyTextColor=
    {read=GetHierarchyTextColor, write=SetHierarchyTextColor};
  __property int HierarchyBackColor=
    {read=GetHierarchyBackColor, write=SetHierarchyBackColor};
};
```

This technique is very pure from an OOP-based point of view, and it is perhaps a more classic and complete example of aggregation than the one I use. However, it is not strictly necessary to create the HierarchyTextColor and HierarchyBackColor properties. Instead, I can make the Hierarchy object public by making it a property of type TVCLHierarchy. The reason this approach is acceptable is because FHierarchy, as well as the FTextColor and FBackColor fields of THierarchy, are all still hidden behind properties.

It would be wrong, however, to make FHierarchy public or to allow users to directly access the FTextColor or FBackColor fields of THierarchy. The reason this is wrong is because it exposes your data to the public, thereby limiting your choices when it comes time to maintain or improve your program.

The technique shown here of exposing TVCLHierarchy via a property shows up everywhere in the VCL. Most notably, it is present in the Items or Lines fields of TListBox, TComboBox, and TMemo. The point here is that you want to use properties to protect your data and your implementation, but you don't want to take things so far that your code becomes needlessly bloated.

However, I do not feel that it would be incorrect or wrong to completely hide FHierarchy from consumers of TForm1 and to instead expose its properties via properties of TForm1. The great advantage of this technique would be that it would allow a seamless aggregation of TForm1 and TVCLHierarchy.

> **NOTE**
>
> If you sense me waffling a bit here, that is because I do not believe there is a hard and fast answer as to what is best in a situation like this. It happens that there are good arguments on both sides. Component design is an art, not a science. The moment it becomes a science, most programmers are going to be out of a job.

I have included the complete source for this program so you can double-check your work against it in case anything goes wrong. The key parts you need to concentrate on are the class declarations in the headers, the declarations for the global variable for the HierarchyForm, and the headers for the various methods used in the forms. The actual implementation of the methods was already cleared up in the HIERARCHY program, so you don't need to check them. The HIERARCHY2 program is shown in Figure 19.6.

FIGURE 19.6.

The HIERARCHY2
program at runtime.

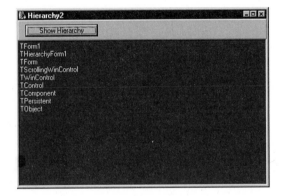

You should spend some time adding controls to the HierarchyForm and watching how they then automatically appear on the main form for the program. Notice that if you move a control on the HierarchyForm, the corresponding control on the main form will also move. If you move a control on the main form, however, that breaks the connection between that control and the corresponding control on the HierarchyForm. To restore the connection, right-click on the control in the main form and choose Revert To Inherited from the menu.

You can disconnect and revert properties one at a time if you wish. For instance, if you move the left side of a component on the main form, that will break the connection for that one property, but it will leave the remaining properties still connected to the HierarchyForm. To restore the Left property, choose that property in the Object Inspector with the right mouse button and select Revert To Inherited from the menu. To test this, you might want to drop a single button in the middle of the HierarchyForm, then switch back to the main form and work on changing just one of the inherited button's properties, such as its Left property or its Caption.

19

INHERITANCE

Summary

In this chapter, you have had a good chance to start working with object-oriented programming. However, there are still several big topics to tackle, including encapsulation and polymorphism. Rather than trying to cover such big topics inside this already lengthy chapter, I have decided to break things up and give them their own chapters where they can have plenty of room to unfold naturally.

Plenty of material was covered in this chapter, including inheritance, virtual methods, aggregation, and form inheritance. If you are new to this material, it would only be natural that some of it did not sink in the first time around. If so, you can either re-read the chapter or go on to the next chapter and see if some of it doesn't start to become clear when you work with new examples that approach the material from a slightly different angle.

Inheritance and virtual methods are everywhere in the BCB, and the more you work with them, the easier it will be to understand the principles involved. However, this is material that you must master if you want to be good at using BCB—and particularly if you want to start creating your own components.

Encapsulation

CHAPTER 20

Overview

In this chapter, you continue the overview of object-oriented programming begun in the last chapter. In particular, the focus is on encapsulation and properties. The next chapter focuses on polymorphism.

This chapter covers the following topics:

- An overview of encapsulation, including the need to hide data and certain parts of the implementation
- An in-depth look at the `private`, `protected`, `public`, and `__published` access specifiers
- Property creation
- The five basic types of properties
- Read-only properties
- Default value declarations for properties

This chapter features some of the syntactical jewels in the BCB treasure chest. In particular, it offers a complete array of scoping directives. These tools enable you to fine-tune access to your objects in a way that helps promote their re-use. Properties are also cutting-edge tools, and their implementation in BCB yields some surprising fruits, such as arrays that are indexed on strings.

Encapsulation

The words *encapsulation* and *object* are closely linked in my mind. Encapsulation is one of the primary and most fundamental aspects of OOP. It is useful because it helps to enlist related methods and data under a single aegis, and to hide the implementation details that don't need to be exposed or that might change in future versions of an object.

The ability to encapsulate methods and data inside an object is important because it helps you design clean, well-written programs. To use a classic example, suppose you were to create an object called `TAirplane`, which would represent (naturally enough) an airplane. This object might have fields such as `Altitude`, `Speed`, and `NumPassengers`; it might have methods such as `TakeOff`, `Land`, `Climb`, and `Descend`. From a design point of view, everything is simpler if you can encapsulate all these fields and methods in a single object, rather than leaving them spread out as individual variables and routines:

```
class TAirplane: public TObject
{
  int Altitude;
  int Speed;
  int NumPassengers;
  void TakeOff();
  void Land();
  void Climb();
  void Descend();
};
```

There is a sleek elegance in this simple object declaration. Its purpose and the means for implementing its functionality are readily apparent.

Consider the class declaration from the current version of the Object3 program:

```
 class THierarchy: public TMyObject
{
  int FTextColor;
  int FBackColor;
protected:
  virtual void SetTextColor(int Color)
    { FTextColor = Color; textcolor(FTextColor); }
  virtual void SetBackColor(int Color)
    { FBackColor = Color; textbackground(FBackColor); }
public:
  THierarchy() : TMyObject() {}
  virtual void PrintString(AnsiString S);
  virtual void ClrScr();
  __property int TextColor={read=FTextColor,write=SetTextColor};
  __property int BackColor={read=FBackColor,write=SetBackColor};
};
```

THierarchy encapsulates a certain amount of functionality, including the ShowHierarchy method it inherits from TMyObject. If you want to call ShowHierarchy, you need to first instantiate an object of type THierarchy and then use that object as a qualifier when you call ShowHierarchy:

```
void main()
{
  THierarchy *H = new THierarchy();
  H->TextColor = YELLOW;
  H->BackColor = BLUE;
  H->ShowHierarchy(H);
  delete H;
}
```

This kind of encapsulation is useful primarily because it makes you treat everything about the THierarchy object as a single unit. There are, however, other advantages to this system, which become apparent when you examine the access specifiers used in the class declaration.

BCB defines four keywords meant to aid in the process of encapsulation by specifying the access levels for the various parts of an object:

> private: Use this directive to declare a section in a class that can be accessed only from inside the current object. The only way around this limitation is to declare a class as a friend.

> protected: Code declared in a protected section can be accessed only by the current object and by descendant objects. The point here is that protected fields and methods are available primarily to other component developers, not to standard consumers of the object.

> public: Code declared in a public section of an object is available to anyone who uses an object of that particular type. Along with the published section, it is the standard interface of the object.

20

ENCAPSULATION

__published: Properties that are declared in the published section are public variables that appear in the Object Inspector. Furthermore, you can discover the type of published properties at runtime; simple published properties can be streamed to disk automatically. Because published properties are for use in the Object Inspector, you should not declare a property as published unless the object descends from TComponent or one of TComponent's children. TComponent is the base object from which all objects that appear on the Component Palette must descend.

All the data in your programs should be declared private and should be accessed only through methods or properties. As a rule, it is a serious design error to ever give anyone direct access to the data of an object. Giving other objects or non-OOP routines direct access to data is a sure way to get into deep trouble when it comes time to maintain or redesign part of a program. To the degree that it's practical, you might even want the object itself to access its own data primarily through properties or public routines.

The whole idea that some parts of an object should remain forever concealed from other programmers is one of the hardest ideas for new OOP programmers to grasp. In fact, in early versions of Turbo Pascal with Objects, this aspect of encapsulation was given short shrift. Experience, however, has shown that many well-constructed objects consist of two parts:

- Data and implementation sections hidden from the programmers who use the object.
- A set of interface routines that enable programmers to talk to the concealed methods and data that form the heart of an object.

Data and implementation sections are hidden so that the developer of the object can feel free to change those sections at a later date. If you expose a piece of data or a method to the world and find a bug that forces you to change the type of that data or the declaration for that method, you are breaking the code of people who rely on that data or that method. Therefore, it's best to keep all your key methods and data hidden from consumers of your object. Give them access to those methods and procedures only through properties and public methods. Keep the guts of your object private, so that you can rewrite it, debug it, or rearrange it at any time.

One way to approach the subject of hiding data and methods is to think of objects as essentially modest beings. An object doesn't want to show the world how it performs some task, and it is especially careful not to directly show the world the data or data structures it uses to store information. The actual data used in an object is a private matter that should never be exposed in public. The methods that manipulate that data should also be hidden from view, because they are the personal business of that object. Of course, an object does not want to be completely hidden from view, so it supplies a set of interface routines that talk to the world—but these interface routines jealously guard the secret of how an object's functionality is actually implemented.

A well-made object is like a beautiful woman who conceals her charms from a prying world. Conversely, a poorly made object should also hide, much like an elderly man who doesn't want the world to see how his youth and virility have faded. These analogies are intentionally a bit whimsical, but they help to illustrate the extremely powerful taboo associated with directly exposing data and certain parts of the implementation.

Of course, the point of hiding data and implementations is not primarily to conceal how an object works, but to make it possible to completely rewrite the core of an object without changing the way it interacts with the world. In short, the previous analogies collapse when it comes to a functional analysis of data hiding, but they serve well to express the spirit of the enterprise.

> **NOTE**
>
> If you have the source code to the VCL, you will find that at least half of most key objects in the BCB code base are declared as `private`. A few complex objects contain several hundred lines of private declarations, and only 20 or 30 methods and properties that serve as an interface for that object. Objects near the top of a hierarchy don't always follow this model, because they usually consist primarily of interface routines. It's the core objects that form the heart of a hierarchy that are currently under discussion.

If you will allow me to mix my metaphors rather egregiously, and to introduce a fairly strong set of images, I can provide one further way to think about the internal and public sections of an object. Rather than thinking of the private parts of an object from a sexual perspective, you can literally think of them as the internal organs of the object. As such, they should, by definition, never be exposed directly to the light of day. Instead, they are covered by skin and bone, which is the public interface of the object.

Our face and hands are the public part of our being, and our internal organs are covered with skin and bone and never see the light of day. The only reason ever to expose these organs is if you are in the hospital—that is, during object maintenance. Furthermore, any object that does expose its private parts to the light of day is incomplete, a monster from Dr. Moreau's island, where gruesome experiments roam free.

Simplicity: The Secret of Good Object Design

Before moving on, I want to talk about the importance of creating easy-to-use interfaces. Notice, for instance, how easy it is to use the `TTable`, `TDataSource`, and `TDBGrid` objects. These are examples of well-constructed objects with easy-to-use interfaces. If you take these objects away,

20

ENCAPSULATION

however, and access the functions in the `DbiProcs.c` directly, you see that `TTable`, `TDBGrid`, and `TDataSource` conceal a great deal of complexity. In other words, if you have to call the raw BDE functions directly to open and view a table, you will find that the process is both tedious and error-prone. Using `TTable`, however, is very easy. You might need to have someone tell you how it works the first time you see it, but after that, the process of getting hooked up to a table and displaying data to the user is trivial. All good programmers should strive to make their objects this easy to use.

In the next few chapters, I discuss component creation. Components are very useful because they help guide you in the process of creating a simple, easy-to-use object. If you can drop an object onto a form and hook it up with just a few clicks in the Object Inspector, you know that you have at least begun to create a good design. If you drop an object onto a form and then need to mess around with it for 15 or 20 minutes before you can use it, you know something is probably wrong. Objects should be easy to use, whether they are placed on the Component Palette or not.

Simplicity is important because it helps people write error-free programs. If you have to complete 30 steps to hook up an object, there are 30 opportunities to make a mistake. If you need to complete only two steps, it is less likely that an error will occur. It is also easier for people to understand how to complete two steps, whereas they often can become confused when trying to learn a 30-step process.

I do not mean to say that the act of creating an object is simple or easy. I have seen great programmers wrestle for months with the overwhelming minutiae of creating a complex object that is easy to use. A good programmer doesn't think the job is done just because the code works. Good code should not only work, but it should also be easy to use! Conversely, I often suspect that an object is poorly designed if it is difficult to use. In most cases, my suspicions turn out to be true, and a complex interface ends up being a wrapper around a buggy and an ineptly coded object.

No hard-and-fast rules exist in the area of object design. However, the presence of an easy-to-use interface is a good sign. If you are working with a component, you should be able to drop it onto a form and hook it up in just a few seconds. If you are working with an object that is not encapsulated in a component, you should be able to initialize and use it by writing just a few lines of code. If hooking up takes more than a few minutes, you often have reason to be suspicious of the entire enterprise.

The private methods of your objects should also be cleanly and logically designed. However, it is not a disaster if your private methods are difficult to understand, as long as your public methods are easy to use. The bottom line is that the private methods should be designed to accomplish a task, and the public methods should be designed to be easy to use. When you look at the design this way, you can see a vast difference between the public and private methods in an object.

The scope of knowledge programmers must master today is huge. Professionals are expected to understand the Windows API, OLE, the Internet, graphics, at least two languages, object design, and database architectures. Some of these fields, such as Internet programming, break down into many complex parts such as ISAPI, CGI, WinINet, TCP/IP, electronic mail, HTTP, and FTP. Learning about all these areas of programming is an enormously complex task. In fact, for all practical purposes, it is impossible. No one person can know everything necessary to write most contemporary programs from scratch. As a result, he or she needs to find easy-to-use objects that encapsulate complexity and make it usable.

The worst mistake an object creator can make is to insist that the consumer of the object knows as much about the subject as its creator. It's not enough to define a set of useful routines that can speed development if you already know a subject inside and out. Instead, you need to create objects that someone can use, even if he or she doesn't understand the details of how a particular subject works.

The trick to good object design, of course, is to simultaneously present an easy-to-use interface, while also giving experienced programmers access to the fine points of a particular area. Once again, `TTable` and `TQuery` serve as an example. `TTable` is an easy-to-use object providing neophytes easy access to data. At the same time, it allows an expert to manipulate one-to-many relationships, lookups, filters, and indices. Add `TQuery` to the mix, and there are few limits to what you can do with these objects in terms of manipulating databases.

`TMediaPlayer` is another example of a component that takes a relatively complex API and makes it easy to use. It is arguable that this component could have a bit more depth, but it allows programmers to run multimedia applications without having to understand `mciSendCommand` and its many complex parameters, structures and constants.

The bottom line is simplicity. If you create an object that is as hard to use as the API it encapsulates, 95 percent of the people who see your object will consider it useless. The reason programmers create objects is to provide an easy, bug-free interface to a particular area of programming.

As you read through the next few chapters, you might consider thinking about the importance of creating a simple interface to your objects. Having a simple interface is particularly important for the top-level objects in your hierarchy.

A Concrete Example

Neither `TMyObject` nor `THierarchy` provides much scope for exploring encapsulation. As a result, it's time to introduce a new class called `TWidget`, which is a descendant of `TCustomControl` and uses a descendant of `THierarchy` through aggregation. In Chapter 21, "Polymorphism," `TWidget` becomes the ancestor of a series of different kinds of widgets that can be stored in a warehouse. In other words, in a computer factory `TWidget` might be the ancestor of several classes of objects such as `TSiliconChip`, `TAddOnBoard`, and `TPowerSupply`. Descendants of these objects might be `TPentiumChip`, `TPentiumProChip`, `TVideoBoard`, and so on.

> **NOTE**
>
> I suppose one could literally think of the `TWidget` descendants as representations of concrete objects or as abstract representations of these objects. The meaning I intend is the latter.
>
> This later, more abstract, technique is similar to the process used in object-oriented databases. Instead of having a table that stores rows of raw data, the table could instead store objects that represent data. When a new 486 chip rolls off the line, a new `T486Chip` object is added to the database to represent this physical object. You could then query the abstract object and ask it questions: "When were you made? What part of the warehouse are you stored in? What is your wholesale price? What is your street price?" Thus, the abstract object would be a computerized representation of something in the real world.
>
> Creating computerized representations of physical objects is a very common use of OOP, but it is not the primary reason for the existence of this technology. The great benefits of OOP are related to the reuse, design, and maintenance of software. Using OOP to represent real-world objects is only one branch of this field of knowledge.

Note that object hierarchies always move from the general to the specific:

```
TWidget
TSiliconChip
TPentiumChip
```

The underlying logic is simple enough:

1. A `TWidget` could be almost any object that is bought and sold.

2. A `TSiliconChip` is some kind of silicon-based entity.

3. A `TPentiumChip` is a specific kind of computer chip that has a real-world counterpart.

The movement is from the abstract to the specific. It is almost always a mistake to embody specific traits of an object in a base class for a hierarchy. Instead, these early building blocks should be so broad in scope that they can serve as parents to a wide variety of related objects or tools.

The main reason for this rule might not become apparent to all readers until they have seen Chapter 21. The condensed explanation, however, looks like this:

■ `TWidget` encapsulates certain basic functionality that applies to all widgets. For instance, all widgets might keep track of the date they were created, whereas only certain types of widgets might support the MX instruction set. Therefore, you can use polymorphism to ask all your widgets certain basic questions, such as when they were created. Conversely, there are certain types of questions you can ask only of widgets that are also computer processors. This system would not work if you did not move from the general to the specific. In short, you want all widgets to have certain basic functionality, and then as you move up the hierarchy, you can provide specific domains of knowledge or functionality to particular types of objects.

The Widget1 program found on the CD that accompanies this book includes a declaration for class TWidget. (See Listing 20.1.) This declaration appears in a file called Widgets.h. TWidget descends from the VCL class called TCustomControl and uses a descendant of THierarchy through aggregation. As a result, you will need to add both MyObject and the new Widgets files to your projects.

I have created a new file called Widgets because I am building a new type of object that is distinct from THierarchy and TMyObject. I could, of course, have put all the objects in one file, but I thought it made more sense to separate the different types of objects into different files. There is no hard-and-fast rule governing this kind of decision, and you can take whichever course makes sense to you on a case-by-case basis.

I have also added a new class to TMyObject:

```
class TListHierarchy: public TMyObject
{
private:
  TStringList *FList;
protected:
  virtual void PrintString(AnsiString S)
    { FList->Add(S); }
public:
  TListHierarchy() { FList = new TStringList(); }
  __fastcall virtual ~TListHierarchy() { delete FList; }
  TStringList *GetHierarchy(TObject *AnObject)
    { ShowHierarchy(AnObject); return FList; }
};
```

As you can see, this class stores its information in a TStringList. You can retrieve the list from the class by using the GetHierarchy method:

```
ListBox1->Items = MyWidget->GetHierarchy();
```

After you make this call, the list box referenced in the code would contain an object hierarchy.

TWidget and Its Destructor

The Widgets unit is very simple at this point. To create it, I went to the files menu and chose New Unit. I then saved the file as Widgets.cpp and edited the header so that it looked like this:

```
//////////////////////////////////////
// Widgets.h
// Learning how to use objects
// Copyright (c) 1997 by Charlie Calvert
//
#ifndef WidgetsH
#define WidgetsH
#include "myobject.h"
```

```
class TWidget: public TCustomControl
{
private:
  TListHierarchy *Hierarchy;
public:
  virtual __fastcall TWidget(TComponent *AOwner): TCustomControl(AOwner)
    { Hierarchy = new TListHierarchy; }
  virtual __fastcall ~TWidget()
    { delete Hierarchy; }
  TStringList *GetHierarchy()
    { return Hierarchy->GetHierarchy(this); }
};
#endif
```

This object uses aggregation to enlist the functionality of the TListHierarchy object for its own purposes. In particular, it declares the object as private data and then allocates memory for it in its constructor, and deallocates memory in its destructor:

```
virtual __fastcall ~TWidget()
    { delete Hierarchy; }
```

NOTE

A destructor is declared by writing the name of the object with a tilde prefaced to it: ~TWidget. You rarely have reason to call a destructor explicitly. Instead, a destructor is called automatically when you use the delete operator on the entire object, when you call Free, or when a local object goes out of scope:

```
delete MyWidget; // Automatically calls the destructor
```

Destructors exist so you can have a place to deallocate any memory associated with an object, or to perform any other cleanup chores. The destructor exists for your convenience and serves no other purpose than to give you a chance to clean up before your object shuts down.

All VCL objects inherit a virtual destructor declared in TObject. If you create a destructor for one of your own VCL objects, it must have the same signature used by the destructor in the TWidget object. That is, it must be declared as virtual __fastcall. This is because of the precedent set by the destructor found in TObject.

The GetHierarchy method of TWidget returns the result of a call to the Hierarchy::GetHierarchy method:

```
TStringList *GetHierarchy()
    { return Hierarchy->GetHierarchy(this); }
```

As you can see, this function hardcodes a reference to the TWidget object into this call. You therefore can't use this version of the Widget object to get the hierarchy of another object, but only for retrieving its own hierarchy.

To make sure you understand how I got started with this new series of files, I have created a very simple program called Widget1 that contains the Widgets unit and a main program that uses it. The code for the program is available on this book's CD, and the output from the program is shown in Figure 20.1.

FIGURE 20.1.

The output from the Widget1 program found on the CD that accompanies this book.

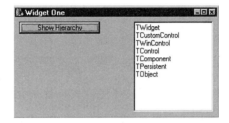

The main program contains one procedure that looks like this:

```
void __fastcall TForm1::ShowHierarchyBtnClick(TObject *Sender)
{
  Memo1->Clear();
  TWidget *W = new TWidget(Memo1);
  Memo1->Lines = W->GetHierarchy();
  delete W;
}
```

If you have questions on how to create this program, go to the Widget1 directory and study the example provided there. After you are set up, you can read the note below and then copy the Widgets.cpp and Widgets.h files to the Utils directory, where CodeBox is kept. This file is used in Widgets2, which is described in the next section of this chapter.

> **NOTE**
>
> Actually, you might want to be careful copying the files. If you are following along by creating copies of the files by hand, then go ahead and copy the files. If you are working from my source, be careful that you don't overwrite my copy of the file when you move the file to the Utils directory.

Working with Widgets

In the last section, you got started with the TWidget object. In the Widget2 program, shown in Listings 20.1 through 20.5, I add data and methods to the object so it can serve as the base class for an object that represents some kind of widget such as a computer chip, a light bulb, a book, or whatever. Because the object could have such a wide range of uses, I keep it very abstract, giving it only a few traits such as a cost, a creation time, the ability to draw itself, and the ability to stream itself.

> **NOTE**
>
> You will find that the Widgets module gets rewritten several times over the course of the next few chapters. As a result, the version of this unit used in the Widget2 program is stored in the Widgets2 directory on the CD that accompanies this book. There is a second version of this unit, stored in the Utils subdirectory, that contains the final version of Widgets.cpp.
>
> If you are working along with this text, creating your own version of the program, it might be best to copy Widgets.cpp out to the Utils directory and update it little by little as the next few chapters unfold. If your efforts get fouled for one reason or another, you can always revert to the versions stored on the CD.

Listing 20.1. The Main unit for the Widget2 program.

```cpp
////////////////////////////////////////
// Main.cpp
// Learning about objects
// Copyright (c) 1997 by Charlie Calvert
//
#include <vcl\vcl.h>
#pragma hdrstop
#include "widgets.h"
#include "Main.h"
#pragma resource "*.dfm"

TForm1 *Form1;
__fastcall TForm1::TForm1(TComponent* Owner)
  : TForm(Owner)
{
}
void __fastcall TForm1::CreateBtnClick(TObject *Sender)
{
  TWidget * Widget= new TWidget(this);
  Widget->Left = ClientWidth / 4 - Widget->Width / 2;
  Widget->Top = (ClientHeight / 2) + Widget->Height;
  Widget->Parent = this;
  Widget->Cost = 3.3;
  Widget->Description = "This is a widget";
  Widget->TimeCreated = Now();
  Memo1->Lines = Widget->GetHierarchy();
  Widget->Show();
  Edit1->Text = Widget->TimeCreated;
  WriteWidgetToStream("Afile.dat", Widget);
}
void __fastcall TForm1::ReadFromStreamBtnClick(TObject *Sender)
{
  TWidget *Widget = ReadWidgetFromStream("AFile.dat");
  Widget->Parent = this;
  Memo1->Lines = Widget->GetHierarchy();
  Widget->Show();
```

```
  Edit1->Text = Widget->TimeCreated;
}
void __fastcall TForm1::FormResize(TObject *Sender)
{
  Memo1->Left = ClientWidth / 2;
}
```

Listing 20.2. The core of the Widget2 program is the Widgets unit. The header for that module is shown here.

```
/////////////////////////////////////////
// Widgets.h
// Learning how to use objects
// Copyright (c) 1997 by Charlie Calvert
//
#ifndef WidgetsH
#define WidgetsH
#include "myobject.h"
class __declspec(delphiclass) TWidget;
namespace Widgets
{
  void __fastcall Register();
}
TWidget *ReadWidgetFromStream(AnsiString StreamName);
void WriteWidgetToStream(AnsiString StreamName, TWidget *Widget);
class TWidget: public TCustomControl
{
private:
  TListHierarchy *Hierarchy;
  Currency FCost;
  TDateTime FTimeCreated;
  AnsiString FDescription;
  void __fastcall SetTimeCreated(AnsiString S);
  AnsiString __fastcall GetTimeCreated();
protected:
  virtual void __fastcall Paint(void);
public:
  __fastcall virtual TWidget(TComponent *AOwner): TCustomControl(AOwner)
    { Hierarchy = new TListHierarchy(); Width = 25; Height = 25; }
  __fastcall virtual TWidget(TComponent *AOwner, int ACol, int ARow);
  __fastcall virtual ~TWidget() { delete Hierarchy; }
  virtual AnsiString GetName() { return "Widgets"; }
  TStringList *GetHierarchy() { return Hierarchy->GetHierarchy(this); }
  void __fastcall WidgetMouseDown(TObject *Sender, TMouseButton Button,
    TShiftState Shift, int X, int Y);
__published:
  __property Currency Cost={read=FCost, write=FCost};
  __property AnsiString TimeCreated={read=GetTimeCreated, write=SetTimeCreated};
  __property AnsiString Description={read=FDescription, write=FDescription};
};
#endif
```

20

ENCAPSULATION

Listing 20.3. The main file for the Widgets units.

```cpp
/////////////////////////////////////
// Widgets.cpp
// Learning how to use objects
// Copyright (c) 1997 by Charlie Calvert
//
#include <vcl\vcl.h>
#include <conio.h>
#pragma hdrstop
#include "widgets.h"
#pragma link "myobject.obj"
void WriteWidgetToStream(AnsiString StreamName, TWidget *Widget)
{
  TFileStream *Stream = new TFileStream(StreamName, fmCreate | fmOpenRead);
  Stream->WriteComponent(Widget);
  delete Stream;
}
TWidget *ReadWidgetFromStream(AnsiString StreamName)
{
  Widgets::Register();
  TFileStream *Stream = new TFileStream(StreamName, fmOpenRead);
  TWidget *Widget = (TWidget *)Stream->ReadComponent(NULL);
  delete Stream;
  return Widget;
}
__fastcall TWidget::TWidget(TComponent *AOwner, int ACol, int ARow)
  : TCustomControl(AOwner)
{
  Hierarchy = new TListHierarchy();
  Left = ACol;
  Top = ARow;
  Width = 25;
  Height = 25;
  OnMouseDown = WidgetMouseDown;
}
AnsiString __fastcall TWidget::GetTimeCreated()
{
  return FTimeCreated.DateTimeString();
}
void __fastcall TWidget::SetTimeCreated(AnsiString S)
{
  FTimeCreated = TDateTime(S);
}
void__fastcall TWidget::Paint()
{
  Canvas->Brush->Color = clBlue;
  Canvas->Rectangle(0, 0, ClientWidth, ClientHeight);
  Canvas->Brush->Color = clYellow;
  Canvas->Ellipse(0, 0, ClientWidth, ClientHeight);
}
void __fastcall TWidget::WidgetMouseDown(TObject *Sender, TMouseButton Button,
    TShiftState Shift, int X, int Y)
{
  ShowMessage(Format("%m", OPENARRAY(TVarRec, (FCost))));
}
namespace Widgets
{
```

```
  void __fastcall Register()
  {
    TComponentClass classes[1] = {__classid(TWidget)};
    RegisterClasses(classes, 0);
  }
}
```

Listing 20.4. The header file for `MyObjects` with the new `TListHiearchy` object added to it.

```
/////////////////////////////////////
// MyObject.h
// Learning how to use objects
// Copyright (c) 1997 by Charlie Calvert
//
#ifndef MyObjectH
#define MyObjectH
#include <conio.h>
#include <vcl\stdctrls.hpp>

class TMyObject :public TObject
{
protected:
  virtual void PrintString(AnsiString S);
public:
  TMyObject() : TObject()  {}
  void ShowHierarchy(TObject *AnObject);
};

class TListHierarchy: public TMyObject
{
private:
  TStringList *FList;
protected:
  virtual void PrintString(AnsiString S)
    { FList->Add(S); }
public:
  TListHierarchy() { FList = new TStringList(); }
  __fastcall virtual ~TListHierarchy() { delete FList; }
  TStringList *GetHierarchy(TObject *AnObject)
    { ShowHierarchy(AnObject); return FList; }
};
class __declspec(delphiclass) TVCLHierarchy;
class THierarchy: public TMyObject
{
  friend TVCLHierarchy;

  int FTextColor;
  int FBackColor;
protected:
  virtual void SetTextColor(int Color)
    { FTextColor = Color; textcolor(FTextColor); }
  virtual void SetBackColor(int Color)
    { FBackColor = Color; textbackground(FBackColor); }
```

continues

Listing 20.4. continued

```cpp
public:
  THierarchy() : TMyObject() {}
  virtual void PrintString(AnsiString S);
  virtual void ClrScr();
  __property int TextColor={read=FTextColor,write=SetTextColor};
  __property int BackColor={read=FBackColor,write=SetBackColor};
};

class TVCLHierarchy : public THierarchy
{
  TMemo *FMemo;
protected:
  virtual void SetTextColor(int Color)
    { FTextColor = Color; FMemo->Font->Color = TColor(FTextColor); }
  virtual void SetBackColor(int Color)
    { FBackColor = Color; FMemo->Color = TColor(FBackColor); }
public:
  TVCLHierarchy(TMemo *AMemo): THierarchy() { FMemo = AMemo; }
  virtual void PrintString(AnsiString S)
    { FMemo->Lines->Add(S); }
  virtual void ClrScr() { FMemo->Clear(); }
};
#endif
```

Listing 20.5. The main file of the MyObject module.

```cpp
/////////////////////////////////////
// MyObject.cpp
// Learning how to use objects
// Copyright (c) 1997 by Charlie Calvert
//
#include <vcl\vcl.h>
#include <conio.h>
#pragma hdrstop
#include "myobject.h"
void TMyObject::PrintString(AnsiString S)
{
  printf("%s\n", S.c_str());
}
void TMyObject::ShowHierarchy(TObject *AnObject)
{
  TClass AClass;
  AnsiString AClassName = AnsiString(AnObject->ClassName()).c_str();
  PrintString(AClassName);
  AClass = AnObject->ClassParent();
  while (True)
  {
    AClassName = AnsiString(AClass->ClassName());
    PrintString(AClassName);
    if (AClassName == "TObject")
      break;
    AClass = AClass->ClassParent();
  }
}
```

```
void THierarchy::PrintString(AnsiString S)
{
  char Temp[250];
  sprintf(Temp, "%s\n\r", S.c_str());
  cputs(Temp);
}
void THierarchy::ClrScr()
{
  clrscr();
}
```

The functionality associated with this program is still severely limited. An object of type TWidget is created, and its hierarchy is shown. The program assigns a price to the widget, and a bare representation of a widget is displayed on the screen. The program also saves and loads the Widget object to disk.

The output from this program is shown in Figure 20.2.

FIGURE 20.2.

The output from the Widget2 program.

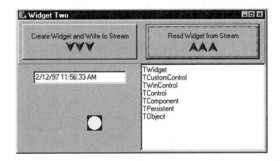

From a user's point of view, this is pretty tame stuff. However, the declaration for class TWidget shows programmers a good deal about how BCB implements encapsulation:

```
class TWidget: public TCustomControl
{
private:
  TListHierarchy *Hierarchy;
  Currency FCost;
  TDateTime FTimeCreated;
  AnsiString FDescription;
  void __fastcall SetTimeCreated(AnsiString S);
  AnsiString __fastcall GetTimeCreated();
protected:
  virtual void __fastcall Paint(void);
public:
  __fastcall virtual TWidget(TComponent *AOwner): TCustomControl(AOwner)
    { Hierarchy = new TListHierarchy(); Width = 25; Height = 25; }
  __fastcall virtual TWidget(TComponent *AOwner, int ACol, int ARow);
  __fastcall virtual ~TWidget() { delete Hierarchy; }
  virtual AnsiString GetName() { return "Widgets"; }
  TStringList *GetHierarchy() { return Hierarchy->GetHierarchy(this); }
  void __fastcall WidgetMouseDown(TObject *Sender, TMouseButton Button,
```

```
    TShiftState Shift, int X, int Y);
__published:
  __property Currency Cost={read=FCost, write=FCost};
  __property AnsiString TimeCreated={read=GetTimeCreated, write=SetTimeCreated};
  __property AnsiString Description={read=FDescription, write=FDescription};
};
```

The private section of TWidget contains several fields of data and two methods:

```
private:
  TListHierarchy *Hierarchy;
  Currency FCost;
  TDateTime FTimeCreated;
  AnsiString FDescription;
  void __fastcall SetTimeCreated(AnsiString S);
  AnsiString __fastcall GetTimeCreated();
```

All of the private data in the program has variable names that begin with the letter F. As stated before, this is a convention and not a syntactical necessity. These variables are called *internal storage*, or *data stores*.

Internal storage should always be declared private, and as such cannot be accessed from outside of this unit. Other objects should never access any of this data directly, but should manipulate it through a predefined interface that appears in the protected, published, or public sections. The F in these variable names stands for *field*. If you want, however, you can think of the F in these names as standing for *forbidden,* as in "it is forbidden to directly access this data!"

Don't step between a mother grizzly bear and her cubs. Don't ask who's buried in Grant's tomb during the middle of a job interview. Don't swim with the sharks if you are bleeding. Don't declare public data in a production-quality program! The problem is not that the error is embarrassing, but that it is going to cause you grief!

The GetTimeCreated and SetTimeCreated functions are also declared private, and you will see that they are accessed through a property. Most objects have many more private methods, but TWidget is relatively bare in this department. The lack of private methods occurs because TWidget is such a simple object that there isn't much need to perform complex manipulations of its data.

The protected section is simple and contains a single virtual method called Paint. This portion of the object can be accessed by descendants of TWidget, but not by an instance of the class. For example, you will have trouble if you write the following code:

```
{
  TWidget *Widget = new TWidget(this);
  Widget->Paint(); // this line won't compile
  delete Widget();
}
```

Only a descendant of TWidget can explicitly call the Paint method.

The methods in the public section of the object make it possible to manipulate the widgets that you declare:

```
public:
    __fastcall virtual TWidget(TComponent *AOwner): TCustomControl(AOwner)
    { Hierarchy = new TListHierarchy(); Width = 25; Height = 25; }
    __fastcall virtual TWidget(TComponent *AOwner, int ACol, int ARow);
    __fastcall virtual ~TWidget() { delete Hierarchy; }
    TStringList *GetHierarchy() { return Hierarchy->GetHierarchy(this); }
    void __fastcall WidgetMouseDown(TObject *Sender, TMouseButton Button,
      TShiftState Shift, int X, int Y);
```

Here, you can see several constructors, a destructor, a routine that lets you iterate through the hierarchy of the object, and a routine that handles mouse clicks on the object. All of these are common activities and need to be declared public.

The first constructor for the object sets up the aggregated THierarchy object and then sets the object's width and height. The second constructor allows you to establish the Left and Top properties for the object.

You have now had an overview of all the code in the Widget program, except for its published properties, which will be discussed in the next section. The discussion so far has concentrated on the BCB object-scoping directives. You have learned about the private, protected, public, and published sections of a program, and have seen why each is necessary.

Properties

Properties provide several advantages:

■ Properties enable you to hide data and implementations.

■ If you write a component and place it in the Component Palette, its published properties appear in the Object Inspector.

■ Some properties can be made available at design-time, and variables are available at runtime only.

■ Properties can have side effects such as not only setting the value of the FWidth variable, but also physically changing the width of the object that appears on the screen.

■ Property access methods can be declared virtual, which gives them more flexibility than simple variables.

The Widget2 program contains three properties, as shown here:

```
__published:
    __property Currency Cost={read=FCost, write=FCost};
    __property AnsiString TimeCreated={read=GetTimeCreated, write=SetTimeCreated};
    __property AnsiString Description={read=FDescription, write=FDescription};
```

Because the TWidget class is a descendant of TComponent, all these properties can be put in the published section, and therefore could be seen from inside the Object Inspector if the object were compiled into BCB's library. It usually does not make sense to create published sections in objects that do not have TComponent in their ancestry.

Remember that properties in the published section have the advantages, and the overhead, associated with a heavy dose of runtime type information. In particular, properties placed in the public section will automatically be streamed to disk!

There is no rule that says which properties should be declared in the published or public sections. In fact, properties often appear in public sections, although there is little reason for them to be in private or protected sections.

The cost and description properties shown here are simple tools that do nothing more than hide data and lay the groundwork for their use inside the Object Inspector.

```
property Currency Cost={read=FCost, write=FCost};
```

The declaration starts with the keyword property, which performs the same type of syntactical chore as class or struct. Every property must be declared as having a certain type, which in this case is Currency.

Most properties can be both read and written. The read directive for the Cost property states that the value to be displayed is FCost and the value to write is FCost. In short, writing

```
{
  Widget->Cost = 2;
  int i = Widget.Cost
}
```

sets FCost to the value 2 and sets i to the value of FCost (again, 2).

The reasons for doing this are twofold:

- To hide data so that it is protected.
- To create a syntax that allows properties to be shown in the Object Inspector. Of course, you won't see these values in the Object Inspector until you metamorphose the object into a component, which is a subject that will be covered in Chapter 22, "Creating Descendants of Existing Components."

The Cost and Description properties provide what is called *direct access;* they map directly to the internal storage field. The runtime performance of accessing data through a direct-access property is exactly the same as accessing the private field directly.

The Cost and Description examples represent the simplest possible case for a property declaration. The TimeCreated property presents a few variations on these themes:

```
property AnsiString TimeCreated={read=GetTimeCreated, write=SetTimeCreated};
```

Rather than reading a variable directly, `TimeCreated` returns the result of a private function:

```
AnsiString __fastcall TWidget::GetTimeCreated()
{
  return FTimeCreated.DateTimeString();
}
```

`SetQuantity`, on the other hand, enables you to change the value of the `FQuantity` variable:

```
void __fastcall TWidget::SetTimeCreated(AnsiString S)
{
  FTimeCreated = TDateTime(S);
}
```

`GetTimeCreated` and `SetTimeCreated` are examples of access methods. Just as the internal storage for direct access variables begins by convention with the letter F, access methods usually begin with either `Set` or `Get`.

Take a moment to consider what is happening here. To use the `Quantity` property, you need to use the following syntax:

```
{
  AnsiString S;
  W->TimeCreated = "1/1/56 02:53:35 AM";
  S = W->TimeCreated;
}
```

Note that when you are writing to the `FTimeCreated` variable, you *don't* write

```
W->TimeCreated(Now());
```

Instead, you use the simple, explicit syntax of a direct assignment:

```
W->TimeCreated = Now();
```

BCB automatically translates the assignment into a function call that takes a parameter. C++ buffs will recognize this as a limited form of operator overloading.

If there were no properties, the previous code would look like this:

```
{
  AnsiString S;
  W->SetTimeCreated(Now());
  S = W->GetTimeCreated;
}
```

Instead of remembering one property name, this second technique requires you to remember two, and instead of the simple assignment syntax, you must remember to pass a parameter. Although it is not the main purpose of properties, it should now be obvious that one of their benefits is that they provide a clean, easy-to-use syntax. Furthermore, they allow you to completely hide the implementation of your `Get` and `Set` methods if you so desire.

Streaming Classes

Published properties allow you to automatically stream the data of your program. In particular, most published properties will be automatically written to your DFM files and restored when they are reloaded.

The following code shows how to explicitly write a component to disk:

```
void WriteWidgetToStream(AnsiString StreamName, TWidget *Widget)
{
  TFileStream *Stream = new TFileStream(StreamName, fmCreate | fmOpenWrite);
  Stream->WriteComponent(Widget);
  delete Stream;
}
```

To call this method, you might write code that looks like this:

```
TWidget * Widget= new TWidget(this);
Widget->Parent = this;
Widget->Left = 10;
Widget->Top = 10;
Widget->Cost = 3.3;
Widget->Description = "This is a widget";
Widget->TimeCreated = Now();
WriteWidgetToStream("Afile.dat", Widget);
```

This code creates an instance of the Widget component, assigns values to its data, and then writes it to disk in the last line of the code quoted here. This creates a persistent version of the object and explicitly preserves each property value.

The TFileStream component can be used to stream anything to disk; however, it has a very useful WriteComponent method that will stream an object automatically, taking care to store the current values of most published properties. In some cases, you might find a property that the VCL does not know how to stream. You can usually convert the property to an AnsiString, which the VCL component will know how to stream. This is what I did in this example, when I found that the VCL didn't want to write a variable of type TDateTime.

To construct an instance of TFileStream, you pass in the name of the file you want to work with and one or more flags specifying the rights you want when you open the file. These flags are listed in the online help and declared in SysUtils.hpp:

```
#define fmOpenRead (Byte)(0)
#define fmOpenWrite (Byte)(1)
#define fmOpenReadWrite (Byte)(2)
#define fmShareCompat (Byte)(0)
#define fmShareExclusive (Byte)(16)
#define fmShareDenyWrite (Byte)(32)
#define fmShareDenyRead (Byte)(48)
#define fmShareDenyNone (Byte)(64)
#define fmClosed (int)(55216)
#define fmInput (int)(55217)
#define fmOutput (int)(55218)
#define fmInOut (int)(55219)
```

FileStreams have a `Handle` property that you can use if you need it for special file operations or if you want to pass it to a handle-based C library file IO routine.

This is not the place to go into a detailed description of how streaming works in the VCL. However, you might want to open up `Classes.hpp` and take a look at the `TReader` and `TWriter` classes, which are helper objects that the VCL uses when it is time to stream an object. These classes have methods such as `ReadInteger`, `WriteInteger`, `ReadString`, `WriteString`, `ReadFloat`, and `WriteFloat`. `TReader` and `TWriter` are for use by the VCL, but I have used these classes for my own purposes on several occasions.

Here is how to read a component from a stream:

```
namespace Widgets
{
  void __fastcall Register()
  {
    TComponentClass classes[1] = {__classid(TWidget)};
    RegisterClasses(classes, 0);
  }
}

TWidget *ReadWidgetFromStream(AnsiString StreamName)
{
  Widgets::Register();
  TFileStream *Stream = new TFileStream(StreamName, fmOpenRead);
  TWidget *Widget = (TWidget *)Stream->ReadComponent(NULL);
  delete Stream;
  return Widget;
}
```

This code first registers the `TWidget` type with the system. This is necessary because the VCL needs to know what type of object you want to stream. Of course, when working with components that are placed on the Component Palette, you can be sure the system has already registered the object for you. However, if you did not drop a component on a form but created it by hand, you might have to register the component before you can stream it.

The `Register` method needs to appear in its own namespace because there will be many register functions in a typical application—at least one for each component. Most of the time this function will be called automatically by the compiler, and it is a bit unusual for you to have to call it explicitly.

Notice that the compiler will automatically construct an object for you if you pass in `NULL` when calling `ReadComponent`:

```
TWidget *Widget = (TWidget *)Stream->ReadComponent(NULL);
```

Alternatively, you can create the component yourself and then pass it to `ReadComponent` so that its properties will be lifted from the stream.

In the last few pages, you had a good look at the Widget2 program. There are several additional traits of properties that should be explored, however, before moving on to the colorful warehouse simulation found in the next chapter.

More on Properties

BCB provides support for five different types of properties:

- Simple properties are declared to be integers, characters, or strings.

- Enumerated properties are declared to be of some enumerated type. When shown in the Object Inspector, you can view them with a drop-down list.

- Set properties are declared to be of type Set. BorderIcons from TForm is an example of this type of property. You can choose only one enumerated value at a time, but you can combine several values in a property of type Set.

- Object properties are declared to be of some object type, such as the Items property from the TListBox component, which is declared to be of type TStrings.

- Array properties are like standard arrays, but you can index on any type, even a string. The classic example of this kind of property is the Strings property in a TStringList.

The PropertyTest program (in Listing 20.6) gives an example of each of the five types of properties. It also gives the TStringList object a fairly decent workout. The program itself is only minimally useful outside the range of a purely academic setting such as this book.

Listing 20.6. The main unit for the PropertyTest program.

```cpp
/////////////////////////////////////////
// Main.cpp
// Learning about properties
// Copyright (c) 1997 by Charlie Calvert
//
#include <vcl\vcl.h>
#pragma hdrstop
#include "Main.h"
#include "propertyobject1.h"
#pragma resource "*.dfm"
TForm2 *Form2;
//-------------------------------------------------------------------
__fastcall TForm2::TForm2(TComponent* Owner)
: TForm(Owner)
{
}
//-------------------------------------------------------------------
void __fastcall TForm2::bCreateObjectsClick(TObject *Sender)
{
  TMyProps *M;
  char Ch;
  int i;
  M = new TMyProps(this);
  M->Parent = this;
  M->SimpleProp = 25;
  M->EnumProp = teEnum;
  M->SetProp = TSetProp() << teEnum << teSet;
  M->StrArrayProp["Jones"] = "Sam, Mary";
  M->StrArrayProp["Doe"] = "John, Johanna";
```

```
    ListBox1->Items->Add(M->StrArrayProp["Doe"]);
    ListBox1->Items->Add(M->StrArrayProp["Jones"]);
    for (i = 0; i < M->ObjectProp->Count; i++)
      ListBox2->Items->Add(M->ArrayProp[i]);
    Ch = M->Default1;
    ListBox1->Items->Add(Ch);
}
```

Listing 20.7. The header file for the `PropertyObject` unit.

```
/////////////////////////////////////
// PropertyObject.h
// Learning about properties
// Copyright (c) 1997 by Charlie Calvert
//
#ifndef PropertyObject1H
#define PropertyObject1H
enum TEnumType {teSimple, teEnum, teSet, teObject, teArray};
typedef Set<TEnumType, teSimple, teArray> TSetProp;
  class TCouple: public TObject
  {
  public:
    AnsiString Husband;
    AnsiString Wife;
    TCouple() {}
  };
  class TMyProps: public TCustomControl
  {
  private:
    int FSimple;
    TEnumType FEnumType;
    TSetProp FSetProp;
    TStringList *FObjectProp;
    char FDefault1;
    AnsiString __fastcall GetArray(int Index);
    AnsiString __fastcall GetStrArray(AnsiString S);
    void SetStrArray(AnsiString Index, AnsiString S);
  protected:
    void virtual __fastcall Paint();
  public:
    virtual __fastcall TMyProps(TComponent *AOwner);
    virtual __fastcall ~TMyProps();
    __property AnsiString ArrayProp[int i]={read=GetArray};
    __property AnsiString StrArrayProp[AnsiString i]=
      {read=GetStrArray,write=SetStrArray};
  __published:
    __property int SimpleProp={read=FSimple, write=FSimple};
    __property TEnumType EnumProp={read=FEnumType, write=FEnumType};
    __property TSetProp SetProp={read=FSetProp, write=FSetProp};
    __property TStringList *ObjectProp={read=FObjectProp, write=FObjectProp};
    __property char Default1={read=FDefault1, write=FDefault1, default= '1'};
  };
#endif
```

Listing 20.8. The source for the PropertyTest unit shows how to work with properties.

```cpp
///////////////////////////////////////
// PropertyObject.cpp
// Learning about properties
// Copyright (c) 1997 by Charlie Calvert
//
#include <vcl\vcl.h>
#pragma hdrstop
#include "PropertyObject1.h"
#include "codebox.h"
__fastcall TMyProps::TMyProps(TComponent *AOwner)
 :TCustomControl(AOwner)
{
  Width = 100;
  Height = 100;
  Left = (((TForm*)(AOwner))->ClientWidth / 2) - (Width / 2);
  Top = (((TForm*)(AOwner))->ClientHeight / 2) - (Height / 2);
  FObjectProp = new TStringList();
  Default1 = '1';
};
__fastcall TMyProps::~TMyProps()
{
  int i;
  for (i = 0; i < FObjectProp->Count; i++)
  {
    FObjectProp->Objects[i]->Free();
  }
  FObjectProp->Free();
}
void __fastcall TMyProps::Paint()
{
  Canvas->Brush->Color = clBlue;
  TCustomControl::Paint();
  Canvas->Rectangle(0, 0, Width, Height);
  Canvas->TextOut(1, 1, "FSimple: " + IntToStr(FSimple));
  Canvas->TextOut(1, Canvas->TextHeight("Blaise"), GetArray(0));
  Canvas->TextOut(1, Canvas->TextHeight("Blaise") * 2, FObjectProp->Strings[1]);
};
AnsiString __fastcall TMyProps::GetArray(int Index)
{
  return FObjectProp->Strings[Index];
}
AnsiString __fastcall TMyProps::GetStrArray(AnsiString S)
{
  TCouple *Couple;
  Couple = (TCouple*)(FObjectProp->Objects[FObjectProp->IndexOf(S)]);
  return Couple->Husband + ", " + Couple->Wife;
}
AnsiString GetHusband(AnsiString S)
{
  return StripLastToken(S, ',');
}
AnsiString GetWife(AnsiString S)
{
  return StripFirstToken(S, ',');
}
void TMyProps::SetStrArray(AnsiString Index, AnsiString S)
{
```

```
    TCouple *Couple;
    Couple = new TCouple();
    Couple->Husband = GetHusband(S);
    Couple->Wife = GetWife(S);
    FObjectProp->AddObject(Index, Couple);
}
```

The structure of the PropertyTest program is simple. There is a main form with a button on it. If you click the button, you instantiate an object of type TMyObject, as shown in Figure 20.3.

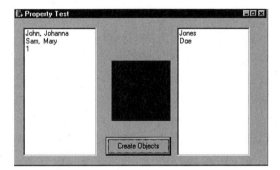

TMyObject has five properties, one for each of the major types of properties. These properties have self-explanatory names:

```
__property int SimpleProp={read=FSimple, write=FSimple};
__property TEnumType EnumProp={read=FEnumType, write=FEnumType};
__property TSetProp SetProp={read=FSetProp, write=FSetProp};
__property TStringList *ObjectProp={read=FObjectProp, write=FObjectProp};
__property AnsiString ArrayProp[int i]={read=GetArray};
```

Before exploring these properties, I should mention that TMyProps is descended from the native VCL object called TCustomControl. TCustomControl is intelligent enough to both display itself on the screen and store itself on the Component Palette. It has several key methods and properties already associated with it, including a Paint method and Width and Height fields.

Because TCustomControl is so intelligent, it is easy to use its Paint method to write values to the screen:

```
void __fastcall TMyProps::Paint()
{
  Canvas->Brush->Color = clBlue;
  TCustomControl::Paint();
  Canvas->Rectangle(0, 0, Width, Height);
  Canvas->TextOut(1, 1, "FSimple: " + IntToStr(FSimple));
  Canvas->TextOut(1, Canvas->TextHeight("Blaise"), GetArray(0));
  Canvas->TextOut(1, Canvas->TextHeight("Blaise") * 2, FObjectProp->Strings[1]);
};
```

Note that you do not need to explicitly call the Paint method. Windows calls it for you whenever the object needs to paint or repaint itself. This means that you can hide the window behind others, and it will repaint itself automatically when it is brought to the fore. Inheriting functionality that you need from other objects is a big part of what OOP is all about.

The first three properties of TMyProps are extremely easy to understand:

```
__property int SimpleProp={read=FSimple, write=FSimple};
__property TEnumType EnumProp={read=FEnumType, write=FEnumType};
__property TSetProp SetProp={read=FSetProp, write=FSetProp};
```

These are direct access properties that simply read to and write from a variable. You can use them with the following syntax:

```
M->SimpleProp = 25;
M->EnumProp = teEnum;
M->SetProp = TSetProp() << teEnum << teSet;
```

> **NOTE**
>
> I once asked one of the developers whether properties such as these didn't waste computer clock cycles. Looking somewhat miffed, he said, "Obviously, we map those calls directly to the variables!"
>
> Chastened, and somewhat the wiser, I nodded sagely as if this were the answer I expected. Then, I ventured, "So they don't cost us any clock cycles?"
>
> "Not at runtime, they don't!" he said, and concentrated once again on his debugger, which hovered over some obscure line in Classes.Pas.

The syntax for using the ObjectProp property is similar to the examples shown previously, but it is a bit harder to fully comprehend the relationship between an object and a property:

```
__property TStringList *ObjectProp={read=FObjectProp, write=FObjectProp};
```

ObjectProp is of type TStringList, which is a descendant of the TStrings type used in the TListBox.Items property or the TMemo.Lines property. I use TStringList instead of TStrings because TStrings is essentially an abstract type meant for use only in limited circumstances. For general purposes, you should always use a TStringList instead of a TStrings object. (In fact, neither TListBox nor TMemo actually uses variables of type TStrings. They actually use descendants of TStrings, just as I do here.)

> **NOTE**
>
> A TStringList has two possible functions. You can use it to store a simple list of strings, and you can also associate an object with each of those strings. To perform the latter task, call AddObject, passing a string in the first parameter and a TObject descendant in the second parameter. You can then retrieve the object by passing in the string you used in the call to AddObject.
>
> TStringLists do not destroy the objects that you store in them—though they will, of course, clean up the strings you hang on them. It is up to you to deallocate the memory of any object you store on a TStringList.
>
> If you want a simple list object that doesn't have all this specialized functionality, use a linked list or the versatile TList object that ships with BCB.

After making the declaration for ObjectProp shown earlier, you can now use it as if it were a simple TStringList variable. This can sometimes be a bit inconvenient, however. For instance, the following syntax retrieves an object that is associated with a string:

```
AnsiString S = "StringConstant";
Couple = (TCouple*)(FObjectProp->Objects[FObjectProp->IndexOf(S)]);
```

While not completely beyond the pale, this is definitely not the kind of code you want to have strewn indiscriminately through a program that is going to be maintained by a mere mortal. Furthermore, you must be sure to allocate memory for the FObjectProp at the beginning of TMyProps's existence, and you must dispose of that memory in the TMyProps destructor:

```
__fastcall TMyProps::TMyProps(TComponent *AOwner)
 :TCustomControl(AOwner)
{
  ... // Code omitted here
  FObjectProp = new TStringList();
};
__fastcall TMyProps::~TMyProps()
{
  int i;
  for (i = 0; i < FObjectProp->Count; i++)
  {
    FObjectProp->Objects[i]->Free();
  }
  FObjectProp->Free();
}
```

The key point is that you must iterate through the string list at the end of the program, deallocating memory for each object you store on the list. Then you must deallocate the memory for the TStringList itself.

There is nothing you can do about the necessity of allocating and deallocating memory for an object of type TStringList. You can, however, use array properties to simplify the act of accessing it, and to simplify the act of allocating memory for each object you store in it. PropertyTest shows how this can be done.

The code entertains the conceit that you are creating a list for a party to which only married couples are invited. Each couple's last name is stored as a string in a TStringList, and their first names are stored in an object that is stored in the TStringList in association with the last name. In other words, PropertyTest calls AddObject with the last name in the first parameter and an object containing their first names in the second parameter. This sounds complicated at first, but array properties can make the task trivial from the user's point of view.

In the PropertyTest program, I store a simple object with two fields inside the TStringList:

```
class TCouple: public TObject
{
public:
  AnsiString Husband;
  AnsiString Wife;
  TCouple() {}
};
```

Note that this object looks a lot like a simple struct. In fact, I would have used a record here, except that TStringLists expect TObject descendants, not simple records. (Actually, you can sometimes get away with storing non-objects in TStringLists, but I'm not going to cover that topic in this book.)

As described earlier, it would be inconvenient to ask consumers of TMyObject to allocate memory for a TCouple object each time it needed to be used. Instead, PropertyTest asks the user to pass in first and last names in this simple string format:

```
"HusbandName, WifeName"
```

PropertyTest also asks them to pass in the last name as a separate variable. To simplify this process, I use a string array property:

```
__property AnsiString StrArrayProp[AnsiString i]=
    {read=GetStrArray,write=SetStrArray};
```

Notice that this array uses a string as an index, rather than a number!

Given the StrArrayProp declaration, the user can write the following code:

```
M->StrArrayProp["Jones"] = "Sam, Mary";
```

This is a simple, intuitive line of code, even if it is a bit unconventional. The question, of course, is how can BCB parse this information?

If you look at the declaration for StrArrayProp, you can see that it has two access methods called GetStrArray and SetStrArray. SetStrArray and its associated functions look like this:

```
AnsiString GetHusband(AnsiString S)
{
  return StripLastToken(S, ',');
}
AnsiString GetWife(AnsiString S)
{
  return StripFirstToken(S, ',');
}
void TMyProps::SetStrArray(AnsiString Index, AnsiString S)
{
  TCouple *Couple;
  Couple = new TCouple();
  Couple->Husband = GetHusband(S);
  Couple->Wife = GetWife(S);
  FObjectProp->AddObject(Index, Couple);
}
```

Note the declaration for SetStrArray. It takes two parameters. The first one is an index of type string, and the second is the value to be stored in the array. So, "Jones" is passed in as an index, and "Sam, Mary" is the value to be added to the array.

SetStrArray begins by allocating memory for an object of type TCouple. It then parses the husband and wife's names from the string by calling two token-based functions from the CodeBox unit that ships with this book. Finally, a call to AddObject is executed. When the program is finished, you must be sure to deallocate the memory for the TCouple objects in the destructor.

The twin of SetStrArray is GetStrArray. This function retrieves a couple's last name from the TStringList whenever the user passes in a last name. The syntax for retrieving information from the StrArray property looks like this:

```
AnsiString S = M->StrArrayProp["Doe"];
```

In this case, S is assigned the value "Sam, Mary". Once again, note the remarkable fact that BCB enables us to use a string as an index in a property array.

The implementation for GetStrArray is fairly simple:

```
AnsiString __fastcall TMyProps::GetStrArray(AnsiString S)
{
  TCouple *Couple;
  Couple = (TCouple*)(FObjectProp->Objects[FObjectProp->IndexOf(S)]);
  return Couple->Husband + ", " + Couple->Wife;
}
```

The code retrieves the object from the TStringList and then performs some simple hand-waving to re-create the original string passed in by the user. Obviously, it would be easy to add additional methods that retrieved only a wife's name, or only a husband's name.

20

ENCAPSULATION

I'm showing you this syntax not because I'm convinced that you need to use TStringLists and property arrays in exactly the manner showed here, but because I want to demonstrate how properties can be used to conceal an implementation and hide data from the user. The last two properties declared in this program show how to use important property types, and they also demonstrate how properties can be used to reduce relatively complex operations to a simple syntax.

Consumers of this object don't need to know that I am storing the information in a TStringList, and they won't need to know if I change the method of storing this information at some later date. As long as the interface for TMyObject remains the same—that is, as long as I don't change the declaration for StrArrayProp—I am free to change the implementation at any time.

There is one other array property used in this program that should be mentioned briefly:

```
__property AnsiString ArrayProp[int i]={read=GetArray};
```

ArrayProp uses the traditional integer as an index. However, note that this array still has a special trait not associated with normal arrays: It is read-only! Because no write method is declared for this property, it cannot be written to; it can be used only to query the TStringList that it ends up addressing:

```
AnsiString __fastcall TMyProps::GetArray(int Index)
{
  return FObjectProp->Strings[Index];
}
```

You can call ArrayProp with this syntax:

```
AnsiString S = M->ArrayProp[0];
```

This is an obvious improvement over writing the following:

```
AnsiString S = M->FObjectProp->Strings[0];
```

Creating a simple interface for an object might not seem important at first, but in day-to-day programming a simple, clean syntax is invaluable. For instance, the PropertyTest program calls ArrayProp in the following manner:

```
for (i = 0; i < M->ObjectProp->Count; i++)
    ListBox2->Items->Add(M->ArrayProp[i]);
```

NOTE

Astute readers might be noticing that BCB is flexible enough to enable you to improve even its own syntax. For instance, if you wanted to, you could create a list box descendant that enables you to write this syntax:

```
ListBox2->AddStr(S);
```

instead of

```
ListBox2->Items->Add(S);
```

In Chapter 22, you will see that you can even replace the `TListBox` object on the component palette with one of your own making! The techniques you are learning in these chapters on the VCL will prove to be the key to enhancing BCB so that it becomes a custom-made tool that fits your specific needs.

If you bury yourself in the BCB source code, eventually you might notice the `default` directive, which can be used with properties:

```
__property char Default1={read=FDefault1, write=FDefault1, default= '1'};
```

Looking at this syntax, one would tend to think that this code automatically sets `FDefault1` to the value `'1'`. However, this is not its purpose. Rather, it tells BCB whether this value needs to be streamed when a form file is being written to disk. If you make `TMyProp` into a component, drop it onto a form, and save that form to disk, BCB explicitly saves that value if it is not equal to `1`, but skips it if it is equal to `1`.

An obvious benefit of the `default` directive is that it saves room in DFM files. Many objects have as many as 25, or even 50, properties associated with them. Writing them all to disk would be an expensive task. As it happens, most properties used in a form have default values that are never changed. The `default` directive merely specifies that default value, and BCB thus knows whether to write the value to disk. If the property in the Object Inspector is equal to the default, BCB just passes over the property when it's time to write to disk. When reading the values back in, if the property is not explicitly mentioned in the DFM file, the property retains the value you assigned to it in the component's constructor.

> **NOTE**
>
> The property is never assigned the default value by BCB. You *must* ensure that you assign the default values to the properties as you indicated in the class declaration. This must be done in the constructor. A mismatch between the declared default and the actual initial value established by the constructor will result in lost data when streaming the component in and out:
>
> ```
> __fastcall TMyProps::TMyProps(TComponent *AOwner)
>  :TCustomControl(AOwner)
> {
>   ... // Code omitted here
>   Default1 = '1';
> };
> ```
>
> Similarly, if you change the initial value of an inherited published property in your constructor, you should also reassert/redeclare (partial declaration) that property in your descendant class declaration to change the declared default value to match the actual initial value.
>
> *continues*

20

continued

The `default` directive does nothing more than give BCB a way of determining whether it needs to write a value to disk. It never assigns a value to any property. You have to do that yourself in your constructor.

Of course, there are times when you want to assign a property a default value at the moment that the object it belongs to is created. These are the times when you wish the `default` directive did what its name implies. However, it does not, and never will, perform this action. To gain this functionality you must use the constructor, as shown in the PropertyTest application.

There are a few occasions when the constructor won't work for you because of the current state of a property. In those cases, you can use the `Loaded` or `SetParent` methods to initialize the value of a property. If you use the `Loaded` method to initialize a property, the results of the initialization won't show up at design-time but will become evident at runtime.

After reading this section, it should be clear that array properties represent one of the more powerful and flexible aspects of BCB programming. Though they are quite similar to operator overloading, they have their own special qualities and advantages.

Summary

That wraps up this introduction to properties and encapsulation. The key items you have explored are the `private`, `protected`, `public`, and `__published` directives, as well as the art of creating useful properties. I have also attempted to browbeat you with the importance of hiding data and methods. Remember that robust, easily maintainable objects never directly expose their data! Instead, they present the user with a simple, custom-designed interface that should usually be easy to use.

In the next chapter, you will learn about polymorphism, which is the crown jewel of object-oriented theory.

Polymorphism

IN THIS CHAPTER

Overview

In this chapter, you will learn about an esoteric but important subject called *polymorphism*. If you use object-oriented programming (OOP) but skip polymorphism, you miss out on a key tool that yields robust, flexible architectures.

You don't need to understand polymorphism or much about objects to program in BCB. However, if you want to be an expert BCB programmer and want to create components, you should master this material.

In this chapter, I take you through several fairly simple programs designed to illustrate key aspects of polymorphism. By the time you're done, you should understand why the simple ability to assign a child object to a parent object is one of the most important features of the entire C++ language.

Polymorphism from 20,000 Feet

Polymorphism can be confusing even to experienced OOP programmers. My explanation of this subject starts with a high-level overview of the theoretical issues that lie at the core of this field of study. The text then moves on to show some real-world examples and finally comes back to a second take on the high-level overview. Don't panic if you don't understand the information in the next few paragraphs right away. I cover this material several times in several different ways, and by the time you finish this chapter, all should be clear to you.

Polymorphism is a technique that allows you to set a parent object equal to one or more of its child objects:

```
Parent = Child;
```

The interesting thing about this technique is that, after the assignment, the parent acts in different ways, depending on the traits of the child that is currently assigned to it. One object, the parent, therefore acts in many different ways—hence the name "polymorphism," which translates literally from its Greek roots to an English phrase similar to "many shapes."

> **NOTE**
>
> I find the words "assign" and "equal" extremely tricky. If I'm speaking off the cuff and use the word "assign" in three consecutive sentences, I will trip over myself for sure! Because this seemingly simple subject is so tricky, I'm going to take a moment to lay out some rules that you can reference while you're reading this chapter.
>
> Consider the following code fragment:
>
> ```
> Parent = Child;
> ```

In this simple statement, the child is assigned to its parent. The parent is not assigned to its child. You could easily argue that this definition could be reversed, but I do not take that approach in this chapter.

When referencing the preceding code fragment, I also say that the parent is set equal to its child. The child is not set equal to its parent. Once again, you can argue that this definition could be reversed, or that the action is reflexive. Throughout this chapter, however, I consistently state that the preceding code sets a parent equal to its child, and not a child equal to its parent.

Because these seemingly simple English phrases are so confusing, at least to me, I try to illustrate exactly what I mean as often as possible. That is, I say the statement in English, insert a colon, and then follow the English phrase with code that provides an example of the meaning of my statement. I find the English phrases ambiguous and confusing, but the code is starkly clear. Don't waste too much time parsing the English; concentrate on the code!

The classic example of polymorphism is a series of objects, all of which do the following:

- Descend from one base class
- Respond to a virtual command called Draw
- Produce different outcomes

For instance, you might have four objects called TRectangle, TEllipse, TCircle, and TSquare. Suppose that each of these objects is a descendant of a base class called TShape, and that TShape has a virtual method called Draw. (This hypothetical TShape object is not necessarily the one that appears on BCB's component palette.) All the children of TShape also have Draw methods, but one draws a circle; one, a square; the next, a rectangle; and the last, an ellipse. You could then assign any of these objects to a variable of type TShape, and that TShape variable would act differently after each assignment. That is, the object of type TShape would draw a square if set equal to a TSquare object:

```
TShape *Shape = Square;
Shape->Draw();   // Draws a square.
```

It would draw an ellipse if set equal to a TEllipse object:

```
TShape *Shape = Ellipse;
Shape->Draw();   // Draws an ellipse;
```

and so on.

Notice that in both these cases the object that does the drawing is of type TShape. In both cases, the same command of TShape is called. You would therefore expect that a call to Shape->Draw() would always produce the same results. Polymorphism puts the lie to this logic. It allows a method of an object to act in many different ways. One object, called Shape, "morphs" from one set of functionality to another, depending on the context of the call. That's polymorphism.

From a conceptual point of view, this description does much to explain what polymorphism is all about. However, I still need to explain one key aspect.

According to the rules of OOP, you can pass all these objects to a single function that takes an object of type TShape as a parameter. That single function can call the Draw method of each of these objects, and each one will behave differently:

```
void DrawIt(TShape *Shape)
{
  Shape->Draw(); // TShape draws different shapes depending on "assignment"
}

void DoSomething()
{
  TRectangle *Rectangle = new TRectangle();
  TSquare *Square = new TSquare();
  TEllipse *Ellipse = new TEllipse();
  DrawIt(Rectangle);          // Draws a rectangle
  DrawIt(Square);             // Draws a square
  DrawIt(Ellipse);            // Draws an ellipse

  delete Rectangle;
  delete Square;
  delete Ellipse;
}
```

When you pass an object of type TRectangle to a function that takes a TShape as a parameter, you are accessing the TRectangle object through an object of type TShape. Or, if you look at the act of passing a parameter from a slightly different angle, you're actually assigning a variable of type TRectangle to a variable of type TShape:

```
Shape = Rectangle;
```

This assignment is the actual hub around which polymorphism revolves. Because this assignment is legal, you can use an object of a single type yet have it behave in many different ways: Once again, that's polymorphism.

NOTE

Grasping the idea behind polymorphism is a bit like grasping the idea behind pointers. Many programmers have a hard time understanding pointers when they first see them. Then, after a time, manipulating pointers becomes as natural as tying their shoes. It no longer requires thought. The same is true of polymorphism. The concept can seem quite opaque at first to many programmers, and then they have a little epiphany. Then wham! Suddenly their coding ability makes the same kind of huge jump forward that occurred when they learned about pointers.

Polymorphism has the same relationship to OOP that pointers have to C or C++. People might say they are C++ programmers, but if they don't understand pointers, they are missing out on at least half of what the language has to offer. The same is true of OOP and polymorphism. Many programmers claim to understand OOP, but if they don't yet see what polymorphism is all about, they are missing at least half the power of technology.

To fully understand the preceding few paragraphs, you have to grasp that children of an object are assignment-compatible with their parents. Consider the following declaration:

```
class TParent
{
}

class TChild: public TParent
{
}
```

Given these declarations, the following is legal:

```
{
  TParent *Parent;
  TChild *Child;
  Parent = Child;
}
```

But this syntax is flagged as a type mismatch; that is, the compiler will complain that it cannot convert a variable of type TParent* to TChild*:

```
{
  TParent *Parent;
  TChild *Child;
  Child = Parent;
}
```

You can't set a child equal to a parent because the child is larger than its parent—that is, it has more methods or fields—and therefore all its fields and methods will not be filled out by the assignment. All other things being equal, you can build a two-story building out of the pieces meant for a three-story building; but you can't build a three-story building out of the pieces meant for a two-story building.

Consider the following hierarchy:

```
class TParent: public TObject
{
  virtual void Draw();
};

class TChild: public TParent
{
  virtual void Draw();
  virtual void ShowHierarchy();
};
```

The issue here is that setting a child equal to a parent is not safe:

```
Child = Parent; // Don't do this!
```

If it were allowed, writing the following would be a disaster:

```
Child->ShowHierarchy();
```

In this hypothetical world, the call might compile, but it would fail at runtime because `Parent` has no `ShowHierarchy` method; therefore, it could not provide a valid address for the function at the time of the assignment operation. I will return to this subject in the next section of this chapter.

If you set a parent equal to a child, all the features of the parent will be filled out properly:

```
Parent = Child;
```

That is, all the functions of `TParent` are part of `TChild`, so you can assign one to the other without fear of something going wrong. The methods that are not part of `TParent` are ignored.

> **NOTE**
>
> When you're thinking about this material, you need to be sure you are reading statements about assigning parents to children correctly. Even if I manage to straighten out my grammar, nothing in the English language makes totally clear which item in an assignment statement is on the left and which is on the right. I could use the terms `lvalue` and `rvalue` in this case, except that they don't quite fit. However, if you take this description as an analogy, you can consider a child to be an `rvalue` and a parent to be an `lvalue`. You can set a parent equal to a child:
>
> ```
> Parent = Child;
> ```
>
> but you can't set a child equal to a parent:
>
> ```
> Child  = Parent;
> ```
>
> You literally can't do this. You get a type mismatch. The compiler replies "Cannot convert `TParent*` to `TChild`." In this sense, `Child` becomes like an `rvalue` in this one case. Even though assigning values to `Child` is ultimately possible, you can't assign a `Parent` to it. In this one case, it might as well be an `rvalue`.
>
> To see this process in action, start a new project in the IDE, drop a button on the form, and write the following code:
>
> ```
> void __fastcall TForm1::Button1Click(TObject *Sender)
> {
>   TForm *Form;
>   TComponent *Component;
> ```

```
    Component = Form;
    Form = Component;
}
```
The compiler will allow the first assignment but object to the second. This objection occurs because TForm is a descendant of TComponent.

Another View of Polymorphism

Here's another way of looking at polymorphism. A base class defines a certain number of functions that are inherited by all its descendants. If you assign a variable of the child type to one of its parents, all the parent's methods are guaranteed to be filled out with valid addresses. The issue here is that the child, by the very fact of its being a descendant object, must have valid addresses for all the methods used in its parent's virtual method table (VMT). As a result, you can call one of these methods and watch as the child's functions get called. However, you cannot call one of the child's methods that does not also belong to the parent. The parent doesn't know about those methods, so the compiler won't let you call them. In other words, the parent may be able to call some of the child's functions, but it is still a variable of the parent type.

> **NOTE**
>
> A virtual method table, or VMT, is a table maintained in memory by the compiler; it contains a list of all the pointers to the virtual methods hosted by an object. If you have an object that is descended from TObject, the VMT for that object will contain all the virtual methods of that object, plus the virtual methods of TObject.

To help you understand this arrangement, picture the VMT for TParent. It has a pointer to a Draw method in it, but no pointer to a ShowHierarchy method. Therefore, an attempt to call its ShowHierarchy method would fail, as would an attempt to fill out a TChild's ShowHierarchy through an assignment with a TParent object.

Consider this schema:

```
Simplified VMT for Parent        Simplified VMT for Child
StartTable                       StartTable
  Draw --------------------------- Draw
EndTable                           ShowHierarchy
                                 EndTable
```

This schema shows a parent being set equal to a child. As you can see, the address of the Draw method for the parent is assigned to the address for the Draw method for the child. No ShowHierarchy method exists in the parent, so it is ignored.

Here's what happens if you try to set the child equal to the parent:

```
Simplified VMT for Child        Simplified VMT for Parent
StartTable                      StartTable
   Draw --------------------------- Draw
   ShowHierarchy ------------------ ????
EndTable                        EndTable
```

As you can clearly see, no method pointer in the parent table can be assigned to the ShowHierarchy method of the child table. Therefore, it is left blank, which means a call to the ShowHierarchy method of the child almost certainly fails.

Because the ShowHierarchy method cannot be filled out properly, assigning TParent to TChild is illegal. In other words, it's not just a legal technicality, it's a literal impossibility. You literally can't successfully assign a parent to a child. You can, however, assign a child to a parent, and it's this assignment that lies at the heart of polymorphism. For the sake of clarity, let me spell it out. Here is the legal assignment:

```
Parent = Child;
```

Here is the illegal assignment:

```
Child = Parent;
```

Needless to say, I wouldn't be placing so much emphasis on this subject if it were not vitally important. You simply won't really understand OOP unless you grasp what has been said in the last few pages.

Virtual Methods and Polymorphism

If some of the methods in a base class are defined as virtual, each of the descendants can redefine the implementation of these methods. The key elements that define a typical case of polymorphism are a base class and the descendants that inherit a base class's methods. In particular, the fanciest type of polymorphism involves virtual methods that are inherited from a base class.

A classic example of polymorphism is evident if you examine the BCB VCL. All these objects are descendants of a single base class called TObject; therefore, they all inherit a virtual destructor. As a result, you can pass all the many hundreds of BCB classes to a routine that takes a parameter of the same type as their base class:

```
void FreeAllClasses(TObject O)
{
  delete O;
}
```

You can pass any VCL object to the `FreeAllClasses` function, and the object will be properly destroyed. The VirtualMethodTest program, shown in Listings 21.1 and 21.2, shows how this process works. You can also find this program on the CD that comes with this book.

Listing 21.1. The header for the VirtualMethodTest program.

```
////////////////////////////////////////
// Main.h
// VirtualMethodTest
// Copyright (c) 1997 by Charlie Calvert
//
#ifndef MainH
#define MainH
#include <vcl\Classes.hpp>
#include <vcl\Controls.hpp>
#include <vcl\StdCtrls.hpp>
#include <vcl\Forms.hpp>

class TParent
{
public:
  TParent() {}
  virtual __fastcall ~TParent()
    { ShowMessage("TParent Destructor"); }
  virtual void Draw() {}
};

class TChild: public TParent
{
public:
  TChild(): TParent() {}
  virtual __fastcall ~TChild()
    { ShowMessage("TChild Destructor"); }
  virtual void Draw() {}
  virtual void ShowHierarchy() {}
};

class TForm1 : public TForm
{
__published:
  TButton *RunTestBtn;
  void __fastcall RunTestBtnClick(TObject *Sender);
private:
  void FreeObjects(TParent *Parent);
public:
  virtual __fastcall TForm1(TComponent* Owner);
};

extern TForm1 *Form1;

#endif
```

Listing 21.2. The main body of the main form for the VirtualMethodTest program.

```
/////////////////////////////////////
// Main.cpp
// VirtualMethodTest
// Copyright (c) 1997 by Charlie Calvert
//
#include <vcl\vcl.h>
#pragma hdrstop
#include "Main.h"
#pragma resource "*.dfm"

TForm1 *Form1;

__fastcall TForm1::TForm1(TComponent* Owner)
: TForm(Owner)
{
}

void TForm1::FreeObjects(TParent *Parent)
{
  delete Parent;
}

void __fastcall TForm1::RunTestBtnClick(TObject *Sender)
{
  TParent *Parent = new TParent();
  TChild *Child = new TChild();
  FreeObjects(Parent);
  FreeObjects(Child);
}
```

From a visual point of view, this program is very unexciting, as you can see from a glance at Figure 21.1.

FIGURE 21.1.

The main form of the VirtualMethodTest program.

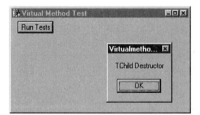

To put this program to work, you need to change the destructors for the TParent and TChild objects so that they are sometimes declared as virtual and sometimes declared as standard, non-virtual methods:

```
class TParent
{
public:
```

```
  TParent() {}
  virtual __fastcall ~TParent() { ShowMessage("TParent Destructor"); }
  virtual void Draw() {}
};

class TParent
{
public:
  TParent() {}
  __fastcall ~TParent() { ShowMessage("TParent Destructor"); }
  virtual void Draw() {}
};
```

In the first case, the destructor is declared as virtual, and in the second, it is not declared as virtual. Notice that I do not make TParent descend from TObject, because all VCL classes must have virtual destructors since TObject itself declares its destructor as virtual.

When you do not declare the destructors as virtual, and you pass the objects to the FreeObjects method, the destructor for TParent is called:

```
void TForm1::FreeObjects(TParent *Parent)
{
  delete Parent;
}
```

If you declare both destructors as virtual, when you pass them to FreeObjects, the destructor for TChild will be called, even though it is being called off an instance of TParent.

If what I'm saying is not clear, start C++Builder and load the VirtualMethodTest program so that you can watch this process in action. Run the program with the destructor declared as virtual and then run it again without the virtual destructor declaration. This material is extremely important. You simply cannot understand what OOP is all about if you do not understand polymorphism.

Remember that passing a parameter to FreeAllClasses is analogous to an assignment statement. In effect, you are writing

```
Parent = Parent;
Parent = Child;
```

You could not, however, write this:

```
void TForm1::FreeObjects(TChild *Child)
{
  delete Child;
}

void __fastcall TForm1::Button1Click(TObject *Sender)
{
  TParent *Parent = new TParent();
  TChild *Child = new TChild();
  FreeObjects(Parent);
  FreeObjects(Child);
}
```

The issue, of course, is that by passing `Parent` to `FreeAllClasses`, you are, in effect, asking BCB to make the following assignment:

```
Child = Parent;
```

BCB is kind enough to tell you that making this assignment is bad practice.

Every object in the VCL can use polymorphism to some degree because they all inherit methods from `TObject`. In particular, they all inherit a virtual destructor. Without this virtual destructor, the whole system would collapse. In particular, the component array hosted by each form is iterated at closing time, and the destructor of each object is called. Doing so would not be possible if the destructors of these objects were not declared virtual. Or, rather, doing so would be possible, but the objects themselves would not be properly destroyed. The reason for the failure is illustrated clearly in the VirtualMethodTest program.

To help illustrate this point, I will implement the classic shape demo example described earlier in this chapter. This program creates a parent object called `TMyShape` and two child objects called `TRectangle` and `TCircle`. All three of these objects have virtual methods called `DrawShape`. You can pass a single instance of this object to a method declared as follows:

```
void TForm1::CallDrawShape(TMyShape *Shape)
{
  Shape->DrawShape();
}
```

If you pass in an instance of `TMyShape`, then the `TMyShape::DrawShape` method will be called, which is what you would expect. However, if you pass in either a `TRectangle` or `TCircle`, then the respective `DrawShape` methods of each object will be called, as shown in Figure 21.2.

FIGURE 21.2.

The ClassicShapeDemo shows how one object can behave in three different ways: on the left it draws a star, in the center a circle, and on the right a square.

The `TForm1::CallDrawShape` method works with a variable of type `TMyShape`. It has only one kind of object in it. It works only with variables of type `TMyShape`. And yet if you pass both a `TRectangle` object and a `TMyShape` object into it, one instance will call the `DrawShape` method of `TRectangle` and the other will call the `DrawShape` method of `TMyShape`. This example illustrates polymorphism in action. The concept here is so important that I have placed this example on disk in a directory called `ClassicShapeDemo` and show it in Listings 21.3 and 21.4.

Listing 21.3. The header for ClassicShapeDemo shows how polymorphism looks in action.

```
///////////////////////////////////
// Main.h
// Classic Shape Demo
// Copyright (c) 1997 by Charlie Calvert
//

#ifndef MainH
#define MainH
#include <vcl\Classes.hpp>
#include <vcl\Controls.hpp>
#include <vcl\StdCtrls.hpp>
#include <vcl\Forms.hpp>
#include <vcl\ExtCtrls.hpp>


class TMyShape: public TCustomControl
{
public:
  virtual __fastcall TMyShape(TComponent *AOwner): TCustomControl(AOwner) {}
  virtual __fastcall TMyShape(TComponent *AOwner, int X, int Y)
    : TCustomControl(AOwner) { Width = 50; Height = 50;  Left = X; Top = Y; }
  virtual void DrawShape()
  { Canvas->Brush->Style = bsClear; Canvas->TextOut(0, 0, "*"); }
};

class TCircle: public TMyShape
{
public:
  virtual __fastcall TCircle(TComponent *AOwner): TMyShape(AOwner) {}
  virtual __fastcall TCircle(TComponent *AOwner, int X, int Y)
    : TMyShape(AOwner) { Width = 50; Height = 50;  Left = X; Top = Y; }
  virtual void DrawShape()
  { Canvas->Brush->Color = clBlue; Canvas->Ellipse(0, 0, Width, Height); }
};

class TRectangle: public TMyShape
{
public:
  virtual __fastcall TRectangle(TComponent *AOwner): TMyShape(AOwner) {}
  virtual __fastcall TRectangle(TComponent *AOwner, int X, int Y)
    : TMyShape(AOwner) { Width = 50; Height = 50;  Left = X; Top = Y; }
  virtual void DrawShape()
  { Canvas->Brush->Color = clLime; Canvas->Rectangle(0, 0, Width, Height); }
};

class TForm1 : public TForm
{
__published:
  TButton *DrawShapesBtn;
  TPanel *Panel1;
  void __fastcall DrawShapesBtnClick(TObject *Sender);
```

continues

Listing 21.3. continued

```
private:
  void TForm1::DrawShape(TMyShape *Shape);
public:
  virtual __fastcall TForm1(TComponent* Owner);
};

extern TForm1 *Form1;

#endif
```

Listing 21.4. The main form for the ClassicShapeDemo program.

```
/////////////////////////////////////
// Main.cpp
// Classic Shape Demo
// Copyright (c) 1997 by Charlie Calvert
//
#include <vcl\vcl.h>
#pragma hdrstop
#include "Main.h"
#pragma resource "*.dfm"
TForm1 *Form1;

__fastcall TForm1::TForm1(TComponent* Owner)
  : TForm(Owner)
{
}

void TForm1::DrawShape(TMyShape *Shape)
{
  Shape->DrawShape();
}

void __fastcall TForm1::DrawShapesBtnClick(TObject *Sender)
{
  TMyShape *Shape = new TMyShape(Panel1, 10, 10);
  Shape->Parent = Panel1;

  TCircle *Circle = new TCircle(Panel1, 50, 10);
  Circle->Parent = Panel1;

  TRectangle *Rectangle = new TRectangle(Panel1, 140, 10);
  Rectangle->Parent = Panel1;

  DrawShape(Shape);
  DrawShape(Circle);
  DrawShape(Rectangle);
}
```

Most of the complexity of this example is a result of the default behavior of VCL objects. Notice that `TMyShape` descends from `TCustomControl`. I chose this lineage because `TCustomControl` has a `Canvas` object ready for use by its consumers. I pay a price for this functionality, because I must create a default constructor with the following signature if I want to suppress valid compiler warnings:

```
virtual __fastcall TMyShape(TComponent *AOwner): TCustomControl(AOwner) {}
```

After I have declared this constructor, I can create a second constructor that suits my own needs:

```
virtual __fastcall TMyShape(TComponent *AOwner, int X, int Y)
: TCustomControl(AOwner) { Width = 50; Height = 50;  Left = X; Top = Y; }
```

Notice that this constructor gives the object a default height and width, and also assigns values to its `Left` and `Top` fields. All these fields are inherited from `TCustomControl` and must be filled out properly if you want to draw the object on the screen.

> **NOTE**
>
> `TCustomControl` is one of the objects from which you can make descendants if you want to create a component. In fact, both of the examples shown here are valid components that could be placed on the Component Palette with only a little more work. However, I will save a complete explanation of `TCustomControl` for the next chapter of this book. For now, all you need to know is that these fairly sophisticated objects come replete with `Left`, `Top`, `Width`, and `Height` properties, as well as an easy-to-use `Canvas` object.

When you create an instance of a VCL control, you need to give it both an owner and a parent:

```
TCircle *Circle = new TCircle(Panel1, 50, 10);
Circle->Parent = Panel1;
```

This code assigns `Panel1` as both the parent and owner of `TCircle`. `Panel1` is just a standard panel to serve as the drawing surface on which the program paints its output.

After you declare constructor objects of type `TMyShape`, `TRectangle`, and `TCircle`, the final step is to pass each of these objects to the `CallDrawShape` method:

```
CallDrawShape(Shape);
CallDrawShape(Circle);
CallDrawShape(Rectangle);
```

When you look at it from this end, the fact that `CallDrawShape` would produce different results depending on the type of object you pass into it makes sense. However, if you look at the `CallDrawShape` method itself, the fact that you can pass objects of different types to it is not at all obvious:

```
void TForm1::CallDrawShape(TMyShape *Shape)
{
  Shape->DrawShape();
}
```

The odd thing about polymorphism is that you can make the assignment of an object of type TRectangle to an object of type TMyShape. Once you understand that you can do that, everything else falls out fairly naturally.

If you have any questions about what's going on in this code, run this program. Step through it with the debugger. Do whatever is necessary to make sense of this very important code. The key point to grasp is that one variable, called Shape, which is of type TMyShape, behaves in three different ways. It's polymorphic—one variable acting in different ways.

Polymorphism in the VCL

One place where BCB uses polymorphism heavily is with the TField objects assigned to the Fields array in a TTable object. The objects in the Fields array are of type TField, but they behave as if they are of type TStringField, TIntegerField, TFloatField, and so on. The issue, of course, is that variables of type TStringField and TIntegerField can all be assigned to the Fields array because you can assign a child object to a variable of its parent type:

```
Parent = Child;
```

Here is the declaration of the Fields property from the TDataSet declaration in DB.hpp:

```
__property TField* Fields[int Index] = {read=GetField, write=SetField};
```

Clearly, this array of objects is of type TField. Suppose, however, that you execute the following method in a simple program containing a TTable object that's pointed to the Biolife table:

```
void __fastcall TForm1::bViewFieldTypesClick(TObject *Sender)
{
  int i;
  for (i = 0; i < Table1->FieldCount; i++)
  {
    ListBox1->Items->Add(Table1->Fields[i]->ClassName());
  }
}
```

According to the declaration of the Fields object, the type of each of the members of the Fields array should be TField. However, the following is what actually gets printed in the program's list box, as you can see in Figure 21.3.

```
TFloatField
TStringField
TStringField
TStringField
TFloatField
TFloatField
TMemoField
TGraphicField
```

Clearly, this isn't really an array of TField objects at all. So what's going on anyway?

FIGURE 21.3.

The PolyFields program shows how polymorphism underlies key parts of the VCL.

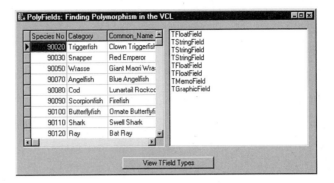

Well, by now the answer should be clear. Somewhere internally, BCB is assigning `TStringField`, `TFloatField`, `TMemoField`, and `TGraphicField` objects to the members of the `TField` array. Why is this legal? Because setting a parent object equal to a child object is always legal! In essence, the following happens:

```
{
  TField *Field;
  TStringField *StringField;
  Field = StringField;  // This is legal!
}
```

Here is the hierarchy of some of the key `TField` descendants:

```
-TField
  -TStringField
  -TNumericField
    -TSmallIntField
    -TWordField
    -TAutoIncField
  -TFloatField
    -TCurrencyField
  -TBlobField
    -TMemoField
    -TGraphicField
```

Given this hierarchy, assigning a `TStringField` or `TFloatField` object to a variable of type `TField` is always legal:

```
{
  TField *Field[3];
  TStringField *StringField;
  TFloatField *FloatField;
  TGraphicField *GraphicField;
  Fields[0] = StringField;    // legal!
  Fields[1] = FloatField;     // legal!
  Fields[2] = GraphicField;   // legal!
};
```

This point is so important that I'm going to include the source code for a program called `PolyFlds.mak` that demonstrates the issue discussed in this section. Listings 21.5 and 21.6 show this source code.

Listing 21.5. The PolyFields program shows how BCB makes practical use of polymorphism.

```
#ifndef MainH
#define MainH
#include <vcl\Classes.hpp>
#include <vcl\Controls.hpp>
#include <vcl\StdCtrls.hpp>
#include <vcl\Forms.hpp>
#include <vcl\DBGrids.hpp>
#include "Grids.hpp"
#include <vcl\DBTables.hpp>
#include <vcl\DB.hpp>
class TForm1 : public TForm
{
__published:
  TDBGrid *DBGrid1;
  TButton *bViewFieldTypes;
  TListBox *ListBox1;
  TTable *Table1;
  TDataSource *DataSource1;
  void __fastcall bViewFieldTypesClick(TObject *Sender);
private:
public:
  virtual __fastcall TForm1(TComponent* Owner);
};
extern TForm1 *Form1;
#endif
```

Listing 21.6. The main form for the PolyFields program.

```
#include <vcl\vcl.h>
#pragma hdrstop
#include "Main.h"
#pragma link "Grids"
#pragma resource "*.dfm"
TForm1 *Form1;

__fastcall TForm1::TForm1(TComponent* Owner)
  : TForm(Owner)
{
}

void __fastcall TForm1::bViewFieldTypesClick(TObject *Sender)
{
  int i;
  for (i = 0; i < Table1->FieldCount; i++)
  {
    ListBox1->Items->Add(Table1->Fields[i]->ClassName());
  }
}
```

This sample program makes clear how important polymorphism is to BCB. The Fields array of TTable is one of the key elements in all of BCB. And what lies at the heart of the whole thing? Polymorphism!

Another important point to grasp here is that very little about BCB is mysterious. If you work with Visual Basic or PowerBuilder, the only explanation for much of the syntax is simply "because." Why does it work that way? Because! With BCB, the explanation is never like that. You can find an explanation for everything in BCB, and you can build any part of the VCL or the environment yourself by using BCB.

Remember: BCB is built into the VCL. You'll find no mysteries here. If you know the language well enough, even the most esoteric parts of the VCL will make sense to you. How can the Fields array be so powerful? How does it do those things? Well, now you know the answer: It's polymorphic!

Polymorphism Encapsulated (Review of Main Points)

I have, at long last, said all I want to say about polymorphism. The key points to remember are these:

■ You can set a parent equal to a child object, but you can't set a child equal to a parent object:

```
Parent = Child;  //  Little set equal to big: OK
Child = Parent;  //  Big set equal to little: Doesn't work
```

Setting a parent equal to a child object is what makes polymorphism tick.

■ The defining elements in polymorphism are the methods of the parent object, particularly those methods that are declared virtual. Even if you assign a child to a parent object

```
Parent = Child;
```

the parent can't call methods of the child that are not also visible in the parent's class declaration. For example, if you assign a TForm instance to a TObject instance, you can't access the form's Caption property from the TObject instance without a typecast.

The point is that you can take a whole slew of hierarchically arranged objects, assign each of them to their parent, call a virtual method belonging to the parent, and watch them all behave in different ways. Polymorphism!

For some readers, I'm sure this information is old hat. Other readers might be new to the subject but have grasped it completely from the descriptions given already. However, most readers probably still have some questions lingering in the backs of their minds.

If you want, just reread the preceding sections as often as necessary. I know from personal experience that as many as three out of four object-oriented programmers don't really understand polymorphism. The subject, however, is not that complicated. Concentrate on these two sentences:

Polymorphism allows you to set one variable of type TParent *equal to a series of child objects. When you call certain virtual methods of that parent, it will behave in different ways, depending on the traits of the currently selected child.*

That's a mouthful, but the concepts set forth are not impossible to comprehend.

So far, all the examples of polymorphism are very stripped-down programs that contain only code directly relevant to the subject at hand. However, the real power of polymorphism won't become clear until you work with a larger program that really taps into the power of OOP. Unfortunately, the example I have for this kind of programming really cries out to be implemented as a set of polymorphic components. Because I have not yet described how to create components, I will have to delay showing you this program until Chapter 23, "Creating Components from Scratch." In that chapter, you will find a sample program called WareHouse that clearly illustrates what polymorphism looks like in a large, and fairly practical, program.

Summary

In this chapter, you have tackled the complex subject of polymorphism. You saw that polymorphism is built on the fact that OOP languages enable you to assign a variable of type child to a variable declared to be of type parent. When you then call a method of the parent type, it will go to the address of the child object's methods. As a result, an object of type TParent, when assigned to four different descendant objects, might react in four different ways. One object, many different faces: polymorphism.

Creating Descendants of Existing Components

IN THIS CHAPTER

Overview

This chapter and the next two cover building components. Component development is one of the most important technologies in contemporary programming, and no C++ environment on the market makes them easier to use or to create than BCB.

You build three types of components in this chapter:

- Descendants that change default settings in existing components.
- Descendants that add features to existing components.
- Tools built on top of abstract component base classes such as TWinControl, TCustomControl, TComponent, and TGraphicControl. You make descendants from these classes if you want to build your own components from the bottom up.

This chapter presents material on building visual components, Chapter 23 focuses on building unique components that are polymorphic, and Chapter 24 explores building nonvisual components. Nonvisual components descend directly from TComponent and appear on the form only at design time.

More specifically, the components built in this chapter fall into two categories:

- The first group is a set of TEdit, TLabel, and TPanel descendants that show how to change default colors, captions, and fonts. This section of the chapter also covers building components that consist of several different child components; that is, this section shows how to group components together to form new components. The specific example included with this book shows a panel that comes with two radio buttons.
- The second tool is a clock component that can be dropped on a form, and stopped and started at will.

In Chapter 24, you will see a nonvisual control that knows how to iterate through subdirectories. You can use it to build programs that search for files, delete all files with a certain extension, and so on.

Besides components, this chapter also briefly covers two related topics:

Property editors are used to edit the properties of components. The classic examples are the common dialogs that pop up when you edit the Color or Font properties that belong to most visible components. The drop-down lists and string-editing capabilities found in the Object Inspector are also property editors.

Component editors are associated not with a single property, but with an entire component. An example is the Fields Editor used with the TTable and TQuery components.

The property editors and component editors are related to a broader topic called the *Tools API*. The Tools API consists of a series of interfaces to the BCB IDE that allows you to build experts, interfaces to version control systems, and similar utilities. The API for property editors and component editors and the Tools API are defined in files with names that end in INTF, which stands for "Interface." For example, the TPropertyEditor class is found in DSGNINTF.HPP.

Components, properties, and events, along with their associated component editors and property editors are perhaps the most important topics in BCB programming. In many ways, this chapter and the next two are the keystones around which this entire book has been designed.

The source for all the components created in this chapter is found in the Chap22 and Utils directories on the CD that accompanies this book. The source on the CD compiles correctly, and all of these components work as described in this chapter. Because of the default behavior of the C++ linker, you might have to run a program called BuildObjs before installing some of these components. This program is in the Utils directory. A description of this program is in the readme file on the CD. If you have any trouble with the code in this chapter, turn to the readme!

Component Theory

BCB components have three outstanding strengths:

- They are native components, built in BCB's language, without recourse to a complicated API such as OLE. You therefore can write, debug, and test your components using the same rules you use in standard BCB programs. You don't need to learn a whole new programming model, as you do when you write ActiveX controls. In short, writing a BCB component is about 10 times easier than writing an OCX or VBX component.

- They are fully object-oriented, which means you can easily change or enhance existing components by creating descendant objects.

- They are small, fast, and light, and can be linked directly into your executables. Native BCB components are orders of magnitude smaller than most ActiveX controls, and they link directly into your programs. In particular, a native BCB component is just a particular kind of object, so it links into your programs naturally, just as any other object would, without any handwaving.

Few people would claim that VBXs aren't groundbreaking, that ActiveX controls aren't going to be very important, or that OLE2 is not an enormously promising architecture. However, BCB components are relatively easy to create and come in a light, easy-to-use package. You can create BCB components that do nearly anything, from serial communications to database links to multimedia. These capabilities give BCB a big advantage over other tools that force you to use large, complex, and unwieldy component models.

> **NOTE**
>
> Most publicly available components cost in the range of $50 to $150. Many of these tools encapsulate functionality that might cost tens of thousands of dollars to produce in-house. For example, a good communication library might take a year to build. However, if a company can sell the library in volume, it can afford to charge $100 or $200 for the same product. That's a real bargain. And most of these tools are easy to use. Building components is a great way for relatively small third-party companies to make money, and buying components is a great way to save time on big projects. These ground-breaking tools are changing everything about the way programs are constructed.

BCB components are flexible tools easily built by anyone who knows OOP and the BCB language. In this package, you have explanations detailing all the prerequisite knowledge that component builders need, from a description of BCB itself, through a description of its language, and on to an overview of its implementation of OOP. From this foundation, you can easily begin building your own components.

Creating Descendants of an Existing Component

In this section, you will see how to create a series of custom TEdit, TPanel, and TLabel controls. The changes made to the standard TEdit and TLabel components involve tweaking their colors, as well as their fonts' colors, names, sizes, and styles. The goal is to show how to create a suite of custom controls that you can place on the Component Palette and use for special effects, or to define the look and feel of a certain set of applications belonging to a particular department or company.

With projects like this, starting with one simple example is best, and then you can move on to more complex components. Listings 22.1 through 22.3 contain a sample component and a program that allows you to test the new component before you place it on the Component Palette. The component is stored in a module called Unleash1. The Unleash1 source code is the first version of a unit that will be expanded later in the chapter. Scan through it and check out its basic structure. Once it is clear to you how to create and test the component, I will briefly discuss how to place it on the Component Palette.

Listing 22.1. The header file for a simple component descending from TEdit.

```
////////////////////////////////////////
// Unleash1.h
// Simple example of creating a component
// Copyright (c) 1997 by Charlie Calvert
//
#ifndef Unleash1H
#define Unleash1H
// - - - - - - - - - - - - - - - - - - - - - - - - - - - - - - - - - - - - - - - - - - - - -
```

```
#include <vcl\sysutils.hpp>
#include <vcl\controls.hpp>
#include <vcl\classes.hpp>
#include <vcl\forms.hpp>
#include <vcl\StdCtrls.hpp>
//-------------------------------------------------------------------
class TSmallEdit : public TEdit
{
private:
protected:
public:
  virtual __fastcall TSmallEdit(TComponent* Owner);
__published:
};
//-------------------------------------------------------------------
#endif
```

Listing 22.2. The code for a simple component descending from TEdit.

```
//////////////////////////////////////
// Unleash1.cpp
// Simple example of creating a component
// Copyright (c) 1997 by Charlie Calvert
//
#include <vcl\vcl.h>
#pragma hdrstop
#include "Unleash1.h"
//-------------------------------------------------------------------
static inline TSmallEdit *ValidCtrCheck()
{
  return new TSmallEdit(NULL);
}
//-------------------------------------------------------------------
__fastcall TSmallEdit::TSmallEdit(TComponent* Owner)
  : TEdit(Owner)
{
  Color = clBlue;
  Font->Color = clYellow;
  Font->Name = "Times New Roman";
  Font->Size = 12;
  Font->Style = TFontStyles() << fsBold << fsItalic;
}
//-------------------------------------------------------------------
namespace Unleash1
{
  void __fastcall Register()
  {
    TComponentClass classes[1] = {__classid(TSmallEdit)};
    RegisterComponents("Unleash", classes, 0);
  }
}
//-------------------------------------------------------------------
```

22

CREATING
DESCENDANTS

Listing 22.3. The main form for the TestUnleash1 program serves as a test bed for the Unleash1 unit.

```cpp
/////////////////////////////////////
// Main.cpp
// Simple example of creating a component
// Copyright (c) 1997 by Charlie Calvert
//
#include <vcl\vcl.h>
#pragma hdrstop
#include "Main.h"
#include "Unleash1.h"
#pragma link "unleash1"
#pragma resource "*.dfm"
TForm1 *Form1;
__fastcall TForm1::TForm1(TComponent* Owner)
  : TForm(Owner)
{
}
void __fastcall TForm1::Button1Click(TObject *Sender)
{
  TSmallEdit *MyEdit = new TSmallEdit(this);
  MyEdit->Parent = this;
  MyEdit->Show();
}
```

This program is designed to test the TSmallEdit control before you add it to the Component Palette. The test program has a single button that responds to clicks. If you click the program's button, the new component appears at the top left of the form, as shown in Figure 22.1. Once again, the goal of the program is to make sure the new edit control is meeting your expectations before trying to compile it as a component.

FIGURE 22.1.

At runtime, the
TestUnleash1 *main*
form features a TButton
and a custom Edit
control called
TSmallEdit.

You can easily create this unit, test it, and compile it as a component that's merged in with the rest of the tools on the Component Palette. To start creating the component, choose File | New and select Component from the first page of the Object Repository. The dialog shown in Figure 22.2 then appears.

FIGURE 22.2.

The Component Wizard dialog.

The Component Wizard is a simple code generator, of the type that any reader of this book who has made it this far should be able to write in an hour or two. It simply asks you for the name of the component you want to create and to then select its parent from a drop-down list. After you define the type of tool you want to create, you can select the page in the Component Palette where you want it to reside. You should fill in the blanks with the following information:

```
Class Name: TSmallEdit
Ancestor type: TEdit
Palette Page: Unleash
```

For your efforts, the Component Expert churns out the code in Listings 22.4 and 22.5, in which everything is boilerplate except for the first line of the class declaration, the constructor, and the parameters passed to the `RegisterComponents` method.

Listing 22.4. The header produced by the standard boilerplate output of the Component Expert.

```
//----------------------------------------------------------------------
#ifndef Unleash1H
#define Unleash1H
//----------------------------------------------------------------------
#include <vcl\sysutils.hpp>
#include <vcl\controls.hpp>
#include <vcl\classes.hpp>
#include <vcl\forms.hpp>
#include <vcl\StdCtrls.hpp>
class TSmallEdit : public TEdit
{
private:
protected:
public:
  virtual __fastcall TSmallEdit(TComponent* Owner);
__published:
};
#endif
```

Listing 22.5. The implementation of `TSmallEdit` as produced by the standard boilerplate output of the Component Expert.

```
//----------------------------------------------------------------------
#include <vcl\vcl.h>
#pragma hdrstop
```

continues

Listing 22.5. continued

```cpp
#include "Unleash1.h"
//---------------------------------------------------------------
static inline TSmallEdit *ValidCtrCheck()
{
  return new TSmallEdit(NULL);
}
//---------------------------------------------------------------
__fastcall TSmallEdit::TSmallEdit(TComponent* Owner)
  : TEdit(Owner)
{
}
//---------------------------------------------------------------
namespace Unleash1
{
  void __fastcall Register()
  {
    TComponentClass classes[1] = {__classid(TSmallEdit)};
    RegisterComponents("Unleash", classes, 0);
  }
}
//---------------------------------------------------------------
```

The Component Expert starts by giving you `#include` directives designed to cover most of the bases you are likely to touch in a standard component:

```cpp
#include <vcl\sysutils.hpp>
#include <vcl\controls.hpp>
#include <vcl\classes.hpp>
#include <vcl\forms.hpp>
#include <vcl\StdCtrls.hpp>
```

The next step is to give you a basic class declaration, in which the name and parent are filled in with the choices you specified in the Component Expert dialog. All this business about the scoping directives is just for your convenience, and you can delete any portion of it that you don't think you'll need.

```cpp
class TSmallEdit : public TEdit
{
private:
  // Private declarations
protected:
  // Protected declarations
public:
  // Public declarations
  virtual __fastcall TSmallEdit(TComponent* Owner);
__published:
  // Published declarations
};
```

Before you can place a component on the Component Palette, you first must register it with the system:

```cpp
void __fastcall Register()
{
```

```
        TComponentClass classes[1] = {__classid(TSmallEdit)};
        RegisterComponents("Unleash", classes, 0);
}
```

Registering a class makes it known to the BCB Component Palette when the unit is compiled into the BCB component library. The `Register` procedure has no impact on programs compiled with this unit. Unless your program calls the `Register` procedure (which it should *never* do), the code for the `Register` procedure will never execute.

This method first creates an array consisting of the types of components you want to register. Recall that `__classid` is one of the new pieces of syntax added to the language. It is discussed in Chapter 2, "Basic Facts About C++Builder." After creating the array, you call `RegisterComponents`, which takes the name of the page you want to use in the Component Palette in the first parameter, the array of metaclasses in the second parameter, and the size of the array in the third parameter. If the page does not exist, it will be created automatically. Here is the declaration for `RegisterComponents`:

```
extern void __fastcall RegisterComponents(const System::AnsiString Page,
    System::TMetaClass* const * ComponentClasses, const int ComponentClasses_Size);
```

Recall that `TMetaClass` is declared in `SysDefs.h` and that it represents a subset of `TObject`. You can get the metaclass of a VCL object by calling the object's `ClassType` method.

If you look back at the source for the whole project, you will see that the `Register` method is placed in its own namespace. This happens because multiple declarations for methods with that name will occur throughout your projects and, indeed, inside BCB itself. As a result, the compiler's need for order must be satiated with a few discreetly placed namespaces. This whole subject will come up again in just a moment, when I talk about recompiling `CmpLib32.ccl`.

After using the Component Expert, you should save the project. Proceed as you normally would by creating a directory for the project and saving `Main.pas` and `TestUnleash1.cpp` inside it. You should not save the new unit that you created into the same directory, however, but you should place it in the `Utils` directory where you store files such as `CodeBox`. This code is now going to come into play as part of your system, and as such you want a single path that leads to all related files of this type. If you have all your components in different subdirectories, you will end up with a source path that is long and unwieldy.

NOTE

`ValidCtrCheck()` verifies that creating an instance of the object at compile time is possible. If you forget to override a pure virtual function, the compilation of the component will fail because the statement "`new foo(0)`" is now invalid. You can test this by creating a component derived from `TCustomGrid` (an abstract class) and installing it without doing any work to change the object.

Because `ValidCtrCheck` is inline and never called, no code will be generated—so there is no runtime cost.

The goal of this project is to give a component of type TEdit a new set of default behaviors so that it starts out with certain colors and certain fonts. To do so, you need to override the Create method and change the fonts inside it. The method declaration itself appears automatically:

```
class TSmallEdit : public TEdit
{
public:
  virtual __fastcall TSmallEdit(TComponent* Owner);
};
```

Notice that in the preceding declaration I have removed the private, __published, and protected directives created by the Component Expert. Making this change is neither here nor there; I do it just to keep the amount of code you need to look at as small as possible.

The Create method for TSmallEdit is declared as public. If you think about the process of creating a component dynamically, you will see that the Create method has to be public. This is one method that must be exposed. Like all VCL constructors, TSmallEdit is declared virtual and __fastcall.

Create is passed a single parameter of type TComponent, which is a base class that encapsulates the minimum functionality needed to be an owner of another component and to place a component on the Component Palette. In particular, whatever form you place a component on usually will be the owner of that component.

The implementation of the Create method is simple:

```
__fastcall TSmallEdit::TSmallEdit(TComponent* Owner)
  : TEdit(Owner)
{
  Color = clBlue;
  Font->Color = clYellow;
  Font->Name = "Times New Roman";
  Font->Size = 12;
  Font->Style = TFontStyles() << fsBold << fsItalic;
}
```

The code first calls Create, passing in the variable AOwner. As I stated previously, the owner of a component will often, though not always, be the form on which the component is to be displayed. In other words, the user will drop the component onto a form, and that form will become the owner of the component. In such a case, AOwner is a variable that points to the form. The VCL uses it to initialize the Owner property, which is one of the fields of all components.

The next step is to define the color and font that you want to use, with Font->Style defined as follows:

```
enum TFontStyle { fsBold, fsItalic, fsUnderline, fsStrikeOut };
typedef Set<TFontStyle, fsBold, fsStrikeOut>  TFontStyles;
```

> **NOTE**
>
> Don't let all this gobbledygook confuse you! All that occurs in this declaration is that a simple enum type is declared, and then you see a Set declaration for the type that ranges from a low value of fsBold to a high value of fsStrikeOut. Piece of cake!

If you want to add the underline and bold style to the text in the edit control, write the following:

```
Font->Style = TFontStyles << fsBold << fsUnderline;
```

If you then want to add the italic style at runtime, write this:

```
Font->Style = Font->Style << fsItalic;
```

To remove the style, write this line:

```
Font->Style = Font->Style >> fsItalic;
```

At this stage, the code is ready to go on the Component Palette. However, most of the time when you write components, you should test them first to see whether they work.

Even on a fast machine, the process of recompiling CmpLib32.ccl and adding your component to the Component Palette takes between 10 seconds and 2 minutes. Perhaps I'm a bit impatient, but that's a little too long a wait for me if all I need to tweak is a few aspects of my code. As a result, I test things first in a small program and then add the component to the IDE.

To test the new class, drop a button on the program's main form, and create an OnClick handler:

```
void __fastcall TForm1::Button1Click(TObject *Sender)
{
  TSmallEdit *MyEdit = new TSmallEdit(this);
  MyEdit->Parent = this;
  MyEdit->Show();
}
```

Don't forget to use View | Project Manager and add the unit to the project. This ensures that the USEUNIT macro is placed in your project source.

This code creates the component and shows it on the main form. this, of course, is the way that TForm1 refers to itself from inside one of its own methods. The owner of the new component is Form1, which will be responsible for disposing of the component when finished with it. This process happens automatically. You never need to worry about disposing of a visible component shown on a form.

The parent of the component is also Form1. The Parent variable is used by Windows when it is trying to decide how to display the form on the screen. If you place a panel on a form and drop a button on the panel, the owner of that button is the form, but the parent is the panel. Ownership determines when and how the component is deallocated, and parental relationships determine where and how the component is displayed. Ownership is fundamentally a BCB issue, whereas parental relationships are primarily concerns of Windows.

NOTE

The next paragraph in this section explains how to recompile CmpLib32.ccl. Remember that you should always keep a backup copy of CmpLib32.ccl on your hard drive. CmpLib32.ccl is stored in the ..\CBUILDER\BIN directory. Beneath this directory, I have created another directory called BACK where I keep a backup copy of CmpLib32.ccl. If worse comes to worst, you can always copy the version of CmpLib32.ccl on your installation CD back into the BIN subdirectory.

My personal experience is that everyone, sooner or later, makes a tasty Mulligan's Stew out of a copy of CmpLib32.ccl. The worst-case scenario is that you're on the road when this mess happens, and that you don't have access to your installation disk. Don't let this situation happen to you. Keep a backup copy of CmpLib32.ccl on your hard drive at all times!

CCL stands for C++Builder Component Library.

After you run the program and test the component, the next step is to put it up on the Component Palette. To do so, choose Components | Install and then click the Add button. Browse through the directories until you find Unleash1.Cpp, select OK, and then close the Install Components dialog by clicking OK. At this point, a project called CmpLib32.cpp is compiled. This project creates a huge DLL called CmpLib32.ccl, which contains all the components in the Component Palette, all the component and property editors associated with those components, the form designer part of the IDE, the experts, and other support modules.

After CmpLib32.ccl finishes recompiling, you can start a new project, turn to the newly created Unleash page, and drop your new component onto a form. It will have a blue background, default to Times New Roman, and have its font style set to bold and its font color to yellow. Notice that all the properties of TEdit have been inherited by TSmallEdit. That's OOP in action. You can see an example of the form that uses this control in Figure 22.3.

FIGURE 22.3.

Using the TSmallEdit
control on a standard
VCL form.

Understanding the Project Source for CmpLib32

You can save the CmpLib32.cpp file used during compilation of CmpLib32.ccl to disk if you choose
Options | Environment | Library | Save Library Source Code. After choosing this option and
recompiling CmpLib32.ccl, you can go to the \CBUILDER\BIN directory and view your copy of
CmpLib32.cpp.

Here is an example of the source code produced by the IDE for use when compiling
CmpLib32.ccl:

```
//------------------------------------------------------------------------
// Component Palette
// Copyright (c) 1996, 1996 by Borland International, All Rights Reserved
//
// Module generated by C++Builder to rebuild the Component
// Palette Library (CmpLib32.ccl).
//------------------------------------------------------------------------
//------------------------------------------------------------------------
// In order to be totally Delphi compatible, the Component palette must be
// built with a namespaced version of the VCL library. Using namespace allows
// us to have multiple functions all called 'Register'.
//------------------------------------------------------------------------
#if !defined(BCB_NAMESPACES)
#define BCB_NAMESPACES
#endif
//------------------------------------------------------------------------
// Include DSTRING.H - Defines AnsiString support class
//------------------------------------------------------------------------
#include <vcl\dstring.h>
//------------------------------------------------------------------------
// The following are expanded inline to avoid pulling in the headers
// and lengthen the compilation time when rebuilding the palette.
//------------------------------------------------------------------------
typedef void* HINSTANCE;
#if !defined(WINAPI)
#define WINAPI __stdcall
#endif
#if !defined(DLL_PROCESS_ATTACH)
#define DLL_PROCESS_ATTACH 1
#endif
#if !defined(DLL_THREAD_ATTACH)
#define DLL_THREAD_ATTACH  2
#endif
#if !defined(DLL_THREAD_DETACH)
#define DLL_THREAD_DETACH  3
#endif
#if !defined(DLL_PROCESS_DETACH)
#define DLL_PROCESS_DETACH 0
#endif
namespace Libmain {
```

```
typedef void __fastcall (*TRegisterProc)(void);
extern  void __fastcall RegisterModule(const System::AnsiString Name,
  TRegisterProc RegisterProc);
}
using namespace Libmain;
namespace System {
extern void __cdecl ProcessAttachTLS(void);
extern void __cdecl ProcessDetachTLS(void);
extern void __cdecl ThreadAttachTLS(void);
extern void __cdecl ThreadDetachTLS(void);
}
using namespace System;
//-------------------------------------------------------------------
// Prototype for each component's 'Register routine. Followed
// by instruction to have linker pull in the OBJ. module which
// implements the Register routine.
//
//   Each component is expected to provide a routine with the
//   following signature:
//
//        extern void __fastcall Register(void);
//
//   This routine must be in a namespace which matches the
//   name of the component itself. Therefore, the routine is
//   actually prototyped as:
//
//        namespace Componentname {
//            extern void __fastcall Register(void);
//        };
//
//   NOTE: The namespace must be in all lowercase characters
//         except for the first one. i.e. Namespacename.
//-------------------------------------------------------------------
namespace Stdreg { extern void __fastcall Register(void); }
namespace Dbreg { extern void __fastcall Register(void); }
namespace Isp { extern void __fastcall Register(void); }
namespace Sysreg { extern void __fastcall Register(void); }
namespace Quickrep { extern void __fastcall Register(void); }
namespace Ocxreg { extern void __fastcall Register(void); }
namespace Olereg { extern void __fastcall Register(void); }
namespace Ddereg { extern void __fastcall Register(void); }
namespace Chartfx { extern void __fastcall Register(void); }
namespace Vcfimprs { extern void __fastcall Register(void); }
namespace Vcfrmla1 { extern void __fastcall Register(void); }
namespace Vcspell { extern void __fastcall Register(void); }
namespace Graphsvr { extern void __fastcall Register(void); }
namespace Ibreg { extern void __fastcall Register(void); }
namespace Win31reg { extern void __fastcall Register(void); }
namespace Sampreg { extern void __fastcall Register(void); }
namespace Unleash1 { extern void __fastcall Register(void); }
// (Search Path for Components (.CPP, .PAS, .OBJ & .LIB)
//   => g:\bcb\LIB;g:\bcb\LIB\OBJ;g:\srcc\punleash\utils
//
// Added to search paths: g:\bcb\LIB
// Added to search paths: g:\bcb\LIB\OBJ
// Added to search paths: g:\srcc\punleash\utils
// Added to project: g:\bcb\bin\cmplib32.cpp FileType: SRC
// Added to project: bcbmm.lib FileType: LIB
```

```
#pragma resource    "StdReg.dcr"  // Link dcr of standard module "StdReg"
// Added to project: g:\bcb\LIB\OBJ\DBReg.obj (From SearchPath) FileType: OBJ
// Added to project: g:\bcb\LIB\OBJ\DBReg.dcr (From SearchPath) FileType: RES
#pragma resource       "ISP.dcr"  // Link dcr of standard module "ISP"
#pragma resource    "SysReg.dcr"  // Link dcr of standard module "SysReg"
#pragma resource "Quickrep.dcr"   // Link dcr of standard module "Quickrep"
#pragma resource    "OLEReg.dcr"  // Link dcr of standard module "OLEReg"
#pragma resource    "DDEReg.dcr"  // Link dcr of standard module "DDEReg"
#pragma resource   "ChartFX.dcr"  // Link dcr of standard module "ChartFX"
#pragma resource  "VCFImprs.dcr"  // Link dcr of standard module "VCFImprs"
#pragma resource  "VCFrmla1.dcr"  // Link dcr of standard module "VCFrmla1"
#pragma resource   "VCSpell.dcr"  // Link dcr of standard module "VCSpell"
#pragma resource  "GraphSvr.dcr"  // Link dcr of standard module "GraphSvr"
#pragma resource     "IBReg.dcr"  // Link dcr of standard module "IBReg"
#pragma resource   "Win31Reg.dcr" // Link dcr of standard module "Win31Reg"
#pragma resource   "SampReg.dcr"  // Link dcr of standard module "SampReg"
// Added to project: g:\srcc\punleash\utils\Unleash1.cpp
//  (From SearchPath) FileType: SRC
//-------------------------------------------------------------------------
// Routine which registers the various modules implementing components
//-------------------------------------------------------------------------
bool
InitCmpLib()
{
  RegisterModule("StdReg", Stdreg::Register);
  RegisterModule("DBReg", Dbreg::Register);
  RegisterModule("ISP", Isp::Register);
  RegisterModule("SysReg", Sysreg::Register);
  RegisterModule("Quickrep", Quickrep::Register);
  RegisterModule("OCXReg", Ocxreg::Register);
  RegisterModule("OLEReg", Olereg::Register);
  RegisterModule("DDEReg", Ddereg::Register);
  RegisterModule("ChartFX", Chartfx::Register);
  RegisterModule("VCFImprs", Vcfimprs::Register);
  RegisterModule("VCFrmla1", Vcfrmla1::Register);
  RegisterModule("VCSpell", Vcspell::Register);
  RegisterModule("GraphSvr", Graphsvr::Register);
  RegisterModule("IBReg", Ibreg::Register);
  RegisterModule("Win31Reg", Win31reg::Register);
  RegisterModule("SampReg", Sampreg::Register);
  RegisterModule("Unleash1", Unleash1::Register);
  return true;
}
//-------------------------------------------------------------------------
// Library's entry point
//-------------------------------------------------------------------------
extern "C"
int WINAPI
DllEntryPoint(HINSTANCE /*hInstance*/, unsigned long reason, void*)
{
  switch (reason) {
    case DLL_PROCESS_ATTACH:
        ProcessAttachTLS();
        InitCmpLib();
        break;
    case DLL_PROCESS_DETACH:
        ProcessDetachTLS();
        break;
```

```
      case DLL_THREAD_ATTACH:
          ThreadAttachTLS();
          break;
      case DLL_THREAD_DETACH:
          ThreadDetachTLS();
          break;
  }
  return 1;
}
```

To understand the unit, start at the bottom, with the DllEntryPoint function. This routine is called when Windows first loads the DLL into memory and each time it is accessed by a BCB thread. ProcessAttachTLS and related routines are all part of the internal system code. This code is none of our business, so we can safely "pay no attention to the man behind the curtain."

InitCmpLib calls the Register method for each of the modules used in the project. If you look at the bottom of the list, you will see where the Register method for Unleash1 is listed. You might think that we don't have enough calls in this section to create the over 100 components found on the Component Palette. The issue here is that some of the Register methods register 20 or 30 different components at one shot. Here, for example, is the Register method from StdReg.pas:

```
procedure Register;
begin
  RegisterComponents(LoadStr(srStandard), [TMainMenu, TPopupMenu, TLabel,
    TEdit, TMemo, TButton, TCheckBox, TRadioButton, TListBox, TComboBox,
    TScrollBar, TGroupBox, TRadioGroup, TPanel]);
  RegisterComponents(LoadStr(srAdditional), [TBitBtn, TSpeedButton,
    TMaskEdit, TStringGrid, TDrawGrid, TImage, TShape, TBevel,
    TScrollBox]);
  RegisterComponents(LoadStr(srWin95), [TTabControl, TPageControl,
    TTreeView, TListView, TImageList, THeaderControl, TRichEdit,
    TStatusBar, TTrackBar, TProgressBar, TUpDown, THotKey]);
  RegisterClasses([TTabSheet]);
  RegisterNoIcon([TMenuItem]);
  RegisterComponentEditor(TMenu, TMenuEditor);
  RegisterComponentEditor(TImage, TGraphicEditor);
  RegisterComponentEditor(TPageControl, TPageControlEditor);
  RegisterComponentEditor(TTabSheet, TPageControlEditor);
  RegisterComponentEditor(TImageList, TImageListEditor);
  RegisterPropertyEditor(TypeInfo(string),
    TCustomMaskEdit, 'EditMask', TMaskProperty);
  RegisterPropertyEditor(TypeInfo(string),
    TCustomMaskEdit, 'Text', TMaskTextProperty);
  RegisterPropertyEditor(TypeInfo(TTabSheet), TPageControl, 'ActivePage',
    TActivePageProperty);
  RegisterPropertyEditor(TypeInfo(TStatusPanels), nil, '',
    TStatusPanelsProperty);
  RegisterPropertyEditor(TypeInfo(THeaderSections), nil, '',
    THeaderSectionsProperty);
  RegisterPropertyEditor(TypeInfo(TListColumns), nil, '',
    TListColumnsProperty);
```

```
    RegisterPropertyEditor(TypeInfo(TListItems), nil, '',
      TListItemsProperty);
    RegisterPropertyEditor(TypeInfo(TTreeNodes), nil, '',
      TTreeNodesProperty);
end;
```

Sorry about bringing Object Pascal code into the book again, but I think it helps to see what is happening behind the scenes in cases like this one. I will talk about `RegisterPropertyEditor` later in this chapter. Notice that the VCL calls `RegisterComponents` just as you do. When you recompile `Cmplib`, you are rebuilding part of BCB itself and simultaneously redefining the way the VCL works.

The DCR files listed in `CmpLib32.cpp` are a series of standard Windows resources that contain bitmaps that are placed in the Component Palette. The bitmaps representing each component come from here. In the case of `TSmallEdit`, it descends from `TEdit`, and so it inherits `TEdit`'s bitmap, unless I create a DCR file for the component. I will create and discuss DCR files later in this chapter and in the next chapter.

The key point to grasp about DCR files is that they are standard Windows resources containing a bitmap. You can build them with the Image Editor that ships with BCB.

Extending the Unleash Unit

In the second version of the `Unleash` unit, a new edit control is added, along with two labels and two panels. The additional edits and labels show how quickly you can build on an idea or object when you understand where you're headed. One of the panels shows how you can get rid of the annoying label that always shows up in the middle of a panel, and the other shows a preliminary take on how you can create a single component that contains other components. Specifically, it shows how to create a panel that comes already equipped with two radio buttons.

The code for the new version of the `Unleash2.cpp` unit is shown in Listings 22.6 and 22.7, and its test bed appears in Listing 22.8. Run `TestBed` first, and make sure the new components are working correctly. If all is well, then add the new components to the Component Palette.

If you have two units on your system, both of which contain instances of `TSmallEdit`, uninstalling the first instance before trying to install the new instance is probably best. For instance, you may have two files on your system, one called `Unleash1.cpp` and the second called `Unleash2.cpp`. Both might contain an instance of `TSmallEdit`. Under such circumstances, it's best to use Component | Install | Remove to remove the first version of `TSmallEdit` before replacing it with a second version. A second alternative is just to rename the second version of the component to `TSmallEditTwo`, which is what I do with the source found on the CD that accompanies this book. If you have only one version of `TSmallEdit`, and you just want to update it, you don't need to remove the first instance before installing the updated instance.

Listing 22.6. The header for the second version of the `Unleash2.cpp` unit contains a class that comes equipped with two radio buttons.

```
///////////////////////////////////////
// Unleash2.h
// Simple components
// Copyright (c) 1997 by Charlie Calvert
//
#ifndef Unleash2H
#define Unleash2H
//-------------------------------------------------------------
#include <vcl\sysutils.hpp>
#include <vcl\controls.hpp>
#include <vcl\classes.hpp>
#include <vcl\forms.hpp>
#include <vcl\StdCtrls.hpp>
//-------------------------------------------------------------
class TSmallEditTwo : public TEdit
{
public:
  virtual __fastcall TSmallEditTwo(TComponent* Owner);
};

class TBigEdit : public TSmallEditTwo
{
public:
  virtual __fastcall TBigEdit(TComponent* Owner)
    :TSmallEditTwo(Owner) { Width = 250; Font->Size = 24; }
};

class TSmallLabel : public TLabel
{
public:
  virtual __fastcall TSmallLabel(TComponent* Owner);
};

class TBigLabel : public TSmallLabel
{
public:
  virtual __fastcall TBigLabel(TComponent *Owner)
    :TSmallLabel(Owner) { Font->Size = 24; }
};

class TEmptyPanel : public TPanel
{
protected:
  void __fastcall Loaded(void);
public:
  virtual __fastcall TEmptyPanel(TComponent *Owner);
  virtual void __fastcall SetParent(TWinControl *AParent);
};

class TRadio2Panel : public TEmptyPanel
{
private:
  TRadioButton *FRadio1;
  TRadioButton *FRadio2;
public:
```

```
   virtual __fastcall TRadio2Panel(TComponent *Owner);
   __property TRadioButton *Radio1={read=FRadio1};
   __property TRadioButton *Radio2={read=FRadio2};
};

//--------------------------------------------------------------------
#endif
```

Listing 22.7. The second version of the `Unleash` unit, called `Unleash2`, contains a class that comes equipped with two radio buttons.

```cpp
/////////////////////////////////////////
// Unleash2.cpp
// Simple components
// Copyright (c) 1997 by Charlie Calvert
//
#include <vcl\vcl.h>
#pragma hdrstop
#include "Unleash2.h"

/////////////////////////////////////////
// TSmallEditTwo /////////////////////////
/////////////////////////////////////////

static inline TSmallEditTwo *ValidCtrCheck()
{
  return new TSmallEditTwo(NULL);
}

__fastcall TSmallEditTwo::TSmallEditTwo(TComponent* Owner)
  : TEdit(Owner)
{
  Color = clBlue;
  Font->Color = clYellow;
  Font->Name = "Times New Roman";
  Font->Size = 12;
  Font->Style = TFontStyles() << fsBold << fsItalic;
}

/////////////////////////////////////////
// TSmallLabel ///////////////////////////
/////////////////////////////////////////

__fastcall TSmallLabel::TSmallLabel(TComponent* Owner)
  : TLabel(Owner)
{
  Color = clBlue;
  Font->Color = clYellow;
  Font->Name = "Times New Roman";
  Font->Size = 12;
```

continues

Listing 22.7. continued

```
  Font->Style = TFontStyles() << fsBold;
}

/////////////////////////////////////////
// TEmptyPanel /////////////////////////////
/////////////////////////////////////////

__fastcall TEmptyPanel::TEmptyPanel(TComponent *Owner)
   :TPanel(Owner)
{
}

void __fastcall TEmptyPanel::Loaded(void)
{
  TPanel::Loaded();
  Caption = "";
}

void __fastcall TEmptyPanel::SetParent(TWinControl *AParent)
{
  TPanel::SetParent(AParent);
  Caption = "";
}


/////////////////////////////////////////
// TRadio2Panel ////////////////////////////
/////////////////////////////////////////

__fastcall TRadio2Panel::TRadio2Panel(TComponent *Owner)
   :TEmptyPanel(Owner)
{
  Width = 175;
  Height = 60;

  FRadio1 = new TRadioButton(this);
  FRadio1->Parent = this;
  FRadio1->Caption = "Radio1";
  FRadio1->Left = 20;
  FRadio1->Top = 10;
  FRadio1->Show();

  FRadio2 = new TRadioButton(this);
  FRadio2->Parent = this;
  FRadio2->Caption = "Radio2";
  FRadio2->Left = 20;
  FRadio2->Top = 32;
  FRadio2->Show();
}

namespace Unleash2
{
```

```
   void __fastcall Register()
   {
     TComponentClass classes[6]={__classid(TSmallEditTwo),
       __classid(TBigEdit), __classid(TSmallLabel), __classid(TBigLabel),
       __classid(TEmptyPanel), __classid(TRadio2Panel)};
     RegisterComponents("Unleash", classes, 5);
   }
}
//------------------------------------------------------------------
```

Listing 22.8. The test bed for the `Unleash2` unit.

```
/////////////////////////////////////////
// Main.cpp
// Simple components: TestUnleash2
// Copyright (c) 1997 by Charlie Calvert
//
#include <vcl\vcl.h>
#pragma hdrstop
#include "Main.h"
#include "Unleash2.h"
#pragma link "Unleash1"
#pragma link "Unleash2"
#pragma resource "*.dfm"
TForm1 *Form1;
__fastcall TForm1::TForm1(TComponent* Owner)
  : TForm(Owner)
{
   TComponentClass classes[1]={__classid(TRadioButton)};
   RegisterClasses(classes, 0);
}
void __fastcall TForm1::TestComponentsBtnClick(TObject *Sender)
{
   TestComponentsBtn->Enabled = False;

   TBigEdit *BigEdit = new TBigEdit(this);
   BigEdit->Parent = this;
   BigEdit->Show();
   TEmptyPanel *E = new TEmptyPanel(this);
   E->Parent = this;
   E->Top = BigEdit->Height + 5;
   E->Show();
   TRadio2Panel *P = new TRadio2Panel(this);
   P->Parent = this;
   P->Top = E->Top + E->Height + 5;
   P->Radio1->Caption = "As you from crimes would pardon'd be ";
   P->Radio1->Width = Canvas->TextWidth(P->Radio1->Caption) + 20;
   P->Radio2->Caption = "Let your indulgence set me free ";
   P->Radio2->Width = Canvas->TextWidth(P->Radio2->Caption) + 20;
   P->Width = max(P->Radio1->Width, P->Radio2->Width) + P->Radio1->Left + 20;
   P->Show();
}
```

You can find this program in the directory called `TestUnleash2` on the CD that accompanies this book. Figure 22.4 shows the program in action.

FIGURE 22.4.

*The TestUnleash2
program demonstrates
how to test a series of
components before
placing them on the
Component Palette.*

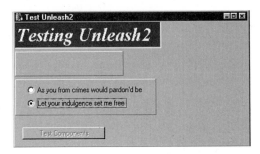

After you've created a component that does something you like, you can easily create children of it. Class `TBigEdit` descends from `TSmallEditTwo`:

```
class TBigEdit : public TSmallEditTwo
{
public:
  virtual __fastcall TBigEdit(TComponent* Owner)
    :TSmallEditTwo(Owner) { Width = 250; Font->Size = 24; }
};
```

It inherits its font nearly unchanged from `TSmallEditTwo`, except that it sets `Font->Size` to 24, a hefty figure that helps the control live up to its name. This elegant syntax is a good example of how OOP can save you time and trouble while still allowing you to write clear code.

The label controls shown in this code work in exactly the same way the edit controls do, except that they descend from `TLabel` rather than from `TEdit`.

The `TEmptyPanel` component rectifies one of the petty issues that sometimes annoys me: Every time you put down a panel, it gets a caption. Most of the time, the first thing you do is delete the caption so that you can place other controls on it without creating a mess!

At first, it would appear that you can change the caption of `TPanel` by overriding its constructor. All you would need to do is set the `Caption` property to an empty string:

```
class TEmptyPanel : public TPanel
{
public:
  virtual __fastcall TEmptyPanel(TComponent *Owner)
    :TPanel(Owner) { Caption = ""; }
};
```

This code should work correctly, but in the first version of C++Builder the caption does not get changed. There are two interesting workarounds for this problem that illustrate interesting facts about the VCL. The first workaround is to override the `Loaded` method:

```
void __fastcall TEmptyPanel::Loaded(void)
{
```

```
  TPanel::Loaded();
  Caption = "";
}
```

The code shown in this overridden `Loaded` method will change the caption of the component at runtime, but not at design time. The `Loaded` method is called after a component has been loaded from a stream but before it is shown to the user. The method exists so that you can set the value of properties that rely on the value of other properties.

A second technique involves overriding the `SetParent` method:

```
void __fastcall TEmptyPanel::SetParent(TWinControl *AParent)
{
  TPanel::SetParent(AParent);
  Caption = "";
}
```

This will fix the problem at both design time and at runtime.

In this example, I am not using `SetParent` for its intended purpose. To understand the method's real purpose, you need to remember that a component is always shown on the surface of its parent. The primary purpose of the `SetParent` method is to give you a chance to change the parent of a component just as it is being made visible to the user. This allows you to store a component in a DFM file with one parent, and to change that parent at runtime. It's unlikely you will ever need to change the parent of a component, but there are occasions when it is useful, and so the VCL gives you that ability.

It is obviously useful to know that you can override the `SetParent` and `Loaded` methods in order to change properties at two different stages in the process of allocating memory for a component. You should note, however, that in this case it is a bit strange that you have to do so, because merely overriding the constructor should have turned the trick.

The last new component in `Unleash2.cpp` enables you to drop down a panel that comes equipped with two radio buttons. This way, you can make a single control out of a set of components that are often combined.

You could create other controls that contain three, four, or more radio buttons. Or you could even create a panel that would populate itself with a specific number of radio buttons.

The declaration for this new radio button is fairly simple:

```
class TRadio2Panel : public TEmptyPanel
{
private:
  TRadioButton *FRadio1;
  TRadioButton *FRadio2;
public:
  virtual __fastcall TRadio2Panel(TComponent *Owner);
  __property TRadioButton *Radio1={read=FRadio1 };
  __property TRadioButton *Radio2={read=FRadio2 };
};
```

The actual radio buttons themselves are declared as private data, and access to them is given by the `Radio1` and `Radio2` properties.

Write access to the radio button properties is not needed because you can modify without it. The following statement performs one read of `RP->Radio1` and one write to the `Caption` property of that radio button:

```
P->Radio1->Caption = "Control one";
```

You don't want write access to the properties either because that would allow the user to assign them garbage (or NULL).

The constructor for the `Radio2Panel` begins by setting the width and height of the panel:

```
__fastcall TRadio2Panel::TRadio2Panel(TComponent *Owner)
  :TEmptyPanel(Owner)
{
  Width = 175;
  Height = 60;
  FRadio1 = new TRadioButton(this);
  FRadio1->Parent = this;
  FRadio1->Caption = "Radio1";
  FRadio1->Left = 20;
  FRadio1->Top = 10;
  FRadio1->Show();
  FRadio2 = new TRadioButton(this);
  FRadio2->Parent = this;
  FRadio2->Caption = "Radio2";
  FRadio2->Left = 20;
  FRadio2->Top = 32;
  FRadio2->Show();
}
```

The next step is to create the first radio button. Notice that the code passes `this` as the owner and sets the parent to the panel itself. The rest of the code in the `Create` method is too trivial to merit comment.

Under some circumstances, you may need to register `TRadioButton`:

```
TComponentClass classes[1]={__classid(TRadioButton)};
RegisterClasses(classes, 0);
```

This event would normally occur when you drop a component on a form. However, in this case a `TRadioButton` is not necessarily ever dropped explicitly on a form. As a result, the safe thing to do is register the component, possibly in the constructor for the class.

When you're ready to test the `TRadio2Panel` object, you can write the following code in the test-bed program to take it through its paces:

```
TRadio2Panel *P = new TRadio2Panel(this);
P->Parent = this;
P->Top = E->Top + E->Height + 5;
P->Radio1->Caption = "As you from crimes would pardon'd be ";
P->Radio1->Width = Canvas->TextWidth(P->Radio1->Caption) + 20;
P->Radio2->Caption = "Let your indulgence set me free ";
```

```
P->Radio2->Width = Canvas->TextWidth(P->Radio2->Caption) + 20;
P->Width = max(P->Radio1->Width, P->Radio2->Width) + P->Radio1->Left + 20;
P->Show();
```

Note that each radio button that belongs to the panel acts exactly as you would expect a normal radio button to act, except you have to qualify it differently before you access it. I use the TextWidth property of Canvas to discover the width needed for the string, and then add 20 to take into account the button itself.

> **NOTE**
>
> If you want, you can surface Radio1 and Radio2 in the Object Inspecter as published properties of TRadio2Panel. However, when you first do so, they will have no property editors available because BCB has no built-in property editors for TRadioButtons. To build your own, you can refer to the DsgnIntf.pas unit that ships with BCB, as well as the upcoming discussion of the Clock component and the Tools API.

The following code is used to register the objects in the Unleash2 unit so they can be placed on the Component Palette:

```
namespace Unleash2
{
  void __fastcall Register()
  {
    TComponentClass classes[6]={__classid(TSmallEditTwo),
      __classid(TBigEdit), __classid(TSmallLabel), __classid(TBigLabel),
      __classid(TEmptyPanel), __classid(TRadio2Panel)};
    RegisterComponents("Unleash", classes, 5);
  }
}
```

Notice how I register multiple components in this example at once by creating an array of type TComponentClass. After registering the objects, you can place them on the Component Palette and use them in a program, as shown in Figures 22.5 and 22.6.

FIGURE 22.5.

The main form of a VCL application that uses some of the components from the Unleash2 *unit.*

FIGURE 22.6.

The new components on the Component Palette, along with some other controls created in later chapters.

> **NOTE**
>
> To create custom bitmaps for components shown on the Component Palette, you need to create a standard resource with the extension .dcr. The Image Editor component that ships with BCB is designed to handle this chore.
>
> I ship a few DCR files in the Utils directory on the CD that accompanies this book. You can study them to see how to proceed, or you can find the DCR files for other components that ship with BCB. To look at a DCR file, open it with the Image Editor.
>
> The DCR file should have the name of the unit that contains the controls, and each small 24×24 bitmap that you create in the file should be named after the component to which it belongs. For example, the DCR file for this unit would be called Unleash2.dcr, and the bitmaps inside it would have names like TBIGEDIT and TEMPTYPANEL.
>
> I will discuss this subject in more depth later in this chapter.

Before closing this section, I'd like to add some notes about how BCB handles streaming chores. The good news is that most of the time you don't have to concern yourself with streaming at all. BCB handles most streaming chores automatically. In particular, it will automatically stream published properties that are simple types. Only under limited circumstances must you explicitly stream the fields of your object.

If a property type is a TComponent or descendant, the streaming system assumes it must create an instance of that type when reading it in. If a property type is TPersistent but not TComponent, the streaming system assumes it is supposed to use the existing instance available through the property and read values into that instance's properties.

The Object Inspector knows to expand the properties of TPersistent but not TComponent descendants. This expansion is not done for TComponent descendants because they are likely to have a lot more properties, which would make navigating the Object Inspector difficult.

Building Components from Scratch

In the previous examples, you created descendants of existing components. Now you're ready to see how to create entirely new components. The main idea to grasp here is that you can make a new component descend from three abstract objects. The term "abstract" can have a

22

specific technical meaning, but here I'm using it to refer to any object that exists only so that you can create descendants of it. In short, the following three objects have built-in functionality that all components need to access, but you would never want to instantiate an instance of any of them:

- TWinControl and TCustomControl are base classes that can be used to produce a Windows control that can receive input focus and that has a standard Windows handle that can be passed to API calls. TWinControl descendants exist inside their own window. TEdit, TListBox, TTabbedNotebook, TNotebook, and TPanel are all examples of this type of control. Most components of this type actually descend from TCustomControl, which is in turn a descendant of TWinControl. The distinction between the two classes is that TCustomControl has a Paint method, and TWinControl does not. If you want to draw the display of your new component, you should make it inherit from TCustomControl. If the object already knows how to draw itself, inherit from TWinControl.

- TGraphicControl is for components that don't need to receive input focus, don't need to contain other components, and don't need a handle. These controls draw themselves directly on their parent's surface, thereby saving Windows resources. Not having a window handle eliminates a lot of Windows management overhead, and that translates into faster display updates. In short, TGraphicControls exist inside their parent's window. They use their parent's handle and their parent's device context. They still have Handle and Canvas fields that you can access, but they actually belong to their parent. TLabel and TShape objects are examples of this type of component. The drawback with this system is that the component can never get the focus!

- TComponent enables you to create nonvisual components. If you want to make a tool such as the TTable, TQuery, TOpenDialog, or TTimer devices, this is the place to start. You can place these components on the Component Palette, but they perform some internal function that you access through code instead of appearing to the user at runtime. A tool such as TOpenDialog can pop up a dialog, but the component itself remains invisible.

Create a TWinControl or TCustomControl descendant whenever the user needs to interact directly with a visible control. If the user doesn't need to interact with a visible component, create a TGraphicControl descendant.

To get a handle on the issues involved here, you should place a TShape or TLabel control on a form and run the program. Clicking or attempting to type on these controls produces no noticeable result. These components don't ever receive the focus. Now place a TEdit control on the form. It responds to mouse clicks, gets the focus, and you can type in it. TEdit controls are descendants of TWinControl, and TShape is a descendant of TGraphicControl.

> **NOTE**
>
> I should add one caveat to the rules about `TGraphicControl` explained previously. In one limited sense, the user can interact with a `TGraphicControl`. For example, these controls do receive mouse messages, and you can set the mouse cursor when the mouse flies over them. They just can't receive keyboard input focus. If an object can't receive focus, it usually seems inert to the user.

If you're having trouble deciding whether you want to make descendants from `TWinControl` or `TCustomControl`, you should always go with `TCustomControl`. It has a real `Paint` method and some other functionality that is useful when creating a component of your own. If you want to wrap an existing Windows control inside a VCL object, you should start with `TWinControl`. Most BCB components that follow this path begin by creating intermediate custom objects, so the hierarchy of `TEdit` looks like this:

```
TWinControl
TCustomEdit
TEdit
```

The hierarchy of `TListBox` looks like this:

```
TWinControl
TCustomListBox
TListBox
```

Of course, BCB wraps all the major Windows controls for you, so you won't need to perform this operation unless you're working with a specialized third-party control of some sort.

Following are the declarations for `TGraphicControl` and `TCustomControl`, as they appear in `Controls.hpp`:

```
class __declspec(delphiclass) TGraphicControl;
class __declspec(pascalimplementation) TGraphicControl : public TControl
{
  typedef TControl inherited;
private:
  Graphics::TCanvas* FCanvas;
  MESSAGE void __fastcall WMPaint(Messages::TWMPaint &Message);
protected:
  virtual void __fastcall Paint(void);
  __property Graphics::TCanvas* Canvas = {read=FCanvas, nodefault};
public:
  __fastcall virtual TGraphicControl(Classes::TComponent* AOwner);
  __fastcall virtual ~TGraphicControl(void);
};
class __declspec(delphiclass) TCustomControl;
class __declspec(pascalimplementation) TCustomControl : public TWinControl
{
  typedef TWinControl inherited;
private:
  Graphics::TCanvas* FCanvas;
  MESSAGE void __fastcall WMPaint(Messages::TWMPaint &Message);
```

```
protected:
  virtual void __fastcall Paint(void);
  virtual void __fastcall PaintWindow(HDC DC);
  __property Graphics::TCanvas* Canvas = {read=FCanvas, nodefault};
public:
  __fastcall virtual TCustomControl(Classes::TComponent* AOwner);
  __fastcall virtual ~TCustomControl(void);
public:
  /* CreateParented */ __fastcall TCustomControl(HWND ParentWindow) :
    Controls::TWinControl(ParentWindow) { }
};
```

You can see that these objects are fairly simple. If you go back one step further in the hierarchy to TControl or TWinControl, you see huge objects. For example, the declaration for class TWinControl is nearly 200 lines long (not the implementation, mind you, just the type declaration).

I'm showing you this source code because component builders should work directly with the source rather than use the online help or the docs. For simple jobs, you can easily create your own components without the source. However, if you have a big project, you have to get the source code if it did not ship with your product. The INT files that ship with all versions of BCB are very helpful, but you'll find no replacement for the actual source. The source is available with the client/server version of BCB and also as an up-sell from Borland.

The Clock Component

You now know enough to build a component from the ground up. The CLOCK unit, as shown in Figure 22.7, is a simple clock that you can pop onto a form, and activate and deactivate at will. In particular, you can start the clock running and then tell it to stop by changing the value of a Boolean property called Running.

FIGURE 22.7.

The CLOCK unit as it appears on its own test bed, before being placed on the Component Palette.

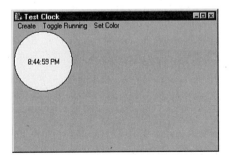

When you're constructing class TClock, the first thing you need to decide is whether the clock is going to descend from TWinControl or TGraphicControl. If you've built a clock in Windows before, you know that one of the best ways to drive it is with a Windows timer. Timers require the presence of a handle so that they can be stopped and started; furthermore, they send their WM_TIMER messages to the window that owns them. Because a TGraphicControl descendant isn't a real window, it will not automatically get the messages. As a result, TGraphicControl is not an ideal choice for this type of object.

Of course, the objections to using TGraphicControl raised in the preceding paragraph aren't insurmountable. If you really want to, you can still make your clock work this way. However, there's no point in expending effort that isn't strictly necessary, so I have opted for the simplest design possible and have made the class a descendant of TCustomControl. I chose TCustomControl rather than TWinControl because I needed a Paint method in which I could draw the clock. (See Figure 22.8.)

FIGURE 22.8.

The TClock and TColorClock controls shown on a form.

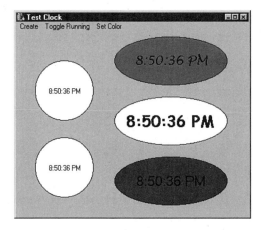

The code, shown in Listings 22.9 through 22.11, also contains a special property editor, as well as a simple component editor. As you will see, neither of these tools is inherently difficult to build.

> **NOTE**
>
> Before installing the clock components, you might need to run the BuildObjs program found in the Utils directory. See the readme file on the CD that accompanies this chapter for additional information.

Listing 22.9. The header for the Clock component contains declarations for the clock and its property and component editors.

```
/////////////////////////////////////
// Clock1.h
// Clock Component
// Copyright (c) 1997 by Charlie Calvert
//
```

```
#ifndef Clock1H
#define Clock1H
#include <vcl\sysutils.hpp>
#include <vcl\controls.hpp>
#include <vcl\classes.hpp>
#include <vcl\forms.hpp>
#include <vcl\dsgnintf.hpp>
#include <vcl\messages.hpp>
#include <vcl\extctrls.hpp>

class TClockAttributes: public TPersistent
{
private:
  TColor FColor;
  TShapeType FShape;
  TComponent *FOwner;
  void __fastcall SetColor(TColor AColor);
  void __fastcall SetShape(TShapeType AShape);
public:
  virtual __fastcall TClockAttributes() : TPersistent() { }
  virtual __fastcall TClockAttributes(TComponent *AOwner)
    : TPersistent() { FOwner = AOwner; }
__published:
  __property TColor Color={read=FColor, write=SetColor};
  __property TShapeType  Shape={read=FShape, write=SetShape};
};

/////////////////////////////////////
// TMyClock /////////////////////////
/////////////////////////////////////
class TMyClock: public TCustomControl
{
private:
  int FTimer;
  Boolean FRunning;
  TClockAttributes *FClockAttributes;
  void __fastcall SetRunning(Boolean ARun);
protected:
  virtual __fastcall ~TMyClock() { delete FClockAttributes; }
  virtual void __fastcall Paint(void);
  void __fastcall WMTimer(TMessage &Message);
  void __fastcall WMDestroy(TMessage &Message);
public:
  virtual __fastcall TMyClock(TComponent* Owner);
__published:
  __property Boolean Running={read=FRunning, write=SetRunning};
  __property Align;
  __property TClockAttributes *ClockAttributes=
    {read=FClockAttributes, write=FClockAttributes };
  __property Font;
BEGIN_MESSAGE_MAP
  MESSAGE_HANDLER(WM_TIMER, TMessage, WMTimer);
  MESSAGE_HANDLER(WM_DESTROY, TMessage, WMDestroy);
```

continues

22

CREATING
DESCENDANTS

Listing 22.9. continued

```cpp
END_MESSAGE_MAP(TCustomControl);
};

/////////////////////////////////////////
// TColorClock /////////////////////////////
/////////////////////////////////////////
class TColorClock: public TMyClock
{
private:
  TColor FFaceColor;
  void __fastcall SetColor(TColor Color);
protected:
  void virtual __fastcall Paint(void);
public:
  virtual __fastcall TColorClock(TComponent *Owner)
    :TMyClock(Owner) { FFaceColor = clGreen; }
__published:
  __property TColor FaceColor={read=FFaceColor, write=SetColor, nodefault};
};

/////////////////////////////////////////
// TClockEditor /////////////////////////////
/////////////////////////////////////////
class TClockEditor: public TComponentEditor
{
protected:
  virtual __fastcall void Edit(void);
public:
  virtual __fastcall TClockEditor(TComponent *AOwner, TFormDesigner *Designer)
    : TComponentEditor(AOwner, Designer) {}
};

/////////////////////////////////////////
// TColorNameProperty /////////////////////
/////////////////////////////////////////
class TColorNameProperty: public TClassProperty
{
public:
  TColorNameProperty(): TClassProperty() {}
  TPropertyAttributes __fastcall GetAttributes(void);
};

#endif
```

Listing 22.10. The code for the Clock component should be kept in the Utils subdirectory where you store CodeBox and other utility units.

```cpp
/////////////////////////////////////////
// Clock1.cpp
// Clock Component
// Copyright (c) 1997 by Charlie Calvert
//
```

```
#include <vcl\vcl.h>
#pragma hdrstop

#include "Clock1.h"

///////////////////////////////////////
// ValidControlCheck
///////////////////////////////////////
static inline TMyClock *ValidCtrCheck()
{
  return new TMyClock(NULL);
}


///////////////////////////////////////
// TColorsProperty
///////////////////////////////////////
void __fastcall TClockAttributes::SetColor(TColor AColor)
{
  FColor = AColor;
  ((TControl *)(FOwner))->Invalidate();
};

void __fastcall TClockAttributes::SetShape(TShapeType AShape)
{
  FShape = AShape;
  ((TControl *)(FOwner))->Invalidate();
};


///////////////////////////////////////
// Constructor
///////////////////////////////////////
__fastcall TMyClock::TMyClock(TComponent* Owner)
  : TCustomControl(Owner)
{
  Width = 100;
  Height = 100;
  FTimer = 1;
  FClockAttributes = new TClockAttributes(this);
  FClockAttributes->Color = clBtnFace;
  FClockAttributes->Shape = stEllipse;
}


///////////////////////////////////////
// SetRunning
///////////////////////////////////////
void __fastcall TMyClock::SetRunning(Boolean Run)
{
  if (Run)
  {
    SetTimer(Handle, FTimer, 50, NULL);
    FRunning = True;
  }
  else
  {
    KillTimer(Handle, FTimer);
```

continues

Listing 22.10. continued

```cpp
    FRunning = False;
  }
}

/////////////////////////////////////
// Paint
/////////////////////////////////////
void __fastcall TMyClock::Paint(void)
{
  Color = ClockAttributes->Color;
  switch (ClockAttributes->Shape)
  {
    int X;

    case stEllipse: Canvas->Ellipse(0, 0, Width, Height); break;
    case stRectangle: Canvas->Rectangle(0, 0, Width, Height); break;
    case stRoundRect:
      Canvas->RoundRect(0, 0, Width, Height, Width - 100, Height);
      break;

    case stSquare:
    {
      if (Width < Height)
      {
        X = Width / 2;
        Canvas->Rectangle(Width - X, 0, Width + X, Width);
      }
      else
      {
        X = Height / 2;
        Canvas->Rectangle((Width / 2) - X, 0, (Width / 2) + X, Height);
      }
      break;
    }

    case stCircle:
    {
      if (Width < Height)
      {
        X = Width / 2;
        Canvas->Ellipse(Width - X, 0, Width + X, Width);
      }
      else
      {
        X = Height / 2;
        Canvas->Ellipse((Width / 2) - X, 0, (Width / 2) + X, Height);
      }
      break;
    }
  }
}

/////////////////////////////////////
// WM_TIMER
/////////////////////////////////////
```

```
void __fastcall TMyClock::WMTimer(TMessage &Message)
{
  AnsiString S = TimeToStr(Time());
  Canvas->Font = Font;
  Canvas->TextOut(Width / 2 - Canvas->TextWidth(S) / 2,
                  Height / 2 - Canvas->TextHeight(S) / 2, S);
}

//////////////////////////////////////
// WM_DESTROY
//////////////////////////////////////
void __fastcall TMyClock::WMDestroy(TMessage &Message)
{
  KillTimer(Handle, FTimer);
  FTimer = 0;
  TCustomControl::Dispatch(&Message);
}

//------------------------------------
//-- TColorClock --------------------
//------------------------------------

//////////////////////////////////////
// WM_DESTROY
//////////////////////////////////////
void __fastcall TColorClock::Paint()
{
  Canvas->Brush->Color = FFaceColor;
  TMyClock::Paint();
}



//////////////////////////////////////
// SetColor
//////////////////////////////////////
void __fastcall TColorClock::SetColor(TColor Color)
{
  FFaceColor = Color;
  InvalidateRect(Handle, NULL, True);
}

//------------------------------------
//-- TClockEditor -------------------
//------------------------------------
void __fastcall TClockEditor::Edit(void)
{
  TColorDialog *C = new TColorDialog(Application);
  if (C->Execute())
    ((TColorClock *)(Component))->FaceColor = C->Color;
}

//------------------------------------
//-- TColorNameProperty -------------
//------------------------------------
TPropertyAttributes __fastcall TColorNameProperty::GetAttributes(void)
{
```

continues

Listing 22.10. continued

```
  return TPropertyAttributes() << paSubProperties;
}

//////////////////////////////////////
// Register
//////////////////////////////////////
namespace Clock1
{
  void __fastcall Register()
  {
    TComponentClass classes[2] = {__classid(TMyClock), __classid(TColorClock)};
    RegisterComponents("Unleash", classes, 1);

    RegisterComponentEditor(__classid(TColorClock), __classid(TClockEditor));
    RegisterPropertyEditor(__typeinfo(TClockAttributes),
      __classid(TMyClock), "Colors", __classid(TColorNameProperty));
  }
}
```

Listing 22.11. The test bed for the `clock` component is stored in the `TestClock` subdirectory.

```
#include <vcl\vcl.h>
#pragma hdrstop
#include "Main.h"
#include "Clock1.h"
#pragma link "Clock1"
#pragma link "sampreg"
#pragma link "ClockProperty1"
#pragma resource "*.dfm"

TForm1 *Form1;

__fastcall TForm1::TForm1(TComponent* Owner)
  : TForm(Owner)
{
}

void __fastcall TForm1::Create1Click(TObject *Sender)
{
  MyClock = new TColorClock(this);
  MyClock->Parent = this;
  MyClock->Show();
}

void __fastcall TForm1::ToggleRunning1Click(TObject *Sender)
{
  MyClock->Running = !MyClock->Running;
}

void __fastcall TForm1::SetColor1Click(TObject *Sender)
{
```

```
if (ColorDialog1->Execute())
{
  MyClock->FaceColor = ColorDialog1->Color;
}
}
```

To run this program, you should first select the menu item that creates the clock and makes it visible on the form. The next logical step is to start the clock running; then, if you'd like, you can also change its color. You get an Access Violation if you click the latter two buttons before selecting the first. The problem is that calling a method or property of the TClock object before the object itself has been created is an error. To prevent this error from happening, you could enable and disable the second two buttons.

The code for the clock components uses inheritance, virtual methods, and properties. TClock has two pieces of private data:

```
int FTimer;
Boolean FRunning;
```

One is an identifier for the timer, and the other is a Boolean value that specifies whether the clock is running.

Windows timers are managed by two Windows API calls. When you want to start a timer, use SetTimer; when you want to stop a timer, use KillTimer. SetTimer takes four parameters:

- Handle is the HWND of your current window.

- IDEvent is an integer identifier that uniquely identifies the timer inside the window that created it. You can make up this value off the top of your head, although I generally set the IDTimer for the first timer in a window to 1, the second timer to 2, and so on. Because you're going to have only one timer in each instance of a TClock window, you can set its IDEvent to 1.

- Elapse is the length of time between calls to the timer, measured in milliseconds.

- TimerFunc is a callback function that is not used in this program. One of the developers' big goals was to create a Windows product that didn't need to use callbacks, and I see no reason to open that can of worms now if I can avoid it. (If you want to create a callback in BCB, you will be able to do so, but it's usually not necessary.)

A typical call to SetTimer looks like this:

```
SetTimer(Handle, FTimer, 50, NULL);
```

50 specifies that the timer is called once every 50 milliseconds. SetTimer returns zero if the call fails. This is a real possibility, so programs that include error checking should inspect this value and put up a MessageBox if the call fails.

22

CREATING
DESCENDANTS

KillTimer takes two parameters, the first being the handle of your window and the second being the unique identifier associated with that timer:

```
KillTimer(Handle, FTimer);
```

When you're not using the callback function, timer events are sent to your window by way of messages:

```
void __fastcall WMTimer(TMessage &Message);
BEGIN_MESSAGE_MAP
  MESSAGE_HANDLER(WM_TIMER, TMessage, WMTimer);
  MESSAGE_HANDLER(WM_DESTROY, TMessage, WMDestroy);
END_MESSAGE_MAP(TCustomControl);
```

This classic dynamic method is of the kind covered in Chapter 4, "Events." The response to this event is a simple procedure that calls TextOut and gets the time from the VCL:

```
void __fastcall TMyClock::WMTimer(TMessage &Message)
{
  AnsiString S = TimeToStr(Time());
  Canvas->TextOut(Width / 2 - Canvas->TextWidth(S) / 2,
                  Height / 2 - Canvas->TextHeight(S) / 2, S);
}
```

The calls to SetTimer and KillTimer are managed primarily through a property called Running:

```
__property Boolean Running={read=FRunning, write=SetRunning};
```

The write mechanism, a procedure called SetRunning, is a fairly straightforward tool:

```
void __fastcall TMyClock::SetRunning(Boolean Run)
{
  if (Run)
  {
    SetTimer(Handle, FTimer, 50, NULL);
    FRunning = True;
  }
  else
  {
    KillTimer(Handle, FTimer);
    FRunning = False;
  }
}
```

If the user sets the Running property to True, this procedure is executed and a call is made to the SetTimer function. If the user sets Running to False, KillTimer is called and the clock immediately stops functioning.

The final issue involving the timer concerns the case in which the user closes a form while the clock is still running. In such a case, you must be sure to call KillTimer before the application exits. If you don't make the call, the timer keeps running even after the application closes. Having the timer running wastes system resources and also uses up one of the dozen or so timers that are available to the system at any one time.

The logical place to call KillTimer is the Destroy method for the TClock object. Unfortunately, the window associated with the clock has already been destroyed by the time this call is made, so no valid handle is available for use when you call KillTimer. As a result, you need to respond to WM_DESTROY messages to be sure the timer is killed before the TClock window is closed:

```
void __fastcall TMyClock::WMDestroy(TMessage &Message)
{
  KillTimer(Handle, FTimer);
  FTimer = 0;
  TCustomControl::Dispatch(&Message);
}
```

Before leaving this description of the TClock object, I should briefly mention the Paint method. Here is the simplest possible version of the paint procedure for the program:

```
void __fastcall TMyClock::Paint(void)
{
  Canvas->Ellipse(0, 0, 100, 100);
}
```

This procedure is called whenever the circle defining the circumference of the clock needs to be repainted. You never have to check for this circumstance, and you never have to call Paint directly. Windows keeps an eye on the TClock window, and if the window needs to be painted, Windows sends you a WM_PAINT message. Logic buried deep in the VCL converts the WM_PAINT message into a call to Paint, the same way TClock translates WM_TIMER messages into calls to TCanvas->TextOut.

The actual paint procedure used in the program looks like this:

```
/////////////////////////////////////
// Paint
/////////////////////////////////////
void __fastcall TMyClock::Paint(void)
{
  Color = ClockAttributes->Color;
  switch (ClockAttributes->Shape)
  {
    int X;

    case stEllipse: Canvas->Ellipse(0, 0, Width, Height); break;
    case stRectangle: Canvas->Rectangle(0, 0, Width, Height); break;
    case stRoundRect:
      Canvas->RoundRect(0, 0, Width, Height, Width - 100, Height);
      break;

    case stSquare:
    {
      if (Width < Height)
      {
        X = Width / 2;
        Canvas->Rectangle(Width - X, 0, Width + X, Width);
      }
```

22

CREATING
DESCENDANTS

```
      else
      {.
        X = Height / 2;
        Canvas->Rectangle((Width / 2) - X, 0, (Width / 2) + X, Height);
      }
      break;
    }

    case stCircle:
    {
      if (Width < Height)
      {
        X = Width / 2;
        Canvas->Ellipse(Width - X, 0, Width + X, Width);
      }
      else
      {
        X = Height / 2;
        Canvas->Ellipse((Width / 2) - X, 0, (Width / 2) + X, Height);
      }
      break;
    }
  }
}
```

This version of the Paint procedure takes into account the ClockAttributes property of TMyClock. TClockAttributes looks like this:

```
class TClockAttributes: public TPersistent
{
private:
  TColor FColor;
  TShapeType FShape;
  TComponent *FOwner;
  void __fastcall SetColor(TColor AColor);
  void __fastcall SetShape(TShapeType AShape);
public:
  virtual __fastcall TClockAttributes() : TPersistent() { }
  virtual __fastcall TClockAttributes(TComponent *AOwner)
    : TPersistent() { FOwner = AOwner; }
__published:
  __property TColor Color={read=FColor, write=SetColor};
  __property TShapeType  Shape={read=FShape, write=SetShape};
};
```

As you can see, it provides a shape and a background color for the clock. The most important aspect of the TClockAttributes type is the property editors I create for it. These editors let you access both properties of this class through a series of special techniques, described later in this chapter. For now, you might want to merely click the ClockAttributes property, open up its two fields, and see how it works.

The `TColorClock` component, which is a descendant of `TClock`, adds color to the face of the control. I made `TColorClock` a separate object, instead of just adding a face color to `TClock`, for two different reasons (both of which are related to design):

■ You might want to create a descendant of `TClock` that doesn't have color or one that implements color differently than `TColorClock` does. By creating two objects, one called `TClock` and the other called `TColorClock`, I enable programmers to have the greatest amount of freedom when creating descendants. This principle has only minimal weight in a simple object such as `TClock`, but it can become extremely important when you're developing large and complex hierarchies. In short, be careful of building too much functionality into one object!

■ `TClock` and `TColorClock` also provide another example of inheritance and vividly demonstrate how this technology can be utilized to your advantage.

`TColorClock` declares a private data store called `FColor` that is of type `TColor`. Users can set the `FColor` variable by manipulating the `Color` property:

```
__property TColor Color={read=FColor, write=SetColor};
```

`SetColor` is a simple procedure that sets the value of `FColor` and calls the Windows API call `InvalidateRect`:

```
void SetColor(TColor Color)
    { FColor = Color; InvalidateRect(Handle, NULL, True); }
```

Just to be sure this information makes sense to you, taking a paragraph or two to provide a refresher course on `InvalidateRect` is worthwhile. Here's the declaration for the routine:

```
BOOL InvalidateRect(
    HWND   hWnd,           // handle of window with changed update region
    CONST RECT  * lpRect,  // address of rectangle coordinates
    BOOL   bErase          // erase-background flag
    );
```

`InvalidateRect` forces the window specified in the first parameter to redraw itself completely if the third parameter is set to `True`. If the third parameter is set to `False`, only the portions of the window that you specifically repaint are changed. The middle parameter is a pointer to the `RECT` structure that can be used to define the area that you want to redraw. Compare this function with the native BCB function called `Invalidate`.

Calls to `InvalidateRect` naturally force calls to the `TColorClick->Paint` method:

```
void __fastcall TColorClock::Paint()
{
  Canvas->Brush->Color = FColor;
  TMyClock::Paint();
}
```

`Paint` sets the brush associated with the window's device context to the color specified by the user; then it calls the `Paint` method defined in `TClock`.

To add this object to the Component Palette, you must first register it:

```
void __fastcall Register()
  {
    TComponentClass classes[2] = {__classid(TMyClock), __classid(TColorClock)};
    RegisterComponents("Unleash", classes, 1);
    ... // Code omitted here
};
```

Here, I specify that the TClock and TColorClock objects should be placed in a group called Unleash.

A number of properties implemented by TCustomControl and its ancestors do not surface automatically. To access these properties from the Component Palette, all you have to do is list them in the __published section of your class declaration:

```
__property Align;
__property Color;
__property Font;
```

These simple declarations give your component the ability to align itself with the surface on which it resides or set its color and font. The color, in this case, is the color of the background of the form, not of the face of the form. In the actual finished version of the control, I ended up replacing the Color property with the TClockAttributes property. Once again, the primary reason for adding the TClockAttributes property was to show you how to work with property editors.

There is, of course, a place where the Align, Color, and Font properties are declared replete with read and write parts. However, after you have declared the property, you can publish it simply by using the two-word declarations shown here.

On the CD that accompanies this book, you will find a program called GoldClock that uses the TClock component to create a small application displaying the time. You can customize the fonts and colors in this program, and the settings you make will be written to the Registry so that they can be preserved for the next run of the program. The main form of the GoldClock application is shown in Figure 22.9.

FIGURE 22.9.

The main form of the GoldClock application.

That's all I'm going to say about `TClock` and `TColorClock`. Overall, these components are fairly simple; they're interesting primarily because they show you how to go about constructing your own controls from scratch. This kind of exercise lies very much at the heart of BCB's architecture, and I expect many readers will be spending most of their time engaged almost exclusively in the business of building components.

Tips on Creating Properties

A standard technique used in component development features base classes that do not publish any properties. Consumers of the component can then inherit the functionality of the class without having to stick with the original developer's choice of published properties.

After a property has been published, there is no good way to "unpublish" it. The solution to this potential problem is to create base classes that do not publish any properties. The functionality is present, but it is not surfaced in a way that it can be viewed in the Object Inspector.

In many cases, the VCL creates classes that do nothing but publish the properties of their immediate ancestors. These classes sport no functions, no methods, nothing but a `__published` section full of declarations like the ones shown in the preceding section for the `Align`, `Color`, and `Font` properties. This architecture lets others inherit the capability of the class while still providing a choice regarding what will be published.

The naming convention used for classes of this type usually involves the word `Custom`: `TCustomImageList`, `TCustomControl`, `TCustomMemoryStream`, `TCustomGroupBox`, `TCustomLabel`, `TCustomEdit`, `TCustomMemo`, `TCustomCheckBox`, and so on. Open `StdCtrls.hpp` to see more explicitly how this system works.

Making descendants from `TEdit` or `TLabel` as I do in this chapter is a perhaps a bit too simplistic. If you really want to create a custom version of the Edit control for your own purposes, you should probably make descendants from `TCustomEdit`. Once again, you would not miss any functionality by doing so because `TEdit` does nothing but surface the "hidden" properties of `TCustomEdit`. It has no methods or data of its own; everything is inherited from `TCustomEdit`. All it does is publish 20-odd properties.

You probably should not declare the read and write parts of a property in a published section because doing so forces consumers of the product to conform with your ideas for the component's interface. Instead, read and write declarations should go in the `public` section of a class that has `Custom` in the name. Then you should create a descendant of that class which actually publishes the property.

Creating Icons for Components

The icon associated with a component and placed in the Component Palette is defined in a file with a `.DCR` extension. If you do not provide this file, BCB uses the icon associated with the object's parent. If no icon is present anywhere in the component's ancestry, a default icon is used.

> **NOTE**
>
> A DCR file is a Windows resource file with the extension changed from `.RES` to `.DCR`. The resource file contains a bitmap resource with the same name as your component. For example, the bitmap resource in a DCR file for a `TCOLOR` component would have a resource ID of `TColor`. This resource should be a 56×28 pixel (or smaller) bitmap that can be edited in the Image Editor. All you need to do is place this DCR file in the same directory as your component, and the images defined therein will show up on the Component Palette. Use the Image Editor to explore the DCR files that ship with BCB. They are stored in the `\CBUILDER\LIB` directory. I also ship some DCR files with this book in the `Utils` subdirectory where `CodeBox` and other files are kept.

Follow these steps to associate your own bitmaps with a particular component.

1. Open the Image Editor from the Tools menu and choose New.
2. Chose File | New | Component Resource from the menu. A dialog called `Untitled1.dcr` appears.
3. Select Resource | New | Bitmap from the menu. A dialog called New Bitmap Attributes appears.
4. Set Colors to 16 colors, because this technology is available on nearly all Windows systems. Set Size in Pixels to 24×24.
5. Save the file as `Clock1.dcr`. Rename the bitmap you have created to `Tmyclock`.

If you don't like the Image Editor, you can create a 24×24 bitmap in `Pbrush.exe` or some other bitmap editor and then create an RC file that looks like this:

```
TMYCLOCK BITMAP clock.bmp
```

Save the file as `Clock1.rc`. Run the Borland Resource Compiler from the command line:

```
brcc32 -r clock.rc
```

The resulting file will be called `Clock1.res`. Rename that file `Clock1.dcr`.

Creating Help Files for Components

BCB enables you to define help files that can ship with your components. These help files can be merged into the help that ships with BCB, so users of your product will feel as though it is a native part of BCB.

The HLP file is a standard Windows help file that contains information about the properties, methods, and events implemented by your component. I strongly recommend that you obtain a third-party tool to aid in the construction of these help files. For example, you might buy a copy of FOREHELP from Borland, or you could turn to Blue Sky software, or some other third party that provides tools to help you create these files. As a last resort, you can use Word, WordPerfect, or even the TRichEdit component, to create RTF files, and then compile these RTF files into HLP files with the HCW.EXE help compiler that ships with BCB in the CBUILDER\HELP\Tools directory. You can also download this file from online sites such as the Microsoft Web site or CompuServe. (The copy of FOREHELP sold by Borland has not been upgraded for Windows 95, but it is still many times better than having no help tool at all. FOREHELP requires that you have a copy of HC.EXE or HCP.EXE on your system. These files ship with many compilers and are available royalty free on CompuServe and the Internet.)

All the tools mentioned here play a peripheral role in the creation of components. They don't require a knowledge of the fascinating syntax used in component creation, but they help to make your tools attractive and easy to use.

The Five Main Tools APIs

Each of the five main Tools APIs is accessible through a separate set of routines that ship with BCB. These APIs enable you to write code that can be linked directly into the BCB IDE. Specifically, you can link your tools into CmpLib32.ccl the same way you link in components. Here is a list of the Tools APIs and the native BCB source files that define them.

Experts: Enable you to write your own experts.

- ExptIntf.hpp
- VirtIntf.hpp
- ToolIntf.hpp: for enumerating the component pages and components installed, adding modules to the project, and so on

Version Control: Enables you to write your own Version Control system or to link in a third-party system.

- VcsIntf.pas: Include this file in your project to generate the HPP file. The Pascal source might not ship with all versions of BCB.
- VirtIntf.hpp.
- ToolIntf.hpp: for opening and closing files in the editor.

Component Editors: Create dialogs associated with a control at design time (for example, the

DataSet Designer is a component editor).

- `DsgnIntf.hpp`

Property Editors: Create editors for use in the Object Inspector.

- `DsgnIntf.hpp`

Editor Interfaces: For use mostly by third-party editor vendors such as Premia, American Cybernetics, and so on.

- `EditIntf.hpp`
- `FileIntf.hpp`

The letters INTF are an abbreviation for the word "Interface." This term was chosen because the Tools API is an interface between your own code and the BCB developers' code.

Needless to say, most people will never use the Tools API. However, it will be important to a small minority of developers, and its existence means that everyone will be able to buy or download tools that extend the functionality of the IDE.

Property Editors

The Tools API for creating property editors is perhaps the most commonly used interface into the heart of the IDE. When you first use BCB and start becoming familiar with the Object Inspector, you are bound to think that it is a static element that never changes. However, by now it should come as no surprise to learn that you can change the functionality of the Object Inspector by adding new property editors to it.

As I mentioned earlier, property editors control what takes place on the right side of the Properties page of the Object Inspector. In particular, when you click the Color property of TEdit, you can select a new color from a drop-down list, from a common dialog, or by typing in a new value. In all three cases, you're using a property editor.

If you want to create a new property editor, you should create a descendant of TPropertyEditor, a class declared in DsgnIntf.hpp. TPropertyEditor has a number of children. Many of these are for handling simple types such as strings and integers. These editors are not very important to BCB programmers, because most simple types have no RTTI associated with them in C++.

Instead of working with simple types, BCB programmers work with properties that are class types. The classic example of a class type of Property is TFont. Note, for instance, that the Font property of a form can be expanded to show the several fields of the TFont object. You can also pop up a dialog to edit the TFont object. This is a complex property editor of the type that will be developed through the remainder of this chapter.

Here is the declaration for the property editor associated with the `ClockAttributes` property of the `TMyClock` component:

```
class TColorNameProperty: public TClassProperty
{
public:
  TColorNameProperty(): TClassProperty() {}
  TPropertyAttributes __fastcall GetAttributes(void);
};
```

`TColorNameProperty` doesn't descend from `TPropertyEditor` directly. Instead, it descends from a child of `TPropertyEditor` called `TClassEditor`. `TClassEditor` is designed for programmers who want to create editors for complex properties that are also classes.

The `TColorNameProperty` editor doesn't pop up any dialogs, although it will in a version of this program shown at the end of this chapter. Instead of creating dialogs, it simply tells the Object Inspector that the `ClockAttributes` class can be edited as two properties. In particular, notice that the `ClockAttributes` class expands out to show a `Color` property and a `Shape` property. You need to click the plus sign in front of the `ClockAttributes` property before you can see these properties.

The `GetAttributes` method is a way of defining what types of property editors you want to have associated with `TColorDialog`:

```
TPropertyAttributes __fastcall TColorNameProperty::GetAttributes(void)
{
  return TPropertyAttributes() << paSubProperties;
}
```

In this case I have set the `paSubProperties` flag, which tells the Object Inspector to place the plus sign before the property so it can be opened up to reveal sub properties.

A property editor that has the `paMultiSelect` flag remains active even if the user has selected more than one component of that type. For example, you can select 10 edit controls and change all their fonts in one step. BCB enables you to make this change because the `TEdit` control has the `paMultiSelect` flag set.

The `paValueList` flag dictates that the property editor drops down a list of values from an enumerated or set type when the user clicks the arrow button at the far right of the editor. This functionality is built into BCB, and you need only set the flag to have it be supported by your property editor.

Finally, `paDialog` states that the property editor pops up a dialog. Ultimately, the `paDialog` flag does little more than assure that the ellipsis button appears at the right of the property editor.

> **NOTE**
>
> When you choose both paDialog and paValuelist in a single component, the property editor button always winds up being a combo drop-down list button. In other words, the dialog button is obscured, even though the functionality is still present. See, for example, the Color property of a TForm or TEdit.

Streaming Properties of Type Class

The ClockAttributes property will not work properly unless it is streamed to disk. In particular, effective use of TClockAttributes depends on whether the two key properties in TClockAttributes get written to the DFM file where the form is stored. To ensure that this happens, all you have to do is declare ClockAttributes as a published property, and then descend TClockAttributes from TPersistent, and make sure that the Shape and Color properties are published.

Here is the declaration for the TClockAttributes:

```
class TClockAttributes: public TPersistent
{
private:
  TColor FColor;
  TShapeType FShape;
  TComponent *FOwner;
  void __fastcall SetColor(TColor AColor);
  void __fastcall SetShape(TShapeType AShape);
public:
  virtual __fastcall TClockAttributes() : TPersistent() { }
  virtual __fastcall TClockAttributes(TComponent *AOwner)
    : TPersistent() { FOwner = AOwner; }
__published:
  __property TColor Color={read=FColor, write=SetColor};
  __property TShapeType  Shape={read=FShape, write=SetShape};
};
```

The key part of this declaration is where the Color and Shape properties are designated as published. This means that they will have RTTI associated with them, and that they will be streamed out to the DFM file automatically.

Here is a text version of the TMyClock component as it appears in a DFM file:

```
object MyClock2: TMyClock
  Left = 112
  Top = 192
  Width = 100
  Height = 100
  ClockAttributes.Color = clBtnFace
  ClockAttributes.Shape = stEllipse
end
```

Note that the two key properties of `ClockAttributes` have been included in the DFM file. I did not have to do anything special to make this happen. Instead, I just made sure that `ClockAttributes` itself was a published property, and that `Color` and `Shape` were published properties of `TClockAttributes`.

Once I was sure the properties were being streamed out, the only thing left to do was tell the Object Inspector to show both values of `TClockAttributes`. To do this, I simply created the simple, do-nothing `TColorNameProperty` class. As you saw, this class descends from `TClassProperty`, which is declared in `Dsdintf.hpp`.

Examining `DsgnIntf.cpp`

The `DsgnIntf` unit is unusual in that it is very carefully documented by the developer who created it. For example, here are excerpts from that unit describing the two methods I call in the descendant of `TPropertyEditor`:

```
Edit
        Called when the '...' button is pressed or the
        property is double-clicked. This can, for example,
        bring up a dialog to allow the editing of the component
        in some more meaningful fashion than by text
        (e.g. the Font property).
GetAttributes
        Returns the information for use in the Object
        Inspector to be able to show the appropriate tools.
        GetAttributes return a set of type TPropertyAttributes.
```

These entries were written by the developers, and they extensively document this important interface to the core code inside the heart of the IDE.

Here are declarations for `Edit` and `GetAttributes`, as well as the other key functions in `TPropertyEditor`:

```
class __declspec(pascalimplementation) TPropertyEditor : public System::TObject
public:
  __fastcall virtual ~TPropertyEditor(void);
  virtual void __fastcall Activate(void);
  virtual bool __fastcall AllEqual(void);
  virtual void __fastcall Edit(void);
  virtual TPropertyAttributes __fastcall GetAttributes(void);
  Classes::TComponent* __fastcall GetComponent(int Index);
  virtual int __fastcall GetEditLimit(void);
  virtual System::AnsiString __fastcall GetName(void);
  virtual void __fastcall GetProperties(TGetPropEditProc Proc);
  Typinfo::PTypeInfo __fastcall GetPropType(void);
  virtual System::AnsiString __fastcall GetValue(void);
  virtual void __fastcall GetValues(Classes::TGetStrProc Proc);
  virtual void __fastcall Initialize(void);
  void __fastcall Revert(void);
  virtual void __fastcall SetValue(const System::AnsiString Value);
  bool __fastcall ValueAvailable(void);
}
```

Once again, all these methods are carefully documented in `DsgnIntf.hpp`. You should study that file carefully in order to add to the knowledge about property and component editors outlined in the remainder of this chapter.

Registering the Property Editors

You must register property editors with the system before compiling them into `CmpLib32.ccl`. To register a property, call `RegisterPropertyEditor` in the `Register` method for your component:

```
RegisterPropertyEditor(__typeinfo(TClockAttributes),
  __classid(TMyClock), "Colors", __classid(TColorNameProperty));
```

The declaration for `RegisterPropertyEditor` looks like this:

```
extern void __fastcall RegisterPropertyEditor(
  Typinfo::PTypeInfo PropertyType,
  System::TMetaClass* ComponentClass,
  const System::AnsiString PropertyName,
  System::TMetaClass* EditorClass);
```

The various parameters are as follow:

- `PropertyType`. The first parameter passed to this function states the type of data handled by the editor. In this case, it is `TClockAttributes`. BCB uses this information as the first in a series of checklists that determine which properties should be associated with this editor. As noted above, this type cannot be a simple value such as an `int` or `TColor`. It must be a class type. If you want to work with simple types, you should either wrap them in a class or switch to Object Pascal.

- `ComponentClass`. The second parameter further qualifies which components will use this editor. In this case, I have narrowed the range down to `TMyClock` and its descendants. If I had written `TComponent` instead of `TMyClock`, or if I had set this parameter to `NULL`, all properties of type `TClockAttributes` would start using that editor. You therefore can build a new editor for fonts or colors, install it on a customer's system, and it would work with all properties of that type. In other words, you don't have to create a component to be able to write an editor for it.

- `PropertyName`. The third parameter limits the scope to properties with the name passed in this string. If the string is empty, the editor is used for all properties that get passed the first two parameters.

- `EditorClass`. This parameter defines the class of editor associated with the properties defined in the first three parameters.

If you want to find out more about this function, refer to the comments in `DsgnIntf.pas`. These comments may not be copied into `DsgnIntf.hpp`, so check both places.

Working with Component Editors

After you have learned how to build property editors, understanding component editors is easy. These tools are descendants of `TComponentEditor`, just as property editors are descendants of `TPropertyEditor`:

```
class TClockEditor: public TComponentEditor
{
protected:
  virtual __fastcall void Edit(void);
public:
  virtual __fastcall TClockEditor(TComponent *AOwner, TFormDesigner *Designer)
    : TComponentEditor(AOwner, Designer) {}
};
```

The `TColorDialog` has a simple editor that pops up a dialog requesting that the user choose a new color:

```
void __fastcall TClockEditor::Edit(void)
{
  TColorDialog *C = new TColorDialog(Application);
  if (C->Execute())
    ((TColorClock *)(Component))->FaceColor = C->Color;
}
```

In this case, I'm popping up the standard `TColorDialog` that appears when you click the ellipsis icon in the Object Inspector for a property of type `TColor`. The difference, of course, is that this is a component editor, not a property editor. In the more complex component editor example shown later in this chapter, you pop open a form that allows the user to make several changes to the component.

It is easy to access the underlying component from inside a component editor. In particular, the component you are editing is available to you in a variable called `Component`.

The `Component` variable referenced in this example is declared globally inside `TComponentEditor` objects. To access it, you merely have to typecast it as desired to get at the component you're currently editing. For example, in this example, I typecast `Component` as a `TColorClock`. I don't bother with a `dynamic_cast` in this example because the conversion has to work, by the very definition of the context of the call.

This component editor, of course, is the simplest possible, but it gets you started working with these useful tools. Figure 22.10 shows the component editor in action.

FIGURE 22.10.

*The first take on the
component editor for
the* TClock *component
pops up a simple*
TColorDialog.

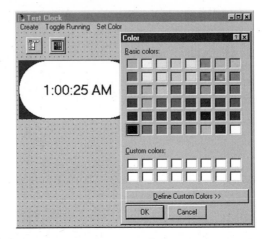

> **NOTE**
>
> Two additional component editors, each one more complex than the last, will be shown
> later in the chapter. In particular, you will see how to pop up a component editor that is
> built on top of a VCL form.

The Register method for TClockEditor looks like this:

```
void __fastcall Register()
{
  . . .
  RegisterComponentEditor(__classid(TMyClock), __classid(TClockEditor));
  . . .
}
}
```

The declaration for this procedure looks like this:

```
extern void __fastcall RegisterComponentEditor(System::TMetaClass* ComponentClass,
                                                System::TMetaClass* ComponentEditor);
```

Clearly, the first parameter specifies the class with which the editor is associated, and the second parameter specifies the class of the editor.

In this section, I introduced you to property editors and component editors. These examples are important primarily because they help focus your attention on DsgnIntf.hpp, which is one of several files that ship with BCB that define the Tools API. If you want to extend the BCB IDE, you should get to know all the files that end in INTF.

Extending the Component and Property Editors

The original component and property editors for TMyClock and TColorClock components are very simple.

Of course, using such simple component and property editors is very limiting. You may use a normal VCL form as an editor. Examples of this type of form are shown in Figures 22.11 and 22.12.

FIGURE 22.11.

The new property editor for ClockAttributes *is a VCL form that gives the user considerable control over the appearance of the clock.*

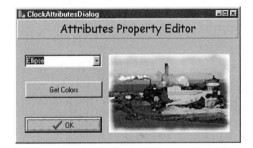

FIGURE 22.12.

This component editor for TClock *uses a standard VCL form and can be as complex as you want.*

To create the form shown in Figure 22.12, I started a new project called TestClock2. I then copied the Clock1 files into a new set of files called Clock2 and changed all the names inside the files to reflect the change. For example, I renamed TMyClock to TMyClock2, TColorClock to TColorClock2, and so on.

I then created a new form called ClockEditor and added several buttons to it, a TColorDialog, and a TImage control. I arranged the controls as shown in Figure 22.12. I then made a few changes to the Edit method of TClockEditor2, and added a button to my main form so that I could test the editor. The source code for this new program is shown in Listings 22.12 through 22.15.

> **NOTE**
>
> Before installing the clock components, you might need to run the BuildObjs program found in the Utils directory. See the readme file on the CD that accompanies this chapter for additional information. In particular, BuildObjs makes sure that ClockAttributes.cpp and ClockEditor.cpp are both compiled into binary form as OBJ files.

Listing 22.12. The header file for the main unit of the TestClock2 program.

```
/////////////////////////////////////
// Main.h
// Project: Testing example of Component editor
// Copyright 1997 by Charlie Calvert
//
#ifndef MainH
#define MainH
#include <vcl\Classes.hpp>
#include <vcl\Controls.hpp>
#include <vcl\StdCtrls.hpp>
#include <vcl\Forms.hpp>
#include "Clock2.h"
#include "Clock1.h"
class TForm1 : public TForm
{
__published:
  TButton *Button1;
  TColorClock2 *ColorClock21;
  void __fastcall Button1Click(TObject *Sender);

private:
public:
  __fastcall TForm1(TComponent* Owner);
};
extern TForm1 *Form1;
#endif
```

Listing 22.13. The main module for the TestClock2 program.

```
/////////////////////////////////////
// Main.cpp
// Project: Testing example of Component editor
// Copyright 1997 by Charlie Calvert
//
#include <vcl\vcl.h>
#pragma hdrstop
#include "Main.h"
#include "ClockEditor.h"
#pragma link "Clock2"
```

```
#pragma link "Clock1"
#pragma resource "*.dfm"
TForm1 *Form1;
__fastcall TForm1::TForm1(TComponent* Owner)
  : TForm(Owner)
{
}
void __fastcall TForm1::Button1Click(TObject *Sender)
{
  RunClockEditorDlg(ColorClock21);
}
```

Listing 22.14. The header for the ColorEditor dialog.

```
///////////////////////////////////////
// ClockEditor.h
// Project: Clock2 example of Component editor
// Copyright 1997 by Charlie Calvert
//
#ifndef ClockEditorH
#define ClockEditorH
#include <vcl\Classes.hpp>
#include <vcl\Controls.hpp>
#include <vcl\StdCtrls.hpp>
#include <vcl\Forms.hpp>
#include <vcl\Dialogs.hpp>
#include "Clock2.h"
#include <vcl\ExtCtrls.hpp>
#include <vcl\Buttons.hpp>

void RunClockEditorDlg(TColorClock2 *Clock);

class TClockEditorDialog : public TForm
{
__published:
  TButton *SetFaceColorBtn;
  TColorDialog *ColorDialog1;
  TButton *SetBackColorBtn;
  TPanel *Panel1;
  TImage *Image1;
  TBitBtn *BitBtn1;
  void __fastcall SetFaceColorBtnClick(TObject *Sender);
  void __fastcall SetBackColorBtnClick(TObject *Sender);
private:
  TColorClock2 *FClock;
public:
  __fastcall TClockEditorDialog(TComponent* Owner);
  __property TColorClock2 *Clock={read=FClock, write=FClock};
};

extern TClockEditorDialog *ClockEditorDialog;

#endif
```

Listing 22.15. The main module for the ColorEditor dialog.

```
//////////////////////////////////////////
// ClockEditor.cpp
// Project: Clock2 example of Component editor
// Copyright 1997 by Charlie Calvert
//
#include <vcl\vcl.h>
#pragma hdrstop
#include "ClockEditor.h"
#include "clock2.h"
#pragma resource "*.dfm"

TClockEditorDialog *ClockEditorDialog;

__fastcall TClockEditorDialog::TClockEditorDialog(TComponent* Owner)
  : TForm(Owner)
{
}

void __fastcall TClockEditorDialog::SetFaceColorBtnClick(TObject *Sender)
{
  if (ColorDialog1->Execute())
  {
    Clock->FaceColor = ColorDialog1->Color;
  }
}

void __fastcall TClockEditorDialog::SetBackColorBtnClick(TObject *Sender)
{
  if (ColorDialog1->Execute())
  {
    Clock->ClockAttributes->Color = ColorDialog1->Color;
  }
}

void RunClockEditorDlg(TColorClock2 *Clock)
{
  ClockEditorDialog = new TClockEditorDialog(Application);
  ClockEditorDialog->Clock = Clock;
  ClockEditorDialog->ShowModal();
  delete ClockEditorDialog;
}
```

Listing 22.16. The header for the VCL form that serves a dialog for editing the ClockAttributes property.

```
//////////////////////////////////////////
// ClockAttributes.h
// Clock Component with Component Editor
// Copyright (c) 1997 by Charlie Calvert
//
#ifndef ClockAttributesH
```

```
#define ClockAttributesH
#include <vcl\Classes.hpp>
#include <vcl\Controls.hpp>
#include <vcl\StdCtrls.hpp>
#include <vcl\Forms.hpp>
#include <vcl\ExtCtrls.hpp>
#include <vcl\Buttons.hpp>
#include "Clock2.h"
#include <vcl\Dialogs.hpp>

void RunClockAttributesDlg(TClockAttribute2 *AClockAttribute);

class TClockAttributesDialog : public TForm
{
__published:
  TPanel *Panel1;
  TComboBox *ComboBox1;
  TBitBtn *GetColorsBtn;
  TBitBtn *BitBtn2;
  TColorDialog *ColorDialog1;
  TImage *Image1;
  void __fastcall GetColorsBtnClick(TObject *Sender);
  void __fastcall BitBtn2Click(TObject *Sender);

private:
  TClockAttribute2 *FClockAttribute;
public:
  __fastcall TClockAttributesDialog(TComponent* Owner);
  __property TClockAttribute2 *ClockAttribute =
    {read=FClockAttribute, write=FClockAttribute};
};

extern TClockAttributesDialog *ClockAttributesDialog;

#endif
```

Listing 22.17. The main source file for the VCL form that serves a dialog for editing the ClockAttributes property.

```
////////////////////////////////////////
// ClockAttributes.cpp
// Clock Component with Component Editor
// Copyright (c) 1997 by Charlie Calvert
//
#include <vcl\vcl.h>
#pragma hdrstop
#include "ClockAttributes.h"
#pragma resource "*.dfm"

TClockAttributesDialog *ClockAttributesDialog;

__fastcall TClockAttributesDialog::TClockAttributesDialog(TComponent* Owner)
  : TForm(Owner)
```

continues

Listing 22.17. continued

```
{
}

void RunClockAttributesDlg(TClockAttribute2 *AClockAttribute)
{
  ClockAttributesDialog = new TClockAttributesDialog(Application);
  ClockAttributesDialog->ClockAttribute = AClockAttribute;
  ClockAttributesDialog->ComboBox1->ItemIndex =  (int)AClockAttribute->Shape;
  ClockAttributesDialog->ShowModal();
  delete ClockAttributesDialog;
}

void __fastcall TClockAttributesDialog::GetColorsBtnClick(TObject *Sender)
{
  if (ColorDialog1->Execute())
  {
    FClockAttribute->Color = ColorDialog1->Color;
  }
}

void __fastcall TClockAttributesDialog::BitBtn2Click(TObject *Sender)
{
  FClockAttribute->Shape = TShapeType(ComboBox1->ItemIndex);
}
```

Listing 22.18. Here is the header for the new version of the clock components.

```
///////////////////////////////////////
// Clock2.h
// Clock Component
// Copyright (c) 1997 by Charlie Calvert
//
//-----------------------------------
#ifndef Clock2H
#define Clock2H
#include <vcl\sysutils.hpp>
#include <vcl\controls.hpp>
#include <vcl\classes.hpp>
#include <vcl\forms.hpp>
#include <vcl\dsgnintf.hpp>
#include <vcl\messages.hpp>

class TClockAttribute2: public TPersistent
{
private:
  TColor FColor;
  TShapeType FShape;
  TComponent *FOwner;
  void __fastcall SetColor(TColor AColor);
  void __fastcall SetShape(TShapeType AShape);
public:
  virtual __fastcall TClockAttribute2(TComponent *AOwner)
    : TPersistent() { FOwner = AOwner; }
```

```cpp
__published:
  __property TColor Color={read=FColor, write=SetColor};
  __property TShapeType  Shape={read=FShape, write=SetShape};
};

/////////////////////////////////////
// TMyClock /////////////////////////
/////////////////////////////////////
class TMyClock2: public TCustomControl
{
private:
  int FTimer;
  Boolean FRunning;
  TClockAttribute2 *FClockAttributes;
  void __fastcall SetRunning(Boolean ARun);
protected:
  virtual void __fastcall Paint(void);
  void __fastcall WMTimer(TMessage &Message);
  void __fastcall WMDestroy(TMessage &Message);
public:
  virtual __fastcall TMyClock2(TComponent* Owner);
__published:
  __property Boolean Running={read=FRunning, write=SetRunning};
  __property Align;
  __property TClockAttribute2 *ClockAttributes=
    {read=FClockAttributes, write=FClockAttributes };
  __property Font;
BEGIN_MESSAGE_MAP
  MESSAGE_HANDLER(WM_TIMER, TMessage, WMTimer);
  MESSAGE_HANDLER(WM_DESTROY, TMessage, WMDestroy);
END_MESSAGE_MAP(TCustomControl);
};

/////////////////////////////////////
// TColorClock //////////////////////
/////////////////////////////////////
class TColorClock2: public TMyClock2
{
private:
  TColor FFaceColor;
  void __fastcall SetColor(TColor Color);
protected:
  void virtual __fastcall Paint(void);
public:
  virtual __fastcall TColorClock2(TComponent *Owner)
    :TMyClock2(Owner) { FFaceColor = clGreen; }
__published:
  __property TColor FaceColor={read=FFaceColor, write=SetColor, nodefault};
};

/////////////////////////////////////
// TClockEditor /////////////////////
/////////////////////////////////////
class TClockEditor2: public TComponentEditor
{
protected:
  virtual __fastcall void Edit(void);
```

continues

Listing 22.18. continued

```
public:
  virtual __fastcall TClockEditor2(TComponent *AOwner, TFormDesigner *Designer)
    : TComponentEditor(AOwner, Designer) {}
};


/////////////////////////////////////////
// TColorNameProperty //////////////////
/////////////////////////////////////////
class TClockAttributeProperty: public TClassProperty
{
public:
  TClockAttributeProperty(): TClassProperty() {}
  TPropertyAttributes __fastcall GetAttributes(void);
  void virtual __fastcall Edit(void);
};


#endif
```

Listing 22.19. The main source file for the new version of the clock components.

```
/////////////////////////////////////////
// Clock2.cpp
// Clock Component with Component Editor
// Copyright (c) 1997 by Charlie Calvert
//
#include <vcl\vcl.h>
#pragma hdrstop
#include "Clock2.h"
#include "ClockEditor.h"
#include "ClockAttributes.h"
#pragma link "ClockEditor.obj"
#pragma link "ClockAttributes.obj"

/////////////////////////////////////////
// ValidControlCheck
/////////////////////////////////////////
static inline TMyClock2 *ValidCtrCheck()
{
  return new TMyClock2(NULL);
}

/////////////////////////////////////////
// TClockAttributes
/////////////////////////////////////////
void __fastcall TClockAttribute2::SetColor(TColor AColor)
{
  FColor = AColor;
  ((TControl *)(FOwner))->Invalidate();
};

void __fastcall TClockAttribute2::SetShape(TShapeType AShape)
{
```

```cpp
    FShape = AShape;
    ((TControl *)(FOwner))->Invalidate();
};


///////////////////////////////////////
// Constructor
///////////////////////////////////////
__fastcall TMyClock2::TMyClock2(TComponent* Owner)
  : TCustomControl(Owner)
{
  Width = 100;
  Height = 100;
  FTimer = 1;
  FClockAttributes = new TClockAttribute2(this);
  FClockAttributes->Color = clBtnFace;
  FClockAttributes->Shape = stEllipse;
}


///////////////////////////////////////
// SetRunning
///////////////////////////////////////
void __fastcall TMyClock2::SetRunning(Boolean Run)
{
  if (Run)
  {
    SetTimer(Handle, FTimer, 50, NULL);
    FRunning = True;
  }
  else
  {
    KillTimer(Handle, FTimer);
    FRunning = False;
  }
}


///////////////////////////////////////
// Paint
///////////////////////////////////////
void __fastcall TMyClock2::Paint(void)
{
  Color = ClockAttributes->Color;
  switch (ClockAttributes->Shape)
  {
    int X;

    case stEllipse: Canvas->Ellipse(0, 0, Width, Height); break;
    case stRectangle: Canvas->Rectangle(0, 0, Width, Height); break;
    case stRoundRect:
      Canvas->RoundRect(0, 0, Width, Height, Width - 100, Height);
      break;

    case stSquare:
    {
      if (Width < Height)
      {
        X = Width / 2;
        Canvas->Rectangle(Width - X, 0, Width + X, Width);
      }
```

continues

Listing 22.19. continued

```cpp
        else
        {
          X = Height / 2;
          Canvas->Rectangle((Width / 2) - X, 0, (Width / 2) + X, Height);
        }
        break;
      }

    case stCircle:
      {
        if (Width < Height)
        {
          X = Width / 2;
          Canvas->Ellipse(Width - X, 0, Width + X, Width);
        }
        else
        {
          X = Height / 2;
          Canvas->Ellipse((Width / 2) - X, 0, (Width / 2) + X, Height);
        }
        break;
      }
  }
}

////////////////////////////////////////
// WM_TIMER
////////////////////////////////////////
void __fastcall TMyClock2::WMTimer(TMessage &Message)
{
  AnsiString S = TimeToStr(Time());
  Canvas->Font = Font;
  Canvas->TextOut(Width / 2 - Canvas->TextWidth(S) / 2,
                  Height / 2 - Canvas->TextHeight(S) / 2, S);
}

////////////////////////////////////////
// WM_DESTROY
////////////////////////////////////////
void __fastcall TMyClock2::WMDestroy(TMessage &Message)
{
  KillTimer(Handle, FTimer);
  FTimer = 0;
  TCustomControl::Dispatch(&Message);
}

//-----------------------------------
//-- TColorClock2 -------------------
//-----------------------------------

////////////////////////////////////////
// WM_DESTROY
////////////////////////////////////////
```

```
void __fastcall TColorClock2::Paint()
{
  Canvas->Brush->Color = FFaceColor;
  TMyClock2::Paint();
}


////////////////////////////////////////
// SetColor
////////////////////////////////////////
void __fastcall TColorClock2::SetColor(TColor Color)
{
  FFaceColor = Color;
  InvalidateRect(Handle, NULL, True);
}


//------------------------------------
//-- TClockEditor -------------------
//------------------------------------
void __fastcall TClockEditor2::Edit(void)
{
  RunClockEditorDlg(((TColorClock2 *)(Component)));
}


//------------------------------------
//-- TColorNameProperty -------------
//------------------------------------
TPropertyAttributes __fastcall TClockAttributeProperty::GetAttributes(void)
{
  return TPropertyAttributes() << paSubProperties << paDialog;
}


void __fastcall TClockAttributeProperty::Edit()
{
  TClockAttribute2 *C = (TClockAttribute2 *)GetOrdValue();
  RunClockAttributesDlg(C);
  Modified();
}


////////////////////////////////////////
// Register
////////////////////////////////////////
namespace Clock2
{
  void __fastcall Register()
  {
    TComponentClass classes[2] = {__classid(TMyClock2), __classid(TColorClock2)};
    RegisterComponents("Unleash", classes, 1);

    RegisterComponentEditor(__classid(TColorClock2), __classid(TClockEditor2));
    RegisterPropertyEditor(__typeinfo(TClockAttribute2),
      __classid(TMyClock2), "ClockAttributes",
      __classid(TClockAttributeProperty));
  }
}
```

When popping up a new form from inside a component editor, you have to create the actual instance of the form and assign it an owner. You need to do so because the form will not be auto-created in your program's project source file.

To handle the chore of creating the form, I created a special method inside the ClockEditor unit. The routine looks like this:

```
void RunClockEditorDlg(TColorClock2 *Clock)
{
  ClockEditorDialog = new TClockEditorDialog(Application);
  ClockEditorDialog->Clock = Clock;
  ClockEditorDialog->ShowModal();
  delete ClockEditorDialog;
}
```

This routine takes an instance of the clock that needs to be edited as its sole parameter. It then creates an instance of the TClockEditorDialog and assigns the clock to an internal data store of the dialog. Finally, the code shows the dialog and cleans up the memory when the user is through making the edits.

To test this dialog, you can simply drop an instance of the clock onto the main form of the application and then call the dialog from a button click response method:

```
void __fastcall TForm1::Button1Click(TObject *Sender)
{
  RunClockEditorDlg(ColorClock21);
}
```

After you're sure that everything is working properly, you can change the TClockEditor2::Edit method so that it calls this dialog when the user double-clicks the component in design mode:

```
void __fastcall TClockEditor2::Edit(void)
{
  RunClockEditorDlg(((TColorClock2 *)(Component)));
}
```

Once again, you can see that the code takes advantage of the Component object that is declared ahead of time by the VCL. All you need to do is typecast the object to the proper type and then pass it on to the ClockEditor object.

Inside the TClockEditorDialog itself, the act of changing the component is trivial:

```
void __fastcall TClockEditorDialog::SetFaceColorBtnClick(TObject *Sender)
{
  if (ColorDialog1->Execute())
  {
    Clock->FaceColor = ColorDialog1->Color;
  }
}
```

This code simply pops up a color dialog and allows the user to choose a new face color. If the user makes a selection, the color is assigned to the relevant property of the TColorClock2 object.

I still need to address one subject in this project. The issue here is that the `TClock2` project now consists of two different modules. The first module contains the `TColorClock` itself, and the second module contains the `TClockEditorDialog`.

When you add the `Clock2.cpp` module to the Component Palette, you also have to find a way to bring in `ClockEditor.cpp`; otherwise, the project will not compile. Unfortunately, you can't add `ClockEditor` directly to the `CmpLib32` project because `ClockEditor` does not have a `Register` method. Without the `Register` method, the component library won't know what to do with the file.

The solution to this problem is provided by a `pragma` that can be added to `Clock2.cpp` to tell the compiler that it must include `ClockEditor.obj` in any projects that use this unit:

```
#pragma link "ClockEditor.obj"
```

After you add this line, `CmpLib32` will know that it has to include `ClockEditor.obj` in the compilation. It will not, however, know to compile the unit from a CPP file into an OBJ file.

NOTE

In the first shipping version of BCB, a problem can occur if you try to recompile `CmpLib32.ccl` and do not provide a precompiled copy of `ClockEditor.obj`. In particular, the compiler does not treat `ClockEditor` as part of the project it is making, so it will not know to make `ClockEditor.obj` from `ClockEditor.cpp`.

One solution to this problem is to start a small project that will compile `ClockEditor.cpp` into `ClockEditor.obj`. For example, the simple `TestClock2` program will create `ClockEditor.obj` each time it is compiled. The BuildObjs file included on the CD will do the same thing.

If you have created a copy of the OBJ file, and the compiler still complains, try touching the unit that uses `ClockEditor`. For example, make a small change to `Clock2.cpp`. Any change will do. You can just add a space to the unit and then remove it. The point is that you need to save the unit so that it has a new date and time. This time, when you recompile and link `CmpLib32`, it will find your new copy of `ClockEditor.obj`.

That's all I'm going to say about component editors. As you have seen, this subject is not complicated, even when you create your own custom form for editing the object. Creating custom forms of this type can be very helpful for the user because it gives you a chance to step him or her through the process of initializing the object. You can even create a little expert that runs when the user double-clicks the component. The expert could take the user by the hand and ensure that he or she sets up your control properly.

The property editor for the ClockAttributes property is very similar to the component editor. The primary difference is in the way you access the underlying value that you want to edit:

```
void __fastcall TClockAttributeProperty::Edit()
{
  TClockAttribute2 *C = (TClockAttribute2 *)GetOrdValue();
  RunClockAttributesDlg(C);
  Modified();
}
```

Instead of having a ready-to-use variable called Component, you need to call the GetOrdValue method of TPropertyEditor. This function was originally intended to retrieve simply ordinal values. It can, however, do double-duty and retrieve pointer values. This is possible because a pointer and an integer both consist of 4 bytes.

In this case, I typecast the value returned from GetOrdValue as a variable of type TClockAttribute. I can then pass this value into my VCL form and edit it as I please. The principle here is exactly the same as in the Component editor, only this time I access the underlying property that I want to edit through GetOrdValue, rather than through a variable named Component.

Inside the ClockAttributes dialog you need to create a routine that will pop open the VCL form:

```
void RunClockAttributesDlg(TClockAttribute2 *AClockAttribute)
{
  ClockAttributesDialog = new TClockAttributesDialog(Application);
  ClockAttributesDialog->ClockAttribute = AClockAttribute;
  ClockAttributesDialog->ComboBox1->ItemIndex  = (int)AClockAttribute->Shape;
  ClockAttributesDialog->ShowModal();
  delete ClockAttributesDialog;
}
```

Most of this code is very routine and does nothing more than allocate memory for a form, show it modally, and then destroy it. Note the line that sets the value of the selected item in the form's combo box:

```
ClockAttributesDialog->ComboBox1->ItemIndex  = (int)AClockAttribute->Shape;
```

This line accesses one of the fields of the TClockAttribute class. It then sets the ItemIndex of the combo box to the currently selected shape. Here are the values displayed in the combo box:

```
Rectangle

Square

RoundRect

RoundSquare

Ellipse

Circle
```

If the technique used here to select an item in the combo box does not make sense to you, you might want to refer to similar code from the ShapeDem2 program in Chapter 2.

Summary

In this chapter, you have learned about building components. Specifically, you learned how to create components that do the following:

- Change an ancestor's default settings. For example, you created TEdit descendants with new default colors and fonts.

- Add functionality not available in an ancestor object. For example, the TColorClock object does things that TClock does not.

- Are built up from scratch so that they can add new functionality to the IDE. For example, the TClock component brings something entirely new to BCB programming that does not exist in any other component that ships with the product.

You also learned about tools and files associated with components, such as the DCR and KWF files. Finally, you learned about the Tools API and specifically about the art of making property editors and component editors.

Creating Components
from Scratch

CHAPTER

23

IN THIS CHAPTER

In this chapter, you learn how to use custom-made components to help create programs that solve at least a minimal set of real-world problems. In particular, the program demonstrated in this chapter provides a minimal implementation of a warehouse-based inventory program. This chapter also covers designing components and screens that mirror objects in the real world, as well as creating your own event handlers.

Much of the material in this chapter follows naturally from the subject matter in the preceding chapter. However, the code shown here is more advanced, and the text looks a little more deeply into the theories involved in creating powerful, reusable components.

A program called Warehouse forms the core of this chapter. Warehouse uses simple graphic objects to depict a warehouse in which several different kinds of widgets are stored. There are seven panels in this warehouse, each containing from 4 to 12 pallets full of widgets. You are able to stock each pallet with new widgets and ask questions about the stock stored in the warehouse.

The program in this chapter builds on the object hierarchy discussed in Chapter 19, "Inheritance," in the program called OBJECT1. The new versions of this hierarchy advances the code to the point where it can be used for the relatively practical tasks just described. OOP, which seems highly theoretical and intangible at first glance, actually turns out to be a natural tool for tracking and depicting the status of real objects, such as the inventory in a warehouse.

Warehouse

As described at the beginning of this chapter, Warehouse is a simulation that features a series of panels arranged in a large room. Each panel has from 4 to 12 pallets on it, and each pallet contains a certain number of widgets. Users can stock additional widgets on the pallets by dragging and dropping them from a central gateway that leads into the warehouse. The idea is that the widgets are being transferred from the point of manufacture to a place where they can be stored before being sold.

> **NOTE**
>
> The Warehouse program shows the outlines of a clean approach to a real-world problem. However, it is not a complete business application. It shows how objects can be used to embody actual entities that we find in day-to-day life, but it's a theoretical example and not a real-world program.
>
> To bring this program up to the point where it might be used in an office would be a considerable chore that would involve adding both features and error checking. However, in the construction of any large project, one key step is the development of a methodology that can support a large application. The foundation for a useful program is found in Warehouse. It shows a lot about the way any good OOP tool should be constructed.

The Warehouse program is stocked with hypothetical widgets named TWidget, TPentium, and TPentiumPro. Another application might have TChairs, TTables, TBureaus, and so on, instead of chips. The issue is not the names or traits of the individual widgets but the fact that a series of different TWidget descendants needs to be created.

You will find that TPentium and TPentiumPro share many traits. This is a somewhat artificial aspect of this program; in a real-world application, each of these objects would be more varied. For instance, a TChair would have an FLegs data store, a TBed would have an FFrame data store, and so on.

> **NOTE**
>
> When studying Warehouse, you will find that the TWidget object has changed slightly from its appearance in OBJECT3. These types of minor structural changes should be expected in OOP. Developers don't start with a base class and build up a hierarchy without ever deciding that changes need to be made to the structures they are creating. Frameworks and hierarchies evolve over time; they do not burst into the world fully formed.
>
> If you are building a certain kind of tool, after the first release, it is very dangerous to go back and start changing the way base classes work. Nevertheless, during development, changes need to be made to the base classes in your hierarchy. This is one of the major "gotchas" of object-oriented programming, and I would be remiss if I didn't lay it out in clear terms. Right now, there are no good remedies for this problem, but the lesson it teaches is clear: *Don't release objects to unsuspecting programmers until you are sure you have the proper design!* If you are looking for some relief, my experience has shown that most major companies don't think beta testers fit the definition of "unsuspecting."
>
> Furthermore, to the best of your ability, you should do everything possible to hide the actual implementation of your object from your user. Use properties heavily. Hide your data. Create public functions or even public objects that call the functions and objects that are part of your real implementation. Nobody ever hides their implementation completely, but it is usually better to err on the side of safety, rather than striving always to save a few bytes of memory.

The Warehouse program features one main form and two child forms used to display reports on the data in the warehouse. The main form depicts the floor of the warehouse, as shown in Figure 23.1. The left-center of the main form contains three widgets you can drag onto the various pallets by using the mouse. To do this, left-click on one of the widgets and drag the mouse over one of the pallets. When you release the mouse, a dialog box pops up prompting you for the number of widgets of a particular type you want to drop on a pallet. You can type in a number and then click OK, as shown in Figure 23.2.

FIGURE 23.1.

The Warehouse form shows the floor of the warehouse.

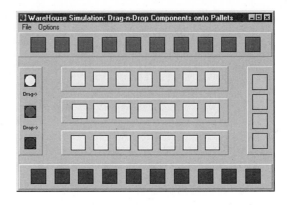

FIGURE 23.2.

Specifying the number of items you want to drop on a particular pallet.

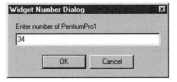

If you select File | Show Table from the menu on the main form, you can see a table that lists all the items in the warehouse, as shown in Figure 23.3. If you select Options | List by Product from the menu, you get a report on all the products in the warehouse, as shown in Figure 23.4. If you select Options | List by Pallet from the menu, you get a report on all the pallets in the warehouse, as shown in Figure 23.5.

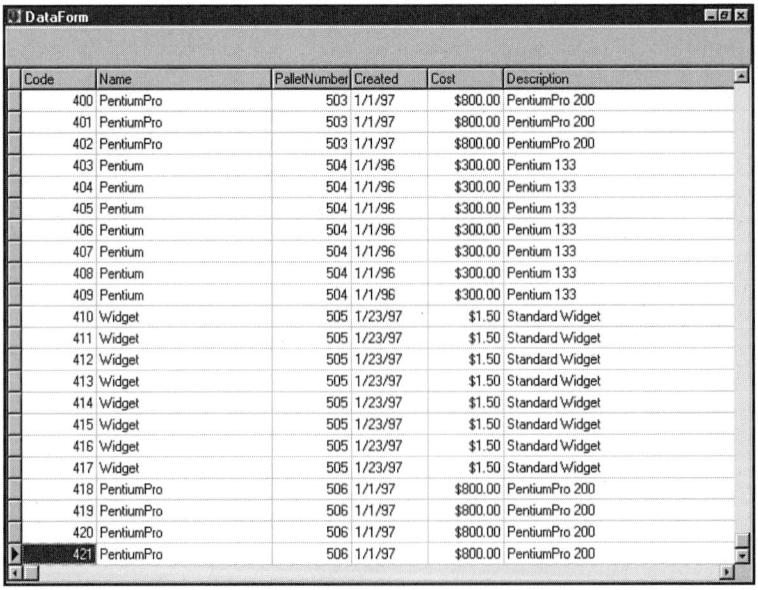

FIGURE 23.3.

The Report form shows the status of the objects on an individual pallet.

Code	Name	PalletNumber	Created	Cost	Description
400	PentiumPro	503	1/1/97	$800.00	PentiumPro 200
401	PentiumPro	503	1/1/97	$800.00	PentiumPro 200
402	PentiumPro	503	1/1/97	$800.00	PentiumPro 200
403	Pentium	504	1/1/96	$300.00	Pentium 133
404	Pentium	504	1/1/96	$300.00	Pentium 133
405	Pentium	504	1/1/96	$300.00	Pentium 133
406	Pentium	504	1/1/96	$300.00	Pentium 133
407	Pentium	504	1/1/96	$300.00	Pentium 133
408	Pentium	504	1/1/96	$300.00	Pentium 133
409	Pentium	504	1/1/96	$300.00	Pentium 133
410	Widget	505	1/23/97	$1.50	Standard Widget
411	Widget	505	1/23/97	$1.50	Standard Widget
412	Widget	505	1/23/97	$1.50	Standard Widget
413	Widget	505	1/23/97	$1.50	Standard Widget
414	Widget	505	1/23/97	$1.50	Standard Widget
415	Widget	505	1/23/97	$1.50	Standard Widget
416	Widget	505	1/23/97	$1.50	Standard Widget
417	Widget	505	1/23/97	$1.50	Standard Widget
418	PentiumPro	506	1/1/97	$800.00	PentiumPro 200
419	PentiumPro	506	1/1/97	$800.00	PentiumPro 200
420	PentiumPro	506	1/1/97	$800.00	PentiumPro 200
421	PentiumPro	506	1/1/97	$800.00	PentiumPro 200

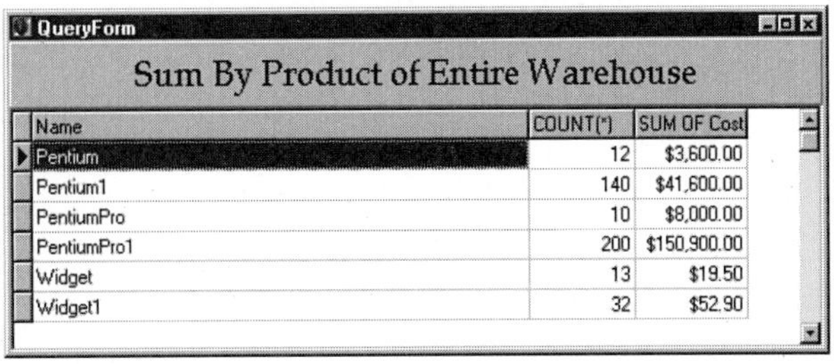

FIGURE 23.4.

A report on all the products in the warehouse, including their count and value.

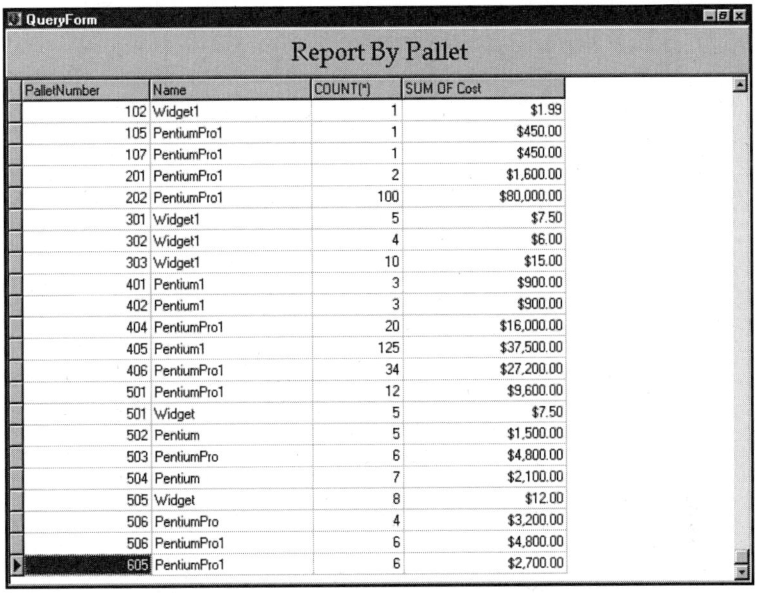

FIGURE 23.5.

A report on all the pallets in the warehouse, including the number of widgets they contain and the value of the widgets.

23

CREATING
COMPONENTS
FROM SCRATCH

If you right-click on a particular pallet, you can bring up a popup menu that lets you explore the contents of a particular pallet. For instance, you can see the items on a pallet, as shown in Figure 23.6, or you can see the value of the items on a particular pallet, as shown in Figure 23.7.

Because of time constraints, I have not added any provisions to the program for selling items. However, you do have a fairly interesting simulation that models a portion of a business.

Perhaps the most interesting thing about the program is the small amount of top-level code needed to create it, as shown in Listing 23.1.

FIGURE 23.6.

A report on the items found on a particular pallet.

Code	Name	PalletNumber	Created	Cost	Description
425	Pentium	301	1/1/96	$300.00	Pentium 133
426	Pentium	301	1/1/96	$300.00	Pentium 133
427	Pentium	301	1/1/96	$300.00	Pentium 133
428	Pentium	301	1/1/96	$300.00	Pentium 133
429	PentiumPro	301	1/1/97	$800.00	PentiumPro 200
430	PentiumPro	301	1/1/97	$800.00	PentiumPro 200
431	PentiumPro	301	1/1/97	$800.00	PentiumPro 200
432	PentiumPro	301	1/1/97	$800.00	PentiumPro 200
433	Pentium	301	1/1/96	$300.00	Pentium 133
434	Pentium	301	1/1/96	$300.00	Pentium 133
435	Pentium	301	1/1/96	$300.00	Pentium 133
436	Pentium	301	1/1/96	$300.00	Pentium 133
437	Pentium	301	1/1/96	$300.00	Pentium 133
438	PentiumPro	301	1/1/97	$800.00	PentiumPro 200
439	PentiumPro	301	1/1/97	$800.00	PentiumPro 200
440	PentiumPro	301	1/1/97	$800.00	PentiumPro 200
441	PentiumPro	301	1/1/97	$800.00	PentiumPro 200
442	PentiumPro	301	1/1/97	$800.00	PentiumPro 200
443	Widget	301	1/23/97	$1.50	Standard Widget
444	Widget	301	1/23/97	$1.50	Standard Widget
445	Widget	301	1/23/97	$1.50	Standard Widget

List of Items on Pallet: 301

FIGURE 23.7.

A report on the value of the items found on a particular pallet.

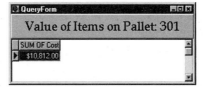

Value of Items on Pallet: 301

SUM OF Cost
$10,812.00

Listing 23.1. The project file for the Warehouse program is listed here; the rest of the program is found on the CD.

```
/////////////////////////////////////
// Warehouse.cpp
// Warehouse example: learning about objects
// Copyright (c) 1997 by Charlie Calvert
//
#include <vcl\vcl.h>
#pragma hdrstop
USEFORM("Main.cpp", Form1);
USERES("WareHouse.res");
USEUNIT("\SrcC\PUnleash\Utils\MyObject.cpp");
USEUNIT("\SrcC\PUnleash\Utils\Widgets.cpp");
USEDATAMODULE("DMod1.cpp", DMod);
USEFORM("DataForm1.cpp", DataForm);
USEFORM("QueryForm1.cpp", QueryForm);
USEFORM("HierarchyDlg1.cpp", HierarchyDlg);
WINAPI WinMain(HINSTANCE, HINSTANCE, LPSTR, int)
{
  try
  {
```

```
    Application->Initialize();
    Application->CreateForm(__classid(TForm1), &Form1);
    Application->CreateForm(__classid(TDMod), &DMod);
    Application->CreateForm(__classid(TDataForm), &DataForm);
    Application->CreateForm(__classid(TQueryForm), &QueryForm);
    Application->CreateForm(__classid(THierarchyDlg), &HierarchyDlg);
    Application->Run();
  }
  catch (Exception &exception)
  {
    Application->ShowException(&exception);
  }
  return 0;
}
```

If you wind your way down the hierarchy of objects used in this program (see Listings 23.2 through 23.15), there is, of course, a considerable amount of complexity. But from the point of view of the application developer, the code for this program is very easy to create. Most of the complexity is in the VCL itself, and some degree of complexity is hidden in the TWidget and TPallet objects created in this chapter, and in some of the earlier chapters. But at the top level, where you find the main modules for this program, almost all the code is sparse, easy to understand, and simple to maintain. This is the right way to leverage objects so they can help you get a lot of high-quality work done quickly.

Listing 23.2. The header file for the main program.

```
/////////////////////////////////////
// Main.h
// Warehouse example: learning about objects
// Copyright (c) 1997 by Charlie Calvert
//
#ifndef MainH
#define MainH
#include <vcl\Classes.hpp>
#include <vcl\Controls.hpp>
#include <vcl\StdCtrls.hpp>
#include <vcl\Forms.hpp>
#include <vcl\ExtCtrls.hpp>
#include <vcl\Buttons.hpp>
#include <vcl\Menus.hpp>
#include "Widgets.h"

class TForm1 : public TForm
{
__published:
  TPanel *Panel1;
  TPanel *Panel2;
  TPanel *Panel3;
  TPanel *Panel4;
  TDataPallet *sp41;
```

continues

Listing 23.2. continued

```cpp
    TDataPallet *Sp42;
    TDataPallet *Sp43;
    TDataPallet *Sp44;
    TDataPallet *Sp45;
    TDataPallet *Sp46;
    TDataPallet *Sp47;
    TDataPallet *Sp48;
    TDataPallet *Sp49;
    TDataPallet *Sp410;
    TPanel *Panel5;
    TDataPallet *DataPallet10;
    TPanel *Panel6;
    TPanel *Panel7;
    TMainMenu *A;
    TMenuItem *List;
    TPentiumPro *PentiumPro;
    TPentium *Pentium;
    TWidget *Widget;
    TDataPallet *DataPallet35;
    TMenuItem *File1;
    TMenuItem *ShowTable1;
    TMenuItem *N1;
    TMenuItem *Exit1;
    TPopupMenu *PopupMenu1;
    TMenuItem *ItemsOnPallet1;
    TMenuItem *ValueofItems1;
    TMenuItem *Options1;
    TMenuItem *ListbyPallet1;
    TMenuItem *GetHierarchy1;
    TLabel *Label1;
    TLabel *Label2;
    void __fastcall SpeedButton1DragOver(TObject *Sender, TObject *Source, int X,
                                    int Y, TDragState State, bool &Accept);
    void __fastcall WidgetMouseDown(TObject *Sender, TMouseButton Button,
                                    TShiftState Shift, int X, int Y);
    void __fastcall Exit1Click(TObject *Sender);
    void __fastcall ShowTable1Click(TObject *Sender);
    void __fastcall DataPallet10MouseDown(TObject *Sender, TMouseButton Button,
                                    TShiftState Shift, int X, int Y);
    void __fastcall ItemsOnPallet1Click(TObject *Sender);
    void __fastcall ValueofItems1Click(TObject *Sender);
    void __fastcall ListClick(TObject *Sender);
    void __fastcall ListbyPallet1Click(TObject *Sender);
    void __fastcall GetHierarchy1Click(TObject *Sender);
private:
public:
    virtual __fastcall TForm1(TComponent* Owner);
};

extern TForm1 *Form1;

#endif
```

Listing 23.3. The main form for the Warehouse program.

```cpp
//////////////////////////////////////
// Main.cpp
// Warehouse example: learning about objects
// Copyright (c) 1997 by Charlie Calvert
//
#include <vcl\vcl.h>
#pragma hdrstop
#include "Main.h"
#include "DMod1.h"
#include "DataForm1.h"
#include "QueryForm1.h"
#include "HierarchyDlg1.h"
#pragma link "Widgets"
#pragma resource "*.dfm"
TForm1 *Form1;

__fastcall TForm1::TForm1(TComponent* Owner)
                                                        : TForm(Owner)
{
}

void __fastcall TForm1::SpeedButton1DragOver(TObject *Sender, TObject *Source,
                        int X, int Y, TDragState State, bool &Accept)
{
 if (!dynamic_cast<TWidget *>(Source))
    Accept = False;
}

void __fastcall TForm1::WidgetMouseDown(TObject *Sender, TMouseButton Button,
                                TShiftState Shift, int X, int Y)
{
  if (!dynamic_cast<TWidget *>(Sender))
    return;

  TWidget *W = (TWidget *)(Sender);

  if (Shift.Contains(ssLeft))
  {
    W->BeginDrag(False);
  }
  else
  {
    HierarchyDlg->ListBox1->Items = W->GetHierarchy();
    HierarchyDlg->ShowModal();
  }
}

void __fastcall TForm1::ShowTable1Click(TObject *Sender)
{
  DataForm->Show();
}
```

continues

Listing 23.3. continued

```cpp
void __fastcall TForm1::Exit1Click(TObject *Sender)
{
  Close();
}

void __fastcall TForm1::DataPallet10MouseDown(TObject *Sender,
  TMouseButton Button, TShiftState Shift, int X, int Y)
{
  if (Shift.Contains(ssLeft))
  {
    if (dynamic_cast<TDataPallet *>(Sender))
    {
      TDataPallet *D = (TDataPallet *)(Sender);
      D->QueryPallet(DMod->WidgetsQuery);
      QueryForm->Panel1->Caption =
        "List of Items on Pallet: " + AnsiString(D->PalletNumber);
      QueryForm->ShowModal();
    }
  }
}

void __fastcall TForm1::ItemsOnPallet1Click(TObject *Sender)
{
  TDataPallet *D = (TDataPallet *)PopupMenu1->PopupComponent;
  DataPallet10MouseDown(D, TMouseButton(), TShiftState() << ssLeft, 0, 0);
}

void __fastcall TForm1::ValueofItems1Click(TObject *Sender)
{
  TDataPallet *D = (TDataPallet *)PopupMenu1->PopupComponent;
  D->QueryPalletSum(DMod->WidgetsQuery);
  QueryForm->Panel1->Caption =
    "Value of Items on Pallet: " + AnsiString(D->PalletNumber);
  QueryForm->ShowModal();
}

void __fastcall TForm1::GetHierarchy1Click(TObject *Sender)
{
  TDataPallet *D = (TDataPallet *)PopupMenu1->PopupComponent;
  HierarchyDlg->ListBox1->Items = D->GetHierarchy();
  HierarchyDlg->ShowModal();
}

void __fastcall TForm1::ListClick(TObject *Sender)
{
  DMod->SumByProduct();
  QueryForm->Panel1->Caption = "Sum By Product of Entire Warehouse";
  QueryForm->ShowModal();
}

void __fastcall TForm1::ListbyPallet1Click(TObject *Sender)
{
  DMod->ReportByPallet();
  QueryForm->Panel1->Caption = "Report By Pallet";
  QueryForm->ShowModal();
}
```

Listing 23.4. The header file for the Widgets unit.

```cpp
/////////////////////////////////////
// Widgets.h
// Learning how to use objects
// Copyright (c) 1997 by Charlie Calvert
//

#ifndef WidgetsH
#define WidgetsH
#include <vcl\dbtables.hpp>
#include "myobject.h"


TCustomControl *ReadWidgetFromStream(AnsiString StreamName);
void WriteWidgetToStream(AnsiString StreamName, TCustomControl *Widget);

class __declspec(delphiclass) TWidget;

namespace Widgets
{
  void __fastcall RegisterShort();
  void __fastcall Register();
}

class TWidget: public TCustomControl
{
private:
  TListHierarchy *Hierarchy;
  Currency FCost;
  TDateTime FTimeCreated;
  AnsiString FDescription;
  void __fastcall SetTimeCreated(AnsiString S);
  AnsiString __fastcall GetTimeCreated();
protected:
  virtual void __fastcall Paint(void);
public:
  __fastcall virtual TWidget(TComponent *AOwner): TCustomControl(AOwner)
    { Hierarchy = new TListHierarchy(); Width = 25; Height = 25; }
  __fastcall virtual TWidget(TComponent *AOwner, int ACol, int ARow);
  __fastcall virtual ~TWidget() { delete Hierarchy; }
  TStringList *GetHierarchy() { return Hierarchy->GetHierarchy(this); }
  void __fastcall WidgetMouseDown(TObject *Sender, TMouseButton Button,
                                  TShiftState Shift, int X, int Y);
__published:
  __property Currency Cost={read=FCost, write=FCost};
  __property AnsiString TimeCreated={read=GetTimeCreated, write=SetTimeCreated};
  __property AnsiString Description={read=FDescription, write=FDescription};
  __property OnDragDrop;
  __property OnMouseDown;
};

class TChip: public TWidget
{
```

continues

Listing 23.4. continued

```
public:
  virtual __fastcall TChip(TComponent *AOwner): TWidget(AOwner) {}
  virtual __fastcall TChip(TComponent *AOwner, int ACol, int ARow)
    : TWidget(AOwner, ACol, ARow) {}
};

class TPentium: public TChip
{
protected:
  virtual void __fastcall Paint(void);
public:
  virtual __fastcall TPentium(TComponent *AOwner): TChip(AOwner) {}
  virtual __fastcall TPentium(TComponent *AOwner, int ACol, int ARow)
    : TChip(AOwner, ACol, ARow) {}
};

class TPentiumPro: public TChip
{
protected:
  virtual void __fastcall Paint(void);
public:
  virtual __fastcall TPentiumPro(TComponent *AOwner): TChip(AOwner) {}
  virtual __fastcall TPentiumPro(TComponent *AOwner, int ACol, int ARow)
    : TChip(AOwner, ACol, ARow) {}
};

class TCustomPallet: public TCustomControl
{
private:
  int FPalletNumber;
  TListHierarchy *FHierarchy;
protected:
  virtual void __fastcall Paint(void);
public:
  virtual __fastcall TCustomPallet(TComponent *AOwner);
  virtual __fastcall ~TCustomPallet(void)
    { delete FHierarchy; }
  TStringList *GetHierarchy() { return FHierarchy->GetHierarchy(this); }
  __property int PalletNumber={read=FPalletNumber, write=FPalletNumber};
};

class TPallet: public TCustomPallet
{
public:
  virtual __fastcall TPallet(TComponent *AOwner): TCustomPallet(AOwner)
    { Width = 25; Height = 25; }
__published:
  __property PalletNumber;
  __property OnDragDrop;
  __property OnDragOver;
  __property Color;
};

class TDataPallet: public TCustomPallet
{
```

```
private:
  TTable *FWidgetsTable;
  TQuery *FWidgetsQuery;
protected:
  void __fastcall PalletDragDrop(TObject *Sender,
    TObject *Source, int X, int Y);
  void __fastcall PalletDragOver(TObject *Sender, TObject *Source,
    int X, int Y, TDragState State, bool &Accept);
  void virtual EnterWidgets(int Total, TWidget *W);
public:
  virtual __fastcall TDataPallet(TComponent *AOwner);
  void __fastcall QueryPallet(TQuery *Query);
  float __fastcall QueryPalletSum(TQuery *Query);
__published:
  __property TTable *WidgetsTable={read=FWidgetsTable, write=FWidgetsTable};
  __property TQuery *WidgetsQuery={read=FWidgetsQuery, write=FWidgetsQuery};
  __property PalletNumber;
  __property Hint;
  __property Color;
  __property TabOrder;
  __property OnMouseDown;
  __property PopupMenu;
};

#endif
```

Listing 23.5. The main source file for the Widgets unit.

```
/////////////////////////////////////
// Widgets.cpp
// Learning how to use objects
// Copyright (c) 1997 by Charlie Calvert
//
#include <vcl\vcl.h>
#include <conio.h>
#pragma hdrstop
#include "widgets.h"

#pragma link "MyObject.obj"

void WriteWidgetToStream(AnsiString StreamName, TCustomControl *Widget)
{
  TFileStream *Stream = new TFileStream(StreamName, fmCreate | fmOpenWrite);
  Stream->WriteComponent(Widget);
  delete Stream;
}

TCustomControl *ReadWidgetFromStream(AnsiString StreamName)
{
  Widgets::RegisterShort();
  TFileStream *Stream = new TFileStream(StreamName, fmOpenRead);
```

continues

Listing 23.5. continued

```cpp
  TWidget *Widget = (TWidget *)Stream->ReadComponent(NULL);
  delete Stream;
  return Widget;
}

__fastcall TWidget::TWidget(TComponent *AOwner, int ACol, int ARow)
  : TCustomControl(AOwner)
{
  Hierarchy = new TListHierarchy();
  Left = ACol;
  Top = ARow;
  Width = 25;
  Height = 25;
  OnMouseDown = WidgetMouseDown;
}

AnsiString __fastcall TWidget::GetTimeCreated()
{
  return FTimeCreated.DateTimeString();
}

void __fastcall TWidget::SetTimeCreated(AnsiString S)
{
  FTimeCreated = TDateTime(S);
}

void __fastcall TWidget::Paint()
{
  Canvas->Brush->Color = clBlue;
  Canvas->Rectangle(0, 0, ClientWidth, ClientHeight);
  Canvas->Brush->Color = clYellow;
  Canvas->Ellipse(0, 0, ClientWidth, ClientHeight);
}

void __fastcall TWidget::WidgetMouseDown(TObject *Sender, TMouseButton Button,
                                         TShiftState Shift, int X, int Y)
{
  ShowMessage(Format("%m", OPENARRAY(TVarRec, (FCost))));
}

void __fastcall TPentium::Paint()
{
  Canvas->Brush->Color = clPurple;
  Canvas->Rectangle(0, 0, ClientWidth, ClientHeight);
  Canvas->Brush->Color = clRed;
  Canvas->Ellipse(0, 0, ClientWidth, ClientHeight);
}

void __fastcall TPentiumPro::Paint()
{
  Canvas->Brush->Color = clGreen;
  Canvas->Rectangle(0, 0, ClientWidth, ClientHeight);
  Canvas->Brush->Color = clBlue;
  Canvas->Ellipse(0, 0, ClientWidth, ClientHeight);
}
```

```
__fastcall TCustomPallet::TCustomPallet(TComponent *AOwner)
  : TCustomControl(AOwner)
{
  Width = 25;
  Height = 25;
  Color = clBlue;
  FHierarchy = new TListHierarchy();
}

void __fastcall TCustomPallet::Paint(void)
{
  Canvas->Brush->Color = Color;
  Canvas->Rectangle(0, 0, ClientWidth, ClientHeight);
}

__fastcall TDataPallet::TDataPallet(TComponent *AOwner)
: TCustomPallet(AOwner)
{
  OnDragOver = PalletDragOver;
  OnDragDrop = PalletDragDrop;
}

void __fastcall TDataPallet::PalletDragOver(TObject *Sender,
  TObject *Source, int X, int Y, TDragState State, bool &Accept)
{
  Accept = dynamic_cast<TWidget *>(Source);
}

void __fastcall TDataPallet::PalletDragDrop(TObject *Sender,
  TObject *Source, int X, int Y)
{
  if (WidgetsTable == NULL)
    ShowMessage("No table assigned to the WidgetsTable property");
  else
  {
    if (dynamic_cast<TWidget *>(Source))
    {
      TWidget *W = (TWidget *)(Source);
      AnsiString S = "Enter number of " + W->Name;
      AnsiString NumWidgets;

      if (InputQuery("Widget Number Dialog", S, NumWidgets))
      {
        EnterWidgets(NumWidgets.ToInt(), W);
      }
    }
  }
}

void TDataPallet::EnterWidgets(int Total, TWidget* W)
{
  int i;

  for (i = 0; i < Total; i++)
  {
```

continues

Listing 23.5. continued

```
    FWidgetsTable->Insert();
    FWidgetsTable->FieldByName("Name")->AsString = W->Name;
    FWidgetsTable->FieldByName("Created")->AsString = W->TimeCreated;
    FWidgetsTable->FieldByName("Description")->AsString = W->Description;
    FWidgetsTable->FieldByName("Cost")->AsCurrency = W->Cost;
    FWidgetsTable->FieldByName("PalletNumber")->AsInteger = PalletNumber;
    FWidgetsTable->Post();
  }
}

void __fastcall TDataPallet::QueryPallet(TQuery *Query)
{
  AnsiString S = "Select * from Widgets where PalletNumber = " +
    AnsiString(PalletNumber);
  Query->SQL->Clear();
  Query->SQL->Add(S);
  Query->Open();
}

float __fastcall TDataPallet::QueryPalletSum(TQuery *Query)
{
  AnsiString S = "Select Sum(Cost) from Widgets where PalletNumber = " +
    AnsiString(PalletNumber);
  Query->SQL->Clear();
  Query->SQL->Add(S);
  Query->Open();
  return Query->Fields[0]->AsFloat;
}

namespace Widgets
{
  void __fastcall RegisterShort()
  {
    TComponentClass classes[4] = {__classid(TWidget),
      __classid(TPentium), __classid(TPentiumPro),
      __classid(TPallet) };
    RegisterClasses(classes, 3);
  }

  void __fastcall Register()
  {
    TComponentClass classes[5] = {__classid(TWidget),
      __classid(TPentium), __classid(TPentiumPro),
      __classid(TPallet), __classid(TDataPallet) };
    RegisterComponents("Unleash", classes, 4);
  }
}
```

Listing 23.6. The final take on the header for the MyObject unit.

```
/////////////////////////////////////
// MyObject.h
// Learning how to use objects
```

```
// Copyright (c) 1997 by Charlie Calvert
//

#ifndef MyObjectH
#define MyObjectH

#include <conio.h>
#include <vcl\stdctrls.hpp>

class TMyObject :public TObject
{
protected:
  virtual void PrintString(AnsiString S);
public:
  TMyObject() : TObject()  {}
  void ShowHierarchy(TObject *AnObject);
};

class TListHierarchy: public TMyObject
{
private:
  TStringList *FList;
protected:
  virtual void PrintString(AnsiString S)
    { FList->Add(S); }
public:
  TListHierarchy() { FList = new TStringList(); }
  __fastcall virtual ~TListHierarchy() { delete FList; }
  TStringList *GetHierarchy(TObject *AnObject)
    { FList->Clear(); ShowHierarchy(AnObject); return FList; }
};

class __declspec(delphiclass) TVCLHierarchy;

class THierarchy: public TMyObject
{
  friend TVCLHierarchy;
  int FTextColor;
  int FBackColor;
protected:
  virtual __fastcall void SetTextColor(int Color)
    { FTextColor = Color; textcolor(FTextColor); }
  virtual __fastcall void SetBackColor(int Color)
    { FBackColor = Color; textbackground(FBackColor); }
public:
  THierarchy() : TMyObject() {}
  virtual void PrintString(AnsiString S);
  virtual void ClrScr();
  __property int TextColor={read=FTextColor,write=SetTextColor};
  __property int BackColor={read=FBackColor,write=SetBackColor};
};

class TVCLHierarchy : public THierarchy
{
```

continues

Listing 23.6. continued

```
  TMemo *FMemo;
protected:
  virtual __fastcall void SetTextColor(int Color)
    { FTextColor = Color; FMemo->Font->Color = TColor(FTextColor); }
  virtual __fastcall void SetBackColor(int Color);

public:
  TVCLHierarchy(TMemo *AMemo): THierarchy() { FMemo = AMemo; }
  virtual void PrintString(AnsiString S)
    { FMemo->Lines->Add(S); }
  virtual void ClrScr() { FMemo->Clear(); }
};

#endif
```

Listing 23.7. The final take on the main source file for the MyObject unit.

```
/////////////////////////////////////
// MyObject.cpp
// Learning how to use objects
// Copyright (c) 1997 by Charlie Calvert
//
#include <vcl\vcl.h>
#include <conio.h>
#pragma hdrstop
#include "myobject.h"

void TMyObject::PrintString(AnsiString S)
{
  printf("%s\n", S.c_str());
}

void TMyObject::ShowHierarchy(TObject *AnObject)
{
  TClass AClass;

  AnsiString AClassName = AnsiString(AnObject->ClassName()).c_str();
  PrintString(AClassName);

  AClass = AnObject->ClassParent();
  while (True)
  {
    AClassName = AnsiString(AClass->ClassName());
    PrintString(AClassName);
    if (AClassName == "TObject")
      break;
    AClass = AClass->ClassParent();
  }
}
```

```
void THierarchy::PrintString(AnsiString S)
{
  char Temp[250];

  sprintf(Temp, "%s\n\r", S.c_str());
  cputs(Temp);
}

void THierarchy::ClrScr()
{
  clrscr();
}

void __fastcall TVCLHierarchy::SetBackColor(int Color)
{
  FBackColor = Color;
  FMemo->Color = TColor(FBackColor);
}
```

Listing 23.8. The header file for the program's data module.

```
//////////////////////////////////////
// DMod1.h
// Warehouse example: learning about objects
// Copyright (c) 1997 by Charlie Calvert
//
#ifndef DMod1H
#define DMod1H
#include <vcl\Classes.hpp>
#include <vcl\Controls.hpp>
#include <vcl\StdCtrls.hpp>
#include <vcl\Forms.hpp>
#include <vcl\DBTables.hpp>
#include <vcl\DB.hpp>

class TDMod : public TDataModule
{
__published:
  TTable *WidgetsTable;
  TDataSource *WidgetsTableSource;
  TQuery *WidgetsQuery;
  TDataSource *WidgetsQuerySource;
  void __fastcall DModCreate(TObject *Sender);
private:
public:
  virtual __fastcall TDMod(TComponent* Owner);
  void __fastcall SumByProduct();
  void __fastcall ReportByPallet();
};

extern TDMod *DMod;

#endif
```

Listing 23.9. The main source file for the data module.

```cpp
/////////////////////////////////////
// DMod1.cpp
// Warehouse example: learning about objects
// Copyright (c) 1997 by Charlie Calvert
//
#include <vcl\vcl.h>
#pragma hdrstop
#include "DMod1.h"
#pragma resource "*.dfm"
TDMod *DMod;

fastcall TDMod::TDMod(TComponent* Owner)
  : TDataModule(Owner)
{
}

void __fastcall TDMod::DModCreate(TObject *Sender)
{
  WidgetsTable->Open();
}

void __fastcall TDMod::SumByProduct()
{
  AnsiString S = "Select Name, Count(*), Sum(Cost) "
                "from Widgets "
                "group by Name;";
  WidgetsQuery->SQL->Clear();
  WidgetsQuery->SQL->Add(S);
  WidgetsQuery->Open();
}

void __fastcall TDMod::ReportByPallet()
{
  AnsiString S = "Select PalletNumber, Name, Count(*), Sum(Cost) "
                "from Widgets "
                "group by PalletNumber, Name;";
  WidgetsQuery->SQL->Clear();
  WidgetsQuery->SQL->Add(S);
  WidgetsQuery->Open();
}
```

Listing 23.10. The header file for the very simple QueryForm.

```cpp
#ifndef QueryForm1H
#define QueryForm1H
#include <vcl\Classes.hpp>
#include <vcl\Controls.hpp>
#include <vcl\StdCtrls.hpp>
#include <vcl\Forms.hpp>
#include <vcl\DBGrids.hpp>
#include "Grids.hpp"
#include <vcl\ExtCtrls.hpp>
```

```
class TQueryForm : public TForm
{
__published:
  TDBGrid *DBGrid1;
  TPanel *Panel1;
private:
public:
  virtual __fastcall TQueryForm(TComponent* Owner);
};

extern TQueryForm *QueryForm;

#endif
```

Listing 23.11. There is no custom code in the QueryForm.

```
/////////////////////////////////////
// QueryForm1.cpp
// Warehouse example: learning about objects
// Copyright (c) 1997 by Charlie Calvert
//
#include <vcl\vcl.h>
#pragma hdrstop
#include "QueryForm1.h"
#include "DMod1.h"
#pragma link "Grids"
#pragma resource "*.dfm"
TQueryForm *QueryForm;

__fastcall TQueryForm::TQueryForm(TComponent* Owner)
  : TForm(Owner)
{
}
```

Listing 23.12. The header for the very simple DataForm.

```
/////////////////////////////////////
// DataForm1.h
// Warehouse example: learning about objects
// Copyright (c) 1997 by Charlie Calvert
//
#ifndef DataForm1H
#define DataForm1H
#include <vcl\Classes.hpp>
#include <vcl\Controls.hpp>
#include <vcl\StdCtrls.hpp>
#include <vcl\Forms.hpp>
#include <vcl\DBGrids.hpp>
#include "Grids.hpp"
#include <vcl\ExtCtrls.hpp>
```

continues

Listing 23.12. continued

```cpp
class TDataForm : public TForm
{
__published:
  TDBGrid *DBGrid1;
  TPanel *Panel1;
private:
public:
  virtual __fastcall TDataForm(TComponent* Owner);
};

extern TDataForm *DataForm;

#endif
```

Listing 23.13. The main module for the `DataForm` contains no custom code.

```cpp
/////////////////////////////////////
// DataForm1.cpp
// Warehouse example: learning about objects
// Copyright (c) 1997 by Charlie Calvert
//
#include <vcl\vcl.h>
#pragma hdrstop
#include "DataForm1.h"
#include "DMod1.h"
#pragma link "Grids"
#pragma resource "*.dfm"
TDataForm *DataForm;

__fastcall TDataForm::TDataForm(TComponent* Owner)
  : TForm(Owner)
{
}
```

Listing 23.14. The header file for a form that provides a list box for displaying the hierarchy of objects.

```cpp
/////////////////////////////////////
// HierarchyDlg.h
// Learning how to use objects
// Copyright (c) 1997 by Charlie Calvert
//
#ifndef HierarchyDlg1H
#define HierarchyDlg1H
#include <vcl\Classes.hpp>
#include <vcl\Controls.hpp>
#include <vcl\StdCtrls.hpp>
#include <vcl\Forms.hpp>
#include <vcl\ExtCtrls.hpp>
#include <vcl\Buttons.hpp>
```

```
class THierarchyDlg : public TForm
{
__published:
  TListBox *ListBox1;
  TPanel *Panel1;
  TBitBtn *BitBtn1;
private:
public:
    __fastcall THierarchyDlg(TComponent* Owner);
};

extern THierarchyDlg *HierarchyDlg;

#endif
```

Listing 23.15. HierarchyDlg has no custom code in it. The form simply provides a list box in which hierarchies can be shown.

```
/////////////////////////////////////
// HierarchyDlg.cpp
// Learning how to use objects
// Copyright (c) 1997 by Charlie Calvert
//
#include <vcl\vcl.h>
#pragma hdrstop
#include "HierarchyDlg1.h"
#pragma resource "*.dfm"
THierarchyDlg *HierarchyDlg;

__fastcall THierarchyDlg::THierarchyDlg(TComponent* Owner)
  : TForm(Owner)
{
}
```

This program creates five forms at application startup:

```
Application->CreateForm(__classid(TForm1), &Form1);
Application->CreateForm(__classid(TDMod), &DMod);
Application->CreateForm(__classid(TDataForm), &DataForm);
Application->CreateForm(__classid(TQueryForm), &QueryForm);
Application->CreateForm(__classid(THierarchyDlg), &HierarchyDlg);
```

Of these forms, the first two contain significant code, while the last three contain nothing but visual elements that can be shown to the user. For instance, the QueryForm provides a TDBGrid that can be filled with the results of SQL statements executed inside the program's data module. THierarchyDlg provides a list box that can be filled with the hierarchy of some of the objects used in the program.

23

CREATING
COMPONENTS
FROM SCRATCH

The Warehouse application also relies heavily on the Widgets and MyObject modules. In fact, the majority of the program is really nothing but a set piece for the classes found in Widgets.cpp. These objects will be explained in the next section of this chapter.

The Hierarchy for the Widget and Pallet Components

Four components lie at the heart of the Warehouse program. These components are called TWidget, TPentium, TPentiumPro, and TDataPallet. All these objects are declared and implemented in Widgets.h and Widgets.cpp. The hierarchies for these components are shown in Figures 23.8 and 23.9.

FIGURE 23.8.

The hierarchy for the Widget controls used to represent chips.

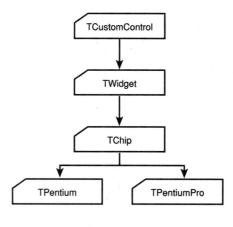

FIGURE 23.9.

The hierarchy for the Pallet controls used to store chips.

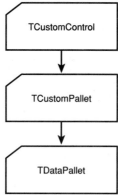

As you can see, all these components descend from `TCustomControl`. The primary reason for choosing this ancestor was that it had a canvas. `TCustomControl` descendants can also contain other controls, which was an option I wanted to keep open in case I desired to build a widget that consisted of several sub-widgets.

> **NOTE**
>
> `TGraphicControl` also has a canvas, but it cannot contain subcontrols or receive the focus. In this case, I made a judgment call and decided that it would be wiser to use the more powerful `TCustomControl` rather than `TGraphicControl`, even though `TCustomControl` uses more resources and takes longer to paint. In the context of this book, it's not really too important which choice I made, so long as I communicate to you the relative virtues of each option.

In Figure 23.10, you can see the hierarchy for the Widget and Pallet controls taken together. For obvious reasons, there is more complexity in this dual hierarchy than there is in either of the single hierarchies shown in Figures 23.8 and 23.9. My point here is simply that the valuable thing about objects is their capability to isolate complexity. As a programmer, you want to find ways to break big, ungainly problems down into smaller, manageable programs. Objects are one of the best ways to achieve this goal.

FIGURE 23.10.

The hierarchy for the Widget and Pallet controls, showing their mutual descent from `TCustomControl`.

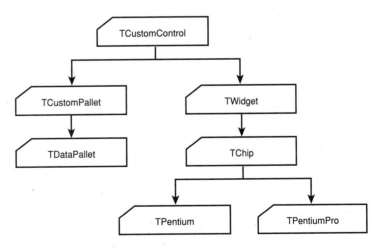

When necessary, break off objects, or object hierarchies, into separate trees and study them alone. Write small test programs that explore the virtues and faults of one object in isolation. Make sure the code you write can be broken up into various smaller programs for testing. For instance, it is easy to take the TPentium component, drop it onto a form, and test it in isolation from the complexity found in the Warehouse program. Components make this kind of testing easy, and that is one of their greatest virtues: They are easily reusable.

Perhaps one of the hardest lessons that beginning programmers have to learn is the value of writing small test programs. If I can't break my programs down into smaller units that can be tested separately, I will generally concede that there is some flaw in my design.

To reiterate: One of the primary goals of OOP is to allow you to build discrete, reusable chunks of code that can be tested in isolation. Components aid in this process enormously, and it is one of the primary reasons why so many components are so robust. The key here is that components are easy to test, and, as a result, a lot of problems get caught that might otherwise be overlooked.

Understanding TWidget, TPentium, and TPentiumPro

The TWidget object provides a base object from which all widgets can descend. The TWidget class provides three basic properties common to all widgets:

```
__property Currency Cost;
__property AnsiString TimeCreated;
__property AnsiString Description;
```

As you saw in Chapter 20, "Encapsulation," widgets can also be saved to disk.

The TChip object is the base class for computer chips. In the implementation of this object I provide here, the TChip object has only minimal functionality:

```
class TChip: public TWidget
{
public:
  virtual __fastcall TChip(TComponent *AOwner): TWidget(AOwner) {}
  virtual __fastcall TChip(TComponent *AOwner, int ACol, int ARow)
    : TWidget(AOwner, ACol, ARow) {}
};
```

If you wanted to have more fun with this object, you could add a wide variety of fields:

```
class TChip: public TWidget
{
private:
  int MHZ;
  bool MMX;
  int Cache;
  int Transistors;
  float Voltage;
  int RegisterSize; // 16, 32, 64?
```

```
public:
  virtual __fastcall TChip(TComponent *AOwner): TWidget(AOwner) {}
  virtual __fastcall TChip(TComponent *AOwner, int ACol, int ARow)
   : TWidget(AOwner, ACol, ARow) {}
};
```

Here you can see an object that contains standard fields for describing the basic attributes of a chip. I hope that in some future version of this program, I will add these features, but for now it is best if I push on and finish the book before my editors tell me what they are *really* thinking about the timeline for this book's development.

Descending from TChip are TPentium and TPentiumPro. As implemented here, the only thing unique about these two objects is their virtual Paint methods:

```
class TPentium: public TChip
{
protected:
  virtual void __fastcall Paint(void);
public:
  virtual __fastcall TPentium(TComponent *AOwner): TChip(AOwner) {}
  virtual __fastcall TPentium(TComponent *AOwner, int ACol, int ARow)
   : TChip(AOwner, ACol, ARow) {}
};

class TPentiumPro: public TChip
{
protected:
  virtual void __fastcall Paint(void);
public:
  virtual __fastcall TPentiumPro(TComponent *AOwner): TChip(AOwner) {}
  virtual __fastcall TPentiumPro(TComponent *AOwner, int ACol, int ARow)
   : TChip(AOwner, ACol, ARow) {}
};
void __fastcall TPentium::Paint()
{
  Canvas->Brush->Color = clPurple;
  Canvas->Rectangle(0, 0, ClientWidth, ClientHeight);
  Canvas->Brush->Color = clRed;
  Canvas->Ellipse(0, 0, ClientWidth, ClientHeight);
}

void __fastcall TPentiumPro::Paint()
{
  Canvas->Brush->Color = clGreen;
  Canvas->Rectangle(0, 0, ClientWidth, ClientHeight);
  Canvas->Brush->Color = clBlue;
  Canvas->Ellipse(0, 0, ClientWidth, ClientHeight);
}
```

In other words, my implementation doesn't do much to differentiate these objects other than to leverage polymorphism to make them appear differently when they are shown on-screen. A nice touch to add to this project would be to show a bitmap of a processor rather than the simple graphic I include here.

As you saw in earlier chapters, all TWidget descendants also have the capability to report on their hierarchy. This feature will play a role in this program when a user right-clicks on a component with the mouse. In particular, if you right-click on any of the Widget objects, a form that shows their hierarchy pops up. I will discuss that aspect of the program later in the chapter.

Because the TWidget components are descendants of TCustomControl, they all can be hung on the Component pallet. The following code from the Widgets unit registers the Widget and Pallet controls:

```
void __fastcall Register()
  {
    TComponentClass classes[5] = {__classid(TWidget),
      __classid(TPentium), __classid(TPentiumPro),
      __classid(TPallet ), __classid(TDataPallet ) };
    RegisterComponents("Unleash", classes, 4);
  }
```

That's all that needs to be said about the technical aspect of the Widget components. When all is said and done, the most important fact about these simple objects is that they all descend from the same parent. As a result, the program will be able to use polymorphism when handling them. This turns out to be very useful, particularly during drag-and-drop operations. The drag-and-drop aspect of the program will be covered over the next few sections of this chapter.

Introducing the Pallet Controls

The TPallet controls are a little more complex than the Widget controls in that they can support drag and drop. In particular, they know how to respond when a user drops a TWidget control onto them.

Before describing the drag-and-drop operation, I should spend a moment covering the heritage of the pallet controls. The TCustomPallet control from which the TDataPallet descends is pretty straightforward:

```
class TCustomPallet : public TCustomControl
{
private:
  int FPalletNumber;
  TListHierarchy *FHierarchy;
protected:
  virtual void __fastcall Paint(void);
public:
  virtual __fastcall TCustomPallet(TComponent *AOwner);
  virtual __fastcall ~TCustomPallet(void)
    { delete FHierarchy; }
  TStringList *GetHierarchy() { return FHierarchy->GetHierarchy(this); }
  __property int PalletNumber={read=FPalletNumber, write=FPalletNumber};
};
```

This object has a field for storing the number of the pallet and, through aggregation, the capability to report on its hierarchy.

> **NOTE**
>
> One of my goals in these chapters is to convince some readers of the merits of aggregation. Multiple inheritance is a powerful tool, but it adds considerable complexity to your program. In the last few chapters, you have had several opportunities to look at aggregation. This technique takes a little more work to implement than multiple inheritance, but I believe it often ends up saving you time in the long run, because it is so much easier to understand and maintain than multiple inheritance.
>
> My point here is not to criticize multiple inheritance, but rather to point out that aggregation is a valuable tool in its own right. There are certain settings in which each technology shines, and good programmers should explore the benefits of both aggregation and multiple inheritance so that they will know when to favor one method over the other.
>
> When you are in doubt, I would suggest using aggregation, because it almost never causes trouble. Multiple inheritance is easier to implement, but under certain circumstances it can cause enormous confusion that leaves even the best programmers feeling frustrated. This is literally true. Some of the best programmers I have ever met have spent days, sometimes even weeks, trying to untie the knots caused by someone else's unintelligent or ill-advised use of multiple inheritance.
>
> Of course, if you use multiple inheritance intelligently, it is a great tool. But one of the prerequisites for using it intelligently is knowing when not to use it. If you are not going to use it, you need to understand the alternatives. There is really only one good alternative to multiple inheritance, and that is aggregation. As a result, all programmers should understand both multiple inheritance and aggregation.

In `Widgets.h`, I declare a direct descendant of `TCustomPallet` called `TPallet`:

```
class TPallet : public TCustomPallet
{
public:
  virtual __fastcall TPallet(TComponent *AOwner): TCustomPallet(AOwner)
    { Width = 25; Height = 25; }
__published:
  __property PalletNumber;
  __property OnDragDrop;
  __property OnDragOver;
  __property Color;
};
```

This object adds no functionality to `TCustomPallet` but only publishes certain of its properties. I place this object here for no other reason than to point out the correct way to design objects from which others may descend. If you want to be sure that you are following the best techniques, you might want to create two classes when it might at first appear that one will do:

1. The first class provides all the functionality needed by an object.

2. The second class descends from the first and publishes the properties you think you will need to use for your particular version of the object.

When you do things this way, others can descend from the first class you created but get the option of deciding which classes they want to publish.

An example of this technology in action is shown by the `TDataPallet`:

```
class TDataPallet : public TCustomPallet
{
private:
  TTable *FWidgetsTable;
  TQuery *FWidgetsQuery;
protected:
  void __fastcall PalletDragDrop(TObject *Sender,
    TObject *Source, int X, int Y);
  void __fastcall PalletDragOver(TObject *Sender, TObject *Source,
    int X, int Y, TDragState State, bool &Accept);
  void virtual EnterWidgets(int Total, TWidget *W);
public:
  virtual __fastcall TDataPallet(TComponent *AOwner);
  void __fastcall QueryPallet(TQuery *Query);
  float __fastcall QueryPalletSum(TQuery *Query);
__published:
  __property TTable *WidgetsTable={read=FWidgetsTable, write=FWidgetsTable};
  __property TQuery *WidgetsQuery={read=FWidgetsQuery, write=FWidgetsQuery};
  __property PalletNumber;
  __property Hint;
  __property Color;
  __property TabOrder;
  __property OnMouseDown;
  __property PopupMenu;
};
```

`TDataPallet` descends from `TCustomPallet`, thereby inheriting certain useful functionality. It then adds its own methods and publishes the properties that it wants to expose in the Object Inspector. The key point here is that `TDataPallet` should have the right to decide which properties it wants to expose!

The `TDataPallet` is smart enough to accept drag and drop, and also to work with objects of type `TTable` and `TQuery`. These are both relatively complex subjects, so I will handle them in their own sections of this chapter.

TDataPallet, and Drag and Drop

Drag and drop is a flashy interface element of the type that I have a natural tendency to resist. I just tend to think that the really hot technology involves the language itself, and particularly the construction of objects and components. However, there is a lot to be said for building programs that are easy to use, and drag and drop can aid in that process.

The one problem with drag and drop is that there are few simple ways to tell the user that the feature is available. When you open up the Warehouse program, there is no way to show users that they can drag components onto the pallets. You have to tell them this in the online help or in some kind of tutorial. The same problem exists in the Explorer, in many of the Zip utilities I've seen, and elsewhere in the application development world.

Lately, I've even seen some programs just write the words *drag and drop* in their captions. Even though the words appear out of context and with no specific reference, this is often enough to allow me to figure out how to use the application. I attempt this same thing with the Warehouse program, as shown in Figure 23.1.

After you get over the initial training period, drag and drop gets a chance to come into its own. It can then provide a very powerful addition to your programs, especially if used in the right context.

The VCL makes drag and drop simple to implement. To make it work, you need to respond to `WM_MOUSEDOWN` events on the component you want to drag:

```
void __fastcall TForm1::WidgetMouseDown(TObject *Sender, TMouseButton Button,
  TShiftState Shift, int X, int Y)
{
  if (!dynamic_cast<TWidget *>(Sender))
    return;
  TWidget *W = (TWidget *)(Sender);

  if (Shift.Contains(ssLeft))
  {
    W->BeginDrag(False);
  }
  else
  {
    HierarchyDlg->ListBox1->Items = W->GetHierarchy();
    HierarchyDlg->ShowModal();
  }
}
```

The relevant code in this example is only three lines long. Stripped of the context of the particular example used in this program, it would look like this:

```
if (dynamic_cast<TWidget *>(Sender))
{
  TWidget *W = (TWidget *)(Sender);
  W->BeginDrag(False);
}
```

Checking to see that the component is really a `Widget` is probably overkill, because you would only associate this code with the `OnMouseMove` event of a control you wanted to drag. Nevertheless, it is often better to be safe than sorry. In particular, you want to know immediately if you accidentally associate the wrong code with the wrong component. In short, error checking is often as much about detecting programmer error as it is about detecting user error. If you decide later that you have a performance problem, you can strip this kind of error checking from your program, or else use assertions, conditional compilation, or some other technology.

> **NOTE**
>
> If you use the Object Inspector to examine TWidget or its descendants, you will notice that one of the two events it publishes is OnMouseDown. Obviously I published this event because I knew it would be needed. I also published the OnDragDrop event, but only because I think the user might need it under certain circumstances never exploited in this program.

After you have safely typecast the object as a Widget, you can begin the drag operation:

```
W->BeginDrag(False);
```

You should set the parameter BeginDrag to false if you want the cursor to change only after a drag operation is begun. For instance, if the user wants to click on a component for some other reason than dragging, you would want to set the parameter to false, so that the cursor will not change if users merely click on a component but only if they click and then start dragging.

Starting a drag-and-drop operation is obviously fairly trivial. The other side of the operation is a bit trickier but still not rocket science:

```
void __fastcall TDataPallet::PalletDragOver(TObject *Sender,
  TObject *Source, int X, int Y, TDragState State, bool &Accept)
{
  Accept = dynamic_cast<TWidget *>(Source);
}
void __fastcall TDataPallet::PalletDragDrop(TObject *Sender,
  TObject *Source, int X, int Y)
{
  if (WidgetsTable == NULL)
    ShowMessage("No table assigned to the WidgetsTable property");
  else
  {
    if (dynamic_cast<TWidget *>(Source))
    {
      TWidget *W = (TWidget *)(Source);
      AnsiString S = "Enter number of " + W->Name;
      AnsiString NumWidgets;

      if (InputQuery("Widget Number Dialog", S, NumWidgets))
      {
        EnterWidgets(NumWidgets.ToInt(), W);
      }
    }
  }
}
```

The first of the two methods shown here is an event handler that is called when the user drags something over the component. If you set the `Accept` parameter to an `OnDragOver` event to `true`, the cursor on the mouse will change to reflect that this object accepts the current type of drag-and-drop operation. The code shown here sets `Accept` to `true` as long as I am sure the object in question is a `Widget`:

```
Accept = dynamic_cast<TWidget *>(Source);
```

This is where polymorphism plays such a key role in the program. The issue here is that polymorphism allows me to safely typecast any object that descends `TWidget` as a `Widget`. This is an enormously powerful concept. By now you are used to the idea that `TWidget`, `TPentium`, and `TPentiumPro` are closely related objects. Nevertheless, they are not the same object, and if I had to write code that worked with three different types of objects, my application would be much more difficult to write and maintain.

> **NOTE**
>
> Polymorphism allows you to treat objects generically, as a type. I can talk not about a specific widget, but about all widgets, regardless of their subtype.
>
> When dealing with real-world objects, the same thing is done all the time. For instance, I explain how to do something to you, the reader of this book, without having to know your name, your race, your sex, or your age. I can just refer to readers in general and know that you will be able to understand the explanation, given the context of the expected audience for this book. If I had to address each copy of this book to a specific person, it would be considerably less useful.
>
> Polymorphism lets the programmer tell a whole class of objects what needs to be done. This book works with all programmers who understand C++ and the basics of OOP. The methods shown here work with all objects that descend from `TWidget`. This capability to generalize, to work with abstractions, is enormously powerful!

When the user actually drops a component on another component, an `OnDragDrop` event occurs:

```
void __fastcall TDataPallet::PalletDragDrop(TObject *Sender, TObject *Source,
                                            int X, int Y)
{
  if (dynamic_cast<TWidget *>(Source))
  {
    TWidget *W = (TWidget *)(Source);
```

The code shown here is a stripped-down version of the response to this event. The component that was dropped is stored in the `Source` parameter of the `OnDragDrop` event. I can simply typecast it as a `TWidget` and then begin calling its methods. Some of the actual methods called, such as `EnterWidgets`, are actually more related to the database part of this equation, so I will explain them in the next section of this chapter.

The final point to notice about these drag-and-drop operations is that the event handlers shown here are not part of the main form of the application but are instead methods of the TDataPallet itself! In particular, notice the constructor for the object:

```
__fastcall TDataPallet::TDataPallet(TComponent *AOwner)
: TCustomPallet(AOwner)
{
  OnDragOver = PalletDragOver;
  OnDragDrop = PalletDragDrop;
}
```

This code sets up event handlers for OnDragDrop and OnDragOver events. In other words, when you drop a TDataPallet onto a form, it is automatically ready to handle drag-and-drop events without any custom coding from the user.

To go any further on this subject would be to start wrestling with the tables used in this project. My plan is to cover that material in the next section of the chapter.

TDataPallet and Databases

In an ideal world, TDataPallet could store itself directly in an object-oriented database. BCB is, in fact, capable of using OOP databases such as Poet, but that is not a feature I want to stress in this book, because few readers will be using such tools.

Instead of using an object-oriented database, I instead use the properties of TDataPallet to allow the user to hook in TTable and TQuery objects. That way TDataPallet can have "carnal knowledge," as it were, of the databases in your application.

> **NOTE**
>
> The relationship between TDataPallet and the TTable objects used in this program is very specific. You can't use just any TTable object with TDataPallet but only the one that contains a particular set of fields.
>
> In many ways, this tight coupling of a particular TTable and the TDataPallet object is less than ideal in terms of OOP design. The problem here is that TDataPallet needs to know too much about the structure of the TTable object you are using with it. There is not a sufficient degree of abstraction here to suit the best principles of OOP design.
>
> The origin of the problem is simply that I can't store TDataPallets and TWidgets directly in an OOP database, nor can I easily descend visible controls from the non-visible TTable object. As a result, I need to come up with a compromise solution to a problem that a later generation of tools will undoubtedly solve for me.
>
> For now, I can come up with a reasonable solution simply by creating a TDataPallet component with a simple, easy-to-use interface. This simple interface makes it easy for the user to see what needs to be done to use the object.

Each TDataPallet has a TWidgetTable property:

```
private:
  TTable *FWidgetsTable;
  TQuery *FWidgetsQuery;
__published:
  __property TTable *WidgetsTable={read=FWidgetsTable, write=FWidgetsTable};
  __property TQuery *WidgetsQuery={read=FWidgetsQuery, write=FWidgetsQuery};
```

These properties can be manipulated via the Object Inspector, as shown in Figure 23.11, which makes it easy for the user to connect the TDataWidget to the appropriate table. Learning to make components interact in this way is a key skill in BCB programming.

FIGURE 23.11.

Using the Object Inspector to connect a TDataPallet *to a table.*

After the table is connected to the data pallet, the consumer of the object need not think about it any further. For instance, when you drag a widget onto a pallet, the method TDataWidget is called in order to enter data into the table:

```
void TDataPallet::EnterWidgets(int Total, TWidget* W)
{
  int i;
  for (i = 0; i < Total; i++)
  {
    FWidgetsTable->Insert();
    FWidgetsTable->FieldByName("Name")->AsString = W->Name;
    FWidgetsTable->FieldByName("Created")->AsString = W->TimeCreated;
    FWidgetsTable->FieldByName("Description")->AsString = W->Description;
    FWidgetsTable->FieldByName("Cost")->AsCurrency = W->Cost;
    FWidgetsTable->FieldByName("PalletNumber")->AsInteger = PalletNumber;
    FWidgetsTable->Post();
  }
}
```

In short, after you hook up the TDataPallet object to the table, the pallet knows how to manage the table. This helps to keep the code for your program clean, by isolating each problem inside of discrete objects.

From the point of view of the consumer of the TDataPallet, all he or she has to do is drop a TDataPallet on a form and then hook it up to a TTable object. After that, all the database and drag-and-drop operations are taken care of automatically! Obviously, it would be better if there were a more pure OOP way to relate the `TTable` and `TDataPallet` objects, but given the limitations of the current technology, the VCL provides a means to implement a very clean, simple solution to the problem. This is what OOP is all about: finding simple, error-free, easy-to-understand solutions to problems that would otherwise be complex and error-prone.

The last point to make about this solution is that it allows the user to simplify the act of data entry. If someone had to enter each of these objects in a database with the keyboard, it would be a very boring, time-consuming task. The Warehouse program completely eliminates the need for any painful data entry other than typing in the single digit specifying the number of components to drop on a pallet.

This kind of solution could be implemented in a wide range of situations. For instance, with a hospital, someone could enter the basic facts about a patient once and then simply drag that patient's icon onto a form in order to transfer the information from the original record to the form. Even better, a fully digital world could equip each patient with a card that would be read on admission to the hospital, so that the basic data on the patient would be imported into the database automatically. Then you could just drag and drop a picture of the patient onto any forms needed by insurance companies or other entities that live on raw data. This type of solution is probably not very widely used at this time, but it seems obvious that it will be over the course of the next few years.

Now that most companies are computerized, the way to be competitive is to provide intuitive, easy-to-use solutions that allow individuals to get a lot of paperwork done quickly. If someone provides clunky, hard-to-use solutions that users dislike and that require a lengthy training period, others can get a competitive advantage by coming in and providing clean, easy-to-use interfaces that workers enjoy and that require only a few minutes of training.

Querying the Database

After you have the drag-and-drop solution to data entry in place, the final step is to use SQL to query the database. I have divided up these chores between two different objects: `TDataPallet` and the `TDataModule`. If a question applies directly to a single `TDataPallet`, I ask the data pallet itself to reply. If the question applies generically to the entire warehouse, I ask the program's data module to answer the question.

Generic questions that apply to the entire warehouse are accessed through the menu at the top of the program, while questions that apply to a particular pallet are accessed through a local menu found by right-clicking on the object, as shown in Figure 23.12.

FIGURE 23.12.

Right-clicking on a pallet to find its local menu.

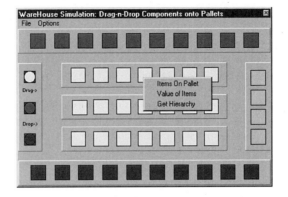

To associate an object with a popup menu, first drag the menu from the Standard page of the Component Palette. Then use the Menu Designer to fill out the menu. Finally, use the PopupMenu property of the component with which you want to associate the menu. For instance, I use the PopupMenu property of TDataPallet to associate the program's popup menu with each pallet. You can multiselect all the TDataPallets on the form and then change their PopupMenu properties globally with one click of the mouse. TDataPallet inherited its PopupMenu property from TCustomControl.

This is probably not the place to get into a long explanation of the SQL that answers the user's questions about the database. However, the following examples from the program's data module provide a sample of how this system works:

```
void __fastcall TDMod::SumByProduct()
{
  AnsiString S = "Select Name, Count(*), Sum(Cost) "
                "from Widgets "
                "group by Name;";
  WidgetsQuery->SQL->Clear();
  WidgetsQuery->SQL->Add(S);
  WidgetsQuery->Open();
}
```

This code provides a report on all the widgets in the database. As you can see, it groups them by name, as shown in Figure 23.4. The query reports on the number of each particular widget (Count(*)) and on the total value of the stock of each particular widget (Sum(Cost)).

The following example shows how to report on the contents of each pallet in the warehouse, as shown in Figure 23.5:

```
void __fastcall TDMod::ReportByPallet()
{
  AnsiString S = "Select PalletNumber, Name, Count(*), Sum(Cost) "
                "from Widgets "
                "group by PalletNumber, Name;";
```

```
    WidgetsQuery->SQL->Clear();
    WidgetsQuery->SQL->Add(S);
    WidgetsQuery->Open();
}
```

As you can see, this query groups the pallets by number and name and reports on the total number of items on the pallet and the total value of the items on the pallet. SQL provides an elegant, simple means of retrieving this data that is vastly superior to trying to retrieve it through a series of loops written in C++.

I don't want to dwell on this subject too much longer, but I will show one method of the TPallet object answering a question from the database:

```
float __fastcall TDataPallet::QueryPalletSum(TQuery *Query)
{
    AnsiString S = "Select Sum(Cost) from Widgets where PalletNumber = " +
        AnsiString(PalletNumber);
    Query->SQL->Clear();
    Query->SQL->Add(S);
    Query->Open();
    return Query->Fields[0]->AsFloat;
}
```

This code returns the value of the items on a particular pallet. You can show the answer to the user either in a custom-made dialog that works with the return value of the function or by showing the results of the query in a TDBGrid.

The user would ask the question answered by the QueryPalletSum method by right-clicking on a particular pallet and bringing up the local popup menu for the pallet. The response method for selecting an item on the menu looks like this:

```
void __fastcall TForm1::ValueofItems1Click(TObject *Sender)
{
    TDataPallet *D = (TDataPallet *)PopupMenu1->PopupComponent;
    D->QueryPalletSum(DMod->WidgetsQuery);
    QueryForm->Panel1->Caption =
        "Value of Items on Pallet: " + AnsiString(D->PalletNumber);
    QueryForm->ShowModal();
}
```

This menu item response method can find the pallet the user clicked on by checking PopupComponent property of the PopupMenu itself:

```
TDataPallet *D = (TDataPallet *)PopupMenu1->PopupComponent;
```

After you have the pallet in your hands, you are free to call its methods, such as the QueryPalletSum method shown earlier.

> **NOTE**
>
> In this case, I probably could skip the step of asking the user to pass the query explicitly to the function, because you can already associate the TQuery object with the TDataPallet object via the Object Inspector. However, I used this technique because it seemed expedient at the time and perhaps allowed me to write code that was easier to read.

After the TDataPallet returns the answer to the query, I use the QueryForm object to display the reply to the user. The QueryForm is a standard VCL form with a TDBGrid on it. The advantage of this system is that I can just pass a query to the QueryForm, and it will display the results to the user, regardless of the type of question being asked.

Looking at Hierarchies

The final thing to point out about this program is that you can right-click on the TWidget and TPallet objects in order to see their hierarchies, as shown in Figures 23.13 and 23.14.

FIGURE 23.13.

The hierarchy of a TWidget *descendant as found by right-clicking on the object.*

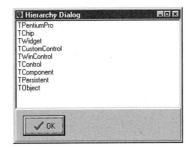

FIGURE 23.14.

The hierarchy of a TCustomPallet *descendant found by right-clicking on a pallet and choosing from a popup menu.*

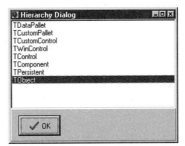

I've come back to the subject of hierarchies at the end of this chapter just for the sake of completeness. As you recall, the discussion of objects was started back in Chapter 19, "Inheritance," by implementing a simple base object that could show its own hierarchy. You've seen a number of sample programs that use that functionality in a variety of different contexts, including this relatively sophisticated program that manages to embody the traits of objects you first started exploring several chapters ago.

The real point of the Warehouse example is not so much to simulate a warehouse as it is to show how objects work. The fact that each of the key objects in the program allows you to see its hierarchy reminds you of the purpose of this program and of its real import.

Summary

One of the goals of OOP is to allow you to create objects that encapsulate functionality in a reusable container that makes applications easy to maintain. To achieve these ends, you use inheritance, encapsulation, and polymorphism in a variety of different contexts. The object hierarchy is, in a sense, a symbol of this power.

In this chapter, you took a look at working examples of object hierarchies, polymorphism, inheritance, and encapsulation. You have seen how to wrap objects inside components and use them in a relatively real-world example.

You have also seen how to use drag and drop and right mouse clicks to provide the user with a simple, easy-to-understand interface to an application. Both drag and drop and right clicks are confusing to the user at first, because their availability is not always clearly broadcast by symbols visible on the interface of the application. However, after the user is clued in to their existence, they add a great deal to the interface of a program. As time goes on, right-clicking and drag and drop will become standard parts of all programs, and users will then be more inclined to search out these features and use them, without having to be specifically alerted to their existence.

Creating Non-Visual Components

IN THIS CHAPTER

CHAPTER 24

Overview

In this chapter, you will learn how to build a non-visual component. In particular, I will emphasize the following topics:

- Descending directly from TComponent
- Using and designing non-visual components
- Using FindFirst and FindNext to iterate through the files in directories
- Creating your own stacks
- Pushing and popping items off a stack

In particular, you will look at one reusable non-visual component called TFindDirs, which is used in a program that will iterate through a series of directories and will archive the names of the files found there into a database. You could, for example, use the program to iterate over all the files on several zip discs of CD-ROMs. You would then have one database that could be searched when you're looking for files that might be located on any of a number of different discs.

Why Create Non-Visual Components?

The program shown in this chapter uses the TFindDirs component to illustrate the concept of component reuse. Write the TFindDirs component once, and you can reuse it in multiple programs. The big bonus here is that TFindDirs is a component and thereby makes a relatively complex task simple enough that you can perform it by just dropping an object onto a form and plugging it into your program.

This short chapter is presented primarily to promote the idea of turning objects that you might not usually think of as components into components. You can easily see why an edit control makes a good component, but the fact that an object used to iterate through directories would make a good component is less obvious. In fact, I first turned this object into a component on a whim. Once I had it around, however, I found that I could plug it into all kinds of applications to aid with one task or another.

Here are some of my applications that use this component:

- A program for iterating through directories to delete files that I no longer need.
- A program for "touching" all the files in a series of directories so that they have the same date.
- A file backup utility for comparing two directory structures to be sure they are identical. This same program will also produce scripts that copy files from one directory structure to the other if a mismatch occurs.

My point here is that writing these utilities became easy after I had the TFindDirs component in place. The core functionality for each of these programs was easy to implement because it was based on a component. As you will see, in just a few seconds you can create a program that uses the component. After you have that much functionality in place, you can easily add more features.

When Should Non-Visual Objects Become Components?

Whether you should turn a particular object into a component is not always clear. For example, the TStringList object has no related component and cannot be manipulated through visual tools. The question then becomes "Why have I taken the TFindDirs object and placed it on the Component Palette?"

As you'll discover, the advantages of placing TFindDirs on the Component Palette are two-fold:

- You might need to tweak several options before you use this object. In particular, you need to decide whether you want to have the lists of directories and files that you find saved to memory in a TStringList. Letting the programmer decide these matters by clicking a property can go a long way toward presenting a clean, easy-to-use interface for an object.

- The TFindDirs object has two features that can be accessed through the Events page. Specifically, custom event handlers can be notified every time a new file or directory has been found. However, constructing an event handler manually can be confusing, particularly if you don't know which parameters will be passed to the functions involved. If you place a component on the Component Palette, you do not need to guess about how to handle an event. All it takes is a quick click on the Events page, and the event handler is created for you automatically!

Creating a component also has the enormous advantage of forcing, or at least encouraging, programmers to design a simple interface for an object. After I have placed an object on the Component Palette, I always want to ensure that the user can hook it into his or her program in only a few short seconds. I am therefore strongly inclined to create a simple, easy-to-use interface. If I don't place the component on the Component Palette, then I find it easier to slip by with a complex interface that takes many lines of code for myself and others to utilize. To my mind, good components are not only bug free, but also very easy to use.

The SearchDirs Program

In this section, you will find the SearchDirs program, which can be used to iterate through the subdirectories on a hard drive looking for files with a particular name or file mask. For example, you could look for `*.cpp` or `m*.cpp` or `ole2.hpp`. This program will put the names of all the files that match the mask into a database, so you can search for the files later.

The SearchDirs program depends on the TFindDirs component, which ships with this book. To use this component, you must first load it onto the Component Palette, using the techniques described in the preceding few chapters. In general, all you have to do is choose Component | Install and then click the Add button. Browse the Utils subdirectory that ships with this book. There you will find the FindDirs2.cpp unit. Add it to CMPLIB32.CCL, and you are ready to build the SearchDirs program. As usual, you might want to run the BuildObjs project once before installing the component. The source for this program is shown in Listings 24.1 through 24.8. A screen shot of the program is shown in Figure 24.1. You need to make sure the CUnleashed alias is in place before running the program. This is a standard Paradox alias that points at the data directory off the root directory where the files from the CD that accompany this book are installed. See both the text right after the listings and also the readme file for more information about the alias.

FIGURE 24.1.

A screen shot of the main form of the SearchDirs program.

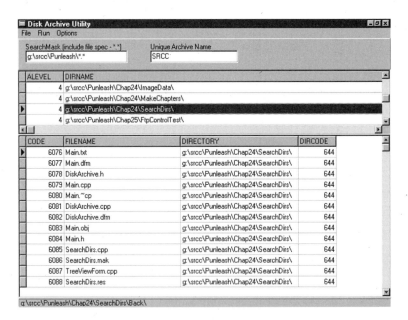

The point here is that TFindDirs, like TTable and TQuery, is a non-visual component. TFindDirs completes your introduction to the basic component types by showing you how to build non-visual components. You already know how to build visual components. After you understand how to build non-visual components, most of the power of BCB will be open to you. The TFindDirs component is also important because it shows you how to create custom event handlers.

Listing 24.1. The header for the main form for the SearchDirs program.

```
////////////////////////////////////////
// Main.h
// SearchDirs
// Copyright (c) 1997 by Charlie Calvert
//
#ifndef MainH
#define MainH
#include <vcl\Classes.hpp>
#include <vcl\Controls.hpp>
#include <vcl\StdCtrls.hpp>
#include <vcl\Forms.hpp>
#include <vcl\Menus.hpp>
#include <vcl\ComCtrls.hpp>
#include <vcl\DBGrids.hpp>
#include <vcl\Grids.hpp>
#include <vcl\DBCtrls.hpp>
#include <vcl\ExtCtrls.hpp>
#include "FindDirs2.h"

class TForm1 : public TForm
{
__published:
  TMainMenu *MainMenu1;
  TMenuItem *File1;
  TMenuItem *Counter1;
  TMenuItem *N1;
  TMenuItem *Exit1;
  TMenuItem *Run1;
  TDBGrid *FileNamesGrid;
  TMenuItem *Options1;
  TMenuItem *Delete1;
  TMenuItem *DisableGrids1;
  TPanel *Panel2;
  TEdit *Edit1;
  TEdit *Edit2;
  TMenuItem *N2;
  TMenuItem *PickArchive1;
  TLabel *Label1;
  TLabel *Label2;
  TStatusBar *StatusBar1;
  TDBGrid *DirNamesGrid;
  TFindDirs *FindDirs1;
  void __fastcall Button1Click(TObject *Sender);
  void __fastcall Exit1Click(TObject *Sender);
  void __fastcall Delete1Click(TObject *Sender);
  void __fastcall PickArchive1Click(TObject *Sender);
  void __fastcall OnFoundDir(AnsiString NewDir);
  void __fastcall FindDirs1FoundFile(AnsiString NewDir);
```

continues

Listing 24.1. continued

```cpp
private:
  int FStartLevel;
  AnsiString FCurrentRoot;
  AnsiString FDiskName;
  void StartRun();
  void EndRun();
public:
  virtual __fastcall TForm1(TComponent* Owner);
};

extern TForm1 *Form1;

#endif
```

Listing 24.2. The main form for the SearchDirs program.

```cpp
//////////////////////////////////////
// Main.cpp
// SearchDirs
// Copyright (c) 1997 by Charlie Calvert
//
#include <vcl\vcl.h>
#pragma hdrstop
#include "Main.h"
#include "DiskArchive.h"
#include "FindDirsDMod.h"
#pragma resource "*.dfm"
TForm1 *Form1;

__fastcall TForm1::TForm1(TComponent* Owner)
  : TForm(Owner)
{
}

int GetLevel(AnsiString Source)
{
  BOOL Done = False;
  int i = 0;
  char S[500];

  strcpy(S, Source.c_str());

  strtok(S, "\\");
  while (!Done)
  {
    if (strtok(NULL, "\\") == NULL)
      Done = True;
    else
      i += 1;
  }
  return i;
}
```

```cpp
void TForm1::StartRun()
{
  DirNamesGrid->DataSource = NULL;
  FileNamesGrid->DataSource = NULL;
  Screen->Cursor = (Controls::TCursor)crHourGlass;
  FindDirs1->StartString = Edit1->Text;
  FDiskName = Edit2->Text;

  FStartLevel = GetLevel(FindDirs1->StartDir);
  DMod->DiskNamesTable->Insert();
  DMod->DiskNamesTable->FieldByName("DiskName")->AsString = FDiskName;
  DMod->DiskNamesTable->Post();
}

void TForm1::EndRun()
{
  Screen->Cursor = (Controls::TCursor)crDefault;
  DirNamesGrid->DataSource = DMod->DirNamesSource;
  FileNamesGrid->DataSource = DMod->FileNamesSource;
}

void __fastcall TForm1::Button1Click(TObject *Sender)
{
  if (MessageBox((HWND)Handle, Edit1->Text.c_str(), "Make Run?", MB_YESNO) ==
ID_YES)
  {
    StartRun();
    FindDirs1->Run();
    EndRun();
  }
}

void __fastcall TForm1::Exit1Click(TObject *Sender)
{
  Close();
}

void __fastcall TForm1::Delete1Click(TObject *Sender)
{
  if (MessageBox((HWND)Handle, "Delete", "Delete Dialog", MB_YESNO) == ID_YES)
    DMod->CascadingDelete();
}

void __fastcall TForm1::PickArchive1Click(TObject *Sender)
{
  ArchiveForm->ShowModal();
}

void __fastcall TForm1::OnFoundDir(AnsiString NewDir)
{
  int i;

  StatusBar1->SimpleText = NewDir;
  StatusBar1->Update();

  FCurrentRoot = NewDir;
```

continues

Listing 24.2. continued

```
  i = GetLevel(FCurrentRoot);
  DMod->DirNamesTable->Insert();
  DMod->DirNamesTable->FieldByName("DirName")->AsString = NewDir;
  DMod->DirNamesTable->FieldByName("ALevel")->AsInteger = i;
  DMod->DirNamesTable->FieldByName("DiskCode")->AsInteger =
  DMod->DiskNamesTable->FieldByName("Code")->AsInteger;
  DMod->DirNamesTable->Post();
}

void __fastcall TForm1::FindDirs1FoundFile(AnsiString NewDir)
{
  AnsiString Temp;

  if (FCurrentRoot.Length() == 0)
    Temp = FindDirs1->StartDir;
  else
    Temp = FCurrentRoot;

  DMod->FileNamesTable->Insert();
  DMod->FileNamesTable->FieldByName("Directory")->AsString = Temp;
  DMod->FileNamesTable->FieldByName("FileName")->AsString =
    ExtractFileName(NewDir);
  DMod->FileNamesTable->Post();
}
```

Listing 24.3. The header for the program's data module.

```
//////////////////////////////////////
// FindDirsDMod.h
// SearchDirs
// Copyright (c) 1997 by Charlie Calvert
//
#ifndef FindDirsDModH
#define FindDirsDModH
#include <vcl\Classes.hpp>
#include <vcl\Controls.hpp>
#include <vcl\StdCtrls.hpp>
#include <vcl\Forms.hpp>
#include <vcl\DB.hpp>
#include <vcl\DBTables.hpp>

class TDMod : public TDataModule
{
__published:
  TDatabase *FileData1;
  TTable *DirNamesTable;
  TTable *FileNamesTable;
  TTable *DiskNamesTable;
  TTable *DiskTypeTable;
  TDataSource *DirNamesSource;
  TDataSource *FileNamesSource;
  TDataSource *DiskNamesSource;
  TDataSource *DiskTypeSource;
  TIntegerField *DirNamesTableALEVEL;
  TStringField *DirNamesTableDIRNAME;
```

```
        TIntegerField *DirNamesTableDISKCODE;
        TIntegerField *FileNamesTableCODE;
        TStringField *FileNamesTableDIRECTORY;
        TStringField *FileNamesTableFILENAME;
        TIntegerField *FileNamesTableDIRCODE;
        TIntegerField *DirNamesTableCODE;
        TQuery *DeleteFileNames;
        TQuery *DeleteDirNames;
        TQuery *DeleteDiskNames;
        TAutoIncField *DiskTypeTableCode;
        TStringField *DiskTypeTableDiskType;
        TIntegerField *DiskTypeTableDiskTypeCode;
        TAutoIncField *DiskNamesTableCode;
        TStringField *DiskNamesTableDiskName;
        TIntegerField *DiskNamesTableType;
        void __fastcall DModCreate(TObject *Sender);



private:
public:
    virtual __fastcall TDMod(TComponent* Owner);
    void CascadingDelete(void);
};

extern TDMod *DMod;

#endif
```

Listing 24.4. The data module for the program.

```
//////////////////////////////////////
// FindDirsDMod.cpp
// SearchDirs
// Copyright (c) 1997 by Charlie Calvert
//
#include <vcl\vcl.h>
#pragma hdrstop
#include "FindDirsDMod.h"
#pragma resource "*.dfm"

TDMod *DMod;

__fastcall TDMod::TDMod(TComponent* Owner)
        : TDataModule(Owner)
{
}

void __fastcall TDMod::DModCreate(TObject *Sender)
{
    DirNamesTable->Open();
    FileNamesTable->Open();
    DiskNamesTable->Open();
    DiskTypeTable->Open();
```

continues

Listing 24.4. continued

```
}

void TDMod::CascadingDelete(void)
{
  DirNamesTable->First();
  DeleteFileNames->Prepare();
  while (!DirNamesTable->Eof)
  {
    DeleteFileNames->ExecSQL();
    DirNamesTable->Delete();
  }
  FileNamesTable->Refresh();

  DirNamesTable->Refresh();

  int i = DiskNamesTableCode->Value;
  DeleteDiskNames->Params->Items[0]->AsInteger = i;
  DeleteDiskNames->ExecSQL();
  DiskNamesTable->Refresh();
}
```

Listing 24.5. The header for the DiskArchive form.

```
/////////////////////////////////////
// DiskArchive.h
// SearchDirs
// Copyright (c) 1997 by Charlie Calvert
//
#ifndef DiskArchiveH
#define DiskArchiveH
#include <vcl\Classes.hpp>
#include <vcl\Controls.hpp>
#include <vcl\StdCtrls.hpp>
#include <vcl\Forms.hpp>
#include <vcl\DBGrids.hpp>
#include <vcl\Grids.hpp>
#include <vcl\ExtCtrls.hpp>
#include <vcl\DBCtrls.hpp>
#include <vcl\Buttons.hpp>

class TArchiveForm : public TForm
{
__published:
  TDBGrid *DBGrid1;
  TPanel *Panel1;
  TDBNavigator *DBNavigator1;
  TBitBtn *BitBtn1;
private:
public:
  virtual __fastcall TArchiveForm(TComponent* Owner);
};

extern TArchiveForm *ArchiveForm;

#endif
```

Listing 24.6. The `DiskArchive` form. This form is used only for displaying data. It has no custom code.

```cpp
/////////////////////////////////////
// DiskArchive.cpp
// SearchDirs
// Copyright (c) 1997 by Charlie Calvert
//
#include <vcl\vcl.h>
#pragma hdrstop
#include "DiskArchive.h"
#include "FindDirsDMod.h"
#pragma resource "*.dfm"

TArchiveForm *ArchiveForm;

__fastcall TArchiveForm::TArchiveForm(TComponent* Owner)
    : TForm(Owner)
{
}
```

Listing 24.7. The header for the `TFindDirs` components.

```cpp
/////////////////////////////////////
// FindDirs2.h
// SearchDirs
// Copyright (c) 1997 by Charlie Calvert
//
#ifndef FindDirs2H
#define FindDirs2H
#ifndef ComCtrlsHPP
#include <vcl\ComCtrls.hpp>
#endif

struct TDirInfo
{
  TSearchRec SearchRec;
  AnsiString CurDirectory;
};

class TDirStack : public TList
{
public:
  TDirStack(): TList() {};
  void Push(TDirInfo *DirInfo);
  TDirInfo *Pop();
};

typedef void __fastcall (__closure *TFoundDirEvent)(AnsiString NewDir);

class TFindDirs : public TComponent
{
private:
  #ifdef DEBUG_FIND_DIRS
  FILE *fp;
```

continues

Listing 24.7. continued

```
  #endif
  AnsiString FStartString;     // Unchanged string passed in by user.
  AnsiString FFileExt;
  AnsiString FStartDir;        // The directory where the search starts
  AnsiString FCurDirectory;    // the current directory
  AnsiString FFileMask;        // The file mask of files to search for
  AnsiString FSearchString;    // Combine last three into a search string
  TDirStack *FDirStack;        // Stack of directories in the current dir
  TFoundDirEvent FOnFoundDir;
  TFoundDirEvent FOnFoundFile;
  void GetAllFiles(AnsiString *StartDir);
  void FoundAFile(TSearchRec *FileData);
  void FoundADir(TSearchRec *FileData);
  void __fastcall Initialize(void);
  void SetupSearchString();
  void GetNextDirectory();
  BOOL SetupFirstDirectory();
protected:
  __fastcall virtual ~TFindDirs();
  virtual void ProcessFile(TSearchRec FileData, AnsiString FileName);
  virtual void ProcessDir(TSearchRec FileData, AnsiString DirName);
  virtual void __fastcall SetStartString(AnsiString AStartString);
public:
  virtual __fastcall TFindDirs(TComponent *AOwner)
    : TComponent(AOwner) { FDirStack = NULL; FOnFoundDir = NULL; }
  virtual __fastcall TFindDirs(TComponent *AOwner, AnsiString AStartString);
  virtual void Run(void);
  __property AnsiString StartDir = {read = FStartDir};
  __property AnsiString CurDirectory = {read = FCurDirectory};
__published:
  __property AnsiString StartString={read=FStartString, write=SetStartString};
  __property TFoundDirEvent OnFoundFile={read=FOnFoundFile, write=FOnFoundFile};
  __property TFoundDirEvent OnFoundDirf={read=FOnFoundDir, write=FOnFoundDir};
};

class TFindDirsList : public TFindDirs
{
private:
  TStringList *FFileList;
  TStringList *FDirList;
protected:
  __fastcall virtual ~TFindDirsList();
  virtual void ProcessFile(TSearchRec FileData, AnsiString FileName);
  virtual void ProcessDir(TSearchRec FileData, AnsiString DirName);
public:
  virtual __fastcall TFindDirsList(TComponent *AOwner): TFindDirs(AOwner) {}
  virtual __fastcall TFindDirsList(TComponent *AOwner, AnsiString AStartString);
__published:
  __property TStringList *FileList = {read = FFileList, nodefault};
  __property TStringList *DirList = {read = FDirList, nodefault};
};

  #endif
```

Listing 24.8. The main source file for the `TFindDirs` component.

```cpp
//////////////////////////////////////
// FindDirs2.cpp
// SearchDirs
// Copyright (c) 1997 by Charlie Calvert
//
#include <vcl\vcl.h>
#include <vcl\ComCtrls.hpp>
#pragma hdrstop
#include "FindDirs2.h"


// -- TDirStack ----------------

void TDirStack::Push(TDirInfo *DirInfo)
{
  Add(DirInfo);
}

TDirInfo *TDirStack::Pop()
{
  void *Temp = Items[0];
  Delete(0);
  return (TDirInfo *)Temp;
}

// -- TFindDirs ----------------

__fastcall TFindDirs::TFindDirs(TComponent *AOwner, AnsiString AStartString)
: TComponent(AOwner)
{
  SetStartString(AStartString); // Don't set data store directly!
  FDirStack = NULL;
  FOnFoundDir = NULL;
}

void __fastcall TFindDirs::SetStartString(AnsiString AStartString)
{
  FStartString = AStartString;
  FStartDir = ExtractFilePath(FStartString);
  FFileExt = ExtractFileExt(FStartString);
}

void __fastcall TFindDirs::Initialize(void)
{
  #ifdef DEBUG_FIND_DIRS
  if ((fp = fopen("c:\searchdirs.txt", "w+")) == NULL)
  {
    ShowMessage("Can't open debug file");
  }
  #endif
  if (FDirStack)
    delete FDirStack;
  FDirStack = new TDirStack;
```

continues

Listing 24.8. continued

```
  FCurDirectory = "";
  FFileMask = "*.*";
  #ifdef DEBUG_FIND_DIRS
  fprintf(fp, "%s %s %s \n", FStartDir.c_str(), FFileMask.c_str(),
FFileExt.c_str());
  #endif
}

__fastcall TFindDirs::~TFindDirs()
{
  #ifdef DEBUG_FIND_DIRS
  fclose(fp);
  #endif
}

void TFindDirs::ProcessFile(TSearchRec FileData, AnsiString FileName)
{
  if (FOnFoundFile != NULL)
    FOnFoundFile(FileName);
  #ifdef DEBUG_FIND_DIRS
  fprintf(fp, "File found: %s\n", FileName);
  #endif
}

void TFindDirs::ProcessDir(TSearchRec FileData, AnsiString DirName)
{
  if (FOnFoundDir != NULL)
    FOnFoundDir(DirName);
  #ifdef DEBUG_FIND_DIRS
  fprintf(fp, "Dir found: %s\n", DirName);
  #endif
}

void TFindDirs::FoundADir(TSearchRec *FileData)
{
  AnsiString FullName;
  #ifdef DEBUG_FIND_DIRS
  fprintf(fp, "Dir found: %s\n", FileData->Name);
  #endif
  if ((FileData->Name != ".") &&
      (FileData->Name != ".."))
  {
    TDirInfo *DirInfo = new TDirInfo;
    DirInfo->CurDirectory = AnsiString(FCurDirectory + FileData->Name + "\\");
    DirInfo->SearchRec = *FileData;
    #ifdef DEBUG_FIND_DIRS
    fprintf(fp, "DirInfo: %s\n", DirInfo->SearchRec.Name);
    fflush(fp);
    #endif
    FDirStack->Push(DirInfo);
  }
}

////////////////////////////////////
// FoundAFile
////////////////////////////////////
```

```
void TFindDirs::FoundAFile(TSearchRec *FileData)
{
  AnsiString FullName;

  if ((FFileExt == ".*") ||
      (UpperCase(ExtractFileExt(FileData->Name)) == UpperCase(FFileExt)))
  {
    FullName = FStartDir + FCurDirectory + FileData->Name;
    ProcessFile(*FileData, FullName);
  }
}

/////////////////////////////////////////
// GetAllFiles
/////////////////////////////////////////
void TFindDirs::GetAllFiles(AnsiString *StartDir)
{
  TSearchRec FileData;
  int Info;

  Info = FindFirst(StartDir->c_str(), faDirectory, FileData);
  while (Info == 0)
  {
    if (FileData.Attr == faDirectory)
      FoundADir(&FileData);
    else
      FoundAFile(&FileData);
    Info = FindNext(FileData);
  }
  FindClose(&FileData.FindData);
}

/////////////////////////////////////////
// SetupSearchString
/////////////////////////////////////////
void TFindDirs::SetupSearchString()
{
  FSearchString = FStartDir + FCurDirectory + FFileMask;
  #ifdef DEBUG_FIND_DIRS
  fprintf(fp, "FSearchString: %s \n", FSearchString);
  #endif
}

/////////////////////////////////////////
// GetNextDirectory
/////////////////////////////////////////
void TFindDirs::GetNextDirectory()
{
  TDirInfo *FDirInfo = FDirStack->Pop();
  FCurDirectory = FDirInfo->CurDirectory;
  #ifdef DEBUG_FIND_DIRS
  fprintf(fp, "Next Directory: %s\n", FCurDirectory);
  fflush(fp);
  #endif
  ProcessDir(FDirInfo->SearchRec, FStartDir + FCurDirectory);
  delete FDirInfo;
}
```

24

CREATING
NON-VISUAL
COMPONENTS

continues

Listing 24.8. continued

```cpp
BOOL TFindDirs::SetupFirstDirectory()
{
  TSearchRec FileData;
  AnsiString SearchStr = FStartDir + FFileMask;

  int Info = FindFirst(SearchStr.c_str(), faDirectory, FileData);
  FindClose(&FileData.FindData);
  if (Info == 0)
  {
    TDirInfo *DirInfo = new TDirInfo;
    DirInfo->CurDirectory = FCurDirectory;
    FileData.Name = FStartDir;
    DirInfo->SearchRec = FileData;
    FDirStack->Push(DirInfo);
    return TRUE;
  }
  else
    return FALSE;
}

////////////////////////////////////////
// Run: FindFilesAndDirs
////////////////////////////////////////
void TFindDirs::Run(void)
{
  BOOL FDone = False;
  BOOL FirstTime = TRUE;

  Initialize();

  if (!SetupFirstDirectory())
  {
    ShowMessage("Invalid Search String");
    return;
  }

  while (!FDone)
  {
    SetupSearchString();
    if (!FirstTime)
      GetAllFiles(&FSearchString);
    if (FDirStack->Count > 0)
      GetNextDirectory();
    else
      FDone = True;
    FirstTime = FALSE;
  }
  FDirStack->Free();
  FDirStack = NULL;
}

////////////////////////////////////////
// TFindDirsList ////////////////////////
////////////////////////////////////////

__fastcall TFindDirsList::TFindDirsList(TComponent *AOwner,
  AnsiString AStartDir): TFindDirs(AOwner, AStartDir)
```

```
{
  FFileList = new TStringList;
  FFileList->Sorted = True;
  FDirList = new TStringList;
  FDirList->Sorted = True;
}

__fastcall TFindDirsList::~TFindDirsList()
{
  FFileList->Free();
  FDirList->Free();
}

void TFindDirsList::ProcessFile(TSearchRec FileData, AnsiString FileName)
{
  FFileList->Add(FileName);
}

void TFindDirsList::ProcessDir(TSearchRec FileData, AnsiString DirName)
{
  FDirList->Add(DirName);
}

namespace Finddirs2
{
  void __fastcall Register()
  {
    TComponentClass classes[2] = {__classid(TFindDirs),
      __classid(TFindDirsList)};
    RegisterComponents("Unleash", classes, 1);
  }
}
```

The database aspects of this program are important. You will find the files used by the program in the Data directory on the CD that ships with this book. As I explain in the readme file that accompanies the CD, you should set up an alias called CUnleashed that points to these files. Needless to say, you should recreate the data directory on your hard drive, and should not use the read-only directory found on the CD, but should make sure they've been copied onto your hard drive. The DatabaseName for the TDatabase object used in my version of the program contains the string FileData, so you might get an error about that alias if you try to run the program. However, you do not want to try to fix the FileData alias, rather the one called CUnleashed. The data module for the program is shown in Figure 24.2.

To use the program, first point it to a subdirectory on your hard disk. Then type in a file mask in the edit control at the top of the form. For example, you might type in c:\temp*.cpp or simply c:\temp*.*. Be sure to type in the file mask. It would cause an error if you typed I:\ instead of I:*.*. (In general, the program is not robust enough to check for many user errors.) When you click the button at the bottom of the program, the code iterates through all the directories beneath the one you pointed to and finds all the files that have the extension you designated. The program then places these files in a list database.

FIGURE 24.2.

*The data module for
the SearchDirs
program.*

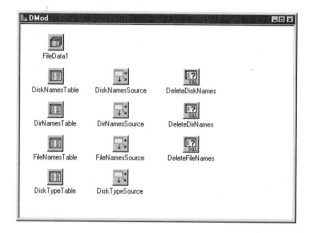

> **NOTE**
>
> I tested the TFindDirs component fairly extensively. For instance, I aimed it at the root of my C drive, which contains 1.12GB of space, with all but about 100MB used. The program ran fine against the thousands of files on that drive. I also aimed the component at nested directories containing long filenames, and again it handled the challenge without incident.
>
> One problem I have had with the component involves sharing violations. If the SearchDirs program is iterating through a series of files, and one of which is locked by the file system, then the TFindDirs component will probably raise a rather unsightly access violation. Check the CD and my Web site to see if I have come up with a fix for this problem. In the meantime, you should make sure other programs are closed before running the SearchDirs program, or be sure to aim the program at drives that do not have open files on them.
>
> Note that running the SearchDirs program against huge drives will create truly monolithic Paradox files containing lists of the files found during the search. For instance, after running against my C drive, the main DB file and its index were both more than 9MB in size. I have not tested the program to see what would happen if I ran out of disk space for the DB file during a run of the program.

To use the FindDirs component, you need do nothing more than assign it a string containing the file mask you want to use. You can do so via a property in the Object Inspector; you can insert the information at runtime:

```
if (MessageBox((HWND)Handle, Edit1->Text.c_str(), "Make Run?", MB_YESNO) ==
ID_YES)
  {

  FindDirs1->StartString = Edit1->Text;
  FindDirs1->Run();
  }
```

That's all you have to do to use the component, other than respond to events when files or directories are found. You can set up these event handlers automatically, as described in the next section.

Iterating Through Directories with `TFindDirs`

The SearchDirs program uses the `TFindDirs` component to iterate through directories. The `TFindDirs` component sends events to your program whenever a new directory or a new file is found. The events include the name of the new directory or file, as well as information about the size and date of the files the component finds. You can respond to these events in any way you want. For example, this program stores the names in a Paradox file.

> **NOTE**
>
> The SearchDirs program tends to create huge database files fairly quickly. The main problem here is that I need to store long filenames, which means I need to set aside large fields in the table. This problem is severe enough that I am going to eventually need to come up with some kind of custom solution to storing these strings. For now, however, I am just living with some very big DB files on my hard drive.
>
> One possible solution to this problem would be to save all the information from a directory in a `TStringList` and then save the `TStringList` as a single string, which is one of the capabilities of this object. I could then save the whole string in a single blob field, which would make a better use of space. When I want to display the directory to a user, I could ask the `TStringList` to read the string in again and store it in a `TMemoryStream`.

The SearchDirs program responds as follows when a file with the proper extension is found:

```
void __fastcall TForm1::FindDirs1FoundFile(AnsiString NewDir)
{
  AnsiString Temp;

  if (FCurrentRoot.Length() == 0)
    Temp = FindDirs1->StartDir;
  else
    Temp = FCurrentRoot;
  DMod->FileNamesTable->Insert();
  DMod->FileNamesTable->FieldByName("Directory")->AsString = Temp;
  DMod->FileNamesTable->FieldByName("FileName")->AsString =
    ExtractFileName(NewDir);
  DMod->FileNamesTable->Post();
}
```

As you can see, the code does nothing more than shove the filename in a table.

To set up this method, you merely have to click the `TFindDirs` `OnFoundFile` event in the Object Inspector. The `OnFoundFile` and `OnFoundDir` events of `TFindDirs` are of type `TFoundDirEvent`:

```
typedef void __fastcall (__closure *TFoundDirEvent)(AnsiString NewDir);
```

I created two private events for TFindDirs that are of this type:

```
TFoundDirEvent FOnFoundDir;
TFoundDirEvent FOnFoundFile;
```

I then make these events into published properties that can be seen in the Object Inspector:

```
__property TFoundDirEvent OnFoundFile={read=FOnFoundFile, write=FOnFoundFile};
__property TFoundDirEvent OnFoundDirf={read=FOnFoundDir, write=FOnFoundDir};
```

If you're unclear about what is happening here, study the code in FindDirs2.h, or turn to the section about creating and using events covered in depth in Chapter 4, "Events."

If you have events like this one set up, then you need merely to click them in the Object Inspector, and the outline for your code will be created for you automatically. The following, for example, is the code BCB will produce if you click the OnFoundDir event:

```
void __fastcall TForm1::FindDirs1FoundFile(AnsiString NewDir)
{
}
```

The great thing about events is that they not only save you time when you're typing, but they also help to show how to use the component. After you see a method like FindDirs1FoundFile, you don't have to worry about going to the online help to find out how to get the directories found by the component! What you're supposed to do is obvious.

The following code in FoundDirs2.cpp calls the event handlers:

```
void TFindDirs::ProcessDir(TSearchRec FileData, AnsiString DirName)
{
  if (FOnFoundDir != NULL)
    FOnFoundDir(DirName);
  #ifdef DEBUG_FIND_DIRS
  fprintf(fp, "Dir found: %s\n", DirName);
  #endif
}
```

This code checks to see whether the FOnFoundDir event is set to NULL. If it is not, the event is called.

NOTE

Notice that the code for the ProcessDir method uses conditional compilation to leave you the option of writing debug output to a file. I used this code when I was creating the unit. My goal was to find a way to write out a list of the directories and files found during a run of the program. I could then study the list to make sure my algorithm was working correctly.

Layering Your Objects

TFindDirs has a descendant object called TFindDirsList. Part of the built-in functionality of the TFindDirsList unit is to maintain lists of the files it finds. After you finish searching all the directories, the list is ready for you to do with as you want. This list is kept in a TStringList object, so you can just assign it to the Items property in a list box, as shown in this code excerpt:

```
ListBox1->Items = FileIterator1->FileList;
```

This idea of layering your components so that you can create different objects, descending from different parents, under different circumstances, is key to object-oriented design. You don't want to push too much functionality up too high in the object hierarchy; otherwise, you will be forced to rewrite the object to get access to a subset of its functionality. For example, if the BCB developers had not created a TDataSet component but had instead created one component called TTable, they would have had to duplicate that same functionality in the TQuery component. This approach is wasteful. The smart thing to do is to build a component called TDataSet and end its functionality at the point at which the specific attributes of TQuery and TTable need to be defined. That way, TQuery and TTable can both reuse the functionality of TDataSet rather than have to rewrite that same functionality for both objects.

Before I close this section, let me reiterate some key points. The TFindDirs object is the brains of this particular operation. It knows how to iterate through directories, how to find all the files in each directory, and how to notify the user when new directories or files are found. The SearchDirs program is just a wrapper around this core functionality.

Iterating Through Directories

The task of iterating through directories has a simple recursive solution. However, recursion is a slow and time-consuming technique that is also wasteful of stack space. As a result, TFindDirs creates its own stacks and pushes the directories it finds onto them.

> **NOTE**
>
> BCB includes some built-in tools for creating stacks and lists. For example, the TList and TStringList objects are available. I use these tools here because they are simple objects specific to the VCL. Another alternative would have been to use the STL.

You can find the following objects in FindDirs2.h:

TDirInfo: This simple structure keeps track of the current directory and of the complete set of information describing a particular file.

TDirStack: I need a place to push each directory after I find it. That leaves me free to iterate through all the files in the directory first and then go back and pop each subdirectory off the stack when I am free to examine it.

TFindDirs: This object provides the ability to iterate through directories.

TFindDirsList: This object adds TStringList objects to TFindDirs. These objects are accessible as properties, and they are maintained automatically by the object. I do not use the TFindDirsList object in the SearchDirs example. However, you'll find it very helpful when you're experimenting with these objects on your own.

To dust off the classic analogy used in these situations, the stacks implemented here are like piles of plates in a kitchen cabinet. You can put one plate down and then add another one to it. When you need one of the plates, you take the first one off either the top or the bottom, depending on whether it's a FIFO or a LIFO stack. Putting a new plate on the top of a stack is called *pushing* the object onto the stack, and removing a plate is called *popping* the object off the stack. For more information on stacks, refer to any book on basic programming theory. Books that cover the STL (Standard Template Library) in depth also usually cover this subject in the process.

Look at the implementation of the following FIFO stack:

```
void TDirStack::Push(TDirInfo *DirInfo)
{
  Add(DirInfo);
}
TDirInfo *TDirStack::Pop()
{
  void *Temp = Items[0];
  Delete(0);
  return (TDirInfo *)Temp;
}
```

The code is so simple because it is built on top of the TList object that is part of the VCL:

```
class TDirStack : public TList
{
public:
  TDirStack(): TList() {};
  void Push(TDirInfo *DirInfo);
  TDirInfo *Pop();
};
```

One look at this simple code, and you can see why I was drawn to the TList object rather than the STL. If I had had any doubt in my mind, then, of course, I would have turned to the VCL, because this book is about BCB, not about the Standard Template Library.

Using FindFirst, FindNext, and FindClose

In this section, I continue the examination of the stacks created in the TFindDirs units. The cores of these stacks are the calls to FindFirst, FindNext, and FindClose that search through directories looking for particular files.

Using FindFirst, FindNext, and FindClose is like typing DIR in a directory at the DOS prompt. FindFirst finds the first file in the directory, and FindNext finds the remaining files. You should call FindClose when you're finished with the process. FindFirst and the others are found in the SysUtils unit.

These calls enable you to specify a directory and file mask, as if you were issuing a command of the following type at the DOS prompt:

```
dir c:\aut*.bat
```

This command would, of course, show all files beginning with aut and ending in .bat. This particular command would typically find AUTOEXEC.BAT and perhaps one or two other files.

When you call FindFirst, you pass in three parameters:

```
extern int __fastcall FindFirst(const System::AnsiString Path,
                        int Attr, TSearchRec &F);
```

The first parameter contains the path and file mask that specify the files you want to find. For example, you might pass in "c:\\BCB\\include\\vcl*.hpp" in this parameter. The second parameter lists the type of files you want to see:

faReadOnly	0x01	Read-only files
faHidden	0x02	Hidden files
faSysFile	0x04	System files
faVolumeID	0x08	Volume ID files
faDirectory	0x10	Directory files
faArchive	0x20	Archive files
faAnyFile	0x3F	Any file

Most of the time, you should pass in faArchive in this parameter. However, if you want to see directories, pass in faDirectory. The Attribute parameter is not a filter. No matter what flags you use, you will always get all normal files in the directory. Passing faDirectory causes directories to be included in the list of normal files; it does not limit the list to directories. You can use OR to concatenate several different fa*XXX* constants, if you want. The final parameter is a variable of type TSearchRec, which is declared as follows:

```
struct TSearchRec {
  int Time;
  int Size;
```

```
    int Attr;
    System::AnsiString Name;
    int ExcludeAttr;
    int FindHandle;
    WIN32_FIND_DATAA FindData; };
```

The most important value in TSearchRec is the Name field, which on success specifies the name of the file found. FindFirst returns zero if it finds a file and nonzero if the call fails. However, I rely heavily on the FindData portion of the record. FindData is the original structure passed back from the operating system. The rest of the fields are derived from it and are presented here in this form so as to present a simple, easy-to-use interface to VCL programmers.

WIN32_FIND_DATA looks like this:

```
typedef struct _WIN32_FIND_DATA { // wfd
    DWORD dwFileAttributes;
    FILETIME ftCreationTime;
    FILETIME ftLastAccessTime;
    FILETIME ftLastWriteTime;
    DWORD    nFileSizeHigh;
    DWORD    nFileSizeLow;
    DWORD    dwReserved0;
    DWORD    dwReserved1;
    TCHAR    cFileName[ MAX_PATH ];
    TCHAR    cAlternateFileName[ 14 ];
} WIN32_FIND_DATA;
```

FindNext works exactly like FindFirst, except that you have to pass in only a variable of type TSearchRec because it is assumed that the mask and file attribute are the same. Once again, FindNext returns zero if all goes well, and a nonzero value if it can't find a file. You should call FindClose after completing a FindFirst/FindNext sequence.

Given this information, here is a simple way to call FindFirst, FindNext, and FindClose:

```
void TFindDirs::GetAllFiles(AnsiString *StartDir)
{
  TSearchRec FileData;
  int Info;
  Info = FindFirst(StartDir->c_str(), faDirectory, FileData);
  while (Info == 0)
  {
    if (FileData.Attr == faDirectory)
      FoundADir(&FileData);
    else
      FoundAFile(&FileData);
    Info = FindNext(FileData);
  }
  FindClose(&FileData.FindData);
}
```

That's all I'm going to say about the basic structure of the TFindDirs object. As I said earlier, you can learn more about stacks by studying a book on basic programming data structures. This book, however, is about BCB, so I'm going to move on to a discussion of creating event handlers.

Summary

The SearchDirs program, along with the `TFindDirs` component, points the way toward an understanding of BCB's greatest strengths. `TFindDirs` is not a particularly difficult piece of code, but it is sufficiently complex to highlight the fact that you can place almost any kind of logic inside a BCB object. If you want to write multimedia code, or code that enables conversations on a network or simulates the behavior of a submarine, you can write a BCB component or set of components that will encapsulate the logic needed to reach your goal. More importantly, these components can then be placed on the Component Palette and dropped onto a form where they can easily be manipulated through the Object Inspector. Objects help you hide complexity and help you reuse code.

The Object Inspector—and its related property editors and component editors—provide an elegant, easy-to-use interface to any object. Component architectures represent one of the most important tools in programming today, and BCB has by far the best implementation of a component architecture currently available in the C++ market. In fact, the VCL is several orders of magnitude better at creating components than any other existing Windows-based technology.

V

PART

Internet and Distributed OLE

Using WININET to Create FTP Applications

IN THIS CHAPTER

Overview

In this chapter, you will look at techniques for building FTP clients. Most of the chapter will be dedicated to a discussion of WININET, which is a relatively simple Windows API for creating FTP, Gopher, and HTTP applications. This API is especially appealing because it is built into the operating system, ships with all versions of Windows after Windows NT 4.0, and allows you to create small, fast applications. If you don't have `WININET.DLL` on your system, you can download it for free from Microsoft's Web site. It works with all 32-bit versions of Windows.

I will also briefly discuss the FTP ActiveX component that ships with BCB. The FTP component provides a wide range of services that are easily accessible. However, it is not as light, nor as flexible, a tool as WININET.

A standard FTP component wrapped around WININET will be the central focus of this chapter. As a result, you will get a chance to take another look at building components. Included in the chapter will be some discussion about how to create components that are easy to use.

Another topic I touch on in this chapter is how to make an owner draw list box. This subject comes up in the course of creating an application that can display the files shown in an FTP directory search.

Requirements

BCB ships with `WININET.h` in the `Include\Win32` directory. `WININET.h` contains manifests, functions, types, and prototypes for the Microsoft Windows Internet extensions. Therefore, you can now easily add FTP, Gopher, and HTTP support to your programs. Microsoft's `WININET.DLL` is freely distributable, and is available from Microsoft if it is not already installed in your `Windows/System` or `Windows/System32` directory. Windows NT 4.0 ships with `WININET.DLL`, as will Windows 97. `WININET.DLL` runs fine on Windows 95.

One of the best places to get help on this subject is in the ActiveX SDK that ships as part of the MSDN and that has frequently been available for downloading from `www.microsoft.com`. Here is how, at the time of this writing, to get the Windows help file for `WININET.h`:

`http://www.microsoft.com/intdev/sdk/docs/WININET/default.htm`

In general, the INTDEV section of the Microsoft Web site is home ground for MS Internet developers.

> **NOTE**
>
> When working with `WININET.h`, you might find that you need to edit some of the code in the file. You should try simply including the file in your project first, and if you have problems, then consider making the following changes.

If you come across a #pragma pack, you can replace it with the pshpack4.h file:

```
// #pragma pack(push, WININET, 4)
#include <pshpack4.h>
```

At the end of the file, you will have to make the following substitutions:

```
// #pragma pack(pop, WININET)
#include <poppack.h>
```

You will need an FTP server of some kind to be able to use this control. Windows NT 4.0 comes with an excellent server, or you can usually download the Personal Web Server from the Microsoft Web site or get it with a copy of FrontPage. Personal Web Server supports FTP and ISAPI, and it runs on Windows 95. I have heard numerous complaints about the Personal Web Server's robustness. These may or may not be well founded, but there is no denying the usefulness of the tool when you are developing an application on a Win95 machine. If need be, you can copy your finished files to a more robust server after you complete the development cycle.

Making Sure FTP Is Working on Your System

If you're connected to the Internet, you should be able to FTP into various sites. For example, to connect to the Borland FTP site, type the following at the command prompt:

```
ftp ftp.borland.com
```

When the system asks for a username, type in anonymous. When it requests a password, type in your e-mail address. Figure 25.1 shows a screen shot of a typical old-fashioned, command-line-based FTP session.

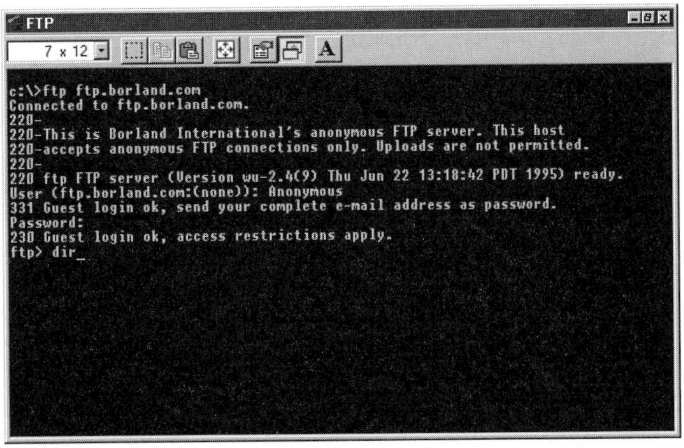

FIGURE 25.1.

FTP from the command line. This chapter will show how to do the same thing in a Windows program that uses graphical controls.

25

USING WININET

If you can't FTP into `borland.com`, `microsoft.com`, or some site on your intranet, something is wrong with your Windows setup. You should clear up that problem first, before tackling the material in this chapter. I provide some help in this regard in Chapter 8, "Database Basics and Database Tools," in the section called "Some Notes on Installing TCP/IP."

Figure 25.2 shows a commercial program that works from inside Windows. The program you will create in this chapter, called WININET, is not quite this fancy, but it does allow you to use standard Windows controls to make and maintain your connections. FTPWININET has provisions for copying files from and to FTP sites, and for using the mouse to navigate through directories.

FIGURE 25.2.

An example of a shareware FTP program logging onto the Borland FTP site.

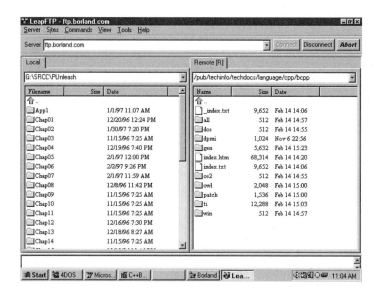

FTP Using WININET

Now you're ready to look at the code needed to use the WININET DLL in an FTP session. This study will not be exhaustive, but it should help to get you up and running. The first fact you need to know about this technology is that some of the functions in `WININET.h` return a pointer variable declared to be of type `HINTERNET`:

```
typedef LPVOID HINTERNET;
```

This pointer acts as a handle to the various Internet services you employ. After retrieving the handle, you will pass it in as the first parameter to many of the other WININET functions you call throughout the life of a single session.

You need to remember to return the handle to the system when you're through using it, usually by calling the WININET function called `InternetCloseHandle`:

```
BOOL InternetCloseHandle(
  HINTERNET hInet  // Valid Internet handle to be closed.
);
```

> **NOTE**
>
> Just hearing this much information should tip you off to the fact that you ought to have an object to use this material and should consider creating a component. The tip-off here is the need to perform housekeeping chores with pointers.
>
> I no longer believe in trying to write complex cleanup code on-the-fly. Most of the time I remember to deallocate memory that I have allocated, and I almost always remember to allocate memory before trying to use it. However, computers aren't very considerate about human weaknesses, even infrequent weaknesses. You want to get these things right all the time, and almost just isn't good enough!
>
> Possible solutions involve using a language such as Java or Visual Basic. These languages generally take allocation chores out of your hands. Of course, you almost always have to pay a price for using tools of that kind, and it generally involves a severe performance penalty. If you want speed and flexibility, working in a language such as C++ is always better.
>
> Objects and components are the tools you can use to make C++ safe. If you build an object properly, it will always take care of chores such as allocating and deallocating memory for you. You get the job done right once or find someone who has done it right once, and then you can reuse the object over and over without concern for petty housekeeping chores.
>
> The key point to absorb is that some developers, myself included, believe that almost any moderately complicated chore that involves allocating and deallocating handles is a strong candidate for wrapping in an object. Even better, put the code in a component; then there is almost no chance you will misuse it. The great thing about BCB components is that they are only marginally larger than regular objects, and they're every bit as fast.

In the next few pages, you will learn how to create a component that wraps the FTP calls found in WININET. I will present the WININET calls to you at the same time that I slowly construct the pieces of a component called `TMyFTP`.

Using `InternetOpen`

To get a WININET session started, you call `InternetOpen`:

```
HINTERNET InternetOpen(
    LPCTSTR lpszAgent,        // Name of app opening the session
```

```
    DWORD dwAccessType,        // The access type, usually set to 0
    LPCTSTR lpszProxyName,     // For use in specifying a proxy, pass 0
    LPCTSTR lpszProxyBypass,   // For use in specifying a proxy, pass NULL
    DWORD dwFlags              // You can set up a callback here.
);
```

The first parameter is the name of the application opening the session. You can pass in any string you want in this parameter. Microsoft documentation states "This name is used as the user agent in the HTTP protocol." The remaining parameters can be set to 0 or NULL.

The following are some options for use in the dwAccessType parameter:

LOCAL_INTERNET_ACCESS	Connects only to local Internet sites.
GATEWAY_INTERNET_ACCESS	Allows connections to any site on the Web.
CERN_PROXY_INTERNET_ACCESS	Uses a CERN proxy to access the Web.

Here are the options as they appear in WININET.h:

```
#define INTERNET_OPEN_TYPE_PRECONFIG   0   // use registry configuration
#define INTERNET_OPEN_TYPE_DIRECT      1   // direct to net
#define INTERNET_OPEN_TYPE_PROXY       3   // via named proxy
#define PRE_CONFIG_INTERNET_ACCESS         INTERNET_OPEN_TYPE_PRECONFIG
#define LOCAL_INTERNET_ACCESS              INTERNET_OPEN_TYPE_DIRECT
#define GATEWAY_INTERNET_ACCESS        2   // Internet via gateway
#define CERN_PROXY_INTERNET_ACCESS         INTERNET_OPEN_TYPE_PROXY
```

As you can see, passing in zero means that you will use information already stored in the Registry. The rest of the parameters are involved with setting up a proxy server, except for the last one, which can be used to set up a callback if you need it. The last parameter has only one possible flag:

```
INTERNET_FLAG_ASYNC
```

Refer to the Microsoft documentation for additional information.

Here is an example of a typical call to InternetOpen:

```
FINet = InternetOpen("WININET1", 0, NULL, 0, 0);
```

Using InternetConnect

After you open the session, the next step is to connect to the server using InternetConnect:

```
HINTERNET InternetConnect(
    HINTERNET hInternetSession,  // Handle from InternetOpen
    LPCTSTR lpszServerName,      // Server: e.g., www.borland.com
    INTERNET_PORT nServerPort,   // Usually 0
    LPCTSTR lpszUsername,        // usually anonymous
    LPCTSTR lpszPassword,        // usually your email address
    DWORD dwService,             // FTP, HTTP, or Gopher?
    DWORD dwFlags,               // Usually 0
    DWORD dwContext              // User defined number for callback
);
```

Here are the three possible self-explanatory and mutually exclusive flags that can be passed in the `dwService` parameter:

```
INTERNET_SERVICE_FTP
INTERNET_SERVICE_GOPHER
INTERNET_SERVICE_HTTP
```

Here is the option for the `dwFlags` parameter:

```
INTERNET_CONNECT_FLAG_PASSIVE
```

This option is valid only if you passed `INTERNET_SERVICE_FTP` in the previous parameter. At this time, no other flags are valid for this parameter.

If the session succeeds, `InternetOpen` returns a valid pointer; otherwise, it returns `NULL`. Remember that you will have to deallocate this memory later. Doing so in the destructor for an object that takes control of the entire FTP session is probably best.

Here are the two sections' methods in `TMyFTP` that use `InternetOpen` and `InternetConnect`:

```
__fastcall TMyFtp::TMyFtp(Classes::TComponent* AOwner)
: TComponent(AOwner)
{
  FCurFiles = new TStringList();
  FINet = InternetOpen("WinINet1", 0, NULL, 0, 0);
}
bool __fastcall TMyFtp::Connect(void)
{
  AnsiString S;
  AnsiString CR1("\x00D\x00A");
  FContext = 255;
  FFtpHandle = InternetConnect(FINet, FServer.c_str(), 0,
   FUserID.c_str(), FPassword.c_str(),
   INTERNET_SERVICE_FTP, 0, FContext);
  if (FFtpHandle == NULL)
  {
    S = "Connection failed" + CR1 +
        "Server: " + FServer + CR1 +
        "UserID: " + FUserID + CR1 +
        "Password: " + FPassword;
    ShowMessage(S);
    return FALSE;
  }
  else
    SetUpNewDir();
  return TRUE;
}
```

Besides calling `InternetOpen`, the constructor also allocates memory for a `TStringList`. This list will be used to hold the names of the files in the directories visited by the FTP session. The connect method provides code that pops up a message explaining exactly what went wrong in case of error. This function would probably be stronger if it contained exception-handling code:

```
void __fastcall TMyFtp::Connect(void)
{
  AnsiString S;
```

```
AnsiString CR1("\x00D\x00A");
FContext = 255;
FFtpHandle = InternetConnect(FINet, FServer.c_str(), 0,
 FUserID.c_str(), FPassword.c_str(),
 INTERNET_SERVICE_FTP, 0, FContext);
if (FFtpHandle == NULL)
{
  S = "Connection failed" + CR1 +
        "Server: " + FServer + CR1 +
        "UserID: " + FUserID + CR1 +
        "Password: " + FPassword;
  throw Exception(S);
}
else
  SetUpNewDir();
}
```

The key difference to note about this new version of the function is that it does not return a value. You don't have to concern yourself with whether the function succeeds because none of the code after the exception is raised will be executed. Your program itself won't end, but you will automatically be popped out of the current process and sent back to the message loop if something goes wrong. The only way to stop that process is to catch the exception. As you learned in Chapter 5, "Exceptions," it is usually best not to try to handle the exception in a catch block, but instead to let the exception-handling process resolve the problem for you automatically.

When you call the Connect function, you might want to do so in a function that looks like this:

```
void __fastcall TForm1::ConnectBtnClick(TObject *Sender)
{
  if (FTPNames->GetConnectionData())
  {
    Application->ProcessMessages();
    Ftp->Server = FTPNames->Server;
    Ftp->UserID = FTPNames->UserID;
    Ftp->Password = FTPNames->Password;
    Screen->Cursor = TCursor(crHourGlass);
    Ftp->Connect();
    Screen->Cursor = TCursor(crDefault);
  }
}
```

The GetConnectionData function makes sure that the Server, UserID, and Password properties are filled in correctly. Notice that the function calls ProcessMessages to be sure that the screen is properly redrawn before handing control over to the system. Care is also taken to put up a cursor that asks the user to wait. Especially if something goes wrong, the system could take a minute or more to return from a call to InternetConnect. While you're waiting for the system to either time out or resolve the call, you want the screen to look right, and you want to tell users that all is well and that they should sit tight.

After Connecting

After you are connected, you can call the GetCurrentDirectory to retrieve the name of the current directory:

```
System::AnsiString __fastcall TMyFtp::GetCurrentDirectory(void)
{
  DWORD Len = 0;
  FtpGetCurrentDirectory(FFtpHandle, FCurDir.c_str(), &Len);
  FCurDir.SetLength(Len);
  FtpGetCurrentDirectory(FFtpHandle, FCurDir.c_str(), &Len);
  return FCurDir;
}
```

This function is declared as follows:

```
BOOL FtpGetCurrentDirectory(
    IN HINTERNET hFtpSession,              // handle from InternetConnect
    OUT LPCTSTR lpszCurrentDirectory,      // directory returned here
    IN OUT LPDWORD lpdwCurrentDirectory    // buf size of 2nd parameter
); // True on success
```

If you set the last parameter to zero, then WININET will use this parameter to return the length of the directory string. You can then allocate memory for your string and call the function a second time to retrieve the directory name. This process is shown earlier in the GetCurrentDirectory method. (Notice the call to SetLength. C++Builder requires that you allocate memory for the new long strings in situations like this. The issue here is that the string will be assigned a value inside the operating system, not inside your C++Builder application. As a result, C++Builder can't perform its usual surreptitious string allocations in these circumstances.)

The following set of functions returns the currently available files in a particular directory:

```
Classes::TStringList* __fastcall TMyFtp::FindFiles(void)
{
  WIN32_FIND_DATA FindData;
  HINTERNET FindHandle;
  AnsiString Temp;
  FCurFiles->Clear();
  FindHandle = FtpFindFirstFile(FFtpHandle, "*.*", &FindData, 0, 0);
  if (FindHandle == NULL)
  {
    return FCurFiles;
  }
  GetFindDataStr(FindData, &Temp);
  FCurFiles->Add(Temp);
  while (InternetFindNextFile(FindHandle, &FindData))
  {
    GetFindDataStr(FindData, &Temp);
    FCurFiles->Add(Temp);
  }
  InternetCloseHandle(FindHandle);
  return FCurFiles;
}
```

The key functions to notice here are FtpFindFirstFile, InternetFindNextFile, and InternetCloseHandle. You use these functions in a manner similar to that employed when calling the C++Builder functions FindFirst, FindNext, and FindClose. In particular, you use FtpFindFirstFile to get the first file in a directory. You then call InternetFindNextFile repeatedly, until the function returns False. After finishing the session, call InternetCloseHandle to inform the operating system that it can deallocate the memory associated with this process.

The following function returns a simple string designating what type of file is retrieved by a call to ftpFindFirstFile or InternetFindNextFile:

```
AnsiString *GetFindDataStr(WIN32_FIND_DATA FindData, AnsiString *S)
{
  AnsiString Temp;
  switch (FindData.dwFileAttributes)
  {
    case FILE_ATTRIBUTE_ARCHIVE:
    {
      *S = 'A';
      break;
    }
    case FILE_ATTRIBUTE_COMPRESSED:
      *S = 'C';
      break;
    case FILE_ATTRIBUTE_DIRECTORY:
      *S = 'D';
      break;
    case FILE_ATTRIBUTE_HIDDEN:
      *S = 'H';
      break;
    case FILE_ATTRIBUTE_NORMAL:
      *S = 'N';
      break;
    case FILE_ATTRIBUTE_READONLY:
      *S = 'R';
      break;
    case FILE_ATTRIBUTE_SYSTEM:
      *S = 'S';
      break;
    case FILE_ATTRIBUTE_TEMPORARY:
      *S = 'T';
      break;
    default:
      *S = IntToStr(FindData.dwFileAttributes);
  }
  *S = *S + GetDots(75);
  S->Insert(FindData.cFileName, 6);
  Temp = IntToStr(FindData.nFileSizeLow);
  S->Insert(Temp, 25);
  return S;
}
```

I use this information to create a simple string I can show to the user explaining the type of file currently under examination. For example, if I find a directory, the string might look like this:

```
D WINDOWS
```

If I find a file, the string might look like this:

```
F AUTOEXEC.BAT
```

One final note: Unlike the functions and structures mentioned in the preceding few paragraphs, WIN32_FIND_DATA is not defined in WININET.h, but instead can be found in WinBase.h and other standard Windows files. Detailed information on this structure is available in the WIN32 help file that ships with C++Builder. A second constant called TWin32FindData mapped to the same value is declared in the \include\vcl\Windows.hpp file that ships with C++Builder.

Retrieving a File

You can use the ftpGetFile function from WININET.h to retrieve a file via FTP:

```
BOOL FtpGetFile(
    IN HINTERNET hFtpSession, // Returned by InternetConnect
    IN LPCTSTR lpszRemoteFile, // File to get
    IN LPCTSTR lpszNewFile, // Where to put it on your PC
    IN BOOL fFailIfExists, // Overwrite existing files?
    IN DWORD dwFlagsAndAttributes, // File attribute-See CreateFile.
    IN DWORD dwFlags, // Binary or ASCII transfer
    IN DWORD dwContext// Usually zero
); // True on success
```

The following is an example of how to use this call:

```
bool __fastcall TMyFtp::GetFile(System::AnsiString FTPFile,  System::AnsiString
                                NewFile)
{
  return FtpGetFile(FFtpHandle, FTPFile.c_str(), NewFile.c_str(),
                  False, FILE_ATTRIBUTE_NORMAL,
                  FTP_TRANSFER_TYPE_BINARY, 0);
}
```

To learn about the parameters that can be passed in the dwFlagsAndAttributes parameter, look up CreateFile in the WIN32 help file that ships with C++Builder. The dwFlags parameter can be set to either FTP_TRANSFER_TYPE_BINARY or FTP_TRANSFER_TYPE_ASCII.

Sending Files to an FTP Server

When you're sending files to an NT site, remember that you probably don't have rights in the default FTP directory. Instead, you should change to another directory where your user has rights. You can usually configure what rights a particular user has on a server through the server-side tools provided for administrating user accounts.

This function copies a file to a server:

```
bool __fastcall TMyFtp::SendFile1(System::AnsiString FTPFile,
                                  System::AnsiString NewFile)
{
```

```
     DWORD Size = 3000;
     AnsiString S;
     BOOL Transfer = FtpPutFile(FFtpHandle,
                        FTPFile.c_str(),
                        NewFile.c_str(),
                        FTP_TRANSFER_TYPE_BINARY, 0);
   if (!Transfer)
   {
     int Error = GetLastError();
     S = Format("Error Number: %d. Hex: %x", OPENARRAY(TVarRec, (Error, Error)));
     ShowMessage(S);
     S.SetLength(Size);
     if (!InternetGetLastResponseInfo(&(DWORD)Error, S.c_str(), &Size))
     {
       Error = GetLastError();
       ShowMessage(Format("Error Number: %d. Hex: %x", OPENARRAY(TVarRec, (Error,
                                                         Error))));
     }
     ShowMessage(Format("Error Number: %d. Hex: %x Info: %s",
               OPENARRAY(TVarRec, (Error, Error, S))));
   }
   else
     ShowMessage("Success");

   return Transfer;
}
```

The core function looks like this:

```
BOOL Transfer = FtpPutFile(FFtpHandle,
                  FTPFile.c_str(),
                  NewFile.c_str(),
                  FTP_TRANSFER_TYPE_BINARY, 0);
```

`FtpPutFile` takes

- The session handle in the first parameter.
- The file to copy from your hard drive in the second parameter.
- The name the file will have on the server in the third parameter.
- Whether to conduct a binary or ASCII transfer in the fourth parameter.
- Information about the context of the transfer. You can usually set this parameter to zero.

The rest of the code in the `SendFile1` function is dedicated to error handling. Call `GetLastError` to retrieve the error code, and call `InternetGetLastResponseInfo` to retrieve a human-readable description of the error.

Deleting Files

The act of deleting a file on a server is extremely simple:

```
bool __fastcall TMyFtp::DeleteFile(System::AnsiString S)
{
```

```
    return FtpDeleteFile(FFtpHandle, S.c_str());
}
```

FtpDeleteFile takes a handle to the current FTP session in the first parameter and a string specifying the file to delete in the second parameter. I find it hard to imagine how the call could be much simpler.

Creating and Removing Directories

WININET makes the process of creating and deleting directories trivial. Each purpose has one function, and each takes HINTERNET for your connection in the first parameter and the name of the directory you want to create or destroy in the second parameter:

```
BOOL FtpCreateDirectory(
    HINTERNET hFtpSession,    // Handle to session
    LPCTSTR lpszDirectory     // Name of directory
);
BOOL FtpRemoveDirectory(
    HINTERNET hFtpSession,    // Handle to session
    LPCTSTR lpszDirectory     // Name of directory
);
```

The following two simple functions demonstrate how to use the routines:

```
bool __fastcall TMyFtp::CreateDirectory(AnsiString S)
{
  return FtpCreateDirectory(FFtpHandle, S.c_str());
}
bool __fastcall TMyFtp::RemoveDir(System::AnsiString S)
{
  return FtpRemoveDirectory(FFtpHandle, S.c_str());
}
```

Assuming the presence of these routines, you can then write a function like the following to provide an interface with which the user can interact:

```
void __fastcall TForm1::RemoveDirectory1Click(TObject *Sender)
{
  AnsiString Title("Delete Directory?");
  AnsiString S = ListBox1->Items->Strings[ListBox1->ItemIndex];
  S = *Ftp->CustomToFileName(&S);
  if (MessageBox((HWND)Handle, S.c_str(), Title.c_str(),
      MB_YESNO | MB_ICONQUESTION) == ID_YES)
  {
    Ftp->RemoveDir(S);
    NewDirClick(NULL);
  }
}
```

This routine first retrieves the name of the directory you want to delete from a list box. It then calls the CustomToFileName routine, which converts the string shown in the list box into a simple directory name by stripping off information about the size of the directory and the time it was created. The MessageBox function is then used to check with the user to be sure that this action is really what he or she wants to do. If the user replies in the affirmative, the directory is deleted, and the new state of the directory is shown to the user.

Here is a similar function used to create a directory:

```
void __fastcall TForm1::CreateDirectory1Click(TObject *Sender)
{
  AnsiString S;
  if (InputQuery("Create Directory", "Directory Name", S))
  {
    Ftp->CreateDirectory(S);
    NewDirClick(NULL);
  }
}
```

In this case, the VCL InputQuery dialog is invoked. This function takes a title in the first parameter, a prompt in the second parameter, and the string you want the user to edit in the third parameter. If the user clicks the OK button in the dialog, then the directory is created, and the user's view of the directory is refreshed by a call to `NewDirClick`.

A Sample FTP Control

You now know the basics about the process of writing an FTP control with WININET. Listings 25.1 and 25.2 show the complete code to a simple control that can set up an FTP session for you. As is, the control lets you use the Object Inspector to define the `RemoteServer`, `UserID`, and `Password`. The code also automatically returns the current directory in a `TStringList` and allows you to perform file transfers.

In Listings 25.3 through 25.6, you will find a sample program that uses the control. The main screen for the program is shown in Figure 25.3, and a form in which users can select FTP connections is shown in Figure 25.4.

> **NOTE**
>
> `FTP2.CPP` has a dependency on `CODEBOX.CPP`. Both files are stored in the `UTILS` directory on the CD-ROM that accompanies this book. Due to the nature of the C++ linker, `CODEBOX.CPP` must be compiled to binary form before you can link the control into the Component Library. To build `CODEBOX.CPP`, compile the `BUILDOBJS.MAK` project in the `UTILS` directory. If you do this, and the linker still complains about `CODEBOX`, then make a small change to `FTP2.CPP`, such as adding and then deleting a space, then save your changes and try to compile the component library again. See the readme file on the CD-ROM that accompanies this book for additional information.
>
> `FTP2.CPP` needs the `CUNLEASHED` alias set up in the database tools. The readme file on the disc discusses this alias at some length. Basically, it's a Paradox alias pointing at the `Data` directory from the CD that accompanies this book. As always, make sure the source code and data are copied from the CD to your hard drive before trying to compile or run this program.

FIGURE 25.3.

The main form for the FTPWININET program. Here I'm connected to `ftp.download.com`, *in the all-important* Games *directory.*

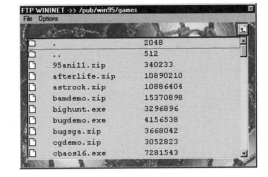

FIGURE 25.4.

A form used by the FTPWININET program to allow users to select an FTP connection from a table.

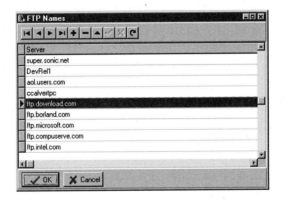

Listing 25.1. The header file for the FTP component.

```
/////////////////////////////////////////
// FTP.h
// FTP Component
// Copyright (c) 1997 by Charlie Calvert
//
#ifndef Ftp2H
#define Ftp2H

class TMyFtp : public Classes::TComponent
{
  typedef Classes::TComponent* inherited;
private:
  int FContext;
  bool FConnected;
  void *FINet;
  void *FFtpHandle;
  Classes::TStringList* FCurFiles;
  System::AnsiString FServer;
  Classes::TNotifyEvent FOnNewDir;
  System::AnsiString FCurDir;
  System::AnsiString FUserID;
  System::AnsiString FPassword;
```

continues

Listing 25.1. continued

```
  System::AnsiString __fastcall GetCurrentDirectory(void);
  void __fastcall SetUpNewDir(void);
protected:
  fastcall virtual ~TMyFtp(void);
public:
  fastcall TMyFtp(Classes::TComponent* AOwner);
  void __fastcall Connect(void);
  Classes::TStringList* __fastcall FindFiles(void);
  bool __fastcall BackOneDir(void);
  bool __fastcall ChangeDir(System::AnsiString *S);
  bool __fastcall ChangeDirCustom(System::AnsiString *S);
  bool __fastcall CreateDirectory(AnsiString S);
  bool __fastcall RemoveDir(System::AnsiString S);
  bool __fastcall RemoveDirCustom(System::AnsiString S);
  bool __fastcall DeleteFile(System::AnsiString S);
  bool __fastcall DeleteFileCustom(System::AnsiString S);
  bool __fastcall GetFile(System::AnsiString FTPFile,  System::AnsiString NewFile);
  bool __fastcall SendFile1(System::AnsiString FTPFile,  System::AnsiString
                            NewFile);
  bool __fastcall SendFile2(System::AnsiString FTPFile,  System::AnsiString
                            NewFile);
  System::AnsiString *__fastcall CustomToFileName(System::AnsiString *S);
__published:
  __property Classes::TStringList* CurFiles = {read=FCurFiles, nodefault};
  __property System::AnsiString CurDir = {read=GetCurrentDirectory, nodefault};
  __property System::AnsiString UserID = {read=FUserID, write=FUserID, nodefault};
  __property System::AnsiString Password = {read=FPassword, write=FPassword,
                                     nodefault};
  __property System::AnsiString Server = {read=FServer, write=FServer, nodefault};
  __property Classes::TNotifyEvent OnNewDir = {read=FOnNewDir, write=FOnNewDir};
};

#endif
```

Listing 25.2. The source for the FTP component.

```
/////////////////////////////////////
// FTP.cpp
// FTP Component
// Copyright (c) 1997 by Charlie Calvert
//
/////////////////////////////////////
// Add a "#pragma comment(lib, "Inet.lib")" statement to the
// module that requires the lib.
// Add a "#pragma link "codebox.obj"" into the module that needs
// an obj.
/////////////////////////////////////
#include <vcl\vcl.h>
#include <wininet.h>
#pragma hdrstop
#pragma comment(lib, "Inet.lib")
#pragma link "codebox.obj"
```

```
#include "codebox.h"
#include "Ftp2.h"

__fastcall TMyFtp::~TMyFtp(void)
{
  if (FINet != NULL)
    InternetCloseHandle(FINet);
  if (FFtpHandle != NULL)
    InternetCloseHandle(FFtpHandle);
}

__fastcall TMyFtp::TMyFtp(Classes::TComponent* AOwner)
: TComponent(AOwner)
{
  FCurFiles = new TStringList();
  FINet = InternetOpen("WinINet1", 0, NULL, 0, 0);
  FFtpHandle = NULL;
  FConnected = False;
}

void __fastcall TMyFtp::Connect(void)
{
  AnsiString S;
  AnsiString CR1("\x00D\x00A");

  FContext = 255;
  FFtpHandle = InternetConnect(FINet, FServer.c_str(), 0,
   FUserID.c_str(), FPassword.c_str(),
   INTERNET_SERVICE_FTP, 0, FContext);
  if (FFtpHandle == NULL)
  {
    S = "Connection failed" + CR1 +
        "Server: " + FServer + CR1 +
        "UserID: " + FUserID + CR1 +
        "Password: " + FPassword;
    throw Exception(S);
  }
  else
  {
    FConnected = True;
    SetUpNewDir();
  }
}

System::AnsiString __fastcall TMyFtp::GetCurrentDirectory(void)
{
  DWORD Len = 0;

  FtpGetCurrentDirectory(FFtpHandle, FCurDir.c_str(), &Len);
  FCurDir.SetLength(Len);
  FtpGetCurrentDirectory(FFtpHandle, FCurDir.c_str(), &Len);
  return FCurDir;
}

void __fastcall TMyFtp::SetUpNewDir(void)
{
```

25

continues

Listing 25.2. continued

```
  FCurDir = GetCurrentDirectory();
  if (FOnNewDir != NULL)
    FOnNewDir(this);
}

AnsiString GetDots(int NumDots)
{
  AnsiString S;
  int i;
  for (i = 1; i <= NumDots; i++)
    S = S + " ";
  return S;
}

AnsiString *GetFindDataStr(WIN32_FIND_DATA FindData, AnsiString *S)
{
  AnsiString Temp;
  switch (FindData.dwFileAttributes)
  {
    case FILE_ATTRIBUTE_ARCHIVE:
    {
      *S = 'A';
      break;
    }

    case FILE_ATTRIBUTE_COMPRESSED:
      *S = 'C';
      break;

    case FILE_ATTRIBUTE_DIRECTORY:
      *S = 'D';
      break;

    case FILE_ATTRIBUTE_HIDDEN:
      *S = 'H';
      break;

    case FILE_ATTRIBUTE_NORMAL:
      *S = 'N';
      break;

    case FILE_ATTRIBUTE_READONLY:
      *S = 'R';
      break;

    case FILE_ATTRIBUTE_SYSTEM:
      *S = 'S';
      break;

    case FILE_ATTRIBUTE_TEMPORARY:
      *S = 'T';
      break;

    default:
      *S = IntToStr(FindData.dwFileAttributes);
  }
```

```
    *S = *S + GetDots(75);
    S->Insert(FindData.cFileName, 6);
    Temp = IntToStr(FindData.nFileSizeLow);
    S->Insert(Temp, 25);
    return S;
}

Classes::TStringList* __fastcall TMyFtp::FindFiles(void)
{
    WIN32_FIND_DATA FindData;
    HINTERNET FindHandle;
    AnsiString Temp;

    FCurFiles->Clear();
    FindHandle = FtpFindFirstFile(FFtpHandle, "*.*", &FindData, 0, 0);
    if (FindHandle == NULL)
    {
        return FCurFiles;
    }

    GetFindDataStr(FindData, &Temp);
    FCurFiles->Add(Temp);

    while (InternetFindNextFile(FindHandle, &FindData))
    {
        GetFindDataStr(FindData, &Temp);
        FCurFiles->Add(Temp);
    }
    InternetCloseHandle(FindHandle);

    return FCurFiles;
}

bool __fastcall TMyFtp::ChangeDir(System::AnsiString *S)
{
    if(!FConnected)
        throw Exception("You must connect first!");
    if (S->Length() != 0)
        if (!FtpSetCurrentDirectory(FFtpHandle, S->c_str()))
        {
            ShowMessage("Could not change to: " + *S);
            return FALSE;
        }
    FindFiles();
    SetUpNewDir();
    return TRUE;
}

System::AnsiString *__fastcall TMyFtp::CustomToFileName(System::AnsiString *S)
{
    const int PreSize = 5;
    AnsiString Temp;
    int TempSize;
```

continues

25

USING
WININET

Listing 25.2. continued

```
    TempSize = S->Length() - PreSize;
    Temp.SetLength(TempSize);
    *S = StripFromFront(*S, PreSize);
    memcpy(Temp.c_str(), S->c_str(), TempSize);
    *S = GetFirstToken(Temp, ' ');
    return S;
}

bool __fastcall TMyFtp::ChangeDirCustom(System::AnsiString *S)
{
  AnsiString Temp = *CustomToFileName(S);
  return ChangeDir(&Temp);
}

bool __fastcall TMyFtp::CreateDirectory(AnsiString S)
{
  return FtpCreateDirectory(FFtpHandle, S.c_str());
}

bool __fastcall TMyFtp::RemoveDir(System::AnsiString S)
{
  return FtpRemoveDirectory(FFtpHandle, S.c_str());
}

bool __fastcall TMyFtp::RemoveDirCustom(System::AnsiString S)
{
  AnsiString Temp = *CustomToFileName(&S);
  return RemoveDir(Temp);
}

bool __fastcall TMyFtp::BackOneDir(void)
{
  AnsiString S;
  S = FCurDir;
  S = StripLastToken(S, '/');
  if (S == '/')
  {
    return FALSE;
  }

  if (S.Length() != 0)
  {
    ChangeDir(&S);
  }
  else
  {
    S = '/';
    ChangeDir(&S);
  }
  return TRUE;
}

bool __fastcall TMyFtp::DeleteFile(System::AnsiString S)
{
  return FtpDeleteFile(FFtpHandle, S.c_str());
}
```

```
bool __fastcall TMyFtp::DeleteFileCustom(System::AnsiString S)
{
  S = *CustomToFileName(&S);
  return DeleteFile(S);
}

bool __fastcall TMyFtp::GetFile(System::AnsiString FTPFile,
  System::AnsiString NewFile)
{
  return FtpGetFile(FFtpHandle, FTPFile.c_str(), NewFile.c_str(),
    False, FILE_ATTRIBUTE_NORMAL, FTP_TRANSFER_TYPE_BINARY, 0);
}

bool __fastcall TMyFtp::SendFile1(System::AnsiString FTPFile,
  System::AnsiString NewFile)
{
  DWORD Size = 3000;
  AnsiString S;

  BOOL Transfer = FtpPutFile(FFtpHandle,
                       FTPFile.c_str(),
                       NewFile.c_str(),
                       FTP_TRANSFER_TYPE_BINARY, 0);
  if (!Transfer)
  {
    int Error = GetLastError();
    S = Format("Error Number: %d. Hex: %x",
      OPENARRAY(TVarRec, (Error, Error)));
    ShowMessage(S);
    S.SetLength(Size);
    if (!InternetGetLastResponseInfo(&(DWORD)Error, S.c_str(), &Size))
    {
      Error = GetLastError();
      ShowMessage(Format("Error Number: %d. Hex: %x",
        OPENARRAY(TVarRec, (Error, Error))));
    }
    ShowMessage(Format("Error Number: %d. Hex: %x Info: %s",
                OPENARRAY(TVarRec, (Error, Error, S))));
  }
  else
    ShowMessage("Success");

  return Transfer;
}

bool __fastcall TMyFtp::SendFile2(System::AnsiString FTPFile,
  System::AnsiString NewFile)
{
  HINTERNET FHandle;

  FHandle = FtpOpenFile(FFtpHandle, "sam.txt", GENERIC_READ,
                        FTP_TRANSFER_TYPE_BINARY, 0);
  if (FHandle != NULL)
    InternetCloseHandle(FHandle);
  else
    ShowMessage("Failed");
```

25

USING
WININET

continues

Listing 25.2. continued

```
  return TRUE;
}

namespace Ftp2
{
  void __fastcall Register()
  {
    TComponentClass classes[1] = {__classid(TMyFtp)};
    RegisterComponents("Unleash", classes, 0);
  }

}
```

Listing 25.3. Header for the main module of the FTPWININET program showing how to use the FTP component.

```
/////////////////////////////////////
// File: Main.h
// Project: FtpWinINet
// copyright (c) 1997 by Charlie Calvert
//
#ifndef MainH
#define MainH
#include <vcl\Classes.hpp>
#include <vcl\Controls.hpp>
#include <vcl\StdCtrls.hpp>
#include <vcl\Forms.hpp>
#include <vcl\ExtCtrls.hpp>
#include <vcl\Buttons.hpp>
#include <vcl\Menus.hpp>
#include <vcl\Dialogs.hpp>
#include "Ftp2.h"

class TForm1 : public TForm
{
__published:
  TListBox *ListBox1;
  TImage *Image1;
  TSpeedButton *SpeedButton1;
  TMainMenu *MainMenu1;
  TMenuItem *File1;
  TMenuItem *Connect1;
  TMenuItem *CopyFile1;
  TMenuItem *N1;
  TMenuItem *Exit1;
  TMenuItem *SendToSite;
  TSaveDialog *SaveDialog1;
  TMenuItem *Options1;
  TMenuItem *ChangeDirectory1;
  TMenuItem *RemoveDirectory1;
  TMenuItem *CreateDirectory1;
  TMenuItem *DeleteFile1;
  TMenuItem *EditConnectionData1;
```

```cpp
  TMyFtp *Ftp;
  void __fastcall ConnectBtnClick(TObject *Sender);
  void __fastcall ListBox1DblClick(TObject *Sender);
  void __fastcall BackOneDirectoryBtnClick(TObject *Sender);
  void __fastcall CopyFileClick(TObject *Sender);
  // void __fastcall NewDirectory(TObject *Sender);
  void __fastcall NewDirClick(TObject *Sender);
  void __fastcall Exit1Click(TObject *Sender);
  void __fastcall SendToSiteClick(TObject *Sender);
  void __fastcall ChangeDirectory1Click(TObject *Sender);
  void __fastcall RemoveDirectory1Click(TObject *Sender);
  void __fastcall CreateDirectory1Click(TObject *Sender);
  void __fastcall DeleteFile1Click(TObject *Sender);
  void __fastcall ListBox1DrawItem(TWinControl *Control, int Index,
  const TRect &Rect, TOwnerDrawState State);
  void __fastcall EditConnectionData1Click(TObject *Sender);
  void __fastcall ListBox1MouseDown(TObject *Sender, TMouseButton Button,
  TShiftState Shift, int X, int Y);
private:
  // TMyFtp *Ftp;
  AnsiString FStartCaption;
  Graphics::TBitmap *FFileBitmap;
  Graphics::TBitmap *FFolderBitmap;
  virtual __fastcall ~TForm1(void);
  void ActivateMenus();
public:
  virtual __fastcall TForm1(TComponent* Owner);
};

extern TForm1 *Form1;

#endif
```

Listing 25.4. The main module of the FTPWININET program showing how to use the FTP component.

```cpp
/////////////////////////////////////////
// File: MAIN.CPP
// Project: FtpWinINet
// copyright (c) 1997 by Charlie Calvert
//
#include <vcl\vcl.h>
#pragma hdrstop
#include "Ftp2.h"
#include "Main.h"
#include "FtpNames1.h"
#pragma link "Ftp2"
#pragma resource "*.dfm"
#pragma resource "listicon.res"

TForm1 *Form1;

__fastcall TForm1::TForm1(TComponent* Owner)
  : TForm(Owner)
{
```

continues

Listing 25.4. continued

```cpp
  FStartCaption = Caption;
  FFolderBitmap = new Graphics::TBitmap;
  FFileBitmap = new Graphics::TBitmap;
  FFolderBitmap->Handle = LoadBitmap((HINSTANCE)HInstance, "FolderBmp");
  FFileBitmap->Handle = LoadBitmap((HINSTANCE)HInstance, "FileBmp");
}


__fastcall TForm1::~TForm1()
{
  FFolderBitmap->Free();
  FFileBitmap->Free();
}

void TForm1::ActivateMenus()
{
  int i;

  for (i = 0; i < ComponentCount; i++)
  {
    if(dynamic_cast<TMenuItem *>(Components[i]))
      dynamic_cast<TMenuItem *>(Components[i])->Enabled = True;
  }
}

void __fastcall TForm1::ConnectBtnClick(TObject *Sender)
{
  Ftp->OnNewDir = NewDirClick;
  if (FTPNames->GetConnectionData())
  {
    Application->ProcessMessages();
    Ftp->Server = FTPNames->Server;
    Ftp->UserID = FTPNames->UserID;
    Ftp->Password = FTPNames->Password;
    Screen->Cursor = TCursor(crHourGlass);
    Ftp->Connect();
    Screen->Cursor = TCursor(crDefault);
    ActivateMenus();
  }
}

void __fastcall TForm1::ListBox1DblClick(TObject *Sender)
{
  int i = ListBox1->ItemIndex;
  AnsiString S = ListBox1->Items->Strings[i];
  Ftp->ChangeDirCustom(&S);
}

void __fastcall TForm1::BackOneDirectoryBtnClick(TObject *Sender)
{
  Screen->Cursor = Controls::TCursor(crHourGlass);
  Ftp->BackOneDir();
  Screen->Cursor = Controls::TCursor(crDefault);
}


void __fastcall TForm1::CopyFileClick(TObject *Sender)
{
```

```
    AnsiString S = ListBox1->Items->Strings[ListBox1->ItemIndex];
    Ftp->CustomToFileName(&S);
    SaveDialog1->FileName = "C:\\" + S;
    if (SaveDialog1->Execute())
      Ftp->GetFile(S, SaveDialog1->FileName);
}

void __fastcall TForm1::NewDirClick(TObject *Sender)
{
  Caption = FStartCaption + " ->> " + Ftp->CurDir;
  ListBox1->Items = Ftp->FindFiles();
}

void __fastcall TForm1::Exit1Click(TObject *Sender)
{
  Close();
}

void __fastcall TForm1::SendToSiteClick(TObject *Sender)
{
  if (SaveDialog1->Execute())
  {
    AnsiString SaveFile(ExtractFileName(SaveDialog1->FileName));
    Ftp->SendFile1(SaveDialog1->FileName, SaveFile);
  }
}

void __fastcall TForm1::ChangeDirectory1Click(TObject *Sender)
{
  AnsiString S;
  if (InputQuery("Change Directory", "Enter Directory", S))
    Ftp->ChangeDir(&S);
}

void __fastcall TForm1::RemoveDirectory1Click(TObject *Sender)
{
  AnsiString Title("Delete Directory?");

  AnsiString S = ListBox1->Items->Strings[ListBox1->ItemIndex];
  S = *Ftp->CustomToFileName(&S);
  if (MessageBox((HWND)Handle, S.c_str(), Title.c_str(),
      MB_YESNO | MB_ICONQUESTION) == ID_YES)
  {
    Ftp->RemoveDir(S);
    NewDirClick(NULL);
  }
}

void __fastcall TForm1::CreateDirectory1Click(TObject *Sender)
{
  AnsiString S;
  if (InputQuery("Create Directory", "Directory Name", S))
  {
    Ftp->CreateDirectory(S);
    NewDirClick(NULL);
  }
}
```

25

USING
WININET

continues

Listing 25.4. continued

```cpp
void __fastcall TForm1::DeleteFile1Click(TObject *Sender)
{
  AnsiString S = ListBox1->Items->Strings[ListBox1->ItemIndex];
  S = *Ftp->CustomToFileName(&S);
  if (MessageBox((HWND)Handle, S.c_str(), "DeleteFile?",
      MB_YESNO | MB_ICONQUESTION) == ID_YES)
  {
    Ftp->DeleteFile(S);
    NewDirClick(NULL);
  }
}

void __fastcall TForm1::ListBox1DrawItem(TWinControl *Control, int Index, const
                                    Windows::TRect &Rect, TOwnerDrawState State)
{
  ListBox1->Canvas->FillRect(Rect);
  AnsiString S = ListBox1->Items->Strings[Index];
  ListBox1->Canvas->TextOut(Rect.Left, Rect.Top, S);
  char ch = S[1];
  if (ch == 'N')
    ListBox1->Canvas->Draw(Rect.Left, Rect.Top, FFileBitmap);
  else
    ListBox1->Canvas->Draw(Rect.Left, Rect.Top, FFolderBitmap);
}

void __fastcall TForm1::EditConnectionData1Click(TObject *Sender)
{
  FTPNames->ShowModal();
}

void __fastcall TForm1::ListBox1MouseDown(TObject *Sender, TMouseButton Button,
                                    TShiftState Shift, int X, int Y)
{
  if (Shift.Contains(ssRight))
  {
    if (ListBox1->ItemIndex >= 0)
      ShowMessage(ListBox1->Items->Strings[ListBox1->ItemIndex]);
  }
}
```

Listing 25.5. The header for the module for picking the next connection from a database.

```cpp
////////////////////////////////////
// FTPNames.h
// Project: FTPWININET
// Copyright (c) 1997 by Charlie Calvert
//
#ifndef FtpNames1H
#define FtpNames1H
#include <vcl\Classes.hpp>
#include <vcl\Controls.hpp>
#include <vcl\StdCtrls.hpp>
```

```
#include <vcl\Forms.hpp>
#include <vcl\DBTables.hpp>
#include <vcl\DB.hpp>
#include <vcl\DBGrids.hpp>
#include <vcl\Grids.hpp>
#include <vcl\ExtCtrls.hpp>
#include <vcl\DBCtrls.hpp>
#include <vcl\Buttons.hpp>

class TFTPNames : public TForm
{
__published:
 TTable *FTPTable;
 TDataSource *FTPSource;
 TAutoIncField *FTPTableCode;
 TStringField *FTPTableServer;
 TStringField *FTPTableUserID;
 TStringField *FTPTablePassword;
 TDBGrid *DBGrid1;
 TPanel *Panel1;
 TDBNavigator *DBNavigator1;
 TPanel *Panel2;
 TBitBtn *BitBtn1;
 TBitBtn *BitBtn2;
private:
  AnsiString FServer;
  AnsiString FUserID;
  AnsiString FPassword;
public:
 virtual __fastcall TFTPNames(TComponent* Owner);
 BOOL GetConnectionData(void);
 __property System::AnsiString Server = {read=FServer};
 __property System::AnsiString UserID = {read=FUserID};
 __property System::AnsiString Password = {read=FPassword};
};

extern TFTPNames *FTPNames;

#endif
```

Listing 25.6. The source for the module that lets the user pick the next FTP connection from a database.

```
/////////////////////////////////////
// FTPNames.cpp
// Project: FTPWININET
// Copyright (c) 1997 by Charlie Calvert
//
#include <vcl\vcl.h>
#pragma hdrstop
#include "FtpNames1.h"
#pragma resource "*.dfm"
TFTPNames *FTPNames;
```

continues

25

USING
WININET

Listing 25.6. continued

```
__fastcall TFTPNames::TFTPNames(TComponent* Owner): TForm(Owner)
{
}

BOOL TFTPNames::GetConnectionData(void)
{
  if (ShowModal() == mrOk)
  {
    FServer = FTPTableServer->Value;
    FUserID = FTPTableUserID->Value;
    FPassword = FTPTablePassword->Value;
    return TRUE;
  }
  else
    return FALSE;
}
```

This component is used in the FTPWININET program found on the CD that comes with this book. To use the component, simply drop it on a form and then use the Object Inspector to fill in the Server, UserID, and Password.

To start a session, simply call the Connect method:

```
void __fastcall TForm1::ConnectBtnClick(TObject *Sender)
{
  MyFtp1->Connect();
}
```

If you choose not to add the component to the Component Palette, you can create and initialize the FTP component with the following code:

```
void __fastcall TForm1::ConnectBtnClick(TObject *Sender)
{
  Ftp = new TMyFtp(this);
  Ftp->OnNewDir = NewDirClick;
  Ftp->Server = "devinci";
  Ftp->UserID = "ccalvert";
  Ftp->Password = "flapper";
  Ftp->Connect();
  ListBox1->Items = Ftp->FindFiles();
}

void __fastcall TForm1::NewDirClick(TObject *Sender)
{
  Caption = FStartCaption + " ->> " + Ftp->CurDir;
  ListBox1->Items = Ftp->FindFiles();
}
```

For this code to work, you must #include ftp2.h at the top of your file, and you must declare the variable Ftp as a field of TForm1: TMyFtp *Ftp. You should also add NewDirClick to your class declaration in the header file.

The difference between these two versions of the `ConnectBtnClick` method shows how much simpler using the RAD paradigm is rather than slogging your way through the old coding techniques. Note in particular the second line in the preceding method; this line explicitly sets up the event handler (closure) for the `OnNewDir` event.

If you respond to the `OnNewDir` event, you can get a directory listing for the current FTP site mirrored in a `ListBox` by writing the following line of code:

```
void __fastcall TForm1::NewDirClick(TObject *Sender)
{
  Caption = FStartCaption + " ->> " + Ftp->CurDir;
  ListBox1->Items = Ftp->FindFiles();
}
```

The first line of code shown here is optional; it does nothing more than show the current directory in the caption of the program. The `FStartCaption` variable is a field of the `TForm` object that is initialized in the constructor for the form:

```
__fastcall TForm1::TForm1(TComponent* Owner)
: TForm(Owner)
{
  FStartCaption = Caption;
}
```

The technique of saving the default caption in a global variable for later reuse is a common one in C++Builder programming.

The `FindFile` method called in the `NewDirClick` routine was explained in the section "After Connecting."

After you have displayed a directory of files, the program still needs to provide a technique for letting the user change directories. One simple method is to respond to double-clicks on a directory name by changing into the selected directory.

Creating User Draw List Boxes

When displaying a list of files to the user, you need to provide some clear way of distinguishing files from directories. One simple way to make this distinction is with an owner draw list box that provides different icons for the different types of files and directories you want to show the user.

To get started creating an owner draw list box, change the `Style` property for the list box to `lbOwnerDrawFixed`. This means that you want all the items in the list box to have the same height. You can now associate a graphic item with the `Object` field of each string in the `TStringList`. Next, you respond to `OnDrawItem` events.

Here is the constructor for the form, which is used to load the bitmaps to be displayed in the list box from a resource:

```
fastcall TForm1::TForm1(TComponent* Owner)
  : TForm(Owner)
```

```
{
  FStartCaption = Caption;
  FFolderBitmap = new Graphics::TBitmap;
  FFileBitmap = new Graphics::TBitmap;
  FFolderBitmap->Handle = LoadBitmap((HINSTANCE)HInstance, "FolderBmp");
  FFileBitmap->Handle = LoadBitmap((HINSTANCE)HInstance, "FileBmp");
}
```

The code shown here explicitly sets the OnDrawItem event to the ListBox1DrawItem method, but, of course, you could also do this visually, from the Events page of the Object Inspector. In particular, you could turn to the Events page for the ListBox1 control; then you could set the OnDrawItem event to ListBox1DrawItem or to some other method that you choose. The only requirement, of course, is that the method be of type TNotifyEvent; that is, it must take TObject Sender as its sole parameter.

The code goes on to create two bitmaps and then loads the bitmaps from a resource with the LoadBitmap function. LoadBitmap is a Windows API routine that takes the HInstance for the program in its first parameter and the name of the resource you want to retrieve in its second parameter. You can then assign the handle returned by LoadBitmap to the handle of the native VCL TBitmap object. After it is assigned to TBitmap, you no longer have to worry about disposing the handle, as it will be cleaned up when TBitmap is destroyed. You will, however, have to explicitly destroy the TBitmap objects in the destructor for the form:

```
__fastcall TForm1::~TForm1()
{
  FFolderBitmap->Free();
  FFileBitmap->Free();
}
```

The custom RC file called LISTICON.RC looks like this:

```
FolderBmp BITMAP "FOLDER.BMP"
FileBmp BITMAP "FILE.BMP"
```

You can include this file in your project by choosing Project | Add to Project and then browsing for RC files and adding your custom file to the project, as shown Figure 25.5. This way, you add the following macro to your project file:

```
USERC("ListIcon.rc");
```

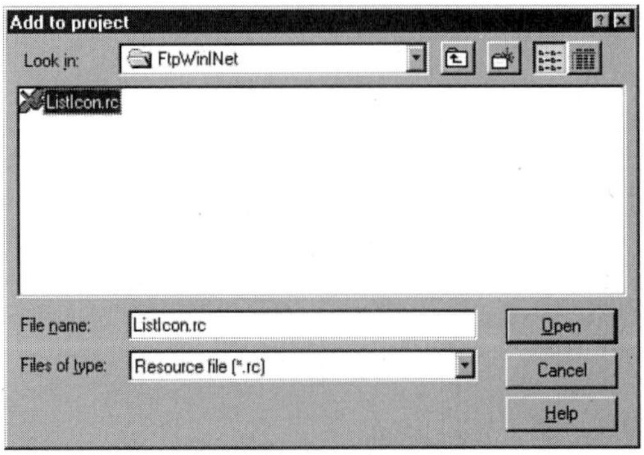

FIGURE 25.5.

*Adding an RC file to a
BCB project.*

Remember that you don't want to add this code into the pre-made RES file that C++Builder makes automatically for your program. Instead, you should create a separate RES file, using the techniques I've described here. The two bitmaps included here are shown in Figure 25.6.

FIGURE 25.6.

The two 16×16 16-color folder and file bitmaps used in FTPWININET.

If you don't want to have the C++Builder IDE add the RC file to your project, you can do so explicitly with only a few seconds' work. Here is how to proceed.

Compile the RC file at the command line by passing it as the sole parameter to the BRCC32.EXE utility that ships with C++Builder.

Add the following code at the top of your main form:

```
#include <vcl\vcl.h>
#pragma hdrstop
#include "Ftp2.h"
#include "Main.h"
#include "FtpNames1.h"
#pragma resource "*.dfm"
#pragma resource "listicon.res"    // Here is the line you should add to your
                                            project!
TForm1 *Form1;
__fastcall TForm1::TForm1(TComponent* Owner)
: TForm(Owner)
{
    ... // etc
```

The only line that is important here is the seventh, but I have shown you additional lines from the program so that you can find the context in which to place the file. Both techniques work fine, though the first is probably preferred.

Now that all the resource issues are finally out of the way, you can write the following code to display the bitmaps in a list box:

```
void __fastcall TForm1::ListBox1DrawItem(TWinControl *Control, int Index,
    const Windows::TRect &Rect, TOwnerDrawState State)
{
    ListBox1->Canvas->FillRect(Rect);
    AnsiString S = ListBox1->Items->Strings[Index];
    ListBox1->Canvas->TextOut(Rect.Left, Rect.Top, S);
    char ch = S[1];
    if (ch == 'N')
        ListBox1->Canvas->Draw(Rect.Left, Rect.Top, FFileBitmap);
    else
        ListBox1->Canvas->Draw(Rect.Left, Rect.Top, FFolderBitmap);
}
```

The header for this method is created automatically for you when you click the TListBox OnDrawItem event in the Object Inspector. Alternatively, you can add the method manually, being sure to modify both the header file and the CPP file. Obviously, you can add additional code if you want to handle distinctions between normal files and system files, and so on.

OnDrawItem event handlers like ListBox1DrawItem get four parameters:

- The first is the TListBox itself.
- The second is the index of the current item into the list of strings shown in the list box. For example, if you have five strings in the list box, this event handler is called five times, with the index set to numbers ranging from 0 to 4.
- The second parameter is the area in the list box in which you are free to draw. Remember that this example covers list boxes of a fixed size. You must respond to OnMeasureItem events if you want to vary the size of the items in the list box.
- The final parameter is of type TOwnerDrawState.

The final TOwnerDrawState parameter is a set used to designate whether the current item is in one of the following states:

```
odSelected: The item is selected.
odDisabled: The entire list box is disabled.
odFocused: The item currently has focus.
```

To find out more about TOwnerDrawState, browse for that value in StdCtrls.hpp.

The code for the event handler first blanks out the Rect in white, so no artifacts appear in the control:

```
ListBox1->Canvas->FillRect(Rect);
```

The code then gets the appropriate string to display from the list box's string list. After the code retrieves the string, the string is displayed with the TextOut function from the Canvas field of the TListBox:

```
AnsiString S = ListBox1->Items->Strings[Index];
ListBox1->Canvas->TextOut(Rect.Left, Rect.Top, S);
```

The TRect structure passed to the OnDrawItem event handler is used to calculate the location in the list box where the information should be displayed. Don't forget that the VCL ensures that the font to be used is already selected in the Canvas property for the list box, so you don't have to worry about that either.

The last step is to actually draw the bitmap to the screen:

```
char ch = S[1];
if (ch == 'N')
  ListBox1->Canvas->Draw(Rect.Left, Rect.Top, FFileBitmap);
else
  ListBox1->Canvas->Draw(Rect.Left, Rect.Top, FFolderBitmap);
```

The strings that I display in the list box begin with either an N or a D, depending on whether they reference a file or a directory. This display would be an aesthetic atrocity, were it not for the fact that the bitmap obliterates this letter, replacing it with a "pretty" image. Keeping the letter in there is nice though, as I can sort the list box on this letter, thereby ensuring that all the directories are displayed at the top of the list box and the files next.

Old hands at Windows are no doubt dreading the moment when they will have to actually use BitBlt to place the bitmap on the screen. However, all the traditional "horror" is taken out of the process by the VCL, which allows you to display the bits through a simple call to the Draw method of the canvas for TListBox. Notice that you can just pass in the TBitmap object made in the form's constructor as the third parameter to Draw. Internally, the VCL will calculate the size of the bitmap and call BitBlt for you.

> **NOTE**
>
> The VCL really shines here. Notice how simple it is to dovetail the TBitmap object with the Windows API LoadBitmap function. Then, after you have the bitmap in your hands, you can just pass it to the ListBox itself when you need to display it. In effect, all you have to say is "Here, Mr. List Box, you take this and draw it to the screen for me." The list box, being a well-designed object, is happy to do your bidding.
>
> The point here is that all the pieces fit together very nicely. The VCL always walks a fine line between making tasks too simple and making them too hard. If the VCL makes the process too simple, the code would almost certainly be inefficient from a memory and performance point of view and also difficult to customize. If this process were too difficult, then programmers would have to spend too much time selecting fonts into device contexts and deciding which resources need to be destroyed and how. The art of the VCL is to take you right down the middle of this obstacle course. It gives you enough control so that you can customize to your liking, but does not leave you with so many details to manage that you are likely to end up with a program that leaks resources like a ship with a bad case of dry rot!
>
> I often study VCL code when I want to pick up tips on how to construct safe, easy-to-use objects. As I mentioned earlier, one of the useful chores an object can do for you is to help with the cleanup of resources. The VCL does this job in many cases, and studying how this job is done is often worthwhile.

This section on owner draw list boxes has turned out to be longer than I expected, but I hope you see that the actual process described is not very difficult. The key here is just to understand a little about resources and bitmaps, and then to understand the parameters passed to the OnDrawItem event. If you have those pieces down, then the rest should fall in place fairly easily.

25

USING
WININET

A Few Words on the FTP OCX Control

If you don't want to create your own FTP component, you can use the TFTP component that resides on the Internet page of the Component Palette. The disadvantages of this system include having to ship a separate OCX file and the fact that OCXs are larger than native components. (The FTP OCX is about 250KB, and the WININET component I built is around 50KB with debug information.) The advantages of using an OCX component are that it is probably already debugged and that a company stands behind it and can give you support.

To get help on the FTP component, right-click it and select Properties. Then click the Help button. A standard Windows help file is launched, with reasonably complete help. These help files are stored in the Windows system directory.

Listings 25.7 and 25.8 contain the source to a test program that uses the OCX controls that ship with BCB. Needless to say, this program will not work correctly unless the OCX controls are installed on the Component Palette. By default, these controls are installed automatically by BCB on the Internet page of the Component Palette.

Listing 25.7. The FTPICP program shows how to use the FTP ActiveX component from the Internet page of the Component Palette.

```
/////////////////////////////////////
// main.h
// FtpIcp: Use Active X Control for Ftp
// Copyright (c) 1997 by Charlie calvert
//
#ifndef MainH
#define MainH
#include <vcl\Classes.hpp>
#include <vcl\Controls.hpp>
#include <vcl\StdCtrls.hpp>
#include <vcl\Forms.hpp>
#include <vcl\ISP.hpp>
#include <vcl\OleCtrls.hpp>
class TForm1 : public TForm
{
__published:
  TFTP *Ftp1;
  TListBox *ListBox1;
  TListBox *ListBox2;
  void __fastcall FormCreate(TObject *Sender);
  void __fastcall FormDestroy(TObject *Sender);
  void __fastcall Ftp1StateChanged(TObject *Sender, short State);
  void __fastcall Ftp1ProtocolStateChanged(TObject *Sender, short ProtocolState);
  void __fastcall Ftp1ListItem(TObject *Sender, const Variant &Item);
private:
public:
  virtual __fastcall TForm1(TComponent* Owner);
};
extern TForm1 *Form1;
#endif
```

Listing 25.8. The main source file for the FTPICP program.

```cpp
/////////////////////////////////////
// main.cpp
// FtpIcp: Use Active X Control for Ftp
// Copyright (c) 1997 by Charlie calvert
//
#include <vcl\vcl.h>
#include "icpbox.h"
#pragma hdrstop
#include "Main.h"
#pragma resource "*.dfm"
TForm1 *Form1;
__fastcall TForm1::TForm1(TComponent* Owner)
  : TForm(Owner)
{
}
void __fastcall TForm1::FormCreate(TObject *Sender)
{
  Ftp1->Connect(Ftp1->RemoteHost, Ftp1->RemotePort);
}
void __fastcall TForm1::FormDestroy(TObject *Sender)
{
  Ftp1->Cancel();
  Ftp1->Quit();
}
void __fastcall TForm1::Ftp1StateChanged(TObject *Sender, short State)
{
  AnsiString S;
  switch(State)
  {
    case prcConnecting: S = "Connecting"; break;
    case prcConnected: S = "Connected"; break;
    case prcResolvingHost: S = "Resolving Host"; break;
    case prcHostResolved: S = "Host Resolved"; break;
    default:
      S = "State Unknown";
  }
  ListBox1->Items->Add(S);
}
void __fastcall TForm1::Ftp1ProtocolStateChanged(TObject *Sender,
                                        short ProtocolState)
{
  AnsiString S;
  switch(ProtocolState)
  {
    case ftpAuthentication:
     S = "Authenticate";
     Ftp1->Authenticate(Ftp1->UserId, Ftp1->Password);
     break;
    case ftpTransaction:
      S = "Transaction";
      Ftp1->List("/");
      break;
  }
```

continues

Listing 25.8. continued

```
   ListBox1->Items->Add(S);
}
void __fastcall TForm1::Ftp1ListItem(TObject *Sender, const Variant &Item)
{
   ListBox2->Items->Add(ParseFtpItem(Item));
}
```

This sample program will automatically connect you to sites on the Internet or intranet where you can download files. Before running it, check to make sure you know which site you will be connected to, as explained in the next few paragraphs.

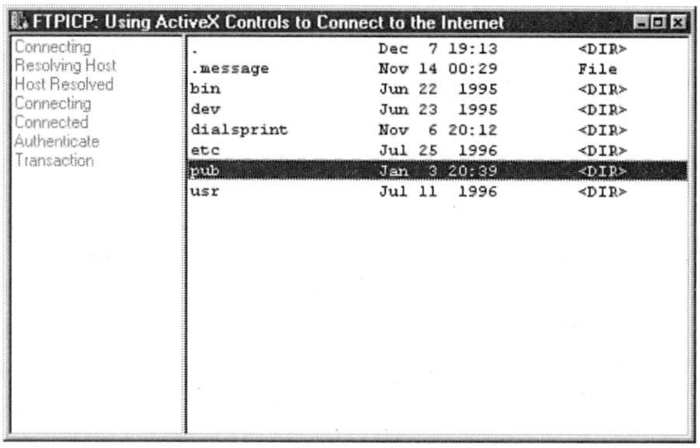

FIGURE 25.7.

The main screen from the FTPICP program that uses an ActiveX control to connect to the Internet via FTP.

You can use the Object Inspector to set the Password, RemoteHost, RemotePort, and UserId for the component. For example, you might set them like this if you want to connect to a server on your current machine:

```
RemoteHost = 127.0.0.1
RemotePort = 21
UserId = Anonymous
Password = ccalvert@wpo.borland.com
```

To connect to Microsoft's FTP site, use ftp.microsoft.com rather than 127.0.0.1. Needless to say, you should enter your own e-mail address, not mine, when you're connecting to a site.

To connect to a server, you write the following:

```
Ftp1->Connect(Ftp1->RemoteHost, Ftp1->RemotePort);
```

When you're finished, you should close out the session:

```
void __fastcall TForm1::FormDestroy(TObject *Sender)
{
  Ftp1->Cancel();
  Ftp1->Quit();
}
```

The Cancel command cancels whatever command might currently be executing. This command is helpful because users will often quit a program when a command is taking too long to execute. Long delays are common in FTP communications, not because the control is slow, but because the Internet is slow.

The FTP control will use events to notify you when events occur. In particular, you can use the OnStateChanged event to keep the user informed about what is happening:

```
void __fastcall TForm1::Ftp1StateChanged(TObject *Sender, short State)
{
  AnsiString S;
  switch(State)
  {
    case prcConnecting: S = "Connecting"; break;
    case prcConnected: S = "Connected"; break;
    case prcResolvingHost: S = "Resolving Host"; break;
    case prcHostResolved: S = "Host Resolved"; break;
    default:
      S = "State Unknown";
  }
  ListBox1->Items->Add(S);
}
```

The State variable passed to the control can be set to one of the following values:

```
#define prcConnecting (unsigned char)(1)
#define prcResolvingHost (unsigned char)(2)
#define prcHostResolved (unsigned char)(3)
#define prcConnected (unsigned char)(4)
#define prcDisconnecting (unsigned char)(5)
#define prcDisconnected (unsigned char)(6)
#define prcConnectTimeout (unsigned char)(1)
#define prcReceiveTimeout (unsigned char)(2)
#define prcUserTimeout (unsigned char)(65)
#define prcGet (unsigned char)(1)
#define prcHead (unsigned char)(2)
#define prcPost (unsigned char)(3)
#define prcPut (unsigned char)(4)
```

You can find these values in ISP.hpp in the Include/VCL subdirectory.

During the process of connecting to the server, you must respond to certain events:

```
void __fastcall TForm1::Ftp1ProtocolStateChanged(TObject *Sender,
  short ProtocolState)
{
  AnsiString S;
  switch(ProtocolState)
  {
    case ftpAuthentication:
      S = "Authenticate";
      Ftp1->Authenticate(Ftp1->UserId, Ftp1->Password);
      break;
    case ftpTransaction:
      S = "Transaction";
      Ftp1->List("/");
      break;
```

```
    }
    ListBox1->Items->Add(S);
}
```

The `ftpAuthentication` protocol can have the following values:

`ftpBase = 0`	The base state before the connection to the server is established.
`ftpAuthorization = 1`	Authorization is performed.
`ftpTransaction = 2`	The client has been successfully identified.

Here you're stepping through the process of signing the user onto the site. You get an `ftpAuthorization` message when it's time to begin the authorization process. In response to this message, you can call `Authenticate`:

```
Ftp1->Authenticate(Ftp1->UserId, Ftp1->Password);
```

Here you pass in the `UserID` and `Password` so that the process of authentication can be completed.

After you have been successfully authenticated, then you get an `ftpTransaction` message. In response to this message, you can show the user a listing of the current directory, which is the root:

```
Ftp1->List("/");
```

This command causes an `OnListItem` event to occur, as long as the `ListItemNotify` property is set to `True`, which is the default state. These events send you a `Variant` with a listing of the current directory in it:

```
void __fastcall TForm1::Ftp1ListItem(TObject *Sender, const Variant &Item)
{
    ListBox2->Items->Add(ParseFtpItem(Item));
}
```

The `Item` contains an object replete with information about each file or directory to be listed. In particular, it lists the filename, size, date, and attributes of the current file or directory. The `OnListItem` event gets fired multiple times until all the files or directories are listed:

I use a custom procedure called `ParseFtp`:

```
AnsiString ParseFtpItem(Variant &V)
{
    AnsiString S;
    AnsiString Result;
    AnsiString Temp;
    S.SetLength(StrLen);
    memset(S.c_str(), ' ', StrLen - 1);
    Temp = V.OleFunction("FileName");
    S.Insert(Temp, 1);
    Temp = V.OleFunction("Date");
    S.Insert(Temp, 20);
```

```
  Temp = V.OleFunction("Attributes");
  if (Temp == "1")
    Temp = "<DIR>";
  if (Temp == "2")
    Temp = "File";
  S.Insert(Temp, 40);

  return S;
}
```

To call the `FileName` function of the object, you can write the following code:

```
Temp = V.OleFunction("FileName");
```

`OleFunction` is a method of the variant object that takes one or more parameters.

That's all I'm going to say about the FTP component. You should now have enough information to get up and running. If you want more details, you might find an example of using the component that ships with BCB in the `Examples\Internet` subdirectory. If the FTP component does not suit your needs, and you don't want to roll your own with WININET, then you can buy a component from a third party. You can usually find components on the Internet. If you're having trouble getting started looking for them, visit my Web site at `users.aol.com/charliecal` and look for links that might help you get started.

Summary

This chapter focuses mostly on WININET and FTP. WININET turns out to be a fairly simple API to use. It provides a great means for creating small, powerful objects that allow you to access the key features of the Internet. You should visit Microsoft's Web site to download additional information about WININET. The DLL that makes this all possible is called, naturally enough, `WININET.DLL`. Starting with Windows NT 4.0, it ships with all versions of Windows, and is freely available for distribution with your applications. It works fine on Windows 95.

Other subjects covered in this chapter include owner draw list boxes, as well as the FTP ActiveX control that ships with BCB. As a rule, it is better to use WININET rather than the ActiveX control because WININET is so small and fast. On the other hand, canned code of the kind you find in the FTP ActiveX is easy to use, and can help you construct safe, reliable programs. Before you decide to rely on a control made by a third party, you should always test it carefully to be sure that it meets your needs.

CHAPTER 26

Extending an Internet Server with ISAPI

IN THIS CHAPTER

Overview

This chapter examines the ISAPI and CGI technologies. You can use CGI to create applications that extend a Web server, and you can use ISAPI to create DLLs that extend a Web server. In particular, ISAPI allows you to write scripts and filters and to interact dynamically with a user of your browser.

ISAPI technology is specific to the Internet Information Server that ships with Windows NT and to the Personal Web Server that ships with Microsoft FrontPage. It is, however, merely a specification, and other servers could conform to it if they wish. Several different vendors, including Borland, have created technology that allows ISAPI-based technology to be used in conjunction with NSAPI, which is a similar technology to ISAPI. (The NSAPI/ISAPI bridge is available in Delphi 3.0, for example.)

ISAPI programming is very similar to CGI programming. The only major difference is that you're creating a DLL instead of an executable. DLLs are advantageous because they can be loaded into the address space of the Web server. This capability gives them a leg up over CGI when you're considering performance. CGI, on the other hand, is a very simple specification to use, and it adapts itself easily to database applications.

ISAPI's reliance on the Windows platform might be a serious limitation in some other context, but because C++Builder also relies on Windows, discussing the topic at length in this book makes sense. Another feature to recommend ISAPI is its extreme simplicity. Friendly, powerful, easy-to-use APIs are the bread and butter of this book, and ISAPI fits the bill beautifully. Writing BCB database applications with ISAPI is, however, a bit tricky.

The first half of this chapter deals with ISAPI, and the second half deals with CGI. I will show how to retrieve data from both ISAPI DLLs and CGI applications, though my treatment of the subject is more complete in the section on CGI. If you are interested primarily in ISAPI, you should also take the time to read about the CGI database applications in the second half of this chapter.

The C++ code in this chapter relies on the presence of several HTML files that are quoted in full in this chapter and that are also available on the CD that ships with this book. However, the C++ code will not function properly unless the HTML files quoted in this chapter are in the correct location on your hard drive. See the README.TXT file that comes with the CD for additional information on setting up your system correctly to run this code. Some of these files are located in the root of the Chap26 directory on the CD. You will also need to use several databases' aliases described in the readme file.

Hardware and Software Requirements

As I implied in the "Overview" section for this chapter, the code discussed here requires one of the following:

- A copy of Microsoft Windows NT 3.51 Server or NT 4.0 or later server with the Internet Information Server loaded
- Windows 95 and a copy of the Personal Web Server that ships with FrontPage

At the time of this writing, it is not clear whether the Personal Web Server (PWS) will be available from other sources besides FrontPage. I downloaded the beta copy I used while writing this book directly from Microsoft's Web site. Checking to see if this copy is still available in that form is probably worthwhile.

You should also check to see if the Netscape or WebSite servers are now supporting the ISAPI API. An unfortunate and rather unseemly economic battle between Microsoft and its various competitors may slow down or even halt the spread of ISAPI as a standard, but checking to see if the battle has cooled somewhat is still worthwhile.

At any rate, the PWS is a useful piece of software for home users to explore. It will turn any Windows 95 machine into a Web server. I'm not sure how robust it will be under the strain of more than a few contiguous users. However, it is ideal if you want to set up a Web server in your home or in a small office. WebSite, from O'Reilly, is another fine product to turn to, particularly if you want to select a well-tested, robust server that can carry a heavy load.

You should also have a second computer equipped with a Web browser. This second computer can be running any operating system and can use virtually any software that supports Web browsing. I can think of no reason why you can't test most of this code on a single machine running a server, of course, but you will hardly get into the spirit of this enterprise if you're limited to that kind of setup.

I assume that most readers working in a business setting will have an intranet setup that will allow them to experiment with this technology. If you're working at home, I cannot stress too often the incredible value of setting up a network in your house. Network cards are very inexpensive these days. One of the ones I use in my home cost about $30 new. Network cable is also inexpensive, and both Windows 95 and Windows NT come equipped with all the software you need to set up a network that supports both file browsing with Windows Explorer and also TCP/IP.

When I first set up a network in my home, I thought I was pushing the extreme edge of modern technology. Now I simply take it for granted and can't understand how in the world I ever got along without it. Old computers don't have to die; they can just become Web servers. Small hard drives are extended easily by sharing storage space across multiple machines. After all, you don't need a separate copy of every application or every file on each machine. You can just share drives back and forth between machines, thereby saving a tremendous amount of space.

Most importantly, you can study and experiment with your network at your leisure and then apply that knowledge at work. A home network is an ideal place to educate yourself regarding this valuable technology.

Getting More Information on ISAPI

The best place to go for information on ISAPI is the Microsoft MSDN or the Microsoft Internet SDK. These two sources provide most of the information you need that can't be found in this book.

Here's a place you can go on the Web if you want to find out more about the ISAPI specification:

```
http://www.microsoft.com/win32dev/apiext/isalegal.htm
```

Of course, I can't guarantee that this Web page will still be in existence when you read this book. However, two relatively stable sites on the Web that should serve as links to this spot are

```
http://www.microsoft.com/intdev/
http://www.microsoft.com/win32dev/
```

Check in at both these sites on fairly regular intervals to get updates on Win32 and Internet technology.

ISAPI

As stated in the Microsoft documentation, ISAPI allows you to "Write server-side scripts and filters to extend the capabilities of Microsoft Internet Information Server and other ISAPI Web servers."

ISAPI is a very easy-to-use yet extremely powerful technology that allows you to extend the reach of the Internet Information Server or the Personal Web Server. This tool allows you to make your Web site do pretty much whatever you want it to do. For example, it provides a means for you to

- Set up interactive responses to user input
- Provide database browsing and updating
- Filter input to your browser to track who signs on and where he or she goes

In the past, the best way to extend a Web server was to create CGI applications. These powerful tools were limited by their executable format. When you sent in a CGI-based request from a browser to a server, the CGI application in question usually had to be loaded into memory, which took a long time. Also, the CGI technology could be a bit awkward to use under some circumstances.

ISAPI is a method of writing DLLs that replace CGI applications. You can also write filters with ISAPI, though this subject is not covered in this book. ISAPI has the advantage of being easier to use than CGI, plus it can be much faster and make much better use of system resources. In particular, the following points help explain why ISAPI DLLs are better than CGI applications:

- ISAPI DLLs live in the same address space as the HTTP server. They can therefore directly access the HTTP services available from the server. They load into memory more quickly and have much less overhead when it comes to making a call from the server. These capabilities can be particularly helpful if you're working under a heavy load.

- You can control when the DLL is loaded or unloaded. For example, you can preload DLLs for fast access on the first try or unload the ISAPI applications DLLs that are not being used to free system resources. You can do the same thing with the CGI executable, but the executable format was not really designed for this kind of manipulation, although this is part of the native capability of DLLs.

In this chapter, I will concentrate on writing DLLs that return datasets or that simply communicate with the user who is running a browser. I will not explore filters at all. For information on filters, you should go to the Microsoft Web site or browse the MSDN.

ISAPI Basics

The file `Httpext.h` contains the key declarations used with ISAPI. This file should ship with C++Builder and is available with versions of the Microsoft SDK dated later than July 1996. It should also appear in the `\include\vcl` directory as `ISAPI.HPP`. Because it is a Windows 95– or Windows NT–based technology, you must be using a 32-bit compiler to access this technology. You can't use it from a 16-bit compiler, nor is it available on Windows 3.1.

`Httpext.h` contains the interface to the ISAPI technology created by Microsoft. At the time of this writing, C++Builder has no custom interface for ISAPI, and I will describe only how to use Microsoft's existing technology. However, ISAPI is extremely easy to use, and the addition of a custom object is not necessary for most users.

Three functions can serve as entry points to ISAPI DLLs. The first two listed here are mandatory, whereas the third is optional:

- `GetExtensionVersion`: This function just does minimal version checking.
- `HttpExtensionProc`: This function is the entry point of the DLL, like the main `begin..end` block in a Delphi application.
- `TerminateExtension`: This optional routine can be used to clean up threads of other memory allocations.

When you're creating an ISAPI DLL, you must export the first two of the three preceding functions. Implementing these two functions is the key to all ISAPI programming.

In C++Builder, DEF files are frowned upon. You should therefore make sure that `Httpext.h` has been modified to export both of these functions with `__declspec(dllexport)`:

```
BOOL WINAPI __declspec(dllexport) GetExtensionVersion(HSE_VERSION_INFO *pVer);
DWORD
WINAPI
__declspec(dllexport) HttpExtensionProc(EXTENSION_CONTROL_BLOCK *pECB);
```

`TerminateExtension` is new in ISAPI 2.0. Its declaration looks like this:

```
BOOL  WINAPI  TerminateExtension( DWORD dwFlags );
```

`TerminateExtension` is called just before a connection is broken. It provides a place for you to deallocate memory allocated inside your DLL.

These three routines all contain the word `Extension`. This term is used because ISAPI DLLs extend the Internet Information Server or the Personal Web Server. (Remember, the Internet Information Server is Microsoft's Web server. If you want to turn an NT Server into a Web server, you use this tool. It ships with NT 4.0 and is installed automatically during the setup of that operating system.)

Using GetExtensionVersion

The `GetExtensionVersion` function must be exported from your DLL; otherwise, the server will not load your DLL. The only job of this function is to report the version of ISAPI that you expect to support.

You can always just cut and paste the `GetExtensionVersion` code into your DLLs. You need to change the function only slightly when you want to change the description passed in the `lpszExtensionDesc` field of the `HSE_VERSION_INFO` struct:

```
BOOL WINAPI GetExtensionVersion(HSE_VERSION_INFO *pVer)
{
  pVer->dwExtensionVersion = MAKELONG(HSE_VERSION_MINOR, HSE_VERSION_MAJOR);
  strcpy(pVer->lpszExtensionDesc, "C++ Builder ISAPI DLL");
  return (TRUE);
};
```

The parameter passed to this function is declared in `Httpext.h` as follows:

```
typedef struct   _HSE_VERSION_INFO {
    DWORD   dwExtensionVersion;                       // Version info
    CHAR    lpszExtensionDesc[HSE_MAX_EXT_DLL_NAME_LEN];  // Description
} HSE_VERSION_INFO, *LPHSE_VERSION_INFO;
```

Extending an Internet Server with ISAPI

CHAPTER 26

1027

26

EXTENDING AN
INTERNET SERVER
WITH **ISAPI**

The two fields of the record are self-explanatory, with the first containing the ISAPI version number and the second holding a user-defined string describing the purpose of the DLL. The following are some constants declared in the DLL that are used in the preceding code:

```
#define    HSE_MAX_EXT_DLL_NAME_LEN   256
#define    HSE_VERSION_MAJOR            1     // major version of this spec
#define    HSE_VERSION_MINOR            0     // minor version of this spec
```

That's all you need to do to set up the first of the two mandatory functions in an ISAPI DLL. The next step, using `HttpExtensionProc`, is a bit more complex, so I will treat it in its own section.

Working with the `HttpExtensionProc`

The `HttpExtensionProc` routine is the entry point for the DLL. It serves the same purpose that the `main()` routine does in a C program, or that the `main begin..end` pair does in a Delphi program.

Here is a very simple example of an `HttpExtensionProc` routine:

```
DWORD WINAPI HttpExtensionProc(EXTENSION_CONTROL_BLOCK *pECB)
{
  char ResultString[500];
  DWORD resultLen;
  char *IsapiLogText = "ISAPI1 - Simple ISAPI Extension DLL";
  strcpy(pECB->lpszLogData, IsapiLogText);
  pECB->dwHttpStatusCode = 200;
  char *HtmlInfo =
    "<HTML>"
    "<HEAD><TITLE>C++ Builder ISAPI DLL </TITLE></HEAD>"
    "<H1>ISAPI1 Test Results</H1>"
    "<BODY bgcolor=\"#0000FF\" text=\"#00FFFF\">"
    "Hello from a C++ Builder ISAPI DLL!<BR></BODY>"
    "</HTML>";
  sprintf(ResultString,
    "HTTP/1.0 200 OK\nContent-Type: text/html\n"
    "Content-Length: %d\nContent:\n\n %s", 500, HtmlInfo);
  resultLen = lstrlen(ResultString);
  fprintf(out, ResultString);
  pECB->WriteClient(pECB->ConnID, ResultString, &resultLen, 0);
  return (HSE_STATUS_SUCCESS);
}
```

If you queried a DLL containing this function from a browser, you would get a page back with this message:

```
ISAPI1 Test Results
Hello from a C++ Builder ISAPI DLL!
```

In the next few paragraphs, I will describe the key points of the code shown here. However, I'll help you develop a complete understanding of this routine slowly in the next few sections of the chapter.

The HTML code for querying the DLL might look something like this:

```
<a href="/scripts/isapi1.dll">ISAPI1 Example</a>
```

Most of the body of the function is taken up with simple HTML code that provides basic information to the user:

```
char *HtmlInfo =
    "<HTML>"
    "<HEAD><TITLE>C++ Builder ISAPI DLL </TITLE></HEAD>"
    "<H1>ISAPI1 Test Results</H1>"
    "<BODY bgcolor=\"#0000FF\" text=\"#00FFFF\">"
    "Hello from a C++ Builder ISAPI DLL!<BR></BODY>"
    "</HTML>";
```

You also need to fill in a few fields of the EXTENSION_CONTROL_BLOCK:

```
char *IsapiLogText = "ISAPI1 - Simple ISAPI Extension DLL";
strcpy(pECB->lpszLogData, IsapiLogText);
pECB->dwHttpStatusCode = 200;
```

The lpszLogData field contains the string that will be written to the log on your server. With the Personal Web Server, this log is kept by default in the Windows directory, though you can change this in the Administration section of the server applet found in the Control Panel.

The status code in this example is set to 200, which means "OK." Other possible values include the following:

```
HTTP_STATUS_BAD_REQUEST
HTTP_STATUS_AUTH_REQUIRED
HTTP_STATUS_FORBIDDEN
HTTP_STATUS_NOT_FOUND
HTTP_STATUS_SERVER_ERROR
HTTP_STATUS_NOT_IMPLEMENTED
```

More information on the EXTENSION_CONTROL_BLOCK is provided in the section called "Working with the EXTENSION_CONTROL_BLOCK."

Notice the function pointer called WriteClient in the struct. You can call this function to send information back to the browser. When calling this function, you use the value in the ConnID field of the EXTENSION_CONTROL_BLOCK struct. ConnID is filled in for you automatically when the HttpExtensionProc function is called.

Before you look at the EXTENSION_CONTROL_BLOCK struct, let me show you a complete ISAPI DLL that uses the HttpExtensionProc function shown in this section.

A Stripped-Down ISAPI Example

The source code in Listing 26.1 shows how to create the simplest possible ISAPI DLL. The goal is to remove all the complications from the code, and just include enough information to make sure everything is working correctly.

Extending an Internet Server with ISAPI

CHAPTER 26

1029

26

EXTENDING AN
INTERNET SERVER
WITH ISAPI

Listing 26.1. The ISAPI1 example.

```cpp
//////////////////////////////////////
// FILE: ISAPI1.CPP
// PROJECT: ISAPI1.DLL
// copyright (3) 1996 by Charlie Calvert
//
// This example shows how to use ISAPI, which is similar to creating a
// CGI application. The code should return a simple string to an HTML
// browser such as the Internet Explorer.
//
// Here is the HTML you output in a browser to call this ISAPI DLL:
//
// <HTML>
// <HEAD>
// <TITLE>CharlieC Home Page</TITLE>
// </HEAD>
// <BODY>
// <H1>My Home Page </H1>
// <P>
// This is the home page for my home computer.
// <P>
// <A HREF="/scripts/isapi1.dll" >ISAPI One</A><BR>
// </BODY>
// </HTML>
#include <vcl\vcl.h>
#include <string.h>
#include <stdio.h>
#pragma hdrstop
#include "..\..\utils\Httpext.h"
USERES("Isapi1.res");
FILE *out;
// GetExtensionVersion callback definition
BOOL WINAPI GetExtensionVersion(HSE_VERSION_INFO *pVer)
{
  fputs("Version", out);
  pVer->dwExtensionVersion = MAKELONG(HSE_VERSION_MINOR, HSE_VERSION_MAJOR);
  strcpy(pVer->lpszExtensionDesc, "C++ Builder ISAPI DLL");
  return (TRUE);
};
DWORD WINAPI HttpExtensionProc(EXTENSION_CONTROL_BLOCK *pECB)
{
  AnsiString ResultString;
  DWORD resultLen;
  AnsiString IsapiLogText = "ISAPI1 - Simple ISAPI Extension DLL";
  strcpy(pECB->lpszLogData, IsapiLogText.c_str());
  AnsiString HtmlInfo =
    "<HTML>"
    "<HEAD><TITLE>C++ Builder ISAPI DLL </TITLE></HEAD>"
    "<H1>ISAPI1 Test Results</H1>"
    "<BODY bgcolor=\"#0000FF\" text=\"#00FFFF\">"
    "You are talking to a C++Builder ISAPI DLL."
    "<BR></BODY>"
    "</HTML>";
  pECB->dwHttpStatusCode = 200;
  ResultString = Format(
    "HTTP/1.0 200 OK\nContent-Type: text/html\n"
```

continues

Listing 26.1. continued

```
      "Content-Length: %d\nContent:\n\n %s",
      OPENARRAY(TVarRec, (HtmlInfo.Length(), HtmlInfo)));
  resultLen = ResultString.Length();
  fprintf(out, ResultString.c_str());
  pECB->WriteClient(pECB->ConnID, ResultString.c_str(), &resultLen, 0);
  return (HSE_STATUS_SUCCESS);
}
#pragma argsused
int WINAPI DllEntryPoint(HINSTANCE hinst, unsigned long reason, void*)
{
  switch (reason)
  {
    case DLL_PROCESS_ATTACH:
      out = fopen("c:\\test.txt", "w+");
      fprintf(out,"hello");
      break;
    case DLL_PROCESS_DETACH:
      fprintf(out,"goodbye");
      fclose(out);
      break;
    default:
      break;
  }
  return (TRUE);
}
```

To use this DLL, you should copy it into a subdirectory of the `scripts` directory beneath the root for your Web. On my NT 4.0 machine, the subdirectory looks like this:

```
c:\winnt\system32\inetsrv\scripts\mystuff\isapi1.dll
```

In this case, I have created the directory called MYSTUFF, and it is used solely for storing ISAPI DLLs I have created. Your mileage may, of course, differ on your machine, depending on where you put the `InetSrv` directory and various other factors.

To call this DLL, you should add the following hyperlink to one of your HTML pages:

```
<A HREF="/scripts/mystuff/isapi1.dll" >ISAPI One</A><BR>
```

For example, here is a complete sample page:

```
<HTML>
<HEAD><TITLE>An ISAPI Page</TITLE></HEAD>
<BODY>
<H1>My ISAPI Page</H1>
<P>This is the home page for ISAPI on my computer.<P>
<A HREF="/scripts/mystuff/isapi1.dll" >ISAPI One</A><BR>
</BODY>
</HTML>
```

When the user clicks the hyperlink, the ISAPI1 DLL will be called and the string `"Hello from C++ Builder"` will appear in the user's browser. If you did not put the ISAPI1.DLL in the MYSTUFF

Extending an Internet Server with ISAPI

CHAPTER **26**

1031

26

EXTENDING AN
INTERNET SERVER
WITH **ISAPI**

directory, then you should change the preceding HTML code to reflect that fact. Notice that the path you assign is relative to the InetSrv directory and does not, and should not, contain the entire path to your DLL.

Note that if you copy the ISAPI1.DLL into the MYSTUFF directory multiple times, you will need to shut down the WWW portion of the Internet server before each copy. The rule is that you can copy the DLL the first time for free, but after you have used it, it belongs to the server, and you need to shut down the WWW services on the server before you can copy an updated version of the file over the first copy. You can use the Internet Service Manager application to shut down the WWW services on the NT Server. This application should be in the Microsoft Internet Server group created in Windows Explorer or Program Manager (NT 3.51) at the time of the installation of the Internet Information Server. You can use the PWS applet in the Control Panel if you're using the Personal Web Server on Windows 95 or on the Windows NT Workstation.

Working with the EXTENSION_CONTROL_BLOCK

By this point in the chapter, you should be able to create your first ISAPI DLL and call it from a Web browser on a second machine. The rest of this chapter explores ISAPI in more depth.

The following fairly complex record is passed as the sole parameter to HttpExtensionProc:

```
typedef struct _EXTENSION_CONTROL_BLOCK {
    DWORD     cbSize;                  // size of this struct.
    DWORD     dwVersion;              // version info of this spec
    HCONN     ConnID;                 // Context number not to be modified!
    DWORD     dwHttpStatusCode;       // HTTP Status code
    CHAR      lpszLogData[HSE_LOG_BUFFER_LEN];// log info
    LPSTR     lpszMethod;             // REQUEST_METHOD
    LPSTR     lpszQueryString;        // QUERY_STRING
    LPSTR     lpszPathInfo;           // PATH_INFO
    LPSTR     lpszPathTranslated;     // PATH_TRANSLATED
    DWORD     cbTotalBytes;           // Total bytes indicated from client
    DWORD     cbAvailable;            // Available number of bytes
    LPBYTE    lpbData;                // pointer to cbAvailable bytes
    LPSTR     lpszContentType;        // Content type of client data
    BOOL (WINAPI * GetServerVariable) ( HCONN      hConn,
                                        LPSTR      lpszVariableName,
                                        LPVOID     lpvBuffer,
                                        LPDWORD    lpdwSize );
    BOOL (WINAPI * WriteClient)   ( HCONN      ConnID,
                                    LPVOID     Buffer,
                                    LPDWORD    lpdwBytes,
                                    DWORD      dwReserved );
    BOOL (WINAPI * ReadClient)    ( HCONN      ConnID,
                                    LPVOID     lpvBuffer,
                                    LPDWORD    lpdwSize );
```

```
    BOOL (WINAPI * ServerSupportFunction)( HCONN      hConn,
                                           DWORD      dwHSERRequest,
                                           LPVOID     lpvBuffer,
                                           LPDWORD    lpdwSize,
                                           LPDWORD    lpdwDataType );
} EXTENSION_CONTROL_BLOCK, *LPEXTENSION_CONTROL_BLOCK;
```

Notice that this record contains the ConnID field referenced previously and passed as the first parameter to WriteClient.

The first parameter of this record is used for version control. It should be set to the size of the EXTENSION_CONTROL_BLOCK. If Microsoft changes this structure, then they can tell which version of the structure they are dealing with by checking the size of the record as recorded in this field. You should never change any of the first three fields of this record; these fields are filled out ahead of time by ISAPI and can only be referenced, not changed, by your program.

The most important field of this record is probably the lpszQueryString, which contains information about the query passed in from the server. For example, suppose you have created a DLL called ISAPI1.DLL. To call this DLL, you would create an HREF that looks like this in one of your browser pages:

```
<A HREF="/scripts/mystuff/test1.dll">Test One</A>
```

If you want to query the DLL, you would edit the preceding line so that it looks like this:

```
<A HREF="/scripts/mystuff/test1.dll?MyQuery">Test One</A>
```

Given the second of the two HTML fragments listed here, your DLL would get called with the string "MyQuery" in the lpszQueryString parameter. Notice in particular the use of the question mark, followed by the query string itself.

You could, of course, change the query string at will. For example, you could write

```
<A HREF="/scripts/mystuff/test1.dll?ServerName">Test One</A>
```

To this query, the DLL might reply with the name of the server. You have no limits on what you can pass in this parameter, but the string after the question mark cannot have any spaces in it. If you need to use spaces, replace them with a plus sign: Instead of "Server Name", write "Server+Name". The string can be anything you want, and it is up to you to parse the information from inside the DLL as you like.

When you return information from the server back to the browser, you use the WriteClient function pointer that is part of this record.

Writers of CGI applications will notice that the syntax for sending query strings is familiar. Indeed, ISAPI follows many of the conventions of CGI, and most of the fields in the EXTENSION_CONTROL_BLOCK are simply borrowed directly to initialize this pointer; it is passed to you gratis by the Internet Information Server.

Another key field in the EXTENSION_CONTROL_BLOCK is the lpbData field, which contains any additional information sent to you by the browser. In particular, it is used to pass information associated with a Submit button. For example, if you have an HTML form with a number of fields in it, the information from these fields will be sent in the pointer called lpbData after the Submit button is clicked. The section of this chapter called "Getting Information from a Submit Button" focuses on how to handle this situation.

So far I have zeroed in on three key fields of the EXTENSION_CONTROL_BLOCK:

- ■ WriteClient: A pointer to a function that allows you to send formatted HTML data back to the browser. This function uses the ConnID field of EXTENSION_CONTROL_BLOCK.

- ■ lpszQueryString: The query passed to you from the browser.

- ■ lpbData: Any additional data being passed to you from the browser. This data is usually the contents of any fields on an HTML form. I discuss this field further in the section on the Submit button.

Mirroring the Fields of the EXTENSION_CONTROL_BLOCK

The best way to get a feeling for how the rest of the fields of EXTENSION_CONTROL_BLOCK work is simply to mirror them back to yourself in a browser. In other words, you can create an HTML page that allows the user to call a custom ISAPI DLL. The purpose of this ISAPI DLL is simply to snag the contents of each field of the EXTENSION_CONTROL_BLOCK, format them in HTML, and send them back to the browser. This will turn your browser into a rather jazzy debugger that shows each of the fields in the EXTENSION_CONTROL_BLOCK. Listing 26.2 contains the source to a DLL called IsapiVars that performs this task.

Listing 26.2. The IsapiVars code that mirrors back the parameters sent in the EXTENSION_CONTROL_BLOCK.

```
////////////////////////////////////
// IsapiVars.cpp
// Mirror back the information sent to an ISAPI DLL by the server
// Copyright (c) 1997 by Charlie Calvert
//
#include <vcl\vcl.h>
#pragma hdrstop
#include "..\..\utils\Httpext.h"

USERES("IsapiVars.res");

BOOL WINAPI GetExtensionVersion(HSE_VERSION_INFO *pVer)
{
  pVer->dwExtensionVersion = MAKELONG(HSE_VERSION_MINOR, HSE_VERSION_MAJOR);
```

continues

Listing 26.2. continued

```cpp
        strcpy(pVer->lpszExtensionDesc, "ISAPI Variables DLL");
        return (TRUE);
};

#define SIZE 2048

DWORD WINAPI HttpExtensionProc(EXTENSION_CONTROL_BLOCK *pECB)
{
    char ResultString[SIZE * 2];
    char HtmlInfo[SIZE];
    char Buffer[SIZE];
    DWORD StrSize;
    DWORD resultLen;

    char *IsapiLogText = "ISAPIVars from C++ Builder";
    strcpy(pECB->lpszLogData, IsapiLogText);
    pECB->dwHttpStatusCode = 200;

    sprintf(HtmlInfo,
        "<HTML><TITLE>Fields of EXTENSION_CONTROL_BLOCK</TITLE>"
        "<H1>Test server results</H1><BODY>"
        "Size = %d<BR>"
        "Version = %.8x<BR>"
        "ConnID = %.8x<BR>"
        "Method = %s<BR>"
        "Query = %s<BR>"
        "PathInfo = %s<BR>"
        "PathTranslated = %s<BR>"
        "TotalBytes = %d<BR>"
        "AvailableBytes = %d<BR>"
        "ContentType = %s<BR><BR>"
        "<H1>Calls to GetServerVariable</H1>",
        pECB->cbSize, pECB->dwVersion, pECB->ConnID,
        pECB->lpszMethod, pECB->lpszQueryString,
        pECB->lpszPathInfo, pECB->lpszPathTranslated,
        pECB->cbTotalBytes, pECB->cbAvailable,
        pECB->lpszContentType);

    StrSize = sizeof(Buffer);
    pECB->GetServerVariable(pECB->ConnID, "REMOTE_ADDR", &Buffer, &StrSize);
    AnsiString VarString("REMOTE_ADDR = " + AnsiString(Buffer) + "<BR>");

    StrSize = sizeof(Buffer);
    pECB->GetServerVariable(pECB->ConnID, "REMOTE_HOST", &Buffer, &StrSize);
    VarString += "REMOTE_HOST = " + AnsiString(Buffer) + "<BR>";

    StrSize = sizeof(Buffer);
    pECB->GetServerVariable(pECB->ConnID, "REMOTE_USER", &Buffer, &StrSize);
    VarString += "REMOTE_USER = " + AnsiString(Buffer) + "<BR>";

    StrSize = sizeof(Buffer);
    pECB->GetServerVariable(pECB->ConnID, "SERVER_NAME", &Buffer, &StrSize);
    VarString += "SERVER_NAME = " + AnsiString(Buffer) + "<BR>";
```

Extending an Internet Server with ISAPI

CHAPTER 26

1035

26

EXTENDING AN
INTERNET SERVER
WITH **ISAPI**

```
  StrSize = sizeof(Buffer);
  pECB->GetServerVariable(pECB->ConnID, "SERVER_PORT", &Buffer, &StrSize);
  VarString += "SERVER_PORT = " + AnsiString(Buffer) + "<BR>";

  StrSize = sizeof(Buffer);
  pECB->GetServerVariable(pECB->ConnID, "SERVER_PROTOCOL", &Buffer, &StrSize);
  VarString += "SERVER_PROTOCOL = " + AnsiString(Buffer) + "<BR>";

  StrSize = sizeof(Buffer);
  pECB->GetServerVariable(pECB->ConnID, "SERVER_SOFTWARE", &Buffer, &StrSize);
  VarString += "SERVER_SOFTWARE = " + AnsiString(Buffer) + "<BR>";

  StrSize = sizeof(Buffer);
  pECB->GetServerVariable(pECB->ConnID, "HTTP_ACCEPT", &Buffer, &StrSize);
  VarString += "HTTP_ACCEPT = " + AnsiString(Buffer) + "<BR>";

  StrSize = sizeof(Buffer);
  pECB->GetServerVariable(pECB->ConnID, "URL", &Buffer, &StrSize);
  VarString += "URL = " + AnsiString(Buffer) + "<BR><BR><BR>";

  StrSize = sizeof(Buffer);
  pECB->GetServerVariable(pECB->ConnID, "ALL_HTTP", &Buffer, &StrSize);
  VarString += "ALL_HTTP = " + AnsiString(Buffer) + "<BR>";


  strcat(HtmlInfo, VarString.c_str());

  sprintf(ResultString,
    "HTTP/1.0 200 OK\nContent-Type: text/html\n"
    "Content-Length: %d\nContent:\n\n %s </HTML>",
    SIZE, HtmlInfo);


  StrSize = strlen(ResultString);
  pECB->WriteClient(pECB->ConnID, ResultString, &StrSize, 0);
  return (HSE_STATUS_SUCCESS);
}

int WINAPI DllEntryPoint(HINSTANCE hinst, unsigned long reason, void*)
{
  return 1;
}
```

To call this DLL, you should create an HTML script that contains the following line:

```
<A HREF="/scripts/mystuff/isapivars.dll">Test One</A> <BR>
```

Of course, the actual path shown in your code may be somewhat different from what I show here.

The HttpExtensionProc for this DLL is broken into two sections. The first retrieves all the main fields from the EXTENSION_CONTROL_BLOCK, and the second goes to town on one particular field, which is a function called GetServerVariable.

The code that parses the main fields of the EXTENSION_CONTROL_BLOCK is fairly straightforward:

```
sprintf(HtmlInfo,
    "<HTML><TITLE>Fields of EXTENSION_CONTROL_BLOCK</TITLE>"
    "<H1>Test server results</H1><BODY>"
    "Size = %d<BR>"
    "Version = %.8x<BR>"
    "ConnID = %.8x<BR>"
    "Method = %s<BR>"
    "Query = %s<BR>"
    "PathInfo = %s<BR>"
    "PathTranslated = %s<BR>"
    "TotalBytes = %d<BR>"
    "AvailableBytes = %d<BR>"
    "ContentType = %s<BR><BR>"
    "<H1>Calls to GetServerVariable</H1>",
    pECB->cbSize, pECB->dwVersion, pECB->ConnID,
    pECB->lpszMethod, pECB->lpszQueryString,
    pECB->lpszPathInfo, pECB->lpszPathTranslated,
    pECB->cbTotalBytes, pECB->cbAvailable,
    pECB->lpszContentType);
```

This code is nothing more than a simple call to `sprintf`. The goal is simply to take the fields of the EXTENSION_CONTROL_BLOCK and mirror them back to the user's browser. To do so, all you need to do is set up a legitimate HTML document and then add a human-readable version of the struct to the body of the form.

The output from this part of the code looks like the screen shot shown in Figure 26.1.

FIGURE 26.1.

The main fields of the
EXTENSION_CONTROL_BLOCK
shown in a browser.

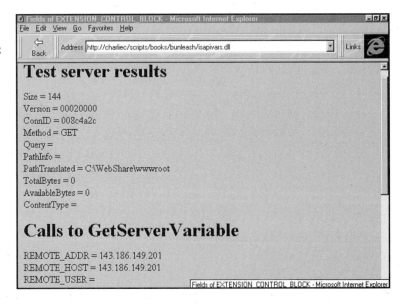

Working with `GetServerVariable` is a bit more complicated. As a result, I will give this description a whole section so that it can have plenty of room in which to knock about.

Extending an Internet Server with ISAPI

CHAPTER **26**

1037

26

EXTENDING AN
INTERNET SERVER
WITH **ISAPI**

The `GetServerVariable` and `ReadClient` Routines

You can use `GetServerVariable` to retrieve information from a server just as you would request information inside a CGI application. Here is an example of calling the routine:

```
#define SIZE 2048;
...
char Buffer[SIZE];
...
StrSize = sizeof(Buffer);
pECB->GetServerVariable(pECB->ConnID, "REMOTE_ADDR", &Buffer, &StrSize);
AnsiString VarString("REMOTE_ADDR = " + AnsiString(Buffer) + "<BR>");
```

This function takes a connection ID in the first parameter, a constant in the second parameter, a buffer in the third parameter, and the length of the buffer in the fourth parameter:

```
BOOL WINAPI GetServerVariable(
 HCONN hConn,
 LPSTR lpszVariableName,
 LPVOID lpvBuffer,
 LPDWORD lpdwSizeofBuffer
);
```

As a rule, you will have to reset the fourth parameter before each call to this function because the function itself returns the length of the string found in the `lpvBuffer` parameter in the `lpdwSizeOfBuffer` parameter. You definitely don't want to raise any exceptions or cause any errors to occur in your DLL, so I suggest playing it safe when calling this function.

The preceding code first sets the length of the buffer that will hold the information retrieved from the server. It then calls the server and asks for information. In this case, it asks for the content length of the information sent by the server.

You can pass the following strings in the second parameter of `GetServerVariable`:

`AUTH_TYPE`	Type of authentication used.
`CONTENT_LENGTH`	Number of bytes you can expect to receive from the client.
`CONTENT_TYPE`	Type of information in the body of a `POST` request.
`PATH_INFO`	Trailing part of the URL after the script name.
`PATH_TRANSLATED`	`PATH_INFO` with any virtual pathname expanded.
`QUERY_STRING`	Info following the "`?`" in the URL.
`REMOTE_ADDR`	IP address of the client (could be a gateway or firewall).
`REMOTE_HOST`	Hostname of the client or agent of the client.
`REMOTE_USER`	Username supplied by the client and authenticated by the server.

UNMAPPED_REMOTE_USER	Username before ISAPI mapped to an NT user account.
REQUEST_METHOD	The HTTP request method.
SCRIPT_NAME	The name of the script program being executed.
SERVER_NAME	The server name.
SERVER_PORT	The TCP/IP port on which the request was received.
SERVER_PORT_SECURE	If the request is on the secure port, then this will be 1; otherwise, it is 0.
SERVER_PROTOCOL	Usually HTTP/1.0.
SERVER_SOFTWARE	The name of the server software.
ALL_HTTP	All headers not already parsed into one of the previous variables.
HTTP_ACCEPT	The special-case HTTP header.
URL	New for version 2.0. The base portion of the URL.

You can find additional information on these variable names in the Microsoft online help.

You can see examples of the type of information returned by calling GetServerVariable in Figure 26.2. Note that this screen shot simply shows the lower half of the window shown in Figure 26.1.

FIGURE 26.2.

The results of making several repeated calls to GetServerVariable.

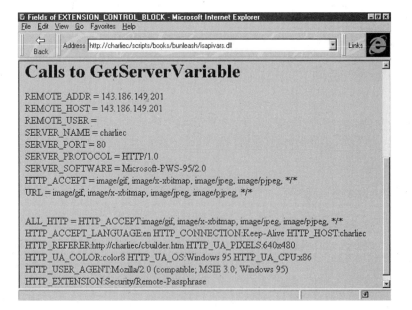

Extending an Internet Server with ISAPI

CHAPTER 26

1039

26

EXTENDING AN
INTERNET SERVER
WITH ISAPI

Note that many of the preceding pieces of information are automatically passed in the EXTENSION_CONTROL_BLOCK record. Therefore, you usually do not need to call GetServerVariable, but you can if you need to, particularly if you want to retrieve information with ReadClient and need to know how much information to read.

Most of the time, you don't need to call ReadClient. However, if the amount of data being sent by the browser is larger than 48KB, you will need to call ReadClient to get the rest of the data.

The DLLEntryPoint

Before completing the discussion of how this DLL works, I want to take a moment to get some housekeeping chores out of the way. In particular, I want to mention the DLLEntryPoint routine, which appears at the bottom of the DLL.

All DLLs have an entry point that is called automatically. You don't have to respond to this entry point, but doing so is usually a good idea. In this case, I simply open a text file for debugging purposes:

```
#pragma argsused
int WINAPI DllEntryPoint(HINSTANCE hinst, unsigned long reason, void*)
{
  switch (reason)
  {
    case DLL_PROCESS_ATTACH:
      out = fopen("c:\\test.txt", "w+");
      fprintf(out,"hello");
      break;
    case DLL_PROCESS_DETACH:
      fprintf(out,"goodbye");
      fclose(out);
      break;
    default:
      break;
  }
  return (TRUE);
}
```

Nothing about the code shown here is mandatory. You don't have to open a text file and write to it; the code serves no other purpose than to give you a simple means of debugging your DLL. In particular, it creates a text file on the server to leave a record of your DLL's behavior. This file is helpful, particularly if you're learning ISAPI and have problems simply creating a valid DLL that exports the key functions.

> **NOTE**
>
> You can debug an ISAPI DLL by using several different means. One rather fancy method is to load the entire server into the stand-alone debugger, load your ISAPI DLL, and then set a break point inside it.
>
> Although effective, the technique described in the preceding paragraph can be overkill. My suggestion is not to be too proud about resorting to the old-fashioned technique of creating a text file and writing to it. You can produce very detailed reports in this fashion, and they can show you exactly what is going on in your DLL. The only flaw in this system is that entering all those `fprintf` statements takes a bit of time.

The example shown here has a more valuable purpose then merely showing one rather simple-minded way to debug an ISAPI DLL. In particular, it reminds you of the proper way to handle the entry point of a DLL. In addition to the `DLL_PROCESS_ATTACH` and `DLL_PROCESS_DETACH` notifications are two others called `DLL_THREAD_ATTACH` and `DLL_THREAD_DETACH`. Because multiple clients could be using your DLL at the same time, `DLL_THREAD_ATTACH` can be a very important entry point to use when you're debugging or constructing your DLL.

Getting Information from a Submit Button

Often you get information sent to you from an HTML form that has a Submit button on it. As long as this information is shorter than 49KB, you can assume that it will be available in the `lpbData` field of `TExtensionControlBlock`. Otherwise, you will need to call `ReadClient`. Here is how you would typically read the information from the pointer passed in this field:

```
AnsiString S;
  if (pECB->lpbData != NULL)
  {
    S = (char *)pECB->lpbData;
    S = Parse(S);
  }
  else
    S = "Error occurred on get from lpbData field";
```

This code first checks to see if `lpbData` is non-`NULL`. This type of conservative coding is a necessity in ISAPI, as you don't want errors to be occurring way over on the server side, where it is hard to see what is going on. The fragment shown here then typecasts `lpbData` so that you can place its contents in a variable of type `AnsiString`. It then passes the string to a user-defined function called `Parse` that handles the string passed by the server. If something goes wrong, the string variable is set equal to an error message and then returned to the user so he or she can view it in a browser.

Extending an Internet Server with ISAPI

CHAPTER 26

1041

26

EXTENDING AN
INTERNET SERVER
WITH ISAPI

If you want to see exactly what information is available in the `lpbData` field, you can use the following two functions to echo the data back to your Web browser:

```
AnsiString SetupHeader(AnsiString &ResultString, AnsiString S, int &Len)
{
  char *HeaderInfo = "HTTP/1.0 200 OK\nContent-Type: text/html\n"
                     "Content-Length: %d\nContent:\n\n %s </HTML>";

  ResultString.SetLength(S.Length() + strlen(HeaderInfo) + 1);
  Len = ResultString.Length();
  sprintf(ResultString.c_str(), HeaderInfo, Len, S);
  return ResultString;
}
//HttpExtensionProc callback definition
DWORD WINAPI HttpExtensionProc(EXTENSION_CONTROL_BLOCK *pECB)
{
  AnsiString ResultString;
  int ResultLen;
  char *IsapiLogText = "Mirror lpbData";
  strcpy(pECB->lpszLogData,IsapiLogText);
  pECB->dwHttpStatusCode = 200;
  AnsiString S;
  if (pECB->lpbData != NULL)
  {
    S = (char *)pECB->lpbData;
  }
  else
    S = "Error occurred get lpbData field";
  SetupHeader(ResultString, S, ResultLen);
  pECB->WriteClient(pECB->ConnID, ResultString.c_str(), &(DWORD)ResultLen, 0);
  return (HSE_STATUS_SUCCESS);
}
```

The first function, called `SetupHeader`, is just a utility routine that automates the process of setting up a header. It forces you to pass in the variable that is sent in the third parameter of `WriteClient`. I do this simply to help remind myself that I have to initialize this variable before passing it to the server.

The second routine simply mirrors the `lpbData` field back to the user of the DLL. On the CD that accompanies this book, you will find a DLL called `MirrorData` and an HTML form called `MirrorDataTest.htm`, which looks like this:

```
<!DOCTYPE HTML PUBLIC "-//IETF//DTD HTML//EN">
<html>
<head>
<meta http-equiv="Content-Type"
content="text/html; charset=iso-8859-1">
<meta name="GENERATOR" content="Microsoft FrontPage 2.0">
<title>MirrorDataTest</title>
</head>
<body bgcolor="#0000FF" text="#00FFFF">
<h1>View lpbData Test</h1>
```

```
<form action="/scripts/Books/BUnleash/MirrorData.dll"
method="POST">
    <p>Enter some information: </p>
    <p><textarea name="SendData" rows="16" cols="74"></textarea></p>
    <p>Enter More Information</p>
    <p><input type="text" size="76" name="SendData"></p>
    <p><input type="submit" name="SendData" value="Submit"></p>
</form>
</body>
</html>
```

You can use this code to test the `HttpExtensionProc` that mirrors back the value of `lpbData`. Note that the HTML form contains two fields for entering text, the first called `SendData` and the second called `MoreData`. If you have only one field and you type `Fast` into it, the DLL would mirror back the following to the user:

```
SendData=Fast&SendData=Submit
```

If you have two fields, as in the HTML code shown here, then the following would be mirrored back if the first field contains `Fast` and the second contains `Loose`:

```
SendData=Fast&MoreData=Loose&SendData=Submit
```

If you break down this text into three separate fields, they would look like this:

```
SendData=Fast
&MoreData=Loose
&SendData=Submit
```

This text says, in effect, the `SendData` field has the word `Fast` in it, the `MoreData` field has the word `Loose` in it, and the SendData button is a Submit button.

Responding to a Submit Button

Assume that you have an HTML form with the code shown in Listing 26.3.

Listing 26.3. The HTML code for a Web page that uses ISAPI to interact with the user.

```
<html>
<head>
<title>Talking ISAPI Test</title>
</head>
<body bgcolor="#0000FF" text="#00FFFF">
<h1>Talking ISAPI Test</h1>
<p>Press this button to see more of the simple ISAPI test:</p>
<form action="/scripts/Books/BUnleash/IsapiTalk.dll"
method="POST">
    <p>Enter your name: <input type="text" size="20"
    name="SendName"></p>
    <p><input type="submit" name="SendName" value="Submit"></p>
</form>
</body>
</html>
```

Extending an Internet Server with ISAPI

CHAPTER 26

1043

26

EXTENDING AN
INTERNET SERVER
WITH **ISAPI**

This code will produce a form that contains a text area where the user can enter his or her name and a button called Submit. Given this form, you can expect the lpbData field to contain the following string, assuming the user enters the word Sammy in the name field:

```
SendName=Sammy&SendName=Submit
```

To understand what is happening here, note the BODY of the HTML statement composed on the server as reflected in the following excerpt from the SetUpResString function shown previously:

```
'<BODY>lpbData = %s </BODY>' +
```

If you study the code in the HttpExtensionProc function, you will see that it uses the Format routine to substitute the value of ECB.lpbData for the %s variable in the preceding piece of code. (If you don't understand how Format works, see the BCB documentation, or my references to this method in Chapter 3, "C++Builder and the VCL.")

After you get the information from the form in the lpbData parameter, you can parse it and return information to the user. For example, you could extract the number 23 from the preceding example and then square it and return it to the user. Doing so would in effect allow you to get information from the user, namely a number, perform a mathematical action on the number, and then return the result to the user. This means you're creating dynamic, interactive Web pages on-the-fly, which is the current *sine qua non* of Internet programming!

Listing 26.4 shows the complete code for a program that will reply to a user who enters his or her name into a page of a Web browser and submits it to the DLL. The HTML that accompanies this program is shown in Listing 26.5.

Listing 26.4. The code for the ISAPITalk DLL.

```cpp
/////////////////////////////////////////
// IsapiTalk.cpp
// Mirror back the information sent to an ISAPI DLL by the server
// Copyright (c) 1997 by Charlie Calvert
//
#include <vcl\vcl.h>
#include <fstream.h>
#include <dir.h>
#pragma hdrstop
#include "..\..\utils\Httpext.h"

USERES("IsapiTalk.res");

BOOL WINAPI GetExtensionVersion(HSE_VERSION_INFO *pVer)
{
  pVer->dwExtensionVersion = MAKELONG(HSE_VERSION_MINOR, HSE_VERSION_MAJOR);
  strcpy(pVer->lpszExtensionDesc, "C++ Builder ISAPI DLL");
  return (TRUE);
};

// Remember: IOStream deals with OS paths, not relative path to server!
BOOL GetResultString(AnsiString &Result, AnsiString Path)
```

continues

Listing 26.4. continued

```
{
  fstream InFile;
  AnsiString FileName(Path + "\\BUnleash\\TalkTest\\TalkReply.htm");
  char ch;
  char S[500];

  InFile.open(FileName.c_str(), ios::in, filebuf::openprot);
  if (!InFile)
  {
    // If we couldn't get file, then what directory were we in?
    Result = "<H>Error reading stream!</H>";
    FileName = ExtractFilePath(FileName);
    if (chdir(FileName.c_str()) == 0)
    {
      getcurdir(0, S);
      Result += S;
    }
    else
      Result += "Could not get file, nor find current directory!";
    return FALSE;
  }
  while (InFile.get(ch))
    Result += ch;
  return TRUE;
}

AnsiString Parse(AnsiString &S)
{
  int i = S.Pos("&");
  S.SetLength(i - 1);
  S = strrev(S.c_str());
  i = S.Pos("=");
  S.SetLength(i - 1);
  S = strrev(S.c_str());
  return S;
}

//HttpExtensionProc callback definition
DWORD WINAPI HttpExtensionProc(EXTENSION_CONTROL_BLOCK *pECB)
{
  AnsiString Header("HTTP/1.0 200 OK\nContent-Type: text/html\nContent-Length:
                    %d\nContent:\n\n");
  AnsiString ResultString;
  int resultLen;

  char *IsapiLogText = "ISAPI Talk";
  strcpy(pECB->lpszLogData,IsapiLogText);
  pECB->dwHttpStatusCode = 200;

  // build the HTML result string
  AnsiString S;
  if (pECB->lpbData != NULL)
  {
    S = (char *)pECB->lpbData;
    S = Parse(S);
  }
```

Extending an Internet Server with ISAPI

CHAPTER 26

1045

26

EXTENDING AN
INTERNET SERVER
WITH ISAPI

```
  else
    S = "Error occurred get lpbData field";

  AnsiString Date(DateToStr(Now()));
  AnsiString Time(TimeToStr(Now()));

  GetResultString(ResultString, pECB->lpszPathTranslated);
  ResultString = Format(ResultString, OPENARRAY(TVarRec, (S, Date, Time)));
  resultLen = ResultString.Length();
  Header = Format(Header, OPENARRAY(TVarRec, (resultLen)));

  pECB->WriteClient(pECB->ConnID, ResultString.c_str(), &(DWORD)resultLen, 0);

  return (HSE_STATUS_SUCCESS);
}

int WINAPI DllEntryPoint(HINSTANCE hinst, unsigned long reason, void*)
{
  return 1;
}
```

Listing 26.5. The HTML file, called `TalkReply.htm`, used in the reply generated by the ISAPITalk DLL.

```
<html>
<head>
<title>This is a simple htm file</title>
</head>
<body bgcolor="#0000FF" text="#00FFFF">
<h1>Talking HTML Reply</h1>
<p> </p>
<p>Welcome, %s, to the talking HTML file!</p>
<p>It's remarkable that you should drop by today, %s, at %s (PST), as
I was just thinking about you. </p>
</body>
</html>
```

This program allows an HTML browser to work interactively with a Web server. Screen shots of before and after a query is made are shown in Figure 26.3 and Figure 26.4, respectively.

When you're working with this program, note that I assume you have placed the `TalkReply.htm` program in the following location relative to the root of your Web:

`\\BUnleash\\TalkTest\\TalkReply.htm`

The ISAPITalk DLL might receive the following string from the user who clicks the Submit button, asking that a number be squared:

`SendName=Sammy&SendName=Submit`

FIGURE 26.3.

Preparing to query the ISAPITalk *DLL.*

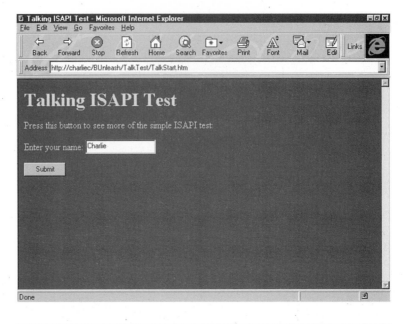

FIGURE 26.4.

The results of querying the ISAPITalk *DLL.*

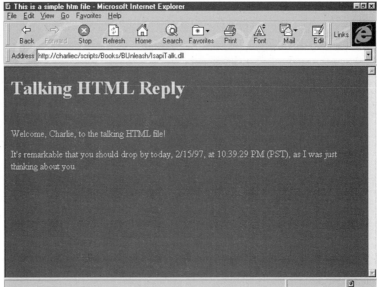

Given this input, the preceding code would return the following string to the user across the Internet:

```
Welcome, Sammy, to the talking HTML file!
It's remarkable that you should drop by today, 2/15/97,
at 10:39:29 PM (PST), as I was just thinking about you.
```

In short, the user enters the string `"Sammy"`, and the ISAPI DLL mirrors this information back and even adds in the current date and time as it is reported on the server side. This process sounds trivial, but the key issue here is that this activity is taking place dynamically on the Internet.

The function that parses the data sent by the user looks like this:

```
AnsiString Parse(AnsiString &S)
{
  int i = S.Pos("&");
  S.SetLength(i - 1);
  S = strrev(S.c_str());
  i = S.Pos("=");
  S.SetLength(i - 1);
  S = strrev(S.c_str());
  return S;
}
```

The code uses the `strrev` function from the Standard C Library to expedite the task of parsing out all the unnecessary data sent by the server.

The ISAPITalk program does not imbed any HTML code inside the C++ code that makes the DLL run. Instead, it reads in an HTML file and uses the VCL `Format` function to fill in the blank fields of the form shown in Listing 26.5.

The code for reading in the HTML file goes to considerable lengths to properly handle any errors that occur:

```
if (!InFile)
{
  // If we couldn't get file, then what directory were we in?
  Result = "<H>Error reading stream!</H>";
  FileName = ExtractFilePath(FileName);
  if (chdir(FileName.c_str()) == 0)
  {
    getcurdir(0, S);
    Result += S;
  }
  else
    Result += "Could not get file, nor find current directory!";
  return FALSE;
}
```

The issue here is that the file you want to load might be missing or might be in another directory than the one you suppose. The code shown here attempts to find the directory in which the DLL expects the HTML file to reside and to mirror that information back to the user on the off chance that an error occurs. This information can help you fix any broken links in your program without too much fussing around.

> **NOTE**
>
> The reason the ISAPITalk program reads in the HTML for the reply form from a file is simply that I don't like embedding HTML code inside C++ code. No technical reason prevents me from embedding HTML inside C++, but doing so does tend to be confusing. In particular, embedding the code makes it difficult for you to generate an attractive form that has just the proper look you want to produce. If you separate the HTML from your C++ code, you can use your favorite HTML editor to produce just the look you want.

The discussion of the ISAPITalk program has one final leg that needs to be completed before the race is done. This last portion of the journey involves getting the proper path to the HTML file that you read in while generating the reply form.

The Server Path Versus the OS Path

When you're writing ISAPI applications, you need to distinguish between the relative path you use when talking to the Web server and the absolute OS path you use when executing functions inside your DLL. Server paths should always be relative to the root of your Web, but OS paths are concerned with the current drive and directory.

If you embed the name of an HTML file in a hyperlink that is part of a Web path, you're dealing with relative server paths. If you call the C library `chdir` or `getcurdir` functions, then you're working with an OS path. For example, I need to pass an OS-based path to the function in the ISAPITalk program that reads an HTML file from disk.

Finding out the current OS path is relatively easy because ISAPI passes the absolute path to the root of the Web in the `lpszPathTranslated` field of the `EXTENSION_CONTROL_BLOCK`. For example, if the root of your Web is `C:\WEBSHARE\WWWROOT`, that path is passed to you in the `lpszPathTranslated` field.

The relative path you use in your Web pages is something that you usually determine while laying out the Web itself. Sometimes you have to refer to this path in your code. In particular, you will often reference this path if you're creating HTML on-the-fly. Most of the time, you simply have to determine the correct path by looking at the position of your files relative to the root of your Web.

Extending an Internet Server with ISAPI

CHAPTER **26**

1049

26

**EXTENDING AN
INTERNET SERVER
WITH ISAPI**

Here is an example of a relative path used in an HTML file:

```
\\BUnleash\\TalkTest\\TalkReply.htm
```

Here is the OS path to the same file:

```
C:\WEBSHARE\WWWROOT\\BUnleash\\TalkTest\\TalkReply.htm
```

Whatever you do, don't ever embed full OS pathnames in either your HTML or your ISAPI DLLs. If you do, then you will have to edit your code and your HTML whenever you change the location of your Web site. That is much too much work. Furthermore, from a security point of view, telling the users of your Web any more than they have to know about the actual layout of your hard drive is probably not a good idea.

To find out more about this subject, you can examine the ISAPITalk DLL on the CD that accompanies this book. This program provides an example of finding out the exact path to a file on the server so that you can load it into your DLL.

That's most of what I want to say about ISAPI in this chapter. This information should be enough to get you up and running and having some fun with this great technology.

Retrieving Data with an ISAPI DLL

In this section you will see a simple example for retrieving data from an ISAPI DLL. The CGI examples featured later in this book go into more depth on database techniques to use in this type of program. You can easily convert the CGI code into code that can be used with ISAPI.

The sample DLL shown in Listing 26.6 retrieves all the data from the Country table in the BCDEMOS database and shows it to the user in an HTML table.

Listing 26.6. The IsapiData program shows how to retrieve data from a database and display it in a browser.

```
/////////////////////////////////////////
// IsapiData
// Return Database rows from an ISAPI DLL
// Copyright (c) 1997 by Charlie Calvert
// Thanks to David Intersimone and Roland Fernandez
//
#include <vcl\vcl.h>
#include "..\..\utils\Httpext.h"
#pragma hdrstop

AnsiString TableToHtml(TDataSet *Table)
{
  int i;
  AnsiString Result;
```

continues

Listing 26.6. continued

```
  Result = "<TABLE BORDER>\n";
  for (i = 0; i < Table->FieldCount; i++)
  {
    Result = Result + Format("<TH>%s</TH>",
      OPENARRAY(TVarRec, (Table->Fields[i]->FieldName.c_str())));
  }

  while (!Table->Eof)
  {
    Result = Result + "<TR>";
    for (i = 0; i < Table->FieldCount; i++)
    {
      Result = Result + Format("<TD>%s</TD>",
        OPENARRAY(TVarRec, (Table->Fields[i]->AsString.c_str())));
    }
    Result = Result + "</TR>\n";
    Table->Next();
  }

  return Result + "</TABLE>\n";
}


AnsiString _stdcall _export GetData()
{
  TTable *Table;
  AnsiString Result;

  Table = new TTable(Application);
  Table->DatabaseName = "DBDEMOS";
  Table->TableName = "Country";
  Table->Open();
  Result = TableToHtml(Table);
  Table->Close();
  delete Table;

  return Result;
}

BOOL WINAPI _export GetExtensionVersion(HSE_VERSION_INFO *pVer)
{
  pVer->dwExtensionVersion = MAKELONG(HSE_VERSION_MINOR, HSE_VERSION_MAJOR);
  strcpy(pVer->lpszExtensionDesc, "ISAPI Variables DLL");
  return (TRUE);
};

void TextWrite(AnsiString S)
{
  FILE *F;
  S = S + "\n";
  F = fopen("c:\\foo.txt", "w+");
```

Extending an Internet Server with ISAPI

CHAPTER **26**

1051

26

EXTENDING AN
INTERNET SERVER
WITH **ISAPI**

```cpp
    fprintf(F, S.c_str());
    fclose(F);
}

void TextAppend(AnsiString S)
{
    FILE *F;
    S = S + "\n";
    F = fopen("c:\\foo.txt", "a+");
    fprintf(F, S.c_str());
    fclose(F);
}

DWORD WINAPI _export HttpExtensionProc(EXTENSION_CONTROL_BLOCK *pECB)
{
    AnsiString Header("HTTP/1.0 200 OK\nContent-Type: text/html\nContent-Length: "
                      " %d\nContent:\n\n");
    AnsiString ResultString;
    int resultLen;

    char *IsapiLogText = "ISAPI1 - Simple BC++ ISAPI Extension DLL";
    strcpy(pECB->lpszLogData,IsapiLogText);
    pECB->dwHttpStatusCode = 200;

    ResultString = GetData();


    Header = Format(Header, OPENARRAY(TVarRec, (ResultString.Length())));
    Header = Header + ResultString;
    resultLen = Header.Length();

    pECB->WriteClient(pECB->ConnID, Header.c_str(), &(DWORD)resultLen, 0);

    return (HSE_STATUS_SUCCESS);
}


int WINAPI DllEntryPoint(HINSTANCE hinst, unsigned long reason, void*)
{
    switch (reason)
    {
      case DLL_PROCESS_ATTACH:
        // TextWrite("DllLoaded");
        break;

      case DLL_PROCESS_DETACH:
        // TextAppend("Dll UnLoaded");
        break;
    }

    return 1;
}
```

BCB makes creating database-centered DLLs very simple. To open a table, all you have to do is write the standard code for creating and opening a database:

```
AnsiString _stdcall _export GetData()
{
  TTable *Table;
  AnsiString Result;

  Table = new TTable(Application);
  Table->DatabaseName = "DBDEMOS";
  Table->TableName = "Country";
  Table->Open();
  Result = TableToHtml(Table);
  Table->Close();
  delete Table;

  return Result;
}
```

In this example I create and open a table, being sure to set up the `DatabaseName` and `TableName` properties. I then call a special routine specifically designed to convert the data in a table into an HTML form. Finally I close and delete the table.

If you wanted to create a simpler test program, you could simply access the first field of data in the table:

```
Result = Table->Fields[0]->AsString.c_str()
```

As you will see in the CGI examples presented next, there is no reason why you cannot add a `DataModule` to this kind of program. In fact, you can extend ISAPI DLLs to the point where they handle relatively complex database chores such as processing queries or editing records. I want to thank David Intersimone and Roland Fernandez for showing me that these applications could be considerably simpler than I thought at first.

Introduction to CGI Programming

CGI programming is similar to ISAPI programming, except that you create executables rather than DLLs, and it works from inside any respectable server, rather than only from Microsoft's servers. To get input from a browser, you read the DOS environment variables.

Here is an example of reading a CGI variable:

```
char * S;
S = getenv("QUERY_STRING");
```

Here is an example of writing to a browser from a CGI application:

```
printf("This string will appear in a browser.");
```

Extending an Internet Server with ISAPI

CHAPTER 26

1053

26

EXTENDING AN
INTERNET SERVER
WITH ISAPI

As you can see, writing this code is not exactly rocket science. Because of its simplicity, I will whip right through several simple examples and then get on to some database applications. I don't mean to denigrate CGI because it is so simple to use. I don't like anything more than simple APIs, and CGI is one of the simplest. This technology is very powerful, and like ISAPI, it can quickly upgrade a Web site from something pretty average to something pretty spectacular.

A Simple CGI Example

CGI is so simple that I almost don't need to include the most basic of possible examples. However, enough things can go wrong with Web-based applications that you need one simple example that you know will work. The code in Listing 26.7 provides that example.

Listing 26.7. The SimpleCGI application.

```
//////////////////////////////////////////
// SimpleHelp.cpp
// Using an object to make CGI easier
// Copyright (3) 1997 by Charlie Calvert
//
#include <vcl\vcl.h>
#pragma hdrstop
  char S[] =
    "TO HIS COY MISTRESS<P>\n"
    "Had we but world enough and time,<BR>\n"
    "This coyness, lady, were no crime.<BR>\n"
    "We would sit down, and think which way<BR>\n"
    "To walk, and pass our long love's day.<BR>\n"
    "Thou by the Indian Ganges' side<BR>\n"
    "Shouldst rubies find: I by the tide<BR>\n"
    "Of Humber would complain. I would<BR>\n"
    "Love you ten years before the Flood:<BR>\n"
    "And you should if you please refuse<BR>\n"
    "Till the conversion of the Jews.<BR>\n"
    "My vegetable love should grow<BR>\n"
    "Vaster than empires, and more slow.<BR>\n"
    "An hundred years should go to praise<BR>\n"
    "Thine eyes, and on thy forehead gaze.<BR>\n"
    "Two hundred to adore each breast:<BR>\n"
    "But thirty thousand to the rest.<BR>\n"
    "An age at least to every part,<BR>\n"
    "And the last age should show your heart.<BR>\n"
    "For lady, you deserve this state;<BR>\n"
    "Nor would I love at lower rate.<BR>\n"
    "But at my back I always hear<BR>\n"
    "Time's winged chariot hurrying near:<BR>\n"
```

continues

Listing 26.7. continued

```
          "And yonder all before us lie<BR>\n"
          "Deserts of vast eternity.<BR>\n"
          "Thy beauty shall no more be found,<BR>\n"
          "Nor, in thy marble vault, shall sound<BR>\n"
          "My echoing song; then worms shall try<BR>\n"
          "That long preserved virginity:<BR>\n"
          "And your quaint honour turn to dust;<BR>\n"
          "And into ashes all my lust.<BR>\n"
          "The grave's a fine and private place,<BR>\n"
          "But none, I think , do there embrace.<BR>\n"
          "Now therefore, while the youthful hue<BR>\n"
          "Sits on thy skin like morning dew,<BR>\n"
          "And while thy willing soul transpires<BR>\n"
          "At every pore with instant fires,<BR>\n"
          "Now let us sport us while we may;<BR>\n"
          "And now, like am'rous birds of prey,<BR>\n"
          "Rather at once our time devour,<BR>\n"
          "Than languish in his slow chapped power<BR>\n"
          "Let us roll all our strength, and all<BR>\n"
          "Our sweetness, up into one ball:<BR>\n"
          "And tear our pleasures with rough strife,<BR>\n"
          "Through the iron gates of life.<BR>\n"
          "Thus, though we cannot make our sun<BR>\n"
          "Stand still, yet we will make him run.<BR>\n"
          "-- Andrew Marvell";

void main(void)
{
  setvbuf(stdout, NULL, _IONBF, 0);
  printf("\nContent-type: text/html\n\n");
  printf("<html>\n");
  printf("<body>\n");
  printf("<body bgcolor=\"\#0000FF\" text=\"\#00FFFF\" link=\"\#FFFF00\""
          "vlink=\"\#00FF00\" alink=\"\#FFFFFF\">");
  printf(S);
  printf("</body>\n");
  printf("</html>\n");
}
```

This console application has no main form; its output appears only in a browser, as shown in Figure 26.5.

To create the SimpleCGI application, start a new project and remove the main form. Save the project file in its own directory, and then choose Options | Project | Linker and set the Application Type to Console Application. You can also use File | New and select Console App from the App Expert dialog.

Extending an Internet Server with ISAPI

CHAPTER 26

1055

26

EXTENDING AN
INTERNET SERVER
WITH ISAPI

FIGURE 26.5.

The SimpleCGI *application.*

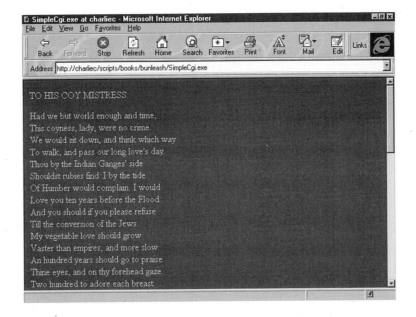

Remove all the WinMain business, and replace it with a simple DOS-style main block:

```
void main(void)
{
  setvbuf(stdout, NULL, _IONBF, 0);
  printf("\nContent-type: text/html\n\n");
  printf("<html>\n");
  printf("<body>\n");
  printf("...the sessions of sweet silent thought...");
  printf("</body>\n");
  printf("</html>\n");
}
```

This complete CGI application needs only be compiled and then copied to a server.

You call a CGI application exactly as you would an ISAPI DLL:

```
<p><a href="/scripts/books/bunleash/SimpleCgi.exe">SimpleCgi.exe</a>
```

Two complete HTML files for use with this chapter are available in the root of the Chap26 directory on the CD that accompanies this book. You might, of course, have to edit the paths shown in these files.

Retrieving the Variables Passed to a CGI Application

The variables passed to a CGI application can be retrieved from the DOS environment. You see these same types of variables when you type Set at the DOS prompt. You can use the getenv or _environ function to retrieve this data.

> **NOTE**
>
> Ghastly function names like getenv and the deplorable _environ are the result of a bygone time when compilers had a limited ability to work with long identifiers. Furthermore, there was a need to try to save every byte in the applications being produced.
>
> Despite the ugly function names, those were romantic and exciting times. It was a period when all PC-based computer technology was new, and the industry was experiencing dynamic growth.
>
> Despite the romance of that era, our much more complex contemporary programming environments require more careful habits. In modern programming, these functions would have easier-to-understand names like GetEnvironment and Environment.
>
> I sometimes catch myself wondering how many wasted hours have been lost, on a global scale, as a result of the horrible naming conventions and ludicrous capitalization standards that used to exist. On the other hand, I also can't help but look back fondly, on the smaller, more manageable APIs that existed in those times, and on the highly charged, and much more friendly, atmosphere that prevailed.

The CGIVars application found on the CD that accompanies this book shows how to iterate through all the environment variables passed to a CGI application. The output from that program is shown in Figure 26.6, and the source for the program is shown in Listing 26.8 through Listing 26.10.

FIGURE 26.6.

The output from the CGIVars application.

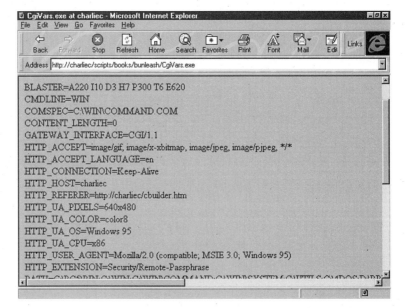

Listing 26.8. The CGIVars application shows how to retrieve all the variables passed to a CGI application.

```cpp
/////////////////////////////////////
// CGIVars.cpp
// Using an object to make CGI easier
// Copyright (c) 1997 by Charlie Calvert
//
#include <vcl\vcl.h>
#pragma hdrstop
#include "CGIHelp1.h"

USEUNIT("..\..\Utils\CGIHelp1.cpp");

void main(void)
{
  TCGIHelp CGI;
  CGI.Header("World Enough and Time");
  CGI.ShowEnv();
}
```

Listing 26.9. The TCGIHelp object provides support for CGI application. This is the header for the module.

```cpp
/////////////////////////////////////
// CGIHelp1.h
// An object to make CGI easier
// Copyright (c) 1997 by Charlie Calvert
//
#ifndef CGIHelp1H
#define CGIHelp1H

enum TColorType {ctLightBlue, ctRedYellow, ctBlueYellow, ctGreenBlack};

class TCGIHelp
{
public:
  TCGIHelp();
  ~TCGIHelp();
  void HTMLHeader();
  void Header(AnsiString S);
  AnsiString GetQuery();
  void Colors(TColorType ColorType);
  void ShowEnv();
};

#endif
```

Listing 26.10. The main source file for the TCGIHelp utility.

```cpp
/////////////////////////////////////
// CGIHelp1.cpp
// An object to make CGI easier
```

continues

Listing 26.10. continued

```cpp
// Copyright (c) 1997 by Charlie Calvert
//
#include <vcl\vcl.h>
#pragma hdrstop
#include "CGIHelp1.h"

TCGIHelp::TCGIHelp()
{
  setvbuf(stdout, NULL, _IONBF, 0);
  printf("\nContent-type: text/html\n\n");
  printf("<html>\n");
  printf("<body>\n");
}

TCGIHelp::~TCGIHelp()
{
  printf("</body>\n");
  printf("</html>\n");
}

void TCGIHelp::Header(AnsiString S)
{
  AnsiString Temp = "<H1>" + S + AnsiString("</H1>");
  printf(Temp.c_str());
}

AnsiString TCGIHelp::GetQuery()
{
  char *Query;
  Query = getenv("QUERY_STRING");
  if (Query)
    return Query;
  else
    return "";
}

void TCGIHelp::Colors(TColorType ColorType)
{
  switch(ColorType)
  {
    case ctLightBlue:
      printf("<body bgcolor=\"\#0000FF\""
          "text=\"\#00FFFF\""
          "link=\"\#FFFF00\""
          "vlink=\"\#00FF00\""
          "alink=\"\#FFFFFF\">");
    break;

    case ctRedYellow:
      printf("<body bgcolor=\"\#FF0000\""
          "text=\"\#FFFF\""
          "link=\"\#FFFF00\""
          "vlink=\"\#00FF00\""
          "alink=\"\#FFFFFF\">");
    break;
```

```
      case ctBlueYellow:
        printf("<body bgcolor=\"\#0000FF\""
               "text=\"\#FFFF\""
               "link=\"\#FFFF00\""
               "vlink=\"\#00FF00\""
               "alink=\"\#FFFFFF\">");
      break;

      case ctGreenBlack:
        printf("<body bgcolor=\"\#00FF00\""
               "text=\"\#000000\""
               "link=\"\#FFFF00\""
               "vlink=\"\#00FF00\""
               "alink=\"\#FFFFFF\">");
      break;

  }
}

void TCGIHelp::ShowEnv()
{
  int i =0;
  while (_environ[i])
    printf("%s<BR>", _environ[i++]);
}
```

The main body of this console application is simple:

```
void main(void)
{
  TCGIHelp CGI;
  CGI.Header("Current Environment");
  CGI.ShowEnv();
}
```

The code is brief because I'm using a small helper object that gets many of the worst chores out of the way for me:

```
class TCGIHelp
{
public:
  TCGIHelp();
  ~TCGIHelp();
  void HTMLHeader();
  void Header(AnsiString S);
  AnsiString GetQuery();
  void Colors(TColorType ColorType);
  void ShowEnv();
};
```

This object performs the basic chores needed to run a CGI application. It is also the kind of simple object that can be improved and enlarged as you see fit. In other words, you should feel free to add methods to this object as you find a need for them.

The constructor for TCGIHelp takes care of sending off a MIME header that browsers examine so they can know what to do with the HTTP code that is being streamed toward them:

```
TCGIHelp::TCGIHelp()
{
  setvbuf(stdout, NULL, _IONBF, 0);
  printf("\nContent-type: text/html\n\n");
  printf("<html>\n");
  printf("<body>\n");
}
```

The equally simple destructor outputs the lines that mark the end of an HTML form:

```
TCGIHelp::~TCGIHelp()
{
  printf("</body>\n");
  printf("</html>\n");
}
```

Other functions perform mundane tasks such as automatically formatting a header:

```
void TCGIHelp::Header(AnsiString S)
{
  AnsiString Temp = "<H1>" + S + AnsiString("</H1>");
  printf(Temp.c_str());
}
```

If you look at the source, you will see a method called colors that sets the background and foreground colors for a form. A simple enumerated type can be passed to the function so that you can set up the colors you need:

```
enum TColorType {ctLightBlue, ctRedYellow, ctBlueYellow, ctGreenBlack};
```

You can create more colors if you like. Each color statement sets the background color, the text color, and the link colors for the times before, during, and after they have been selected:

```
printf("<body bgcolor=\"\#0000FF\""
       "text=\"\#00FFFF\""
       "link=\"\#FFFF00\""
       "vlink=\"\#00FF00\""
       "alink=\"\#FFFFFF\">");
```

The numbers representing the colors work just like the standard Windows RGB colors:

```
#0000FF: Blue
#00FF00: Green
#FF0000: Red
```

You can find more details in Chapter 7, "Graphics."

The method that actually iterates through the environment is extremely simple:

```
void TCGIHelp::ShowEnv()
{
  int i =0;
  while (_environ[i])
    printf("%s<BR>", _environ[i++]);
}
```

Extending an Internet Server with ISAPI

CHAPTER 26

1061

26

EXTENDING AN
INTERNET SERVER
WITH ISAPI

Not much I can say about that one. It's just simple C 101 code from your first programming course.

If you want to retrieve an individual item from the environment, you can use this method:

```
AnsiString TCGIHelp::GetQuery()
{
  char *Query;
  Query = getenv("QUERY_STRING");
  if (Query)
    return Query;
  else
    return "";
}
```

The main purpose of this code is to return a friendly AnsiString rather than force the user to gamble on using a NULL-terminated string. This place would, of course, be a particularly bad one to try to shave a few clock cycles off an application by using NULL-terminated strings rather than AnsiStrings. The reasons for this are twofold:

1. If you do make a mistake using a NULL-terminated string, you will raise an exception, which will stop your application dead in the water because it is running on another machine. Often the only way to recover is to reboot the server. Later in the chapter, I will discuss how to treat exceptions raised in CGI applications.

2. CGI applications are slow by their very nature because they run over the network. As a result, nobody is going to notice if you shave a few nanoseconds here and a few nanoseconds there. As a result, you should use safe techniques for handling strings and think about other techniques for improving performance.

Given these considerations, I chose to return AnsiStrings from this method.

If no environment variable called QUERY_STRING exists, then the GetQuery method returns an empty AnsiString; otherwise, it returns the string retrieved from the system. getenv returns NULL if it cannot find the environment string you request. The server is the one that sets up the environment that will prevail inside the session where your application is launched.

NOTE

This section is not the place for me to get into the whole subject of creating CGI applications that are as small and as efficient as possible. You should be aware, however, that considerable thought has gone into sensible ways of creating applications that will stay in memory so that they do not have to be launched each time they are called. You can find books on this subject, or you can turn to third parties such as HREF: www.href.com.

Creating Simple CGI Database Applications

You can easily create a BCB-based CGI application that handles databases. All you have to do is allocate memory for a table, open it, and wrap its contents inside HTML statements. An example is shown Figure 26.7.

FIGURE 26.7.

The output for the CGIData application.

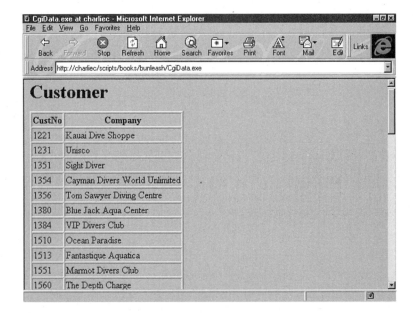

On the CD that accompanies this book, I include two applications that show the basics of working with the TTable object inside a CGI application. I also include one slightly more complex example that shows how to work with TQuery, TDatamodule, and InterBase from inside a CGI application.

NOTE

For the code shown in this section, I assume that you have the BDE set up on your server and that you or the installation program has created a BCDEMOS alias for the BDE.

Later, I will show an application running against InterBase tables. In that case, you will need to have both InterBase and the BDE running on your server. You could run the local InterBase server in this case because you can, if you want, query InterBase from the same machine on which the server resides. In other words, you can run both the local InterBase and your Web server on the same machine.

If you're using InterBase, Oracle, or other SQL servers, you will find a limit to the number of simultaneous connections you can support, depending on the nature of the license for your database server. You can still have multiple connections to your Web server, but you might be able to service only a limited number of requests for data at any one time.

Extending an Internet Server with ISAPI

CHAPTER 26

1063

26

EXTENDING AN
INTERNET SERVER
WITH ISAPI

The source for the first of the CGI-based database applications is shown in Listing 26.11. This program depends on the TCGIHelp object shown in Listing 26.9.

Listing 26.11. The source for the simplest possible case example of using a database code in a CGI application.

```cpp
/////////////////////////////////////////
// IsapiVars.cpp
// Mirror back the information sent to an ISAPI DLL by the server
// Copyright (c) 1997 by Charlie Calvert
//
#include <vcl\vcl.h>
#pragma hdrstop
#include "..\..\utils\Httpext.h"

USERES("IsapiVars.res");

BOOL WINAPI GetExtensionVersion(HSE_VERSION_INFO *pVer)
{
  pVer->dwExtensionVersion = MAKELONG(HSE_VERSION_MINOR, HSE_VERSION_MAJOR);
  strcpy(pVer->lpszExtensionDesc, "ISAPI Variables DLL");
  return (TRUE);
};

#define SIZE 2048

DWORD WINAPI HttpExtensionProc(EXTENSION_CONTROL_BLOCK *pECB)
{
  char ResultString[SIZE * 2];
  char HtmlInfo[SIZE];
  char Buffer[SIZE];
  DWORD StrSize;
  DWORD resultLen;

  char *IsapiLogText = "ISAPIVars from C++ Builder";
  strcpy(pECB->lpszLogData, IsapiLogText);
  pECB->dwHttpStatusCode = 200;

  sprintf(HtmlInfo,
    "<HTML><TITLE>Fields of EXTENSION_CONTROL_BLOCK</TITLE>"
    "<H1>Test server results</H1><BODY>"
    "Size = %d<BR>"
    "Version = %.8x<BR>"
    "ConnID = %.8x<BR>"
    "Method = %s<BR>"
    "Query = %s<BR>"
    "PathInfo = %s<BR>"
    "PathTranslated = %s<BR>"
    "TotalBytes = %d<BR>"
    "AvailableBytes = %d<BR>"
    "ContentType = %s<BR><BR>"
    "<H1>Calls to GetServerVariable</H1>",
    pECB->cbSize, pECB->dwVersion, pECB->ConnID,
    pECB->lpszMethod, pECB->lpszQueryString,
    pECB->lpszPathInfo, pECB->lpszPathTranslated,
```

continues

Listing 26.11. continued

```
      pECB->cbTotalBytes, pECB->cbAvailable,
      pECB->lpszContentType);

  StrSize = sizeof(Buffer);
  pECB->GetServerVariable(pECB->ConnID, "REMOTE_ADDR", &Buffer, &StrSize);
  AnsiString VarString("REMOTE_ADDR = " + AnsiString(Buffer) + "<BR>");

  StrSize = sizeof(Buffer);
  pECB->GetServerVariable(pECB->ConnID, "REMOTE_HOST", &Buffer, &StrSize);
  VarString += "REMOTE_HOST = " + AnsiString(Buffer) + "<BR>";

  StrSize = sizeof(Buffer);
  pECB->GetServerVariable(pECB->ConnID, "REMOTE_USER", &Buffer, &StrSize);
  VarString += "REMOTE_USER = " + AnsiString(Buffer) + "<BR>";

  StrSize = sizeof(Buffer);
  pECB->GetServerVariable(pECB->ConnID, "SERVER_NAME", &Buffer, &StrSize);
  VarString += "SERVER_NAME = " + AnsiString(Buffer) + "<BR>";

  StrSize = sizeof(Buffer);
  pECB->GetServerVariable(pECB->ConnID, "SERVER_PORT", &Buffer, &StrSize);
  VarString += "SERVER_PORT = " + AnsiString(Buffer) + "<BR>";

  StrSize = sizeof(Buffer);
  pECB->GetServerVariable(pECB->ConnID, "SERVER_PROTOCOL", &Buffer, &StrSize);
  VarString += "SERVER_PROTOCOL = " + AnsiString(Buffer) + "<BR>";

  StrSize = sizeof(Buffer);
  pECB->GetServerVariable(pECB->ConnID, "SERVER_SOFTWARE", &Buffer, &StrSize);
  VarString += "SERVER_SOFTWARE = " + AnsiString(Buffer) + "<BR>";

  StrSize = sizeof(Buffer);
  pECB->GetServerVariable(pECB->ConnID, "HTTP_ACCEPT", &Buffer, &StrSize);
  VarString += "HTTP_ACCEPT = " + AnsiString(Buffer) + "<BR>";

  StrSize = sizeof(Buffer);
  pECB->GetServerVariable(pECB->ConnID, "URL", &Buffer, &StrSize);
  VarString += "URL = " + AnsiString(Buffer) + "<BR><BR><BR>";

  StrSize = sizeof(Buffer);
  pECB->GetServerVariable(pECB->ConnID, "ALL_HTTP", &Buffer, &StrSize);
  VarString += "ALL_HTTP = " + AnsiString(Buffer) + "<BR>";


  strcat(HtmlInfo, VarString.c_str());

  sprintf(ResultString,
    "HTTP/1.0 200 OK\nContent-Type: text/html\n"
    "Content-Length: %d\nContent:\n\n %s </HTML>",
    SIZE, HtmlInfo);


  StrSize = strlen(ResultString);
  pECB->WriteClient(pECB->ConnID, ResultString, &StrSize, 0);
  return (HSE_STATUS_SUCCESS);
}
```

```
int WINAPI DllEntryPoint(HINSTANCE hinst, unsigned long reason, void*)
{
  return 1;
}
```

Because you're working in an application, as opposed to a DLL, the `TApplication` object is available to you. This object helps set up the `TSessions` object that is required by database applications. As a result, the conservative and safe thing to do is to make sure that the `Application->Initialize` method is called so that the database tools are set up properly:

```
Application->Initialize();
```

> **NOTE**
>
> This step makes ISAPI database applications a bit tricky. ISAPI runs in a DLL, and you have to be careful setting up database code in a DLL. In particular, you have to be sure the `Sessions` object is properly initialized and that each table is assigned a `Session`.

After setting up the `Application` and `Sessions` objects, you are free to open up a table. This application has no data module and no form, so you must do all the work yourself:

```
Table = new TTable(Application);
Table->DatabaseName = "BCDEMOS";
Table->TableName = "Customer";
Table->Open();
```

This code allocates memory for the table, specifies the database and table the application wants to use, and finally opens the table.

After the table is open, you can start retrieving data immediately. However, you might want to put off this step just long enough to set up an HTML table:

```
printf("<TABLE BORDER>\n");
printf("<TH>%s</TH><TH>%s</TH>",
  Table->Fields[0]->FieldName.c_str(),
  Table->Fields[1]->FieldName.c_str());
```

This code calls the `FieldName` property of the `TField` object to retrieve the name of each column in the database. This information is displayed in the top row of the HTML table. As you can see, this example works with only the first two columns. The CGIData2 program, shown in Listing 26.12, provides a generic solution for converting any table to HTML.

The following code iterates through the database, displaying all the data from the first two fields to the user:

```
while (!Table->Eof)
{
  printf("<TR><TD>%s</TD><TD>%s</TD></TR>\n",
```

```
   Table->Fields[0]->AsString.c_str(),
   Table->Fields[1]->AsString.c_str());
  Table->Next();
}
```

After the data is shown, I close the HTML table, close the TTable object, and then delete the TTable object:

```
printf("</TABLE>\n");
Table->Close();
delete Table;
```

CGI database programming is obviously simple. You can, however, make the process even easier. I will demonstrate these techniques in the next section.

Converting a Table to HTML

The CGIData2 application shows a technique for converting any arbitrary table to HTML. The program also shows how to pass information to a CGI application so that the user can choose the table he or she wants to display. The combination of these two traits gives the user the ability to browse any table on your system over the Internet.

The output from the CGIData2 program is shown Figure 26.8, and the source for the program is shown in Listings 26.12 through 26.14. Note the URL passed to the application in Figure 26.8. The information after the question mark specifies which table the user wants to browse.

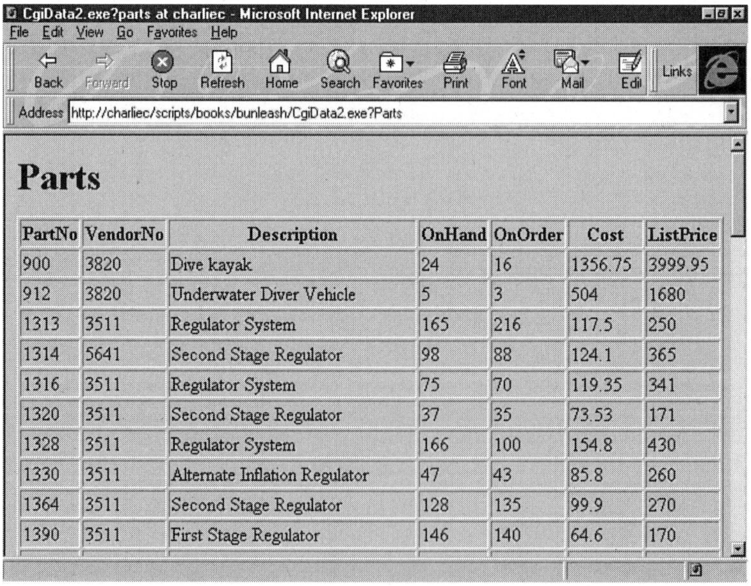

FIGURE 26.8.

The output from the CGIData2 application while looking at the Parts table from BCDEMOS.

Parts

PartNo	VendorNo	Description	OnHand	OnOrder	Cost	ListPrice
900	3820	Dive kayak	24	16	1356.75	3999.95
912	3820	Underwater Diver Vehicle	5	3	504	1680
1313	3511	Regulator System	165	216	117.5	250
1314	5641	Second Stage Regulator	98	88	124.1	365
1316	3511	Regulator System	75	70	119.35	341
1320	3511	Second Stage Regulator	37	35	73.53	171
1328	3511	Regulator System	166	100	154.8	430
1330	3511	Alternate Inflation Regulator	47	43	85.8	260
1364	3511	Second Stage Regulator	128	135	99.9	270
1390	3511	First Stage Regulator	146	140	64.6	170

Listing 26.12. The source for the main module in the CGIData2 application.

```cpp
///////////////////////////////////////
// CGIData2.cpp
// Databases and CGI
// Copyright (c) 1997 by Charlie Calvert
//
#include <vcl\vcl.h>
#pragma hdrstop
#include "cgiDBhelp1.h"

USEUNIT("..\..\Utils\CGIHelp1.cpp");
USEUNIT("..\..\Utils\CGIDBHelp1.cpp");

void main(void)
{
  TCGIDBHelp CGI;
  CGI.Colors(ctGreenBlack);
  char *Query;

  TTable *Table;

  Query = getenv("QUERY_STRING");

  if (Query)
  {
    Application->Initialize();
    Table = new TTable(Application);
    Table->DatabaseName = "BCDEMOS";
    Table->TableName = Query;
    try
    {
      Table->Open();
      CGI.Header(Table->TableName);
      CGI.PrintTable(Table);
      Table->Close();
      delete Table;
    }
    catch(Exception &E)
    {
      printf("Could not open table: %s", E.Message.c_str());
    }
    catch(...)
    {
      printf("Could not open table");
    }
  }
  else
  {
    printf("<H1>No query string available</H1>\n");
  }
  Application->Run();
}
```

Listing 26.13. The header for the `TCGIDBHelp` file.

```
/////////////////////////////////////
// CGIDBHelp1.h
// An object to make CGI easier
// Copyright (c) 1997 by Charlie Calvert
//
#ifndef CGIDBHelp1H
#define CGIDBHelp1H
#include "CGIHelp1.h"

class TCGIDBHelp: public TCGIHelp
{
public:
  void PrintTable(TDataSet *Table);
};

#endif
```

Listing 26.14. The `TCGIDBHelp` object provides support for CGI database applications.

```
/////////////////////////////////////
// CGIDBHelp1.cpp
// An object to make CGI easier
// Copyright (c) 1997 by Charlie Calvert
//
#include <vcl\vcl.h>
#pragma hdrstop
#include "CGIDBhelp1.h"

void TCGIDBHelp::PrintTable(TDataSet *Table)
{
  int i;

  printf("<TABLE BORDER>\n");
  for (i = 0; i < Table->FieldCount; i++)
  {
    printf("<TH>%s</TH>", Table->Fields[i]->FieldName.c_str());
  }
  while (!Table->Eof)
  {
    printf("<TR>");
    for (i = 0; i < Table->FieldCount; i++)
    {
      printf("<TD>%s</TD>", Table->Fields[i]->AsString.c_str());
    }
    printf("</TR>\n");
    Table->Next();
  }
  printf("</TABLE>\n");
}
```

This application is designed to allow the user to interact with it dynamically. In particular, this application retrieves the name of the table the user wants to see from the environment variable called QUERY_STRING:

```
Query = getenv("QUERY_STRING");
if (Query)
{
  ... // Code omitted here
  Table->TableName = Query;
}
else
{
  printf("<H1>No query string available</H1>\n");
}
```

These strings are passed to the application if you append a question mark to the URL that calls the CGI script and then append data after the question mark. For example, the following HTML code would call this script without specifying any table name:

```
<a href="/scripts/books/bunleash/CgiData2.exe">CGIData2.exe</a>
```

You might have to change the path specified in this code, but it shows the general formula for the code you should write. If you click the reference listed here, the program would report an error, as shown in Figure 26.9.

FIGURE 26.9.

The CGIData2 program returns an error like this if the user does not specify the name of a table he or she wants to view.

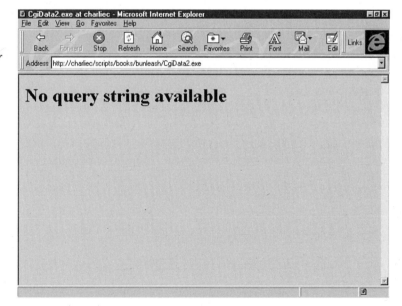

If you want to ask about the Customer database, you can edit the string so that it looks like this:

```
/scripts/books/bunleash/CgiData2.exe?Customer">CGIData2.exe
```

This request retrieves the `Customer` table from the database. You do not, of course, have to hard-code the name of each table you want to query into your form. In fact, in this particular example, you don't even have to use an HTML form at all. If you want, you can merely edit the raw HTML string in the `Address` field of your browser, appending different files after the question mark to retrieve different sets of data. For example, you could ask for the `Customer`, `Orders`, `Items`, `Events`, `Parts`, or `BioLife` tables.

If CGIData2 finds a valid query string in the global environment, it tries to open a table. If it can't find a string, then it prints a message to the user explaining the problem:

```
printf("<H1>No query string available</H1>\n");
```

Figure 26.10 shows the message that the CGIData2 program returns to the browser when the user enters an invalid table name.

FIGURE 26.10.

The output from the CGIData2 program when the user asks for a nonexistent table.

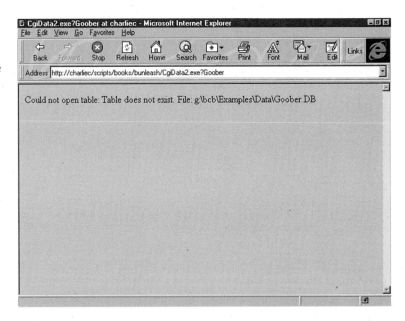

As you can see, the big danger here is that the user will pass in an invalid string. If this happens, an exception will be raised, which can hang your server, at least until you use a Task Manager to shut down the service.

Extending an Internet Server with ISAPI

CHAPTER 26

1071

26

EXTENDING AN
INTERNET SERVER
WITH ISAPI

NOTE

One way to ease the chore of debugging CGI applications is to run against a server on your own system. For example, if you are on Windows 95 and you use the Personal Web Server, then exceptions raised by your application appear in message boxes that you can read directly on your screen. You can then just click the OK button on the message so that the application will terminate. This option is not available if you're running against an NT server that resides on a separate machine. In fact, exceptions never appear on the screen on most servers, and your application will hang, with no way for you to click the OK button.

I'm sure most readers can guess that try..catch blocks are the way to handle exceptions that occur on a server. In particular, the following code catches exceptions that occur when you try to open a table or during the process of iterating through the records of a table:

```
try
{
  Table->Open();
  CGI.Header(Table->TableName);
  CGI.PrintTable(Table);
  Table->Close();
  delete Table;
}
catch(Exception &E)
{
  printf("Could not open table: %s", E.Message.c_str());
}
catch(...)
{
  printf("Could not open table");
}
}
```

In this case, I am assuming that all errors will be caused because the user passed in an invalid string. However, the code will trap any VCL error and return a string specifying what went wrong. On the off chance that the exception is not raised by the VCL, I have a generic catch block that simply states that something went wrong and that the table could not be opened. For more information, see Chapter 5, "Exceptions."

Notice that I also call Application->Run(). Calling this method appears to be necessary if you want to handle exceptions properly in a database application.

The last chunk of code to look at from this application is the bit that converts a table to HTML:

```
void TCGIDBHelp::PrintTable(TDataSet *Table)
{
  int i;

  printf("<TABLE BORDER>\n");
  for (i = 0; i < Table->FieldCount; i++)
  {
```

```
      printf("<TH>%s</TH>", Table->Fields[i]->FieldName.c_str());
    }
    while (!Table->Eof)
    {
      printf("<TR>");
      for (i = 0; i < Table->FieldCount; i++)
      {
        printf("<TD>%s</TD>", Table->Fields[i]->AsString.c_str());
      }
      printf("</TR>\n");
      Table->Next();
    }
    printf("</TABLE>\n");
}
```

This code is part of an object designed to work with database CGI applications. I separate it from the TCGIHelp object because database code adds so much to the size of a file. My theory is that you should include this file in your project only if you're explicitly using database objects; otherwise, stick with the smaller TCGIHelp file. TCGIDBHelp is a direct descendant of TCGIHelp, so it inherits all of methods from TCGIHelp.

The code shown here starts by iterating through all the fields in the database and places their names in the header for the table:

```
printf("<TABLE BORDER>\n");
for (i = 0; i < Table->FieldCount; i++)
{
  printf("<TH>%s</TH>", Table->Fields[i]->FieldName.c_str());
}
```

With this task out of the way, the code then iterates through the entire table, filling out each row in its entirety:

```
for (i = 0; i < Table->FieldCount; i++)
{
  printf("<TD>%s</TD>", Table->Fields[i]->AsString.c_str());
}
```

That's all I'm going to say about the CGIData2 program. Once again, you can see that publishing data over the Web is an easy operation. If you own BCB and run on an NT Server, you can publish data all day long with very little effort. If you have a smaller clientele, you can do the same thing with Windows 95 and the Personal Web Server, or else you can turn to more powerful tools such as the WebSite Server provided by O'Reilly.

O'Reilly is located at www.ora.com. Try http://www.ora.com/catalog/webpro/ for the professional version of the product and http://www.ora.com/catalog/web1.1/ for the inexpensive standard edition.

Using Queries, Data Modules, and InterBase over the Web

The real power of CGI applications is made clear when you start running SQL queries against data. For example, I took the Music.gdb database from Chapter 16, "Advanced InterBase Concepts," and let the user run some queries against it, as shown in Figure 26.11 and Figure 26.12. In

Extending an Internet Server with ISAPI

CHAPTER 26

1073

26

EXTENDING AN
INTERNET SERVER
WITH ISAPI

particular, this application calls some stored procedures designed to quickly pump out data that answers complex questions about a database. The stored procedures in question were discussed in Chapter 16. Remember that this is an InterBase database, and that you must set up the alias for it as described in the readme file on the CD that accompanies this book. I have hardcoded the password "masterkey" into the Params property of the TDatabase object in the program's data module.

FIGURE 26.11.

Running a query against the Music *database to see albums rated as* PEACEFUL.

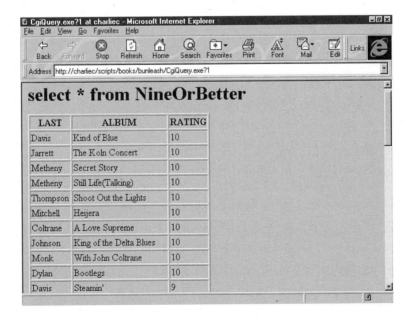

FIGURE 26.12.

Running a query against the Music *database to see albums with very high ratings.*

The source for the CGIQuery program is shown in Listing 26.15. A special HTML page is needed to query this application. A screen shot of the page is shown in Figure 26.13, and the HTML source for the page is shown in Listing 26.16.

FIGURE 26.13.

The HTML page used to query the CGIQuery application.

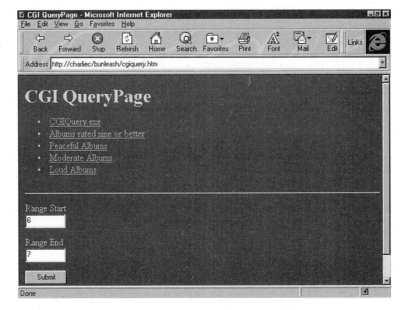

Listing 26.15. The CGIQuery application lets the user ask a number of questions of the database.

```cpp
///////////////////////////////////////
// CGIQuery.cpp
// An object to make CGI easier
// Copyright (c) 1997 by Charlie Calvert
//
#include <vcl\vcl.h>
#pragma hdrstop
#include "DMod1.h"
#include "CGIDBHelp1.h"

USERES("CGIQuery.res");
USEDATAMODULE("DMod1.cpp", DMod);
USEUNIT("\SrcC\PUnleash\Utils\CGIDBHelp1.cpp");
USEUNIT("\SrcC\PUnleash\Utils\CGIHelp1.cpp");

AnsiString ParseQuery(AnsiString S)
{
  int i = S.Pos("&");
  S.SetLength(i - 1);
  S = strrev(S.c_str());
  i = S.Pos("=");
  S.SetLength(i - 1);
```

```
    S = strrev(S.c_str());
    return S.c_str();
}

AnsiString ParseQuery1(AnsiString S)
{
    S = strrev(S.c_str());
    int i = S.Pos("=");
    S.SetLength(i - 1);
    return S.c_str();
}

/////////////////////////////////////////
// If user pressed a button on the HTML
// form, them must parse input.
// String will look like this:
//    Query=6&Query1=7
/////////////////////////////////////////
AnsiString GetButtonQuery(AnsiString S)
{
    AnsiString Query = ParseQuery(S);
    AnsiString Query1= ParseQuery1(S);
    try
    {
        return Format("select * from RatingRange(%s, %s)",
            OPENARRAY(TVarRec, (Query, Query1)));
    }
    catch(...)
    {
        return "You entered invalid data";
    }
}

bool GetLetters(AnsiString(S))
{
    int i;
    FILE * out;

    out = fopen("c:\\sam.txt", "w+");
    for (i = 0; i < S.Length(); i++)
    {
        fprintf(out, "Letters: %c\n", S[i]);
    }
    fclose(out);
    return True;
}

void RunQueries()
{
    int i;
    TCGIDBHelp CGI;

    AnsiString S = CGI.GetQuery();

    if (S.Length() == 0)
        S = "0";
```

continues

Listing 26.15. continued

```
if (S[1] != 'Q') // Did user press button? If so first letter is 'Q'
{
  if (S != "")
    i = S.ToInt();
  else
    i = 0;

  switch(i)
  {
    case 0: S = "select * from Album"; break;
    case 1: S = "select * from NineOrBetter"; break;
    case 2: S = "select * from GetLoudness(1)"; break;
    case 3: S = "select * from GetLoudness(2)"; break;
    case 4: S = "select * from GetLoudness(3)"; break;
    default:
      S = "select * from Artist";
  }
}
else
  S = GetButtonQuery(S);

DMod->Query1->SQL->Add(S);
try
{
  DMod->Query1->Open();
  CGI.Header(DMod->Query1->SQL->Strings[0]);
  CGI.PrintTable(DMod->Query1);
  DMod->Query1->Close();
}
catch(...)
{
  printf("Invalid Query: %s", S.c_str());
}
}

WINAPI WinMain(HINSTANCE, HINSTANCE, LPSTR, int)
{
  try
  {
    Application->Initialize();
    Application->CreateForm(__classid(TDMod), &DMod);
    RunQueries();
    Application->Run();
  }
  catch (Exception &exception)
  {
    Application->ShowException(&exception);
  }
  return 0;
}
```

Listing 26.16. The HTML file used to query the CGIQuery application.

```
<HTML>
<TITLE>CGI QueryPage</TITLE>
<HEAD>
<H1>CGI QueryPage</H1>
</HEAD>
<body bgcolor="#0000FF" text="#00FFFF" link="#FFFF00"
vlink="#00FF00" alink="#FFFFFF">
<BODY>
<UL>
<LI><a href="/scripts/books/bunleash/CgiQuery.exe">CGIQuery.exe</a>
<LI><a href="/scripts/books/bunleash/CgiQuery.exe?1">
  Albums rated nine or better</a>
<LI><a href="/scripts/books/bunleash/CgiQuery.exe?2">Peaceful Albums</a>
<LI><a href="/scripts/books/bunleash/CgiQuery.exe?3">Moderate Albums</a>
<LI><a href="/scripts/books/bunleash/CgiQuery.exe?4">Loud Albums</a>
</UL>
<HR>
<FORM METHOD="GET" ACTION="/scripts/books/bunleash/CGIQuery.exe">
Range Start<BR>
<INPUT TYPE = "text" NAME="Query" SIZE=10 defaultvalue="1"><BR><BR>
Range End<BR>
<INPUT TYPE = "text" NAME="Query1" SIZE=10 defaultvalue="2"><BR><BR>
<INPUT TYPE = "submit" VALUE="Submit">
<HR>
</BODY>
</HTML>
```

The most interesting thing about the CGIQuery application is that it uses a TDataModule, as shown in Figure 26.14. The data module allows you to access all the visual database tools that can make BCB programming so simple. For example, you can drop down a TDataBase object, connect to a database, set up your password in the Params property, and open up the database. Performing these tasks visually is much easier than doing them in code. You can also set up a one-to-many relationship or perform filters and lookups.

FIGURE 26.14.

The data module for the CGIQuery application. Using a data module in a CGI application allows you to leverage the power of the BCB RAD environment.

When you're using a data module, giving up altogether on the idea of using a `Console` application is probably simplest. Instead, keep the standard `WinMain` block set up by BCB:

```
WINAPI WinMain(HINSTANCE, HINSTANCE, LPSTR, int)
{
  try
  {
    Application->Initialize();
    Application->CreateForm(__classid(TDMod), &DMod);
    RunQueries();
    Application->Run();
  }
  catch (Exception &exception)
  {
    Application->ShowException(&exception);
  }
  return 0;
}
```

This code calls `Application::Initialize`, `CreateForm`, and `Run`. As you can see, I do not include a standard `TForm` object in the application, which means that it has no visual interface. It just runs silently in the background, without ever showing its face to the user. Once again, notice that I call `Run`, which appears to be necessary when you include a data module and exception handling in your application.

I should perhaps add that during application development, I often include a form so that I can test my queries at design time or sometimes even at runtime. The form usually need not contain anything but a `TDBGrid` in which to display the results of the query. I include a `TDataSource` on the data module for use with a form during program testing. It will be deleted during the final phases of project development. Furthermore, you can simply remove the entire test form from your project when it's time to distribute your application.

The key point to emphasize here is that you can leverage the visual tools during CGI development, even if you end up stripping them out of the application when you ship. This capability helps show why BCB is the best environment to use even when you're not producing standard RAD applications.

> **NOTE**
>
> I once again want to stress that you can design CGI applications in a number of ways. I mean for the techniques I show here to be an introduction to the subject and to show you how to get a lot of work done quickly. If you find that this subject interests you, you should consider turning to third parties that have developed custom VCL components to make this task simpler and more efficient.

Extending an Internet Server with ISAPI

CHAPTER 26

1079

26

EXTENDING AN
INTERNET SERVER
WITH ISAPI

Using a Browser to Ask Questions

To understand the CGI Query application, you should first look at the HTML code that calls it:

```
<LI><a href="/scripts/books/bunleash/CgiQuery.exe">CGIQuery.exe</a>
<LI><a href="/scripts/books/bunleash/CgiQuery.exe?1">
  Albums rated nine or better</a>
<LI><a href="/scripts/books/bunleash/CgiQuery.exe?2">Peaceful Albums</a>
<LI><a href="/scripts/books/bunleash/CgiQuery.exe?3">Moderate Albums</a>
<LI><a href="/scripts/books/bunleash/CgiQuery.exe?4">Loud Albums</a>
```

These options pass in various query strings, depending on the user's interests. For example, if the query string "1" is passed in, the following code gets called:

```
case 1: S = "select * from NineOrBetter"; break;
```

This line sets up a SQL statement that calls the stored procedure called NineOrBetter. The code for the stored procedure looks like this:

```
begin
  for
  select Artist.Last, Album.Album, Album.Rating
  from Album, Artist
  where Album.GroupCode = Artist.Code and Album.Rating >= 9
  Order By Album.Rating Desc
  into :Last, :Album, :Rating
  do
    suspend;
end
```

As I said earlier, you can turn to Chapter 16 for an in-depth explanation of this code. The key point is that it retrieves a list of albums rated 9 or better.

The code that runs the query looks like this:

```
DMod->Query1->SQL->Add(S);
try
{
  DMod->Query1->Open();
  CGI.Header(DMod->Query1->SQL->Strings[0]);
  CGI.PrintTable(DMod->Query1);
  DMod->Query1->Close();
}
catch(...)
{
  printf("Invalid Query: %s", S.c_str());
}
```

The first line here sets up the query string. The TQuery object is then run, and the data from it is processed by the TCGIDBHelp object, as described in the examination of the CGIData2 application.

Besides calling the NineOrBetter stored procedure, the user's other choices include selecting a query that retrieves data about the relative volume of the albums in the database:

```
case 2: S = "select * from GetLoudness(1)"; break;
case 3: S = "select * from GetLoudness(2)"; break;
case 4: S = "select * from GetLoudness(3)"; break;
```

The `GetLoudness` stored procedure looks like this:

```
begin
  for
  select Artist.Last, Album.Album, Album.Rating, Loudness.Loudness
  from Album, Artist, Loudness
  where Album.GroupCode = Artist.Code and
  Album.Loudness = :LoudnessValue and
  Loudness.Code = :LoudnessValue
  Order By Album.Album Desc
  into :Last, :Album, :Rating, :LoudnessStr
  do
    suspend;
end
```

This SQL code depends on the values from the `Loudness` table. The `Loudness` table contains three records, stating that `Peaceful` records have a code of `1`, `Moderate` records have a code of `2`, and `Loud` records have a code of `3`. The stored procedure does a lookup into this table, retrieves the string specifying the loudness of a particular album, and displays it to the user.

Now that you understand how the system works, you can see that calling `GetLoudness(1)` retrieves a list of the `Peaceful` records, `GetLoudness(2)` gets the records of `Moderate` volume, and so on. All this information is then wrapped up in an HTML table and shown to the user, as shown in Figure 26.11.

Submit Buttons and CGI Applications

The final point I want to make about this program is that it allows you to run queries based on data typed in by the user, as shown Figure 26.14. In particular, the user can type in a starting and ending range for the ratings of albums. If he or she then clicks the Submit button, a query will be formulated based on the user's input.

The standard HTML code that allows the user to submit the question looks like this:

```
<HR>
<FORM METHOD="GET" ACTION="/scripts/books/bunleash/CGIQuery.exe">
Range Start<BR>
<INPUT TYPE = "text" NAME="Query" SIZE=10 defaultvalue="1"><BR><BR>
Range End<BR>
<INPUT TYPE = "text" NAME="Query1" SIZE=10 defaultvalue="2"><BR><BR>
<INPUT TYPE = "submit" VALUE="Submit">
<HR>
```

The `FORM METHOD` statement tells the browser what to do when the user clicks the Submit button. In particular, it says that the `CGIQuery` application should be called. The HTML then defines two edit controls and the Submit button itself.

When the user clicks the button, a string like the following is automatically generated and passed to the application after the question mark in the URL:

```
Query=6&Query1=7
```

Extending an Internet Server with ISAPI

CHAPTER 26

1081

26

EXTENDING AN
INTERNET SERVER
WITH ISAPI

This string specifies that the user wants to see records that have a rating between 6 and 7.

I write some very ugly code that checks to see if the user is passing in a string to query the ratings of a table:

```
AnsiString S = CGI.GetQuery();

if (S.Length() == 0)
  S = "0";
if (S[1] != 'Q') // Did user press button? If so first letter is 'Q'
{
    ... // Handle queries against Loudness table, etc.
}
else
  S = GetButtonQuery(S);
```

As you can see, I've actually commented my code in this case, because there is no logical way for the reader to figure out why I am checking for the letter Q. Once you understand the system, you can see that the check is made because all but one type of query from the browser will consist of a simple integer. That one exceptional query is the kind that asks for record albums and CDs in a particular range, and I can identify that type of query because it always begins with a Q. This is, as I readily confess, horrible code, even by my standards. However, in this case I ask for your indulgence because of the rather primitive nature of all CGI technology.

> **NOTE**
>
> When I say that CGI technology is primitive, I am, of course, aware that network-based technology in and of itself is quite remarkable. However, the interface between a browser and an application is still very rudimentary, and will probably continue to be so in the foreseeable future. Because of the shortcomings of this technology, I take up DCOM in the next chapter. Of course, DCOM also has its limitations. In fact, sometimes DCOM shines, and sometimes CGI and ISAPI shine. The key point is knowing all the available technologies so that you can choose the best ones for a particular situation.

That's all I'm going to say about the CGIQuery program. You might want to examine parts of the application on your own. For example, you should take a look at the code that handles exceptions and make sure you understand what I'm doing when I parse the query string received from the browser.

I should perhaps add that various available technologies can relieve you of the task of parsing query strings and of retrieving strings from the environment. Much of the time, these tasks are so simple that you don't need complex code to get the job done. However, if you need to create really big, complex CGI applications, then you should get on the Web and see whether you can examine your available options for offloading some of these chores.

Summary

In this chapter, you learned about ISAPI and CGI. These technologies allow you to enhance a server with custom C++ code. In particular, they both allow you to access databases over the World Wide Web.

You saw that ISAPI is a DLL-based technology that runs inside the address space of the server. As a result, it is very highly optimized from a performance standpoint. CGI technology, on the other hand, is based on executables rather than DLLs. CGI applications, therefore, are usually slower than ISAPI applications. They are, on the other hand, much simpler to write, or more specifically, simpler to debug.

The key point to grasp about these technologies is that they can be used to make Web sites interactive. Though its performance is a bit slow, the Web can be a very powerful means of reaching a large audience that can extend across the entire globe. Many of the most exciting Web sites are powered by CGI or ISAPI, and BCB enables you to easily participate in this process.

Distributed COM

CHAPTER 27

IN THIS CHAPTER

Overview

The Distributed Component Object Model (DCOM) allows you to share objects easily over a network. In this chapter, you will see how to use BCB to implement DCOM. In particular, you will see how to create two applications that can control one another across a network and how to create distributed database applications. In the process of describing this technology, I will also show you how to create local OLE Automation objects.

BCB and Windows NT 4.0 provide full support for DCOM. You can also easily add DCOM client support to Windows 95. If you want, you can also add DCOM server support to Windows 95, though this option has some drawbacks and limitations.

The following subjects are covered in this chapter:

- An overview of DCOM technology
- Some caveats and general comments about DCOM, including a brief overview of competing technologies such as DSOM and CORBA
- Using `TAutoObject` to implement a DCOM server
- Creating a DCOM client
- Reviewing some key points about the Registry
- Working with remote datasets
- Using DCOM to access a database server on a different system without loading any database tools on your current system

At the time of this writing, DCOM is not built into Windows 95, although it is built into Windows NT 4.0. To add DCOM support to Windows 95, you can download Windows 95 DCOM from the Microsoft Web server. You should start looking for it in the OleDev section: `www.microsoft.com/oledev`. Alternatively, you can purchase a product called OLE Enterprise (OLEnterprise) from Borland.

What Is DCOM?

Before I begin describing the fairly simple technical steps involved in implementing DCOM, perhaps I should talk about this technology from a high level so that all the key ideas will be clear to everyone. If you already understand DCOM and just want to see how to implement it in BCB, you can skip this section.

Distributed COM is important because it allows applications to talk to one another across a network. In particular, it allows you to share objects that reside on two separate machines. You therefore can create an object in one application or DLL and then call the methods of that object from an application or DLL that resides on a different computer.

DCOM is built on top of COM, which is the technology that underlies both OLE and ActiveX. The relationship between COM and OLE is a bit confusing, and the boundaries separating the two technologies seem to shift at times, depending on the vagaries of the Microsoft marketing machine. In general, I can safely say that OLE is a subset of COM. That is, everything that is part of OLE is also part of COM, but not everything that is part of COM is a part of OLE. Many people, however, use the words "COM" and "OLE" virtually interchangeably, and indeed, the two technologies are very closely bound together.

COM is simply a specification for defining an object hierarchy. In particular, it lays out a set of rules for defining objects that can be used across applications and languages. DCOM extends this specification to allow objects on separate machines to talk to one another.

One of the most important aspects of this technology is that it allows you to distribute the load of a task across several machines. For example, if you have a complex database query to run, you can use DCOM to ask an object on a separate machine to run it. That way, your current processor will not have to expend any clock cycles on the task, nor will any large database-related tools be loaded into memory on your own machine. You are therefore free to continue playing DOOM or Quake while your server loses clock cycles and precious RAM to your background task.

You need to understand that the COM specification, as the name itself implies, is really only a set of rules for defining an object hierarchy. These rules include defining the names and methods of many of the key objects in the hierarchy, as well as the specific techniques for structuring the objects themselves. (When you think of the definition this way, you might find some value in regarding OLE as an implementation of certain parts of the COM specification.)

The COM specification can be compared to the specification for other object hierarchies such as VCL, OWL, or MFC. For example, all COM objects descend from a base class called IUnknown, just as all VCL objects descend from a base class called TObject. COM supports polymorphism and encapsulation, and it uses a series of unique interfaces to achieve the same ends as traditional inheritance in standard object-oriented languages. Unlike OWL or VCL, however, COM is not tied to any particular language, nor is it bound by application boundaries.

In short, COM is an alternative to the VCL, OWL, or MFC that attempts to go these object hierarchies one better by allowing you to use COM objects across language, application, and now even machine boundaries. As a result, you can write a COM object in Object Pascal, extend it in BCB, and then use it in a third language such as Visual Basic. You can call methods of the object from inside a single application, from one application that is calling into a DLL, or from one application that is calling an object in a separate application. What DCOM brings to the picture is the capability to call objects that reside in applications located on separate machines. It allows you to "distribute" the objects across the network. In particular, this capability allows you to divide up the load of running a major task across several machines.

If you already understand COM, then you are ready to use DCOM without any further work. DCOM works exactly the same way that COM works. You can, in fact, at least theoretically convert existing COM objects into DCOM objects with no change to your code. This system works great between two Windows NT machines, but Windows 95 requires that you switch from Share Level to User Level access, which might crimp your style in some cases. In particular, User Level sharing requires that an NT machine or some other source of user access lists be available on your network.

> **NOTE**
>
> You can switch from Share Level access to User Level access via the Network applet found in the Control Panel. To then help configure your server, you can use the `DComCfg.exe` application freely available from Microsoft's Web server.

If you don't want to switch to User Level access, you can choose an alternative that will allow you to run DCOM as a client service on Windows 95 machines. In that case, you need to add only a single new parameter to your calls into an OLE function named `CoGetClassObject`. I'll explain more in the technical section of this chapter.

> **NOTE**
>
> Consider these three points:
>
> - In most cases, User Level access controls require that you have an NT machine in your network.
> - NT machines don't require any special configuration to be able to act as a DCOM server.
> - You cannot remotely launch an OLE server that resides on a Windows 95 machine. The process must be in memory before you can call it. This is not true of NT machines, which can automatically launch a server if it is not already in memory.
>
> The upshot of this point is that you can't set up a DCOM server unless you have an NT machine on your network, and even under the best circumstances, a Windows 95 box is crippled as a server. Given these facts, I prefer to have the NT machine act as my DCOM server and to let the Windows 95 machines act only as clients.
>
> When connecting the two via DCOM for the first time, sign on to both machines with the same name and password. The simplest way to do this is to create a new user on the server with the same name and password you use on your Win95 box. Then sign on to the NT server with this name and password and sign on to your Windows 95 machine with the same name and password. Once you get things working this way, then you can try connecting with more stringent security.

The key point to grasp here is that DCOM is really nothing more than a new capability added to the already-existing COM technology. If you have working COM objects, upgrading them to work with DCOM is easy.

At the time of this writing (February '97), DCOM has been working on Windows NT 4.0 for over six months, but Microsoft has only just released DCOM for Windows 95. Microsoft has stated that, in the future, COM and DCOM will be ported to other platforms such as UNIX and the Mac.

Why Is COM Controversial?

Having, in a sense, made the case for COM and DCOM in the preceding section, I should perhaps step back for a moment and describe some competing systems. In this technical chapter, I'm not interested in advocating any particular system. However, describing the current state of this technology is probably worthwhile so that you can put this chapter in perspective.

COM is a Microsoft technology that is competing with similar technologies such as CORBA and DSOM, which are created by other corporations or groups of corporations. Adherents of these alternative technologies can rally numerous arguments regarding who implemented what first and who has designed the most sophisticated technology. Furthermore, many people have invested themselves heavily in technologies such as OWL or MFC that can be seen as "competing," in some sense, with COM. OWL, MFC, and the VCL don't have the same capabilities as COM, DSOM, OPENDOC, or CORBA, but you still get a feeling that the technologies are to some degree competing for the mind share of contemporary programmers. There is no specific reason that you can't use COM and VCL in the same program, and indeed that is the approach I take in this chapter.

My point here is not to advocate any particular solution, but only to make it clear that this controversial topic tends to excite strong opinions. If you're considering using COM in your projects, you might also want to look at CORBA and SOM. Conversely, if you hear criticisms of COM from other members working in the industry, you might check to see whether they are so heavily invested in some alternative technology that they are perhaps somewhat unfairly predisposed to be critical of COM and DCOM.

DCOM, IDispatch, Marshaling, and OLE Automation

BCB programmers can use the `IDispatch` COM interface to gain easy access to the capabilities of DCOM. This interface is encapsulated inside the BCB `TAutoObject` class. If you understand `TAutoObject` and the theory behind `IDispatch` and `IMarshal`, you can probably skip this section and move on to the next.

27

DISTRIBUTED COM

OLE Automation is a technique that allows you to control one application from inside a second application. In particular, it allows you to control an object placed inside one application from the code of a second application.

The key to OLE Automation is a COM object called `IDispatch`. All OLE technologies are based on COM, and in this particular case the functionality behind OLE Automation is implemented by `IDispatch`. In short, OLE Automation is really just a marketing term for publicizing the technology found in `IDispatch`. Or, more charitably, OLE Automation is an implementation of the `IDispatch` specification.

`IDispatch` is not difficult to understand, but it can be a bit awkward at times to implement. To help simplify the use of `IDispatch`, the VCL has a class called `TAutoObject` that encapsulates all the functionality of `IDispatch` inside an easy-to-use and highly leveraged technology.

In this chapter, I focus much of the technical content on an analysis of `TAutoObject`. However, you can automate any COM object, not just `IDispatch`. I have chosen to concentrate on this one technology at the exclusion of others because it provides a simple workaround to the difficult problem of trying to marshal code and data back and forth between two applications.

Marshaling is a COM-specific term for the technique used to transfer data or function calls back and forth between two applications that reside in separate processes. For example, if you have to pass a parameter to a function between two applications, you have to be sure that it is treated properly by both applications. For example, if you declare the parameter as an `Integer` in Pascal, that means you're passing a four-byte ordinal value. How do you express that same concept in C? How do you do it Visual Basic? The answers to these questions are expressed in COM by a complex interface called `IMarshal` that is beyond the scope of this chapter. Indeed, `IMarshal` is notorious for being difficult to implement.

Here is how the Microsoft documentation defines `IMarshal`: "'Marshaling' is the process of packaging data into packets for transmission to a different process or machine. 'Unmarshaling' is the process of recovering that data at the receiving end. In any given call, method arguments are marshaled and unmarshaled in one direction, while return values are marshaled and unmarshaled in the other." This is all good and well. Unfortunately, as I stated earlier, the `IMarshal` interface is very hard to implement.

If you're using a standard COM object, you don't have to implement `IMarshal` because these interfaces will be marshaled for you automatically by the system. In other words, if you're implementing an instance of `IDispatch`, `IUnknown`, `IClassFactory`, `IOleContainer`, or any other predefined COM class, you don't have to worry about marshaling. Microsoft will take care of this job for you. However, if you're creating a custom object of your own, you need to implement `IMarshal` or come up with some alternative scheme.

Because of the complexity of `IMarshal`, C programmers also generally choose not to attempt an implementation of `IMarshal`. Instead, they rely on an intermediate language called Interface Definition Language (IDL) that can be compiled into source code by a Microsoft-created program called `MIDL.EXE`. The IDL is a special language meant to allow people to define interfaces in a neutral language that can be compiled into source that can be used by multiple languages such as Pascal, C, and Visual Basic.

In other words, you can theoretically write your COM object in C or Pascal, use IDL to define its interface, and then use MIDL to turn that interface into a set of files that can be used by any language. In other words, MIDL automatically takes care of the `IMarshal` business for you as long as you first describe your interface in IDL.

This approach is quite reasonable, but I will not treat it in this current book, in part because BCB does not ship with MIDL. It is, however, available from the Microsoft SDKs and may be freely available via their Web site. You should also note that Delphi 3.0 includes tools that automate this process without your having to learn IDL or work with MIDL.

For now, however, I will back away from both `IMarshal` (because it is so complex) and MIDL (because it doesn't ship with BCB). This situation would appear to leave no good way to handle DCOM, were it not for the power of `IDispatch` and `TAutoObject`. `IDispatch` is a COM interface designed to make controlling one application from inside a second application easy. In implementing this code, Microsoft provided an alternative means for solving the whole problem of marshaling data between applications. In `TAutoObject`, the VCL provides a very simple means of using `IDispatch`.

Thinking About IDispatch

Here is how Microsoft defines `IDispatch`: "`IDispatch` is a COM interface that is designed in such a way that it can call virtually any other COM interface." In other words, if you put a COM object in an application, you can call its methods from a second application by using `IDispatch`. This way, OLE Automation allows you to control one application from inside a second application. (In particular, `IDispatch` was created to help make COM programming easier from inside the limited confines of a Visual Basic application.)

To understand why `IDispatch` works, you need to remember that marshaling is taken care of for you automatically as long as you're using an existing COM interface. In other words, you don't have to implement marshaling for `IDispatch` because it is a standard COM object, not a custom object designed by yourself or someone on your team. `IDispatch` exists to allow you to call the methods of any legal COM object. In other words, it is designed to solve the whole problem of marshaling data. As such, it is the perfect solution for BCB programmers who want to use DCOM without engaging in too much manual labor.

Before closing this section, I should emphasize that you don't have to use `IDispatch`. If you prefer, you can use other predefined COM objects, or you can implement `IMarshal`, or you can attempt to use MIDL. BCB has none of the limitations found in languages like Visual Basic, so you don't need to be confined to using `IDispatch` unless you find its relative simplicity appealing.

Using TAutoObject to Implement a DCOM Server

Now you're ready to move away from theoretical issues and to concentrate instead on technical matters. Ironically, the theory behind this technology is much harder to understand than the technology itself. In short, in this section and the next, I outline a simple technique for using DCOM that can be used by any intermediate-level BCB programmer.

You learned in the preceding sections that TAutoObject is BCB's wrapper around IDispatch. IDispatch is the COM object that makes OLE Automation possible. In this section, I show you how to implement OLE Automation that works not only between two applications, but also between two applications that reside on separate machines.

If you go to the File menu in BCB and choose New, you can pop up the Object Repository. On the first page of the Object Repository is an icon you can select if you want to create an Automation object. After selecting the Automation Object icon, you are presented with a dialog, as shown in Figure 27.1.

FIGURE 27.1.

Selecting the Automation object from the Object Repository.

You can fill in the fields of this dialog as you like, or you can put in the following default values:

```
Class Name: TMyDCOM
OLE Class Name: MyProj.MyDCom
Description: My DCOM Object
Instancing: Multiple Instance
```

When you're done, BCB spits out two pages of code as shown in Listing 27.1 and Listing 27.2. As you can see, I have, for the sake of fidelity to the compiler's output and contrary to habit, left in the mystifying series of dashes inserted by the compiler.

Listing 27.1. The header file produced by the BCB OLE Automation Wizard.

```
//-------------------------------------------------------------------
#ifndef Unit1H
#define Unit1H
```

```
//------------------------------------------------------------
#include <vcl\OleAuto.hpp>
#include <vcl\Classes.hpp>
//------------------------------------------------------------
class TMyDCom : public TAutoObject
{
private:
public:
    __fastcall TMyDCom();
__automated:
};
//------------------------------------------------------------
#endif
```

Listing 27.2. The main source file produced by the OLE Automation Wizard.

```
//------------------------------------------------------------
#include <vcl\vcl.h>
#pragma hdrstop
#include "Unit1.h"
//------------------------------------------------------------
__fastcall TMyDCom::TMyDCom()
    : TAutoObject()
{
}
//------------------------------------------------------------
void __fastcall RegisterTMyDCom()
{
  TAutoClassInfo AutoClassInfo;
  AutoClassInfo.AutoClass = __classid(TMyDCom);
  AutoClassInfo.ProgID = "MyProj.MyDCom";
  AutoClassInfo.ClassID = "{FCB9F540-87FF-11D0-BCD7-0080C80CF1D2}";
  AutoClassInfo.Description = "My DCOM Object";
  AutoClassInfo.Instancing = acMultiInstance;
  Automation->RegisterClass(AutoClassInfo);
}
//------------------------------------------------------------
#pragma startup RegisterTMyDCom
//------------------------------------------------------------
```

The RegisterTMyDCOM procedure is used to register your object with the system—that is, to list it in the Registry. The details of this process are described in the section called "Registration Issues." For now, you need only take note of the ClassID assigned to your object because you will need this ID when you try to call the object from another machine, as described in the next section.

The act of registering the object is not something you necessarily have to understand because it will occur automatically whenever you run the client application of which TMyDCOM is a part.

27

DISTRIBUTED
COM

NOTE

The object will be registered repeatedly, whenever you run the program, which ensures that you will find it easy to register the object, while simultaneously requiring very little overhead in terms of system resources. If you move the application to a new location, you can register this change with the system by running it once. This capability guarantees that the old items associated with your CLSID will be erased, and new items will be filled in their place. Registering a class ID multiple times does not mean that you will end up with multiple items in the Registry because each registration of a CLSID will overwrite the previous registration. All OLE servers worth their name provide this service. For example, Word and Excel update the Registry each time they are run.

Besides the registration procedure, the other key part of the code generated by the Automation expert is the class definition found at the top of the header:

```
class TMyDCom : public TAutoObject
{
private:
public:
    __fastcall TMyDCom();
__automated:
};
```

This code has two sections, one called `private` and the other called `automated`. In the `__automated` section, you can declare methods or properties that you want to call across program or machine boundaries. In other words, any methods or properties that you declare in this space will automatically be marshaled for you by the underlying `IDispatch` object encapsulated by `TAutoObject`.

Consider the following code fragments:

```
class TSimpleDCOM : public TAutoObject
{
private:
public:
    virtual __fastcall TSimpleDCOM();
__automated:
  AnsiString __fastcall GetName();
  int __fastcall Square(int A);
};
AnsiString __fastcall TSimpleDCOM::GetName()
{
  return "SimpleDCOM";
}
int __fastcall TSimpleDCOM::Square(int A)
{
  return A * A;
}
```

This object has two methods: one that states the name of the object and one that can square an integer. These two methods are declared in the automated section of the object, so they can be accessed from another program via another program.

The TSimpleDCOM object exports two methods that IDispatch will automatically marshal for you across application or machine boundaries. You can go on adding methods to this object as you like. Any data that you want to add to the object should go in the private section, and any methods or properties that you don't want to export should also go in the private section. All methods that you want to call from inside another application should go in the automated section. You should declare these exported methods as __fastcall.

Some limits to the marshaling will be done for you by IDispatch. In particular, the following types are legal to use in the declarations for the methods or properties in the automated section:

```
int,
float,
double,
Currency,
TDateTime,
AnsiString,
WordBool
Short
String
unsigned short
Variant
```

The following types are illegal to use in the declarations for the methods or properties in the automated section:

```
arrays
char *
void *
structs
```

For additional information, see the "Automating properties and methods" section in the online help for the VCL.

The apparent limitations created by the lack of support from IDispatch for custom types can be considerably mitigated by an intelligent use of variant arrays. These structures can be so helpful that I have added a section later in this chapter called "Using Variant Arrays to Pass Data" to describe their use.

The complete source for a simple DCOM server is shown in Listing 27.3 through Listing 27.6. Notice that OleAuto is included in this project. This unit is essential to OLE Automation programming with the VCL.

Listing 27.3. The heading for the `SimpleObject` file from the EasyDCOM project.

```
///////////////////////////////////////
// SimpleObject.h
// EasyDCOM
// Copyright (c) 1997 by Charlie Calvert
//
#ifndef SimpleObjectH
#define SimpleObjectH
#include <vcl\oleauto.hpp>
#include <vcl\Classes.hpp>

class TSimpleDCOM : public TAutoObject
{
private:
public:
    virtual __fastcall TSimpleDCOM();
__automated:
  AnsiString __fastcall GetName();
  int __fastcall Square(int A);
};

#endif
```

Listing 27.4. The main source file of an OLE Automation object.

```
///////////////////////////////////////
// SimpleObject.cpp
// EasyDCOM
// Copyright (c) 1997 by Charlie Calvert
//
#include <vcl\vcl.h>
#pragma hdrstop
#undef RegisterClass
#include "SimpleObject.h"

int Initialization();

static int Initializer = Initialization();

__fastcall TSimpleDCOM::TSimpleDCOM()
  : TAutoObject()
{
}

AnsiString __fastcall TSimpleDCOM::GetName()
{
  return "SimpleDCOM";
}

int __fastcall TSimpleDCOM::Square(int A)
{
  return A * A;
}

void __fastcall RegisterTSimpleDCOM()
```

```
{
  TAutoClassInfo AutoClassInfo;

  AutoClassInfo.AutoClass = __classid(TSimpleDCOM);
  AutoClassInfo.ProgID = "EasyDCOM.SimpleDCOM";
  AutoClassInfo.ClassID = "{E2674A60-2DF2-11D0-92C5-000000000000}";
  AutoClassInfo.Description = "Easiest possible DCOM program";
  AutoClassInfo.Instancing = acMultiInstance;

  Automation->RegisterClass(AutoClassInfo);
}

int Initialization()
{
  RegisterTSimpleDCOM();
  return 0;
}
```

Listing 27.5. The header for the main source file for the EasyDCOM OLE server.

```
#ifndef MainH
#define MainH
#include <vcl\Classes.hpp>
#include <vcl\Controls.hpp>
#include <vcl\StdCtrls.hpp>
#include <vcl\Forms.hpp>

class TForm1 : public TForm
{
__published:
  TLabel *Label1;
private:
public:
  virtual __fastcall TForm1(TComponent* Owner);
};

extern TForm1 *Form1;

#endif
```

Listing 27.6. The main source file for the EasyDCOM OLE server.

```
#include <vcl\vcl.h>
#pragma hdrstop
#include "Main.h"
#pragma resource "*.dfm"
TForm1 *Form1;

__fastcall TForm1::TForm1(TComponent* Owner)
  : TForm(Owner)
{
}
```

This program is meant to be run from a client. As such, it has no controls on it and no public interface other than the OLE object itself. I do, however, give the main form a distinctive look, as you can see in Figure 27.2.

FIGURE 27.2.

The main form for the EasyDCOM program.

Of course, there is no reason that a single program could not simultaneously have an OLE server interface and a set of standard controls. For example, Word and Excel are both OLE servers, and standard applications run through a set of menus and other controls. In fact, the same application can work as a server, a standard application, and as a client.

Note that, by using two different approaches, you can ensure that the application is registered each time it is run. One technique involves including an initialization procedure:

```
int Initialization()
{
  RegisterTSimpleDCOM();
  return 0;
}
```

The second technique, shown earlier in the chapter, involves a `pragma`:

```
#pragma startup RegisterTSimpleDCom
```

Both technologies achieve the same effect. As a rule, you don't have to think about this part of the process because the code will be inserted automatically by the Automation Wizard. Needless to say, nothing is magic about the Automation expert, and you can simply create the code yourself by typing it in. In that case, you are free to use either technique, though the `pragma` is probably easier to write.

That's all I'm going to say for now about creating the server side of a BCB DCOM project. Remember that this code will not work unless you first register the `TSimpleDCOM` object with the system by running the server once. After you run the server the first time, you never have to run it again, as it will be called automatically by the client program described in the next section. Let me repeat that the whole point of this exercise is that the client program can be located on a separate machine.

Creating the DCOM Client

The GetDCOM program found on the CD that accompanies this book will call the functions in the server program described in the preceding section. In particular, GetDCOM can automatically launch the server program and then call its `GetName` and `Square` functions.

> **NOTE**
>
> When I say that GetDCOM can automatically launch the server, I'm assuming that the server is either on the current system (in which case, it is launched via COM) or on an NT machine (in which case, it is launched via DCOM). DCOM cannot launch an application residing on a remote Windows 95 box.

You can run this application in two different modes. You can run it as a client to a local Automation server or as a client to a remote Automation server. If you look at the main form for the program, shown in Figure 27.3, you can see that it has three buttons: one for launching the server remotely, one for launching it locally, and a third that will be used to call a simple function on the server.

FIGURE 27.3.

The main form for the GetDCOM application.

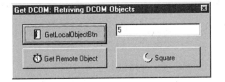

The source for the GetDCOM program is shown in Listing 27.7 and Listing 27.8. This program uses a routine called `CreateRemoteObject` that is declared in the `CodeBox` unit found in the `Utils` subdirectory on the CD that accompanies this book. You need to add the `CodeBox` unit to your project; otherwise, it will not compile. I do not include the entire `CodeBox` unit in this chapter, but it is available on the CD, and I do include the `CreateRemoteObject` function in its entirety later in this chapter. Notice also that this project includes the `OleAuto` unit to call `CreateOleObject` to retrieve a local instance of `IDispatch`.

When using this program, please note that I have hard coded the IP address of my server into the source. You will need to change this so that it works with your server. When making the connection between a Windows 95 and Windows NT machine, you should start by calling from the Windows 95 machine to the Windows NT machine; that is, put the client on the Windows 95 machine. You should also start by signing on to both machines with the same name and password. That way you don't have to worry about security issues on the server while you are first getting the technology up and running. Also, give yourself all possible rights on the server. Make yourself an administrator.

Listing 27.7. The header for the GetDCOM OLE client application.

```
//////////////////////////////////////
// Main.h
// Project: GetDCOM
```

continues

Listing 27.7. continued

```cpp
// Copyright (c) 1997 by Charlie Calvert
//
#ifndef MainH
#define MainH
#include <vcl\Classes.hpp>
#include <vcl\Controls.hpp>
#include <vcl\StdCtrls.hpp>
#include <vcl\Forms.hpp>
#include <vcl\Buttons.hpp>
class TForm1 : public TForm
{
__published:
  TBitBtn *GetLocalObjectBtn;
  TBitBtn *GetRemoteObjectBtn;
  TEdit *Edit1;
  TBitBtn *SquareBtn;
  void __fastcall GetLocalObjectBtnClick(TObject *Sender);
  void __fastcall GetRemoteObjectBtnClick(TObject *Sender);
  void __fastcall SquareBtnClick(TObject *Sender);
  void __fastcall FormDestroy(TObject *Sender);
private:
  Variant V;
public:
  virtual __fastcall TForm1(TComponent* Owner);
};
extern TForm1 *Form1;
#endif
```

Listing 27.8. The main source file for the GetDCOM application.

```cpp
/////////////////////////////////////
// Main.cpp
// Project: GetDCOM
// Copyright (c) 1997 by Charlie Calvert
//
#include <vcl\vcl.h>
#include <vcl\OleAuto.hpp>
#include <vcl\ole2.hpp>
#include <initguid.h>
#pragma hdrstop
#include "Main.h"
#include "codebox.h"
#pragma resource "*.dfm"

TForm1 *Form1;

__fastcall TForm1::TForm1(TComponent* Owner)
  : TForm(Owner)
{
```

```
    CoInitialize(NULL);
}

void __fastcall TForm1::GetLocalObjectBtnClick(TObject *Sender)
{
  V = CreateOleObject("EasyDCOM.SimpleDCOM");
  ShowMessage(V.OleFunction("GetName"));
}

DEFINE_GUID(ClassID, 0xE2674A60, 0x2DF2, 0x11D0, 0x92,0xC5,
  0x00,0x00,0x00,0x00,0x00,0x00);

void __fastcall TForm1::GetRemoteObjectBtnClick(TObject *Sender)
{
  Screen->Cursor = crHourGlass;

  if (CreateRemoteObject(ClassID, "143.186.149.228", V))
  {
    ShowMessage(V.OleFunction("GetName"));
  }
  else
  {
    ShowMessage("Failed");
  }
  Screen->Cursor = crDefault;
}

void __fastcall TForm1::SquareBtnClick(TObject *Sender)
{
  try
  {
    ShowMessage(V.OleFunction("Square", Edit1->Text));
  }
  catch(Exception &E)
  {
    ShowMessage(E.Message);
  }
}

void __fastcall TForm1::FormDestroy(TObject *Sender)
{
  CoUninitialize();
}
```

The code declares the CLSID created by the BCB Automation expert in the preceding section of this chapter:

```
DEFINE_GUID(ClassID, 0xE2674A60, 0x2DF2, 0x11D0, 0x92,0xC5,
            0x00,0x00,0x00,0x00,0x00,0x00);
```

This is the CLSID associated with the server half of this DCOM project, and you need to include it here in the client program. Additional information about CLSIDs and the registration process will be presented later in this chapter.

> **NOTE**
>
> You need to include the standard Windows API `initguids.h` file in projects that use GUIDs.

The actual call to automate the object is nearly identical to the call you would make if you wanted to automate an object on your local machine. The only difference is that you call `CreateRemoteOleObject` rather than `CreateOleObject`. Here is the way to call the object locally:

```
void __fastcall TForm1::GetLocalObjectBtnClick(TObject *Sender)
{
  V = CreateOleObject("EasyDCOM.SimpleDCOM");
  ShowMessage(V.OleFunction("GetName"));
}
```

This code assumes that the variable `V`, of type `Variant` is a field of `TForm1`. The code calls a built-in function of the VCL called `CreateOleObject`. This function takes the `ProgID` of an object, looks up its CLSID in the Registry, finds the place on the hard drive where the program that owns the object is located, launches the program, and retrieves the object in a `Variant`.

The code then uses the `OleFunction` method of the `Variant` object to call one of the methods of the OLE server. `OleFunction` takes one or more parameters, specifying the name of the function you want to call and any parameters you want to pass to it. BCB does not have support for named parameters.

Later in the program, you can call the `Square` method of the Automation server:

```
void __fastcall TForm1::SquareBtnClick(TObject *Sender)
{
  try
  {
    ShowMessage(V.OleFunction("Square", Edit1->Text));
  }
  catch(Exception &E)
  {
    ShowMessage(E.Message);
  }
}
```

Again, I use the `OleFunction` method to make the call to the `Square` method via `OleAutomation`. As you can see, I wrap the function call in a `try..except` block because chances are good that the user might click the Square button before initializing the object with a call to `CreateOleObject` or `CreateRemoteOleObject`. Notice that this time `OleFunction` takes two parameters, one stating the name of the OLE server method to be called and the second specifying a parameter to be passed to that method.

Here is the method of `GetDCOM` that I use to summon the remote server:

```
void __fastcall TForm1::GetRemoteObjectBtnClick(TObject *Sender)
{
  Screen->Cursor = crHourGlass;
```

```
  if (CreateRemoteObject(ClassID, "143.186.149.228", V))
  {
    ShowMessage(V.OleFunction("GetName"));
  }
  else
  {
    ShowMessage("Failed");
  }
  Screen->Cursor = crDefault;
}
```

This function is no different in substance from the GetDCOM routine that retrieves the local object. The only difference is that I call CreateRemoteObject rather than CreateOleObject. Remember that you can call CreateOleObject to retrieve remote objects if you are on an NT machine or if you have set the Windows 95 server machine into User Access mode via the Network applet in the Control Panel.

> **NOTE**
>
> Let me just reiterate that you need to pass in the IP address, or server name, of the machine on which your server is located. Here I type in the IP address of my NT server: 143.186.149.228. You replace this number with the name or number of your server. If you're confused by the topic of IP addresses, you might be able to glean some information from the discussion of TCP/IP in Chapter 8, "Database Basics and Database Tools."

CreateRemoteObject is a custom function I have written; it looks like this:

```
BOOL CreateRemoteObject(GUID ClassID, char *Server, Variant &V)
{
  Ole2::IClassFactory *ClassFactory;
  Ole2::IUnknown *Unknown1;
  COSERVERINFO Info;
  OLECHAR Dest[MAX_PATH];
  int i = MultiByteToWideChar(CP_ACP, 0, Server, -1, Dest, MAX_PATH);
  if (i <= 0)
    return FALSE;
  ClassFactory = NULL;
  Info.dwReserved1 = 0;
  Info.pAuthInfo = NULL;
  Info.dwReserved2 = 0;
  Info.pwszName = Dest;
  HRESULT hr = CoGetClassObject(ClassID, CLSCTX_REMOTE_SERVER, &Info,
                 Ole2::IID_IClassFactory, (void **)&ClassFactory);
  OleCheck(hr);

  if (ClassFactory != NULL)
  {
    hr = ClassFactory->CreateInstance(NULL,
      Ole2::IID_IUnknown, (void **)&Unknown1);
    OleCheck(hr);
    V = VarFromInterface(Unknown1);
    ClassFactory->Release();
```

```
    if (VarType(V) != varNull)
      return True;
    else
      return False;
  }
  return FALSE;
}
```

This routine is declared in the `CodeBox` unit found in the `Utils` subdirectory on the CD that accompanies this book. As I stated earlier, you need to add the `CodeBox` unit to your project; otherwise, it will not compile. Alternatively, you can simply copy this routine into your project. However, keeping it in a separate unit makes sense because you might want to call it from multiple applications.

Whether you understand this routine is not really important. You can just plug it into your applications the same way you do `CreateOleObject`. However, I will talk about it briefly for those who are interested.

The `CreateRemoteObject` routine takes three parameters. The first contains the ID of the object you want to obtain, and the second contains the name of the server where the object resides. The last parameter contains a variant that will hold the instance of `IDispatch` retrieved from the system. (Sometimes you might have to use the IP address itself rather than the name of the server.) `CreateRemoteObject` returns a variant that "contains" a copy of the object that you want to call. You can use this variant to call all the methods in the `automated` section of your object.

Variants are special BCB types that can contain a wide variety of data types, including OLE objects. I discussed variants at some length in Chapter 3, "C++Builder and the VCL."

When you call the methods of an OLE object off a variant, no runtime checking for the calls occurs. BCB just assumes you know what you're doing, and if the call fails, you won't know until runtime. This problem is addressed in Delphi 3, and so I assume it will be addressed in future releases of C++Builder.

The key call in `CreateRemoteOleObject` is to `CoGetClassObject`:

```
HRESULT hr = CoGetClassObject(ClassID, CLSCTX_REMOTE_SERVER, &Info,
                              Ole2::IID_IClassFactory, (void **)&ClassFactory);
OleCheck(hr);
```

This routine has long been a part of COM, but it has been altered slightly to support DCOM. Here is how the routine is currently declared in `ObjBase.h`:

```
WINOLEAPI  CoGetClassObject(
  REFCLSID rclsid,      // The ID of the object you want
  DWORD dwClsContext,   // In process, local or remote server?
  LPVOID pvReserved,    // Previously reserved, now used for CoServerInfo
  REFIID riid,          // Usually IID_IClassFactory
  LPVOID FAR* ppv);     // Where the class factory is returned
```

The function returns an HRESULT variable containing information on the outcome of the call. If HRESULT is set to zero, then the call succeeded. Most other values represent an error in the form of a number. You can retrieve a human-readable string by passing that number to a VCL function called OleCheck.

The third parameter to CoGetClassObject, previously reserved, is now the place where you pass in the name of the server you want to access. The server is usually designated with either a string or a literal IP address, such as 143.186.149.111. You would pass in the IP address in the form of a string. That is, don't try to pass a number; just put the IP address in quotation marks and pass it in as a string. Here is the new declaration for CoGetClassObject, as found in the MSDN:

```
STDAPI CoGetClassObject(
  REFCLSID rclsid,            //CLSID associated with the class object
  DWORD dwClsContext,         //Context for running executable code
  COSERVERINFO * pServerInfo, // Machine on which object is to be instantiated
  REFIID riid,                //Reference to the identifier of the interface
  LPVOID * ppv                //Indirect pointer to the interface
);
```

In particular, here is the record you pass in for the third parameter:

```
typedef struct _COSERVERINFO {
  DWORD      dwSize;   // must be set to sizeof(COSERVERINFO)
  OLECHAR*   pszName;  // machine name
} COSERVERINFO;
```

The first field of this record is just a version check field that should contain the size of the TCoServerInfo record. The second parameter contains a Unicode string that has the name of the server or its IP address embedded in it. Use the MultiByteToWideChar Windows API function to convert a standard BCB string into a Unicode string:

```
OLECHAR Dest[MAX_PATH];
int i = MultiByteToWideChar(CP_ACP, 0, Server, -1, Dest, MAX_PATH);
if (i <= 0)
  return FALSE;
```

The call to CoGetClassObject retrieves a ClassFactory. After you have the ClassFactory back from the server, you can use it to retrieve an instance of the object you want to call. What you retrieve back, of course, is an instance of IDispatch. You can convert this instance into a variant by calling the BCB routine VarFromInterface, which is found in the OleAuto unit that ships with BCB.

If you want, you can simplify this call by using CoCreateInstanceEx. CoCreateInstanceEx is superior to CoGetClassObject because it retrieves the object you want with only one call instead of having to first get the ClassFactory and then call CreateInstance on the ClassFactory. In short, CoCreateInstanceEx executes faster than CoGetClassObject. (Remember, all calls between objects on separate machines are going to have a considerable overhead associated with them!) Another advantage of `CoCreateInstanceEx` is that it takes a `MultiQI` structure that can contain a list of multiple objects to retrieve. That way, you can retrieve multiple objects through a single call. Again, using this method will save considerable time.

Before I close this section, let me review the key points covered so far:

- DCOM allows you to call objects located in one application or DLL on one machine from inside a separate application on a separate machine.
- You can use `TAutoObject` to create the server side of your application.
- You can use the custom `CreateRemoteObject` to call the server from a client program located on a second server.

Registration Issues

Before going further, I want to mention a few issues about CLSIDs and the Registry. If you already understand the Registry, you can skip this section. I covered some aspects of the Registry in Chapter 13, "Flat-File, Real-World Databases." However, I will go over this material again here from the perspective of an OLE application.

The Registry is a place where information can be stored. It's a database.

CLSIDs are statistically unique numbers that can be used by the operating system to reference an OLE object. CLSIDs are stored in the Registry.

In this case, visiting the actual perpetrator in its native habitat is probably best. In the example explained here, I'm assuming that you have a copy of Word loaded on your system.

To get started, use the Run menu on the Windows taskbar to launch the RegEdit program that ships with Windows NT. Just type `RegEdit` and click OK. Search through the `HKEY_CLASSES_ROOT` for the `Word.Basic` entry, as shown in Figure 27.4. When you find it, you can see that it's associated with the following CLSID:

```
{000209FE-0000-0000-C000-000000000046}
```

This unique class ID is inserted into the Registry of all machines that contain a valid, and properly installed, copy of Word for Windows. The only application that uses this ID is Word for Windows. It belongs uniquely to that application.

Now go further up `HKEY_CLASSES_ROOT` and look for the CLSID branch. Open it and search for the CLSID shown above. When you find it, you can see two entries associated with it: one is called `LocalServer`, or `LocalServer32`, and the other is called `ProgID`. The `ProgID` is set to `word.basic`. The `LocalServer` entry looks something like this:

```
C:\WINWORD\WINWORD.EXE /Automation
```

FIGURE 27.4.

If you run the Windows program Regedit.exe, *then you can see the registration database entry for* Word.Basic *under* HKEY_CLASSES_ROOT.

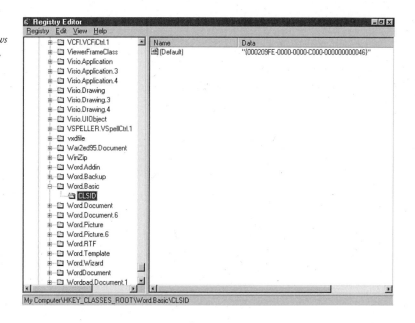

If you look at this command, you can begin to grasp how Windows can translate the CLSID passed to CoGetClassObject into the name of an executable. In particular, Windows looks up the CLSID in the Registry and then uses the LocalServer32 entry to find the directory and name of the executable or DLL you want to launch.

Having these kinds of entries in the registration database does not mean that the applications in question are necessarily Automation servers. For example, many applications with LocalServer and ProgID entries are not Automation servers. However, all Automation servers do have these two entries. Note, further, that this is a reference to the Automation server in Word, not a reference to Word as a generic application. It references an Automation object inside Word, not Word itself. (The Automation object is an instance of IDispatch. It was not created with TAutoObject, but it has all the same attributes.)

The same basic scenario outlined here takes place when you call CoGetClassObject and specify the CLSID of an object on another machine. In particular, Windows contacts the specified machine, asks it to look up the CLSID in the Registry, and then marshals information back and forth between the two machines.

CLSIDs are said to be statistically unique. You can create a new CLSID by calling CoCreateGuid. The following code shows one way to make this call:

```
CoInitialize(NULL);
CoCreateGuid(GUID);
// eventually you should call CoUninitialize;
```

The code shown here begins by calling `CoInitialize`, which is usually unnecessary in BCB because the `OLE2` unit will call this function automatically when your program is launched; that is, it will do so if you include `OLE2` in the `uses` clause of one of your units.

`CoCreateGuid` is the call that retrieves the new CLSID from the system. This ID is guaranteed to be unique as long as you have a network card on your system. Each network card has a unique number on it, and this card number is combined with the date and time and other random bits of information to create a unique number that could only be generated on a machine with your network card at a particular date and time. Rumors that the phase of the moon and current age of Bill Gates's children are also factored in are probably not true. At any rate, the result is a number that is guaranteed to be statistically unique, within the tolerance levels for your definition of that word given your faith in mathematicians in general and Microsoft-based mathematicians in particular.

The `StringFromCLSID` routine converts a CLSID into a string. The `ParseGuid` routine is a custom function I wrote to convert a string of type

```
{FC41CC90-C01D-11CF-8CCD-0080C80CF1D2}
```

into a record of type `GUID` that can be used in a BCB application as defined in `Wtypes.h`:

```
typedef struct   _GUID
    {
    DWORD Data1;
    WORD Data2;
    WORD Data3;
    BYTE Data4[ 8 ];
    } GUID;
```

That's all I want to say about the Registry for now. This subject can appear a bit tricky at first, but ultimately it is not complicated.

Using Variant Arrays to Pass Data

BCB enables you to create variant arrays, which are the VCL version of the safe arrays used in OLE Automation. You can use variant arrays to pass large chunks of data back and forth between COM objects. For example, you can pass a bitmap, AVI file, or text file between two applications using variant arrays. In short, this type can help you avoid the shortcomings created by the limited types supported by `IDispatch`.

Variant arrays (and safe arrays) are costly in terms of memory and CPU cycles, so you normally would not use them except in automation or DCOM code, or in special cases in which they provide obvious benefits over standard arrays. For example, the database code makes some use of variant arrays.

The Variant class type, found in SysDefs.h and covered in Chapter 3 has constructors for creating variant arrays:

```
// constructor for array of variants of type varType
__fastcall Variant(const int* bounds, const int boundsSize,
                    Word varType);
// constructor for one-dimensional array of type Variant
__fastcall Variant(const Variant* values, const int valuesSize);
```

If you know the type of the elements to be used in an array, you can set the VarType parameter to that type. For example, if you know you're going to be working with integers, you can write the following:

```
Variant MyVariant(OPENARRAY(int, (0, 5)), varInteger);
```

You cannot use varString in the last parameter; instead, use varOleStr. Remember that an array of Variant takes up 16 bytes for each member of the array, and other types might take up less space.

Arrays of Variant can be resized with the VarArrayRedim function:

```
extern void __fastcall VarArrayRedim(Variant &A, int HighBound);
```

The variable to be resized is passed in the first parameter, and the number of elements to be contained in the resized array is held in the second parameter.

You declare a two-dimensional array like this:

```
Variant MyVariant(OPENARRAY(int, (0, 5, 0, 5)), varInteger);
```

This array has two dimensions, each with six elements. To access a member of this array, you write code that looks like the following:

```
for (i = 0; i < 6; i++)
    for (j = 0; j < 6; j++)
        MyVariant.PutElement(i * j, i, j);
  for (i = 0; i < 6; i++)
  {
    for (j = 0; j < 6; j++)
    {
      S = S + " " + MyVariant.GetElement(i, j);
    }
    S = S + '\r';
  }
```

The following code fragment shows how to use a one-dimensional array and how to query an array to find out about its composition:

```
AnsiString TForm1::GetInfo(Variant &V)
{
  int Count, HighBound, LowBound, i;
  AnsiString S;
  Count = VarArrayDimCount(V);
```

```
S = AnsiString("\nDimension Count: ") + IntToStr(Count) + '\n';
for (i = 1; i <= Count; i++)
{
  HighBound = VarArrayHighBound(V, i);
  LowBound = VarArrayLowBound(V, i);
  S = S + "LowBound: " + IntToStr(LowBound) + '\n';
  S = S + "HighBound: " + IntToStr(HighBound) + '\n';
}
return S + '\n';
}

void __fastcall TForm1::bOneDimClick(TObject *Sender)
{
  AnsiString S;
  int i;
  S = "";
  Variant MyVariant(OPENARRAY(int, (0, 5)), varInteger);
  for (i = 0; i <= 5; i++)
    MyVariant.PutElement(i * 2, i);
  for (i = 0; i <= 5; i++)
    S = S + " " + MyVariant.GetElement(i);
  S = GetInfo(MyVariant) + S;
  ShowMessage(S);
}
```

The GetInfo method demonstrates how to work with a variant array passed as a parameter. Notice that you don't have to do anything special to access a variant as an array. The type travels with the variable.

If you try to pass a variant with a VType of varInteger to this function, BCB raises an exception when you try to treat the variant as an array. In short, the variant must have a VType of VarArray; otherwise, the call to GetInfo will fail. You can use the VarType function to check the current setting for the VType of a variant, or you can call VarIsArray, which returns a Boolean value.

You can use the VarArrayHighBound, VarArrayLowBound, and VarArrayDimCount functions to find out about the number of dimensions in your array and about the bounds of each dimension. The following GetInfo function creates a string showing the number of dimensions in a variant array, as well as the high and low values for each dimension:

```
AnsiString TForm1::GetInfo(Variant &V)
{
  int Count, HighBound, LowBound, i;
  AnsiString S;

  Count = VarArrayDimCount(V);
  S = AnsiString("\nDimension Count: ") + IntToStr(Count) + '\n';
  for (i = 1; i <= Count; i++)
  {
    HighBound = VarArrayHighBound(V, i);
    LowBound = VarArrayLowBound(V, i);
    S = S + "LowBound: " + IntToStr(LowBound) + '\n';
    S = S + "HighBound: " + IntToStr(HighBound) + '\n';
  }

  return S + '\n';
}
```

This routine starts by getting the number of dimensions in the array. It then iterates through each dimension, retrieving its high and low values. If you create an array with the call

```
Variant MyVariant(OPENARRAY(int, (0, 5, 1, 3)), varInteger);
```

the `GetInfo` function produces the following output if passed `MyVariant`:

```
Dimension Count: 2
HighBound: 5
LowBound: 0
HighBound: 3
LowBound: 1
```

`GetInfo` raises an exception if you pass in a variant that causes `VarIsArray` to return `False`.

A certain amount of overhead is involved in working with variant arrays. If you want to process the arrays quickly, you can use two functions called `VarArrayLock` and `VarArrayUnlock`. The first of these routines returns a pointer to the data stored in an array. In particular, `VarArrayLock` takes a variant array and returns a standard Pascal array. For it to work, the array must be explicitly declared with one of the standard types listed earlier in the chapter. The type used in the variant array and the type used in the Pascal array must be identical.

Here is an example of using `VarArrayLock` and `VarArrayUnlock`:

```
Variant GetArrayData()
{
  int i, j;
  Variant V(OPENARRAY(int, (1, Max, 1, Max)), varInteger);

  for (i = 1; i < Max; i++)
    for (j = 1; j < Max; j++)
      V.PutElement(i * j, j, i);
  return V;
}
void __fastcall TForm1::LockedArray1Click(TObject *Sender)
{
  int Data[Max][Max];
  int i, j;
  Variant V;
  V = GetArrayData();
  void *P = VarArrayLock(V);
  memcpy(Data, P, sizeof(Data));
  for (i = VarArrayLowBound(V, 1); i < VarArrayHighBound(V, 1); i++)
    for (j = VarArrayLowBound(V, 2); j < VarArrayHighBound(V, 2); j++)
      Grid->Cells[i-1][j-1] = Data[i-1][j-1];
  VarArrayUnlock(V);
}
```

Notice that this code first locks down the array and then accesses it as a pointer to a standard array. Finally, it releases the array when the operation is finished. You must remember to call `VarArrayUnlock` when you're finished working with the data from the array:

```
for (i = VarArrayLowBound(V, 1); i < VarArrayHighBound(V, 1); i++)
  for (j = VarArrayLowBound(V, 2); j < VarArrayHighBound(V, 2); j++)
    Grid->Cells[i-1][j-1] = Data[i-1][j-1];
VarArrayUnlock(V);
```

Remember that the point of using `VarArrayLock` and `VarArrayUnlock` is that they speed access to the array. The actual code you write is more complex and verbose, but the performance is faster.

If you don't want to lock down an array, you can still access the data. You have to do so by brute-force means, however, and can't use vast pointer-manipulation routines such as `memcpy`. The following `NormalArray1Click` method shows how to proceed if you don't lock down the data:

```
void __fastcall TForm1::NormalArray1Click(TObject *Sender)
{
  int i, j;
  Variant V = GetArrayData();
  for (i = 1; i < VarArrayHighBound(V, 1); i++)
    for (j = 1; j < VarArrayHighBound(V, 2); j++)
      Grid->Cells[i-1][j-1] = V.GetElement(i, j);
}
```

One of the most useful reasons for using a variant array is to transfer binary data to and from a server. If you have a binary file, say a WAV file or an AVI file, you can pass it back and forth between your program and an OLE server using variant arrays. Such a situation would present an ideal time for using `VarArrayLock` and `VarArrayUnlock`. You would, of course, use `VarByte` as the second parameter to `VarArrayCreate` when you're creating the array. That is, you would be working with an array of `Byte` and accessing it directly by locking down the array before moving data into and out of the structure. Such arrays are not subject to translation while being marshaled across boundaries.

The next program in this chapter shows how to pass data back and forth between programs using this technique. Listing 27.9 and Listing 27.10 contain a single sample program that encapsulates most of the ideas that you have seen in this section on variant arrays. The program from which this code is excerpted is called VarArray, and you can find it in the `Chap27` directory on the disk. Some screen shots from the program are shown in Figure 27.5 and Figure 27.6.

FIGURE 27.5.

Using the VarArray program to view information about a two-dimensional array.

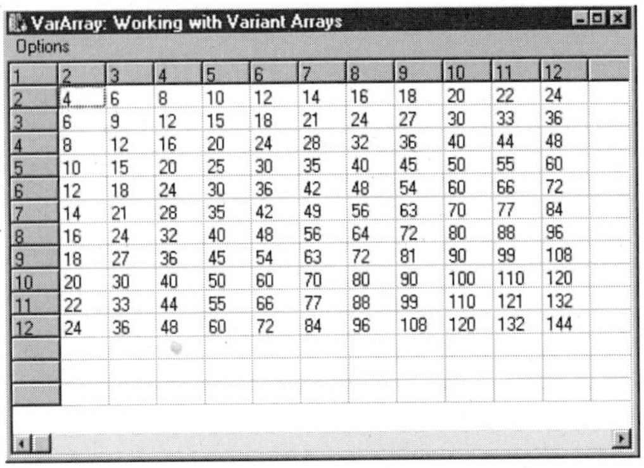

1	2	3	4	5	6	7	8	9	10	11	12
2	4	6	8	10	12	14	16	18	20	22	24
3	6	9	12	15	18	21	24	27	30	33	36
4	8	12	16	20	24	28	32	36	40	44	48
5	10	15	20	25	30	35	40	45	50	55	60
6	12	18	24	30	36	42	48	54	60	66	72
7	14	21	28	35	42	49	56	63	70	77	84
8	16	24	32	40	48	56	64	72	80	88	96
9	18	27	36	45	54	63	72	81	90	99	108
10	20	30	40	50	60	70	80	90	100	110	120
11	22	33	44	55	66	77	88	99	110	121	132
12	24	36	48	60	72	84	96	108	120	132	144

FIGURE 27.6.
Viewing a two-dimensional array that is locked down to get fast access to its data.

Listing 27.9. The header for the VarArray program. VarArray is designed to show how to use variant arrays.

```
///////////////////////////////////////
// Main.cpp
// Project: VarArray
// Copyright (c) 1997 by Charlie Calvert
//
#ifndef MainH
#define MainH
#include <vcl\Classes.hpp>
#include <vcl\Controls.hpp>
#include <vcl\StdCtrls.hpp>
#include <vcl\Forms.hpp>
#include "Grids.hpp"
#include <vcl\Menus.hpp>
class TForm1 : public TForm
{
__published:
  TStringGrid *Grid;
  TMainMenu *MainMenu1;
  TMenuItem *Options1;
  TMenuItem *CreateOneDimensionalArray1;
  TMenuItem *CreateTwoDimensionalArray1;
  TMenuItem *NormalArray1;
  TMenuItem *LockedArray1;
  void __fastcall bOneDimClick(TObject *Sender);
  void __fastcall bTwoDimClick(TObject *Sender);
  void __fastcall NormalArray1Click(TObject *Sender);
  void __fastcall LockedArray1Click(TObject *Sender);
private:
  AnsiString GetInfo(Variant &V);
public:
  __fastcall TForm1(TComponent* Owner);
};
extern TForm1 *Form1;
#endif
```

Listing 27.10. The main source file for the VarArray program.

```cpp
/////////////////////////////////////////
// Main.cpp
// Project: VarArray
// Copyright (c) 1997 by Charlie Calvert
//
#include <vcl\vcl.h>
#pragma hdrstop
#include "Main.h"
#pragma link "Grids"
#pragma resource "*.dfm"
#define Max 13

TForm1 *Form1;

__fastcall TForm1::TForm1(TComponent* Owner)
  : TForm(Owner)
{
}

AnsiString TForm1::GetInfo(Variant &V)
{
  int Count, HighBound, LowBound, i;
  AnsiString S;

  Count = VarArrayDimCount(V);
  S = AnsiString("\nDimension Count: ") + IntToStr(Count) + '\n';
  for (i = 1; i <= Count; i++)
  {
    HighBound = VarArrayHighBound(V, i);
    LowBound = VarArrayLowBound(V, i);
    S = S + "LowBound: " + IntToStr(LowBound) + '\n';
    S = S + "HighBound: " + IntToStr(HighBound) + '\n';

  }
  return S + '\n';
}

void __fastcall TForm1::bOneDimClick(TObject *Sender)
{
  AnsiString S;
  int i;

  S = "";
  Variant MyVariant(OPENARRAY(int, (0, 5)), varInteger);
  for (i = 0; i <= 5; i++)
    MyVariant.PutElement(i * 2, i);
  for (i = 0; i <= 5; i++)
    S = S + " " + MyVariant.GetElement(i);

  S = GetInfo(MyVariant) + S;
  ShowMessage(S);
}

void __fastcall TForm1::bTwoDimClick(TObject *Sender)
{
```

```
    int i, j;
    AnsiString S;

    Variant MyVariant(OPENARRAY(int, (0, 5, 0, 5)), varInteger);

    for (i = 0; i < 6; i++)
      for (j = 0; j < 6; j++)
        MyVariant.PutElement(i * j, i, j);

    for (i = 0; i < 6; i++)
    {
      for (j = 0; j < 6; j++)
      {
        S = S + " " + MyVariant.GetElement(i, j);
      }
      S = S + '\r';
    }

    S = GetInfo(MyVariant) + S;
    ShowMessage(S);
}

Variant GetArrayData()
{
  int i, j;

  Variant V(OPENARRAY(int, (1, Max, 1, Max)), varInteger);

  for (i = 1; i < Max; i++)
    for (j = 1; j < Max; j++)
      V.PutElement(i * j, j, i);

  return V;
}

void __fastcall TForm1::NormalArray1Click(TObject *Sender)
{
  int i, j;
  Variant V = GetArrayData();

  for (i = 1; i < VarArrayHighBound(V, 1); i++)
    for (j = 1; j < VarArrayHighBound(V, 2); j++)
      Grid->Cells[i-1][j-1] = V.GetElement(i, j);
}

void __fastcall TForm1::LockedArray1Click(TObject *Sender)
{
  int Data[Max][Max];
  int i, j;
  Variant V;

  V = GetArrayData();
  void *P = VarArrayLock(V);
  memcpy(Data, P, sizeof(Data));
  for (i = VarArrayLowBound(V, 1); i < VarArrayHighBound(V, 1); i++)
    for (j = VarArrayLowBound(V, 2); j < VarArrayHighBound(V, 2); j++)
      Grid->Cells[i-1][j-1] = Data[i-1][j-1];
  VarArrayUnlock(V);
}
```

This program has two menu items:

■ One enables you to look at the dimensions and bounds of two different variant arrays. The first array has one dimension, and the second has two.

■ The second pop-up menu enables you to display an array in a string grid using two different methods. The first method accesses the array through standard techniques, and the second lets you lock down the data before accessing it.

Remember that variant arrays are of use only in special circumstances. They are powerful tools, especially when you're making calls to OLE automation objects. However, they are slower and bulkier than standard BCB arrays and should be used only when necessary.

Using Remote Datasets with DCOM

The DataCom directory on the CD that accompanies this book contains two programs. One is an OLE Automation server, and the other is an OLE Automation client. I will talk about the server first. The code for the server is shown in Listing 27.11 through Listing 27.17. The interface for the server isn't very important from the perspective of this book, but you can see it in Figure 27.7. Note that the Globals.h and Globals.cpp files used by both the client and server applications are stored in the client application's directory.

FIGURE 27.7.

The DataServer OLE Automation server allows you to view the data and test the routines that will be exported to other applications.

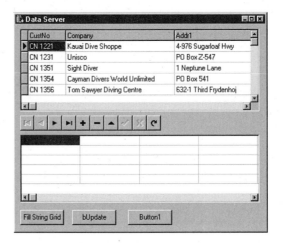

Listing 27.11. The header for the main module in the DataServer OLE Automation program.

```
/////////////////////////////////////////
// Main.h
// Project: DataServer
// Copyright (c) 1997 by Charlie Calvert
//
#ifndef MainH
#define MainH
```

```cpp
#include <vcl\Classes.hpp>
#include <vcl\Controls.hpp>
#include <vcl\StdCtrls.hpp>
#include <vcl\Forms.hpp>
#include <vcl\DBGrids.hpp>
#include "Grids.hpp"
#include <vcl\DBCtrls.hpp>
#include <vcl\ExtCtrls.hpp>

class TForm1 : public TForm
{
__published:
  TDBGrid *DBGrid1;
  TButton *bFillStrGrid;
  TStringGrid *Grid;
  TButton *bUpdate;
  TDBNavigator *DBNavigator1;
  void __fastcall bFillStrGridClick(TObject *Sender);
  void __fastcall bUpdateClick(TObject *Sender);
private:
public:
  __fastcall TForm1(TComponent* Owner);
  Variant __fastcall GetData();
  WordBool __fastcall DoUpdate(Variant V);
  void __fastcall UpdateParams(AnsiString CustNo, AnsiString Company,
    AnsiString Address, AnsiString City, AnsiString State, AnsiString Zip);
};

extern TForm1 *Form1;

#endif


#endif
```

Listing 27.12. The main source file for the DataServer application.

```cpp
////////////////////////////////////////
// Main.cpp
// Project: DataServer
// Copyright (c) 1997 by Charlie Calvert
//
#include <vcl\vcl.h>
#pragma hdrstop
#include "Main.h"
#include "DMod1.h"
#pragma link "Grids"
#pragma resource "*.dfm"

TForm1 *Form1;

__fastcall TForm1::TForm1(TComponent* Owner)
  : TForm(Owner)
```

continues

Listing 27.12. continued

```
{
}

Variant __fastcall TForm1::GetData()
{
  TCustomerRecord *Customer = new TCustomerRecord();
  void *P;

  DMod->GetCustAry(*Customer);

  Variant V(OPENARRAY(int, (0, sizeof(TCustomerRecord))), varByte);
  P = VarArrayLock(V);
  memcpy(P, Customer, sizeof(TCustomerRecord));
  VarArrayUnlock(V);
  return V;
}

// This function merely tests GetData to make sure it is working
void __fastcall TForm1::bFillStrGridClick(TObject *Sender)
{
  TCustomerRecord *Customer = new TCustomerRecord();
  void *P;
  int i;

  Variant V = GetData();
  P = VarArrayLock(V);
  memcpy(Customer, P, sizeof(TCustomerRecord));
  VarArrayUnlock(V);
  Grid->RowCount = Customer->Count;
  for (i = 0; i < Customer->Count; i++)
  {
    Grid->Cells[0][i] = Customer->CustAry[i].CustNo;
    Grid->Cells[1][i] = Customer->CustAry[i].Company;
    Grid->Cells[2][i] = Customer->CustAry[i].Address;
    Grid->Cells[3][i] = Customer->CustAry[i].City;
    Grid->Cells[4][i] = Customer->CustAry[i].State;
    Grid->Cells[5][i] = Customer->CustAry[i].Zip;
  }
}

WordBool __fastcall TForm1::DoUpdate(Variant V)
{
  void *P;
  TCustomer C;
  try
  {
    P = VarArrayLock(V);
    memcpy(&C, P, sizeof(TCustomer));
    VarArrayUnlock(V);
    ShowMessage("Ok");
    DMod->Update(C);
  }
  catch(...)
  {
    return False;
  }
```

```
    return True;
}

void __fastcall TForm1::UpdateParams(AnsiString CustNo, AnsiString Company,
  AnsiString Address, AnsiString City, AnsiString State, AnsiString Zip)
{
  TCustomer Customer;

  strcpy(Customer.CustNo, CustNo.c_str());
  strcpy(Customer.Company, Company.c_str());
  strcpy(Customer.Address, Address.c_str());
  strcpy(Customer.City, City.c_str());
  strcpy(Customer.State, State.c_str());
  strcpy(Customer.Zip, Zip.c_str());
  DMod->Update(Customer);
}

void __fastcall TForm1::bUpdateClick(TObject *Sender)
{
  TCustomer Customer;
  AnsiString CustNo;

  CustNo = "";
  InputQuery("CustNo of Record to Edit", "Enter CustNo: ", CustNo);
  strcpy(Customer.Company, "Company");
  strcpy(Customer.Address, "Address");
  strcpy(Customer.City, "City");
  strcpy(Customer.State, "State");
  strcpy(Customer.Zip, "Zip");
  strcpy(Customer.CustNo, CustNo.c_str());

  void *P;

  Variant V(OPENARRAY(int, (0, sizeof(TCustomer))), varByte);
  P = VarArrayLock(V);
  memcpy(P, &Customer, sizeof(TCustomer));
  VarArrayUnlock(V);

  DoUpdate(V);
}
```

27

DISTRIBUTED
COM

Listing 27.13. The header for the data module for the DataServer application.

```
///////////////////////////////////////
// DMod1.h
// Project: DataServer
// Copyright (c) 1997 by Charlie Calvert
//
#ifndef DMod1H
#define DMod1H
#include <vcl\Classes.hpp>
#include <vcl\Controls.hpp>
#include <vcl\StdCtrls.hpp>
```

continues

Listing 27.13. continued

```cpp
#include <vcl\Forms.hpp>
#include <vcl\DBTables.hpp>
#include <vcl\DB.hpp>
#include "Globals.h"

class TDMod : public TDataModule
{
__published:
  TTable *CustomerTable;
  TFloatField *CustomerTableCustNo;
  TStringField *CustomerTableCompany;
  TStringField *CustomerTableAddr1;
  TStringField *CustomerTableAddr2;
  TStringField *CustomerTableCity;
  TStringField *CustomerTableState;
  TStringField *CustomerTableZip;
  TStringField *CustomerTableCountry;
  TStringField *CustomerTablePhone;
  TStringField *CustomerTableFAX;
  TFloatField *CustomerTableTaxRate;
  TStringField *CustomerTableContact;
  TDateTimeField *CustomerTableLastInvoiceDate;
  TDataSource *CustomerSource;
  TQuery *UpdateQuery;
private:
public:
  __fastcall TDMod(TComponent* Owner);
  void GetCustAry(TCustomerRecord &Customer);
  void Update(TCustomer Customer);
};

extern TDMod
 *DMod;

#endif
```

Listing 27.14. The data module for the DataServer application.

```cpp
///////////////////////////////////////
// DMod1.cpp
// Project: DataServer
// Copyright (c) 1997 by Charlie Calvert
//
#include <vcl\vcl.h>
#include <vcl\bde.hpp>
#pragma hdrstop
#include "DMod1.h"
#pragma resource "*.dfm"

TDMod *DMod;

__fastcall TDMod::TDMod(TComponent* Owner)
  : TDataModule(Owner)
{
```

```
    CustomerTable->Open();
}

void TDMod::GetCustAry(TCustomerRecord &Customer)
{
  int i = 0;
  Variant V;
  Double Num;

  CustomerTable->First();
  CustomerSource->Enabled = False;
  while (!CustomerTable->Eof)
  {
    Num = CustomerTable->FieldByName("CustNo")->AsFloat;
    sprintf(Customer.CustAry[i].CustNo, "%f", Num);
    strcpy(Customer.CustAry[i].Company, CustomerTableCompany->AsString.c_str());
    strcpy(Customer.CustAry[i].Address, CustomerTableAddr1->AsString.c_str());
    strcpy(Customer.CustAry[i].City, CustomerTableCity->AsString.c_str());
    strcpy(Customer.CustAry[i].State, CustomerTableState->AsString.c_str());
    strcpy(Customer.CustAry[i].Zip, CustomerTableZip->AsString.c_str());
    i++;
    CustomerTable->Next();
  }
  Customer.Count = i - 1;
  CustomerSource->Enabled = True;
}

void TDMod::Update(TCustomer Customer)
{
  float Value;

  UpdateQuery->Close();
  UpdateQuery->Params->Items[0]->AsString = Customer.Company;
  UpdateQuery->Params->Items[1]->AsString = Customer.Address;
  UpdateQuery->Params->Items[2]->AsString = Customer.City;
  UpdateQuery->Params->Items[3]->AsString = Customer.State;
  UpdateQuery->Params->Items[4]->AsString = Customer.Zip;
  Value = StrToFloat(Customer.CustNo);
  UpdateQuery->Params->Items[5]->AsFloat = Value;
  UpdateQuery->ExecSQL();
}
```

Listing 27.15. The header for the OLE Automation object in the DataServer application.

```
/////////////////////////////////////
// DataObject.h
// Project: DataServer
// Copyright (c) 1997 by Charlie Calvert
//
#ifndef DataObjectH
#define DataObjectH
```

continues

Listing 27.15. continued

```cpp
#include <vcl\OleAuto.hpp>
#include <vcl\Classes.hpp>

class TDataServer : public TAutoObject
{
private:
public:
  __fastcall TDataServer();
__automated:
  AnsiString __fastcall GetName();
  Variant __fastcall TDataServer::GetData();
  WordBool __fastcall UpdateRecord(Variant V);
  void __fastcall UpdateParams(AnsiString CustNo, AnsiString Company,
    AnsiString Address, AnsiString City, AnsiString State, AnsiString Zip);
};

#endif
```

Listing 27.16. The main source file for the OLE Automation object in the DataServer application.

```cpp
////////////////////////////////////////
// DataObject.cpp
// Project: DataServer
// Copyright (c) 1997 by Charlie Calvert
//
#include <vcl\vcl.h>
#pragma hdrstop
#include "DataObject.h"
#include "DMod1.h"
#include "Main.h"

__fastcall TDataServer::TDataServer()
  : TAutoObject()
{
}

AnsiString __fastcall TDataServer::GetName()
{
  return AnsiString("TDataServer: ") + Now();
}

Variant __fastcall TDataServer::GetData()
{
  return Form1->GetData();
}

WordBool __fastcall TDataServer::UpdateRecord(Variant V)
{
  return Form1->DoUpdate(V);
}

void __fastcall TDataServer::UpdateParams(AnsiString CustNo, AnsiString Company,
    AnsiString Address, AnsiString City, AnsiString State, AnsiString Zip)
{
```

```
  Form1->UpdateParams(CustNo, Company, Address, City, State, Zip);
}


void __fastcall RegisterTDataServer()
{
  TAutoClassInfo AutoClassInfo;

  AutoClassInfo.AutoClass = __classid(TDataServer);
  AutoClassInfo.ProgID = "DataServer.DataServer";
  AutoClassInfo.ClassID = "{34BADDC0-884F-11D0-BCD7-0080C80CF1D2}";
  AutoClassInfo.Description = "DCOM DataServer ";
  AutoClassInfo.Instancing = acMultiInstance;

  Automation->RegisterClass(AutoClassInfo);
}

#pragma startup RegisterTDataServer
```

Listing 27.17. The Globals unit contains some declarations used by both the DataServer and the GetData client applications. It is stored in the GetData directory.

```
///////////////////////////////////////
// Globals.h
// Project: GetData
// Copyright (c) 1997 by Charlie Calvert
//
#ifndef GlobalsH
#define GlobalsH

  struct TCustomer {
    char CustNo[256];
    char Company[256];
    char Address[256];
    char City[256];
    char State[256];
    char Zip[256];
  };

  typedef TCustomer TCustAry[100];

  struct TCustomerRecord
  {
    int Count;
    TCustAry CustAry;
  };

#endif
```

This program exports the entire Customer table to remote clients. It also allows the clients to edit a particular row of data. This way, you can both view and edit the data from a database without ever loading any database tools on your machine.

> **NOTE**
>
> Understanding that remote datasets give you many of the advantages of the Web without the slow performance of the Internet and the limited interface capabilities of HTML is very important. For example, you can access remote datasets via DCOM without having to load any database tools. All that you need on your system is the subset of OLE DLLs that concern COM. All these DLLs, and more, are loaded whenever you launch the Internet Explorer. Both Web browsers (via ISAPI and CGI) and DCOM give you access to remote datasets. DCOM, however, is a more efficient, albeit platform-specific, solution.
>
> DCOM is also limited in terms of its range because it works best on an intranet but might not currently be a viable solution if you're trying to access data halfway around the world. Once again, the key is to know the available technologies and to use the one that makes sense in a particular context.

Understanding the ServerData Program

ServerData is fairly long, but the important sections of code are really fairly brief, and not particularly difficult to understand. I include the whole program so you can follow the logic of the entire application at your leisure, but I will focus mostly on a few key elements.

Here is the declaration for the `Automation` class:

```
class TDataServer : public TAutoObject
{
private:
public:
  __fastcall TDataServer();
__automated:
  AnsiString __fastcall GetName();
  Variant __fastcall GetData();
  WordBool __fastcall UpdateRecord(Variant V);
  void __fastcall UpdateParams(AnsiString CustNo, AnsiString Company,
    AnsiString Address, AnsiString City, AnsiString State, AnsiString Zip);
};
#endif
```

The `GetName` function is provided primarily so that you can test your connection to the server. If you can call `GetName`, then you know that you have access to the server.

The `GetData` function retrieves a variant array that contains an entire dataset. At any rate, I grab the key fields from a dataset and iterate through all the records of the dataset to get the information I need.

The `UpdateRecord` and `UpdateParams` functions are used by the client when it wants to update data on the server. For example, the user might edit one particular record and then send the edits back to the server via these functions.

27

> **NOTE**
>
> At the time of this writing, the first versions of BCB out of the dock apparently will not handle `UpdateRecord` properly, although they will handle `UpdateParams`. The problem with the `UpdateRecord` function has to do with what appears to be a bug in how BCB handles variants that are passed as parameters. In short, you simply cannot pass a variant to a procedure or function by value; you must pass it by reference. OLE Automation cannot handle parameters that are passed by reference; you must pass them by value. As a result, you cannot pass variants as parameters between BCB `TAutoObject`-based automation clients and servers. You can, however, return a variant from any BCB method, including BCB Automation methods.
>
> If you contemplate this bug for a second, you can see that it has absolutely nothing to do with OLE Automation. That part of the equation is handled fine by BCB and the VCL. The problem shown here is completely a BCB bug involving its implementation of variants, and it has nothing to do with the VCL, and nothing to do with OLE Automation.
>
> I'm sure this bug will be fixed very quickly, and you should check to see whether your version of BCB handles it correctly, or if you can download patches to fix the problem. I, of course, have not been able to properly test `UpdateRecord` because of this bug, but I believe that it will work when the BCB problem is cleaned up.

The `GetData` method looks like this:

```
Variant __fastcall TDataServer::GetData()
{
  return Form1->GetData();
}
```

As you can see, I delegate the actual implementation of `GetData` to the main form. This practice is common in OLE Automation because the Automation object is supposed to be a wrapper around the built-in functionality of your server. For example, ServerData provides access to the `Customer` table. The goal of the Automation server is simply to export that functionality to other programs. As a result, the fact that the Automation object would simply wrap methods already existing in the program makes sense.

The `TForm1` implementation of `GetData` looks like this:

```
Variant __fastcall TForm1::GetData()
{
  TCustomerRecord *Customer = new TCustomerRecord();
  void *P;
  DMod->GetCustAry(*Customer);
  Variant V(OPENARRAY(int, (0, sizeof(TCustomerRecord))), varByte);
  P = VarArrayLock(V);
  memcpy(P, Customer, sizeof(TCustomerRecord));
  VarArrayUnlock(V);
  return V;
}
```

This method asks the data module to retrieve a custom structure that contains the data from the Customer table. I will explain how that process works in one moment. For now, just concentrate on the fact that the GetData method converts the custom structure into a variant array by using VarArrayLock and VarArrayUnlock. This process was described earlier in the chapter, in the section on the VarArray program.

The custom data structure used by this program consists of an array of TCustomer structures:

```
struct TCustomer {
  char CustNo[256];
  char Company[256];
  char Address[256];
  char City[256];
  char State[256];
  char Zip[256];
};
typedef TCustomer TCustAry[100];
```

The program takes this array and hides inside a custom structure that defines the number of records in the array:

```
struct TCustomerRecord
{
  int Count;
  TCustAry CustAry;
};
```

Clearly, I could find more memory-efficient ways to store this data, but I wanted to keep this part of the program simple so that you would be able to follow the logic of the program without getting bogged down by a mass of irrelevant pointer manipulation. The important point of this program is how it handles OLE Automation; finding the best way to store data in memory is really another subject altogether.

After you declare the data structures, you simply need to fill them out in the data module for the application:

```
void TDMod::GetCustAry(TCustomerRecord &Customer)
{
  int i = 0;
  Variant V;
  Double Num;
  CustomerTable->First();
  CustomerSource->Enabled = False;
  while (!CustomerTable->Eof)
  {
    Num = CustomerTable->FieldByName("CustNo")->AsFloat;
    sprintf(Customer.CustAry[i].CustNo, "%f", Num);
    strcpy(Customer.CustAry[i].Company, CustomerTableCompany->AsString.c_str());
    strcpy(Customer.CustAry[i].Address, CustomerTableAddr1->AsString.c_str());
    strcpy(Customer.CustAry[i].City, CustomerTableCity->AsString.c_str());
    strcpy(Customer.CustAry[i].State, CustomerTableState->AsString.c_str());
    strcpy(Customer.CustAry[i].Zip, CustomerTableZip->AsString.c_str());
    i++;
```

```
  CustomerTable->Next();
  }
  Customer.Count = i - 1;
  CustomerSource->Enabled = True;
}
```

This code simply iterates through the entire dataset, using brute-force methods to copy the data into the array. Notice that I disable the DataSource for the module so that the program does not waste time updating the visual display for a program that is, after all, running on a remote server.

The data module also provides a method for updating the dataset when the user sends back a record with new data:

```
void TDMod::Update(TCustomer Customer)
{
  float Value;
  UpdateQuery->Close();
  UpdateQuery->Params->Items[0]->AsString = Customer.Company;
  UpdateQuery->Params->Items[1]->AsString = Customer.Address;
  UpdateQuery->Params->Items[2]->AsString = Customer.City;
  UpdateQuery->Params->Items[3]->AsString = Customer.State;
  UpdateQuery->Params->Items[4]->AsString = Customer.Zip;
  Value = StrToFloat(Customer.CustNo);
  UpdateQuery->Params->Items[5]->AsFloat = Value;
  UpdateQuery->ExecSQL();
}
```

The preceding is just standard TQuery code, of the type that was explained in depth in Chapter 10, "SQL and the TQuery Object."

The SQL for the UpdateQuery looks like this:

```
update
  Customer
set
  Company = :Company,
  Addr1 = :Address,
  City = :City,
  State = :State,
  Zip = :Zip
where
  CustNo = :CustNo
```

As you can see, the code will update an existing record given its CustNo. However, this program makes no provisions for inserting new data. Obviously, adding that functionality to the program would not be hard, but I have not done so in this example. In particular, all you would have to do is insert the new record rather than just update it. You would, however, have to provide a technique for providing a valid CustNo.

That's all I'm going to say about the ServerData program. You will probably want to study a few other parts of the program on your own, but overall this program is not a complex piece of work. One of the great advantages of DCOM and OLE Automation is that both technologies are easy to use.

GetData: The Client Program for Remote Datasets

The GetData application, found on the CD that accompanies this book, shows how to access a remote dataset from a client application. A simple menu allows you to retrieve a dataset from either a local OLE Automation server or from a remote DCOM Automation server. In both cases, the server is the ServerData application explained in the preceding section of this chapter.

After the user connects to the data, it is displayed in the main form of the program, as shown in Figure 27.8. The user can then edit the data in a custom form, as shown in Figure 27.9.

FIGURE 27.8.

Viewing the data retrieved over the network from a remote server.

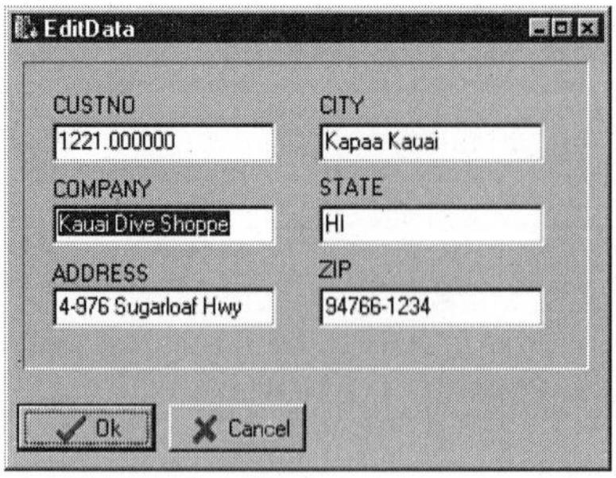

FIGURE 27.9.

Editing a row of data before sending it back to the server.

The code for the GetData program is shown in Listing 27.18 through Listing 27.21. I do not show the Globals unit here because it was included in the listings for the ServerData program. I also omit the CodeBox unit, which is found in the Utils directory on the CD that accompanies this book. I bring in the CodeBox unit because I need to call CreateRemoteObject. I supplied the full source for CreateRemoteObject previously in the section "Creating the DCOM Client."

Listing 27.18. The header file for the main module of the GetData application. GetData is an OLE client that retrieves a database table from a server via OLE Automation.

```
/////////////////////////////////////
// Main.h
// Project: GetData
// Copyright (c) 1997 by Charlie Calvert
//
#ifndef MainH
#define MainH
#include <vcl\Classes.hpp>
#include <vcl\Controls.hpp>
#include <vcl\StdCtrls.hpp>
#include <vcl\Forms.hpp>
#include "Grids.hpp"
#include <vcl\Buttons.hpp>
#include <vcl\Menus.hpp>
#include "globals.h"
class TForm1 : public TForm
{
__published:
  TStringGrid *Grid;
  TMainMenu *MainMenu1;
  TMenuItem *File1;
  TMenuItem *MakeConnection1;
  TMenuItem *MakeConnectionLocal1;
  TMenuItem *N1;
  TMenuItem *Exit1;
  TMenuItem *Options1;
  TMenuItem *Edit1;
  TMenuItem *UpdateData1;
  void __fastcall MakeConnectionBtnClick(TObject *Sender);
  void __fastcall ShowDataClick(TObject *Sender);
  void __fastcall Edit1Click(TObject *Sender);
  void __fastcall UpdateData1Click(TObject *Sender);
  void __fastcall MakeConnection1Click(TObject *Sender);
private:
  Variant V;
  TCustomerRecord FCustomerRecord;
  void FillGrid();
public:
  __fastcall TForm1(TComponent* Owner);
};
extern TForm1 *Form1;
#endif
```

Listing 27.19. The main module for the GetData program.

```cpp
//////////////////////////////////////
// Main.cpp
// Project: GetData
// Copyright (c) 1997 by Charlie Calvert
//
#include <vcl\vcl.h>
#pragma hdrstop
#include "Main.h"
#include "OleAuto.hpp"
#include "Globals.h"
#include "codebox.h"
#include "EditData1.h"
#include "initguid.h"
#pragma link "Grids"
#pragma resource "*.dfm"
TForm1 *Form1;

__fastcall TForm1::TForm1(TComponent* Owner)
  : TForm(Owner)
{
}

void __fastcall TForm1::MakeConnectionBtnClick(TObject *Sender)
{
  V = CreateOleObject("DataServer.DataServer");
  ShowDataClick(NULL);
}

DEFINE_GUID(CLSID_IDATASERVER, 0x34BADDC0, 0x884F, 0x11D0,
            0xBC,0xD7,0x00,0x80,0xC8,0x0C,0xF1,0xD2);

void __fastcall TForm1::MakeConnection1Click(TObject *Sender)
{
  CreateRemoteObject(CLSID_IDATASERVER, "143.186.149.228", V);
  ShowDataClick(NULL);
}

void TForm1::FillGrid()
{
  int i;

  Grid->RowCount = FCustomerRecord.Count;
  for (i = 0; i < FCustomerRecord.Count; i++)
  {
    Grid->Cells[0][i] = FCustomerRecord.CustAry[i].CustNo;
    Grid->Cells[1][i] = FCustomerRecord.CustAry[i].Company;
    Grid->Cells[2][i] = FCustomerRecord.CustAry[i].Address;
    Grid->Cells[3][i] = FCustomerRecord.CustAry[i].City;
    Grid->Cells[4][i] = FCustomerRecord.CustAry[i].State;
    Grid->Cells[5][i] = FCustomerRecord.CustAry[i].Zip;
  }
}

void __fastcall TForm1::ShowDataClick(TObject *Sender)
{
```

```
  Variant Data;
  void *P;

  Data = V.OleFunction("GetData");
  P = VarArrayLock(Data);
  memcpy(&FCustomerRecord, P, sizeof(TCustomerRecord));
  VarArrayUnlock(Data);
  FillGrid();
}

void __fastcall TForm1::Edit1Click(TObject *Sender)
{
  /*  if (EditData->EditCustomer(FCustomerRecord.CustAry[Grid->Selection.Top]) ==
        mrOk)
  {
    FillGrid();
    Variant Temp = EditData->GetCustomerAsVariant();
    V.OleFunction("UpDateRecord", Temp);
  } */
  if (EditData->EditCustomer(FCustomerRecord.CustAry[Grid->Selection.Top]) == mrOk)
  {
    FillGrid();
    EditData->SendCustomerAsStrings(V);
  }
}

void __fastcall TForm1::UpdateData1Click(TObject *Sender)
{
  ShowDataClick(NULL);
}
```

Listing 27.20. The EditData module provides a form for editing an individual record. This is the header file for the unit.

```
/////////////////////////////////////////
// EditData.h
// Project: GetData
// Copyright (c) 1997 by Charlie Calvert
//
#ifndef EditData1H
#define EditData1H
#include <vcl\Classes.hpp>
#include <vcl\Controls.hpp>
#include <vcl\StdCtrls.hpp>
#include <vcl\Forms.hpp>
#include <vcl\ExtCtrls.hpp>
#include <vcl\Buttons.hpp>
#include "globals.h"

class TEditData : public TForm
{
__published:
  TLabel *Label1;
```

continues

Listing 27.20. continued

```cpp
  TLabel *Label2;
  TLabel *Label3;
  TLabel *Label4;
  TLabel *Label5;
  TLabel *Label6;
  TBevel *Bevel1;
  TEdit *ECompany;
  TEdit *EAddress;
  TEdit *ECity;
  TEdit *EState;
  TEdit *EZip;
  TEdit *ECustNo;
  TBitBtn *BitBtn1;
  TBitBtn *BitBtn2;
  void __fastcall BitBtn1Click(TObject *Sender);
private:
  TCustomer FCustomer;
public:
  __fastcall TEditData(TComponent* Owner);
  Variant GetCustomerAsVariant();
  void GetCustomer();
  void FillCustomer();
  int EditCustomer(TCustomer &ACustomer);
  void SendCustomerAsStrings(Variant &V);
};

extern TEditData *EditData;

#endif
```

Listing 27.21. The EditData module provides a form for editing an individual record. You can then send the updated data back to the server via OLE Automation.

```cpp
///////////////////////////////////////
// EditData.cpp
// Project: GetData
// Copyright (c) 1997 by Charlie Calvert
//
#include <vcl\vcl.h>
#pragma hdrstop
#include "EditData1.h"
#pragma resource "*.dfm"

TEditData *EditData;

__fastcall TEditData::TEditData(TComponent* Owner)
  : TForm(Owner)
{
}

Variant TEditData::GetCustomerAsVariant()
```

```
{
  void *P;

  GetCustomer();
  Variant V(OPENARRAY(int, (0, sizeof(TCustomer))), varByte);
  P = VarArrayLock(V);
  memcpy(P, &FCustomer, sizeof(TCustomer));
  VarArrayUnlock(V);
  return V;
}

void TEditData::SendCustomerAsStrings(Variant &V)
{
  GetCustomer();
  V.OleProcedure("UpdateParams", FCustomer.CustNo, FCustomer.Company,
                 FCustomer.Address,
    FCustomer.City, FCustomer.State, FCustomer.Zip);
}

void TEditData::GetCustomer()
{
  strcpy(FCustomer.CustNo, ECustNo->Text.c_str());
  strcpy(FCustomer.Company, ECompany->Text.c_str());
  strcpy(FCustomer.Address, EAddress->Text.c_str());
  strcpy(FCustomer.City, ECity->Text.c_str());
  strcpy(FCustomer.State, EState->Text.c_str());
  strcpy(FCustomer.Zip, EZip->Text.c_str());
}

void TEditData::FillCustomer()
{
  ECustNo->Text = FCustomer.CustNo;
  ECompany->Text = FCustomer.Company;
  EAddress->Text = FCustomer.Address;
  ECity->Text = FCustomer.City;
  EState->Text = FCustomer.State;
  EZip->Text = FCustomer.Zip;
}

int TEditData::EditCustomer(TCustomer &ACustomer)
{
  FCustomer = ACustomer;
  FillCustomer();
  int Result = ShowModal();
  if (Result == mrOk)
    ACustomer = FCustomer;
  return Result;
}

void __fastcall TEditData::BitBtn1Click(TObject *Sender)
{
  GetCustomer();
}
```

This program starts out by retrieving the server either locally or remotely:

```
void __fastcall TForm1::MakeConnectionBtnClick(TObject *Sender)
{
  V = CreateOleObject("DataServer.DataServer");
  ShowDataClick(NULL);
}
DEFINE_GUID(CLSID_IDATASERVER, 0x34BADDC0, 0x884F, 0x11D0,
            0xBC,0xD7,0x00,0x80,0xC8,0x0C,0xF1,0xD2);
void __fastcall TForm1::MakeConnection1Click(TObject *Sender)
{
  CreateRemoteObject(CLSID_IDATASERVER, "143.186.149.228", V);
  ShowDataClick(NULL);
}
```

I described all the code shown here in some depth earlier in the chapter. Notice that I use the GUID from the OLE server to retrieve the program from a remote location. As I mentioned earlier, you can use the DComCfg.exe application to access remote servers using the same techniques used with local servers. However, you'll experience some drawbacks using this system when Windows 95 is involved in the equation. Figure 27.10 shows DComCfg.exe running on an NT server.

FIGURE 27.10.

You can use the DComCfg.exe utility to make remote servers appear as local servers so that you can call them with CreateOleObject.

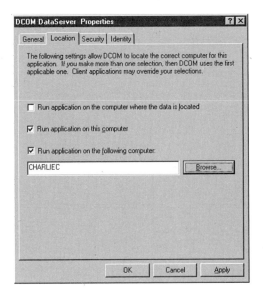

After you connect to the server, you can ask it for a copy of the dataset from the Customer table and then display the data to the user:

```
void __fastcall TForm1::ShowDataClick(TObject *Sender)
{
  Variant Data;
  void *P;
```

```
Data = V.OleFunction("GetData");
P = VarArrayLock(Data);
memcpy(&FCustomerRecord, P, sizeof(TCustomerRecord));
VarArrayUnlock(Data);
FillGrid();
}
```

This code calls the GetData function of the ServerData program. It then locks down the variant array returned by the server and extracts the custom record from it. This operation is the reverse of the operation performed in the ServerData, where you say how to pack the custom data into a variant array.

The FillGrid method simply displays the data in a string grid:

```
void TForm1::FillGrid()
{
  int i;

  Grid->RowCount = FCustomerRecord.Count;
  for (i = 0; i < FCustomerRecord.Count; i++)
  {
    Grid->Cells[0][i] = FCustomerRecord.CustAry[i].CustNo;
    Grid->Cells[1][i] = FCustomerRecord.CustAry[i].Company;
    Grid->Cells[2][i] = FCustomerRecord.CustAry[i].Address;
    Grid->Cells[3][i] = FCustomerRecord.CustAry[i].City;
    Grid->Cells[4][i] = FCustomerRecord.CustAry[i].State;
    Grid->Cells[5][i] = FCustomerRecord.CustAry[i].Zip;
  }
}
```

The Cells property of the TStringGrid object allows you to access the array of data underlying the grid.

Now that the user can see the remote dataset, the only thing left to do is give him or her a chance to edit it. The following line of code retrieves the currently selected row from the string grid:

```
if (EditData->EditCustomer(FCustomerRecord.CustAry[Grid->Selection.Top])
   == mrOk)
```

The key point to grasp here is that Grid->Selection.Top designates the currently selected row in the grid.

Inside the TEditData form, only one routine is of any real interest. This routine is called GetCustomerAsVariant:

```
Variant TEditData::GetCustomerAsVariant()
{
  void *P;
  GetCustomer();
  Variant V(OPENARRAY(int, (0, sizeof(TCustomer))), varByte);
  P = VarArrayLock(V);
```

27

DISTRIBUTED COM

```
    memcpy(P, &FCustomer, sizeof(TCustomer));
    VarArrayUnlock(V);
    return V;
}
```

This code uses the `GetCustomer` function, which follows, to retrieve the newly edited data from the `TEditData` form. It then moves the data into a variant array by first locking down the array and then moving some bytes around via a call to `memcpy`. Here is the simple `GetCustomer` method used to retrieve the data from the visual controls in the `TEditForm`:

```
void TEditData::GetCustomer()
{
    strcpy(FCustomer.CustNo, ECustNo->Text.c_str());
    strcpy(FCustomer.Company, ECompany->Text.c_str());
    strcpy(FCustomer.Address, EAddress->Text.c_str());
    strcpy(FCustomer.City, ECity->Text.c_str());
    strcpy(FCustomer.State, EState->Text.c_str());
    strcpy(FCustomer.Zip, EZip->Text.c_str());
}
```

If you don't want to pass the data back to the server using a variant array, you can just pass the strings of the record back directly:

```
void TEditData::SendCustomerAsStrings(Variant &V)
{
    GetCustomer();
    V.OleProcedure("UpdateParams", FCustomer.CustNo, FCustomer.Company,
        FCustomer.Address, FCustomer.City, FCustomer.State, FCustomer.Zip);
}
```

This code retrieves the text that the user has edited and then calls the `UpdateParams` procedure of the OLE server. `UpdataParams` will execute a SQL update statement to insert the new data into the `Customer` table.

That's all I'm going to say about remote datasets. They're one of the more powerful aspects of DCOM, and I'm sure you can imagine many other ways to use this technology. If you want to extend this technology with a set of robust tools, you should look into Entera, a remote client/server technology provided by Borland.

Summary

In this chapter, you learned how to use BCB to build applications that take advantage of the Distributed Component Object Model, or DCOM. You have seen that combining BCB, DCOM, and OLE Automation provides a simple method for allowing one application to control or use another application that resides on a second machine.

People who are interested in this field should look at Borland's Entera and OLEnterprise products, as well as the very powerful OLE-based tools found in Delphi 3.0. The plan at the time of this writing is for all the tools in Delphi 3.0 to appear in future versions of BCB.

Windows programmers have seen so many extraordinary technical developments in the last few years that it's difficult to single out any one technology and say that it is significantly more important than the rest. Nevertheless, DCOM appears to be a viable solution to one of the major problems faced by contemporary programmers. In short, we can now easily distribute the workload of a particular product across multiple machines. Just how much impact this technology will have on the industry is hard to say at this early stage, but DCOM (and related technologies such as CORBA) certainly have the potential to change the way we build applications.

VI

PART

Win32 and Multimedia

Game Programming

IN THIS CHAPTER

Overview

In this chapter and the next, you'll examine multimedia and game objects. In particular, you will see the following:

■ A simple two-dimensional graphics engine that uses DirectDraw

■ A simple game engine

■ Examples of how to use both objects

■ Various comments on object design

■ The opening portions of a strategy game called Byzantium

The graphics engine used in this chapter is implemented on disk both in C++ and in Object Pascal, and it appears to BCB programmers as a set of simple components. The game engine, shown in the next chapter, is implemented in C++, and it appears to the user as a set of objects. In short, the graphics engine consists of components, and the game engine consists of simple objects.

You can use all the code found in this book in your own programs, but you cannot use the art or designs found in this chapter and the next. My objection is to distributing the art in your own programs. You are free to use the art in your own home or at your company, but you cannot distribute it to others in any form. You can use the game engine to build your own games, but it must be distinct from the game you find in the next chapter. The world must be different, and so should the art.

I hope that many readers are specifically interested in developing and using game engines. If you're not interested in that subject, I still think that you will find these chapters among the most interesting in the book. In particular, in these pages you will see how to create complex sets of objects and use them in real-world programs that have to perform complex tasks.

The DirectX technology shown in these chapters can be used in a wide variety of applications. For example, you can use the graphics engine shown here to create the following:

■ Games

■ Simulations

■ Presentations

■ Advanced graphical features of all kinds

Besides describing the raw graphics tools in this chapter, I also show you how to create complex object hierarchies, how to plan and design the functionality of an object properly, how to divide groups of objects into specific engines, and how to get the engines to work together.

The overriding theme of these chapters is the importance of object design. You have to learn how to create objects that are reusable and how to design object hierarchies that are simple enough to meet the needs of real programmers.

In the end, everything comes down to design. If you design the right kinds of objects, you can accomplish almost anything. Furthermore, as you will see, the judicious use of objects can help you dig yourself out of almost any hole. Objects are the Holy Grail of contemporary programming, and if you understand how to use them correctly, they will help you complete project after project on time.

Just understanding the basics of object technology is not enough. Just knowing about polymorphism, inheritance, and encapsulation is not enough. You also need to know how to design objects that you can use and that other people can use. This section of the book is about designing these kinds of objects. Of course, on the way, you will also have the chance to engage in a good deal of fun with graphics, games, and multimedia.

Game Resources

Game programming is more complicated than most standard Windows programming tasks for many reasons. The root of this complexity is the need to use special graphics tools such as DirectX. Another complication that many first-time game programmers underestimate involves creating art.

Many books are available on game programming and on producing art for games. Two that I have found useful are

> *Tricks of the Game Programming Gurus*, LaMothe, Ratcliff, et al., Sams Publishing
>
> *The Ultimate Game Developers Sourcebook*, Ben Sawyer, Coriolis Group Books

You will also need a paint program. I find that the inexpensive shareware program called Paint Shop Pro meets most of my needs, though many other powerful programs such as Fractal Paint (`www.fractal.com`) are available. Here's the contact information for Paint Shop Pro:

JASC, Inc.

P.O. Box 44997

Eden Prairie, MN 55344

930-9171

`www.jasc.com`

Other key paint programs that I use often include TrueSpace (`www.caligari.com`) and VistaPro from Virtual Reality Laboratories in San Luis Obispo. TrueSpace allows you to create three-dimensional objects, and VistaPro allows you to create landscapes. The background scenes that show rolling hills, mountains, and trees in the figures for this chapter and the next were created in VistaPro (Virtual Reality Laboratories in San Luis Obispo, CA, 805-545-8515, e-mail: `VRLI@aol.com`, WWW: `http://www.romt.com`). (See the files called `Backgrd1.bmp` and `Backgrd2.bmp` on the CD that comes with this book for examples of VistaPro files that have gone through a color reduction so that they could fit on a 256-color palette.)

You might find additional game components, links, or code available at these sites:

```
http://www.silvercrk.com/directx/
http://www.spinlogic.com/GameDev/
http://users.aol.com/charliecal
```

Many other Web sites are of interest to game developers, but you can find links to most of them from the sites listed here. On CompuServe, type GO GAMEDEV to find the game developers' forum.

As I stated previously, game programming is an extremely complex undertaking. The biggest mistake you can make is to try to create your own tools from scratch. Use the tools included in this book to get some sense of what you can gain from a graphics engine and a set of gaming tools. Then go out and search the Web and your local bookstores for ready-made graphics and game engines. Build your games using these tools; don't try to create your own tools from scratch unless you're sure, double-sure, and then triple-sure you know what you're doing and why.

If you have never built a game before, then don't even consider building one from scratch. Build your first game with someone else's engine. Then, after you understand something about the tools that are available, you might finally be in a position to consider creating some of your own tools. Even then, however, I would still recommend turning around and using someone else's tools rather than trying to create your own. The *Ultimate Game Developers Sourcebook*, mentioned previously, offers a great deal of information on finding third-party game engines.

Where We're Headed: Object Overview

In this part of the book, you'll create two sets of objects. Using the first set of objects, you can encapsulate DirectX multimedia functionality inside easy-to-use components. The second set of objects allows you to create games, simulations, or multimedia tools using the game engine.

The classic mistake to make in this process is to find or create the objects that give you access to the multimedia and DirectX interfaces and to then think you're ready to create a program. This error is fatal—and very common.

Suppose that you have a set of objects that give you full access to DirectDraw. The mistake many programmers make is to assume that they can directly use these objects when creating a game or simulation. Indeed, in some cases, that may be possible. However, most of the time you need to create a second set of objects tailored specifically for games or simulations. In particular, you need a TGameEngine object. Furthermore, this object is not necessarily a direct descendant of any of your graphics-based objects. It may use them via aggregation but probably does not descend directly from them. The same applies for simulations: You need a TSimulation object that uses your graphics objects but presents a different interface to the user. A game object, for example, needs items such as TPlayer, TBoard, THero, TScene, and so on. Your graphic objects don't know anything about those kinds of objects.

To get a handle on this issue, you need to think in terms of specific *problem domains*. One problem domain involves using DirectDraw to create fast graphics. A second problem domain involves creating a game engine, and a third problem domain involves creating a specific game. You need to draw firm lines between these domains so that the complexity of one problem domain does not creep into another domain. As a rule, you should not allow any direct calls to your graphics objects by the users of your TGameEngine object. TGameEngine calls the graphics objects, but it does so via private interfaces that TGameEngine users can never see.

> **NOTE**
>
> An example might be helpful here. In DirectX, you can write text to the screen using device contexts. You get the DC for a device, copy objects into it, and then use TextOut to write to the screen. Having the game engine use these same objects is probably not wise. Instead, you should hide the underlying technology and provide a routine with a name such as WriteXY or WriteLn or printf or Say that will let you write to the screen. Internally, your implementation of WriteXY will use device contexts, but that fact should be hidden from the user. This will allow you to switch your game from Windows to DOS to the Mac without having to change its code. Only the interface to the graphics engine changes, but your game code remains untouched.

One way to help design these objects correctly is to ensure that a user of TGameEngine would have to do nothing more than recompile if you were to switch your game engine technology from one set of graphics objects to another. In other words, the users of TGameEngine should not have to know anything about the tools you use to create fast graphics. You can tell them, "Hey, I use DirectDraw," or "I use WinG," but the actual technology involved should not matter to them in the sense that their code will still compile if you switch the background engine. Users of TGameEngine should not have to know whether TGameEngine uses DirectDraw or WinG. Users of TGameEngine never call the graphics objects directly, and they don't even have to conceive of the fact that such a thing as an IDirectDraw object exists.

Obviously, one of the important benefits of this system is that you can change from WinG to DirectDraw without having to rewrite your game or game engine. But this capability is not the primary benefit that interests me. What I like about this system is that it creates domains for problems. If I'm working with the TGameEngine object and find that it's not drawing things correctly because of some error in the way I access DirectDraw, then I can put the TGameEngine object away, open the graphics engine, and find out what is wrong. My game engine and my game cannot be the cause of the problem because they don't talk to the IDirectDraw interface. They don't know anything about the IDirectDraw interface!

Another benefit of this system is that it allows you to improve one part of your code without affecting existing parts of your code. For example, I could drastically rewrite the graphics engine without having to change the way TGameEngine operates. In these situations, rewriting the graphics engine without changing its interface is best, but even if you do change it, you can still buffer your game from these changes because it talks to `TGameEngine`, not to the graphics engine. However, the best thing to do is to never change a public interface after you create it.

> **NOTE**
>
> I will concede that some of the theory I am describing here is a bit idealized. In practice, I rarely achieve precisely the degree of object independence described in the preceding paragraphs. However, the closer I can get to it, the better off I am. Aiming as high as possible is always best, thereby limiting as much as possible the amount of trouble you will have if your architecture needs to be upgraded.
>
> Furthermore, the process of learning to design good objects is incremental at best. The first time I tried to create a complex set of objects, I failed miserably. The second time, I took to heart some of the ideas I am describing here and came closer to achieving my goal. The third time out I made yet fewer gross design errors, and so on, till finally I was starting to produce complex object hierarchies that could actually be used and maintained.

Creating Public Interfaces

The last paragraph of the preceding section introduces a second key rule of object-oriented design. Creating problem domains is the most important step, but a second crucial condition is creating public interfaces that have little to do with your underlying technology.

When you're creating the public interface for the graphics engine, you should take off your `IDirectDraw` expert hat and put on one that helps you pretend you are the user of this object. What will a user of this object want to see? A user doesn't want to hear about the nitty-gritty of using `IDirectDraw`; instead, he or she wants to be able to work with broad concepts such as `TBackground`, `TSprite`, and `TWindow`.

Managing Complexity: Create Humble Objects

Before going further, I want to talk just a little more about limiting the problem domain.

One of the most important jobs that objects can do for you is to help manage complexity. In the first chapter of this book, I stressed the importance of being humble when you program. Here, that theme can really start to pay off.

The worst mistake you can make as a programmer is to decide "Hey, I'm so smart, so cool, that I can make this object stunningly complex and efficient and still be able to use it." In the process, you might end up continually collapsing one object into another and continually finding fast, clever ways to get tasks done in the fewest possible moves. All this cleverness is good and well, if you can simultaneously produce objects that you and others can use and maintain.

Putting all the logic into one set of objects has the following problems:

- Any hope of code reuse is obliterated. If one small set of objects forms the whole game, how can you separate the reusable part of the code for a second game that has similar characteristics?

- Maintaining it is a nightmare. If something goes wrong anywhere in the game, you have no way of localizing a problem and testing it separately from the rest of the application. If all you have are a few big, complex objects, when something goes wrong, *all* the lines of code in your program are suspect, and you cannot separate out the code you need to test and repair. This monumental problem is likely to sink most projects completely. You have to be able to break down a program into its various components and test each part separately.

- Teaching someone how to work with the code for a game is extremely hard if he or she has to understand the entire game to be able to work on any part of it. Under-standing one huge, complex object is difficult. The paradigm is innately complex. You have a much simpler task getting someone up to speed on some code if you can say, "Here, we need to make these changes to this 500-line object. Please get to work right away; time is of the essence." The nightmare scenario sounds like this: "Welcome aboard. We have 200,000 lines of code here, and we need to make some changes to it. Please spend the next six months becoming familiar with our code base, and then I would like you to make some changes to a few small portions of it. Tell me when you're up to speed."

Putting all the logic in clearly delineated sets of objects has the following advantages, which are the converse of the disadvantages laid out in the preceding three points.

- Code reuse is supported. A well-designed graphics engine can be reused in almost any graphics-based game. A subset of those objects can be used in virtually any multimedia venture that requires DirectDraw. The same is true with the GameEngine code. It's all in one place and can be reused. Conversely, the code that is specific to Byzantium is all in one place.

- Maintaining it is easy. If something goes wrong in the code, you can isolate the problem in a few distinct objects that you can test separately. Problems in one part of the code don't automatically percolate into other, related domains. Instead, they are isolated in one section of the code. This problem is like a leak in a submarine: If one section of the ship is damaged, you can seal it off from the rest of the ship. It won't affect the whole program; it is isolated in one area. You can then concentrate on fixing that area without worrying about the ramifications of those repairs on the rest of the program.

■ Understanding it is easy. You know exactly what is going on in the graphics engine components because the problem domain is manageable. You can explain the basic structure of the program to someone in five minutes because each part plays a distinct, easy-to-understand role.

The theme underlying all these points is humility. To be a good programmer, you have to admit that a certain level of complexity simply overwhelms you. Your only bulwark against that confusion is to break down the project into manageable chunks that you can understand.

Humble programmers produce real programs. Hotshots are going to produce fantastic programs Real Soon Now. I know that's true because those hotshots have been telling me about their program ideas for years.

The DirectX Game Engine

In the next few sections of the chapter, I describe a set of components that make up a simple graphics engine. The key components in this graphics engine are described in Table 28.1.

Table 28.1. The key objects in the graphics engine.

Component	Purpose
THermes	Get into and out of DirectX Exclusive mode
TScene	Draw the background of a graphics scene
TSpriteScene	Draw the background of a graphics scene that supports sprites
THermesChart	Create a tiled game scene

After I describe the graphics engine, I will describe the game engine that can be used in conjunction with these objects.

THermes: Getting Into and Out of Exclusive Mode

DirectX is a Microsoft technology that allows you to write high-performance gaming, simulation, and multimedia programs. In this chapter, I focus on the IDirectDraw interface, which is a portion of DirectX that gives you the ability to write directly to the video buffer.

The first thing you find when working with DirectX is that, to take full advantage of it, you need to switch into a special video mode called *Exclusive mode*. For the purposes of this book, this mode has a 640×480 screen dimension and 256 colors. Actually, other screen sizes and color resolutions are available to you as a DirectX programmer, but THermes gives you access only to this one screen mode.

The first object in the graphics engine is designed to switch you into and out of this mode. The class declaration for this object is shown in Listing 28.1. You can find the full source for the code shown here in a file called `Mercury2.cpp` in the `Utils` directory on the CD that accompanies this book.

The `Mercury` unit relies on `Creatures.pas`, which ships with this book, and `DDraw.h`, which ships in the included directory with BCB. You will also find a Pascal version of the `Mercury` unit in the `Units` subdirectory on the CD that accompanies this book.

NOTE

To find some Web sites of interest to DirectX programmers and full Pascal translations of DirectX 3.X headers, go to the following:

`http://www.dkw.com/bstone/`

When you're looking at this code, keep these points in mind:

- I do not quote the entire source until the end of the chapter. Throughout the main body of this chapter, I quote only the class declarations, one at a time as needed so that you can use them to grasp the structure of the portion of code currently under discussion. At the end of the chapter, I quote the entire object.

- You can install all the key objects in these units as components and use them directly in BCB, just as you would use any of the other components discussed in this book.

- You don't really have to understand this code, but you do need to know how to use the components created when these objects are installed on the Component Palette.

Listing 28.1. `Mercury2.cpp` **contains logic for handling sprites, backgrounds, and DirectX. The key object in this file is THermes.**

```
class THermes : public Classes::TComponent
{
  typedef Classes::TComponent inherited;
  friend THermesChart;
  friend TDraw;

private:
  bool FActive;
  Creatures1::TFileCreatureList* FCreatureList;
  HWND FHandle;
  bool FTimerOdd;
  int FTimerInterval;
  bool FExclusive;
  Classes::TNotifyEvent FPaintProc;
  TScene* FScene;
  bool FUseTimer;
```

continues

28

GAME
PROGRAMMING

Listing 28.1. continued

```
    bool FFirstTime;
    IDirectDraw* FDirectDraw;
    IDirectDrawSurface* FBackSurface;
    IDirectDrawClipper* FClipper;
    IDirectDrawSurface* FPrimarySurface;
    bool __fastcall CreatePrimary(void);
    void __fastcall DDTest(long hr,  System::AnsiString S);
    void __fastcall InitBaseObjects(void);
    bool __fastcall MakeItSo(long DDResult);
    void __fastcall SetScene(TScene* Scene);
    bool __fastcall SetUpBack(void);
    protected:
    void __fastcall DrawBitmaps(void);
    virtual long __fastcall RestoreSurfaces(void);
public:
    __fastcall virtual THermes(Classes::TComponent* AOwner);
    __fastcall virtual ~THermes(void) {}
    void __fastcall EndExclusive(void);
    void __fastcall ErrorEvent( System::AnsiString S);
    void __fastcall Flip(void);
    virtual void __stdcall InitObjects(void);
    virtual void __fastcall Run(void);
    __property bool Active = {read=FActive, write=FActive, nodefault};
    __property IDirectDrawSurface* BackSurface =
       {read=FBackSurface, write=FBackSurface, nodefault};
    __property Classes::TNotifyEvent OnDrawBitmap =
       {read=FPaintProc, write=FPaintProc};

__published:
    __property Creatures1::TFileCreatureList* CreatureList =
       {read=FCreatureList, write=FCreatureList, nodefault};
    __property bool Exclusive = {read=FExclusive, write=FExclusive, nodefault};
    __property TScene* Scene = {read=FScene, write=SetScene, nodefault};
    __property int TimerInterval =
       {read=FTimerInterval, write=FTimerInterval, nodefault};
    __property bool UseTimer = {read=FUseTimer, write=FUseTimer, nodefault};
};
```

To install THermes and the other graphics engine objects, choose Component | Install. Click the Add button, and then browse the Units directory from the CD that accompanies this book. Install both Creatures1.pas and Mercury2.cpp.

To use THermes, start a new project, drop a THermes object on it, and create an OnKeyDown handler that closes the form if any key is pressed. The code for such a project is shown in Listings 28.2 and 28.3.

Listing 28.2. The HermesTest1 project shows how to use THermes. The header for the main unit is shown here.

```
/////////////////////////////////////////
// Main.h
// Testing the THermes object
```

```
// Copyright (c) 1997 by Charlie Calvert
//
#ifndef MainH
#define MainH
#include <vcl\Classes.hpp>
#include <vcl\Controls.hpp>
#include <vcl\StdCtrls.hpp>
#include <vcl\Forms.hpp>
#include "..\..\utils\Mercury2.h"
#include <vcl\Menus.hpp>

class TForm1 : public TForm
{
__published:
  THermes *Hermes1;
  TMainMenu *MainMenu1;
  TMenuItem *Run1;
  void __fastcall FormKeyDown(TObject *Sender, WORD &Key, TShiftState Shift);
  void __fastcall Run1Click(TObject *Sender);
private:
  void __fastcall MyExceptions(TObject *Sender, Exception *E);
public:
  __fastcall TForm1(TComponent* Owner);
};

extern TForm1 *Form1;

#endif
```

Listing 28.3. The source for the main unit in the HermesTest1 project.

```
//////////////////////////////////////
// Main.cpp
// The TestHermes project tests the THermes component
// Copyright (c) 1997 by Charlie Calvert
//
#include <vcl\vcl.h>
#pragma hdrstop
#include "Main.h"
#pragma link "Mercury2"
#pragma resource "*.dfm"

TForm1 *Form1;

__fastcall TForm1::TForm1(TComponent* Owner)
  : TForm(Owner)
{
  Application->OnException = MyExceptions;
}

void __fastcall TForm1::FormKeyDown(TObject *Sender, WORD &Key,
  TShiftState Shift)
{
```

continues

Listing 28.3. continued

```
  if ((Shift.Contains(ssAlt)) && (Key == 'E'))
    throw Exception("Some Exception");
  else
    if (!Shift.Contains(ssAlt))
      Close();
}

void __fastcall TForm1::Run1Click(TObject *Sender)
{
  Hermes1->Run();
}

void __fastcall TForm1::MyExceptions(TObject *Sender,
  Exception *E)
{
  Hermes1->EndExclusive();
  ShowMessage(E->Message);
}
```

You should note that this project probably will not run correctly unless you add `Creatures.pas` to it, as shown in the USEUNIT statement from the project source:

```
//---------------------------------------------------------------------------
#include <vcl\vcl.h>
#pragma hdrstop
//---------------------------------------------------------------------------
USEFORM("Main.cpp", Form1);
USERES("HermesTest1.res");
USEUNIT("..\..\Units\creatures1.pas");
//---------------------------------------------------------------------------
WINAPI WinMain(HINSTANCE, HINSTANCE, LPSTR, int)
{
  try
  {
    Application->Initialize();
    Application->CreateForm(__classid(TForm1), &Form1);
    Application->Run();
  }
  catch (Exception &exception)
  {
    Application->ShowException(&exception);
  }
  return 0;
}
//---------------------------------------------------------------------------
```

Run the project once with Exclusive set to False. Click the Run button once to switch on DirectX. In this mode, you should see the color of the main form change, but nothing else very special will happen.

Go back into design mode, and check once to make sure that you have not placed any components on the main form other than the menu and the THermes. The rest of the form must be free of visual controls so that you can detect keystrokes directly on the surface of the form.

Set Exclusive to True and run the program again. Click the Run menu item, and the whole screen should go blank as you switch into Exclusive mode. To get out of the mode, simply press any key.

If you want, you can change the code for the OnKeyDown event:

```
void __fastcall TForm1::FormKeyDown(TObject *Sender, WORD &Key,
  TShiftState Shift)
{
  if ((Shift.Contains(ssAlt)) && (Key == 'X'))
    Close();
}
```

With this code in place, you will be able to press Alt+Tab to move away from the main window of the program and switch out of Exclusive mode. You can then press Alt+Tab to move back to the program and press Alt+X to exit. When you're pressing these keys, the actual picture drawn on your screen when in Exclusive mode is undefined because THermes does not control the output in Exclusive mode; it controls only the act of entering and exiting Exclusive mode.

DirectX allows you to run applications in a *windowed mode*. That is, you don't have to slip into Exclusive mode to run DirectX applications. However, windowed mode is not very good in terms of performance. In fact, you'll find little advantage to a windowed mode DirectX application over a GDI-based standard Windows program.

I give you access to windowed mode primarily because it is valuable when you're debugging an application. In short, you should run your DirectX applications in windowed mode while you're debugging them so that you can step through the debugger while viewing your application's output. After you set up your application correctly, switch into Exclusive mode and test it.

If an exception happens when you're in Exclusive mode, that is a bad thing. In particular, your program will appear to lock up, and you may be forced to reboot. Following the steps outlined in the preceding paragraphs helps you eliminate the possibility that this will happen. However, you cannot be sure that an exception will not be raised in your application. As a result, you might want to override the exception handler for your application in this case:

```
__fastcall TForm1::TForm1(TComponent* Owner)
  : TForm(Owner)
{
  Application->OnException = MyExceptions;
}

void __fastcall TForm1::MyExceptions(TObject *Sender,
  Exception *E)
{
  Hermes1->EndExclusive();
  ShowMessage(E->Message);
}
```

28

GAME PROGRAMMING

The constructor for the main form designates a custom routine called `MyExceptions` to handle all the exceptions that occur in this application. Whenever an unhandled exception occurs, it will be passed to this routine. When I get the exception, I call `Hermes1->EndExclusive`, which pops the application out of `Exclusive` mode, therefore making it possible to open the dialog box that shows the error message.

> **NOTE**
>
> This system will not do you any good, of course, unless you turn off the Break On Exception option, which you can find by choosing Options | Environment | Preferences. If you are in Exclusive mode, and the IDE tries to take you to the line of code in your application where an exception occurred, your system will appear to lock up.

As a rule, I will not show you the underlying Object Pascal code that makes this component work. However, in this one case, I will show you what goes on:

```
procedure THermes.EndExclusive;
begin
  if (FDirectDraw <> nil) then begin
    FDirectDraw.FlipToGDISurface;
    if FExclusive then
      FDirectDraw.SetCooperativeLevel(FHandle, DDSCL_Normal);
  end;
end;
```

This code first flips away from DirectX to GDI mode and then cuts out of Exclusive mode by setting the cooperative level to normal. When I take the application into Exclusive mode, I make the same call but with different parameters:

```
DDTest(DirectDrawCreate(nil, FDirectDraw, nil), 'InitObjects1');
if not FExclusive then
  Flags := DDSCL_NORMAL
else
  Flags := DDSCL_EXCLUSIVE or DDSCL_FULLSCREEN;
DDTest(FDirectDraw.SetCooperativeLevel(FHandle, Flags),'SetCooperativeLevel');
if FExclusive then begin
  hr := FDirectDraw.SetDisplayMode(640, 480, 8);
  if(hr <> DD_OK) then
    raise EDDError.CreateFmt('THermes.InitObjects: %d %s',
      [hr, GetOleError(hr)]);
end;
```

Notice that my `EndExclusive` method makes no attempt to set the display mode back to the dimensions and bit depth selected by the user in his or her system configuration. Instead, I just leave it to the user to close the application, which will return the screen to its normal resolution. My goal in using `EndExclusive` is just to keep the system from hanging.

TScene: Drawing a Background

After you know how to get into and out of `Exclusive` mode, the next step is to learn how to draw a picture to the screen. Most games consist of many pictures, but I start out showing you how to use a simple object that just displays a single bitmap. For most people, this object is not really very useful, in that there is no point in using DirectX if you want to show only one picture. However, `TScene` serves as a base class for other objects that handle more complex tasks. I will therefore spend a few moments showing you how to use it so that you will understand the class on which the other objects are built.

You can find the declaration for the class and some code that uses it in Listings 28.4 through 28.6. Again, I show only the class declarations for the Pascal code and give the complete listings for the C++ code.

Listing 28.4. The class declaration for the key parts of the TScene and TDraw objects.

```
class TDraw;
class TDraw : public Classes::TComponent
{
  typedef Classes::TComponent inherited;
  friend THermesTiler;
  friend THermesChart;
  friend TScene;
  friend TSpriteScene;

private:
  AnsiString FDLLName;
  THermes* FHermes;
  HANDLE FLib;
  IDirectDrawPalette* FPalette;
  int FTransparentColor;
  bool __fastcall CreateDDSurface(IDirectDrawSurface* &DDS,
    System::AnsiString BitmapName, bool UsePalette);
  IDirectDrawSurface* __fastcall CreateSurface(HANDLE Bitmap);
  HANDLE __fastcall GetDib(HANDLE Instance,  System::AnsiString S);
  IDirectDrawPalette* __fastcall LoadPalette(HANDLE Instance,
    const System::AnsiString BitmapName);

public:
  __fastcall virtual TDraw(Classes::TComponent* AOwner);
  __fastcall virtual ~TDraw(void);
    void __fastcall WriteXY(int X, int Y,  System::AnsiString S);
  __property int TransparentColor =
    {read=FTransparentColor, write=FTransparentColor, nodefault};

__published:
  __property AnsiString DLLName =
```

continues

Listing 28.4. continued

```
    {read=FDLLName, write=FDLLName};
};

class TScene : public TDraw
{
  typedef TDraw inherited;
  friend THermes;
private:
  System::AnsiString FBackgroundBitmap;
  Graphics::TColor FBackColor;
  RECT FBackRect;
  tagPOINT FBackOrigin;
  bool FBlankScene;
  bool FShowBitmap;
  IDirectDrawSurface* FWorkSurface;
  Classes::TNotifyEvent FOnSetupSurfaces;
  Classes::TNotifyEvent FOnDrawScene;

public:
  __fastcall virtual TScene(Classes::TComponent* AOwner);
  virtual void __fastcall DestroyObjects(void);
  virtual void __fastcall DrawScene(void);
  virtual long __fastcall RestoreSurfaces(void);
  virtual void __fastcall SetupSurfaces(System::TObject* Sender);

__published:
  __property System::AnsiString BackgroundBitmap =
    {read=FBackgroundBitmap, write=FBackgroundBitmap, nodefault};
  __property bool BlankScene = {read=FBlankScene, write=FBlankScene, nodefault};
  __property long OriginX ={read=FBackOrigin.x, write=FBackOrigin.x, nodefault};
  __property long OriginY ={read=FBackOrigin.y, write=FBackOrigin.y, nodefault};
  __property bool ShowBitmap = {read=FShowBitmap, write=FShowBitmap, default=1};
  __property Classes::TNotifyEvent OnDrawScene =
    {read=FOnDrawScene, write=FOnDrawScene};
  __property Classes::TNotifyEvent OnSetupSurfaces =
    {read=FOnSetupSurfaces, write=FOnSetupSurfaces};
  __property Graphics::TColor BackColor =
    {read=FBackColor, write=FBackColor, nodefault};
  __property TransparentColor ;
public:
  __fastcall virtual ~TScene(void) { }
};
```

Listing 28.5. The header for the unit from the SceneTest1 project that tests the TScene object.

```
//////////////////////////////////////
// Main.h
// Test the TScene object
// Copyright (c) 1997 by Charlie Calvert
//
#ifndef MainH
#define MainH
#include <vcl\Classes.hpp>
#include <vcl\Controls.hpp>
```

```
#include <vcl\StdCtrls.hpp>
#include <vcl\Forms.hpp>
#include <vcl\Menus.hpp>
#include "Mercury2.h"

class TForm1 : public TForm
{
__published:
  TScene *Scene1;
  THermes *Hermes1;
  TMainMenu *MainMenu1;
  TMenuItem *Run1;
  void __fastcall Run1Click(TObject *Sender);
  void __fastcall FormKeyDown(TObject *Sender, WORD &Key, TShiftState Shift);
private:
public:
  __fastcall TForm1(TComponent* Owner);
};

extern TForm1 *Form1;

#endif
```

Listing 28.6. The main form for the unit that tests the TScene object.

```
/////////////////////////////////////
// Main.cpp
// Test the TScene object
// Copyright (c) 1997 by Charlie Calvert
//
#include <vcl\vcl.h>
#pragma hdrstop
#include "Main.h"
#pragma link "Mercury2"
#pragma resource "*.dfm"

TForm1 *Form1;

__fastcall TForm1::TForm1(TComponent* Owner)
  : TForm(Owner)
{
}

void __fastcall TForm1::Run1Click(TObject *Sender)
{
  Hermes1->Run();
}

void __fastcall TForm1::FormKeyDown(TObject *Sender, WORD &Key,
  TShiftState Shift)
{
  if ((Shift.Contains(ssAlt)) && (Key == 'X'))
    Close();
}
```

The program shown here can switch you into `Exclusive` mode and show a picture like the one shown in Figure 28.1.

FIGURE 28.1.

The main screen of the TestScene1 program in windowed mode.

To get started with the `TScene` object, drop both it and the `THermes` object on a form. Use the `Scene` property of `THermes` to connect it to the `TScene` object. Click the `TScene` object, and select a background bitmap by browsing the `Chap28/Media` directory included on the CD that accompanies this book. Select any bitmap that is smaller than or equal to 640×480 and that has 256 colors in it. For example, you might choose `BackGrd2.bmp`. Set the Transparent color to black, which will appear at offset zero on the bitmaps. Set the `BackColor` property of the bitmap to the same shade, and set `BlankScene` to `True`:

```
TransparentColor = 0;
BackColor = clBlack;
BlankScene = True;
```

> **NOTE**
>
> `TransparentColor` refers to the color in a bitmap that will be transparent. That is, the areas in the bitmap where this color is present become transparent. You need a transparent color when you want to blit an irregularly shaped bitmap on top of a background bitmap. For example, if you have a picture of a bird that you want to blit onto a picture of the sky, just set the background area in the picture of the bird to the transparent color, and it will not show up when the bird is blitted to the screen. In other words, the picture of the sky will

show through the transparent area, so the bird will appear directly against the sky, with no intervening border.

You choose the selected transparent color from an offset in the palette of the bitmap you're using. For example, if you set `TransparentColor` to `0`, the first color in the bitmap's palette will be the transparent color. Most good paint programs will show you the palette for a picture. For example, Paint Shop Pro provides this service.

If you select a prominently used color from a picture as the transparent color, the portions of the picture with that color in them will look strange at runtime. To avoid this situation, set the `BackColor` property of `TScene` and the `TransparentColor` for the picture to the same shade. Also set `BlankScene` to `True`. This way, the transparent color will look through onto a background that is the same shade as the color you're making transparent.

The `BlankScene` property blanks the background of the `TScene` object to the color found in the `BackColor` property. This capability can be useful in the current situation and also when you have a small bitmap that you want to show against a blank window set to some particular color.

When you're creating multimedia applications in Windows, the palette of your bitmaps is very important. In particular, you should usually create the same 256-color palette for all your bitmaps. Use a program such as Paint Shop Pro to set up these bitmaps. Most of the bitmaps included in the `Chap28/Media` directory on the CD that comes with this book have a palette designed for pictures that have lots of green fields, brown earth, and a range of skin tones.

When you're working with only one bitmap in a scene, all this business about palettes seems unnecessarily complicated. However, after you start adding sprites to the scene, you will be glad that you have some way to set up background colors and to set up `TransparentColor`. I explain more about palettes in the next section of this chapter.

The `TScene` object also has a built-in timer that will continually redraw the picture at preset intervals. This capability is not particularly useful in the case of a program that blits only one picture to the screen. However, when you start working with multiple bitmaps, some of which are animated, this capability becomes a key feature. In particular, DirectX allows you to draw to an offscreen buffer, which is then blitted to the screen almost instantly. Using this method is an excellent way to achieve smooth animation.

Instead of using a timer, you can also handle the `TApplication::OnIdle` event, and then call `Hermes1->Flip` inside that event handler. The `OnIdle` event will be called whenever the CPU is not otherwise occupied.

To get the `TScene` object set up correctly, you should turn on the timer and set the `TimerInterval` property to some reasonable value, such as 250 milliseconds. Setting this property will cause the picture to be refreshed four times a second. This number is too slow for animation, but it works fine for the simple scene created here. In particular, if you press Alt+Tab to move away from the DirectX program, the timer will automatically restore the picture when you press Alt+Tab to move back to the main scene.

On the CD that accompanies this book, you will find a program called TestScene1. The source for this program is shown in Listings 28.5 and 28.6. You can use this code as a guide for using the TScene object. Remember that TScene is not really meant to be used in a real program. It is just a base object from which other, more useful objects can descend.

Art and Palettes

In Windows and DOS games, you almost always work with a 256-color palette. Someday this will change, but for now you should get used to working with these palettes and come to understand them well. An in-depth description of palettes is available in some of the books and Web sites mentioned in the section called "Games Resources" at the beginning of this chapter.

Using Paint Shop Pro, you can save a palette to disk as a text file:

```
JASC-PAL
0100
256
0 0 0
128 0 0
0 128 0
128 128 0
0 0 128
128 0 128
0 128 128
192 192 192
176 136 72
216 192 160
… // Many numbers omitted here…
240 224 208
160 160 164
128 128 128
255 0 0
0 255 0
255 255 0
0 0 255
255 0 255
0 255 255
255 255 255
```

Here is how to decode the first few lines of this file:

```
JASC-PAL
0100
256
0 0 0
```

JASC-PAL identifies the palette as belonging to Paint Shop Pro. The second line defines the number of entries in the palette in hexadecimal format. The third line has the number of entries in base ten notation. The fourth line is the first member of the palette in RGB format, with all values set to 0, which is black.

Notice that my palette runs through various shades:

```
118 102 237
117 116 240
129 113 249
155 110 239
107 144 140
115 144 140
123 136 140
123 148 140
111 148 148
```

Clearly, I'm interested in this area of the palette.

Obviously, you don't want to have to work with raw numbers like this. Paint Shop Pro will let you view a palette as an array of colors, as shown in Figure 28.2. Having some kind of tool that will help you design your palette is essential. You should also find books, such as this one and the ones mentioned previously, that include sample palettes.

FIGURE 28.2.

Using Paint Shop Pro to view an array of shades that make up a 256-color palette.

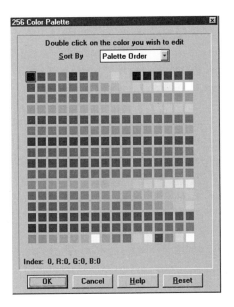

Working with TSpriteScene

Now that you know how to show a simple picture in DirectX mode, and now that you know a bit about palettes, you're ready to start working with sprites. The sprite support I have at this time is very rudimentary, as you can see in Listings 28.7 through 28.9. You could, however, use these base sprite classes to create sprites that are more full-featured. You should also check my Web site for updates to this code.

Listing 28.7. The declarations for the TSpriteScene and TScene classes.

```
 class TSprite : public Classes::TComponent
{
  typedef Classes::TComponent inherited;
  friend TSpriteScene;

private:
  System::AnsiString FBitmap;
  tagPOINT FPosition;
  IDirectDrawSurface* FSurface;
  RECT FRect;

public:
  bool __fastcall IsHit(int X, int Y);
  __property IDirectDrawSurface* Surface=
      {read=FSurface, write=FSurface, nodefault};
  __property RECT Rect = {read=FRect, write=FRect};

  __published:
  __property System::AnsiString Bitmap={read=FBitmap, write=FBitmap, nodefault};
  __property long XPos = {read=FPosition.x, write=FPosition.x, nodefault};
  __property long YPos = {read=FPosition.y, write=FPosition.y, nodefault};
public:
  __fastcall virtual TSprite(Classes::TComponent* AOwner)
    : Classes::TComponent(AOwner) { }
  __fastcall virtual ~TSprite(void) { }
};

class TSpriteScene : public TScene
{
  typedef TScene inherited;

private:
  Classes::TList* FSpriteList;

protected:
  __fastcall virtual ~TSpriteScene(void);
  virtual void __fastcall SetupSurfaces(System::TObject* Sender);

public:
  __fastcall virtual TSpriteScene(Classes::TComponent* AOwner);
  virtual void __fastcall DestroyObjects(void);
  void __fastcall AddSprite(TSprite* Sprite);
  virtual void __fastcall DrawScene(void);
  virtual long __fastcall RestoreSurfaces(void);
  __property Classes::TList* SpriteList = {read=FSpriteList, write=FSpriteList,
                                    nodefault};

  __published:
  __property TransparentColor;
};
```

Listing 28.8. The header for the SpriteTest1 program.

```cpp
/////////////////////////////////////
// Main.h
// Project: SpriteTest1
// Copyright (c) 1997 by Charlie Calvert
//
#ifndef MainH
#define MainH
#include <vcl\Classes.hpp>
#include <vcl\Controls.hpp>
#include <vcl\StdCtrls.hpp>
#include <vcl\Forms.hpp>
#include <vcl\Menus.hpp>
#include "Mercury2.h"

class TForm1 : public TForm
{
__published:
  THermes *Hermes1;
  TSpriteScene *SpriteScene1;
  TSprite *Sprite1;
  TSprite *Sprite2;
  TMainMenu *MainMenu1;
  TMenuItem *Run1;
  void __fastcall SpriteScene1SetupSurfaces(TObject *Sender);
  void __fastcall Run1Click(TObject *Sender);
  void __fastcall FormKeyDown(TObject *Sender, WORD &Key, TShiftState Shift);
private:
public:
  __fastcall TForm1(TComponent* Owner);
};

extern TForm1 *Form1;

#endif
```

Listing 28.9. The main form for the TestSprite1 program.

```cpp
/////////////////////////////////////
// Main.cpp
// Project: SpriteTest1
// Copyright (c) 1997 by Charlie Calvert
//
#include <vcl\vcl.h>
#pragma hdrstop
#include "Main.h"
#pragma link "Mercury2"
#pragma resource "*.dfm"

TForm1 *Form1;

__fastcall TForm1::TForm1(TComponent* Owner)
  : TForm(Owner)
```

continues

Listing 28.9. continued

```
{
}

void __fastcall TForm1::SpriteScene1SetupSurfaces(TObject *Sender)
{
  SpriteScene1->SpriteList->Add(Sprite1);
  SpriteScene1->SpriteList->Add(Sprite2);
}

void __fastcall TForm1::Run1Click(TObject *Sender)
{
  Hermes1->Run();
}

void __fastcall TForm1::FormKeyDown(TObject *Sender, WORD &Key,
  TShiftState Shift)
{
  if ((Shift.Contains(ssAlt)) && (Key == 'X'))
    Close();
}
```

Don't forget that when using this program, you will probably have to explicitly add `Creatures1.pas` to your project:

```
//-----------------------------------------------------------------------
#include <vcl\vcl.h>
#pragma hdrstop
//-----------------------------------------------------------------------
USEFORM("Main.cpp", Form1);
USERES("SpriteTest1.res");
USEUNIT("..\..\Units\creatures1.pas");
//-----------------------------------------------------------------------
WINAPI WinMain(HINSTANCE, HINSTANCE, LPSTR, int)
{
  try
  {
    Application->Initialize();
    Application->CreateForm(__classid(TForm1), &Form1);
    Application->Run();
  }
  catch (Exception &exception)
  {
    Application->ShowException(&exception);
  }
  return 0;
}
```

Figure 28.3 shows the TestSpriteScene program in action. In this program, I make no attempt to animate the sprites. To do so, you can merely change the x- and y-coordinates at which they are shown and then wait for the screen to be updated automatically by the timer.

FIGURE 28.3.

The TestSpriteScene program shows a background bitmap with two sprites placed on it.

To work with the TSpriteScene object, you should drop a THermes, a TSpriteScene, and one or more TSprite objects on a form. Connect the THermes object to the sprite scene. Pick a background bitmap and a transparent color for the sprite scene. In the sample program, I use BackGrd2.bmp for the background and 254 for the transparent color.

For the bitmaps that ship in the Chap28/Media directory, I assume that the background color is the 254 element in the palette of the background bitmap. This color is a robin's egg blue, which means that this particular shade of blue cannot be used in any of the bitmaps except for areas that you want to be transparent. Don't forget that if a particular RGB pattern such as 255, 0, 255 is designated as the transparent color, you can change any one value to get a nearby color that is not going to appear as transparent. For example, you can choose 255, 1, 255, which is virtually identical in shade to 255, 0, 255, but it will not be transparent to the user and can be shown in your bitmaps.

Connect the TSprite objects to a bitmap. I connect the first sprite to Queen2.bmp and the second sprite to Monk2.bmp.

NOTE

These graphical figures were created by Kari Marcussen and, like all the artwork in this book, are copyrighted and cannot be used in your own programs. You can, of course, use the art in the "privacy of your own home," but you cannot distribute programs of any kind, even free programs, that contain this art.

28

GAME
PROGRAMMING

The XPos and YPos positions for the first sprite are 100×200, whereas the second sprite is 400×200. You don't have to be concerned with the size of the sprite itself, as the components will calculate the size automatically at runtime.

You need to have some way of telling the TSpriteScene object about the sprites that it owns. I use a simple event handler of TSpriteScene called OnSetupSurface for this purpose:

```
void __fastcall TForm1::SpriteScene1SetupSurfaces(TObject *Sender)
{
  SpriteScene1->SpriteList->Add(Sprite1);
  SpriteScene1->SpriteList->Add(Sprite2);
}
```

SpriteList is a simple TList descendant. Keeping all the child sprites in a list allows for easy deallocation of memory:

```
void __fastcall TSpriteScene::DestroyObjects(void)
{
  if(FSpriteList != NULL)
  {
    for(int i = 0; i < FSpriteList->Count; i++)
      ((TSprite*)(FSpriteList->Items[i]))->Surface->Release();

    FSpriteList->Clear();
  }
}
```

This kind of routine is important because you might want to switch between numerous TScene descendants during the course of a program. In other words, your game may have more than one scene in it. I will explain this process in more depth later in the chapter. However, the quick overview is that you can simply write code that looks like this:

```
Hermes1->Scene = Scene1;
... // Code omitted here.
Hermes1->Scene = Scene2;
```

In this case, the program starts by showing Scene1 and then at some later point switches to Scene2. When you switch scenes, the DestroyObjects method for the previous scene is called, thereby deallocating all the memory associated with background and sprite bitmaps. At the same time, new memory is allocated for the bitmaps used in Scene2.

The SpriteList also is important when you switch away from a program in Exclusive mode and then press Alt+Tab to move back to it. At those times, the following routine is called:

```
long __fastcall TSpriteScene::RestoreSurfaces(void)
{
  TSprite *Sprite;
  HRESULT Result;

  Result = TScene::RestoreSurfaces();
  if(Result == DD_OK)
  {
      for(int i = 0; i < FSpriteList->Count; i++)
    {
      Sprite = (TSprite *)FSpriteList->Items[i];
```

```
        Result = Sprite->Surface->Restore();
        if(Result == DD_OK)
          DDReloadBitmapLib(FLib, Sprite->Surface, Sprite->Bitmap);
        else
          break;  // Exit on error
    }
  }
```

This routine iterates through all the bitmaps in the SpriteList and restores each surface. This process occurs so quickly that the user simply sees the scene being restored all at once and is not aware that a list of objects is being re-created.

You can now run the program, trying it first in windowed mode, where the output will appear a bit muddy because the transparent color probably won't work correctly. After you're sure everything is running correctly, you can try the program in Exclusive mode. When in Exclusive mode, you can press Alt+Tab to move away from the main game window and view some other program such as the Windows Explorer. You can then press Alt+Tab to go back to the game window. This capability is one of the key features of DirectX.

If you're concerned about the TransparentColor not working right in windowed mode, you can try using a common color such as black for your TransparentColor. It might work correctly, or you can play with the Windows palette system to make sure the right palette is selected when your program appears in a window. For now, however, my graphics engine assumes that you want to run your program in Exclusive mode, and support for windowed mode is available only so that you can easily debug your programs. After all, DirectX doesn't really provide many advantages over GDI in windowed mode. The whole point of this process is to switch into Exclusive mode where you can get the following:

28

GAME PROGRAMMING

- High performance
- Control over the size of the palette
- Control over the dimensions of the screen

When I say that DirectX offers high performance, I mean that in Exclusive mode you can write directly to the video buffer, thereby obtaining the same kind of performance you would expect from a DOS program. The actual degree of performance improvement you get is dependent on the amount of RAM on your video card and on the bus between RAM and your video card. The ideal situation is to have a video card with enough RAM in it to hold all the bitmaps used by any one scene. Therefore, 2MB of memory on your video card is pretty much a minimum, and a strong argument can be made in favor of having 4MB. The code that ships with this book will work fine, however, with a small amount of RAM such as 524KB.

The actual system for drawing to the video buffer involves a process called *flipping*. When using this technology, the program draws the image you want to show the user to an offscreen buffer and then flips that offscreen buffer into the part of video memory the user sees. The user therefore never sees the relatively lengthy process of drawing to the buffer but sees only the finished picture when it is blitted, or "flipped," onto the screen. The core job of the graphics engine presented in this chapter is to automate this process so you don't have to think about it.

THermesChart: Working with a Tiled World

Some of the most interesting games consist of large worlds that fill up screen after screen with information. Classic examples of this kind of game are Heroes of Might and Magic, WarCraft, and Civilization. The THermesChart component shows how to work with one of these worlds.

Tiled worlds are made up of bitmaps that consist of lots of tiny tiles that can be combined in various ways to create maps. A picture of one of the tiled bitmaps is shown in Figure 28.4, and a small portion of the world created from these tiles is shown in Figure 28.5.

FIGURE 28.4.

The tiles from which a tiled world is made.

FIGURE 28.5.

A tiled world created by the THermesChart *component from the bitmaps shown in Figure 28.4.*

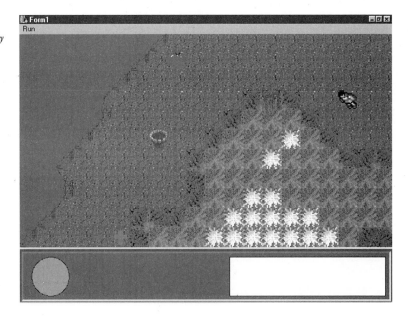

The declaration for the THermesChart component is shown in Listing 28.10, although the test program for it is shown in Listings 28.11 and 28.12.

Listing 28.10. The declaration for the THermesChart class and its parent.

```
struct TSpecialRect
{
  bool IsCreature;
  RECT R1;
  RECT R2;
};

class THermesTiler : public TScene
{
  typedef TScene inherited;
  friend THermesChart;

  private:
  int FMaxMapRows;
  int FMaxMapCols;
  int FBitmapWidth;
  int FBitmapHeight;
  System::AnsiString FTileMap;
  IDirectDrawSurface* FTileSurface;

protected:
  __fastcall virtual ~THermesTiler(void);
  virtual void __fastcall DrawScene(void);
  virtual void __fastcall SetupSurfaces(System::TObject* Sender);
  virtual TSpecialRect __fastcall GetRect(int Col, int Row) = 0;
  virtual bool __fastcall MoveGrid(int Col, int Row, bool CallFlip) = 0;

  public:
  __fastcall virtual THermesTiler(Classes::TComponent* AOwner);
  virtual void __fastcall DestroyObjects(void);
  Windows::TRect __fastcall MapTypeToTileRect(int MapType);
  virtual long __fastcall RestoreSurfaces(void);

  __published:
  __property System::AnsiString TileMap =
    {read=FTileMap, write=FTileMap, nodefault};
  __property int BitmapWidth =
    {read=FBitmapWidth, write=FBitmapHeight, nodefault};
  __property int BitmapHeight =
    {read=FBitmapHeight, write=FBitmapHeight, nodefault};
};

typedef void __fastcall (__closure *TMoveHeroEvent)(System::TObject* Sender,
                         const tagPOINT &NewPos, int NewType, bool &MoveOk);

class THermesChart : public THermesTiler
{
  typedef THermesTiler inherited;

private:
  Creatures1::TCreature* FHero;
  bool FHeroActive;
```

continues

Listing 28.10. continued

```
  TMoveHeroEvent FOnHeroMove;
  bool __fastcall CheckHeroPos(Creatures1::TCreatureList* HeroList,
    int Col, int Row);
  Windows::TRect __fastcall MapTypeToCreature(int Col, int Row);
  virtual TSpecialRect __fastcall GetRect(int Col, int Row);
  virtual bool __fastcall MoveGrid(int Col, int Row, bool CallFlip);
  protected:
  void __fastcall MoveHero(int NewCol, int NewRow);
  virtual void __fastcall SetupSurfaces(System::TObject* Sender);

public:
  __fastcall virtual ~THermesChart(void);
  void __fastcall Move(int Value);

  __published:
  __property bool HeroActive = {read=FHeroActive, write=FHeroActive, nodefault};
  __property TMoveHeroEvent OnHeroMove = {read=FOnHeroMove, write=FOnHeroMove};
public:
  __fastcall virtual THermesChart(Classes::TComponent* AOwner)
    : Mercury2::THermesTiler(AOwner) { }
};
```

Listing 28.11. The header file for the TilerTest program.

```
////////////////////////////////////
// Main.h
// Project: TilerTest1
// Copyright (c) 1997 by Charlie Calvert
//
#ifndef MainH
#define MainH
#include <vcl\Classes.hpp>
#include <vcl\Controls.hpp>
#include <vcl\StdCtrls.hpp>
#include <vcl\Forms.hpp>
#include "Creatures1.hpp"
#include <vcl\Menus.hpp>
#include "Mercury2.h"

class TForm1 : public TForm
{
__published:
  THermes *Hermes1;
  THermesChart *HermesChart1;
  TFileCreatureList *FileCreatureList1;
  TMainMenu *MainMenu1;
  TMenuItem *Run1;
  void __fastcall Run1Click(TObject *Sender);
  void __fastcall FormKeyDown(TObject *Sender, WORD &Key, TShiftState Shift);
private:
```

```
public:
    __fastcall TForm1(TComponent* Owner);
};

extern TForm1 *Form1;

#endif
```

Listing 28.12. The main source for the TestTiler program.

```
///////////////////////////////////////
// Main.cpp
// Project: TilerTest1
// Copyright (c) 1997 by Charlie Calvert
//
#include <vcl\vcl.h>
#pragma hdrstop
#include "Main.h"
#pragma link "Creatures1"
#pragma link "Mercury2"
#pragma resource "*.dfm"

TForm1 *Form1;

__fastcall TForm1::TForm1(TComponent* Owner)
    : TForm(Owner)
{
}

void __fastcall TForm1::Run1Click(TObject *Sender)
{
  Hermes1->Run();
}

void __fastcall TForm1::FormKeyDown(TObject *Sender, WORD &Key,
                                    TShiftState Shift)
{
  if (Shift.Contains(ssAlt) && (Key == 'X'))
    Close();
  else
    HermesChart1->Move(Key);
}
```

By now, you should be getting used to the fact that these components are very easy to use. The only custom code you have to write is to define how to exit the program:

```
if (Shift.Contains(ssAlt) && (Key == 'X'))
  Close();
```

Other than this one simple statement, all the other "coding" involves nothing more than changing a few properties.

This particular example uses bitmaps that are stored in a DLL called `BitDll.dll`. To create a DLL of this type, simply build a resource file containing the bitmaps you want to use and then add the RC file to a DLL project. You can create a DLL by choosing File | New | DLL from the BCB menu.

Here is the RC code for a sample resource that contains multiple bitmaps:

```
Back BITMAP "PANEL4.BMP"
TileMap BITMAP "TILEMAP.BMP"
City BITMAP "FLOOR1.BMP"
Dirs BITMAP "COMPDIRS.BMP"
Treasure BITMAP "TREASURE.BMP"
Sage1 BITMAP "SAGE1.BMP"
```

You can access the various bitmaps in the DLL by name. For example, you should set the `BackgroundBitmap` property of the `THermesChart` to `Back` and the `TileMap` property to `TileMap`. As long as the `DLLName` property is pointing to a valid DLL, you need do nothing else. All `TScene` descendants know how to read bitmaps from either a file on disk or from a DLL.

You'll discover several obvious advantages to using a DLL rather than a raw BMP file:

- You can ship one file with your game rather than a series of files.
- The DLL helps to conceal your bitmaps from prying eyes. Other developers will know how to get at them, but most users won't be able to find them.
- You can ship a series of DLLs with your projects and then load and unload the DLLs as needed to access various different bitmaps. If you switch scenes during the run of a program, the DLL associated with one scene will be unloaded from memory, and the DLL associated with the new scene will be loaded.

The tiled world that you create depends on two interrelated binary files. One binary file contains the screen map that you create, and the second contains a list of creatures that inhabit the map.

The screen map is simply an array 255×252 characters wide. At this time, the map you make must be this size, though I will provide alternative sizes at a later date. Check my Web site for updates.

Each element in the bitmap containing the tiles has a number associated with it. These numbers are described in the following enumerated type:

```
enum TMapType {mtGrass, mtWater, mtMountain, mtRoad, mtWater2,
               mtFootHill, mtNorthShore, mtWestShore, SouthShore, mtEastShore,
               mtSWShore, mtSEShore, mtNWShore, mtNEShore,
               mtWNWShore, mtWSEShore, mtESEShore, mtENEShore,
               mtBlank1, mtBlank2, mtBlank3, mtBlank4, mtAllSnow,
               mtSnowyMountain, mtSouthMtn, mtWestMtn, mtNorthMtn, mtEastMtn,
               mtSEMtn, mtSWMtn, mtNWMtn, mtNEMtn, mtNWFootHill,
               mtNEFootHill, mtSEFootHill, mtSWFootHill,
               mtNorthFootHill, mtEastFootHill, mtSouthFootHill,
               mtWestFootHill, mtNEDiagShore, mtSEDiagShore,
               mtSWDiagShore, mtNWDiagShore, mtSWBendShore, mtSEBendShore,
```

```
                mtNWBendShore, mtNEBendShore, mtENBendShore, mtWNBendShore,
                mtWSBendShore, mtESBendShore, mtCity, mtCreature};
```

mtGrass is element 0 in this enumerated type. mtWater is element 1; mtMountain, element 2; and so on. This type is not used in the TestTiler1 program, but it will come in handy later in the chapter.

Here is a simple two-dimensional array that encodes a small world:

```
1 1 1 1 1
1 1 0 1 1
1 0 2 0 1
1 1 0 1 1
1 1 1 1 1
```

This world consists of a small island with a mountain in the center of it. The entire island is surrounded by water. Of course, this world is tiny and cannot be used by the THermesChart component. To find a world that can be used by THermesChart, look in the Media directory on the CD that accompanies this book. There you will find a textual representation of a world in a file called Screen.txt and binary translation of that file called Screen.dta.

A simple program called TextToBinary found on the CD will translate the textual representation of a world to a binary file. The code that does so takes only a few lines:

```
__fastcall TForm1::TForm1(TComponent* Owner)
  : TForm(Owner)
{
  FMapPointList = new TMapPointList();
}

void __fastcall TForm1::FormDestroy(TObject *Sender)
{
  FMapPointList->Free();
}

void __fastcall TForm1::Button1Click(TObject *Sender)
{
  int X, Y;

  if (OpenDialog1->Execute())
  {
    FMapPointList->ReadBinary(OpenDialog1->FileName, X, Y);
    AnsiString S = ChangeFileExt(OpenDialog1->FileName, ".txt");
    FMapPointList->WriteText(S, X, Y);
  }
}

void __fastcall TForm1::Button2Click(TObject *Sender)
{
  if (OpenDialog1->Execute())
  {
    FMapPointList->ReadText(OpenDialog1->FileName);
    AnsiString S = ChangeFileExt(OpenDialog1->FileName, ".dta");
    FMapPointList->WriteBinary(S,
      FMapPointList->StartX, FMapPointList->StartY);
  }
}
```

The constructor and destructor for this program create an object of type `TMapPointList`. You can find the `TMapPointList` object in a file called `Creatures1.pas` on the CD. To translate a binary file to text, simply call the methods of `TMapPointList` called `ReadBinary` and `WriteText`. To reverse the process, call `ReadText` and `WriteBinary`.

> **NOTE**
>
> I don't really expect you to create a world by editing a text file. The file is not ready at the time of this writing, but the CD that ships with this book may contain a program in the `Chap28` directory that will allow you to edit a map from inside Windows by using the mouse. Check my Web site for updates to this program.
>
> In particular, note that there are methods in `Creatures1.pas` that make it easy to create this type of program. For instance, note the following methods of `TCreatureList`:
>
> ```
> function NameFromLocation(ACol, ARow: Integer): string;
> function TypeFromLocation(ACol, ARow: Integer): string;
> function CreatureFromLocation(ACol: Integer; ARow: Integer): TCreature;
> ```
>
> Methods like this allow you to quickly identify the tile at a particular location. You can then use the `Map` array property from the same object to change these tiles.

Besides the screen file, you also need to maintain a file that tracks the creatures shown on your tiled world. In the sample programs that ship with this book, this file is called `Creatures.dta`.

You can edit `Creatures.dta` with a simple program called Entity. Most of this program is written in Pascal, so I won't discuss its code here. However, it compiles fine in C++Builder.

> **NOTE**
>
> I apologize for including so much Pascal code in this chapter. For various reasons, I need to have these objects working in both C++Builder and Delphi, and the simplest way to do that is to write the core objects and utilities in Object Pascal. In this particular case, I have taken a Delphi program and swapped out the Pascal version of the project source and substituted a version written in BCB. That way, I could get the program to compile in C++Builder by merely changing a few lines of code, all of which are generated automatically by the IDE. In short, I started a new project, removed the main form, and added the main form from the Pascal version of the Entities program. That was all I had to do to translate the program from Delphi to C++Builder.

The Entity program tracks the creature and screen file that it edits through the Registry. To do so, it uses the same technique I discussed in Chapter 13, "Flat-File, Real-World Databases." In particular, the following code should jog your memory as to how I retrieve the current creature and screen file from the Registry:

```
RegFile := TRegIniFile.Create('Software\Charlie''s Stuff\Entities');
FCreatureFile := RegFile.ReadString('FileNames', 'CreatureFile', '');
FScreenFile := RegFile.ReadString('FileNames', 'ScreenFile', '');
```

Running the program once places the proper entries in the Registry. You can then edit the Registry to enter in the names of the actual files you want to use. In particular, you should use the Windows utility called `RegEdit.exe` to edit the area under `HKEY_CURRENT_USER\Charlie's Stuff\Entities`.

The creatures file contains a number of creature profiles, as shown in Figure 28.6 and Figure 28.7.

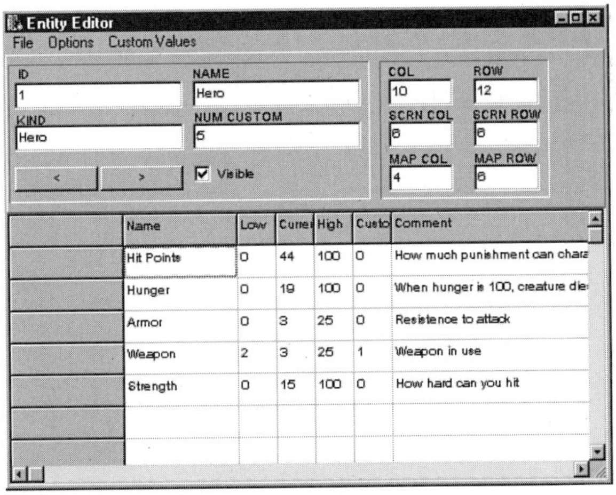

FIGURE 28.6.

The hero's profile as shown in the Entity program.

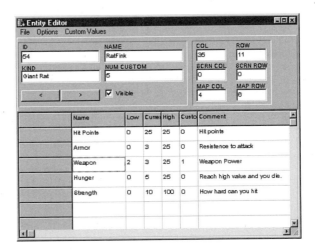

FIGURE 28.7.

A hostile creature's profile as shown in the Entity program.

When you first open the screen, be sure that the hero is located at column 11 and row 11. To set this up properly, you need to edit the Col and Row fields, as well as the Scrn Col, Scrn Row, Map Col, and Map Row. You need all these values because you can never see the whole map at one time. Instead, you see a window into the entire grid. You therefore need to track where the window is on the grid, where the character is on the grid, and where the character is on the window currently opened onto the grid. You have three pairs of values, all of which are tracked for you automatically by the THermesChart object.

Now that you've examined the screen and creature files, you're ready to run the TestTiler program. Go ahead and run it once in windowed mode to make sure that you're reaching all the files in question. Then run the program again in Exclusive mode.

NOTE

You can possibly mangle the screen file by exiting the TilerTest1 program incorrectly. In other words, if TilerTest1 crashes in mid-run and you reboot, you can lose the contents of the screen file. To check whether you've lost the contents, check that your screen file is equal to 64,276 bytes. If it is some other value, the file is probably corrupt and should be refreshed from the file on the CD that accompanies the book. If you have this problem, you will probably get a Range error when trying to run the program.

The only point left for you to learn is how to move the character on the screen and how to scroll around through the world. To do so, simply modify the OnKeyDown event for TilerTest1:

```
void __fastcall TForm1::FormKeyDown(TObject *Sender, WORD &Key,
                                    TShiftState Shift)
{
  if (Shift.Contains(ssAlt) && (Key == 'X'))
    Close();
  else
    HermesChart1->Move(Key);
}
```

This code will exit the program if the user presses Alt+X; otherwise, it will pass the current keystroke on the HermesChart object. This object responds to presses on the arrow keys by moving either the main character or by scrolling the entire map. Press the Insert key to switch between these two modes. Figure 28.8 shows the main character walking on the map.

FIGURE 28.8.

The main character exploring the shore of a lake, with mountains nearby.

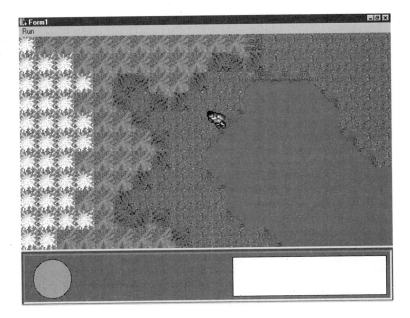

The Mercury2 Source Code

The source for `Mercury2.cpp` is shown in Listings 28.13 and 28.14. Please note that several stand-alone functions right at the top of `Mercury2.cpp` are only slightly modified versions of code that appears in the `DDUtils.cpp` file that ships with the DirectDraw SDK. I could not let you use the original functions, available on the Microsoft Web site, because they do not take into account the possibility that the user might want to store bitmaps in a DLL.

Listing 28.13. The header for the `Mercury2` unit.

```
#ifndef Mercury2H
#define Mercury2H
#include <Creatures1.hpp>
#include <ddraw.h>
#include <DsgnIntf.hpp>
#include <OLE2.hpp>
#include <Graphics.hpp>
#include <Forms.hpp>
#include <Controls.hpp>
#include <Classes.hpp>
#include <Windows.hpp>
#include <System.hpp>

namespace Mercury2
{
```

continues

Listing 28.13. continued

```
//-- type declarations -------------------------------------------------
typedef tagPALETTEENTRY T256PalEntry[256];

typedef tagRGBQUAD TRGB[256];

typedef TRGB *PRGB;

class THermes;
class TScene;
class THermesTiler;
class THermesChart;
class TSpriteScene;

class TDraw;
class TDraw : public Classes::TComponent
{
  typedef Classes::TComponent inherited;
  friend THermesTiler;
  friend THermesChart;
  friend TScene;
  friend TSpriteScene;

private:
  AnsiString FDLLName;
  THermes* FHermes;
  HANDLE FLib;
  IDirectDrawPalette* FPalette;
  int FTransparentColor;
  bool __fastcall CreateDDSurface(IDirectDrawSurface* &DDS,
    System::AnsiString BitmapName, bool UsePalette);
  IDirectDrawSurface* __fastcall CreateSurface(HANDLE Bitmap);
  HANDLE __fastcall GetDib(HANDLE Instance,  System::AnsiString S);
  IDirectDrawPalette* __fastcall LoadPalette(HANDLE Instance,
    const System::AnsiString BitmapName);

public:
  __fastcall virtual TDraw(Classes::TComponent* AOwner);
  __fastcall virtual ~TDraw(void);
  void __fastcall WriteXY(int X, int Y,  System::AnsiString S);
  __property int TransparentColor =
    {read=FTransparentColor, write=FTransparentColor, nodefault};

__published:
  __property AnsiString DLLName =
    {read=FDLLName, write=FDLLName};
};

class TScene : public TDraw
{
  typedef TDraw inherited;
  friend THermes;
private:
  System::AnsiString FBackgroundBitmap;
  Graphics::TColor FBackColor;
  RECT FBackRect;
```

```
      tagPOINT FBackOrigin;
      bool FBlankScene;
      bool FShowBitmap;
      IDirectDrawSurface* FWorkSurface;
      Classes::TNotifyEvent FOnSetupSurfaces;
      Classes::TNotifyEvent FOnDrawScene;

  public:
      __fastcall virtual TScene(Classes::TComponent* AOwner);
      virtual void __fastcall DestroyObjects(void);
      virtual void __fastcall DrawScene(void);
      virtual long __fastcall RestoreSurfaces(void);
      virtual void __fastcall SetupSurfaces(System::TObject* Sender);

  __published:
      __property System::AnsiString BackgroundBitmap =
        {read=FBackgroundBitmap, write=FBackgroundBitmap,  nodefault};
      __property bool BlankScene = {read=FBlankScene, write=FBlankScene, nodefault};
      __property long OriginX ={read=FBackOrigin.x, write=FBackOrigin.x, nodefault};
      __property long OriginY ={read=FBackOrigin.y, write=FBackOrigin.y, nodefault};
      __property bool ShowBitmap = {read=FShowBitmap, write=FShowBitmap, default=1};
      __property Classes::TNotifyEvent OnDrawScene =
        {read=FOnDrawScene, write=FOnDrawScene};
      __property Classes::TNotifyEvent OnSetupSurfaces =
        {read=FOnSetupSurfaces, write=FOnSetupSurfaces};
      __property Graphics::TColor BackColor =
        {read=FBackColor, write=FBackColor, nodefault};
      __property TransparentColor ;
  public:
      __fastcall virtual ~TScene(void) { }
  };

  class THermes : public Classes::TComponent
  {
    typedef Classes::TComponent inherited;
    friend THermesChart;
    friend TDraw;

  private:
    bool FActive;
    Creatures1::TFileCreatureList* FCreatureList;
    HWND FHandle;
    bool FTimerOdd;
    int FTimerInterval;
    bool FExclusive;
    Classes::TNotifyEvent FPaintProc;
    TScene* FScene;
    bool FUseTimer;
    bool FFirstTime;
    IDirectDraw* FDirectDraw;
    IDirectDrawSurface* FBackSurface;
    IDirectDrawClipper* FClipper;
    IDirectDrawSurface* FPrimarySurface;
    bool __fastcall CreatePrimary(void);
    void __fastcall DDTest(long hr,  System::AnsiString S);
    void __fastcall InitBaseObjects(void);
```

28

GAME
PROGRAMMING

continues

Listing 28.13. continued

```cpp
    bool __fastcall MakeItSo(long DDResult);
    void __fastcall SetScene(TScene* Scene);
    bool __fastcall SetUpBack(void);
protected:
    void __fastcall DrawBitmaps(void);
    virtual long __fastcall RestoreSurfaces(void);
public:
    __fastcall virtual THermes(Classes::TComponent* AOwner);
    __fastcall virtual ~THermes(void) {}
    void __fastcall EndExclusive(void);
    void __fastcall ErrorEvent( System::AnsiString S);
    void __fastcall Flip(void);
    virtual void __stdcall InitObjects(void);
    virtual void __fastcall Run(void);
    __property bool Active = {read=FActive, write=FActive, nodefault};
    __property IDirectDrawSurface* BackSurface =
      {read=FBackSurface, write=FBackSurface, nodefault};
    __property Classes::TNotifyEvent OnDrawBitmap =
      {read=FPaintProc, write=FPaintProc};

__published:
    __property Creatures1::TFileCreatureList* CreatureList =
      {read=FCreatureList, write=FCreatureList,    nodefault};
    __property bool Exclusive = {read=FExclusive, write=FExclusive, nodefault};
    __property TScene* Scene = {read=FScene, write=SetScene, nodefault};
    __property int TimerInterval =
      {read=FTimerInterval, write=FTimerInterval, nodefault};
    __property bool UseTimer = {read=FUseTimer, write=FUseTimer, nodefault};
};

struct TSpecialRect
{
  bool IsCreature;
  RECT R1;
  RECT R2;
};

class THermesTiler : public TScene
{
  typedef TScene inherited;
  friend THermesChart;

  private:
  int FMaxMapRows;
  int FMaxMapCols;
  int FBitmapWidth;
  int FBitmapHeight;
  System::AnsiString FTileMap;
  IDirectDrawSurface* FTileSurface;

protected:
    __fastcall virtual ~THermesTiler(void);
    virtual void __fastcall DrawScene(void);
    virtual void __fastcall SetupSurfaces(System::TObject* Sender);
```

```
      virtual TSpecialRect __fastcall GetRect(int Col, int Row) = 0;
      virtual bool __fastcall MoveGrid(int Col, int Row, bool CallFlip) = 0;

public:
   __fastcall virtual THermesTiler(Classes::TComponent* AOwner);
   virtual void __fastcall DestroyObjects(void);
   Windows::TRect __fastcall MapTypeToTileRect(int MapType);
   virtual long __fastcall RestoreSurfaces(void);

__published:
   __property System::AnsiString TileMap =
      {read=FTileMap, write=FTileMap, nodefault};
   __property int BitmapWidth =
      {read=FBitmapWidth, write=FBitmapHeight, nodefault};
   __property int BitmapHeight =
      {read=FBitmapHeight, write=FBitmapHeight, nodefault};
};

typedef void __fastcall (__closure *TMoveHeroEvent)(System::TObject* Sender,
   const tagPOINT &NewPos, int NewType, bool &MoveOk);

class THermesChart : public THermesTiler
{
   typedef THermesTiler inherited;

private:
   Creatures1::TCreature* FHero;
   bool FHeroActive;
   TMoveHeroEvent FOnHeroMove;
   bool __fastcall CheckHeroPos(Creatures1::TCreatureList* HeroList,
      int Col, int Row);
   Windows::TRect __fastcall MapTypeToCreature(int Col, int Row);
   virtual TSpecialRect __fastcall GetRect(int Col, int Row);
   virtual bool __fastcall MoveGrid(int Col, int Row, bool CallFlip);
   protected:
   void __fastcall MoveHero(int NewCol, int NewRow);
   virtual void __fastcall SetupSurfaces(System::TObject* Sender);

public:
   __fastcall virtual ~THermesChart(void);
   void __fastcall Move(int Value);

   __published:
   __property bool HeroActive = {read=FHeroActive, write=FHeroActive, nodefault};
   __property TMoveHeroEvent OnHeroMove = {read=FOnHeroMove, write=FOnHeroMove};
public:
   __fastcall virtual THermesChart(Classes::TComponent* AOwner)
      : Mercury2::THermesTiler(AOwner) { }
};

class TSprite;
class TSprite : public Classes::TComponent
{
```

28

GAME
PROGRAMMING

continues

Listing 28.13. continued

```cpp
  typedef Classes::TComponent inherited;
  friend TSpriteScene;

private:
  System::AnsiString FBitmap;
  tagPOINT FPosition;
  IDirectDrawSurface* FSurface;
  RECT FRect;

public:
  bool __fastcall IsHit(int X, int Y);
  __property IDirectDrawSurface* Surface=
    {read=FSurface, write=FSurface, nodefault};
  __property RECT Rect = {read=FRect, write=FRect};

  __published:
  __property System::AnsiString Bitmap={read=FBitmap, write=FBitmap, nodefault};
  __property long XPos = {read=FPosition.x, write=FPosition.x, nodefault};
  __property long YPos = {read=FPosition.y, write=FPosition.y, nodefault};
public:
  __fastcall virtual TSprite(Classes::TComponent* AOwner)
    : Classes::TComponent(AOwner) { }
  __fastcall virtual ~TSprite(void) { }
};

class TSpriteScene : public TScene
{
  typedef TScene inherited;

private:
  Classes::TList* FSpriteList;

protected:
  __fastcall virtual ~TSpriteScene(void);
  virtual void __fastcall SetupSurfaces(System::TObject* Sender);

public:
  __fastcall virtual TSpriteScene(Classes::TComponent* AOwner);
  virtual void __fastcall DestroyObjects(void);
  void __fastcall AddSprite(TSprite* Sprite);
  virtual void __fastcall DrawScene(void);
  virtual long __fastcall RestoreSurfaces(void);
  __property Classes::TList* SpriteList = {read=FSpriteList, write=FSpriteList,
                                           nodefault};

  __published:
  __property TransparentColor;
};

////////////////////////////////////////
// TSceneEditor ////////////////////////
////////////////////////////////////////
class TSceneEditor: public TComponentEditor
{
protected:
  virtual __fastcall void Edit(void);
```

```
public:
  virtual __fastcall TSceneEditor(TComponent *AOwner, TFormDesigner *Designer)
    : TComponentEditor(AOwner, Designer) {}
};


//-- var, const, procedure -------------------------------------------
#define Timer1 (Byte)(1)
extern void __fastcall Register(void);

}/* namespace Mercury1 */
#if !defined(NO_IMPLICIT_NAMESPACE_USE)
using namespace Mercury2;
#endif
//-- end unit --------------------------------------------------------
#endif // Mercury2
```

Listing 28.14. The main source file for the Mercury2 module.

```
/////////////////////////////////////
// Mercury2.cpp
// DirectX Graphics
// Copyright (c) 1997 by Charlie Calvert
// Thanks to John Thomas, Stuart Fullmar and Jeff Cottingham
/////////////////////////////////////
#include <vcl\vcl.h>
#pragma hdrstop
#include "Mercury2.h"
#include "errors1.h"
#include "SceneEditor1.h"
#pragma link "Errors1.obj"
#pragma link "SceneEditor1.obj"


/*{ ---------------------- }
  { --- THermes ----------- }
  { ---------------------- } */

THermes *AHermes;

void Timer2Timer(HWND H, UINT Msg, UINT Event, DWORD Time)
{
  if (AHermes->Active)
    AHermes->Flip();
}

namespace Mercury2
{
  // Slightly modified version of code from DDUtils.cpp
  HRESULT DDCopyBitmap(IDirectDrawSurface *pdds,
    HBITMAP hbm, int x, int y, int dx, int dy)
  {
    HDC               hdcImage;
    HDC               hdc;
```

continues

28

GAME
PROGRAMMING

Listing 28.14. continued

```
    BITMAP              bm;
    DDSURFACEDESC       ddsd;
    HRESULT             hr;

    if (hbm == NULL ¦¦ pdds == NULL)
        return E_FAIL;

    //
    // make sure this surface is restored.
    //
    pdds->Restore();

    //
    //  select bitmap into a memoryDC so we can use it.
    //
    hdcImage = CreateCompatibleDC(NULL);
    if (!hdcImage)
        OutputDebugString("createcompatible dc failed\n");
    SelectObject(hdcImage, hbm);

    //
    // get size of the bitmap
    //
    GetObject(hbm, sizeof(bm), &bm);      // get size of bitmap
    dx = dx == 0 ? bm.bmWidth  : dx;      // use the passed size, unless zero
    dy = dy == 0 ? bm.bmHeight : dy;

    //
    // get size of surface.
    //
    ddsd.dwSize = sizeof(ddsd);
    ddsd.dwFlags = DDSD_HEIGHT ¦ DDSD_WIDTH;
    pdds->GetSurfaceDesc(&ddsd);

    if ((hr = pdds->GetDC(&hdc)) == DD_OK)
    {
        StretchBlt(hdc, 0, 0, ddsd.dwWidth, ddsd.dwHeight, hdcImage, x, y, dx, dy,
                   SRCCOPY);
        pdds->ReleaseDC(hdc);
    }

    DeleteDC(hdcImage);

    return hr;
}

// Slightly modified version of code from DDUtils.cpp
void DDReloadBitmapLib(HANDLE Lib, IDirectDrawSurface *Surface,
  const AnsiString BitmapName)
{
    HBITMAP Bitmap;

    if (Lib)
      Bitmap = LoadImage(Lib, BitmapName.c_str(),
        IMAGE_BITMAP, 0, 0, LR_CREATEDIBSECTION);
    else
```

```
    Bitmap = LoadImage(GetModuleHandle(NULL), BitmapName.c_str(),
      IMAGE_BITMAP, 0, 0, LR_CREATEDIBSECTION);

  if (!Bitmap)
    Bitmap = LoadImage(0, BitmapName.c_str(), IMAGE_BITMAP,
      0, 0, LR_LOADFROMFILE ¦ LR_CREATEDIBSECTION);

  if (!Bitmap)
    throw Exception("Unable to load bitmap %s",
      OPENARRAY(TVarRec, (BitmapName)));

  DDCopyBitmap(Surface, Bitmap, 0, 0, 0, 0);
  DeleteObject(Bitmap);
}


// Slightly modified version of code from DDUtils.cpp
IDirectDrawSurface *DDCreateSurface(IDirectDraw *DD, DWORD Width, DWORD Height,
                                    bool SysMem, bool Trans, DWORD dwColorKey)

{
  DDSURFACEDESC SurfaceDesc;
  HRESULT hr;
  DDCOLORKEY ColorKey;
  IDirectDrawSurface *Surface;

  // fill in surface desc
  memset(&SurfaceDesc, 0, sizeof(DDSURFACEDESC));
  SurfaceDesc.dwSize = sizeof(SurfaceDesc);
  SurfaceDesc.dwFlags = DDSD_CAPS ¦ DDSD_HEIGHT ¦ DDSD_WIDTH;

  SurfaceDesc.ddsCaps.dwCaps = DDSCAPS_OFFSCREENPLAIN;

  SurfaceDesc.dwHeight = Height;
  SurfaceDesc.dwWidth = Width;

  hr = DD->CreateSurface(&SurfaceDesc, &Surface, NULL);

  // set the color key for this bitmap
  if (hr == DD_OK)
  {
    if (Trans)
    {
      ColorKey.dwColorSpaceLowValue = dwColorKey;
      ColorKey.dwColorSpaceHighValue = dwColorKey;
      Surface->SetColorKey(DDCKEY_SRCBLT, &ColorKey);
    }
  }
  else
    throw EDDError("CreateSurface Failed in DDCreateSurface");

  return Surface;
} // DDCreateSurface

IDirectDrawClipper *CreateClipper(IDirectDraw *DD, HWND Handle)
{
```

continues

28

GAME
PROGRAMMING

Listing 28.14. continued

```
    HRESULT hr;
    IDirectDrawClipper *lpClipper;

    hr = DD->CreateClipper(0, &lpClipper, NULL);

    if (hr != DD_OK)
    {
      throw EDDError("No Clipper");
    }

    hr = lpClipper->SetHWnd(0, Handle);

    if (hr != DD_OK)
    {
      throw EDDError("Can''t set clipper window handle");
    }

    return lpClipper;
  }
}


__fastcall THermes::THermes(TComponent* AOwner)
:TComponent(AOwner)
{
  FHandle = ((TWinControl *)(AOwner))->Handle;
  FFirstTime = true;
}// THermes


void __fastcall THermes::EndExclusive()
{
  FDirectDraw->FlipToGDISurface();
  if (FExclusive)
    FDirectDraw->SetCooperativeLevel(FHandle, DDSCL_NORMAL);
}// EndExclusive

void __fastcall THermes::ErrorEvent(String S)
{
  FActive = false;
  EndExclusive();
  throw EDDError(S);
}// ErrorEvent

void __fastcall THermes::Run()
{
  InitObjects();
  Flip();
}// Run

void __fastcall THermes::DDTest(long hr,  System::AnsiString S)
{
  if (!Windows::Succeeded(hr))
```

```
      throw EDDError("DDTest Error: %s $%x %s",
        OPENARRAY(TVarRec, (S, int(hr), AnsiString(GetOleError(hr)))));

}// DDTest

///////////////////////////////////////////////////
// Create the primary surface
///////////////////////////////////////////////////
bool __fastcall THermes::CreatePrimary(void)
{
  DDSURFACEDESC SurfaceDesc;
  HResult hr;
  bool Result = true;

  memset(&SurfaceDesc, 0, sizeof(SurfaceDesc));
  SurfaceDesc.dwSize = sizeof(SurfaceDesc);

  if (!FExclusive){
    SurfaceDesc.dwFlags = DDSD_CAPS;
    SurfaceDesc.ddsCaps.dwCaps = DDSCAPS_PRIMARYSURFACE;
  }
  else{
    SurfaceDesc.dwFlags = DDSD_CAPS | DDSD_BACKBUFFERCOUNT;
    SurfaceDesc.ddsCaps.dwCaps = DDSCAPS_PRIMARYSURFACE |
                                 DDSCAPS_FLIP |
                                 DDSCAPS_COMPLEX;
    SurfaceDesc.dwBackBufferCount = 1;
  };

  hr = FDirectDraw->CreateSurface(&SurfaceDesc, &FPrimarySurface, NULL);
  if (hr != DD_OK)
    throw EDDError("THermes.CreatePrimary: %d %s",
      OPENARRAY(TVarRec, (int(hr), GetOleError(hr))));
  else
    return Result;
}// CreatePrimary

void __fastcall THermes::SetScene(TScene *Scene)
{
  if (Scene)
    Scene->DestroyObjects();

  FScene = Scene;
}// SetScene

bool __fastcall THermes::SetUpBack(void)
{
  bool Result = false;
  HResult hr;
  DDSCAPS DDSCaps;
  if (!FExclusive)
  {
    FBackSurface =
      Mercury2::DDCreateSurface(FDirectDraw, 640, 480, false, false, 0);
```

28

GAME
PROGRAMMING

continues

Listing 28.14. continued

```
      if (FBackSurface == NULL)
        throw EDDError("Can''t set up back surface");

    FClipper = Mercury2::CreateClipper(FDirectDraw, FHandle);
    hr = FPrimarySurface->SetClipper(FClipper);
    if( hr != DD_OK )
      throw EDDError("Can''t attach clipper to front buffer");
  }
  else
  {
    memset(&DDSCaps, 0, sizeof(DDSCaps));
    DDSCaps.dwCaps = DDSCAPS_BACKBUFFER;
     hr = FPrimarySurface->GetAttachedSurface(&DDSCaps, &FBackSurface);
    if (hr != DD_OK)
      throw EDDError("TSpeedDraw.SetUpBack: %d %s",
        OPENARRAY(TVarRec, (int(hr), GetOleError(hr))));
    else
      Result = true;
  };
  return Result;
}// SetUpBack

void __fastcall  THermes::InitBaseObjects()
{
  DWORD Flags;
  HResult hr;
  DDTest(DirectDrawCreate(NULL, &FDirectDraw, NULL), "InitObjects1");

  if (!FExclusive)
    Flags = DDSCL_NORMAL;
  else
    Flags = DDSCL_EXCLUSIVE | DDSCL_FULLSCREEN;

  DDTest(FDirectDraw->SetCooperativeLevel(FHandle, Flags),"SetCooperativeLevel");
  if (FExclusive)
  {
    hr = FDirectDraw->SetDisplayMode(640, 480, 8);
    if(hr != DD_OK)
      throw EDDError("TSpeedDraw.InitObjects: %d %s",
        OPENARRAY(TVarRec, (int(hr), GetOleError(hr))));
  };

  CreatePrimary();
  SetUpBack();
  if (FCreatureList != NULL) FCreatureList->ReadFiles();
}// InitBaseObjects


/* Here are the steps in the initialization:
    Create DirectDraw Object
    SetCooperativeLevel
    if Exclusive then SetDisplayMode
    CreatePrimary
    SetupBack
```

```
      Create the work surface
      Set Active to true */
void __stdcall THermes::InitObjects(void)
{
  AHermes = this;

  if (FFirstTime)
  {
    InitBaseObjects();
    FFirstTime = false;
  };

  if ((Scene) && (Scene->FBackgroundBitmap != ""))
    Scene->SetupSurfaces(this);
  if (FUseTimer)
    SetTimer(FHandle, Timer1, FTimerInterval, (FARPROC)Timer2Timer);

  FActive = true;
}// InitObjects


void __fastcall THermes::DrawBitmaps()
{
  if (Scene) Scene->DrawScene();
}

bool __fastcall THermes::MakeItSo(HResult DDResult)
{
  bool Result;

  switch(DDResult)
  {
    case DD_OK:
      Result = true;
      break;
    case DDERR_SURFACELOST:
      Result = (RestoreSurfaces() == DD_OK);
      break;
    default:
      Result = DDResult != DDERR_WASSTILLDRAWING;
      break;
  };
  return Result;
} // MakeItSo

long __fastcall THermes::RestoreSurfaces()
{
  HRESULT Result;
  Result = FPrimarySurface->Restore();
  if ((Result == DD_OK) && (Scene))
    Result = Scene->RestoreSurfaces();
  return Result;
}// RestoreSurfaces

void __fastcall THermes::Flip(void)
{
```

continues

Listing 28.14. continued

```
  RECT R1, R;
  FTimerOdd = !FTimerOdd;

  if (!FActive)
    return;

  if (!FExclusive)
  {
    try
    {
      DrawBitmaps();
      GetWindowRect(FHandle, &R);
      R1 = Rect(0, 0, 640, 480);
      DDTest(FPrimarySurface->Blt(&R, FBackSurface, &R1, 0, NULL), "Flip");
    }
    catch(Exception &E)
    {
      ErrorEvent("Flipping");
    };
  }
  else
  {
    try
    {
      if (FActive)
      {
        do
        {
          Application->ProcessMessages();
        } while(!MakeItSo(FPrimarySurface->Flip(NULL, DDFLIP_WAIT)));

        DrawBitmaps();
      }
    }
    catch(...)
    {
      ErrorEvent("Flipping");
    }
  }
}// Flip


/////////////////////////////////////////
// TDraw /////////////////////////////////
/////////////////////////////////////////

__fastcall TDraw::TDraw(Classes::TComponent* AOwner)
  : TComponent(AOwner)
{
}

__fastcall TDraw::~TDraw(void)
{
  if (FLib != NULL)
```

```
      FreeLibrary(FLib);
}
bool __fastcall TDraw::CreateDDSurface(IDirectDrawSurface* &DDS,
  System::AnsiString BitmapName, bool UsePalette)
{
  bool Result;
  DDCOLORKEY ColorKey;
  HRESULT hr;
  HANDLE Dib;

  if (UsePalette)
  {
    FPalette = LoadPalette(FLib, BitmapName.c_str());
    if (!FPalette)
      throw EDDError("LoadPalette Failed");

    FHermes->FPrimarySurface->SetPalette(FPalette);
  }

  Dib = GetDib(FLib, BitmapName);
  DDS = CreateSurface(Dib);

  if (!DDS)
    throw EDDError("CreateSurface Failed");

  ColorKey.dwColorSpaceLowValue = FTransparentColor;
  ColorKey.dwColorSpaceHighValue = FTransparentColor;
  hr = DDS->SetColorKey(DDCKEY_SRCBLT, &ColorKey);
  if (hr != DD_OK)
    throw EDDError("TSpeedDraw.CreateDDSurface: %d %s",
      OPENARRAY(TVarRec, (int(hr), GetOleError(hr))));
  else
    Result = True;

  return Result;
}

IDirectDrawSurface* __fastcall TDraw::CreateSurface(HANDLE Bitmap)
{
  DDSURFACEDESC SurfaceDesc;
  Windows::TBitmap BM;
  IDirectDrawSurface *Result;

  if (Bitmap == 0)
    throw Exception("No Bitmap in CreateSurface");

  try
  {
    GetObject(Bitmap, sizeof(BM), &BM);

    memset(&SurfaceDesc, 0, sizeof(SurfaceDesc));
    SurfaceDesc.dwSize = sizeof(SurfaceDesc);
    SurfaceDesc.dwFlags = DDSD_CAPS | DDSD_HEIGHT | DDSD_WIDTH;
    SurfaceDesc.ddsCaps.dwCaps = DDSCAPS_OFFSCREENPLAIN;
```

28

continues

Listing 28.14. continued

```
    SurfaceDesc.dwWidth = BM.bmWidth;
    SurfaceDesc.dwHeight = BM.bmHeight;

    if (FHermes->FDirectDraw->CreateSurface(&SurfaceDesc, &Result, NULL) != DD_OK)
      throw Exception("CreateSurface failed");

    DDCopyBitmap(Result, Bitmap, 0, 0, 0, 0);
  }
  catch(Exception &E)
  {
    FHermes->ErrorEvent("TSpeedDraw.CreateSurface: " + E.Message);
  }

  return Result;
}

HANDLE __fastcall TDraw::GetDib(HANDLE Instance,  System::AnsiString S)
{
  HANDLE Result;
  UINT Flags;

  if (Instance != 0)
    Flags = LR_CREATEDIBSECTION;
  else
    Flags = LR_LOADFROMFILE | LR_CREATEDIBSECTION;

  Result = LoadImage((HANDLE)Instance, S.c_str(), IMAGE_BITMAP,
              0, 0, Flags);
  if (Result == 0)
    FHermes->ErrorEvent("TSpeedDraw.GetDib: Could not load bitmap");

  return Result;
}

IDirectDrawPalette* __fastcall TDraw::LoadPalette(HANDLE Instance,
    const System::AnsiString BitmapName)
{
  IDirectDrawPalette* ddpal;
  int                 i;
  int                 n;
  int                 fh;
  HRSRC               h;
  LPBITMAPINFO        BitmapInfo;
  PALETTEENTRY        ape[256];
  RGBQUAD *           RGBQuad;

  //
  // build a 332 palette as the default.
  //
  for (i=0; i<256; i++)
  {
      ape[i].peRed   = (BYTE)(((i >> 5) & 0x07) * 255 / 7);
      ape[i].peGreen = (BYTE)(((i >> 2) & 0x07) * 255 / 7);
```

```
        ape[i].peBlue  = (BYTE)(((i >> 0) & 0x03) * 255 / 3);
        ape[i].peFlags = (BYTE)0;
}

if (BitmapName == "")
  FHermes->ErrorEvent("No bitmapname in LoadPalette");


//
// get a pointer to the bitmap resource.
//
if (Instance)
{
  h = FindResource(Instance, BitmapName.c_str(), RT_BITMAP);
  if (h)
  {
    BitmapInfo = (LPBITMAPINFO)LockResource(LoadResource(Instance, h));
    if (!BitmapInfo)
      throw EDDError("No LockResouce: " + this->ClassName());

    RGBQuad = (RGBQUAD*)BitmapInfo->bmiColors;

    if (BitmapInfo == NULL || BitmapInfo->bmiHeader.biSize <
        sizeof(BITMAPINFOHEADER))
        n = 0;
    else if (BitmapInfo->bmiHeader.biBitCount > 8)
        n = 0;
    else if (BitmapInfo->bmiHeader.biClrUsed == 0)
        n = 1 << BitmapInfo->bmiHeader.biBitCount;
    else
        n = BitmapInfo->bmiHeader.biClrUsed;


    //
    //  a DIB color table has its colors stored BGR not RGB
    //   so flip them around.
    //
    for(i=0; i<n; i++ )
    {
      ape[i].peRed   = RGBQuad[i].rgbRed;
      ape[i].peGreen = RGBQuad[i].rgbGreen;
      ape[i].peBlue  = RGBQuad[i].rgbBlue;
      ape[i].peFlags = 0;
    }
  }
}
else
{
  fh = _lopen(BitmapName.c_str(), OF_READ);
  if (fh != -1)
  {
    BITMAPFILEHEADER bf;
    BITMAPINFOHEADER bi;

    _lread(fh, &bf, sizeof(bf));
    _lread(fh, &bi, sizeof(bi));
```

continues

Listing 28.14. continued

```
            _lread(fh, ape, sizeof(ape));
            _lclose(fh);

            if (bi.biSize != sizeof(BITMAPINFOHEADER))
              n = 0;
            else if (bi.biBitCount > 8)
              n = 0;
            else if (bi.biClrUsed == 0)
              n = 1 << bi.biBitCount;
            else
              n = bi.biClrUsed;

            //
            //  a DIB color table has its colors stored BGR not RGB
            //  so flip them around.
            //
            for(i=0; i<n; i++ )
            {
                BYTE r = ape[i].peRed;
                ape[i].peRed  = ape[i].peBlue;
                ape[i].peBlue = r;
            }
        }
    }

    FHermes->FDirectDraw->CreatePalette(DDPCAPS_8BIT, ape, &ddpal, NULL);

    return ddpal;
}

void __fastcall TDraw::WriteXY(int X, int Y,  System::AnsiString S)
{
  HDC DC;

  FHermes->BackSurface->GetDC(&DC);
  SetBkMode(DC, TRANSPARENT);
  TextOut(DC, X, Y, S.c_str(), S.Length());
  FHermes->BackSurface->ReleaseDC(DC);
}


// -----------------------
// -- TScene ------------
// -----------------------

__fastcall TScene::TScene(TComponent *AOwner) : TDraw(AOwner)
{
  ShowBitmap = true;
}

void __fastcall TScene::DestroyObjects(void)
{
```

```
  if(FWorkSurface != NULL)
    FWorkSurface->Release();

  FWorkSurface = NULL;
}

long _fastcall TScene::RestoreSurfaces(void)
{
  long Result;
  Result = FWorkSurface->Restore();
  if(Result == DD_OK)
    DDReloadBitmapLib(FLib, FWorkSurface, FBackgroundBitmap);

  return(Result);
}

void __fastcall TScene::SetupSurfaces(System::TObject *Sender)
{
  AnsiString ErrStr = "TSpeedDraw.SetupWorkSurface: No Surface Desc %d %s";
  DDSURFACEDESC SurfaceDesc;
  HRESULT hr;

  FHermes = dynamic_cast <THermes *>(Sender);
  if(FDLLName != "")
  {
    if(!FLib)
      FLib = LoadLibrary(FDLLName.c_str());
    if(int(FLib) < 32)
      throw EDDError("No Library");
  }

  if(!CreateDDSurface(FWorkSurface, FBackgroundBitmap, True))
    throw EDDError("TSpeedDraw.SetupWorkSurface: No WorkSurface: " +
      FBackgroundBitmap);
    else
  {
    SurfaceDesc.dwSize = sizeof(SurfaceDesc);
    hr = FWorkSurface->GetSurfaceDesc(&SurfaceDesc);
    if(hr != DD_OK)
      throw EDDError(ErrStr, OPENARRAY(TVarRec, (int(hr), GetOleError(hr))));
    FBackRect = Rect(0, 0, SurfaceDesc.dwWidth, SurfaceDesc.dwHeight);
  }

  if(FOnSetupSurfaces)
  FOnSetupSurfaces(this);
}

void _fastcall TScene::DrawScene()
{
  AnsiString ErrStr = "TSpeedDraw.BackGroundBlits: $%x \r %s \r %s";
  HRESULT hr;
  HDC DC;
  HBRUSH OldBrush, Brush;

  if (FBlankScene)
  {
```

continues

Listing 28.14. continued

```
      FHermes->BackSurface->GetDC(&DC);                    // Don't step through!!
      Brush = CreateSolidBrush(FBackColor);
      OldBrush = SelectObject(DC, Brush);
      Rectangle(DC, 0, 0, 640, 480);
      SelectObject(DC, OldBrush);
      DeleteObject(Brush);
      FHermes->BackSurface->ReleaseDC(DC);
    }
    if (FShowBitmap)
    {
      hr = AHermes->BackSurface->BltFast(FBackOrigin.x, FBackOrigin.y,
           FWorkSurface, &FBackRect,
           DDBLTFAST_WAIT | DDBLTFAST_SRCCOLORKEY);
      if (!Windows::Succeeded(hr))
        throw EDDError(ErrStr, OPENARRAY(TVarRec,
          (int(hr), GetOleError(hr), "Check BackRect, BackOrigin???")));
    }
    if (FOnDrawScene)
      FOnDrawScene(this);
}


/////////////////////////////////////////
// THermesTiler /////////////////////////
/////////////////////////////////////////
__fastcall THermesTiler::THermesTiler(Classes::TComponent* AOwner)
 :TScene(AOwner)
{
  FBitmapWidth = 32;
  FBitmapHeight = 32;
  FMaxMapRows = 12;
  FMaxMapCols = 20;
}


__fastcall THermesTiler::~THermesTiler(void)
{
  DestroyObjects();
}


void __fastcall THermesTiler::DrawScene(void)
{
  TScene::DrawScene();

  int i, j, k;
  TSpecialRect SpR;

  if (FTileSurface == NULL)
    return;

  k = 1;
  for (j = 1; j <= FMaxMapRows; j++)
    for (i = 1; i <= FMaxMapCols; i++)
    {
      SpR = GetRect(i + FHermes->CreatureList->MapCol, j + FHermes->CreatureList-
                   >MapRow);
```

```
        FHermes->BackSurface->BltFast(FBitmapWidth * (k - 1),
          FBitmapHeight * (j - 1), FTileSurface, &SpR.R1, DDBLTFAST_SRCCOLORKEY);
        if (SpR.IsCreature) // There's a character or building here
          FHermes->BackSurface->BltFast(FBitmapWidth * (k - 1),
            FBitmapHeight * (j - 1), FTileSurface, &SpR.R2, DDBLTFAST_SRCCOLORKEY);

      if ((i % 20) == 0)
        k = 1;
      else
        k++;
    }
}

void __fastcall THermesTiler::SetupSurfaces(System::TObject* Sender)
{
  TScene::SetupSurfaces(Sender);
  if (FTileMap != "")
    if (!CreateDDSurface(FTileSurface, FTileMap, True))
      throw Exception("THermesTiler.InitObjects");
}

void __fastcall THermesTiler::DestroyObjects(void)
{
  if (FTileMap != "")
    if (FTileSurface != NULL)
      FTileSurface->Release();
  FTileSurface = NULL;
}

Windows::TRect __fastcall THermesTiler::MapTypeToTileRect(int MapType)
{
  int X, Y = 0;

  if ((MapType > 19) && (MapType < 41))
  {
    Y = FBitmapHeight;
    X = (MapType - 21) * FBitmapWidth;
  }
  else if (MapType > 39)
  {
    Y = 64;
    X = (MapType - 41) * FBitmapWidth;
  }
  else
  {
    X = MapType * FBitmapWidth;
  }

  return Rect(X, Y, X + FBitmapWidth, FBitmapHeight + Y);
}

long __fastcall THermesTiler::RestoreSurfaces(void)
{
  long Result = TScene::RestoreSurfaces();
  if (Result == DD_OK)
  {
```

28

GAME
PROGRAMMING

continues

Listing 28.14. continued

```
    Result = FTileSurface->Restore();
    if (Result == DD_OK)
      if (FTileMap != "")
        DDReloadBitmapLib(FLib, FTileSurface, FTileMap);
  }
  return Result;
}


/////////////////////////////////////
// THermesChart /////////////////////////
/////////////////////////////////////

bool __fastcall THermesChart::CheckHeroPos(Creatures1::TCreatureList* HeroList,
                                           int Col, int Row)
{
  int NewPosType;
  TPoint NewPos;
  bool MoveOk = True;

  if (OnHeroMove != NULL)
  {
    NewPos.x = FHero->TrueCol + Col;
    NewPos.y = FHero->TrueRow + Row;
    NewPosType = HeroList->GetMapType(NewPos.x, NewPos.y);
    OnHeroMove(this, NewPos, NewPosType, MoveOk);
  }
  return MoveOk;
}

Windows::TRect __fastcall THermesChart::MapTypeToCreature(int Col, int Row)
{
  TCreature *Creature = FHermes->CreatureList->CreatureFromLocation(Col, Row);

  if (Creature->TypeStr == "Hero")
    return MapTypeToTileRect(3);
  else
    return MapTypeToTileRect(StrToInt(Creature->ID));
}


TSpecialRect __fastcall THermesChart::GetRect(int Col, int Row)
{
  Byte MapType;
  TSpecialRect Result;

  MapType = FHermes->CreatureList->Map[Col][Row];
  if ((FHermes->FTimerOdd == True) && (MapType == 1 /*mtWater*/))
    MapType = 4; // mtWater2;

  if (BitOn(7, MapType))
  {
    Result.IsCreature = True;
    SetBit(7, 0, MapType);
    Result.R1 = MapTypeToTileRect(MapType);
    Result.R2 = MapTypeToCreature(Col, Row);
  }
  else
  {
```

```
      Result.IsCreature = False;
      Result.R1 = MapTypeToTileRect(MapType);
  }
  return Result;
}

bool __fastcall THermesChart::MoveGrid(int Col, int Row, bool CallFlip)
{
  TPoint P;

  if (CheckHeroPos(FHermes->CreatureList, Col, Row))
  {
    P.x = FHermes->CreatureList->MapCol + Col;
    P.y = FHermes->CreatureList->MapRow + Row;
    if ((P.x < 0) ||
        (P.x > (FHermes->CreatureList->MaxCols - FMaxMapCols)) ||
        (P.y < 0) ||
        (P.y > (FHermes->CreatureList->MaxRows - FMaxMapRows)))
      return False;
    FHermes->CreatureList->MapCol = P.x;
    FHermes->CreatureList->MapRow = P.y;
    FHermes->CreatureList->MoveCreature(FHero, Col, Row);
    FHermes->Flip();
    return True;
  }
  return False;
}

__fastcall THermesChart::~THermesChart(void)
{
}

void __fastcall THermesChart::MoveHero(int NewCol, int NewRow)
{
  TPoint P;

  if (!CheckHeroPos(FHermes->CreatureList, NewCol, NewRow))
    return;

  P.x = FHero->ScreenCol + NewCol;
  P.y = FHero->ScreenRow + NewRow;
  if ((P.x <= 0) || (P.x > (FMaxMapCols)) ||
      (P.y <= 1) || (P.y > FMaxMapRows))
    return;

  FHero->ScreenCol = P.x;
  FHero->ScreenRow = P.y;

  FHermes->CreatureList->MoveCreature(FHero, NewCol, NewRow);
  FHermes->Flip();
}

void __fastcall THermesChart::SetupSurfaces(System::TObject* Sender)
{
  THermesTiler::SetupSurfaces(Sender);

  if (FHermes->CreatureList == NULL)
    throw EDDError("CreatureList cannot be blank.");
```

continues

28

GAME
PROGRAMMING

Listing 28.14. continued

```cpp
  FHeroActive = True;
  FHero = FHermes->CreatureList->CreatureFromName("Hero");
}

void __fastcall THermesChart::Move(int Value)
{
  if (Value == VK_INSERT)
    HeroActive = !HeroActive;
  else if (HeroActive)
    switch (Value)
    {
      case VK_RIGHT: MoveHero(1, 0); break;
      case VK_LEFT: MoveHero(-1, 0); break;
      case VK_DOWN: MoveHero(0, 1); break;
      case VK_UP: MoveHero(0, -1); break;
    }
  else
    switch(Value)
    {
      case VK_RIGHT: MoveGrid(1, 0, False); break;
      case VK_LEFT: MoveGrid(-1, 0, False); break;
      case VK_DOWN: MoveGrid(0, 1, False); break;
      case VK_UP: MoveGrid(0, -1, False); break;
    }
}

/* ---------------------- */
/* -- TSprite ------------ */
/* ---------------------- */

bool __fastcall TSprite::IsHit(int X, int Y)
{
  X = X - XPos;
  Y = Y - YPos;

  if ((X >= 0) && (Y >= 0) && (X <= Rect.right) && (Y <= Rect.bottom))
    return true;
  else
    return false;
}

/* ---------------------- */
/* -- TSpriteScene ------- */
/* ---------------------- */

__fastcall TSpriteScene::TSpriteScene(TComponent *AOwner)
  : TScene(AOwner)
{
  FSpriteList = new TList();
}

__fastcall TSpriteScene::~TSpriteScene()
{
```

```
  DestroyObjects();
    delete FSpriteList;
}

void __fastcall TSpriteScene::DestroyObjects(void)
{
  if(FSpriteList != NULL)
  {
    for(int i = 0; i < FSpriteList->Count; i++)
      ((TSprite*)(FSpriteList->Items[i]))->Surface->Release();

    FSpriteList->Clear();
  }
}

void __fastcall TSpriteScene::AddSprite(TSprite *Sprite)
{
  SpriteList->Add(Sprite);
}

void __fastcall TSpriteScene::DrawScene(void)
{
  const char ErrStr[] = "TSpriteScene.DrawScene";
  HResult hr;
  TSprite *Sprite;

  TScene::DrawScene();
  for(int i = 0; i < FSpriteList->Count; i++)
  {
    Sprite = (TSprite *)FSpriteList->Items[i];
    hr = FHermes->BackSurface->BltFast(Sprite->XPos, Sprite->YPos,
      Sprite->Surface, &Sprite->FRect, DDBLTFAST_WAIT | DDBLTFAST_SRCCOLORKEY);
    if(!Windows::Succeeded(hr))
      throw(EDDError(ErrStr, OPENARRAY(TVarRec, (int(hr), GetOleError(hr),
        "Check BackRect, BackOrigin???"))));
  }
}

long __fastcall TSpriteScene::RestoreSurfaces(void)
{
  TSprite *Sprite;
  HRESULT Result;

  Result = TScene::RestoreSurfaces();
  if(Result == DD_OK)
  {
        for(int i = 0; i < FSpriteList->Count; i++)
    {
      Sprite = (TSprite *)FSpriteList->Items[i];
      Result = Sprite->Surface->Restore();
      if(Result == DD_OK)
        DDReloadBitmapLib(FLib, Sprite->Surface, Sprite->Bitmap);
```

continues

Listing 28.14. continued

```
          else
            break; // Exit on error
    }
  }

  return((long)Result);
}

void __fastcall TSpriteScene::SetupSurfaces(TObject *Sender)
{
  IDirectDrawSurface *Surface;
  TSprite *Sprite;
  DDSURFACEDESC SurfaceDesc;
  HRESULT hr;

  TScene::SetupSurfaces(Sender);
  if(SpriteList == NULL)
    return;
  for(int i = 0; i < SpriteList->Count; i++)
  {
    Sprite = (TSprite *)SpriteList->Items[i];
    if(!CreateDDSurface(Surface, Sprite->Bitmap, False))
      throw EDDError("Could not create surface");
    SurfaceDesc.dwSize = sizeof(SurfaceDesc);
    hr = Surface->GetSurfaceDesc(&SurfaceDesc);
    if(hr == DD_OK)
      Sprite->Rect = Rect(0, 0, SurfaceDesc.dwWidth, SurfaceDesc.dwHeight);
    else
      throw EDDError("No SurfaceDesc");
    Sprite->Surface = Surface;
  }
}

void __fastcall TSceneEditor::Edit(void)
{
  RunSceneEditorDlg((TScene *)Component);
}

namespace Mercury2
{
  void __fastcall Register()
  {
    TComponentClass classes[5] = {__classid(THermes), __classid(TScene),
      __classid(THermesChart), __classid(TSpriteScene), __classid(TSprite)};
    RegisterComponents("Unleash", classes, 4);

    RegisterComponentEditor(__classid(TScene), __classid(TSceneEditor));
  }
}
```

Summary

In this chapter, you learned how to create a simple graphics engine that gives you access to DirectX. In particular, you learned how to do the following:

- Get into and out of Exclusive mode
- Restore surfaces when the user switches away from a DirectX application
- Create backgrounds and sprites
- Work with a tiled world that expands far beyond the reaches of the screen

In the next chapter, I add a simple game engine to this graphics engine and then give a simple example of how to use these tools to create the elements of a strategy game.

Game Engines

Overview

In this chapter, you will see how to implement the key pieces of a simple strategy game called Byzantium. In particular, you will see how to define problem domains that assure that graphics-based problems are confined to the graphics engine and that game-based problems are confined to the game engine.

There are no hard and fast rules defining where the lines between problem domains should be drawn. The particular scope of a problem domain can be decided only by the individuals involved in any one project. The key is not necessarily seeking out the ideal problem domains, but rather creating certain reasonable domains and then rigorously enforcing their sovereignty.

Unlike the code in the preceding chapter, all the code in this chapter is written in C++. In particular, you will see two base objects called TCharacter and TGame, each of which can be used in a wide variety of projects. Descending from these broad, abstract tools are two classes called TByzCharacter and TByzGame. These objects will help to define the character of the particular game implemented in this chapter.

Creating the Framework for a Simple Game

In the preceding chapter, you learned how to develop a graphics engine. Now you're ready to go on and create the framework for a simple game. I have not had time to complete the entire game for this book, but I can give you the basic tools you need to start creating it. In other words, I will give you a game engine, but not a complete game. I hope that you will find this reasonable, because games are plentiful and game engines are in short supply.

The partially complete game called Byzantium described in this chapter uses all the elements in the graphics engine you learned about in the preceding chapter. This game is a rudimentary version of the type of strategy game you find in the old hack games that used to circulate on the Net, and it is also remotely related to WarCraft, Heroes of Might and Magic, and Civilization. Byzantium is not nearly as fancy as those games, but it has some of the same underlying architectural features, albeit only in nascent form.

The game has three main screens, shown in Figures 29.1 through 29.3. The first scene is the introduction to the game, the second is the main playing field, and in the third you can have battles between the hero and various nefarious opponents. The hero can find food and medical kits as he wanders around, and the game tracks his hunger and strength.

FIGURE 29.1.

The introductory scene to Byzantium.

Press Alt-B to Start
Press Alt-X to Exit

FIGURE 29.2.

The main playing field for Byzantium. An apple is visible near the top of the screen, and a medical kit near the bottom. In the center are the hero and an opponent.

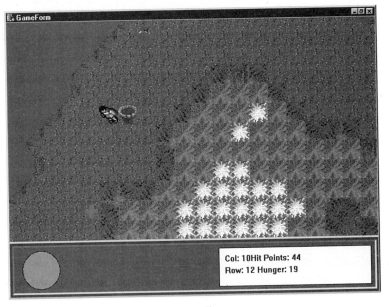

Col: 10 Hit Points: 44
Row: 12 Hunger: 19

FIGURE 29.3.

A battle occurs between the hero and an evil queen.

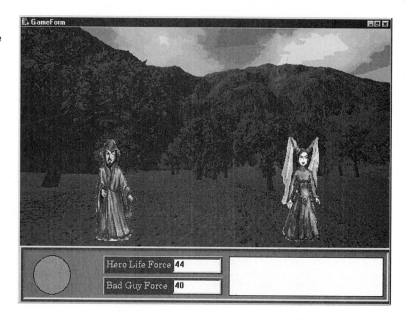

> **CAUTION**
>
> You are free to play around with these game elements to whatever degree you want. If you create your own games for public distribution with these tools, you must devise your own map, using your own art. In other words, the world found here, with mountains, grass, and ocean in particular locations, cannot be used in your own games. You can, however, use the tools provided with this book to create your own world, with different mountains, grass, and lakes and different bitmaps used to depict them. You can use both the graphics engine and game engine in any way you see fit. It's the art and the world I have created that I want to reserve for my own use.

The source for Byzantium is divided into three parts:

- The graphics engine, which was explained in the preceding chapter
- The game engine, which is described in this chapter
- The game itself, which consists of a set of objects resting on top of both the graphics engine and the game engine

In Listings 29.1 through 29.9, you will find the source for the game engine in a set of files called `GameEngine1.cpp` and `GameEngine1.h`. You can find the game itself primarily in `ByzEngine.cpp`, `ByzEngine1.h`, `GameForm1.cpp`, `GameForm1.h`, `FightClass1.cpp`, and `FightClass1.h`. I have a few other related files, such as one that contains a set of global constants and types, but the heart of the game is located in the files described here. Besides the main form, one global object called ByzGame is available to all the modules of the program. This object encapsulates the game engine itself.

Listing 29.1. The header file for the game engine.

```
/////////////////////////////////////
// File: GameEngine1.h
// Project: GameObjects
// Copyright (c) 1997 by Charlie Calvert

#ifndef GameEngine1H
#define GameEngine1H
#include <vcl\Forms.hpp>
#include "gameform1.h"
#include "creatures1.hpp"

class TGame;

class TCharacter : public TObject
{
private:
  AnsiString Bitmaps;
  TGame *FGame;
  TCreature *FCreature;
  int GetRow(void);
  int GetCol(void);
  AnsiString GetName(void);
  TStringList *FCustomFeatures;
  TStringList *GetCustomFeatures(void);
protected:
  virtual __fastcall ~TCharacter(void);
public:
  virtual __fastcall TCharacter(TGame *AGame);
  __property TGame *Game={read=FGame, write=FGame, nodefault};
  __property int Row={read=GetRow, nodefault};
  __property int Col={read=GetCol, nodefault};
  __property TCreature *Creature={read=FCreature, write=FCreature, nodefault};
  __property AnsiString Name={read=GetName, nodefault};
  __property TStringList *CustomFeatures={read=GetCustomFeatures, nodefault};
  void Move(int Key);
};

class TScoreCard : public TObject
{
};

// typedef void __fastcall (__closure *TSetSceneProc)(int NextScene);

class TGame : public TObject
{
private:
  TCreatureList *FCreatureList;
  TCharacter *FHero;
```

continues

Listing 29.1. continued

```
  TCharacter *FBadGuy;
  AnsiString FCreatureFile;
  AnsiString FScreenFile;
  TGameForm *FCurrentGameForm;
  int FCurrentScene;
  void SetHero(TCharacter *Hero);
  void SetBadGuy(TCharacter *ABadGuy);
protected:
  virtual void CreateCharacters(void);
  virtual __fastcall ~TGame(void);
public:
  virtual __fastcall TGame(void);
  void Initialize(TGameForm *AOwner, TCreatureList *ACreatureList);
  void SetScene(TGameForm *AOwner, HANDLE MainHandle);
  void UpdateMap();
// properties
  __property TCharacter *Hero=
    {read=FHero, write=SetHero, nodefault};
  __property TCharacter *BadGuy=
    {read=FBadGuy, write=SetBadGuy, nodefault};
  __property AnsiString CreatureFile=
    {read=FCreatureFile, write =FCreatureFile, nodefault};
  __property AnsiString ScreenFile=
    {read=FScreenFile, write=FScreenFile};
  __property TGameForm *CurrentGameForm=
    {read=FCurrentGameForm, write=FCurrentGameForm};
  __property int CurrentScene=
    {read=FCurrentScene, write=FCurrentScene, nodefault};
  __property TCreatureList *CreatureList=
    {read=FCreatureList, write=FCreatureList};
};
#endif
```

Listing 29.2. The main source for the game engine.

```
/////////////////////////////////////
// File: GameEngine1.cpp
// Project: GameObjects
// Copyright (c) 1997 by Charlie Calvert
//
#include <vcl.h>
#pragma hdrstop
#include "GameEngine1.h"

/////////////////////////////////////
// Constructor
/////////////////////////////////////
__fastcall TGame::TGame(void)
{
  FCreatureList = NULL;
```

```
  FHero = NULL;
  FBadGuy = NULL;
}

////////////////////////////////////
// Destructor
////////////////////////////////////
__fastcall TGame::~TGame(void)
{
}

////////////////////////////////////
// Initialize
////////////////////////////////////
void TGame::Initialize(TGameForm *AOwner, TCreatureList *ACreatureList)
{
  if (FCreatureList == NULL)
  {
    CurrentGameForm = AOwner;
    FCreatureList = ACreatureList;
    CreateCharacters();
    FHero->Creature = FCreatureList->CreatureFromName("Hero");
  }
}


void TGame::CreateCharacters(void)
{
  FHero = new TCharacter(this);
  FBadGuy = new TCharacter(this);
}

////////////////////////////////////
// SetHero
////////////////////////////////////
void TGame::SetHero(TCharacter *AHero)
{
  FHero = AHero;
  FHero->Game = this;
}

void TGame::SetBadGuy(TCharacter *ABadGuy)
{
  FBadGuy = ABadGuy;
  FBadGuy->Game = this;
}

void TGame::SetScene(TGameForm *AOwner, HANDLE MainHandle)
{
  CurrentGameForm = AOwner;
  CurrentScene = AOwner->ShowModal();
  PostMessage(MainHandle, WM_NEXTSCENE, 0, 0);
}

void TGame::UpdateMap()
{
```

29

GAME ENGINES

continues

Listing 29.2. continued

```
  FCreatureList->UpdateMap();
}


// -----------------------------------
// -- TCharacter ------------------
// -----------------------------------

/////////////////////////////////////////
// Constructor
/////////////////////////////////////////

__fastcall TCharacter::TCharacter(TGame *AGame)
{
  FGame = AGame;
  FCustomFeatures = new TStringList();
}


__fastcall TCharacter::~TCharacter(void)
{
  FCustomFeatures->Free();
}

int TCharacter::GetRow(void)
{
  return Creature->TrueRow;
}

int TCharacter::GetCol(void)
{
  return Creature->TrueCol;
//   return Game->CurrentGameForm->Tiler->Hero->TrueCol;
}

AnsiString TCharacter::GetName(void)
{
  if (FCreature)
    return FCreature->CreatureName;
  else
    return "Creature not initialized";
}

TStringList *TCharacter::GetCustomFeatures(void)
{
  int i;

  FCustomFeatures->Clear();
  for (i = 0; i < FCreature->GetCustomCount() - 1; i++)
  {
    FCustomFeatures->Add(FCreature->GetCustom(i)->ValueName);
  }
```

```
      return FCustomFeatures;
}

void TCharacter::Move(int Key)
{
  if (Name == "Hero")
    Game->CurrentGameForm->HermesChart1->Move(Key);
}
```

Listing 29.3. The header file for the game objects specific to Byzantium.

```
///////////////////////////////////////
// File: ByzEngine1.h
// Project: GameObjects
// Copyright (c) 1997 by Charlie Calvert
//
#ifndef ByzEngine1H
#define ByzEngine1H
#include "gameengine1.h"

class TByzCharacter : public TCharacter
{
private:
  int FArmor;
  int FWeapon;
  int FHitPoints;
  int FHunger;
  int FStrength;
  bool FVisible;
  int GetArmor(void);
  void SetArmor(int Value);
  int GetHitPoints(void);
  void SetHitPoints(int Value);
  int GetHunger(void);
  void SetHunger(int Value);
  int GetWeapon(void);
  void SetWeapon(int Value);
  int GetStrength(void);
  void SetStrength(int Value);
protected:
  virtual __fastcall ~TByzCharacter(void);
public:
  virtual __fastcall TByzCharacter(TGame *AGame);
  bool DefendYourself(TByzCharacter *Attacker);
  void SetVisible(bool Value);
  __property int Armor={read=GetArmor, write=SetArmor, nodefault};
  __property int Hunger={read=GetHunger, write=SetHunger, nodefault};
  __property int HitPoints={read=GetHitPoints, write=SetHitPoints, nodefault};
```

continues

29

GAME ENGINES

Listing 29.3. continued

```
  __property int Weapon={read=GetWeapon, write=SetWeapon, nodefault};
  __property int Strength={read=GetStrength, write=SetStrength, nodefault};
// __property bool Visible={read=FVisible, write=SetVisible, nodefault);
};

class THero : public TByzCharacter
{
public:
  __fastcall THero(TGame *AGame): TByzCharacter(AGame) {}
};

class TBadGuy : public TByzCharacter
{
public:
  __fastcall TBadGuy(TGame *AGame): TByzCharacter(AGame) {}
};


class TByzGame : public TGame
{
protected:
  virtual void CreateCharacters(void);
public:
  __fastcall TByzGame(void): TGame() {}
};

extern TByzGame *ByzGame;

#endif
```

Listing 29.4. The main source for the game objects specific to Byzantium.

```
///////////////////////////////////////
// File: ByzEngine1.cpp
// Project: GameObjects
// Copyright (c) 1997 by Charlie Calvert
//
#include <vcl.h>
#pragma hdrstop
#include "ByzEngine1.h"

TByzGame *ByzGame;

void TByzGame::CreateCharacters(void)
{
  Hero = new THero(this);
  BadGuy = new TBadGuy(this);
}

__fastcall TByzCharacter::TByzCharacter(TGame *AGame)
```

```
  : TCharacter(AGame)
{
}

__fastcall TByzCharacter::~TByzCharacter(void)
{
}

int TByzCharacter::GetArmor(void)
{
  return Creature->GetCustomInt("Armor");
}

void TByzCharacter::SetArmor(int Value)
{
  Creature->SetCustomInt("Armor", Value);
}

int TByzCharacter::GetHitPoints(void)
{
  return Creature->GetCustomInt("Hit Points");
}

void TByzCharacter::SetHitPoints(int Value)
{
  Creature->SetCustomInt("Hit Points", Value);
}

int TByzCharacter::GetHunger(void)
{
  return Creature->GetCustomInt("Hunger");
}

void TByzCharacter::SetHunger(int Value)
{
  Creature->SetCustomInt("Hunger", Value);
}

int TByzCharacter::GetWeapon(void)
{
  return Creature->GetCustomInt("Weapon");
}

void TByzCharacter::SetWeapon(int Value)
{
  Creature->SetCustomInt("Weapon", Value);
}

int TByzCharacter::GetStrength(void)
{
  return Creature->GetCustomInt("Strength");
}

void TByzCharacter::SetStrength(int Value)
{
```

continues

Listing 29.4. continued

```cpp
  Creature->SetCustomInt("Strength", Value);
}

void TByzCharacter::SetVisible(bool Value)
{
  Creature->Visible = Value;
  FVisible = Value;
  if (!Value)
    ByzGame->UpdateMap();
}

int GetResistanceChance()
{
  int i = random(49);
  i -= (24);
  return i;
}

int GetWeaponChance()
{
  return 0;
}

void PlaySound(AnsiString S)
{
  sndPlaySound(S.c_str(), SND_ASYNC);
}

bool TByzCharacter::DefendYourself(TByzCharacter *Attacker)
{
  int Resistance = (Strength - Attacker->Strength) + (Armor - Attacker->Weapon);

  if (Resistance + GetResistanceChance() < 0)
  {
    HitPoints -= (Attacker->Weapon - GetWeaponChance());
    PlaySound("..\\media\\bang.wav");
    return False;
  }
  else
  {
    PlaySound("..\\media\\rev.wav");
    return True;
  }
}
```

Listing 29.5. The header file for the game form.

```cpp
/////////////////////////////////////////
// GameForm1.h
// Byzantium Project
// Copyright (c) 1997 by Charlie Calvert
//
```

```cpp
#ifndef GameForm1H
#define GameForm1H
#include <Classes.hpp>
#include <Controls.hpp>
#include <StdCtrls.hpp>
#include <Forms.hpp>
#include "globals.h"
#include "Creatures1.hpp"
#include "FightClass1.h"
#include "Mercury2.h"

class TGameForm : public TForm
{
__published:
  THermes *Hermes1;
  THermesChart *HermesChart1;
  TFileCreatureList *FileCreatureList1;
  TScene *Scene1;
  TSpriteScene *SpriteScene1;
  TSprite *Hero1;
  TSprite *BadQueen1;
  void __fastcall FormShow(TObject *Sender);
  void __fastcall FormKeyDown(TObject *Sender, WORD &Key, TShiftState Shift);

  void __fastcall FormDestroy(TObject *Sender);
  void __fastcall HermesChart1DrawScene(TObject *Sender);
  void __fastcall SpriteScene1SetupSurfaces(TObject *Sender);
  void __fastcall FormMouseMove(TObject *Sender, TShiftState Shift, int X,
                                  int Y);
  void __fastcall SpriteScene1DrawScene(TObject *Sender);
  void __fastcall FormMouseDown(TObject *Sender, TMouseButton Button,
                                  TShiftState Shift, int X, int Y);

  void __fastcall Scene1DrawScene(TObject *Sender);
  void __fastcall HermesChart1HeroMove(TObject *Sender, const tagPOINT &NewPos,
                                  int NewType, bool &MoveOk);
private:
//  TNotifyEvent FHitCreatureProc;
  TFightClass *FFightClass;
  MESSAGE void StartShow(TMessage &Msg);
public:
  virtual __fastcall TGameForm(TComponent* Owner);
  void Run(void);
BEGIN_MESSAGE_MAP
  MESSAGE_HANDLER(WM_STARTSHOW, TMessage, StartShow);
END_MESSAGE_MAP(TForm);

};

extern TGameForm *GameForm;

#endif
```

Listing 29.6. The main source for the game form.

```cpp
///////////////////////////////////////////
// GameForm1.cpp
// Byzantium Project
// Copyright (c) 1997 by Charlie Calvert
//
#include <vcl.h>
#pragma hdrstop
#include "Globals.h"
#include "ByzEngine1.h"
#include "GameForm1.h"
#pragma link "Creatures1"
#pragma link "Mercury2"
#pragma resource "*.dfm"

TGameForm *GameForm;

__fastcall TGameForm::TGameForm(TComponent* Owner)
  : TForm(Owner)
{
  FFightClass = NULL;
  ByzGame = new TByzGame();
  ByzGame->CurrentScene = mrIntroMap;
}

void __fastcall TGameForm::FormDestroy(TObject *Sender)
{
  delete ByzGame;
}

///////////////////////////////////////////
// Run
///////////////////////////////////////////
void TGameForm::Run(void)
{
  if (FFightClass)
  {
    delete FFightClass;
    FFightClass = NULL;
  }

  switch(ByzGame->CurrentScene)
  {
    case mrWorldMap:
      Hermes1->Scene = HermesChart1;
      break;
    case mrIntroMap:
      Hermes1->Scene = Scene1;
      break;
    case mrFightMap:
      Hermes1->Scene = SpriteScene1;
      FFightClass = new TFightClass(Handle, SpriteScene1);
      break;
  }

  Hermes1->InitObjects();
  ByzGame->Initialize(this, Hermes1->CreatureList);
```

```
    Hermes1->Flip();
}

void __fastcall TGameForm::FormShow(TObject *Sender)
{
    PostMessage(Handle, WM_STARTSHOW, 0, 0);
}

void TGameForm::StartShow(TMessage &Msg)
{
    Run();
}

void __fastcall TGameForm::FormKeyDown(TObject *Sender, WORD &Key,
                                       TShiftState Shift)
{
    if ((Shift.Contains(ssAlt)) && (Key=='X'))
    {
        if (Hermes1->Exclusive)
            Hermes1->EndExclusive();
        Close();
    }
    else if ((Shift.Contains(ssAlt)) && (Key=='A'))
    {
        ByzGame->CurrentScene = mrIntroMap;
        Run();
    }
    else if ((Shift.Contains(ssAlt)) && (Key=='B'))
    {
        ByzGame->CurrentScene = mrWorldMap;
        Run();
    }
    else if (ByzGame)
        dynamic_cast<THero*>(ByzGame->Hero)->Move(Key);
}
void __fastcall TGameForm::HermesChart1DrawScene(TObject *Sender)
{
    AnsiString S;
    S = "Col: " + IntToStr(ByzGame->Hero->Col);
//  S = S + " Scr Col: " + IntToStr(ByzGame->Hero->Creature->ScreenCol);
//  S = S + " Map Col: " + IntToStr(Hermes1->CreatureList->MapCol);
    S = S + "Hit Points: " + dynamic_cast<TByzCharacter*>(ByzGame->Hero)->HitPoints;
    HermesChart1->WriteXY(370, 410, S);
    S = "Row: " + IntToStr(ByzGame->Hero->Row);
//  S = S + " Scr Row: " + IntToStr(ByzGame->Hero->Creature->ScreenRow);
//  S = S + " Map Row: " + IntToStr(Hermes1->CreatureList->MapRow);
    S = S + " Hunger: " + dynamic_cast<TByzCharacter*>(ByzGame->Hero)->Hunger;
    HermesChart1->WriteXY(370, 430, S);
}

void __fastcall TGameForm::SpriteScene1SetupSurfaces(TObject *Sender)
{
    SpriteScene1->AddSprite(Hero1);
```

29

GAME ENGINES

continues

Listing 29.6. continued

```
    SpriteScene1->AddSprite(BadQueen1);
}

void __fastcall TGameForm::FormMouseMove(TObject *Sender, TShiftState Shift,
                                         int X, int Y)
{
  if (ByzGame->CurrentScene == mrFightMap)
  {
    if (BadQueen1->IsHit(X, Y))
      Screen->Cursor = crCross;
    else
      Screen->Cursor = crDefault;
  }
}

void __fastcall TGameForm::SpriteScene1DrawScene(TObject *Sender)
{
  if (FFightClass)
    FFightClass->ShowData();
}

void __fastcall TGameForm::FormMouseDown(TObject *Sender, TMouseButton Button,
                                         TShiftState Shift, int X, int Y)
{
  if (ByzGame->CurrentScene == mrFightMap)
  {
    if (BadQueen1->IsHit(X, Y))
      FFightClass->PerformHit(this);
  }
}

void __fastcall TGameForm::Scene1DrawScene(TObject *Sender)
{
  Scene1->WriteXY(375, 405, "Press Alt-B to Start");
  Scene1->WriteXY(375, 430, "Press Alt-X to Exit");
}

void __fastcall TGameForm::HermesChart1HeroMove(TObject *Sender,
    const tagPOINT &NewPos, int NewType, bool &MoveOk)
{
  switch (TMapType(NewType))
  {
    case mtGrass:
      MoveOk = True;
      break;

    case mtCreature:
      MoveOk = False;
      ByzGame->BadGuy->Creature =
        ByzGame->CreatureList->CreatureFromLocation(NewPos.x, NewPos.y);
      if (ByzGame->BadGuy->Creature->Kind == "Food")
      {
        dynamic_cast<TByzCharacter*>(ByzGame->Hero)->Hunger += 3;
```

```
            dynamic_cast<TByzCharacter*>(ByzGame->BadGuy)->SetVisible(False);
          }
          else if (ByzGame->BadGuy->Creature->Kind == "Medicine")
          {
            dynamic_cast<TByzCharacter*>(ByzGame->Hero)->HitPoints += 3;
            dynamic_cast<TByzCharacter*>(ByzGame->BadGuy)->SetVisible(False);
          }
          else
          {
            ByzGame->CurrentScene = mrFightMap;
            Run();
          }
          break;

      default:
        MoveOk = False;
    }
}
```

Listing 29.7. A header file containing some global declarations.

```
/////////////////////////////////////
// Globals.h
// Byzantium Project
// Copyright (c) 1997 by Charlie Calvert
//
#ifndef GlobalsH
#define GlobalsH
#define mrHitCreature 0x5001
#define mrGameOver    0x5002

#define mrWorldMap    0x6001
#define mrFightMap    0x6002
#define mrIntroMap    0x6003

#define WM_NEXTSCENE  WM_USER + 1
#define WM_STARTSHOW  WM_USER + 2

enum TMapType {mtGrass, mtWater, mtMountain, mtRoad, mtWater2,
               mtFootHill, mtNorthShore, mtWestShore, mtSouthShore, mtEastShore,
               mtSWShore, mtSEShore, mtNWShore, mtNEShore,
               mtWNWShore, mtWSEShore, mtESEShore, mtENEShore,
               mtBlank1, mtBlank2, mtBlank3, mtBlank4, mtAllSnow,
               mtSnowyMountain, mtSouthMtn, mtWestMtn, mtNorthMtn, mtEastMtn,
               mtSEMtn, mtSWMtn, mtNWMtn, mtNEMtn, mtNWFootHill,
               mtNEFootHill, mtSEFootHill, mtSWFootHill,
               mtNorthFootHill, mtEastFootHill, mtSouthFootHill,
               mtWestFootHill, mtNEDiagShore, mtSEDiagShore,
               mtSWDiagShore, mtNWDiagShore, mtSWBendShore, mtSEBendShore,
               mtNWBendShore, mtNEBendShore, mtENBendShore, mtWNBendShore,
               mtWSBendShore, mtESBendShore, mtCity, mtCreature};

#endif
```

Listing 29.8. The header file for the fight class.

```
/////////////////////////////////////
// Fightclass.h
// Project: Byzantium
// Copyright (c) 1997 by Charlie Calvert
//
#ifndef FightClass1H
#define FightClass1H
#include "Mercury1.hpp"

class TFightClass
{
private:
  AnsiString FBadGuyName;
  AnsiString FDisplayString;
  HWND FHandle;
  TScene *FScene;
  bool FHitInProcess;
  void Button1Click(void);
  bool BadGuyAttacks(void);
  bool CheckCharacters(void);
  bool HeroAttacks(void);
  void DisplayData(AnsiString S);
public:
  TFightClass(HWND AHandle, TScene *AScene);
  void PerformHit(TObject *Sender);
  void ShowData();
  __property AnsiString BadGuyName={read=FBadGuyName};
};

#endif
```

Listing 29.9. The main source file for the fight class.

```
/////////////////////////////////////
// Fightclass.cpp
// Project: Byzantium
// Copyright (c) 1997 by Charlie Calvert
//
#include <vcl\vcl.h>
#include <time.h>
#pragma hdrstop
#include "Creatures1.hpp"
#include "FightClass1.h"
#include "ByzEngine1.h"
#include "Mercury2.h"

TFightClass::TFightClass(HWND AHandle, TScene *AScene)
{
  FHandle = AHandle;
  FHitInProcess = False;
```

```
    FScene = AScene;
    FBadGuyName = ByzGame->BadGuy->Name;
}

void TFightClass::DisplayData(AnsiString S)
{
    TCustomValue *CustomValue;
    AnsiString DisplayValue;

    CustomValue = ByzGame->Hero->Creature->FindCustomByName("Hit Points");
    DisplayValue = CustomValue->CurrentValue;
    FScene->WriteXY(270, 405, DisplayValue);

    CustomValue = ByzGame->BadGuy->Creature->FindCustomByName("Hit Points");
    DisplayValue = CustomValue->CurrentValue;
    FScene->WriteXY(270, 440, DisplayValue);

    FScene->WriteXY(375, 410, FDisplayString);
}

void TFightClass::ShowData()
{
    DisplayData("Hit Points");
    if (ByzGame->BadGuy->Creature)
        DisplayData("Hit Points");
}

void TFightClass::Button1Click()
{
    ShowMessage(ByzGame->Hero->Name + " retreats. Receives 5 points damage.");
    dynamic_cast<TByzCharacter *>(ByzGame->Hero)->HitPoints -= 5;
    if (CheckCharacters());
}

void WaitTime(int Delay)
{
    time_t t1, t2;

    t1 = time(NULL);
    while (True)
    {
        Application->ProcessMessages();
        t2 = time(NULL);
        if (t2 - t1 >= Delay)
            return;
    }
}

bool TFightClass::CheckCharacters(void)
{
    TBadGuy *B = dynamic_cast<TBadGuy*>(ByzGame->BadGuy);

    if (B->HitPoints <= 0)
    {
        ByzGame->CreatureList->HideCreature(B->Name, False);
        FDisplayString = "Victory is sweet!";
```

continues

Listing 29.9. continued

```cpp
      WaitTime(1);
      ByzGame->CurrentScene = mrWorldMap;
      PostMessage(FHandle, WM_STARTSHOW, 0, 0);
      return False;
    }

  if (dynamic_cast<THero*>(ByzGame->Hero)->HitPoints <= 0)
    {
      FDisplayString = "Defeat is bitter ashes!";
      WaitTime(1);
      ByzGame->CurrentScene = mrIntroMap;
      PostMessage(FHandle, WM_STARTSHOW, 0, 0);
      return False;
    }
    return True;
}

bool TFightClass::BadGuyAttacks(void)
{
  THero *H = dynamic_cast<THero*>(ByzGame->Hero);
  TBadGuy *B = dynamic_cast<TBadGuy*>(ByzGame->BadGuy);


  FDisplayString = H->Name + " Under attack!";
  WaitTime(1);
  if (H->DefendYourself(B))
    {
      FDisplayString = H->Name + ": No damage!";
    }
  else
    FDisplayString = H->Name + " is hit!";

  WaitTime(1);

  return CheckCharacters();
}

bool TFightClass::HeroAttacks(void)
{
  TBadGuy *B = dynamic_cast<TBadGuy*>(ByzGame->BadGuy);
  THero *H = dynamic_cast<THero*>(ByzGame->Hero);

  FDisplayString = B->Name + " Under attack!";
  WaitTime(1);
  if (B->DefendYourself(H))
    FDisplayString = B->Name + ": No damage!";
  else
    FDisplayString = B->Name + " is hit!";
  WaitTime(1);

  return CheckCharacters();
}

void TFightClass::PerformHit(TObject *Sender)
{
  if (FHitInProcess)
```

```
    return;
  FHitInProcess = True;

  if (HeroAttacks())
    BadGuyAttacks();

  FHitInProcess = False;
  FDisplayString = "Waiting...";
}
```

As it is implemented here, Byzantium is a very simple game. When the program is first launched, you see a main form with a picture of a bucolic landscape. A window in the form states that you can start the game by pressing Alt+B, or you can press Alt+X to exit.

If you press Alt+B, then you can see the hero standing on a tiled world map. You can use the arrow keys to move the hero, pushing the Insert key to toggle back and forth between moving the hero alone, or moving the entire landscape.

The hero can interact with various objects on the tiled surface. For example, the hero can eat bits of food, thereby alleviating his hunger. He also can pick up medical kits to restore the hit points or his health.

The hero can also encounter various bad guys, most of whom live in castles or stone turrets. If you bump into a bad guy, you will be switched to a third scene where the hero can engage in combat with the bad guy.

When in fight mode, the hero, dressed as a monk, appears on the left. The villain, who is always a wicked queen, is standing on the right. If you move the mouse cursor over the queen, the cursor changes shape; that is, it moves into attack mode. When the cursor is in attack mode, you can left-click the wicked queen to attack her. The hero gets a chance to do some damage to her, and she in turn will have a chance to attack the hero.

> **NOTE**
>
> I feel the need to defend myself against possible charges of sexism. As I develop this game further, I will give the user a chance to choose whether the main character is a man or woman. It was perhaps not wise of me to pick the word "Hero" as a field of the TGame object, but it seemed to me more concise and easy to understand than a phrase like "MainCharacter."
>
> The fact that the villain is a queen is mostly a function of my artist's inclination when she produced her first evil character for me to use. As the game matures, it will have more evil characters, some male, some female.
>
> In short, the game is not intended to contain any political messages about sexuality, and a more egalitarian world view will emerge as the game matures.

29

GAME ENGINES

The game is designed so that the hero can easily withstand several fights with the bad guys. Eventually, however, he will be worn down and will need to find more food or medical kits or else perish. The condition for losing the game is to run out of hit points before killing all the bad guys.

As I stated earlier, this game is not complete. My goal was just to give you enough pieces so that you could begin to construct your own game with its own rules. Where you take the game from the point at which I have left it is up to you. You might, however, want to check my Web site to see whether I have found time to actually complete a full game.

Understanding the Technology Behind Byzantium

Now you can take a closer look at Byzantium. In the next few sections of the book, I help you examine the technology behind the game, showing the way it was put together and giving hints about ways in which the game could be expanded.

This program uses all the graphics engine components introduced in the preceding chapter. I lay them out on the main form, as shown in Figure 29.4. The properties of these objects are filled out almost exactly as they were in Chapter 28, "Game Programming," only this time I'm using all the components at once. To see the details of which properties are connected to which values, you should launch the game and study the main form.

FIGURE 29.4.

The graphics components used in the Byzantium program as they appear on the main form at design time.

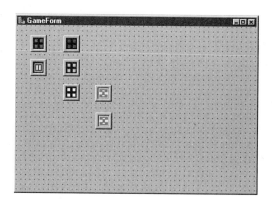

On top of the graphics components I lay a game engine that consists of two main objects called TCharacter and TGame. These objects are meant to be base classes from which you can make descendants of the characters and games that you want to create.

The key fact to understand about TGame and TCharacter is that they know how to work with the graphics engine and shield the user from the graphics engine's complexity. In short, the user should feel most of the time as though he or she is manipulating a game or character that simply knows how to draw him, her, or itself to the screen. In short, the programmer can stay inside the problem domain defined by the game itself and can ignore the problems inherent in implementing a graphics engine.

For example, the user can simply ask the character to move, hide, state its name, or keep track of its health, hit points, and so on. The technical implementation of all these traits should not be a concern to the programmer. It doesn't matter how a character moves, hides, or is drawn to the screen. When you're writing a game, you don't want to have to think about those kinds of issues. You just want to design a game.

Furthermore, you want to be sure that problems with the graphics engine can occur only if a mistake is made in `Mercury1.pas` or in `Creatures1.pas`. Graphics-based problems should never be caused by errors in the game engine because the game engine shouldn't contain any graphics-based code. Conversely, problems with the logic of the game should not ever occur in the graphics engine because it should contain no game logic. Game-based problems are put in the game engine, and graphics-based problems are put in the graphics engine. If you want to have a maintainable code base, then setting up clearly defined problem domains is important.

> **NOTE**
>
> Once again, I have to ask myself how completely I have managed to achieve my goals. Can you really afford to forget about what goes on in `Mercury1.pas` when you're working with the game objects? Well, in all truthfulness, you probably can't completely ignore the graphics engine or its implementation. However, it is hidden well enough that you can forget about it at times, and a clearly defined partition exists between the game objects and the graphics objects.
>
> The only time you might have to bridge the gap between the game engine and graphics engine would be if something went wrong, that is, when you find a bug. At such times, you have to decide whether the bug is in the game engine or in the graphics engine, and then you have to implement the fix in the right place. Though it might not seem likely from this perspective, fixing the graphics engine by putting some kind of patch in the game engine, or vice versa, can be very tempting. You should avoid this temptation whenever possible.

Understanding the TGame Object

The game object, implemented in `GameEngine1.cpp`, has five key properties:

```
__property TCharacter *Hero;
__property TCharacter *BadGuy;
__property TGameForm *CurrentGameForm;
__property int CurrentScene;
__property TCreatureList *CreatureList;
```

In Byzantium, `CurrentScene` can be set to one of the following values:

```
#define mrWorldMap    0x6001
#define mrFightMap    0x6002
#define mrIntroMap    0x6003
```

Each of these values represents one of the possible scenes that can be displayed by the Byzantium game. Notice that these values are defined as part of Byzantium itself and are not declared inside the game engine. You therefore can make up as many of these constants as you need to implement your game. In short, the `TGame` object knows that you will need to define constants specifying the name and type of the current scene. It does not know or care, however, about the specific value or meaning of these constants.

In almost all cases, the game will have only one main form on which a series of different scenes will be drawn. But the fact that a programmer would want to have more than one form is conceivable, so I provide for that possibility.

The `CreatureList` is implemented in `Creatures1.pas`. It is needed internally by the `TGame` object and is made available to the user in case it might come in handy. Allowing the user to access the `CreatureList` directly in this manner is not very wise from a design point of view, but I found it the most practical solution to a series of potential problems. The `CreatureList` is made available in the `TGame` object not through multiple inheritance, but through aggregation.

The hero is probably the most important feature of the `TGame` object. From both the user's and game programmer's point of view, the hero is the center of the game. One of the primary goals of the game engine is to allow the user and programmer to access the hero freely and to treat him as a stand-alone entity with his own autonomous existence. The hero is really stored on the `CreatureList`. One of the goals of the `TGame` object is to allow the programmer to access the hero without having to think about the `CreatureList` or the hero's position in it.

The fact that the `CreatureList` is a public property of `TGame` shows that I am not sure the game object automatically provides all necessary access to the creatures on the `CreatureList`. As a result, I hedge my bets by giving the user direct access to the `CreatureList`, just in case it is needed.

Understanding the TCharacter Object

The `THermes`, `TScene`, and `THermesChart` objects give you access to characters that can be moved on a tiled surface. However, these characters have no separate existence apart from the technology that implements them, and in particular, they are hung on the `CreatureList` object, which is a bit unwieldy to use.

The `TCharacter` object is designed to give you some meaningful way to access the characters that live on a tiled grid. In particular, notice that you can use the Entities program to define characters, to give them names, and to give them traits such as Hit Points, Hunger, Speed, Weapons, and so on. You can use the Entities program to add as many characters and traits as you want to the tiled world implemented by THermesChart.

TCharacter exists in order to lift the characters out of their tiled world and give them a specific, easy-to-recognize identity. In particular, note the following traits of the TCharacter object:

```
__property int Row={read=GetRow, nodefault};
__property int Col={read=GetCol, nodefault};
__property TCreature *Creature={read=FCreature, write=FCreature, nodefault};
__property AnsiString Name={read=GetName, nodefault};
__property TStringList *CustomFeatures={read=GetCustomFeatures, nodefault};
```

Each character can have a position, as defined by the Row and Col properties. Furthermore, it can have a name and a set of CustomFeatures. The Creature property is like the CreatureList property associated with the game. In particular, it is implemented by Creatures1.pas and should, from the point of view of an ideal design, be entirely hidden from the programmer. However, I cover it here in case it is needed by the programmer.

The CustomFeatures listed in the properties of the TCharacter object can be defined by the Entities program, as shown in Figure 29.5. Notice that the properties at the top of the form, such as Name and Kind, are core properties that belong to all characters. The properties in the grid at the bottom of the form are custom properties that can be created by the user. To edit one of the custom properties, just double-click the appropriate row in the grid.

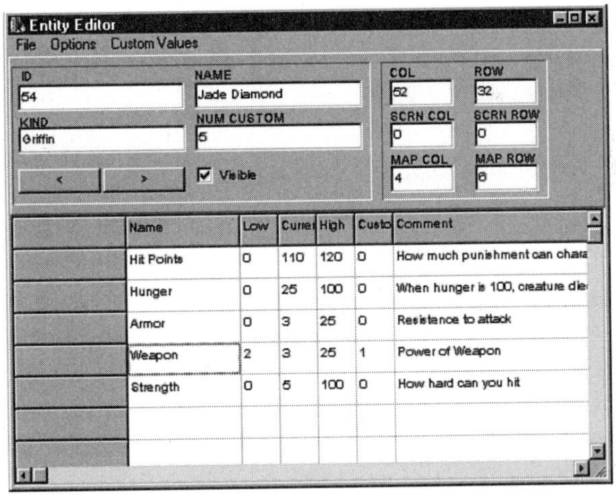

FIGURE 29.5.

Here is a list of the features associated with the hero. All the properties shown in the grid at the bottom of the form are custom properties defined by the user at runtime.

29

GAME ENGINES

Working with the TByzCharacter Object

The TCharacter object is an abstraction that can be used in any game. The TByzCharacter object is a descendant of the TCharacter object designed for use in Byzantium. TByzCharacter is implemented in ByzEngine1.cpp.

In addition to the properties it inherits from TCharacter, TByzCharacter has the following traits:

```
__property int Armor={read=GetArmor, write=SetArmor, nodefault};
__property int Hunger={read=GetHunger, write=SetHunger, nodefault};
__property int HitPoints={read=GetHitPoints, write=SetHitPoints, nodefault};
__property int Weapon={read=GetWeapon, write=SetWeapon, nodefault};
__property int Strength={read=GetStrength, write=SetStrength, nodefault};
```

Each of these properties is a custom property surfaced by TByzCharacter so that it can be easily accessed by the programmer. The key point you need to grasp here is that the TCreature object found in Creatures1.pas has a few simple traits such as a name, a column, and a row. In addition, it has a series of custom properties that can be defined by the user via the Entities program. The type and number of these custom properties can be defined by the user.

In Byzantium, I have decided that the hero and each of the bad guys will have five key traits called Armor, Hunger, HitPoints, Weapon, and Strength. These properties are given to the individual creatures in the tiled map through the good graces of the Entities program. The game programmer can find out about the traits of any one creature at runtime by accessing the TByzCharacter object, which is one of the fields of the game object.

Here is the code that TByzCharacter uses to define the armor of a character:

```
int TByzCharacter::GetArmor(void)
{
  return Creature->GetCustomInt("Armor");
}

void TByzCharacter::SetArmor(int Value)
{
  Creature->SetCustomInt("Armor", Value);
}
```

As you can see, these methods are just wrappers around the Creature object defined in Creatures1.pas. You can retrieve an individual creature by finding where it is stored on the CreatureList.

TByzCharacter hides complexity. For example, if this object did not exist, then you could find out the hero's current armor value only be iterating through the CreatureList till you found the creature called Hero. Then you would have to ask that creature for a custom value called Armor. The game engine objects allow you to avoid all this confusion; instead, you can write simple code along these lines:

```
int Armor = ByzGame->Hero->Armor;
ByzGame->Hero->Armor = 3;
```

The Character in Battle Against the Queen

Another key trait of the TByzCharacter object is that it helps define how a character performs in battle:

```
int GetResistanceChance()
{
```